Global Competition Law and Economics

Second Edition

Einer Elhauge
and
Damien Geradin

·HART·
PUBLISHING

OXFORD AND PORTLAND, OREGON

Published in the United Kingdom by Hart Publishing Ltd
16C Worcester Place, Oxford, OX1 2JW
Telephone: +44 (0)1865 517530
Fax: +44 (0)1865 510710
E-mail: mail@hartpub.co.uk
Website: http://www.hartpub.co.uk

British Library Cataloguing in Publication Data
Data Available

ISBN: 978-1-84946-044-6

Printed and bound in Great Britain by
TJ International Ltd, Padstow, Cornwall

PREFACE TO THE SECOND EDITION (2011)

In the four years since the first edition, the increased globalization of antitrust law has continued apace. China, the world's third largest economy after the EU and US, has adopted an antitrust law. Many other nations have continued to modify and modernize their antitrust regimes and step up enforcement. Nor have things been static in the EU and US. The EU has adopted a new EU Treaty and new guidelines on multiple issues, and the US has experienced important new Supreme Court cases and a significant revision of its merger guidelines that reflects modern economic approaches to merger analysis.

Given these developments, this second edition expands and updates the globalized approach to antitrust law and economics that was pioneered in the first edition. The edition updates coverage of the antitrust laws in the US, EU, Australia, Brazil, Canada, Israel, Japan, South Africa, and South Korea. It also expands coverage to add not only China's new antitrust law, but also the antitrust laws of Argentina, Chile, Colombia, Egypt, India, Indonesia, New Zealand, Peru, Russia, Saudi Arabia, Singapore, Taiwan, Thailand, Turkey, and Venezuela. Antitrust laws in all the nations that have the world's leading GDPs are now covered. The US updates include the 2010 U.S. Merger Guidelines and the U.S. Supreme Court's 2009 *Linkline* decision and 2010 *American Needle* decision. The EU updates include the new EU Treaty, the new EU guidelines on abuse of dominance, the new EU guidelines on nonhorizontal mergers, and the new EU regulations and guidelines on vertical agreements.

PREFACE TO THE FIRST EDITION (2007)

No one would think of writing a casebook on Massachusetts Antitrust Law. It has long been too obvious that such a book would be parochial in at least two senses. First, markets (not to mention legal practices) generally span regions far larger than any state. Second, antitrust analysis has a common methodology applicable across the states, and thus does not benefit from a state-centric focus.

Yet antitrust casebooks continue to be parochial in the sense that they focus on the antitrust and competition law of only one nation. That perspective is rapidly becoming as outmoded as a state-centric approach would be. Markets are increasingly becoming global or at least multinational. A typical merger between large U.S. corporations must get approval not just in the United States but also by the European Community (the "EC"), for their activities often affect both markets. Likewise for large European corporations. Cartels in one nation affect supply in others. And countries are increasingly entering into treaties with each other about the content or enforcement of competition laws. Thus, businessmen, lawyers, and lawmakers can no longer content themselves with understanding only the antitrust and competition law of their nation. They must also understand the other regimes that form part of the overall legal framework that regulates competitive behavior.

Modern antitrust law is thus global antitrust law. (We shall use "antitrust" law to refer to what other nations generally call "competition" or "anti-monopoly" law.) Modern antitrust law also differs from traditional antitrust law in that it now reflects the dominance of the economic model of analyzing antitrust and competition policy. This is a shift that has occurred both in the U.S. and EC, where legal models that once included political, formalistic, corporatist, or autonomy-based notions of "competition" have embraced an exclusively economic methodology based on maximizing consumer welfare, and have done so in a way that is common to the diverging political viewpoints in each. There remain important differences between the U.S. and EC, and differing political viewpoints, but they no longer have as much to do with different values as with different presumptions about how to resolve theoretical or empirical ambiguities raised by a common framework of antitrust economics. The same is true for most other developed nations, as well as for the developing nations that increasingly borrow from the antitrust frameworks of the U.S. or EC.

These two key aspects of modern antitrust law are highly related, for the common economic methodology used in the U.S. and EC means both are amenable to analysis by a common body of scholarship that speaks an increasingly common language of antitrust economics. It differs from pure economics in that it must crucially concern itself with the administrability and implementation of economic concepts in a world where information is limited, decision-makers are imperfect, adjudication is lengthy and costly, and parties are strategic both in litigation and in responding to different substantive rules. But those realities are common across nations, and thus this modern methodology means that antitrust and competition scholars are, whether they recognize it or not, now part of a global community and that ideas generated on one continent cannot safely be cabined and ignored on the others.

We thus organize this casebook as a study of global antitrust law and economics. Major U.S. and EC laws and cases will be presented and analyzed on each major antitrust topic. Although we also briefly summarize in each section the competition laws of other jurisdictions, our focus is on the U.S. and EC for several reasons. First, as a practical matter, the lion's share of global antitrust enforcement is done by the U.S. and EC. Second, as a conceptual matter, nations outside those jurisdictions by and large borrow the basic statutory frameworks of either the U.S. and EC and employ similar methods of antitrust analysis. Knowing how the U.S. and EC jurisdictions have grappled with the standard set of antitrust problems thus goes a long way to understanding how antitrust analysis is done in the rest of the world too. We discuss other nations in a bit more length where they seem to clearly raise a "third way" of addressing an important antitrust issue.

This is not a book on comparative law in the narrow sense of analyzing comparisons purely in order to shed light on laws that are really national in application. Rather we write with the conviction that this combination of laws from varying nations in actual practice presents a truer picture of the overall regime of competition law that now faces multinational market players. But it is surely a delightful side-benefit that this juxtaposition provides important comparative insights into differing possible approaches and their benefits and drawbacks, which will also aid analysis even in purely national markets. Nor is this a book on international antitrust law in the narrow sense of analyzing how nations resolve legal conflicts between their antitrust regimes. Such topics will certainly command attention in our final chapter, but our dominant perspective is that the antitrust laws of multiple nations are legally relevant to modern antitrust law and practice. Thus, this is not a book on comparative or international antitrust law any more than a casebook on contracts law that includes cases from multiple states is a book on comparative or interstate contracts law. It is rather a book designed to replace more parochial books on basic antitrust law by giving a more realistic sense of the range of issues and analyses relevant to modern antitrust law wherever practiced.

ACKNOWLEDGEMENTS

American Law Institute, Restatement of the Foreign Relations Law of the United States, Third, Copyright © 1987 by The American Law Institute. Reprinted with permission of The American Law Institute.

Elhauge, Defining Better Monopolization Standards. A full version of this work previously appeared in the *Stanford Law Review* at 56 Stan. L. Rev. 253 (2003). When possible and appropriate, please cite to that version.

Elhauge, Why Above-Cost Price Cuts to Drive out Entrants Do Not Signal Predation or Even Market Power—and the Implications for Defining Costs. This excerpt is derived from an Article previously published in *The Yale Law Journal*. See 112 Yale Law Journal 681 (2003).

Damien Geradin and Nicolas Petit, Price Discrimination under EC Law: Another Doctrine in Search of Limiting Principles. This excerpt is derived from an Article previously published in *The Journal of Competition Law and Economics*. 2 J. Competition L. & Econ. 479 (2005).

Damien Geradin and Nicolas Petit, Article 230 EC annulment proceedings against competition law decisions in the light of the "modernisation" process. This excerpt is derived from an Article previously published in Barry Hawk, Ed., International Antitrust Law & Policy: Fordham Corporate Law 2005.

Damien Geradin and Michel Kerf, "Levelling the Playing Field: Is the World Trade Organization Adequately Equipped to Prevent Anti Competitive Practices in Telecommunications?". This excerpt is derived from an Article previously published D. Geradin and D. Luff, Eds., The WTO and Global Convergence in Telecommunications and Audio Visual Services 130 62 (Cambridge University Press 2004).

Einer Elhauge would like to thank his wife Julia, and his children Dash, Kristina, and Nicholas, for their love and patience while this book took precious time away from them. He would also like to thank all the research and administrative assistants who provided so much help in the preparation of this book, especially in researching antitrust laws outside the US and EU.

Damien Geradin would like to thank his wife Mercedes and his daughters Ana and Emma for their love and unquestioning patience and support during the writing of this book. He would also like to thank his colleague Nicolas Petit for his invaluable research assistance.

SUMMARY OF CONTENTS

CHAPTER 8   Markets That Span Multiple Antitrust Regimes 1137

TABLE OF CONTENTS

TABLE OF CASES

Principal cases are in bold type. Non-principal cases are in roman type. References are to Pages.

GLOBAL ANTITRUST LAW AND ECONOMICS

CHAPTER 1

INTRODUCTION

A. THE FRAMEWORK OF LEGAL ISSUES RAISED BY BASIC ANTITRUST ECONOMICS

How the Basic Economics Explains the Core Legal Concerns. In a world of perfect competition, life is good. Firms can enter and exit markets instantly and without cost, products are homogeneous, and everyone is perfectly informed. Firms are so numerous that none of them is large enough to influence prices by altering output and all act independently. Supplier competition for sales thus drives prices for products and services down to the costs of providing them. (Costs here should be understood to include capital and risk-bearing costs, and thus incorporates a normal profit that reflects the capital market rate of return necessary to induce investment in firms given the risk level.) Any firm that tried to charge more than costs would be undercut by another firm that would charge less because they would gain sales whose revenue exceeded costs. Lower cost producers would thus underprice and displace higher cost producers. Their output would be purchased whenever market buyers found that the value of the product to them exceeded its price/cost but not otherwise.

If demand increased or costs decreased so that suppliers would earn supranormal profits if their output remained constant, then the existence or prospect of those supranormal profits would induce supplier expansion or entry, increasing supply until it drove prices back down toward costs. If demand decreased or costs increased so that suppliers would earn sub-standard profits if their output remained constant, then they would con-tract or exit the market, shifting any moveable capital to more profitable ventures and reducing supply until prices rise to meet costs. The nice result is to allocate societal resources towards those markets where they can best provide value to buyers. Even nicer, it does not have to be the case that suppliers are omniscient, or even know what they're doing—the market will winnow out those who guess wrong regardless.

In the real world, life is regrettably imperfect. Entry, exit or expansion are costly and take time. Products vary by brand or attributes and information is imperfect. Economies of scale mean many markets cannot sustain a large enough number of firms to leave each without any incentive to consider the effect of its decisions on market prices. But despite such unavoidable realities, typical markets are workably competitive in the sense that they produce results that are fairly close to perfect competition, at least in the long run. In any event, perfect competition provides an aspiration and useful benchmark that helps identify the sort of interfer-ences with market mechanisms that should most concern antitrust law. The economic literature analyzing such issues can be frightfully complicat-

1

ed and mystifying. Luckily the essential regulatory issues flow in a simple straightforward way from the basics outlined above.

The first major concern is that firms might agree to avoid competing with each other, thus elevating prices above cost and increasing their profits to supracompetitive levels. Price-fixing agreements among competitors is a classic example. Similar results can be obtained by agreements to restrict output or divide markets or impede entry. The legal responses to such concerns about agreements to restrict competition will occupy us in Chapter 2.

A second concern is that one firm might individually be large enough to raise prices by reducing output. In the pure case of monopoly, there is only one firm and entry is impossible. Such a monopolist need not worry that, if it raises prices, it will lose business to rivals. Instead, it has incentives to raise prices above costs, up to the point that the extra profits earned from the customers willing to pay the higher price are offset by the profits lost from diminished sales to other customers who aren't willing to pay that price. The result is higher prices, lower output, and many customers who inefficiently do not get the product even though they value it more than it costs to provide. A single buyer, called a monopsonist, raises the parallel problem that it has incentives to suppress prices below competitive levels, which suppresses output from suppliers.

True monopolists are rare. More typical is what economists call a dominant firm, which is a firm that is much larger than the other firms because it has lower costs or a better product. A dominant firm also has incentives to price above cost, but is somewhat constrained by the ability of the other firms to offer the product at their costs. The dominant firm faces what is called the residual demand that results when one subtracts from total market demand the output that the other less efficient firms provide at any given price. The dominant firm effectively faces no competition for this residual demand, and thus has similar incentives to a monopolist to increase prices above its costs. A similar result follows even if rivals are not less efficient but would have difficulty expanding or entering in response to an increase in prices.

The mere possession of monopoly or dominant power need not, however, be a concern. If a firm makes a better mousetrap, and the world beats a path to its door, it may drive out all rivals and establish a monopoly; but that is a good result, not a bad one. Dominant market power normally reflects the fact that a firm is more efficient because of some cost or quality advantage over its rivals. If a firm has acquired that efficiency advantage through productive investments in innovation, physical capital, or organization, then the additional profits it is able to earn might reasonably be thought to provide the right reward for that investment, especially since any price premium it charges cannot exceed its efficiency advantage over other prevailing market options.

Typically the antitrust laws are instead focused on anticompetitive conduct that is used to obtain or maintain monopoly or dominant market power at levels that were not earned through productive efforts. A dominant firm has incentives to use anticompetitive conduct to exclude rivals from the market, impair rival efficiency, or impede the sort of rival expansion and entry that would drive down prices toward more competitive levels. So does a firm that, while not yet dominant, thinks such anticompetitive conduct will help it obtain dominance. Because a firm that obtains or maintains monopoly or dominant market power can exploit it unilaterally, it also has incentives to engage in such anticompetitive conduct unilaterally, rather than requiring agreement or coordination with rivals. Chapter 3 will address how the law seeks to identify such unilateral anticompetitive conduct and distinguish it from procompetitive unilateral conduct.

Firms with market power might likewise have incentives to enter into agreements with suppliers or buyers to try to exclude rivals, diminish their efficiency, or impede their expansion or entry. Because these agreements are up or down the supply chain, they are generally called "vertical" agreements, in contrast to the "horizontal" agreements entered into by rivals at the same level. They thus involve concerted action but also involve firms who use such vertical agreements to obtain or maintain single firm market power. Chapter 4 addresses these sets of cases.

Firms might also engage in unilateral conduct or vertical agreements that antitrust law fears will impede competition among downstream firms. One form of unilateral conduct that some laws seek to condemn on this score is price discrimination among buyers that distorts their ability to compete downstream. Similar concerns have been raised about vertical agreements to restrain resale by buyers, including agreements to fix the prices that distributors can charge downstream, or to limit where or to whom they can sell. As we will see, legal liability for such conduct or agreements has been the subject of strong economic critique, based mainly on the observation that firms typically have little incentive to impede competition among downstream firms. Such issues will be addressed in Chapter 5.

Chapter 6 then addresses how to prove the existence of an agreement, and addressed a third concern: that some markets have few enough firms that each has an influence on prices and output. and can notice and respond to the actions of each other. If so, then even without an explicit agreement, such firms may be able to coordinate to restrict output and raise prices. This is called oligopolistic coordination. The big difficulty this raises is whether such coordination can be condemned without proof of an agreement, especially when oligopolistic firms cannot avoid knowing that their pricing and output decisions will affect the behavior of other firms.

The final major concern, addressed in Chapter 7, is that rivals might merge or combine into one firm. Horizontal mergers can have anticompetitive effects if the resulting firm has monopoly or dominant market power, or the structure of the rest of the market means the merger will create an oligopoly or exacerbate its ability to coordinate on higher prices. The difficulty is determining when this is the effect of a merger and whether the merger is justified by any greater efficiencies it might create. Vertical mergers between firms up and down the supply chain raise issues similar to vertical agreements that might exclude or impair rival competition. Mergers between firms that are not related horizontally or vertically are called conglomerate mergers, which raise issues if they eliminate potential horizontal competition or enable the merged firm to engage in anticompetitive exclusionary conduct.

In addressing all the above issues, antitrust courts and regulators must also face the problem that many markets span multiple antitrust regimes. In particular, on global markets, firms are subject to regulation under U.S. and EU antitrust law. As we shall see throughout the book, those laws often vary significantly from each other and from antitrust regulation in other nations, which offers a useful lens for analyzing the relevant issues. But when should a nation regulate conduct that either occurs or has effects extraterritorially, and what does one do about the international conflicts in antitrust regimes that result when multiple nations seek to regulate the same conduct? Further, what does one do with conduct that anticompetitively harms markets (typically outside the U.S. and EU) in a way that no individual antitrust authority has strong incentives to pursue? Chapter 8 addresses those topics.

Graphing the Basic Economics. The prior section explains the basic relevant economics using simple words. But some might find graphical depictions more helpful. In a competitive market, the situation is represented by Figure 1. The X-axis indicates the market quantity Q. The Y-axis indicates the market price P. The line marked D is the demand curve, which indicates what quantity buyers would demand at each price. As price (P) goes up, the quantity demanded (Q) goes down because making a product more expensive means fewer buyers will find the value of the product worth the price. That is why the demand curve goes down. The line marked MC indicates the marginal cost of production. It generally increases as quantity goes up, mainly because increasing market quantity generally requires bidding away resources from other markets or because seller's plants are operating at output levels where their marginal costs of operation would increase if they made more. The MC curve is also the same as the supply curve, S, which indicates the quantity the market would supply at each price, because in a competitive market suppliers should be willing to supply output at any price that exceeds their marginal cost. If they didn't, then a rival seller would take away the sale at any P > MC because that would be more profitable to the rival than losing that sale.

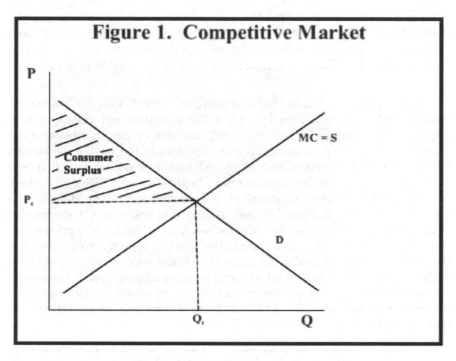

Figure 1. Competitive Market

The intersection of the demand and supply curves is the competitive market equilibrium, where buyer willingness to pay matches supplier willingness to provide, and P_c and Q_c are, respectively, the competitive market price and quantity. If the price dipped below P_c, then quantity supplied would dip below Q_c but that would leave some buyer demand unsatisfied because some buyers are willing to pay a higher price, and thus they would bid up the price until it reached P_c again. If a supplier tried to charge above P_c then the quantity demanded would go below Q_c, but that would leave an opportunity for a rival seller to win sales by charging a lower price. Thus rival sellers would bid down the price until it reached P_c again.

This competitive market equilibrium has many wonderful features. Goods are never provided to buyers if the marginal cost of doing so exceeds the value buyers would put on it, as indicated by buyer willingness to pay. Goods are provided whenever buyer valuation does exceed marginal cost. If demand increases (such as if rainy weather increases the need for umbrellas), then the demand curve will shift to the right (at each price, more quantity demanded), but then a new equilibrium arises, with a higher P_c and Q_c, that again provides the good whenever buyer valuation exceeds market cost. If costs increase (such as if increased metal costs make it more expensive to make umbrellas), then the supply curve will go up, resulting in a higher P_c and lower Q_c, but again the product will be supplied whenever buyer valuation exceeds the new marginal cost. And the whole thing works in reverse if market demand or costs decrease.

Further, only the marginal buyer (the buyer on the demand curve whose willingness to pay just equals P_c) pays a price that equals her valuation of the product. All the inframarginal buyers (buyers on the demand curve to the left of Q_c) value the product more highly than P_c, and thus enjoy a consumer surplus that reflects the difference between their valuation and P_c. The total consumer surplus is the shaded area in Figure 1.

Now suppose that instead of a competitive market, we have a monopoly market with only one supplier. Then the situation will instead reflect Figure 2. The monopolist will not simply increase its output whenever the market price exceeds its marginal cost. The reason is that the monopolist knows that if it increases output to sell to the marginal buyer, it will decrease prices to all its inframarginal buyers as well. Thus, for every increased unit of output, its marginal revenue, marked by the MR curve, is lower than the market price because selling that unit gains it the market price on the marginal unit, but also causes it to suffer a lower price on all the inframarginal units. (In a competitive market, sellers ignore this effect because the inframarginal units are sold to other sellers.) Thus, instead of setting its market output at where price equals marginal cost, a monopolist will maximize profits by setting its market output at where price equals its marginal revenue, or at Q_m. At this subcompetitive level of output, market demand will lead to a supracompetitive price, P_m.

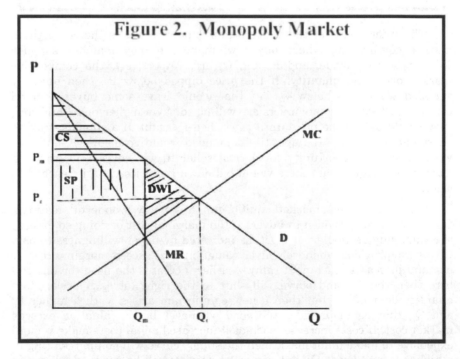

Figure 2. Monopoly Market

At this monopoly price there will be an allocative inefficiency, called a dead weight loss, which is marked DWL on the graph. This reflects the fact that many buyers who value the product more than it would cost to make it (all the buyers on the demand curve between Q_m and Q_c) would not get it. It is called an allocative inefficiency because it reflects an inefficient allocation of resources. The supracompetitive profits would equal the quantity produced (Q_m) times the difference between P_m and P_c, which is represented by the box marked SP. The consumer surplus would be reduced to the area marked CS on the graph. Thus, the monopoly pricing would both be inefficient and reduce consumer welfare.

In a cartel, rivals agree to make decisions about price or output together, and thus collectively act like a monopolist, maximizing their profits by agreeing to fix a price above the competitive level, or by agreeing to fix an output below the competitive level. Either strategy amounts to the same thing. Both strategies require the cartel members to reach some sort of understanding about how to allocate the market quantity among the various rivals, because all of the sales earn supracompetitive profits and thus every rival will want them.

A dominant firm prices in a way similar to a monopolist, but against a residual demand curve. Suppose, for example, a firm enjoys dominant market power because the rest of the market is capacity-constrained; rivals are making as much as they can and cannot make any more. Then the situation can be illustrated by Figure 3. D_{mkt} indicates overall market demand. At any price, the dominant firm knows that its rivals can produce no more than their capacity cap, marked as Q_{riv}. Thus, the dominant firm faces the residual demand curve, marked D_{res}. Against that residual demand curve, the dominant firm will price just like a monopolist, producing price and quantity P_{dom} and Q_{dom}. If rivals' ability to expand output is not totally blocked, but is limited so that they are more willing to expand supply at higher prices, then Q_{riv} will get larger at higher prices. This will make the residual demand curve flatter, but will not eliminate it unless rivals' supply is perfectly elastic—that is, unless rivals can expand instantly to supply the whole market if prices go above competitive levels. A firm can have such market power even if it does not have a huge share of the market if rival ability to expand output is sufficiently limited.

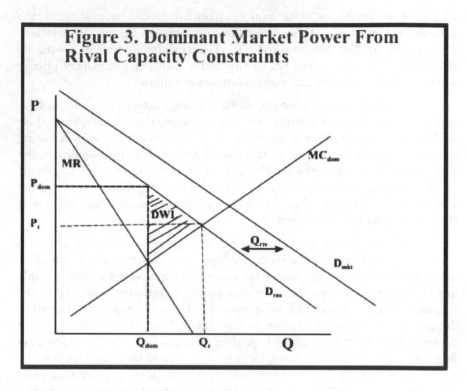

Figure 3. Dominant Market Power From Rival Capacity Constraints

The situation is a bit more complicated, but similar, where a dominant firm enjoys market power because it is more efficient than its rivals. Suppose a dominant firm has marginal costs that are lower than its rivals. Then the situation can be described by Figure 4. We can ascertain the residual demand curve faced by the dominant firm by asking what quantity its rivals would supply at each price given their higher costs, and then subtracting that quantity from the market demand. For example, at price P_A, rivals operating at marginal cost will make enough output to satisfy all market demand, leaving the dominant firm with zero residual demand. At price P_B, rivals will make zero output, so that residual demand equals the entire market demand at that price, or Q_B. For any price between P_A and P_B, the residual demand available to the dominant firm is the line that connects point $(P_A, 0)$ and point (P_B, Q_B). The residual demand at each price reflects the difference between the quantity rivals will supply at that price and the quantity the market would demand at that price, which is the difference between MC_{riv} and D_{mkt}, marked as $\longleftrightarrow$ on the graph. Against that residual demand curve, the dominant firm prices just like a monopolist. Again, a firm can have such market power even if it does not have a huge market share.

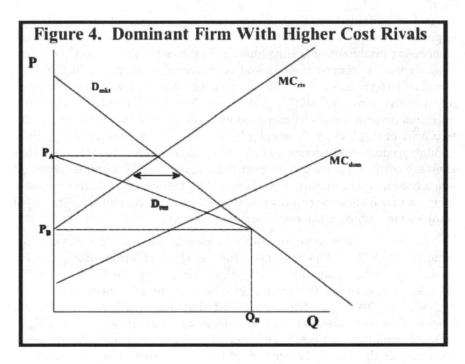

Figure 4. Dominant Firm With Higher Cost Rivals

Mere possession of monopoly or market power is not a concern because it may merely indicate the fruits of investment in building more capacity or becoming more efficient than rivals. If a firm lowers its marginal costs, it is said to increase its productive efficiency, and such an increase in productive efficiency can offset any reduction in allocative efficiency. Indeed, in the above cases, buyers are clearly better off if the dominant firm exists or has lower costs, than if it did not, because if it did not then prices would be higher and quantity lower. However, agreements that create cartels that have monopoly or market power are a concern because they create no offsetting efficiencies. Likewise, anticompetitive conduct that restricts rival competitiveness, by limiting their ability to expand output or by raising rival costs, can enhance monopoly or market power without offsetting efficiencies and thus are also an anticompetitive concern.

If there are not many firms, they may be able to coordinate on prices that are above competitive levels without reaching an actual agreement. Such coordination can achieve results similar to monopoly or dominant firm pricing if the coordinating firms collectively have monopoly or market power. Mergers are often condemned because they make such coordination possible or easier. Mergers may also be condemned because they create a firm that will enjoy unilateral market power or because they make it easier for the merged firm to engage in anticompetitive conduct that impairs rival efficiency.

However, mergers and other conduct may create both productive efficiencies and allocative inefficiencies, and sometimes the former might offset the latter. Consider Figure 5. Suppose that before a merger (or some alleged misconduct), a firm is constrained to price at marginal cost, depicted as MC_{pre}. The merger (or conduct) both lowers its marginal costs (increasing productive efficiency) and gives it market power, so it now acts as a monopolist against the demand curve, creating allocative inefficiency. Consider two cases. In case 1, the merger (or conduct) lowers marginal cost all the way down to MC_{post1}. The firm then sets output at where its marginal revenue equals its marginal costs, meaning at Q_{post1}, which results in a price of P_{post1}, which is actually lower than the initial price of P_{pre}. Here enough productive efficiency was passed on to consumers that they are that they are better off after the conduct than before, and the firm is better off since it earns higher profits than before. The merger (or conduct) in case 1 increased both consumer welfare and producer welfare, and thus increased total welfare, which is the combination of the two.

In case 2, the merger (or conduct) lowers marginal cost down somewhat less, to MC_{post2}. The firm then produces Q_{post2}, at a price of P_{post2}, which is actually higher than the initial price of P_{pre}. Now we have conflicting effects. Compared to the initial situation, there is a deadweight loss, indicated by DWL_{post2}, reflecting the fact that output is lower than it was before. However, there is also an efficiency gain, indicated by EG_{post2}, reflecting the fact that costs are lower. If, as here the size of the efficiency gain exceeds the size of the dead weight loss, then there is a net increase in efficiency and total welfare. However, consumer welfare has decreased, not only because of the deadweight loss, but also because buyers pay a higher price on the output they still buy. However, the firm gains both the latter higher prices and the efficiency gain, so the increase to producer welfare exceeds the loss to consumer welfare. Thus, conduct might simultaneously decrease consumer welfare and increase total welfare, raising the issue of which to favor. As we shall see, so far antitrust law generally favors a consumer welfare standard, perhaps on the notion that producers could always convert a total welfare gain into a consumer welfare gain by transferring some of their increased profits back to consumers. But the issue remains controversial, particularly for mergers of firms that mainly export to other nations.

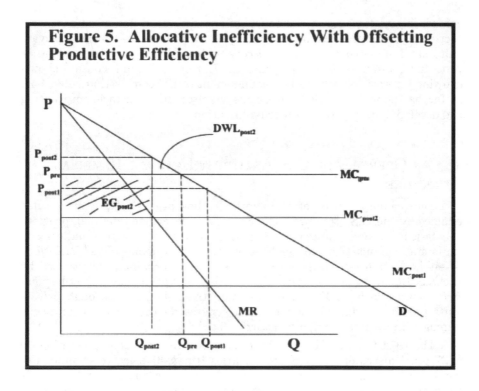

Figure 5. Allocative Inefficiency With Offsetting Productive Efficiency

B. THE REMEDIAL STRUCTURE

Understanding all the above issues requires some understanding of the basic remedial structure of U.S. and EU law. Indeed, one recurring issue throughout this book is whether differences in remedies between the United States and Europe suggest the desirability of having different substantive rules about which conduct merits a remedy. While more detail follows below, the basic differences between the U.S. and EU can be plainly stated.

In the U.S., the basic antitrust laws are enforced not only by governmental actions for injunctive relief, but by criminal penalties and by private suits brought by injured parties (or by states on their behalf) for treble damages, injunctive relief, and attorney fees. The exception is the Federal Trade Commission Act, which is enforceable only through injunctive relief in cases brought by the Federal Trade Commission (FTC) and subject to judicial approval. Most U.S. antitrust cases are brought by private parties seeking damages rather than by centralized government agencies.

In the EU, in contrast, virtually all enforcement is done by the European Commission (or national competition agencies) in a way roughly analogous to the Federal Trade Commission in the United States. EU competition law does not provide for criminal sanctions, although the competition laws of some of the Member States, such as the United Kingdom, contain criminal penalties. Although in theory any violation of EU competition law would also be subject to a private suit for (untrebled) compensatory damages in the courts of any European nation on a general tort theory, as a practical matter this option is seldom used because private suits are hampered by lack of discovery, fee-shifting statutes and other procedural obstacles. In recent years, the European Commission has shown growing interest for private law enforcement of EU competition rules, but, so far, has done very little to overcome the procedural obstacles preventing the development of private antitrust litigation.

1. AN OVERVIEW OF U.S. ANTITRUST LAWS AND REMEDIAL STRUCTURE

The primary source of U.S. antitrust law are a handful of statutes enacted by the U.S. Congress. The Sherman Act, enacted in 1890, provides the basic laws condemning (in § 1) anticompetitive agreements and (in § 2) unilateral conduct that monopolizes or attempts to monopolize.[1] Violations of either section constitute a felony that can be criminally prosecuted by the U.S. Department of Justice (DOJ). Other provisions make the Sherman Act enforceable by DOJ actions for injunctive relief, and through private suits brought by injured parties (or by states on their behalf) for treble damages, injunctive relief, and attorney fees.[2]

The 1914 Clayton Act added more specific antitrust laws governing (in § 2) price discrimination in commodities, (in § 3) sales of commodities conditioned on the buyer not dealing with the seller's rivals, and (in §§ 7–8) mergers and interlocking directorates. Clayton Act § 3 remains in its original form, but the provision on price discrimination was amended in 1936 by the Robinson–Patman Act, and the provision on mergers was amended in 1950 by the Celler–Kefauver Act and supplemented in 1976 by the Hart–Scott–Rodino Act which provides for pre-merger notification to U.S. enforcement agencies.[3] These Clayton Act provisions are not enforceable by criminal penalties, but are otherwise enforceable by the DOJ and private suits in the same way as the Sherman Act.[4] They are also enforceable through prospective cease-or-desist orders by the FTC, unless the conduct occurs in an industry regulated by a special federal agency, in which case the special agency has that authority.[5]

The 1914 Congress also enacted FTC Act § 5, which generally prohibits all "unfair methods of competition."[6] (This provision also prohibits unfair or deceptive practices, which are addressed by a separate consumer protection branch of the FTC.) The vagueness of the "unfair" language has

---

1. *See* 15 U.S.C. §§ 1–2.

2. *See* 15 U.S.C. §§ 4, 12, 15–15c, 25–26.

3. *See* 15 U.S.C. §§ 13–14, 18–19.

4. *See* 15 U.S.C. §§ 12, 15–15c, 25–26. Robinson–Patman Act § 3 imposes criminal penalties up to $5000 and a year in prison for knowingly price discriminating with an anticompetitive purpose, *see* 15 U.S.C. § 13a, but this provision is seldom enforced.

5. *See* 15 U.S.C. § 21. The special agencies are the Federal Communications Commission, the Federal Reserve Board, the Department of Transportation and the Surface Transportation Board. *Id.*

6. *See* 15 U.S.C. § 45(a).

been cabined by a 1994 amendment, which provides that the FTC cannot deem conduct "unfair unless the act or practice causes or is likely to cause substantial injury to consumers which is not reasonably avoidable by consumers themselves and not outweighed by countervailing benefits to consumers or to competition."[7] The FTC Act is not enforceable by private suits, nor by the DOJ, nor by any retroactive penalties.[8] Instead, it is enforceable only by the FTC itself, whose only remedy is to issue a prospective order to cease and desist the activity, which is in turn subject to review by the federal courts of appeals.[9] The FTC can also go to court to seek a preliminary injunction pending a final resolution by itself and the courts.[10] Although the FTC may have authority to adopt prospective rules defining the conduct it regards as an unfair method of competition, it has not exercised such authority as a matter of practice.[11]

The FTC does not have jurisdiction to enforce Sherman Act violations, *see* 15 U.S.C. § 21, but this is of little practical importance in cases seeking injunctive relief because anything that violates the Sherman Act could also be deemed an unfair method of competition actionable under FTC Act

---

7. 15 U.S.C. § 45(n).

8. *See* 15 U.S.C. § 12 (defining "antitrust laws" enforceable in those ways to exclude the FTC Act); 15 U.S.C. § 56(a) (vesting the FTC with exclusive enforcement authority over the FTC Act with limited exceptions).

9. *See* 15 U.S.C. § 45.

10. 15 U.S.C. § 53(b).

11. The legal issue is surprisingly unsettled. Before 1973, it was seriously doubted that the FTC Act gave the FTC authority to issues substantive rules. *See* K. Davis, Administrative Law Text 130 (3d ed. 1972); Marinelli, *The Federal Trade Commission's Authority to Determine Unfair Practices and Engage in Substantive Rulemaking*, 2 Ohio N.U.L. Rev. 289, 295–96 & n.75 (1974). Then, in National Petroleum Refiners Ass'n v. FTC, 482 F.2d 672, 673–78 (D.C.Cir. 1973), Judge Skelly Wright interpreted 15 U.S.C. § 46(g) to give the FTC authority to adopt substantive rules defining "unfair methods of competition" and "unfair and deceptive trade practices." But that was a debatable interpretation because § 46(g) could be read to just authorize creating procedural rules for carrying out the FTC's cease and desist powers. It was also dicta as applied to rules defining "unfair methods of competition" because the case was actually about a rule defining an "unfair and deceptive trade practice," namely the failure to disclose octane levels on gas pumps. The House initially passed a bill that said the FTC had authority to enact rules defining deceptive trade practices but not unfair methods of competition; however, the House compromised with the Senate on a statute that did the former but did not purport to alter whether or not authority existed to enact rules defining unfair methods of competition. *See* 15 U.S.C. § 57a(2); H.R. Rep. No. 1107, 93d Cong., 2d Sess. 49–50 (1974), reprinted in 4 U.S. Code Cong. & Ad. News 7702, 7727 (1974); S. Rep. No. 1408, 93d Cong., 2d Sess. 32 (1974) (conference report), reprinted in 4 U.S. Code Cong. & Ad. News 7755, 7764 (1974). Thus, it appears there were insufficient legislative votes for either the proposition that the FTC could enact rules defining anticompetitive practices or the proposition that it could not. The FTC rules on its rulemaking procedure seem to carefully limit its rulemaking to deceptive practices (Rule 1.7) or special areas where it has express statutory authority to adopt rules, such as defining whether certain conduct constitutes illegal price discrimination (Rule 1.23–1.24) unless the reference in Rule 1.2.1 to "unlawful trade practices" is intended to cut more broadly. The only substantive rule related to competition that the FTC ever enacted was pursuant to its special authority to define price discrimination under 15 U.S.C. § 13(a), and has since been rescinded. *See* 58 Fed. Reg. 35907–01. The FTC does not appear to have adopted any substantive rule that purported to define "unfair methods of competition" that were not deceptive nor any procedural rule that claims general authority to enact rules defining "unfair methods of competition" that are not deceptive.

§ 5.[12] Thus, the DOJ and FTC effectively have concurrent jurisdiction over most industries when seeking injunctive relief. However, especially for mergers, they have adopted a practice of informally dividing their jurisdiction by concentrating on different industries, though an effort to adopt a written agreement that would more precisely define this division was withdrawn in the face of Congressional opposition.[13]

Federal courts have exclusive jurisdiction over federal antitrust claims.[14] Antitrust cases brought by anyone other than the FTC (or special agency) are brought in the U.S. federal district courts for a trial to adjudicate the facts and determine the relevant law,[15] and citations to their opinions are marked "F. Supp." Appeals from decisions of the district courts are generally first brought to the U.S. Courts of Appeals (noted "F.2d" or "F.3d" in citations), which are often called the circuit courts because there is a different one for each region of the country. Most are numbered (e.g., "1st Cir." is New England, "9th Cir." comprises certain West Coast states) except for the D.C. Circuit, which sits in Washington, D.C. and tends to handle appeals from federal agency decisions. Appeals are on questions of law, though this can include such legal questions as whether there was sufficient evidence to support the factual findings and whether those findings suffice to meet the legal standard. Losing parties can then seek review before the U.S. Supreme Court (marked "U.S." in citations), but although that Court was formerly obligated to take any appeal that presented a "substantial" federal question, it now has discretion to decide when to take a case (called taking "certiorari"), which it generally does only when the circuit courts are split on an important relevant legal issue.[16]

In addition, many states have their own antitrust statutes. These statutes tend to be less vigorously enforced, in part because they generally borrow U.S. antitrust standards and are usually brought as ancillary claims to U.S. antitrust claims that can be brought only in federal court. Plus, state antitrust enforcement is usually left to the understaffed offices of state attorneys general. However, state antitrust law is free to prohibit

---

12. *See* FTC v. Cement Institute, 333 U.S. 683, 689–95 (1948).

13. *See* Baer, Feinstein & Shaheen, *Taking Stock: Recent Trends in U.S. Merger Enforcement*, 18 ANTITRUST 15, 20–21 (Spring 2004).

14. *See* Marrese v. American Academy of Orthopaedic Surgeons, 470 U.S. 373, 379 (1985).

15. At the FTC, the general procedure is instead (1) the five commissioners issue a complaint, (2) that complaint is adjudicated by an administrative law judge (ALJ) within the FTC, (3) that ALJ decision is appealed to the five commissioners who decide whether to issue the cease and desist order, and (4) that FTC decision is appealed directly to the Courts of Appeal, and from there to the Supreme Court where appropriate. *See* 15 U.S.C. §§ 21, 45. The exception is that the FTC must bring a claim for a preliminary injunction to a federal district court, 15 U.S.C. § 53(b), which generally must be done in merger cases to prevent the merger from occurring. At any step along the way, the FTC (like the DOJ) can instead settle with the parties and enter into a consent decree limiting their conduct or merger in some way, which is in fact how the bulk of cases are ultimately handled.

16. Historically, there were special statutes that provided for antitrust trials by 3 judge district courts and direct appeal to the U.S. Supreme Court, which was true in some of the cases in this book. But today direct appeal from district court to the U.S. Supreme Court is exceedingly rare, though possible in extreme cases. *See* 15 U.S.C. § 29.

conduct that federal antitrust law allows,[17] and in the rare cases where it does so, it can have important effects. And occasionally the state attorneys general indicate a willingness to pursue a case beyond where the federal authorities think is appropriate even under the same antitrust standards, as happened in the Microsoft case where some states did not agree to the U.S.'s settlement and thus continued to pursue the states' claims.

i. Criminal Penalties. The criminal penalties for violating the Sherman Act have changed over time, and currently provide for punishment "by fine not exceeding $100,000,000 if a corporation, or, if any other person, $1,000,000, or by imprisonment not exceeding 10 years, or by both said punishments, in the discretion of the court." *See* 15 U.S.C. §§ 1–2. In addition, general U.S. criminal law allows for an alternative fine equal to twice the defendant's pecuniary gain or the victims' pecuniary loss. *See* 15 U.S.C. § 3571(d).

The Supreme Court has held that defendants can be criminally liable even for rule of reason offenses.[18] However, proving a criminal violation of the Sherman Act requires proving a criminal intent (called *mens rea*), which necessitates proof that the conduct either (1) had "anticompetitive effects" and was "undertaken with knowledge of its probable consequences" or (2) had "the purpose of producing anticompetitive effects . . . , even if such effects did not come to pass."[19] Thus, criminal violations require proof either of an anticompetitive intent or of knowledge that anticompetitive effects were probable and in fact ensued. The Supreme Court has explained that the reason for adding these elements in a criminal suit, even though the same elements would not be required in civil suit alleging a violation under the very same statutory language, was the concern that, compared to civil penalties, criminal penalties would produce greater "overdeterrence" of "procompetitive conduct lying close to the borderline of impermissible conduct."[20]

The Department of Justice (DOJ) brings criminal prosecutions, and indeed most of the DOJ's cases are criminal cases. The DOJ Manual generally limits enforcement to conduct that is clearly unlawful, known to be unlawful, intended to suppress competition, or a repeat offense.[21] The DOJ does not limit its enforcement to per se violations, and indictments have even been sustained against agreements that other district courts found legal under the rule of reason.[22] But as a matter of practice, virtually all the criminal prosecutions are for patently per se illegal horizontal agreements like price-fixing between unrelated competitors. These cases thus tend to raise few interesting legal issues in their adjudication. More interesting are the enforcement policy implications arising from the facts that the size of criminal penalties and number of criminal cases have both

---

17.   *See* California v. ARC America Corp., 490 U.S. 93, 104–05 (1989).

18.   See Nash v. United States, 229 U.S. 373, 376–78 (1913).

19.   United States v. United States Gypsum, 438 U.S. 422, 444 & n.21 (1978).

20.   *Id.* at 441.

21.   II PHILLIP E. AREEDA, ROGER D. BLAIR, & HERBERT HOVENKAMP, ANTITRUST LAW ¶ 303, at 29 (2d ed. 2000).

22.   See *id.* at 29–30 & n.9.

increased over time, that these cases are increasingly focused on foreign-based conspirators, and that the DOJ has had increasing success by offering leniency to the first conspirator who reveals the conspiracy or implicates the other conspirators.

ii.   Treble Damages. The most distinctive feature of U.S. antitrust enforcement is that it provides actions for treble damages that mean government enforcement is supplemented, and in many areas dominated, by private suits. "[A]ny person who shall be injured in his business or property by reason of anything forbidden in the antitrust laws" can sue the violator for three times their damages plus litigation costs, including reasonable attorney fees.[23] The requirement of an injury to "business or property" excludes claims for physical injury but includes any claim of monetary injury.[24] If a court concludes the defendant has improperly delayed the antitrust suit, it can also award interest covering the period from the time the plaintiff filed suit to the time of judgment.[25]

Treble damages often sound excessive because, at first cut, single damages should be adequate to deter any conduct whose harm exceeds its benefits. However, in fact treble damages are not as draconian as they sound because they are reduced by the fact that: (a) plaintiffs cannot collect pre-suit interest and usually cannot collect prejudgment interest, (b) plaintiffs have difficulty proving harm from the fact that the anticompetitive overcharge caused them not to buy the product at all (that is, the deadweight loss triangle usually cannot be collected), and (c) in many courts, plaintiffs cannot recover damages for the harmful umbrella effect an overcharge causes by increasing the prices of rivals or substitutes. It has been calculated that the combination of these three factors reduces treble damages to single damages on average.[26] Further, single damages are likely to underdeter anticompetitive conduct because it is often difficult to detect or prove. Some conduct (like a cartel) is hard to detect, but once detected is easy to prove to be anticompetitive. Other conduct may be easier to detect, but harder to prove it is anticompetitive, such as a tie of some computer software to other software. High litigation costs may also deter many claims. Because expected damages will be the actual damages times the odds of detection and adjudicated punishment, they may well be less than the gains of conduct that inflicts greater costs than benefits.

Damage claims can be brought not only by private parties but by governments injured in their own "business or property," though foreign governments are limited to single damages unless they themselves were not eligible for foreign sovereign immunity from antitrust claims because they

---

23. *See* 15 U.S.C. § 15. "Antitrust laws" are defined to include the Sherman and Clayton Acts (as amended by later acts) but not the FTC Act or Robinson–Patman Act § 3. *See* 15 U.S.C. § 12; Nashville Milk v. Carnation Co., 355 U.S. 373, 378–79 (1958). The former is enforceable just by injunctive claims by the FTC and the latter just by criminal actions by the DOJ, which are rarely brought.

24. Reiter v. Sonotone Corp., 442 U.S. 330, 339 (1979).

25. *See* 15 U.S.C. § 15.

26. *See* Robert H. Lande, *Five Myths About Antitrust Damages,* 40 U.S.F. L. Rev. 651 (2006).

were engaged in commercial activities.[27] In addition, states can bring a treble damages action on behalf of its residents (called a "parens patriae" action) for monetary injuries they suffered from a Sherman Act violation, unless those residents opt out of such litigation.[28] In such a parens patriae case, the district court can either distribute the damages to the injured parties or deem the damages a civil penalty and deposit them in the state treasury.[29] Few parens patriae are in fact brought, which probably reflects not only the uncertainty of gain to the state treasury but also a provision that makes the state liable for the defendant's attorney fees if the court determines the action was in bad faith.[30]

To prove damages, a party must show: (1) that the antitrust violation was a material but-for cause of its injury; (2) that its injury flowed from the anticompetitive effects of the violation; (3) that the link between the violation and injury was sufficiently direct or proximate; and (4) the amount of damages it suffered from the injury.

(1) Material But–For Causation. Like any plaintiff seeking damages, an antitrust plaintiff must show the violation was the "but-for" cause of its injury. This does not mean the plaintiff must show that the injury definitely would not have occurred but for the violation nor that other factors did not contribute to the likelihood or extent of that injury. The plaintiff need only show the violation was a "material cause" of its injury or "materially contributed" to that injury.[31] Under this standard, "It is therefore enough that the antitrust violation contributes significantly to the plaintiff's injury even if other factors amounted in the aggregate to a more substantial cause."[32] Lower courts have interpreted this to mean that there need only be a "reasonable probability" defendants' antitrust violation caused plaintiffs' injury; plaintiffs "need not rule out 'all possible alternative sources of injury.'"[33] In short, to show but-for material causation, a plaintiff need only show that, but for the violation, the probability or extent of its injury would have been significantly lower. Just what constitutes "significantly lower" is not clear, but it is clear that the violation does not have to be more than 50% responsible for the probability or extent of injury.

---

27. *See* 15 U.S.C. § 15a (authoring federal suits); State of Georgia v. Evans, 316 U.S. 159 (1942) (holding that states are "persons" authorized to sue under the statute); 15 U.S.C. § 15(b) (limiting damage claims of foreign nations).

28. *See* 15 U.S.C. § 15c.

29. *See* 15 U.S.C. § 15e.

30. *See* 15 U.S.C. § 15c(d).

31. Zenith Radio Corp. v. Hazeltine Research, Inc. (Zenith I), 395 U.S. 100, 114 & n.9 (1969) ("It is enough that the illegality is shown to be a material cause of the injury; a plaintiff need not exhaust all possible alternative sources of injury in fulfilling his burden of proving compensable injury."); Continental Ore v. Union Carbide, 370 U.S. 690, 702 (1962) (enough that violation "materially contributed" to the harm).

32. II Areeda et al., *supra* note 21, at ¶ 338a, at 317.

33. Catlin v. Washington Energy Co., 791 F.2d 1343, 1347 (9th Cir.1986); *see also* Virginia Vermiculite, Ltd. v. W.R. Grace & Co.–Conn., 156 F.3d 535, 539 (4th Cir. 1998); Advanced Health–Care Servs., Inc. v. Radford Community Hosp., 910 F.2d 139, 149 (4th Cir. 1990).

Further, a defendant cannot defeat causation by arguing that it *could* have caused the same injury through lawful conduct.[34] Nor can it defeat causation by arguing that others would have chosen to act in the same way absent an anticompetitive restraint that dictated that choice.[35] The basic rationale is twofold. First, where defendants themselves thought they needed to restrain a certain market choice, it is highly likely that their restraint was in fact necessary to prevent that choice because defendants are unlikely to adopt restraints that they think have no purpose or effect. Second, any inquiry into whether defendants and others would have engaged in the same conduct absent a restraint that dictated that conduct involves a highly burdensome and counterfactual inquiry into a state of affairs that never existed. Because it is defendants' own fault that this unrestrained state of affairs did not exist, antitrust courts and plaintiffs should not bear the burden on this hypothetical inquiry.

(2) Antitrust Injury. An antitrust plaintiff seeking damages must also show that its injury constituted *"antitrust* injury, which is to say injury of the type the antitrust laws were intended to prevent and that flows from that which makes defendants' acts unlawful. The injury should reflect the anticompetitive effect either of the violation or of anticompetitive acts made possible by the violation."[36] In short, a plaintiff must allege an injury that results from an anticompetitive aspect of the antitrust violation rather than from a procompetitive aspect of the challenged conduct. The basic point of this requirement is to preclude actions by antitrust plaintiffs that would suffer no injury unless the challenged conduct were actually procompetitive.[37]

Thus, the Supreme Court has twice found no antitrust injury for rivals challenging horizontal mergers because the mergers would hurt the rival only if they *decreased* market prices to more competitive levels.[38] It has also found no antitrust injury for rivals challenging nonpredatory price-fixing or output restrictions (whether horizontal or vertical) because the challenged agreement would benefit the rival if they raised prices and thus could injure the rival only by bringing prices closer to competitive levels.[39] On the other hand, when a rival is an unwilling participant in the conspiracy and is punished or threatened with punishment for deviating from it, then it

---

34. *Virginia Vermiculite,* 156 F.3d at 540; Lee–Moore Oil Co. v. Union Oil Co., 599 F.2d 1299, 1302 (4th Cir.1979); Irvin Indus. v. Goodyear Aerospace Corp., 974 F.2d 241, 245–46 (2d Cir. 1992). *Cf.* In re Cardizem CD Antitrust Litigation, 332 F.3d 896, 914 (6th Cir. 2003) (in Sixth Circuit, defendant can defeat causation by showing that legal conduct *would* have caused the same injury even without any antitrust violation).

35. *See* United Shoe v. United States, 258 U.S. 451, 462 (1922); X Areeda, Elhauge & Hovenkamp, Antitrust Law ¶ 1753c, at 294–96 (1996) (collecting cases).

36. Brunswick Corp. v. Pueblo Bowl–O–Mat, 429 U.S. 477, 489 (1977) (emphasis in original).

37. See Los Angeles Memorial Coliseum v. NFL, 791 F.2d 1356, 1364 (9th Cir. 1986) ("[T]he *Brunswick* standard is satisfied 'on a showing that the injury was caused by a reduction, rather than an increase, in competition flowing from the defendant's acts.' ")

38. *See Brunswick*; Cargill, Inc. v. Monfort of Colorado, Inc., 479 U.S. 104 (1986).

39. Matsushita Electric v. Zenith Radio, 475 U.S. 574, 586 (1986); Atlantic Richfield v. U.S.A Petroleum, 495 U.S. 328 (1990).

does suffer antitrust injury and has standing to sue.[40] Indeed, even a plaintiff that voluntarily agreed to an anticompetitive restraint can bring an antitrust claim, if the plaintiff was injured by the anticompetitive aspects of that restraint or by its enforcement against the plaintiff and if the plaintiff was not equally responsible for the restraint.[41]

This antitrust injury doctrine provides an enormously useful function: it screens out those plaintiffs whose anticompetitive motives make litigation unlikely to benefit consumer welfare. This not only saves litigation costs but also lowers the risk that antitrust courts will mistakenly impose liability that deters procompetitive conduct. Thus, like the *mens rea* requirement in criminal cases, this doctrine is an important part of reducing the overdeterrence of procompetitive conduct that antitrust law inevitably creates given errors or difficulties in distinguishing such conduct from anticompetitive conduct.

(3) Proximate Causation. An antitrust plaintiff seeking damages must also show that its injury was sufficiently direct or proximate. This generally, but not always, precludes antitrust claims by a plaintiff that claims the antitrust violation harmed an intervening party that passed the harm on to it. For example, if an antitrust violation harms a corporation, then its shareholders, employees and creditors cannot bring an antitrust suit. However, the Supreme Court has held that whether it terms an injury "direct" or "indirect" turns not on formalisms, such as whether an intervening party exists but rather on the application of three policy factors.[42] Those factors are: (1) whether a more directly injured party could bring the same cause of action to vindicate the interest in statutory enforcement; (2) whether allowing suit by the indirect party would require complicated apportionment of damages to avoid duplicative damages; and (3) whether indirectness makes the causal inquiry too speculative.[43] The Court interprets these factors to foster, rather than frustrate, enforcement by concentrating the antitrust claim in the hands of the private party with the best incentives to vigorously enforce the statute.[44] The goal is to pick the best plaintiff, not to bar all plaintiffs.

---

40. *See, e.g.,* NCAA v. Board of Regents, 468 U.S. 85 (1984).

41. *See* Perma Life Mufflers v. International Parts Corp., 392 U.S. 134, 138–141 (1968); *id.* at 143–48 (White, J., concurring). Because Justice White was the fifth vote for the Court opinion, his concurring opinions would seem to limit language in the Court opinion that suggested a plaintiff could sue even if it were equally responsible.

42. Associated General Contractors of Cal. v. California State Council of Carpenters, 459 U.S. 519, 536 n.33 (1983) (rejecting the "directness of the injury" test, stating that instead "courts should analyze each situation in light of the factors set forth in the text"); Holmes v. SIPC, 503 U.S. 258, 272 n.20 (1992) (interpreting the antitrust standard for incorporation to RICO cases and concluding, "Thus, our use of the term 'direct' should merely be understood as a reference to the proximate-cause enquiry that is informed by the concerns set out in the text.")

43. *Associated General,* 459 U.S. at 538–45; *Holmes,* 503 U.S. at 269, 273 n.20.

44. *See Associated General,* 459 U.S. at 542 (noting that the Court does not deny standing when that is "likely to leave a significant antitrust violation undetected or unremedied" and inquiring into "existence of an identifiable class of persons whose self-interest would normally motivate them to vindicate the public interest in antitrust enforcement."); Kansas v. UtiliCorp, 497 U.S. 199, 214 (1990) ("our interpretation of [Clayton Act] § 4 must promote the vigorous enforcement of the antitrust laws.").

Thus, in *Associated General Contractors,* the Court denied antitrust standing to unions complaining that (a) the defendants had boycotted landowners and general contractors who used unionized subcontractors, (b) who in turn may (to some extent) have declined to use unionized subcontractors, (c) who in turn may have passed on some (unspecified) harm onto unionized employees, (d) who in turn may have passed on some (unspecified) harm to the unions who were the plaintiffs.[45] The Court concluded that this causal chain was too speculative, rife with possibilities for duplicative or hard to apportion damages, and that more direct plaintiffs existed. On the other hand, the Court stated that the unionized subcontractors allegedly injured at step (b) would have standing even though they were indirectly injured.[46] Why? Because the three factors were met for those plaintiffs. (1) Although more directly injured, the landowners and general contractors would have had little incentive to sue because they could avoid the harm by declining to use unionized subcontractors. (2) The unionized subcontractors' injury of lost business was distinct from the harm to landowners and general contractors of not being able to choose their preferred subcontractors. (3) The causal connection was not unduly speculative, especially since the harm to the unionized subcontractors was clearly intended and foreseeable.

Likewise, *McCready* found antitrust standing for patients complaining that a conspiracy to withhold coverage for psychologist services in the insurance sold to their employers meant that the patients were unable to obtain reimbursement for psychologist services.[47] Why did the patients have standing even though they did not directly purchase from the defendants? Because they met the three policy factors. (1) No more direct party could sue for these damages because only the patients paid the medical bills.[48] (2) There was no difficulty apportioning to avoid duplicative damages since the harm to the patients was distinct from harm to employers or to psychologists, the latter of which could also sue for their separate (also indirect) injury of lost business from other patients who (to avoid losing reimbursement) switched to psychiatrists.[49] (3) Causation was not too speculative (even though the intervening employers could have changed insurers) because the insurance contracts meant the patients' medical costs could be ascertained to the penny.[50]

In *Illinois Brick,* the Supreme Court dealt with a more commonly occurring type of case, a claim that price-fixing injured indirect purchasers because the direct purchasers passed on some of the supracompetitive prices to their downstream customers.[51] The Court concluded that generally the indirect purchasers could not sue, reasoning that the direct purchasers had adequate incentives to sue and that allowing suits by both direct

---

45.   459 U.S. at 538–45.

46.   *Id.* at 541–42.

47.   *See* Blue Shield v. McCready, 457 U.S. 465 (1982).

48.   *Id.* at 475, 483.

49.   *Id.* at 483.

50.   *Id.* at 475 n.11 & 480 n.17.

51.   Illinois Brick v. Illinois, 431 U.S. 720 (1977).

and indirect purchasers would require complicated and difficult inquiries into the extent to which the inflated prices were passed on. Such a complicated and difficult inquiry would increase the evidentiary burdens on plaintiffs and thus discourage statutory enforcement.[52] Thus, it concluded "that the antitrust laws will be more effectively enforced by concentrating the full recovery ... in the direct [party]."[53] In the same decision, the Court recognized that indirect purchasers may have standing if they bought under pre-existing, cost-plus contracts.[54] Why? Because none of the policy factors indicate that the latter sort of indirect claim should be barred if the direct purchaser has a cost-plus contract that fixes quantity. (1) The more direct party has no incentive to sue because the cost-plus contract meant it suffered no injury. (2) The cost-plus contract also eliminates any difficulty in apportioning to avoid duplicative damages. (3) The cost-plus contract further means causation is not at all speculative.[55] On the other hand, when the cost-plus contract does not specify the quantity, then the direct purchaser is given standing instead of the indirect purchaser because supracompetitive prices would harm the direct purchaser by reducing output.[56]

In the wake of *Illinois Brick*, many states enacted "*Illinois Brick* repealer" statutes that authorized indirect purchasers to bring suit under state antitrust law. Indeed, this is the main area where state antitrust law differs significantly from federal antitrust law. In *ARC America*, the Supreme Court held that such statutes are not preempted by federal antitrust law, holding that there is no duplication problem necessitating apportionment where damages under state antitrust law might duplicate federal antitrust damages because there is no "federal policy against states imposing liability in addition to that imposed by federal law."[57]

(4) Proving the Amount of Damages. Proving antitrust damages is often very difficult because it requires comparing what actually happened

---

52. *See id.* at 737 (rejecting apportionment option because "it would add whole new dimensions of complexity to treble-damage suits and seriously undermine their effectiveness"); *id.* at 745–46 (doctrine concentrating claims in most directly injured party supports "the longstanding policy of encouraging vigorous enforcement of the antitrust laws" because they thus are "not only spared the burden of litigating the intricacies of pass-on but also are permitted to recover the full amount of the overcharge"); *id.* at 732 (trying to trace complex economic adjustments through a second market level would "reduce the effectiveness of already protracted treble-damages proceedings"). *See also McCready*, 457 U.S. at 475 n.11 (task of disentangling overlapping damages would "discourage vigorous enforcement of the antitrust laws by private suit"); *Associated General*, 459 U.S. at 545 (agreeing that apportionment must be rejected because it "undermines the effectiveness of treble-damage suits."); *California*, 490 U.S. at 104 ("*Illinois Brick* was concerned that requiring direct and indirect purchasers to apportion the recovery under a single statute—§ 4 of the Clayton Act—would result in no one plaintiff having a sufficient incentive to sue under that statute.")

53. *Illinois Brick v. Illinois*, 431 U.S. at 735.

54. *Id.* at 736.

55. *See also California*, 490 U.S. at 102 n.6 ("*Illinois Brick* ... was concerned ... that at least some party have sufficient incentive to bring suit. Indeed, we implicitly recognized as much in noting that indirect purchasers might be allowed to bring suit in cases in which it would be easy to prove the extent to which the overcharge was passed on to them.").

56. *Utilicorp*, 497 U.S. at 220.

57. *Id.* at 104–05.

to a but-for world that never occurred. Unless we gain the ability to observe parallel universes, courts can never be certain just what would have happened in the but-for world. The U.S. Supreme Court has responded by adopting a "traditional rule excusing antitrust plaintiffs from an unduly rigorous standard of proving antitrust injury."[58] This traditional rule has two elements. First, proof of injury can be more uncertain in an antitrust case than in other cases. This reflects the practical fact that antitrust damages are inherently more difficult to prove because they rest on counterfactual claims about what would have happened in the market absent defendants' restraint of trade.[59] Second, once the plaintiff establishes the *fact* of antitrust damages (that is, material proximate causation) by a preponderance of the evidence, then it can collect damages even though the *amount* of antitrust damages is uncertain.[60] The rationale for this doctrine is that antitrust defendants should not be permitted to profit from the uncertainty created by their own antitrust violations.[61] It suffices that some "reasonable inference" can be made about damages "although the result be only approximate."[62]

In short: "The Court has repeatedly held that in the absence of more precise proof, the factfinder may 'conclude as a matter of just and reasonable inference from the proof of defendants' wrongful acts and their tendency to injure plaintiffs' business, and from the evidence of the decline in prices, profits and values, not shown to be attributable to other causes, that defendants' wrongful acts had caused damage to the plaintiffs.' "[63] In practice, what this typically means is that the antitrust plaintiff first comes

---

58. J. Truett Payne Co. v. Chrysler Motors Corp., 451 U.S. 557, 565 (1981).

59. *J. Truett*, 451 U.S. at 566 ("Our willingness to accept a degree of uncertainty in these cases rests in part on the difficulty of ascertaining business damages as compared, for example, to damages resulting from a personal injury or from condemnation of a parcel of land."); *Zenith I*, 395 U.S. at 123 (damages resulting "from a partial or total exclusion from a market ... are rarely susceptible of the kind of concrete detailed proof of injury which is available in other contexts.")

60. Story Parchment Co. v. Paterson Parchment Paper Co., 282 U.S. 555, 562 (1931) ("there is a clear distinction between the measure of proof necessary to establish the fact that petitioner had sustained some damage, and the measure of proof necessary to enable the jury to fix the amount. The rule which precludes the recovery of uncertain damages applies to such as are not the certain result of the wrong, not to those damages which are definitely attributable to the wrong and only uncertain in respect of their amount.").

61. Bigelow v. RKO Radio Pictures, 327 U.S. 251, 265 (1946) ("The most elementary conceptions of justice and public policy require that the wrongdoer shall bear the risk of the uncertainty which his own wrong has created."); *Story Parchment*, 282 U.S. at 563 ("Where the tort itself is of such a nature as to preclude the ascertainment of the amount of damages with certainty, it would be a perversion of fundamental principles of justice to deny all relief to the injured person, and thereby relieve the wrongdoer from making any amend for his acts"); Eastman Kodak Co. v. Southern Photo Materials Co., 273 U.S. 359, 379 (1927) ("a defendant whose wrongful conduct has rendered difficult the ascertainment of the precise damages suffered by the plaintiff, is not entitled to complain that they cannot be measured with the same exactness and precision as would otherwise be possible."); *J. Truett,*, 451 U.S. at 566 ("Any other rule would enable the wrongdoer to profit by his wrongdoing at the expense of his victim.... [I]t does not 'come with very good grace' for the wrongdoer to insist upon specific and certain proof of the injury which it has itself inflicted."); *Zenith I*, 395 U.S. at 124 (same).

62. *Story Parchment,* 282 U.S. at 563; *J. Truett*, 451 U.S. at 565–66; *Zenith I*, 395 U.S. at 123; *Bigelow*, 327 U.S. at 264.

63. *Zenith I*, 395 U.S. at 123–24 (collecting cases).

forward with (a) evidence showing that it suffered the sort of injury that the proven antitrust violation tends to create and (b) some rough method of approximating the amount of damages it suffered. Although this burden does not require the plaintiff to disprove the possibility that other causal factors also contributed to the injury, the defendant then has an opportunity (and burden) to prove that the other causal factors in fact created all or some portion of the alleged injury. In the typical case involving injured firms claiming lost profits, antitrust defendants usually employ various "blame the victim" arguments that the injured firm would have lost profits anyway because it was poorly managed, poorly located, had a bad product, or was less efficient than other firms in some other way. In cases claiming inflated prices, the defendants will typically argue either that prices actually went down or would have increased anyway because of increased costs or other market factors.

Under this rough-approximation-of-damages standard, the Supreme Court has approved awarding lost profits damages based on assumptions that, absent the antitrust violation, the plaintiff would have (1) acquired the same market share as it had in another nation, (2) made the same profits as another firm, (3) made the same profits as it made in the past, or (4) enjoyed the same prices as it enjoyed in the past.[64] One cannot really know whether, absent an antitrust violation, a firm would have done as well as another or as it did in a different nation, nor that past profits or prices will continue into the future. But such crude assumptions are permitted to deal with the uncertainty caused by defendant's antitrust violation.

Thus, the typical method allowed is to pick some contemporaneous or past baseline where or when markets or firms were not affected by the anticompetitive conduct and assume that any difference between the baseline and reality was caused by the anticompetitive conduct. Unfortunately, contemporaneous or past baselines may be inaccurate because of different costs or demand, because they were also affected by the same anticompetitive conduct, or because the firms in those baselines differ in their efficiency or other features. The past can also be a poor baseline in the typical case where a monopolist is engaging in anticompetitive conduct precisely to slow down the inevitable erosion of a monopoly power it initially earned.[65] In such cases, using a past baseline may falsely suggest the conduct caused no damages even though the conduct did anticompetitively make prices higher than they would have been in the but-for world without that conduct.

Plaintiffs thus often must base their cases on expert projections about what prices or profits would have been but for the anticompetitive conduct in a way that accounts for differences between the but-for world and the posited baseline. One possible method is to run a regression analysis that correlates various features of the market and firms with prices or profit levels to predict what prices or profits would have been but for the anticompetitive conduct, in a way that accounts for differences in market

---

64. *Zenith I*, 395 U.S. at 124–25; *Bigelow*, 327 U.S. at 259–65; *Kodak*, 273 U.S. at 379; *Story Parchment*, 282 U.S. at 562–66.

65. Einer R. Elhauge, *Defining Better Monopolization Standards*, 56 Stan. L. Rev. 253, 337–39 (2003).

features or firms.[66] Where the claim involves future lost profits, a present value calculation must also be conducted to reduce the stream of future lost profits into a current damage amount.[67]

Often, it is attractive to build a model of how prices are set in the relevant industry, and then use it to predict what but-for prices would have been absent some change caused by the conduct. This can lead to conflicting results because models with different assumptions can lead to quite different results. One promising modern approach, called the New Empirical Industrial Organization (NEIO) approach, is to use empirical analysis to estimate the conduct parameters rather than assume them.[68] In particular, with empirical estimates of (1) the relevant demand-elasticities, (2) seller concentration levels, and (3) producer price-cost margins, one can calculate (4) the extent to which firms in the market act competitively ("the conduct parameter").[69] One could then use such data to calculate the extent to which that conduct parameter changed with the relevant conduct and how much that change affected prices. Or one might calculate the extent to which changes in seller concentration levels might alter prices if the conduct parameter remained constant. Or one might be able to assume, say

66. II AREEDA ET AL., *supra* note 21, at ¶ ¶ 393, 394b.

67. *Id.* ¶ 392c.

68. *See*, *e.g.*, Timothy F. Bresnahan, *Empirical Methods for Industries with Market Power*, in 2 HANDBOOK OF INDUSTRIAL ORGANIZATION (Richard Schmalensee & Robert Willig eds., North Holland 1989); Timothy F. Bresnahan & Valerie Y. Suslow, *Oligopoly Pricing with Capacity Constraints*, 15/16 ANNALES D'ECONOMIE ET DE STATISTIQUE 267–89 (1989); Jonathan B. Baker & Daniel L. Rubinfeld, *Empirical Methods in Antitrust Litigation: Review and Critique*, 1 AM. L. & ECON. REV. 386, 427–29 (1999).

69. For example, as we shall see in Chapter 7, the Cournot Model of competition predicts that (without any collusion or coordination), $(P–MC)/P = HHI/\epsilon$, assuming the products are homogeneous and marginal costs are constant, where P is price, MC is marginal cost, HHI is the sum of squares of the market shares of the firms, and ϵ equals the absolute value of the marketwide demand elasticity. In contrast, the Bertrand Model predicts that prices will equal marginal cost even in a duopoly. Finally, monopoly models predict that a cartel (or perfectly coordinating oligopoly) would set prices at $(P–MC)/P = 1/\epsilon$. Rather, than assuming a particular model is true, one could simply set $(P–MC)/P = HHI(1+k)/\epsilon$, where k is the conduct parameter, which could vary from –1 (where the Bertrand prediction holds) to 0 (if Cournot holds) or to positive numbers (where collusion or coordination is true) up to $k = (1–HHI)/HHI$ (where collusion or coordination is perfect). With a conduct parameter calculated from data rather than assumed by model, one could then calculate what the change in conduct parameter must have been between two periods if one has the data on price, cost, market shares and demand elasticity in the two periods, and then calculate what effect that change in conduct parameter had given current prices, costs and market shares. Or, if one wants to calculate the effects of a merger, one might calculate the current conduct parameter, conservatively assume that it would not be any higher after the merger (i.e., that the merger would not increase the degree of oligopolistic coordination), and then calculate what the change in market prices would be.

Other models can be used to calculate the predicted price effects of a merger if one instead assumes Bertrand competition on differentiated markets. Assuming the merged firms are closest to each other in the relevant product space, one need simply calculate the cross-elasticities of demand between the firms and the aggregate elasticity of the alleged product space using current price-output data, and then (with varying assumptions about the shape of the demand curve) predict the prices that the merged firm would charge, and thus the extent to which those prices would be higher than premerger levels. Using this method, one can even calculate the extent to which a posited decrease in marginal costs would offset any tendency toward increased prices.

in a cartel case, that the conduct parameter was at maximum anticompetitive levels, and then calculate one of the other missing variables.

Where a plaintiff can show that prices were inflated by the defendants' anticompetitive conduct, it is entitled to recover the amount of the price overcharge times the quantity it purchased.[70] Notwithstanding arguments that business purchasers should be limited to the lost profits that more accurately measure their injury, they are entitled to recover for the full overcharge because the *Illinois Brick* doctrine concentrates the antitrust claim in their hands rather than allowing indirect purchasers to sue for any overcharge that was passed on downstream. However, this does seem to undercompensate for the total harm inflicted by the violation, which will include not only this overcharge but the deadweight loss caused because the price increase will diminish output and crowd some purchasers out of the market. In theory, a plaintiff should be able to satisfy the requisite standards on causation and damages by showing that it would have bought a greater amount but for the antitrust violation, or (if it purchased nothing) that it would have been a direct purchaser but for the antitrust violation. But proof of that will usually be difficult. This undercompensation problem is to some extent offset by trebling damages.

(5) Allocating Damages Among Defendants. When multiple firms engage in a conspiracy that causes anticompetitive harm, their liability is joint and several.[71] This means that, although a plaintiff can sue all the defendant co-conspirators, the plaintiff also has the option to sue just one (or some) of the defendant co-conspirators for the entire amount of the injury resulting from the conspiracy.[72] The plaintiff need not even *name* the co-conspirators in its complaint,[73] though in some cases specificity might be necessary to adequately allege the conspiracy. The fact that the plaintiff actually did not buy from the defendant does not matter as long as the price at which the plaintiff bought was fixed by the conspiracy.[74] Indeed, if the defendant and his co-conspirators fixed prices in a way that caused market prices to rise generally, a plaintiff should be able to recover even if the plaintiff did not buy from a co-conspirator at all, on the ground that the illegal conspiracy did materially contribute to the higher prices the plaintiff paid in a way that directly flowed from the anticompetitive aspects of the conduct. However, the cases are somewhat split on this last point.[75]

---

70. *See* Chattanooga Foundry & Pipe Works v. City of Atlanta, 203 U.S. 390, 396 (1906).

71. *See* Texas Industries v. Radcliff Materials, 451 U.S. 630, 646 (1981).

72. *See* Burlington Indus. v. Milliken & Co., 690 F.2d 380, 392 n.8 (4th Cir. 1982); MacMillan Bloedel Limited v. Flintkote Co., 760 F.2d 580, 584–85 (5th Cir. 1985); In re Uranium Antitrust Litigation, 617 F.2d 1248, 1257 (7th Cir. 1980).

73. *See Texas Industries*, 451 U.S. at 632–33 (plaintiff complaint allowed to proceed that did not even name who defendant's horizontal co-conspirators were).

74. *See Chattanooga Foundry*, 203 U.S. at 396 (upholding antitrust verdict against horizontal co-conspirator of actual seller, even though actual seller was not sued). Thus, a plaintiff who alleges it paid retail prices that were fixed by an illegal vertical price-fixing agreement between a manufacturer and dealer can elect to sue just the manufacturer or just the dealer or both. *See* II Areeda et al., *supra* note 21, at ¶ 346h, at 369; VII Areeda, Antitrust Law ¶ 1459b4, at 186–87 (1986).

75. *See* II Areeda et al., *supra* note 21, at ¶ 347, at 384–85.

The Supreme Court has also held that a defendant cannot even seek contribution from its co-conspirators for their share of the damages caused.[76] This does not mean that a plaintiff can get double recovery by separately suing each defendant for the full amount of its loss. Rather, each defendant is entitled to a defense of payment for any amount previously paid by other co-conspirators.[77] However, the non-contribution rule does create incentives for plaintiffs to settle early with some co-defendants for less than their pro-rata share of damages in order to fund the rest of the litigation and minimize the downside risk, confident that the remaining co-defendants are still on the hook for all other damages. It also creates corresponding incentives for co-defendants to settle early to avoid being the nonsettling defendant left exposed to a disproportionate share of the liability risk.

iii. Injunctive Relief. Claims for injunctive relief to prevent Sherman or Clayton Act violations can be brought not only by the Department of Justice, but also by private parties injured by those violations.[78] The FTC can also seek or impose injunctive relief as noted above for Clayton and FTC Act violations.[79] "In a Government case the proof of the violation of law may itself establish sufficient public injury to warrant relief."[80] In contrast, a private plaintiff must prove "threatened loss or damage," in other words that the violation threatens to have a material causal link to an injury that would constitute antitrust injury.[81] Thus, two of the elements necessary to prove damages have parallels in private injunctive claims. The other two do not. A private plaintiff seeking injunctive relief need not prove that any causal link is proximate because an injunction poses no danger of duplicative or speculative damages.[82] And obviously the plaintiff seeking injunctive relief need not prove the amount of its damages. Rather, it must generally show the opposite: that damages do not provide it an adequate remedy, which is true whenever some portion of its injury is too difficult to quantify in damages.[83] Thus, a private plaintiff will typically seek damages and injunctive relief in the alternative because denial of the former supports the latter. Often a plaintiff will be able to quantify past

---

76. *Texas Industries*, 451 U.S. at 646–47.

77. *See* Zenith Radio Corp. v. Hazeltine Research, Inc. (Zenith II), 401 U.S. 321, 348 (1971); *Burlington Indus.*, 690 F.2d at 391–92.

78. *See* 15 U.S.C. §§ 4, 25–26.

79. *See* 15 U.S.C. §§ 21, 45, 53(b).

80. *See* California v. American Stores, 495 U.S. 271, 295 (1990). However, as shown below, if the government is not simply seeking injunctive relief to prevent or undo the anticompetitive conduct, but also seeks affirmative injunctive relief to undo the anticompetitive effects or force disgorgement of anticompetitive gains, it must show a material causal link between the defendant's conduct and those anticompetitive effects or gains.

81. *See id.;* 15 U.S.C. § 26; *Cargill*, 479 U.S. at 111 (private plaintiff seeking injunction must prove antitrust injury); *Zenith I*, 395 U.S. at 130 (injunctive "remedy is characteristically available even though the plaintiff has not yet suffered actual injury; he need only demonstrate a significant threat of injury from an impending violation of the antitrust laws or from a contemporary violation likely to continue or recur" to show the requisite causal connection); II AREEDA ET AL., *supra* note 21, at ¶ 337b, 310–13.

82. *Cargill*, 479 U.S. at 110–111 n.6.

83. *See* Blue Cross v. Marshfield Clinic, 152 F.3d 588, 591 (7th Cir.1998) (Posner, J.).

but not future damages, in which case it should get a damage award for the past, and injunctive relief for the future. Subject to the above limitations, private parties have the same right to seek extraordinary injunctive relief like divestiture as the government does, though district courts are not obligated to order such remedies in every case where the government could obtain it.[84] If a private party "substantially prevails" on a claim for injunctive relief, it is also entitled to have the defendant reimburse its litigation costs and reasonable attorneys' fees.[85]

Injunctive relief should be awarded not only (1) to prevent or undo the anticompetitive conduct but also (2) to undo any anticompetitive effects the conduct had on the market and (3) to deny the defendant the fruits of its antitrust violations.[86] Thus, injunctive relief need not be limited to either prohibiting illegal conduct nor to returning the market to the status quo ante, but can include more affirmative relief to undo anticompetitive effects or gains.[87] District courts have considerable discretion to fashion remedies to achieve these goals, including orders requiring firms to: divest or create companies, share access to physical or intellectual property, enter into contracts or modify them, or refrain from certain businesses or practices even though they are normally legal.[88]

Injunctive relief cannot be punitive in the sense of seeking to inflict hardships on the defendant that are unnecessary to accomplish the above three goals, but it is also true that defendant hardships cannot relegate the plaintiff to injunctive relief that is less effective at accomplishing those three goals.[89] When the injunctive relief sought does not simply seek to prevent or undo antitrust violations, a material causal connection must generally be shown between the anticompetitive conduct and the anticompetitive effects it seeks to undo or the fruits it seeks to take away, even in a suit brought by the government.[90]

Injunctions to undo the conduct's anticompetitive effects can include conduct regulation designed to influence markets far into the future: in *Ford Motor* the Supreme Court awarded injunctive relief designed to affect how the market would look like ten years in the future, and stressed that drafting an antitrust decree by necessity "involves predictions and assump-

---

84.   *See American Stores*, 495 U.S. at 295–96.

85.   *See* 15 U.S.C. § 26.

86.   *See* United States v. Microsoft, 253 F.3d 34, 103 (D.C.Cir.2001) (en banc) ("'[A] remedies decree in an antitrust case must seek to 'unfetter a market from anticompetitive conduct' [and] . . . deny to the defendant the fruits of its statutory violation . . .'") (citing Ford Motor v. United States, 405 U.S. 562, 577 (1972), and United States v. United Shoe, 391 U.S. 244, 250 (1968)); Schine Chain Theatres, Inc. v. United States, 334 U.S. 110, 128–29 (1948) (injunctive relief "serves several functions: (1) It puts an end to the combination or conspiracy when that is itself the violation. (2) It deprives the antitrust defendants of the benefits of their conspiracy. (3) It is designed to break up or render impotent the monopoly power which violates the Act.")

87.   *See* Professional Engineers v. United States, 435 U.S. 679, 697–98 (1978); United States v. Loew's, 371 U.S. 38, 53 (1962); *Ford Motor*, 405 U.S. at 573 n.8; *American Stores*, 495 U.S. at 283–84.

88.   *See* II AREEDA ET AL., *supra* note 21, ¶ 325a, at 248 (collecting cases).

89.   *See* United States v. E.I. du Pont de Nemours & Co., 366 U.S. 316, 326–27 (1961).

90.   *See Microsoft*, 253 F.3d at 106.

tions concerning future economic and business events."[91] Courts can also modify injunctions many years after trial (whether or not the court expressly retained jurisdiction in the original decree) if subsequent evidence indicates the earlier injunction was not completely effective.[92]

Injunctions to deprive the defendant of the fruits of its anticompetitive conduct should include injunctions ordering the defendant to divest property:

> "if the property was acquired . . . as a result of practices which constitute unreasonable restraints of trade. Otherwise, there would be reward from the conspiracy through retention of its fruits. Hence the problem of the District Court does not end with enjoining continuance of the unlawful restraints nor with dissolving the combination which launched the conspiracy. Its function includes undoing what the conspiracy achieved. . . . [T]he requirement that the defendants restore what they unlawfully obtained is no more punishment than the familiar remedy of restitution."[93]

This language would appear broad enough to authorize the government to bring antitrust claims seeking the disgorgement of any supracompetitive profits causally related to antitrust violations.[94] Although not yet frequently sought as a remedy, the FTC has sought disgorgement as injunctive relief and had its authority to do so upheld,[95] as has the DOJ.[96] Further, the Sherman Act gives the DOJ express authority to obtain forfeiture of any property owned by or pursuant to any antitrust conspiracy that crosses state or national boundaries.[97] This can be done in a civil action rather than criminal prosecution.[98]

Governments and private parties can also obtain preliminary injunctions to prevent conduct from occurring or continuing pending litigation under the normal standards that balance the likelihood of ultimate success on the merits, the harm the preliminary injunction would cause the defendant, and whether any injury to the plaintiff or public from allowing the conduct would be irreparable later.[99] Such preliminary injunctions are typically the remedy sought in the biggest area of antitrust practice: suits to prevent mergers from occurring.

iv. Consent Decrees and the Interplay Between Public and Private Enforcement. Treble damages compensate for the underdeterrence problems that might otherwise result because it is often hard to

---

91. 405 U.S. at 578.

92. United States v. United Shoe, 391 U.S. 244, 251–52 (1968).

93. United States v. Paramount Pictures, 334 U.S. 131, 171–72 (1948).

94. *See* II AREEDA ET AL., *supra* note 21, at ¶ 325a, at 245 ("equity relief may include . . . the disgorgement of improperly obtained gains"); Elhauge, *Disgorgement as an Antitrust Remedy*, 76 Antitrust L.J. 79 (2009).

95. *See* FTC v. Mylan Labs., 62 F. Supp. 2d 25, 36–37 (D.D.C. 1999) (collecting cases upholding authority of FTC to seek disgorgement as an injunctive relief).

96. See U.S. v. Keyspan Corp., 2011 WL 338037 (S.D.N.Y. 2011).

97. *See* 15 U.S.C. §§ 6, 11.

98. 28 U.S.C. § 2461(a).

99. *See* 15 U.S.C. §§ 4, 25–26, 53(b).

detect antitrust violations and costly and risky to bring antitrust actions. The regime is thus often said to enlist "private attorneys general" to aid antitrust enforcement. This can result in tension because private parties often pursue cases that government agencies view as wrongheaded. Further, private suits are an omnipresent factor in judicial interpretation because courts interpreting a U.S. antitrust statute (other than the FTC Act) know that they cannot simply adopt broad interpretations to give disinterested government agencies authority to root out all possible undesirable conduct, confident that they will typically exercise their prosecutorial discretion to avoid bringing cases that involve overinclusive applications of that interpretation. Instead, courts know that any such overinclusive applications will be pursued by private litigants whenever it is profitable to do so. The antitrust injury requirement helps reduce this overdeterrence problem by barring suits by private plaintiffs that could not suffer any injury unless the alleged conduct were procompetitive, but it remains a serious problem given the difficulties of accurately sorting out procompetitive conduct. This makes courts inclined to interpret U.S. antitrust statutes more narrowly than they might if the statutes authorized only government suits.

However, government agencies also rely on private enforcement to supplement their efforts. Indeed, sometimes agencies will decline to pursue cases precisely because they believe that the incentives for private suit are adequate, and thus the agencies conclude that they should allocate their scarce resources to those areas where private suits are less likely. Agencies also sensibly focus their energies on cases that have the most general impact, leaving to private litigation issues that are of relevance to a more limited set of parties. Thus, a governmental decision not to bring suit after investigation does not create an adverse inference about private litigation over the same matter. In contrast, if the government obtains a judgment after obtaining testimony, then that judgment has preclusive effect in subsequent private lawsuits, unless the judgment constitutes a consent decree entered before testimony was obtained.[100] The statute of limitations for private suits is also suspended pending the government suit.[101] And even if the government loses its litigation, subsequent parties may be able to benefit from the discovery the government collected. Accordingly, potential plaintiffs often lobby the government agencies to bring the cases first, and defendants often enter into consent decrees in order to avoid adverse effects on subsequent private suits.

To be effective, governmental consent decrees must be approved by courts under the Tunney Act after others have had sixty days notice to comment.[102] The rather vague statutory standard is the court can approve

---

100. Although the antitrust statutes state that the prior government judgment only constitutes prima facie evidence of a violation, *see* 15 U.S.C. § 16(a), modern developments in collateral estoppel law give prior litigated judgments (whether in public or private suits) preclusive effect, effectively mooting this provision. *See* II Areeda et al., *supra* note 21, ¶ 319c, at 204.

101. *See* 15 U.S.C. § 16(i).

102. *See* 15 U.S.C. § 16(b)–(h)

the consent decree only if it determines it is in the "public interest."[103] However, courts cannot review the government's decision to simply dismiss a case without any consent judgment.[104] Nor can a judge refuse to accept a consent decree based on facts that the government's complaint never alleged and were never tested by the adversary process and appeal.[105] Given that the government generally files its complaints and corresponding consent decrees at the same time, this means that the government can generally avoid any meaningful review of pre-litigation settlements by simply tailoring its factual allegations closely to its consent decree relief. Even without these limitations, one suspects that courts would generally approve consent decrees because it is difficult to make a reluctant agency prosecute a case effectively and the courts can hardly take over the prosecution of a case themselves. The main utility of the Tunney Act is to provide better information about such consent decrees and to avoid unintended adverse consequences for other parties or markets that might be caused by the decree's terms.

v. **Statute of Limitations.** Whether brought by a private or public actor, antitrust claims seeking injunctive relief have no statute of limitations, but claims seeking damages must be brought within four years from when the claim accrued.[106] However, suits seeking injunctive relief can be barred by the doctrine of laches when suit is unjustifiably delayed, though this doctrine normally does not apply to government suits and some courts seem drawn to four years as a baseline measure of unjustifiable delay.[107] Criminal antitrust cases fall within the general five-year statute of limitations for criminal prosecutions.[108]

A cause of action "accrues" in a way that begins the limitations period when a defendant commits a violation that injures a plaintiff.[109] That is, *both* requirements must be fulfilled: misconduct and injury. The limitations period can be tolled not only by a prior government suit, as noted above, but by three other doctrines.

(1) The Fraudulent Concealment Doctrine. The statute of limitations is tolled during any period where the defendant fraudulently concealed the violation, as long as the plaintiff was unaware of the concealed violation despite due diligence.[110]

(2) The Continuing Conduct Doctrine. When a defendant engages in a continuing series of anticompetitive conduct, then each act that is part of the violation and injures the plaintiff restarts the period of limitations, even though the plaintiff knew the illegality began much earlier.[111] Howev-

---

103. 15 U.S.C. § 16(e).

104. *See* In re IBM Corp., 687 F.2d 591, 600–03 (2d Cir. 1982).

105. *See* United States v. Microsoft Corp., 56 F.3d 1448 (D.C.Cir.1995).

106. 15 U.S.C. § 15b.

107. *See* II Areeda et al., *supra* note 21, at ¶ 320g, 237–39.

108. 18 U.S.C. § 3282.

109. *Zenith II,* 401 U.S. at 338.

110. *See* II Areeda et al., *supra* note 21, at ¶ 320e, at 231–35.

111. *See* Klehr v. A.O. Smith Corp., 521 U.S. 179, 189 (1997).

er, although this doctrine allows the plaintiff to sue for conduct that began more than four years ago, it can recover only for injuries suffered from those acts that occurred within the last four years.[112] To illustrate, if defendants engage in a continuous course of horizontal price-fixing from 2000 to 2004, then a plaintiff can bring suit in 2006, even though it knew the price-fixing began in 2000, because each sale at the fixed price restarts the statute of limitations period. However, unless some other tolling doctrine applied, the plaintiff could not recover for the inflated prices it paid before 2002.

(3) The Speculative Injury Doctrine. Even if the misconduct and injury have occurred, the statute does not begin to run until the injury becomes sufficiently non-speculative to form the basis for reasonably ascertainable damages.[113] The logic is fairly straightforward: a plaintiff cannot be penalized for delaying suit if an earlier suit would have been barred on the grounds that its damages had not yet become reasonably ascertainable. For example, if the exclusionary conduct started producing injury to rivals in 2000, but the magnitude was not reasonably measurable until 2003, then the limitations period would not start until 2003, and thus a lawsuit could still be brought in 2006 for all injury since 2000.

vi. Class Actions. Antitrust cases are often particularly well-suited for resolution by class action because antitrust aims to protect marketwide competition, not individual firms or buyers, and therefore necessarily requires resolution of issues that are marketwide and thus common to any class of persons in that market. This includes market definition, market power, market shares, foreclosure shares, characterization of the conduct, whether the conduct had anticompetitive effects, whether it had procompetitive effects, whether there was less restrictive alternative, whether it caused injury, whether that injury constituted antitrust injury, and what the total damages were. Because those issues are all common to any class of persons in that market, requiring separate litigation of those issues would be greatly duplicative. Also, where there are many persons in the market, each may lack a sufficient incentive to litigate given their individual stakes and the large costs of antitrust litigation. These problems are worsened by collective action problems that make every person in the market prefer to have others bear the burden of litigation and free ride on those efforts either by enjoying the benefits of an injunction for the market or through later collateral estoppel in their own damages claim.

The main obstacle to class actions has been finding a common methodology for distributing those total damages among different persons in the market who may have bought on varying terms or have varying preferences. These problems can be overstated because these variances exist not only in the actual world but also in the but-for world without the anticompetitive conduct, so they generally cancel out using the method of rough approximation allowed to calculate antitrust damages when a violation has been proven.[114] Still, problems with proving individual damages sometimes

---

112. *Id.*

113. *Zenith II*, 401 U.S. at 339–40.

114. Suppose, for example, that a monopolist has engaged in anticompetitive foreclosure that has raised market prices, but each buyer pays somewhat different prices because they

causes courts to balk at certifying an antitrust class action on damages under Federal Rule of Civil Procedure 23. However, even in such cases, a class can often be certified on all other issues, including the existence of liability and the appropriateness of injunctive relief, leaving only proof of individual damages to separate trials. In addition, modern economic methods of measuring damages and the increasing computerization of sales data makes it easier and easier to devise common methods for calculating individuated damages from the common market injury.

Even when a private class action cannot be certified under Rule 23, states continue to have the right to bring "parens patriae" actions that are effectively class actions on behalf of their residents.[115] Where it is too difficult to distribute individuated damages to the injured parties, an antitrust statute allows the problem to be avoided by simply depositing the damages in the state treasury.[116] Another provision specifies that, in a parens patriae action challenging price-fixing, damages can be shown through aggregate statistical methods without need to prove individual damages.[117]

vii. Personal Jurisdiction and Venue. Antitrust suits against corporations "may be brought not only in the judicial district whereof it is an inhabitant, but also in any district wherein it may be found or transacts business; and all process in such cases may be served in the district of which it is an inhabitant, or wherever it may be found."[118] The latter clause is understood to allow worldwide service of process,[119] but the courts are split on whether that process provision depends on showing venue under the first clause.[120]

If the clauses are independent, then the service of process clause confers personal jurisdiction in any district court, which allows suit to be

---

have varying negotiating ability. This would be no obstacle to measuring classwide damages because that variance in negotiating ability would exist in *both* the actual world and the but-for world, and thus cancels out. That is, suppose each buyer pays a price for the product in the actual world of $P_{actual} + N_i$, where P_{actual} is the average market price in the actual world with the defendant's conduct, and N_i reflects the varying negotiating of each of i buyers, being negative for buyers that have the negotiating ability or power to get reductions from the average and positive for buyers who are sufficiently lacking in ability or power that they pay above the average. Such an ability or inability to negotiate for favorable pricing presumably would also hold in the but-for world, and can reasonably be approximated to be about the same in magnitude in both the actual and but-for worlds. Thus, the price the ith buyer pays in the but-for world would be $P_{butfor} + N_i$, where P_{butfor} is the average price each buyer would have paid in the but-for world. The injury to each buyer will accordingly equal: $(P_{actual} + N_i) - (P_{butfor} + N_i) = P_{actual} - P_{butfor}$. Because each buyer's varying negotiating ability or power cancels out, each buyer is injured by the difference in the average price between the actual and but-for worlds. If separate trials were conducted, that would require duplicating this same inquiry about the difference in average prices at each trial.

115. *See* 15 U.S.C. § 15c.

116. *See* 15 U.S.C. § 15e.

117. *See* 15 U.S.C. § 15d.

118. *See* 15 U.S.C. § 22; Go–Video, Inc. v. Akai Elec. Co., 885 F.2d 1406, 1414–16 (9th Cir. 1989).

119. *See, e.g., Go–Video,* 885 F.2d at 1413.

120. *See* Daniel v. American Bd. of Emergency Medicine, 428 F.3d 408, 422–23 (2d Cir. 2005) (collecting the conflicting cases).

brought in any district against corporations because a general venue state allows suit in any district that a corporation is subject to personal jurisdiction (and against aliens in any district) as long as they have minimum contacts with the United States.[121] If the process clause does depend on the venue clause, then the worldwide service of process provision applies only if the case is brought in a district where the corporation is an inhabitant, may be found, or transacts business. This "dependent" interpretation does not bar showing venue under the general provisions of 28 U.S.C. §§ 1391, but normal service of process limitations would apply if that is the basis of venue, which usually require a state long-arm statute and minimum contacts with the state in which the district court sits.[122]

This split may not matter much, however. Even under the "dependent clause" interpretation, if a defendant is not subject to jurisdiction in any state because it lacks sufficient contacts with any one state, then Federal Rule of Civil Procedure 4(k)(2) allows worldwide service of process based on nationwide contacts. Thus, neither interpretation allows a foreign firm to avoid personal jurisdiction in the United States as long as it has minimum contacts with the nation as a whole. The main effect of the "dependent clause" interpretation is that, in cases where a corporate defendant has minimum contacts with some states and not with others, the plaintiff cannot bring the case in a district located in a state where the defendant has no contacts. But even under the "independent clause" interpretation, if a plaintiff brings a case in such a forum, the defendant should be able to get the case transferred to some district where it does have minimum contacts under the doctrine of forum non conveniens.[123] Thus, under either interpretation, a plaintiff can bring suit in some U.S. district as long as the defendant has minimum contacts with the United States as a whole, but the plaintiff's ability to forum-shop among the districts will be constrained where the defendant has contacts with some states but not others.

Noncorporate antitrust defendants are not subject to any special antitrust service of process provision and are subject either to the general venue provisions or under the antitrust venue provision to suit "in any district court of the United States in the district in which the defendant resides or is found or has an agent." 15 U.S.C. § 15. Antitrust venue thus does not extend to any district in which a noncorporate defendant "transacts business," but it does extend to any district in which such a defendant may be "found." Under the general venue statute, aliens may be sued in any district,[124] subject to ordinary service of process limits, which (as we have seen) allow worldwide service if the alien would not otherwise be subject to suit in any district.

---

121. *See* 28 U.S.C. § 1391(c)–(d); *Go–Video*, 885 F.2d at 1408–16; Icon Indus. Controls Corp. v. Cimetrix, Inc., 921 F.Supp. 375, 376 (W.D.La.1996); Kingsepp v. Wesleyan Univ., 763 F.Supp. 22, 24–25 (S.D.N.Y.1991) *But see* Cumberland Truck Equipment Co. v. Detroit Diesel Corp., 401 F. Supp. 2d 415 (E.D. Pa. 2005).

122. *See Daniel,* 428 F.2d at 427.

123. *See* 28 U.S.C. § 1404(a); United States v. National City Lines, 337 U.S. 78 (1949); Capital Currency Exchange v. National Westminster Bank, 155 F.3d 603 (2d Cir. 1998).

124. 28 U.S.C. §§ 1391(d) ("An alien may be sued in any district.")

However, for both corporate and noncorporate defendants, if service is only feasible in a foreign nation, then it is only valid if it complies with foreign or international law or is expressly authorized by some other federal law.[125] Thus, theoretically worldwide service of process might be restricted by foreign prohibitions, though this is not usually an obstacle because foreign nations typically want firms to be amenable to service for other purposes.

viii.   Limits on Antitrust. Application of U.S. antitrust laws is limited in three ways. First, the statute has been interpreted to exclude certain conduct, like state legislation or petitioning for governmental action, even though it results in fixed prices or other anticompetitive effects. Second, in some areas, federal statutes explicitly or implicitly exempt specific industries or conduct from antitrust liability. Third, the statute requires some trivial effect on interstate commerce, and does not cover foreign restraints that have no substantial effect on U.S. markets.

(1) State Action and Petitioning Immunity. The antitrust statutes have been interpreted not to apply to "state action" on the ground that Congress did not intend to interfere with the traditional state power to regulate markets, even though such regulation often fixes prices, restrains output, and restricts entry.[126] Nor do the antitrust statutes apply to private petitioning efforts that are designed to obtain such anticompetitive government regulation, even though such genuine petitioning efforts might incidentally impose direct anticompetitive effects.[127]

a.   STATE ACTION IMMUNITY. Antitrust state action doctrine employs three different tiers of immunity depending on who has set the terms of the challenged anticompetitive restraint.

1.   Top of Three Branches of Government—An anticompetitive restraint is per se immune from antitrust scrutiny if the terms of that restraint were set by the state legislature, the highest state court acting legislatively, or (probably) the governor.[128] However, even though such state efforts are immune from antitrust scrutiny, they do face dormant commerce clause review if they exploit out-of-staters.[129]

2.   State Agencies and Municipalities—Public entities that are subordinate to the top levels of state government, like state agencies or municipalities, enjoy antitrust immunity if their restraints are clearly authorized by one of the entities that acts directly for the state (such as the state legislature, supreme court, or governor).[130] The "clear authorization" test

---

125. *See* Fed. Rule Civ. Proc. 4(f), (h)(2); Prewitt Enterprises, Inc. v. OPEC, 353 F.3d 916 (11th Cir. 2003).

126. Parker v. Brown, 317 U.S. 341, 350–52 (1943); *see generally* Elhauge, *The Scope of Antitrust Process,* 104 HARV. L. REV. 667 (1991) (synthesizing the caselaw and explaining its underlying theory).

127. Eastern R.R. Pres. Conf. v. Noerr Motor Freight, 365 U.S. 127 (1961); *see generally* Elhauge, *Making Sense of Antitrust Petitioning Immunity,* 80 CALIF. L. REV. 1177 (1992).

128. See Hoover v. Ronwin, 466 U.S. 558, 567–69 (1984). The Supreme Court's approach suggests that the actions of state governors will also be per se immune, but it has left the issue open. *See id.* at 568 n.17.

129. *See* Elhauge, *supra* note 126, at 732.

130. See Southern Motor Carriers Rate Conference, Inc. v. United States, 471 U.S. 48, 57, 60–61, 62–63 (1985); Town of Hallie v. City of Eau Claire, 471 U.S. 34, 38–40, 46–47 &

is something of a misnomer because it does not require much clarity or authority. As for clarity, it suffices that the state has given the agency or municipality some general regulatory authority that could foreseeably be exercised to suppress competition, even though the state never contemplated either those anticompetitive effects or the specific restraint being challenged.[131] As for authority, municipalities and state agencies have been found immune even when their specific restraints were literally *un*authorized because they exceeded the scope of their regulatory authority.[132]

In short, if a disinterested municipality or state agency has been given general regulatory authority, it enjoys antitrust immunity when adopting any regulation that—whether or not actually authorized—has the sorts of anticompetitive effects one could have foreseen from the regulatory authority that was granted, whether or not any of the top three branches of government actually approved or contemplated those effects. The word "disinterested" is included in the last sentence because the caselaw makes clear that even someone that has been formally designated a state official or agent will be deemed a "private" actor (and thus governed by the third tier below) if they operate businesses that are financially interested in the terms of the challenged restraint.[133] More generally, state action immunity may not apply when a municipality or state agency acts as a commercial participant rather than just as a regulator, especially when it furthers the financial interests of its residents by imposing extraterritorial costs.[134]

Although *City of Boulder* might suggest a more narrow immunity because it held that municipal home rule authority did not constitute a sufficiently clear authorization to merit antitrust immunity,[135] a later decision held that municipal regulation of this sort could be subject to review only as unilateral conduct under Sherman Act § 2, thus effectively limiting antitrust review to cases where the municipality had the sort of market power over outsiders that would give it a financial interest in the regulation.[136] Further, the Local Government Antitrust Act of 1984 has

n.10 (1985); *Hoover*, 466 U.S. at 568–69; Community Communications Co. v. City of Boulder, 455 U.S. 40, 50–54 (1982).

131. *See* City of Columbia v. Omni Outdoor Advertising, 499 U.S. 365, 372–73 (1991); *Hallie*, 471 U.S. at 41–42; *Southern Motor Carriers*, 471 U.S. at 64; Elhauge, *supra* note 126, at 691–92.

132. *See City of Columbia*, 499 U.S. at 370–72; Elhauge, *supra* note 126, at 692.

133. Goldfarb v. Virginia State Bar, 421 U.S. 773, 776 & n.2, 789–92 (1975) (state bar enjoyed no antitrust immunity even though it was a statutorily designated state agency exercising an authority granted by the state); Continental Ore Co. v. Union Carbide & Carbon Corp., 370 U.S. 690, 703 n.11, 706–07 (1962) (defendant enjoyed no antitrust immunity even though the Canadian government had appointed the defendant its official agent and delegated to it "discretionary agency power to purchase and allocate to Canadian industries all vanadium products."); *see also* Allied Tube & Conduit Corp. v. Indian Head, Inc. 486 U.S. 492, 501 (1988) (citing *Goldfarb* and *Continental Ore* for the proposition that "persons with economic incentives to restrain trade" are not state actors who enjoy antitrust immunity); Elhauge, *supra* note 126, at 683–91.

134. *See City of Columbia*, 499 U.S. at 374, 379; City of Lafayette v. Louisiana Power & Light Co., 435 U.S. 389, 403–04 (1978); Elhauge, *supra* note 126, at 732–33.

135. 455 U.S. 40.

136. Fisher v. City of Berkeley, 475 U.S. 260 (1986); Elhauge, *supra* note 126, at 734–35.

eliminated damage claims in cases involving municipal action, thus leaving antitrust review of municipal action that imposes extraterritorial costs out-of-town much the same as dormant commerce clause review of state action that imposes extraterritorial costs out-of-state.[137]

3. Private Actors—Anticompetitive restraints by "private" persons are immune only if those restraints are both (1) clearly authorized and (2) actively supervised by the state, which can include supervision by municipalities or state agencies.[138] As the Court has interpreted the active supervision requirement, it effectively requires evidence that some disinterested state or municipal official exercised substantive control over the terms of the relevant restraint.[139] Mere rubberstamping by a public official does not suffice: the official must make a substantive decision in favor of the restraint's terms.[140] Nor can the substantive approval come after-the-fact: the public official must make the substantive decision before the restraint is imposed on the market.[141] When disinterested public officials do not control the terms of the relevant restraint, then no state action immunity applies even if a state statute explicitly allows or even requires private actors to adopt such restraints.[142] On the other hand, when disinterested public officials do substantively control the terms of the restraint, then antitrust immunity applies whether or not they "conspired" with the regulated private actors.[143]

4. Combining the Three Tiers—Given how the cases define clear authorization and active supervision, one can simplify these complex tiers into one test: "restraints are immune from antitrust review whenever financially disinterested and politically accountable persons control and make a substantive decision in favor of the terms of the challenged restraint before it is imposed on the market."[144]

b. PETITIONING IMMUNITY. Petitioning immunity clearly applies when the complaint is that the petitioning led some disinterested public lawmaker to impose an anticompetitive restraint, even if the petitioner "conspired" with the lawmaker.[145] In such a case, the petitioning immunity

---

137. 15 U.S.C. §§ 35–36; Elhauge, *supra* note 126, at 735.

138. California Retail Liquor Dealers Association v. Midcal Aluminum, Inc., 445 U.S. 97, 105–06 & n.9 (1980); Patrick v. Burget, 486 U.S. 94, 101–03 (1988) (evaluating whether supervision by various state agencies was sufficiently active). An additional prong applies when a facial challenge is brought against a state statute or municipal ordinance. If the state action doctrine does not provide immunity, the statute or ordinance is facially preempted only if it authorizes or mandates conduct that per se violates the antitrust laws. *See Fisher*, 475 U.S. at 264–65; Rice v. Norman Williams Co., 458 U.S. 654, 661 (1982). This prong does not apply when plaintiffs challenge a statute or ordinance as applied. *See Fisher*, 475 U.S. at 270 n.2; *Rice*, 458 U.S. at 662 & nn.7–8.

139. *Patrick*, 486 U.S. at 101; 324 Liquor Corp. v. Duffy, 479 U.S. 335, 344–45 & n.7 (1987).

140. FTC v. Ticor Title Insurance Co., 504 U.S. 621 (1992); *Patrick*, 486 U.S. at 100–01.

141. *See* Elhauge, *supra* note 126, at 714–15.

142. See *324 Liquor*, 479 U.S. at 343–45; *Midcal*, 445 U.S. at 105–06; Schwegmann Bros. v. Calvert Distillers Corp., 341 U.S. 384, 389 (1951).

143. *See City of Columbia*, 499 U.S. at 374–79; Elhauge, *supra* note 126, at 704–06.

144. Elhauge, *supra* note 126, at 671, 696. Here, "politically accountable" means that the authority of the public official can be traced to an election, appointment by elected officials, or through some chain of appointment starting with elected officials. *Id.* at 671 n.10. A judge is thus politically accountable within the meaning used here.

145. *See City of Columbia*, 499 U.S. at 379–84; United Mine Workers v. Pennington, 381 U.S. 657, 660–61, 669–72 (1965).

could be deemed derivative of the state action immunity that applies to the challenged restraint. By the same token, petitioning immunity clearly does not apply to efforts to persuade a financially interested market participant to impose an anticompetitive restraint that would not enjoy state action immunity.[146] Nor does petitioning immunity apply if a financially interested market participant imposes the challenged market restraint in order to coerce government action.[147]

The difficulty is with dual effect cases where the same private activity both (a) indirectly helps procure government action and (b) directly restrains trade in a way that would cause anticompetitive effects whether or not the government made a favorable substantive decision. Petitioners are always immune for the former effects given state action immunity,[148] and are also immune for the latter direct effects when they are incidental to genuine petitioning efforts that are valid by the standards of the relevant governmental process.[149] Immunity for the direct effects is thus denied if the alleged input into public decisionmaking was a "sham" in the sense that the activity was not genuinely designed to influence government action,[150] or if the direct effects were inflicted by a restraint that was in fact separate from the valid effort to influence the government and thus was not "incidental" to any such petitioning.[151] Such cases are not true dual effect cases because one of the effects is a sham or the duality does not really exist because the effects are severable.

Even in true dual effect cases, immunity for the direct effects is also denied if the restraint violates the prevailing standards for providing input to the relevant government decisionmaking process.[152] Under the no-holds-barred standards for providing input to the political process, this can protect even deceptive and unethical speech.[153] Under the more stringent standards for providing input into the adjudicative process, immunity can be lost for the direct effects of conduct that violates the legal standards applicable to litigation.[154] This does not mean immunity is lost for the

---

146. *See Allied Tube,* 486 U.S. at 501; *Continental Ore,* 370 U.S. at 707–08; Elhauge, *supra* note 126, at 1200–03.

147. *See* FTC v. Superior Court Trial Lawyers Ass'n, 493 U.S. 411, 421–25, 427 (1990); *Allied Tube,* 486 U.S. at 503; Elhauge, *supra* note 127, at 1206–11, 1237–40.

148. *See Allied Tube,* 486 U.S. at 499; *Noerr,* 365 U.S. at 135–36; *City of Columbia,* 499 U.S. at 378–79; Elhauge, *supra* note 127, at 1213, 1220, 1240–42.

149. *See Noerr,* 365 U.S. at 142–44; Elhauge, *supra* note 127, at 1213–37.

150. Professional Real Estate Investors v. Columbia Pictures Indus., 508 U.S. 49, 58–61 (1993); *City of Columbia,* 499 U.S. at 380; *Allied Tube,* 486 U.S. at 500 n.4, 508 n.10; *Noerr,* 365 U.S. at 144.

151. Elhauge, *supra* note 127, at 1215–19 (collecting cases).

152. *See id.* at 1219–21.

153. *See Noerr,* 365 U.S. at 140–41 & n.20 (stressing that the challenged activity was in widespread use and apparently not prohibited by the laws applicable to lobbying); Elhauge, *supra* note 127, at 1223–26.

154. *See Allied Tube,* 486 U.S. at 499–500; California Motor Transp. Co. v. Trucking Unlimited, 404 U.S. 508, 512–13 (1972); *Professional Real Estate,* 508 U.S. at 62–66 (judging whether conduct constitutes an abuse of process under traditional litigation standards).

results of a favorable court decision obtained by invalid litigation conduct, just that there is no immunity for the direct effects that flow regardless of whether substantive judicial approval obtained, such as the litigation costs imposed by the process itself.[155] Immunity is also denied to a firm that procures a patent by filing false information with the Patent Office, a holding that can be explained on the grounds that, because the Patent Office does not check the accuracy of filings before issuing a patent, it has effectively delegating factual determinations to the financially interested applicant, thus making this a direct effect of financially interested decision-making.[156]

(2) Federal Antitrust Exemptions and Limitations

a. IMPLIED EXEMPTIONS OR LIMITATIONS. A federal statute enacted subsequent to an antitrust statute is always free to partially repeal the antitrust laws by exempting particular industries. However, important canons of interpretation adopt powerful presumptions against interpreting any federal statute to create an antitrust exemption and for narrowly construing any exemption that does exist.[157]

Absent an explicit antitrust exemption, an antitrust exemption can be "implied only if necessary to make the [non-antitrust statute] work, and even then only to the minimum extent necessary."[158] This test does not require a showing that the specific challenged conduct or rule is necessary for the regulatory scheme to function, but rather a conclusion that the regulatory system could not work properly if antitrust liability could conflict with regulatory determinations about the desirability of the conduct.[159] The doctrine generally denies an exemption if the agency either (a) lacks the power to authorize, require, or prohibit the relevant sort of conduct, or (b) has such power but has not exercised it, unless the decision not to exercise such a power reflects a regulatory judgment to allow the challenged sort of conduct despite consideration of its potential anticompetitive effects.[160]

---

155. See Professional Real Estate, 508 U.S. at 60–61; City of Columbia, 499 U.S. at 380; Elhauge, supra note 127, at 1228–29, 1249–50.

156. Walker Process Equip. Co. v. Food Mach. & Chem. Corp., 382 U.S. 172 (1965); Elhauge, supra note 127, at 1248–50.

157. E.g., National Gerimedical Hosp. & Gerontology Ctr. v. Blue Cross, 452 U.S. 378, 389 (1981); Group Life & Health Ins. Co. v. Royal Drug Co., 440 U.S. 205, 231 (1979).

158. Silver v. NYSE, 373 U.S. 341, 357 (1963); Nat'l Gerimedical, 452 U.S. at 389.

159. See Gordon v. NYSE, 422 U.S. 659, 662, 683 (1975); United States v. NASD, 422 U.S. 694, 726–28 (1975); Nat'l Gerimedical, 452 U.S. at 389.

160. See Nat'l Gerimedical, 452 U.S. at 389–90; NASD, 422 U.S. at 726–28; Georgia v. Pennsylvania R.R., 324 U.S. 439 (1945); United States v. Borden, 308 U.S. 188 (1939); Nader v. Allegheny Airlines, 426 U.S. 290, 301 (1976); McLean Trucking Co. v. United States, 321 U.S. 67 (1944). In addition, even without any implicit antitrust exemption, regulators are sometimes held to have primary jurisdiction in the sense that antitrust courts should defer their adjudications until the agency has had a chance to address the issue first, generally either because the agency has an expertise advantage in determining the facts relevant to the antitrust claim or because agency resolution might affect whether an antitrust exemption existed. See id. at 301–04; Ricci v. Chicago Mercantile Exch., 409 U.S. 289, 305, 307 (1973); Carnation Co. v. Pacific Westbound Conf., 383 U.S. 213, 222 (1966); Far East Conf. v. United States, 342 U.S. 570, 574–75 (1952). However, other cases have somewhat inconsistently held

In *Credit Suisse,* the Court held that federal securities law precludes antitrust law when the two are "clearly incompatible" given "(1) the existence of regulatory authority under the securities law to supervise the activities in question; (2) evidence that the responsible regulatory entities exercise that authority; ... (3) a resulting risk that the securities and antitrust laws, if both applicable, would produce conflicting guidance, requirements, duties, privileges, or standards of conduct," and that "(4) ... the possible conflict affected practices that lie squarely within an area of financial market activity that the securities law seeks to regulate."[161] The Court emphasized that the possible conflict need not be a present one: even if the federal securities agency currently prohibits precisely the same conduct that antitrust law prohibits, it suffices for an antitrust exemption that, in the future: (a) the agency could create a conflict by choosing to exercise its regulatory authority differently, or (b) the agency and antitrust courts might interpret or apply their similar prohibitions differently.[162]

This test uses factors similar to those considered by prior implied exemption cases, but goes beyond them to suggest an affirmative test of when an antitrust exemption would be implied. If generalizable beyond securities cases, it indicates that an implied antitrust exemption applies if: (1) a federal non-antitrust agency has an exercised power to regulate the relevant conduct, and (2) current or future agency choices about how to exercise or apply that power might create a risk of a conflict with antitrust standards on conduct that is squarely within the core area covered by the non-antitrust law. Two features indicated, however, that the Court was trying to cabin this implied exemption doctrine a bit. First, the limitation of implied exemption to the core areas covered by non-antitrust laws indicated a potential narrowing of implied exemption law. Second, the Court suggested in several places that the potential-conflict exemption test might be unique to securities law.[163]

One can see why the Court might be worried about applying this standard outside of securities cases. Given the extent of modern federal regulation, it may well be the case that, in most of our economy, some agency has an exercised power to regulate some conduct that might also constitute an antitrust violation. If all such conduct were exempt from antitrust scrutiny, there could well be little left to the antitrust laws. Further, usually Congress has authorized the relevant agency to regulate the conduct in some more limited way, or based on more limited standards that are unrelated to competitive concerns. It seems implausible that in all such cases that Congress really meant to oust antitrust review, or that doing so would be socially desirable. Instead, Congress may well have intended to express even more concern about the relevant conduct, by

---

that agencies should hold off until an antitrust court has addressed the relevant issue. *See* California v. FPC, 369 U.S. 482 (1962). Perhaps the best resolution is that the latter was a merger case brought a federal antitrust agency, which generally both requires a quick decision (and thus makes deferring impracticable) and means the agency in the antitrust suit has an equal or greater claim to expertise.

161. Credit Suisse Securities v. Billing, 551 U.S. 264, 275 (2007).

162. *Id.* at 271–73, 278–82.

163. *Id.* at 269, 275.

indicating it was undesirable not only under competition standards, but under other normative standards as well. If these concerns prove persuasive, it may be the case that *Credit Suisse* does not generate a new broad general doctrine of implied exemption, but rather has defined a "securities exemption" that, like the labor and insurance exemptions discussed below, is a special exemption doctrine with its own elements that do not extend to other sorts of cases.

The filed rate doctrine differs from an exemption in that it provides only that a party may not collect damages (in antitrust or otherwise) based on an overcharge that reflected a rate filed with and approved by a federal regulator.[164] This doctrine does not provide an exemption because it bars only some damage claims and not others, and bars no claims for injunctive relief or criminal penalties.[165] Unlike with state action immunity, rubberstamp approval by a federal regulator suffices for the filed rate doctrine even absent evidence that the agency considered any anticompetitive conduct.[166] However, a filed rate that the agency either disapproves or lacks authority to regulate can form the basis for an antitrust action.[167] The filed rate doctrine bars only claims that seek damages on the grounds that the rate reflected an overcharge, and thus does not bar claims that seek damages from a requirement to buy the product or service,[168] or from a filed rate that excluded rivals (because it reflected a price squeeze or predatory price) and thus resulted in lost profits to that rival.[169]

U.S. government agencies enjoy sovereign immunity from antitrust liability unless there is a statutory waiver, and even when a general waiver exists, are not deemed "persons" eligible to be defendants under the antitrust statutes unless the agency statute explicitly provides otherwise.[170]

b. EXPLICIT EXEMPTIONS OR LIMITATIONS. Congress has also frequently enacted explicit exemptions or alterations of antitrust standards. These include exemptions that:

---

164. *See* Square D Co. v. Niagara Frontier Tariff Bureau, 476 U.S. 409, 415–420 (1986).

165. *See id.* at 418–19, 422.

166. *See* Mississippi Power & Light v. Mississippi, 487 U.S. 354, 374 (1988); *Square D*, 476 U.S. at 47 n.19. Some lower courts have extended the filed rate doctrine to rates approved by state agencies, but it seems unlikely the Supreme Court would approve such an extension because the Court has (1) expressed doubts about the wisdom of this doctrine and adhered to it only because it was statutory precedent that Congress left unaltered, *id.* at 420, 423–24, and (2) denied state action immunity to state agencies that engage in the sort rubberstamp approvals that receive protection under the filed rate doctrine, *see Ticor Title*, 504 U.S. 621.

167. *See* Litton Sys., Inc. v. American Tel. & Tel. Co., 700 F.2d 785, 820 (2d Cir.1983); Florida Municipal Power Agency v. Florida Power & Light, 64 F.3d 614 (11th Cir. 1995).

168. *See Litton*, 700 F.2d at 820.

169. *See* Cost Management Service v. Washington Natural Gas, 99 F.3d 937, 944–45 (9th Cir. 1996); City of Kirkwood v. Union Elec. Co., 671 F.2d 1173, 1178 (8th Cir. 1982).

170. *See* United States Postal Service v. Flamingo Indus. (U.S.A) Ltd., 540 U.S. 736 (2004). An earlier case had held that the United States was not a "person" who could be an antitrust damages plaintiff or defendant, *see* United States v. Cooper Corp., 312 U.S. 600, 607–09, 614 (1941), and Congress had responded with a statute that did not make the United States a "person" who could sue and be sued, but rather simply gave the United States standing to sue for antitrust damages, *see* 15 U.S.C. § 15a.

1. Allow those who farm and fish to form cooperatives without those cooperatives being considered agreements in restraint of trade, although the Secretary of Agriculture has authority to enjoin cooperatives that unduly enhance prices.[171] This exemption does not extend to agreements with nonexempt persons, nor to exclusionary conduct by cooperatives against rivals or other nonmembers.[172]

2. Exempt certain mergers and television agreements by sports leagues.[173] Baseball also enjoys a special judicially-created antitrust exemption, other than for conduct that affects the employment of ballplayers,[174] which is instead governed by the labor exemption described below.

3. Immunize charitable gift annuities or charitable remainder trusts.[175]

4. Exempt the medical resident matching program.[176]

5. Provide more generous antitrust standards for mergers and agreements between newspapers when one is a failing firm.[177]

6. Exempt professional review bodies from antitrust damages for actions that are based on the quality of a physician's care and may adversely affect the physician's hospital privileges or society memberships, provided the actions were based on a reasonable belief that they would enhance the quality of health care and were made after reasonable investigation and process.[178]

7. Exempt collective rate making that is known and approved by the Interstate Commerce Commission.[179]

8. Exempt shipper conduct that is already prohibited by the Shipping Act of 1984.[180]

9. Exempt agreements that the President finds vital to national defense.[181]

10. Exempt joint research and development that has been approved by the Small Business Administration.[182]

11. Provide more generous antitrust standards for judging bank mergers.[183]

---

171. See 15 U.S.C. § 17, 7 U.S.C. § 291; 15 U.S.C. § 521.

172. See United States v. Borden, 308 U.S. 188, 194, 205 (1939); Maryland & Va. Milk Producers Ass'n v. United States, 362 U.S. 458, 466–68, 471–72 (1960).

173. See 15 U.S.C. §§ 1291–95.

174. See Flood v. Kuhn, 407 U.S. 258, 282 (1972); 15 U.S.C. § 26b.

175. See 15 U.S.C. § 37.

176. See 15 U.S.C. § 37b.

177. See 15 U.S.C. § 1803.

178. See 42 U.S.C. § 11111–12, 11151(9)–(11).

179. See 49 U.S.C. § 10706.

180. See 46 U.S.C. § 1706(c)(2).

181. See 50 U.S.C. § 2158. See also 15 U.S.C. § 640.

182. See 15 U.S.C. § 638.

183. 12 U.S.C. § 1828(c).

All of these exemptions require examination of the detailed statutory requirements. Two other exemptions require a bit more discussion because of their importance and doctrinal development.

   c. STATE–REGULATED INSURANCE ACTIVITIES. The McCarran–Ferguson Act exempts insurance practices that are regulated by state laws unless the practices involve boycotts.[184] To receive this exemption, all of the following three requirements must be met:

   1. The Practice Involves the Business of Insurance—To merit this exemption, it is not enough that the defendant is an insurer. Rather, the challenged practice itself must involve the "business of insurance" under a doctrine that considers three factors, all of which are relevant but none of which are determinative: "*first*, whether the practice has the effect of transferring or spreading a policyholder's risk; *second*, whether the practice is an integral part of the policy relationship between the insurer and the insured; and *third*, whether the practice is limited to entities within the insurance industry."[185] Thus, the exemption does not cover insurer practices that are not integral to the transfer or spread of risk, such as (i) health insurer agreements with pharmacies on the prices charged to fill prescriptions, or (ii) insurer peer review of the reasonableness of professional fees or treatment.[186]

   2. The Practice Is Regulated By State Laws—The McCarran–Ferguson Act governs more than just antitrust. It states:

> "No Act of Congress shall be construed to invalidate, impair, or supersede any law enacted by any State for the purpose of regulating the business of insurance ... unless such Act specifically relates to the business of insurance: *Provided*, That after June 30, 1948, ... the Sherman Act, ... the Clayton Act, and ... the Federal Trade Commission Act ... shall be applicable to the business of insurance to the extent that such business is not regulated by State law."[187]

Read literally, the second clause provides no freestanding antitrust exemption, but rather *limits* the first clause's exemption in cases involving antitrust statutes, which means that an antitrust exemption should require a showing that the antitrust statute would "impair" the state regulation in addition to the factors in the second clause. However, based on certain legislative history, the Supreme Court has traditionally read the second clause as an independent affirmative grant of immunity from federal

---

   184. *See* 15 U.S.C. §§ 1011–1103; Group Life & Health Ins. v. Royal Drug, 440 U.S. 205, 210 n.4, 220 (1979).

   185. Hartford Fire Ins. Co. v. California, 509 U.S. 764, 781–82 (1993); Union Labor Life Ins. Co. v. Pireno, 458 U.S. 119, 129 (1982).

   186. *See Group Life*, 440 U.S. 205; *Pireno*, 458 U.S. at 129–31. On similar logic, most courts also hold the exemption inapplicable to insurer decisions to limit or exclude reimbursement for nonphysician services. *See* Virginia Academy of Clinical Psychologists v. Blue Shield, 624 F.2d 476, 484 (4th Cir. 1980); Hahn v. Oregon Physicians Serv., 689 F.2d 840 (9th Cir. 1982). *But see* Health Care Equalization Comm. v. Iowa Med. Socy., 851 F.2d 1020 (8th Cir. 1988).

   187. 15 U.S.C. § 1012(b).

antitrust law for insurance practices that are regulated by state law.[188] Still, the most recent Supreme Court opinion more accurately describes the second clause as an exception to the first,[189] suggesting that future courts may instead follow the plain meaning of the statute and require a showing of impairment. This would also be more consistent with the statutory canon requiring narrow interpretation of any antitrust exemption, as well as with the full legislative history.[190]

Leaving aside the possible future addition of this impairment test, the traditional regulated-by state-law standard does not require proof that the state "effectively" enforces its regulation of the practice as long as the state "authorizes enforcement through a scheme of administrative supervision."[191] This element is also satisfied if the state regulator permits or authorizes the relevant practice, like collective ratemaking, even though the regulator does not substantively control those rates, as long as the practice is open and supervised by the state regulator.[192] Although the

---

188. *See* F.T.C. v. National Casualty Co., 357 U.S. 560, 563 n.3 (1958).

189. *See Hartford Fire*, 509 U.S. at 780. If it does, this would narrow the exemption because, in non-antitrust cases, the Court has found such impairment only when the federal claim would directly conflict with state regulation or frustrate a declared state policy. *See* Humana Inc. v. Forsyth, 525 U.S. 299, 311–12 (1999). The main difference is that, unlike the regulated-by-state-law standard, the impairment standard does not preclude federal prohibitions of the same sort of conduct prohibited by state law. For example, state regulation of deceptive insurance practices does not preclude RICO efforts to penalize such deception under the impairment standard, *id.*, but does preclude FTC efforts to penalize such deception under the regulated-by-state-law standard. *See National Casualty*, 357 U.S. at 563.

One might wonder whether reading the second clause as an exception renders it superfluous on the ground that federal antitrust law could never impair state law when the matter is not regulated by state law. But the impairment clause applies to any state law enacted for the "purpose" of regulating insurance whether or not it actually does so. Thus, a plain meaning interpretation would not create superfluity because under it the federal antitrust laws would apply when they impair a state law that has the purpose of regulating insurance but does not actually do so. It is unclear the extent to which such state laws actually exist, but it is not superfluous for Congress to provide for the possibility. In any event, superfluous language in statutes is in fact commonplace, and the canon against superfluous language is not followed when it conflicts with the most sensible reading of statutory language.

190. Of the legislative history cited in *National Casualty*, the only part that actually supports its statutory reading is that Senator McCarran did state that state regulation would oust federal antitrust liability. *See* 91 Cong. Rec. 1443. However, given the context, he may have simply been assuming a case where the antitrust liability would impair the state regulation, especially since what the Senators mainly had in mind was state regulations authorizing collective ratemaking by insurers subject to state supervision. *See id.* at 1444, 1481, 1484. Other Senators supporting the statute read the language to mere be a "positive declaration" of when antitrust applied notwithstanding the impairment clause, *see id.* at 1444 (Sen. O'Mahoney), or stressed that state regulation would preclude antitrust liability only when the state regulation was "in conflict" with antitrust law or affirmatively "permitted" conduct that would otherwise violate antitrust law, *id.* at 1481 (Sen. Murdock), which is quite similar to the impairment standard. None of the legislative history suggested that the antitrust laws would be deemed inapplicable when they did not conflict with state law or some declared state policy, and thus none of it conflicts with applying the impairment standard to antitrust cases.

191. *See* St. Paul Fire & Marine Ins. Co. v. Barry, 438 U.S. 531, 551 (1978); *National Casualty*, 357 U.S. at 564–65; Lawyers Title Co. v. St. Paul Title Ins. Corp., 526 F.2d 795, 797 (8th Cir. 1975).

192. *Group Life*, 440 U.S. at 223; *St. Paul Fire*, 438 U.S. at 548 n.21, 549; *Pireno,* 458 U.S. at 129; Ohio AFL–CIO v. Insurance Rating Board, 451 F.2d 1178, 1181 (6th Cir. 1971).

occasional court mistakenly thinks it suffices that *insurers* are generally regulated by the state, in fact the test is whether the particular *insurance practice* is regulated by the state in that it either (a) prohibits undesirable instances of the practice and has some system of enforcement, or (b) has made a considered regulatory judgment to permit the practice subject to ongoing public monitoring.[193] This is less rigorous than the state action immunity requirement that the regulator actually substantively approve the terms of any immune restraint, but comes fairly close to the standards for determining whether a federal statute creates an implicit antitrust exemption.

Further, for the McCarran–Ferguson antitrust exemption, the practice must both occur in *and* have effects in the state that regulates the practice; there is thus no federal antitrust immunity for conduct that is regulated by the state in which the insurer exists and committed the practice but has effects in other states.[194] Even if immune from federal antitrust law, insurance practices remain subject to state antitrust law unless it provides otherwise.

3. The Practice Does Not Constitute a "Boycott."—The insurance exemption has an exception which states that nothing in the McCarran–Ferguson Act "shall render the ... Sherman Act inapplicable to any agreement to boycott, coerce, or intimidate, or act of boycott, coercion, or intimidation."[195] This creates an interesting interpretive question because a "boycott" is a concerted refusal to deal, and one could think of any agreement in restraint of trade as a concerted refusal to deal on anything other than at the restrained terms. Indeed, in defining the substantive law of antitrust, the Supreme Court has characterized a concerted refusal to deal at less than a fixed price as a "boycott" even though it noted it could also be considered a price-fixing agreement.[196] And yet the McCarran–Ferguson Act was intended to allow insurers to collectively agree on insurance prices and terms (subject to state monitoring) and thus must have been using a more narrow understanding of the word "boycott."

Accordingly, the Supreme Court has held that the "boycott" element of the insurance exemption requires a concerted refusal to deal that went

---

193. *See* sources collected in last two notes. The claim that any state regulation of insurers ousts all federal antitrust regulation of nonboycott insurer practices is inconsistent with the statutory text, which makes clear that federal antitrust laws continue to apply "to the extent" insurers are not regulated by states, 15 U.S.C. § 1012(b), rather than "only if" insurers are not regulated by states. This claim is also inconsistent with the legislative history. It was specifically rejected by Senator McCarran, who agreed with Senator White that the federal antitrust laws "shall be applicable to whatever extent the State fails to occupy the ground and engage in regulation.... If ... the state goes only to the point indicated, then these Federal statutes apply throughout the whole field beyond the scope of the State's activity." *See* 91 Cong. Rec. 1444. Senator McCarran even agreed with Senator Barkley that "where States attempt to occupy the field—but do it inadequately—... these [federal antitrust] acts still would apply." *Id.*

194. *See* FTC v. Travelers Health Ass'n, 362 U.S. 293, 297–99 (1960). The Court left open the question whether the exemption might apply if all the states in which the conduct had effects also effectively regulated it. *Id.* at 298 n.4.

195. *See* 15 U.S.C. § 1013(b).

196. See *Trial Lawyers*, 493 U.S. at 422–23, 432–36 & n.19.

beyond refusing to deal on other than desired terms.[197] This includes an absolute concerted refusal to deal with a party (either entirely or on some transactions) in order to punish that party for its past conduct.[198] It also includes a conditioned refusal to deal that is designed to coerce the party to change its future conduct to meet the condition, but only if the scope of the refusal includes matters "unrelated" or "collateral" to the desired terms in the transaction with the refused party.[199] Under this standard, if a conspiracy sought to sell an insurance product at $10 or only on term X, then a concerted refusal to sell that product to any buyer for less than $10 or terms worse than X would not be a boycott. But it would be a boycott to have a concerted refusal to sell that product (on nondiscriminatory terms) to buyers based on their *other* transactions (such as with noncomplying sellers) or to refuse to buy or sell some *other* product (on nondiscriminatory terms) to firms that don't buy or sell the first product at $10 or on term X.

d. The Labor Exemptions. Without a labor exemption, ordinary union activities like strikes or setting labor prices in collective bargaining agreements would be horizontal boycotts and price-fixing agreements subject to the risk of antitrust liability. To avoid this, Congress has enacted statutes that provide antitrust exemptions for, and bar injunctions against, such ordinary labor union activities as collective refusals to supply labor or agreements not to compete on wages or other employment terms.[200] This explicit statutory exemption protects agreements among labor employees, but not among independent contractors who collectively engage in boycotts or price-fixing.[201] The explicit statutory exemption extends only to conduct and agreements by employees and their unions, and not to their agreements with non-labor groups.[202]

The Court has also recognized what it calls a "nonstatutory exemption" for agreements between unions and employers, but only to the extent necessary to make the collective bargaining process work.[203] It would be more accurate to call this exemption "implicit" rather than "nonstatutory"

---

197. *See Hartford Fire*, 509 U.S. at 801–03. Although in substantive antitrust law, the Court sometimes uses "boycott" to refer to those concerted refusals to deal that are per se unlawful, the boycott exception to the insurance exemption does not require that the concerted refusal be per se unlawful. *See St. Paul Fire*, 438 U.S. at 542.

198. *Hartford Fire*, 509 U.S. at 801.

199. *Id.* at 801–803, 806, 810–11.

200. *See* 15 U.S.C. § 17; 29 U.S.C. §§ 52, 101–115.

201. *See* AMA v. United States, 317 U.S. 519, 526–27, 536 (1943) (physicians); United States v. National Ass'n of Real Estate Boards, 339 U.S. 485, 489 (1950) (real estate brokers); Columbia River Packers Ass'n v. Hinton, 315 U.S. 143 (1942) (fisherman). Those employees who are considered managers, which generally includes professionals who have any supervisory responsibilities, are also not eligible to form labor unions and bargain collectively. *See* NLRB v. Health Care & Retirement Corp., 511 U.S. 571 (1994) (licensed practical nurses); FHP, Inc., 274 N.L.R.B. 1141, 1142–43 (1985) (physicians who were HMO employees).

202. United States v. Hutcheson, 312 U.S. 219, 232 (1941).

203. Connell Constr. Co., Inc. v. Plumbers & Steamfitters Local Union No. 100, 421 U.S. 616, 622 (1975); *see also Pennington*, 381 U.S. at 662 (collecting cases); Allen Bradley Co. v. Local Union No. 3, IBEW, 325 U.S. 797, 810 (1945) ("the same labor union activities may or may not be in violation of the Sherman Act, dependent upon whether the union acts alone or in combination with business groups.").

given that it is in fact implied from the statute. The Court has interpreted this nonstatutory (implicit) labor exemption to extend even to horizontal agreements among employers on the other side of the same collective bargaining process about the terms they will offer as part of that process or impose if the union does not agree, on the grounds that such immunity is necessary to make multi-employer collective bargaining work.[204] In short, the labor exemption allows the competition model favored by antitrust to be replaced with the model of bilateral collective bargaining between sellers and buyers that is favored by labor law. In the latter type of case, the process is policed by the National Labor Relations Board rather than by antitrust courts.[205]

The nonstatutory (implicit) labor exemption is limited to activities that are legitimately within the collective bargaining process about wages, hours, and other employment terms. Even collective bargaining agreements between union and businesses can lose their immunity when used to suppress competition from a rival business[206] or to restrain competition by employers in their product markets.[207] *A fortiori,* this doctrine offers no immunity when a union and business impose a direct restraint on market competition outside any collective bargaining agreement.[208] Accordingly, the courts have repeatedly held that alleged conspiracies between unions and businesses to suppress competition from another business enjoy no antitrust exemption.[209] For example, *Connell* involved an agreement between a union and general contractor that the general contractor would award subcontracts only to firms that had a contract with the union.[210] The Court held that this was not exempted because it involved a direct restraint on a business market, rather than being part of a collective bargaining agreement limited to the standardization of wages and working conditions.[211] It did not matter that the union's only goal was the legal one of organizing as many subcontractors as possible because the method violated antitrust law.[212] In *Pennington,* the allegation was that the union and large coal operators conspired to exclude small coal operators from the market by

---

204. *See* Brown v. Pro Football, 518 U.S. 231 (1996).

205. *Id.* at 242.

206. *See Pennington,* 381 U.S. at 662–69 (holding that this lack of immunity applied even when the restraint involves a compulsory subject of collective bargaining).

207. *See id.* at 662–63; Amalgamated Meat Cutters v. Jewel Tea Co., 381 U.S. 676 (1965).

208. *See* A.L. Adams Constr. Co. v. Georgia Power Co., 733 F.2d 853, 855–56 (11th Cir.1984) (no exemption if Agreement was not part of a collective bargaining relationship); C & W Constr. Co. v. Brotherhood of Carpenters, 687 F.Supp. 1453, 1464 (D. Hawai'i 1988) (union-business refusal to deal that was outside any collective bargaining agreement was per se outside the labor exemption).

209. *See Connell Constr.,* 421 U.S. at 623–26; *Pennington,* 381 U.S. at 662–69; *Allen,* 325 U.S. at 809–810; United States v. Employing Plasterers Assn., 347 U.S. 186, 190 (1954); Philadelphia Record v. Manufacturing Photo–Engravers Assn., 155 F.2d 799, 803 (3d Cir. 1946); Gilmour v. Wood, Wire & Metal Lathers Intern., 223 F.Supp. 236, 248 (N.D. Ill. 1963).

210. 421 U.S. at 618–19.

211. *Id.* at 623–26.

212. *Id.* at 625.

imposing an agreed-upon wage on smaller coal operators.[213] The Court concluded that, although those wages were a compulsory subject of bargaining, the agreement to impose those wage levels on other employers outside the bargaining unit stated an antitrust claim.[214]

The inapplicability of the labor exemption does not eliminate the need to prove the nonexempt conduct actually violates antitrust law. Nor does the inapplicability of the nonstatutory exemption to an agreement between unions and employers remove the statutory exemption for agreements among union members. Rather, where the nonstatutory exemption does not apply, the horizontal agreement among union members remains exempt under the statutory exemption and the only issue is whether the union's nonexempt vertical agreement with the employer violates antitrust law. For example, when *Connell* held the nonstatutory labor exemption inapplicable, it remanded for a determination of whether the vertical "agreement between Local 100 and Connell.... restrains trade," not whether the horizontal agreement among union members of Local 100 did.[215] Likewise, *Pennington* removed only the nonstatutory exemption for the vertical "agreement between [United Mine Workers] and the large operators," not the statutory exemption for the horizontal agreement among members of United Mine Workers. In cases where the nonstatutory labor exemption does not apply, the situation comes close to treating the union as a single entity, but is distinct from it because any union decision to offer a wage or refuse to deal with an employer would remain immune under the statutory labor exemption even when the union collectively has monopoly power that would, if it were a single business entity, make such decisions reviewable as predatory pricing or unilateral refusal to deals when certain conditions are met.

(3) Effect on U.S. Interstate Commerce. Finally, the U.S. antitrust statutes require some effect on U.S. interstate commerce. This imposes three limitations. First, the effects of the conduct cannot be limited to one state, but must have some interstate effects. However, the required effect is so trivial that this rarely poses a practical barrier. Second, for foreign restraints, U.S. law requires some substantial effect on U.S. markets or exporters. Third, the restraint or anticompetitive effect must be on "commerce" rather than on some noncommercial activity.

a.   EFFECT ON INTERSTATE COMMERCE. All of the U.S. antitrust statutes require that the challenged conduct involve or affect interstate commerce.[216] But while this requirement was historically important, it has been narrowly interpreted in a way that makes it practically irrelevant. Even a restraint of a highly local market within one state has the requisite interstate effects as long as lawyers remember to dutifully plead that some sort of business is transacted across state lines by either the defendants or any firms in the market directly affected by the defendant's conduct.[217] It is

---

213.   381 U.S. at 664.

214.   *Id.* at 665–69.

215.   421 U.S. at 637.

216.   *See* 15 U.S.C. §§ 1–2, 12(a), 13, 14, 18, 44–45.

217.   *See* Summit Health v. Pinhas, 500 U.S. 322, 329–33 (1991); McLain v. Real Estate Board of New Orleans, 444 U.S. 232, 235–36; 241–46 (1980).

hard to know how one could ever fail to satisfy this requirement unless one had an odd market where no sellers or buyers ever made interstate sales, purchases, loans, or phone calls. Indeed, at least one prominent judge has concluded that the requirement is so trivial that merely pleading the bare conclusion that interstate commerce was affected should suffice.[218] The U.S. Supreme Court has held the interstate commerce requirement satisfied in a case where the defendants allegedly conspired to deny staff privileges in a Los Angeles hospital to a single surgeon.[219] The Court has also interpreted the Sherman Act to extend to the furthest reaches of congressional power to regulate interstate commerce,[220] which itself covers even a farmer's decision to grow wheat for his farm's own consumption.[221]

b. EFFECT ON U.S. COMMERCE. Unless it has a sufficient effect on U.S. commerce or exporters, the U.S. antitrust laws do not cover restraints on foreign soil or domestic restraints on export trade. Further, even with sufficient effects on U.S. commerce, the reach of U.S. antitrust law may be limited by principles of comity (where foreign law is in conflict) or by sovereign immunity and the act of state doctrine (when the conduct involves foreign governmental action). The complex set of rules on this topic is addressed in Chapter 8, which generally deals with the problem of coordinating antitrust jurisdictions on global markets.

c. EFFECT ON COMMERCE. To be covered by U.S. antitrust law, the restraint or anticompetitive effect must be on "commerce," which is to say on some market that involves the sale of goods, services or property in exchange for valuable consideration. A restraint on a donative activity, such as an agreement between two charities that one will provide or solicit donations in the eastern United States and the other in the western United States, would not be a restraint on commerce.[222] This does not mean that charities or nonprofit *entities* are not covered by the antitrust laws. To the contrary, nonprofits are covered whenever they restrain some commercial market, such as providing medical care or college education in exchange for money.[223] Further, even noncommercial activities, like donations or promulgating safety standards, are restraints on commerce if their terms

---

218. Hammes v. AAMCO Transmissions, Inc., 33 F.3d 774, 778–79 (7th Cir. 1994) (Posner, J.)

219. *Summit*, 500 U.S. 322.

220. *Summit*, 500 U.S. at 328–29 & n.8, 332–33; *McLain*, 444 U.S. at 241. Other cases have held that the Clayton Act and Robinson–Patman Act did not go quite so far because they did not apply to any conduct that affected interstate commerce but rather required that the defendants and their activities be "in" interstate commerce, *see* United States v. American Bldg. Maintenance Indus., 422 U.S. 271, 275–84 (1975); Gulf Oil Corp. v. Copp Paving Co., 419 U.S. 186, 194–203 (1974). However, Congress amended Clayton Act § 7 to include persons and conduct affecting interstate commerce, *see* 15 U.S.C. § 15, and amended FTC Act § 5 to include conduct in or affecting commerce, *see* 15 U.S.C. § 45, and the FTC has authority to enforce the Clayton and Robinson–Patman Act. In addition, the Sherman Act likely covers any anticompetitive conduct covered by Clayton Act §§ 3,7, *see infra* Chapters 4, 7.

221. Wickard v. Filburn, 317 U.S. 111 (1942).

222. *See* Dedication & Everlasting Love to Animals v. Humane Society, 50 F.3d 710, 712 (9th Cir. 1995).

223. *See id.* at 713; *infra* Chapter 2.

affect some commercial market.[224] However, Congress has enacted specific exemptions for charitable gift annuities and charitable remainder trusts.[225]

2.   An Overview of EU Competition Laws and Remedial Structure

i.   The EU Competition Provisions and Enforcement Architecture

(1) Origins, Content and Basic Institutional Framework. The sources of European competition law can historically be traced back to the 1951 European Coal and Steel (ECSC) Treaty. This treaty initiated a process of deep economic integration in the steel and coal sectors between Belgium, Italy, Luxembourg, France and the Netherlands. Besides a number of legal and economic provisions organizing the trade of steel and coal between its Member States, the treaty contained a few competition law provisions which had been drafted by several antitrust experts, among them Robert Bowie, then a Harvard Law Professor.[226] These competition provisions were threefold: a prohibition of cartels, a ban on the "misuse" of economic power and a system of merger control.

A few years later, the Members of the ECSC decided to extend the scope of their economic integration to a larger number of sectors by establishing the European Communities (hereafter the "EC"). Convinced of the merits of economic competition, the drafters of the EC Treaty found a useful source of reference in the competition provisions of the ECSC Treaty. It is therefore not surprising that the EC Treaty, signed in Rome in 1957, holds undistorted competition as one of its fundamental objectives,[227] and lays down a complete set of competition provisions. With the entry into force of the Lisbon Treaty on December 1, 2009, the EC Treaty was amended and renamed the Treaty on the Functioning of the European Union (TFEU). This led to a renumbering of the provisions that were initially contained in the EC Treaty. The main competition provisions of the EC Treaty can now be found at Article 101 to Article 109 TFEU. As will be seen below, the name of the Court of First Instance, which plays an important role as it is the Court that reviews the appeals lodged by private

---

224. *See* American Soc'y v. Hydrolevel, 456 U.S. 556, 560–62 (1982) (nonprofit liable for issuing a letter that, without any financial benefit to the nonprofit, interpreted a safety standard in a way that restrained trade); *Allied Tube*, 486 U.S. at 501 (antitrust rule of reason applies to safety standard setting by disinterested nonprofit associations); *Virginia Vermiculite*, 156 F.3d 535 (donation of land by mining company with restrictive covenants prohibiting its use for mining was an agreement in restraint of commerce); Ozee v. American Council, 110 F.3d 1082, 1093 (5th Cir. 1997) (donation to charity is treated as a commercial transaction when the donor receives an "annuity, substantial tax advantage, and the satisfaction of having given to charity.")

225. *See* 15 U.S.C. § 37.

226. *See* David J. Gerber, *Law and Competition in Twentieth Century Europe—Protecting Prometheus*, Clarendon Press Oxford, 1998 at p.340.

227. Commission Regulation 330/2010 of 20 April 2010 on the application of Article 101(3) of the Treaty on the Functioning of the European Union to categories of vertical agreements and concerted practices, O.J. L 102/1.

parties against decisions of the European Commission, has also been changed to "General Court". Given the fact these changes entered into force very recently, the vast majority of the materials we use in this casebook refer to the old numbering system. In order to avoid confusion, we will either refer to the new numbers and replace the old numbers with the new numbers in the documents examined below or leave the old numbers unchanged but add the new numbers to which they correspond between brackets. While Articles 101 and 102 of the TFEU respectively prohibit restrictive agreements between firms and abuses of a dominant position, the TFEU also contain rules aimed at preventing its Member States from taking measures that distort competition. Article 106, for instance, prevents Member States from adopting measures vis-à-vis public (i.e., State-owned) firms and firms in charge of services of general economic interest that would *inter alia* violate competition rules. Similarly, Article 107 prevents Member States from granting State aids that restrict competition and affect intra-EU trade to firms. Articles 106 and 107 of the TFEU find no equivalent in U.S. antitrust law. Throughout this book, we will thus focus on the prohibitions imposed by Articles 101 and 102.

As far as the EU institutional framework is concerned, a number of authorities are in charge of applying EU competition rules. First, at the EU level the Commission is in charge of ensuring the application of such rules. Within the Commission, there is a special "directorate" that has been entrusted with the enforcement of EU competition rules, i.e. DG Competition (also known as "DG COMP"), which comprises several hundred officials (lawyers and economists) who operate under the leadership of a Director General. Within the College of Commissioners (the political body which formally adopts the decisions prepared by DG COMP), there is one Commissioner in charge of competition policy.

Second, at the national level, all Member States set up national competition authorities (often referred to as "NCAs"), which are in charge of applying EU and national competition rules. Some of these authorities, such as the Office of Fair Trading in the UK and the Bundeskartellamt in Germany, enjoy staff and resources that are considerably larger than the Commission. National courts are also entitled to apply EU and national competition rules. Depending on a number of factors, such as the rapidity of the procedure or the possibility to ask for compensatory damages, plaintiffs will start proceedings before the NCAs or the national courts and even in some cases before both. When anticompetitive practices produce effects in several Member States, plaintiffs may initiate legal proceedings in several Member States, the authorities of which will then have to coordinate to decide which of them will investigate the matter.[228]

(2) Other Competition Law Provisions adopted by the Council or by the Commission. Besides the TFEU competition law provisions, secondary sources of EU competition law can be found in Regulations adopted by the Council of Ministers (a body which comprises the relevant ministers of the different Member States), as well as in a range of legal acts adopted by the

---

228. Commission Regulation No 1218/2010 of 14 December 2010 on the application of Article 101(3) of the Treaty to categories of specialisation agreements, O.J. L 335/43.

Commission such as Block Exemption Regulations, Guidelines, Notices, Guidance letters, etc.

a.   THE EU MERGER REGULATION. The now defunct EC Treaty contained no provision establishing a merger control system. In 1989, however, the Council and adopted Regulation 4064/89, establishing an EU Merger Control regime. The Regulation was subsequently revised in 1997 and in 2004 (it is now Regulation 139/2004).[229] A noticeable feature of the EU Merger Regulation is that it provides for a "one stop shop", whereby all transactions crossing the turnover thresholds contained in the Regulation fall within the exclusive jurisdiction of the European Commission. Below these thresholds, the Commission has no jurisdiction to examine the merger (since it has no "Community dimension"). It is thus left to the jurisdiction of national authorities.

b.   ADOPTION OF BLOCK EXEMPTION REGULATIONS FOR CERTAIN SECTORS/CATEGORIES OF AGREEMENTS. Pursuant to Article 101(3), agreements "improving the production or distribution of goods or ... promoting technical or economic progress" are exempted from the Article 101(1) prohibition, provided a number of conditions are met. It did not take long for the Commission to realize that the vast majority of the agreements entered into by firms (cooperation agreements, licensing agreements, etc.) fulfilled these conditions. Thus, the Council (under the authority of Article 103), or the Commission (under delegated authority from the Council) adopted so-called "block exemption regulations." Under these regulations, certain categories of agreements or agreements concluded in specific sectors automatically benefit from the Article 101(3) exemption. Examples of the former include transfer of technology agreements,[230] distribution agreements,[231] specialization agreements,[232] and research and development agreements.[233] Examples of the latter include motor vehicle distribution agreements[234] and agreements in the insurance sector.[235]

c.   PROLIFERATION OF SOFT LAW INSTRUMENTS. In recent years, the increased complexity of competition law, both in terms of substance (increased economically-driven approach) and procedure (by virtue of the

---

229.   *See* Council Regulation 139/2004 of 20 January 2004 on the control of concentrations between undertakings, O.J. 2004, L 24/1.

230.   *See* Commission Regulation 772/2004 of 27 April 2004 on the application of Article 81(3) of the Treaty to categories of technology transfer agreements, O.J. 2004, L 123/11.

231.   Commission Regulation 330/2010 of 20 April 2010 on the application of Article 101(3) of the Treaty on the Functioning of the European Union to categories of vertical agreements and concerted practices, O.J. L 102/1.

232.   Commission Regulation No 1218/2010 of 14 December 2010 on the application of Article 101(3) of the Treaty to categories of specialisation agreements, O.J. L 335/43.

233.   Commission Regulation No 1217/2010 of 14 December 2010 on the application of Article 101(3) of the Treaty on the functioning of the European Union to categories of research and development agreements, O.J. L 335/36.

234.   Commission Regulation (EU) No 461/2010 of 27 May 2010 on the application of Article 101(3) of the Treaty on the Functioning of the European Union to categories of vertical agreements and concerted practices in the motor vehicle sector, O.J. 2010, L 129/1.

235.   Commission Regulation (EU) No 267/2010 of 24 March 2010 on the application of Article 101(3) of the Treaty on the Functioning of the European Union to certain categories of agreements, decisions and concerted practices in the insurance sector, O.J. 2010, L 83/1.

complex decentralization process) has induced the Commission to adopt numerous soft law instruments, so as to clarify its approaches with respect to an heterogeneous set of issues. These instruments, often labeled "Guidelines" or "Notices", do not bind courts. They, however, bind the Commission and are thus very helpful for firms and their counsel seeking to determine whether their conduct is likely or unlikely to be challenged by the Commission. Examples of such documents include Guidelines on Vertical Restraints,[236] Guidelines on Technology Transfer Agreements,[237] or Guidelines on the Assessment of Horizontal Mergers.[238]

(3) Case-law of the European Court of Justice and of the General Court. A final source of EC competition law emerges from the case-law of the European Court of Justice (the "ECJ") and the General Court (the "GC") of the European Union. All institutions in charge of applying EU competition law (see our discussion below) are bound to follow the interpretations of the ECJ, whose pronouncements on EU law have the same interpretative value as those of the U.S. Supreme Court on U.S. law.

(4) National Competition Laws. Besides EU competition rules, all Member States have adopted national competition rules. These rules are closely patterned on EU competition law and contain provisions that are (nearly) identical to Articles 101 and 102 TFEU. The application of national competition laws must not lead to the prohibition of agreements or concerted practices that are not prohibited under EU competition law.[239] Member States may, however, apply stricter competition rules to unilateral conduct.[240]

ii.   The EU Enforcement System and Remedial Structure

(1) Regulation 17's Conferral of Enforcement Authority on the European Commission. Council Regulation 17/62 centralized the enforcement of Article 101 and 102 within the hands of the Commission, giving it far reaching investigative and regulatory powers.[241] In addition, it required firms to notify all agreements falling within the scope of Article 101 to the Commission. If the agreement was contrary to Article 101(1), the Commission had sole jurisdiction to deliver an exemption on the basis of Article 101(3). In contrast, existing National Competition Authorities (hereafter "NCAs") and national courts only played a marginal role in the implementation of EU competition rules.

(2) Reform of the Enforcement System in 2003. In the early 2000s, the Commission concluded that the notification procedure had considerably overloaded its staff and resources, preventing it, in turn, from focusing on

---

236. Guidelines on Vertical Restraints, O.J. 2010, C 130/01.

237. *See* Guidelines on the application of Article 81 of the EC Treaty [now 101 of the TFEU] to technology transfer agreements, O.J. 2004, C 101/2.

238. *See* Guidelines on the assessment of horizontal mergers under the Council Regulation on the control of concentrations between undertakings, O.J. 2004, C 31/5.

239. *See* Article 3(2) of Regulation 1/2003, Council Regulation (EC) No 1/2003 of 16 December 2002 on the implementation of the rules on competition laid down in Articles 81 and 82 of the EC Treaty [now articles 101 and 102 of the TFEU], O.J. 2003, L 1/1.

240. *Id.*

241. Regulation 17/62/main implementing Regulation, O.J. Spec. ed., 1959–62, 87.

the most serious violations of EU competition rules, such as hardcore cartels.[242] Meanwhile, most Member States had set up NCAs and entrusted them with the mandate to apply national competition statutes, drafted in language close to the now defunct EC Treaty. The combination of these two evolutions induced the Commission to ask the Council to (i) abolish the notification procedure, and (ii) entrust NCAs and national courts with the application of Article 101(3).

The Council followed the Commission's proposals and adopted Regulation 1/2003, which replaced Regulation 17/62 effective May 1, 2004. Regulation 1/2003 sets out a decentralized system where NCAs and national Courts are at the forefront of the enforcement of EU competition rules. The increased decentralization achieved in turn allows the Commission to redeploy its resources in other directions. The Commission now focuses its investigations on sectors "where there are only a few players, where cartel activity is recurrent, or where abuses of market power are generic." In addition, the Commission increasingly monitors the action of NCAs and retains the possibility to intervene in cases dealt with at the national level.

(3) Administrative vs. Judicial Remedies. Unlike U.S. antitrust law where remedies are generally obtained through court litigation, EU competition law is mostly enforced through administrative remedial mechanisms (before the Commission or before NCAs). An important feature of the European competition law enforcement system is that it is based upon administrative agencies whose powers go beyond the mere seeking of injunctive relief. In contrast with U.S. agencies (DOJ and FTC), the Commission and the NCAs do not need litigation before courts of law to obtain a finding of infringement, negotiate behavioral and/or structural remedies and impose fines. These competition agencies enjoy important decision powers of their own and thus offer attractive remedies to complainants.

In contrast, judicial remedial mechanisms (i.e. before national courts) are traditionally left unexplored by plaintiffs. This is the case for a number of reasons.[243] First, unlike before U.S. Courts, rules of discovery are underdeveloped in Europe. This means that in most Member States, parties are under no obligation to produce relevant information and often will only be ordered to do so when the requesting party can identify the individual document he seeks, which in many cases will simply not be possible. Second, plaintiffs' incentives to bring court actions are less obvious than in the U.S., as in most cases national courts do not grant punitive/treble damages. They merely provide compensation/restitution and often, judges are reluctant to assess the damage caused by an anti-competitive practice. Third, in most Member States, the rules governing legal cost provide that the loser pays costs (although these can be divided in cases of partial

---

242. *See* 1999 White Paper on the Modernisation of the Rules implementing Article 81 and 82 EC [now 101 and 102 of the TFEU], COM (1999) 101 final. Of course, the burden on the Commission had been slightly reduced through the adoption of block exemption regulations, notices, guidelines and comfort letters.

243. These reasons have been empirically identified in a Comparative Report by Ashurst, *Study on the conditions of claims for damages in case of infringement of EC competition rules*, 31 August 2004.

success). However, it is often the case that fees are not fully recoverable in practice. Combined with the substantial costs of litigating antitrust issues, this generates a clear disincentive for private parties to initiate judicial proceedings.

On December 19, 2005, the European Commission published a Green Paper on how to facilitate actions for damages caused by violations of EU competition rules' ban on restrictive business practices and abuse of dominant market positions (Articles 101 and 102 respectively).[244] The Green Paper notes that violations of these rules, in particular by price fixing cartels, can cause considerable damage to companies and consumers but numerous obstacles can hinder actions for damages by injured parties in national courts. The Green Paper identifies certain of these obstacles, such as access to evidence and the quantification of damages, and presents various options for debate for their removal. This Green Paper was followed up by a White Paper on "Damages Actions for Breach of the EC antitrust rules"[245] suggesting a new model for achieving compensation for consumers and businesses who are the victims of antitrust violations.[246] The White Paper comprises various suggestions to ensure that victims of competition law infringements have access to truly effective mechanisms for claiming full compensation for the harm they have suffered, whilst ensuring respect for European legal systems and traditions. The model outlined by the Commission is based on compensation through single damages for the harm suffered. The White Paper's other key recommendations cover collective redress, disclosure of evidence and the effect of final decisions of competition authorities in subsequent damages actions. The European Commission is now expected to propose directive on private damages for breach of antitrust rules.

(4) Administrative Remedies—Actions by the Commission and the NCAs

a.   THE DIVISION OF COMPETENCIES BETWEEN THE NCAS AND THE COMMISSION. The NCAs and the Commission form an integrated network of agencies (referred to as the "European Competition Network"). They act in a complementary fashion and hold distinct duties.

On the low end of the network, the decentralized enforcement framework established by Regulation 1/2003 entrusts NCAs with the bulk of Article 101 and 102 cases. As there are more than 25 NCAs in the EU, the allocation of jurisdiction between national agencies may be a delicate issue, in particular for practices affecting several Member States' territories. In principle, the NCA that should have jurisdiction to inquire into a specific practice should prove that it is "well placed" to act. For a NCA to be "well placed", three conditions should be fulfilled.[247] First, the agreement or

---

244.   Green Paper, Damages actions for breach of the EC antitrust rules, 19 December 2005; Commission Staff Working Paper, Damages actions for breach of the EC antitrust rules, COM (2005) 672 final, 19 December 2005.

245.   COM (2008) 165, 2 April 2008.

246.   See "Antitrust: Commission presents policy paper on compensating consumer and business victims of competition breaches" IP/08/515, 3 April 2008.

247.   *See* Commission Notice on cooperation within the Network of Competition Authorities, O.J. C 101 of 27 April 2004, pp. 43–53.

practice must have substantial direct actual or foreseeable effects on competition within its territory and must be implemented within or must originate from its territory. Second, the NCA must be able to effectively bring to an end the entire infringement, i.e. it must be able to adopt a cease-and-desist order the effect of which will be sufficient to bring an end to the infringement and it must be able, where appropriate, to sanction the infringement adequately. Third, it must be able to gather, possibly with the assistance of other authorities, the evidence required to prove the infringement.[248]

On the high end of the network, the Commission holds a wider range of roles. First, it intervenes with respect to the most serious infringements (i.e. hardcore cartels or severe abuse of dominance cases)[249] or agreements and practices with important cross border effects, that is those that have effects on competition in more than three Member States.[250] Second, the Commission defines EU competition policy through the adoption of guidelines, notices, guidance letters, etc. Recent initiatives in that respect have, for instance, led the Commission to focus on a number of sectors (through the opening of inquiries in the energy and banking fields, etc.) or on a specific provision of the TFEU (*e.g.*, Article 102). Third, the Commission holds an assistance mission to the NCAs when the latter apply EU competition law.[251] Finally, the Commission acts as the watchdog of the European Competition Network. It monitors actions taken by the NCAs on the basis of EU competition rules. Ultimately, it enjoys the power to remove a case from a NCA (taking over the case in question) on the basis of Article 11(6) of Regulation 1/2003, if for instance the national authority is not applying EU rules in a correct fashion.

    b. Remedies Before the European Commission.

    1. Initiation of Proceedings by the European Commission. The Commission may initiate proceedings following (1) a complaint, (2) a request or transfer of a NCA or (3) simply acting of its own motion (after an investigation or information received through any channel, such as trade journals, etc.).

    (i) Action upon complaint.—Plaintiffs can lodge formal complaints before the Commission.[252] Article 7 of Regulation 1/2003 provides that "natural or legal persons who can show a legitimate interest" can lodge a complaint before the Commission. Any person who can show that she is

---

    248. A number of other cooperation mechanisms are provided for, when several NCAs open parallel proceedings or where a NCA that considered it was "well placed" is, in fact, not "well placed" to deal with a practice. *See id.* at §§ 18–19.

    249. *See* Recital 3 of Regulation 1/2003, supra note 235.

    250. *See* § 14 of Commission Notice on cooperation within the Network of Competition Authorities, supra note 224.

    251. *See* Article 11(5) of Regulation 1/2003, supra note 229, where the NCAs can consult the Commission when applying EU Competition law. This assistance duty is also addressed to national courts, where the latter can request the Commission to provide them with information it holds or with an opinion on a point of law. See Article 15 of Regulation 1/2003.

    252. *See,* on the following, Commission Notice on the handling of complaints by the Commission under Articles 81 and 82 of the EC Treaty [now 101 and 102 of the TFEU], O.J. 2004, C 101/65.

suffering or likely to suffer injury or loss from the alleged infringement has a legitimate interest for lodging a complaint before the Commission (party to a terminated agreement, actual or potential competitors facing predatory behavior, consumer associations, etc.). In addition, the potential plaintiff can lodge "informal" or anonymous complaints to the Commission, the main difference being the procedural duties bearing on the Commission. When dealing with a formal complaint, the Commission is under a duty to examine the complaint with "vigilance" (i.e. it has to "consider attentively all the matter of facts and law which the complainant brings to its attention").[253] Furthermore, it has to answer to the complaint within a reasonable time frame, provide an opportunity to the complainant to be heard (if the Commission envisions rejecting the application), and give sufficiently precise and detailed reasons in case it actually rejects the complaint.

(ii) Action on the basis of request or transfer of a NCA.—Pursuant to Article 11 of Regulation 1/2003, the Commission and NCAs cooperate with each other through extensive exchange of information protocols. The information circulated by NCAs may trigger the initiation of proceedings by the European Commission, in which case NCAs are relieved of their competence to apply Article 101 or 102 to a given practice.[254]

(iii) Initiation of proceedings by the Commission on its own motion.— The Commission can initiate proceedings on its own motion, on the basis of any information which it considers sufficient to that end. The Commission may open procedures when, for instance, "the trend of trade between Member States, the rigidity of prices or other circumstances suggest that competition may be restricted or distorted within the common market."[255]

2. *Powers and Remedies Available at the Commission Level*

(i) Cease and Desist Orders.—Pursuant to Article 7 of Regulation 1/2003, the Commission, if it "finds that there is an infringement of Article [101] or of Article [102] of the Treaty, [. . .] may by decision require the undertakings and associations of undertakings concerned to bring such infringement to an end." If the agreement or abusive behavior has already been terminated, the Commission may nonetheless issue a declaration that it constituted an infringement.

(ii) Behavioral and Structural Remedies.—In order to bring an infringement to an end, the Commission enjoys the power to impose behavioral and structural remedies on the parties. For instance, in an illegal refusal to supply case, the Commission is entitled to order the supply of the product concerned,[256] or the conclusion of licensing agreements on the intellectual property right at hand.[257] Regulation 1/2003 brings, however, a qualification with respect to structural remedies:

---

253. *See* ECJ C–119/97, *UFEX v. Commission* [1999] ECR I–1341 at § 86.

254. *See* Article 11(6) of Regulation 1/2003, supra note 229.

255. *Id. at* Article 17.

256. *See e.g.*, ECJ, 6–7/73, *Commercial Solvents v. Commission*, [1974] ECR–223.

257. *See e.g.*, ECJ 241–242/91, *RTE and ITP v. Commission*, [1995] ECR II–1439.

"Structural remedies can only be imposed either where there is no equally effective behavioural remedy or where any equally effective behavioural remedy would be more burdensome for the undertaking concerned than the structural remedy."

The explicit possibility for the Commission to adopt structural remedies is a novelty introduced by Regulation 1/2003. It seems that these remedies are only available to bring an abusive behavior to an end. In contrast, structural remedies do not seem available to correct the consequences of illegal exclusionary behavior so as to reestablish a *statu quo ante* (for instance, through ordering a dominant firm to divest the share of products gained after having successfully forced its competitors out of the market).

(iii) Interim Measures.—Regulation 17/62 did not explicitly envisage the possibility for the Commission to order interim measures. However, following an extensive interpretation of Article 3 of that regulation in its *Camera Care* order, the ECJ did bestow upon the Commission the power to order such measures.[258] In practice, though, most interim measures were ordered upon the request of undertakings rather than by the Commission acting on its own initiative.[259] This power has since then been codified at Article 8(1) of Regulation 1/2003.[260]

(iv) Settlements and Commitments.—In the course of its investigations and prior to adopting a cease an desist order, the Commission has the possibility to terminate or suspend proceedings because the agreement or conduct at hand is terminated or amended by the parties (who wish to comply with EU competition rules). The Commission does not need to adopt a formal decision. The vast majority of the cases brought before the Commission are settled without the adoption of a formal decision. Often, the parties offer commitments to meet the anticompetitive concerns identified by the Commission during its preliminary assessment. Pursuant to Regulation 1/2003, the Commission enjoys the possibility to make these commitments binding on the parties by adopting a decision which concludes that there is no longer ground for action.[261]

The Commission may nonetheless reopen proceedings if (i) there has been a material change in any of the facts on which the decision was based; (ii) the firms concerned have disregarded their commitments; or (iii) where the decision was based on incomplete, incorrect or misleading information provided by the parties.[262]

---

258. *See* Order of the European Court of Justice, Case C–792/79, *Camera Care v. Commission*, [1980] ECR, 119 at para. 18.

259. *See*, for a well-known example, Commission decision of 3 July 2001, *NDC Health/ IMS Health*, (2003) O.J. L. 268/69.

260. *See* Article 8(1) of Regulation 1/2003, supra note 235: "In cases of urgency due to the risk of serious and irreparable damage to competition, the Commission, acting on its own initiative may by decision, on the basis of a prima facie finding of infringement, order interim measures."

261. *See* Article 9 of Regulation 1/2003, supra note 235.

262. *Id.*

Given that commitment decisions or settlements do not establish the existence of an infringement to EU competition rules, NCAs and national courts keep the possibility of adopting decisions finding an infringement of Article 81 or 82.[263]

(v) Fines.—Regulation 1/2003, empowers the Commission to fine a firm up to 10% of its total turnover in the preceding business year where, intentionally or negligently: "they infringe Article 101 or Article 102 of the Treaty; or they contravene a decision ordering interim measures [. . .]; or they fail to comply with a commitment made binding by a decision [. . .]."[264] Fines represent the main EU legal instrument to remedy and deter violations of competition law. The ECJ indicated in *Musique Diffusion France*, that the underlying rationale for the imposition of fines is to ensure the implementation of Community competition policy and, in particular, to ensure (i) the suppression of illegal activity and (ii) the prevention of recidivism.[265]

In fixing the amount of the fine, the Commission should take into account the gravity and the duration of the infringement.[266] The calculation method follows a four step process.[267] First, a "basic amount" for the fine is calculated based on (i) the qualification of the infringement as minor, serious or very serious and (ii) of an assessment of the duration of the infringement as short, medium or long. Second, the Commission examines whether it should reduce or increase the basic amount with reference to any aggravating or mitigating circumstances.[268] The factors that can be held as aggravating encompass recidivism, leading role, retaliatory measures against other undertakings, refusal to co-operate, etc. Attenuating circumstances on the other hand include passive role, non-implementation of the offending agreement, and termination of the infringement as soon as the Commission intervened. Third, the Commission determines whether the company under inquiry can benefit from the principles set out in the leniency notice, which may reduce the fines or even lead to the non-imposition of fines.[269] Fourth, the Commission can adjust up or down the amount of fines to reflect that an undertaking manufactures a wide portfolio of products or to reflect the economic or financial benefit derived from the anti-competitive conduct or their ability to pay.[270] Finally, during its step-by-step construction of the final fine the Commission must also bear in mind that it must stay within the confines of the statutory ceiling of 10% of the world-wide turnover of the undertaking in question.

---

263. *Id. at* Recital 13.

264. *Id. at* Article 23(2).

265. *See* Damien Geradin & David Henry, *The EC Fining Policy for Violations of Competition Law: An Empirical Review of the Commission Decisional Practice and the Case-Law of the European Courts*, 1 *European Competition Journal*, 2005, 401.

266. *See* Article 23(3) of Regulation 1/2003, supra note 236.

267. *See* Guidelines on the method of setting fines, O.J. C 9 of 14 January 1998.

268. *Id.* at Sections 2 and 3.

269. *See* Commission Notice on the non-imposition or reduction of fines, published in O.J. C 45 of 19 February 2002.

270. Guidelines, supra note 261, at Section 5.

In June 2006, the European Commission adopted new Guidelines on the method of setting fines that increase their deterrent effect on violations of EU competition rules in three ways.[271] First, the revised Guidelines provide that fines may be based on up to 30% of the company's annual sales to which the infringement relates, multiplied by the number of years of participation in the infringement, subject to the Council Regulation 1/2003 limit that companies may be fined only up to 10% of their total annual turnover. Second, for seriously illegal conduct like cartels, a part of the fine may be imposed irrespective of the duration of the infringement. In other words, the mere fact that a company enters into a cartel could "cost" it at least 15 to 25% of its yearly turnover in the relevant product. Third, the new Guidelines introduce important changes with regard to aggravating and mitigating circumstances, the most significant of which concerns repeat offenders. Up to now, the Commission's practice is to increase a fine by 50% where the undertaking has been found to have been previously involved in one or more similar infringements. The new Guidelines change this approach in 3 ways: (i) the Commission will take into account not only its own previous decisions, but also those of National Competition Authorities applying Articles 101 or 102; (ii) the increase may be up to 100%; and (iii) each prior infringement will justify an increase of the fine.

While subject to a certain degree of codification, the Guidelines nonetheless leave a margin of maneuver to the European Commission when setting fines. This, in turn, is giving rise to two related phenomena. First, the Commission has been freely developing a heavy handed fining policy that recently culminated with the levying of a €497.2 million fine on Microsoft for alleged abuses of a dominant position.[272] As noted above, this increase in the fines imposed by the Commission may, however, be warranted by the need to deter firms from violating EU competition law. Second, firms are increasingly challenging Commission decisions before the GC in order to obtain a reduction of the fines imposed by the European Commission.[273]

(vi) Guidance Letters.—Conscious of the importance of legal certainty for the business community, the Commission allows firms in doubt with respect to the legality of an agreement or practice to solicit its views.[274] A request for Commission guidance will only be admissible if it fulfills the following cumulative conditions: it raises a novel question in law; guidance is useful for the case at hand; and the information provided by the company is sufficient for the Commission to provide guidance (no further investigative measures are needed).[275] The legal value of guidance letters is unclear.

---

271. Guidelines on the method of setting fines imposed pursuant to Article 23(2)(a) of Regulation No 1/2003 (text with EEA relevance), June 2006.

272. *See* Commission Decision, Microsoft, Case COMP/C–3/37/792, not published yet.

273. *See* Damien Geradin and Nicolas Petit, "Judicial Remedies under EC Competition Law: Complex Issues arising from the 'Modernisation' Process", Fordham Corporate Law Institute, forthcoming 2005.

274. *See* Recital 38 of Regulation 1/2003, supra note 235.

275. *See* Commission Notice on informal guidance relating to novel questions concerning Articles 81 and 82 of the EC Treaty [now Articles 101 and 102 TFEU] that arise in individual cases, O.J. 2004, C 101/78, at § 8.

The Commission notice on guidance letters takes the view that the issuance of a guidance letter does not prejudge its assessment of subsequent cases.[276] However, it is clear that the Commission could be found to violate the general principle of legitimate expectations if it ignored its pronouncements with respect to a practice covered by a guidance letter. As far as NCAs and national courts are concerned, the notice provides that they are not formally bound by Commission guidance letters.[277]

c. REMEDIES BEFORE NCAs. The remedies which can be offered by NCAs are provided for by national statutes adopted by the Member States. It would be out of the scope of the present casebook to analyze in detail the various remedies offered under national laws. Regulation 1/2003 seeks nonetheless to ensure a minimal amount of homogeneity among national remedies. It provides that, when applying Article 101 and 102 of the TFEU, NCAs shall be able to take the following decisions:

> "requiring that an infringement be brought to an end; ordering interim measures; accepting commitments; imposing fines, periodic penalty payments or any other penalty provided for in their national law."[278]

(5) Judicial Remedies at the National Level. National courts can also apply Article 101 and 102.[279] In spite of the fact that they can neither act of their own motion nor impose fines on companies infringing EU competition law, the initiation of proceedings before national courts presents several advantages over the system of administrative remedies described above. First, national courts can award damages for losses incurred as a result of a violation of Articles 101 or 102.[280] Second, in complex litigation matters, the initiation of proceedings before a national court enables plaintiffs to combine claims related to the application of national competition law with claims based on EU competition provisions. Third, unlike the Commission and competition authorities, national courts cannot drop complaints (or refuse to launch an investigation) and are required to take a judgment on the merits of the claims advanced before it.

The settings in which EU competition law is invoked before national courts are generally twofold. A first setting (usually referred to as the "Euro-defense" setting) arises when Articles 101 or 102 are invoked by a defendant in a national procedure as a shield against a complainant seeking to enforce an agreement/practice that infringes EU competition law.[281] For instance, a licensee may seek to escape the payment of royalties demanded

---

276. *Id.* at § 24.

277. *Id.* at § 25.

278. *See* Article 5 of Regulation 1/2003, *supra* note 236.

279. *Id. at* Article 6.

280. *Id. at* Recital 7.

281. *See* ECJ, C–453/99, 20 September 2001, *Courage Ltd. v. Bernard Crehan and Bernard Crehan v. Courage Ltd. and Others*, [2001] ECR I–6297 at § 24 "[. . .] any individual can rely on a breach of Article 85(1) of the Treaty before a national court even where he is a party to a contract that is liable to restrict or distort competition within the meaning of that provision."

by a patent holder by arguing that the license agreement infringes Article 101 and does not benefit from an exemption under Article 101(3).

A second setting (usually referred to as the "Euro-offense" setting) arises when a claimant seeks to obtain injunctive relief, remedies or the attribution of damages by arguing that the defendant has forced him to enter into an anti-competitive agreement or abused a dominant position. In *Courage vs. Crehan*, for instance, the ECJ upheld the possibility for a pub owner to lodge a counter-claim for damages against a brewery, which had forced the former to enter into an anticompetitive exclusive purchase agreement.[282]

Regulation 1/2003 lays down a number of mechanisms that seek to ensure that national courts apply Article 101 and 102 in a proper and consistent fashion. First, national courts must avoid taking decisions that could run contrary to a decision adopted by the Commission.[283] They must also avoid adopting decisions which would conflict with a decision contemplated by the Commission in proceedings it has initiated. To that effect, national courts may decide to stay proceedings until the Commission adopts a decision.

Second, national courts shall forward to the Commission a copy of any written judgment deciding on the application of Article 101 or Article 102 TFEU.[284] This duty is of a purely informative nature.

Third, in a fashion similar to the *amicus curiae* procedure under U.S. law, both the NCAs and the Commission can, acting on their own initiative, submit written observations to the national courts of their Member State on issues relating to the application of Articles 101 or 102 of the Treaty.[285] With the permission of the court in question, they may also submit oral observations.

Finally, in proceedings involving Articles 101 or 102, national courts may ask the Commission to transmit to them information in its possession or its opinion on questions concerning the application of the Community competition rules.[286]

iii. Judicial Review of Commission's Decisions

(1) Annulment Proceedings Pursuant to Article 304. Article 304 of the TFEU allows natural or legal persons to bring annulment proceedings against Commission decisions before the GC on all points of facts and appeal in law before the ECJ. In the field of Articles 101 and 102 infringements, firms often appeal Commission decisions. However, annulment actions against Commission decisions banning mergers have for a long time been rare. This was explained by the fact that parties to a forbidden merger had no incentives to bring their case to the European courts as proceedings were too long (on average 21 months) to give them a

---

282. In *Courage v. Crehan*, the ECJ held that the contracting party entitled to damages from an anticompetitive contract was the one with the weakest bargaining power. See § 33.

283. *See* Article 16 of Regulation 1/2003, supra note 236.

284. *Id.* at Article 15(2).

285. *Id.* at Article 15(3).

286. *Id.* at Article 15(1).

chance to resume their transaction in case of an annulment. This situation was problematic as it gave the Commission a final say on any merger transaction. The Commission only prohibited a small number of mergers (19 in total since 1989). Yet, it made extensive use of the threat of a prohibition to extract substantial commitments from the merging parties. This situation has recently evolved as a result of two distinct events. First, in order to effectively ameliorate the effectiveness of its control of the Commission's merger decisions, the GC's Rules of Procedure were amended in December 2000 to introduce a "fast track" procedure.[287] Second, the GC handed down, in 2002, a series of judgments where it annulled several high profile merger control decisions, which it found illegal under EU law.[288] These cases addressed a signal to the business community that the GC was ready to carry out an extensive control of the Commission's review of mergers. The combination of these two events induced merging parties to increasingly appeal Commission's mergers decisions before the GC and the Commission to make a more careful assessment of the mergers notified to it.

(2) Revision of Fines Imposed by the European Commission. Article 31 of Regulation 1/2003 allows the GC and the ECJ to "cancel, reduce or increase the fine or periodic penalty imposed" by the European Commission in the application of EU competition rules. Thus far, the GC has exercised its control with moderation. The GC does not repeat the whole assessment process. It restrains itself to assessing whether the factors linked to duration and gravity, leniency and methodology have been correctly applied. The implementation of these principles has, nonetheless, allowed the GC to substantially reduce the fines imposed by the Commission in a range of decisions. On the other hand, the GC has never revised a fine upwards. Several authors have cast doubts on the possibility of the GC and ECJ to do so. Insofar as an appeal to revise a fine is brought by the undertaking being sanctioned, any increase in the fine would involve giving a ruling on points that the applicant did not raise. The GC has however dismissed this argument in the *Graphite Electrodes* cases where it confirmed the possibility for the EU courts to revise a fine upwards.[289]

(3) Suspensive Orders and Interim Relief. The introduction of annulment proceedings before the GC has in principle no suspensive effect on a Commission decision. However, the TFEU allows plaintiffs to obtain either (i) the suspension of the contested decision pursuant to Article 278, or (ii) the ordering of interim measures pursuant to Article 279, in parallel with the introduction of an annulment action on the basis of Article 263. Suspensive orders and interim relief are granted by the President of the GC (with a possible appeal before the President of the ECJ). To obtain the

---

287. *See* Amendments to the Rules of Procedure of the Court of First Instance [Now General Court] of the European Communities, O.J. 2000, L 322/4.

288. *See* Case T–342/99, *Airtours v. Commission*, [2002] ECR II–2585; Case T–310/01, *Schneider Electric v. Commission*, [2002] ECR II–4071; Case T–5/02, *Tetra Laval v. Commission*, [2002] ECR II–4381.

289. *See* Joined Cases T–236/01, T–239/01, T–244/01 to T–246/01, T–251/01 and T–252/01, *Tokai Carbon Co. Ltd. and others v. Commission*, 29 April 2004, not yet reported at para. 165.

granting of interim relief a plaintiff must satisfy two conditions.[290] First, the plaintiff must bring evidence of a *fumus boni juris*, i.e. a *prima facie* case against the challenged decision. Second, the plaintiff has to show that there is "urgency" in obtaining the interim relief, in order to prevent "serious and irreparable harm" to the applicant. Only if these conditions are met, will the President consider the granting of interim relief. In general, however, the President additionally balances the interests at stake (the plaintiffs interests versus the interests which the Commission was trying to attain through the adoption of its decision) in order to decide on whether or not granting the requested measures.

(4) Possibility to Introduce Claims for Compensation for Illegal Action by the European Commission. Article 340(2) allows parties which would have suffered a damage resulting from the action of an EU institution to seek to obtain damages by initiating a proceeding before the GC.[291] This also applies to decisions in the field of competition law. Such an action could for instance be launched when the Commission has been shown to have acted illegally by wrongly prohibiting a conduct or a merger between undertakings. In the past, this provision was almost never used in the field of competition law. However, in recent times, the virulence of the statements formulated by the GC in its *Airtours*, *Schneider* and *Tetra Laval* annulment judgments and the serious consequences resulting from the Commission's prohibition decisions (abandonment of the mergers in question) encouraged a number of firms to introduce actions based on Article 340(2).[292]

Three conditions must be met for such actions to succeed. First, the relevant institution must have committed a sufficiently serious breach of a legal rule designed to confer rights on individuals. The assessment of the factor "sufficiently serious breach" must be carried out in the light of two parameters. On the one hand, it depends on the extent of discretion possessed by the EU institution in question and, on the other, on the complexity of the situation under consideration. Following a sliding-scale approach, the greater the degree of institutional discretion, the more serious the illegality must be to make that institution liable. Second, the applicant must have suffered real and definite harm. In line with classic tort law principles, the harm may consist in a damnum emergens (material damage) or a lucrum cessans (loss of profits). In principle, the burden of establishing the amount of the actual damage rests on the applicant. Finally, the applicant must prove that there is a direct and immediate causal link between the damage and the act of the institution.

To date, private applicants have only in one case successfully obtained compensation for a breach of Community law by the Commission.[293] The

---

290. *See* Article 104(2) of the CFI's rules of procedures, supra note 281.

291. This provision states: "[. . .] the Community shall, in accordance with the general principles common to the laws of the Member States, make good any damage caused by its institutions or by its servants in the performance of their duties."

292. *See* Case T–342/99, *Airtours v. Commission*, [2002] ECR II–2585; Case T–310/01, *Schneider Electric v. Commission*, [2008] ECR II–4071; Case T–5/02, *Tetra Laval v. Commission*, [2002] ECR II–4381.

293. See Case T–351/03, *Schneider Electric SA v. Commission*, [2007] ECR II–2237.

reason for the limited number of successful application for damages is that the three conditions laid down in the case-law are very difficult to satisfy. Holcim v. Commission amply demonstrates this. In this case the Commission fined various undertakings in its Cement decision for operating a cartel. The decision eventually came before the GC. The latter partially annulled the Commission's decision as a result of finding that two undertakings, Alsen and Nordcement, had not violated Article 101.[294] These undertakings, which had given bank guarantees in order not to pay the relevant fine immediately, requested the Commission to reimburse the fees paid to obtain these guarantees. After their request was rejected by the Commission, the undertakings (which in the meantime had merged giving rise to a new undertaking Holcim) lodged a fresh appeal for indemnity before the GC. They claimed that the illegal Commission decision caused them harm through having to pay bank fees. The GC carried out an examination to see whether the three conditions had been fulfilled. It considered that the first condition was not satisfied insofar as:

> "regard being had to the fact that Cement was a particularly complex case, involving a very large number of undertakings and almost the entire European cement industry, to the fact that the structure of Cembureau made the investigation difficult owing to the existence of direct and indirect members, and to the fact that it was necessary to analyse a great number of documents, including in the applicant's specific situation, it must be held that the defendant was faced with complex situations to be regulated. Last, it is necessary to take account of the difficulties in applying the provisions of the EC Treaty in matters relating to cartels. Those practical difficulties were all the greater because the factual elements of the case in question, including in the part of the decision concerning the₁ applicant, were numerous. On all of those grounds, it must be held that the breach of Community law found in the Cement judgment as regards the part of the decision concerning the applicant is not sufficiently serious."

The appeal was therefore rejected. The above passage reveals the extremely cautious approach followed by the Court when dealing with action for damages. In insisting on the difficulties of applying the provisions of the Treaty with respect to cartel agreements (which are amongst some of the most clear and precise rules in the field of competition law), the GC also casts serious doubt on the possibility to successfully lodge an appeal for indemnity against an illegal Commission intervention in a field as complex and speculative as, for example, merger control.

In its *Schneider v. Commission* ruling, the GC, however, found the Commission liable for damages incurred as a result of its unlawful prohibition of a notified merger case. In 2001, the Commission had adopted a decision declaring the merger of Schneider and Legrand as incompatible with the common market. The Commission then adopted a further decision ordering Schneider to divest Legrand. The parties, however, appealed this decision and, in 2002, the GC annulled both of the Commission's decisions on incompatibility and divestiture. The Commission then began a second

---

294.   See Case T–28/03, *Holcim v. Commission*, [2005] ECR II–1357.

review of the transaction and closed its file after Schneider completed its divestment of Legrand. Schneider agreed to sell Legrand to a third party at a reduced price (because a long delay between signing and completion was agreed). The GC ordered the EU to compensate Schneider for (i) the expenses incurred by Schneider during the Commission's second review of the transaction and (ii) the reduction in the sale price of Legrand.[295]

Although Schneider obtained compensation, the GC's judgment does not reverse its traditionally reluctant approach towards indemnity applications in the field of competition law. In *Schneider v. Commission*, the Court identified an egregious infringement of Schneider's rights of defence which in turn had inflicted a serious damage to the applicant.[296] The Court, however, did not provide guidance on the thornier question of whether substantive legal and economic errors made by the Commission in its decision entitled the parties to obtain compensation. The GC merely indicated that "manifestly serious breaches vitiating the underlying economic analysis" can in principle give rise to a right of damages.[297] However, it sounded a note of caution in recalling that the Commission must enjoy a wide margin of discretion in its assessment of complex economic issues.

Subsequent to its *Schneider* judgment, the GC confirmed its cautious approach with respect to actions for damages as it dismissed the claim for damages against the European Commission brought by MyTravel. In 1999, the Commission had prohibited the merger between MyTravel (then Airtours) and First Choice plc, on the basis that the transaction would create a collective dominant position on the market for UK short-haul holiday packages. MyTravel brought an appeal and in 2002 the GC annulled the prohibition decision. MyTravel then initiated proceedings at the GC pursuant to which it claimed compensation from the Commission for the damage it alleged to have suffered as a result of the overturned decision.

In its judgment, the GC recalled that "[w]here the unlawfulness of a legal measure is relied on as a legal basis for action for damages, that measure, in order to be capable of causing the Community to incur non-contractual liability, must constitute a sufficiently serious breach of a rule of law intended to confer rights on individuals."[298] In this respect, the GC stated that the annulment of the *Airtours* decision of the Commission due to a series of errors of assessment could not be equated without further analysis with a "sufficiently serious breach" of a rule of law.[299] Otherwise this "would risk compromising the capacity of the Commission fully to function as regulator of competition, a task entrusted to it by the EC Treaty [now the TFEU], as a result of the inhibiting effect that the risk of having to bear the losses alleged by the undertakings concerned might have

---

295. The ECJ, however, partly annulled the judgment of the GC on this point. It upheld the CFI's order in respect to (i) above and annulled its order in respect to (ii). The ECJ ruled that the reduction in the transfer price for Legrand was not a direct result of the Commission's procedural irregularity. See E.C.J., case C–440/07 P, not yet reported.

296. See § 129.

297. Id.

298. Id. at § 37.

299. Id. at §§ 41–42.

on the control of concentrations."[300] The right to compensation for damage resulting from the conduct of an institution would only become available "when such conduct takes the form of action manifestly contrary to the rule of law and seriously detrimental to the interests of persons outside the institution and cannot be justified or accounted for by the particular constraints to which the staff of the institution, operating normally, are objectively subject."[301] In light of the facts of the case, the GC concluded that the various errors it established in its judgment annulling the *Airtours* decision of the Commission were not sufficiently serious to give rise to the non-contractual liability of the Community.

The GC nevertheless recognized and somewhat developed the position it had adopted in *Schneider* that "[i]n the field of non-contractual liability, the possibility cannot be ruled out in principle that manifest and grave defects affecting the economic analysis which underlies [merger control decisions] could constitutes breaches that are sufficiently serious to give rise to the non-contractual liability of the Community for the purposes of the case-law".[302] The GC, however, noted that economic analysis in competition cases involved generally "complex and difficult intellectual exercises, which inadvertently contain some inadequacies, such as approximations, inconsistencies, or indeed certain omissions."[303] These inadequacies where "all the more likely to occur where, as in the case of the control of concentrations, the analysis has a prospective element."[304] The Court also recalled that the Commission enjoys a broad discretion in maintaining control over EU competition policy and that it included the choice of the analytical tools it would use in a given matter.[305] The GC then observed that the factors described above had to be taken into account in assessing whether the Commission committed a sufficiently serious breach in analyzing the effects of the *Airtours/First Choice* merger.[306]

The GC's dismissal of MyTravel's claim is not entirely surprising as the GC probably wanted to avoid that the Commission be frightened in the future to prohibit a problematic merger due to the risk of liability and damages in case its decision was subsequently struck down as illegal. This would obviously damage the Commission's ability to control mergers with negative consequences resulting for consumers. Now, given the wide latitude left to the Commission by the GC, the circumstances where the prohibition by the Commission of a merger that is subsequently annulled due to the fact its draw the wrong conclusion on the merits of the case will lead to a successful action for damages on the part of the affected parties are likely to be very limited. As illustrated by the GC's decision in *Schneider*, claims for indemnity are more likely to succeed for blatant infringement procedural or basic due process requirements.

---

300.   Id. at § 42.

301.   Id. at § 43.

302.   Id. at § 80.

303.   Id. at § 81.

304.   Id. at § 82.

305.   Id. at § 83.

306.   Id. at § 84.

iv. Limits on EU Competition Law

(1) Application of EU Competition Law to Public Entities. EU competition law applies *ratione personae* to all "undertakings," regardless of their legal status. As long as an entity is engaged into an economic activity, i.e. the offering of goods and services on a given market, it falls within the scope of Article 101 and 102. Thus, public entities may be found liable of a violation of EU competition law provided they carry out an economic activity. A public employment agency was, for instance, found violating Article 102 in *Höfner and Elser*.[307] On the other hand, a public entity that confines itself to the exercise of noneconomic activities (such as, for instance, the control and supervision of air space in *Eurocontrol*) does not fall within the scope of EU competition law.[308]

(2) State Compulsion Defense. A distinct situation arises, however, when a Member State uses its legislative or regulatory powers in such a way that it leads firms to infringe EU competition rules. This can be the case, for instance, when public authorities impose the conclusion of a price agreement to firms operating in a given sector. In such situations, the ECJ has ruled that these firms will only escape a finding of a violation of Article 101 if State intervention effectively required companies to act in a particular manner and left them no "breathing space" for competing in the market.[309] In sum, the possibility for firms to escape the application of Article 101 by invoking the state compulsion defense is a narrow one. They have to prove that the state intervention left them absolutely no margin of maneuver on the market.

(3) Act of State Offense? Under EU law, the Commission may challenge Member States' actions violating the purpose and impeding the effectiveness of TFEU[310] In the field of competition law, the Commission has not yet challenged States' measures frustrating the *"effet utile"*(in other words, the effectiveness) of Articles 101 and 102.[311] The reluctance of the Commission may be explained by political reasons. In addition to being in charge of implementing EU competition rules, the Commission is also a political institution proposing EU legislation in a wide number of sectors. However, this legislation has to be approved by the Council (and in some cases by the European Parliament) to become binding law. The Commission is thus always cautious when it deals with Member States because aggressive legal actions against their measures could be subject to retaliation within the legislative process.

The ECJ recently gave a strong impetus for the eradication of public restrictions on competition in the *Consorzio Industrie Fiammiferi* case.[312]

---

307. *See* ECJ, C–41/90, *Höfner and Elser v. Macrotron GmbH*, [1991] ECR I–1979.

308. *See* ECJ, C–364/92, *SAT Fluggesellschaft mbH v. Eurocontrol*, [1994] ECR I–43.

309. *See* D. Goyder, *EC Competition Law*, 4th ed., at p. 479. *See* ECJ, 240–242, 260–262, 268–269/82, *Stichting Sigarettenindustrie and others v. Commission*, [1985] ECR 3831.

310. Through the initiation of infringements proceedings pursuant to Article 226 on the basis of Article 10 of the Treaty (duty of loyal cooperation of Member States) combined with either Article 81 or 82.

311. The only case in which the Commission acted on this basis being: ECJ, C–35/96, *Commission v. Italy*, ECR [1998] I–3851.

312. *See* ECJ, C–198/01, *Consorzio Industrie Fiammiferi v. Autorità Garante della Concorrenza e del Mercato*, [2003] ECR I–8055.

The Court concluded that the application of the then Article 10 of the EC Treaty (now repealed) combined with Article 101 or 102 required NCAs to declare inapplicable any piece of national legislation contrary to EU competition law. As a result, market operators facing legislation likely to violate EC competition law may turn to their NCA to obtain confirmation that it is indeed contrary to Article 101 or 102 and thus should not be applied.

(4) Limited Application of Competition Rules in Specific Sectors

a. AGRICULTURAL SECTOR AND COMMON AGRICULTURAL POLICY. The first sector that falls only partly under EU competition rules is agriculture. The belief that the agricultural sector fulfills special social and cultural functions in Europe led the drafters of the now defunct EC Treaty to include Article 36 [now Article 42 TFEU] pursuant to which: "The provisions of the chapter relating to rules on competition shall apply to production of and trade in agricultural products only to the extent determined by the Council."

In accordance with Article 36 [now Article 42 TFEU], the Council adopted Regulation 26/62, which made Articles 101 and 102 applicable to a large number of agricultural products. However, this Regulation provided that Article 101 would be inapplicable to agreements, decisions and practices that:

> "form an integral part of a national market organisation or are necessary for attainment of the objectives set out in Article 39 of the Treaty. In particular, it shall not apply to agreements, decisions and practices of farmers, farmers' associations, or associations of such associations belonging to a single Member State which concern the production or sale of agricultural products or the use of joint facilities for the storage, treatment or processing of agricultural products, and under which there is no obligation to charge identical prices, *unless the Commission finds that competition is thereby excluded or that the objectives of Article 39 of the Treaty are jeopardised.*"[313]

The Commission enjoys exclusive jurisdiction to decide which agreements, decisions and practices benefit from the above exception.[314] Article 102 and the EU Merger Regulation, however, apply in full to markets for agricultural products.

b. TRANSPORT. The fact that Title V of the now defunct EC Treaty laid down a "Common Transport Policy" did not prevent the ECJ, in the seminal *Asjes* case, from holding that absent explicit provisions enacting a specific competition regime for the transport sector, the competition rules of the Treaty could apply as such.[315] However, as far as competition rules

---

313. *See* Council Regulation 26 applying certain rules of competition to production of and trade in agricultural products, O.J. 1962, p. 993.

314. *Id.* at Article 2(2) (emphasis added).

315. *See* ECJ, Joined cases 209 to 213/84, *Criminal proceedings against Lucas Asjes and others, Andrew Gray and others, Andrew Gray and others, Jacques Maillot and others and Léo Ludwig and others*, [1986] ECR–1425. Note that Regulation 1/2003 at Recital 36 repealed Council Regulation 141 of 26 November 1962 exempting transport from the application of Regulation 17/62, and led to the revision of the various procedural specificities laid down by

are concerned, the transport sector has two distinctive features. First, Regulation 1/2003 does not apply to:

"(a) international tramp vessel services as defined in Article 1(3)(a) of Regulation 4056/86; (b) a maritime transport service that takes place exclusively between ports in one and the same Member State as foreseen in Article 1(2) of Regulation 4056/86; (c) air transport between Community airports and third countries."

Second, the enforcement of the EU competition rules in the transport sector is shared between DG COMP and the Directorate General for Transport of the Commission. This, on some occasions, led to internal conflicts.

c. Defense Industry. In principle, EU competition rules apply to the defense industry. However, Article 346 TFEU allows Member States to refuse to disclose information if that disclosure could run "contrary to the essential interests of [their] security." In addition, Member States may take measures that are considered "necessary for the protection of the essential interests of [their] security which are connected with the production of or trade in arms, munitions and war material." This provision thus allows Member States to limit the application of EU competition rules when they establish that it prejudices their security interests. Article TFEU insists nonetheless on the fact that these exceptions shall be strictly limited to products that are intended for "specifically military purposes".[316]

In practice, this provision has only rarely been invoked by the Member States. In the context of the *Matra/Aérospatiale* merger, the French authorities enjoined the parties to abstain from notifying the aspects of the transaction relating to missiles and missiles system.[317] The Commission checked whether the conditions of Article 346 were fulfilled. It came to the conclusion that the measures taken by the French authorities were necessary for the protection of the essential interests of its security and that they did not encroach upon non military product markets.[318]

(5) Effect on Trade Between Member States. EU competition provisions will only apply provided the agreement or abuse at hand "may affect trade between Member States." The purpose of this condition is to set out a jurisdictional threshold for the prohibitions contained in Articles 101 and 102 to apply.[319] Only those anticompetitive practices that are likely to produce a cross-border effect fall within the scope of the TFEU. Absent an effect on intermember trade, the practice is not necessarily left unchecked, as it may fall within the jurisdiction of a national competition legislation.

---

and Regulations 1017/68 (rail, road and inland waterways), 4056/86 (maritime transport) and 3975/87 (air transport).

316. *See* Article 306 TFEU: "[...] such measures shall not adversely affect the conditions of competition in the common market regarding products which are not intended for specifically military purposes."

317. *See* Commission Decision *Matra/Aérospatiale* of 28 April 1999, IV/M.1309.

318. Id. at § 16.

319. A similar effect is achieved, in the field of Merger Control, with the turnover thresholds established by Regulation 139/2004 at Article 1(2) and 1(3).

Pursuant to Regulation 1/2003, the finding that a practice has an effect on trade between member states produces important legal consequences on NCAs and national courts as they are obliged to apply, in addition to national competition law, Articles 101 and 102 of the Treaty to agreements and practices which may affect trade between Member States.[320] Absent such a solution, NCAs and national courts could apply national law to cross-border matters and stray from EU competition law.

The case-law of the Court of Justice as well as the Commission "Guidelines on the effect on trade concept" clarify how to assess whether a given practice affects trade between Member States within the meaning of Article 101 and 102 of the TFEU. Traditionally, the ECJ has broadly interpreted this requirement, requiring only that "it must be possible to foresee with a sufficient degree of probability on the basis of a set of objective factors of law or of fact that the agreement in question may have an influence, direct or indirect, actual or potential, on the pattern of trade between Member States."[321] The ECJ has accordingly concluded that agreements between firms operating in the same Member States satisfy this test if they have an impact, however remote, on intra-Community trade.[322] Moreover, even an agreement that increases trade between Member States can nevertheless fall within the scope of Article 101(1) as what the ECJ considers determinative is not so much whether the agreement in question increases or decreases the flows of goods or services between Member States, but whether it can "distort" trade between Member States in the sense that it affects what would have been the normal pattern of trade absent such an agreement.[323] Recent ECJ cases may signal a narrower approach to the definition of the notion of impact on trade,[324] but it remains true that in the vast majority of cases the condition of impact on trade between Member States is not likely to be a major obstacle to the application of EU competition law.

3.   A Brief Overview of Antitrust Laws and Remedies in Other Nations

Over 100 nations currently have antitrust laws—many adopted in the 1990s—and others are in the process of drafting their laws. Some nations have a single agency with both investigative and adjudicative powers, whereas other split that task between multiple government bodies. These agencies generally have authority to investigate and obtain injunctions and often fines. Many nations also impose criminal imprisonment for some

---

320. *See* Recital 8 and Article 3 of Regulation 1/2003, supra note 229.

321. Case 56/65, Société La Technique Minière Ulm v. Maschinenbau, [1966] ECR 235, 249.

322. Case 322/81, Michelin v. Commission, [1983] ECR 3461.

323. Cases 56 & 58/64, Etablissements Consten SA & Grundig–Verkaufs–GmbH v. Commission, [1966] ECR 299 at 341–42.

324. Joined cases C–215/96 and C–216/96, Carlo Bagnasco and Others v. Banca Popolare di Novara soc. coop. arl. (BNP) and Cassa di Risparmio di Genova e Imperia SpA (Carige), [1999] ECR I–135.

antitrust violations, including Canada, India, Indonesia, Israel, Japan, Russia, South Africa, South Korea, Taiwan, and Thailand.[325]

Many nations also explicitly provide for private antitrust enforcement, but often limit it in various ways. Canada authorizes (1) private damage suits for criminal antitrust violations and (2) private injunctive suits against noncriminal violations if the Canada Competition Bureau is not investigating and the Competition Tribunal grants leave to sue.[326] Japan allows private parties to bring (1) antitrust damage suits after the JFTC has found an antitrust violation, (2) antitrust suits for injunctive relief, or (3) tort suits for damages caused by antitrust violations.[327] Chile, India, Mexico, Peru, Singapore, South Africa, and Turkey allow private actions for damages from violations established in a prior agency proceeding.[328] Without requiring any agency finding or approval, Australia, Brazil, China, and Taiwan allow private actions for both damages and injunctions, while Saudi Arabia and South Korea do so for damages but not injunctions.[329] Even when nations do not provide for direct private enforcement of their antitrust statute, they often allow private suits based on a theory that a violation of antitrust law that injures others constitutes a tort.[330]

No other nation appears to automatically treble damages for all antitrust violations like the U.S. does. However, a discretion to impose treble damages can be exercised by the India Competition Commission for cartel violations, by Taiwan courts for intentional violations, and by Turkey courts for illegal agreements or gross negligence.[331] Several nations have enacted clawback statutes authorizing actions to recover any excess over single damages paid because of a foreign judgment for multiple damages.[332]

---

325. Canada Competition Act Part VI; India Competition Act Chapter VI; Indonesia Competition Law Art. 47–49; Israel Restrictive Trade Practices Law § 47; Japan Antimonopoly Act §§ 89–98 (2009); Russia Criminal Code § 178(1); South Africa Competition Act Chapter 7; South Korea Fair Trade Act Chapter XIV; Taiwan Fair Trade Act Chpt. VI; Thailand Trade Competition Act § 51.

326. Canada Competition Act §§ 36(1), 103.1.

327. Japan Antimonopoly Act §§ 24–26 (2009); Japan Civil Code § 709. Unlike in the U.S., indirect purchasers can bring claims for damages in Japan. *See* Tokyo Toyu, 41 Minshu No. 5, 785 (Japan Supreme Court July 2, 1987).

328. OECD, Competition Law and Policy in Latin America 210 (2006) (Chile); India Competition Act § 53N; Mexico Federal Economic Competition Law Art. 38; Peru Competition Law 1034, Art. 49; Singapore Competition Act § 86; South Africa Competition Act § 65; Turkey Competition Law Arts. 57–58; Turkey 19th Chamber of Supreme Court of Appeals, Decision 2007/10677.

329. Australia Trade Practices Act §§ 80–82; Brazil Antitrust Law 8884/94, Art.29; China Anti–Monopoly Law Art. 50; Taiwan Fair Trade Act Chpt. V; Saudi Arabia Competition Law Art. 18; South Korea Fair Trade Act Art. 56 (allowing private damages); Case No. 2001 Gahap 60373, Seoul Central District Court Judgment, August 1, 2003 (disallowing private injunctive relief). *See also* Argentina Competition Law Art. 51 (allowing private damages for cartel violations).

330. *See, e.g.,* Israel Restrictive Trade Practices Law § 50; Egypt Civil Code Art. 163.

331. India Competition Act § 27(b); Taiwan Fair Trade Act Art. 32; Turkey Competition Law Art. 58.

332. *See* Chapter 8.

Class actions have so far been relatively rare in other nations, but China and Israel authorize them, as do many Canadian provinces.[333]

Questions on Remedies

1. Should people go to prison for antitrust violations? Why can't they be sufficiently deterred by damage claims? Is prison more likely to effectively deter corporate managers?

2. Should antitrust laws be enforced by private rights of actions? By class actions? Why wouldn't government enforcement to protect markets suffice? Do government enforcers have sufficient incentives? Are they likely to know about all the violations private parties would know about? Do injured private parties have enough incentives to complain without the prospect of damages?

3. Should treble damages be used? If only single damages are imposed, wouldn't it be tempting to engage in anticompetitive conduct because you can keep the supracompetitive profits if you don't get caught and just pay successful litigants out of those profits if you do? If the odds of an antitrust violation being detected and successfully proven are 33%, aren't treble damages necessary to deter those violations? On the other hand, won't treble damages deter conduct that might mistakenly be judged anticompetitive but actually constitutes desirable aggressive competition?

---

333. *See* China Civil Procedure Law Art. 54–55; ISRAEL RESTRICTIVE TRADE PRACTICES LAW § 46A; ABA, COMPETITION LAWS OUTSIDE THE UNITED STATES at Canada 25 (First Supp. 2005). Some European nations use forms of aggregate litigation that could be used in antitrust cases. *See* Richard A. Nagareda, *Aggregate Litigation Across the Atlantic and the Future of American Exceptionalism*, 62 Vand. L. Rev. 1. 21–25 (2009) (Denmark, England, Finland, France, Italy, Norway and Sweden).

CHAPTER 2

WHICH HORIZONTAL AGREEMENTS ARE ILLEGAL?

A. RELEVANT LAWS AND BASIC LEGAL ELEMENTS

Horizontal agreements are agreements between firms who operate at the same market level. Vertical agreements are agreements between firms that are in some supply relation. For example, suppose we have a steel market with two firms that supply steel to two car manufacturers, which in turn sell cars to consumers. Then, an agreement between the two steel suppliers would be a horizontal agreement, as would an agreement between the two car makers. An agreement between a steel supplier and car maker would be a vertical agreement. Where effects at both market levels are relevant, the steel market would be called the upstream market and the car market the downstream market, with the market closest to the ultimate consumer the downstream one. The topic of this chapter shall be horizontal agreements, with vertical agreements deferred until Chapters 4 and 5. Mergers between competitors could be considered horizontal agreements, but raise distinctive issues that will be deferred until Chapter 7. This chapter shall instead focus on agreements between firms that continue to operate separately at the same market level.

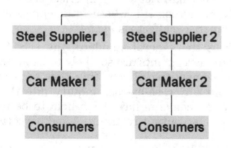

1. RELEVANT U.S. LAWS AND GENERAL LEGAL STANDARDS

Three statutes cover horizontal agreements. The most important is Sherman Act § 1:

Sherman Act § 1, 15 U.S.C. § 1

Every contract, combination in the form of trust or otherwise, or conspiracy, in restraint of trade or commerce among the several States, or with foreign nations, is declared to be illegal.

The statute's reference to a "contract, combination in the form of trust or otherwise, or conspiracy" has been interpreted to require some sort of agreement. Just what constitutes an "agreement" will prove to be a big question in many cases, but those issues are deferred until Chapter 6, with this section assuming an agreement has been proven and focusing on the application to horizontal agreements. The statute also contains an inter-state commerce requirement (as do all the U.S. antitrust statutes), but as Chapter 1 details, this requirement is trivial to establish, although it technically remains necessary to dutifully plead an effect on interstate commerce in any complaint.

Thus, leaving aside the reference to foreign nations, which we address in the international effects discussion in Chapter 8, the statute effectively reads: "Every agreement in restraint of trade or commerce is declared to be illegal." The word "every" was the subject of much hand-wringing in the early days of the interpretation of the Sherman Act, with the ultimate judicial resolution being that the word "every" could not be taken literally, otherwise every contract or partnership would be unlawful. Thus, the traditional view was that the statute must instead mean to condemn only "unreasonable" restraints of trade, with an unreasonable restraint being one whose anticompetitive effects outweigh its procompetitive ones.[1] But there is an alternative textual interpretation that could likewise avoid functional irrationality without committing the linguistic violence of reading a new word into the statute and effectively reading the word "every" out. Under this alternative, one could instead say that the word "restraint" inherently suggests some *net* restraint of trade, for trade could hardly be said to be restrained if it were increased. Thus, if a challenged agreement on balance increases competition and trade output, it is not really in restraint of trade at all.[2] Whatever interpretive path one chooses, the fact remains that today Sherman Act § 1 is in effect read to adopt the general standard that "Every agreement whose anticompetitive effects on trade outweigh its procompetitive effects is illegal."

But while this is the general standard, the U.S. Supreme Court has also held that certain agreements are so likely to be anticompetitive, and so unlikely to have procompetitive effects, that they are condemned "per se," which means without any case-by-case inquiry into their net effect.[3] The following horizontal agreements have been held to be per se illegal: price-fixing,[4] market divisions,[5] output restraints,[6] and boycotts.[7] When an agree-

---

1. *See* Standard Oil Co. v. United States, 221 U.S. 1, 59–68 (1911); Chicago Board of Trade v. United States, 246 U.S. 231, 238 (1918); United States v. Topco Associates, 405 U.S. 596, 606–07 (1972); National Soc'y of Prof'l Eng'rs v. United States, 435 U.S. 679, 687–90 (1978); Arizona v. Maricopa County Med. Soc'y, 457 U.S. 332, 342–43 (1982); NCAA v. Board of Regents, 468 U.S. 85, 98, 103 (1984); Texaco Inc. v. Dagher, 547 U.S. 1, 5 (2006).

2. Indeed, language in the old *Standard Oil* case that created the rule of reason does in fact focus on whether an agreement constitutes a "restraint of trade" within the meaning of the statute. 211 U.S. at 63–64.

3. Northern Pacific R. Co. v. United States, 356 U.S. 1, 5 (1958); *Topco*, 405 U.S. at 607; *Maricopa*, 457 U.S. at 344–45.

4. United States v. Socony–Vacuum Oil Co., 310 U.S. 150, 218 (1940); *Northern Pacific*, 356 U.S. at 5; *Maricopa*, 457 U.S. at 345–48; *Dagher*, 126 S.Ct. at 1279.

5. *Northern Pacific*, 356 U.S. at 5; Palmer v. BRG, 498 U.S. 46 (1990); *Topco*, 405 U.S. at 608–09.

ment is per se illegal, the Court says it will consider neither any procompetitive justifications the defendant might offer nor whether anticompetitive effects actually occurred.[8]

If a per se rule does not apply, then general "rule of reason" review applies. Under the rule of reason, courts consider on a case by case basis whether the agreement has a plausible procompetitive justification. If it does, then the plaintiff must prove an anticompetitive effect either through direct proof or by showing market power that can be used to infer the anticompetitive effect. If the anticompetitive effect is shown, the defendant must prove the procompetitive justification empirically and that the challenged restraint is the least restrictive means of accomplishing that procompetitive virtue. If that is proven, the court must determine whether the anticompetitive effects outweigh the procompetitive effects.

This way of framing the distinction between per se and rule of reason scrutiny has, however, been eroded by two doctrinal developments. First, the Supreme Court has stated that, even if a horizontal agreement "literally" constitutes price-fixing, an output restraint or a boycott, it will not be deemed to fall within such per se illegal categories when a procompetitive justification in fact exists for the agreement in question.[9] Second, the Court has held that, even if a restraint falls within the rule of reason, it will be condemned summarily as a "naked" restraint if no procompetitive justification is offered for it.[10] This has led some to conclude that the distinction is incoherent. On this view, the rule of reason is really being applied in all cases; it is just that the rule can be applied quite quickly in cases where no plausible procompetitive justification has been offered. Others have more charitably concluded that what the cases actually stand for is that certain defenses are excluded, such as: (a) the claim that the defendants tried to fix prices or restrict output but lacked the market power to have the anticompetitive effect; or (b) the claim that the fixed prices were reasonable because market prices would be too high or too low.[11]

An alternative way that might offer a clearer way of understanding the pattern of case results is to keep in mind a distinction between horizontal agreements among unrelated firms and those among firms that are in a productive business relationship. When firms are in some business relationship where their joint efforts produce some tangible product or service, then it makes sense to apply some rule of reason to see whether the

---

6. *NCAA*, 468 U.S. at 99–101.

7. FTC v. Superior Court Trial Lawyers Association, 493 U.S. 411 (1990); Klor's Inc. v. Broadway–Hale Stores, Inc., 359 U.S. 207 (1959); Fashion Originators' Guild of Am. v. FTC, 312 U.S. 457 (1941); *Northern Pacific*, 356 U.S. at 5.

8. *See Socony–Vacuum*, 310 U.S. at 218, 226 n.59; *Maricopa*, 457 U.S. at 345, 351.

9. *NCAA*, 468 U.S. at 101–04; Broadcast Music, Inc. v. CBS, 441 U.S. 1, 8–9, 13, 20–21 (1979); Northwest Wholesale Stationers v. Pacific Stationery & Printing, 472 U.S. 284, 294–98 (1985). And even when it has said the per se rule applies and precludes consideration of procompetitive justifications, it has nonetheless gone ahead to consider and reject those justifications. *See Maricopa*, 457 U.S. at 351–54.

10. FTC v. Indiana Federation of Dentists, 476 U.S. 447, 459 (1986); *NCAA*, 468 U.S. at 109–110; *Professional Engineers*, 435 U.S. at 693–95.

11. *See* Krattenmaker, *Per se Violations in Antitrust Law*, 77 Geo. L.J. 165 (1988).

restraint creates benefits to their ability to produce that outweigh any anticompetitive costs. Indeed, it is hard to see how it could be otherwise since the Supreme Court was driven to adopt the rule of reason precisely to avoid condemning every partnership that might be formed, and yet every partnership could be said to result in the partners fixing prices, restraining output, and boycotting others when the partnership makes decisions about what price, output, suppliers and customers to choose. In contrast, when firms are unrelated by any productive business collaboration, then the per se rules do have bite, for it is only in cases involving productive joint ventures that the Court has stated that procompetitive justifications can take a restraint out of per se rules. The Court will not listen to claims by unrelated horizontal businesses that their restraints have procompetitive justifications, even though such justifications might exist and suggest market failures that would merit government regulation of price or output. Because such cases do not involve joint business efforts but rather effective market regulation, disinterested and politically accountable government agencies might be thought per se better suited than financially interested and unaccountable businesses to determine whether the regulation is merited. As we shall see, the pattern of Supreme Court cases largely tracks the above distinction.

The distinction between agreements between productively related and unrelated rivals suggests two sorts of limitations. First, sometimes a productive business collaboration might exist, but the price-fixing agreement in question is unrelated to its advancement, or the productive business collaboration is nothing more than a fig leaf to avoid per se scrutiny. In such cases, the courts generally apply the per se rule notwithstanding the technical existence of a productive business collaboration.[12] Second, professionals have traditionally engaged in self-regulation designed to correct the sort of market failures that government agencies normally regulate in nonprofessional business markets. Consistent with this, courts have been less willing to condemn per se professional efforts to self-regulate through horizontal agreements that are not ancillary to any productive business collaboration, but rather have allowed such efforts subject to rule of reason review.[13]

Sherman Act § 2 is also relevant. It provides:

Sherman Act § 2, 15 U.S.C. § 2

Every person who shall monopolize, or attempt to monopolize, or combine or conspire with any other person or persons, to monopolize any part of the trade or commerce among the several States, or with foreign nations, shall be deemed guilty of a felony....

The statute is generally targeted at unilateral conduct and thus does not require proof of an agreement, other than for proving a conspiracy to monopolize. However, agreements or combinations to form a corporation or

---

12. *See Palmer*, 498 U.S. 46; *Maricopa*, 457 U.S. at 356–57. Similarly, in *Dagher*, the Court rejected application of the per se rule both because there the joint venture was not a "sham," 126 S.Ct. at 1280 n.1, and the challenged agreement involved a core activity of the joint venture rather than one unrelated to the venture, *id.* at 1280–81.

13. *See* California Dental Ass'n v. FTC, 526 U.S. 756 (1999).

cartel that exercises monopoly power have long been held to constitute monopolization in violation of § 2 as well as an agreement in restraint of trade that violates § 1.[14] Since any agreement that creates monopoly power would surely also be an agreement in restraint of trade, this adds little to the law on horizontal agreements, but will prove relevant (in Chapter 3) to assessing unsuccessful attempts to form cartel agreements. Further, the provision on conspiracies to monopolize may have different elements than those for agreements in restraint of trade. See Chapter 3.

Finally, Federal Trade Commission Act § 5 provides:

Federal Trade Commission Act § 5, 15 U.S.C. § 45

"Unfair methods of competition in or affecting commerce ... are hereby declared unlawful."

This general prohibition of unfair methods of competition clearly extends beyond horizontal agreements but does authorize the FTC to bring actions against any anticompetitive horizontal agreements.

2. Relevant EU Laws and General Legal Standards

In the EU, horizontal agreements (and more generally all agreements between competitors) have to be examined under Article 101 TFEU.

Article 101 TFEU

1. The following shall be prohibited as incompatible with the common market: all agreements between undertakings,[15] decisions by associations of undertakings and concerted practices which may affect trade between Member States and which have as their object or effect the prevention, restriction or distortion of competition within the common market, and in particular those which:

> (a) directly or indirectly fix purchase or selling prices or any other trading conditions;

> (b) limit or control production, markets, technical development, or investment;

> (c) share markets or sources of supply;

> (d) apply dissimilar conditions to equivalent transactions with other trading parties, thereby placing them at a competitive disadvantage;

> (e) make the conclusion of contracts subject to acceptance by the other parties of supplementary obligations which, by their nature or according to commercial usage, have no connection with the subject of such contracts.

---

14. See, e.g., United States v. Grinnell Corp., 384 U.S. 563, 576 (1966); American Tobacco Co. v. United States, 328 U.S. 781, 783–84, 808–09, 813–14 (1946); Standard Oil Co. v. United States, 221 U.S. 1, 70–75 (1911); Lorain Journal Co. v. United States, 342 U.S. 143 (1951).

15. [Editor's Note: "Undertakings" is the European terminology for an entity that engages in an economic activity, or what in the United States is called a business or firm.]

2.   Any agreements or decisions prohibited pursuant to this Article shall be automatically void.

3.   The provisions of paragraph 1 may, however, be declared inapplicable in the case of:

—any agreement or category of agreements between undertakings;

—any decision or category of decisions by associations of undertakings;

—any concerted practice or category of concerted practices,

which contributes to improving the production or distribution of goods or to promoting technical or economic progress, while allowing consumers a fair share of the resulting benefit, and which does not:

(a) impose on the undertakings concerned restrictions which are not indispensable to the attainment of these objectives;

(b) afford such undertakings the possibility of eliminating competition in respect of a substantial part of the products in question.

The European Court of Justice (ECJ) has traditionally interpreted Article 101(1) broadly. However, the vast majority of agreements that infringe Article 101(1) can be justified under Article 101(3). Agreements that infringe Article 101(1) and cannot be justified under Article 101(3) are void under Article 101(2).

Enforcement Rules. Article 101 can be enforced by a variety of institutions, but at the EU level, enforcement is by the European Commission. *See* Chapter 1. In 1962, Regulation 17 required that all agreements that could fall within Article 101(1) had to be notified to the Commission, which had the sole authority to grants exemptions under Article 101(3).[16] This created strong incentives to notify agreements to the Commission but created anomalies, such as the fact that firms sued in national court for a contract violation could argue in defense that the contract was void under Article 101(1) without the court being able to consider whether the contract was justifiable under Article 101(3).

It also created immense administrative overload, leading to various responses to reduce the number of notifications requiring formal Commission resolution. First, the Commission began to adopt block exemptions that declared Article 101(1) inapplicable to certain categories of practices. Agreements that fell under these block exemptions did not have to be notified to the Commission. Second, the Commission began issuing "comfort" letters notifying undertakings that their agreements did not fall within 101(1) or qualified for an 101(3) exemption without having to go through the heavy procedural obligations of making a formal decision. Third, the Commission tried to encourage a more decentralized system for processing complaints by both national competition authorities and nation-

---

16.   [1959–62] O.J. Spec. Ed. 87.

al courts.[17] However, the latter generally failed to induce complainants to initiate procedures at the national level, in part because defendants subject to national proceedings could still notify their agreements to the Commission, causing the national competition authorities to lose jurisdiction and often inducing national courts to stay their proceedings.

Finally, Regulation No 1/2003 was adopted, which abolished both the notification process and the Commission's monopoly over granting Article 101(3) exemptions.[18] Today, the Commission, as well as national courts and authorities, can all resolve whether an agreement falls within 101(3) or is exempted by 101(3) and do so after a dispute arises.

Article 101(1). In addition to the relatively easy requirement of showing a possible effect on trade between member states, *see* Chapter 1, Article 101(1) has two elements. *First*, the challenged activity must be an "agreement" or "concerted practice" by firms or a decision by an association of firms. We address that issue in Chapter 6, focusing here on cases where the agreement is clear. *Second*, the agreement must have the "object or effect" of restricting competition. Article 101(1) lists various agreements that can satisfy this test, but that list is not exhaustive.

The term "object" does not refer to the subjective intention of the parties, but to the objective meaning and purpose of the agreement.[19] An agreement deemed to have the "object" of restricting competition (like a price-fixing agreement) infringes Article 101(1) without having to establish its effects.[20] The Commission guidelines on the application of article 101(3) state that:

> "[n]on-exhaustive guidance on what constitutes restrictions by object can be found in Commission block exemption regulations, guidelines and notices. Restrictions that are black-listed in block exemptions or identified as hardcore restrictions in guidelines and notices are generally considered by the Commission to constitute restrictions by object.[21] In the case of horizontal agreements restrictions of competition by object include price fixing, output limitation and sharing of markets and customers."

---

17. Commission Notice of 13 February 1993 on cooperation between national courts and the Commission in applying Articles [101] and [102] of the EC Treaty, O.J. 1993, C 39; Commission notice on cooperation between national competition authorities and the Commission in handling cases falling within the scope of Articles [101] and [102], O.J. 1997, C 313.

18. Council Regulation (EC) No 1/2003 of 16 December 2002 on the implementation of the rules on competition laid down in Articles [101] and [102] of the Treaty, O.J. 2003, L 1/1.

19. Case T 213/00, CMA CGM—FETTSCA, [2003] E.C.R., p. II–913, at § 183.

20. Cases 56 & 58/64, Etablissements Consten SA & Grundig–Verkaufs–GmbH v. Commission, [1966] E.C.R. 299, at 342 ("... there is no need to take account of the concrete effects of an agreement once it appears that it has as its object the prevention, restriction or distortion of competition").

21. [Editors Note: See, for instance, the obligations that are blacklisted in Article 4 of No 1218/2010 of 14 December 2010 on the application of Article 101(3) of the Treaty to categories of specialisation agreements, O.J. L 335/43 and Article 5 of Commission Regulation No 1217/2010 of 14 December 2010 on the application of Article 101(3) of the Treaty on the functioning of the European Union to categories of research and development agreements, O.J. L 335/36].

If an agreement does not have an anticompetitive object, then it infringes Article 101(1) only if it has anticompetitive effects. This effects test requires an examination *in concreto* of the economic conditions prevailing on the market(s) concerned and of the effects of the agreement on competition.[22]

One important feature of Article 101(1) relates to the so-called agreements of "minor importance." In its 1969 decision in *Völk v. Vervaecke*, the ECJ stated that a restraint of competition and its effects on trade must be "appreciable" for the restraint to fall within the prohibition of Article 101(1).[23] Although this requirement of appreciability is not stated in the text of Article 101(1), the ECJ probably found it convenient to ensure that not too many agreements would infringe Article 101(1) and require notification back then, before the notification process was abolished. The ECJ has not defined what suffices to show such appreciability, however in its so-called "de minimis" Notice, the Commission states that agreements do not appreciably restrict competition if:

(1) the agreeing firms have fewer than 250 employees and either an annual revenue less than 50 million euros or an annual balance-sheet total less than 43 million euros, *or*

(2) the aggregate market shares held by the parties do not exceed:

(a) 10% in the case of horizontal agreements or mixed horizontal/vertical agreements;

(b) 15% in the case of vertical agreements; or

(c) 5% in the case of agreements having a cumulative effect, which may exist when more than 30% of the relevant market is covered by parallel agreements having similar effects.[24]

However, the Commission's "de minimis" Notice states that the quantitative thresholds below which it deems agreements to lack an appreciable impact:

"do not apply to agreements containing any of the following hardcore restrictions:

... as regards agreements between competitors ..., restrictions which, directly or indirectly, in isolation or in combination with other factors under the control of the parties, have as their object:

(a) the fixing of prices when selling the products to third parties;

(b) the limitation of output or sales;

---

22. See Case 56/65, *Société Technique Minière c. Maschinenbau Ulm*, [1966] E.C.R. 337; Case 26/76, *Metro c. Commission*, [1977] E.C.R. 1875; Case 258/78, *Nungesser c. Commission*, [1982] E.C.R. 2015; Case 262/81, *Coditel SA, Compagnie générale pour la diffusion de la télévision, et autres contre Ciné-Vog Films SA et autres*, [1982] E.C.R. 3381.

23. Case 5/69, Völk v. Vervaecke, [1969] E.C.R. 295.

24. Notice on agreements of Minor Importance which do not Appreciably Restrict Competition, 2001 O.J., C 372/5.

(c) the allocation of markets or customers."[25]

This passage indicates that the EU appreciability test does not apply to horizontal agreements that have the objective purpose of fixing price or output or dividing markets. This parallels U.S. law., which makes such agreements per se illegal regardless of how small the firms are that engage in it.

Leaving aside such hardcore horizontal cartel agreements, the appreciability test amounts to a rule of per se *legality* for agreements between small firms. Although the EU's de minimis market share rule has no direct parallel under U.S. law, a similar rule could be thought to govern restraints judged under the U.S. rule of reason, for a court will ordinarily dismiss such a claim unless the agreeing firms have some significant market share. The difference is that the U.S. rule of reason remains open to proof that market share is an inaccurate proxy for market power,[26] or that the challenged agreement had actual anticompetitive effects that obviate any need to inquire into market power. Further, the U.S. rule of reason dispenses with any need to show market share or power in cases where the defendant cannot even articulate a procompetitive justification. Which rule is preferable turns on which is greater: (a) the errors of underenforcement caused from using a market share in those cases where either markets are inaccurately defined or anticompetitive effects are possible despite low market shares; or (b) the errors of overenforcement caused by mistaken assessments of market power or anticompetitive effects or by the inabilities of defendants to articulate procompetitive theories for their agreements or of tribunals to understand those theories.

The above rationale does not, however, justify extending such a rule of per se legality to firms that are small in number of employees or revenue even when their market share is great because they are in a small market. This rule has no parallel under U.S. law, which generally deems anticompetitive effects to be of antitrust concern no matter how puny the market in question. Still, factors such as a small absolute size no doubt often guide the prosecutorial discretion of U.S. agencies. Further, a rule categorically immunizing nonhardcore agreements by such small firms can be justified on the ground that the adjudication costs of assessing such agreements would likely exceed the financial magnitude of any anticompetitive injury such agreements could cause, especially when one considers the firms are unlikely to have a high market share and that assessing their market shares would itself be costly.

A recent General Court decision makes clear that Article 101(1) does not embody a rule of reason inquiry that balances anticompetitive effects against procompetitive justifications.[27] However, such justifications may be considered under Article 101(3).

---

25. Commission Notice on agreements of minor importance, O.J. 2001, C 368/13, at § 11.

26. See Chapter 3 (explaining why market share is often an inaccurate proxy for market power).

27. *See* Case T–328/03, O2 (Germany), GmbH & Co. OHG v. Commission, [2006] E.C.R. 11–1231.

Article 101(3). Agreements that infringe Article 101(1) can generally still be justified under Article 101(3) provided four conditions are met. Two of these conditions are positive in that the agreement: (i) must contribute to improving the production or distribution of goods or to promoting technical or economic progress and (ii) must allow consumers a fair share of the resulting benefit. The other two conditions are negative in that the agreement cannot: (i) impose restrictions that are broader than necessary to attain the positive objectives and (ii) or eliminate competition in respect of a substantial part of the products in question.

Whether an agreement satisfies the conditions of Article 101(3) essentially turns whether its procompetitive features outweigh its anticompetitive features under an inquiry similar to, but somewhat distinct from, the U.S. rule of reason. As the Commission stated in its Notice on the Application of Article 101(3):

> "The aim of the Community competition rules is to protect competition on the market as a means of enhancing consumer welfare and of ensuring an efficient allocation of resources. Agreements that restrict competition may at the same time have pro-competitive effects by way of efficiency gains. Efficiencies may create additional value by lowering the cost of producing an output, improving the quality of the product or creating a new product. When the pro-competitive effects of an agreement outweigh its anti-competitive effects the agreement is on balance pro-competitive and compatible with the objectives of the Community competition rules. The net effect of such agreements is to promote the very essence of the competitive process, namely to win customers by offering better products or better prices than those offered by rivals."[28]

Thus, cooperation agreements like specialization or research and development agreements can be justified under Article 101(3) when their pro-competitive efficiencies outweigh their negative effects on competition.

However, agreements that generate substantial efficiencies will only be exempted if they also meet the other three conditions. The second condition, that consumers must get a "fair share" of those efficiencies, has been interpreted to adopt a consumer welfare standard, requiring that any efficiencies created by a restraint must be passed on to consumers in sufficient size as to offset the costs to them of any anticompetitive effects.[29] That is, while consumers are not entitled to a particular share of any efficiency gain, the restraint cannot leave consumers as a group worse off, though particular consumers might be. U.S. antitrust law today seems to also embody a consumer welfare standard,[30] though some have argued that

---

28. Communication from the Commission Notice—Guidelines on the application of Article [101](3) of the Treaty, O.J. 2004, C 101/97.

29. *See* Commission Guidelines on [101](3) ¶¶ 43, 85–87.

30. *See NCAA*, 468 at 107 ("Congress designed the Sherman Act as a 'consumer welfare prescription.'") (quoting Reiter v. Sonotone Corp., 442 U.S. 330, 343 (1979)); Brooke Group Ltd. v. Brown & Williamson Tobacco Corp., 509 U.S. 209, 221 (1993) (describing "antitrust laws' traditional concern" as "consumer welfare"); FTC–DOJ, Antitrust Guidelines for Collaborations among Competitors § 3.37 (2000) (agencies "determine the agreement's overall

it should instead be interpreted to embody a total welfare standard that would allow restraints that harmed consumers as long as the size of that harm were smaller than the efficiency gain to producers.[31]

The third condition, that the challenged restraint must be truly necessary to achieve the alleged efficiencies, parallels the "no less restrictive alternative" test under U.S. law. The usual difficulty is just how to determine whether a restraint is necessary and whether the alternatives are really less restrictive of competition.

The fourth condition, that the agreement cannot eliminate competition in a substantial part of the products in question, has no parallel under U.S. law. One might think the provision refers to the elimination of particular competitors. However, that interpretation seems inconsistent with the text referring to the elimination of "competition" and with EU caselaw stressing that EU competition law aims to protect "competition, not competitors." On the other hand, if it does not refer to eliminating particular competitors, then its meaning is unclear because, if the product market has been properly defined, competition cannot be eliminated for a substantial part of that market without eliminating it for the entire market. *See* Chapter 3. Perhaps this condition thus means only that efficiencies cannot justify the creation of a combination with a 100% market share. However, that would be a trivially small exception. And even that narrow interpretation seems questionable on policy grounds because the existence of such efficiencies suggests the market may be a natural monopoly and consumers might be worse off with two less efficient firms than one efficient combination.

The Distinction Between Hard–Core Restraints and Cooperation Agreements. Although in theory Article 101(3) could apply even to hard-core cartels, in practice it is very unlikely that such hard-core agreements could ever be justified under Article 101(3). As with U.S. law, the difficulty is that not all horizontal agreements on price, output or market division fall into the hard-core category. Rather, when horizontal rivals are

---

actual or likely effect on competition in the relevant market" by "consider[ing] whether cognizable efficiencies likely would be sufficient to offset the potential of the agreement to harm consumers in the relevant market, for example, by preventing price increases.")

31. *Compare* Lande, *Wealth Transfers as the Original and Primary Concern of Antitrust: The Efficiency Interpretation Challenged*, 34 Hastings L.J., 65, 68, 74–77, 82–106, 142–51 (1982) (concluding antitrust laws were intended to protect consumer surplus even at the sacrifice of overall efficiency), *with* R. Bork, the Antitrust Paradox 90–91, 107–115 (1978) (concluding antitrust laws were intended to promote wealth-maximization even at the sacrifice of consumer welfare). *See generally* Elhauge, *Tying, Bundled Discounts, and the Death of the Single Monopoly Profit Theory*, 123 Harvard Law Review 397, 436–442 (2009) (concluding that antitrust law embodies a consumer welfare standard, and that this standard is justifiable because: (1) ex ante dissipation of expected monopoly profits can make consumer welfare a better measure of ex ante total welfare, (2) transactions that increase ex post total welfare can generally be restructured to improve consumer welfare, (3) given concurrent international antitrust jurisdiction, the decisive enforcers will likely be importing nations who have incentives to apply a consumer welfare standard accurately, and (4) a consumer welfare standard has desirable distributional effects); Wickelgren, *Issues in Antitrust Enforcement*, in Research Handbook on the Economics of Antitrust Law (forthcoming 2011) (adding that a consumer welfare standard can also (1) drive firms to choose the action that increases total welfare the most rather than the most profitable action that increases total welfare, and (2) maximize total welfare if firms have private information about their efficiencies).

in a "cooperation agreement" whereby they jointly produce some tangible business product or service, their agreements on price, output and market division are not necessarily hard-core. This parallels the pattern of U.S. caselaw, which applies a per se rule to horizontal agreements among unrelated firms but not to firms that are in a productive relationship.

Unlike U.S. law, EU competition law has adopted block exemption regulations that are designed to specifically regulate horizontal cooperation agreements. The block exemptions on specialization agreements and research and development agreements take into account the market shares of the agreeing firms.[32] These regulations have been supplemented by the Commission guidelines on horizontal cooperation agreements, whose principles also apply to other categories of horizontal cooperation agreements, including joint purchasing, joint selling, standardization, and environmental agreements.[33] Under these exemptions and guidelines, the 101(3) inquiry first asks if the relevant agreements contain certain sorts of restrictions that are excluded from the regulations or guidelines. If not, then the agreements are presumptively exempted if market shares of the participants fall below a stated threshold, which is 20% for specialization agreements, 25% for R&D agreements, or 15% for joint buying or selling agreements. If those thresholds are exceeded, then the four conditions must be applied.

3.   OTHER NATIONS

Anticompetitive horizontal agreements are illegal in virtually all nations that have adopted antitrust laws. Nations usually distinguish between horizontal agreements that are anticompetitive per se and those whose anticompetitive nature is judged only after considering all effects and justifications in a rule of reason inquiry. Most nations use a per se rule that bars inquiries both into justifications *and* into effects for horizontal agreements on price, output, or market division that are not reasonably necessary to further a productive business collaboration. These nations include Australia, Canada, Egypt, India, Israel, Indonesia, Mexico, Peru, South Africa, South Korea, Taiwan, Thailand, Turkey, and Venezuela.[34] Some of

---

32. Commission Regulation No 1218/2010 of 14 December 2010 on the application of Article 101(3) of the Treaty to categories of specialisation agreements, O.J. L 335/43; Commission Regulation No 1217/2010 of 14 December 2010 on the application of Article 101(3) of the Treaty on the functioning of the European Union to categories of research and development agreements, O.J. L 335/36.

33. Commission Regulation No 1218/2010 of 14 December 2010 on the application of Article 101(3) of the Treaty to categories of specialisation agreements, O.J. L 335/43; Commission Regulation No 1217/2010 of 14 December 2010 on the application of Article 101(3) of the Treaty on the functioning of the European Union to categories of research and development agreements, O.J. L 335/36.

34. Australia Trade Practices Act § 44ZZRD; Canada Competition Act §§ 45, 47; Egypt Competition Law Art. 6; India Competition Act § 3(3); Israel Restrictive Trade Practices Law § 2(b); Indonesia Competition Law Arts. 5, 7, 9, 11, 22; Mexico Competition Law Art. 9; Peru Competition Law Art. 8, 11.2; South Africa Competition Act § 4(1)(b); South Korea Guidelines on Reviewing Cartel Activities IV.1.A (2009); Taiwan Fair Trade Act Art. 7; Thailand Trade

these nations allow parties to petition an agency or tribunal for an exemption, but nonetheless apply such a per se rule to agreements that lack this advance authorization.[35]

Other nations, including Argentina, Chile, and Japan, condemn horizontal agreements only if substantial anticompetitive effects are shown or seem likely because of market power, thus effectively creating a rule of per se legality for horizontal agreements that cover a small market share even if they are between unrelated firms and lack a procompetitive justification.[36] However, these statutes do not seem to allow justifications for horizontal agreements between unrelated firms when market power is present, so these nations appear to use a *partial* per se rule that excludes justifications but allows evidence of lack of anticompetitive effect. China allows firms to defend their horizontal agreements with justifications even when market power is present.[37] Because China does not appear to allow a defense of lack of market power for horizontal agreements fixing prices and output or dividing markets, China thus seems to apply a *different* partial per se rule that allows justifications but excludes evidence on lack of anticompetitive effect.

B. HORIZONTAL PRICE-FIXING

United States v. Trenton Potteries

273 U.S. 392 (1927).

■ MR. JUSTICE STONE delivered the opinion of the Court.

Respondents, twenty individuals and twenty-three corporations, were convicted ... of violating the Sherman Anti–Trust Law.... The indictment

---

Competition Act § 27; Turkey Competition Act Art. 4; Venezuela Regulation No.1 of the Procompetition Act, Art. 7.

35. Australia Trade Practices Act §§ 88, 90; India Competition Act § 54; Israel Restrictive Trade Practices Law §§ 7–10; South Korea Fair Trade Act Art. 19(2); Taiwan Fair Trade Act Art. 14; Turkey Competition Act Art. 5; Thailand Trade Competition Act § 27 (Commission can authorize agreements other than price-fixing when commercially necessary).

36. Argentina Competition Law Arts. 1–2 (requiring that the agreement "lessen, restrict or distort competition ... in a manner that may result in damage to the general economic interest"); Chile Competition Law Art. 3 (requiring market power); Japan Antimonopoly Act § 2(6) (requiring "a substantial restraint of competition").

Some nations require evidence of either market power or an anticompetitive purpose. *See* Brazil Antitrust Law No. 8,884, Arts. 20–21 (must show anticompetitive purpose or capacity to produce effects); Saudi Arabia Competition Law Art. 4 (requiring that the firms have a "dominant status" to qualify for per se condemnation, and otherwise requiring an anticompetitive purpose or effect). These nations might have a pure rule of per se illegality if the requisite anticompetitive purpose can be inferred from a horizontal agreement on prices, output or market division between unrelated firms. However, if instead a lack of anticompetitive purpose can be inferred from a lack of market power, then these nations would effectively have a rule of per se legality when market power is absent.

Saudi Arabia also allows firms to apply to the Council for an exemption by showing efficiencies, but requires advance authorization. *See* Saudi Arabia Competition Law Art. 4; Saudi Arabia Executive Regulation Art.5. This law thus does not apply a rule of reason, which would instead allow parties to engage in the conduct and defend it after the fact by showing the efficiencies outweighed any anticompetitive effects.

37. China Anti–Monopoly Law Arts. 13, 15.

. . . charged a combination to fix and maintain uniform prices for the sale of sanitary pottery. . . . On appeal, the court of appeals for the second circuit reversed the judgment of conviction on both counts on the ground that there were errors in the conduct of the trial. . . .

Respondents, engaged in the manufacture or distribution of 82 per cent. of the vitreous pottery fixtures produced in the United States for use in bathrooms and lavatories, were members of a trade organization known as the Sanitary Potters' Association. . . . There is no contention here that the verdict was not supported by sufficient evidence that respondents, controlling some 82 per cent. of the business of manufacturing and distributing in the United States vitreous pottery of the type described, combined to fix prices and to limit sales in interstate commerce to jobbers. . . .

The trial court charged, in submitting the case to the jury, that if it found the agreements or combination complained of, it might return a verdict of guilty without regard to the reasonableness of the prices fixed, or the good intentions of the combining units, whether prices were actually lowered or raised or whether sales were restricted . . . since [the] agreements of themselves were unreasonable restraints. . . . In particular the court refused the request to charge the following: "The essence of the law is injury to the public. It is not every restraint of competition and not every restraint of trade that works an injury to the public; it is only an undue and unreasonable restraint of trade that has such an effect and is deemed to be unlawful." . . . [T]he trial judge plainly and variously charged the jury that the combinations alleged in the indictment, if found, were violations of the statute as a matter of law, saying: ". . . the law is clear that an agreement on the part of the members of a combination controlling a substantial part of an industry, upon the prices which the members are to charge for their commodity, is in itself an undue and unreasonable restraint of trade and commerce; . . ." . . .

The question therefore to be considered here is whether the trial judge correctly withdrew from the jury the consideration of the reasonableness of the particular restraints charged.

That only those restraints upon interstate commerce which are unreasonable are prohibited by the Sherman Law was the rule laid down by the opinions of this Court in the *Standard Oil* and *Tobacco* cases. But it does not follow that agreements to fix or maintain prices are reasonable restraints and therefore permitted by the statute, merely because the prices themselves are reasonable. Reasonableness is not a concept of definite and unchanging content. Its meaning necessarily varies in the different fields of the law, because it is used as a convenient summary of the dominant considerations which control in the application of legal doctrines. Our view of what is a reasonable restraint of commerce is controlled by the recognized purpose of the Sherman Law itself. Whether this type of restraint is reasonable or not must be judged in part at least in the light of its effect on competition, for whatever difference of opinion there may be among economists as to the social and economic desirability of an unrestrained competitive system, it cannot be doubted that the Sherman Law and the judicial decisions interpreting it are based upon the assumption that the public interest is best protected from the evils of monopoly and price control by the maintenance of competition.

The aim and result of every price-fixing agreement, if effective, is the elimination of one form of competition. The power to fix prices, whether reasonably exercised or not, involves power to control the market and to fix arbitrary and unreasonable prices. The reasonable price fixed today may through economic and business changes become the unreasonable price of tomorrow. Once established, it may be maintained unchanged because of the absence of competition secured by the agreement for a price reasonable when fixed. Agreements which create such potential power may well be held to be in themselves unreasonable or unlawful restraints, without the necessity of minute inquiry whether a particular price is reasonable or unreasonable as fixed and without placing on the government in enforcing the Sherman Law the burden of ascertaining from day to day whether it has become unreasonable through the mere variation of economic conditions. Moreover, in the absence of express legislation requiring it, we should hesitate to adopt a construction making the difference between legal and illegal conduct in the field of business relations depend upon so uncertain a test as whether prices are reasonable—a determination which can be satisfactorily made only after a complete survey of our economic organization and a choice between rival philosophies. . . .

[U]niform price-fixing by those controlling in any substantial manner a trade or business in interstate commerce is prohibited by the Sherman Law, despite the reasonableness of the particular prices agreed upon. . . .

The charge of the trial court, viewed as a whole, fairly submitted to the jury the question whether a price-fixing agreement as described in the first count was entered into by the respondents. Whether the prices actually agreed upon were reasonable or unreasonable was immaterial. . . .

Questions on *Trenton Potteries*

1. If only unreasonable restraints of trade are illegal, why shouldn't defendants be able to introduce evidence that their restraint was reasonable? What was the Court concerned about?

2. Is the Court's decision based on (a) the position that any price fixed by horizontal agreement is unreasonable on principle or (b) the view that it would be administratively too difficult for courts to determine the reasonableness of prices, or (c) both?

3. If the contrary rule were adopted, how would judges or juries determine whether fixed prices were reasonable?

a. Would they have principled criteria for assessing reasonableness other than whether the prices were set by competition?

b. If they did have such criteria, could they handle the factual issues and monitor them as market conditions changed?

4. What would such a general reasonableness standard do to:

a. the incentives of government or private actors to bring suit?

    b.   the ability of firms to ascertain and comply with the law?

    5.   Why not let defendants introduce the defense that their price-fixing agreement had no effect at all—that is, that it was unsuccessful in changing prices from those that would have prevailed without it?

    a.   Would allowing the defense prevent the law from discouraging any desirable conduct?

    b.   Is there anything to be lost by allowing such a defense if courts can perfectly and costlessly ascertain whether price-fixing agreements had an effect? What if proving such an effect is costly and sometimes results in erroneous conclusions that no such effect existed?

    c.   Can we infer from the act of price-fixing that the defendants must have had the purpose of altering market prices and thought they had the power to have that effect? Are business firms usually better placed to decide whether they have the power to have such an effect than judges and juries?

    d.   Should the rule against allowing the defense that price-fixing has no effect apply even if the defendants comprise only 1% of the market? Would such an exception raise concerns if market definition is sometimes hard to prove or incorrectly assessed? If the law allowed the defense when market shares were only 1%, should it also allow it at 10%? 20%? 30%? Would anything be gained by allowing such a defense? Anything lost?

Broadcast Music, Inc. (BMI) v. Columbia Broadcasting System

441 U.S. 1 (1979).

■ MR. JUSTICE WHITE delivered the opinion of the Court.

    This case involves an action under the antitrust and copyright laws brought by respondent Columbia Broadcasting System, Inc. (CBS), against petitioners, American Society of Composers, Authors and Publishers (AS-CAP) and Broadcast Music, Inc. (BMI), and their members and affiliates. The basic question presented is whether the issuance by ASCAP and BMI to CBS of blanket licenses to copyrighted musical compositions at fees negotiated by them is price fixing *per se* unlawful under the antitrust laws.

I

    CBS operates one of three national commercial television networks, supplying programs to approximately 200 affiliated stations and telecasting approximately 7,500 network programs per year. Many, but not all, of these programs make use of copyrighted music recorded on the soundtrack. CBS also owns television and radio stations in various cities. . . .

    Since 1897, the copyright laws have vested in the owner of a copyrighted musical composition the exclusive right to perform the work publicly for profit, but the legal right is not self-enforcing. In 1914, Victor Herbert and a handful of other composers organized ASCAP because those who performed copyrighted music for profit were so numerous and widespread, and most performances so fleeting, that as a practical matter it was impossible for the many individual copyright owners to negotiate with and license the users and to detect unauthorized uses. . . . As ASCAP operates today, its 22,000 members grant it nonexclusive rights to license nondramatic performances of their works, and ASCAP issues licenses and distributes royalties to copyright owners in accordance with a schedule reflecting the nature and amount of the use of their music and other factors.

BMI, a nonprofit corporation owned by members of the broadcasting industry,[4] was organized in 1939, is affiliated with or represents some 10,000 publishing companies and 20,000 authors and composers, and operates in much the same manner as ASCAP. Almost every domestic copyrighted composition is in the repertory either of ASCAP, with a total of three million compositions, or of BMI, with one million.

Both organizations operate primarily through blanket licenses, which give the licensees the right to perform any and all of the compositions owned by the members or affiliates as often as the licensees desire for a stated term. Fees for blanket licenses are ordinarily a percentage of total revenues or a flat dollar amount, and do not directly depend on the amount or type of music used. Radio and television broadcasters are the largest users of music, and almost all of them hold blanket licenses from both ASCAP and BMI. Until this litigation, CBS held blanket licenses from both organizations for its television network on a continuous basis since the late 1940's and had never attempted to secure any other form of license from either ASCAP[5] or any of its members.

. . . After an 8–week trial, . . . the [trial] court dismissed the complaint, rejecting again the claim that the blanket license was price fixing and a *per se* violation of § 1 of the Sherman Act, and holding that since direct negotiation with individual copyright owners is available and feasible there is no undue restraint of trade, illegal tying, misuse of copyrights, or monopolization. . . [T]he Court of Appeals held that the blanket license issued to television networks was a form of price fixing illegal *per se* under the Sherman Act. This conclusion, without more, settled the issue of liability under the Sherman Act, . . . and required reversal of the District Court's judgment, as well as a remand to consider the appropriate remedy. . . . Because we disagree with the Court of Appeals' conclusions with respect to the *per se* illegality of the blanket license, we reverse. . . .

II

In construing and applying the Sherman Act's ban against contracts, conspiracies, and combinations in restraint of trade, the Court has held that certain agreements or practices are so "plainly anticompetitive," and so often "lack . . . any redeeming virtue," that they are conclusively presumed illegal without further examination under the rule of reason generally applied in Sherman Act cases. This *per se* rule is a valid and useful tool of antitrust policy and enforcement.[11] And agreements among

---

4. CBS was a leader of the broadcasters who formed BMI, but it disposed of all of its interest in the corporation in 1959.

5. Unless the context indicates otherwise, references to ASCAP alone in this opinion usually apply to BMI as well.

11. "This principle of *per se* unreasonableness not only makes the type of restraints which are proscribed by the Sherman Act more certain to the benefit of everyone concerned,

competitors to fix prices on their individual goods or services are among those concerted activities that the Court has held to be within the *per se* category. But easy labels do not always supply ready answers.

A

To the Court of Appeals and CBS, the blanket license involves "price fixing" in the literal sense: the composers and publishing houses have joined together into an organization that sets its price for the blanket license it sells.[13] But this is not a question simply of determining whether two or more potential competitors have literally "fixed" a "price." As generally used in the antitrust field, "price fixing" is a shorthand way of describing certain categories of business behavior to which the *per se* rule has been held applicable. The Court of Appeals' literal approach does not alone establish that this particular practice is one of those types or that it is "plainly anticompetitive" and very likely without "redeeming virtue." Literalness is overly simplistic and often overbroad. When two partners set the price of their goods or services they are literally "price fixing," but they are not *per se* in violation of the Sherman Act. See *United States v. Addyston Pipe & Steel Co.*, 85 F. 271, 280 (CA6 1898), aff'd, 175 U.S. 211 (1899). Thus, it is necessary to characterize the challenged conduct as falling within or without that category of behavior to which we apply the label "*per se* price fixing." That will often, but not always, be a simple matter.

Consequently, . . . "[i]t is only after considerable experience with certain business relationships that courts classify them as *per se* violations. . . ." We have never examined a practice like this one before; indeed, the Court of Appeals recognized that "[i]n dealing with performing rights in the music industry we confront conditions both in copyright law and in antitrust law which are *sui generis.*" And though there has been rather intensive antitrust scrutiny of ASCAP and its blanket licenses, that experience hardly counsels that we should outlaw the blanket license as a *per se* restraint of trade.

B

. . . In separate complaints in 1941, the United States charged that the blanket license, which was then the only license offered by ASCAP and BMI, was an illegal restraint of trade. . . . The case was settled by a consent decree that imposed tight restrictions on ASCAP's operations. . . . Under

---

but it also avoids the necessity for an incredibly complicated and prolonged economic investigation into the entire history of the industry involved, as well as related industries, in an effort to determine at large whether a particular restraint has been unreasonable—an inquiry so often wholly fruitless when undertaken." *Northern Pac. R. Co. v. United States,* 356 U.S. 1, 5 (1958).

13. CBS also complains that it pays a flat fee regardless of the amount of use it makes of ASCAP compositions and even though many of its programs contain little or no music. We are unable to see how that alone could make out an antitrust violation or misuse of copyrights: "Sound business judgment could indicate that such payment represents the most convenient method of fixing the business value of the privileges granted by the licensing agreement. . . . Petitioner cannot complain because it must pay royalties whether it uses Hazeltine patents or not. What it acquired by the agreement into which it entered was the privilege to use any or all of the patents and developments as it desired to use them." *Automatic Radio Mfg. Co. v. Hazeltine Research, Inc.,* 339 U.S. 827, 834 (1950).

the amended decree, which still substantially controls the activities of ASCAP, members may grant ASCAP only nonexclusive rights to license their works for public performance. Members, therefore, retain the rights individually to license public performances, along with the rights to license the use of their compositions for other purposes.[38] ASCAP itself is forbidden to grant any license to perform one or more specified compositions in the ASCAP repertory unless both the user and the owner have requested it in writing to do so. ASCAP is required to grant to any user making written application a nonexclusive license to perform all ASCAP compositions either for a period of time or on a per-program basis. ASCAP may not insist on the blanket license, and the fee for the per-program license, which is to be based on the revenues for the program on which ASCAP music is played, must offer the applicant a genuine economic choice between the per-program license and the more common blanket license. If ASCAP and a putative licensee are unable to agree on a fee within 60 days, the applicant may apply to the District Court for a determination of a reasonable fee, with ASCAP having the burden of proving reasonableness.

The 1950 decree, as amended from time to time, continues in effect, and the blanket license continues to be the primary instrument through which ASCAP conducts its business under the decree. The courts have twice construed the decree not to require ASCAP to issue licenses for selected portions of its repertory. It also remains true that the decree guarantees the legal availability of direct licensing of performance rights by ASCAP members; and the District Court found, and in this respect the Court of Appeals agreed, that there are no practical impediments preventing direct dealing by the television networks if they so desire. Historically, they have not done so. Since 1946, CBS and other television networks have taken blanket licenses from ASCAP and BMI. It was not until this suit arose that the CBS network demanded any other kind of license.

Of course, a consent judgment, even one entered at the behest of the Antitrust Division, does not immunize the defendant from liability for actions, including those contemplated by the decree, that violate the rights of nonparties. . . . But it cannot be ignored that the Federal Executive and Judiciary have carefully scrutinized ASCAP and the challenged conduct, have imposed restrictions on various of ASCAP's practices, and, by the terms of the decree, stand ready to provide further consideration, supervision, and perhaps invalidation of asserted anticompetitive practices. In these circumstances, we have a unique indicator that the challenged practice may have redeeming competitive virtues and that the search for those values is not almost sure to be in vain.[24] Thus, although CBS is not bound by the Antitrust Division's actions, the decree is a fact of economic and legal life in this industry, and the Court of Appeals should not have ignored it completely in analyzing the practice. That fact alone might not

---

38. [Editor's Note: Although members retained this right to individually license the use of their songs, members of ASCAP or BMI could not license their songs to another performance rights organization. *See* United States v. Broadcast Music, Inc. and RKO General, Inc., 1966 Trade Cas. (CCH) ¶ 71,141, at Consent Decree § VI.A.]

24. Moreover, unthinking application of the *per se* rule might upset the balancing of economic power and of procompetitive and anticompetitive effect presumably worked out in the decree.

remove a naked price-fixing scheme from the ambit of the *per se* rule, but, as discussed *infra,* Part III, here we are uncertain whether the practice on its face has the effect, or could have been spurred by the purpose, of restraining competition among the individual composers. . . .

Finally, we note that Congress itself, in the new Copyright Act, has chosen to employ the blanket license and similar practices. Congress created a compulsory blanket license for secondary transmissions by cable television systems . . . 17 U.S.C. App. § 111(d)(5)(A). And the newly created compulsory license for the use of copyrighted compositions in jukeboxes is also a blanket license, which is payable to the performing-rights societies such as ASCAP unless an individual copyright holder can prove his entitlement to a share. § 116(c)(4). Moreover, in requiring noncommercial broadcasters to pay for their use of copyrighted music, Congress again provided that "[n]otwithstanding any provision of the antitrust laws" copyright owners "may designate common agents to negotiate, agree to, pay, or receive payments." § 118(b). Though these provisions are not directly controlling, they do reflect an opinion that the blanket license, and ASCAP, are economically beneficial in at least some circumstances. . . .

III

Of course, we are no more bound than is CBS by the views of the Department of Justice, the results in the prior lower court cases, or the opinions of various experts about the merits of the blanket license. But while we must independently examine this practice, all those factors should caution us against too easily finding blanket licensing subject to *per se* invalidation.

A

As a preliminary matter, we are mindful that the Court of Appeals' holding would appear to be quite difficult to contain. If, as the court held, there is a *per se* antitrust violation whenever ASCAP issues a blanket license to a television network for a single fee, why would it not also be automatically illegal for ASCAP to negotiate and issue blanket licenses to individual radio or television stations or to other users who perform copyrighted music for profit? Likewise, if the present network licenses issued through ASCAP on behalf of its members are *per se* violations, why would it not be equally illegal for the members to authorize ASCAP to issue licenses establishing various categories of uses that a network might have for copyrighted music and setting a standard fee for each described use?

Although the Court of Appeals apparently thought the blanket license could be saved in some or even many applications, it seems to us that the *per se* rule does not accommodate itself to such flexibility and that the observations of the Court of Appeals with respect to remedy tend to impeach the *per se* basis for the holding of liability.[27]

---

27. The Court of Appeals would apparently not outlaw the blanket license across the board but would permit it in various circumstances where it is deemed necessary or sufficiently desirable. It did not even enjoin blanket licensing with the television networks, the relief it realized would normally follow a finding of *per se* illegality of the license in that context. Instead, as requested by CBS, it remanded to the District Court to require ASCAP to offer in addition to blanket licensing some competitive form of per-use licensing. But per-use licensing

CBS would prefer that ASCAP be authorized, indeed directed, to make all its compositions available at standard per-use rates within negotiated categories of use. But if this in itself or in conjunction with blanket licensing constitutes illegal price fixing by copyright owners, CBS urges that an injunction issue forbidding ASCAP to issue any blanket license or to negotiate any fee except on behalf of an individual member for the use of his own copyrighted work or works. Thus, we are called upon to determine that blanket licensing is unlawful across the board. We are quite sure, however, that the *per se* rule does not require any such holding.

B

In the first place, the line of commerce allegedly being restrained, the performing rights to copyrighted music, exists at all only because of the copyright laws. Those who would use copyrighted music in public performances must secure consent from the copyright owner or be liable at least for the statutory damages for each infringement and, if the conduct is willful and for the purpose of financial gain, to criminal penalties.... Although the copyright laws confer no rights on copyright owners to fix prices among themselves or otherwise to violate the antitrust laws, we would not expect that any market arrangements reasonably necessary to effectuate the rights that are granted would be deemed a *per se* violation of the Sherman Act. Otherwise, the commerce anticipated by the Copyright Act and protected against restraint by the Sherman Act would not exist at all or would exist only as a pale reminder of what Congress envisioned.[32]

C

More generally, in characterizing this conduct under the *per se* rule,[33] our inquiry must focus on whether the effect and, here because it tends to show effect, the purpose of the practice are to threaten the proper operation of our predominantly free-market economy—that is, whether the practice facially appears to be one that would always or almost always tend to restrict competition and decrease output, and in what portion of the

---

by ASCAP, as recognized in the consent decrees, might be even more susceptible to the *per se* rule than blanket licensing.

The rationale for this unusual relief in a *per se* case was that "[t]he blanket license is not simply a 'naked restraint' ineluctably doomed to extinction." To the contrary, the Court of Appeals found that the blanket license might well "serve a market need" for some. This, it seems to us, is not the *per se* approach, which does not yield so readily to circumstances, but in effect is a rather bobtailed application of the rule of reason, bobtailed in the sense that it is unaccompanied by the necessary analysis demonstrating why the particular licensing system is an undue competitive restraint.

32. Because a musical composition can be "consumed" by many different people at the same time and without the creator's knowledge, the "owner" has no real way to demand reimbursement for the use of his property except through the copyright laws *and* an effective way to enforce those legal rights. It takes an organization of rather large size to monitor most or all uses and to deal with users on behalf of the composers. Moreover, it is inefficient to have too many such organizations duplicating each other's monitoring of use.

33. The scrutiny occasionally required must not merely subsume the burdensome analysis required under the rule of reason, or else we should apply the rule of reason from the start. That is why the *per se* rule is not employed until after considerable experience with the type of challenged restraint.

market, or instead one designed to "increase economic efficiency and render markets more, rather than less, competitive."

The blanket license, as we see it, is not a "naked restrain[t] of trade with no purpose except stifling of competition," but rather accompanies the integration of sales, monitoring, and enforcement against unauthorized copyright use. . . . ASCAP and the blanket license developed together out of the practical situation in the marketplace: thousands of users, thousands of copyright owners, and millions of compositions. Most users want unplanned, rapid, and indemnified access to any and all of the repertory of compositions, and the owners want a reliable method of collecting for the use of their copyrights. Individual sales transactions in this industry are quite expensive, as would be individual monitoring and enforcement, especially in light of the resources of single composers. Indeed, as both the Court of Appeals and CBS recognize, the costs are prohibitive for licenses with individual radio stations, nightclubs, and restaurants, and it was in that milieu that the blanket license arose.

A middleman with a blanket license was an obvious necessity if the thousands of individual negotiations, a virtual impossibility, were to be avoided. Also, individual fees for the use of individual compositions would presuppose an intricate schedule of fees and uses, as well as a difficult and expensive reporting problem for the user and policing task for the copyright owner. Historically, the market for public-performance rights organized itself largely around the single-fee blanket license, which gave unlimited access to the repertory and reliable protection against infringement. When ASCAP's major and user-created competitor, BMI, came on the scene, it also turned to the blanket license.

With the advent of radio and television networks, market conditions changed, and the necessity for and advantages of a blanket license for those users may be far less obvious than is the case when the potential users are individual television or radio stations, or the thousands of other individuals and organizations performing copyrighted compositions in public.[34] But even for television network licenses, ASCAP reduces costs absolutely by creating a blanket license that is sold only a few, instead of thousands, of times, and that obviates the need for closely monitoring the networks to see that they do not use more than they pay for.[36] ASCAP also provides the necessary resources for blanket sales and enforcement, resources unavailable to the vast majority of composers and publishing houses. Moreover, a bulk license of some type is a necessary consequence of the integration necessary to achieve these efficiencies, and a necessary consequence of an aggregate license is that its price must be established.

D

This substantial lowering of costs, which is of course potentially beneficial to both sellers and buyers, differentiates the blanket license from individual use licenses. The blanket license is composed of the individual

---

34. And of course changes brought about by new technology or new marketing techniques might also undercut the justification for the practice.

36. To operate its system for distributing the license revenues to its members, ASCAP relies primarily on the networks' records of which compositions are used.

compositions plus the aggregating service. Here, the whole is truly greater than the sum of its parts; it is, to some extent, a different product. The blanket license has certain unique characteristics: It allows the licensee immediate use of covered compositions, without the delay of prior individual negotiations[37] and great flexibility in the choice of musical material. Many consumers clearly prefer the characteristics and cost advantages of this marketable package, and even small-performing rights societies that have occasionally arisen to compete with ASCAP and BMI have offered blanket licenses.[39] Thus, to the extent the blanket license is a different product, ASCAP is not really a joint sales agency offering the individual goods of many sellers, but is a separate seller offering its blanket license, of which the individual compositions are raw material.[40] ASCAP, in short, made a market in which individual composers are inherently unable to compete fully effectively.

E

Finally, we have some doubt—enough to counsel against application of the *per se* rule—about the extent to which this practice threatens the "central nervous system of the economy," *United States v. Socony–Vacuum Oil Co.*, 310 U.S. 150, 226 n. 59 (1940), that is, competitive pricing as the free market's means of allocating resources. Not all arrangements among actual or potential competitors that have an impact on price are *per se* violations of the Sherman Act or even unreasonable restraints. Mergers among competitors eliminate competition, including price competition, but they are not *per se* illegal, and many of them withstand attack under any existing antitrust standard. Joint ventures and other cooperative arrangements are also not usually unlawful, at least not as price-fixing schemes, where the agreement on price is necessary to market the product at all.

Here, the blanket-license fee is not set by competition among individual copyright owners, and it is a fee for the use of any of the compositions covered by the license. But the blanket license cannot be wholly equated with a simple horizontal arrangement among competitors. ASCAP does set the price for its blanket license, but that license is quite different from anything any individual owner could issue. The individual composers and

---

37. See Timberg, The Antitrust Aspects of Merchandising Modern Music: The ASCAP Consent Judgment of 1950, 19 Law & Contemp.Prob. 294, 297 (1954) ("The disk-jockey's itchy fingers and the bandleader's restive baton, it is said, cannot wait for contracts to be drawn with ASCAP's individual publisher members, much less for the formal acquiescence of a characteristically unavailable composer or author"). Significantly, ASCAP deals only with nondramatic performance rights. Because of their nature, dramatic rights, such as for musicals, can be negotiated individually and well in advance of the time of performance. The same is true of various other rights, such as sheet music, recording, and synchronization, which are licensed on an individual basis.

39. See also Garner, *United States v. ASCAP*: The Licensing Provisions of the Amended Final Judgment of 1950, 23 Bull.Copyright Soc. 119, 149 (1975) ("no performing rights are licensed on other than a blanket basis in any nation in the world").

40. Moreover, because of the nature of the product—a composition can be simultaneously "consumed" by many users—composers have numerous markets and numerous incentives to produce, so the blanket license is unlikely to cause decreased output, one of the normal undesirable effects of a cartel. And since popular songs get an increased share of ASCAP's revenue distributions, composers compete even within the blanket license in terms of productivity and consumer satisfaction.

authors have neither agreed not to sell individually in any other market nor use the blanket license to mask price fixing in such other markets. Moreover, the substantial restraints placed on ASCAP and its members by the consent decree must not be ignored. The District Court found that there was no legal, practical, or conspiratorial impediment to CBS's obtaining individual licenses; CBS, in short, had a real choice.

With this background in mind, which plainly enough indicates that over the years, and in the face of available alternatives, the blanket license has provided an acceptable mechanism for at least a large part of the market for the performing rights to copyrighted musical compositions, we cannot agree that it should automatically be declared illegal in all of its many manifestations. Rather, when attacked, it should be subjected to a more discriminating examination under the rule of reason. It may not ultimately survive that attack, but that is not the issue before us today. . . .

Questions on *BMI*

1. Why isn't this case simply resolved by the per se rule against price fixing?

a. Does this agreement fix sale prices to networks? The prices paid to composers? Are the members of ASCAP and BMI horizontally fixing prices? Or are they engaged in a productive joint venture that buys inputs and creates a different product whose price the joint venture unilaterally sets?

b. If the Court believes this is literally price-fixing, then why doesn't the per se rule apply? If this were covered by a per se rule because it was literally price-fixing, wouldn't all partnerships that fix the price of their product be per se unlawful?

c. Is the position of CBS and the Court of Appeals on remedies consistent with the position that the per se rule condemns all literal fixing of prices by ASCAP or BMI?

2. Does the Court's meta-test for determining whether the per se rule applies turn on. . . .

a. the fact that the restraint here is ancillary to a productive rival collaboration and integration of business activities?

b. the notion that here ASCAP and BMI are producing a "different product" from their members? Would that exception explain the inapplicability of the per se rule to prices fixed by ordinary partnerships?

c. an assessment that here the procompetitive justifications look strong and the anticompetitive effects weak? Does that assessment really differ from applying the rule of reason itself?

3. Why does application of the Court's meta-test for determining which rule to apply indicate that the rule of reason should apply here?

a. Do negotiation, monitoring, and enforcement costs require collective organization? Does that collective organization require a blanket license?

i.   Why couldn't organizations (instead or also) allow each composer to post her own price for each song? Does this issue go to whether the per se rule applies, or rather to whether a less restrictive alternative exists under rule of reason analysis?

ii.   Do the blanket licenses here eliminate the need to measure use of individual compositions? Don't the organizations still need to measure use to decide how to distribute revenue among composers? Do the blanket licenses make monitoring usage easier? Why?

iii.   Do the blanket licenses also require banning members from licensing their songs to rival performance rights organizations?

iv.   Does modern technology change these conclusions? Suppose the advent of the computer and the internet provides a cheap, reliable way for determining what compositions every television network has used, and for each composer to list the price she wishes to charge for her songs, in a way that networks could easily check on the internet. Would the case then come out differently under footnote 34?

b.   How do the organizations determine the price paid to individual composers? Does that method allow a lesser known composer to compete on price by offering to license her songs for less than more famous composers? Is any restriction on such price competition by composers necessary to further the procompetitive purposes of the organizations?

c.   How are the prices of the blanket licenses determined? Doesn't judicial review of this issue require courts to determine what price is reasonable?

4.   How should rule of reason analysis come out on remand?

a.   Was the lower court right that the ability to negotiate individual licenses eliminates any anticompetitive effect?

i.   What does the procompetitive justification suggest about the feasibility of individual negotiation? If it is unfeasible, would that also eliminate any anticompetitive effect from the restraint?

ii.   Doesn't a similar possibility of direct negotiation exist for every price-fixing cartel because a cartel cannot legally restrict negotiation with individual cartel members?

b.   Why isn't it a less restrictive alternative for BMI or ASCAP to do what they actually did, but to (also or instead) offer individual composition prices set by composers? If that were feasible and preferable, why hasn't it already occurred?

c.   Do the procompetitive justifications justify grouping all compositions into two organizations with 75% and 25% of the market respectively? Why wouldn't it be a less restrictive alternative to group composers into 5–10 competing organizations, each selling their own blanket licenses?

5.   Suppose two corporations, Microhard and Orange have the only competing operating systems, and decide to give copyright licenses to sell those operating systems to the OS Licensing Corporation, which in turn sells to computer users a blanket license to use either operating system, with the resulting revenues distributed to Microhard and Orange based on usage. Is this agreement per se unlawful or subject to the rule of reason?

   a.   Is the procompetitive justification the same as in *BMI*?

   b.   Are the anticompetitive effects the same?

   c.   Do your answers turn on whether Microhard and Orange gave an exclusive license to the OS Licensing Corporation or a nonexclusive one that gives them the right to continue to license their operating system directly? On whether Microhard and Orange retain control over the OS Licensing Corporation?

   d.   Suppose Microhard and Orange retained control over the OS Licensing Corporation and gave it nonexclusive licenses. If the OS Licensing Corporation set a high cartel price for the blanket license, would Microhard and Orange have adequate incentives to undercut it with lower prices for direct licenses? Does the *BMI* case differ on this front?

   e.   If this agreement is not per se illegal, does it violate the rule of reason? Would one need a very elaborate inquiry to resolve that issue?

Arizona v. Maricopa County Medical Soc'y

457 U.S. 332 (1982).

■ Justice Stevens delivered the opinion of the Court.

   The question presented is whether § 1 of the Sherman Act ... has been violated by agreements among competing physicians setting, by majority vote, the maximum fees that they may claim in full payment for health services provided to policyholders of specified insurance plans. The United States Court of Appeals for the Ninth Circuit held that the question could not be answered without evaluating the actual purpose and effect of the agreements at a full trial. Because the undisputed facts disclose a violation of the statute, we ... reverse....

II

   The Maricopa Foundation for Medical Care is a nonprofit Arizona corporation composed of licensed doctors of medicine, osteopathy, and podiatry engaged in private practice. Approximately 1,750 doctors, representing about 70% of the practitioners in Maricopa County, are members.

   The Maricopa Foundation was organized in 1969 for the purpose of promoting fee-for-service medicine and to provide the community with a competitive alternative to existing health insurance plans. The foundation performs three primary activities. It establishes the schedule of maximum fees that participating doctors agree to accept as payment in full for services performed for patients insured under plans approved by the foundation. It reviews the medical necessity and appropriateness of treatment provided by its members to such insured persons. It is authorized to draw checks on insurance company accounts to pay doctors for services performed for covered patients. In performing these functions, the foundation is considered an "insurance administrator" by the Director of the Arizona Department of Insurance. Its participating doctors, however, have no financial interest in the operation of the foundation.

The Pima Foundation for Medical Care, which includes [30–80% of the doctors in Pima County], performs similar functions. For the purposes of this litigation, the parties seem to regard the activities of the two foundations as essentially the same. No challenge is made to their peer review or claim administration functions. Nor do the foundations allege that these two activities make it necessary for them to engage in the practice of establishing maximum-fee schedules.

At the time this lawsuit was filed, each foundation made use of "relative values" and "conversion factors" in compiling its fee schedule. The conversion factor is the dollar amount used to determine fees for a particular medical specialty.... The relative value schedule provides a numerical weight for each different medical service—thus, an office consultation has a lesser value than a home visit. The relative value was multiplied by the conversion factor to determine the maximum fee. The fee schedule has been revised periodically. The foundation board of trustees would solicit advice from various medical societies about the need for change in either relative values or conversion factors in their respective specialties. The board would then formulate the new fee schedule and submit it to the vote of the entire membership.[10]

The fee schedules limit the amount that the member doctors may recover for services performed for patients insured under plans approved by the foundations. To obtain this approval the insurers—including self-insured employers as well as insurance companies[11]—agree to pay the doctors' charges up to the scheduled amounts, and in exchange the doctors agree to accept those amounts as payment in full for their services. The doctors are free to charge higher fees to uninsured patients, and they also may charge any patient less than the scheduled maxima. A patient who is insured by a foundation-endorsed plan is guaranteed complete coverage for the full amount of his medical bills only if he is treated by a foundation member. He is free to go to a nonmember physician and is still covered for charges that do not exceed the maximum-fee schedule, but he must pay any excess that the nonmember physician may charge.

The impact of the foundation fee schedules on medical fees and on insurance premiums is a matter of dispute. The State of Arizona contends that the periodic upward revisions of the maximum-fee schedules have the effect of stabilizing and enhancing the level of actual charges by physicians, and that the increasing level of their fees in turn increases insurance premiums. The foundations, on the other hand, argue that the schedules impose a meaningful limit on physicians' charges, and that the advance agreement by the doctors to accept the maxima enables the insurance

---

10. The parties disagree over whether the increases in the fee schedules are the cause or the result of the increases in the prevailing rate for medical services in the relevant markets. There appears to be agreement, however, that 85–95% of physicians in Maricopa County bill at or above the maximum reimbursement levels set by the Maricopa Foundation.

11. Seven different insurance companies underwrite health insurance plans that have been approved by the Maricopa Foundation, and three companies underwrite the plans approved by the Pima Foundation. The record contains no firm data on the portion of the health care market that is covered by these plans. The State relies upon a 1974 analysis indicating that insurance plans endorsed by the Maricopa Foundation had about 63% of the prepaid health care market, but the respondents contest the accuracy of this analysis.

carriers to limit and to calculate more efficiently the risks they underwrite and therefore serves as an effective cost-containment mechanism that has saved patients and insurers millions of dollars. . . . [W]e must assume that the respondents' view of the genuine issues of fact is correct [because the question here is whether the district court was right to enter summary judgment finding liability]. . . .

III

The respondents recognize that our decisions establish that price-fixing agreements are unlawful on their face. But they argue that the *per se* rule does not govern this case because the agreements at issue are horizontal and fix maximum prices, are among members of a profession, are in an industry with which the judiciary has little antitrust experience, and are alleged to have procompetitive justifications. . . .

A

Section 1 of the Sherman Act of 1890 literally prohibits *every* agreement "in restraint of trade." In *United States v. Joint Traffic Assn.*, 171 U.S. 505 (1898), we recognized that Congress could not have intended a literal interpretation of the word "every"; since *Standard Oil Co. of New Jersey v. United States*, 221 U.S. 1 (1911), we have analyzed most restraints under the so-called "rule of reason." As its name suggests, the rule of reason requires the factfinder to decide whether under all the circumstances of the case the restrictive practice imposes an unreasonable restraint on competition.

The elaborate inquiry into the reasonableness of a challenged business practice entails significant costs. Litigation of the effect or purpose of a practice often is extensive and complex. Judges often lack the expert understanding of industrial market structures and behavior to determine with any confidence a practice's effect on competition. And the result of the process in any given case may provide little certainty or guidance about the legality of a practice in another context.

The costs of judging business practices under the rule of reason, however, have been reduced by the recognition of *per se* rules. Once experience with a particular kind of restraint enables the Court to predict with confidence that the rule of reason will condemn it, it has applied a conclusive presumption that the restraint is unreasonable. As in every rule of general application, the match between the presumed and the actual is imperfect. For the sake of business certainty and litigation efficiency, we have tolerated the invalidation of some agreements that a fullblown inquiry might have proved to be reasonable.[16]

Thus the Court in *Standard Oil* recognized that inquiry under its rule of reason ended once a price-fixing agreement was proved, for there was "a

---

16. . . . The Court made the same point in *Continental T.V., Inc. v. GTE Sylvania Inc.*, 433 U.S. at 50, n.16: "*Per se* rules thus require the Court to make broad generalizations about the social utility of particular commercial practices. The probability that anticompetitive consequences will result from a practice and the severity of those consequences must be balanced against its procompetitive consequences. Cases that do not fit the generalization may arise, but a *per se* rule reflects the judgment that such cases are not sufficiently common or important to justify the time and expense necessary to identify them."

conclusive presumption which brought [such agreements] within the statute." 221 U.S., at 65. By 1927, the Court was able to state that "it has ... often been decided and always assumed that uniform price-fixing by those controlling in any substantial manner a trade or business in interstate commerce is prohibited by the Sherman Law." *Trenton Potteries*....

Thirteen years later, the Court could report that "for over forty years this Court has consistently and without deviation adhered to the principle that price-fixing agreements are unlawful *per se* under the Sherman Act and that no showing of so-called competitive abuses or evils which those agreements were designed to eliminate or alleviate may be interposed as a defense." *United States v. Socony–Vacuum Oil Co.*, 310 U.S. 150, 218 (1940). In that case a glut in the spot market for gasoline had prompted the major oil refiners to engage in a concerted effort to purchase and store surplus gasoline in order to maintain stable prices. Absent the agreement, the companies argued, competition was cutthroat and self-defeating. The argument did not carry the day:

> "Any combination which tampers with price structures is engaged in an unlawful activity. Even though the members of the price-fixing group were in no position to control the market, to the extent that they raised, lowered, or stabilized prices they would be directly interfering with the free play of market forces. The Act places all such schemes beyond the pale and protects that vital part of our economy against any degree of interference. Congress has not left with us the determination of whether or not particular price-fixing schemes are wise or unwise, healthy or destructive. It has not permitted the age-old cry of ruinous competition and competitive evils to be a defense to price-fixing conspiracies. It has no more allowed genuine or fancied competitive abuses as a legal justification for such schemes than it has the good intentions of the members of the combination. If such a shift is to be made, it must be done by the Congress. Certainly Congress has not left us with any such choice. Nor has the Act created or authorized the creation of any special exception in favor of the oil industry. Whatever may be its peculiar problems and characteristics, the Sherman Act, so far as price-fixing agreements are concerned, establishes one uniform rule applicable to all industries alike." *Id.* at 221–222.

The application of the *per se* rule to maximum-price-fixing agreements in *Kiefer–Stewart Co. v. Joseph E. Seagram & Sons, Inc.*, 340 U.S. 211 (1951), followed ineluctably from *Socony–Vacuum:*

> "For such agreements, no less than those to fix minimum prices, cripple the freedom of traders and thereby restrain their ability to sell in accordance with their own judgment. We reaffirm what we said in *Socony–Vacuum*, 310 U.S. at 223: 'Under the Sherman Act a combination formed for the purpose and with the effect of raising, depressing, fixing, pegging, or stabilizing the price of a commodity in interstate or foreign commerce is illegal *per se.*' " 340 U.S., at 213.

Over the objection that maximum-price-fixing agreements were not the "economic equivalent" of minimum-price-fixing agreements, *Kiefer–Stewart* was reaffirmed in *Albrecht v. Herald Co.*, 390 U.S. 145 (1968)....

B

Our decisions foreclose the argument that the agreements at issue escape *per se* condemnation because they are horizontal and fix maximum prices. *Kiefer–Stewart* and *Albrecht* place horizontal agreements to fix maximum prices on the same legal—even if not economic—footing as agreements to fix minimum or uniform prices.[18] The *per se* rule "is grounded on faith in price competition as a market force [and not] on a policy of low selling prices at the price of eliminating competition." In this case the rule is violated by a price restraint that tends to provide the same economic rewards to all practitioners regardless of their skill, their experience, their training, or their willingness to employ innovative and difficult procedures in individual cases. Such a restraint also may discourage entry into the market and may deter experimentation and new developments by individual entrepreneurs. It may be a masquerade for an agreement to fix uniform prices, or it may in the future take on that character.

Nor does the fact that doctors—rather than nonprofessionals—are the parties to the price-fixing agreements support the respondents' position. In *Goldfarb v. Virginia State Bar*, 421 U.S. 773, 788, n.17 (1975), we stated that the "public service aspect, and other features of the professions, may require that a particular practice, which could properly be viewed as a violation of the Sherman Act in another context, be treated differently." The price-fixing agreements in this case, however, are not premised on public service or ethical norms. The respondents do not argue ... that the quality of the professional service that their members provide is enhanced by the price restraint. The respondents' claim for relief from the *per se* rule is simply that the doctors' agreement not to charge certain insureds more than a fixed price facilitates the successful marketing of an attractive insurance plan. But the claim that the price restraint will make it easier for customers to pay does not distinguish the medical profession from any other provider of goods or services.

We are equally unpersuaded by the argument that we should not apply the *per se* rule in this case because the judiciary has little antitrust experience in the health care industry.[19] The argument quite obviously is inconsistent with *Socony–Vacuum*. In unequivocal terms, we stated that, "[w]hatever may be its peculiar problems and characteristics, the Sherman Act, so far as price-fixing agreements are concerned, establishes one uniform rule applicable to all industries alike." 310 U.S. at 222. We also stated that "[t]he elimination of so-called competitive evils [in an industry] is no legal justification" for price-fixing agreements, *id.* at 220, yet the Court of

---

18. It is true that in *Keifer–Stewart*, as in *Albrecht*, the agreement involved a vertical arrangement in which maximum resale prices were fixed. But the case also involved an agreement among competitors to impose the resale price restraint. In any event, horizontal restraints are generally less defensible than vertical restraints....

19. The argument should not be confused with the established position that a *new per se* rule is not justified until the judiciary obtains considerable rule-of-reason experience with the particular type of restraint challenged....

Appeals refused to apply the *per se* rule in this case in part because the health care industry was so far removed from the competitive model.[20] Consistent with our prediction in *Socony–Vacuum,* 310 U.S. at 221, the result of this reasoning was the adoption by the Court of Appeals of a legal standard based on the reasonableness of the fixed prices,[21] an inquiry we have so often condemned. Finally, the argument that the *per se* rule must be rejustified for every industry that has not been subject to significant antitrust litigation ignores the rationale for *per se* rules, which in part is to avoid "the necessity for an incredibly complicated and prolonged economic investigation into the entire history of the industry involved, as well as related industries, in an effort to determine at large whether a particular restraint has been unreasonable—an inquiry so often wholly fruitless when undertaken." *Northern Pacific,* 356 U.S. at 5.

The respondents' principal argument is that the *per se* rule is inapplicable because their agreements are alleged to have procompetitive justifications. The argument indicates a misunderstanding of the *per se* concept. The anticompetitive potential inherent in all price-fixing agreements justifies their facial invalidation even if procompetitive justifications are offered for some.[23] Those claims of enhanced competition are so unlikely to prove significant in any particular case that we adhere to the rule of law that is justified in its general application. Even when the respondents are given every benefit of the doubt, the limited record in this case is not inconsistent with the presumption that the respondents' agreements will not significantly enhance competition.

The respondents contend that their fee schedules are procompetitive because they make it possible to provide consumers of health care with a uniquely desirable form of insurance coverage that could not otherwise exist. The features of the foundation-endorsed insurance plans that they stress are a choice of doctors, complete insurance coverage, and lower

---

20. "The health care industry, moreover, presents a particularly difficult area. The first step to understanding is to recognize that not only is access to the medical profession very time consuming and expensive both for the applicant and society generally, but also that numerous government subventions of the costs of medical care have created both a demand and supply function for medical services that is artificially high. The present supply and demand functions of medical services in no way approximate those which would exist in a purely private competitive order. An accurate description of those functions moreover is not available. Thus, we lack baselines by which could be measured the distance between the present supply and demand functions and those which would exist under ideal competitive conditions." 643 F.2d at 556.

21. "Perforce we must take industry as it exists, absent the challenged feature, as our baseline for measuring anticompetitive impact. The relevant inquiry becomes whether fees paid to doctors under that system would be less than those payable under the FMC maximum fee agreement. Put differently, confronted with an industry widely deviant from a reasonably free competitive model, such as agriculture, the proper inquiry is whether the practice enhances the prices charged for the services. In simplified economic terms, the issue is whether the maximum fee arrangement better permits the attainment of the monopolist's goal, viz., the matching of marginal cost to marginal revenue, or in fact obstructs that end." *Ibid.*

23. "Whatever economic justification particular price-fixing agreements may be thought to have, the law does not permit an inquiry into their reasonableness. They are all banned because of their actual or potential threat to the central nervous system of the economy." *United States v. Socony–Vacuum Oil Co.,* 310 U.S. 150, 226 n.59 (1940).

premiums. The first two characteristics, however, are hardly unique to these plans. Since only about 70% of the doctors in the relevant market are members of either foundation, the guarantee of complete coverage only applies when an insured chooses a physician in that 70%. If he elects to go to a nonfoundation doctor, he may be required to pay a portion of the doctor's fee. It is fair to presume, however, that at least 70% of the doctors in other markets charge no more than the "usual, customary, and reasonable" fee that typical insurers are willing to reimburse in full. Thus, in Maricopa and Pima Counties as well as in most parts of the country, if an insured asks his doctor if the insurance coverage is complete, presumably in about 70% of the cases the doctor will say "Yes" and in about 30% of the cases he will say "No."

It is true that a binding assurance of complete insurance coverage—as well as most of the respondents' potential for lower insurance premiums[25] —can be obtained only if the insurer and the doctor agree in advance on the maximum fee that the doctor will accept as full payment for a particular service. Even if a fee schedule is therefore desirable, it is not necessary that the doctors do the price fixing.... [I]nsurers are capable not only of fixing maximum reimbursable prices but also of obtaining binding agreements with providers guaranteeing the insured full reimbursement of a participating provider's fee....

The most that can be said for having doctors fix the maximum prices is that doctors may be able to do it more efficiently than insurers. The validity of that assumption is far from obvious,[28] but in any event there is no reason to believe that any savings that might accrue from this arrangement would be sufficiently great to affect the competitiveness of these kinds of insurance plans. It is entirely possible that the potential or actual power of the foundations to dictate the terms of such insurance plans may more than offset the theoretical efficiencies upon which the respondents' defense ultimately rests.[29]

---

25. We do not perceive the respondents' claim of procompetitive justification for their fee schedules to rest on the premise that the fee schedules actually reduce medical fees and accordingly reduce insurance premiums, thereby enhancing competition in the health insurance industry. Such an argument would merely restate the long-rejected position that fixed prices are reasonable if they are lower than free competition would yield. It is arguable, however, that the existence of a fee schedule, whether fixed by the doctors or by the insurers, makes it easier—and to that extent less expensive—for insurers to calculate the risks that they underwrite and to arrive at the appropriate reimbursement on insured claims.

28. In order to create an insurance plan under which the doctor would agree to accept as full payment a fee prescribed in a fixed schedule, someone must canvass the doctors to determine what maximum prices would be high enough to attract sufficient numbers of individual doctors to sign up but low enough to make the insurance plan competitive. In this case that canvassing function is performed by the foundation; the foundation then deals with the insurer. It would seem that an insurer could simply bypass the foundation by performing the canvassing function and dealing with the doctors itself....

29. In this case it appears that the fees are set by a group with substantial power in the market for medical services, and that there is competition among insurance companies in the sale of medical insurance. Under these circumstances the insurance companies are not likely to have significantly greater bargaining power against a monopoly of doctors than would individual consumers of medical services.

C

Our adherence to the *per se* rule is grounded not only on economic prediction, judicial convenience, and business certainty, but also on a recognition of the respective roles of the Judiciary and the Congress in regulating the economy. Given its generality, our enforcement of the Sherman Act has required the Court to provide much of its substantive content. By articulating the rules of law with some clarity and by adhering to rules that are justified in their general application, however, we enhance the legislative prerogative to amend the law. The respondents' arguments against application of the *per se* rule in this case therefore are better directed to the Legislature. Congress may consider the exception that we are not free to read into the statute.

IV

Having declined the respondents' invitation to cut back on the *per se* rule against price fixing, we are left with the respondents' argument that their fee schedules involve price fixing in only a literal sense. For this argument, the respondents rely upon *Broadcast Music, Inc.*

In *Broadcast Music* ... the ... so-called "blanket license" was entirely different from the product that any one composer was able to sell by himself. Although there was little competition among individual composers for their separate compositions, the blanket-license arrangement did not place any restraint on the right of any individual copyright owner to sell his own compositions separately to any buyer at any price. But a "necessary consequence" of the creation of the blanket license was that its price had to be established....

This case is fundamentally different. Each of the foundations is composed of individual practitioners who compete with one another for patients. Neither the foundations nor the doctors sell insurance, and they derive no profits from the sale of health insurance policies. The members of the foundations sell medical services. Their combination in the form of the foundation does not permit them to sell any different product. Their combination has merely permitted them to sell their services to certain customers at fixed prices and arguably to affect the prevailing market price of medical care.

The foundations are not analogous to partnerships or other joint arrangements in which persons who would otherwise be competitors pool their capital and share the risks of loss as well as the opportunities for profit. In such joint ventures, the partnership is regarded as a single firm competing with other sellers in the market. The agreement under attack is an agreement among hundreds of competing doctors concerning the price at which each will offer his own services to a substantial number of consumers. It is true that some are surgeons, some anesthesiologists, and some psychiatrists, but the doctors do not sell a package of three kinds of services. If a clinic offered complete medical coverage for a flat fee, the cooperating doctors would have the type of partnership arrangement in which a price-fixing agreement among the doctors would be perfectly proper. But the fee agreements disclosed by the record in this case are among independent competing entrepreneurs. They fit squarely into the horizontal price-fixing mold....

Questions on *Maricopa*

1. Suppose the case had involved naked maximum price-fixing among unrelated firms. Why should maximum price-fixing be within the per se rule at all? Isn't lowering prices good for consumers?

a. Is a maximum likely to be a target price for a minimum?

b. Does a maximum price likely reduce market output or quality?

c. Does a maximum price likely reduce entry?

2. Why is the *Maricopa* case within the per se rule given *BMI*?

a. Isn't this a new arrangement with which the Court lacks experience?

b. The dissent argued that the Foundation was offering a "different product" consisting of "maximum-fee scheduling service." Is that argument persuasive? If so, couldn't any price-fixing agreement be deemed a different product? What criteria make sense to define a "different product" exception?

c. In *BMI*, the Court seemed to accept the claim that the procompetitive purposes served by collective monitoring and enforcement may require collective price-setting. Why in *Maricopa* doesn't the Court accept the parallel claim that collective peer review and insurance claim administration may require collective price-setting, or at least that the issue is debatable enough to justify rule of reason scrutiny? Why isn't setting a price reasonably related to the insurance review and administration purposes of the Foundation? Did the defendants claim it was?

d. Haven't procompetitive justifications (limiting physician charges and insurer risk) been offered? Are they excluded? Presumptively? Rejected on the merits? Should they have been rejected on the merits?

e. Would a rule of reason inquiry in this case have required an inquiry into the reasonableness of the price?

f. Should the inquiry turn on whether this agreement reduced or increased prices in fact? Would that be consistent with the Court's views on maximum price-fixing?

3. Is the alternative of insurer-fixed prices preferable?

a. Would it be per se illegal for insurers to agree with physicians to pay them a fixed fee in order to offer care at a set price to employers? How is that different from the actual case?

b. Is having insurers set physician fees to limit their charges and reduce risk a less restrictive alternative to having physicians do it?

c. Why do you think insurers in the actual case were willing to leave the task of fixing maximum prices to physicians?

i. Is it likely that physicians have greater expertise on price setting that insurers have or could obtain?

ii. Might it reflect the market power of the doctor combination?

iii.   Suppose an insurer independently set maximum fees that most doctors refused to accept. Would insurance that failed to provide complete coverage at most physicians be as attractive to consumers?

iv.   Might insurers have been attracted to an agreement among physicians because it provides an effective agreement among insurers about how much they will pay doctors?

v.   Do insurers have the same interests as patients in avoiding price increases for health care? Do they care as long as those prices are equally increased for all insurers? Don't increased medical bills just increase demand for health insurance to cover those bills?

d.   What if physicians formed an insurer? Would their agreement to form the insurer be per se illegal? A violation of the rule of reason? Does antitrust doctrine encourage excessive integration?

Texaco Inc. v. Dagher

547 U.S. 1 (2006).

■ JUSTICE THOMAS delivered the opinion of the Court.

From 1998 until 2002, petitioners Texaco Inc. and Shell Oil Co. collaborated in a joint venture, Equilon Enterprises, to refine and sell gasoline in the western United States under the original Texaco and Shell Oil brand names. Respondents, a class of Texaco and Shell Oil service station owners, allege that petitioners engaged in unlawful price fixing when Equilon set a single price for both Texaco and Shell Oil brand gasoline. We granted certiorari to determine whether it is per se illegal under § 1 of the Sherman Act, for a lawful, economically integrated joint venture to set the prices at which the joint venture sells its products. We conclude that it is not, and accordingly we reverse the contrary judgment of the Court of Appeals.

I

Historically, Texaco and Shell Oil have competed with one another in the national and international oil and gasoline markets. Their business activities include refining crude oil into gasoline, as well as marketing gasoline to downstream purchasers, such as the service stations represented in respondents' class action.

In 1998, Texaco and Shell Oil formed a joint venture, Equilon, to consolidate their operations in the western United States, thereby ending competition between the two companies in the domestic refining and marketing of gasoline. Under the joint venture agreement, Texaco and Shell Oil agreed to pool their resources and share the risks of and profits from Equilon's activities. Equilon's board of directors would comprise representatives of Texaco and Shell Oil, and Equilon gasoline would be sold to downstream purchasers under the original Texaco and Shell Oil brand names. The formation of Equilon was approved by consent decree, subject to certain divestments and other modifications, by the Federal Trade Commission, as well as by the state attorneys general of California, Hawaii,

Oregon, and Washington. Notably, the decrees imposed no restrictions on the pricing of Equilon gasoline. . . .

II

. . . Price-fixing agreements between two or more competitors, otherwise known as horizontal price-fixing agreements, fall into the category of arrangements that are per se unlawful. These cases do not present such an agreement, however, because Texaco and Shell Oil did not compete with one another in the relevant market—namely, the sale of gasoline to service stations in the western United States—but instead participated in that market jointly through their investments in Equilon.[1] In other words, the pricing policy challenged here amounts to little more than price setting by a single entity—albeit within the context of a joint venture—and not a pricing agreement between competing entities with respect to their competing products. Throughout Equilon's existence, Texaco and Shell Oil shared in the profits of Equilon's activities in their role as investors, not competitors. When "persons who would otherwise be competitors pool their capital and share the risks of loss as well as the opportunities for profit . . . such joint ventures [are] regarded as a single firm competing with other sellers in the market." *Maricopa*. As such, though Equilon's pricing policy may be price fixing in a literal sense, it is not price fixing in the antitrust sense. See *BMI* ("When two partners set the price of their goods or services they are literally 'price fixing,' but they are not per se in violation of the Sherman Act").

This conclusion is confirmed by respondents' apparent concession that there would be no per se liability had Equilon simply chosen to sell its gasoline under a single brand. We see no reason to treat Equilon differently just because it chose to sell gasoline under two distinct brands at a single price. As a single entity, a joint venture, like any other firm, must have the discretion to determine the prices of the products that it sells, including the discretion to sell a product under two different brands at a single, unified price. If Equilon's price unification policy is anticompetitive, then respondents should have challenged it pursuant to the rule of reason. But it would be inconsistent with this Court's antitrust precedents to condemn the internal pricing decisions of a legitimate joint venture as per se unlawful.[3]

The court below reached the opposite conclusion by invoking the ancillary restraints doctrine. That doctrine governs the validity of restric-

---

1. We presume for purposes of these cases that Equilon is a lawful joint venture. Its formation has been approved by federal and state regulators, and there is no contention here that it is a sham. As the court below noted: "There is a voluminous record documenting the economic justifications for creating the joint ventures. [T]he defendants concluded that numerous synergies and cost efficiencies would result" by creating Equilon as well as a parallel venture, Motiva Enterprises, in the eastern United States, and "that nationwide there would be up to $800 million in cost savings annually." Had respondents challenged Equilon itself, they would have been required to show that its creation was anticompetitive under the rule of reason. See *Copperweld*.

3. Respondents alternatively contend that petitioners should be held liable under the quick look doctrine. To be sure, we have applied the quick look doctrine to business activities that are so plainly anticompetitive that courts need undertake only a cursory examination before imposing antitrust liability. But for the same reasons that per se liability is unwarranted here, we conclude that petitioners cannot be held liable under the quick look doctrine.

tions imposed by a legitimate business collaboration, such as a business association or joint venture, on nonventure activities. See, e.g., *NCAA;* Citizen Publishing Co. v. United States, 394 U.S. 131, 135–136 (1969). Under the doctrine, courts must determine whether the nonventure restriction is a naked restraint on trade, and thus invalid, or one that is ancillary to the legitimate and competitive purposes of the business association, and thus valid. We agree with petitioners that the ancillary restraints doctrine has no application here, where the business practice being challenged involves the core activity of the joint venture itself-namely, the pricing of the very goods produced and sold by Equilon. And even if we were to invoke the doctrine in these cases, Equilon's pricing policy is clearly ancillary to the sale of its own products. Judge Fernandez, dissenting from the ruling of the court below, put it well:

> "In this case, nothing more radical is afoot than the fact that an entity, which now owns all of the production, transportation, research, storage, sales and distribution facilities for engaging in the gasoline business, also prices its own products. It decided to price them the same, as any other entity could. What could be more integral to the running of a business than setting a price for its goods and services?"

See also *BMI* ("Joint ventures and other cooperative arrangements are . . . not usually unlawful, at least not as price-fixing schemes, where the agreement on price is necessary to market the product at all").

Because the pricing decisions of a legitimate joint venture do not fall within the narrow category of activity that is per se unlawful under § 1 of the Sherman Act, respondents' antitrust claim cannot prevail. . . .

Questions on *Texaco v. Dagher*

1. Given this decision, could *BMI* have been resolved on the simple theory that, because the formation of the joint venture was not alleged to be anticompetitive, its agreement to fix the price of its joint product—the blanket license—could not violate the per se rule? Or does *Dagher* turn on the fact that Texaco and Shell no longer competed at all in the Western United States market, whereas in *BMI* the individual composers could compete to license their compositions?

a. If the latter was the theory, shouldn't the Court have required a finding that the Western United States was a properly defined market?

b. Even if it was a proper market, doesn't the latter theory beg the question whether the agreement not to compete separately in that market was a per se illegal market division?

2. Is the Court right in footnote 3 that the reasons to reject the per se rule also support rejecting abbreviated rule of reason scrutiny? Wouldn't the per se rule also exclude justifications, whereas the abbreviated rule of reason applies only if the defendants themselves cannot articulate any justification for their decision? Do the reasons for considering justifications dictate declining to condemn an agreement when the defendants have no justifications? Isn't the better distinction that here there were undisputed justifications for the joint venture, see footnote 1, and the agreement here was a necessary part of that joint venture?

3. If Texaco and Shell had no separate operations in the relevant market, was this joint venture really an effective merger of Texaco and Shell in this market? If so, should they have been deemed a single entity incapable of agreeing and thus not subject to review even under the rule of reason? *See* Chapter 6. Aren't Texaco and Shell still potential separate entrants to this market? Doesn't that mean the agreement can still have an anticompetitive effect that would not exist if they were truly merged?

4. If the joint venture had produced a single brand of gasoline, would there have been any way for it to have set different prices? Is there any reason to treat the joint venture differently because it sold two different brands?

5. Even if the joint venture fixed *different* prices for Texaco and Shell brand gasoline, wouldn't their agreement still involve horizontal price-fixing? If two unrelated rivals agreed on the prices each would charge, wouldn't that agreement be per se illegal even if their prices differed? Isn't this the real main distinction, that here collective price-setting was an *unavoidable* feature of the joint venture, so there was no way to distinguish condemnation of the pricing from condemnation of the joint venture? Isn't that why more analysis was necessary in *BMI*, where the defendant joint ventures could have collectively monitored and enforced licenses but let composers set the prices for each distinctive composition?

Horizontal Price–Fixing Under EU Law

Article 101(1)(a) prohibits agreements or concerted practices that "directly or indirectly fix purchase or selling prices." As price competition is one of the most important forms of competition, price-fixing cartels have been very severely condemned by the Commission. These agreements are considered as having as their object to restrict competition and thus are typically submitted to a per se rule.

Article 101(1)(a) prohibits agreements between firms to fix prices, but also a variety of price agreements, which, without going as far as setting the price of a product, restrict price competition. Such agreements include:

— the setting of minimum,[39] maximum[40] or mutually acceptable[41] prices;

— informal consultation on the dates and amounts of price increases;[42]

— exchange of price information;[43]

---

39. See, e.g., Commission Decision of 2 April 2003, PO/Viandes Bovines Françaises, O.J. 2003, L 209/12.

40. See, e.g., Commission Decision of 30 November 1994, Cement, O.J. 1994, L 343/1.

41. See, e.g., Commission Decision of 26 October 1999, Nederlandse Federatieve EG, O.J. L 39/1.

42. See, e.g., Cases 48/69 et al., ICI v. Commission, [1972] E.C.R. 619.

43. See, e.g., Case C–194/99, Thyssen Stahl, [2003] E.C.R. I–10821.

— agreement not to deviate from published prices;[44]

— jointly setting recommended sales prices;[45]

Commission Decision of 23 April 1986 No 86/398/EEC, Polypropylene

O.J. 1986, L 230/1.

.... II.   The Nature and Structure of the "Agreement"

From 1977 the producers of polypropylene supplying the [EU] have been party to a whole complex of schemes, arrangements and measures decided in the framework of a system of regular meetings and continuous contact. The overall plan of the producers was to meet and reach agreement upon specific matters, including at various times:

— the fixing of target prices,

— the modalities of price initiatives,

— the sharing of markets according to annual quota schemes or volume targets,

— at times where no definitive quota was in operation, temporary measures to control or monitor sales volumes,

— the exchange of detailed information on their individual activities of a kind normally considered a business secret so as to facilitate coordination of their behaviour....

IV.   The Object and Effect of the Agreement

Article [101(1)] expressly mentions as restrictive of competition agreements which directly or indirectly fix selling prices or share markets between producers, the essential characteristics of the agreements under consideration in the present case. In the present case, the basic purpose behind the institution of the system of regular meetings and the continuing collusion of the producers was to achieve price increases by means of a complex of agreements and arrangements. By planning common action on price initiatives with target prices for each grade and national currency effective from an agreed date, the producers aimed to eliminate the risks which would be involved in any unilateral attempt to increase prices.

The various quota systems and other mechanisms designed to accommodate the divergent interests of the established producers and the newcomers all had as their ultimate objective the creation of artificial conditions of "stability" favourable to price rises. In pursuit of these objectives, the producers were aiming at the organization of the polypropylene market on a basis which substituted for the free operation of competitive forces an institutionalized and systematic collusion between producers and amounted to a cartel. The fact that the polypropylene market was characterized over

---

44.   See, e.g., Decision of the Commission 83/546, Cast Iron and Steel Rolls, O.J. 1983, L 317/1.

45.   See, e.g., Decision of the Commission of 21 October 1988, Pre–Insulated Pipes, O.J. 1999, L24/1.

a period of several years by under-utilization of capacity, with attendant losses by the producers, does not relieve the agreement of its anticompetitive object.

It is not strictly necessary, for the application of Article [101(1)], given the overtly anticompetitive object of the agreement, for an adverse effect upon competition to be demonstrated. However, in the present case the evidence shows that the agreement did in fact produce an appreciable effect upon competitive conditions.

The agreement in meetings of target prices for each grade and national currency was implemented by the producers all issuing price instructions to their national sales offices or agents which then had to inform customers of the new price levels.

The customers were thus faced as a result of these concerted price initiatives with a uniform basic price in each currency for each major grade. Individual customers might benefit from special conditions or discounts and some producers might delay the planned increase or make concessions. Some producers might fix their actual prices for some grades or in some countries slightly below the targets while still determining such prices in the context of a general move by all the other producers ("shaving" the cartel price). The setting however of a particular price level which was then presented to the market as "the list price" or "the official price" meant that the opportunities for customers to negotiate with producers were already circumscribed and they were deprived of many of the benefits which would otherwise be available from the free play of competitive forces. The documentary evidence, including the market reports of the producers themselves, thus shows the existence in the market place of concerted price initiatives involving all producers and the close link between these initiatives and the system of regular meetings.

It is true that the achieved price level generally lagged behind the "targets" and that price initiatives tended to run out of momentum, sometimes eventually resulting in a sharp drop in prices. However the graphs relied upon by the producers themselves show a regular pattern over the years of close parallel movement of target and actual levels. During the period covered by known price initiatives the price achieved each month moved up toward the agreed target. When there was a sudden price "collapse" (for example, when propylene prices fell) this was arrested by fixing a new and much lower target and the upward trend was re-established. . . .

It was also argued that the changes in the market share of some producers since 1977 were evidence of "unrestricted" competition. This argument overlooks the fact that quotas or targets were agreed so as to take account of the ambitions of the newcomers and the larger firms were willing to accept some reduction in their own market share in the interests of increasing price levels.

The fact that in practice the cartelization of the market was incomplete and did not entirely exclude the operation of competitive forces does not preclude application of Article [101]. Given the large number of producers, their divergent commercial interests and the absence of any enforceable measures of constraint in the event of non-compliance by a producer with agreed arrangements, no cartel could control totally the activities of the participants.

The Commission does not accept the argument implicit in the written and oral observations of several of the producers and in the econometric study which they commissioned that in the absence of their arrangements market developments would have been the same. What might have occurred had there been no agreement is a matter of speculation but it is significant that the producers themselves acknowledged the effectiveness of their meetings in rejecting the suggestion in May 1982 that they cease to meet, since it was considered better, if supply and demand were in equilibrium, to take "active steps" to move prices up rather than leave it to the market.

Questions on *Polypropylene*

1. Given that the agreement on "target" prices left some degree of pricing flexibility, should it be deemed price-fixing?

2. Is the fact that cartel members sometimes deviate from cartel prices and quotas inconsistent with the existence of a cartel? Do price-fixing cartels create incentives for cartel members to cheat on the cartel? Does some cheating mean the cartel is not affecting prices in fact?

3. Was the Commission right to reject the defense that the polypropylene market was unprofitable and had excess capacity?

a. Given that cartels raise prices by restricting output below the competitive level, would you expect a cartel that charges supracompetitive prices to be characterized by excess capacity? If a competitive market already has excess capacity, and a cartel is organized to raise prices, won't that reduce market output and thus increase the amount of excess capacity?

b. Should an agreement designed to prevent firms from making losses be prohibited in the same way as an agreement designed to increase the profits of the cartel participants?

 i. On a competitive market, do producers have any incentive to produce output if the marginal cost of production exceeds market prices?

 ii. Thus, when firms say they are losing money on a competitive market, don't they have to mean that even though prices are at or above marginal costs, they are below the average total cost, which includes the sunk costs of building that capacity? Is that the sort of profit loss that should trouble us?

 iii. If market capacity exceeds market demand, don't we want firms to be unprofitable so they won't rebuild capacity as it ends its useful life? Don't we want firms to leave the market or shrink capacity over time to shift resources to other markets where there is more market demand? Isn't that the normal competitive outcome of a market situation characterized with excess capacity?

iv.   If a cartel induces firms to continue to keep excess capacity in operation in order to maintain their quota of the product sold at the supracompetitive cartel price, doesn't that result in waste and inefficiency?

c.   Should producers be able to defend their cartel by arguing that unless prices are propped up, all producers will shut down their unused capacity, and next year there will be insufficient capacity when demand rises again?

i.   If the producers foresee that demand will rise again next year, won't they have adequate incentives to individually decide not to close capacity this year? Why then does this claim justify collective agreement instead of such individual action?

ii.   Does it seem likely producers on a competitive market would abruptly close capacity if prices exceed marginal costs but are lower than average total costs? Isn't it more likely that they would simply decline to rebuild capacity when it reaches the end of its useful life, thus making any capacity reduction gradual?

Commission Decision 85/77/EEC of 10 December 1984, Uniform Eurocheques

O.J. 1985, L 35/43.

... I.   THE FACTS ...

The Eurocheque organization was created in 1968 on the private initiative of European financial bodies. Its aim is to meet the need for international payment systems resulting from the growth of tourism and business travel within Europe, by making available a means of payment which customers may use both in their country of origin and in other countries.

The Eurocheque system is open to all European banks. It is based on two instruments: the Eurocheque and the Eurocheque card.... [Consumers who want Eurocheques pay a commission to the issuing (or drawee) bank, which gives the consumers their Eurocheques and a cheque guarantee card. Consumers can then cash those Eurocheques for their face value (without any commission) at any participating European bank by showing their Eurocheque card, which guarantees the cashing (or payee) bank payment by the issuing (or drawee) bank. The cashing bank charges a commission to the issuing bank to compensate the cashing bank for its services. The agreements at issue in this case fixed (1) the maximum amount of each Eurocheque and (2) the commissions the issuing banks pay the cashing banks. They did not fix the commissions issuing banks charge consumers for Eurocheques.] ...

One of the main objectives of the Eurocheque Community which brings together the issuing institutions, is to encourage credit institutions to issue uniform cheques and cheque cards rather than the other, non-uniform instruments that may be used in the system, in order to encourage widespread recognition and acceptance of Eurocheques by traders in a large number of countries. . . .

II.   LEGAL ASSESSMENT . . .

B.   ARTICLE [101(1)] . . .

The agreements and decisions within the Eurocheque system, which have as their object the fixing of the price of a service, represent restrictive practices explicitly caught by the general prohibition contained in article [101(1)] of the EEC Treaty. They have as their effect the prevention of competition between the banks in any country and in particular in any Member State in the encashing of uniform Eurocheques drawn on banks in other countries. The [EU] working group decides in a direct and uniform manner on the amount of commission to be charged or received by banks for the encashment of guaranteed cheques drawn on foreign banks within the Eurocheque system. . . .

Competition is also prevented between issuing banks in the same Member State as to the maximum guaranteed amount. No bank may offer its customers a guaranteed amount larger than that adopted by the national Eurocheque organization in agreement with the Eurocheque assembly, which applies to all uniform Eurocheques drawn in that country. . . .

C.   ARTICLE [101(3)]

The four criteria for exemption under article [101(3)] are met in this case, for the reasons set out below.

1.   Improvement of the payment system

The Eurocheque system . . . and the agreements [at issue] contribute to improving payment facilities within the Common Market.

(a) Cheques guaranteed under the Eurocheque system may be drawn outside the country of the institution which issued them and cashed at banks established in several foreign countries, including the Community Member States.

(b) In their uniform format, adopted by the majority of issuing institutions, Eurocheques may be drawn in the local currencies of several countries, including the Community Member States. Under the agreements [at issue], these uniform Eurocheques are, subject to certain exceptions now paid in full, without deduction of any commission, by the payee banks, which makes them more acceptable to the trading sector. In the case of certain banks which only apply the agreements in part, bearers of Eurocheques are or will be informed, in any event, of the cost of encashing a foreign uniform Eurocheque.

(c) Centralized clearing makes it easier for the payee banks to obtain reimbursement of the foreign uniform Eurocheques which they accept. This advantage is particularly important to credit institutions in countries with a heavy tourist trade.

2. Benefit to users

The users of the Eurocheque system obtain a fair share of the resulting benefit.

(a) In practice all European currencies are made available to holders of Eurocheques. They may draw cash as needed from credit institutions in any foreign country they are visiting. For such transactions they enjoy the benefit of the guarantee provided by their own bank.

(b) They also enjoy the benefit of a period of interest-free credit before the cheque drawn abroad is cleared.

(c) Holders of uniform Eurocheques may also use them to pay their expenses direct in the trading sector of foreign countries. The Eurocheque will be honoured to the amount drawn in local currency, with no deduction made except in special cases. The drawer will, in principle, obtain a better rate of exchange since the conversion into his own currency is made at the market rate by the clearing centre in his country. In the case of certain banks which only apply the agreements in part, bearers of Eurocheques are or will be informed, in any event, of the cost of encashing a foreign uniform Eurocheque.

(d) Traders who accept these cheques also benefit from the guarantee by the drawee bank. They also have the assurance that uniform Eurocheques will be reimbursed to them in full by banks in their country, without any commission being charged for cashing them except in special cases. Their commercial activities are stimulated by the possibility of direct payment by Eurocheques.

3. Indispensable restrictions

The restrictions imposed on the issuing and accepting credit institutions are indispensable to the proper functioning of the Eurocheque system.

(a) The encashment in a foreign country of a cheque drawn on a particular bank is a service that the latter cannot provide unless it has branches or correspondents in that foreign country. By accepting cheques issued by banks situated abroad, the payee banks are providing to persons who are neither their own customers nor those of other banks in that country a service which is neither balanced nor compensated by an equivalent reciprocal service. When such a service is provided collectively by all the banks in one country to the customers of banks in other countries, it is indispensable that the terms and conditions for accepting and clearing the cheques concerned be determined in common between the issuing and the accepting institutions of the various centres involved.

(b) Within the framework of such an agreement, the common and uniform determination of the remuneration for this service, and for the drain of cash which it involves for the payee banks, is inherent in and ancillary to the cooperation between the banks and their national clearing centres and between the clearing centres, which enables the acceptance and international clearing of cheques drawn abroad. Variations in commissions from one bank to another would imply bilateral negotiations between the 15,000 banks which are parties to the scheme so that each accepting bank may agree with each issuing bank the remuneration it wishes to receive.

Any centralized clearing would thus be made impossible and the cost of processing Eurocheques would substantially increase.

(c) The obligation of the accepting banks not to exceed the maximum rates of commission laid down is essential in order to preclude the levying of additional charges or commissions, such as [value-added tax], local tax, stamp duty, collection fee and the like.

(d) The uniform fixing of the maximum guaranteed amount in a given country is indispensable in order to avoid unnecessarily complicating the system and making centralized, simplified clearing virtually impossible. The system would be unworkable if every person accepting a uniform Eurocheque—in the banking sector and particularly in the non-banking sector—had to make sure each time that the specific maximum amount guaranteed by the issuing institution concerned had not been exceeded.

This decision does not cover any national agreements between banks or decisions by national banking associations to fix the level of commission that individual issuing institutions in the country concerned should charge to their customers. National agreements or decisions of that type, which would eliminate residual competition between institutions issuing uniform Eurocheques, could not in any circumstances be regarded as indispensable within the meaning of article [101(3)(a) TFEU].

4. Scope for competition

The agreements and decisions concerned do not afford the credit institutions which issue uniform Eurocheques the possibility of eliminating competition in respect of a substantial part of international means of payment. Any person travelling to a foreign country generally has a choice between several means of payment, such as:

— cash in the currency of the country visited, the country of origin or other countries,

— travellers' cheques denominated in one or other of these currencies,

— postal payment orders,

— credit cards,

— cards for automatic teller machines, which can be used in more than one country, and

— Eurocheques.

The agreements and decisions in question do not govern relations between the drawee banks and their customers. Scope for competition therefore remains in the relations between each issuing institution and its customers. The extent to which commissions are passed on to the customers is left to the discretion of the drawee bank. The amount of commission charged to the customer may thus, in theory at least, be lower than the commissions remunerating the services of the foreign payee bank and of the drawee bank's clearing centre.

However, the above assessment applies only if the agreements and decisions in question are not supplemented by national agreements or decisions of associations governing relations between the banks and their customers on the question of commissions. The customer must be free to approach the credit institution of his choice to open an account and obtain a cheque-book. This freedom of choice of the customer would be illusory if all credit institutions in the same country provided the same service at the same price. . . .

Questions on *Uniform Eurocheques*

1. Is the European Commission right that the fees that issuing banks charge consumers might be lower than the fees charged by the cashing bank and clearing house? If that were so, wouldn't it be unprofitable to be an issuing bank? Given this, isn't there a good argument that any agreement fixing the fees paid to cashing banks effectively does fix the minimum price that issuing banks will charge customers buying the Eurocheque?

2. Why not allow the member banks to fix the maximum interbank fee but not a minimum? The Commission's conclusion appears to be that you need some figure to avoid endless negotiations, but why not instead allow the member banks to set only a default price that governs unless firms are willing to negotiate, thus preserving the option of individual negotiation as was the case in *BMI*?

a. Would it make sense to allow cashing banks to charge the issuing banks a lower fee if they want? Would cashing banks who did so be any more likely to attract customers who do not pay that fee? Does anything in the agreement prohibit cashing banks from giving consumers a rebate gift, or other inducement to attract them? Would this tend to reduce any tendency for the fee to be excessive?

b. Would it make sense to allow issuing banks to say they will pay less than the default fee for the cashing of their checks? Would that complicate a cashing bank's decision about which Eurocheques to cash? What if they simply printed on their Eurocheques that they should be cashed only by banks willing to take a lower fee? Would that undermine the brand reputation of Eurocheques for universal acceptability? Do individual issuers have incentives to free ride on the brand reputation, enjoying the business of customers who come to their bank expecting Eurocheques with universal acceptability, but giving them Eurocheques with more limited acceptability?

c. Would allowing either cashing or issuing banks to opt out impose additional burdens on the clearinghouse?

d. Are we safe in assuming member banks won't fix too high a fee because Eurocheques must compete with other financial instruments?

3. Does the maximum amount on each Eurocheque really matter given that a customer can just buy more Eurocheques?

4. Is the EU law approach of allowing price-fixing agreements of the kind considered here under Article 101(3) better than systematically applying a per se rule? Is it any different from the U.S. approach of holding that the per se rule does not apply when the price-fixing is ancillary to the procompetitive purposes of a productive rival collaboration?

Agreements Fixing Other Trade Conditions

Article 101(1)(a) prohibits not only agreements to fix prices, but also agreements fixing "any other trading conditions." This term has been interpreted to include any agreements fixing credit or service terms.[46]

U.S. law likewise condemns, under the per se rule, a horizontal agreement between unrelated rivals on credit terms or similar conditions of trade. *See* Catalano, Inc. v. Target Sales, Inc., 446 U.S. 643 (1980).

Other Nations' Regulation of Horizontal Price–Fixing

As noted in Section A, most nations apply a per se rule to horizontal price-fixing between unrelated firms that excludes both procompetitive justifications and evidence of lack of anticompetitive effect. However, some of these nations (such as Japan) appear to apply a partial per se rule that excludes justifications but allows evidence that anticompetitive effects are unlikely because the firms lacked market power. Further, some nations (like China) appear to apply a different partial per se rule that allows justifications but excludes evidence of lack of market power for horizontal price-fixing that lacks such a justification.

1.   Some think that no per se rule can ever really exclude evidence of justifications, on the grounds that justifications are always admissible because they affect whether the agreement falls within the category covered by the per se rule. They often cite cases like *BMI* for this proposition, and thus conclude that really a rule of reason is being applied to all cases, and those that look per se are just cases where the defendant has no legitimate procompetitive justification. On this view, no matter what the nations say, they really all apply a rule of reason to all cases.

The alternative view, developed above, is that cases like *BMI* allow procompetitive justifications only when they are ancillary to business collaborations and not when unrelated firms horizontally agree on prices. On this view, the per se rule does have bite when applied to horizontal agreements that do not further a productive business collaboration, and thus there is a real difference between using a per se rule for those agreements and applying a rule of reason to all agreements.

To see where this difference in views makes a difference in outcome, consider the following sort of case. Suppose the firms in a market do not engage in any business collaboration but instead simply decide to enter into a horizontal agreement that regulates an arguable market failure in a way that they argue procompetitively increases output. Can they introduce such a justification? If the first view were correct, then the firms can. If the alternative view is correct, then the firms cannot because this is a horizontal agreement between unrelated firms.

To make this a bit more concrete, suppose that the law does not recognize any intellectual property rights to a certain type of innovation (say new dress designs), which leads other firms to free ride by copying the innovation of others, which in turn deters that innovation. The firms

---

46.   See Commission Decision 78/670, Fedetab O.J. 1978, L 224/29, on appeal Joint Cases 205–15 & 217/78, Heinen van Landewijck SARL v. Commission, [1980] ECR 3125.

horizontally agree not to copy each other's legally unprotected innovations, and wish to defend their horizontal agreement by arguing that it furthers the procompetitive goal of increasing innovation. Under the first view, they can, whereas under the alternative view, they cannot. Which view is better?

The argument in favor of the first view is that the agreement might procompetitively increase market output, and the courts can always use the rule of reason to invalidate any agreements that do not. The argument in favor of the latter view is that, although this is true, by hypothesis we have a case where the parties are alleging a market failure that the government has chosen not to regulate, which suggests that the government has not been convinced that the regulatory restraint was desirable. Further, government regulation seems preferable to regulation by the firms because the government regulators will be financially disinterested and politically accountable, whereas the firms will be neither. Instead, the firms have might act idiosyncratically or to further their self-interest by adopting restraints that are undesirable. Financially self-interested firms might also be overzealous in finding violations of those restraints or in imposing punishments. Although courts could review all such agreements under the rule of reason, that would allow the restraint to be imposed on markets pending often lengthy court review and would impose a large adjudicatory burden. Moreover, it seems better to invalidate financially-interested self-regulation in order to channel regulatory activities into a more disinterested politically accountable process. In contrast, agreements that are ancillary to a productive business collaboration should be allowed when they further the procompetitive purposes of that collaboration, because such agreements are ubiquitous among garden-variety business partnerships and because we cannot say that having the government run those business collaborations would be a more effective alternative. Which side do you find more persuasive?

2. Suppose the firms actually offer no plausible procompetitive justification for their horizontal agreement. Is there any reason to inquire into anticompetitive effects? It would seem not because we know in such cases that either there are anticompetitive effects, in which case condemning the agreement is affirmatively desirable, or there are none, in which case there is still no harm to condemning the agreement because it has no procompetitive justification either. There is thus little to gain from an inquiry because if the inquiry mistakenly fails to find anticompetitive effects, we will underdeter harmful conduct, whereas if the inquiry mistakenly finds anticompetitive effects, it will deter conduct that has no effect in either direction, which is not harmful.

3. A similar analysis applies to the question of whether a lack of market power should provide an exception to the per se rule against naked horizontal price-fixing agreements between unrelated firms. Such an exception would raise tough line-drawing questions about when the firms have market power. The costs and uncertainties created at the boundaries will sometimes result in mistaken judgments that firms lack market power, which will underdeter price-fixing between firms that do have market power. Further, there is nothing procompetitive we can say about price-fixing between unrelated firms that have no market power. Thus, having a per se rule without exceptions creates no concerns about overdeterrence. Accordingly, eliminating any exception for lack of market power from a per se rule for naked horizontal price-fixing would reduce underdeterrence without increasing overdeterrence. Do you agree that this means all nations would be better off with per se rules for naked horizontal price-fixing that had no exception for cases where market power is lacking or anticompetitive effects seem unlikely?

C. HORIZONTAL OUTPUT RESTRICTIONS

Given any particular market demand curve, every output level implies a price and every price implies an output level. Thus, horizontal agreements to restrict output below the competitive level are just the flip side of horizontal agreements to fix prices. Indeed, a horizontal agreement on output production is generally necessary for any price-fixing agreement, otherwise members of the cartel might increase production to gain a greater market share at the cartel price and, if left with unsold product, would be tempted to undercut the cartel price to unload it. Restrictions on output might also well be more effective because they can be easier to verify, more clearly allocate market share among participants, and lead ineluctably to increased market prices while allowing the precise level of those inflated prices to vary with changing market demand. Prominent cartels like OPEC thus often focus on agreements to restrict output rather than fix prices.

Thus, like price-fixing, horizontal agreements to restrict output are typically regarded as per se illegal under U.S. and EU law.[47] Indeed, what is generally considered one of the most famous U.S. cases on horizontal price-fixing was in fact a case to take output off the market in order to raise prices.[48] But as with price-fixing, an output restraint might be viewed as reasonably necessary to some productive rival collaboration, such as when a partnership decides how much output to produce. This thus raises similar issues to those we saw above for price fixing, regarding when an agreement that literally restricts output should nonetheless be characterized as falling outside the per se rule.

NCAA v. Board of Regents of Univ. of Oklahoma

468 U.S. 85 (1984).

■ JUSTICE STEVENS delivered the opinion of the Court. . . .

[The NCAA is an association of colleges that, among other things, sets the rules for collegiate football. It collectively negotiated television rights for college football games with two television networks, CBS and ABC, setting the maximum number of total televised games and the minimum aggregate price each network had to pay college teams, limiting any

---

47. *See NCAA*, 468 U.S. at 99–101; Article 101(1)(b); Commission Decision 84/405 of 6 August 1984, Zinc Partner Group, O.J. 1984, L220/27.

48. *Socony*, 310 U.S. 150.

individual school to no more than six televised games (four nationally televised), and requiring that each network televise at least 82 colleges in each two-year period. The University of Oklahoma and other major football colleges organized the College Football Association (CFA), which signed a contract with NBC that gave them more television appearances and increased their revenue. The NCAA threatened disciplinary action against CFA members, prompting an antitrust suit that resulted in a ruling that the NCAA had violated Sherman Act § 1, which was affirmed by the Court of Appeals.]

II

There can be no doubt that the challenged practices of the NCAA constitute a "restraint of trade" in the sense that they limit members' freedom to negotiate and enter into their own television contracts. In that sense, however, every contract is a restraint of trade, and as we have repeatedly recognized, the Sherman Act was intended to prohibit only unreasonable restraints of trade.

It is also undeniable that these practices share characteristics of restraints we have previously held unreasonable. The NCAA is an association of schools which compete against each other to attract television revenues, not to mention fans and athletes. As the District Court found, the policies of the NCAA with respect to television rights are ultimately controlled by the vote of member institutions. By participating in an association which prevents member institutions from competing against each other on the basis of price or kind of television rights that can be offered to broadcasters, the NCAA member institutions have created a horizontal restraint—an agreement among competitors on the way in which they will compete with one another. A restraint of this type has often been held to be unreasonable as a matter of law. Because it places a ceiling on the number of games member institutions may televise, the horizontal agreement places an artificial limit on the quantity of televised football that is available to broadcasters and consumers. By restraining the quantity of television rights available for sale, the challenged practices create a limitation on output; our cases have held that such limitations are unreasonable restraints of trade. Moreover, the District Court found that the minimum aggregate price in fact operates to preclude any price negotiation between broadcasters and institutions, thereby constituting horizontal price fixing, perhaps the paradigm of an unreasonable restraint of trade.

Horizontal price fixing and output limitation are ordinarily condemned as a matter of law under an "illegal per se" approach because the probability that these practices are anticompetitive is so high; a per se rule is applied when "the practice facially appears to be one that would always or almost always tend to restrict competition and decrease output." In such circumstances a restraint is presumed unreasonable without inquiry into the particular market context in which it is found. Nevertheless, we have decided that it would be inappropriate to apply a per se rule to this case. This decision is not based on a lack of judicial experience with this type of arrangement,[21] on the fact that the NCAA is organized as a nonprofit

---

21. While judicial inexperience with a particular arrangement counsels against extending the reach of per se rules, the likelihood that horizontal price and output restrictions are

entity,[22] or on our respect for the NCAA's historic role in the preservation and encouragement of intercollegiate amateur athletics.[23] Rather, what is critical is that this case involves an industry in which horizontal restraints on competition are essential if the product is to be available at all.

. . . What the NCAA and its member institutions market in this case is competition itself—contests between competing institutions. Of course, this would be completely ineffective if there were no rules on which the competitors agreed to create and define the competition to be marketed. A myriad of rules affecting such matters as the size of the field, the number of players on a team, and the extent to which physical violence is to be encouraged or proscribed, all must be agreed upon, and all restrain the manner in which institutions compete. Moreover, the NCAA seeks to market a particular brand of football—college football. The identification of this "product" with an academic tradition differentiates college football from and makes it more popular than professional sports to which it might otherwise be comparable, such as, for example, minor league baseball. In order to preserve the character and quality of the "product," athletes must not be paid, must be required to attend class, and the like. And the integrity of the "product" cannot be preserved except by mutual agreement; if an institution adopted such restrictions unilaterally, its effectiveness as a competitor on the playing field might soon be destroyed. Thus, the NCAA plays a vital role in enabling college football to preserve its character, and as a result enables a product to be marketed which might otherwise be unavailable. In performing this role, its actions widen consumer choice—not only the choices available to sports fans but also those available to athletes—and hence can be viewed as procompetitive.

Broadcast Music squarely holds that a joint selling arrangement may be so efficient that it will increase sellers' aggregate output and thus be procompetitive. . . . Respondents concede that the great majority of the NCAA's regulations enhance competition among member institutions. Thus, despite the fact that this case involves restraints on the ability of member institutions to compete in terms of price and output, a fair evaluation of their competitive character requires consideration of the NCAA's justifications for the restraints.

Our analysis of this case under the Rule of Reason, of course, does not change the ultimate focus of our inquiry. Both per se rules and the Rule of Reason are employed "to form a judgment about the competitive significance of the restraint." . . . Per se rules are invoked when surrounding

---

anticompetitive is generally sufficient to justify application of the per se rule without inquiry into the special characteristics of a particular industry.

22. There is no doubt that the sweeping language of § 1 applies to nonprofit entities, *Goldfarb*, 421 U.S. at 786–787, and in the past we have imposed antitrust liability on nonprofit entities which have engaged in anticompetitive conduct, American Society of Mechanical Engineers, Inc. v. Hydrolevel Corp., 456 U.S. 556, 576 (1982). Moreover, the economic significance of the NCAA's nonprofit character is questionable at best. Since the District Court found that the NCAA and its member institutions are in fact organized to maximize revenues, it is unclear why petitioner is less likely to restrict output in order to raise revenues above those that could be realized in a competitive market than would be a for-profit entity. . . .

23. While as the guardian of an important American tradition, the NCAA's motives must be accorded a respectful presumption of validity, it is nevertheless well settled that good motives will not validate an otherwise anticompetitive practice.

circumstances make the likelihood of anticompetitive conduct so great as to render unjustified further examination of the challenged conduct. But whether the ultimate finding is the product of a presumption or actual market analysis, the essential inquiry remains the same—whether or not the challenged restraint enhances competition. . . .

III

Because it restrains price and output, the NCAA's television plan has a significant potential for anticompetitive effects.[28] The findings of the District Court indicate that this potential has been realized. The District Court found that if member institutions were free to sell television rights, many more games would be shown on television, and that the NCAA's output restriction has the effect of raising the price the networks pay for television rights. Moreover, the court found that by fixing a price for television rights to all games, the NCAA creates a price structure that is unresponsive to viewer demand and unrelated to the prices that would prevail in a competitive market. And, of course, since as a practical matter all member institutions need NCAA approval, members have no real choice but to adhere to the NCAA's television controls.

The anticompetitive consequences of this arrangement are apparent. Individual competitors lose their freedom to compete. Price is higher and output lower than they would otherwise be, and both are unresponsive to consumer preference. This latter point is perhaps the most significant, since "Congress designed the Sherman Act as a 'consumer welfare prescription.' " Reiter v. Sonotone Corp., 442 U.S. 330, 343 (1979). A restraint that has the effect of reducing the importance of consumer preference in setting price and output is not consistent with this fundamental goal of antitrust law.[34] Restrictions on price and output are the paradigmatic examples of restraints of trade that the Sherman Act was intended to prohibit. At the same time, the television plan eliminates competitors from the market, since only those broadcasters able to bid on television rights covering the entire NCAA can compete. Thus, as the District Court found, many telecasts that would occur in a competitive market are foreclosed by the NCAA's plan.

Petitioner argues, however, that its television plan can have no significant anticompetitive effect since the record indicates that it has no market power—no ability to alter the interaction of supply and demand in the market.[38] We must reject this argument for two reasons, one legal, one factual.

As a matter of law, the absence of proof of market power does not justify a naked restriction on price or output. To the contrary, when there

---

28. In this connection, it is not without significance that Congress felt the need to grant professional sports an exemption from the antitrust laws for joint marketing of television rights. See 15 U.S.C. §§ 1291–1295. The legislative history of this exemption demonstrates Congress' recognition that agreements among league members to sell television rights in a cooperative fashion could run afoul of the Sherman Act. . . .

34. . . . ". . . Many games for which there is a large viewer demand are kept from the viewers, and many games for which there is little if any demand are nonetheless televised."

38. Market power is the ability to raise prices above those that would be charged in a competitive market.

is an agreement not to compete in terms of price or output, "no elaborate industry analysis is required to demonstrate the anticompetitive character of such an agreement."[39] Petitioner does not quarrel with the District Court's finding that price and output are not responsive to demand. Thus the plan is inconsistent with the Sherman Act's command that price and supply be responsive to consumer preference. We have never required proof of market power in such a case. This naked restraint on price and output requires some competitive justification even in the absence of a detailed market analysis.

As a factual matter, it is evident that petitioner does possess market power. The District Court employed the correct test for determining whether college football broadcasts constitute a separate market—whether there are other products that are reasonably substitutable for televised NCAA football games. Petitioner's argument that it cannot obtain supra-competitive prices from broadcasters since advertisers, and hence broadcasters, can switch from college football to other types of programming simply ignores the findings of the District Court. It found that intercollegiate football telecasts generate an audience uniquely attractive to advertisers and that competitors are unable to offer programming that can attract a similar audience. These findings amply support its conclusion that the NCAA possesses market power. Indeed, the District Court's subsidiary finding that advertisers will pay a premium price per viewer to reach audiences watching college football because of their demographic characteristics is vivid evidence of the uniqueness of this product.[47] Moreover, the District Court's market analysis is firmly supported by our decision in International Boxing Club of New York, Inc. v. United States, 358 U.S. 242 (1959), that championship boxing events are uniquely attractive to fans[48] and hence constitute a market separate from that for non-championship events.[49] Thus, respondents have demonstrated that there is a separate

---

39. "The fact that a practice is not categorically unlawful in all or most of its manifestations certainly does not mean that it is universally lawful. For example, joint buying or selling arrangements are not unlawful per se, but a court would not hesitate in enjoining a domestic selling arrangement by which, say, Ford and General Motors distributed their automobiles nationally through a single selling agent. Even without a trial, the judge will know that these two large firms are major factors in the automobile market, that such joint selling would eliminate important price competition between them, that they are quite substantial enough to distribute their products independently, and that one can hardly imagine a pro-competitive justification actually probable in fact or strong enough in principle to make this particular joint selling arrangement 'reasonable' under Sherman Act § 1. The essential point is that the rule of reason can sometimes be applied in the twinkling of an eye." P. Areeda, The "Rule of Reason" in Antitrust Analysis: General Issues 37–38 (Federal Judicial Center, June 1981) (parenthetical omitted)

47. . . . the most analogous programming in terms of the demographic characteristics of its audience is professional football, and as a condition of its limited exemption from the antitrust laws the professional football leagues are prohibited from telecasting games at times that conflict with intercollegiate football. See 15 U.S.C. § 1293.

48. We approved of the District Court's reliance on the greater revenue-producing potential and higher television ratings of championship events as opposed to other events to support its market definition.

49. For the same reasons, it is also apparent that the unique appeal of NCAA football telecasts for viewers means that "from the standpoint of the consumer—whose interests the

market for telecasts of college football which "rest[s] on generic qualities differentiating" viewers. It inexorably follows that if college football broadcasts be defined as a separate market—and we are convinced they are—then the NCAA's complete control over those broadcasts provides a solid basis for the District Court's conclusion that the NCAA possesses market power with respect to those broadcasts. . . .

Thus, the NCAA television plan on its face constitutes a restraint upon the operation of a free market, and the findings of the District Court establish that it has operated to raise prices and reduce output. Under the Rule of Reason, these hallmarks of anticompetitive behavior place upon petitioner a heavy burden of establishing an affirmative defense which competitively justifies this apparent deviation from the operations of a free market. We turn now to the NCAA's proffered justifications.

IV

Relying on *Broadcast Music*, petitioner argues that its television plan constitutes a cooperative "joint venture" which assists in the marketing of broadcast rights and hence is procompetitive. While joint ventures have no immunity from the antitrust laws, as *Broadcast Music* indicates, a joint selling arrangement may "mak[e] possible a new product by reaping otherwise unattainable efficiencies." The essential contribution made by the NCAA's arrangement is to define the number of games that may be televised, to establish the price for each exposure, and to define the basic terms of each contract between the network and a home team. The NCAA does not, however, act as a selling agent for any school or for any conference of schools. The selection of individual games, and the negotiation of particular agreements, are matters left to the networks and the individual schools. Thus, the effect of the network plan is not to eliminate individual sales of broadcasts, since these still occur, albeit subject to fixed prices and output limitations. Unlike *Broadcast Music*'s blanket license covering broadcast rights to a large number of individual compositions, here the same rights are still sold on an individual basis, only in a noncompetitive market.

The District Court did not find that the NCAA's television plan produced any procompetitive efficiencies which enhanced the competitiveness of college football television rights; to the contrary it concluded that NCAA football could be marketed just as effectively without the television plan. There is therefore no predicate in the findings for petitioner's efficiency justification. Indeed, petitioner's argument is refuted by the District Court's finding concerning price and output. If the NCAA's television plan produced procompetitive efficiencies, the plan would increase output and reduce the price of televised games. The District Court's contrary findings accordingly undermine petitioner's position. In light of these findings, it cannot be said that "the agreement on price is necessary to market the product at all." *Broadcast Music*. In *Broadcast Music*, the

---

statute was especially intended to serve," there can be no doubt that college football constitutes a separate market for which there is no reasonable substitute. Thus we agree with the District Court that it makes no difference whether the market is defined from the standpoint of broadcasters, advertisers, or viewers.

availability of a package product that no individual could offer enhanced the total volume of music that was sold. Unlike this case, there was no limit of any kind placed on the volume that might be sold in the entire market and each individual remained free to sell his own music without restraint. Here production has been limited, not enhanced.[54] No individual school is free to televise its own games without restraint. The NCAA's efficiency justification is not supported by the record. . . .

V

Throughout the history of its regulation of intercollegiate football telecasts, the NCAA has indicated its concern with protecting live attendance. This concern, it should be noted, is not with protecting live attendance at games which are shown on television; that type of interest is not at issue in this case. Rather, the concern is that fan interest in a televised game may adversely affect ticket sales for games that will not appear on television.[56]

Although . . . studies in the 1950's provided some support for the thesis that live attendance would suffer if unlimited television were permitted, the District Court found that there was no evidence to support that theory in today's market. Moreover, as the District Court found, the television plan has evolved in a manner inconsistent with its original design to protect gate attendance. Under the current plan, games are shown on television during all hours that college football games are played. The plan simply does not protect live attendance by ensuring that games will not be shown on television at the same time as live events.

There is, however, a more fundamental reason for rejecting this defense. The NCAA's argument that its television plan is necessary to protect live attendance is not based on a desire to maintain the integrity of college football as a distinct and attractive product, but rather on a fear that the product will not prove sufficiently attractive to draw live attendance when faced with competition from televised games. At bottom the NCAA's position is that ticket sales for most college games are unable to compete in a free market.[60] The television plan protects ticket sales by limiting output—just as any monopolist increases revenues by reducing output. By seeking to insulate live ticket sales from the full spectrum of competition because of its assumption that the product itself is insufficiently attractive to consumers, petitioner forwards a justification that is inconsistent with the basic policy of the Sherman Act. "[T]he Rule of Reason

---

54. Ensuring that individual members of a joint venture are free to increase output has been viewed as central in evaluating the competitive character of joint ventures.

56. The NCAA's plan is not even arguably related to a desire to protect live attendance by ensuring that a game is not televised in the area where it is to be played. No cooperative action is necessary for that kind of "blackout." The home team can always refuse to sell the right to telecast its game to stations in the immediate area. The NCAA does not now and never has justified its television plan by an interest in assisting schools in "blacking out" their home games in the areas in which they are played.

60. Ironically, to the extent that the NCAA's position has merit, it rests on the assumption that football telecasts are a unique product. If, as the NCAA argues, all television programming is essentially fungible, it would not be possible to protect attendance without banning all television during the hours at which intercollegiate football games are held.

does not support a defense based on the assumption that competition itself is unreasonable."

VI

Petitioner argues that the interest in maintaining a competitive balance among amateur athletic teams is legitimate and important and that it justifies the regulations challenged in this case. We agree with the first part of the argument but not the second.

Our decision not to apply a per se rule to this case rests in large part on our recognition that a certain degree of cooperation is necessary if the type of competition that petitioner and its member institutions seek to market is to be preserved. It is reasonable to assume that most of the regulatory controls of the NCAA are justifiable means of fostering competition among amateur athletic teams and therefore procompetitive because they enhance public interest in intercollegiate athletics. The specific restraints on football telecasts that are challenged in this case do not, however, fit into the same mold as do rules defining the conditions of the contest, the eligibility of participants, or the manner in which members of a joint enterprise shall share the responsibilities and the benefits of the total venture.

The NCAA does not claim that its television plan has equalized or is intended to equalize competition within any one league.[62] The plan is nationwide in scope and there is no single league or tournament in which all college football teams complete. There is no evidence of any intent to equalize the strength of teams in Division I–A with those in Division II or Division III, and not even a colorable basis for giving colleges that have no football program at all a voice in the management of the revenues generated by the football programs at other schools. The interest in maintaining a competitive balance that is asserted by the NCAA as a justification for regulating all television of intercollegiate football is not related to any neutral standard or to any readily identifiable group of competitors.

The television plan is not even arguably tailored to serve such an interest. It does not regulate the amount of money that any college may spend on its football program, nor the way in which the colleges may use the revenues that are generated by their football programs, whether derived from the sale of television rights, the sale of tickets, or the sale of concessions or program advertising. The plan simply imposes a restriction on one source of revenue that is more important to some colleges than to others. There is no evidence that this restriction produces any greater measure of equality throughout the NCAA than would a restriction on alumni donations, tuition rates, or any other revenue-producing activity. At

---

62. It seems unlikely, for example, that there would have been a greater disparity between the football prowess of Ohio State University and that of Northwestern University in recent years without the NCAA's television plan. The District Court found that in fact the NCAA has been strikingly unsuccessful if it has indeed attempted to prevent the emergence of a "power elite" in intercollegiate football. Moreover, the District Court's finding that there would be more local and regional telecasts without the NCAA controls means that Northwestern could well have generated more television income in a free market than was obtained under the NCAA regime.

the same time, as the District Court found, the NCAA imposes a variety of other restrictions designed to preserve amateurism which are much better tailored to the goal of competitive balance than is the television plan, and which are "clearly sufficient" to preserve competitive balance to the extent it is within the NCAA's power to do so. And much more than speculation supported the District Court's findings on this score. No other NCAA sport employs a similar plan, and in particular the court found that in the most closely analogous sport, college basketball, competitive balance has been maintained without resort to a restrictive television plan.

Perhaps the most important reason for rejecting the argument that the interest in competitive balance is served by the television plan is the District Court's unambiguous and well-supported finding that many more games would be televised in a free market than under the NCAA plan. The hypothesis that legitimates the maintenance of competitive balance as a procompetitive justification under the Rule of Reason is that equal competition will maximize consumer demand for the product. The finding that consumption will materially increase if the controls are removed is a compelling demonstration that they do not in fact serve any such legitimate purpose.[68] ... *Affirmed.*

Questions on *NCAA*

1. Why isn't this agreement per se illegal? Though the fact that the product is competition between college teams requires some agreements on the rules of football competition, does that imply any need to agree on television contracts? Why isn't that just unrelated to the productive rival collaboration? Did the NCAA argue that the television contracts were reasonably necessary to achieve the procompetitive purposes of their productive joint collaboration regarding a collegiate brand and football parity? Is that the difference from *Maricopa*, where the defendants did not argue that their agreement was necessary for their insurance administration functions?

2. The dissent argued that the agreement produced "exclusive TV rights" that fit within the "new product" exception of *BMI*. If that is so, could the "new product" exception cover any output restriction? How can we tell what qualifies as a new product?

3. Is the Court's summary rule of reason analysis here any different from its per se analysis in *Maricopa*?

4. Why aren't the following justifications valid? Are there less restrictive alternatives to them?

  a. Protecting live attendance from competition with televised college football. Is the goal to protect attendance at televised games or untelevised games?

---

68. This is true not only for television viewers, but also for athletes. The District Court's finding that the television exposure of all schools would increase in the absence of the NCAA's television plan means that smaller institutions appealing to essentially local or regional markets would get more exposure if the plan is enjoined, enhancing their ability to compete for student athletes.

i. If the former, isn't this a valid concern because empty stadiums would discourage television viewers? Is there a less restrictive alternative?

ii. If the latter, is the goal procompetitive or anticompetitive? Does the NCAA plan really advance it at all?

b. Evening out TV revenue/exposure of different schools to increase parity on the football field.

i. Is regulating the amount that teams spend on football a less restrictive alternative? Doesn't that alternative restrict output in the relevant input markets? Would equal spending alter the fact that greater television exposure helps recruit the best athletes?

ii. Why does parity justify grouping so many schools in one division? Why wouldn't parity among CFA members suffice?

iii. Did the NCAA plan in fact create parity on football field or in television exposure and revenue? Would there be greater parity with more regional telecasts?

c. Reducing TV exposure/revenue to protect amateurism.

i. Why should exposure and college revenue alter the amateurism of players?

ii. Are academic eligibility requirements a less restrictive alternative? Might the restraint aid enforcement of those requirements by lowering the gains for evading them?

5. What is the relevant output? Televised games? Television viewers? The sum of live attendees and television viewers? Advertising revenue? Should the answer depend on whether the question is what was restricted, in which case the answer is televised games, or instead whether a justification exists, in which case the number of viewers or advertising revenue may matter more?

6. If we know output has been restricted, should courts bother to consider evidence on market power or efficiency justifications?

Commission Decision 84/380/EEC of 4 July 1984, Synthetic Fibres

O.J. 1984, L 207/17.

I.   The facts . . .

The products covered by the agreement are the following synthetic textile fibres: polyamide textile yarn, polyamide carpet yarn, polyester textile yarn, polyamide staple, polyester staple and acrylic staple. . . . At the time the agreement was signed, the signatories held about 70% of total synthetic-fibre capacity in Western Europe and about 85% of installed capacity in the EEC.

3.   Origin of the agreement and state of the industry

The parties to the agreement see the difficulties being experienced by the European synthetic-fibres industry as due to an imbalance between supply and demand. This imbalance stems partly from adverse market trends characterized by weak demand and increased import penetration and partly from the existence of increasing surplus capacity in the industry.

The polyester-staple sector had already run into these difficulties in 1972. Increased import penetration and the need to design much larger plants to reap economies of scale had contributed to a situation of overcapacity and low prices. The main producers of polyester staple notified to the commission an agreement to coordinate investment and rationalize production in order to eliminate present and prevent future overcapacity. However, in the face of the commission's opposition to the agreement, which would have affected the production and sales policies of those involved, the producers eventually withdrew the notification.

From 1975 onwards the overcapacity in synthetic fibres became more and more unmanageable and began to jeopardize profitability. By 1977 plant was operating at an average of only 70% of capacity.

In 1978, with prices continuing to depress profitability and the installation of new capacity imminent, the producers concluded a new agreement covering all the products listed . . . above.

The aims of the 1978 agreement were twofold: to bring supply and demand gradually back into balance by 1981 by means of an orderly reduction in capacity of approximately 13% and to restore a reasonable level of capacity utilization. The Commission again refused to exempt this agreement under article [101(3)] because it too contained unacceptable clauses providing for production and delivery quotas. Between 1979 and 1981 the parties made various changes to the original agreement, but without securing the Commission's formal approval.

Meanwhile, in July 1977, the Commission had called upon Member State governments to avoid aggravating the overcapacity problem by granting any form of state aid to the sector. The aid discipline introduced in 1977 is still in operation.

The 1978 agreement was provisionally implemented pending a Commission decision and the capacity-reduction target was in fact greatly exceeded: by the end of 1981, installed capacity had been cut by an average of 20% from 1977 levels.

Nevertheless, after a thorough reappraisal of the situation on both the European and the international markets, the same producers concluded that there was still no prospect of a significant upturn in demand between 1982 and 1985 and that any increase in capacity during this period would continue to be damaging to the industry.

For these reasons, and in order to create favourable conditions for long-term research and development to enable the industry to offer consumers improved products and face third-country competition, the producers agreed to carry out a further round of capacity reductions and, to that end signed the agreement of 21 October 1982 which is the subject of this decision.

That agreement was notified on 10 November 1982 and was subsequently amended on 9 March and 19 July 1983 in response to observations made by the Commission.

4.   The present content of the agreement

The size of the projected capacity reductions has been based on the following assumptions:

— capacity must be operated at at least 85% to be economic,

— sales will stabilize at 1981 levels by 1986.

The signatories' sales of all the products covered by the agreement in 1981 totalled 1,373,000 tonnes. On the basis of a minimum capacity-utilization ratio of 85%, capacity still needs to be brought down to 1,640,-000 tonnes. The agreement therefore calls for cuts totalling 354,000 tonnes in the signatories' combined production capacity for synthetic fibres by the end of 1985 ...

The other main provisions of the agreement are as follows:

(a) The participating companies commit themselves to achieving their individually determined capacity targets by the dates they have announced.

They must lodge details of the capacities they intend to cut and of the implementation of the cuts with an independent trustee body. They will be subject to checks by independent experts. The obligation not to exceed the capacity to which they have committed themselves is not satisfied by selling or otherwise transferring capacity to third parties for use within Western Europe.

(b) The participating companies undertake not to increase their capacities during the currency of the agreement, e.g., until the end of 1985.

(c) The parties will endeavour, as far as possible, to secure the retraining and redeployment of any labour displaced in the process of restructuring their operations and undertake to observe their statutory and/or contractual obligations existing in this regard in their respective countries.

(d) The Commission will be kept informed of any decisions or recommendations arising from the agreement and of its results in both the economic and social fields.

(e) Any non-signatory company established in the [EU] or elsewhere in Western Europe can accede to the agreement on terms to be determined in each case.

(f) A trustee body with powers to carry out on-the-spot inspections will periodically check on the accuracy of the information the parties have supplied concerning their capacity.

(g) In the event of major changes in the situation (involving, for example, the behaviour of European non-signatories on the European market, imports from non-European sources or the collapse of export markets), the parties will consult together to find solutions to the problem.

(h) In the event of transfers of activities or rights, the rights and obligations under the agreement will continue to vest in the parties benefiting from such transfers.

If a party purchases production capacity either from another party or from a non-signatory, its capacity will be adjusted appropriately.

A party wishing to sell or assign the use of some or all of its capacity to a non-signatory must endeavour to secure an undertaking from the purchaser to observe the principles of the agreement, except where the capacity is transferred outside Western Europe.

In the event of a party's non-compliance with its obligation to scrap or not to increase capacity, the party will be liable to pay damages of 2,000 [Euro] per tonne of excess annual capacity and a further sum of the same amount for each year of delay. Violations of the agreement will be dealt with under an arbitration procedure.

5.   Clauses deleted from the agreement

The notified draft of the agreement contained some clauses which have been deleted at the insistence of the commission. They include the following:

— a ban on investment leading to increases in capacity without the consent of all other parties. This clause has been deleted; increases in signatories' capacity now come under the clause providing for consultations in the event of major changes.

— a clause providing that the commission would use its good offices in the event of difficulties arising from implementation of the agreement. This clause has been deleted.

— a clause providing for the transmission of information on deliveries to the trustee body ... and a clause whereby the operation of plant at over 95% of the party's declared capacity would be taken as casting doubt on the correctness of the capacity declaration. These clauses would have made it possible to monitor output and deliveries and have been deleted.

The expiry of the agreement was also brought forward from 30 June 1986 to 31 December 1985. . . .

III.   Legal assessment

A.   Article [101(1)]

The notified agreement is an agreement between undertakings which has the object and effect of restricting competition within the common market.

By committing themselves to reduce capacity, the parties accept restrictions on the scale of their production facilities and hence on their investment. This commitment involves an obligation on each party to draw up and implement a capacity reduction plan showing, by product and plant, the size and timetable of the cuts to be made by the party. . . .

B.   Article [101(3)]

1.   The question whether the agreement meets the conditions set out in Article [101(3)] must be considered against the background of the overcapacity that existed in the synthetic-fibres industry in 1982 and that

is still running at a high level (around 30%) despite some reduction in capacity in the past few years.

The overcapacity is mainly a result of rapid technological advances (introduction of the rapid spinning process, building of larger production units to take advantage of scale economies) and a demand trend which, though not actually falling, has failed to rise as much as expected.

2(a) The purpose of the agreement is to reduce capacity so that the capacity that remains can be operated at a more economic level.

In a free market economy it ought to be principally a matter for the individual undertaking to judge the point at which overcapacity becomes economically unsustainable and to take the necessary steps to reduce it.

In the present case, however, market forces by themselves had failed to achieve the capacity reductions necessary to re-establish and maintain in the longer term an effective competitive structure within the Common Market.

The producers concerned therefore agreed to organize for a limited period and collectively, the needed structural adjustment.

As major producers, many of them would have been unwilling to go ahead with capacity cuts on their own without the certain knowledge that their competitors would follow suit and that no new capacity would be installed for the period of the agreement.

The fact that some of the parties, particularly the more diversified ones, may, for their own peculiar economic, technical or social reasons, have cut back their capacity further than others does not diminish the effectiveness of these collective arrangements in securing the capacity reductions required.

By reducing its capacity, the industry will shed the financial burden of keeping underutilized excess capacity open without incurring any loss of output, since the remaining capacity can be operated more intensively. The capacity reductions also provide the undertakings with an opportunity to develop their particular strengths, since each has selected for closure those of its plants which are less profitable or competitive because of their obsolescence or small size.

By concentrating on the production of particular products and giving up the production of others, the signatories will tend to become more specialized. Specialization on products for which they have the best plant and more advanced technology will help the parties to achieve optimum plant size and improve their technical efficiency. It will also help them to develop better-quality products more in tune with the user's requirements. The elimination of the capital and labour costs of unprofitable activities will make resources available for the capacity that remains in production.

The eventual result should be to raise the profitability and restore the competitiveness of each party. It is worth noting that the total losses of the European synthetic-fibres industry are reported to have been down to DM 500,000,000 in 1983 from an estimated DM 1,200,000,000 in 1981.

The coordination of plant closures will also make it easier to cushion the social effects of the restructuring by making suitable arrangements for the retraining and redeployment of workers made redundant.

It can be concluded then that the agreement contributes to improving production and promoting technical and economic progress.

(b) Article [101(3)] also requires that an agreement afford consumers a fair share of the resulting benefit. In the present case, consumers stand to gain from the improvement in production, in that the industry which eventually emerges will be healthier and more competitive and able to offer them better products thanks to greater specialization, whilst in the short term they will continue to enjoy the benefits of competition between the parties. The agreement also ensures that the shake-out of capacity will eliminate the non-viable and obsolete plant that could only have survived at the expense of the profitable plant through external subsidies or loss financing within a group, and will leave the competitive plants and businesses in operation.

The number of producers remaining for each product (signatories and non-signatories) is big enough to leave users a choice of supplier and security of supply and to preclude the danger of monopolies developing on national markets....

Textile manufacturer users of the products covered by the agreement have expressed fears about future price levels.

It is true that a capacity reduction agreement may lead to a short-term increase in prices to the user. However, in the present case this tendency may be expected to be limited by the special features of the synthetic-fibres market where each signatory faces considerable pressure in his pricing from synthetic-fibre users, who because they are now operating on a very competitive market and have difficulties of their own resist price increases which they regard as unjustified. Users could also switch to other sources of supply in Europe or elsewhere if the signatories tried to charge exorbitant prices.

(c) Another important consideration for the application of article [101(3)] is whether or not all the planned arrangements for effecting the capacity cutbacks are indispensable to that end.

The agreement is concerned solely with reducing excess capacity and is of limited duration. It does not interfere with the parties' freedom to determine their output or deliveries. Clauses which might have done so have been deleted....

The agreement's success depends on each party strictly observing the closure timetable it has announced. Hence, it is essential that pecuniary sanctions may be imposed if a party fails to discharge this basic obligation.

The adjustment of parties' obligations in the event of transfers of capacity between them and the extension of the obligations to non-signatories to which capacity is sold are necessary to ensure that all capacity set down for scrapping is actually scrapped.

Finally, the restrictions on the scale of the parties' production facilities are also indispensable for the attainment of the objectives in view.

(d) For article 101(3) to be applicable, the agreement must further not afford the undertakings the possibility of eliminating competition for a substantial part of the products in question.

In determining whether this condition is met, account must be taken of the features of the market, the duration of the agreement and the provisions contained in it.

The signatories are not the only suppliers of the products covered by the agreement on the community market. A number of other producers, including subsidiaries of North American companies and American producers importing direct from the United States, also operate on the market and are in strong competition with the signatories.

The products covered by the agreement are in competition with natural fibres (cotton and wool) and cellulosics. Although normally used together, these fibres are all to some extent interchangeable and therefore competing materials, the degree of competition between them depending on their relative prices.

The limited duration of the agreement, which is due to expire on 31 December 1985, obliges the signatories to take account in the dispositions they make while it is in force of the imminent disappearance of the restrictions at the scheduled date. Moreover, there is no provision in the agreement for any coordination of the signatories' commercial behaviour, and the coordinated capacity reductions involve but one element of the undertakings' competitive strategies.

Questions on *Synthetic Fibres*

1. In this case, the Commission exempted a horizontal agreement to reduce capacity, but not any horizontal agreement to restrict output. Coupled with the 1986 holding in *Polypropylene*, the cases suggest that in the mid–1980s the Commission's position was that excess capacity was no defense for an agreement to fix prices or output, but could be a defense for an agreement to reduce capacity, at least if it were sufficiently temporary and left substantial excess capacity on the market. Does this position make sense? Consider the following.

2. Is a horizontal agreement to restrict output likely to be more inefficient than an agreement to restrict capacity?

a. Suppose, as typical, the output restricting agreement allocates that output among cartel members based on their capacity? What does that do to the incentives of cartel members to phase out unnecessary capacity? Can an agreement to restrict capacity avoid a similarly wasteful maintenance of unneeded capacity?

b. Suppose that all firms are equally efficient and their marginal costs are flat until they get to full capacity, at which point they rise sharply. Under those assumptions, would an industry where all firms were at 85% capacity have a price and output that differs at all from one at 70% capacity?

i. Is your answer different if marginal costs are increasing over the range from 70 to 85% capacity?

ii. What if in fact some firms are or become more efficient than others? Would restricting all firms to 85% capacity impede the shift of production from the less efficient firms to the more efficient ones?

iii. What if demand increases substantially? Would it be more likely to raise prices if the industry was at 85% capacity than if it were at 70%? Is that problem avoided or mitigated by only allowing temporary agreements to restrict capacity? Was the agreement here that temporary?

3. Even if a horizontal agreement to restrict capacity is less inefficient than one to restrict output, is it affirmatively efficient or procompetitive in any way? Why do firms need a collective agreement to reduce unneeded capacity? Why wouldn't each firm have individual incentives to do so if running such capacity is unprofitable? Consider the four causes the Commission cites for the existence of large excess capacity on the market.

a. Technological developments that offered economies of scale for building larger plants.

i. Did anyone force the firms to build these larger plants? Aren't they the ones best positioned to judge when doing so will be profitable and when it won't?

ii. Don't firms also have full incentives to take into account that others have built additional capacity when they decide whether to follow suit or mothball existing less efficient small-scale capacity? Is the agreement necessary to give them the opportunity to make this choice?

iii. Won't the agreement inefficiently slow the transition to larger, more efficient, plants? Isn't the result that some portion of market output will be produced less efficiently than it otherwise would have been? Is this ameliorated by the Commission decision to delete the clause requiring the consent of other firms for new investments in capacity? Does that suffice given the continued agreement to consult about such new investments and to reduce overall capacity?

b. Increased import penetration.

i. Don't the firms in the market have full incentives to take this into account when they decide whether to reduce or grow their own capacity?

ii. If the agreement reduces capacity less than the free market would, will it further its purported justification?

iii. If the agreement reduces capacity more than the free market would, won't that if anything increase import penetration?

c. Demand that did not increase as much as predicted.

i. Should firms be bailed out when they make faulty predictions by allowing them to restrain trade? Or should consumers enjoy the windfall? Isn't the latter more consistent with a consumer welfare standard?

ii. If demand had instead increased more than predicted, so that demand exceeded capacity, what would happen to prices and profits? Would the firms then be likely to engage in a restraint to restore those profits to consumers? If firms enjoy supranormal profits if demand increases more than expected, and antitrust law allows them to enter into restraints to avoid losses when demand increases less than expected, won't this create *ex ante* incentives to be excessively optimistic in deciding when to build capacity?

iii. The Commission says that the firms needed a collective agreement to act on marketwide excess capacity because: "As major producers, many of them would have been unwilling to go ahead with capacity cuts on their own without the certain knowledge that their competitors would follow suit and that no new capacity would be installed for the period of the agreement." If the excess capacity is unprofitable, why wouldn't each producer be delighted if its rivals suffered losses by refusing to shed unprofitable capacity? Won't producers be reluctant only if they think demand will increase enough in the future to make use of the currently unused capacity of their rivals? Why shouldn't such decisions be left to individual firm decisions?

d. Government subsidies. The Commission noted that one cause of market overcapacity was government subsidies by European Member States, which it had been getting Member States to reduce. The fact that part of the European Commission's mandate is to reduce government subsidies on European markets is an important difference from U.S. antitrust courts. Does it make sense for the Commission to accept an agreement to restrict capacity on the grounds that otherwise political pressures would have eventually produced even less efficient government subsidies? Would it make sense for U.S. antitrust courts to take such political consequences into account?

4. Are consumers made better off by this agreement?

a. Would there be any purpose to this agreement unless it made output lower than it otherwise would be? If without the restraint, market output were the same as with it, wouldn't firms already have incentives to close this unprofitable capacity?

b. Does the Commission deny that short-term prices are likely to increase because of this agreement? Aren't the long-run effects if anything likely to be worse if demand increases?

c. Can the Commission take into account that consumers are also taxpayers and thus likely to be made better off if this agreement staves off even more inefficient government subsidies?

5. The Commission also cites benefits to workers as a justification for the agreement.

a. Is it legitimate to favor worker interests over consumer interests given that Article 101(3) explicitly refers to the latter but not the former?

b. Isn't reducing capacity likely to *reduce* employment? How could that be good for workers?

c. Might an agreement to have all firms equally reduce capacity affect the distribution of unemployment? Should antitrust law favor an agreement that spreads unemployment more equally among firms even when it reduces total employment, efficiency, and consumer welfare? Might an unequal distribution that focuses unemployment on certain areas be more likely to provoke government subsidies that create greater inefficiency?

6. The *Synthetic Fibres* decision is sometimes said to embrace a doctrine permitting "crisis cartels." During the Depression, the U.S. Supreme Court sustained what might also be regarded as a crisis cartel to address an overcapacity problem faced by coal producers. *See* Appalachian Coals v. United States, 288 U.S. 344 (1933). Today, that decision is legally regarded as an aberration and implicitly overruled by United States v. Socony–Vacuum Oil Co., 310 U.S. 150 (1940), and its progeny. Economic scholarship has also concluded that permitting cartels exacerbated the Depression. The reason is that while cartels might ameliorate certain symptoms of an economic downturn—namely low prices and profits—cartels can do so only if they reduce output (and thus employment) below the levels that would exist without the cartel, which worsens the underlying economic downturn. Should the U.S. courts re-embrace *Appalachian Coals*? Should the EU overrule *Synthetic Fibres*? Do you think the EU would rule the same way today?

Other Nations' Regulation of Horizontal Output Restraints

Other nations apply the same approach to horizontal output restraints that they apply to price-fixing, given that each is the flip side of the other.[49] As with price-fixing, these nations may apply a pure per se rule, a rule of reason, or a partial per se rule that excludes evidence on justifications or lack of anticompetitive effects but not the other. Although they vary in their standards, these nations apply the same standards to horizontal output restrictions that they apply to horizontal price fixing.

On the issue of crisis cartels, the new China law not only allows firms to defend all agreements with evidence of procompetitive efficiencies, but also allows the defense that the agreement has "the purpose of mitigating the severe decrease of sales volume or obviously excessive production during economic recessions."[50] However, the China law makes this defense

---

49. *See* Argentina Competition Law Art. 2(b); Australia Trade Practices Act § 44ZZRD; Brazil Antitrust Law No. 8,884, Art. 21; Canada Competition Act §§ 45(1)(c); Chile Competition Law Art. 3; China Anti–Monopoly Law Arts. 13, 15; Colombia Decree 2153/92, Art. 47; Egypt Competition Law Art. 6; India Competition Act § 3(3); Israel Restrictive Trade Practices Law § 2(b); Indonesia Competition Law Art. 11; Japan Antimonopoly Act § 2(6); Mexico Competition Law Art. 9; Peru Competition Law Art. 11.2(b); Saudi Arabia Competition Law Art. 4; Singapore Competition Act § 34(2)(b); South Korea Fair Trade Act Art. 19(1)(iii); South Korea Guidelines on Reviewing Cartel Activities IV.1.A (2009); Taiwan Fair Trade Act Art. 7; Thailand Trade Competition Act § 27; Turkey Competition Act Art. 4; Venezuela Procompetition Act Art. 10; Venezuela Regulation No.1 of the Procompetition Act, Art. 7. *See also* Competition Commission v. Patensie Sitrus Beherend Beperk, 37/CR/JUN01, at ¶ 35 (interpreting South Africa Competition Act § 4(1)(b)'s prohibition on agreements "directly or indirectly fixing a purchase or selling price or any other trading condition" to include horizontal agreements on output.).

50. China Anti–Monopoly Law Art. 15.

contingent on proof that the agreement (1) "shall not substantially restrict competition," and (2) "can enable the consumers to share the benefits of the agreement."[51] It is unclear these conditions could ever be satisfied for any agreement that furthered the stated purpose. Any agreement that mitigates a decrease in sales volume will raise prices and any agreement that mitigates "excessive" production will decrease production, either of which would substantially lessen competition. Nor would achieving these goals produce benefits that are shared with consumers, who would be better off with lower prices and higher output. The conditions thus seem to contradict the goal, and it is unclear how the China authorities will resolve the contradiction.

The temptation to allow cartels in moments of crisis is hardly unique to China. The U.S. and EU have allowed them, as noted above. Likewise, several other nations have provisions that seem to allow, or permit agencies to authorize, "crisis cartels" in special circumstances for limited periods of time.[52] Should these provisions be eliminated because the cartels they allow are counterproductive and harm consumers? Should courts narrowly interpret these provisions?

D.   HORIZONTAL MARKET DIVISIONS

Horizontal agreements between unrelated rivals to divide a market are per se illegal. Such market divisions generally involve territorial divisions, where each firm agrees to limit itself to a geographic area different from the other firm. But customers can also be divided in other ways, such as having one rival sell to commercial users and another to regular consumers, or by having firms agree to restrict themselves to different products or lines of commerce. Bid rigging is also a form of market division, where the conspirators agree that only one of them will really bid for each particular job. Similar to the above sections, the question is whether and when horizontal market divisions might be taken out of the per se rule on the grounds that they are incidental to some productive rival collaboration.

Horizontal market divisions can be even more anticompetitive than price-fixing or output-restrictions. They allow cartels to avoid the difficulties of fixing and monitoring prices and output, and of allocating market share among the cartel members. The cartel need simply monitor where or to whom firms are selling. Further, market divisions end all forms of competition between the firms, including on quality and service. Thus,

---

51.   China Anti–Monopoly Law Art. 15.

52.   See UNCTAD, Model Law on Competition, TD/B/RBP/CONF.5/7/Rev.2, at 27 (2004) (Japan and Venezuela); South Africa Competition Act § 10(3) (Commission can exempt agreements that contribute to "the economic stability of any industry designated by the Minister, after consulting the Minister responsible for that industry."); South Korea Fair Trade Act Art. 19(2) (allowing the KFTC to permit horizontal agreements for the purpose of "industry rationalization," "overcoming economic depression," or "industrial restructuring");Taiwan Fair Trade Act Art. 14 (FTC may temporarily authorize horizontal restrictions of output or price during times of economic downturn when the price of products falls below the average production cost).

unlike price and output restraints, market divisions cannot be undermined by nonprice competition.

Palmer v. BRG

498 U.S. 46 (1990).

■ PER CURIAM opinion:

In preparation for the 1985 Georgia Bar Examination, petitioners contracted to take a bar review course offered by respondent BRG of Georgia, Inc. (BRG). In this litigation they contend that the price of BRG's course was enhanced by reason of an unlawful agreement between BRG and respondent Harcourt Brace Jovanovich Legal and Professional Publications (HBJ), the Nation's largest provider of bar review materials and lecture services. The central issue is whether the 1980 agreement between respondents violated § 1 of the Sherman Act.

HBJ began offering a Georgia bar review course on a limited basis in 1976, and was in direct, and often intense, competition with BRG during the period from 1977–1979. BRG and HBJ were the two main providers of bar review courses in Georgia during this time period. In early 1980, they entered into an agreement that gave BRG an exclusive license to market HBJ's material in Georgia and to use its trade name "Bar/Bri." The parties agreed that HBJ would not compete with BRG in Georgia and that BRG would not compete with HBJ outside of Georgia. Under the agreement, HBJ received $100 per student enrolled by BRG and 40% of all revenues over $350. Immediately after the 1980 agreement, the price of BRG's course was increased from $150 to over $400.

. . . [The Court of Appeals held] that per se unlawful horizontal price fixing required an explicit agreement on prices to be charged or that one party have the right to be consulted about the other's prices. . . . [It also held] that to prove a per se violation under a geographic market allocation theory, petitioners had to show that respondents had subdivided some relevant market in which they had previously competed. . . .

In United States v. Socony–Vacuum Oil Co., 310 U.S. 150 (1940), we held that an agreement among competitors to engage in a program of buying surplus gasoline on the spot market in order to prevent prices from falling sharply was unlawful, even though there was no direct agreement on the actual prices to be maintained. We explained that "under the Sherman Act a combination formed for the purpose and with the effect of raising, depressing, fixing, pegging, or stabilizing the price of a commodity in interstate or foreign commerce is illegal per se."

The revenue-sharing formula in the 1980 agreement between BRG and HBJ, coupled with the price increase that took place immediately after the parties agreed to cease competing with each other in 1980, indicates that this agreement was "formed for the purpose and with the effect of raising" the price of the bar review course. It was, therefore, plainly incorrect for the District Court to enter summary judgment in respondents' favor. Moreover, it is equally clear that the District Court and the Court of Appeals erred when they assumed that an allocation of markets or submarkets by competitors is not unlawful unless the market in which the two previously competed is divided between them.

In United States v. Topco Associates, Inc., 405 U.S. 596 (1972), we held that agreements between competitors to allocate territories to minimize competition are illegal:

> "One of the classic examples of a per se violation of § 1 is an agreement between competitors at the same level of the market structure to allocate territories in order to minimize competition.... This Court has reiterated time and time again that 'horizontal territorial limitations ... are naked restraints of trade with no purpose except stifling of competition.' Such limitations are per se violations of the Sherman Act."

The defendants in Topco had never competed in the same market, but had simply agreed to allocate markets. Here, HBJ and BRG had previously competed in the Georgia market; under their allocation agreement, BRG received that market, while HBJ received the remainder of the United States. Each agreed not to compete in the other's territories. Such agreements are anticompetitive regardless of whether the parties split a market within which both do business or whether they merely reserve one market for one and another for the other. Thus, the 1980 agreement between HBJ and BRG was unlawful on its face.

The petition for writ of certiorari is granted, the judgment of the Court of Appeals is reversed, and the case is remanded for further proceedings consistent with this opinion.

■ JUSTICE MARSHALL, dissenting. Although I agree that the limited information before us appears to indicate that the Court of Appeals erred in its decision below, I continue to believe that summary dispositions deprive litigants of a fair opportunity to be heard on the merits and significantly increase the risk of an erroneous decision. I therefore dissent from the Court's decision today to reverse summarily the judgment below.

Questions on *Palmer v. BRG*

1. Does this agreement constitute price-fixing?

a. Is the purpose-or-effect test consistent with the per se rule against price-fixing that was used in *Maricopa*?

i. Doesn't a purpose-or-effect test amount to a rule of reason inquiry?

ii. Does the combination of this case and *Maricopa* suggest that, if a purpose and effect to alter prices exists, an explicit agreement on prices need not be proven, but that if an explicit agreement on prices is proven, such a purpose and effect need not be shown?

b. How do we know the purpose or effect here was to raise prices?

i. Why couldn't the agreement be justified by the agreement to license high-quality Bar/Bri materials? Couldn't that explain the revenue-sharing? The price increase for BRG?

ii.   The lower court found that, in 1979, BRG was charging low prices because it was getting free test-marketed West materials, and HBJ charged low prices to compete with BRG but was losing money. The district court concluded the 1980 price increase was as likely caused by West's decision to stop its free test-market as by the challenged agreement.

(1) Does this evidence and finding undermine the Supreme Court's assumption that the plain effect of the agreement was to raise prices?

(2) Does it give an independent motive for why BRG wanted to obtain HBJ materials and thus undermine the Court's assumption that the plain purpose was to raise prices?

(3) Does the Supreme Court's failure to address these facts suggest that perhaps it acted precipitously in adjudicating this case on the petitions for certiorari without the benefit of briefing on the merits?

2.   Even if the agreement were not deemed price fixing, should it be deemed per se illegal as a horizontal market division?

a.   The lower court thought the per se prohibition on horizontal market divisions applied only when firms divide and stay in the same market, but isn't an agreement to become and stay monopolists in separate markets even more anticompetitive?

b.   The lower court found that, at about the same time that BRG lost access to free West materials, the lawyer who had been in charge of HBJ in Georgia had a heart attack, and HBJ said it decided to leave the Georgia market then, which was months before it reached its agreement with BRG. Given this evidence, is it so clear this agreement should be classified as a horizontal territorial restraint that ended horizontal competition that otherwise would have existed? Does this evidence suggest the agreement may have had a purpose and effect other than raising prices and reducing competition? Do you think the Supreme Court would have come out the same way if it had taken into account this evidence of an independent purpose?

c.   Even if the agreement were deemed horizontal, why shouldn't the agreement in *Palmer* be deemed outside the per se rule because it is related to the productive business collaboration of licensing bar review materials? Does this case overturn *BMI*? *NCAA*? Is the problem here that the agreement is not reasonably necessary to the productive business collaboration?

d.   Given that the territorial division was part of HBJ's agreement to license bar materials to BRG, why isn't the agreement (as the defendants argued below) vertical rather than horizontal? (A vertical agreement between a supplier and distributor that restricts the territory in which the distributor can do business is subject to rule of reason review under U.S. law, even when the supplier chooses to itself distribute in other territories. *See* Chapter 5). Is it relevant that the agreement here did not limit just the distribution of Harcourt Brace materials but any competition by BRG outside of Georgia? Might a supplier have procompetitive reasons to want its distributor to focus on a particular region?

e. Do you think this case would have come out the same way if 10 equally sized firms were left in the Georgia bar review market after the agreement?

i. If yes, isn't it implausible that the purpose of the agreement would be anticompetitive on such a market, so that the agreement must have had a procompetitive purpose?

ii. If not, then can we really call this a per se test if it turns on market shares and structure?

iii. The lower court found there were actually two other bar review firms in the Georgia market: NORD and PMBR. There was no evidence on the record about what happened to their prices from 1979 to 1980. Plaintiffs' expert opined that HBJ or BRG combined had over 80% of University of Georgia law students who took a bar review course in Athens, Georgia in 1979, but the district court held that the expert improperly defined the market as limited to Athens during the winter academic term. The district court concluded the proper market was instead statewide, on which the HBJ–BRG market share was unclear but presumably lower. Does the existence of these two state-wide competitors help suggest the purpose of the agreement may have been procompetitive rather than anticompetitive? Might taking this evidence into account have changed the Supreme Court's conclusions?

3. Suppose . . .

a. HBJ had never entered the Georgia market, but rather from the beginning just licensed BRG to sell Bar/Bri materials in Georgia with the same territorial agreement. Is that per se illegal or legitimate franchising?

i. Isn't the resulting agreement and end result precisely the same as in the actual case? Might the agreement affect potential competition?

ii. Does the anticompetitive effect differ from the effect in the actual case inside or outside Georgia? Does the likelihood of a procompetitive justification differ?

b. BRG had never existed before the agreement, but rather was created as part of the deal.

i. Isn't the resulting agreement and end result precisely the same as in the actual case and the last hypothetical?

ii. Does the anticompetitive effect of this hypothetical differ, inside or outside Georgia, from that of the actual case or the last hypothetical? Does strength of the procompetitive justification differ?

c. BRG had been in the bar review market in Alabama but never in Georgia, and reached the same agreement except it continued operating with its own materials in the Alabama market?

i. Isn't the end result here the same as the actual case and other hypotheticals, other than in Alabama?

ii. How do the anticompetitive effects inside or outside Georgia here compare to the last two hypotheticals? The procompetitive effects?

U.S. DOJ/FTC, Antitrust Guidelines for Collaborations Among Competitors

(2000).

... **1.1 Purpose and Definitions** ... A "competitor collaboration" comprises a set of one or more agreements, other than merger agreements, between or among competitors to engage in economic activity, and the economic activity resulting therefrom. "Competitors" include firms that are actual or potential competitors[6] in a relevant market. Competitor collaborations involve one or more business activities, such as research and development ("R&D"), production, marketing, distribution, sales or purchasing. Information sharing and various trade association activities also may take place through competitor collaborations. ...

1.3 Competitor Collaborations Distinguished from Mergers. The competitive effects from competitor collaborations may differ from those of mergers due to a number of factors. Mergers completely end competition between the merging parties in the relevant market(s). By contrast, most competitor collaborations preserve some form of competition among the participants. This remaining competition may reduce competitive concerns, but also may raise questions about whether participants have agreed to anticompetitive restraints on the remaining competition.

Mergers are designed to be permanent, while competitor collaborations are more typically of limited duration. Thus, participants in a collaboration typically remain potential competitors, even if they are not actual competitors for certain purposes (e.g., R&D) during the collaboration. The potential for future competition between participants in a collaboration requires antitrust scrutiny different from that required for mergers.

Nonetheless, in some cases, competitor collaborations have competitive effects identical to those that would arise if the participants merged in whole or in part. The Agencies treat a competitor collaboration as a horizontal merger in a relevant market and analyze the collaboration pursuant to the *Horizontal Merger Guidelines* if: (a) the participants are competitors in that relevant market; (b) the formation of the collaboration involves an efficiency-enhancing integration of economic activity in the relevant market; (c) the integration eliminates all competition among the participants in the relevant market; and (d) the collaboration does not terminate within a sufficiently limited period[11] by its own specific and express terms.

---

6. A firm is treated as a potential competitor if there is evidence that entry by that firm is reasonably probable in the absence of the relevant agreement, or that competitively significant decisions by actual competitors are constrained by concerns that anticompetitive conduct likely would induce the firm to enter.

11. In general, the Agencies use ten years as a term indicating sufficient permanence to justify treatment of a competitor collaboration as analogous to a merger. The length of this

. . . **3.2 Agreements Challenged as Per Se Illegal.** Agreements of a type that always or almost always tends to raise price or reduce output are per se illegal. The Agencies challenge such agreements, once identified, as per se illegal. Typically these are agreements not to compete on price or output. Types of agreements that have been held per se illegal include agreements among competitors to fix prices or output, rig bids, or share or divide markets by allocating customers, suppliers, territories or lines of commerce. The Department of Justice prosecutes participants in such hard-core cartel agreements criminally. Because the courts conclusively presume such hard-core cartel agreements to be illegal, the Department of Justice treats them as such without inquiring into their claimed business purposes, anticompetitive harms, procompetitive benefits, or overall competitive effects.

If, however, participants in an efficiency-enhancing integration of economic activity enter into an agreement that is reasonably related to the integration and reasonably necessary to achieve its procompetitive benefits, the Agencies analyze the agreement under the rule of reason, even if it is of a type that might otherwise be considered per se illegal.[19] . . . In an efficiency-enhancing integration, participants collaborate to perform or cause to be performed (by a joint venture entity created by the collaboration or by one or more participants or by a third party acting on behalf of other participants) one or more business functions, such as production, distribution, or R&D, and thereby benefit, or potentially benefit, consumers by expanding output, reducing price, or enhancing quality, service, or innovation. Participants in an efficiency-enhancing integration typically combine, by contract or otherwise, significant capital, technology, or other complementary assets to achieve procompetitive benefits that the participants could not achieve separately. The mere coordination of decisions on price, output, customers, territories, and the like is not integration, and cost savings without integration are not a basis for avoiding per se condemnation. The integration must promote procompetitive benefits that are cognizable under the efficiencies analysis set forth in Section 3.36 below. Such procompetitive benefits may enhance the participants' ability or incentives to compete and thus may offset an agreement's anticompetitive tendencies.

An agreement may be "reasonably necessary" without being essential. However, if the participants could achieve an equivalent or comparable efficiency-enhancing integration through practical, significantly less restrictive means, then the Agencies conclude that the agreement is not reasonably necessary.[20] In making this assessment, except in unusual circumstances, the Agencies consider whether practical, significantly less restrictive means were reasonably available when the agreement was en-

---

term may vary, however, depending on industry-specific circumstances, such as technology life cycles.

   19. See *Maricopa* (finding no integration).

   20. See *id.* at 352–53 (observing that even if a maximum fee schedule for physicians' services were desirable, it was not necessary that the schedule be established by physicians rather than by insurers); *Broadcast Music*, 441 U.S. at 20–21 (setting of price "necessary" for the blanket license).

tered into, but do not search for a theoretically less restrictive alternative that was not practical given the business realities.

Before accepting a claim that an agreement is reasonably necessary to achieve procompetitive benefits from an integration of economic activity, the Agencies undertake a limited factual inquiry to evaluate the claim.[21] Such an inquiry may reveal that efficiencies from an agreement that are possible in theory are not plausible in the context of the particular collaboration. Some claims—such as those premised on the notion that competition itself is unreasonable—are insufficient as a matter of law,[22] and others may be implausible on their face. In any case, labeling an arrangement a "joint venture" will not protect what is merely a device to raise price or restrict output; the nature of the conduct, not its designation, is determinative. . . .

3.36 Identifying Procompetitive Benefits of the Collaboration
. . . If the Agencies conclude that the relevant agreement has caused, or is likely to cause, anticompetitive harm, they consider whether the agreement is reasonably necessary to achieve "cognizable efficiencies." "Cognizable efficiencies" are efficiencies that have been verified by the Agencies, that do not arise from anticompetitive reductions in output or service, and that cannot be achieved through practical, significantly less restrictive means. Cognizable efficiencies are assessed net of costs produced by the competitor collaboration or incurred in achieving those efficiencies. . . . Some asserted efficiencies, such as those premised on the notion that competition itself is unreasonable, are insufficient as a matter of law. . . .

4.2 Safety Zone for Competitor Collaborations in General.
Absent extraordinary circumstances, the Agencies do not challenge a competitor collaboration when the market shares of the collaboration and its participants collectively account for no more than twenty percent of each relevant market in which competition may be affected. The safety zone, however, does not apply to agreements that are per se illegal, or that would be challenged without a detailed market analysis, or to competitor collaborations to which a merger analysis is applied. . . .

Questions on FTC–DOJ Guidelines

1. Does the analysis in the guidelines to determine whether the per se rule applies differ significantly from just applying the rule of reason?

2. How would *Palmer* come out under these guidelines? Wouldn't it get rule of reason scrutiny because the firms were engaged in economic integration unless perhaps a "limited factual inquiry" led to the conclusion that per se analysis was appropriate?

---

21. See *Maricopa*, 457 U.S. at 352–53, 356–57 (scrutinizing the defendant medical foundations for indicia of integration and evaluating the record evidence regarding less restrictive alternatives).

22. See *Indiana Dentists*, 476 U.S. at 463–64; *NCAA*, 468 U.S. at 116–17; *Prof'l. Eng'rs*, 435 U.S. at 693–96. Other claims, such as an absence of market power, are no defense to per se illegality. See *Trial Lawyers*, 493 U.S. at 434–36; *Socony*, 310 U.S. at 224–26 & n.59.

3. How would *NCAA* and *Maricopa* come out under these guidelines? Is the only difference between them that in *Maricopa* the Court decided to apply the per se rule after "limited factual inquiry" whereas in *NCAA* the same sort of "limited factual inquiry" occurred under the rule of reason? If so, is there any difference between the per se rule and rule of reason at all? Isn't a better distinction that in *NCAA* the restraint was alleged to be reasonably necessary to the productive business collaboration and in *Maricopa* no such allegation was made?

4. Does it make sense to have a safety zone of effective per se legality when market shares are small and some integrative efficiency exists? Does the answer depend on how accurate a proxy market shares are for market power?

EU Law on Horizontal Market Divisions

Article 101(1)(c) TFEU specifically prohibits agreements which "share markets and sources of supply." Market-sharing has been generally considered a very severe infringement of competition by the Commission and the Community courts and very heavy fines have been generally imposed on infringers. In the majority of the cases, market sharing takes the form of the "home market" rule whereby each producer will concentrate on its country of origin and refrain from selling in the other Member States. Besides territorial restrictions, the Commission has also condemned agreements whereby firms divided markets by type of customer[53] or type of product.[54]

While the anti-competitive effects of geographic market sharing agreements are well known, there is an additional reason why the Commission and Community courts have been very severe with agreements: they go against the most fundamental objectives of the TFEU, which is the establishment of a Common market. This objective is particularly perceptible in the *Soda Ash* decision of the Commission.

Commission Decision 91/227 of 19 December 1990, Soda–Ash–Solvay/ICI

O.J. 1991, L 152/1.

PART I   THE FACTS

... From at least 1 January 1973 Solvay and ICI, the two major producers of soda-ash in the Community, participated in a concerted practice contrary to Article [101 TFEU] by knowingly continuing ... a restrictive market-sharing agreement dating from 1945 ... by avoiding all competition with each other and by confining their soda-ash activities in the Community to their traditional home markets namely continental

---

53. See, e.g., Decision of the Commission 5 Sept. 1979, BP Kemi/DDSF, O.J. 1979, L 286/32.

54. See, e.g., Decision of the Commission, Welded Steel Mesh, O.J. 1989, L 260/1. On appeal, Cases T–141, 142, 143, 144, 145, 147, 148, 149, 150, 151 and 152/89, [1995] E.C.R. II–791.

western Europe for Solvay and the United Kingdom for ICI.... Solvay is the market leader with almost 60% of the total Community market and sales in all Member States except for the United Kingdom and Ireland.

After three years of stagnant demand in the mid–1980s, sales of soda-ash in western Europe began to increase substantially in 1987. In 1988 and 1989 producers worked at full capacity. The west European market for soda-ash is still characterized by separation along national lines. The producers tend to concentrate their sales on those Member States where they possess production facilities, although since about 1981 or 1982 the smaller producers—CFK, M & W and AKZO—have increased their sales outside their "home" markets. There is no competition between Solvay and ICI, each limiting its Community sales to its traditional "spheres of influence" in continental western Europe and the British Isles respectively. Both ICI and Solvay have substantial export business to non-European overseas markets which are supplied from the [EU]. A large part of ICI's exports in fact consist of material supplied to it by Solvay for this purpose....

Over many years all the soda-ash producers in Europe accepted and acted upon the "home market" principle as the basis on which their commercial operations were determined. Under this principle each producer limited its sales to (a) the country or countries in which it had established production facilities, (b) export markets in which there was no domestic producer. The other producers reciprocated by not selling into the "home market" of that producer. In the event of incursions by an outsider into what a producer considered its home market, it was entitled and expected to "retaliate" by selling an equivalent tonnage on the intruder's home market.

The documents obtained at several producers show that the protection of home markets by this means was for many years the subject of a general consensus in the soda-ash industry. Indeed the concept of "retaliation" as a means of defending the home market was expressly provided for in a market-sharing agreement made between Solvay and Nederlande Soda Industrie (now AKZO) in 1956 (which is not the subject of any proceedings under Article [101]). The "home market" rule was strictly observed by all producers until the 1970s when declining demand and the appearance in continental western Europe of United States natural ash and east European material provided some element of competition. AKZO also began selling in the German market in the late 1970s since the Netherlands was too small a market to fill its available production capacity. Solvay had apparently indicated to AKZO its acceptance of this development without first obtaining the agreement of the smaller German producers. One of those affected therefore indicated to AKZO that it would begin to sell in the Netherlands and continue to do so as long as AKZO sold in Germany. In general, however, deliveries to customers across national borders (as opposed to co-producer sales) are still apparently considered by producers as an exception....

An important aspect of the close ICI–Solvay relationship was ICI's practice of purchasing substantial tonnage of soda-ash from Solvay in order to meet medium-and long-term commitments in its traditional markets.

These arrangements—referred to as "purchase for resale" or "PFR"—followed ICI's closure of its Wallerscote works in 1984. The reduction in capacity meant that for several years ICI was unable to meet the whole domestic demand in the United Kingdom and Ireland, let alone continue to supply its major export market in South Africa. One of the basic tenets of ICI's commercial policy being the maintenance of its control over the United Kingdom market, it was prepared neither to see any other producer take up the shortfall on its home market nor to allow customers to begin importing directly themselves. For several years ICI purchased substantial tonnages from Solvay for resale to United Kingdom customers (who were not apparently aware of the origin of the material).... Solvay is also the principal source of soda-ash sold in South Africa by ICI, which does not itself produce any of the material it sells in that market....

[A]n ICI memorandum ... [indicates that these PFRs were designed to help ICI] maintain its control over the United Kingdom market and prevent any perception that its "sovereignty" had been weakened by the planned capacity reduction.... Although ICI seems originally to have presented these arrangements to Solvay as intended simply to overcome short-term production problems, it must soon have been apparent to Solvay that their purpose was to support ICI's long-term position in particular countries and thereby preserve the existing separation of markets between the two groups.

PART II   LEGAL ASSESSMENT

... Arrangements between producers which have the object or effect of protecting national markets are expressly prohibited by subparagraph (c) of Article [101](1). Such protection is in fundamental conflict with one of the basic objectives of the Treaty, namely the creation of a common market. Given the size of the two undertakings concerned and their importance in the market for soda-ash, there can be no doubt that the arrangement had an appreciable effect upon trade between Member States.

... [To support the conclusion that a heavy fine was appropriate, the Commission stated that] the infringement was of considerable gravity. Over a long period of time the two major producers of soda-ash in the Community have knowingly concerted their commercial policies so as to avoid all competition between them in an important industrial product and a market worth some [Euro] 900 million annually. But for the discovery of the relevant evidence by the Commission, there is every likelihood that they would have continued their anti-competitive cooperation in some form for an indefinite period.

The division of markets on national lines by means of collusive arrangements constitutes an infringement which is contrary to the most fundamental objectives of the [TFEU], namely the creation of a single market between Member States.

The protection of home markets allows the producers involved to pursue a commercial policy in their own market which is insulated from competition from other Member States. The complete absence of imports to the United Kingdom from other Member States has undoubtedly contributed to the maintenance of ICI's dominant position (over 90% market share).

Solvay was also protected from any competitive pressure from the second largest Community producer. The absence of competition between the two major Community producers to a large extent ensured that the market for soda-ash was partitioned along national boundaries. It must also have been an important factor in the maintenance of the substantial price differences which exist between the United Kingdom and the Member States in continental western Europe for this product. . . .

Questions on Soda–Ash

1. Why would a market division cartel like ICI–Solvay adopt a purchase for resale system?

a. Suppose a single firm had a Europewide capacity that was sufficiently shy of European demand to maximize profits, but had a plant in France that produced far more than French demand and a plant in Britain that produced so much less than British demand that it failed to produce the profit-maximizing amount of British output. Would it be more profitable for it to (a) engage in a costly expansion of capacity in Britain or (b) transfer output from its French plant to Britain sales in a way that left profit-maximizing levels of excess demand in both France and Britain?

b. Can you see why the same sort of profit analysis might make purchases for resale profit-maximizing for a cartel?

2. Suppose a similar agreement between two small firms that have 100 similarly sized rivals in Britain and in France but that do not have the resources to distribute their products in each other's country. Would this agreement be likely to generate anticompetitive effects? Could it have some procompetitive justifications, perhaps similar to those invoked to justify vertical agreements?

3. In this case, the Commission considers the infringement particularly egregious since it divides market along national lines.

a. Are market-sharing agreements dividing a Member State into two zones objectively less restrictive than those dividing market across national lines? Why does the Commission seem to consider the second form of agreement more serious that the first?

b. Would a U.S. federal court conclude that horizontal market divisions are particularly bad, and thus deserve a very heavy fine, when they divides markets along state lines?

4. What is the relevance of the evidence that others firms also sell only in their home markets? Is this evidence equally consistent with the propositions that (a) home-selling is efficient, and (b) these firms are part of the conspiracy or are coordinating with those who are? If home-selling were just more efficient, would there be any reason for ICI and Solvay to enter into a market-division agreement?

5. Given the evidence in this case that ICI and Solvay exported to non-European overseas markets, is it likely transportation costs explained why each stayed within their home markets?

Specialization Agreements Under EU Law

As already noted, naked product division agreements generally have the same anticompetitive effects as other market divisions, and receive the same condemnation. However, EU competition law has adopted a favorable view to specialization agreements that couple a product division with an agreement to supply the product in which one firm "specializes" to the other. As the Commission stated in the 6th and 7th recitals of Regulation 1218/2010:

> Agreements on specialisation in production are most likely to contribute to improving the production or distribution of goods if the parties have complementary skills, assets or activities, because they can concentrate on the manufacture of certain products and thus operate more efficiently and supply the products more cheaply. The same can generally be said about agreements on specialisation in the preparation of services. Given effective competition, it is likely that consumers will receive a fair share of the resulting benefits.

> Such advantages can arise from agreements whereby one party fully or partly gives up the manufacture of certain products or preparation of certain services in favour of another party (unilateral specialisation), from agreements whereby each party fully or partly gives up the manufacture of certain products or preparation of certain services in favour of another party (reciprocal specialisation) and from agreements whereby the parties undertake to jointly manufacture certain products or prepare certain services (joint production). In the context of this Regulation, the concepts of unilateral and reciprocal specialisation do not require a party to reduce capacity, as it is sufficient if they reduce their production volumes. The concept of joint production, however, does not require the parties to reduce their individual production activities outside the scope of their envisaged joint production arrangement.

Because they generate efficiencies, Article 2 of Regulation 2658/2000 provides that, pursuant to Article 101(3), Article 101(1) shall not apply to "specialisation agreements", which, according to Article 1, include unilateral specialisation agreements, reciprocal specialization agreements and joint production agreements.

Pursuant to Article 3, the Article 2 exemption applies only when the parties' combined market share does not exceed 20%. Moreover, Article 4 makes this exemption inapplicable to agreements that contain severe anticompetitive restrictions, which is to say agreements that involve:

(a) the fixing of prices when selling the products to third parties with the exception of the fixing of prices charged to immediate customers in the context of joint distribution;

(b) the limitation of output or sales with the exception of:

(i) provisions on the agreed amount of products in the context of unilateral or reciprocal specialisation agreements or the setting of the capacity and production volume in the context of a joint production agreement; and

(ii) the setting of sales targets in the context of joint distribution;

(c) the allocation of markets or customers.

The inclusion of any of these restrictions excludes the entire agreement (not just the offensive provisions) from the benefit of the block exemption.

Other Nations' Regulation of Horizontal Market Divisions and Bid–Rigging

Other nations generally apply the standards they use for judging horizontal price-fixing to judge horizontal market divisions and bid-rigging as well.[55] Some nations allow the advance authorization of specialization agreements whereby the firms each agree to specialize in different products or services if the agreements generate offsetting efficiencies and the firms have received advance approval by a court or agency.[56]

E.   Horizontal Agreements Not to Deal With Particular Firms

Horizontal agreements between unrelated rivals not to do business with another firm are considered per se illegal boycotts under U.S. and EU antitrust law. As with the other per se offenses, the per se rule against boycotts tends not to apply when the rivals are related in a productive rival collaboration that is furthered by the agreement. Rather, a more nuanced analysis is used to determine when it is unlawful for members of a productive rival collaboration to agree to refuse to admit other competitors

---

55. *See* Australia Trade Practices Act § 44ZZRD; Argentina Competition Law Art. 2; Brazil Antitrust Law No. 8,884, Art. 21; Canada Competition Act §§ 45, 47; Chile Competition Law Art. 3; Colombia Decree 2153/92, Art. 47; Egypt Competition Law Art. 6; India Competition Act § 3(3); Indonesia Competition Law Arts. 9, 22; Israel Restrictive Trade Practices Law § 2(b); Japan Distribution Guidelines Ch. 4 (1991); China Anti–Monopoly Law Arts. 13, 15; Mexico Competition Law Art. 9; Peru Competition Law Art. 11(2)(c); Singapore Competition Act § 34(2)(c); Singapore Guidelines on § 34, Prohibition § 3.2; South Africa Competition Act § 4(1)(b); South Korea Fair Trade Act Art. 19(1); South Korea Guidelines on Reviewing Cartel Activities IV.1.A (2009); Saudi Arabia Competition Law Art. 4; Taiwan Fair Trade Act Art. 7; Thailand Trade Competition Act § 27(1); Venezuela Regulation No.1 of the Procompetition Act, Art. 7.

56. Canada Competition Act §§ 85–86 (approval by the Tribunal); Taiwan Fair Trade Act Art. 14 (approval by the Taiwan FTC).

into their collaboration, or to expel them after they were previously admitted.

But horizontal boycotts do have some consistent thematic differences from other per se offenses such as fixing prices or output or dividing markets. First, boycotts are often aimed at harming particular competitors, rather than competition in general. This raises an issue whether such activity should be condemned by antitrust given that it is often said that antitrust laws aim to protect "competition, not competitors."[57] But the context in which such statements are made is almost always when a claim is made to protect competitors at the expense of competition and efficiency. If competitors are being harmed without any benefit to competition or efficiency, then there seems little reason to tolerate the abuse. This seems especially true when the conduct might create anticompetitive effects that are costly or difficult to ascertain accurately.

Second, boycotts are more likely to have plausible noneconomic justifications, such as punishing particular bad actors. But this also raises a parallel new noneconomic objection: the concern that firms might abuse any extra-governmental power conferred on them because of their collective market position to further views that are self-interested, politically unaccountable, and possibly idiosyncratic.

1.   BOYCOTTS BY UNRELATED RIVALS

Klor's Inc. v. Broadway–Hale Stores, Inc.

359 U.S. 207 (1959).

■ MR. JUSTICE BLACK delivered the opinion of the Court.

Klor's, Inc., operates a retail store on Mission Street, San Francisco, California; Broadway–Hale Stores, Inc., a chain of department stores, operates one of its stores next door. The two stores compete in the sale of radios, television sets, refrigerators and other household appliances. Claiming that Broadway–Hale and 10 national manufacturers and their distributors have conspired to restrain and monopolize commerce in violation of §§ 1 and 2 of the Sherman Act, Klor's brought this action for treble damages and injunction in the United States District Court.

In support of its claim Klor's made the following allegations: . . . Klor's is as well equipped as Broadway–Hale to handle all brands of appliances. Nevertheless, manufacturers and distributors of such well-known brands as General Electric, RCA, Admiral, Zenith, Emerson and others have conspired among themselves and with Broadway–Hale either not to sell to Klor's or to sell to it only at discriminatory prices and highly unfavorable terms. Broadway–Hale has used its "monopolistic" buying power to bring

---

57. *See, e.g.,* Brooke Group Ltd. v. Brown & Williamson Tobacco Corp., 509 U.S. 209, 224 (1993); Copperweld Corp. v. Independence Tube Corp., 467 U.S. 752, 768 n.14 (1984); Brunswick Corp. v. Pueblo Bowl–O–Mat, Inc., 429 U.S. 477, 488 (1977); Brown Shoe Co. v. United States, 370 U.S. 294, 320 (1962).

about this situation.... The concerted refusal to deal with Klor's has seriously handicapped its ability to compete and has already caused it a great loss of profits, goodwill, reputation and prestige.

The defendants did not dispute these allegations, but sought summary judgment and dismissal of the complaint for failure to state a cause of action. They submitted unchallenged affidavits which showed that there were hundreds of other household appliance retailers, some within a few blocks of Klor's who sold many competing brands of appliances, including those the defendants refused to sell to Klor's.... [T]he District Court concluded that the controversy was a "purely private quarrel" between Klor's and Broadway–Hale, which did not amount to a "public wrong proscribed by the (Sherman) Act." On this ground the complaint was dismissed and summary judgment was entered for the defendants. The Court of Appeals for the Ninth Circuit affirmed the summary judgment. It stated that "a violation of the Sherman Act requires conduct of defendants by which the public is or conceivably may be ultimately injured." It held that here the required public injury was missing since "there was no charge or proof that by any act of defendants the price, quantity, or quality offered the public was affected, nor that there was any intent or purpose to effect a change in, or an influence on, prices, quantity, or quality * * *." The holding, if correct, means that unless the opportunities for customers to buy in a competitive market are reduced, a group of powerful business-men may act in concert to deprive a single merchant, like Klor, of the goods he needs to compete effectively....

We think Klor's allegations clearly show one type of trade restraint and public harm the Sherman Act forbids, and that defendants' affidavits provide no defense to the charges.... In the landmark case of *Standard Oil*, this Court read § 1 to prohibit those classes of contracts or acts which the common law had deemed to be undue restraints of trade and those which new times and economic conditions would make unreasonable.... The effect ... the Court said, was to adopt the common-law proscription of all "contracts or acts which it was considered had a monopolistic tendency * * * "and which interfered with the "natural flow" of an appreciable amount of interstate commerce. The Court recognized that there were some agreements whose validity depended on the surrounding circum-stances. It emphasized, however, that there were classes of restraints which from their "nature or character" were unduly restrictive, and hence forbidden by both the common law and the statute. As to these classes of restraints, the Court noted, Congress had determined its own criteria of public harm and it was not for the courts to decide whether in an individual case injury had actually occurred.

Group boycotts, or concerted refusals by traders to deal with other traders, have long been held to be in the forbidden category. They have not been saved by allegations that they were reasonable in the specific circum-stances, nor by a failure to show that they "fixed or regulated prices, parcelled out or limited production, or brought about a deterioration in quality." *Fashion Originators'. Cf. Trenton Potteries.* Even when they operated to lower prices or temporarily to stimulate competition they were banned. For, ... "such agreements, no less than those to fix minimum prices, cripple the freedom of traders and thereby restrain their ability to sell in accordance with their own judgment."

Plainly the allegations of this complaint disclose such a boycott. This is not a case of a single trader refusing to deal with another, nor even of a manufacturer and a dealer agreeing to an exclusive distributorship. Alleged in this complaint is a wide combination consisting of manufacturers, distributors and a retailer. This combination takes from Klor's its freedom to buy appliances in an open competitive market and drives it out of business as a dealer in the defendants' products. It deprives the manufacturers and distributors of their freedom to sell to Klor's at the same prices and conditions made available to Broadway–Hale and in some instances forbids them from selling to it on any terms whatsoever. It interferes with the natural flow of interstate commerce. It clearly has, by its "nature" and "character," a "monopolistic tendency." As such it is not to be tolerated merely because the victim is just one merchant whose business is so small that his destruction makes little difference to the economy. Monopoly can as surely thrive by the elimination of such small businessmen, one at a time, as it can by driving them out in large groups. In recognition of this fact the Sherman Act has consistently been read to forbid all contracts and combinations which "tend to create a monopoly," whether "the tendency is a creeping one" or "one that proceeds at full gallop." ... [R]eversed ...

Questions on *Klor's*

1. Is the Court correct to hold that the Sherman Act makes horizontal boycotts illegal without proof of any effect on market price, output or quality? Is that interpretation of the Sherman Act compelled by its language? By sensible legal policy?

2. Did the manufacturers here have any independent incentive to agree to eliminate a retailer? If each agreed only because of Broadway–Hale's buyer market power, why would a horizontal agreement be necessary? Why wouldn't a series of vertical agreements be enough?

3. Assuming this was a horizontal boycott, what harm did it likely cause? Is there harm to Klor's? To consumer choice? To market prices, output or quality? Is it really plausible this is the first step to an incipient monopoly?

4. Was any procompetitive justification offered for the agreement here? Might that explain the summary condemnation?

5. If the courts allowed the defense of an absence of effect on market prices, output, quality, what would that likely do to the litigation costs and difficulties of proving effects when market power is marginal or hard to prove? Could there possibly be some local market power on Mission Street here? If not, could we cabin the application of such a defense so it did not apply in more marginal cases? Would allowing such a defense increase the underdeterrence of agreements that did harm consumers and markets?

6. Can't we infer some anticompetitive motive for an agreement that lacks any procompetitive justification, unless it is motivated by irrational motives like spite? Do we have to worry that condemning naked group boycotts like this might increase the overdeterrence of any desirable conduct?

Fashion Originators' Guild of Am. v. FTC

312 U.S. 457 (1941).

■ Mr. Justice Black delivered the opinion of the Court.

The Circuit Court of Appeals . . . affirmed a Federal Trade Commission decree ordering petitioners to cease and desist from certain practices found to have been done in combination and to constitute "unfair methods of competition" tending to monopoly. . . .

Some of the members of the combination design, manufacture, sell and distribute women's garments—chiefly dresses. Others are manufacturers, converters or dyers of textiles from which these garments are made. Fashion Originators' Guild of America (FOGA), an organization controlled by these groups, is the instrument through which petitioners work to accomplish the purposes condemned by the Commission. The garment manufacturers claim to be creators of original and distinctive designs of fashionable clothes for women, and the textile manufacturers claim to be creators of similar original fabric designs. After these designs enter the channels of trade, other manufacturers systematically make and sell copies of them, the copies usually selling at prices lower than the garments copied. Petitioners call this practice of copying unethical and immoral, and give it the name of "style piracy." And although they admit that their "original creations" are neither copyrighted nor patented, and indeed assert that existing legislation affords them no protection against copyists, they never-theless urge that sale of copied designs constitutes an unfair trade practice and a tortious invasion of their rights. Because of these alleged wrongs, petitioners, while continuing to compete with one another in many re-spects, combined among themselves to combat and, if possible, destroy all competition from the sale of garments which are copies of their "original creations." They admit that to destroy such competition they have in combination purposely boycotted and declined to sell their products to retailers who follow a policy of selling garments copied by other manufac-turers from designs put out by Guild members. As a result of their efforts, approximately 12,000 retailers throughout the country have signed agree-ments to "cooperate" with the Guild's boycott program, but more than half of these signed the agreements only because constrained by threats that Guild members would not sell to retailers who failed to yield to their demands—threats that have been carried out by the Guild practice of placing on red cards the names of non-cooperators (to whom no sales are to be made), placing on white cards the names of cooperators (to whom sales are to be made), and then distributing both sets of cards to the manufactur-ers.

The one hundred and seventy-six manufacturers of women's garments who are members of the Guild occupy a commanding position in their line of business. In 1936, they sold in the United States more than 38% of all women's garments wholesaling at $6.75 and up, and more than 60% of those at $10.75 and above. The power of the combination is great; competition and the demand of the consuming public make it necessary for most retail dealers to stock some of the products of these manufacturers. And the power of the combination is made even greater by reason of the affiliation of some members of the National Federation of Textiles, Inc.— that being an organization composed of about one hundred textile manufacturers, converters, dyers, and printers of silk and rayon used in making women's garments. Those members of the Federation who are affiliated with the Guild have agreed to sell their products only to those garment manufacturers who have in turn agreed to sell only to cooperating retailers.

The Guild maintains a Design Registration Bureau for garments, and the Textile Federation maintains a similar Bureau for textiles. The Guild employs "shoppers" to visit the stores of both cooperating and non-cooperating retailers, "for the purpose of examining their stocks, to determine and report as to whether they contain ... copies of registered designs.... " An elaborate system of trial and appellate tribunals exists, for the determination of whether a given garment is in fact a copy of a Guild member's design. In order to assure the success of its plan of registration and restraint, and to ascertain whether Guild regulations are being violated, the Guild audits its members' books. And if violations of Guild requirements are discovered, as, for example, sales to red-carded retailers, the violators are subject to heavy fines....

If the purpose and practice of the combination of garment manufacturers and their affiliates runs counter to the public policy declared in the Sherman and Clayton Acts, the Federal Trade Commission has the power to suppress it as an unfair method of competition.... And among the many respects in which the Guild's plan runs contrary to the policy of the Sherman Act are these: it narrows the outlets to which garment and textile manufacturers can sell and the sources from which retailers can buy; subjects all retailers and manufacturers who decline to comply with the Guild's program to an organized boycott; takes away the freedom of action of members by requiring each to reveal to the Guild the intimate details of their individual affairs; and has both as its necessary tendency and as its purpose and effect the direct suppression of competition from the sale of unregistered textiles and copied designs. In addition to all this, the combination is in reality an extra-governmental agency, which prescribes rules for the regulation and restraint of interstate commerce, and provides extra-judicial tribunals for determination and punishment of violations, and thus "trenches upon the power of the national legislature and violates the statute." ...

Petitioners, however, argue that the combination cannot be contrary to the policy of the Sherman and Clayton Acts, since the Federal Trade Commission did not find that the combination fixed or regulated prices, parcelled out or limited production, or brought about a deterioration in quality. But action falling into these three categories does not exhaust the types of conduct banned by the Sherman and Clayton Acts.... [I]t was the object of the Federal Trade Commission Act to reach not merely in their fruition but also in their incipiency combinations which could lead to these and other trade restraints and practices deemed undesirable. In this case, the Commission found that the combination exercised sufficient control and power in the women's garments and textile businesses "to exclude from the industry those manufacturers and distributors who do not conform to the rules and regulations of said respondents, and thus tend to create in themselves a monopoly in the said industries." While a conspiracy to fix prices is illegal, an intent to increase prices is not an ever-present essential of conduct amounting to a violation of the policy of the Sherman and Clayton Acts; a monopoly contrary to their policies can exist even though a combination may temporarily or even permanently reduce the price of the articles manufactured or sold. For as this Court has said, "Trade or commerce under those circumstances may nevertheless be badly and unfortunately restrained by driving out of business the small dealers and worthy men whose lives have been spent therein, and who might be unable to readjust themselves to their altered surroundings. Mere reduction in the price of the commodity dealt in might be dearly paid for by the ruin of such a class, and the absorption of control over one commodity by an all-powerful combination of capital."

But petitioners further argue that their boycott and restraint of interstate trade is not within the ban of the policies of the Sherman and Clayton Acts because "the practices of FOGA were reasonable and necessary to protect the manufacturer, laborer, retailer and consumer against the devastating evils growing from the pirating of original designs and had in fact benefited all four." The Commission declined to hear much of the evidence that petitioners desired to offer on this subject. As we have pointed out, however, the aim of petitioners' combination was the intentional destruction of one type of manufacture and sale which competed with Guild members. The purpose and object of this combination, its potential power, its tendency to monopoly, the coercion it could and did practice upon a rival method of competition, all brought it within the policy of the prohibition declared by the Sherman and Clayton Acts.... Under these circumstances it was not error to refuse to hear the evidence offered, for the reasonableness of the methods pursued by the combination to accomplish its unlawful object is no more material than would be the reasonableness of the prices fixed by unlawful combination. Nor can the unlawful combination be justified upon the argument that systematic copying of dress designs is itself tortious, or should now be declared so by us. In the first place, whether or not given conduct is tortious is a question of state law.... In the second place, even if copying were an acknowledged tort under the law of every state, that situation would not justify petitioners in combining together to regulate and restrain interstate commerce in violation of federal law.... *Affirmed.*

Questions on *Fashion Originators'*

1.   If stopping copying is procompetitive, would the agreement still be per se illegal?

a.   If we allow copying, won't there be fewer original clothing designs? Isn't increasing the output of clothing designs procompetitive?

b.   Doesn't the government often recognize intellectual property rights that bar copying in order to avoid the market failure that would otherwise result if investments in creating new innovations were freely copied by others? When the government does so, isn't the effect of increasing innovation considered procompetitive? Why should the Fashion Originators be barred from advancing the same sort of procompetitive justifications that a government regulator could pursue?

2. Does the agreement here prohibit copying only when it is illegal? Should the agreement have to be so limited to survive antitrust scrutiny?

a. Why can't the Fashion Originators act to procompetitively encourage original clothing designs in the meantime before the government acts?

b. Would any concerns be better addressed by having government regulators rather than producers identify when copying should be banned? Do the Fashion Originators have the right incentives to disinterestedly decide whether any procompetitive effects on encouraging the creation original clothing designs outweigh any anticompetitive effects on reducing free competition in the production and distribution of each design?

c. Would those concerns be mooted by having antitrust courts review whether they agree with the producers that banning the copying at issue would create net procompetitive effects?

    i. Wouldn't that amount to court creation of a new species of intellectual property enforceable by group boycotts? Is that sort of decision better left to legislatures or regulators?

    ii. Would it make sense to have an intellectual property right that was enforceable only when innovators happened to already possess the organized market power to enforce their right through a boycott?

    iii. Wouldn't a decentralized system of antitrust adjudication about when the procompetitive effects outweighed the anticompetitive ones make the existence of this intellectual property right turn on the happenstance of the judge and jury drawn in the antitrust case?

3. If copying original clothing designs were illegal, would this case come out any differently? Why not? What objection could the court have to the Fashion Originators enforcing a legal ban on copying?

a. What concerns might such private enforcement raise about the accuracy of determinations about whether a clothing design was original and whether it was copied? About the amount of penalties imposed for violations? Do the Fashion Originators have disinterested incentives in making such determinations?

b. Would those concerns be mooted by having antitrust courts determine whether they agreed both that illegal copying occurred and that the penalty was appropriate? Would antitrust adjudication of such issues to decide whether a boycott was illegal be better than court adjudication of a complaint seeking to enforce whatever law banned copying? Does the fact that such antitrust review would come after the penalties are imposed by private action matter?

4. How is this case any different from the collective effort to stop copying allowed in *BMI*?

a. Do they differ on who determines whether and what copying is harmful? On who adjudicates whether such copying occurs and enforces the penalties?

b. Was the agreement here ancillary to the sort of productive business collaboration the government regulators normally do not provide? Or does it just offer a means of private regulation that replaces what government regulators could do? Which was the case in *BMI*?

5. Is there any anticompetitive effect here given the lack of any finding of an effect on output, price or quality?

a. Does the case indicate that a harmful effect on competitors suffices?

b. Does it seem likely the defendants would have engaged in this conduct if they thought it had no effect on prices?

Commission Decision 1999/60 of 21 October, Pre–Insulated Pipe Cartel

O.J. 1999, L 241/1.

[Many illegal boycotts are not pure boycotts, but rather involve the use of boycotts to coerce others to comply with a cartel. This was such a case. The cartel members made district heating pipes. They asked their only substantial non-member, Powerpipe, to stay out of the German market in exchange for higher prices in Sweden, and demanded that it engage in bid-rigging once it entered the German market. Powerpipe refused. The cartel retaliated by boycotting Powerpipe's customers and suppliers. They withheld component parts that Powerpipe did not make, but that were necessary for a subcontractor called DSD to install piping. They also pressured suppliers of plastic not to supply Powerpipe.]

... The Commission ... rejects the argument advanced by most of the producers—Lgstr, Henss/Isoplus, Pan–Isovit, Starpipe, Tarco and Brugg—that they did not participate "in any agreement to damage Powerpipe".

Their contention is unsustainable in law. The producers involved seek to divide the various manifestations of the cartel into totally separate infringements of Article [101]. This analysis is entirely artificial, since the plan to damage or eliminate Powerpipe was an integral part of the schemes for cartellising the European and German markets in which they were all deeply involved.

In any case, the factual evidence belies their claims. From the time when Powerpipe entered the German market, there had been concerted efforts by Lgstr, Henss/Isoplus (as well as ABB) to keep it out or induce it to enter the cartel. All the undertakings making this argument were present at the meeting [where the agreement to boycott was reached.] The main advocates of the boycott may have been ABB and Henss, but all those present at the meeting knew of and acquiesced in the plan.

Nor does it matter that in the implementation of the boycott the leading role fell to ABB and Lgstr; these were by force of circumstance the two producers best placed to approach Powerpipe's sub-contractors or suppliers.

It is, of course, not possible to state with certainty that the refusal of these producers to supply the DSD order was motivated solely by the intention to damage Powerpipe: they may well have been unable to meet an order of this type or size and in any case they are not legally obliged to contract. Nevertheless the annotation on the order enquiry found at Pan–Isovit confirms that ABB, Henss and Pan–Isovit (the three members of the unsuccessful consortium) were in contact about this order; that Pan–Isovit at least was pleased that DSD was in difficulties finding supplies; and that the question was discussed in the directors' club.

The express instructions given by ABB to KWH not to supply Power-pipe and the discussions in the directors' meetings of 5 May and 13 June 1995 confirm that the plan to eliminate that competitor was a settled policy of the cartel.

Given the common design and common objective which the producers steadily pursued, namely of eliminating competition in the district heating industry, the Commission considers that the joint enterprise constituted a continuing infringement of Article [101(1)] beginning in late 1990 in which each of the producers played its part.

Although, considered as a whole, the complex of arrangements between the producers could be regarded as presenting the characteristics of a full "agreement", the conduct in question also comprises factual elements some of which could aptly be described as a concerted practice. . . .

Questions on *Pre–Insulated Pipe*

1. What are the common points and differences between the facts of this case and those at play in *Klor's* or *Fashion Originators*?

2. Why did the members of the pre-insulated pipe cartel try to eliminate Powerpipe? Was it for the same reasons the infringers in *Klor's* and *Fashion Originators* decided to engage in boycotts?

3. What did the Commission seek to protect by banning this boycott? Powerpipe? The buyers of pre-insulated pipes? Or both?

2. EXCLUSIONS AND EXPULSIONS FROM A PRODUCTIVE COLLABORATION OF RIVALS

United States v. Terminal Railroad Ass'n
224 U.S. 383 (1912).

■ MR. JUSTICE LURTON delivered the opinion of the court:

[Jay Gould and various railroad companies formed the Terminal Rail-road Association of St. Louis (the "terminal company"), which acquired and combined into one unitary system not only the only three ways of getting railroad cars across the Mississippi river between St. Louis to East St. Louis—the Eads bridge, the Merchant's bridge, and the Wiggins Ferry Company—but also every terminal that connected those bridges and ferry to railroads terminating on either side of the river. The United States sued, alleging monopolization in violation of the Sherman Act.]

The consequences to interstate commerce of this combination cannot be appreciated without a consideration of natural conditions greatly affecting the railroad situation at St. Louis. Though twenty-four lines of railway converge at St. Louis, not one of them passes through. About one half of these lines have their termini on the Illinois side of the river. The others, coming from the west and north, have their termini either in the city or on its northern edge.... The cost of construction and maintenance of railroad bridges over so great a river makes it impracticable for every road desiring to enter or pass through the city to have its own bridge. The obvious solution is the maintenance of toll bridges open to the use of any and all lines, upon identical terms. And so the commercial interests of St. Louis sought to solve the question, the system of carferry transfer being inadequate to the growing demands of an ever-increasing population.... [But though the toll bridges could] be used by all upon equal terms, [they were] accessible only by means of the several terminal companies operating lines connecting it with the railroad termini.... Now, it is evident that these lines connecting railroad termini with the railroad bridges dominated the situation. They stood, as it were, just outside the gateway, and none could enter, though the gate stood open, who did not comply with their terms....

The result of the geographical and topographical situation is that it is, as a practical matter, impossible for any railroad company to pass through, or even enter St. Louis, so as to be within reach of its industries or commerce, without using the facilities entirely controlled by the terminal company.... Not is this effect denied; for the learned counsel representing the proprietary companies, as well as the terminal company, say in their filed brief: "There indeed is compulsion, but it is inherent in the situation. The other companies use the terminal properties because it is not possible to acquire adequate facilities for themselves. The cost to any one company is prohibitive." Obviously, this was not true before the consolidation of the systems of the Wiggins Ferry Company and the Merchants' Bridge Company with the system theretofore controlled by the terminal company. That the nonproprietary companies might have been compelled to use the instrumentalities of one or the other of the three systems then available, and that the advantages secured might not have been so great as those offered by the unified system now operated by the terminal company, must be admitted. But that there existed before the three terminal systems were combined a considerable measure of competition for the business of the other companies, and a larger power of competition, is undeniable. That the fourteen proprietary companies did not then have the power they now have to exclude either existing roads not in the combination, or new companies, from acquiring an independent entrance into the city, is also indisputable....

... The fact that the terminal company is not an independent corporation at all is of the utmost significance. There are twenty-four railroads converging at St. Louis. The relation of the terminal company is not one of impartiality to each of them. It was organized in 1889, at the instance of six of these railroad companies, for the purpose of acquiring all existing terminal instrumentalities for the benefit of the combination, and such other companies as they might thereafter admit to joint ownership by unanimous consent, and upon a consideration to be agreed upon. From time to time other companies came to an agreement with the original proprietors until, at the time this bill was filed, the properties unified were held for the joint use of the fourteen companies made defendants.... [T]he proprietary companies prescribe that the charges of the company shall be so adjusted as to produce no more revenue than shall equal the fixed charges, operating and maintenance expenses....

We fail to find in either of the contracts referred to any provision abrogating the requirement of unanimous consent to the admission of other companies to the ownership of the terminal company, though counsel say that no such company will now find itself excluded from joint use or ownership upon application. That other companies are permitted to use the facilities of the terminal company upon paying the same charges paid by the proprietary companies seems to be conceded. But there is no provision by which any such privilege is accorded....

[The Court concluded that the mere combination of properties into the terminal company was not an illegal merger because it allowed for a more efficient system of transport.] ...

It cannot be controverted that, in ordinary circumstances, a number of independent companies might combine for the purpose of controlling or acquiring terminals for their common but exclusive use. In such cases other companies might be admitted upon terms or excluded altogether. If such terms were too onerous, there would ordinarily remain the right and power to construct their own terminals. But the situation at St. Louis is most extraordinary, and we base our conclusion in this case, in a large measure, upon that fact. The "physical or topographical condition peculiar to the locality," which is advanced as a prime justification for a unified system of terminals, constitutes a most obvious reason why such a unified system is an obstacle, a hindrance, and a restriction upon interstate commerce, unless it is the impartial agent of all who, owing to conditions, are under such compulsion, as here exists, to use its facilities. The witness upon whom the defendants chiefly rely to uphold the advantages of the unified system which has been constructed, Mr. Albert L. Perkins, gives this as his unqualified judgment.... From his study of the local situation he expresses the opinion that the terminals of railway lines in any large city should be unified as far as possible, and that such unification may be of the greatest public utility and of immeasurable advantage to commerce, state and interstate.... The witness, however, points out that such a terminal company should be the agent of every company, and, furthermore, that its service should not be for profit or gain. In short, that every railroad using the service should be a joint owner and equally interested in the control and management. This, he thinks, will serve the greatest possible economy, and will give the most efficient service without discrimination....

The terminal properties in question are not so controlled and managed, in view of the inherent local conditions, as to escape condemnation as a restraint upon commerce. They are not under a common control and ownership. Nor can this be brought about unless the prohibition against the admission of other companies to such control is stricken out and provision made for the admission of any company to an equal control and management upon an equal basis with the present proprietary companies.

There are certain practices of this terminal company which operate to the disadvantage of the commerce which must cross the river at St. Louis, and of nonproprietary railroad lines compelled to use its facilities. [These included special charges to cross the river for traffic originating in a hundred-mile area around St. Louis that were not imposed on traffic that originated in a certain Green Line territory or that originated in East St. Louis and was thus bound west rather than east. This had the effect of imposing a discriminatory burden on short haul traffic, and on merchants in St. Louis who were not in the Green Line territory compared to East St. Louis merchants.] . . .

We come now to the remedy. . . . If, as we have already said, the combination of two or more mere terminal companies into a single system does not violate the prohibition of the statute against contracts and combinations in restraint of interstate commerce, it is because such a combination may be of the greatest public utility. But when, as here, the inherent conditions are such as to prohibit any other reasonable means of entering the city, the combination of every such facility under the exclusive ownership and control of less than all of the companies under compulsion to use them violates both the first and second sections of the act, in that it constitutes a contract or combination in restraint of commerce among the states, and an attempt to monopolize commerce among the states which must pass through the gateway at St. Louis.

The government has urged a dissolution of the combination between the terminal company, the Merchants' Bridge Terminal Company, and the Wiggins Ferry Company. That remedy may be necessary unless one equally adequate can be applied. . . . Plainly the combination which has occurred would not be an illegal restraint under the terms of the statute if it were what is claimed for it, a proper terminal association acting as the impartial agent of every line which is under compulsion to use its instrumentalities. If, as we have pointed out, the violation of the statute, in view of the inherent physical conditions, grows out of administrative conditions which may be eliminated and the obvious advantages of unification preserved, such a modification of the agreement between the terminal company and the proprietary companies as shall constitute the former the bona fide agent and servant of every railroad line which shall use its facilities, and an inhibition of certain methods of administration to which we have referred, will amply vindicate the wise purpose of the statute, and will preserve to the public a system of great public advantage. . . .

[The case was remanded with instructions to dissolve the combination unless the parties agreed to a reorganization that included the following elements.]

First. By providing for the admission of any existing or future railroad to joint ownership and control of the combined terminal properties, upon such just and reasonable terms as shall place such applying company upon a plane of equality in respect of benefits and burdens with the present proprietary companies.

Second. Such plan of reorganization must also provide definitely for the use of the terminal facilities by any other railroad not electing to become a joint owner, upon such just and reasonable terms and regulations as will, in respect of use, character, and cost of service, place every such company upon as nearly an equal plane as may be with respect to expenses and charges as that occupied by the proprietary companies. . . .

Associated Press v. United States

326 U.S. 1 (1945).

■ MR. JUSTICE BLACK delivered the opinion of the Court.

[Associated Press (AP) had 1,200 newspapers as its members. In addition to collecting news via AP employees, each member furnished AP with any news it had from its area, and AP then distributed the collective results to every member. Each member thus received the local news generated by every other member without having to have staff in each area. AP members comprised 65% of U.S. newspapers and 83% of U.S. circulation.

AP bylaws prohibited members from providing news to non-members. The AP board could admit without payment any new member that did not compete with any existing member. But if an applicant did compete with an existing member, then under the bylaws the applicant had to either (1) obtain that member's permission to join or (2) get the approval of a majority of AP members and pay AP 10% of the total amount paid by members in that area since 1900.]

The District Court found that the By–Laws in and of themselves were contracts in restraint of commerce in that they contained provisions designed to stifle competition in the newspaper publishing field. The court also found that AP's restrictive By–Laws had hindered and impeded the growth of competing newspapers. This latter finding, as to the *past* effect of the restrictions, is challenged. We are inclined to think that it is supported by undisputed evidence, but we do not stop to labor the point. For the court below found, and we think correctly, that the By–Laws on their face, and without regard to their past effect, constitute restraints of trade. Combinations are no less unlawful because they have not as yet resulted in restraint. An agreement or combination to follow a course of conduct which will necessarily restrain or monopolize a part of trade or commerce may violate the Sherman Act, whether it be "wholly nascent or abortive on the one hand, or successful on the other." For these reasons the argument, repeated here in various forms, that AP had not yet achieved a complete monopoly is wholly irrelevant. Undisputed evidence did show, however, that its By–Laws had tied the hands of all of its numerous publishers, to the extent that they could not and did not sell any part of their news so that it could reach any of their non-member competitors. In this respect the court did find, and that finding cannot possibly be challenged, that AP's By–Laws had hindered and restrained the sale of interstate news to non-members who competed with members.

Inability to buy news from the largest news agency, or any one of its multitude of members, can have most serious effects on the publication of competitive newspapers, both those presently published and those which, but for these restrictions, might be published in the future. This is illustrated by the District Court's finding that, in 26 cities of the United States, existing newspapers already have contracts for AP news and the same newspapers have contracts with United Press and International News Service under which new newspapers would be required to pay the contract holders large sums to enter the field.[11] The net effect is seriously to limit the opportunity of any new paper to enter these cities. Trade restraints of this character, aimed at the destruction of competition, tend to block the initiative which brings newcomers into a field of business and to frustrate the free enterprise system which it was the purpose of the Sherman Act to protect.

Nor can we treat this case as though it merely involved a reporter's contract to deliver his news reports exclusively to a single newspaper, or an exclusive agreement as to news between two newspapers in different cities. For such trade restraints might well be "reasonable," and therefore not in violation of the Sherman Act. But however innocent such agreements might be, standing alone, they would assume quite a different aspect if utilized as essential features of a program to hamper or destroy competition. It is in this light that we must view this case.

It has been argued that the restrictive By–Laws should be treated as beyond the prohibitions of the Sherman Act, since the owner of the property can choose his associates and can, as to that which he has produced by his own enterprise and sagacity, efforts or ingenuity, decide for himself whether and to whom to sell or not to sell. While it is true in a very general sense that one can dispose of his property as he pleases, he cannot "go beyond the exercise of this right, and by contracts or combinations, express or implied, unduly hinder or obstruct the free and natural flow of commerce in the channels of interstate trade." The Sherman Act was specifically intended to prohibit independent businesses from becoming "associates" in a common plan which is bound to reduce their competitor's opportunity to buy or sell the things in which the groups compete. Victory of a member of such a combination over its business rivals achieved by such collective means cannot consistently with the Sherman Act or with practical, everyday knowledge be attributed to *individual* "enterprise and sagacity"; such hampering of business rivals can only be attributed to that which really makes it possible—the collective power of an unlawful combination. That the object of sale is the creation or product of a man's ingenuity does not alter this principle. *Fashion Originators'*. It is obviously fallacious to view the By–Laws here in issue as instituting a program to

---

11. INS and UP make so-called "asset value" contracts under which if another newspaper wishes to obtain their press services, the newcomer shall pay to the competitor holding the UP or INS contract the stipulated "asset value."

encourage and permit full freedom of sale and disposal of property by its owners. Rather, these publishers have, by concerted arrangements, pooled their power to acquire, to purchase, and to dispose of news reports through the channels of commerce. They have also pooled their economic and news control power and, in exerting that power, have entered into agreements which the District Court found to be "plainly designed in the interest of preventing competition."[15]

It is further contended that since there are other news agencies which sell news, it is not a violation of the Act for an overwhelming majority of American publishers to combine to decline to sell their news to the minority. But the fact that an agreement to restrain trade does not inhibit competition in all of the objects of that trade cannot save it from the condemnation of the Sherman Act. It is apparent that the exclusive right to publish news in a given field, furnished by AP and all of its members, gives many newspapers a competitive advantage over their rivals. Conversely, a newspaper without AP service is more than likely to be at a competitive disadvantage. The District Court stated that it was to secure this advantage over rivals that the By–Laws existed. It is true that the record shows that some competing papers have gotten along without AP news, but morning newspapers, which control 96% of the total circulation in the United States, have AP news service. And the District Court's unchallenged finding was that "AP is a vast, intricately reticulated organization, the largest of its kind, gathering news from all over the world, the chief single source of news for the American press, universally agreed to be of great consequence."

. . . [The district court had enjoined AP from discriminating against applicants that competed with existing members, which the Supreme Court held was not unduly vague. The Supreme Court also upheld the district court's decision not to enjoin the ban on furnishing news to non-members standing alone, noting that the district court retained jurisdiction to alter that decision if the injunction against discriminatory admissions proved insufficient.]

Questions on *Terminal RR* and *Associated Press*

1. Is the result in *Associated Press* dictated by *Terminal R.R.?*

a. Did Associated Press have the same degree of monopoly power as Terminal RR?

b. Did Terminal RR acquire its power through the same sort of skill and foresight as Associated Press?

c. Do these factors help explain why *Terminal RR* imposed a duty to admit all rivals, whereas *Associated Press* only imposed a duty to have nondiscriminatory rules about their admission?

---

15. Even if additional purposes were involved, it would not justify the combination, since the Sherman Act cannot "be evaded by good motives. The law is its own measure of right and wrong, of what it permits, or forbids, and the judgment of the courts cannot be set up against it in a supposed accommodation of its policy with the good intention of parties, and it may be, of some good results." Standard Sanitary Mfg. Co. v. United States, 226 U.S. 20, 49.

2. Suppose two authors combine to make a great antitrust casebook that drives every other casebook out of the market. Do they have to license that casebook to all rivals? How is that different from what Terminal RR and Associated Press did? Do the casebook hypothetical and these cases differ in their effect on existing or potential competition between the joint venturers? In the ability of excluded rivals to duplicate the valuable property or service created by the joint venture?

3. What precisely is the illegal agreement in *Terminal R.R.* and *Associated Press*?

a. Is it the formation of each organization? Is there a procompetitive purpose to that formation agreement in each case? Are there economies of scale in a railroad system? In newsgathering?

b. Is it the agreement to discriminate against applicants who are competitors? What anticompetitive effect does such an agreement have? Does it further the procompetitive purposes of the productive collaboration?

4. What does the admission of competing newspapers do to the incentives of members to share their news with Associated Press? If they do share, what does this do to their incentives to invest efforts in getting news scoops? Are there less restrictive alternatives to addressing those problems? Are such problems with having competitors share access to the common facility equally present in *Terminal R.R.*?

5. What does a duty to admit competing applicants do to initial incentives to create something like Terminal RR or Associated Press? Would firms invest in the formation of each unless doing so gave them a competitive advantage over rivals?

6. What does a duty to admit competing applicants do to the incentives of others to form (or join) rivals to Terminal RR or Associated Press?

a. Was it possible to form a rival to Terminal RR given the relevant geography?

b. Was it possible to form a rival in the market for news-gathering agencies? Didn't UPI and INS in fact form such rivals? Would *Associated Press* come out the same way if Associated Press had signed up only 25% of newspapers in the nation? Does this decision invalidate the similar bylaws of UPI and INS that required applicants who competed with an existing member to pay an additional fee to that member?

7. Does Associated Press have to admit applicants:

a. who initially declined to join Associated Press? Can Associated Press charge a higher price to new members to compensate for past investments and risks? If so, do courts have any principled mechanism to determine how much can be charged for this?

b. if AP reaches a size where too many members clog the lines? If so, can Associated Press charge a higher price to new members to take account of the fact that it has reached a size where it has diseconomies of scale? Do courts have any principled mechanism to determine how much can be charged for this?

c. Would either of those problems justify a rule that admitted new members for free unless they ran competing newspapers?

8. Can Associated Press:

a. Charge higher fees to applicants who compete with existing members on the theory that such applicants will add relatively little incremental news because they operate in cities that AP members already cover?

b. exclude new applicants by saying that they are poor news sources? Do courts have the capacity to meaningfully review whether independent good reasons exist to exclude any new applicants who compete with existing members?

9. Should the by-law requiring members to provide their own news exclusively to Associated Press be illegal standing alone? Suppose some towns are only large enough to support one newspaper, and that newspapers in such monopoly towns already decided to join the first news-gathering agency, Associated Press. What would that do to the ability of a rival news-gathering agency to get full geographic coverage and offer an equally desirable product? Is this bylaw necessary to advance the procompetitive purposes of the productive collaboration?

Northwest Wholesale Stationers v. Pacific Stationery

472 U.S. 284 (1985).

■ JUSTICE BRENNAN delivered the opinion of the Court. . . .

Because the District Court ruled on cross-motions for summary judgment after only limited discovery, this case comes to us on a sparse record. Certain background facts are undisputed. Petitioner Northwest Wholesale Stationers is a purchasing cooperative made up of approximately 100 office supply retailers in the Pacific Northwest States. The cooperative acts as the primary wholesaler for the retailers. Retailers that are not members of the cooperative can purchase wholesale supplies from Northwest at the same price as members. At the end of each year, however, Northwest distributes its profits to members in the form of a percentage rebate on purchases. Members therefore effectively purchase supplies at a price significantly lower than do nonmembers.[2] Northwest also provides certain warehousing facilities. The cooperative arrangement thus permits the participating retailers to achieve economies of scale in purchasing and warehousing that would otherwise be unavailable to them. In fiscal 1978 Northwest had $5.8 million in sales.

Respondent Pacific Stationery & Printing Co. sells office supplies at both the retail and wholesale levels. Its total sales in fiscal 1978 were approximately $7.6 million; the record does not indicate what percentage of revenue is attributable to retail and what percentage is attributable to wholesale. Pacific became a member of Northwest in 1958. In 1974 Northwest amended its bylaws to prohibit members from engaging in both retail and wholesale operations. A grandfather clause preserved Pacific's mem-

---

2. Although this patronage rebate policy is a form of price discrimination, § 4 of the Robinson–Patman Act specifically sanctions such activity by cooperatives. . . .

bership rights. In 1977 ownership of a controlling share of the stock of Pacific changed hands, and the new owners did not officially bring this change to the attention of the directors of Northwest. This failure to notify apparently violated another of Northwest's bylaws.

In 1978 the membership of Northwest voted to expel Pacific. Most factual matters relevant to the expulsion are in dispute. No explanation for the expulsion was advanced at the time, and Pacific was given neither notice, a hearing, nor any other opportunity to challenge the decision. Pacific argues that the expulsion resulted from Pacific's decision to maintain a wholesale operation. Northwest contends that the expulsion resulted from Pacific's failure to notify the cooperative members of the change in stock ownership. The minutes of the meeting of Northwest's directors do not definitively indicate the motive for the expulsion. It is undisputed that Pacific received approximately $10,000 in rebates from Northwest in 1978, Pacific's last year of membership. Beyond a possible inference of loss from this fact, however, the record is devoid of allegations indicating the nature and extent of competitive injury the expulsion caused Pacific to suffer.

Pacific brought suit ... The gravamen of the action was that Northwest's expulsion of Pacific from the cooperative without procedural protections was a group boycott that limited Pacific's ability to compete and should be considered *per se* violative of § 1. On cross-motions for summary judgment the District Court rejected application of the *per se* rule and held instead that rule-of-reason analysis should govern the case. Finding no anticompetitive effect on the basis of the record as presented, the court granted summary judgment for Northwest.

The Court of Appeals for the Ninth Circuit reversed ...

The decision of the cooperative members to expel Pacific was certainly a restraint of trade in the sense that every commercial agreement restrains trade. Whether this action violates § 1 of the Sherman Act depends on whether it is adjudged an *unreasonable* restraint. Rule-of-reason analysis guides the inquiry unless the challenged action falls into the category of "agreements or practices which because of their pernicious effect on competition and lack of any redeeming virtue are conclusively presumed to be unreasonable and therefore illegal without elaborate inquiry as to the precise harm they have caused or the business excuse for their use."

This *per se* approach permits categorical judgments with respect to certain business practices that have proved to be predominantly anticompetitive. Courts can thereby avoid the "significant costs" in "business certainty and litigation efficiency" that a full-fledged rule-of-reason inquiry entails. *Maricopa*. The decision to apply the *per se* rule turns on "whether the practice facially appears to be one that would always or almost always tend to restrict competition and decrease output ... or instead one designed to 'increase economic efficiency and render markets more, rather than less, competitive.' " *BMI. See also NCAA* ("*Per se* rules are invoked when surrounding circumstances make the likelihood of anticompetitive conduct so great as to render unjustified further examination of the challenged conduct").

This Court has long held that certain concerted refusals to deal or group boycotts are so likely to restrict competition without any offsetting efficiency gains that they should be condemned as *per se* violations of § 1 of the Sherman Act. See *Klor's;* United States v. General Motors Corp., 384 U.S. 127 (1966); Radiant Burners, Inc. v. Peoples Gas Light & Coke Co., 364 U.S. 656 (1961); *Associated Press*; *Fashion Originators'*; Eastern States Retail Lumber Dealers' Assn. v. United States, 234 U.S. 600 (1914). The question presented in this case is whether Northwest's decision to expel Pacific should fall within this category of activity that is conclusively presumed to be anticompetitive. The Court of Appeals held that the exclusion of Pacific from the cooperative should conclusively be presumed unreasonable on the ground that Northwest provided no procedural protections to Pacific. . . .

[Silver v. NYSE, 373 U.S. 341 (1963), had held that the Securities Exchange Act provided antitrust immunity to self-regulation by the stock exchange only when the exchange provided procedural protections. But those procedural protections under *Silver* were, the Court held, relevant only to the scope of that regulatory immunity and were not affirmatively imposed by antitrust law.]

. . . [T]he absence of procedural safeguards can in no sense determine the antitrust analysis. If the challenged concerted activity of Northwest's members would amount to a *per se* violation of § 1 of the Sherman Act, no amount of procedural protection would save it. If the challenged action would not amount to a violation of § 1, no lack of procedural protections would convert it into a *per se* violation because the antitrust laws do not themselves impose on joint ventures a requirement of process. . . .

This case therefore turns not on the lack of procedural protections but on whether the decision to expel Pacific is properly viewed as a group boycott or concerted refusal to deal mandating *per se* invalidation. "Group boycotts" are often listed among the classes of economic activity that merit *per se* invalidation under § 1. Exactly what types of activity fall within the forbidden category is, however, far from certain. . . . Some care is therefore necessary in defining the category of concerted refusals to deal that mandate *per se* condemnation.

Cases to which this Court has applied the *per se* approach have generally involved joint efforts by a firm or firms to disadvantage competitors by "either directly denying or persuading or coercing suppliers or customers to deny relationships the competitors need in the competitive struggle." See, e. g., *Silver* (denial of necessary access to exchange members); *Radiant Burners* (denial of necessary certification of product); *Associated Press* (denial of important sources of news); *Klor's* (denial of wholesale supplies). In these cases, the boycott often cut off access to a supply, facility, or market necessary to enable the boycotted firm to compete, *Silver; Radiant Burners*, and frequently the boycotting firms possessed a dominant position in the relevant market. e. g., *Silver; Associated Press; Fashion Originators'*. In addition, the practices were generally not justified by plausible arguments that they were intended to enhance overall efficiency and make markets more competitive. Under such circumstances the

likelihood of anticompetitive effects is clear and the possibility of countervailing procompetitive effects is remote.

Although a concerted refusal to deal need not necessarily possess all of
these traits to merit *per se* treatment, not every cooperative activity
involving a restraint or exclusion will share with the *per se* forbidden
boycotts the likelihood of predominantly anticompetitive consequences. For
example, we recognized last Term in *NCAA* that *per se* treatment of the
NCAA's restrictions on the marketing of televised college football was
inappropriate—despite the obvious restraint on output—because the "case
involves an industry in which horizontal restraints on competition are
essential if the product is to be available at all."

Wholesale purchasing cooperatives such as Northwest are not a form of
concerted activity characteristically likely to result in predominantly anticompetitive effects. Rather, such cooperative arrangements would seem to
be "designed to increase economic efficiency and render markets more,
rather than less, competitive." *BMI*. The arrangement permits the participating retailers to achieve economies of scale in both the purchase and
warehousing of wholesale supplies, and also ensures ready access to a stock
of goods that might otherwise be unavailable on short notice. The cost
savings and order-filling guarantees enable smaller retailers to reduce
prices and maintain their retail stock so as to compete more effectively with
larger retailers.

Pacific, of course, does not object to the existence of the cooperative
arrangement, but rather raises an antitrust challenge to Northwest's
decision to bar Pacific from continued membership.[6] It is therefore the
action of expulsion that must be evaluated to determine whether *per se*
treatment is appropriate. The act of expulsion from a wholesale cooperative
does not necessarily imply anticompetitive animus and thereby raise a
probability of anticompetitive effect. Wholesale purchasing cooperatives
must establish and enforce reasonable rules in order to function effectively.
Disclosure rules, such as the one on which Northwest relies, may well
provide the cooperative with a needed means for monitoring the creditworthiness of its members.[7] Nor would the expulsion characteristically be likely
to result in predominantly anticompetitive effects, at least in the type of
situation this case presents. Unless the cooperative possesses market power
or exclusive access to an element essential to effective competition, the
conclusion that expulsion is virtually always likely to have an anticompeti-

---

6. Because Pacific has not been wholly excluded from access to Northwest's wholesale
operations, there is perhaps some question whether the challenged activity is properly
characterized as a concerted refusal to deal. To be precise, Northwest's activity is a concerted
refusal to deal with Pacific on substantially equal terms. Such activity might justify *per se*
invalidation if it placed a competing firm at a severe competitive disadvantage.

7. Pacific argues, however, that this justification for expulsion was a pretext because the
members of Northwest were fully aware of the change in ownership despite lack of formal
notice. According to Pacific, Northwest's motive in the expulsion was to place Pacific at a
competitive disadvantage to retaliate for Pacific's decision to engage in an independent
wholesale operation. Such a motive might be more troubling. If Northwest's action were not
substantially related to the efficiency-enhancing or procompetitive purposes that otherwise
justify the cooperative's practices, an inference of anticompetitive animus might be appropriate. But such an argument is appropriately evaluated under the rule-of-reason analysis.

tive effect is not warranted. Absent such a showing with respect to a cooperative buying arrangement, courts should apply a rule-of-reason analysis. At no time has Pacific made a threshold showing that these structural characteristics are present in this case.

The District Court appears to have followed the correct path of analysis—recognizing that not all concerted refusals to deal should be accorded *per se* treatment and deciding this one should not. The foregoing discussion suggests, however, that a satisfactory threshold determination whether anticompetitive effects would be likely might require a more detailed factual picture of market structure than the District Court had before it. Nonetheless, in our judgment the District Court's rejection of *per se* analysis in this case was correct. A plaintiff seeking application of the *per se* rule must present a threshold case that the challenged activity falls into a category likely to have predominantly anticompetitive effects. The mere allegation of a concerted refusal to deal does not suffice because not all concerted refusals to deal are predominantly anticompetitive. When the plaintiff challenges expulsion from a joint buying cooperative, some showing must be made that the cooperative possesses market power or unique access to a business element necessary for effective competition. Focusing on the argument that the lack of procedural safeguards required *per se* liability, Pacific did not allege any such facts. Because the Court of Appeals applied an erroneous *per se* analysis in this case, the court never evaluated the District Court's rule-of-reason analysis rejecting Pacific's claim. A remand is therefore appropriate for the limited purpose of permitting appellate review of that determination. . . .

Questions on *Northwest Stationers*

1.   Why doesn't the per se rule apply? Is it because here the concerted refusal to deal is arguably ancillary to a productive rival collaboration or because here there is no market power over a necessary input and a plausible procompetitive justification exists?

a.   Would the Court also require proof of market power in the case of a boycott among unrelated firms? Would that be consistent with *Klor's*?

b.   In what sense would the rule against boycotts still be a per se test if it depended on market power and a lack of procompetitive justification?

2.   What is the procompetitive justification for the buying association?

a.   Does that justification justify the expulsion here? Does it justify the rule requiring disclosure of a change in member ownership? Might such a disclosure rule be relevant to a joint venture wishing to know facts relevant to the creditworthiness of its members?

b.   Is there any procompetitive purpose to expelling members who compete with the joint venture?

　　　i.   Is discriminating against rivals of the joint venture the same as discriminating against the rivals of members? Isn't this more like *Associated Press* refusing to admit UPI? Might a joint venture legitimately want to exclude its own rivals as members, so as to avoid strategic use of the joint venture's capacity or resources? Does a rival wholesaler have much of an argument that it needs access to the wholesale facilities provided by the joint venture in order to compete downstream at retail?

   ii.   Was the expulsion here justified on the grounds that the joint venture wanted to exclude members who competed with it?

   c.   Should the mere offering of a plausible procompetitive justification be enough to escape per se scrutiny?

   d.   Under the rule of reason, would the court determine whether the actual defendant motive was to expel wholesale rivals? Or would the lack of market power and any plausible anticompetitive effect end the inquiry?

   3.   Should the standards for proving an illegal expulsion be harder or easier to satisfy than the standards for proving an illegal refusal to admit?

   a.   Does *Northwest* set a looser standard for condemning expulsions in that it requires only proof of market power over an input used by rivals, not (as in the *AP* case on refusals to admit) dominance over a facility vital to competition that rivals cannot practically duplicate?

   b.   As a practical matter, would you expect it is easier in an expulsion case (compared to a nonadmission case) to determine whether a joint venture was discriminating on the basis of rivalry? In which sort of case will it likely be easier for a court to determine: (a) whether the rival is an appropriate member; (b) whether there are legitimate diseconomies of scale to including more members; and (c) what the terms of membership should be for that rival?

   4.   Should any procedural protections given to expulsion decisions change the competitive analysis?

   a.   Would a lack of due process imply an anticompetitive motive if the joint venture generally denies due process?

   b.   Does giving due process help if an anticompetitive motive drives decisionmaking?

Joined Cases 96–102, 104, 105, 108 and 110/82, NV IAZ International Belgium and others v. Commission (ANSEAU)

[1983] E.C.R. 3369.

[Manufacturers of dishwashers and washing machines often appoint one exclusive distributor per European nation, called the "official" or "sole" importer. While EU law permits vertical agreements that bar such distributors from actively marketing their products outside their territory, it prohibits vertical agreements that bar those distributors from passively responding to purchase requests coming from other territories. See Chapter 5. Thus, in many markets, including those in this case, parallel importers buy products in low-price nations (generally from the official distributor in that nation) and resell in high-priced nations like Belgium.

Belgian law required that appliances satisfy certain standards to be hooked up to the water-supply, leaving the responsibility for compliance to

ANSEAU, an association of 31 water-supply companies. ANSEAU had previously carried out this duty with a system of checks based on lists setting out which types of appliances satisfied these standards. But it decided to replace such checks by entering into an agreement with FCAE and CEG, groups that included manufacturers and their sole importers of electrical appliances into Belgium, whereby CEG would put a conformity label on appliances, and ANSEAU would refuse to install any appliances that did not have such a label. Parallel importers were not permitted to join this agreement or obtain a label, even though they were selling precisely the same appliances.

The Commission found that the provisions precluding parallel importers from getting a conformity label violated Article 101.]

ANSEAU and Miele [one of the manufacturers] contend that in its decision the Commission has not provided adequate legal proof that the purpose of the agreement was to restrict competition. In that regard they maintain first that the true purpose of the agreement was to ensure that conformity checks were carried out and to reduce the administrative costs involved and secondly that not all the parties intended to restrict competition.

As regards the first part of the applicant's argument, it must be stated that the agreement, regard being had to its content, its origin and the circumstances in which it was implemented, clearly expresses the intention of treating parallel imports less favourably than official imports with a view to hindering the former.

That conclusion stems, in the first place, from the fact that the agreement is based on a single system of checks involving the use of conformity labels which replaced an earlier system of checks based on lists of authorized appliances, and that only manufacturers and sole importers may obtain those labels. That conclusion is also based on certain statements made by the CEG and by the FCAE at the preliminary meetings. During those meetings, the CEG stated that it wished to obtain for its members preferential treatment as against non-members and that it regarded the proposed agreement as a "weapon" against parallel imports. Moreover, the FCAE emphasized that the disadvantage of the system of listing authorized appliances was that parallel importers also benefited from the verification obtained by the official importer without having to share in the costs. Finally, the intention of hindering parallel imports is also apparent from the steps taken by the CEG and ANSEAU after the conclusion of the agreement in order to put dealers and consumers on their guard against the sale and purchase respectively of appliances not bearing a conformity label.

Therefore, the purpose of the agreement, regard being had to its terms, the legal and economic context in which it was concluded and the conduct of the parties, is appreciably to restrict competition within the common market, notwithstanding the fact that it also pursues the objective of protecting public health and reducing the cost of conformity checks. That finding is not invalidated by the fact that it has not been established that it was the intention of all the parties to the agreement to restrict competition.

ANSEAU and Miele also contend that, contrary to the findings set out in the decision, the agreements had no restrictive effect on competition.

It is clear from the foregoing considerations that the agreement is of such a kind as to make parallel imports of washing machines and dishwashers more difficult, if not impossible, and that it is therefore capable of affecting trade between Member States. In view of the fact that, according to the observations submitted in these proceedings, signatory undertakings' share of the market is approximately 90% and is therefore very considerable, the conclusion must be drawn that the agreement had a restrictive effect on competition.

It also follows from those considerations that, contrary to the objections raised by ANSEAU, the agreement affects intra-community trade to an extent which must be regarded as appreciable.

This group of submissions must therefore also be dismissed.

Questions on *ANSEAU*

1. Was the CEG's refusal to grant a label to the parallel importers of washing machines and dishwashers motivated by the same objective as the discriminatory access given by Associated Press to the newspapers competing with its members? Were the effects of the discriminatory measures in question similar?

2. Should competition law allow private industry associations to hold powers, such as the granting of labels which are necessary for competing manufacturers or distributors to sell their products on a given market?

3. An important effect of the agreement here was to deny labels to parallel importers and thus decrease competition from them.

a. Is that effect anticompetitive or procompetitive?

b. Why would manufacturers want to decrease distributor competition for the marketing of their goods? Unless there were some procompetitive gains from the exclusivity, wouldn't manufacturers want to minimize the retail markup so they get a bigger share of price paid by consumers? Might they do so in response to the demands of powerful distributors?

c. If the EU really wants to encourage a more economically-integrated common market across Europe, why doesn't it ban the exclusive distributorships themselves? If the exclusive distributors are considered sufficiently procompetitive to allow, does it make sense to ban vertical agreements that try to enforce that exclusivity? To ban horizontal agreements that do so?

4. The Commission refused to exempt this agreement under Article 101(3) because it was not notified as required under the pre–2003 procedure. If the parties had properly notified the agreement to the Commission, should it have granted an exemption?

a. Was there a procompetitive justification for the agreement to set a standard conformity label? Should such decisions be left in the hands of industry participants with a financial self-interest in excluding their rivals?

b. Was discriminatorily denying a conformity label to parallel import-ers reasonably necessary to advance any procompetitive justification?

i. Was there any reason to believe that all goods distributed by parallel importers in fact failed to conform to the technical require-ments in the Royal Decrees?

ii. Is it administratively easier to just give conformity labels to the official distributors who are known to sell conforming products rather than to check each appliance to make sure it is conforming? Do those administrative savings justify adopting a general rule to give conformity labels only to official distributors?

iii. Did the Court believe that any procompetitive justification actually motivated the agreement? Should the case turn on what the subjective purpose of the agreement was, or only on whether it can be objectively justified? If the former, is it enough that most or some participants had a bad subjective purpose?

5. The decision sustained the Commission decision on the grounds that this boycott had an appreciable anticompetitive purpose and effect, citing a 90% market share in favor of the latter conclusion. Does that mean that there is no per se rule against horizontal boycotts under EU law? Or only that there is none when there is some procompetitive purpose to the joint venture as a whole?

6. Suppose that the Massachusetts Association of Manufacturers of Washing Machines and Dishwashers (MAMAWASH) adopted a quality label that was much easier to obtain by its members than by manufacturers from other states.

a. Would this give a cause of action under Section 1 of the Sherman Act?

b. Would U.S. judges analyze it under a per se rule or the rule of reason?[58] Is there any procompetitive justification for creating a quality label designed to provide information to consumers? To making it easier for Massachusetts firms to obtain the label?

c. Would the case turn on:

i. whether the only effect of the quality label was whatever information it provided to consumers?

ii. whether MAMAWASH had market power in the market for providing quality labels?

iii. whether access to a MAMAWASH label was as a practical matter necessary to survive on the market?

iv. whether excluded rivals could reasonably develop their own quality label?

---

58. In *Radiant Burners, Inc. v. Peoples Gas Light & Coke Co.,* 364 U.S. 656 (1961), the Court held that the per se rule applied to an association's refusal to give a safety seal of approval to the plaintiff's gas burner, but in that case the association members that sold gas could not supply gas for use in an unapproved burner, so that the agreement amounted to a collective refusal to supply gas. *Id.* at 659–60.

v.   whether the exclusion was based on a legitimate quality concern or on the basis of rivalry?

vi.   whether MAMAWASH had 50 members who vigorously competed? On whether the exclusion of other rivals had any adverse price
or output effect on the market that harmed consumer welfare?

vii.   whether the excluded rivals were denied initial admission or
expelled after being admitted?

Other Nations' Regulation of Boycotts

A few other nations apply a per se rule to horizontal agreements not to
deal with particular firms.[59] Most nations do not. Canada makes a refusal
to deal illegal if (1) it substantially injures a business (2) the business
cannot obtain the product elsewhere on usual market terms because of a
lack of competition among suppliers, (3) the business is willing to pay the
supplier's usual trade terms, (4) the defendants have an ample supply of
the product, and (5) the refusal will likely cause an anticompetitive effect.[60]
This test thus requires market power and an anticompetitive effect. In
Japan, a concerted refusal to deal with a rival (or to deal with those who
deal with rivals) is illegal as an unfair trade practice if it lacks a "proper
justification" and "tends to impede competition."[61] However, the JFTC
guidelines state that boycotts generally tend to impede competition, so are
illegal even when they do not cause a substantial restraint of competition.[62]
Argentina and Chile make boycotts illegal when the firms have market
power.[63] China makes boycotts illegal unless they are justified, share their
benefits with consumers, and do not substantially restrict competition.[64]
Mexico makes boycotts illegal when they aim to exclude or hamper firms
and the defendants have market power, unless any anticompetitive effects
are offset by efficiencies.[65] Brazil, Peru, and South Korea likewise applies
various forms of rule of reason review.[66] Should concerted refusals to deal

---

59.   *See e.g.*, Australia Trade Practices Act §§ 4D, 45(1)(a), 45DB, 45DD (other than
consumer, environmental or labor boycotts); Turkey Competition Act Art. 4(d); Venezuela
Procompetition Act, Art. 7. However, nations may not apply their per se rule if the parties got
advance approval from an agency or tribunal. Australia Trade Practices Act §§ 88, 90; Turkey
Competition Act Art. 5.

60.   *See* Canada Competition Act § 75. Canada also allows the Tribunal to enjoin a
person from refusing to deal with another person because of the low pricing policy of that
person. See *id.* § 76(1).

61.   See Japan Antimonopoly Act § 2(9); Japan Designations of Unfair Trade Practices
§ 1.

62.   Japan Distribution Guidelines Ch. 2 (1991).

63.   Argentina Competition Law Arts. 1–2; Chile Competition Law Art. 3. *See also* Saudi
Arabia Competition Law Art. 4 (requiring that the firms have a "dominant status" to qualify
for condemnation, and otherwise requiring an anticompetitive purpose or effect, but allowing
application for exemption).

64.   China Anti–Monopoly Law Arts. 13 & 15.

65.   *See* Mexico Competition Law Arts. 10, 11.

66.   *See* Brazil Antitrust Law No. 8,884, Art.21(VI); Brazil CADE Resolution 20, Attachment I (1999); Peru Competition Law, Arts. 9, 11(1)(g); South Korea Guidelines on Reviewing
Unfair Trade Practices V.1.A.(3) (2009).

be governed by a general rule of reason, even when they are between firms unrelated by any productive business collaboration?

F.   ARE SOCIAL WELFARE JUSTIFICATIONS ADMISSIBLE?

Social welfare justifications often exist for restraining unfettered competition. Few, for example, would quarrel with the government ban on baby-selling, even though it does restrain a form of competition. But the questions raised in antitrust law are not whether and when it might be in the public interest for government lawmakers to regulate competition. The questions rather focus on: (1) whether private market actors can be trusted to exercise their collective market power to restrain competition in public interest, and to properly trade off any noncompetitive benefits against competitive ones; (2) whether, if such private actors cannot be trusted, review by antitrust courts of such issues suffices to make sure that private regulation of this sort will be in the public interest; (3) whether it makes sense to instead have such issues resolved by government lawmakers or regulators when the restraints are not ancillary to a productive business collaboration; (4) whether, even if one thinks such private regulation might make sense, the relevant laws permit it or rather reflect a contrary policy judgment; and (5) whether any resolution of the first four issues should be modified when the private actors in question are professionals or nonprofit corporations.

National Society of Professional Engineers v. United States

435 U.S. 679 (1978).

■ MR. JUSTICE STEVENS delivered the opinion of the Court.

This is a civil antitrust case brought by the United States to nullify an association's canon of ethics prohibiting competitive bidding by its members. The question is whether the canon may be justified under the Sherman Act because it was adopted by members of a learned profession for the purpose of minimizing the risk that competition would produce inferior engineering work endangering the public safety. The District Court rejected this justification without making any findings on the likelihood that competition would produce the dire consequences foreseen by the association. The Court of Appeals affirmed. We granted certiorari to decide whether the District Court should have considered the factual basis for the proffered justification before rejecting it. Because we are satisfied that the asserted defense rests on a fundamental misunderstanding of the Rule of Reason frequently applied in antitrust litigation, we affirm.

I

Engineering is an important and learned profession. There are over 750,000 graduate engineers in the United States, of whom about 325,000 are registered as professional engineers.... About half of those who are registered engage in consulting engineering on a fee basis. They perform services in connection with the study, design, and construction of all types of improvements to real property—bridges, office buildings, airports, and factories are examples. Engineering fees, amounting to well over $2 billion each year, constitute about 5% of total construction costs. In any given facility, approximately 50% to 80% of the cost of construction is the direct result of work performed by an engineer concerning the systems and equipment to be incorporated in the structure.

The National Society of Professional Engineers (Society) was organized in 1935 to deal with the nontechnical aspects of engineering practice, including the promotion of the professional, social, and economic interests of its members. Its present membership of 69,000 resides throughout the United States and in some foreign countries. Approximately 12,000 members are consulting engineers who offer their services to governmental, industrial, and private clients. Some Society members are principals or chief executive officers of some of the largest engineering firms in the country.

... This case does not ... involve any claim that the National Society has tried to fix specific fees, or even a specific method of calculating fees. It involves a charge that the members of the Society have unlawfully agreed to refuse to negotiate or even to discuss the question of fees until after a prospective client has selected the engineer for a particular project. Evidence of this agreement is found in ... the Society's Code of Ethics, [which prohibited competitive bidding, defined as the submission of price information that would allow clients to compare engineers on price, but did not prohibit submitting recommended fee schedules prepared by engineering societies. Instead, members had to use] ... the traditional method, [whereby] the client initially selects an engineer on the basis of background and reputation, not price [and then either negotiates a fee agreement with that engineer or, if unable to do so, selects a new engineer to negotiate with.]

... [T]he Society admitted the essential facts alleged by the Government and pleaded [the] ... defense ... that the standard set out in the Code of Ethics was reasonable because competition among professional engineers was contrary to the public interest. It was averred that [competitive bidding would: (1) inevitably result in engineers offering their services at the lowest possible price, which would cause them to spend insufficient effort and instead design unnecessarily expensive structures; (2) cause buyers to pick engineers purely on price rather than quality, thus endangering public safety.]

... The District Court did not ... make any finding on the question whether, or to what extent, competition had led to inferior engineering work which, in turn, had adversely affected the public health, safety, or welfare. That inquiry was considered unnecessary because the court was convinced that the ethical prohibition against competitive bidding was "on its face a tampering with the price structure of engineering fees in violation of § 1 of the Sherman Act." ...

II

In Goldfarb v. Virginia State Bar, 421 U.S. 773, the Court held that a bar association's rule prescribing minimum fees for legal services violated § 1 of the Sherman Act. In that opinion the Court ... said:

"The fact that a restraint operates upon a profession as distinguished from a business is, of course, relevant in determining whether that particular restraint violates the Sherman Act. It would be unrealistic to view the practice of professions as interchangeable with other business activities, and automatically to apply to the professions anti-trust concepts which originated in other areas. The public service aspect, and other features of the professions, may require that a particular practice, which could properly be viewed as a violation of the Sherman Act in another context, be treated differently...."

Relying heavily on this footnote, and on some of the major cases applying a Rule of Reason ... petitioner argues that its attempt to preserve the profession's traditional method of setting fees for engineering services is a reasonable method of forestalling the public harm which might be produced by unrestrained competitive bidding....

A.   The Rule of Reason

One problem presented by the language of § 1 of the Sherman Act is that it cannot mean what it says. The statute says that "every" contract that restrains trade is unlawful. But, as Mr. Justice Brandeis perceptively noted, restraint is the very essence of every contract; read literally, § 1 would outlaw the entire body of private contract law. Yet it is that body of law that establishes the enforceability of commercial agreements and enables competitive markets—indeed, a competitive economy—to function effectively.

Congress, however, did not intend the text of the Sherman Act to delineate the full meaning of the statute or its application in concrete situations. The legislative history makes it perfectly clear that it expected the courts to give shape to the statute's broad mandate by drawing on common-law tradition. The Rule of Reason, with its origins in common-law precedents long antedating the Sherman Act, has served that purpose. It has been used to give the Act both flexibility and definition, and its central principle of antitrust analysis has remained constant. Contrary to its name, the Rule does not open the field of antitrust inquiry to any argument in favor of a challenged restraint that may fall within the realm of reason. Instead, it focuses directly on the challenged restraint's impact on competitive conditions.

This principle is apparent in even the earliest of cases applying the Rule of Reason, *Mitchel v. Reynolds*[, 24 Eng. Rep. 347 (1711)]. *Mitchel* involved the enforceability of a promise by the seller of a bakery that he would not compete with the purchaser of his business. The covenant was for a limited time and applied only to the area in which the bakery had operated. It was therefore upheld as reasonable, even though it deprived the public of the benefit of potential competition. The long-run benefit of enhancing the marketability of the business itself—and thereby providing incentives to develop such an enterprise—outweighed the temporary and limited loss of competition.

The Rule of Reason suggested by *Mitchel* has been regarded as a standard for testing the enforceability of covenants in restraint of trade which are ancillary to a legitimate transaction, such as an employment contract or the sale of a going business. Judge (later Mr. Chief Justice) Taft so interpreted the Rule in his classic rejection of the argument that competitors may lawfully agree to sell their goods at the same price as long as the agreed-upon price is reasonable. United States v. Addyston Pipe & Steel Co., 85 F. 271, 282–283 (CA6 1898), aff'd, 175 U.S. 211. That case, and subsequent decisions by this Court, unequivocally foreclose an interpretation of the Rule as permitting an inquiry into the reasonableness of the prices set by private agreement.

The early cases also foreclose the argument that because of the special characteristics of a particular industry, monopolistic arrangements will better promote trade and commerce than competition. That kind of argument is properly addressed to Congress and may justify an exemption from the statute for specific industries, but it is not permitted by the Rule of Reason. As the Court observed in *Standard Oil*, "restraints of trade within the purview of the statute ... [can] not be taken out of that category by indulging in general reasoning as to the expediency or nonexpediency of having made the contracts, or the wisdom or want of wisdom of the statute which prohibited their being made."

The test prescribed in *Standard Oil* is whether the challenged contracts or acts "were unreasonably restrictive of competitive conditions." Unreasonableness under that test could be based either (1) on the nature or character of the contracts, or (2) on surrounding circumstances giving rise to the inference or presumption that they were intended to restrain trade and enhance prices. Under either branch of the test, the inquiry is confined to a consideration of impact on competitive conditions.[16] ... [T]he inquiry mandated by the Rule of Reason is whether the challenged agreement is one that promotes competition or one that suppresses competition....

There are, thus, two complementary categories of antitrust analysis. In the first category are agreements whose nature and necessary effect are so plainly anticompetitive that no elaborate study of the industry is needed to establish their illegality—they are "illegal per se." In the second category are agreements whose competitive effect can only be evaluated by analyzing the facts peculiar to the business, the history of the restraint, and the reasons why it was imposed. In either event, the purpose of the analysis is to form a judgment about the competitive significance of the restraint; it is not to decide whether a policy favoring competition is in the public interest, or in the interest of the members of an industry. Subject to exceptions defined by statute, that policy decision has been made by the Congress.

B.   The Ban on Competitive Bidding

Price is the "central nervous system of the economy," *Socony–Vacuum*, and an agreement that "interfere[s] with the setting of price by free market forces" is illegal on its face. United States v. Container Corp., 393 U.S. 333, 337. In this case we are presented with an agreement among

---

16. ... "This standard ... makes obsolete once prevalent arguments, such as, whether monopoly arrangements would be socially preferable to competition in a particular industry, because, for example, of high fixed costs or the risks of 'cut-throat' competition or other similar unusual conditions."

competitors to refuse to discuss prices with potential customers until after negotiations have resulted in the initial selection of an engineer. While this is not price fixing as such, no elaborate industry analysis is required to demonstrate the anticompetitive character of such an agreement. . . .

The Society's affirmative defense confirms rather than refutes the anticompetitive purpose and effect of its agreement. The Society argues that the restraint is justified because bidding on engineering services is inherently imprecise, would lead to deceptively low bids, and would thereby tempt individual engineers to do inferior work with consequent risk to public safety and health. The logic of this argument rests on the assumption that the agreement will tend to maintain the price level; if it had no such effect, it would not serve its intended purpose. The Society nonetheless invokes the Rule of Reason, arguing that its restraint on price competition ultimately inures to the public benefit by preventing the production of inferior work and by insuring ethical behavior. As the preceding discussion of the Rule of Reason reveals, this Court has never accepted such an argument.

It may be, as petitioner argues, that competition tends to force prices down and that an inexpensive item may be inferior to one that is more costly. There is some risk, therefore, that competition will cause some suppliers to market a defective product. Similarly, competitive bidding for engineering projects may be inherently imprecise and incapable of taking into account all the variables which will be involved in the actual performance of the project. Based on these considerations, a purchaser might conclude that his interest in quality—which may embrace the safety of the end product—outweighs the advantages of achieving cost savings by pitting one competitor against another. Or an individual vendor might independently refrain from price negotiation until he has satisfied himself that he fully understands the scope of his customers' needs. These decisions might be reasonable; indeed, petitioner has provided ample documentation for that thesis. But these are not reasons that satisfy the Rule; nor are such individual decisions subject to antitrust attack.

The Sherman Act does not require competitive bidding; it prohibits unreasonable restraints on competition. Petitioner's ban on competitive bidding prevents all customers from making price comparisons in the initial selection of an engineer, and imposes the Society's views of the costs and benefits of competition on the entire marketplace. It is this restraint that must be justified under the Rule of Reason, and petitioner's attempt to do so on the basis of the potential threat that competition poses to the public safety and the ethics of its profession is nothing less than a frontal assault on the basic policy of the Sherman Act.

The Sherman Act reflects a legislative judgment that ultimately competition will produce not only lower prices, but also better goods and services. "The heart of our national economic policy long has been faith in the value of competition." *Standard Oil*. The assumption that competition is the best method of allocating resources in a free market recognizes that all elements of a bargain—quality, service, safety, and durability—and not just the immediate cost, are favorably affected by the free opportunity to select among alternative offers. Even assuming occasional exceptions to the presumed consequences of competition, the statutory policy precludes inquiry into the question whether competition is good or bad.

The fact that engineers are often involved in large-scale projects significantly affecting the public safety does not alter our analysis. Exceptions to the Sherman Act for potentially dangerous goods and services would be tantamount to a repeal of the statute. In our complex economy the number of items that may cause serious harm is almost endless—automobiles, drugs, foods, aircraft components, heavy equipment, and countless others, cause serious harm to individuals or to the public at large if defectively made. The judiciary cannot indirectly protect the public against this harm by conferring monopoly privileges on the manufacturers.

By the same token, the cautionary footnote in *Goldfarb* ... cannot be read as fashioning a broad exemption under the Rule of Reason for learned professions. We adhere to the view expressed in *Goldfarb* that, by their nature, professional services may differ significantly from other business services, and, accordingly, the nature of the competition in such services may vary. Ethical norms may serve to regulate and promote this competition, and thus fall within the Rule of Reason.[22] But the Society's argument in this case is a far cry from such a position. We are faced with a contention that a total ban on competitive bidding is necessary because otherwise engineers will be tempted to submit deceptively low bids. Certainly, the problem of professional deception is a proper subject of an ethical canon. But, once again, the equation of competition with deception, like the similar equation with safety hazards, is simply too broad; we may assume that competition is not entirely conducive to ethical behavior, but that is not a reason, cognizable under the Sherman Act, for doing away with competition.

In sum, the Rule of Reason does not support a defense based on the assumption that competition itself is unreasonable. Such a view of the Rule would create the "sea of doubt" on which Judge Taft refused to embark in *Addyston*, and which this Court has firmly avoided ever since.

III

The judgment entered by the District Court, as modified by the Court of Appeals, prohibits the Society from adopting any official opinion, policy statement, or guideline stating or implying that competitive bidding is unethical. Petitioner argues that this judgment abridges its First Amendment rights. We find no merit in this contention.... Just as an injunction against price fixing abridges the freedom of businessmen to talk to one another about prices, so too the injunction in this case must restrict the Society's range of expression on the ethics of competitive bidding.... Affirmed.

---

22.   Courts have, for instance, upheld marketing restraints related to the safety of a product, provided that they have no anticompetitive effect and that they are reasonably ancillary to the seller's main purpose of protecting the public from harm or itself from product liability. See, e. g., Tripoli Co. v. Wella Corp., 425 F.2d 932 (CA3 1970) (en banc); cf. *GTE Sylvania*.

Questions on *Professional Engineers*

1.   Why isn't this agreement per se illegal?

a.   Did the agreement fix prices? What about the fact that the only pre-bid price information engineers were allowed to give were the recommended fee schedules prepared by engineering societies?

b.   Wasn't the absence of an agreement on specific fixed prices rejected as unnecessary to apply the per se rule in *Socony* and *Palmer*?

c.   How could the agreement to ban competitive bidding affect prices given that buyers could always withdraw from their selection of a particular engineer if they were unable to negotiate a satisfactory fee? Does the agreement alter the pricing information buyers get? The transaction costs of making a choice based on price?

d.   According to the defendant's own argument, isn't the clear purpose and effect of the agreement to alter prices? If it didn't, how could the ethical rule further the alleged safety justification?

2.   Does it matter whether the per se rule or rule of reason applies?

a.   Either way, can procompetitive justifications be offered under *BMI*?

b.   Either way, aren't justifications that are unrelated to competition excluded?

c.   Is the difference that the Court seems to implicitly allow professionals (unlike other businesses) to offer procompetitive justifications that are not necessarily ancillary to a joint business collaboration?

3.   In deciding whether a justification is admissible, what does the Court mean by "competition": a competitive result or process?

a.   if result, then does this understanding conflict with cases rejecting the need to prove anticompetitive effects in a price-fixing case?

b.   if process, then does this understanding conflict with *BMI*, which seemed to allow a noncompetitive process because it produced procompetitive results? Why is it a procompetitive justification to overcome the difficulty of monitoring copyright use in *BMI*, but not one to overcome the difficulty of monitoring the quality of engineering here in *Professional Engineers*?

c.   Does it help to ask whether the process was calculated to expand market output or would, if it had any effect at all, decrease output? To ask whether the agreements expanded or contracted market options?

4.   Is the Court disputing the factual claim that price-fixing is necessary to achieve quality in this case, or rejecting the claim on principle and categorically for all cases?

a.   Wouldn't marginal producers be tempted to cut quality at *any* price?

b.   Isn't one purpose of competition to allow buyers to make their *own* quality/price tradeoffs? Does it seem likely that buyers in this market would be sufficiently sophisticated and informed to do so?

c. If this defense were allowed, couldn't one offer it in *every* price-fixing case? Would you, for example, be inclined to accept a defense that the quality of bar preparation courses will be too low unless prices are fixed high?

5. Could the Court consider the justification offered here without having to inquire into the reasonableness of market prices?

6. Is the Court saying that competitive bidding is desirable? Or just that engineers should not be able to collectively decide whether it is offered?

7. Suppose the National Society of Professional Engineers agreed not to build any homes with polyvinyl conduit because they considered it unsafe, and are sued on the grounds that this agreement restrains competition.

a. Would their claim that polyvinyl conduit is unsafe be an inadmissible justification under the general test that "the inquiry is confined to a consideration of impact on competitive conditions"?

b. Would their claim be admissible under footnote 22, or not because here there would be an anticompetitive effect by preventing consumers from buying the product they otherwise would choose? Wouldn't that anticompetitive effect also exist in the case of a marketing restraint, or does it not exist because such an agreement would be vertical? Would a seller of a product have any financial interest in reducing sales of its product by restraining its marketing?

c. Would a ban on using polyvinyl conduit be more or less worrisome than a ban on competitive bidding?

    i. Which seems more overbroad relative to the safety concern?

    ii. Which seems more likely to be distorted by the financial interest of the engineers?

FTC v. Indiana Federation of Dentists
476 U.S. 447 (1986).

■ JUSTICE WHITE delivered the opinion of the Court.

[Dental insurers try to contain costs by using x rays and other information to review whether the dental care provided was unnecessary or more expensive than equally effective alternative care. Typically, the initial review is done by lay examiners, who either approve payment or refer the claim to dentists hired by the insurer to make a final determination. Fearing a loss of money and professional independence, the Indiana Dental Association initially organized dentists to agree not to submit x rays to insurers. It stopped doing so under an FTC consent decree, but another group of dentists split off and formed the Indiana Federation of Dentists to continue this denial of x rays.]

Although the Federation's membership was small, numbering less than 100, ... [it] succeeded in enlisting nearly 100% of the dental specialists in the Anderson area, and approximately 67% of the dentists in and around

Lafayette. In the areas of its strength, the Federation was successful in continuing to enforce the Association's prior policy of refusal to submit x rays to dental insurers.

[T]he Federal Trade Commission ... ruled that the Federation's policy constituted a violation of § 5 ... [because it] amounted to a conspiracy in restraint of trade that was unreasonable and hence unlawful under the standards for judging such restraints developed in this Court's precedents interpreting § 1 of the Sherman Act.... The ... Court of Appeals for the Seventh Circuit ... vacated the order.... We now reverse....

The policy of the Federation with respect to its members' dealings with third-party insurers resembles practices that have been labeled "group boycotts": the policy constitutes a concerted refusal to deal on particular terms with patients covered by group dental insurance. Although this Court has in the past stated that group boycotts are unlawful *per se,* we decline to resolve this case by forcing the Federation's policy into the "boycott" pigeonhole and invoking the *per se* rule. As we observed last Term in *Northwest Stationers,* the category of restraints classed as group boycotts is not to be expanded indiscriminately, and the *per se* approach has generally been limited to cases in which firms with market power boycott suppliers or customers in order to discourage them from doing business with a competitor—a situation obviously not present here. Moreover, we have been slow to condemn rules adopted by professional associations as unreasonable *per se,* see *Professional Engineers,* and, in general, to extend *per se* analysis to restraints imposed in the context of business relationships where the economic impact of certain practices is not immediately obvious, see *BMI.* Thus, as did the FTC, we evaluate the restraint at issue in this case under the Rule of Reason rather than a rule of *per se* illegality.

Application of the Rule of Reason to these facts is not a matter of any great difficulty. The Federation's policy takes the form of a horizontal agreement among the participating dentists to withhold from their customers a particular service that they desire—the forwarding of x rays to insurance companies along with claim forms.... A refusal to compete with respect to the package of services offered to customers, no less than a refusal to compete with respect to the price term of an agreement, impairs the ability of the market to advance social welfare by ensuring the provision of desired goods and services to consumers at a price approximating the marginal cost of providing them. Absent some countervailing procompetitive virtue—such as, for example, the creation of efficiencies in the operation of a market or the provision of goods and services, see *BMI; Chicago Board of Trade;* cf. *NCAA*—such an agreement limiting consumer choice by impeding the "ordinary give and take of the market place," *Professional Engineers,* cannot be sustained under the Rule of Reason. No credible argument has been advanced for the proposition that making it more costly for the insurers and patients who are the dentists' customers to obtain information needed for evaluating the dentists' diagnoses has any such procompetitive effect.

The Federation advances three principal arguments for the proposition that, notwithstanding its lack of competitive virtue, the Federation's policy of withholding x rays should not be deemed an unreasonable restraint of trade. First, ... the Federation suggests that in the absence of specific findings by the Commission concerning the definition of the market in which the Federation allegedly restrained trade and the power of the Federation's members in that market, the conclusion that the Federation unreasonably restrained trade is erroneous as a matter of law, regardless of whether the challenged practices might be impermissibly anticompetitive if engaged in by persons who together possessed power in a specifically defined market. This contention, however, runs counter to the Court's holding in *NCAA* that "[a]s a matter of law, the absence of proof of market power does not justify a naked restriction on price or output," and that such a restriction "requires some competitive justification even in the absence of a detailed market analysis." Moreover, even if the restriction imposed by the Federation is not sufficiently "naked" to call this principle into play, the Commission's failure to engage in detailed market analysis is not fatal to its finding of a violation of the Rule of Reason. The Commission found that in two localities in the State of Indiana (the Anderson and Lafayette areas), Federation dentists constituted heavy majorities of the practicing dentists and that as a result of the efforts of the Federation, insurers in those areas were, over a period of years, actually unable to obtain compliance with their requests for submission of x rays. Since the purpose of the inquiries into market definition and market power is to determine whether an arrangement has the potential for genuine adverse effects on competition, "proof of actual detrimental effects, such as a reduction of output," can obviate the need for an inquiry into market power, which is but a "surrogate for detrimental effects." 7 P. Areeda, Antitrust Law ¶ 1511, p. 429 (1986). In this case, we conclude that the finding of actual, sustained adverse effects on competition in those areas where IFD dentists predominated, viewed in light of the reality that markets for dental services tend to be relatively localized, is legally sufficient to support a finding that the challenged restraint was unreasonable even in the absence of elaborate market analysis.

Second, the Federation ... argues that a holding that its policy of withholding x rays constituted an unreasonable restraint of trade is precluded by the Commission's failure to make any finding that the policy resulted in the provision of dental services that were more costly than those that the patients and their insurers would have chosen were they able to evaluate x rays in conjunction with claim forms. This argument, too, is unpersuasive. Although it is true that the goal of the insurers in seeking submission of x rays for use in their review of benefits claims was to minimize costs by choosing the least expensive adequate course of dental treatment, a showing that this goal was actually achieved through the means chosen is not an essential step in establishing that the dentists' attempt to thwart its achievement by collectively refusing to supply the requested information was an unreasonable restraint of trade. A concerted and effective effort to withhold (or make more costly) information desired by consumers for the purpose of determining whether a particular purchase is cost justified is likely enough to disrupt the proper functioning of the price-setting mechanism of the market that it may be condemned even absent proof that it resulted in higher prices or, as here, the purchase of higher priced services, than would occur in its absence. *Professional Engineers*. Moreover, even if the desired information were in fact completely useless to the insurers and their patients in making an informed choice regarding the least costly adequate course of treatment—or, to put it another way, if the costs of evaluating the information were far greater than the cost savings resulting from its use—the Federation would still not be justified in deciding on behalf of its members' customers that they did not need the information: presumably, if that were the case, the discipline of the market would itself soon result in the insurers' abandoning their requests for x rays. The Federation is not entitled to pre-empt the working of the market by deciding for itself that its customers do not need that which they demand.

Third, the Federation complains that the Commission erred in failing to consider, as relevant to its Rule of Reason analysis, noncompetitive "quality of care" justifications for the prohibition on provision of x rays to insurers in conjunction with claim forms. . . . The gist of the claim is that x rays, standing alone, are not adequate bases for diagnosis of dental problems or for the formulation of an acceptable course of treatment. Accordingly, if insurance companies are permitted to determine whether they will pay a claim for dental treatment on the basis of x rays as opposed to a full examination of all the diagnostic aids available to the examining dentist, there is a danger that they will erroneously decline to pay for treatment that is in fact in the interest of the patient, and that the patient will as a result be deprived of fully adequate care.

The Federation's argument is flawed both legally and factually. The premise of the argument is that, far from having no effect on the cost of dental services chosen by patients and their insurers, the provision of x rays will have too great an impact: it will lead to the reduction of costs through the selection of inadequate treatment. Precisely such a justification for withholding information from customers was rejected as illegitimate in the *Professional Engineers* case. The argument is, in essence, that an unrestrained market in which consumers are given access to the information they believe to be relevant to their choices will lead them to make unwise and even dangerous choices. Such an argument amounts to "nothing less than a frontal assault on the basic policy of the Sherman Act." *Professional Engineers*. Moreover, there is no particular reason to believe that the provision of information will be more harmful to consumers in the market for dental services than in other markets. Insurers . . . are themselves in competition for the patronage of the patients—or, in most cases, the unions or businesses that contract on their behalf for group insurance coverage—and must satisfy their potential customers not only that they will provide coverage at a reasonable cost, but also that that coverage will be adequate to meet their customers' dental needs. There is thus no more reason to expect dental insurance companies to sacrifice quality in return for cost savings than to believe this of consumers in, say, the market for engineering services. Accordingly, if noncompetitive quality-of-service justifications are inadmissible to justify the denial of information to consumers in the latter market, there is little reason to credit such justifications here.

In any event, the Commission did not, as the Federation suggests, refuse even to consider the quality-of-care justification for the withholding of x rays.... The Commission was amply justified in concluding on the basis of ... conflicting evidence that even if concern for the quality of patient care could under some circumstances serve as a justification for a restraint of the sort imposed here, the evidence did not support a finding that the careful use of x rays as a basis for evaluating insurance claims is in fact destructive of proper standards of dental care.

In addition to arguing that its conspiracy did not effect an unreasonable restraint of trade, the Federation appears to renew its argument ... that the conspiracy to withhold x rays is immunized from antitrust scrutiny by virtue of a supposed policy of the State of Indiana against the evaluation of dental x rays by lay employees of insurance companies. Allegedly, such use of x rays by insurance companies—even where no claim was actually denied without examination of an x ray by a licensed dentist—would constitute unauthorized practice of dentistry by the insurance company and its employees. The Commission found that this claim had no basis in any authoritative source of Indiana law, and the Federation has not identified any adequate reason for rejecting the Commission's conclusion. Even if the Commission were incorrect in its reading of the law, however, the Federation's claim of immunity would fail. That a particular practice may be unlawful is not, in itself, a sufficient justification for collusion among competitors to prevent it. See *Fashion Originators'*.... [A]ccordingly, whether or not the policy the Federation has taken upon itself to advance is consistent with the policy of the State of Indiana, the Federation's activities are subject to Sherman Act condemnation.... *Reversed.*

Questions on *Indiana Dentists*

1. Do you agree with the Court's holdings that this was not a per se illegal boycott, but that the absence of a procompetitive justification made it a naked restraint illegal under the rule of reason?

a. Why isn't it per se illegal given that it is a horizontal boycott without any procompetitive justification?

i. Is the Court's reference to market power consistent with *Klor's*? Does it make sense to limit the per se rule to cases where the agreement involves a secondary boycott: that is, a boycott that targets third parties to stop them from doing business with rivals? Does it make sense to exempt professional associations from per se rules?

ii. Is it a better distinction that this case really involves a refusal to provide a product at all, not a refusal to deal with particular businesses to harm them? Is this like an agreement not to use polyvinyl conduit?

b. Is the holding here any different from holding that the absence of a procompetitive justification makes any agreement a naked restraint that can be condemned summarily under the rule of reason? Is the difference that, because the per se rule does not apply here given this holding, the dentists at least have the opportunity to offer a procompetitive justification even though the restraint is not ancillary to any productive rival collaboration?

2. Do you agree with the Court's alternative holding that direct proof of anticompetitive effects obviates any need to prove market definition or power?

a. Why should it?

b. Were anticompetitive effects directly proven?

c. Why doesn't the lack of proof that dental prices were altered mean that no anticompetitive effect was shown?

3. Why isn't the quality-of-care justification procompetitive? Is it implausible insurers would misuse x-ray information? Would the case come out the same way if insurers did not use dentists to make any denial decisions?

4. Could dentists conclude that some type of dental polish is harmful and agree to stop using it? Is that different from dentists agreeing that x-rays will be used in an unsafe manner by insurers and agreeing to stop giving them?

FTC v. Superior Court Trial Lawyers Ass'n
493 U.S. 411 (1990).

■ JUSTICE STEVENS delivered the opinion of the Court.

[Under the D.C. Criminal Justice Act (CJA), private lawyers were appointed to represent indigent criminal defendants at rates of $30/hr. for court time and $20/hr. for other time. Most such appointments went to about 100 lawyers, called CJA regulars, who derived almost all their income from representing the indigent. Through the Superior Court Trial Lawyers Association (SCTLA), they tried to persuade D.C. to raise the rate to $35/hr., but were unsuccessful. At a SCTLA meeting, the CJA regulars then agreed decided to stop taking cases unless their rates were raised. They also publicized their boycott. D.C. was unable to find other lawyers to accept these cases, and concluded its criminal justice system was on the brink of collapse. D.C. then agreed to raise the rate to $35/hr. and the boycott ended. The Administrative Law Judge (ALJ) found that it was the shortage of lawyers, rather than the publicity, that caused D.C. to capitulate.

The FTC concluded this conduct violated Sherman Act § 1, and thus violated FTC Act § 5, and enjoined future such boycotts. The Court of Appeals held the First Amendment immunized the boycott unless the defendants were on remand found to have market power.]

.... Respondents' boycott may well have served a cause that was worthwhile and unpopular. We may assume that the preboycott rates were unreasonably low, and that the increase has produced better legal representation for indigent defendants. Moreover, given that neither indigent criminal defendants nor the lawyers who represent them command any special appeal with the electorate, we may also assume that without the boycott there would have been no increase in District CJA fees.... These assumptions do not control the case, for it is not our task to pass upon the social utility or political wisdom of price-fixing agreements.

As the ALJ, the FTC, and the Court of Appeals all agreed, respondents' boycott "constituted a classic restraint of trade within the meaning of Section 1 of the Sherman Act." As such, it also violated the prohibition against unfair methods of competition in § 5 of the FTC Act. Prior to the boycott CJA lawyers were in competition with one another, each deciding independently whether and how often to offer to provide services to the District at CJA rates. The agreement among the CJA lawyers was designed to obtain higher prices for their services and was implemented by a concerted refusal to serve an important customer in the market for legal services and, indeed, the only customer in the market for the particular services that CJA regulars offered. "This constriction of supply is the essence of 'price-fixing,' whether it be accomplished by agreeing upon a price, which will decrease the quantity demanded, or by agreeing upon an output, which will increase the price offered." The horizontal arrangement among these competitors was unquestionably a "naked restraint" on price and output. *See NCAA.*

It is of course true that the city purchases respondents' services because it has a constitutional duty to provide representation to indigent defendants. It is likewise true that the quality of representation may improve when rates are increased. Yet neither of these facts is an acceptable justification for an otherwise unlawful restraint of trade. As we have remarked before, the "Sherman Act reflects a legislative judgment that ultimately competition will produce not only lower prices, but also better goods and services." *Professional Engineers.* This judgment "recognizes that all elements of a bargain—quality, service, safety, and durability—and not just the immediate cost, are favorably affected by the free opportunity to select among alternative offers." *Ibid.* That is equally so when the quality of legal advocacy, rather than engineering design, is at issue.

The social justifications proffered for respondents' restraint of trade thus do not make it any less unlawful. The statutory policy underlying the Sherman Act "precludes inquiry into the question whether competition is good or bad." *Ibid.* Respondents' argument, like that made by the petitioners in *Professional Engineers*, ultimately asks us to find that their boycott is permissible because the price it seeks to set is reasonable. But it was settled shortly after the Sherman Act was passed that it "is no excuse that the prices fixed are themselves reasonable." *See, e. g., Trenton Potteries.* Respondents' agreement is not outside the coverage of the Sherman Act simply because its objective was the enactment of favorable legislation. . . .

The Court of Appeals, however, crafted a new exception to the per se rules, and it is this exception which provoked the FTC's petition to this Court. The Court of Appeals derived its exception from United States v. O'Brien, 391 U.S. 367 (1968). In that case O'Brien had burned his Selective Service registration certificate on the steps of the South Boston Courthouse. He did so before a sizable crowd and with the purpose of advocating his antiwar beliefs. We affirmed his conviction. We held that the governmental interest in regulating the "nonspeech element" of his conduct adequately justified the incidental restriction on First Amendment freedoms. Specifically, we concluded that the statute's incidental restriction on O'Brien's freedom of expression was no greater than necessary to further the Government's interest in requiring registrants to have valid certificates continually available.

However, the Court of Appeals held that, in light of *O'Brien*, the expressive component of respondents' boycott compelled courts to apply the antitrust laws "prudently and with sensitivity," with a "special solicitude for the First Amendment rights" of respondents. The Court of Appeals concluded that the governmental interest in prohibiting boycotts is not sufficient to justify a restriction on the communicative element of the boycott unless the FTC can prove, and not merely presume, that the boycotters have market power. Because the Court of Appeals imposed this special requirement upon the Government, it ruled that per se antitrust analysis was inapplicable to boycotts having an expressive component.

There are at least two critical flaws in the Court of Appeals' antitrust analysis: it exaggerates the significance of the expressive component in respondents' boycott and it denigrates the importance of the rule of law that respondents violated. Implicit in the conclusion of the Court of Appeals are unstated assumptions that most economic boycotts do not have an expressive component, and that the categorical prohibitions against price fixing and boycotts are merely rules of "administrative convenience" that do not serve any substantial governmental interest unless the price-fixing competitors actually possess market power.

It would not much matter to the outcome of this case if these flawed assumptions were sound. *O'Brien* would offer respondents no protection even if their boycott were uniquely expressive and even if the purpose of the per se rules were purely that of administrative efficiency. We have recognized that the Government's interest in adhering to a uniform rule may sometimes satisfy the *O'Brien* test even if making an exception to the rule in a particular case might cause no serious damage. United States v. Albertini, 472 U.S. 675, 688 (1985) ("The First Amendment does not bar application of a neutral regulation that incidentally burdens speech merely because a party contends that allowing an exception in the particular case will not threaten important government interests"). The administrative efficiency interests in antitrust regulation are unusually compelling. The per se rules avoid "the necessity for an incredibly complicated and prolonged economic investigation into the entire history of the industry involved, as well as related industries, in an effort to determine at large whether a particular restraint has been unreasonable." *Northern Pacific*. If small parties "were allowed to prove lack of market power, all parties would have that right, thus introducing the enormous complexities of market definition into every price-fixing case." R. Bork, The Antitrust Paradox 269 (1978). . . .

In any event, however, we cannot accept the Court of Appeals' characterization of this boycott or the antitrust laws. Every concerted refusal to do business with a potential customer or supplier has an expressive component. At one level, the competitors must exchange their views about their objectives and the means of obtaining them. The most blatant, naked price-fixing agreement is a product of communication, but that is surely not a reason for viewing it with special solicitude. At another level, after the terms of the boycotters' demands have been agreed upon, they must be communicated to its target: "We will not do business until you do what we ask." That expressive component of the boycott conducted by these respondents is surely not unique. On the contrary, it is the hallmark of every effective boycott.

At a third level, the boycotters may communicate with third parties to enlist public support for their objectives; to the extent that the boycott is newsworthy, it will facilitate the expression of the boycotters' ideas. But this level of expression is not an element of the boycott. Publicity may be generated by any other activity that is sufficiently newsworthy. Some activities, including the boycott here, may be newsworthy precisely for the reasons that they are prohibited: the harms they produce are matters of public concern. Certainly that is no reason for removing the prohibition.

In sum, there is thus nothing unique about the "expressive component" of respondents' boycott. A rule that requires courts to apply the antitrust laws "prudently and with sensitivity" whenever an economic boycott has an "expressive component" would create a gaping hole in the fabric of those laws. Respondents' boycott thus has no special characteristics meriting an exemption from the per se rules of antitrust law.

Equally important is the second error implicit in respondents' claim to immunity from the per se rules. In its opinion, the Court of Appeals assumed that the antitrust laws permit, but do not require, the condemnation of price fixing and boycotts without proof of market power. The opinion further assumed that the per se rule prohibiting such activity "is only a rule of 'administrative convenience and efficiency,' not a statutory command." This statement contains two errors. The per se rules are, of course, the product of judicial interpretations of the Sherman Act, but the rules nevertheless have the same force and effect as any other statutory commands. Moreover, while the per se rule against price fixing and boycotts is indeed justified in part by "administrative convenience," the Court of Appeals erred in describing the prohibition as justified only by such concerns. The per se rules also reflect a long-standing judgment that the prohibited practices by their nature have "a substantial potential for impact on competition." *Jefferson Parish . . . .*

The per se rules in antitrust law serve purposes analogous to per se restrictions upon, for example, stunt flying in congested areas or speeding. Laws prohibiting stunt flying or setting speed limits are justified by the State's interest in protecting human life and property. Perhaps most violations of such rules actually cause no harm. No doubt many experienced drivers and pilots can operate much more safely, even at prohibited speeds, than the average citizen.

If the especially skilled drivers and pilots were to paint messages on their cars, or attach streamers to their planes, their conduct would have an expressive component. High speeds and unusual maneuvers would help to draw attention to their messages. Yet the laws may nonetheless be enforced against these skilled persons without proof that their conduct was actually harmful or dangerous.

In part, the justification for these per se rules is rooted in administrative convenience. They are also supported, however, by the observation that every speeder and every stunt pilot poses some threat to the community. An unpredictable event may overwhelm the skills of the best driver or pilot, even if the proposed course of action was entirely prudent when initiated. A bad driver going slowly may be more dangerous that a good driver going quickly, but a good driver who obeys the law is safer still.

So it is with boycotts and price fixing. Every such horizontal arrangement among competitors poses some threat to the free market. A small participant in the market is, obviously, less likely to cause persistent damage than a large participant. Other participants in the market may act quickly and effectively to take the small participant's place. For reasons including market inertia and information failures, however, a small conspirator may be able to impede competition over some period of time. Given an appropriate set of circumstances and some luck, the period can be long enough to inflict real injury upon particular consumers or competitors. . . .

Of course, some boycotts and some price-fixing agreements are more pernicious than others; some are only partly successful, and some may only succeed when they are buttressed by other causative factors, such as political influence. But an assumption that, absent proof of market power, the boycott disclosed by this record was totally harmless—when overwhelming testimony demonstrated that it almost produced a crisis in the administration of criminal justice in the District and when it achieved its economic goal—is flatly inconsistent with the clear course of our antitrust jurisprudence. Conspirators need not achieve the dimensions of a monopoly, or even a degree of market power any greater than that already disclosed by this record, to warrant condemnation under the antitrust laws. . . .

The judgment of the Court of Appeals is accordingly reversed insofar as that court held the *per se* rules inapplicable to the lawyers' boycott[19]. . . .

Questions on *Trial Lawyer's Ass'n*

1. Isn't any boycott against selling at rates below $35 the same as a price-fixing agreement to charge $35?

2. Even if other social welfare justifications are inadmissible, should the justification that an agreement aims to further a constitutional right be inadmissible too?

   a. Does this case fall into the general rule that one cannot argue that prices should be elevated to achieve quality?

   b. Is there any way to assess the justification here without inquiring into the reasonableness of prices?

---

19. In response to JUSTICE BRENNAN's opinion, and particularly to its observation that some concerted arrangements that might be characterized as "group boycotts" may not merit *per se* condemnation, we emphasize that this case involves not only a boycott but also a horizontal price-fixing arrangement—a type of conspiracy that has been consistently analyzed as a *per se* violation for many decades. . . .

c. Would it be better to leave constitutional issues to adjudication rather than private enforcement? Do the defendants here have neutral incentives in deciding whether a violation of constitutional rights exists and what penalties should be imposed if it does?

3. Should a boycott be deemed outside of antitrust law or protected by the First Amendment if it was intended to have only a symbolic effect? Should the Court have to examine the defendants' market power to determine whether the boycott was symbolic?

a. What is the Court concerned would happen if it did?

b. Could that defense be cabined to particular cases?

c. Does this case cut back on any suggestion in *Northwest Stationers* that boycotts are per se illegal only if market power is shown, at least where as here the agreement is not ancillary to any productive business collaboration? Or does this case turn on the fact that the boycott here could also be characterized as price-fixing?

d. Does this case cut back on any suggestion in *Indiana Dentists* that the per se rule is limited to secondary boycotts or does not apply to professionals, at least where as here the boycotters have no procompetitive justification?

4. Does it seem plausible to you that the defendants did not have market power? Do we have any evidence of anticompetitive effects from which market power could be inferred, like any shortages in output or changes in prices? Is the District of Columbia the only purchaser of legal services, or does it compete with other cities and clients to buy legal services? If the District of Columbia were the only possible buyer of legal services, would that justify a price-fixing agreement by sellers to counter-vail D.C.'s buyer market power?

California Dental Ass'n v. FTC

526 U.S. 756 (1999).

■ JUSTICE SOUTER delivered the opinion of the Court.

[About 75% of California dentists belonged to the California Dental Association (CDA), and agreed to abide by its code of ethics. The CDA interpreted its provision against false or misleading advertising to prohibit: (1) advertising the quality of services, on the ground that those services are not susceptible to measurement or verification; and (2) price advertising that uses vague terms like "low fees" or "as low as" and does not fully disclose all variables, like the dollar amount of the undiscounted fee for each service, the amount of the discount, the length of time the discount is offered, and any other limitations. The FTC concluded this CDA position constituted an agreement to restrain advertising of quality and price that violated Sherman Act § 1, and thus violated FTC Act § 5, and the Court of Appeals affirmed under a truncated rule of reason analysis.

The FTC Act covers both for-profits and nonprofits that carry on business for the profit of their members, and the Supreme Court concluded the CDA fell into the latter category because it] provides substantial economic benefit to its for-profit members. [The court also concluded] that where, as here, any anticompetitive effects of given restraints are far from intuitively obvious, the rule of reason demands a more thorough enquiry into the consequences of those restraints than the Court of Appeals performed. . . .

In *NCAA* we held that a "naked restraint on price and output requires some competitive justification even in the absence of a detailed market analysis." Elsewhere, we held that "no elaborate industry analysis is required to demonstrate the anticompetitive character of" horizontal agreements among competitors to refuse to discuss prices, *Professional Engineers*, or to withhold a particular desired service, *Indiana Dentists*. In each of these cases, which have formed the basis for what has come to be called abbreviated or "quick-look" analysis under the rule of reason, an observer with even a rudimentary understanding of economics could conclude that the arrangements in question would have an anticompetitive effect on customers and markets. In *NCAA*, the league's television plan expressly limited output (the number of games that could be televised) and fixed a minimum price. In *Professional Engineers*, the restraint was "an absolute ban on competitive bidding." In *Indiana Dentists*, the restraint was "a horizontal agreement among the participating dentists to withhold from their customers a particular service that they desire." As in such cases, quick-look analysis carries the day when the great likelihood of anticompetitive effects can easily be ascertained.

The case before us, however, fails to present a situation in which the likelihood of anticompetitive effects is comparably obvious. Even on JUSTICE BREYER'S view that bars on truthful and verifiable price and quality advertising are prima facie anticompetitive, and place the burden of procompetitive justification on those who agree to adopt them, the very issue at the threshold of this case is whether professional price and quality advertising is sufficiently verifiable in theory and in fact to fall within such a general rule. Ultimately our disagreement with JUSTICE BREYER turns on our different responses to this issue. Whereas he accepts, as the Ninth Circuit seems to have done, that the restrictions here were like restrictions on advertisement of price and quality generally, it seems to us that the CDA's advertising restrictions might plausibly be thought to have a net procompetitive effect, or possibly no effect at all on competition. The restrictions on both discount and nondiscount advertising are, at least on their face, designed to avoid false or deceptive advertising in a market characterized by striking disparities between the information available to the professional and the patient.[10] Cf. Carr & Mathewson, The Economics of Law Firms: A Study in the Legal Organization of the Firm, 33 J. Law & Econ. 307, 309 (1990) (explaining that in a market for complex professional services,

---

10. "The fact that a restraint operates upon a profession as distinguished from a business is, of course, relevant in determining whether that particular restraint violates the Sherman Act. It would be unrealistic to view the practice of professions as interchangeable with other business activities, and automatically to apply to the professions antitrust concepts which originated in other areas. The public service aspect, and other features of the professions, may require that a particular practice, which could properly be viewed as a violation of the Sherman Act in another context, be treated differently." Goldfarb v. Virginia State Bar, 421 U.S. 773, 788–789, n.17 (1975).

"inherent asymmetry of knowledge about the product" arises because "professionals supplying the good are knowledgeable [whereas] consumers demanding the good are uninformed"); Akerlof, The Market for "Lemons": Quality Uncertainty and the Market Mechanism, 84 Q.J. Econ. 488 (1970) (pointing out quality problems in market characterized by asymmetrical information). In a market for professional services, in which advertising is relatively rare and the comparability of service packages not easily established, the difficulty for customers or potential competitors to get and verify information about the price and availability of services magnifies the dangers to competition associated with misleading advertising.

What is more, the quality of professional services tends to resist either calibration or monitoring by individual patients or clients, partly because of the specialized knowledge required to evaluate the services, and partly because of the difficulty in determining whether, and the degree to which, an outcome is attributable to the quality of services (like a poor job of tooth-filling) or to something else (like a very tough walnut). Patients' attachments to particular professionals, the rationality of which is difficult to assess, complicate the picture even further. The existence of such significant challenges to informed decisionmaking by the customer for professional services immediately suggests that advertising restrictions arguably protecting patients from misleading or irrelevant advertising call for more than cursory treatment as obviously comparable to classic horizontal agreements to limit output or price competition.

The explanation proffered by the Court of Appeals for the likely anticompetitive effect of the CDA's restrictions on discount advertising began with the unexceptionable statements that "price advertising is fundamental to price competition," and that "[r]estrictions on the ability to advertise prices normally make it more difficult for consumers to find a lower price and for dentists to compete on the basis of price." The court then acknowledged that, according to the CDA, the restrictions nonetheless furthered the "legitimate, indeed procompetitive, goal of preventing false and misleading price advertising." The Court of Appeals might, at this juncture, have recognized that the restrictions at issue here are very far from a total ban on price or discount advertising, and might have considered the possibility that the particular restrictions on professional advertising could have different effects from those "normally" found in the commercial world, even to the point of promoting competition by reducing the occurrence of unverifiable and misleading across-the-board discount advertising. Instead, the Court of Appeals confined itself to the brief assertion that the "CDA's disclosure requirements appear to prohibit across-the-board discounts because it is simply infeasible to disclose all of the information that is required," followed by the observation that "the record provides no evidence that the rule has in fact led to increased disclosure and transparency of dental pricing."

But these observations brush over the professional context and describe no anticompetitive effects. Assuming that the record in fact supports the conclusion that the CDA disclosure rules essentially bar advertisement of across-the-board discounts, it does not obviously follow that such a ban would have a net anticompetitive effect here.

Whether advertisements that announced discounts for, say, first-time customers, would be less effective at conveying information relevant to competition if they listed the original and discounted prices for checkups, X-rays, and fillings, than they would be if they simply specified a percentage discount across the board, seems to us a question susceptible to empirical but not a priori analysis. In a suspicious world, the discipline of specific example may well be a necessary condition of plausibility for professional claims that for all practical purposes defy comparison shopping. It is also possible in principle that, even if across-the-board discount advertisements were more effective in drawing customers in the short run, the recurrence of some measure of intentional or accidental misstatement due to the breadth of their claims might leak out over time to make potential patients skeptical of any such across-the-board advertising, so undercutting the method's effectiveness. Cf. Akerlof, 84 Q.J. Econ., at 495 (explaining that "dishonest dealings tend to drive honest dealings out of the market"). It might be, too, that across-the-board discount advertisements would continue to attract business indefinitely, but might work precisely because they were misleading customers, and thus just because their effect would be anticompetitive, not procompetitive. Put another way, the CDA's rule appears to reflect the prediction that any costs to competition associated with the elimination of across-the-board advertising will be outweighed by gains to consumer information (and hence competition) created by discount advertising that is exact, accurate, and more easily verifiable (at least by regulators). As a matter of economics this view may or may not be correct, but it is not implausible, and neither a court nor the Commission may initially dismiss it as presumptively wrong.[12]

In theory, it is true, the Court of Appeals neither ruled out the plausibility of some procompetitive support for the CDA's requirements nor foreclosed the utility of an evidentiary discussion on the point. The court indirectly acknowledged the plausibility of procompetitive justifications for the CDA's position when it stated that "the record provides no evidence that the rule has in fact led to increased disclosure and transparency of dental pricing." But because petitioner alone would have had the incentive to introduce such evidence, the statement sounds as though the Court of Appeals may have thought it was justified without further analysis to shift a burden to the CDA to adduce hard evidence of the procompetitive nature of its policy; the court's adversion to empirical evidence at the moment of this implicit burden-shifting underscores the leniency of its enquiry into evidence of the restrictions' anticompetitive effects.

---

12. JUSTICE BREYER suggests that our analysis is "of limited relevance" because "the basic question is whether this ... theoretically redeeming virtue in fact offsets the restrictions' anticompetitive effects in this case." He thinks that the Commission and the Court of Appeals "adequately answered that question," but the absence of any empirical evidence on this point indicates that the question was not answered, merely avoided by implicit burden-shifting of the kind accepted by JUSTICE BREYER. The point is that before a theoretical claim of anticompetitive effects can justify shifting to a defendant the burden to show empirical evidence of procompetitive effects, as quick-look analysis in effect requires, there must be some indication that the court making the decision has properly identified the theoretical basis for the anticompetitive effects and considered whether the effects actually are anticompetitive. Where, as here, the circumstances of the restriction are somewhat complex, assumption alone will not do.

The Court of Appeals was comparably tolerant in accepting the sufficiency of abbreviated rule-of-reason analysis as to the nonprice advertising restrictions. The court began with the argument that "[t]hese restrictions are in effect a form of output limitation, as they restrict the supply of information about individual dentists' services." Although this sentence does indeed appear as cited, it is puzzling, given that the relevant output for antitrust purposes here is presumably not information or advertising, but dental services themselves. The question is not whether the universe of possible advertisements has been limited (as assuredly it has), but whether the limitation on advertisements obviously tends to limit the total delivery of dental services. The court came closest to addressing this latter question when it went on to assert that limiting advertisements regarding quality and safety "prevents dentists from fully describing the package of services they offer," adding that "[t]he restrictions may also affect output more directly, as quality and comfort advertising may induce some customers to obtain nonemergency care when they might not otherwise do so." This suggestion about output is also puzzling. If quality advertising actually induces some patients to obtain more care than they would in its absence, then restricting such advertising would reduce the demand for dental services, not the supply; and it is of course the producers' supply of a good in relation to demand that is normally relevant in determining whether a producer-imposed output limitation has the anticompetitive effect of artificially raising prices.[13]

Although the Court of Appeals acknowledged the CDA's view that "claims about quality are inherently unverifiable and therefore misleading," it responded that this concern "does not justify banning all quality claims without regard to whether they are, in fact, false or misleading." As a result, the court said, "the restriction is a sufficiently naked restraint on output to justify quick look analysis." The court assumed, in these words, that some dental quality claims may escape justifiable censure, because they are both verifiable and true. But its implicit assumption fails to explain why it gave no weight to the countervailing, and at least equally plausible, suggestion that restricting difficult-to-verify claims about quality or patient comfort would have a procompetitive effect by preventing misleading or false claims that distort the market. It is, indeed, entirely possible to understand the CDA's restrictions on unverifiable quality and comfort advertising as nothing more than a procompetitive ban on puffery, cf. *Bates*, 433 U.S., at 366 (claims relating to the quality of legal services "probably are not susceptible of precise measurement or verification and, under some circumstances, might well be deceptive or misleading to the public, or even false"); id., at 383–384, ("[A]dvertising claims as to the

---

13. JUSTICE BREYER wonders if we "mea[n] this statement as an argument against the anticompetitive tendencies that flow from an agreement not to advertise service quality." But as the preceding sentence shows, we intend simply to question the logic of the Court of Appeals's suggestion that the restrictions are anticompetitive because they somehow "affect output," presumably with the intent to raise prices by limiting supply while demand remains constant. We do not mean to deny that an agreement not to advertise service quality might have anticompetitive effects. We merely mean that, absent further analysis of the kind JUSTICE BREYER undertakes, it is not possible to conclude that the net effect of this particular restriction is anticompetitive.

quality of services . . . are not susceptible of measurement or verification; accordingly, such claims may be so likely to be misleading as to warrant restriction'') . . .

The point is not that the CDA's restrictions necessarily have the procompetitive effect claimed by the CDA; it is possible that banning quality claims might have no effect at all on competitiveness if, for example, many dentists made very much the same sort of claims. And it is also of course possible that the restrictions might in the final analysis be anticompetitive. The point, rather, is that the plausibility of competing claims about the effects of the professional advertising restrictions rules out the indulgently abbreviated review to which the Commission's order was treated. The obvious anticompetitive effect that triggers abbreviated analysis has not been shown.

In light of our focus on the adequacy of the Court of Appeals's analysis, JUSTICE BREYER's thorough-going, de novo antitrust analysis contains much to impress on its own merits but little to demonstrate the sufficiency of the Court of Appeals's review. The obligation to give a more deliberate look than a quick one does not arise at the door of this Court and should not be satisfied here in the first instance. Had the Court of Appeals engaged in a painstaking discussion in a league with JUSTICE BREYER's (compare his 14 pages with the Ninth Circuit's 8), and had it confronted the comparability of these restrictions to bars on clearly verifiable advertising, its reasoning might have sufficed to justify its conclusion. Certainly JUSTICE BREYER's treatment of the antitrust issues here is no "quick look." Lingering is more like it, and indeed JUSTICE BREYER, not surprisingly, stops short of endorsing the Court of Appeals's discussion as adequate to the task at hand.

Saying here that the Court of Appeals's conclusion at least required a more extended examination of the possible factual underpinnings than it received is not, of course, necessarily to call for the fullest market analysis. Although we have said that a challenge to a "naked restraint on price and output" need not be supported by "a detailed market analysis" in order to "requir[e] some competitive justification," *NCAA*, it does not follow that every case attacking a less obviously anticompetitive restraint (like this one) is a candidate for plenary market examination. The truth is that our categories of analysis of anticompetitive effect are less fixed than terms like "per se," "quick look," and "rule of reason" tend to make them appear. We have recognized, for example, that "there is often no bright line separating per se from Rule of Reason analysis," since "considerable inquiry into market conditions" may be required before the application of any so-called "per se" condemnation is justified. *Id.* . . . As the circumstances here demonstrate, there is generally no categorical line to be drawn between restraints that give rise to an intuitively obvious inference of anticompetitive effect and those that call for more detailed treatment. What is required, rather, is an enquiry meet for the case, looking to the circumstances, details, and logic of a restraint. The object is to see whether the experience of the market has been so clear, or necessarily will be, that a confident conclusion about the principal tendency of a restriction will follow from a quick (or at least quicker) look, in place of a more sedulous one. And of course what we see may vary over time, if rule-of-reason analyses in case after case reach identical conclusions. For now, at least, a less quick look was required for the initial assessment of the tendency of these professional advertising restrictions. Because the Court of Appeals did not scrutinize the assumption of relative anticompetitive tendencies, we vacate the judgment and remand the case for a fuller consideration of the issue....

■ JUSTICE BREYER, with whom JUSTICE STEVENS, JUSTICE KENNEDY, and JUSTICE GINSBURG join, concurring in part and dissenting in part....

... I would not simply ask whether the restraints at issue are anticompetitive overall. Rather, like the Court of Appeals (and the Commission), I would break that question down into four classical, subsidiary antitrust questions: (1) What is the specific restraint at issue? (2) What are its likely anticompetitive effects? (3) Are there offsetting procompetitive justifications? (4) Do the parties have sufficient market power to make a difference?

A

The most important question is the first: What are the specific restraints at issue? Those restraints do not include merely the agreement to which the California Dental Association's (Dental Association or Association) ethical rule literally refers, namely, a promise to refrain from advertising that is " 'false or misleading in any material respect.' " Instead, the Commission found a set of restraints arising out of the way the Dental Association implemented this innocent-sounding ethical rule in practice, through advisory opinions, guidelines, enforcement policies, and review of membership applications. As implemented, the ethical rule reached beyond its nominal target, to prevent truthful and nondeceptive advertising. In particular, the Commission determined that the rule, in practice:

> (1) "precluded advertising that characterized a dentist's fees as being low, reasonable, or affordable,"

> (2) "precluded advertising ... of across the board discounts," and

> (3) "prohibit[ed] all quality claims,"....

B

Do each of the three restrictions mentioned have "the potential for genuine adverse effects on competition"? *Indiana Dentists*. I should have thought that the anticompetitive tendencies of the three restrictions were obvious. An agreement not to advertise that a fee is reasonable, that service is inexpensive, or that a customer will receive a discount makes it more difficult for a dentist to inform customers that he charges a lower price. If the customer does not know about a lower price, he will find it more difficult to buy lower price service. That fact, in turn, makes it less likely that a dentist will obtain more customers by offering lower prices. And that likelihood means that dentists will prove less likely to offer lower prices....

The restrictions on the advertising of service quality also have serious anticompetitive tendencies. This is not a case of "mere puffing," as the FTC recognized.... [S]ome parents may ... want to know that a particular dentist makes a point of "gentle care." Others may want to know about

1–year dental work guarantees. To restrict that kind of service quality advertisement is to restrict competition over the quality of service itself, for, unless consumers know, they may not purchase, and dentists may not compete to supply that which will make little difference to the demand for their services. That, at any rate, is the theory of the Sherman Act. And it is rather late in the day for anyone to deny the significant anticompetitive tendencies of an agreement that restricts competition in any legitimate respect, let alone one that inhibits customers from learning about the quality of a dentist's service....

C

... The Association, the argument goes, had to prevent dentists from engaging in the kind of truthful, nondeceptive advertising that it banned in order effectively to stop dentists from making unverifiable claims about price or service quality, which claims would mislead the consumer.

The problem with this or any similar argument is an empirical one. Notwithstanding its theoretical plausibility, the record does not bear out such a claim.... [T]he Court of Appeals wrote, in respect to the price restrictions, that "the record provides no evidence that the rule has in fact led to increased disclosure and transparency of dental pricing." With respect to quality advertising, the Commission stressed that the Association "offered no convincing argument, let alone evidence, that consumers of dental services have been, or are likely to be, harmed by the broad categories of advertising it restricts." Nor did the Court of Appeals think that the Association's unsubstantiated contention that "claims about quality are inherently unverifiable and therefore misleading" could "justify banning all quality claims without regard to whether they are, in fact, false or misleading."

With one exception, my own review of the record reveals no significant evidentiary support for the proposition that the Association's members must agree to ban truthful price and quality advertising in order to stop untruthful claims. The one exception is the obvious fact that one can stop untruthful advertising if one prohibits all advertising. But since the Association made virtually no effort to sift the false from the true, that fact does not make out a valid antitrust defense.

In the usual Sherman Act § 1 case, the defendant bears the burden of establishing a procompetitive justification. See *Professional Engineers*.... And the Court of Appeals was correct when it concluded that no such justification had been established here.

D

I shall assume that the Commission must prove one additional circumstance, namely, that the Association's restraints would likely have made a real difference in the marketplace. The Commission ... found that the Association did possess enough market power to make a difference. In at least one region of California, the mid-Peninsula, its members accounted for more than 90% of the marketplace; on average they accounted for 75%. In addition, entry by new dentists into the market place is fairly difficult. Dental education is expensive (leaving graduates of dental school with

$50,000–$100,000 of debt), as is opening a new dentistry office (which costs $75,000–$100,000). And Dental Association members believe membership in the Association is important, valuable, and recognized as such by the public.

These facts, in the Court of Appeals' view, were sufficient to show "enough market power to harm competition through [the Association's] standard setting in the area of advertising." And that conclusion is correct. Restrictions on advertising price discounts in Palo Alto may make a difference because potential patients may not respond readily to discount advertising by the handful (10%) of dentists who are not members of the Association. And that fact, in turn, means that the remaining 90% will prove less likely to engage in price competition. Facts such as these have previously led this Court to find market power—unless the defendant has overcome the showing with strong contrary evidence. *See, e.g., Indiana Dentists*. I can find no reason for departing from that precedent here.

... [In] *Indiana Dentists* ... the Court found that an agreement by dentists not to submit dental X rays to insurers violated the rule of reason. The anticompetitive tendency of that agreement was to reduce competition among dentists in respect to their willingness to submit X rays to insurers—a matter in respect to which consumers are relatively indifferent, as compared to advertising of price discounts and service quality, the matters at issue here. The redeeming virtue in *Indiana Dentists* was the alleged undesirability of having insurers consider a range of matters when deciding whether treatment was justified—a virtue no less plausible, and no less proved, than the virtue offered here. The "power" of the dentists to enforce their agreement was no greater than that at issue here (control of 75% to 90% of the relevant markets). It is difficult to see how the two cases can be reconciled....

Questions on *California Dental*

1. Why isn't this a naked restraint? What does the Court mean by saying anticompetitive effects must be "intuitively obvious"?

a. Does it mean that anticompetitive effects must be empirically proven? If so, when would abbreviated rule-of-reason review ever apply?

b. Does it mean that the agreement must be a restraint on output or price?

c. Does it mean that the agreement must not have a theoretically plausible procompetitive justification, that is some theory that might explain why the restraint would increase market output?

2. Was there a plausible procompetitive justification here? What was it?

a. Was this justification ancillary to any productive business collaboration? Even if the restraint here did procompetitively cure a market for lemons problem, should professionals be able to regulate their own market failures like this? Are they financially disinterested when they do so? Politically accountable?

b. Why isn't a less restrictive alternative:

i.   having the Association give consumers more information, such as giving a seal of approval for nondeceptive dentists?

ii.   having the voluminous disclosure made to the Association, rather than to consumers, so that the Association could determine whether the price and quality claims made in advertisements were accurate?

iii.   having the government decide whether to regulate to address any market failure?

3.   Is *Indiana Dentists* distinguishable?

a.   Did the defendants in *Indiana Dentists* offer any procompetitive justification?

b.   Was it accurate to say the restraint in *Indiana Dentists* was on the output of a service, whereas here it was only on advertising? Is information sometimes a product and sometimes not?

4.   Given that the majority and dissent seem to agree that the restraints in theory have both anticompetitive potential and a plausible procompetitive justification, what do they actually disagree about? How would each allocate the burdens and orders of proof?

Burdens and Orders of Theory and Proof after *California Dental*

After *California Dental,* the U.S. caselaw appears to adopt the following complex order in which theoretical and empirical claims must be made under Sherman Act § 1.

Step 1. Plaintiff must allege an agreement that theoretically has anticompetitive potential. If it does, the court goes to step 2.

Step 2. Defendants must respond by articulating a theoretically plausible claim that there exists a procompetitive justification for which the restraint was reasonably necessary.

a.   If the defendants fail to do so, they lose summarily, and it doesn't really matter whether we call it a per se rule or a naked restraint under the rule of reason. *See Trenton Potteries; Klor's; Professional Engineers; Indiana Dentists; Trial Lawyers.*

b.   If the defendants can articulate a theoretically plausible procompetitive justification for which the restraint is reasonably necessary, then treatment varies depending on other factors:

i.   If the restraint at issue is reasonably necessary to advance the procompetitive purposes of productive business collaboration among those defendants (that is, a collaboration that actually has some business product), then the court moves to step 3, which is the beginning of full scale rule of reason review. *See BMI; Northwest Stationers; Dagher.*

ii.   If the restraint is not alleged to be reasonably necessary to advance the procompetitive purposes of any productive business collaboration *and* is on price (or on a output level that would affect price), then the procompetitive justification is inadmissible, and the agreement is condemned under the per se rule. *See Maricopa.*

iii. For other restraints that are not reasonably necessary for any productive business collaboration, treatment likely varies depending on whether the defendants are professionals that traditionally engage in market self-regulation or are financially disinterested in the restraint.

(1) Professionals apparently get rule of reason review for such self-regulation even when they have a financial self-interest, at least when the regulation is directed at informational market defects, and thus can get to step 3 by articulating a procompetitive justification for which their restraint is reasonably necessary. *See California Dental.*

(2) Nonprofessionals probably do not enjoy the same rule of reason review for self-regulation unrelated to productive business collaborations, at least not if they are financially interested, and instead the agreement is summarily condemned under the per se rule. *See Fashion Originators.* But they may well enjoy rule of reason review and be able to go onto step 3 when they are financially disinterested in their restraint.

Step 3. If both sides have articulated theoretically plausible anti-and procompetitive effects in a way that triggers full-scale rule of reason review, then the plaintiff has the burden of producing empirical evidence of the anticompetitive effects under the rule of reason. *See California Dental.* Such anticompetitive effects can be shown by direct evidence or inferred from market power. *See Indiana Dentists.* If the plaintiff does prove anticompetitive effects, then the court moves to step 4.

Step 4. Given evidence of actual anticompetitive effects, the defendant has the burden of producing empirical evidence to support the claimed procompetitive effects and to show that less restrictive alternatives could not equally achieve those procompetitive effects. *See California Dental.* If the defendant does, then the court moves to step 5.

Step 5. In the final stage, the tribunal weighs the anticompetitive and procompetitive evidence to determine which is greater. The plaintiff has the burden of persuasion on whether the net effect is anticompetitive.

Less Restrictive Alternatives. The issue of whether a less restrictive alternative exists is often considered a separate step, but really it can come up at both steps 2 and 4, because it bears on whether theoretically or empirically the restraint was reasonably necessary to advance the claimed procompetitive justification. Step 2 should be used to consider theoretical arguments that the restraint is not reasonably necessary to advance the procompetitive justification because a less restrictive alternative exists that could equally advance that justification. But often such arguments are controverted by theoretical arguments that the posited alternative was not feasible, would not equally advance the justification, or would not be less restrictive. Such a theoretical conflict suffices to show a plausible enough theoretical relationship between the justification and the restraint to survive step 2. Step 4 should be used to resolve such a theoretical conflict with empirical evidence about whether the posited alternatives are in fact feasible, useful and less restrictive.

Appropriate Litigation Stage. Although lower courts have not been entirely consistent, generally steps 1 and 2 should be conducted at the motion to dismiss stage, given that they are purely theoretical and do not require the costly development of evidence. Steps 3 and 4 should be conducted at the stage of summary judgment, because they turn on whether the empirical evidence demonstrates sufficient evidence of anti- and procompetitive effects. Step 5 should be conducted at trial because it turns on how that evidence is weighed by the factfinder.

Case C–309–99, Wouters

2002 E.C.R. I–1577

Pursuant to Article 28 of the Advocatenwet, the [Dutch bar authorities] adopted ... the 1993 Regulation ... [which prohibits practicing lawyers from entering into partnerships with accountants. The Supervisory Boards of the Rotterdam and Amsterdam Bars found two lawyers in violation of this provision for proposing to be part of partnerships that included both practicing lawyers and accounts. The lawyers appealed this decision up to the Dutch High Court, which referred various questions to the European Court of Justice.] ...

[T]he national court seeks, essentially, to ascertain whether a regulation such as the 1993 Regulation which, in order to guarantee the independence and loyalty to the client of members of the Bar who provide legal assistance in conjunction with members of other liberal professions, adopts universally binding rules governing the formation of multi-disciplinary partnerships, has the object or effect of restricting competition within the common market and is likely to affect trade between Member States.

In the alternative, the appellants in the main proceedings claim that, irrespective of its object, the 1993 Regulation produces effects that are restrictive of competition.

They maintain that multi-disciplinary partnerships of members of the Bar and accountants would make it possible to respond better to the needs of clients operating in an ever more complex and international economic environment.

Members of the Bar, having a reputation as experts in many fields, would be best placed to offer their clients a wide range of legal services and would, as partners in a multi-disciplinary partnership, be especially attractive to other persons active on the market in legal services.

Conversely, accountants would be attractive partners for members of the Bar in a professional partnership. They are experts in fields such as legislation on company accounts, the tax system, the organisation and restructuring of undertakings, and management consultancy. There would be many clients interested in an integrated service, supplied by a single provider and covering the legal as well as financial, tax and accountancy aspects of a particular matter.

The prohibition at issue in the main proceedings prohibits all contractual arrangements between members of the Bar and accountants which provide in any way for shared decision-making, profit-sharing or for the use of a common name, and this makes any form of effective partnership difficult.

By contrast, the Luxembourg Government claimed at the hearing that a prohibition of multi-disciplinary partnerships such as that laid down in the 1993 Regulation had a positive effect on competition. It pointed out that, by forbidding members of the Bar to enter into partnership with accountants, the national rules in issue in the main proceedings made it possible to prevent the legal services offered by members of the Bar from being concentrated in the hands of a few large international firms and, consequently, to maintain a large number of operators on the market.

It appears to the Court that the national legislation in issue in the main proceedings has an adverse effect on competition and may affect trade between Member States.

As regards the adverse effect on competition, the areas of expertise of members of the Bar and of accountants may be complementary. Since legal services, especially in business law, more and more frequently require recourse to an accountant, a multi-disciplinary partnership of members of the Bar and accountants would make it possible to offer a wider range of services, and indeed to propose new ones. Clients would thus be able to turn to a single structure for a large part of the services necessary for the organisation, management and operation of their business (the one-stop shop advantage).

Furthermore, a multi-disciplinary partnership of members of the Bar and accountants would be capable of satisfying the needs created by the increasing interpenetration of national markets and the consequent necessity for continuous adaptation to national and international legislation.

Nor, finally, is it inconceivable that the economies of scale resulting from such multi-disciplinary partnerships might have positive effects on the cost of services.

A prohibition of multi-disciplinary partnerships of members of the Bar and accountants, such as that laid down in the 1993 Regulation, is therefore liable to limit production and technical development within the meaning of Article [101(1)(b) TFEU].

It is true that the accountancy market is highly concentrated, to the extent that the firms dominating it are at present known as the big five and the proposed merger between two of them, Price Waterhouse and Coopers & Lybrand, gave rise to Commission Decision ... declaring a concentration to be compatible with the common market and the functioning of the EEA Agreement ...

On the other hand, the prohibition of conflicts of interest with which members of the Bar in all Member States are required to comply may constitute a structural limit to extensive concentration of law-firms and so reduce their opportunities of benefiting from economies of scale or of entering into structural associations with practitioners of highly concentrated professions.

In those circumstances, unreserved and unlimited authorisation of multi-disciplinary partnerships between the legal profession, the generally decentralised nature of which is closely linked to some of its fundamental features, and a profession as concentrated as accountancy, could lead to an overall decrease in the degree of competition prevailing on the market in legal services, as a result of the substantial reduction in the number of undertakings present on that market.

Nevertheless, in so far as the preservation of a sufficient degree of competition on the market in legal services could be guaranteed by less extreme measures than national rules such as the 1993 Regulation, which prohibits absolutely any form of multi-disciplinary partnership, whatever the respective sizes of the firms of lawyers and accountants concerned, those rules restrict competition.

As regards the question whether intra-Community trade is affected, it is sufficient to observe that an agreement, decision or concerted practice extending over the whole of the territory of a Member State has, by its very nature, the effect of reinforcing the partitioning of markets on a national basis, thereby holding up the economic interpenetration which the Treaty is designed to bring about.

That effect is all the more appreciable in the present case because the 1993 Regulation applies equally to visiting lawyers who are registered members of the Bar of another Member State, because economic and commercial law more and more frequently regulates transnational transactions and, lastly, because the firms of accountants looking for lawyers as partners are generally international groups present in several Member States.

However, not every agreement between undertakings or every decision of an association of undertakings which restricts the freedom of action of the parties or of one of them necessarily falls within the prohibition laid down in Article [101(1) TFEU]. For the purposes of application of that provision to a particular case, account must first of all be taken of the overall context in which the decision of the association of undertakings was taken or produces its effects. More particularly, account must be taken of its objectives, which are here connected with the need to make rules relating to organisation, qualifications, professional ethics, supervision and liability, in order to ensure that the ultimate consumers of legal services and the sound administration of justice are provided with the necessary guarantees in relation to integrity and experience. It has then to be considered whether the consequential effects restrictive of competition are inherent in the pursuit of those objectives. . . .

As regards members of the Bar, it has consistently been held that, in the absence of specific Community rules in the field, each Member State is in principle free to regulate the exercise of the legal profession in its territory. For that reason, the rules applicable to that profession may differ greatly from one Member State to another.

The current approach of the Netherlands, where Article 28 of the Advocatenwet [the law on lawyers] entrusts the Bar of the Netherlands with responsibility for adopting regulations designed to ensure the proper practice of the profession, is that the essential rules adopted for that purpose are, in particular, the duty to act for clients in complete independence and in their sole interest, the duty, mentioned above, to avoid all risk of conflict of interest and the duty to observe strict professional secrecy....

Thus, they require of members of the Bar that they should be in a situation of independence *vis-à-vis* the public authorities, other operators and third parties, by whom they must never be influenced. They must furnish, in that respect, guarantees that all steps taken in a case are taken in the sole interest of the client.

By contrast, the profession of accountant is not subject, in general, and more particularly, in the Netherlands, to comparable requirements of professional conduct.

As the Advocate General has rightly pointed out ..., there may be a degree of incompatibility between the advisory activities carried out by a member of the Bar and the supervisory activities carried out by an accountant. The written observations submitted by the respondent in the main proceedings show that accountants in the Netherlands perform a task of certification of accounts. They undertake an objective examination and audit of their clients' accounts, so as to be able to impart to interested third parties their personal opinion concerning the reliability of those accounts. It follows that in the Member State concerned accountants are not bound by a rule of professional secrecy comparable to that of members of the Bar, unlike the position under German law, for example.

The aim of the 1993 Regulation is therefore to ensure that, in the Member State concerned, the rules of professional conduct for members of the Bar are complied with, having regard to the prevailing perceptions of the profession in that State. The Bar of the Netherlands was entitled to consider that members of the Bar might no longer be in a position to advise and represent their clients independently and in the observance of strict professional secrecy if they belonged to an organisation which is also responsible for producing an account of the financial results of the transactions in respect of which their services were called upon and for certifying those accounts....

A regulation such as the 1993 Regulation could therefore reasonably be considered to be necessary in order to ensure the proper practice of the legal profession, as it is organised in the Member State concerned.

Furthermore, the fact that different rules may be applicable in another Member State does not mean that the rules in force in the former State are incompatible with [EU] law. Even if multi-disciplinary partnerships of lawyers and accountants are allowed in some Member States, the Bar of the Netherlands is entitled to consider that the objectives pursued by the 1993 Regulation cannot, having regard in particular to the legal regimes by which members of the Bar and accountants are respectively governed in the Netherlands, be attained by less restrictive means.

In light of those considerations, it does not appear that the effects restrictive of competition such as those resulting for members of the Bar practising in the Netherlands from a regulation such as the 1993 Regulation go beyond what is necessary in order to ensure the proper practice of the legal profession.

Having regard to all the foregoing considerations, the answer to be given to the second question must be that a national regulation such as the 1993 Regulation adopted by a body such as the Bar of the Netherlands does not infringe Article [101(1) TFEU], since that body could reasonably have considered that that regulation, despite the effects restrictive of competition that are inherent in it, is necessary for the proper practice of the legal profession, as organised in the Member State concerned.

Questions on *Wouters*

1.   Would it not have been more correct for the ECJ to conclude that the Dutch bar regulations fell within Article 101(1) (as they clearly restricted competition), but that they could be exempted under Article 101(3)? If the ECJ had considered that the regulations in question fell under Article 101(1), would the Dutch bar authorities have been able to demonstrate that the conditions to benefit from an exemption under Article 101(3) were met? Consider especially the first condition that the agreement must contribute "to improving the production or distribution of goods or to promoting technical or economic progress"?

2.   Does this case amount to a separate EU test for professional self-regulation?

3.   Couldn't there be less restrictive alternatives to continue to ensure the independence and professional secrecy of lawyers integrated in multidisciplinary partnerships?

4.   How would this case be treated if U.S. antitrust law applied? Although the case involves professional self-regulation, would U.S. courts conclude the justification was not procompetitive because it amounts to an argument that competition should be decreased to increase quality?

Other Nations' Treatment of Social Welfare Justifications

China allows otherwise illegal agreements if they protect the environment, provide disaster relief, help deal with recession, or advance trade interests, but these social welfare justifications require proof that the benefits are shared with consumers and that competition is not substantially restricted, unless the justification is advancing China's trade interests.[67] It is not clear whether this law would permit any agreement that actually harmed consumer welfare to advance social welfare justifications other than China's trade interests. Some other nations have antitrust laws whose stated purpose is to further not just efficiency or consumer welfare, but also other social welfare goals like promoting employment or equalizing business opportunities.[68] However, because these nations' statutes do not prioritize these varied purposes, it is unclear how they would treat an

---

67.   China Anti–Monopoly Law Art. 15(4).

68.   *See* Indonesia Competition Law Art. 2–3 (equalizing business opportunities); South Africa Competition Act § 2 (equalizing business opportunities, promoting employment, and increasing the ownership stakes of historically disadvantaged persons).

agreement that harms consumer welfare to promote other social welfare concerns.

Many nations allow a government agency or tribunal to provide advance authorization for an anticompetitive agreement on public interest grounds other than competition.[69] Other nations more narrowly exempt agreements by associations of professionals, small entrepreneurs, or consumers, when they meet certain conditions that might be deemed to advance social welfare concerns.[70]

Should social welfare concerns unrelated to competition or consumer welfare be considered? If so, which approach for considering them seems best?

The Policy Relevance of Nonprofit Status

It is sometimes argued that nonprofit firms should, like professionals, be treated more deferentially by antitrust law. Proper consideration of this issue requires us to put aside two misconceptions. First, notwithstanding their name, nonprofit firms *can* make a profit. Their organizational form bars them from *distributing* profits to investors, not from making profits, and they might spend those profits in ways that benefit their members or

---

69. *See* Australia Trade Practices Act §§ 88, 90 (if provides a public benefit); Colombia Competition Law Art. 1 (to defend stability of basic sectors producing goods or services of interest for the general economy); India Competition Act § 54 (if necessary in public interest or national security); Israel Restrictive Trade Practices Law §§ 9–10 (if in public interest, including protecting employment, improving balance of payments by reducing imports or import prices or increasing exports, preventing damage to industry important to national economy); New Zealand Commerce Act §§ 58, 61(6) (if public benefits outweighs lessening of competition); Singapore Competition Act Third Schedule § 4 (if "exceptional and compelling reasons of public policy"); South Africa Competition Act § 10(3)(b) (if promotes exports, stops industry decline, protects economic stability, or promotes small businesses or firms owned by historically disadvantaged persons); South Korea Fair Trade Act Art. 19(2) (if overcomes depression, restructures industry, rationalizes trade, or enhances small businesses); Taiwan Fair Trade Act, Article 14 (if beneficial to economy and public interest and either advances trade interests, strengthens small businesses, or reduces output to address fact that economic downturn has driven prices below production cost).

Brazil also allows a government agency to authorize otherwise illegal agreements if they are in the public interest or benefit the Brazilian economy, but only if they do not harm consumer welfare and meet at least three of the following four conditions: the agreement (1) produces efficiencies, (2) fairly shares those efficiencies with consumers; (3) does not eliminate competition in a substantial portion of the market, or (4) is the least restrictive alternative for achieving those efficiencies. *See* Brazil Antitrust Law No. 8,884, Art.54. Meeting those conditions would normally survive the U.S. rule of reason even though the U.S. rule excludes social welfare concerns.

70. *See* Indonesia Competition Law Art 50 (exempting "small-scale" businesses and cooperative business associations serving only members); Japan Antimonopoly Act § 22 (where associations neither engage in unfair trade practices nor substantially restrain competition in a way that unjustly increases prices, their actions are exempt if (i) the association is voluntarily formed for the purpose of providing mutual aid among small-scale entrepreneurs or consumers; (ii) members have equal voting rights and freedom to join or withdraw; and (iii) any profit distribution is specified); South Africa Competition Act Schedule 1 (Competition Commission can exempt professional association rules that are reasonably required to maintain professional standards). Canada does not exempt professional associations. *See* Calvin S. Goldman, *The Competition Act and the Professions* (1999), available at http://www.competition bureau.gc.ca/.

employees. Second, nonprofits *can* run a business. Indeed, most nonprofits are commercial (e.g., hospitals) in the sense that they get most of their revenue from sales. Some nonprofits are donative; that is, they get virtually all their revenue from donations, like the Red Cross. Others are mixed, like universities, which both charge for education and raise money through donations.

The argument for treating nonprofits differently than other firms turns on the premise that they evidence a behavioral difference that merits different treatment. One theory is that nonprofits are different because they don't run their businesses to maximize profits. This has been disputed factually, with the extent of the behavioral difference sufficiently unclear that vigorous debate has developed in the empirical literature about whether nonprofit hospitals act any differently than for-profit hospitals, with some studies suggesting they provide similar amounts of uncompensated care. If the premise is factually accurate, then the implications for antitrust review remain disputed. Should the courts apply more lax antitrust scrutiny because nonprofits are less motivated by profit-maximization? Or should courts apply tougher antitrust scrutiny because nonprofits remain financially interested in reducing competition and may dislike competition on ideological grounds as well as selfish grounds?

Another theory is that nonprofits do run businesses to maximize profits, but should be subjected to less strict antitrust scrutiny because they use their revenue more charitably. One question this raises is whether this is true, or whether they effectively distribute profits to members or employees. A prominent theory of nonprofit hospitals, for example, claims they are run to maximize the financial interests of medical staff. Even if empirically true, the issue remains whether on principle this justifies different treatment. Many firms could claim that their owners or stockholders use their profits charitably. Indeed, the famous *Standard Oil* case involved a corporation owned by John Rockefeller, who was famous for donating his profits to foundations and worthy causes. Likewise, the fact that Bill Gates has become a great philanthropist has not caused any different standards to be applied in this generation's *Microsoft* litigation. One might also think that this theory relies on social welfare justifications of the sort rejected in *Professional Engineers*.

The Legal Treatment of Nonprofits Under U.S. and EU Law

U.S. Antitrust Law. Under U.S. law, the Sherman Act applies to nonprofits. *See NCAA.* The Supreme Court has declined to adopt any presumption that nonprofits are not maximizing revenue, *id.,* and while some demonstrable behavioral difference might bear on the legality of their conduct, the Supreme Court has repeatedly made clear that good motives are insufficient, and the inquiry remains limited to competitive concerns. *Id.; Professional Engineers.* The Sherman Act, however, applies only to restraints on "trade or commerce." Thus, while the Act fully governs restraints a nonprofit might impose on any commercial activity involving the sale of products or services, it does not cover restraints on donative activities.

Other U.S. antitrust statutes do treat nonprofits differently. As explained in *California Dental*, the FTC Act doesn't cover a nonprofit unless it is carrying on activities that profit its members. The Robinson Patman Act exempts purchases by nonprofits for their own use.[71] Clayton Act § 7, the merger statute, refers to the FTC jurisdictional limitation, and thus might not apply to nonprofits, but most courts have held it does because it refers only to a jurisdictional limit in Clayton Act § 11 that excludes business regulated by other agencies.[72] In any event, Sherman Act § 1 probably provides the same merger review standards as Clayton Act § 7.[73]

EU Competition Law. The TFEU provisions on competition law apply to all "undertakings," which the ECJ has held "encompasses every entity engaged in an economic activity, regardless of the legal status of the entity and the way in which it is financed."[74] An "economic activity" is "any activity consisting in offering goods and services on a given market."[75] As long as they are engaged in such an economic activity, the Treaty covers corporations (public or private, for-profit or non-profit), partnerships, natural persons, professionals, industry associations, agricultural cooperatives, sport clubs or federations, or state agencies.

The ECJ has, however, adopted some limitations to its extensive definition of the notion of undertakings. First, the ECJ has concluded that entities involved in the performance of "a task in the public interest which forms part of the essential functions of the State" should not be deemed undertakings, such as an organization that provides air traffic control services pursuant to state delegation under an international convention.[76] Second, the ECJ has concluded that entities are not undertakings if they are engaged in a social function, like a sickness or welfare fund that provides "statutory benefits bearing no relation to the amount of the contributions."[77] Where the benefits provided do depend on the contributions made, then this exception does not apply.[78] Third, the ECJ has concluded that Article 106(2) can exempt firms, like post offices or electric utilities, that are obliged to provide universal services throughout the territory, at uniform tariffs and on similar quality conditions, and on terms which may not vary save in accordance with objective criteria applicable to customers.[79] This exemption applies only when the defendant shows (a)

---

71. *See* 15 U.S.C. § 13c.

72. United States v. Rockford Memorial Corp., 898 F.2d 1278, 1280 (7th Cir.1990); FTC v. University Health, 938 F.2d 1206, 1214–17 (11th Cir.1991).

73. 898 F.2d at 1281–82.

74. Case C–41/90, Klaus Höfner and Fritz Elser v. Macrotron GmbH, [1991] E.C.R. I–1979.

75. Case C–35/96, Commission v. Italy, [1998] E.C.R. I–3851.

76. Case C–364/92, Eurocontrol, [1994] E.C.R.I–43. See also Case C–343/95, Diego Cali, [1997] E.C.R. I–547.

77. Case C–159/91, Poucet et Pistre v. Assurances Générales de France, [1993] E.C.R. I–637.

78. Case C–244/94, Fédération Française des Sociétés d'Assurances and Others v. Ministère de l'Agriculture et de la Pêche, [1995] E.C.R. I–4013; Case C–67/96, Albany International BV v. Stichting Bedrijfspensioenfonds Textielindustrie, [1999] E.C.R. I–5751.

79. Case C–320/91, Criminal Proceedings against Paul Corbeau, [1993] E.C.R. I–2533, § 15; Case C–393/92, Municipality of Almelo and others v. NV Energiebedrijf Ijsselmij, [1994] E.C.R. I–1477, at § 48.

that applying EU competition law would make it impossible or unfeasible to perform such services,[80] and (b) the challenged restrictions on competition are absolutely necessary to performing such services and no less restrictive alternatives are available.[81]

United States v. Brown University

5 F.3d 658 (3d Cir. 1993).

■ COWEN, CIRCUIT JUDGE. . . .

I. FACTUAL AND PROCEDURAL BACKGROUND

. . . In 1958, MIT and the eight Ivy League schools formed the "Ivy Overlap Group" to collectively determine the amount of financial assistance to award to commonly admitted students. The facts concerning this Agreement are essentially undisputed. The Ivy Overlap Group expressly agreed that they would award financial aid only on the basis of demonstrated need. Thus, merit-based aid was prohibited. To ensure that aid packages would be comparable, the participants agreed to share financial information concerning admitted candidates and to jointly develop and apply a uniform needs analysis for assessing family contributions. . . .

[Congress has promulgated a method for calculating family contributions, from which schools may deviate as long as a student receiving federal aid does not receive more than under the Congressional Methodology]. The Ivy Overlap group . . . differed from the Congressional Methodology in several significant respects. . . . Each deviation resulted in less generous aid packages than under the Congressional Methodology.

Although each Ivy Overlap institution employed the same analysis to compute family contributions, discrepancies in the contribution figures still arose. To eliminate these discrepancies, the Overlap members agreed to meet in early April each year to jointly determine the amount of the family contribution for each commonly admitted student. Prior to this conference, the Overlap schools independently determined the family contribution of each student they admitted. . . .

At the two-day spring Overlap conference, the schools compared their family contribution figures for each commonly admitted student. Family contribution differences of less than $500 were ignored. When there was a disparity in excess of $500, the schools would either agree to use one school's figure or meet somewhere in the middle. Due to time constraints, the schools spent only a few minutes discussing an individual and the agreed upon figures were more a result of compromise than of a genuine effort to accurately assess the student's financial circumstances.

All Ivy Overlap Group institutions understood that failing to comply with the Overlap Agreement would result in retaliatory sanctions. Consequently, noncompliance was rare and quickly remedied. For example, in

---

80. Id. at § 49.

81. Case C–320/91, Criminal Proceedings against Paul Corbeau, [1993] E.C.R. I–2533, § 16–18.

1986, Princeton began awarding $1,000 research grants to undergraduates based on academic merit. After a series of complaints from other Overlap institutions who viewed these grants as a form of scholarship, Princeton terminated this program.

Stanford represented the Overlap schools' only meaningful competition for students. The Ivy Overlap Group, fearful that Stanford would lure a disproportionate number of the highest caliber students with merit scholarships, attempted to recruit Stanford into the group. Stanford declined this invitation.

In 1991, the Antitrust Division of the Justice Department brought this civil suit alleging that the Ivy Overlap Group unlawfully conspired to restrain trade in violation of section one of the Sherman Act, by (1) agreeing to award financial aid exclusively on the basis of need; (2) agreeing to utilize a common formula to calculate need; and (3) collectively setting, with only insignificant discrepancies, each commonly admitted students' family contribution toward the price of tuition. The Division sought only injunctive relief. All of the Ivy League institutions signed a consent decree with the United States, and only MIT proceeded to trial....

The district court entered judgment in favor of the Division....

II.   TRADE OR COMMERCE

... Section one, by its terms, does not apply to all conspiracies, but only to those which restrain "trade or commerce...."

The exchange of money for services, even by a nonprofit organization, is a quintessential commercial transaction. Therefore, the payment of tuition in return for educational services constitutes commerce. MIT concedes as much by acknowledging that its determination of the full tuition amount is a commercial decision.

We thus come to the crux of the issue—is providing financial assistance solely to needy students a selective reduction or "discount" from the full tuition amount, or a charitable gift? If this financial aid is a component of the process of setting tuition prices, it is commerce. See Catalano, Inc. v. Target Sales, Inc., 446 U.S. 643, 648 (1980) (agreement to eliminate discounts violates section one). If it is pure charity, it is not.

When MIT admits an affluent student, that student must pay approximately $25,000 annually (tuition plus room, board and incidental expenses) if he or she wishes to enroll at MIT. If MIT accepts a needy student and calculates that it will extend $10,000 in financial aid to that student, the student must pay approximately $15,000 to attend MIT. The student certainly is not free to take the $10,000 and apply it toward attendance at a different college. The assistance package is only available in conjunction with a complementary payment of approximately $15,000 to MIT. The amount of financial aid not only impacts, but directly determines the amount that a needy student must pay to receive an education at MIT. The financial aid therefore is part of the commercial process of setting tuition.

MIT suggests that providing aid exclusively to needy students and setting the amount of that aid is not commercial because the price needy students are charged is substantially below the marginal cost of supplying a year of education to an undergraduate student. Because profit maximizing companies would not engage in such economically abnormal behavior, MIT concludes that such activity must be noncommercial. MIT's concession, however, that setting the full tuition amount is a commercial decision subject to antitrust scrutiny undermines this argument. The full tuition figure, like the varying amounts charged to needy students, is significantly below MIT's marginal cost. Therefore, whether the price charged for educational services is below marginal cost is not probative of the commercial or noncommercial nature of the methodology utilized to determine financial aid packages.

The fact that MIT is not obligated to provide any financial aid does not transform that aid into charity. Similarly, discounting the price of educational services for needy students is not charity when a university receives tangible benefits in exchange. Regardless of whether MIT's motive is altruism, self-enhancement or a combination of the two, MIT benefits from providing financial aid. MIT admits that it competes with other Overlap members for outstanding students. By distributing aid, MIT enables exceptional students to attend its school who otherwise could not afford to attend. The resulting expansion in MIT's pool of exceptional applicants increases the quality of MIT's student body. MIT then enjoys enhanced prestige by virtue of its ability to attract a greater portion of the "cream of the crop." The Supreme Court has recognized that nonprofit organizations derive significant benefit from increased prestige and influence. See American Society of Mechanical Engineers, Inc. v. Hydrolevel Corp., 456 U.S. 556, 576. Although MIT could fill its class with students able to pay the full tuition, the caliber of its student body, and consequently the institution's reputation, obviously would suffer. Overlap affords MIT the benefit of an overrepresentation of high caliber students, with the concomitant institutional prestige, without forcing MIT to be responsive to market forces in terms of its tuition costs. By immunizing itself through the Overlap from competition for students based on a price/quality ratio, MIT achieves certain institutional benefits at a bargain....

III.   RESTRAINT OF TRADE ...

A.   *Is Overlap Illegal Per Se?*

The district court found that the "Ivy Overlap Group members, which are horizontal competitors, agreed upon the price which aid applicants and their families would have to pay to attend a member institution to which that student had been accepted." Based on this finding, the Division argues that MIT's conduct was per se unlawful price fixing. We disagree....

Per se rules of illegality are judicial constructs, and are based in large part on economic predictions that certain types of activity will more often than not unreasonably restrain competition. The economic models of behavior that spawn these predictions are not equally applicable in all situations. The fact that Overlap may be said to involve price-fixing in "a literal sense," therefore, does not mean that it automatically qualifies as per se illegal price-fixing. *BMI*....

Antitrust analysis is based largely on price theory, which "assures us that economic behavior ... is primarily directed toward the maximization of profits." R. Bork, The Antitrust Paradox 116 (1978). The rationale for treating professional organizations differently is that they tend to vary somewhat from this economic model. Specifically, while professional organizations aim to enhance the profits of their members, they and the professionals they represent may have greater incentives to pursue ethical, charitable, or other non-economic objectives that conflict with the goal of pure profit maximization. While it is well settled that good motives themselves "will not validate an otherwise anticompetitive practice," *NCAA*, courts often look at a party's intent to help it judge the likely effects of challenged conduct. Thus, when bona fide, non-profit professional associations adopt a restraint which they claim is motivated by "public service or ethical norms," economic harm to consumers may be viewed as less predictable and certain. In such circumstances, it is proper to entertain and weigh procompetitive justifications proffered in defense of an alleged restraint before declaring it to be unreasonable.

The same rationale counsels against declaring Overlap per se unreasonable. As a qualified charitable organization under 26 U.S.C. § 501(c)(3), MIT deviates even further from the profit-maximizing prototype than do professional associations. While non-profit professional associations advance the commercial interests of their for-profit constituents, MIT is, as its 501(c)(3) status suggests, an organization "operated exclusively for ... educational purposes ... no part of the net earnings of which inures to the benefit of any private shareholder or individual." 26 U.S.C. § 501(c)(3). This does not mean, of course, that MIT and other bona fide charitable organizations lack incentives to increase revenues. Nor does it necessarily mean that commercially motivated conduct of such organizations should be immune from per se treatment. Like the defendant associations in *Indiana Dentists* and *Professional Engineers*, however, MIT vigorously maintains that Overlap was the product of a concern for the public interest, here the undisputed public interest in equality of educational access and opportunity, and alleges the absence of any revenue maximizing purpose.

This alleged pure altruistic motive and alleged absence of a revenue maximizing purpose contribute to our uncertainty with regard to Overlap's anti-competitiveness, and thus prompts us to give careful scrutiny to the nature of Overlap, and to refrain from declaring Overlap per se unreasonable. We thus agree with the district court that Overlap must be judged under the rule of reason.

B.   *The Rule of Reason*

... MIT does not dispute that the stated purpose of Overlap is to eliminate price competition for talented students among member institutions. Indeed, the intent to eliminate price competition among the Overlap schools for commonly admitted students appears on the face of the Agreement itself. In addition to agreeing to offer financial aid solely on the basis of need and to develop a common system of needs analysis, the Overlap members agreed to meet each spring to compare data and to conform one another's aid packages to the greatest possible extent. Because the Overlap

Agreement aims to restrain "competitive bidding" and deprive prospective students of "the ability to utilize and compare prices" in selecting among schools, it is anticompetitive "on its face." *Professional Engineers....* We therefore agree [with the district court] that Overlap initially "requires some competitive justification even in the absence of a detailed market analysis." *Indiana Dentists* (quoting *NCAA*); see *Professional Engineers....*

At trial, MIT maintained that Overlap had the following procompetitive effects: (1) it improved the quality of the educational program at the Overlap schools; (2) it increased consumer choice by making an Overlap education more accessible to a greater number of students; and (3) it promoted competition for students among Overlap schools in areas other than price. The district court rejected each of these alleged competitive virtues, summarily concluding that they amounted to no more than non-economic social welfare justifications.

On appeal, MIT first contends that by promoting socio-economic diversity at member institutions, Overlap improved the quality of the education offered by the schools and therefore enhanced the consumer appeal of an Overlap education. The Supreme Court has recognized improvement in the quality of a product or service that enhances the public's desire for that product or service as one possible procompetitive virtue. See *NCAA*. The district court itself noted that it cannot be denied "that cultural and economic diversity contributes to the quality of education and enhances the vitality of student life"....

MIT also contends that by increasing the financial aid available to needy students, Overlap provided some students who otherwise would not have been able to afford an Overlap education the opportunity to have one. In this respect, MIT argues, Overlap enhanced consumer choice. The policy of allocating financial aid solely on the basis of demonstrated need has two obvious consequences. First, available resources are spread among more needy students than would be the case if some students received aid in excess of their need. Second, as a consequence of the fact that more students receive the aid they require, the number of students able to afford an Overlap education is maximized. In short, removing financial obstacles for the greatest number of talented but needy students increases educational access, thereby widening consumer choice. Enhancement of consumer choice is a traditional objective of the antitrust laws and has also been acknowledged as a procompetitive benefit. See *NCAA*.

Finally, MIT argues that by eliminating price competition among participating schools, Overlap channelled competition into areas such as curriculum, campus activities, and student-faculty interaction. As the Division correctly notes, however, any competition that survives a horizontal price restraint naturally will focus on attributes other than price. This is not the kind of procompetitive virtue contemplated under the Act, but rather one mere consequence of limiting price competition.

MIT next claims that beyond ignoring the procompetitive effects of Overlap, the district court erroneously refused to consider compelling social welfare justifications. MIT argues that by enabling member schools to maintain a steadfast policy of need-blind admissions and full need-based aid, Overlap promoted the social ideal of equality of educational access and opportunity....

The district court was not persuaded by the alleged social welfare values proffered for Overlap because it believed the Supreme Court's decisions in *Professional Engineers* and *Indiana Dentists* required a persuasive procompetitive justification, or a showing of necessity, neither of which it believed that MIT demonstrated.... Both the public safety justification rejected by the Supreme Court in *Professional Engineers* and the public health justification rejected by the Court in *Indiana Dentists* were based on the defendants' faulty premise that consumer choices made under competitive market conditions are "unwise" or "dangerous." Here MIT argues that participation in the Overlap arrangement provided some consumers, the needy, with additional choices which an entirely free market would deny them. The facts and arguments before us may suggest some significant areas of distinction from those in *Professional Engineers* and *Indiana Dentists* in that MIT is asserting that Overlap not only serves a social benefit, but actually enhances consumer choice. Overlap is not an attempt to withhold a particular desirable service from customers, as was the professional combination in Indiana Dentists, but rather it purports only to seek to extend a service to qualified students who are financially "needy" and would not otherwise be able to afford the high cost of education at MIT. Further, while Overlap resembles the ban on competitive bidding at issue in *Professional Engineers*, MIT alleges that Overlap enhances competition by broadening the socio-economic sphere of its potential student body. Thus, rather than suppress competition, Overlap may in fact merely regulate competition in order to enhance it, while also deriving certain social benefits. If the rule of reason analysis leads to this conclusion, then indeed Overlap will be beyond the scope of the prohibitions of the Sherman Act.

We note the unfortunate fact that financial aid resources are limited even at the Ivy League schools. A trade-off may need to be made between providing some financial aid to a large number of the most needy students or allowing the free market to bestow the limited financial aid on the very few most talented who may not need financial aid to attain their academic goals. Under such circumstances, if this trade-off is proven to be worthy in terms of obtaining a more diverse student body (or other legitimate institutional goals), the limitation on the choices of the most talented students might not be so egregious as to trigger the obvious concerns which led the Court to reject the "public interest" justifications in *Professional Engineers* and *Indiana Dentists*. However, we leave it for the district court to decide whether full funding of need may be continued on an individual institutional basis, absent Overlap, whether tuition could be lowered as a way to compete for qualified "needy" students, or whether there are other imaginable creative alternatives to implement MIT's professed social welfare goal.

We note too, however, that another aspect of the agreements condemned in *Professional Engineers* and *Indiana Dentists* was that those agreements embodied a strong economic self-interest of the parties to them. In *Professional Engineers*, the undisputed objective of the ban on competitive bidding was to maintain higher prices for engineering services than a free competitive market would sustain. The engineers' public safety justification "rest[ed] on the assumption that the agreement [would] tend to maintain price level; if it had no such effect, it would not serve its intended purpose." Likewise, the Court in *Indiana Dentists* characterized the dentists' agreement to withhold x-rays as an "attempt to thwart" the goal of "choosing the least expensive adequate course of dental treatment." Though not singled out by the Court in these two cases, the nature of the agreements made any public interest argument greatly suspect. To the extent that economic self-interest or revenue maximization is operative in Overlap, it too renders MIT's public interest justification suspect.... In the case sub judice, the quest for economic self-interest is professed to be absent, as it is alleged that the Overlap agreement was intended, not to obtain an economic profit in the form of greater revenue for the participating schools, but rather to benefit talented but needy prospective students who otherwise could not attend the school of their choice.

The nature of higher education, and the asserted procompetitive and pro-consumer features of the Overlap, convince us that a full rule of reason analysis is in order here....

It is most desirable that schools achieve equality of educational access and opportunity in order that more people enjoy the benefits of a worthy higher education. There is no doubt, too, that enhancing the quality of our educational system redounds to the general good. To the extent that higher education endeavors to foster vitality of the mind, to promote free exchange between bodies of thought and truths, and better communication among a broad spectrum of individuals, as well as prepares individuals for the intellectual demands of responsible citizenship, it is a common good that should be extended to as wide a range of individuals from as broad a range of socio-economic backgrounds as possible. It is with this in mind that the Overlap Agreement should be submitted to the rule of reason scrutiny under the Sherman Act.

We conclude that the district court was obliged to more fully investigate the procompetitive and noneconomic justifications proffered by MIT than it did when it performed the truncated rule of reason analysis. Accordingly, we will remand this case to the district court with instructions to evaluate Overlap using the full-scale rule of reason analysis outlined above....

Even if an anticompetitive restraint is intended to achieve a legitimate objective, the restraint only survives a rule of reason analysis if it is reasonably necessary to achieve the legitimate objectives proffered by the defendant.... The district court "questioned" whether the Overlap Agreement was "a necessary ingredient" to achieve the social welfare objectives offered by MIT. The district court implicitly concluded, and we agree, that to some extent the Overlap Agreement promoted equality of access to higher education and economic and cultural diversity. It thus turned directly to the second inquiry—whether a substantially less restrictive alternative, the free market coupled with MIT's institutional resolve, could achieve the same benefits. In a conclusory statement, the court found "no evidence supporting MIT's fatalistic prediction that the end of the Ivy

Overlap Group necessarily would sound the death knell of need-blind admissions or need-based aid." Although the district court acknowledged that the end of Overlap could herald the end of full need-based aid at MIT, it also observed that this was not an inevitability if indeed MIT counted full need-based aid among its priority institutional goals.

On remand if the district court, under a full scale rule of reason analysis, finds that MIT has proffered a persuasive justification for the Overlap Agreement, then the Antitrust Division of the Justice Department, the plaintiff in this case, must prove that a reasonable less restrictive alternative exists. The district court should consider, if and when the issue arises, whether the Antitrust Division has shown, by a preponderance of the evidence, that another viable option, perhaps the free market, can achieve the same benefits as Overlap.

Questions on *United States v. Brown*

1. Why is this a restraint on trade or commerce rather than on the distribution of charitable aid?

a. Is financial aid the same as price discrimination?

b. Or is it charity because the price of college is less than its costs? Does the answer turn on whether faculty are employees or de facto owners of the university? If the latter, is it accurate to call money spent on faculty "costs" rather than profit distributions?

c. Are students consumers or, instead, inputs to producing prestige for the university? Is prestige rather than profits what universities maximize? If universities do maximize prestige, does that cut in favor of the universities, or just suggest they are trying to fix monopsonistic low prices for the inputs they need to maximize their prestige?

2. Why doesn't the per se rule apply?

a. Isn't the effect and undisputed purpose here "to eliminate price competition for talented students"?

b. Isn't this a price-fixing agreement that isn't ancillary to any productive collaboration?

c. Should nonprofits have the same self-regulation powers (subject to court antitrust review) as professionals? Does this decision go beyond the professional cases because it allows restraints directly on price?

3. Would the court reach the same conclusion if Cambridge apartment owners agree to form cartel that price discriminates based on the wealth of tenant? What is the difference?

4. Does this agreement increase the total amount of financial aid?

a. If so, why is the aid always less generous than the Congressional methodology?

b. If it does, is that procompetitive?

5. Does the agreement alter the distribution of aid? From which students to which?

    a.   Does such redistribution increase consumer choice for all students or just some? Is this effect procompetitive?

    b.   Could the universities agree to fix faculty salaries and devote saved resources to financial aid? What's the difference between that hypothetical and this case?

    6.   Is it procompetitive to make students pick solely on educational grounds?

    a.   Why don't students have the same right to trade off price and quality as buyers of engineering services?

    b.   Doesn't all price-fixing leave only nonprice competition?

    7.   Does the agreement improve quality by increasing diversity?

    a.   Assuming schools agree diversity increases quality, doesn't that just mean diversity is part of merit? Why wouldn't schools have adequate incentives to individually pursue such merit without any agreement?

    b.   Doesn't the agreement prevent competition in offering merit scholarships to diversity applicants?

    8.   Would the following be a better argument for why this agreement might be procompetitive? Suppose the result of decreasing merit aid and increasing need-based aid is that those who otherwise would have received merit but not need-based aid will still go to college (because they can afford to) and in addition some who otherwise wouldn't have gone to college will go because of the increased need-based aid. If so, this agreement either increases the total output of students educated or increases the quality of the student body, if the universities do not expand their student body but instead become more selective. Further, to the extent that the quality of education turns on the quality of other students, increasing the quality of the student body by admitting more qualified needy students has positive externalities for other students as well. Is this argument any different than saying price discrimination can increase output? Is there more of an argument here that students who would have paid less (got more merit aid) without the agreement received a net benefit from the agreement?

    9.   This case was originally brought under the first Bush Administration. After the Third Circuit's decision, it was settled under the Clinton Administration. Under the settlement, MIT and the Ivy League schools cannot discuss or agree with other schools on the financial aid offered individual students, but can exchange financial data about each applicant, agree on general principles for determining financial aid, and have independent auditors review awards and report any gross disparities that might indicate a university was deviating from those principles. However, universities could only enter into the latter sorts of agreements if they adopted "need-blind and full-need" admission policies, which Harvard President Rudenstine complained would include only "a very small handful" of universities, excluding Brown University and perhaps other Ivy League universities. See William Honan, "M.I.T. Wins Right to Share Financial Aid Data in Antitrust Accord," N.Y. Times Dec. 23, 1993 at A13.

    a.   Should the government have agreed to this settlement? Could it have done better if the case had gone to the Supreme Court?

b.   Is this settlement likely to curb university coordination restraining price competition for students, when universities can agree on a general pricing policy and have an independent auditor report aggregate but not individual discrepancies? Wouldn't such a mechanism normally suffice for a cartel?

c.   What does President Rudenstine's stated concern about the financial implications of the settlement on aid expenditures suggest about whether the original agreement was increasing or reducing total university expenditures on aid?

d.   Is there any antitrust policy justifying the Antitrust Division's insistence that the Universities adopt more generous financial aid policies than they already had? Is that just a social welfare justification outside the confines of antitrust? Or is it a guarantee that the agreement was fulfilling its procompetitive purpose, rather than anticompetitively restraining the total amount of aid?

10.   After this settlement, Congress enacted a statute that gives universities that admit all students on a need-blind basis an antitrust exemption for using a common methodology or application for determining need, or for exchanging financial aid information through a third party, but no immunity for agreeing on the financial aid award of any individual student. *See* IMPROVING AMERICA'S SCHOOLS ACT OF 1994 § 568, 108 Stat. 4060 (1994). The initial three year provision was renewed for four years in 1997, for 7 more years in 2001, and for 7 more years in 2008. *See* NEED-BASED EDUCATIONAL AID ACT of 2008, 122 Stat. 3566 (2008). Should this antitrust exemption continue to get renewed? Was the statute right to effectively extend the settlement to universities with need-blind admissions that did not fully fund all need?

G.   DOES INTELLECTUAL PROPERTY LAW JUSTIFY AN ANTICOMPETITIVE RESTRAINT?

Many commentators on the patent-antitrust intersection frame the issue as raising an inherent tension because antitrust law aims to protect competition, whereas patent law creates monopolies that aim to eliminate competition in order to reward invention.[82] Under this framing, adjudicators must reconcile this tension as best they can, by determining which restraints desirably increase the reward the patent holder gets for its innovation, and whether that benefit offsets any anticompetitive effect.[83] This approach presumes that patent rights merit special treatment compared to other property rights.

This approach raises internal difficulties. The extent to which patent rewards are necessary to incentivize invention is unclear, and it is even less clear what incentive effect comes from any incremental increase in reward that would be produced by restraints associated with patents. One thus

---

82.   *See, e.g.,* Louis Kaplow, *The Patent–Antitrust Intersection: A Reappraisal*, 97 HARV. L. REV. 1813, 1817 (1984).

83.   *Id.* at 1816.

might doubt whether adjudicators have the capacity to balance any incremental incentives to innovate against the anticompetitive effects of the restraints at issue. Further, the actual doctrinal distinctions are often unclear or poorly related to such policy concerns. For example, why does U.S. law (as we shall see) treat licensing a patent with price conditions differently than selling the patented product with price conditions? Why does it treat licensing a patent with a price condition differently than licensing with a tying condition?

More fundamentally, one might dispute this entire way of framing the issue and instead conclude that patents are just another form of property right and should be treated no better or worse than any other property right.[84] Patent rights in fact do not necessarily create economic monopolies or ban competition. They merely provide a right to exclude others from a particular innovation. Such patent rights often compete with other patents or methods of accomplishing the same goal, and thus may or may not enjoy any monopoly or market power. Whether a patent confers monopoly power depends entirely on how much value the patent has compared to other market options. This is likewise true for other intellectual property rights, like copyright. The copyright to prevent others from copying this book, for example, confers no monopoly power on its authors (much as we wish it did), as long as competing antitrust books are regarded as reasonable substitutes by a sufficient number of buyers (hard as that possibility may be to fathom for our loyal reader).

One could say precisely the same about physical property rights, like the right to exclude rivals from a firm's plant. Such rights to exclude may or may not preclude competition or confer monopoly power, depending on how valuable that plant is compared to other market options. Whichever sort of property right we are talking about, its ability to preclude competition or create monopoly power turns on its economic value compared to the property rights held by others, not on some metaphysical distinction between the natures of the property rights. If a firm has one of the 50 patents that exist for making widgets, it will have no market power. If a firm owns the only plant capable of making widgets in the world, it likely has monopoly power.

To be sure, it may be the case that some patent restrictions have greater procompetitive effect or less anticompetitive effect than a comparable restriction on other property rights because of particular facts regarding the patent. But those facts must be identified rather than assumed. The courts have, however, sometimes struggled with this problem.

United States v. General Electric

272 U.S. 476 (1926).

■ MR. CHIEF JUSTICE TAFT delivered the opinion of the Court.

This is a bill in equity, brought by the United States ... to enjoin ... General Electric [and Westinghouse] ... from further violation of the Anti–

---

84. See Elhauge, *Defining Better Monopolization Standards*, 56 STANFORD LAW REVIEW 253, 304–05 (2003).

Trust Act ... [T]he case involves the validity of a license granted ... by [General Electric] to the Westinghouse Company to make, use, and sell lamps under the patents owned by the former. It was charged that the license in effect provided that the Westinghouse Company would follow prices and terms of sale from time to time fixed by [General Electric] and observed by it.... The District Court upon a full hearing dismissed the bill....

The General Electric Company is the owner of three patents.... These three patents cover completely the making of the modern electric lights with the tungsten filaments, and secure to the General Electric Company the monopoly of their making, using, and vending.

The total business in electric lights for the year 1921 was $68,300,000, and the relative percentages of business done by the companies were: General Electric, 69 percent.; Westinghouse, 16 percent.; other licensees, 8 percent.; and manufacturers not licensed, 7 percent....

... Conveying less than title to the patent or part of it, the patentee may grant a license to make, use, and vend articles under the specifications of his patent for any royalty, or upon any condition the performance of which is reasonably within the reward which the patentee by the grant of the patent is entitled to secure. It is well settled ... that where a patentee makes the patented article, and sells it, he can exercise no future control over what the purchaser may wish to do with the article after his purchase. It has passed beyond the scope of the patentee's rights.

But the question is a different one which arises when we consider what a patentee who grants a license to one to make and vend the patented article may do in limiting the licensee in the exercise of the right to sell. The patentee may make and grant a license to another to make and use the patented articles but withhold his right to sell them. The licensee in such a case acquires an interest in the articles made. He owns the material of them and may use them. But if he sells them he infringes the right of the patentee, and may be held for damages and enjoined. If the patentee goes further and licenses the selling of the articles, may he limit the selling by limiting the method of sale and the price? We think he may do so provided the conditions of sale are normally and reasonably adapted to secure pecuniary reward for the patentee's monopoly. One of the valuable elements of the exclusive right of a patentee is to acquire profit by the price at which the article is sold. The higher the price, the greater the profit, unless it is prohibitory. When the patentee licenses another to make and vend and retains the right to continue to make and vend on his own account, the price at which his licensee will sell will necessarily affect the price at which he can sell his own patented goods. It would seem entirely reasonable that he should say to the licensee, "Yes, you may make and sell articles under my patent but not so as to destroy the profit that I wish to obtain by making them and selling them myself." He does not thereby sell outright to the licensee the articles the latter may make and sell or vest absolute ownership in them. He restricts the property and interest the licensee has in the goods he makes and proposes to sell....

... [I]n ... Motion Picture Patents Co. v. Universal Film Co., 243 U. S. 502, [t]he patent ... covered a part of the mechanism used in motion picture exhibiting machines for feeding a film through the machine with a regular uniform and accurate movement so as not to expose the film to excessive strain or west. The license agreement contained a covenant on the part of the licensee that every machine sold by it should be sold under the restriction and condition that such exhibiting or projecting machines should be used solely for exhibiting or projecting motion pictures of the Motion Picture Patents Company. The [covenant was invalidated] . . . on the ground that the grant of the patent was of the exclusive right to use the mechanism and produce the result with any appropriate material and that the materials or pictures upon which the machine was operated were no part of the patented machine, or of the combination which produced the patented result.

. . . The price at which a patented article sells is certainly a circumstance having a more direct relation and is more germane to the rights of the patentee than the unpatented material with which the patented article may be used. Indeed, as already said, price fixing is usually the essence of that which secures proper reward to the patentee.

Nor do we think that the decisions of this court holding restrictions as to price of patented articles invalid apply to a contract of license like the one in this case. These cases really are only instances of the application of the principle . . . that a patentee may not attach to the article made by him or with his consent a condition running with the article in the hands of purchasers limiting the price at which one who becomes its owner for full consideration shall part with it. They do not consider or condemn a restriction put by a patentee upon his licensee as to the prices at which the latter shall sell articles which he makes and only can make legally under the license. . . .

For the reasons given, we sustain the validity of the license granted by [General Electric] to the Westinghouse Company. The decree of the District Court dismissing the bill is affirmed.

Questions on *General Electric*

1. *The Test:* The Court's decision appears to create a rule of per se *legality* whenever a patentee licenses its patent on any condition "the performance of which is reasonably within the reward" granted by the patent statute. How do we know imposing a price-fixing condition on the licensee is reasonably within the patent reward? Why isn't it beyond the scope of the exclusive power the patent confers?

2. *The License/Sale Distinction:* Why isn't it also within that reward to sell patented lamps to dealers on the condition that dealers charge no less than GE's dealerships do? Why does the first sale exhaust the patentee's interest but not the first license?

3. *The Pricing/Tying Distinction*: Why isn't it also within that reward to license the patent on the condition that the licensee purchase unpatented switches from GE? Couldn't the sale of unpatented items sometimes be the best way to measure the value of the patent and thus price discriminate in a way that most rewards the patentee?

4. *The Patent/Normal Property Distinction:* Is it also per se legal for GE to lease one of its 7 lamp-making plants to Westinghouse on the condition Westinghouse charges the same prices for lamps as GE? Why isn't that within the reward provided by real estate property law?

5. Can this case be resolved by the reasoning that the greater power not to license includes the lesser power to license on condition?

a. Would that be consistent with the Court's own doctrines that the greater power not to license does not include the lesser power to license with tying conditions, and that the greater power not to sell does not include the lesser power to sell on conditions restricting resale?

b. Would that be consistent with the implicit holding in *Palmer v. BRG* that the greater power not to license copyrights does not include the lesser power to license copyrights on the condition that the licensee not compete in the same geographic market as the licensor?

6. What are the possible procompetitive motives for licensing a patent to make lamps?

a. Why is it necessary to impose a price condition to advance those legitimate motives? Why couldn't GE just charge a royalty at or above its manufacturing profit margin?

b. If GE preferred a license with a pricing condition to a license with a high royalty, doesn't that prove the former must have been more profitable? And won't that increase the reward for innovation in a desirable way?

7. What are the possible anticompetitive effects of licensing lamps with a pricing condition?

a. If it could not license with the pricing condition what do you think GE would have done: (1) not license at all or (2) license without the pricing condition?

b. If Westinghouse were denied a license, what would do you think Westinghouse have done: (1) not produce lamps; or (2) produce a lamp without this patent? Does the answer depend on the value of the patent?

8. How can a court define which rewards are within the proper scope of the property right?

a. If Westinghouse already has or could develop a way of making lamps without the patent, isn't precluding that competition (and earning extra profits by doing so) outside the legitimate scope of the patent?

b. If Westinghouse does not have a way of making lamps without the patent, then isn't any pricing condition just choosing the profit-maximizing way of exploiting GE's patent (and rewarding the investment that created it) and thus within its legitimate scope?

c. Which is more likely here?

9. Couldn't we say the same for physical property rights? Suppose again that GE leases one of its 7 lamp-making plants to Westinghouse on the condition that Westinghouse charges the same prices for lamps as GE.

a. If Westinghouse already has or could develop a way of making lamps without that plant, isn't precluding that competition outside the legitimate scope of the real estate property right?

b. If Westinghouse does not have a way of making lamps without the plant, then isn't any pricing condition just choosing the profit-maximizing way of exploiting GE's real estate property right (and rewarding the investments in that property that made it so valuable) and thus within its legitimate scope?

c. Which would seem more likely in this sort of case? Would that be the case for all physical property leases one could imagine?

United States v. New Wrinkle, Inc.

342 U.S. 371 (1952).

■ MR. JUSTICE REED delivered the opinion of the Court.

This suit against New Wrinkle, Inc., and The Kay & Ess Co. was instituted . . . by the United States as a civil proceeding. . . . Defendants are charged with . . . conspiring to fix uniform minimum prices and to eliminate competition throughout substantially all of the wrinkle finish industry[3] of the United States by means of patent license agreements. . . . The District Court . . . entered separate judgments as to each defendant dismissing the complaint. . . .

In granting the motions of defendants, the District Court, of course, treated the allegations of the complaint as true. In substance the complaint charges that prior to and during 1937, defendant Kay & Ess was engaged in litigation with a named coconspirator, the Chadeloid Chemical Co., in regard to certain patents covering manufacture of wrinkle finish enamels, varnishes and paints. Each company claimed it controlled the basic patents on wrinkle finish, contending that the patents of the other were subservient to its own. Negotiations throughout 1937 resulted in a contract entered into by Kay & Ess and Chadeloid on November 2, 1937. This contract made provision for the organization of a new corporation, the defendant New Wrinkle. Both Kay & Ess and Chadeloid agreed to accept stock in the new company in exchange for assignments of their wrinkle finish patents. New Wrinkle was to grant patent licenses, incorporating agreements which fixed the minimum prices at which all licensed manufacturers might sell, to the manufacturers in the wrinkle finish industry, including Kay & Ess and Chadeloid. The price-fixing schedules were not to

---

3. " 'Wrinkle' finishes . . . are defined as enamels, varnishes and paints which have been compounded from such materials and by such methods as to produce when applied and dried, a hard wrinkled surface on metal or other material. Wrinkle finishes are widely used as coverings for the surfaces of typewriters, cash registers, motors, adding machines, and many other articles of manufacture. They have the following advantages over smooth finishes such as ordinary enamels and varnishes: a. One coat of wrinkle finish is sufficient for many purposes for which two or more coats of smooth finish would be required; b. Surfaces to which wrinkle finishes are to be applied need not be prepared as carefully as those which are to receive smooth finishes, since the wrinkle finishes cover small imperfections; and c. The original appearance of wrinkle-finished articles can be maintained with less cleaning and polishing than that of smooth-finished articles."

become operative until twelve of the principal producers of wrinkle finishes had subscribed to the minimum prices prescribed in the license agreements.

Pursuant to this arrangement, the complaint charges New Wrinkle was incorporated, and the patent rights of Kay & Ess and Chadeloid were transferred to it. In conjunction with other named companies and persons, the defendants and Chadeloid thereafter worked together to induce makers of wrinkle finishes to accept the price-fixing patent licenses which New Wrinkle had to offer. These prospective licensees were advised of the agreed-upon prices, terms and conditions of sale in the New Wrinkle licenses, and they were assured that like advice was being given to other manufacturers "in order to establish minimum prices throughout the industry." After May 7, 1938, when the requisite twelve leading manufacturing companies had accepted New Wrinkle licenses, the price schedules became operative. By September 1948, when the complaint was filed in this action, more than two hundred, or substantially all, manufacturers of wrinkle finishes in the United States held nearly identical ten-year extendable license agreements from New Wrinkle. These agreements required, among other things, that a licensee observe in all sales of products covered by the licensed patents a schedule of minimum prices, discounts and selling terms established by the licensor New Wrinkle. Upon thirty days' notice in writing, New Wrinkle might alter any or all of the terms of the price schedule, but such prices, terms and discounts as New Wrinkle might establish were to bind the licensee only if imposed at the same time and in the same terms upon the licensor and all other licensees. Termination provisions in the agreements required a licensee to give three months' written notice and allowed the licensor to terminate the license if a licensee failed to remedy a violation of the agreement within thirty days after written notice thereof by the licensor. A 5 cent per gallon royalty was made payable on all wrinkle finish sold or used by a licensee, said royalty to be reduced to the same figure as that contained in any subsequent license granted at a lower royalty charge.... [Appendix A set forth the minimum prices that New Wrinkle set for the sale of wrinkle finish, which ranged from $2.55–4.00/gallon.]

Appellees argue ... that the principles of *General Electric* control here.... *General Electric* ... allow[s] a patentee to license a competitor in commerce to make and vend with a price limitation controlled by the patentee. When we examined the rule in 1948, the holding of the *General Electric* case was left as stated above. But it was pointed out that "the possession of a valid patent or patents does not give the patentee any exemption from the provisions of the Sherman Act beyond the limits of the patent monopoly." United States v. Line Material Co., 333 U.S. 287, 310. We said that: "two or more patentees in the same patent field may [not] legally combine their valid patent monopolies to secure mutual benefits for themselves through contractual agreements, between themselves and other licensees, for control of the sale price of the patented devices." Price control through cross-licensing was barred as beyond the patent monopoly.

On the day of the *Line Material* decision, this Court handed down United States v. United States Gypsum Co., 333 U.S. 364. The *Gypsum* case was based on facts similar to those here alleged except that the patent owner was also a manufacturer.... [W]e consider the fact that New Wrinkle is exclusively a patent-holding company of no significance as a defense to the alleged violation of the Sherman Act. We said in *Gypsum* that: "industry-wide license agreements, entered into with knowledge on the part of licensor and licensees of the adherence of others, with the control over prices and methods of distribution through the agreements and the bulletins, were sufficient to establish a *prima facie* case of conspiracy."

On remand, the prima facie case resulted in a final judgment, affirmed by this Court. In discussing the *General Electric* case, the Court was unanimous in saying that it:

> "gives no support for a patentee, acting in concert with all members of an industry, to issue substantially identical licenses to all members of the industry under the terms of which the industry is completely regimented, the production of competitive unpatented products suppressed, a class of distributors squeezed out, and prices on unpatented products stabilized.... it would be sufficient to show that the defendants, constituting all former competitors in an entire industry, had acted in concert to restrain commerce in an entire industry under patent licenses in order to organize the industry and stabilize prices."

We see no material difference between the situation in *Line Material* and *Gypsum* and the case presented by the allegations of this complaint. An arrangement was made between patent holders to pool their patents and fix prices on the products for themselves and their licensees. The purpose and result plainly violate the Sherman Act. The judgment below must be *Reversed*.

Questions on *New Wrinkle*

1. Can we infer anything from just the provisions requiring that the pricing condition is binding only if imposed on others and that they will get any lower royalty charged another? Doesn't every licensee want terms no worse than other licensees are getting?

2. What can we infer from the provision that makes the pricing condition effective only when the 12 biggest manufacturers signed up? If the value of the license came from the patent, rather than from the pricing condition, wouldn't licensees want the *fewest* other manufacturers to sign up?

3. Does it make a difference:

    a. that the royalty is quite small compared to minimum price fixed? Doesn't that suggest the licensees don't value the patent that much?

    b. whether the licensees discontinued any unpatented production of wrinkle finish?

    c. whether the alternative prior methods of producing wrinkle finish were just as good and inexpensive as the patented one?

4. Some read the combination of *GE* and *New Wrinkle* as adopting a distinction between individual licensing with pricing conditions, which *GE* allows, and multiple licensing with pricing conditions, which *New Wrinkle* prohibits on the apparent theory that a horizontal conspiracy among licensees can be inferred. Does such a distinction make any sense?

a. Don't the possible procompetitive and anticompetitive effects turn more on: (1) the value the patent had and the impact that has on the likelihood that rivals would have competed without it; and (2) the percentage of the market the licensees cover?

b. If General Electric had imposed similar pricing conditions on its other licensees,[85] could one really infer a horizontal conspiracy among the licensees? Might they not all have accepted independently simply because they needed the patent? If they and Westinghouse could not sell lamps without the patent, could the conditioned licenses cause any anticompetitive harm? Would a price-conditioned license to Westinghouse with 16% of the market have any different effect than price-conditioned licenses to two firms with 8% of the market each?

c. If General Electric had licensed some trivial enamel finish patent to Westinghouse (at 5 cents a lamp) that was not necessary to make lamps on the condition that Westinghouse charged at least $3/lamp, do you think the *General Electric* case would have come out the same way?

Case 27/87, Sprl Louis Erauw–Jacquery v. La Hesbignonne Sc.

1988 E.C.R. 1919.

... [T]he Tribunal de commerce (commercial court), Liège, referred to the Court ... a question concerning the interpretation of Article [101(1) TFEU] with a view to the assessment of the compatibility with that provision of the Treaty of certain provisions of an agreement granting a licence to propagate and sell certain varieties of cereal seed protected by plant breeders' rights.

That question was raised in proceedings relating to certain provisions of an agreement whereby the company Louis Erauw–Jacquery, which is the owner, or the licensee from the owners, of certain plant breeders' rights (hereinafter referred to as "the breeder"), authorized La Hesbignonne, a cooperative, (hereinafter referred to as "the licensee") to propagate basic seed and to sell seed of the first or second generation produced from that basic seed and intended for cereal production (hereinafter referred to as "seed for propagation").

Under the agreement, the licensee, undertook ...:

"... (i) not to sell certified seed of any species, varieties and classes in respect of which the breeder is the holder or the agent of the holder of the plant breeders' rights below the minimum selling prices to be stipulated by the breeder."

---

85. In fact, the other GE licenses restricted output but not prices. See A. BRIGHT, THE ELECTRIC LAMP INDUSTRY Chapter 9 (1949).

In a circular letter ... addressed to all the growers including the licensee, the breeder notified the minimum prices at which the protected varieties were to be sold. As regards E3 seed of Gerbel multi-row winter barley ... the minimum price was fixed at BFR 1 825 per 100 kilograms. The licensee did not abide by that price and ... offered that seed for sale at the price of BFR 1,750 per 100 kilograms. In Belgium, although E3 seed is basic seed, it is sold almost entirely to farmers for the production of cereals for consumption.

In the breeder's view, that sale obliged the other growers to lower their prices, thereby causing them to incur loss for which they are claiming compensation. In the main proceedings the breeder wishes to pass on that claim, which is estimated at BFR 15,000,000, to the licensee....

Article [101(1) TFEU] expressly mentions as being incompatible with the Common Market agreements which "directly or indirectly fix purchase or selling prices or any other trading conditions." According to the judgment of the national court the plaintiff in the main proceedings concluded with other growers agreements identical to the contested agreement, as a result of which those agreements have the same effects as a price system fixed by a horizontal agreement. In such circumstances the object and effect of such a provision is to restrict competition within the Common Market....

However, it must be recalled that an agreement is subject to the prohibition contained in Article [101] only if it appreciably affects trade between Member States. In this respect it must be stressed that the impact of the contested agreement on intra-community trade depends, in particular, on whether it forms part of a cluster of similar agreements concluded between the breeder and other licensees, on the breeder's market share in respect of the seed concerned and on the ability of the producers bound by those agreements to export that seed.

It is for the national court to decide, on the basis of the relevant information at its disposal and taking into account the economic and legal context of the agreement of 26 February 1982, whether that agreement is capable of affecting trade between Member States to an appreciable degree.

Therefore, the answer to ... the question referred by the national court must be that a provision, in an agreement such as that described above, which obliges the grower to comply with minimum prices fixed by the other party falls within the prohibition set out in Article [101(1) TFEU] only if it is found, having regard to the economic and legal context of the agreement containing the provision in question, that the agreement is capable of affecting trade between member states to an appreciable degree.

Questions on Erauw–Jacquery

1. Is the factual scenario in this case closer to the *GE* or the *New Wrinkle* case? Was the outcome of this case similar to the outcome of the comparable U.S. case?

2. The ECJ states that "the plaintiff in the main proceedings concluded with other growers agreements identical to the contested agreement, as a result of which those agreements have the same effects as a price system fixed by a horizontal agreement." Are we really talking about an horizontal price-fixing agreement, or is it more like a vertical agreement? Does the answer turn on whether the licensees could get seeds for the species in question from other sources?

3.   Is a vertical price-fixing agreement likely to have an appreciable impact on competition if it involves:

a.   a patent without any market power with licensees who collectively lack market power downstream?

b.   a patent that does have market power but the agreement is with only one licensee among many who has no downstream market power?

c.   a patent without which no firm could compete downstream?

d.   a patent licensed to firms that otherwise would not have competed downstream?

U.S. DOJ/FTC, Antitrust Guidelines for the Licensing of Intellectual Property (1995)

. . . **1.   Intellectual property protection and the antitrust laws**. . . . The intellectual property laws and the antitrust laws share the common purpose of promoting innovation and enhancing consumer welfare. The intellectual property laws provide incentives for innovation and its dissemination and commercialization by establishing enforceable property rights for the creators of new and useful products, more efficient processes, and original works of expression. In the absence of intellectual property rights, imitators could more rapidly exploit the efforts of innovators and investors without compensation. Rapid imitation would reduce the commercial value of innovation and erode incentives to invest, ultimately to the detriment of consumers. The antitrust laws promote innovation and consumer welfare by prohibiting certain actions that may harm competition with respect to either existing or new ways of serving consumers.

2.   General principles . . . These Guidelines embody three general principles: (a) for the purpose of antitrust analysis, the Agencies regard intellectual property as being essentially comparable to any other form of property; (b) the Agencies do not presume that intellectual property creates market power in the antitrust context; and (c) the Agencies recognize that intellectual property licensing allows firms to combine complementary factors of production and is generally procompetitive.

2.1.   Standard Antitrust Analysis Applies to Intellectual Property. The Agencies apply the same general antitrust principles to conduct involving intellectual property that they apply to conduct involving any other form of tangible or intangible property. That is not to say that intellectual property is in all respects the same as any other form of property. Intellectual property has important characteristics, such as ease of misappropriation, that distinguish it from many other forms of property. These characteristics can be taken into account by standard antitrust analysis, however, and do not require the application of fundamentally different principles.

Although there are clear and important differences in the purpose, extent, and duration of protection provided under the intellectual property regimes of patent, copyright, and trade secret, the governing antitrust principles are the same. Antitrust analysis takes differences among these forms of intellectual property into account in evaluating the specific market circumstances in which transactions occur, just as it does with other particular market circumstances.

Intellectual property law bestows on the owners of intellectual property certain rights to exclude others. These rights help the owners to profit from the use of their property. An intellectual property owner's rights to exclude are similar to the rights enjoyed by owners of other forms of private property. As with other forms of private property, certain types of conduct with respect to intellectual property may have anticompetitive effects against which the antitrust laws can and do protect. Intellectual property is thus neither particularly free from scrutiny under the antitrust laws, nor particularly suspect under them. . . .

2.2. Intellectual Property and Market Power. Market power is the ability profitably to maintain prices above, or output below, competitive levels for a significant period of time. The Agencies will not presume that a patent, copyright, or trade secret necessarily confers market power upon its owner. Although the intellectual property right confers the power to exclude with respect to the *specific* product, process, or work in question, there will often be sufficient actual or potential close substitutes for such product, process, or work to prevent the exercise of market power. . . .

2.3. Procompetitive Benefits of Licensing. Intellectual property typically is one component among many in a production process and derives value from its combination with complementary factors. Complementary factors of production include manufacturing and distribution facilities, workforces, and other items of intellectual property. The owner of intellectual property has to arrange for its combination with other necessary factors to realize its commercial value. Often, the owner finds it most efficient to contract with others for these factors, to sell rights to the intellectual property, or to enter into a joint venture arrangement for its development, rather than supplying these complementary factors itself.

Licensing, cross-licensing, or otherwise transferring intellectual property (hereinafter "licensing") can facilitate integration of the licensed property with complementary factors of production. This integration can lead to more efficient exploitation of the intellectual property, benefiting consumers through the reduction of costs and the introduction of new products. Such arrangements increase the value of intellectual property to consumers and to the developers of the technology. By potentially increasing the expected returns from intellectual property, licensing also can increase the incentive for its creation and thus promote greater investment in research and development.

Sometimes the use of one item of intellectual property requires access to another. An item of intellectual property "blocks" another when the second cannot be practiced without using the first. For example, an improvement on a patented machine can be blocked by the patent on the machine. Licensing may promote the coordinated development of technologies that are in a blocking relationship.

Field-of-use, territorial, and other limitations on intellectual property licenses may serve procompetitive ends by allowing the licensor to exploit its property as efficiently and effectively as possible. These various forms of exclusivity can be used to give a licensee an incentive to invest in the commercialization and distribution of products embodying the licensed intellectual property and to develop additional applications for the licensed property. The restrictions may do so, for example, by protecting the licensee against free-riding on the licensee's investments by other licensees or by the licensor. They may also increase the licensor's incentive to license, for example, by protecting the licensor from competition in the licensor's own technology in a market niche that it prefers to keep to itself. These benefits of licensing restrictions apply to patent, copyright, and trade secret licenses, and to know-how agreements. . . .

3.   Antitrust concerns and modes of analysis

3.1.   Nature of the concerns. While intellectual property licensing arrangements are typically welfare-enhancing and procompetitive, antitrust concerns may nonetheless arise. For example, a licensing arrangement could include restraints that adversely affect competition in goods markets by dividing the markets among firms that would have competed using different technologies. *See, e.g.*, Example 7. An arrangement that effectively merges the research and development activities of two of only a few entities that could plausibly engage in research and development in the relevant field might harm competition for development of new goods and services. An acquisition of intellectual property may lessen competition in a relevant antitrust market. The Agencies will focus on the actual effects of an arrangement, not on its formal terms.

The Agencies will not require the owner of intellectual property to create competition in its own technology. However, antitrust concerns may arise when a licensing arrangement harms competition among entities that would have been actual or likely potential competitors in a relevant market in the absence of the license (entities in a "horizontal relationship"). A restraint in a licensing arrangement may harm such competition, for example, if it facilitates market division or price-fixing. In addition, license restrictions with respect to one market may harm such competition in another market by anticompetitively foreclosing access to, or significantly raising the price of, an important input, or by facilitating coordination to increase price or reduce output. When it appears that such competition may be adversely affected, the Agencies will follow the analysis set forth below. . . .

3.4.   Framework for evaluating licensing restraints . . . To determine whether a particular restraint in a licensing arrangement is given per se or rule of reason treatment, the Agencies will assess whether the restraint in question can be expected to contribute to an efficiency-enhancing integration of economic activity. In general, licensing arrangements promote such integration because they facilitate the combination of the licensor's intellectual property with complementary factors of production owned by the licensee. A restraint in a licensing arrangement may further such integration by, for example, aligning the incentives of the licensor and the licensees to promote the development and marketing of the licensed technology, or by substantially reducing transactions costs. If there is no efficiency-enhancing integration of economic activity and if the type of restraint is one that has been accorded per se treatment, the Agencies will challenge the restraint under the per se rule. Otherwise, the Agencies will apply a rule of reason analysis.

Application of the rule of reason generally requires a comprehensive inquiry into market conditions. However, that inquiry may be truncated in certain circumstances. If the Agencies conclude that a restraint has no likely anticompetitive effects, they will treat it as reasonable, without an elaborate analysis of market power or the justifications for the restraint. Similarly, if a restraint facially appears to be of a kind that would always or almost always tend to reduce output or increase prices, and the restraint is not reasonably related to efficiencies, the Agencies will likely challenge the restraint without an elaborate analysis of particular industry circumstances.

Example 7

Situation: Gamma, which manufactures Product X using its patented process, offers a license for its process technology to every other manufacturer of Product X, each of which competes worldwide with Gamma in the manufacture and sale of X. The process technology does not represent an economic improvement over the available existing technologies. Indeed, although most manufacturers accept licenses from Gamma, none of the licensees actually uses the licensed technology. The licenses provide that each manufacturer has an exclusive right to sell Product X manufactured using the licensed technology in a designated geographic area and that no manufacturer may sell Product X, however manufactured, outside the designated territory.

Discussion: The manufacturers of Product X are in a horizontal relationship in the goods market for Product X. Any manufacturers of Product X that control technologies that are substitutable at comparable cost for Gamma's process are also horizontal competitors of Gamma in the relevant technology market. The licensees of Gamma's process technology are technically in a vertical relationship, although that is not significant in this example because they do not actually use Gamma's technology.

The licensing arrangement restricts competition in the relevant goods market among manufacturers of Product X by requiring each manufacturer to limit its sales to an exclusive territory. Thus, competition among entities that would be actual competitors in the absence of the licensing arrangement is restricted. Based on the facts set forth above, the licensing arrangement does not involve a useful transfer of technology, and thus it is unlikely that the restraint on sales outside the designated territories contributes to an efficiency-enhancing integration of economic activity. Consequently, the evaluating Agency would be likely to challenge the arrangement under the per se rule as a horizontal territorial market allocation scheme and to view the intellectual property aspects of the arrangement as a sham intended to cloak its true nature.

If the licensing arrangement could be expected to contribute to an efficiency-enhancing integration of economic activity, as might be the case if the licensed technology were an advance over existing processes and used by the licensees, the Agency would analyze the arrangement under the rule of reason applying the analytical framework described in this section.

In this example, the competitive implications do not generally depend on whether the licensed technology is protected by patent, is a trade secret or other know-how, or is a computer program protected by copyright; nor do the competitive implications generally depend on whether the allocation of markets is territorial, as in this example, or functional, based on fields of use. . . .

4.3.   Antitrust "safety zone." Because licensing arrangements often promote innovation and enhance competition, the Agencies believe that an antitrust "safety zone" is useful in order to provide some degree of certainty and thus to encourage such activity. Absent extraordinary circumstances, the Agencies will not challenge a restraint in an intellectual property licensing arrangement if (1) the restraint is not facially anticompetitive and (2) the licensor and its licensees collectively account for no more than twenty percent of each relevant market significantly affected by the restraint. This "safety zone" does not apply to those transfers of intellectual property rights to which a merger analysis is applied.

Whether a restraint falls within the safety zone will be determined by reference only to goods markets unless the analysis of goods markets alone would inadequately address the effects of the licensing arrangement on competition among technologies or in research and development.

If an examination of the effects on competition among technologies or in research development is required, and if market share data are unavailable or do not accurately represent competitive significance, the following safety zone criteria will apply. Absent extraordinary circumstances, the Agencies will not challenge a restraint in an intellectual property licensing arrangement that may affect competition in a technology market if (1) the restraint is not facially anticompetitive and (2) there are four or more independently controlled technologies in addition to the technologies controlled by the parties to the licensing arrangement that may be substitutable for the licensed technology at a comparable cost to the user. Absent extraordinary circumstances, the Agencies will not challenge a restraint in an intellectual property licensing arrangement that may affect competition in an innovation market if (1) the restraint is not facially anticompetitive and (2) four or more independently controlled entities in addition to the parties to the licensing arrangement possess the required specialized assets or characteristics and the incentive to engage in research and development that is a close substitute of the research and development activities of the parties to the licensing agreement. . . .

5.   Application of general principles . . .

5.1.   Horizontal restraints . . .

Example 9

Situation: Two of the leading manufacturers of a consumer electronic product hold patents that cover alternative circuit designs
for the product. The manufacturers assign their patents to a
separate corporation wholly owned by the two firms. That corporation licenses the right to use the circuit designs to other consumer
product manufacturers and establishes the license royalties. None
of the patents is blocking; that is, each of the patents can be used
without infringing a patent owned by the other firm. The different
circuit designs are substitutable in that each permits the manufacture at comparable cost to consumers of products that consumers
consider to be interchangeable. One of the Agencies is analyzing
the licensing arrangement.

Discussion: In this example, the manufacturers are horizontal
competitors in the goods market for the consumer product and in
the related technology markets. The competitive issue with regard
to a joint assignment of patent rights is whether the assignment
has an adverse impact on competition in technology and goods
markets that is not outweighed by procompetitive efficiencies, such
as benefits in the use or dissemination of the technology. Each of
the patent owners has a right to exclude others from using its
patent. That right does not extend, however, to the agreement to
assign rights jointly. To the extent that the patent rights cover
technologies that are close substitutes, the joint determination of
royalties likely would result in higher royalties and higher goods
prices than would result if the owners licensed or used their
technologies independently. In the absence of evidence establishing
efficiency-enhancing integration from the joint assignment of patent rights, the Agency may conclude that the joint marketing of
competing patent rights constitutes horizontal price fixing and
could be challenged as a per se unlawful horizontal restraint of
trade. If the joint marketing arrangement results in an efficiency-
enhancing integration, the Agency would evaluate the arrangement under the rule of reason. However, the Agency may conclude
that the anticompetitive effects are sufficiently apparent, and the
claimed integrative efficiencies are sufficiently weak or not reasonably related to the restraints, to warrant challenge of the arrangement without an elaborate analysis of particular industry circumstances (*see* section 3.4). . . .

5.5.   Cross-licensing and pooling arrangements

Cross-licensing and pooling arrangements are agreements of two or
more owners of different items of intellectual property to license one
another or third parties. These arrangements may provide procompetitive
benefits by integrating complementary technologies, reducing transaction
costs, clearing blocking positions, and avoiding costly infringement litiga-

tion. By promoting the dissemination of technology, cross-licensing and pooling arrangements are often procompetitive.

Cross-licensing and pooling arrangements can have anticompetitive effects in certain circumstances. For example, collective price or output restraints in pooling arrangements, such as the joint marketing of pooled intellectual property rights with collective price setting or coordinated output restrictions, may be deemed unlawful if they do not contribute to an efficiency-enhancing integration of economic activity among the participants. When cross-licensing or pooling arrangements are mechanisms to accomplish naked price fixing or market division, they are subject to challenge under the per se rule. *See New Wrinkle.*

Settlements involving the cross-licensing of intellectual property rights can be an efficient means to avoid litigation and, in general, courts favor such settlements. When such cross-licensing involves horizontal competitors, however, the Agencies will consider whether the effect of the settlement is to diminish competition among entities that would have been actual or likely potential competitors in a relevant market in the absence of the cross-license. In the absence of offsetting efficiencies, such settlements may be challenged as unlawful restraints of trade. *Cf. United States v. Singer Manufacturing Co.,* 374 U.S. 174 (1963) (cross-license agreement was part of broader combination to exclude competitors).

Pooling arrangements generally need not be open to all who would like to join. However, exclusion from cross-licensing and pooling arrangements among parties that collectively possess market power may, under some circumstances, harm competition. *Cf. Northwest Stationers* (exclusion of a competitor from a purchasing cooperative not per se unlawful absent a showing of market power). In general, exclusion from a pooling or cross-licensing arrangement among competing technologies is unlikely to have anticompetitive effects unless (1) excluded firms cannot effectively compete in the relevant market for the good incorporating the licensed technologies and (2) the pool participants collectively possess market power in the relevant market. If these circumstances exist, the Agencies will evaluate whether the arrangement's limitations on participation are reasonably related to the efficient development and exploitation of the pooled technologies and will assess the net effect of those limitations in the relevant market.

Another possible anticompetitive effect of pooling arrangements may occur if the arrangement deters or discourages participants from engaging in research and development, thus retarding innovation. For example, a pooling arrangement that requires members to grant licenses to each other for current and future technology at minimal cost may reduce the incentives of its members to engage in research and development because members of the pool have to share their successful research and development and each of the members can free ride on the accomplishments of other pool members. However, such an arrangement can have procompetitive benefits, for example, by exploiting economies of scale and integrating complementary capabilities of the pool members, (including the clearing of blocking positions), and is likely to cause competitive problems only when the arrangement includes a large fraction of the potential research and development in an innovation market.

Example 10

Situation: As in Example 9, two of the leading manufacturers of a consumer electronic product hold patents that cover alternative circuit designs for the product. The manufacturers assign several of their patents to a separate corporation wholly owned by the two firms. That corporation licenses the right to use the circuit designs to other consumer product manufacturers and establishes the license royalties. In this example, however, the manufacturers assign to the separate corporation only patents that are blocking. None of the patents assigned to the corporation can be used without infringing a patent owned by the other firm.

Discussion: Unlike the previous example, the joint assignment of patent rights to the wholly owned corporation in this example does not adversely affect competition in the licensed technology among entities that would have been actual or likely potential competitors in the absence of the licensing arrangement. Moreover, the licensing arrangement is likely to have procompetitive benefits in the use of the technology. Because the manufacturers' patents are blocking, the manufacturers are not in a horizontal relationship with respect to those patents. None of the patents can be used without the right to a patent owned by the other firm, so the patents are not substitutable. As in Example 9, the firms are horizontal competitors in the relevant goods market. In the absence of collateral restraints that would likely raise price or reduce output in the relevant goods market or in any other relevant antitrust market and that are not reasonably related to an efficiency-enhancing integration of economic activity, the evaluating Agency would be unlikely to challenge this arrangement....

5.7. Acquisition of intellectual property rights.... The Agencies will apply a merger analysis to an outright sale by an intellectual property owner of all of its rights to that intellectual property and to a transaction in which a person obtains through grant, sale, or other transfer an exclusive license for intellectual property (i.e., a license that precludes all other persons, including the licensor, from using the licensed intellectual property)....

Commission Regulation (EC) No 772/2004 of 27 April 2004 on the Application of Article [101(3) TFEU] to Categories of Technology Transfer Agreements

O.J. 2004, L 123/11.

Technology transfer agreements concern the licensing of technology. Such agreements will usually improve economic efficiency and be pro-competitive as they can reduce duplication of research and development, strengthen the incentive for the initial research and development, spur incremental innovation, facilitate diffusion and generate product market competition.

The likelihood that such efficiency-enhancing and pro-competitive effects will outweigh any anti-competitive effects due to restrictions contained in technology transfer agreements depends on the degree of market power of the undertakings concerned and, therefore, on the extent to which those undertakings face competition from undertakings owning substitute technologies or undertakings producing substitute products.

This Regulation should only deal with agreements where the licensor permits the licensee to exploit the licensed technology, possibly after further research and development by the licensee, for the production of goods or services. It should not deal with licensing agreements for the purpose of subcontracting research and development. It should also not deal with licensing agreements to set up technology pools, that is to say, agreements for the pooling of technologies with the purpose of licensing the created package of intellectual property rights to third parties.

For the application of Article 101(3) by regulation, it is not necessary to define those technology transfer agreements that are capable of falling within Article 101(1). In the individual assessment of agreements pursuant to Article 101(1), account has to be taken of several factors, and in particular the structure and the dynamics of the relevant technology and product markets.

The benefit of the block exemption established by this Regulation should be limited to those agreements which can be assumed with sufficient certainty to satisfy the conditions of Article 101(3). In order to attain the benefits and objectives of technology transfer, the benefit of this Regulation should also apply to provisions contained in technology transfer agreements that do not constitute the primary object of such agreements, but are directly related to the application of the licensed technology.

For technology transfer agreements between competitors it can be presumed that, where the combined share of the relevant markets accounted for by the parties does not exceed 20% and the agreements do not contain certain severely anti-competitive restraints, they generally lead to an improvement in production or distribution and allow consumers a fair share of the resulting benefits. . . .

There can be no presumption that above th[is] market-share [threshold] technology transfer agreements do fall within the scope of Article [101(1)]. For instance, an exclusive licensing agreement between non-competing undertakings does often not fall within the scope of Article [101(1)]. There can also be no presumption that, above th[is] market-share [threshold], technology transfer agreements falling within the scope of Article [101(1)] will not satisfy the conditions for exemption. However, it can also not be presumed that they will usually give rise to objective advantages of such a character and size as to compensate for the disadvantages which they create for competition.

This Regulation should not exempt technology transfer agreements containing restrictions which are not indispensable to the improvement of production or distribution. In particular, technology transfer agreements containing certain severely anti-competitive restraints such as the fixing of prices charged to third parties should be excluded from the benefit of the block exemption established by this Regulation irrespective of the market shares of the undertakings concerned. In the case of such hardcore restrictions the whole agreement should be excluded from the benefit of the block exemption.

In order to protect incentives to innovate and the appropriate application of intellectual property rights, certain restrictions should be excluded from the block exemption. In particular exclusive grant back obligations for severable improvements should be excluded. Where such a restriction is included in a licence agreement only the restriction in question should be excluded from the benefit of the block exemption.

The market-share thresholds, the non-exemption of technology transfer agreements containing severely anti-competitive restraints and the excluded restrictions provided for in this Regulation will normally ensure that the agreements to which the block exemption applies do not enable the participating undertakings to eliminate competition in respect of a substantial part of the products in question. . . .

This Regulation is without prejudice to the application of Article 102 TFEU.

Commission Guidelines on the Application of Article [101 TFEU] to Technology Transfer Agreements

O.J. 2004, C101/2.

I. INTRODUCTION

These guidelines set out the principles for the assessment of technology transfer agreements under Article [101 TFEU]. Technology transfer agreements concern the licensing of technology where the licensor permits the licensee to exploit the licensed technology for the production of goods or services, as defined in . . . Commission Regulation (EC) No 773/2004 on the application of Article [101(3) TFEU] to categories of technology transfer agreements (the TTBER). The purpose of the guidelines is to provide guidance on the application of the TTBER as well as on the application of Article [101] to technology transfer agreements that fall outside the scope of the TTBER. The TTBER and the guidelines are without prejudice to the possible parallel application of Article [102 TFEU] to licensing agreements.

The standards set forth in these guidelines must be applied in light of the circumstances specific to each case. This excludes a mechanical application. Each case must be assessed on its own facts and the guidelines must be applied reasonably and flexibly. . . .

The present guidelines are without prejudice to the interpretation of Article [101] and the TTBER that may be given by the Court of Justice and the [General Court].

II. GENERAL PRINCIPLES

1. Article [101] and intellectual property rights

The aim of Article [101] as a whole is to protect competition on the market with a view to promoting consumer welfare and an efficient allocation of resources....

Intellectual property laws confer exclusive rights on holders of patents, copyright, design rights, trademarks and other legally protected rights. The owner of intellectual property is entitled under intellectual property laws to prevent unauthorised use of his intellectual property and to exploit it, inter alia, by licensing it to third parties....

The fact that intellectual property laws grant exclusive rights of exploitation does not imply that intellectual property rights are immune from competition law intervention. Articles [101] and [102] are in particular applicable to agreements whereby the holder licenses another undertaking to exploit his intellectual property rights. Nor does it imply that there is an inherent conflict between intellectual property rights and the Community competition rules. Indeed, both bodies of law share the same basic objective of promoting consumer welfare and an efficient allocation of resources. Innovation constitutes an essential and dynamic component of an open and competitive market economy. Intellectual property rights promote dynamic competition by encouraging undertakings to invest in developing new or improved products and processes. So does competition by putting pressure on undertakings to innovate. Therefore, both intellectual property rights and competition are necessary to promote innovation and ensure a competitive exploitation thereof.

In the assessment of licence agreements under Article [101] it must be kept in mind that the creation of intellectual property rights often entails substantial investment and that it is often a risky endeavour. In order not to reduce dynamic competition and to maintain the incentive to innovate, the innovator must not be unduly restricted in the exploitation of intellectual property rights that turn out to be valuable. For these reasons the innovator should normally be free to seek compensation for successful projects that is sufficient to maintain investment incentives, taking failed projects into account. Technology licensing may also require the licensee to make significant sunk investments in the licensed technology and production assets necessary to exploit it. Article [101] cannot be applied without considering such ex ante investments made by the parties and the risks relating thereto. The risk facing the parties and the sunk investment that must be committed may thus lead to the agreement falling outside Article [101(1)] or fulfilling the conditions of Article [101(3)], as the case may be, for the period of time required to recoup the investment.

In assessing licensing agreements under Article [101], the existing analytical framework is sufficiently flexible to take due account of the dynamic aspects of technology licensing. There is no presumption that intellectual property rights and licence agreements as such give rise to competition concerns. Most licence agreements do not restrict competition and create pro-competitive efficiencies. Indeed, licensing as such is pro-competitive as it leads to dissemination of technology and promotes innovation. In addition, even licence agreements that do restrict competition may often give rise to pro-competitive efficiencies, which must be considered under Article [101(3)] and balanced against the negative effects on competition. The great majority of licence agreements are therefore compatible with Article [101].

2.   The general framework for applying Article [101]

Article [101(1)] prohibits agreements which have as their object or effect the restriction of competition. Article [101(1)] applies both to restrictions of competition between the parties to an agreement and to restrictions of competition between any of the parties and third parties. The assessment of whether a licence agreement restricts competition must be made within the actual context in which competition would occur in the absence of the agreement with its alleged restrictions. In making this assessment it is necessary to take account of the likely impact of the agreement on inter-technology competition (i.e. competition between undertakings using competing technologies) and on intra-technology competition (i.e. competition between undertakings using the same technology). Article [101(1)] prohibits restrictions of both inter-technology competition and intra-technology competition. It is therefore necessary to assess to what extent the agreement affects or is likely to affect these two aspects of competition on the market. . . .

Restrictions of competition by object are those that by their very nature restrict competition. These are restrictions which in light of the objectives pursued by the Community competition rules have such a high potential for negative effects on competition that it is not necessary for the purposes of applying Article [101(1)] to demonstrate any actual effects on the market. Moreover, the conditions of Article [101(3)] are unlikely to be fulfilled in the case of restrictions by object. The assessment of whether or not an agreement has as its object a restriction of competition is based on a number of factors. These factors include, in particular, the content of the agreement and the objective aims pursued by it. It may also be necessary to consider the context in which it is (to be) applied or the actual conduct and behaviour of the parties on the market. In other words, an examination of the facts underlying the agreement and the specific circumstances in which it operates may be required before it can be concluded whether a particular restriction constitutes a hardcore restriction of competition. The way in which an agreement is actually implemented may reveal a restriction by object even where the formal agreement does not contain an express provision to that effect. Evidence of subjective intent on the part of the parties to restrict competition is a relevant factor but not a necessary condition. For licence agreements, the Commission considers that the restrictions covered by the list of hardcore restrictions of competition contained in Article 4 of the TTBER are restrictive by their very object.

If an agreement is not restrictive of competition by object it is necessary to examine whether it has restrictive effects on competition. Account must be taken of both actual and potential effects. In other words the agreement must have likely anti-competitive effects. For licence agreements to be restrictive of competition by effect they must affect actual or potential competition to such prices, output, innovation or the variety or quality of competition must be appreciable. Appreciable anticompetitive effects are likely to occur when at least one of the parties has or obtains some degree of market power and the agreement contributes to the creation, maintenance or strengthening of that market power or allows the parties to exploit such market power. Market power is the ability to maintain prices above competitive levels or to maintain output in terms of product quantities, product quality and variety or innovation below competitive levels for a not insignificant period of time. The degree of market power normally required for a finding of an infringement under Article [101(1)] is less than the degree of market power required for a finding of dominance under Article [102].

For the purposes of analysing restrictions of competition by effect it is normally necessary to define the relevant market and to examine and assess, inter alia, the nature of the products and technologies concerned, the market position of the parties, the market position of existence of potential competitors and the level of entry barriers. In some cases, however, it may be possible to show anti-competitive effects directly by analysing the conduct of the parties to the agreement on the market. It may for example be possible to ascertain that an agreement has led to price increases.

Licence agreements, however, also have substantial pro-competitive potential. Indeed, the vast majority of licence agreements are pro-competitive. Licence agreements may promote innovation by allowing innovators to earn returns to cover at least part of their research and development costs. Licence agreements also lead to a dissemination of technologies, which may create value by reducing the production costs of the licensee or by enabling him to produce new or improved products. Efficiencies at the level of the technology with the assets and technologies of the licensee. Such integration of complementary assets and technologies may lead to a cost/output configuration that would not otherwise be possible. For instance, the combination of an improved technology of the licensor with more efficient production or distribution assets of the licensee may reduce production costs or lead to the production of a higher quality product. Licensing may also serve the pro-competitive purpose of removing obstacles to the development and exploitation of the licensee's own technology. In particular in sectors where large numbers of patents are prevalent licensing often occurs in order to create design freedom by removing the risk of infringement claims by the licensor. When the licensor agrees not to invoke his intellectual property rights to prevent the sale of the licensee's products, the agreement removes an obstacle to the sale of the licensee's product and thus generally promotes competition.

In cases where a licence agreement is caught by Article [101(1)] the pro-competitive effects of the agreement must be balanced against its restrictive effects in the context of Article [101(3)]. When all four conditions of Article [101(3)] are satisfied, the restrictive licence agreement in question is valid and enforceable, no prior decision to that effect being required. Hardcore restrictions of competition only fulfil the conditions of Article [101(3)] in exceptional circumstances. Such agreements generally fail (at least) one of the first two conditions of Article [101(3)]. They generally do not create objective economic benefits or benefits for consumers. Moreover, these types of agreements generally also fail the indispensability test under the third condition. For example, if the parties fix the price at which the products produced under the licence must be sold, this will generally lead to a lower output and a misallocation of resources and higher prices for consumers. The price restriction is also not indispensable to achieve the possible efficiencies resulting from the availability to both competitors of the two technologies.

Questions on the U.S. Guidelines and EU Regulation 772/2004 and its Accompanying Guidelines

1. Is there a conflict between intellectual property rights and antitrust law? Does the granting of intellectual property rights pursue the same objective as the one pursued by antitrust law? Should intellectual property be treated just like any other property right?

2. What is the general attitude of the U.S. and EU antitrust authorities regarding the licensing of intellectual property? Is such licensing generally anticompetitive or procompetitive? Can some licenses be per se illegal despite the general procompetitive aspects of licensing? Do the guidelines help much in resolving difficult cases about how to classify or resolve cases?

3. Is the level of market shares held by the licensor and the licensee a relevant factor in the antitrust analysis of licensing agreements? If so, why?

4. Does it make sense to provide a safety zone below 20% market share for agreements that are not per se illegal?

a. What are the possible downsides?

b. Should it be an absolute safe harbor or just a presumption that can be rebutted in exceptional cases?

c. Should any safety zone be extended to private suits?

d. Should any safety zone be extended to per se illegal restraints too? In a case involving patent licensing, isn't there always a plausible enough procompetitive justification that associated restrictions should be allowed if market power seems implausible?

e. If 20% is good, why not 25%?

Other Nations' Treatment of the Antitrust–Intellectual Property Intersection

Like the U.S., Canada applies the same competition law principles to intellectual property as to any other form of property.[86] Other nations, including China, India, Japan, South Korea, and Taiwan, provide that exercising intellectual property rights is not an antitrust violation, but that abusing those rights or imposing unreasonable conditions can be.[87] Some

---

86. *See* Canada Competition Bureau Intellectual Property Enforcement Guidelines, Part 1 (2000).

87. *See* China Anti–Monopoly Law Art. 55; India Competition Act § 3(5)(i); Japan Antimonopoly Act § 21; Japan Guidelines for the Use of Intellectual Property under the Antimonopoly Act Part 2 (2007); Japan Guidelines on Standardization and Patent Pool Arrangements Part 2(2) (2005); South Korea Fair Trade Act Art. 59; South Korea Guidelines

nations simply exempt agreements licensing intellectual property.[88] Other nations require interested parties to apply to the competition agency for an antitrust exemption of an agreement involving the exercise of intellectual property rights.[89] Some nations provide for presumptive safe harbors for agreements licensing intellectual property rights between firms without large market shares.[90] Finally, some nations provide for compulsory licensing of patents as a possible penalty for an antitrust violation.[91] Which approach seems best to you?

H. Buyer Cartels

Mandeville Island Farms v. American Crystal Sugar

334 U.S. 219 (1948).

■ Mr. Justice Rutledge delivered the opinion of the Court.

[Because of their bulk and perishability, sugar beets grown in northern California could be sold only to one of three refiners located there, which processed those beets into sugar that they then sold on an interstate market. Each refiner had paid beetgrowers based on a formula that combined the beet's sugar content and the refiner's profits per hundred pounds of sugar. Then the three refiners all agreed to instead use their average profits to calculate beet prices, which resulted in all three paying the same price for beets. Respondent was the most efficient refiner, and thus the petitioner-farmers who sold beets to it received lower prices than they would have received if prices were calculated based on individual refiner profits.]

In our judgment the amended complaint states a cause of action arising under the Sherman Act, §§ 1 and 2, and the complaint was improperly dismissed [by the lower courts]....

It is clear that the agreement is the sort of combination condemned by the Act, even though the price-fixing was by purchasers, and the persons specially injured under the treble damage claim are sellers, not customers or consumers. And even if it is assumed that the final aim of the conspiracy was control of the local sugar beet market, it does not follow that it is outside the scope of the Sherman Act. For monopolization of local business,

---

on Reviewing Undue Exercise of Intellectual Property Rights (2000); Taiwan Fair Trade Act Art. 45; Taiwan FTC Guidelines on Technology Licensing Arrangements; Taiwan Guidelines on Copyright, Trademark and Patent Rights. *See also* New Zealand Commerce Act § 45 (exercising or licensing intellectual property rights are immune from antitrust liability except from those provisions that prohibit taking advantage of market power and resale price maintenance).

88. Indonesia Competition Law Arts. 50(b); Israel Restrictive Trade Practices Law § 3(2).

89. *See* South Africa Competition Act § 10(4).

90. *See* Singapore Guidelines on the Treatment of Intellectual Property Rights § 3.14 (presumptive safe harbor for licensing agreements between horizontal rivals with less than 25% market share or vertically related firms with less than 35%).

91. *See* Brazil Antitrust Law No. 8,884, Art. 24 (IV.a).

when achieved by restraining interstate commerce, is condemned by the Act. And a conspiracy with the ultimate object of fixing local retail prices is within the Act, if the means adopted for its accomplishment reach beyond the boundaries of one state.

The statute does not confine its protection to consumers, or to purchasers, or to competitors, or to sellers. Nor does it immunize the outlawed acts because they are done by any of these. The Act is comprehensive in its terms and coverage, protecting all who are made victims of the forbidden practices by whomever they may be perpetrated.

Nor is the amount of the nation's sugar industry which the California refiners control relevant, so long as control is exercised effectively in the area concerned ... Congress' power to keep the interstate market free of goods produced under conditions inimical to the general welfare may be exercised in individual cases without showing any specific effect upon interstate commerce.

... [U]nder the facts characterizing this industry's operation and the tightening of controls in this producing area by the new agreements and understandings, there can be no question that their restrictive consequences were projected substantially into the interstate distribution of the sugar, as the amended complaint repeatedly alleges....

Even without the uniform price provision and with full competition among the three refiners, their position is a dominating one. The growers' only competitive outlet is the one which exists when the refiners compete among themselves. There is no other market. The farmers' only alternative to dealing with one of the three refiners is to stop growing beets. They can neither plant nor sell except at the refiners' pleasure and on their terms. The refiners thus effectively control the quantity of beets grown, harvested and marketed, and consequently of sugar sold from the area in interstate commerce, even when they compete with each other. They dominate the entire industry. And their dominant position, together with the obstacles created by the necessity for large capital investment and the time required to make it productive, makes outlet through new competition practically impossible. Upon the allegations, it is absolutely so for any single growing season. A tighter or more all-inclusive monopolistic position hardly can be conceived.

When therefore the refiners cease entirely to compete with each other in all stages of the industry prior to marketing the sugar, the last vestige of local competition is removed and with it the only competitive opportunity for the grower to market his product. Moreover it is inconceivable that the monopoly so created will have no effects for the lessening of competition in the later interstate phases of the over-all activity or that the effects in those phases will have no repercussions upon the prior ones, including the price received by the growers.

There were indeed two distinct effects flowing from the agreement for paying uniform growers' prices, one immediately upon the price received by the grower rendering it devoid of all competitive influence in amount; the other, the necessary and inevitable effect of that agreement, in the setting of the industry as a whole, to reduce competition in the interstate distribution of sugar.

The idea that stabilization of prices paid for the only raw material consumed in an industry has no influence toward reducing competition in the distribution of the finished product, in an integrated industry such as this, is impossible to accept. By their agreement the combination of refiners acquired not only a monopoly of the raw material but also and thereby control of the quantity of sugar manufactured, sold and shipped interstate from the northern California producing area. In substance and roughly, if not precisely, they allocated among themselves the market for California beets substantially upon the basis of quotas competitively established among them at the time the uniform price arrangement was agreed upon. It is hardly likely that any refiner would have entered into an agreement with its only competitors, the effect of which would have been to drive away its growers, or therefore that many of the latter would have good reason to shift their dealings within the closed circle. Thus control of quantity in the interstate market was enhanced.

This effect was further magnified by the fact that the widely scattered location of sugar beet growing regions and their different accessibilities to market give the refiners of each region certainly some advantage over growers and refiners in other regions, and undoubtedly large ones over those most distant from the segment of the interstate market served by reason of being nearest to hand.

Finally, the interdependence and inextricable relationship between the interstate and the intrastate effects of the combination and monopoly are shown perhaps most clearly by the provision of the uniform price agreement which ties in the price paid for beets with the price received for sugar. The percentage factor of interstate receipts from sugar which the grower's contract specifies shall enter his price for beets makes that price dependent upon the price of sugar sold interstate. The uniform agreement's effect, when added to this, is to deprive the grower of the advantage of the individual efficiency of the refiner with which he deals, in this case the most efficient of the three, and of the price that refiner receives. It is also to reflect in the grower's price the consequences of the combination's effects for reducing competition among the refiners in the interstate distribution of sugar.

In sum, the restraint and its monopolistic effects were reflected throughout each stage of the industry, permeating its entire structure. This was the necessary and inevitable effect of the agreement among the refiners to pay uniform prices for beets, in the circumstances of this case. Those monopolistic effects not only deprived the beet growers of any competitive opportunity for disposing of their crops by the immediate operation of the uniform price provision; they also tended to increase control over the quantity of sugar sold interstate; and finally by the tie-in provision they interlaced those interstate effects with the price paid for the beets.

These restrictive and monopolistic effects, resulting necessarily from the practices allegedly intended to produce them, fall squarely within the

Sherman Act's prohibitions, creating the very injuries they were designed to prevent, both to the public and to private individuals.

It does not matter, contrary to respondent's view, that the growers contracting with the other two refiners may have been benefited, rather than harmed, by the combination's effects, even if that result is assumed to have followed. It is enough that these petitioners have suffered the injuries for which the statutory remedy is afforded. For the test of the legality and immunity of such a combination, in view of the statute's policy, is not that some others than the members of the combination have profited by its operation. It is rather whether the statute's policy has been violated in a manner to produce the general consequences it forbids for the public and the special consequences for particular individuals essential to the recovery of treble damages. Both types of injury are present in this case, for in addition to the restraints put upon the public interest in the interstate sale of sugar, enhancing the refiner's controls, there are special injuries affecting the petitioners resulting from those effects as well as from the immediate operation of the uniform price arrangement itself ... [R]eversed.

■ MR. JUSTICE JACKSON, with whom MR. JUSTICE FRANKFURTER joins, dissenting. It appears to me that the Court's opinion is based on assumptions of fact which the petitioner disclaimed in the court below.... On hearing, the trial judge apparently considered that a cause of action would be stated only if the complaint alleged that the growing contracts affected the price of sugar in interstate commerce. But the contracts accompanying the pleadings indicated that the effects ran in the other direction. The market price of interstate sugar was the base on which the price of beets was to be figured. The latter price was derived from the income which respondent and others received from sugar sold in the open market over the period of a year. The trial judge therefore suggested that the references to restraint of trade in sugar in interstate commerce created an ambiguity in the complaint. Accordingly, the plaintiff, at the suggestion of the court and for the specific purpose of this appeal, filed an amended complaint which completely eliminated the charge that the agreements complained of affected the price of sugar in interstate commerce.... Despite the deletion from the complaint of the allegation concerning the price of sugar, the Court assumes, without allegation or evidence, that the price of sugar is affected and on that basis builds its thesis that the Sherman Act has been violated.... I would affirm the judgment of the District Court.

Questions on *Mandeville*

1. Much of the opinion focuses on whether the interstate commerce requirement of the statute has been met, an issue that has largely receded into unimportance as subsequent Supreme Court decisions made that requirement trivial to prove. *See* Chapter 1. But the issue of continuing relevance is that here the adverse intrastate effects were only on the sugar beet producers who sold in the local market, and consumers could not be harmed unless there were some adverse effect on the national (interstate) market for buying sugar. Should the statute be interpreted to require some adverse effect on consumers?

a.   Would requiring proof of harm to downstream consumers be more consistent with a consumer welfare standard?

b.   Is there any harm in protecting producers from anticompetitive buying cartels that have no effect on consumers?

c.   Would you rule the same way if upstream producers were harmed by a restraint and downstream consumers benefited?

2.   Suppose the local buying cartel has simply set a subcompetitive low price for sugar beets.

a.   What would the effect be on the local output of sugar beets?

b.   What would the effect be on the downstream sugar output of the California sugar beet refiners?

c.   If California sugar beet refiners produce a significant share of the nation's sugar, what would a change in their output do to national sugar prices? What does this suggest about whether downstream consumers are likely to benefit from upstream buying cartels?

d.   If California sugar beet refiners produce an insignificant share of the nation's sugar and other national sugar refiners could easily expand to offset any reduction in California output, would a change in the output of California sugar beet refiners alter national sugar prices? Would the California sugar beet refiners still have incentives to fix subcompetitive low prices for sugar beets if they thought that would be the case? To answer, consider the case where local sugar beet supply is inelastic, that is a great reduction in sugar beet prices does not reduce local sugar beet output by much.

3.   Are Justices Jackson and Frankfurter correct that the fact that here the agreements based the local sugar beet prices on a share of national sugar profits (which reflect national sugar prices) alters the above conclusions? Suppose all the nation's sugar beet refiners agreed that instead of getting 50% of national sugar profits, sugar beet producers would get only 1%.

a.   What would that do to sugar beet output?

b.   In turn, what would that do to the output of refined sugar?

c.   And finally, what would that do to national sugar prices?

4.   Are the above conclusions altered by the fact that here the buying cartel apparently did not lower the share of sugar profits given to sugar beet producers, but rather fixed sugar beet prices based on an average of the sugar profits of all three local sugar beet refiners?

a.   Does this agreement lower the average price paid for sugar beets in California? If not, would it alter the total output of sugar beets in California?

b.   Did this lower the price paid to sugar beet producers who contracted with the most profitable (i.e., most efficient) California sugar refiner? Raise the price paid to sugar beet producers who contracted with the other two California sugar refiners? Why should we care about such mixed effects?

c. Before the buying cartel, when all the producers were apparently paying the same share of varying sugar profits, why did any sugar beet producers ever sell to the two less efficient sugar refiners at a lower price than they could have sold to the most efficient sugar refiner?

i. Is it probably because some sugar beet producers were located further from the most efficient producer than others?

ii. Doesn't that mean the local sugar beet markets are smaller than northern California?

iii. Should antitrust weigh harmful effects on market prices in one local producer market against beneficial effects on market prices in another market? Or should it condemn restraints that create anticompetitive effects in any market?

d. If the most efficient sugar refiner lowered the price it paid to sugar beet producers, and the two less efficient sugar refiners raised the price they paid, what would that likely do to the output sold to each? What effect is shifting output from the most efficient to the less efficient refiner likely to have on downstream sugar prices?

e. Why would the California sugar refiners want to enter into an agreement that would raise the prices two of them paid and take away the ability of the more efficient third firm to pay a higher price to reflect the higher profits it could earn on sugar beets? Would that agreement make any sense unless they were trying to maintain some sort of collusion on downstream sugar prices or output?

Commission Decision 80/917 of 9 July 1980, National Sulphuric Acid Association

O.J. 1980, L 260/24.

I. The Facts

. . . Sulphuric acid is one of the most widely used of all manufactured chemical products. . . . The principal products involving the use of sulphuric acid are phosphate fertilizers, paint, fibres, detergents and soap, sulphate of ammonia and various chemicals. . . .

The principal raw material used for the manufacture of sulphuric acid in the United Kingdom is sulphur. . . . Approximately one tonne of sulphur produces three tonnes of sulphuric acid.

Elemental sulphur is a homogeneous commodity and there is a relatively small number of major world producers, currently about eight. The market is a world market and prices for sulphur are largely determined by the balance between world supply and world demand. . . .

In 1979 the UK imported more than one million tonnes of elemental sulphur for sulphuric acid production, accounting for more than 95% of the sulphur used in the production of sulphuric acid. The remaining tonnage came from indigenous sources, mainly recovered as a by-product from oil refinery processes. . . .

In the early 1960s there were still substantially only three sources of supply of elemental sulphur available, namely Sulexco in the USA, Mexico, and ... France. Sulexco was the preponderant supplier. One other source which had been recently discovered, the sour gas fields of the western provinces of Canada, was not really an economic source of supply for the United Kingdom because of high freight rates. . . .

Until 1964 all elemental sulphur shipped to the UK was shipped in solid form on ordinary cargo ships chartered by the Pool. However technical developments ... enabled sulphur to be delivered in molten form both overland using road or rail tanker and by sea using specially constructed bulk tankers discharging at special terminals.

Liquid sulphur has many advantages over solid sulphur. Solid sulphur has to be liquified by a melting process before use; it is more expensive to handle; it has to be stored by the user; and it is more liable to cause pollution. But all the advantages of liquid sulphur were denied to the United Kingdom as long as there were no terminals at which the sulphur-carrying vessels could discharge.

Negotiations with Sulexco having come to nothing, the Mexican and French suppliers indicated their willingness to construct their own liquid sulphur terminals at Immingham once they were satisfied that they were likely to achieve an offtake of about 150,000 tonnes per annum from their respective terminals. Separate French and Mexican terminals were duly constructed at Immingham, the French terminal opening in 1964 and the Mexican terminal in 1965. At terminals such as these the sulphur is piped out of the tanker into heated pipes and thence into the supplier's storage tanks which are also heated. Further shipments from the supplier keep the storage tanks "topped up." From the storage tanks the sulphur is collected by the user by road tanker, often daily unless a company has facilities to receive direct through pipelines.

By the end of the 1960's a new possible source of supply had presented itself, namely Poland. Shipments were first taken from the Polish State trading company Ciech in 1969 and by 1972 Poland ranked after France and Mexico as the Pool's third largest supplier. But all Polish shipments were solid sulphur because Ciech had no liquid terminal. In 1972/73, however, Ciech opened a liquid terminal at Runcorn on the Manchester Ship Canal with an annual throughput of 350,000 tonnes initially, later building up to 400,000 tonnes.

By 1973, therefore, there were three main sources of supply of liquid sulphur in the United Kingdom, the French and the Mexican discharging at Immingham and the Polish discharging from Runcorn. The Immingham and Runcorn areas together include 15 plants representing about 60% of the UK production of sulphuric acid. This geographic proximity of liquid sulphur terminals to the premises of liquid sulphur users is, in view of the high road transport costs involved, a necessary requirement for the economic viability of any such terminal. Indeed, the costs are such that were the liquid sulphur to be carried more than a fairly short distance by road, about 40 miles (60 kilometres), a more economic alternative would be sought. . . .

Solid sulphur is shipped from France, Poland and Canada. Canadian sulphur is sold mainly through the Canadian export company Cansulex and by Shell Canada. Solid sulphur is shipped into a number of ports, in as close proximity as possible to the plant of the users concerned but road transport costs are not as important to the situation of the terminal as for liquid sulphur. The price paid for solid sulphur by the Pool is generally lower than that paid for liquid, reflecting the additional handling and melting costs associated with solid sulphur. Pool members requiring solid sulphur thus pay slightly less for their raw material than liquid users. . . .

The membership of the [National Sulphuric Acid] Association consists of all major manufacturers of sulphuric acid in the United Kingdom and Ireland, accounting for virtually the total manufacturing capacity in these two countries.

In 1956 the members of the Association formed . . . a joint buying pool for the purchase of elemental sulphur for all members who also wished to be members of the Pool. . . .

The Rules for the Sulphur Pool contain the following provisions.

(a) The price paid by members for sulphur purchased through the Pool is fixed by the management committee. . . .

(e) The sulphur is resold to the members on a no-profit, no-loss basis.

(f) Each member notifies the Pool of the tonnage of sulphur for which he wishes a contract entered into on his behalf for the ensuing period of six months commencing 1 January or 1 July. This tonnage is the member's "stated requirement" and the member undertakes to purchase on the terms referred to in the Rules and discussed at (a) to (e) above.

(g) Each member is required to purchase from the Pool at least 25% of the total sulphur acquired by him in any calendar year. Should any member purchase less than 25% of his annual requirements from the Pool, he shall be deemed to have withdrawn from the Pool from the end of that year. Such a purchaser may apply to rejoin the Pool commencing 1 July or 1 January on giving 12 months notice of his intention to do so. . . .

II.   Applicability of Article [101(1) TFEU]

. . . The Rules of the buying pool have the effect of restricting competition between the members of the Pool.

Each member of the Pool, to the extent he is committed to purchasing through the Pool, is prevented from competing with other Pool members to obtain more favourable terms from the suppliers than those obtained by the management committee.

To whatever amount the member is committed, he is deprived of the choice to negotiate terms and conditions with the suppliers which could include, as regards e.g. length of contract and rebates, those terms which would meet the needs of the individual member concerned more specifically than could be obtained by a body acting for a variety of sulphur users with widely varying requirements.

More particularly, individual members, to the extent that they are tied to the Pool, cannot purchase sulphur should prices become lower than those paid by the Pool or benefit from a particularly advantageous situation, e.g. where a supplier may have encountered contractual difficulties with another user or where a user wishes to sell surplus stocks. A member may also be unable to use his geographical location to best advantage as regards transport costs since the choice of port is in the hands of the Pool and any port used for a cargo is unlikely to be of equal advantage to all users of that cargo.

About 30% of the sulphuric acid manufactured by the Pool members is sold commercially to third parties and since sulphur accounts for up to 80% of the production cost of sulphuric acid, the equalising effect the Pool Rules have on the price of sulphur paid by the acid producers is felt in the price of sulphuric acid itself and, at least to some extent, in the prices of the numerous products which require, to a greater or lesser degree, sulphuric acid as a constituent chemical. This is true whether these acid-based products are manufactured by Pool members or by those to whom sulphuric acid is sold. Thus price competition, to the extent that the members purchase through the Pool (i.e. between 25 and 100% of requirements), is largely eliminated between Pool members selling sulphuric acid, a homogeneous product for which little other competition is possible....

II.   Applicability of Article [101(3) TFEU] ...

A.   Improvements in production and distribution

Although the management committee of the Pool dictates to its members the port at which the sulphur is to be discharged and this may not always be the nearest port to the destination of at least part of the cargo, nevertheless the fact that the Pool deals with a number of suppliers and knows its members' requirements leads to the operation of a flexible distribution system acceptable to the members. By contrast to an individual member, especially one with a small sulphur requirement, the Pool can request a supplier with whom it has a contract to deliver a full cargo of sulphur to a particular port. This port will be in the optimum situation for access to most of the various users for whom the sulphur is intended. If liquid sulphur is being purchased, then the supplier with a terminal in the best location, taking into account the destination of the sulphur, would be requested to deliver the required quantity.

In view of the very high transport costs for the carriage of liquid sulphur, in particular by road, from the dockside terminal to the users' plant, the choice of port is very important in any calculation of the price to be paid by a user for delivery at his plant.

The advantages to a user of liquid sulphur over solid are detailed ... above, but the fact that United Kingdom sulphur users have been able to obtain those benefits for so long is in no small measure due to the existence of the Pool and the fact that it could guarantee to the suppliers the purchase of at least the minimum quantity of liquid sulphur to make the installation of the required terminals economically viable.

In addition, the Pool, as a result of its longterm contracts with different suppliers, can have liquid sulphur supplied at the four terminals in the United Kingdom operated by the suppliers. It therefore has the ability, in the event of a shortage of liquid sulphur at one terminal, to provide, with the supplier's agreement and where transport costs allow, supplies from other terminals to avoid the effects of shortages at members' plants. . . .

The Pool's operation therefore allows a considerable degree of flexibility in the distribution of both solid and liquid sulphur. This is of advantage to the members and would be difficult, if not impossible, for any member acting individually to achieve since few, if any, Pool members would be in a position to deal with more than one supplier at a time.

In general, demand has tended to exceed supply on the market for elemental sulphur and purchasers of large quantities have thus been more likely to obtain security of supply and the most advantageous prices. The Pool, therefore, as potentially one of the largest single purchasers of elemental sulphur in the Community, has been in the position of negotiating with all of the relatively few suppliers in the world from a position of strength. This has generally meant that even in times of shortage the Pool has been able to supply its members with at worst a considerable proportion of their individual requirements and no member has had to stop production of sulphuric acid owing to a lack of availability of sulphur.

The existence of the Pool provides price and other advantages to the 14 members who manufacture relatively small quantities of sulphuric acid and have correspondingly small requirements in sulphur. It is likely, especially in periods when demand outstrips supply, that these purchasers of small quantities, accounting for more than half the Pool's membership, would have difficulty in interesting the suppliers in furnishing them with their individual requirements at a reasonable price or even at all. Only when their sulphur needs are aggregated, giving the Pool a strong negotiating position with quantities of a size to interest the suppliers, are they assured of obtaining their requirements and at a reasonable price.

B.   Consumer benefits

The result of these benefits in cost, flexibility in distribution and security of supply of the elemental sulphur is that members of the Pool are assured of obtaining, at a reasonable price, adequate supplies of the raw material to which up to 80% of the cost of manufacturing sulphuric acid is attributable. Since 30% of the total quantity of sulphuric acid manufactured by Pool members is sold to third parties, competition between Pool members on the market for sulphuric acid is ensured. In addition, the consumer, i.e. both the user of the sulphuric acid and the user of a product in the manufacture of which sulphuric acid is required, receives the benefit resulting from the activities of the Pool of regular supplies of both sulphuric acid and the many products in the various sectors for which the acid is used at a cost which reflects the price obtained by the Pool for the raw sulphur. These products, which include fertilizers, paint, fibres, detergents and soap, are, as is sulphuric acid itself, sold on markets in which there is competition between Pool members and between Pool members and other manufacturers of the products. This competition ensures that the consumer receives the cost benefits attributable to the Pool's activities both on purchasing sulphuric acid and on any downstream products. If at any time the conditions at which the Pool obtains sulphur are less advantageous than those which could be obtained by members individually, consumers should receive the cost benefits resulting from members being free to purchase up to 75% of their sulphur requirements from sources outside the Pool.

C.   Indispensability of restrictions

Although the Commission is aware of the benefits of the joint buying pool in terms of improvements in the distribution of sulphur and the production of sulphuric acid, the associated technical and economic progress and resulting consumer benefits, it must at the same time establish that the Pool Rules contain no restrictions on competition which are not indispensable to the attainment of their objectives and which would eliminate competition in respect of the products concerned.

For the Pool to function effectively, it must have a knowledge of the quantities of sulphur which its members wish it to purchase. This knowledge must be available to the Pool in good time to allow meaningful negotiations with the suppliers for specific quantities, albeit usually within certain margins, and for a fixed term. Thus the Pool's task would be greatly hindered if it did not know its members' tonnage requirements for at least the ensuing six month period. That these requirements must amount to a minimum of 25% of a member's total requirements for any calendar year is a restriction without which the Pool's strong negotiating position with the suppliers would be eroded to too great an extent. This commitment by the members gives the Pool credibility in its negotiations with the suppliers which it would otherwise lack, since the suppliers are well aware of the total manufacturing capacity the Pool represents. Thus, to allow the Pool to attain its objectives or indeed for the Pool to continue to function effectively in the face of relatively few suppliers in a situation where demand frequently outstrips supply, its credibility with the suppliers is of great importance.

D.   Elimination of competition

In order that the Pool can be certain that its members are adhering to the Rules as regards the commitment to purchase at least 25% of requirements through the Pool, members are required to inform the Pool of purchases of imported sulphur other than through the Pool. Members can, of course, continue to be members of the Pool while purchasing up to 75% of their imported requirements from other sources. In addition, one of the largest producers of sulphuric acid in the UK, using about 11% of the sulphur imported into the UK, is not a member of the Pool. Thus competition in respect of a substantial part of the products concerned is not eliminated. . . .

Questions on National Sulphuric Acid Association

1. What are the similarities and differences between the factual scenario present in this case and the one present in *Mandeville*?

2.   Do you agree that there were efficiencies to the joint purchasing pool? What were they? If those efficiencies benefited small buyers, why did the large buyers agree? Should this pool have been deemed per se illegal?

3.   Why does it matter that members limit their purchase through the pool to 25% of their total sulphur requirements?

4.   Was the fact that sulphur represents around 80% of the costs of production of sulphuric acid significant in this case? Would things have been different if sulphur represented only 10% of the costs of production of sulphuric acid?

5.   How can the Commission be sure that any efficiency gains will be passed on downstream to consumers of sulphuric acid?

6.   Did the fact that the market for the product of sulphur was oligopolistic play a role in this case? Would things have been different if the producers of sulphur had been numerous?

The EU Safe Harbor

It should be noted that the joint purchasing agreements of the kind described above are covered by the Commission guidelines on the applicability of Article 101 to horizontal cooperation agreements. The Commission once again applies the "safe harbour" approach we have seen applied to specialization, R&D, and transfer of technology agreements. The guidelines provide at paragraphs 208–209:

> There is no absolute threshold above which it can be presumed that the parties to a joint purchasing arrangement have market power so that the joint purchasing arrangement is likely to give rise to restrictive effects on competition within the meaning of Article 101(1). However, in most cases it is unlikely that market power exists if the parties to the joint purchasing arrangement have a combined market share not exceeding 15% on the purchasing market or markets as well as a combined market share not exceeding 15% on the selling market or markets. In any event, if the parties' combined market shares do not exceed 15% on both the purchasing and the selling market or markets, it is likely that the conditions of Article 101(3) are fulfilled.

> A market share above that threshold in one or both markets does not automatically indicate that the joint purchasing arrangement is likely to give rise to restrictive effects on competition. A joint purchasing arrangement which does not fall within that safe harbour requires a detailed assessment of its effects on the market involving, but not limited to, factors such as market concentration and possible countervailing power of strong suppliers.

Countervailing Power and the Problem of the Second Best

As *Trial Lawyers* indicates, U.S. antitrust law recognizes no exception to its per se rule for cases where a cartel is organized to counteract market power. Congress has provided some antitrust exemptions (such as for farmer cooperatives and collective bargaining by labor) that might in part be based on such a theory. Absent such an antitrust exemption, the defense that current prices are unreasonable is inadmissible even if that claim is based on the argument that current prices are uncompetitive. Indeed, this per se rule applies even if the defendants can show that their counterparts on the other side of the market acquired their market power illegally, such as through a cartel.[92] Likewise, there does not appear to be any EU authority that has accepted a countervailing power argument as an efficiency defense. However, some authority in the U.S. and EU suggests that buyer sophistication or market power might be relevant to assessing the degree of market power possessed by defendants.[93] This does not matter for per se claims that exclude evidence of market power, but might be important for antitrust claims where the existence or degree of market power is an element.

Some scholars have argued that antitrust law should be altered to include a countervailing power defense.[94] They can draw some support from the economic theory of the second best, which demonstrates that if a market is inefficient along any dimension, it is indeterminate whether creating another inefficiency will decrease or increase market efficiency.[95] What do you think should be the law in the U.S. and EU on countervailing power? Consider the following hypothetical.

Suppose there are ten local miners of vermiculite, a mineral found in the ground that must be transported to a local processor because it is too heavy to transport long distances before processing. These miners face one local processor who takes advantage of his buyer market power by offering subcompetitive prices. The miners thus decide to form a joint sales agency to bargain as unified group to increase prices. Is this undesirable?

1.   What if the buyer market power is illegal because acquired in violation of antitrust law? If so, is the best remedy antitrust enforcement against the buyer rather than entrenching anticompetitive market power on both sides of the market? Once the courts allow a seller cartel, wouldn't they have to allow a buyer cartel to countervail it if buyer entry occurred in the future?

2.   What if the buyer market power is legal but correctable by market forces, such as by entry encouraged by supracompetitive prices? Wouldn't it be better to have the buyer market power corrected by such market forces rather than to entrench market power on the other side?

---

92.   See Joseph F. Brodley, *Joint Ventures and Antitrust Policy*, 95 HARV. L. REV. 1521, 1569 (1982); Joel Davidow, *Antitrust, Foreign Policy, and International Buying Cooperation*, 84 YALE L.J. 268, 270–71 (1974); LAWRENCE SULLIVAN, HANDBOOK OF THE LAW OF ANTITRUST § 75, at 204 (1977).

93.   *See* Chapter 7.A.6.

94.   *See* Warren S. Grimes, *The Sherman Act's Unintended Bias Against Lilliputians*, 69 ANTITRUST L.J. 195 (2001); Barabara Ann White, *Countervailing Power–Different Rules for Different Markets?*, 41 DUKE L.J. 1045 (1992).

95.   R.G. Lipsey & Kelvin Lancaster, *The General Theory of Second Best*, 24 REV. ECON. STUD. 11 (1956).

3. What if the buyer market power was acquired legally through investment (such a building the processing plant) but is uncorrectable by market forces?

a. If the buyer market power is really uncorrectable by market forces, doesn't that necessarily mean the buyer is a natural monopoly?

b. In that case, isn't it better to remedy market power with utility-type rate regulation rather than to entrench an avoidable market power on the other side? Can antitrust adjudicators reasonably provide the sort of prospective and constantly updated guidance on pricing that utility rate regulators provide?

c. If the government has declined to adopt utility rate-regulation, do antitrust adjudicators have any warrant to do so through the guise of antitrust law by allowing the creation of buyers with market power in the hopes they will impose a form of rate regulation of their own?

4. What if the buyer market power is legal, reflects a natural monopoly uncorrectable by market forces, and for some reason is not amendable to utility-type rate regulation?

a. Even in that case, aren't the *ex ante* effects of permitting a countervailing cartel likely to be undesirable?

    i. Don't any extra returns resulting from buyer market power reflect a desirable return for the investment in the local area that created that market power?

    ii. Won't forcing the buyer to share those returns with miners who did not make that investment necessarily discourage such local investments at the margin, by preventing firms from building costly processing plants in areas that can only support one plant, where the costs of that investment can only be recouped if the builder is allowed to exploit the resulting local market power it earned by its investment?

    iii. Shouldn't we distinguish between market power earned through productive investments and market power created by anticompetitive combinations that reduce market options?

b. Even if we assume away those *ex ante* effects, do we know for sure that sellers allowed to use a cartel to create market power will exercise it to try to countervail the buyer? Don't the vermiculte miners also have incentives to collude with the vermiculite processor to enhance their mutual market power against downstream buyers of processed vermiculite and split the supracompetitive profits?[96]

5. Even if we assume all the above problems do not apply, aren't the *ex post* efficiency effects of permitting a cartel that tries to exercise countervailing power at best indeterminate under the theory of the second best? That is, a countervailing cartel might increase or decrease market output.

6. Given all the above, which doctrine is best given that it is unambiguously better to correct any buyer market with legal and market remedies in situations 1–4, ambiguous whether allowing countervailing

---

96. It turns out that sometimes they do. *See* Chapter 4.

market power will improve market efficiency in residual situation 5, and adjudicators are likely to have difficulty identifying with perfect accuracy which cases fall within residual situation 5?

a.   Isn't the underdeterrence created by mistakenly allowing the defense in situations 1–4 likely to be greater than the overdeterrence created by denying the defense in situation 5 to those cases where it turned out that countervailing market power would have reduced allocative inefficiency?

    i.   Even in the rare and ambiguous situation fitting within residual situation 5, couldn't any change in industry costs, technology or demand end the buyer's "natural" monopoly and thus allow correction by market forces? Thus, even in this case, wouldn't future market results probably be worsened by entrenching anticompetitive market power on both sides?

    ii.   Even in situation 5, don't we still have the offsetting inefficiency that a seller cartel will have to allocate mining production across miners in a way that reduces productive efficiency and decreases miner incentives to increase their productive efficiency in the future?

b.   Wouldn't the underdeterrence problem created by allowing the defense be even greater if we take into account litigation costs and likely inaccurate conclusions about ascertaining whether buyer market power exists at all?

    i.   Wouldn't allowing such a defense lead all cartels to claim there is buyer market power whenever that is at all plausible?

    ii.   Wouldn't that lessen the certainty of the per se rule and thus reduce the rule's ability to deter undesirable cartels?

c.   Even if courts could with perfect accuracy decide when cases falling within residual category 5 existed, wouldn't allowing this defense require antitrust adjudicators to decide when countervailing power improves the market outcome? Can that be distinguished from asking antitrust adjudicators to inquire into the reasonableness of the price? Are antitrust adjudicators likely to be accurate in making such judgments? Do adjudicators have the administrative capacity to keep updating those judgments as market conditions change over time, and with each new bargain between the seller cartel and powerful buyer?

d.   Would these problems exist if adjudicators could perfectly and costlessly determine and constantly update conclusions about: (1) the existence of market power, (2) which cases fell within residual case 5, and (3) which exercises of countervailing market power increased overall market efficiency notwithstanding the creation of seller productive inefficiencies and the possibility that changing market conditions would alter the analysis? Do we enjoy such a world?

Other Nations' Regulation of Buyer Cartels

Most other nations' provisions on horizontal price-fixing explicitly treat buyer cartels the same as seller cartels.[97] Some nations cover buyer cartels under more general provisions.[98] New Zealand makes its per se rule against horizontal price-fixing inapplicable to actual joint purchasing.[99] Which legal doctrine seems best?

---

97. *See* Argentina Competition Law Arts. 2; Australia Trade Practices Act § 44ZZRD; Canada Competition Act § 45; Chile Competition Law Art. 3; Egypt Competition Law Art. 6; India Competition Act § 3(3); Israel Restrictive Trade Practices Law § 2(b); Mexico Competition Law Art. 9; Singapore Competition Law § 34(2); South Africa Competition Act § 4(1)(b); Thailand Trade Competition Act § 27; Turkey Competition Act Art. 4.

98. For example, although Brazil's price-fixing provisions only refers to seller cartels, *see* Brazil Antitrust Law No. 8,884, Art.21(I), its more general Article 20 prohibition of anticompetitive conduct has been interpreted to cover buyer cartels as well. See Cases No. 08012.002493/2005–16 and 08012.008372/99–14.

99. *See* New Zealand Commerce Act § 33.

CHAPTER 3

WHAT UNILATERAL CONDUCT IS ILLEGAL?

A. RELEVANT LAWS & BASIC LEGAL ELEMENTS

1. U.S. LAWS AND LEGAL ELEMENTS

Three U.S. statutes cover anticompetitive unilateral conduct. The most important is Sherman Act § 2 because it is both general and enforceable by private parties who can seek big damages and bring most of the U.S. lawsuits.

Sherman Act § 2, 15 U.S.C. § 2

"Every person who shall monopolize, or attempt to monopolize, or combine or conspire with any other person or persons, to monopolize any part of the trade or commerce among the several States, or with foreign nations, shall be deemed guilty of a felony...."

Later provisions add to this criminal penalty the standard set of damage and injunctive claims, including private actions for treble damages. See Chapter 1. Courts have interpreted this statute to embody three separate offenses. All of them require an effect on interstate commerce that is trivial to prove and rarely relevant, as well as sufficient effects on U.S. commerce. *See* Chapters 1 & 8.

Monopolization. The offense of monopolization "has two elements: (1) the possession of monopoly power in the relevant market and (2) the willful acquisition or maintenance of that power as distinguished from growth or development as a consequence of a superior product, business acumen, or historic accident."[1] This is generally simplified to say the two elements are (1) monopoly power and (2) anticompetitive or exclusionary conduct.[2] Although this standard covers any horizontal agreement to combine into a monopoly,[3] what it adds to Sherman Act § 1 is that it covers unilateral conduct as well. The result is a very general substantive rule forbidding a firm with monopoly power from engaging in any anticompetitive unilateral conduct to obtain, maintain, or enhance that power.

---

1. United States v. Grinnell Corp., 384 U.S. 563, 570–571 (1966).

2. See Verizon Communications v. Law Offices of Curtis V. Trinko, 540 U.S. 398, 407 (2004); Aspen Skiing Co. v. Aspen Highlands Skiing Corp., 472 U.S. 585, 595–96, 602, 605 & n.32 (1985).

3. See, e.g., *Grinnell*, 384 U.S. at 576; American Tobacco Co. v. United States, 328 U.S. 781, 783–84, 808–09, 813–14 (1946); Standard Oil Co. v. United States, 221 U.S. 1, 70–75 (1911) (same).

Attempted Monopolization. The offense of attempted monopolization requires proof "(1) that the defendant has engaged in predatory or anticompetitive conduct with (2) a specific intent to monopolize and (3) a dangerous probability of achieving monopoly power."[4] This offense thus adds a specific intent element but lowers the monopoly power requirement to a dangerous probability of obtaining such power. Further, specific intent is understood to be an objective intent inferable from conduct that is palpably anticompetitive. The result is to provide a general substantive rule banning palpably anticompetitive unilateral conduct that might realistically lead to monopoly power.

Conspiracy to Monopolize. The offense of a conspiracy to monopolize requires evidence of (1) a conspiracy (2) a specific intent to monopolize and (3) an overt act in furtherance of the conspiracy.[5] Although this provision does not regulate unilateral conduct, it covers the overlapping issue of agreements that seek to create the sort of monopoly power that is the target of the regulations of unilateral conduct. This provision is not limited to the sort of per se violations covered by Sherman Act § 1, and its elements do not require proof of actual market power or the existence of anticompetitive effects. Many courts have thus concluded that, with the requisite specific intent to monopolize, an agreement might violate Sherman Act § 2 even though it doesn't violate Sherman Act § 1.[6] However, the Supreme Court has more recently suggested the possibility that a dismissal of a Sherman Act § 1 claim for failure to allege a per se violation or anticompetitive effects might require dismissal of a conspiracy to monopolize claim, though it remanded the issue for further consideration.[7]

Unfair Trade Practices. Another U.S. statute governing unilateral conduct is Federal Trade Commission § 5, whose language is even more general but whose enforcement is more limited.

Federal Trade Commission Act § 5, 15 U.S.C. § 45

"Unfair methods of competition in or affecting commerce ... are hereby declared unlawful."

This provision is more general because it covers unilateral anticompetitive conduct even by a firm without monopoly power. As discussed in Chapter 6, this helps cover unilateral conduct that facilitates oligopolistic coordination. More relevant here, this language covers unilateral anticompetitive conduct by firms that have enough market power to create unilateral anticompeti-

---

4. Spectrum Sports v. McQuillan, 506 U.S. 447 (1993).

5. United States v. Yellow Cab Co., 332 U.S. 218, 225–26 (1947); *American Tobacco Co.*, 328 U.S. at 789.

6. See International Distribution Centers, Inc. v. Walsh Trucking Co., 812 F.2d 786, 795 (2d Cir. 1987); United States v. Consolidated Laundries Corp., 291 F.2d 563, 573 (2d Cir. 1961); Stewart Glass & Mirror v. U.S. Auto Glass Disc. Ctrs., 200 F.3d 307, 316 (5th Cir. 2000); United States v. National City Lines, Inc., 186 F.2d 562, 566–68 (7th Cir. 1951); Baxley–DeLamar Monuments, Inc. v. American Cemetery Ass'n, 843 F.2d 1154, 1157 (8th Cir. 1988); Alexander v. National Farmers Organization, 687 F.2d 1173, 1182 (8th Cir.1982); Monument Builders of Greater Kansas City, Inc. v. American Cemetery Ass'n, 891 F.2d 1473, 1484 (10th Cir.1989); Levine v. Central Florida Medical Affiliates, Inc., 72 F.3d 1538, 1555–56 (11th Cir.1996).

7. NYNEX Corp. v. Discon, Inc., 525 U.S. 128, 139 (1998).

tive effects, but not enough power to find monopoly power or a dangerous probability of obtaining it. However, this provision can be enforced only through actions for prospective relief brought by the Federal Trade Commission. *See* Chapter 1. The net result is that, compared to Sherman Act § 2, the FTC Act lowers the power requirement and makes any anticompetitive conduct by a firm with market power potentially actionable, but also limits enforcement to prospective relief sought by a disinterested government agency.

Anticompetitive Price Discrimination. Finally, the Robinson–Patman Act prohibits one particular type of unilateral conduct—anticompetitive price discrimination.

Robinson–Patman Act, 15 U.S.C. § 13(a)

"It shall be unlawful for any person engaged in commerce, in the course of such commerce, either directly or indirectly, to discriminate in price between different purchasers of commodities of like grade and quality ... where the effect of such discrimination may be substantially to lessen competition or tend to create a monopoly in any line of commerce, or to injure, destroy, or prevent competition with any person who either grants or knowingly receives the benefit of such discrimination, or with customers of either of them."

This statute does not prohibit all price discrimination, but only price discrimination that threatens anticompetitive effects either in the defendant's market or to downstream markets. Brooke Group Ltd. v. Brown & Williamson Tobacco, 509 U.S. 209, 220 (1993). Such anticompetitive effects are proven if there is "a reasonable possibility" of substantial injury to competition. *Id.* at 222. The statute also has exceptions for where the price discrimination is justified by cost differences, changing market conditions, or good faith efforts to meet competition. *Id.*; 15 U.S.C. § 13. The result is to provide a lower standard of proving anticompetitive effects than Sherman Act § 2 but for a much more limited range of conduct. This chapter addresses only the application of this Act to conduct that causes anticompetitive effects in the defendant's market, deferring claims based on downstream effects until Chapter 5.

The Mix of Regulatory Strategies. One might wonder why a single nation would have antitrust laws with multiple differing standards for judging anticompetitive unilateral conduct. Presumably, there is a better reason than deep indecisiveness. To begin to see the answer, consider whether it would be any better to simply have one statute that created a private action for treble damages against any unilateral anticompetitive conduct by any firm, or at least by any firm with market power. Such a statute would certainly deter more anticompetitive unilateral conduct than does existing U.S. law. However, it would also deter more procompetitive unilateral conduct that might mistakenly be judged to be anticompetitive, which is a particular concern because a rule that covers unilateral conduct would include any conduct a firm might engage in and thus is harder for firms to avoid. The decision by the U.S. (and other nations) not to adopt such a uniformly sweeping rule with treble damages is consistent with a belief that any reduction in underdeterrence of anticompetitive conduct from such a rule would not be worth the increase in overdeterrence of procompetitive conduct.

The question then becomes what set of legal rules would achieve the optimal result by minimizing the total harm from underdeterrence and overdeterrence.[8] If we have a rule limited to firms with some high degree of market power, then it excludes the bulk of firms that have less power and might otherwise be overdeterred and focuses on the set of firms for which the concern about underdeterring undesirable conduct is greatest. For this set of firms, a sweeping rule that covers any of their anticompetitive conduct and imposes high penalties might minimize the total under- and overdeterrence, which would justify the U.S. law on monopolization. If we have another rule that extends to firms with medium levels of market power, then our concern about overdeterrence increases and our concern about underdeterrence decreases. It thus might make sense to reduce overdeterrence concerns by adding an intent requirement to limit the rule to the most palpably anticompetitive conduct, which would fit U.S. law on attempted monopolization. Another strategy might be to limit the rule to specifically defined anticompetitive conduct that is undesirable and can easily be avoided, which arguably fits U.S. law on price discrimination that causes anticompetitive effects in the defendant's market. However, we might still be concerned that firms with modest degrees of market power might remain underdeterred from engaging in anticompetitive unilateral conduct. To address this concern without unduly increasing overdeterrence concerns, we might want a rule that covers any such conduct, but that limits enforcement to prospective relief by a financially disinterested government agency, which (unlike private parties) should exercise its discretion to avoid attacking desirable conduct and when it errs will not create the chilling risk of treble damages or retroactive penalties.

As the above suggests, it may be best to employ a mix of strategies to fully optimize the tradeoff between over- and underdeterrence. If so, it makes sense not to define one single offense of anticompetitive unilateral conduct, but rather to have various offenses, each of which adopts a different strategy. We can understand the separate provisions regulating agreements and unilateral conduct as further evidencing such a mixed strategy.

How the Conspiracy to Monopolize Offense Fits Into the Mix. Where the offense of a conspiracy to monopoly fits into this mix of strategies is an interesting question. If, as one recent case suggested might be true, failure to prove a § 1 claim dictates dismissal of a conspiracy to monopolize claim, then that would make the "conspiracy to monopolize" provision entirely superfluous. This would effectively eliminate the conspiracy to monopolize offense from the U.S. statute and override a lot of prior precedent. However, even if that might be sound antitrust policy, such an interpretation would violate the canon of statutory construction that, if

---

8. For a general discussion of the various possible legal strategies for optimizing the tradeoff between overdeterrence and underdeterrence, including using rules versus standards or varying the type or level of sanctions, see Elhauge, *Sacrificing Corporate Profits in the Public Interest,* 80 N.Y.U. LAW REVIEW 733, 747–56 (2005); Stephen Bundy & Einer Elhauge, *Knowledge About Legal Sanctions,* 92 MICH. L. REV. 261, 267–79 (1993).

possible, courts should not interpret statutes in a way that renders some statutory language superfluous.[9]

Under that canon, the issue would seem to be whether, when we do not have an ordinary conspiracy but one with the specific intent of monopolizing a market, Congress might have reasonably thought that the mix of overdeterence/underdeterrence concerns was sufficiently different that it makes sense to drop the proof of market power or anticompetitive effects typically necessary to prove a conspiracy was unreasonable. This seems possible because, compared to ordinary agreements, such a conspiracy to monopolize would seem to raise (a) fewer overdeterrence concerns given the specific intent and the goal and (b) greater underdeterrence concerns because, if successful, the harm is greater. Likewise, Congress might have reasonably thought that, where we do not have an ordinary attempt to monopolize but a conspiracy to further it, the overdeterrence/underdeterrence concerns are sufficiently different to drop the proof of a dangerous probability of acquiring a monopoly that is necessary to show attempted monopolization. Overdeterrence concerns would be different because it is easier to avoid a conspiracy than to avoid unilateral conduct, and underdeterrence concerns would be greater because conspiracies are generally more dangerous than unilateral conduct.

One might thus make a reasonable argument for a separate conspiracy to monopolize claim. However, one might instead think that the lack of any need to prove market power or anticompetitive effects creates such overdeterrence problems, and the underdeterrence problems are sufficiently small given the other antitrust provisions regulating this area, that no separate conspiracy to monopolize claim should exist. Even if one thinks the latter, though, it may not be a reasonable reading of the statute because it effectively requires reading some words out of the enactment.

Assuming a conspiracy to monopolize claim does not require the same level of proof on anticompetitive effects or market power as is required for a § 1 claim or an attempted monopolization claim, a separate issue is whether such a claim requires some evidence of market definition. Many courts have indicated that a conspiracy to monopolize claim does not even require proof of market definition.[10] These cases implicitly hold it suffices that the conspirators believed that there was a market they were trying to monopolize and that they could cause the anticompetitive effect of monopolizing it. Other courts have held that proof of market definition is required.[11] The latter cases thus implicitly hold that there must be objective proof that there was a properly defined market that the defendants could have intended to monopolize, thus providing some objective basis for thinking that a successful conspiracy could have created some monopoly power and anticompetitive harm. This legal conflict may not matter much

---

9. South Carolina v. Catawba Indian Tribe, Inc., 476 U.S. 498, 510 n.22 (1986) (collecting sources).

10. *See* cases cited *supra* note 6.

11. See Doctor's Hosp. of Jefferson, Inc. v. Southeast Med. Alliance, Inc., 123 F.3d 301, 311 (5th Cir.1997); Bill Beasley Farms, Inc. v. Hubbard Farms, 695 F.2d 1341, 1343 (11th Cir.1983). These decisions may, however, have been superseded by subsequent decisions in those circuits. See sources cited *supra* note 6.

because a factfinder is unlikely to find specific intent to monopolize if the market and any potential for causing anticompetitive harm seem implausible. The main practical impact is thus likely to be which side bears the costly burden of producing sufficient evidence to survive summary judgment on the issue of market definition. Although the burdens of proof on market definition are normally borne by antitrust plaintiffs, one could conclude that the burden of production on that issue should be satisfied by proof that the defendants conspired with the specific intent of having the enormous anticompetitive effect of monopolizing a market, thus justifying a shift in the burden of production onto the defendants.

2. EU LAW AND LEGAL ELEMENTS

The central provision is Article 102 of the TFEU, which provides:

Article 102 of the TFEU

"Any abuse by one or more undertakings of a dominant position within the common market or in a substantial part of it shall be prohibited as incompatible with the common market in so far as it may affect trade between Member States. Such abuse may, in particular, consist in:

(a) directly or indirectly imposing unfair purchase or selling prices or other unfair trading conditions;

(b) limiting production, markets or technical development to the prejudice of consumers;

(c) applying dissimilar conditions to equivalent transactions with other trading parties, thereby placing them at a competitive disadvantage;

(d) making the conclusion of contracts subject to acceptance by the other parties of supplementary obligations which, by their nature or according to commercial usage, have no connection with the subject of such contracts.

Article 102 thus requires proof of: (1) a dominant position within the common market or a substantial part of it; and (2) an abuse of that position that impacts trade between Member States."

The dominant position element requires some proof of market power. The statutory language has also been interpreted to cover situations where more than one firm holds a dominant position, which is called "collective dominance." The abuse element covers not only "exclusionary" abuses (through which a dominant firm seeks to anticompetitively impair rival competition or growth) but also "exploitative abuses" (through which dominant firms exploit their market power against customers).

The standard on exclusionary abuses is conduct "which, through recourse to methods different from those governing normal competition in products or services on the basis of the transactions of commercial operators, has the effect of hindering the maintenance of the degree of competition still existing in the market or the growth of that competition." Case

T203/01 Manufacture Française des Pneumatiques Michelin v. Commission (Michelin II), ¶ 54, [2003] ECR II–4071. There is no generic standard defining when a given behavior by a dominant firm amounts to an exploitative abuse. Article 102(a), however, expressly states that an abuse may, in particular, consist of unfair prices or output limitations. For instance, in *United Brands*, the Court of Justice ruled that excessive prices would violate Article 102 where they bore no reasonable relation to the economic value of the product supplied and resulted in harm being caused to consumers. [1978] E.C.R. 207. In *Tetra Pak II*, the Commission concluded that a clause obliging the payment of a rent, which amounted to almost the value of the machine, was considered unfair as it would force the consumer to pay as much as if it had purchased the machine without securing any of the legal benefits of being owner. O.J. 1992, L 72/1, ¶¶ 135–38. Because it is extremely difficult in practice to determine when a price is excessive and because the Commission does not want to engage in price control, there has been relatively little examination of high prices and other exploitative behavior by the Commission. The bulk of cases actually brought under Article 102 are for exclusionary abuses rather than exploitative abuses.

General Similarities and Differences Between EU and U.S. Regulatory Strategy on Unilateral Conduct. Like U.S. law, EU law covers unilateral conduct by firms holding some degree of market power. It is not entirely clear the extent to which the requisite degree of market power differs. U.S. law on monopolization does use the term "monopoly power" whereas EU competition law uses "dominant position." This may reflect the fact that the U.S. enacted the Sherman Act in 1890, before the modern economic literature on dominant firms, whereas EU competition law on the topic is of more recent vintage. (The EU terminology is more technically accurate because U.S. courts use the term "monopoly power" to include large firms that do have some smaller rivals, which would be called dominant firms in the modern economic literature. *See* Chapter 1.) However, as shown below, EU cases have allowed a dominant position to be proven with smaller market shares than those necessary to prove monopoly power under U.S. law. On the other hand, U.S. law requires less than monopoly power to prove a claim of attempted monopolization, price discrimination, or a violation of the FTC Act. Thus, the power necessary to show a dominant position under EU law may lie somewhere between these various shades of market power required by varying U.S. laws.

U.S. and EU law are also similar in that neither makes it illegal to simply possess the requisite degree of market power. Rather, both require in addition some form of bad conduct. But whether one imposes tougher standards than the other cannot be gleaned by the abstract meanings of the terms "exclusionary," "anticompetitive," or "abusive"—that depends on how those terms are applied to concrete cases, as we shall see below. Further, the U.S. laws vary the conduct standard with the degree of market power at issue, with a tougher standard requiring intent being applied to a firm that has a dangerous probability of acquiring monopoly power but has not yet obtained it, a weaker standard being applied to firms with mere market power who are only regulated prospectively by the FTC, and a standard limited to certain forms of price discrimination being applied to firms who have merely "a reasonable possibility" of achieving anticompetitive effects. The European conduct standard may thus be more lenient than some of these standards and tougher than others.

A more important linguistic difference between U.S. and European law may lie in the required connection between the illicit conduct and requisite market power. U.S. law prohibits not only anticompetitive conduct that helps maintain or enhance monopoly power a firm already has, but with its "-ize" suffix has been interpreted to also prohibit anticompetitive conduct that creates monopoly power or a dangerous probability of acquiring it. EU law has no parallel requirement, prohibiting only abuse "of" a dominant position that already exists, and in that sense seems narrower because it does not appear to cover conduct that helps create, and even less threatens to create, such dominance. On the other hand, EU law seems broader in that it prohibits exploitative abuses of a dominant position, such as unfair prices or output reductions, regardless of whether that conduct had any causal connection to the likelihood of maintaining, enhancing or obtaining dominant market power. U.S. antitrust law, in contrast, leaves completely unrestrained the prices or output of a firm that acquired and maintained its market power without anticompetitive conduct. But this last difference is smaller in practice than in theory because the European Commission brings few cases of exploitative abuses of a dominant position.

Perhaps the biggest difference is that, unlike in the U.S., the dominant form of enforcement is by the European Commission, which can seek fines but largely uses injunctive remedies. *See* Chapter 1. Given that, like the U.S. FTC, the European Commission is a disinterested administrative agency pursuing less punitive remedies, it might thus make sense for Article 102 to cover firms with lower degrees of power than U.S. monopolization doctrine and to have substantive standards that cover a broader range of conduct, which as we shall see EU caselaw arguably does. It is less clear that it makes sense to have a competition authority prohibit the unilateral conduct of excessive prices or output limitations, which would seem to be inherent features of dominant market power. Normally that sort of utility rate regulation is limited to cases of natural monopoly where the monopolies are not earned and cannot be corrected by the market and special expert agencies can prospectively set rates. This may explain why the EU law against excessive pricing is so rarely enforced. But if a rule effectively providing for utility rate regulation of any firm with dominant market power does make sense, it certainly makes far more sense when the enforcement lies within the power of a single expert agency that largely acts prospectively rather than in a system (like the U.S.) that relies on retroactive actions for treble damages adjudicated years later by randomly selected lay jurors and judges who may lack economic expertise.

How Collective Dominance Fits In. Article 102 on its face covers "[a]ny abuse by one *or more undertakings* of a dominant position," and thus covers the situation where firms act as a cartel and possess a collective dominant position that they abuse.[12] Like U.S. caselaw, EU caselaw does

---

12. *See* DG Competition Discussion Paper on the Application of Article 82 of the Treaty [now 102 TFEU] to Exclusionary Abuses § 4.3, at ¶¶ 43–45, § 5.4, at ¶¶ 74–76 (Dec. 2005) (collecting cases).

not equate an oligopoly with a cartel because it does not deem oligopolistic coordination sufficient to satisfy the agreement requirement. *See* Chapter 6. However, because early EU merger law only covered mergers that created a dominant position, EU cases extended the concept of collective dominance to cover well-functioning oligopolies, so that mergers that created anticompetitive oligopolies could be prohibited for creating a "collective dominant position." *See* Chapter 7. The 2005 Discussion Paper by the EU Directorate–General for Competition extends this concept even further, concluding that firms which belong to an oligopoly that holds a collective dominant position can be liable under Article 102 for abusing that position.[13] If so, that raises interesting questions because it would seem to make oligopoly pricing actionable as excessive pricing under Article 102, which would seem in some tension with the policy grounds for refusing to treat oligopolies as cartels, though perhaps the Commission only has in mind that unilateral acts that facilitate oligopolistic coordination might be covered. *See* Chapter 6. It would also suggest that when the members of an oligopoly coordinate on exclusionary conduct of the sort covered below, such conduct might be condemned as an abuse of a dominant position under Article 102, though as the Discussion Paper observes, so far the EU caselaw has only dealt with cases where the firms have a "strong structural link" that goes beyond mere oligopolistic coordination.[14] However, in the U.S., a claim of predatory pricing by an oligopoly was held to state a valid legal claim under the Robinson–Patman Act, although not one established by the facts of that case.[15] The Discussion Paper may have in mind that similar claims could be made under Article 102.

3. OTHER NATIONS

Virtually all the antitrust laws issued by the different nations cover unilateral conduct by firms holding some degree of market power. Generally they describe the violation as abuse of a "monopoly" or "dominant position," as anticompetitive "control" of a market, or as "taking advantage" of market power.[16] In most nations, the requirements for finding illegality are both: (1) the existence of sufficient market power, *and* (2) an act that is abusive, anticompetitive or exclusionary.[17] Some nations explicit-

---

13. *Id.* § 4.3, at ¶¶ 46–50, § 5.4, at ¶¶ 74–76 (Dec. 2005).

14. *Id.* at ¶ 76.

15. *Brooke,* 509 U.S. at 227–30.

16. Brazil Antitrust Law No. 8,884, Art.20; Canada Competition Act §§ 78–79; China Anti–Monopoly Law Art. 17; Colombia Decree 2153/92, Art. 45; India Competition Act § 4; Israel Restrictive Trade Practices Law §§ 26, 29A; Peru Competition Law, Art. 7; New Zealand Commerce Act § 36; Singapore Competition Act §§ 47–53; South Africa Competition Act § 8; Taiwan Fair Trade Act Art. 10; South Korea Fair Trade Act Art. 3–2; Venezuela Procompetition Act Art. 13.

17. Australia Trade Practices Act § 46 (requiring a substantial degree of power and conduct taking advantage of that power with a purpose to substantially damage rivals, entrants or deter competitive conduct); New Zealand Commerce Act § 36 (same); Canada Competition Act § 79(1) (requiring substantial control of a market and anticompetitive acts that are likely to prevent or lessen competition substantially); China Anti–Monopoly Law Art. 17 (requiring a dominant market position and an abusive act); India Competition Act § 4

ly allow an efficiency defense,[18] though in other nations efficiencies generally remain implicitly relevant to assessing whether the conduct had net anticompetitive effects. Some nations parallel the EU in covering "collective dominance" situations,[19] but other nations do not. Some jurisdictions cover not only exclusionary behavior, but also (like the EU) exploitative conduct against consumers like excessive pricing.[20]

A few nations also regulate the possession of high market power even if it is not coupled with anticompetitive conduct. Indonesia prohibits the mere possession of sufficient market power to control the production or marketing of any good or service in a way that *"can* cause monopolistic practices and/or unfair business competition."[21] Thus, Indonesia does not seem to require evidence of anticompetitive conduct but rather condemns the possession of market power that could be exercised anticompetitively. Such market power is presumed to exist if a firm has a market share over 50%.[22] Although Japan and Thailand do not prohibit the possession of high market power outright, those nations do authorize commissions to break up firms with high market power without requiring proof of any anticompetitive conduct. Japanese law authorizes the JFTC to impose special remedies to undo the existence of a "monopolistic situation," defined to exist when a firm has a market share over 50% (or two firms have over 75%), entry is extremely difficult, and prices or profits seem excessive.[23] The Thailand Trade Competition Commission can require a business with more than 75% market share to "suspend, cease or vary the market share."[24] Finally, South Korea law requires the KFTC to "establish and implement action plans to promote competition in markets where monopo-

---

(same); Russia Competition Law Arts. 4(10), 10 (same); Taiwan Fair Trade Act Art. 10 (same); Turkey Competition Act Art. 6 (same); Israel Restrictive Trade Practices Law § 29A (requiring monopoly power and an abuse that might reduce competition); Mexico Competition Law Arts. 10–11 (requiring substantial market power and conduct whose aim or effect is to exclude or hamper rivals); Peru Competition Law, Art. 10(1) (requiring a dominant position and conduct restricting competition); Saudi Arabia Competition Law, Art. 5 (same); Singapore Competition Act § 47; Singapore Guidelines on the Section 47 Prohibition § 4 (2007). *See also* Egypt Competition Law Art. 8 (prohibiting certain specific acts by a firm with a dominant position); Brazil Competition Law Article20 (prohibiting conduct that has the purpose or capacity to: (i) restrain competition; (ii) control a market; (iii) increase profits on a discretionary basis; or (iv) abuse market control.)

18. Mexico Competition Law Art. 10; South Africa Competition Act § 8; Peru Competition Law Arts. 9, 10(4).

19. Canada Competition Act § 79(1); Canada Competition Bureau, Enforcement Guidelines on the Abuse of Dominance Provisions § 3.2.1(e) (2001); China Anti–Monopoly Law Arts. 17 & 19; Israel Restrictive Trade Practices Law § 26(d); Russia Competition Law Arts. 4(10), 5; Singapore Competition Act § 47; Singapore Guidelines on Section 47 §§ 3.16–3.17; Turkey Competition Art. 6; Taiwan Fair Trade Act, Arts. 5 & 5–1; Venezuela Procompetition Act Art. 14(2).

20. *See infra* Chapter 3.C.3.

21. Indonesia Competition Law Art. 17(1) (emphasis added).

22. *Id.* Art. 17(2).

23. Japan Antimonopoly Act §§ 2(7), 8–4 (2009). Such remedies may not be used if the JFTC finds that (i) the remedies may reduce economies of scale in a way that sharply increases the firm's costs and undermines its financial position and international competitiveness, or (ii) alternative measures would suffice to restore competition. *Id.* § 8–4.

24. Thailand Trade Competition Act § 30.

lies or oligopolies have existed for an extended period."[25] Are the approaches in this paragraph preferable to requiring both high market power and anticompetitive conduct? One concern is that these approaches would deter desirable efforts to innovate or invest to create products that are so much better than existing market options that they enjoy high market power. One possible answer would be to limit the approaches in this paragraph to cases where the firm did not earn its high market power with desirable innovation or investments. But the desirability of such an approach might turn on how confident we are in judgments about whether a firm earned its high market power.

Some nations also regulate unilateral anticompetitive conduct without requiring separate proof of high market power, although usually one could say some market power can be inferred from the ability to impose the requisite anticompetitive effects. Japan prohibits "private monopolization," defined as business activities that exclude or control the business activities of others in a way that substantially restrains competition.[26] This provision imposes no separate market power requirement, although proving that the conduct excludes or controls other businesses could be deemed to demonstrate such market power. Further, like the U.S. FTC Act, Japan condemns unfair trade practices that tend to impede competition, thus covering unilateral anticompetitive conduct by any firm that has enough market power to create unilateral anticompetitive effects, without requiring separate proof of market power.[27] Likewise, South Korea condemns various unfair business practices that are likely to impede fair trade without requiring proof of market power.[28] Brazil condemns "any act in any way intended or otherwise able ... to limit, restrain or in any way injure open competition or free enterprise" and does so "even if any such effects are not achieved."[29] Colombia prohibits two specific types of unilateral conduct even in absence of a dominant position: (i) influencing firms to raise prices or avoid price decreases; and (ii) refusing to deal or otherwise discriminating against a firm for the purposes of retaliation.[30] Are the approaches in this paragraph preferable to requiring both high market power and anticompetitive conduct? One argument for them is that, if a firm engaged in anticompetitive conduct that had anticompetitive effects, there is no need for a market power screen. Indeed, we can infer the firm must have had sufficient market power to impose the undesirable anticompetitive effects. On the other hand, we might be concerned that erroneous judgments might be made about whether anticompetitive unilateral conduct with anticompetitive effects occurred, which would create overdeterrence problems. The answer might thus turn on the extent of overdeterrence created by the relevant nation's error rates and remedies for violations.

---

25. ActSouth Korea Fair Trade Act Art. 3.
26. Japan Antimonopoly Act §§ 2(5), 3 (2009).
27. *See id.* §§ 2(9), 19.
28. South Korea Fair Trade Act 23.
29. Brazil Competition Law Article 20.
30. Colombia, Art. 48 of Decree 2153/92.

B.   THE POWER ELEMENT

Why ever require proof of some degree of market power for an antitrust claim? After all, if conduct had no anticompetitive effect, then it would not merit condemnation regardless of how much market power the defendant possessed. And if conduct does have an anticompetitive effect, it should be condemned and an inquiry into whether defendant market power existed seems superfluous.

The answer is that it is often difficult to determine whether conduct had an anticompetitive effect, so that adjudication of that issue is often costly or erroneous, and sometimes both. If every act by every firm were subject to potential antitrust liability if it were later determined to have had an anticompetitive effect, then firms would be deterred from engaging in much desirable conduct that they fear would lead to costly antitrust scrutiny and a risk of mistaken antitrust liability. Legal review of business conduct would also be ubiquitous, imposing a large burden on adjudicators.

Thus, one important reason for a market power requirement is to provide a screen on antitrust review, limiting it to the cases where firms are most likely to impose anticompetitive effects. Such a legal screen is most useful when the biggest concern is mistaken or costly appraisal of conduct. Accordingly, the market power screen is especially important for unilateral conduct cases because without any screen every firm would face an omnipresent risk of antitrust review for all its business conduct.

The legal screen imposed by a market power requirement is most harmful when the biggest concern is instead mistaken or costly appraisals of market power, for then firms might engage in anticompetitive conduct either because they know the enforcement costs of proving market power will prevent them from being sued, or because they figure that the odds of mistaken conclusions that they lack market power make the liability risk lower than the anticompetitive gain. Thus, such a screen is least important for agreements that have no conceivable procompetitive purpose because there is little downside to deterring such conduct, a big downside to underdeterring such conduct when it is anticompetitive, and firms can easily avoid entering into such conduct.

In addition to being a screen, though, market power can also be a sword. Again, the root reason lies in the costs or difficulties of proving anticompetitive effects. Because direct proof of anticompetitive effects is so difficult, courts generally conclude that anticompetitive effects can also be inferred from the combination of defendant market power with conduct that is likely to have anticompetitive effects when engaged in by an actor with such power. This alternative is likely to be more attractive the more costly or erroneous direct proof of anticompetitive effects is, and the more confidence we have in conclusions about market power. In short, the utility of market power as a screen or sword depends on a relative assessment of whether it is more difficult to determine market power or anticompetitive effects.

1. ECONOMIC AND LEGAL TESTS OF MARKET POWER GENERALLY

Before we get into the degree of market power necessary to trigger the above antitrust laws, it is useful to first identify what constitutes market power at all. Perhaps the most common definition used by economists is that market power is a power to raise prices above marginal cost, which is the incremental cost of producing the last unit of output.[31] This definition is normally useful. In a perfectly competitive market, all products are sold at marginal cost. An inability to profitably increase prices above marginal cost would certainly indicate the absence of market power, and a persistent ability to charge above long-run marginal costs would typically indicate market power. The degree of market power under this definition is often measured by the Lerner Index, which is the difference between price and marginal cost divided by price.[32] And yet, despite this intuitive appeal and support by economists, courts and enforcement agencies have not adopted the above marginal cost test as the definition of market power.[33] Why?

The main reason usually cited is the notorious difficulty of accurately measuring true marginal costs. But a moment's thought reveals some serious theoretical limitations as well. Suppose, for example, we have a competitive market with numerous sellers with small output who cannot expand quickly, and there is a sudden increase in market demand. Prices will increase sharply, above marginal and average costs, and yet each individual seller is a price taker that cannot itself significantly affect market output or prices. Instead, the price premium they earn over their costs is called an economic rent. Such situations may call for rent control— indeed, the New York rent control laws were initially enacted to deal with the increase in housing demand during World War II. But whether or not rent control is merited, these situations do not suggest an anticompetitive market or that any seller has market power.

Further, firms on competitive markets have constant incentives to improve their products or efficiency of production. Whenever a firm succeeds in doing so, the fact that it has cheaper production or offers a better product than rivals will give it some discretion to price above marginal cost. But if other firms are also constantly improving their own products or efficiency, such an advantage might be short-lived or overcome through competition. Such back-and-forth competition in obtaining efficiency advantages is generally viewed as the essence of competition rather than an

---

31. *See* PHILLIP AREEDA & LOUIS KAPLOW, ANTITRUST ANALYSIS 556 (5th ed. 1997); CARLTON & PERLOF, MODERN INDUSTRIAL ORGANIZATION 92 (3d ed. 1999); JEAN TIROLE, THE THEORY OF INDUSTRIAL ORGANIZATION 284 (1988); DON E. WALDMAN & ELIZABETH J. JENSEN, INDUSTRIAL ORGANIZATION 40, 437, 667 (2d ed. 2001); William M. Landes & Richard A. Posner, *Market Power in Antitrust Cases*, 94 HARV. L. REV. 937, 939 (1981); Krattenmaker, Lande & Salop, *Monopoly Power and Market Power in Antitrust Law*, 76 GEO. L.J. 241, 247 (1987).

32. Or to put it mathematically, the Lerner Index = (P–MC)/P, where P is price and MC is marginal cost.

33. *See* Elhauge, *Why Above–Cost Price Cuts to Drive out Entrants Do Not Signal Predation or Even Market Power—and the Implications for Defining Costs*, 112 YALE L.J. 681, 727 n.137 (2003).

indication of the sort of market or monopoly power that triggers antitrust concerns.

The above problems suggest we may have to add a duration element requiring that any ability to price above marginal cost persist over time. But even a long-lasting ability to price above marginal cost raises conceptual difficulties. If production requires not just marginal costs but fixed costs to be in the market at all, economic models show that firms will price above marginal cost because new firms will not enter unless they can earn enough to cover fixed and marginal costs.[34] Likewise, if firms have differentiated products with varying attributes, brand image, or location of sale, then each firm can have some local market power to charge above marginal cost to customers who are close to it in location or quality or brand preferences.[35] Economists call both sorts of situations cases of "monopolistic competition," to distinguish them from our ideal case of perfect competition, but since fixed costs or product differentiation are a reality in most markets, this is the type of competition the law typically means and can at most aspire to have. Moreover, in such markets, firms can be numerous and prices will equal average cost in the long run. One can call these cases of market power, and perhaps they may usefully be regulated in some affirmative fashion. However, assuming prices equal long-run costs, this is not the sort of power that usefully invites antitrust scrutiny to prevent conduct that might exclude or impede competition, and thus not the sort of market power we mean in antitrust law.[36]

For example, brands of orange juice, coffee, beer and similar products have prices that are 25–67% higher than marginal cost, which would indicate monopoly power by this definition, yet these are understood to be competitive rather than monopoly markets by antitrust law and even by proponents of a marginal cost-based definition of market power.[37] Likewise, economics concludes that price discrimination must signal some degree of economic market power because it means the firm must have a downward sloping demand curve and be pricing some sales above cost.[38] Yet, because such price discrimination is ubiquitous on markets that antitrust deems competitive, it does not alone suffice to prove market power for antitrust purposes.[39]

---

34. *See* Carlton & Perloff, *supra* note 31, at 201–206.

35. *Id.* at 215–225.

36. *See* United States v. E.I. du Pont de Nemours & Co., 351 U.S. 377, 392–93 (1956) (concluding that cases where firms engage in "monopolistic competition" do not involve "the power that makes an illegal monopoly" even though each firm may enjoy "power over the price and production of his own product" and "may have in one sense a monopoly on certain trade because of location, as an isolated country store or filling station, or because no one else makes a product of just the quality or attractiveness of his product, as for example in cigarettes.")

37. *See* Elhauge, *Defining Better Monopolization Standards*, 56 STANFORD LAW REVIEW 253, 260 (2003).

38. See Carlton & Perloff, *supra* note 31, at 277; Waldman & Jensen, *supra* note 31, at 436; Hal R. Varian, Price Discrimination, in 1 Handbook of Industrial Organization 599 (Richard Schmalensee & Robert D. Willig eds., 1989).

39. *See* Illinois Tool Works Inc. v. Independent Ink, Inc., 547 U.S. 28, 44–45 (2006) (concluding that price discrimination does not necessarily indicate market power for antitrust

Another common definition, used in many cases, is that market power is the power to price above competitive levels.[40] This definition may be more apt for antitrust purposes because it posits a more competitive baseline world where prices would be lower if some diminishment of competition were prevented. But there remain conceptual and practical problems.

One conceptual problem is that a firm might have achieved market power *through* competitive behavior, such as making a better or cheaper product than other firms and driving them out of the market. The resulting prices it charges could thus in a sense be said to reflect a competitive level, and yet the firm would have the sort of power over market prices and output we typically mean by market power. We might instead define a competitive market to be what the market would look like with many firms, but this raises other conceptual problems: if there are economies of scale or other efficiencies to large size, then a competitive market with many firms might have higher costs and prices even at the same output level. The use of a competitive price baseline is thus hard to disentangle from questions about just what degree of competition is optimal.

We could define the competitive baseline as what market prices would have been without the anticompetitive conduct being challenged. This seems more promising, but unfortunately conflates the market power element into the supposedly separate element of whether the defendant engaged in anticompetitive conduct that made prices worse than they would have been but for that misconduct. Such a conflation would eliminate any screening benefit the market power element is meant to provide.

The practical problem is that we generally cannot observe the competitive baseline in monopoly cases because, by definition, the hypothesis under investigation is that we do not have a competitive market. We may thus have to guess what those competitive prices would have been based on prices in analogous competitive markets or what prices were back when the market was more competitive. But either contemporaneous or historical analogies will be inapt to the extent costs differ between those analogous markets and the current one. Further, if, as typical, marginal costs for an industry increase with output, then a competitive market that expands output will have higher marginal costs than an equally efficient monopolist that produces lower output. Comparing current prices to competitive price levels would thus understate market power relative to a comparison between current prices and current marginal costs. To avoid these problems, one might instead infer the competitive baseline from costs in the current

purposes because it often exists on competitive markets). For various theoretical explanations of why firms on competitive markets often engage in price discrimination that entails some prices above marginal cost even though total revenue does not exceed total costs, see Elhauge, *supra* note 29, at 735–43.

40. For cases using this sort of definition, see Jefferson Parish Hospital v. Hyde, 466 U.S. 2, 27 n.46 (1984); NCAA v. Board of Regents of the Univ. of Okla., 468 U.S. 85, 109 n.38 (1984); Brooke Group Ltd. v. Brown & Williamson Tobacco Corp., 509 U.S. 209, 235 (1993). *See also* United States Steel Corp. v. Fortner Enterprises, 429 U.S. 610, 620 (1977) (defining market power as the power to "to raise prices or to require purchasers to accept burdensome terms that could not be exacted in a completely competitive market. In short, the question is whether the seller has some advantage not shared by his competitors . . .").

market. But then we are back at the problems with a test that asks whether prices are above marginal cost.

A final definition, used in other cases, is that market power is the power to constrain total market output in order to raise market prices and profits.[41] This definition focuses less on whether prices are above some baseline than on the causal connection between defendant output decisions and market price levels. If a defendant's output is a sufficiently small share of the market, or rivals would expand or enter quickly to make up for any constraint in defendant output, then the defendant lacks the requisite market power. If the contrary is true, then a defendant output restriction would predictably increase not only defendant prices but rival prices as well.

This sort of test often best captures the relevant concerns. But it too faces difficulties. The practical difficulty is that, if the defendant is already at the monopoly price, then any further output restriction would lead sufficient buyers to switch to other products to make any output restriction and price increase unprofitable and thus constrain it. Thus, if we are already at the monopoly price and output, we would not see any current evidence of the defendant raising market prices by restricting output. But we might be able to infer such a power by evidence that the firm's output decisions do affect market prices and that it varies output accordingly.

The conceptual difficulty is that this definition presupposes we know what the "market" is so that we can determine not just whether the defendant can change its own output and prices but whether it can change total market output and prices. If a market is characterized by monopolistic competition, then one could imagine defining the market to be just the defendant's brand because it has some short-term discretion to alter its prices by altering its output. Here the economic literature provides little assistance because: "The issue of how markets should be defined from the viewpoint of economic theory has never been answered definitively. Economic theorists generally take the market as a given."[42] This is not so surprising because the question of how best to define markets is a question not just of economics but of legal policy, which depends on both the functional goals that antitrust law is trying to accomplish and judgments about which rules are most administrable. As we shall see, functional and administrative concerns heavily influence the way antitrust law defines a market, but market definition is often bedeviled by the same sort of baseline issues that bedevil efforts to measure market power.

Whichever way we use to define the existence of market power, one way often used to measure the *degree* of that market power is with the elasticity of demand for the defendant's products.[43] Demand is more "elastic" the more that the quantity demanded changes in response to a

---

41.   For cases using this sort of definition, see Eastman Kodak Co. v. Image Technical Servs., Inc., 504 U.S. 451, 464 (1992); Fortner Enters. v. United States Steel Corp., 394 U.S. 495, 503 (1969); *see also* Benjamin Klein, *Market Power in Antitrust: Economic Analysis After Kodak*, 3 SUP. CT. ECON. REV. 43, 44, 71–85, 88–92 (1993).

42.   *See* Carlton & Perloff, *supra* note 31, at 146.

43.   *Kodak*, 504 U.S. at 469 n.15.

change in price, and more "inelastic" the less that the quantity demanded changes if prices are increased. That is, the more inelastic demand is, the less that buyers are willing to change what they buy in response to price increases. In the usual graphs that plot quantity on the X-axis and price on the Y-axis, a steeper demand curve is more inelastic, and a flatter demand curve is more elastic. More precisely, elasticity is the percentage change in quantity divided by the percentage change in price that produces that quantity change. If a 1% price increase changes output by more than 1%, then elasticity is greater than 1, and demand is defined to be "elastic." If a 1% price increase changes output by less than 1%, then elasticity is lower than 1, and demand is defined to be "inelastic."

Firm-specific demand elasticity, the extent to which a firm's own output responds to an increase in its prices, should be sharply distinguished from market-price demand elasticity. Firm-specific demand elasticity helps measure a single-firm's market power, whereas market-price demand elasticity helps measure the extent to which all the firms on the market combined could raise prices. Marketwide demand for a product can be quite inelastic, so that any reduction in marketwide output sharply raises market prices, even though each firm in that market has highly elastic demand, so that any effort by it to reduce output will not significantly raise prices but simply cause buyers to buy elsewhere. On the other hand, if marketwide demand for a product is highly elastic, so that any increase in market prices for that product would cause buyers to purchase other products, then the firm-specific demand elasticities for every firm in that market must also be highly elastic because no single firm that only sells some of the product in that market can enjoy more power than the whole market would. That is, firm-specific demand elasticity can be much higher than marketwide demand elasticity, but not lower.

In a perfectly competitive market, each firm faces an absolutely flat, perfectly elastic, demand curve, so that none can raise prices without losing all its customers. No firm in such a market has market power, and the firm-specific demand elasticity of each is infinite. This does not necessarily mean that we can identify market power and determine its degree by simply measuring a firm's current firm-specific demand elasticity. To begin with, under the conditions of monopolistic competition that probably constitute most workable competition we actually see, every firm has a downward sloping demand curve, at least in the short run. In such a market, each firm faces a somewhat inelastic demand curve, even though none may have the sort of market power that antitrust law seeks to regulate.

Further, demand elasticity generally is different at different price and output levels. This point is often obscured by the tendency to measure elasticity at current prices and output and then apply it to other price and output levels. In fact, demand elasticity varies with price and output, which is highly important because economic analysis shows that even an absolute monopolist would never set a price that leaves it on the inelastic portion of its demand curve.[44] The reason is simple: if a monopolist were on the

---

44.   *See* Carlton & Perloff, *supra* note 31, at 93.

inelastic portion of its demand curve, then by definition a 1% price increase would reduce its output by less than 1%. This has to be profitable even if its output is entirely costless, and thus surely would be profitable under the more reasonable assumption that there are some marginal costs of production that it avoided by reducing output. Accordingly, a monopolist on the inelastic portion of its demand curve would keep profitably increasing prices (and thus lowering output) until it reached a portion of its demand curve where demand was sufficiently elastic to make further price increases unprofitable. Elastic demand at current levels of price and output is precisely what we would expect from an absolute monopoly that was pricing at the monopoly price. We thus cannot infer an absence of market or monopoly power from the fact that demand is elastic at current prices.

We can conclude that a firm will tend to have greater market power the greater the proportion of its demand curve that is inelastic, and the more inelastic its demand is for that portion. Unfortunately, since a firm with market power will not operate on any inelastic portion of its demand curve, this generally cannot be observed directly, but will have to be inferred from other means.

However, if we assume each firm is pricing at the short-run profit-maximizing level, we can use firm-specific demand elasticity at current prices to determine the degree to which a firm is pricing over its marginal costs because a profit-maximizing firm will raise prices until the marginal revenue lost from diminished sales equals the marginal revenue gained from an increased margin between prices and costs. Indeed, a profit-maximizing firm's Lerner Index equals the inverse of its firm-specific demand elasticity.[45] Thus, to the extent that the Lerner Index is relevant to measuring market power, firm-specific demand elasticity can be used to derive it and, given that prices are generally known, to indirectly determine marginal costs. For example, if firm-specific demand elasticity is 2, then the Lerner index is 1/2, which means the firm's prices are double its marginal cost.[46] A current firm-specific demand elasticity of 2 thus should be regarded as low, and indicative of market power for antitrust purposes where cost-based tests seem appropriate, even though standard economics calls such demand "elastic."

While legal tests often focus on whether the degree of market power suffices to constitute monopoly power, economic models do not really define monopoly power in that way. Rather, in economic models a monopolist is a firm that is literally the only producer of a product for which there are no substitutes that it need ever take into account when setting prices or output. A dominant firm is a firm that faces some rivals, but whose rivals are much smaller and less efficient. Economic models show that such a dominant firm is effectively a monopolist with respect to the "residual"

---

45. A firm that takes into account only its own costs and demand curve will maximize profits by setting price so that $(P-MC)/P = -1/\epsilon$, where ϵ is the firm-specific demand elasticity.

46. Mathematically, a firm-specific demand elasticity of 2 means $(P-MC)/P = 1/2$, which means $P = 2MC$. Note that demand elasticities are almost always negative because an increase in price decreases quantity, but are generally expressed without bothering to express the negative sign. So an "elasticity of 2" generally means -2 must be used in a mathematical formula.

demand curve that is derived by taking the total market demand curve and subtracting from it the output that would be produced by the rivals at each price.[47] Thus, while a dominant firm is somewhat constrained by the existence of rivals, it will still price above its marginal costs and restrict market output below efficient levels. Such a dominant firm is generally what antitrust law means by a monopolist.

Using such a dominant firm model, one can derive the firm-specific demand elasticity of a dominant firm (which can be difficult to ascertain directly) from the marketwide elasticity of demand, the market share of the firm being assessed, and the elasticity of rival supply, which is the percentage change in output supplied by rivals in response to a 1% increase in price. Basically a firm's ability to raise prices will be constrained by both the tendency of buyers to exit the market (the marketwide demand elasticity) and their ability to shift purchases to any increased output supplied by its rivals (which reflects a combination of rival elasticity of supply and their initial market share.)[48] The higher the marketwide demand elasticity or the supply elasticity of rivals, the higher the firm-specific elasticity of demand for the dominant firm, and thus the lower its market power.

Further, if we hold marketwide demand elasticity and rival supply elasticity constant, then the higher a firm's market share, the lower its firm-specific demand elasticity and thus the higher its market power. The reason is twofold. A high firm market share reduces the proportion of its output that it must reduce to create a decrease in marketwide output: a firm with 50% of the market must reduce its output by 20% to reduce market output by 10%, whereas a firm with 90% market share can do so by reducing its output by 11%. A high firm market share also leaves a lower market share to rivals and thus reduces the output expansion they can produce with a given supply elasticity: if a firm lowers market output by 10%, rivals with a market share of 50% can offset that by increasing their output by 20% whereas rivals with a market share of 10% must increase their output by 100% to do so. Unfortunately, it may be hard to ascertain the marketwide demand elasticity and rival supply elasticity necessary to know what inference about market power to make from market shares.

2.   LEGAL TESTS OF MONOPOLY POWER OR A DOMINANT POSITION

The U.S. Supreme Court defines "monopoly power" as "the power to

---

47. *See* Carlton & Perloff, *supra* note 31, at 107–118.

48. Mathematically, if we call ϵ_{dom} the firm-specific demand elasticity of the dominant firm, call ϵ_{mkt} the marketwide demand elasticity, call $\epsilon_{rivsupp}$ the supply elasticity of rivals, and call S the share of the dominant firm (which of course means 1–S is the share of all the other firms), then it can be shown that $\epsilon_{dom} = \epsilon_{mkt}/S + \epsilon_{rivsupp}(1–S)/S$. See Landes & Posner, *supra* note 31, at 944–45, 985–86. If rivals cannot expand output over the relevant period, or if each firm sets prices under the Cournot assumption that the output of rivals is fixed, then $\epsilon_{rivsupp}$ = 0 and the equation reduces to $\epsilon_{dom} = \epsilon_{mkt}/S$. *See id.* at 952 n.30, 954 n.32 see also Chapter 7 (discussing Cournot competition). Thus, under fixed rival output or Cournot competition, $1/\epsilon_{dom} = S/\epsilon_{mkt}$, and since $1/\epsilon_{dom}$ equals the Lerner index, this means $S/\epsilon_{mkt} = (P–MC)/P$. This provides a way of calculating marginal cost from market price, share and demand elasticity where rival output is fixed or firms set their output under the assumption it is. It also provides a way to calculate how changes in market shares or the various elasticities would alter the price-cost margin.

control prices or exclude competition."[49] Given that the economic definitions of any "market power" all involve some discretion over pricing, one
might think that any firm with market power necessarily has "control"
over its prices and thus must be a monopolist. But this is not what the
Court in fact means because it has stressed: "Monopoly power under § 2
requires, of course, something greater than market power under § 1."[50]
The Court appears to mean that monopoly power is a relatively high degree
of market power, though it has left undefined just what that degree is.

The portion of this test about the power to "exclude competition" is
problematic because the second element of monopolization is exclusionary
conduct. Thus, in any case where a firm has in fact engaged in exclusionary
conduct satisfying the second element, one would think that would necessarily mean that the firm must have had the power to exclude rivals, thus
satisfying the first element. Such a conclusion could logically be defended.
If a firm engages in inefficient exclusionary conduct, one could reasonably
infer that it must have market power from which it derives gains because
otherwise such inefficient conduct would be unprofitable. But adopting that
logic would largely conflate what are supposed to be separate legal elements, thus eliminating any screening effect from the market power
element.[51] The Court, however, appears to define such a power to exclude
rivals to exist only when such exclusion allows the firm to raise prices, thus
suggesting that some degree of pricing discretion must also be shown.[52]
One possible reconciliation is that an ability to raise price might result
from constricting either (1) a firm's own output or (2) other firms' outputs
(by excluding rivals or impairing their efficiency), and that the "control
prices" test refers to the former and the "exclude competition" test refers
to latter alternative.[53]

In actual practice, though, U.S. courts tend to determine the existence
of monopoly or market power without requiring direct evidence of control
over pricing *or* power to exclude rivals. Instead, U.S. courts tend to use the
alternative of inferring monopoly or market power from firm market
shares, at least when coupled with evidence that entry barriers to that
market are relatively high.[54] The precise dividing line is unclear. The

---

49. *Kodak*, 504 U.S. at 481 (quoting United States v. E.I. du Pont de Nemours & Co.,
351 U.S. 377, 391 (1956)); *Grinnell*, 384 U.S. at 571 (same).

50. *See Kodak*, 504 U.S. at 481.

51. It would not completely conflate those two elements because, as we will see,
exclusionary conduct satisfying the second element must be improper or anticompetitive,
whereas the power to exclude rivals that satisfies the first element need not be. For example, a
firm may enjoy patents that it earned through productive investments and that enable it to
exclude all rivals from a product market. Such a firm would have a power to exclude and thus
have monopoly power. But the exercise of its patents would not constitute improper exclusionary conduct that satisfies the second element. Still, the problem remains that when conduct
does satisfy the second element, it would seem the first element would always be satisfied.

52. *See duPont*, 351 U.S. at 392 ("Price and competition are so intimately entwined that
any discussion of theory must treat them as one. It is inconceivable that price could be
controlled without power over competition or vice versa.")

53. *See* Krattenmaker, Lande & Salop, *supra* note 31, at 248–49.

54. *See Jefferson Parish*, 466 U.S. at 17; *Kodak*, 504 U.S. at 469 n.15; United States v.
Grinnell Corp., 384 U.S. 563, 571 (1966); United States v. Microsoft, 253 F.3d 34, 51 (D.C. Cir.
2001) (en banc).

Supreme Court has indicated that market shares above 66% indicate monopoly power without clearly specifying the lower bound.[55] Lower court cases have generally required a market share of at least 50% to constitute monopoly power.[56] As for market power, the Supreme Court has held that, standing alone, a 30% market share was insufficient to establish the kind of market power necessary to trigger the per se rule against tying, but stressed this differed from general notions of market power because in a tying case finding market power would preclude further inquiry into actual anticompetitive effects.[57]

A similar path seems to have been followed in the European Union. *United Brands v. Commission* in 1978 defined a dominant position as: "a position of economic strength enjoyed by an undertaking which enables it to prevent effective competition being maintained on the relevant market by giving it the power to behave to an appreciable extent independently of its competitors, customers and ultimately of consumers." This definition of dominance contains two elements—the ability to prevent competition and the ability to behave independently—without, however, explaining precisely either element nor how the two relate one another. This seems quite parallel to the U.S. formulation of a power to exclude competition or control prices, and raises similar issues.

More modern EU cases have stated that the basic test of a dominant position is whether a firm has the "power to behave to an appreciable extent independently of [its] competitors or to gain an appreciable influence on the determination of prices without losing market share".[58] This general test thus focuses on pricing discretion in a way that seems to render it similar to economic definitions of market power. Note, however, that this definition is not limited to the special set of circumstances that constitute a true dominant position in economic models. Moreover, in both *Michelin* cases the Commission relied on Michelin's allegedly abusive practices as themselves indicators of market power, noting that "as is often the case in situations such as that being examined here, the finding of a dominant position is supported inter alia by the evidence relating to the abuse of that position." This raises problems similar to those noted above for the U.S. test that makes a "power to exclude" one way of proving monopoly power.

Like in the United States, in practice the EU cases do not often directly address such issues, but instead generally infer the requisite power from market shares. Very high market shares will generally provide pre-

---

55. *See duPont*, 351 U.S. at 379 (observing that "du Pont produced almost 75% of the cellophane sold in the United States" and that "If cellophane is the 'market' . . ., it may be assumed it does have monopoly power over that 'market' under its test"); *Kodak*, 504 U.S. at 481 (holding that proving a 80–95% market share is enough to survive summary judgment, and describing a prior case as holding that "over two-thirds of a market is a monopoly"); *Grinnell*, 384 U.S. at 571 ("The existence of such [monopoly] power ordinarily may be inferred from the predominant share of the market. . . ." In *American Tobacco,* we said that "over two-thirds of the entire domestic field of cigarettes, and . . . over 80% of the field of comparable cigarettes" constituted "a substantial monopoly." In the present case, 87% [share of the business] leaves no doubt that . . . defendants have monopoly power . . . if that business is the relevant market.).

56. *See* Elhauge, supra note 37, at 336.

57. *See Jefferson Parish*, 466 U.S. at 26–29.

58. See Case T–102/96, Gencor v. Commission, [1999] E.C.R. II–753.

sumptive proof that a firm is dominant. In *Hoffman–La Roche*, the ECJ stated that "[t]he existence of a dominant position may derive from several factors which taken separately are not necessarily determinative but among these factors a highly important one is the existence of very large market shares.... Although the importance of the market shares may vary from one market to another, the view may legitimately be taken that very large market shares are in themselves, and save in exceptional circumstances, evidence of the existence of a dominant position."[59] In *Hoffman*, the defendant held a dominant position was shown by very high shares of a number of vitamin markets, ranging from approximately 75% to approximately 87%. In *Akzo*, however, the ECJ referred to the passage quoted above and indicated that a market share of 50% could be considered as very large and thus, save exceptional circumstances, will create a presumption that a firm with such a market share is dominant.[60] This affirmation was confirmed in subsequent judgments. By contrast, market shares between 25% and 50% will generally fail to conclusively indicate a presence or absence of dominance. In such cases, the analysis will turn on a range of structural factors, including the presence of barriers to entry, the existence of sunk costs and barriers to expansion, the presence of economies of scale and/or scope and/or network effects, the possession of superior technology, the control of essential assets, etc.[61] Conversely, low market shares establish the opposite presumption that a firm does not occupy a dominant position. A firm with a market share below 25% is very unlikely to have a dominant position. In *Saba II*, the ECJ found that a dominant position was virtually impossible with a market share of only 10%.[62]

The U.S. enforcement agencies have so far declined to issue any guidelines to clarify what constitutes monopoly power or exclusionary conduct. The Bush Administration DOJ did issue a monopolization report, but it was rejected by the FTC and withdrawn by the Obama Administration. In the EU, however, the Directorate–General for Competition has recently issued a Guidance Paper on Article 82 [now 102 TFEU], which although it cannot be considered as a set of guidelines (it merely defines the Commission's enforcement priorities), nevertheless gives an indication of what it currently understands to be the operative principles. The portions on defining single firm dominance are excerpted below.

Guidance on the Commission's Enforcement Priorities in Applying Article 82 EC Treaty [now 102 TFEU] to Abusive Exclusionary Conduct by Dominant Undertakings

(Dec. 2008).

The assessment of whether an undertaking is in a dominant position and of the degree of market power it holds is a first step in the application

---

59. Case 85/76, Hoffmann–La Roche v. Commission, [1979] E.C.R. 461.

60. Case C–62/86, AKZO Chemie BV v. Commission, [1991] E.C.R. I–3359.

61. For a good review of these factors, see Damien Geradin et al., "The Concept of Dominance", GCLC Research Papers on Article 82 [now Article 102 TFEU] (June 2005).

62. Case 75/84, Metro v. Commission, [1986] E.C.R. 3021.

of Article [102]. According to the case-law, holding a dominant position confers a special responsibility on the firm concerned, the scope of which must be considered in the light of the specific circumstances of each case.

Dominance has been defined under [EU] law as a position of economic strength enjoyed by an undertaking, which enables it to prevent effective competition being maintained on a relevant market, by affording it the power to behave to an appreciable extent independently of its competitors, its customers and ultimately of consumers. This notion of independence is related to the degree of competitive constraint exerted on the undertaking in question. Dominance entails that these competitive constraints are not sufficiently effective and hence that the firm in question enjoys substantial market power over a period of time. This means that the undertaking's decisions are largely insensitive to the actions and reactions of competitors, customers and, ultimately, consumers. The Commission may consider that effective competitive constraints are absent even if some actual or potential competition remains. In general, a dominant position derives from a combination of several factors which, taken separately, are not necessarily determinative.

The Commission considers that an undertaking which is capable of profitably increasing prices above the competitive level for a significant period of time does not face sufficiently effective competitive constraints and can thus generally be regarded as dominant. In this document, the expression "increase prices" includes the power to maintain prices above the competitive level and is used as shorthand for the various ways in which the parameters of competition—such as prices, output, innovation, the variety or quality of goods or services—can be influenced for the profit of the dominant undertaking and to the detriment of consumers.

The assessment of dominance will take into account the competitive structure of the market, and in particular the following factors:

- constraints imposed by the existing supplies from, and the position on the market of, actual competitors (the market position of the dominant undertaking and its competitors);
- constraints imposed by the credible threat of future expansion by actual competitors or entry by potential competitors (expansion and entry);
- constraints imposed by the bargaining strength of the undertaking's customers (countervailing buyer power).

a) Market position of the dominant undertaking and its competitors

Market shares provide a useful first indication for the Commission of the market structure and of the relative importance of the various undertakings active on the market. However, the Commission will interpret market shares in the light of the relevant market conditions, and in particular of the dynamics of the market and of the extent to which products are differentiated. The trend or development of market shares over time may also be taken into account in volatile or bidding markets.

The Commission considers that low market shares are generally a good proxy for the absence of substantial market power. The Commission's experience suggests that dominance is not likely if the undertaking's market share is below 40% in the relevant market. However, there may be specific cases below this threshold where competitors are not in a position to constrain effectively the conduct of a dominant undertaking, for example where they face serious capacity limitations. Such cases may also deserve attention on the part of the Commission.

Experience suggests that the higher the market share and the longer the period of time over which it is held, the more likely it is that it constitutes an important preliminary indication of the existence of a dominant position and, in certain circumstances, of possible serious effects of abusive conduct, justifying an intervention by the Commission under Article [102]. However, as a general rule, the Commission will not come to a final conclusion on the opportunity to pursue a case without examining all the factors which may be sufficient to constrain the behaviour of the undertaking.

b) Expansion or entry

Competition is a dynamic process and an assessment of the competitive constraints on an undertaking cannot be based solely on the existing market situation. The potential impact of expansion by actual competitors or entry by potential competitors, including the threat of such expansion or entry, is also relevant. An undertaking can be deterred from increasing prices if expansion or entry is likely, timely and sufficient. For the Commission to consider expansion or entry likely it must be sufficiently profitable for the competitor or entrant, taking into account factors such as the barriers to expansion or entry, the likely reactions of the allegedly dominant undertaking and other competitors, and the risks and costs of failure. For expansion or entry to be considered timely, it must be sufficiently swift to deter or defeat the exercise of substantial market power. For expansion or entry to be sufficient, it cannot be simply small-scale entry, for example into some market niche, but must be of such a magnitude as to be able to deter any attempt to increase prices by the putatively dominant undertaking in the relevant market.

Barriers to expansion or entry can take various forms. They may be legal barriers, such as tariffs or quotas, or they may take the form of advantages specifically enjoyed by the dominant undertaking, such as economies of scale and scope, privileged access to essential inputs or natural resources, important technologies or an established distribution and sales network. They may also include costs and other impediments, for instance resulting from network effects, faced by customers in switching to a new supplier. The dominant undertaking's own conduct may also create barriers to entry, for example where it has made significant investments which entrants or competitors would have to match, or where it has concluded long term contracts with its customers that have appreciable foreclosing effects. Persistently high market shares may be indicative of the existence of barriers to entry and expansion.

c) Countervailing buyer power

Competitive constraints may be exerted not only by actual or potential competitors but also by customers. Even an undertaking with a high market share may not be able to act to an appreciable extent independently of customers with sufficient bargaining strength. Such countervailing buying power may result from the customers' size or their commercial significance for the dominant undertaking, and their ability to switch quickly to competing suppliers, to promote new entry or vertically integrate, and to credibly threaten to do so. If countervailing power is of a sufficient magnitude, it may deter or defeat an attempt by the undertaking to profitably increase prices. Buyer power may not, however, be considered a sufficiently effective constraint if it only ensures that a particular or limited segment of customers is shielded from the market power of the dominant undertaking.

Questions on the Commission's Guidance Paper on Article 102

1. The Guidance Paper says that the Commission considers that market shares are generally a good proxy to determine the presence or absence of substantial market power, but that it will also look at a wider range of factors to determine whether the undertaking in question is sufficiently constrained.

a. Is this the right approach? Wouldn't it be simpler to use a market share threshold?

b. What does the Guidance Paper mean when it states that the Commission will seek to determine whether an undertaking is "sufficiently constrained"? Constrained in what sense?

2. Among the factors the Commission will be looking at to determine whether a firm is sufficiently constrained is the presence of "countervailing buyer power".

a. Could you cite two industries where countervailing buyer power is likely to be observable?

b. Why do you consider that countervailing buyer power is likely to be observable in these industries? What are the relevant factors?

3. The Guidance Paper does not seem to consider that dominance could be inferred from the abusive conduct itself. Should it have?

4. The Guidance Paper does not address the issue of "collective dominance". Should an oligopoly be deemed to hold a collective dominant position under Article 102, thus subjecting unilateral conduct by those oligopolists to review under abuse of dominance standards?

The Power Element in Other Nations

Other nations usually require some level of market power to condemn unilateral conduct, at least for some violations.[63] Although most nations call the requisite market power "dominance,"[64] others call it "monopoly"

---

63. *See supra* Chapter 3.A.3.

64. *See* Argentina Competition Law Art. 1; Brazil Antitrust Law No. 8,884, Art.20(3); Chile Competition Law Art. 3(b); China Anti–Monopoly Law Art. 17; Colombia Decree 2153/92, Art. 45; Egypt Competition Law Art. 4; India Competition Act § 4; Peru Competition

power[65] or "substantial" market power,[66] and Canada refers to whether the firm completely or substantially "controls" a market, which its courts have interpreted to mean "market power."[67] Whatever the wording, nations adopt a range of tests of how to prove the requisite market power that is similar to the range of tests used in the U.S. and EU. For example, South Africa adopts a combination of U.S. and EU tests, defining the power element as "the power of a firm to control prices, or to exclude competition or to behave to an appreciable extent independently of its competitors, customers or suppliers."[68] Canada specifies that the requisite power is proven by showing the defendant can profitably sustain prices above competitive levels.[69] Finally, as in the U.S. and EU, many nations use market share thresholds to infer the existence or absence of the requisite market power (absent other countervailing factors like especially low or high barriers to entry or rival expansion), setting thresholds that range from 20% to 65% for inferring that a firm has the requisite market power.[70]

Law Art. 7; Russia Competition Law Art. 4(10); Saudi Arabia Competition Law, Art. 2; Singapore Competition Act § 47; South Africa Competition Act §§ 7–8; South Korea Fair Trade Act Art. 3–2; Turkey Competition Act Art. 3; Venezuela Procompetition Act Art. 13.

65. Israel Restrictive Trade Practices Law § 26. Some nations effectively equate monopoly power with a dominant position. *See* Taiwan Fair Trade Act Article 5 (a firm is a "monopolistic enterprise" when it has a "dominant position.").

66. *See* Australia Trade Practices Act § 46; Mexico Federal Economic Competition Law Art. 13; New Zealand Commerce Act § 36.

67. *See* Canadian Competition Act § 79(1); Canada v. Canada Pipe, 2006 FCA 236, at ¶ 10. The Canadian courts have also stressed that "The required degree of market power . . . comprises 'control' and not simply the ability to behave independently of the market." *Id.* ¶ 52. This seems to reject the way the EU expresses the dominance test, *see United Brands*, but this nominal difference probably has little practical effect since both essentially focus on market power.

68. South Africa Competition Act § 1(1)(xiv).

69. See *Canada Pipe*, 2006 FCA 236, at ¶ 23; Canada Competition Bureau, Enforcement Guidelines on the Abuse of Dominance Provisions § 3.2.1(d) (2001).

70. *See* Brazil Antitrust Law No. 8,884, Art. 20(3) (dominance is presumed from a 20% market share); Canada Competition Bureau, Enforcement Guidelines on the Abuse of Dominance Provisions § 3.2.1(d) (2001) (dominance presumed unlikely below a 35% share, and shares above that will prompt further inquiry); *Canada Pipe*, 2006 FCA 236, at ¶¶ 23–24 (requisite market control may be inferred from market shares unless suggested otherwise by low barriers to entry or expansion and countervailing buyer power); China Anti–Monopoly Law Art. 19 (dominant market position presumed if one firm's market share exceeds 50%, two firms' shares together exceeds 66.6%, or three firms' shares together exceed 75%, although a firm that is below 10% shall not be considered dominant in the last two cases); Israel Restrictive Trade Practices Law § 26 (monopoly if have more than 50% of the market); Egypt Competition Law Art.4 (dominance requires a 25% market share as well as an effective power over prices or output that rivals cannot limit); Indonesia Competition Law Art 17 (sufficient market control if have a market share over 50%); Russia Competition Law Art. 5 (single firm dominance presumed if market share is above 50% and presumed absent if market share is below 35%; collective dominance presumed if stable market shares of two or three largest firms exceeds 50% or of four or five firms exceeds 70%); Saudi Arabia Executive Regulation Art. 7(a) (in merger cases, presuming dominance from 40% market share); Singapore Guidelines on the Section 47 Prohibition § 3.8 (2007) (market shares above 60% likely indicate dominance); South Africa Competition Act § 7 (market share over 45% conclusively presumed dominant, share between 35–45% presumed dominant but rebuttable, and market share below 35% presumed nondominant unless enforcer proves otherwise); South Korea Fair Trade Act Art. 4 (dominance presumed if one firm has a market share of 50% or more, or if three firms

How would you define the requisite market power and what market share threshold should be used? Does your answer turn on the nation's antitrust remedies?

3.   MARKET DEFINITION

Because courts and regulators in the U.S., EU and other nations largely rely on market shares, they must define the relevant markets in order to determine the share of that market that a defendant possesses. This raises two sorts of general framing questions. First, how does the law define markets? Second, why does the law rely on evidence of market share rather than just relying on direct evidence of pricing discretion or market power? As we will see, one important economic concept that courts utilize in defining markets is the cross-elasticity of demand, which is the extent to which a price increase in one item leads to increased sales of another item. Again, an important but often obscured issue is what baseline price one should use. If the cross-elasticity of demand is very high for small price increases over costs or the competitive level, then the two items can be grouped in the same product market because no monopolist in one of the items could exploit it by charging prices significantly above costs or the competitive level without causing a large amount of buyers to switch to the other item. But can we assume the same if the cross-elasticity of demand is high for small price increases over current levels, where those current prices are themselves alleged to be produced by monopoly power? And if we can't rely on current levels as our baseline, can we independently derive a reliable baseline for costs or what the competitive level would be? Consider the following.

United States v. du Pont & Co. (The Cellophane Case)

351 U.S. 377 (1956).

■ MR. JUSTICE REED delivered the opinion of the Court....

... du Pont produced almost 75% of the cellophane sold in the United States, and cellophane constituted less than 20% of all "flexible packaging material" sales.... The court below found that the "relevant market for determining the extent of du Pont's market control is the market for flexible packaging materials," and that competition from those other materials prevented du Pont from possessing monopoly powers in its sales of cellophane.

---

have a market share of 75% or more, excluding firms with a market share of less than 10%); Taiwan Fair Trade Act Article 5-1 (presuming the absence of monopolistic power unless the single firm market share is 50% or higher, the market share of the two largest firms is 66.6% or higher, *or* the market share of the three largest firms is 75% or higher, and providing that firms with less than 10% market share cannot be deemed to have monopolistic power). Some nations consider market shares along with other factors but do not specify any market share thresholds. *See* India Competition Act § 19(4); Mexico Competition Law Art. 13; Mexico Competition Regulation Arts. 11–14.

The Government asserts that cellophane and other wrapping materials are neither substantially fungible nor like priced. For these reasons, it argues that the market for other wrappings is distinct from the market for cellophane and that the competition afforded cellophane by other wrappings is not strong enough to be considered in determining whether du Pont has monopoly powers. Market delimitation is necessary under du Pont's theory to determine whether an alleged monopolist violates § 2. The ultimate consideration in such a determination is whether the defendants control the price and competition in the market for such part of trade or commerce as they are charged with monopolizing. Every manufacturer is the sole producer of the particular commodity it makes but its control in the above sense of the relevant market depends upon the availability of alternative commodities for buyers: i.e., whether there is a cross-elasticity of demand between cellophane and the other wrappings. This interchangeability is largely gauged by the purchase of competing products for similar uses considering the price, characteristics and adaptability of the competing commodities. The court below found that the flexible wrappings afforded such alternatives. This Court must determine whether the trial court erred in its estimate of the competition afforded cellophane by other materials.

The burden of proof, of course, was upon the Government to establish monopoly. This the trial court held the Government failed to do ... For the United States to succeed in this Court now, it must show that erroneous legal tests were applied to essential findings of fact or that the findings themselves were "clearly erroneous" ... We do not try the facts of cases de novo. . . .

[The court below also found that du Pont did not obtain its market position through exclusionary conduct, but the Supreme Court never reached that issue because it concluded the evidence did not prove monopoly power.]

Our cases determine that a party has monopoly power if it has, over "any part of the trade or commerce among the several states", a power of controlling prices or unreasonably restricting competition. . . . If cellophane is the "market" that du Pont is found to dominate, it may be assumed it does have monopoly power over that "market." Monopoly power is the power to control prices or exclude competition. It seems apparent that du Pont's power to set the price of cellophane has been limited only by the competition afforded by other flexible packaging materials. Moreover, it may be practically impossible for anyone to commence manufacturing cellophane without full access to du Pont's technique [over which it held patents]. However, du Pont has no power to prevent competition from other wrapping materials. The trial court consequently had to determine whether competition from the other wrappings prevented du Pont from possessing monopoly power in violation of § 2. Price and competition are so intimately entwined that any discussion of theory must treat them as one. It is inconceivable that price could be controlled without power over competition or vice versa. . . .

If a large number of buyers and sellers deal freely in a standardized product, such as salt or wheat, we have complete or pure competition. Patents, on the other hand, furnish the most familiar type of classic monopoly. As the producers of a standardized product bring about significant differentiations of quality, designed, or packaging in the product that permit differences of use, competition becomes to a greater or less degree incomplete and the producer's power over price and competition greater over his article and its use, according to the differentiation he is able to create and maintain. A retail seller may have in one sense a monopoly on certain trade because of location, as an isolated country store or filling station, or because no one else makes a product of just the quality or attractiveness of his product, as for example in cigarettes. Thus one can theorize that we have monopolistic competition in every nonstandardized commodity with each manufacturer having power over the price and production of his own product. However, this power that, let us say, automobile or soft-drink manufactures have over their trademarked products is not the power that makes an illegal monopoly. Illegal power must be appraised in terms of the competitive market for the product.

Determination of the competitive market for commodities depends on how different from one another are the offered commodities in character or use, how far buyers will go to substitute one commodity for another. For example, one can think of building materials as in commodity competition but one could hardly say that brick competed with steel or wood or cement or stone in the meaning of Sherman Act litigation; the products are too different. This is the interindustry competition emphasized by some economists. On the other hand, there are certain differences in the formulae for soft drinks but one can hardly say that each one is an illegal monopoly. Whatever the market may be, we hold that control of price or competition establishes the existence of monopoly power under § 2.... Our next step is to determine whether du Pont has monopoly power over cellophane: that is, power over its price in relation to or competition with other commodities....

When a product is controlled by one interest, without substitutes available in the market, there is monopoly power. Because most products have possible substitutes, we cannot ... give "that infinite range" to the definition of substitutes. Nor is it a proper interpretation of the Sherman Act to require that products be fungible to be considered in the relevant market.

The Government argues:

"we do not here urge that in no circumstances may competition of substitutes negative possession of monopolistic power over trade in a product. The decisions make it clear at the least that the courts will not consider substitutes other than those which are substantially fungible with the monopolized product and sell at substantially the same price."

But where there are market alternatives that buyers may readily use for their purposes, illegal monopoly does not exist merely because the product said to be monopolized differs from others. If it were not so, only physically identical products would be a part of the market. To accept the Government's argument, we would have to conclude that the manufactures of plain as well as moistureproof cellophane were monopolists, and so with films such as Pliofilm, foil, glassine, polyethylene, and Saran, for each of these wrapping materials is distinguishable. These were all exhibits in the case. New wrappings appear, generally similar to cellophane, is each a monopoly? What is called for is an appraisal of the "cross-elasticity" of demand in the trade.... In considering what is the relevant market for determining the control of price and competition, no more definite rule can be declared than that commodities reasonably interchangeable by consumers for the same purposes make up that "part of the trade or commerce", monopolization of which may be illegal. As respects flexible packaging materials, the market geographically is nationwide.

... Illegal monopolies under § 2 may well exist over limited products in narrow fields where competition is eliminated.... In determining the market under the Sherman Act, it is the use or uses to which the commodity is put that control. The selling price between commodities with similar uses and different characteristics may vary, so that the cheaper product can drive out the more expensive. Or, the superior quality of higher priced articles may make dominant the more desirable. Cellophane costs more than many competing products and less than a few. But whatever the price, there are various flexible wrapping materials that are bought by manufacturers for packaging their goods in their own plants or are sold to converters who shape and print them for use in the packaging of the commodities to be wrapped.

Cellophane differs from other flexible packaging materials. From some it differs more than from others. The basic materials from which the wrappings are made ... are aluminum, cellulose acetate, chlorides, wood pulp, rubber hydrochloride, and ethylene gas. It will adequately illustrate the similarity in characteristics of the various products by noting here Finding 62 as to glassine. Its use is almost as extensive as cellophane, and many of its characteristics equally or more satisfactory to users.[25]

It may be admitted that cellophane combines the desirable elements of transparency, strength and cheapness more definitely than any of the others. Comparative characteristics have been noted thus:

"Moistureproof cellophane is highly transparent, tears readily but has high bursting strength, is highly impervious to moisture and gases, and is resistant to grease and oils. Heat sealable, printable, and adapted to use on wrapping machines, it makes an excellent packaging material for both display and protection of commodities.

"Other flexible wrapping materials fall into four major categories: (1) opaque nonmoistureproof wrapping paper designed primarily for convenience and protection in handling packages; (2) moisture-

---

25. ... "Glassine is, in some types, about 90% transparent, so printing is legible through it. Glassine affords low cost transparency. Moisture protection afforded by waxed or lacquered glassine is as good as that or moistureproof cellophane. Glassine has greater resistance to tearing and breakage than cellophane. Glassine runs on packaging machinery with ease equal to that of cellophane. Glassine can be printed faster than cellophane, and can be run faster than moistureproof cellophane on bag machines. Glassine has greater resistance than cellophane to rancidity-inducing ultraviolet rays. Glassine has dimensional stability superior to cellophane. Glassine is more durable in cold weather than cellophane. Printed glassine can be sold against cellophane on the basis of appearance. Glassine may be more easily laminated than cellophane. Glassine is cheaper than cellophane in some types, comparable in others."

proof films of varying degrees of transparency designed primarily either to protect, or to display and protect, the products they encompass; (3) nonmoistureproof transparent films designed primarily to display and to some extent protect, but which obviously do a poor protecting job where exclusion or retention of moisture is important; and (4) moistureproof materials other than films of varying degrees of transparency (foils and paper products) designed to protect and display." ...

But, despite cellophane's advantages it has to meet competition from other materials in every one of its uses.... Food products are the chief outlet, with cigarettes next. The Government makes no challenge to Finding 283 that cellophane furnishes less than 7% of wrappings for bakery products, 25% for candy, 32% for snacks, 35% for meats and poultry, 27% for crackers and biscuits, 47% for fresh produce, and 34% for frozen foods. Seventy-five to eighty percent of cigarettes are wrapped in cellophane. Thus, cellophane shares the packaging market with others. The over-all result is that cellophane accounts for 17.9% of flexible wrapping materials, measured by the wrapping surface.

Moreover a very considerable degree of functional interchangeability exists between these products ... [E]xcept as to permeability to gases, cellophane has no qualities that are not possessed by a number of other materials. Meat will do as an example of interchangeability. Although du Pont's sales to the meat industry have reached 19,000,000 pounds annually, nearly 35%, this volume is attributed "to the rise of self-service retailing of fresh meat." In fact, since the popularity of self-service meats, du Pont has lost "a considerable proportion" of this packaging business to Pliofilm. Pliofilm is more expensive than cellophane, but its superior physical characteristics apparently offset cellophane's price advantage. While retailers shift continually between the two, the trial court found that Pliofilm is increasing its share of the business. One further example is worth noting. Before World War II, du Pont cellophane wrapped between 5 and 10% of baked and smoked meats. The peak year was 1933. Thereafter du Pont was unable to meet the competition of Sylvania and of greaseproof paper. Its sales declined and the 1933 volume was not reached again until 1947. It will be noted that greaseproof paper, glassine, waxed paper, foil and Pliofilm are used as well as cellophane....

An element for consideration as to cross-elasticity of demand between products is the responsiveness of the sales of one product to price changes of the other. If a slight decrease in the price of cellophane causes a considerable number of customers of other flexible wrappings to switch to cellophane, it would be an indication that a high cross-elasticity of demand exists between them; that the products compete in the same market. The court below held that the "(g)reat sensitivity of customers in the flexible packaging markets to price or quality changes" prevented du Pont from possessing monopoly control over price. The record sustains these findings
...

We conclude that cellophane's interchangeability with the other materials mentioned suffices to make it a part of this flexible packaging material market.

The Government stresses the fact that the variation in price between cellophane and other materials demonstrates they are noncompetitive.... Cellophane costs two or three times as much, surface measure, as its chief competitors for the flexible wrapping market, glassine and greaseproof papers. Other forms of cellulose wrappings and those from other chemical or mineral substances, with the exception of aluminum foil, are more expensive. The uses of these materials ... are largely to wrap small packages for retail distribution. The wrapping is a relatively small proportion of the entire cost of the article. Different producers need different qualities in wrappings and their need may vary from time to time as their products undergo change. But the necessity for flexible wrappings is the central and unchanging demand. We cannot say that these differences in cost gave du Pont monopoly power over prices in view of the findings of fact ... [that: (1) du Pont lowered cellophane prices to compete with cheaper wrapping materials like glassine and wax paper; (2) some customers switched between types of materials in response to price changes; and (3) du Pont prices tended to track changes in its cost.]

The facts above considered dispose also of any contention that competitors have been excluded by du Pont from the packaging material market. That market has many producers and there is no proof du Pont ever has possessed power to exclude any of them from the rapidly expanding flexible packaging market.... The record shows the multiplicity of competitors and the financial strength of some with individual assets running to the hundreds of millions. Indeed, the trial court found that du Pont could not exclude competitors even from the manufacture of cellophane, an immaterial matter if the market is flexible packaging material. Nor can we say that du Pont's profits, while liberal (according to the Government 15.9% net after taxes on the 1937—1947 average), demonstrate the existence of a monopoly without proof of lack of comparable profits during those years in other prosperous industries. Cellophane was a leader over 17%, in the flexible packaging materials market. There is no showing that du Pont's rate of return was greater or less than that of other producers of flexible packaging materials.

The "market" which one must study to determine when a producer has monopoly power will vary with the part of commerce under consideration. The tests are constant. That market is composed of products that have reasonable interchangeability for the purposes for which they are produced—price, use and qualities considered. While the application of the tests remains uncertain, it seems to us that du Pont should not be found to monopolize cellophane when that product has the competition and interchangeability with other wrappings that this record shows....

■ MR. CHIEF JUSTICE WARREN, with whom MR. JUSTICE BLACK and MR. JUSTICE DOUGLAS join, dissenting.... The majority ... admit that "cellophane combines the desirable elements of transparency, strength and cheapness more definitely than any of" a host of other packaging materials....

During the period covered by the complaint (1923–1947) cellophane enjoyed phenomenal growth. ... Yet throughout this period the price of cellophane was far greater than that of glassine, waxed paper or sulphite paper.... We cannot believe that buyers, practical businessmen, would have bought cellophane in increasing amounts over a quarter of a century if close substitutes were available at from one-seventh to one-half cellophane's price. That they did so is testimony to cellophane's distinctiveness.

The inference yielded by the conduct of cellophane buyers is reinforced by the conduct of sellers other than du Pont.... Sylvania, the only other cellophane producer, absolutely and immediately followed every du Pont price change, even dating back its price list to the effective date of du Pont's change. Producers of glassine and waxed paper, on the other hand, displayed apparent indifference to du Pont's repeated and substantial price cuts.... [F]rom 1924 to 1932 du Pont dropped the price of plain cellophane 84%, while the price of glassine remained constant. And during the period 1933–1946 the prices for glassine and waxed paper actually increased in the face of a further 21% decline in the price of cellophane....

Certainly du Pont itself shared our view. From the first, du Pont [documents indicated] that it need not concern itself with competition from other packaging materials.... In 1929, while it was still the sole domestic producer of cellophane, du Pont won its long struggle to raise the tariff from 25% to 60%, ad valorem, on cellophane imports, substantially foreclosing foreign competition. ... If close substitutes for cellophane had been commercially available, du Pont, an enlightened enterprise, would not have gone to such lengths to control cellophane....

A confidential du Pont report shows that during the period 1937–1947, despite great expansion of sales, du Pont's "operative return" (before taxes) averaged 31%, while its average "net return" (after deduction of taxes, bonuses, and fundamental research expenditures) was 15.9%. [The dissent cited an article showing that du Pont's returns in rayon were 32% when the rayon market had two firms like cellophane, but that average market returns were only 5% when the rayon market had 20 firms.]

... The trial judge thought that, if du Pont raised its price, the market would "penalize" it with smaller profits as well as lower sales. Du Pont proved him wrong. When 1947 operating earnings dropped below 26% for the first time in 10 years, it increased cellophane's price 7% and boosted its earnings in 1948. Du Pont's division manager then reported that "If an operative return of 31% is considered inadequate then an upward revision in prices will be necessary to improve the return." It is this latitude with respect to price, this broad power of choice, that the antitrust laws forbid. Du Pont's independent pricing policy and the great profits consistently yielded by that policy leave no room for doubt that it had power to control the price of cellophane. The findings of fact cited by the majority cannot affect this conclusion. For they merely demonstrate, that during the period covered by the complaint, du Pont was a "good monopolist," i.e., ... that it chose to maximize profits by lowering price and expanding sales. Proof of enlightened exercise of monopoly power certainly does not refute the existence of that power.

The majority opinion purports to reject the theory of "interindustry competition." Brick, steel, wood, cement and stone, it says, are "too different" to be placed in the same market. But cellophane, glassine, wax papers, sulphite papers, greaseproof and vegetable parchment papers, aluminum foil, cellulose acetate, Pliofilm and other films are not "too different," the opinion concludes. The majority approach would apparently enable a monopolist of motion picture exhibition to avoid Sherman Act consequences by showing that motion pictures compete in substantial measure with legitimate theater, television, radio, sporting events and other forms of entertainment. Here, too, "shifts of business" undoubtedly accompany fluctuations in price and "there are market alternatives that buyers may readily use for their purposes"....

The majority hold in effect that, because cellophane meets competition for many end uses, those buyers for other uses who need or want only cellophane are not entitled to the benefits of competition within the cellophane industry. For example, ... the largest single use of cellophane in 1951 was for wrapping cigarettes, and ... 75 to 80% of all cigarettes are wrapped with cellophane....

du Pont (The Cellophane Case) and Various Bases for Defining Markets

The *du Pont* case, usually called the *Cellophane* case, has two major legal holdings. First, it held that "Monopoly power is the power to control prices or exclude competition." Issues regarding that test have already been discussed in the introduction. Second, the case held that the test of whether two items are in the same market is whether they are "reasonably interchangeable" by buyers. Issues about how to apply this "reasonably interchangeable" test are discussed next.

1. *Physical/Functional Differences and Similarities.* The Court held that the fact that cellophane and other flexible wrapping materials had physical differences that conferred different functional advantages did not alone prove a separate product market. This holding makes economic sense because such differences and advantages would not necessarily prevent customers from switching between the items if a monopolist in one item tried to raise prices for one of the items above competitive levels. Physical or functional differences are thus not alone enough to show that power over the item would confer any power to raise prices.

On the other had, one also cannot infer a single product market from evidence that two items have enough functional similarities that there is a substantial overlap in end uses. If one could, that would lead to odd conclusions, like that bricks and wood are in the same market because both are used for construction or that televisions and radios are in the same market because both are used for entertainment. The reason one cannot infer a single market is that the existence of an overlap in end uses does not necessarily mean that the degree of buyer substitution between the items is high enough to restrain a monopolist in one of the items from raising prices above competitive levels. Thus, an overlap in end use cannot alone disprove the possibility that power over one item would confer power to raise prices.

But does a high *degree* of physical difference determine the issue? The Court seemed to think so when, in dicta, the Court stated that bricks and wood could not be in the same market regardless of substitution between them because they are "too different." This statement suggests the holding may have turned in part on court intuitions about whether cellophane feels more like other flexible packaging materials than bricks feel like wood, suggesting that if cellophane looked more different (like, say, tupperware) the conclusion might have been different even if the cross-elasticities were the same. However, such a reliance on intuitions about physical differences makes little economic sense because items can physically be very different even though substitution between them constrains any power to raise prices in one of the items.

Likewise, the Court suggested in dicta that different retailers or brands of a product that was very physically similar could not be in different markets even if substitution between them does not suffice to prevent each retailer or brand from having pricing discretion. As we shall see, this dicta was later disapproved by the Supreme Court in *Kodak*. Whether the dicta makes economic sense may depend on the reason for the pricing discretion. On the one hand, suppose the firms are engaged in monopolistic competition, where each firm has discretion to price above marginal cost, but recurring fixed costs mean that no firm makes supracompetitive profits. In such a case, it makes antitrust policy sense to conclude that no firm has monopoly power (even though market power exists in a technical economic sense) because the situation does not mean a firm can raise prices over the more competitive levels we might hope for without exclusionary conduct. One the other hand, if the market is differentiated, so that each retailer or brand has discretion to charge not only above marginal cost, but also above average costs, then it is not clear why the law should regard their market power as less than those of other firms with similar demand curves, just because the products or brands are physically similar or even identical. A firm with such retailer or brand power might still be able to raise prices above competitive levels if it can impair rivals with exclusionary conduct.

The functional power to charge above the competitive level that a well-functioning market could achieve is the relevant policy concern, and thus the real question is what effect any physical differences or similarities have on buyer willingness to substitute in response to price increases over competitive levels. Absent empirical evidence, courts may rely on intuitions about whether physical differences or similarities seem likely to lead to a degree of buyer substitution that would prove or disprove separate markets, but such intuitions should be rejected if they are contrary to empirical evidence about actual buyer substitution rates. Although the occasional court still gets misled by intuitions about physical characteristics, modern courts (and certainly expert agencies) generally focus instead on whether actual buyer substitution rates would eliminate any significant discretion to raise prices above competitive levels. Absent such empirical evidence, should courts at least presume that high degrees of physical/functional differences indicate separate markets and high degrees of physical/functional similarities indicate a single market, as long as that presumption can be rebutted?

2. *Price Differences.* The Court also held that evidence that cellophane sold for a significantly higher price than many of the alleged substitutes did not alone prove separate markets. This holding also makes economic sense because a price difference between two items does not necessarily mean a monopolist in one item would have power to raise prices above competitive levels. Suppose, for example, the price for cellophane is 2 cents and the price for wax paper is 1 cent. Suppose further that cellophane costs 2 cents to make and that any price increase over 2 cents would lead all buyers to switch to 1 cent wax paper. Then, cellophane and wax paper should be considered to be in the same market because the possibility of substitution to wax paper would constrain a nominal monopolist in cellophane to price at cost.

Likewise, the Court rejected the claim that separate products are proven if one item has a significantly lower price than substitutes that are alleged to have advantages over it. To see why this also makes economic sense, suppose the price and cost for cellophane is again 2 cents, the price for Pilofilm is 4 cents, and Pilofilm has functional advantages over cellophane that would cause all buyers to switch to Pilofilm if cellophane prices ever exceeded 2 cents. Then cellophane and Pilofilm should be deemed in the same market because substitution to Pilofilm would constrain a nominal monopolist in cellophane to price at cost.

In short, while a price difference indicates that buyers value the items differently, a price difference may not necessarily mean monopoly power if the price difference equals the cost difference between the items. Thus, a price difference does not necessarily show separate products. On the other hand, it may make sense to conclude that price differences should be deemed presumptive evidence of separate products absent evidence that the price difference equaled the cost difference. Would you favor such a presumption?

3.   *Cross–Elasticities at Current Prices: The Cellophane Fallacy.* Although the above analysis indicates the Court was right to focus on buyer substitution rather than physical or price differences, the Court committed a now well-known economic error when it held that one could infer a single product market from evidence that the cross-elasticities of demand are high at *current* prices. The problem is that current prices may already be at monopoly levels, which are where the monopolist maximizes profits and thus by definition mean a monopolist could not profitably raise prices any further. For example, suppose cellophane prices were 2 cents and any further increase in price would lead to rapid switching to wax paper or Pilofilm, thus indicating a high cross-elasticity of demand, but that cellophane actually costs 0.1 cent to make. This high cross-elasticity at current prices would not mean a monopolist in cellophane had no market power, because the possibility of substituting to wax paper or Pilofilm did not prevent the firm from pricing twenty times its costs. More generally, a monopolist would predictably keep increasing prices until its prices did create significant substitution to other products.

Inferring a single product from substitution at current prices was thus a major error in the Court analysis, which is now so well-recognized that it is commonly referred to as "the Cellophane fallacy." What we really want to know is what buyer substitution rates would be if prices were elevated from competitive levels, which will differ from current levels if monopoly power actually exists. Given this, high cross-elasticities at current prices cannot really disprove the possibility that a separate market exists in which a firm is already exercising monopoly power. As we will, the government guidelines and later Supreme Court decision in *Kodak* appear to reject the Cellophane fallacy.

However, a high cross-elasticity at *competitive* price levels (if measurable) would indicate a single market. Further, low cross-elasticity rates (at current or competitive prices) could prove separate markets. A low cross-elasticity at current prices would suggest that prices could be increased significantly if greater market power were obtained in one of those markets, although it would also suggest that much of that potential market power is not being exercised currently. A low cross-elasticity at competitive prices that does not exist at current prices would suggest that monopoly power is already being exercised.

4.   *Price Trends.* Another method for defining markets focuses on the extent to which prices for the items moved in the same way over time. For example, one might think one can infer separate products from evidence that prices for two items failed to move in the same way over time. If A and B are in the same market, a decrease in prices for A would cause buyers to switch to A, thus decreasing demand for B unless producers of B also decreased prices. Thus, one might ordinarily expect B prices to fall with A prices if they are in the same market. However, if the B firms are already pricing at costs that do not decrease with smaller industry output, then the B firms would be unable to lower their prices in response to a decline in A prices. In such a case, we would expect A to capture more sales, but B's price would remain the same, and thus their price trends would differ even though they are in the same market. On the other hand, if a drop in prices for A results *neither* in a drop in prices for B nor a shift in sales to A, that would seem to indicate that A and B are in separate markets. Thus, even if one cannot infer separate products solely from a difference in price trends, one might think one could have inferred separate products in the *Cellophane* case from evidence that, despite a drop in cellophane prices of over 80% and flat or increasing prices for other flexible packaging materials, cellophane was only able to capture 18% of purchases. This evidence suggests a low cross-elasticity of demand.

Likewise, one might think one can infer a single market from evidence that prices for two items did move in the same way over time. However, parallel price trends might simply reflect the fact that input costs for both items increased. Suppose, for example, that plants for making both cellophane and cars both use electricity. Then, an increase in electricity prices would predictably increase the cost of making both cellophane and cars and thus increase the prices of both, but this common price trend would not put cellophane and cars in the same product market.

On the other hand, it may make sense to at least presume that varying price trends indicate separate markets, and parallel price trends indicate a single market, with that presumption being rebuttable by evidence that the price trends can be explained by diverging or common cost factors like those noted above. Would you favor such a presumption?

5.   *Submarkets.* Even if cellophane had reasonably interchangeable substitutes for most uses, one might think that the Court should have defined a cigarette "submarket" because 75–80% of cigarette manufacturers used cellophane and they were less able to substitute other flexible packaging materials. However, if du Pont tried to sell cellophane at a higher price to cigarette manufacturers than to other buyers, it is quite possible cigarette makers would have responded by buying cellophane through brokers or from other buyers to get the low prices. If so, then even if cigarette makes are particularly dependent on cellophane, a cellophane monopolist could not raise prices to them without also raising them to other buyers of cellophane. Proving such a submarket would thus generally also requires evidence that du Pont could effectively price discriminate by distinguishing who is buying for cigarette manufacturers and preventing other buyers from reselling to them. Sustainable submarkets are thus now generally called "price discrimination" markets to make this clear.

6. *Profits.* Without engaging in market definition, is the dissent right that one can infer monopoly power from the evidence that du Pont profits for cellophane averaged 31% (15.9% after-taxes) for a long period of time and that these profits were far higher than for rayon, where du Pont faced competition? The Court rejected this conclusion, suggesting we would also need evidence that profits were lower for other makers of flexible packaging materials. Both sides have a point. High profits, if sustained, can indicate market power, because a price-taking firm would be unable to price significantly above long-run marginal costs. Indeed, high profits seem directly relevant to whether a firm is exercising a power to raise prices. However, given that workable competition often involves monopolistic competition given fixed costs, it can be hard to determine just how high a profit margin a competitive firm should have. The comparison to a rayon baseline is thus helpful, but profit margins of other flexible packaging materials producers, if they are in competitive segments, may be even a better baseline. However, selecting the right baseline is difficult because the various materials differ in costs and demand and risks.

More generally, one might worry about relying on any profits test because of the difficulty of measuring costs and whether profits exceed risk-adjusted normal returns. It is often difficult to measure economically relevant costs and the extent to which profits exceeded a normal rate of return given the relevant risks. Further, unless sustained for a long period, high profits could reflect short term capacity constraints or economic rents in a competitive market rather than monopoly power. Moreover, a lack of profits could simply indicate that a monopolist is inefficient or has gamed its reporting of joint production costs to allocate them to its monopoly products.

Thus, high profits may neither be sufficient nor necessary to indicate monopoly power. Courts and agencies are thus usually leery of relying solely on profit levels. However, in some cases, profit levels may provide more useful information than the alternatives. Should courts and agencies focus more on profit levels than on the other factors noted above?

7. *Self–Characterizations.* Should one infer separate markets from evidence that du Pont documents themselves stated cellophane was in a separate market? On the one hand, one might reasonably think that du Pont would know better than anyone whether the markets are separate. On the other hand, businesses may use the term "market" in a colloquial fashion that differs from the term's strict antitrust meaning. Further, employees might have incentives to be overzealous in internal memos about their product's lack of competition, especially if their bonuses or promotions are tied to performance. Considering market characterizations by employees also raises the issue of whether characterization by any du Pont employee should suffice or whether we need evidence that characterization was approved at the highest firm levels. The involves the usual difficulty with relying on firm admissions: it is often unclear who speaks for the firm. Given these considerations, courts generally hold that such self-characterizations do not dictate a separate markets conclusion, but are relevant and admissible on the issue.

Should courts infer a single market from internal documents that declared cellophane was in a broader market? The problem is that, if courts did so, then firms will in the future start writing internal documents with broad market definitions in order to minimize antitrust scrutiny. Thus, usually courts put greater weight on internal documents that "admit" narrow market definitions than on documents that embrace broad ones. A one-way ratchet ends up being the effect, where internal documents can hurt defendants but rarely help them. Such a one-way ratchet may seem somewhat unfair to defendants, but in practice it results in very bland internal documents that refer to "market segments" rather than "markets."

8. *Inferring from Conduct.* A more solid basis than mere self-characterization would be evidence that the firm engaged in conduct that makes economic sense only if the firm believed a separate market existed. For example, here the dissent cited evidence that du Pont invested in lobbying for higher import tariffs on foreign cellophane. However, the relevance of this evidence may turn on how large the lobbying costs were. If lobbying costs were very high, such a lobbying investment would probably be economically irrational if du Pont did not have some degree of market power. If lobbying costs are relatively low, then even a firm in a locally competitive market might fear being undercut by foreign cellophane makers that had lower costs. However, if du Pont did not think cellophane was a separate market, it probably makes little economic sense for du Pont to seek tariffs on only foreign cellophane rather than on all foreign flexible packaging materials, unless foreign cellophane was the only low-cost foreign producer of flexible packaging materials. This evidence thus does support a separate market. However, such lobbying need not indicate monopoly power, as long as the firm has sufficient market power to realize enough gain from the reduced competition to cover the lobbying costs.

9. *Possible Limitations on the Holding.* Given that some of the statements in *du Pont* seem economically erroneous or overstated, it is important to consider whether the holding might be more limited than such language suggests or be explained by the circumstances of that case. One possible limitation is that the government had the burden of proof, and the government argued only that differences in physical/functional attributes and prices sufficed to prove separate products. Given that this government position was economically erroneous for reasons noted above, it is not surprising that the Court rejected that position, and limiting the holding to rejecting the government position would eliminate any economic difficulties.

Another possible limitation is that this case was decided at a time when, as the majority stated in unexcerpted portions of the opinion, monopoly power created a presumption of intent to monopolize and sufficed to find liability absent a possible (but not certain) exception for a monopoly that had been "thrust upon" the monopolist. Under a regime with such a lax conduct requirement, one would expect courts to make it harder to find monopoly power. The laxer the conduct element, the tighter the monopoly power screen must be to avoid excessive overderrence. Likewise, the laxer the monopoly power screen, the tighter the conduct standard must be.

Should *du Pont* be limited to rejecting only the government position in that case or to stating a monopoly power test that applies only when the exclusionary conduct standard is very lax?

U.S. DOJ/FTC, Horizontal Merger Guidelines
(2010).

[Although U.S. enforcement agencies have not issued guidelines on how to determine monopoly power or define markets in a monopolization case, they have issued influential guidelines on how they define markets for purposes of merger enforcement, which are also relevant to monopolization cases. The main difference is that in a merger case the question is whether the merger will increase prices from the levels that would prevail without the merger, whereas in a monopolization case the question is whether market power already exists.]

4. Market Definition .... Market definition focuses solely on demand substitution factors, i.e., on customers' ability and willingness to substitute away from one product to another in response to a price increase or a corresponding non-price change such as a reduction in product quality or service. The responsive actions of suppliers are also important in competitive analysis. They are considered in these Guidelines in the sections addressing the identification of market participants, the measurement of market shares, the analysis of competitive effects, and entry.

Customers often confront a range of possible substitutes for the products of the merging firms. Some substitutes may be closer, and others more distant, either geographically or in terms of product attributes and perceptions. Additionally, customers may assess the proximity of different products differently. When products or suppliers in different geographic areas are substitutes for one another to varying degrees, defining a market to include some substitutes and exclude others is inevitably a simplification that cannot capture the full variation in the extent to which different products compete against each other. The principles of market definition outlined below seek to make this inevitable simplification as useful and informative as is practically possible. Relevant markets need not have precise metes and bounds.

Defining a market broadly to include relatively distant product or geographic substitutes can lead to misleading market shares. This is because the competitive significance of distant substitutes is unlikely to be commensurate with their shares in a broad market. Although excluding more distant substitutes from the market inevitably understates their competitive significance to some degree, doing so often provides a more accurate indicator of the competitive effects of the merger than would the alternative of including them and overstating their competitive significance as proportional to their shares in an expanded market.

Example 4: Firms A and B, sellers of two leading brands of motorcycles, propose to merge. If Brand A motorcycle prices were to rise, some buyers would substitute to Brand B, and some others would substitute to cars. However, motorcycle buyers see Brand B motorcycles as much more similar to Brand A motorcycles than are cars. Far more cars are sold than motorcycles. Evaluating shares in a market that includes cars would greatly underestimate the competitive significance of Brand B motorcycles in constraining Brand A's prices and greatly overestimate the significance of cars.

Market shares of different products in narrowly defined markets are more likely to capture the relative competitive significance of these products, and often more accurately reflect competition between close substitutes. As a result, properly defined antitrust markets often exclude some substitutes to which some customers might turn in the face of a price increase even if such substitutes provide alternatives for those customers. However, a group of products is too narrow to constitute a relevant market if competition from products outside that group is so ample that even the complete elimination of competition within the group would not significantly harm either direct customers or downstream consumers. The hypothetical monopolist test (see Section 4.1.1) is designed to ensure that candidate markets are not overly narrow in this respect.

The Agencies implement these principles of market definition flexibly when evaluating different possible candidate markets. Relevant antitrust markets defined according to the hypothetical monopolist test are not always intuitive and may not align with how industry members use the term "market."

Section 4.1 describes the principles that apply to product market definition, and gives guidance on how the Agencies most often apply those principles. Section 4.2 describes how the same principles apply to geographic market definition. Although discussed separately for simplicity of exposition, the principles described in Sections 4.1 and 4.2 are combined to define a relevant market, which has both a product and a geographic dimension. In particular, the hypothetical monopolist test is applied to a group of products together with a geographic region to determine a relevant market.

4.1 Product Market Definition. When a product sold by one merging firm (Product A) competes against one or more products sold by the other merging firm, the Agencies define a relevant product market around Product A to evaluate the importance of that competition. Such a relevant product market consists of a group of substitute products including Product A. Multiple relevant product markets may thus be identified.

4.1.1 The Hypothetical Monopolist Test. The Agencies employ the hypothetical monopolist test to evaluate whether groups of products in candidate markets are sufficiently broad to constitute relevant antitrust markets. The Agencies use the hypothetical monopolist test to identify a set of products that are reasonably interchangeable with a product sold by one of the merging firms.

The hypothetical monopolist test requires that a product market contain enough substitute products so that it could be subject to post-merger exercise of market power significantly exceeding that existing absent the merger. Specifically, the test requires that a hypothetical profit-maximizing firm, not subject to price regulation, that was the only present and future seller of those products ("hypothetical monopolist") likely would impose at least a small but significant and non-transitory increase in price ("SSNIP") on at least one product in the market, including at least one product sold by one of the merging firms. For the purpose of analyzing this issue, the terms of sale of products outside the candidate market are held constant. The SSNIP is employed solely as a methodological tool for performing the hypothetical monopolist test; it is not a tolerance level for price increases resulting from a merger.

Groups of products may satisfy the hypothetical monopolist test without including the full range of substitutes from which customers choose. The hypothetical monopolist test may identify a group of products as a relevant market even if customers would substitute significantly to products outside that group in response to a price increase.

Example 5: Products A and B are being tested as a candidate market. Each sells for $100, has an incremental cost of $60, and sells 1200 units. For every dollar increase in the price of Product A, for any given price of Product B, Product A loses twenty units of sales to products outside the candidate market and ten units of sales to Product B, and likewise for Product B. Under these conditions, economic analysis shows that a hypothetical profit-maximizing monopolist controlling Products A and B would raise both of their prices by ten percent, to $110. Therefore, Products A and B satisfy the hypothetical monopolist test using a five percent SSNIP, and indeed for any SSNIP size up to ten percent. This is true even though two-thirds of the sales lost by one product when it raises its price are diverted to products outside the relevant market.

When applying the hypothetical monopolist test to define a market around a product offered by one of the merging firms, if the market includes a second product, the Agencies will normally also include a third product if that third product is a closer substitute for the first product than is the second product. The third product is a closer substitute if, in response to a SSNIP on the first product, greater revenues are diverted to the third product than to the second product.

Example 6: In Example 5, suppose that half of the unit sales lost by Product A when it raises its price are diverted to Product C, which also has a price of $100, while one-third are diverted to Product B. Product C is a closer substitute for Product A than is Product B. Thus Product C will normally be included in the relevant market, even though Products A and B together satisfy the hypothetical monopolist test.

The hypothetical monopolist test ensures that markets are not defined too narrowly, but it does not lead to a single relevant market. The Agencies may evaluate a merger in any relevant market satisfying the test, guided by the overarching principle that the purpose of defining the market and measuring market shares is to illuminate the evaluation of competitive effects. Because the relative competitive significance of more distant substitutes is apt to be overstated by their share of sales, when the Agencies rely on market shares and concentration, they usually do so in the smallest relevant market satisfying the hypothetical monopolist test. . . .

4.1.2 Benchmark Prices and SSNIP Size. The Agencies apply the SSNIP starting from prices that would likely prevail absent the merger. If prices are not likely to change absent the merger, these benchmark prices can reasonably be taken to be the prices prevailing prior to the merger.[5] If prices are likely to change absent the merger, e.g., because of innovation or entry, the Agencies may use anticipated future prices as the benchmark for the test. If prices might fall absent the merger due to the breakdown of pre-merger coordination, the Agencies may use those lower prices as the benchmark for the test. In some cases, the techniques employed by the Agencies to implement the hypothetical monopolist test focus on the difference in incentives between pre-merger firms and the hypothetical monopolist and do not require specifying the benchmark prices.

The SSNIP is intended to represent a "small but significant" increase in the prices charged by firms in the candidate market for the value they contribute to the products or services used by customers. This properly directs attention to the effects of price changes commensurate with those that might result from a significant lessening of competition caused by the merger. This methodology is used because normally it is possible to quantify "small but significant" adverse price effects on customers and analyze their likely reactions, not because price effects are more important than non-price effects.

The Agencies most often use a SSNIP of five percent of the price paid by customers for the products or services to which the merging firms contribute value. However, what constitutes a "small but significant" increase in price, commensurate with a significant loss of competition caused by the merger, depends upon the nature of the industry and the merging firms' positions in it, and the Agencies may accordingly use a price increase that is larger or smaller than five percent. Where explicit or implicit prices for the firms' specific contribution to value can be identified with reasonable clarity, the Agencies may base the SSNIP on those prices.

Example 8: In a merger between two oil pipelines, the SSNIP would be based on the price charged for transporting the oil, not on the price of the oil itself. If pipelines buy the oil at one end and sell it at the other, the price charged for transporting the oil is implicit, equal to the difference between the price paid for oil at the input end and the price charged for oil at the output end. The relevant product sold by the pipelines is better described

---

5. Market definition for the evaluation of non-merger antitrust concerns such as monopolization or facilitating practices will differ in this respect if the effects resulting from the conduct of concern are already occurring at the time of evaluation.

as "pipeline transportation of oil from point A to point B" than as "oil at point B."

Example 9: In a merger between two firms that install computers purchased from third parties, the SSNIP would be based on their fees, not on the price of installed computers. If these firms purchase the computers and charge their customers one package price, the implicit installation fee is equal to the package charge to customers less the price of the computers.

Example 10: In Example 9, suppose that the prices paid by the merging firms to purchase computers are opaque, but account for at least ninety-five percent of the prices they charge for installed computers, with profits or implicit fees making up five percent of those prices at most. A five percent SSNIP on the total price paid by customers would at least double those fees or profits. Even if that would be unprofitable for a hypothetical monopolist, a significant increase in fees might well be profitable. If the SSNIP is based on the total price paid by customers, a lower percentage will be used.

4.1.3   Implementing the Hypothetical Monopolist Test. The hypothetical monopolist's incentive to raise prices depends both on the extent to which customers would likely substitute away from the products in the candidate market in response to such a price increase and on the profit margins earned on those products. The profit margin on incremental units is the difference between price and incremental cost on those units. The Agencies often estimate incremental costs, for example using merging parties' documents or data the merging parties use to make business decisions. Incremental cost is measured over the change in output that would be caused by the price increase under consideration.

In considering customers' likely responses to higher prices, the Agencies take into account any reasonably available and reliable evidence, including, but not limited to:

- how customers have shifted purchases in the past in response to relative changes in price or other terms and conditions;

- information from buyers, including surveys, concerning how they would respond to price changes;

- the conduct of industry participants, notably:

- sellers' business decisions or business documents indicating sellers' informed beliefs concerning how customers would substitute among products in response to relative changes in price;

- industry participants' behavior in tracking and responding to price changes by some or all rivals;

- objective information about product characteristics and the costs and delays of switching products, especially switching from products in the candidate market to products outside the candidate market;

- the percentage of sales lost by one product in the candidate market, when its price alone rises, that is recaptured by other products in the candidate market, with a higher recapture percentage making a price increase more profitable for the hypothetical monopolist;

• evidence from other industry participants, such as sellers of complementary products;

• legal or regulatory requirements; and

• the influence of downstream competition faced by customers in their output markets.

When the necessary data are available, the Agencies also may consider a "critical loss analysis" to assess the extent to which it corroborates inferences drawn from the evidence noted above. Critical loss analysis asks whether imposing at least a SSNIP on one or more products in a candidate market would raise or lower the hypothetical monopolist's profits. While this "breakeven" analysis differs from the profit-maximizing analysis called for by the hypothetical monopolist test in Section 4.1.1, merging parties sometimes present this type of analysis to the Agencies. A price increase raises profits on sales made at the higher price, but this will be offset to the extent customers substitute away from products in the candidate market. Critical loss analysis compares the magnitude of these two offsetting effects resulting from the price increase. The "critical loss" is defined as the number of lost unit sales that would leave profits unchanged. The "predicted loss" is defined as the number of unit sales that the hypothetical monopolist is predicted to lose due to the price increase. The price increase raises the hypothetical monopolist's profits if the predicted loss is less than the critical loss.

The Agencies consider all of the evidence of customer substitution noted above in assessing the predicted loss. The Agencies require that estimates of the predicted loss be consistent with that evidence, including the pre-merger margins of products in the candidate market used to calculate the critical loss. Unless the firms are engaging in coordinated interaction (see Section 7), high pre-merger margins normally indicate that each firm's product individually faces demand that is not highly sensitive to price.[6] Higher pre-merger margins thus indicate a smaller predicted loss as well as a smaller critical loss. The higher the pre-merger margin, the smaller the recapture percentage necessary for the candidate market to satisfy the hypothetical monopolist test. . . .

4.1.4 Product Market Definition with Targeted Customers. If a hypothetical monopolist could profitably target a subset of customers for price increases, the Agencies may identify relevant markets defined around those targeted customers, to whom a hypothetical monopolist would profitably and separately impose at least a SSNIP. Markets to serve targeted customers are also known as price discrimination markets. In practice, the Agencies identify price discrimination markets only where they believe there is a realistic prospect of an adverse competitive effect on a group of targeted customers.

Example 11: Glass containers have many uses. In response to a price increase for glass containers, some users would substitute substantially to plastic or metal containers, but baby food manufacturers would not. If a hypothetical monopolist could price separately and limit arbitrage, baby

---

6.   While margins are important for implementing the hypothetical monopolist test, high margins are not in themselves of antitrust concern.

food manufacturers would be vulnerable to a targeted increase in the price of glass containers. The Agencies could define a distinct market for glass containers used to package baby food.

The Agencies also often consider markets for targeted customers when prices are individually negotiated and suppliers have information about customers that would allow a hypothetical monopolist to identify customers that are likely to pay a higher price for the relevant product. If prices are negotiated individually with customers, the hypothetical monopolist test may suggest relevant markets that are as narrow as individual customers (see also Section 6.2 on bargaining and auctions). Nonetheless, the Agencies often define markets for groups of targeted customers, i.e., by type of customer, rather than by individual customer. By so doing, the Agencies are able to rely on aggregated market shares that can be more helpful in predicting the competitive effects of the merger.

4.2 Geographic Market Definition. The arena of competition affected by the merger may be geographically bounded if geography limits some customers' willingness or ability to substitute to some products, or some suppliers' willingness or ability to serve some customers. Both supplier and customer locations can affect this. The Agencies apply the principles of market definition described here and in Section 4.1 to define a relevant market with a geographic dimension as well as a product dimension.

The scope of geographic markets often depends on transportation costs. Other factors such as language, regulation, tariff and non-tariff trade barriers, custom and familiarity, reputation, and service availability may impede long-distance or international transactions. The competitive significance of foreign firms may be assessed at various exchange rates, especially if exchange rates have fluctuated in the recent past.

In the absence of price discrimination based on customer location, the Agencies normally define geographic markets based on the locations of suppliers, as explained in subsection 4.2.1. In other cases, notably if price discrimination based on customer location is feasible as is often the case when delivered pricing is commonly used in the industry, the Agencies may define geographic markets based on the locations of customers, as explained in subsection 4.2.2.

4.2.1 Geographic Markets Based on the Locations of Suppliers. Geographic markets based on the locations of suppliers encompass the region from which sales are made. Geographic markets of this type often apply when customers receive goods or services at suppliers' locations. Competitors in the market are firms with relevant production, sales, or service facilities in that region. Some customers who buy from these firms may be located outside the boundaries of the geographic market.

The hypothetical monopolist test requires that a hypothetical profit-maximizing firm that was the only present or future producer of the relevant product(s) located in the region would impose at least a SSNIP from at least one location, including at least one location of one of the merging firms. In this exercise the terms of sale for all products produced elsewhere are held constant. A single firm may operate in a number of different geographic markets, even for a single product.

Example 12: The merging parties both have manufacturing plants in City X. The relevant product is expensive to transport and suppliers price their products for pickup at their locations. Rival plants are some distance away in City Y. A hypothetical monopolist controlling all plants in City X could profitably impose a SSNIP at these plants. Competition from more distant plants would not defeat the price increase because supplies coming from more distant plants require expensive transportation. The relevant geographic market is defined around the plants in City X.

When the geographic market is defined based on supplier locations, sales made by suppliers located in the geographic market are counted, regardless of the location of the customer making the purchase.

In considering likely reactions of customers to price increases for the relevant product(s) imposed in a candidate geographic market, the Agencies consider any reasonably available and reliable evidence, including:

• how customers have shifted purchases in the past between different geographic locations in response to relative changes in price or other terms and conditions;

• the cost and difficulty of transporting the product (or the cost and difficulty of a customer traveling to a seller's location), in relation to its price;

• whether suppliers need a presence near customers to provide service or support;

• evidence on whether sellers base business decisions on the prospect of customers switching between geographic locations in response to relative changes in price or other competitive variables;

• the costs and delays of switching from suppliers in the candidate geographic market to suppliers outside the candidate geographic market; and

• the influence of downstream competition faced by customers in their output markets.

4.2.2 Geographic Markets Based on the Locations of Customers.
When the hypothetical monopolist could discriminate based on customer location, the Agencies may define geographic markets based on the locations of targeted customers.[7] Geographic markets of this type often apply when suppliers deliver their products or services to customers' locations. Geographic markets of this type encompass the region into which sales are made. Competitors in the market are firms that sell to customers in the specified region. Some suppliers that sell into the relevant market may be located outside the boundaries of the geographic market.

The hypothetical monopolist test requires that a hypothetical profit-maximizing firm that was the only present or future seller of the relevant product(s) to customers in the region would impose at least a SSNIP on some customers in that region. A region forms a relevant geographic market if this price increase would not be defeated by substitution away

---

7. For customers operating in multiple locations, only those customer locations within the targeted zone are included in the market.

from the relevant product or by arbitrage, e.g., customers in the region travelling outside it to purchase the relevant product. In this exercise, the terms of sale for products sold to all customers outside the region are held constant.

Example 13: Customers require local sales and support. Suppliers have sales and service operations in many geographic areas and can discriminate based on customer location. The geographic market can be defined around the locations of customers.

Example 14: Each merging firm has a single manufacturing plant and delivers the relevant product to customers in City X and in City Y. The relevant product is expensive to transport. The merging firms' plants are by far the closest to City X, but no closer to City Y than are numerous rival plants. This fact pattern suggests that customers in City X may be harmed by the merger even if customers in City Y are not. For that reason, the Agencies consider a relevant geographic market defined around customers in City X. Such a market could be defined even if the region around the merging firms' plants would not be a relevant geographic market defined based on the location of sellers because a hypothetical monopolist controlling all plants in that region would find a SSNIP imposed on all of its customers unprofitable due to the loss of sales to customers in City Y.

When the geographic market is defined based on customer locations, sales made to those customers are counted, regardless of the location of the supplier making those sales.

Example 15: Customers in the United States must use products approved by U.S. regulators. Foreign customers use products not approved by U.S. regulators. The relevant product market consists of products approved by U.S. regulators. The geographic market is defined around U.S. customers. Any sales made to U.S. customers by foreign suppliers are included in the market, and those foreign suppliers are participants in the U.S. market even though located outside it. . . .

5. Market Participants, Market Shares, and Market Concentration . . . . Market shares can directly influence firms' competitive incentives. For example, if a price reduction to gain new customers would also apply to a firm's existing customers, a firm with a large market share may be more reluctant to implement a price reduction than one with a small share. Likewise, a firm with a large market share may not feel pressure to reduce price even if a smaller rival does. Market shares also can reflect firms' capabilities. For example, a firm with a large market share may be able to expand output rapidly by a larger absolute amount than can a small firm. Similarly, a large market share tends to indicate low costs, an attractive product, or both.

5.1 Market Participants. All firms that currently earn revenues in the relevant market are considered market participants. Vertically integrated firms are also included to the extent that their inclusion accurately reflects their competitive significance. Firms not currently earning revenues in the relevant market, but that have committed to entering the market in the near future, are also considered market participants.

Firms that are not current producers in a relevant market, but that would very likely provide rapid supply responses with direct competitive impact in the event of a SSNIP, without incurring significant sunk costs, are also considered market participants. These firms are termed "rapid entrants." Sunk costs are entry or exit costs that cannot be recovered outside the relevant market. Entry that would take place more slowly in response to adverse competitive effects, or that requires firms to incur significant sunk costs, is considered in Section 9.

Firms that produce the relevant product but do not sell it in the relevant geographic market may be rapid entrants. Other things equal, such firms are most likely to be rapid entrants if they are close to the geographic market.

Example 16: Farm A grows tomatoes halfway between Cities X and Y. Currently, it ships its tomatoes to City X because prices there are two percent higher. Previously it has varied the destination of its shipments in response to small price variations. Farm A would likely be a rapid entrant participant in a market for tomatoes in City Y.

Example 17: Firm B has bid multiple times to supply milk to School District S, and actually supplies milk to schools in some adjacent areas. It has never won a bid in School District S, but is well qualified to serve that district and has often nearly won. Firm B would be counted as a rapid entrant in a market for school milk in School District S.

More generally, if the relevant market is defined around targeted customers, firms that produce relevant products but do not sell them to those customers may be rapid entrants if they can easily and rapidly begin selling to the targeted customers.

Firms that clearly possess the necessary assets to supply into the relevant market rapidly may also be rapid entrants. In markets for relatively homogeneous goods where a supplier's ability to compete depends predominantly on its costs and its capacity, and not on other factors such as experience or reputation in the relevant market, a supplier with efficient idle capacity, or readily available "swing" capacity currently used in adjacent markets that can easily and profitably be shifted to serve the relevant market, may be a rapid entrant.[8] However, idle capacity may be inefficient, and capacity used in adjacent markets may not be available, so a firm's possession of idle or swing capacity alone does not make that firm a rapid entrant.

5.2 Market Shares. The Agencies normally calculate market shares for all firms that currently produce products in the relevant market, subject to the availability of data. The Agencies also calculate market shares for other market participants if this can be done to reliably reflect their competitive significance.

Market concentration and market share data are normally based on historical evidence. However, recent or ongoing changes in market conditions may

---

8. If this type of supply side substitution is nearly universal among the firms selling one or more of a group of products, the Agencies may use an aggregate description of markets for those products as a matter of convenience.

indicate that the current market share of a particular firm either under-states or overstates the firm's future competitive significance. The Agencies consider reasonably predictable effects of recent or ongoing changes in market conditions when calculating and interpreting market share data. For example, if a new technology that is important to long-term competi-tive viability is available to other firms in the market, but is not available to a particular firm, the Agencies may conclude that that firm's historical market share overstates its future competitive significance. The Agencies may project historical market shares into the foreseeable future when this can be done reliably.

The Agencies measure market shares based on the best available indicator of firms' future competitive significance in the relevant market. This may depend upon the type of competitive effect being considered, and on the availability of data. Typically, annual data are used, but where individual transactions are large and infrequent so annual data may be unrepresenta-tive, the Agencies may measure market shares over a longer period of time.

In most contexts, the Agencies measure each firm's market share based on its actual or projected revenues in the relevant market. Revenues in the relevant market tend to be the best measure of attractiveness to customers, since they reflect the real-world ability of firms to surmount all of the obstacles necessary to offer products on terms and conditions that are attractive to customers. In cases where one unit of a low-priced product can substitute for one unit of a higher-priced product, unit sales may measure competitive significance better than revenues. For example, a new, much less expensive product may have great competitive significance if it sub-stantially erodes the revenues earned by older, higher-priced products, even if it earns relatively few revenues. In cases where customers sign long-term contracts, face switching costs, or tend to re-evaluate their suppliers only occasionally, revenues earned from recently acquired customers may better reflect the competitive significance of suppliers than do total revenues.

In markets for homogeneous products, a firm's competitive significance may derive principally from its ability and incentive to rapidly expand production in the relevant market in response to a price increase or output reduction by others in that market. As a result, a firm's competitive significance may depend upon its level of readily available capacity to serve the relevant market if that capacity is efficient enough to make such expansion profitable. In such markets, capacities or reserves may better reflect the future competitive significance of suppliers than revenues, and the Agencies may calculate market shares using those measures. Market participants that are not current producers may then be assigned positive market shares, but only if a measure of their competitive significance properly comparable to that of current producers is available. When market shares are measured based on firms' readily available capacities, the Agencies do not include capacity that is committed or so profitably em-ployed outside the relevant market, or so high-cost, that it would not likely be used to respond to a SSNIP in the relevant market.

Example 18: The geographic market is defined around customers in the United States. Firm X produces the relevant product outside the United States, and most of its sales are made to customers outside the United

States. In most contexts, Firm X's market share will be based on its sales to U.S. customers, not its total sales or total capacity. However, if the relevant product is homogeneous, and if Firm X would significantly expand sales to U.S. customers rapidly and without incurring significant sunk costs in response to a SSNIP, the Agencies may base Firm X's market share on its readily available capacity to serve U.S. customers.

When the Agencies define markets serving targeted customers, these same principles are used to measure market shares, as they apply to those customers. In most contexts, each firm's market share is based on its actual or projected revenues from the targeted customers. However, the Agencies may instead measure market shares based on revenues from a broader group of customers if doing so would more accurately reflect the competitive significance of different suppliers in the relevant market. Revenues earned from a broader group of customers may also be used when better data are thereby available.

Note on the U.S. Market Definition Guidelines

To simplify, the Guidelines conclude that a proposed market is sufficiently broad if an absolute monopolist of the posited market would likely find it profit-maximizing to impose a nontransitory price increase of at least 5%, though other percentages can be used as the SSNIP benchmark. To assess this issue, one must assess *buyer* substitution (the extent to which buyers would turn to other products or regions in response to a price increase) and profit margins (the amount of profits the firm would lose from buyer substitution compared to the profits it would gain from the price increase). The fact that *some* buyer substitution occurs is not enough to conclude the market should be broadened. If a hypothetical monopolist in the posited market would find it profit-maximizing to increase prices by at least 5%, then the market definition is sufficiently broad; if not, then the market definition must be broadened to include possible buyer substitutes until we have a posited market that satisfies the test.

The Guidelines make clear that: "The hypothetical monopolist test ensures that markets are not defined too narrowly, but it does not lead to a single relevant market." Instead, agency analysis can use "any relevant market satisfying the test, guided by the overarching principle that the purpose of defining the market and measuring market shares is to illuminate the evaluation of competitive effects." For example, suppose that a monopolist in town A would likely increase prices by 10% before being constrained by suppliers in town B, but a monopolist in both towns A and B would likely increase prices by 20% before being constrained by suppliers outside of A or B. In assessing a merger between firms in town A, then town A would be the relevant geographic market. But in assessing a merger between firms in town A and town B, then A–B would be the relevant geographic market because here the merger could produce a significant price increase even though a merger in an even smaller market could also produce a significant price increase. There is no single, inherently correct, market definition; it all depends on the anticompetitive effects theory that the market definition is trying to illuminate.

Even more counterintuitively, the proper market definition may not run equally in both directions if either the substitution rates or baseline profit margins differ. For example, suppose a monopolist in A would profitably raise prices by 6% given substitution to B, but a monopolist in B could profitably raise prices by only 4% given substitution to A. Then in assessing conduct in A, the proper market definition is A, but in assessing conduct in B, the proper market definition is A–B combined. Again, the reason is that the focus is functional, on the degree of actual power to raise prices that might be created by anticompetitive conduct or mergers.

The Guidelines also clarify that the focus is on the price increase a hypothetical monopolist would likely impose. For example, it could well be that a hypothetical monopolist in a posited market would find a price increase of 5% unprofitable but would find a price increase of 20% profitable. (This might be true if demand is elastic for a 5% price increase but after that goes down as the market focuses on the really inelastic buyers.) In that case, the posited market is valid, even though a 5% price increase is unprofitable, because a 20% price increase would profitably be imposed. This is why the agencies focus on the price increases that would likely be profitable rather than on "critical loss" analysis of the profitability of a 5% price increase.

Supply substitution is taken into account not in market definition, but rather in defining which firms and capacity are in that defined market. Such firms are deemed to include not only firms that already operate in the posited market, but also firms who operate in another market *if* they would likely enter the posited market rapidly without incurring significant sunk costs in response to any SSNIP. Thus, a similar SSNIP test is used to assess supply substitution.

One might wonder why supply substitution is not simply deemed part of market definition. After all, if the practical import of supply substitution considerations is that sales of product B are being included in market A, aren't the market shares the same as if we defined the market to include A and B? The answer is "no" if only some of the production of B could be easily switched to making A. Further, even if the market share numbers would be the same, the competitive analysis of those share numbers might differ depending on the market definition.

Suppose, for example, the relevant anticompetitive concern was whether a merger would increase the risk of oligopolistic coordination by leaving product market A with three firms, but a fourth firm that makes product B could easily switch to making product A. Then, all four firms should be deemed part of product market A for purposes of considering whether four such firms are likely to oligopolistically coordinate. But one should not dismiss that likelihood on the ground that a product market that includes both A and B is not sufficiently homogeneous to allow such coordination to succeed; the reason is that the inability of buyers to reasonably interchange A and B means that coordination on A will be enough.

Likewise, suppose the anticompetitive concern was instead that a defendant with a very high share of product market A was foreclosing rivals by requiring buyers to buy all their product A from the defendant. Then one should take into account the fact that makers of product B can easily switch to make product A in order to determine whether the defendant has market power in market A. But the relevant *foreclosure* share is not undermined if the defendant allows buyers to buy product B from others because buyers (by definition) do not find product B reasonably interchangeable for A.

Because the Guidelines are focused on whether proposed mergers would worsen market performance, rather than on whether monopoly or market power already exists, the Guidelines "apply the SSNIP starting from prices that would likely prevail absent the merger," which usually "can reasonably be taken to be the prices prevailing prior to the merger." However, in footnote 5, the Guidelines acknowledge that this approach is inappropriate to assess "monopolization or facilitating practices" where monopoly power or anticompetitive effects already exist. Thus, the Guidelines seem to reject the "Cellophane fallacy" of relying on substitution rates at price levels that already monopoly power. In such a case, one must instead ask whether a hypothetical monopolist could impose a SSNIP above a "competitive price" baseline, which requires one to know what that competitive price baseline is.

Is Market Definition Necessary?

The normal rationale for relying on market share is that market power is difficult to measure directly and that market share data coupled with evidence of significant barriers to entry provides a reasonable proxy for market power. But this rationale is undermined by three considerations.

(1) If we think it is difficult to determine whether an *actual* alleged monopolist can raise prices significantly over competitive levels, it is unclear why we would think it easier to calculate market shares that require us to define a market by determining whether a *hypothetical* monopolist could raise prices significantly above competitive levels. For some market definitions, the answer might be that it is obvious that no reasonable substitute exists and thus obvious that a hypothetical monopolist would thus have significant pricing discretion. But the hypothetical monopolist test arguably provides no help in any monopolization case where there is a genuine conflict about the market definition.

(2) Market share is a fairly unreliable proxy for market power. If a firm has 75% of a market, but rivals would expand immediately to make up for any output restriction, the firm has no pricing discretion. If a firm has 18% of a market, but rivals are completely unable to expand or enter, the firm has substantial pricing discretion. Thus, we at least also need to know the rival supply elasticity.

(3) Market share conclusions are distorted by the all-or-nothing judgments used to define markets. Suppose, for example, that substitution to other flexible packaging materials means a cellophane monopolist would maximize profits by increasing prices by 4% over competitive levels. Then, under the Guidelines, flexible packaging materials would be included in the product market definition, producing a market share of 18%. But 18% understates du Pont's market power compared to the power du Pont would

have if the other 82% were really perfect substitutes, because in the latter case du Pont could not increase prices by even 1%.

Likewise, suppose instead that there is slightly less substitution to flexible packaging materials, so that a cellophane monopolist would maximize profits by increasing prices by 6% over competitive levels. Then, under the Guidelines, flexible packaging materials would be excluded from the product market, producing a market share of 75%. But 75% overstates du Pont's market power compared to what it would be if there were no flexible materials to turn to no matter how much du Pont raised prices.

Accordingly, in these cases the real answer seems to be neither 18% and 75%, but something in between. More precisely, to assess the degree of market power we really need to know the marketwide demand elasticity, which will reflect the precise degree of switching to possible substitutes, and not make categorical judgments about whether that demand elasticity will lead to prices increases that are higher or lower than some SSNIP threshold.

Varying the Weight Given to Market Shares. Some argue that courts should respond to these problems by adjusting the weight they attach to market shares based on both (1) judgments about the likely expandability of rivals and (2) awareness about any judgment calls made in defining the market. However, this approach would seem to undermine any apparent precision from market share data and make cases turn really on intuitive judgments. Further, we would need to measure the rival supply elasticity and the marketwide demand elasticity to really determine the degree of market power suggested by any market shares. And if we had that information for any posited market, we could calculate the degree of such pricing discretion from market shares without ever resolving whether the posited market was in some abstract sense "correct." Defining the market narrowly would increase the market share, but that would not matter because a narrow definition would also increase the market demand elasticity (by increasing the likelihood of demand substitution out of the market) and increase rival supply elasticity (by making it more likely other firms would enter into the market to expand supply).[71] Likewise, a broad market definition would have the offsetting effect of lowering market demand elasticity and rival supply elasticity. As long as one takes into account that the market definition alters not only market share, but also market demand elasticity and rival supply elasticity, then one should reach the same conclusion no matter what market definition one uses.

Moreover, there seems to be little reason to think we are generally more likely to have data on rival supply elasticity and the marketwide demand elasticity than on more direct measures of defendant pricing discretion, such as the degree to which defendant prices exceed their costs or competitive levels, defendant's firm-specific demand elasticity, or defendant behavior that makes economic sense only if market power exists. We

---

71. *See* Landes & Posner, *supra* note 31, at 962–63. Recall that $\epsilon_{dom} = \epsilon_{mkt}/S + \epsilon_{rivsupp}$ $(1-S)/S$. *See supra* note 48. Thus, anything that increases or decreases S in parallel with ϵ_{mkt} and $\epsilon_{rivsupp}$ will have offsetting effects. Further, this equation holds true no matter what market definition is used as long as one takes into account that S, ϵ_{mkt} and $\epsilon_{rivsupp}$ are all functions of how the market is defined.

might thus be better off focusing on those direct measures. As we will see in Chapter 7, in other portions of the Merger Guidelines, the U.S. agencies stress that in merger analysis they often focus on direct measures of anticompetitive effects rather than on market definition and inferences from market shares.

Other Reasons Why Market Shares Might Have Economic Significance. Market shares provide such an imperfect proxy for market power and pricing discretion that one might wonder why market shares are used at all. However, market shares might have economic significance for other reasons.[72] The fact that one firm has a dominant share of a market can help indicate whether that firm is likely to be able to act as a unitary actor who either can exploit collective action problems among buyers or enter into a collusive agreement with a powerful buyer that exploits buyers further downstream. Market shares can also help indicate whether a firm is likely to be able to foreclose enough of the market to create anticompetitive effects, to have incentives to invest in such foreclosure, and/or whether it is likely to have efficiency justifications for foreclosing such a large share of the market. This might help explain why high market shares are used in assessing exclusionary conduct in Chapters 3 and 4.

Further, high market shares held by a few firms can help indicate whether a market has few enough firms to make possible oligopolistic coordination on prices. This might explain why market shares are used when considering oligopolistic coordination in Chapters 6 and 7.

Case 27/76, United Brands v. Commission

[1978] E.C.R. 207, 215 (ECJ).

[United Brands was the world's largest producer of bananas. The Commission found that its European subsidiary, United Brands Continental (UBC), had abused its dominant position on the banana market by engaging in excessive and discriminatory pricing, and refusal to supply. UBC challenged the Commission's decision before the ECJ. One of its arguments was that the Commission had been wrong in identifying a separate market for bananas.]

As far as the product market is concerned it is first of all necessary to ascertain whether, as the applicant maintains, bananas are an integral part of the fresh fruit market, because they are reasonably interchangeable by consumers with other kinds of fresh fruit such as apples, oranges, grapes, peaches, strawberries, etc. or whether the relevant market consists solely of the banana market which includes both branded bananas and unlabelled bananas and is a market sufficiently homogeneous and distinct from the market of other fresh fruit.

The applicant submits in support of its argument that bananas compete with other fresh fruit in the same shops, on the same shelves, at prices which can be compared, satisfying the same needs: consumption as a dessert or between meals. The statistics produced show that consumer

---

72. *See* Elhauge, *supra* note 37, at 334–337.

expenditure on the purchase of bananas is at its lowest between June and December when there is a plentiful supply of domestic fresh fruit on the market. Studies carried out by the food and agriculture organization (FAO) (especially in 1975) confirm that banana prices are relatively weak during the summer months and that the price of apples for example has a statistically appreciable impact on the consumption of bananas in the federal republic of Germany. Again according to these studies some easing of prices is noticeable at the end of the year during the "orange season". The seasonal peak periods when there is a plentiful supply of other fresh fruit exert an influence not only on the prices but also on the volume of sales of bananas and consequently on the volume of imports thereof. The applicant concludes from these findings that bananas and other fresh fruit form only one market . . .

The commission maintains that there is a demand for bananas which is distinct from the demand for other fresh fruit especially as the banana is a very important part of the diet of certain sections of the community. The specific qualities of the banana influence customer preference and induce him not to readily accept other fruits as a substitute. The Commission draws the conclusion from the studies quoted by the applicant that the influence of the prices and availabilities of other types of fruit on the prices and availabilities of bananas on the relevant market is very ineffective and that these effects are too brief and too spasmodic for such other fruit to be regarded as forming part of the same market as bananas or as a substitute therefore.

For the banana to be regarded as forming a market which is sufficiently differentiated from other fruit markets it must be possible for it to be singled out by such special features distinguishing it from other fruits that it is only to a limited extent interchangeable with them and is only exposed to their competition in a way that is hardly perceptible.

The ripening of bananas takes place the whole year round without any season having to be taken into account. Throughout the year production exceeds demand and can satisfy it at any time. Owing to this particular feature the banana is a privileged fruit and its production and marketing can be adapted to the seasonal fluctuations of other fresh fruit which are known and can be computed. There is no unavoidable seasonal substitution since the consumer can obtain this fruit all the year round. Since the banana is a fruit which is always available in sufficient quantities the question whether it can be replaced by other fruits must be determined over the whole of the year for the purpose of ascertaining the degree of competition between it and other fresh fruit.

The studies of the banana market on the Court's file show that on the latter market there is no significant long term cross-elasticity any more than—as has been mentioned—there is any seasonal substitutability in general between the banana and all the seasonal fruits, as this only exists between the banana and two fruits (peaches and table grapes) in one of the countries (west Germany) of the relevant geographic market.

As far as concerns the two fruits available throughout the year (oranges and apples) the first are not interchangeable and in the case of the second there is only a relative degree of substitutability. This small degree of substitutability is accounted for by the specific features of the banana and all the factors which influence consumer choice.

The banana has certain characteristics, appearance, taste, softness, seedlessness, easy handling, a constant level of production which enable it to satisfy the constant needs of an important section of the population consisting of the very young, the old and the sick.

As far as prices are concerned two FAO studies show that the banana is only affected by the prices—falling prices—of other fruits (and only of peaches and table grapes) during the summer months and mainly in July and then by an amount not exceeding 20%.

Although it cannot be denied that during these months and some weeks at the end of the year this product is exposed to competition from other fruits, the flexible way in which the volume of imports and their marketing on the relevant geographic market is adjusted means that the conditions of competition are extremely limited and that its price adapts without any serious difficulties to this situation where supplies of fruit are plentiful.

It follows from all these considerations that a very large number of consumers having a constant need for bananas are not noticeably or even appreciably enticed away from the consumption of this product by the arrival of other fresh fruit on the market and that even the personal peak periods only affect it for a limited period of time and to a very limited extent from the point of view of substitutability. Consequently the banana market is a market which is sufficiently distinct from the other fresh fruit markets.

Questions on *United Brands*

1. Do you agree with the ECJ that "the influence of the prices and availabilities of other types of fruit on the prices and availabilities of bananas on the relevant market is very ineffective and that these effects are too brief and too spasmodic for such other fruit to be regarded as forming part of the same market as bananas or as a substitute therefore"?

a. Should a price effect of 20% be dismissed as too small to be taken into consideration in defining the relevant market? Should such effects be dismissed because they only take place during the summer months?

b. If summer bananas are priced 20% lower than they are in other seasons, doesn't that mean there is a separate summer market because prices in other seasons are not sufficiently constrained by the prices of these summer bananas, perhaps because storage costs are too high given the perishable nature of bananas to keep the bananas to sell in the higher priced season?

    i. Does it make sense to define separate seasonal markets (where justified by storage costs) as one would a separate geographical market (where justified by transportation costs)? Or would this violate the ordinary duration requirement to show significant market power?

ii.   If so, could one say United Brand was a dominant firm on the non-summer markets and reach the same conclusion?

2.   Does the fact that bananas are especially valuable to the very young, the old and the sick mean that bananas constitute a separate market product?

a.   Won't a banana maker's ability to raise banana prices be constrained by the fact that it would lose the marginal buyers who don't have a special need for bananas, unless price discrimination between the two sets of buyers is feasible?

b.   Do we see supermarkets charge buyers different prices for bananas depending on who is ultimately going to eat them? Would it be feasible for them to do so?

Commission Notice on the Definition of the Relevant Market for the Purposes of Community Competition Law

1997 O.J. C 372.

... The main purpose of market definition is to identify in a systematic way the competitive constraints that the undertakings involved face. The objective of defining a market in both its product and geographic dimension is to identify those actual competitors of the undertakings involved that are capable of constraining their behaviour and of preventing them from behaving independently of an effective competitive pressure. It is from this perspective, that the market definition makes it possible, inter alia, to calculate market shares that would convey meaningful information regarding market power ...

It follows from the above, that the concept of relevant market is different from other concepts of market often used in other contexts. For instance, companies often use the term market to refer to the area where it sells its products or to refer broadly to the industry or sector where it belongs....

The Commission's interpretation of the notion of relevant market is without prejudice to the interpretation which may be given by the Court of Justice or the [General Court] of the European Communities.

DEFINITION OF RELEVANT MARKET

Definition of relevant product and relevant geographic market

The regulations based on Articles [101] and [102] of the Treaty, in particular in section 6 of Form A/B with respect to Regulation 17, as well as in section 6 of Form CO with respect to regulation 4064/89 on the control of concentrations of a Community dimension have laid down the following definitions. Relevant product markets are defined as follows:

"A relevant product market comprises all those products and/or services which are regarded as interchangeable or substitutable by the consumer, by reason of the products' characteristics, their prices and their intended use."

Relevant geographic markets are defined as follows:

"The relevant geographic market comprises the area in which the undertakings concerned are involved in the supply and demand of products or services, in which the conditions of competition are sufficiently homogeneous and which can be distinguished from neighbouring areas because the conditions of competition are appreciably different in those areas".....

Basic principles for market definition

Competitive constraints. Firms are subject to three main sources of competitive constraints: demand substitutability, supply substitutability and potential competition. From an economic point of view, for the definition of the relevant market, demand substitution constitutes the most immediate and effective disciplinary force on the suppliers of a given product, in particular in relation to their pricing decisions. A firm or a group of firms cannot have a significant impact on the prevailing conditions of sale, such as prices, if its customers are in a position to switch easily to available substitute products or to suppliers located elsewhere. Basically, the exercise of market definition consists in identifying the effective alternative sources of supply for the customers of the undertakings involved, both in terms of products/services and geographic location of suppliers.

The competitive constraints arising from supply side substitutability other then those described [below] and from potential competition are in general less immediate and in any case require an analysis of additional factors. As a result such constraints are taken into account at the assessment stage of competition analysis.

Demand substitution. The assessment of demand substitution entails a determination of the range of products which are viewed as substitutes by the consumer. One way of making this determination can be viewed, as a thought experiment, postulating a hypothetical small, non-transitory change in relative prices and evaluating the likely reactions of customers to that increase. The exercise of market definition focuses on prices for operational and practical purposes, and more precisely on demand substitution arising from small, permanent changes in relative prices. This concept can provide clear indications as to the evidence that is relevant to define markets.

Conceptually, this approach implies that starting from the type of products that the undertakings involved sell and the area in which they sell them, additional products and areas will be included into or excluded from the market definition depending on whether competition from these other products and areas affect or restrain sufficiently the pricing of the parties' products in the short term.

The question to be answered is whether the parties' customers would switch to readily available substitutes or to suppliers located elsewhere in response to an hypothetical small (in the range 5%–10%), permanent relative price increase in the products and areas being considered. If substitution would be enough to make the price increase unprofitable because of the resulting loss of sales, additional substitutes and areas are included in the relevant market. This would be done until the set of products and geographic areas is such that small, permanent increases in relative prices would be profitable. . . . .

A practical example of this test can be provided by its application to a merger of, for instance, soft drink bottlers. An issue to examine in such a case would be to decide whether different flavours of soft drinks belong to the same market. In practice, the question to address would be if consumers of flavour A would switch to other flavours when confronted with a permanent price increase of 5% to 10% for flavour A. If a sufficient number of consumers would switch to, say, flavour B, to such an extent that the price increase for flavour A would not be profitable due to the resulting loss of sales, then the market would comprise at least flavours A and B. The process would have to be extended in addition to other available flavours until a set of products is identified for which a price rise would not induce a sufficient substitution in demand.

Generally, and in particular for the analysis of merger cases, the price to take into account will be the prevailing market price. This might not be the case where the prevailing price has been determined in the absence of sufficient competition. In particular for investigation of abuses of dominant positions, the fact that the prevailing price might already have been substantially increased will be taken into account.

Supply substitution. Supply-side substitutability may also be taken into account when defining markets in those situations in which its effects are equivalent to those of demand substitution in terms of effectiveness and immediacy. This requires that suppliers be able to switch production to the relevant products and market them in the short term[4] without incurring significant additional costs or risks in response to small and permanent changes in relative prices. When these conditions are met, the additional production that is put on the market will have a disciplinary effect on the competitive behaviour of the companies involved. Such an impact in terms of effectiveness and immediacy is equivalent to the demand substitution effect.

These situations typically arise when companies market a wide range of qualities or grades of one product; even if for a given final customer or group of consumers, the different qualities are not substitutable, the different qualities will be grouped into one product market provided that most of the suppliers are able to offer and sell the various qualities under the conditions of immediacy and absence of significant increase in costs described above. In such cases, the relevant product market will encompass all products that are substitutable in demand and supply, and the current sales of those products will be summed to calculate the total value or volume of the market. The same reasoning may lead to group different geographic areas.

A practical example of the approach to supply side substitutability when defining product markets is to be found in the case of paper. Paper is usually supplied in a range of different qualities, from standard writing paper to high quality papers to be used for instance to publish art books.

---

4. I.e. the period which does not imply a significant adjustment of existing tangible and intangible assets (see [below]).

From a demand point of view, different qualities of paper cannot be used for a specific use, i.e. an art book or a high quality publication cannot be based on lower quality papers. However, paper plants are prepared to manufacture the different qualities, and production can be adjusted with negligible costs and in a short time frame. In the absence of particular difficulties in distribution, paper manufacturers are able therefore to compete for orders of the various qualities, in particular if orders are passed with a sufficient lead time to allow to modify production plans. Under such circumstances, the Commission would not define a separate market for each quality of paper and respective usage. The various qualities of paper are included in the relevant market, and their sales added up to estimate total market value and volume.

When supply side substitutability would imply the need to adjust significantly existing tangible and intangible assets, additional investments, strategic decisions or time delays, it will not be considered at the stage of market definition. Examples where supply side substitution did not lead the Commission to enlarge the market are offered in the area of consumer products, in particular for branded beverages. Although bottling plants may in principle bottle different beverages, there are costs and lead times involved (in terms of advertising, product testing and distribution) before the products can actually be sold. In these cases, the effects of supply side substitutability and other forms of potential competition would then be examined at a later stage.

Potential competition. The third source of competitive constraint, potential competition, is not taken into account when defining markets, since the conditions under which potential competition will actually represent an effective competitive constraint depend on the analysis of specific factors and circumstances related to the conditions of entry. If required, this analysis is only carried out at a subsequent stage, in general once the position of the companies involved in the relevant market has already been ascertained, and such position is indicative of concerns from a competition point of view.

EVIDENCE RELIED UPON TO DEFINE RELEVANT MARKETS....

Evidence to define markets—Product dimension

An analysis of the product characteristics and its intended use allows the Commission, in a first step, to limit the field of investigation of possible substitutes. However, product characteristics and intended use are insufficient to conclude whether two products are demand substitutes. Functional interchangeability or similarity in characteristics may not provide in themselves sufficient criteria because the responsiveness of customers to relative price changes may be determined by other considerations also. For example, there may be different competitive constraints in the original equipment market for car components and in spare parts, thereby leading to a distinction of two relevant markets. Conversely, differences in product characteristics are not in themselves sufficient to exclude demand substitutability, since this will depend to a large extent on how customers value different characteristics.

The type of evidence the Commission considers relevant to assess whether two products are demand substitutes can be categorised as follows:

Evidence of substitution in the recent past. In certain cases, it is possible to analyse evidence relating to recent past events or shocks in the market that offer actual examples of substitution between two products. When available, this sort of information will normally be fundamental for market definition. If there have been changes in relative prices in the past (all else being equal), the reactions in terms of quantities demanded will be determinant in establishing substitutability. Launches of new products in the past can also offer useful information, when it is possible to precisely analyse which products lost sales to the new product.

There are a number of quantitative tests that have specifically been designed for the purpose of delineating markets. These tests consist of various econometric and statistical approaches: estimates of elasticities and cross-price elasticities for the demand of a product, tests based on similarity of price movements over time, the analysis of causality between price series and similarity of price levels and/or their convergence. The Commission takes into account the available quantitative evidence capable of withstanding rigorous scrutiny for the purposes of establishing patterns of substitution in the past.

Views of customers and competitors. The Commission often contacts the main customers and competitors of the companies involved in its enquiries, to gather their views on the boundaries of the product market as well as most of the factual information it requires to reach a conclusion on the scope of the market. Reasoned answers of customers and competitors as to what would happen if relative prices for the candidate products would increase in the candidate geographic area by a small amount (for instance of 5%–10%) are taken into account when they are sufficiently backed by factual evidence.

Consumer preferences. In cases of consumer goods, it might be difficult for the Commission to gather the direct views of end consumers about substitute products. Marketing studies that companies have commissioned in the past and that are used by companies in their own decision making as to pricing of their products and/or marketing actions may provide useful information for the Commission's delineation of the relevant market. Consumer surveys on usage patterns and attitudes, data from consumer's purchasing patterns, the views expressed by retailers and more generally, market research studies submitted by the parties and their competitors are taken into account to establish whether an economically significant proportion of consumers consider two products as substitutable, taking also into account the importance of brands for the products in question. The methodology followed in consumer surveys carried out ad-hoc by the undertakings involved or their competitors for the purposes of a merger procedure or a procedure under Regulation 17 will usually be scrutinized with utmost care. Unlike pre-existing studies, they have not been prepared in the normal course of business for the adoption of business decisions.

Barriers and costs associated with switching demand to potential substitutes. There are a number of barriers and costs that might prevent the Commission from considering two prima facie demand substitutes as belonging to one single product market. It is not possible to provide an exhaustive list of all the possible barriers to substitution and of switching costs. These barriers or obstacles might have a wide range of origins, and in its decisions, the Commission has been confronted with regulatory barriers or other forms of State intervention, constraints arising in downstream markets, need to incur specific capital investment or loss in current output in order to switch to alternative inputs, the location of customers, specific investment in production process, learning and human capital investment, retooling costs or other investments, uncertainty about quality and reputation of unknown suppliers, and others.

Different categories of customers and price discrimination. The extent of the product market might be narrowed in the presence of distinct groups of customers. A distinct group of customers for the relevant product may constitute a narrower, distinct market when such group could be subject to price discrimination. This will usually be the case when two conditions are met: a) it is possible to identify clearly which group an individual customer belongs to at the moment of selling the relevant products to him, and b) trade among customers or arbitrage by third parties should not be feasible.

Evidence to define markets—Geographic dimension

The type of evidence the Commission considers relevant to reach a conclusion as to the geographic market can be categorised as follows:

Past evidence of diversion of orders to other areas. In certain cases, evidence on changes in prices between different areas and consequent reactions by customers might be available. Generally, the same quantitative tests used for product market definition might as well be used in geographic market definition, bearing in mind that international comparisons of prices might be more complex due to a number of factors such as exchange rate movements, taxation and product differentiation.

Basic demand characteristics. The nature of demand for the relevant product may in itself determine the scope of the geographical market. Factors such as national preferences or preferences for national brands, language, culture and life style, and the need for a local presence have a strong potential to limit the geographic scope of competition.

Views of customers and competitors. Where appropriate, the Commission will contact the main customers and competitors of the parties in its enquiries, to gather their views on the boundaries of the geographic market as well as most of the factual information it requires to reach a conclusion on the scope of the market when they are sufficiently backed by factual evidence.

Current geographic pattern of purchases. An examination of the customers' current geographic pattern of purchases provides useful evidence as to the possible scope of the geographic market. When customers purchase from companies located anywhere in the EU or the EEA on similar terms, or they procure their supplies through effective tendering procedures in which companies from anywhere in the EU or the EEA do submit bids, the geographic market will be usually considered to be Community-wide.

Trade flows/pattern of shipments. When the number of customers is so large that it is not possible to obtain through them a clear picture of geographic purchasing patterns, information on trade flows might be used alternatively, provided that the trade statistics are available with a sufficient degree of detail for the relevant products. Trade flows, and above all, the rational behind trade flows provide useful insights and information for the purpose of establishing the scope of the geographic market but are not in themselves conclusive.

Barriers and switching costs associated to divert orders to companies located in other areas. The absence of transborder purchases or trade flows, for instance, does not necessarily mean that the market is at most national in scope. Still, barriers isolating the national market have to be identified before concluding that the relevant geographic market in such a case is national. Perhaps the clearest obstacle for a customer to divert its orders to other areas is the impact of transport costs and transport restrictions arising from legislation or from the nature of the relevant products. The impact of transport costs will usually limit the scope of the geographic market for bulky, low value products, bearing in mind that a transport disadvantage might also be compensated by a comparative advantage in other costs (labour costs or raw materials). Access to distribution in a given area, regulatory barriers still existing in certain sectors, quotas and custom tariffs might also constitute barriers isolating a geographic area from the competitive pressure of companies located outside that area. Significant switching costs in procuring supplies from companies located in other countries constitute additional sources of such barriers. . . .

CALCULATION OF MARKET SHARES

The definition of the relevant market in both its product and geographic dimensions allows to identify the suppliers and the customers/consumers active on that market. On that basis, a total market size and market shares for each supplier can be calculated on the basis of their sales of the relevant products on the relevant area. In practice, the total market size and market shares are often available from market sources, i.e. companies' estimates, studies commissioned to industry consultants and/or trade associations. When this is not the case, or also when available estimates are not reliable, the Commission will usually ask each supplier in the relevant market to provide its own sales in order to calculate total market size and market shares.

If sales are usually the reference to calculate market shares, there are nevertheless other indications that, depending on the specific products or industry in question, can offer useful information such as, in particular, capacity, the number of players in bidding markets, units of fleet as in aerospace, or the reserves held in the case of sectors such as mining.

As a rule of thumb, both volume sales and value sales provide useful information. In cases of differentiated products, sales in value and their associated market share will usually be considered to better reflect the relative position and strength of each supplier.

ADDITIONAL CONSIDERATIONS

There are certain areas where the application of the principles above has to be undertaken with care. This is the case when considering primary and secondary markets, in particular, when the behaviour of undertakings at a point in time has to be analysed under Article [102]. The method to define markets in these cases is the same, i.e. to assess the responses of customers based on their purchasing decisions to relative price changes, but taking into account as well constraints on substitution imposed by conditions in the connected markets. A narrow definition of market for secondary products, for instance, spare parts, may result when compatibility with the primary product is important. Problems of finding compatible secondary products together with the existence of high prices and a long life time of the primary products may render relative price increases of secondary products profitable. A different market definition may result if significant substitution between secondary products is possible or if the characteristics of the primary products make quick and direct consumer responses to relative price increases of the secondary products feasible.

In certain cases, the existence of chains of substitution might lead to the definition of a relevant market where products or areas at the extreme of the market are not directly substitutable. An example might be provided by the geographic dimension of a product with significant transport costs. In such cases, deliveries from a given plant are limited to a certain area around each plant by the impact of transport costs. In principle, such area could constitute the relevant geographic market. However, if the distribution of plants is such that there are considerable overlaps between the areas around different plants, it is possible that the pricing of those products will be constrained by a chain substitution effect, and lead to define a broader geographic market. The same reasoning may apply if product B is a demand substitute for products A and C. Even if products A and C are not direct demand substitutes they might be found to be in the same relevant product market since their respective pricing might be constrained by substitution to B.

From a practical perspective, the concept of chains of substitution has to be corroborated by actual evidence, for instance related to price interdependence at the extremes of the chains of substitution, in order to lead to an extension of the relevant market in an individual case. Price levels at the extremes of the chains would have to be as well of the same magnitude.

Note and Questions on the Commission Notice

The Notice does not have binding legal force, but presumably indicates the approach the Commission uses defining markets. Although the EU courts are obviously free to refer to these documents, nothing prevents them from relying on distinct tests and principles when they define markets for the purpose of competition law. In its Article 102 case-law, the ECJ continues to refer to other "less quantitative" factors, such as product characteristics, intended use and consumer preference.

1. How would the ECJ judgment in *United Brands* fare under the standards set by the Commission Notice? Would the latter define a separate bananas market:

a. because of the special attraction of bananas to the old, sick, and young?

b. because the ability of other fruit to constrain banana prices is seasonal?

2. Why do merger cases and abuse of dominance cases raise different issues about whether current prices can be used as a baseline?

3. The Commission Notice uses a 5–10% presumptive SSNIP test rather than the 5% test relied upon in the U.S. guidelines. Is this difference significant? What could be its practical implications?

4. Does the Commission Notice differ much from the U.S. guidelines in their willingness to refer to supply substitution when defining markets? In how quick supply substitution has to be before a potentially substituting firm would be deemed in the relevant market?

5. The Commission Notice does not refer to the SSNIP test when it discusses supply substitution. Is this test only relevant when it comes to assessing the presence of demand substitution or is it also relevant in the assessment of supply substitution?

6. Does the European Commission still preserve a role for qualitative factors such as product characteristics, intended use and consumer preference? Should it?

7. In many EU cases, markets are still being defined as "national" rather than EU-wide.

a. Does this reflect the fact that the EU has been focused on trade between Member States as well as rules of competition? Will the growing level of economic integration progressively taking place between EU Member States likely have an impact on the geographic scope of markets?

b. Do you see why different product prices in different nations help demonstrate not only separate geographic markets but also that other products are not reasonable substitutes?

Technical Methods Used in Market Definition

Critical Elasticity of Demand. A popular method of defining markets involves calculating a critical elasticity of demand. This is the highest marketwide elasticity that would make it profitable for a hypothetical monopolist to raise prices by the SSNIP amount of 5–10%, depending on whether U.S. or EU guidelines are used. If this critical elasticity is higher than the actual elasticity of demand for the posited market, then that supports the market definition, for it suggests a monopolist could raise prices by the SSNIP amount over competitive prices. If the critical elasticity is lower than actual elasticity, then that cuts against the market definition.

As with other methods, the difficulties concern the right baselines to use when conducting such an analysis, here most importantly at what price levels to measure the critical and actual elasticities. The typical approach is to go where the data is: using current prices and profit margins as the baseline from which to consider whether a 5–10% price increase would be profitable to a hypothetical monopolist given the sales it would lose. The higher current profit margins are, the smaller the critical elasticity will be because a hypothetical monopolist would lose more profits from any lost sales resulting from a given price increase, making rejection of the posited market definition more likely because it is less likely that the current elasticity would be below that figure.[73]

This approach raises several conceptual issues. The first is that the more a market already reflects an anticompetitive market structure, the higher current prices and profit margins will be, which will both lower the calculated critical elasticity of demand and make it likely that prices have already been raised until demand is elastic. For example, if a monopolist already dominates a market, its profit margins will be high, and it will already be pricing at a monopoly price, which by definition is its profit-maximizing price, thus making any further price increase unprofitable. Literal application of such a method would thus indicate that a monopoly market could never be defined. More generally, high profit margins mean a high Lerner Index and likely market power, which indicates the more narrow market is meaningful, yet under this test high profit margins are used to define the market more broadly and to infer a likely absence of market power.

Both U.S. and EU guidelines indicate that competitive price levels should be used as the baseline instead of prevailing prices if the prevailing prices have already been increased by market power or coordination. But because the very reason to do market definition analysis is to help determine whether market power or coordination seems likely, it seems circular to presume that prevailing prices either do or do not reflect such market power or coordination. What we really want to know as a policy matter is what the profit margin and demand elasticity would be at competitive price levels and whether (given that competitive margin and elasticity) a hypothetical monopolist could profitably impose a 5–10% increase above that competitive level. If so, then there is some functional reason to worry about market power or coordination on that market, otherwise not. But we won't

---

73. To define this mathematically, let m be the current profit margin = (P–MC)/P, which is .5 if prices are twice marginal costs and .75 if prices are 4 times marginal costs. Let t be the SSNIP test percentage used, which is .05 if the test is 5% and .10 if the test is 10%. Then, assuming a linear demand curve and constant marginal costs, it can be shown that a hypothetical monopolist could increase prices by t without losing profits if the current demand elasticity is at least $1/(m + t)$ and that a price increase of t or greater would be profit-maximizing for the hypothetical monopolist if the current demand elasticity is $1/(m + 2t)$ or greater. Thus, if the current profit margin is 50% and the test percentage is 5%, the critical demand elasticity would be $1/.55 = 1.82$ if the question is whether a monopolist could profitably impose a 5% price increase and $1/.6 = 1.67$ if the question is whether a profit-maximizing monopolist would impose a price increase of at least 5%. If instead the current profit margin is 75%, then the critical demand elasticity would be $1/.8 = 1.25$ if the question is whether a 5% increase would be profitable and $1/.85 = 1.18$ if the question is whether a profit-maximizing monopolist would impose at least a 5% increase. Thus, the higher current profit margins, the lower the critical demand elasticity, and the harder it will be to show that current elasticity is low enough to support the market definition under this approach.

have the data on competitive price levels or on what margins or elasticity would be at such levels unless we assume that current prices are competitive, and that assumption assumes away precisely the possibility that is being investigated, which is whether the market is narrow enough that market power or coordination is plausible. Thus critical demand elasticities calculated at current prices will be too low and define markets too narrowly to the extent that markets are not already competitive.

The second issue is that marginal costs are typically unavailable, so that critical demand elasticities are often calculated using *average* profit margins rather than the *marginal* profit margin associated with the final units of output. Average profit margins will reflect the difference between prices and the average variable cost of producing all units, which is the average total cost minus any fixed costs of being in business. But if (as typical) marginal costs increase with increasing output, then marginal costs will likely be higher than average variable costs, meaning that the marginal profit margin will be lower. Using the average profit margin rather than the true marginal profit margin thus likely inflates the profits that a hypothetical monopolist would lose by imposing a 5–10% price increase, and thus makes the critical elasticity of demand lower than it should be. Thus critical demand elasticities calculated using average profit margins will tend to be too low and define markets too narrowly.

The third issue is that critical demand elasticity depends heavily on what assumption one makes about the shape of the demand curve. If one assumes a linear demand curve rather than constant elasticity, then the critical elasticity of demand will be much lower.[74] Indeed, at a profit margin of 50% this seemingly innocuous assumption about the shape of the demand curve can alter the critical elasticity calculated by over 20%.[75] Furthermore, elasticity will sometimes decrease with higher prices because the price increase will drive out marginal customers and leave only customers with very inelastic demand. If so, using the elasticity of demand at current prices will tend to understate the ability of a hypothetical monopolist to profitably impose a 5–10% price increase and thus will tend to make market definition too narrow. Unfortunately, there will often be little

---

74. It might seem that since the slope of a linear demand curve is constant, it must have constant elasticity. But this is not so because the slope (or dQ/dP) measures the the extent to which the *amount* of quantity changes in response to a change in the *amount* of price. Elasticity, in contrast, measures the *percentage* change in quantity over the *percentage* change in price, or $(dQ/Q)/(dP/P)$, which is the same as the slope times P/Q. Thus, a linear demand curve is more elastic as Q is small in relation to P (the lefthand side of a linear demand curve) and less elastic as Q is large in relation to P (the righthand side of a linear demand curve). The intuitive way to see this is that, with a constant slope, a $1 price increase will always produce a constant reduction in the *amount* of Q, and this must produce a higher *percentage* reduction in Q as Q gets smaller and a lower *percentage* increase in P as P gets larger, so that the ratio of those percentages will get larger as Q gets smaller and P larger. A demand curve with constant elasticity would have to be a curve that is steep on the lefthand side (where Q is small in relation to P) and flatter on the righthand side (where Q is large in relation to P).

75. If elasticity is constant, the critical elasticity that would make a price increase of at least t profit-maximizing is $(1 + t)/(m + t)$ whereas it is $1/(m + 2t)$ if demand is linear. Assuming t = .10 and the profit margin is 50%, then the critical elasticity is 1.1/.6 = 1.83 under an assumption of constant elasticity and 1/.7 = 1.43 under an assumption of linear demand. Both results assume constant marginal costs.

information on what the demand curve would look like at prices and output different from the ones that prevailed recently.

Finally, the critical elasticity one calculates turns out to vary depending on whether the question asked is (a) whether a hypothetical monopolist *could* profitably impose a 5–10% price increase, or instead (b) whether a profit-maximizing hypothetical monopolist *would* impose at least a 5–10% price increase. The first asks whether such a price increase would be at least as profitable as the current price. The second asks whether such a price increase would also be more profitable than price increases of less than 5–10%. Since the latter standard is more demanding, it results in a lower critical elasticity and thus leads to more narrow market definitions than the former standard. For example, if the current profit margin is 50%, the latter standard lowers the critical elasticity by 8% under an assumption of linear demand.[76]

The U.S. guidelines adopt the latter standard, asking whether a hypothetical "profit-maximizing" monopolist "likely would impose at least" a SSNIP. In contrast, the EU guidelines seem to embrace the former standard, framing the test as whether "substitution would be enough to make the price increase unprofitable because of the resulting loss of sales." However, the EU guidelines compensate by suggesting that a 10% SSNIP test might be used rather than the 5% SSNIP test presumptively favored by the U.S. guidelines.

Should the standard be whether a hypothetical monopolist could or would impose the relevant price increase? Is there any basis for deciding this issue other than a general policy judgment about how aggressive one wants to make antitrust enforcement? Isn't that the same policy judgment necessary to determine whether to use a 5 or 10% SSNIP test? Is this complicated approach to defining markets, in order to calculate a market share that in turn is used to imperfectly infer market power, really any easier or less problematic than directly estimating market power?

Critical Sales Loss. The critical sales loss is the percentage of sales a hypothetical monopolist would have to lose to make a SSNIP unprofitable. If a court concludes that a 5–10% price increase would cause a higher percentage of sales to switch to other products or areas, then that supports a broader market definition. If a lower percentage would switch, then that supports the more narrow market definition.

This approach raises the four issues noted above for critical elasticities. (1) If prices already reflect market power, then the current price baseline and current profit margin will be inflated. This will misleadingly lower the critical sales loss figure calculated as it inflates profit margins and the predicted percentage of sales that would switch in response to further price increases.[77] (2) Using average rather than marginal profit margins will

---

76.   *See supra* note 73.

77.   Mathematically, it can be shown that the critical sales loss that would prevent a profit-maximizing monopolist from raising prices by at least t equals $t/(m + 2t)$ if demand is linear but is different under different demand assumptions. The critical sales loss that would make a price increase of t actually lose profits equals $t/(m + t)$ for any demand curve. Again, all these results assume constant marginal costs.

likewise likely inflate profit margins and thus misleadingly lower the critical sales loss figure. (3) The critical sales loss calculated can turn on the shape of the demand curve assumed, and in any event conclusions about how many sales will be lost with a given price increase will depend on assumptions about the demand curve. (4) The critical sales loss figure calculated will be higher if the question asked is whether the sales loss would make the entire price increase unprofitable than if the question asked is whether the sales loss would suffice to make a lower price increase more profitable.

In addition to these problems, the use of critical sales loss figures can raise a fifth difficulty because, as the U.S. guidelines note, the "breakeven" approach used by critical loss analysis differs from the profit-maximizing approach used by the hypothetical monopolist test. A 5–10% price increase might produce a critical sales loss figure that is lower than the lost sales that would be produced by such a price increase, yet an even larger price increase (like 25%) might produce a critical sales loss figure that is higher than the lost sales from the larger price increase. That is, a 5–10% price increase might be unprofitable even though a 25% price increase would be. In that case, a hypothetical monopolist would raise prices by 25%, which would justify the more narrow market definition, and yet the critical sales loss figure calculated for a 5–10% price increase would indicate the market definition should be broadened.

Assumptions About Effect of Price Increase on Other Products. The current U.S. guidelines ask whether a hypothetical monopolist would likely impose at least a 5% price increase despite substitution to other products or locations *if* one assumes that "the terms of sale of products outside the candidate market are held constant." But in fact, if a price increase leads buyers to switch to other products or locations, that will likely drive up the price of those substitutes to some extent, which will reduce the amount of substitution. Assuming away this effect on substitute prices thus tends to make market definition broader than it otherwise would be. The assumption that a price increase would not alter substitute prices differs from the EU guidelines, which make no such assumption. This factor, standing alone, would tend to make market definition narrower in the EU. This may be another reason why the EU guidelines use a 5–10% test rather than a 5% test, which cuts in the opposite direction.

Summary. While calculations of critical elasticities and critical sales losses may seem merely technical, in fact the methods for their calculation implicate important underlying issues about antitrust policy. Failure to be attentive to those issues can obscure the policy choices being made or produce misleading results in particular cases.

Market Definition in Other Nations

As in the U.S. and EU, other nations generally define product and geographic markets by applying a SSNIP test, with the price increase thresholds used varying from 5–15%.[78] Many nations expressly take into

---

78. *See, e.g.,* Australia Merger Guidelines §§ 4.19–4.21 (2008) (5% for the foreseeable future); Brazil Horizontal Merger Guidelines ¶ 30 n.7 (2001) (5%, 10%, or 15% depending on

account the "cellophane fallacy", that is whether the current price is already above the competitive level.[79] Like the U.S., Canada excludes supply substitution for purposes of market definition, but calculates market shares by including any production by firms outside the market that would respond to a 5% price increase by switching to the relevant market without incurring significant sunk costs within in year.[80]

4. AFTERMARKETS

Eastman Kodak v. Image Technical Servs.

504 U.S. 451 (1992).

■ JUSTICE BLACKMUN delivered the opinion of the Court....

The principal issue here is whether a defendant's lack of market power in the primary equipment market precludes—as a matter of law—the possibility of market power in derivative aftermarkets.

Petitioner Eastman Kodak Company manufactures and sells photocopiers and micrographic equipment. Kodak also sells service and replacement parts for its equipment. Respondents are 18 independent service organizations (ISO's) that in the early 1980's began servicing Kodak copying and micrographic equipment. Kodak subsequently adopted policies to limit the availability of parts to ISO's and to make it more difficult for ISO's to compete with Kodak in servicing Kodak equipment....

Because this case comes to us on petitioner Kodak's motion for summary judgment, "[t]he evidence of [respondents] is to be believed, and all justifiable inferences are to be drawn in [their] favor." ... Kodak parts are not compatible with other manufacturers' equipment, and vice versa. Kodak equipment, although expensive when new, has little resale value.

Kodak provides service and parts for its machines to its customers. It produces some of the parts itself; the rest are made to order for Kodak by independent original-equipment manufacturers (OEM's). Kodak does not sell a complete system of original equipment, lifetime service, and lifetime parts for a single price. Instead, Kodak provides service after the initial

---

case); Canada Competition Bureau, Enforcement Guidelines on the Abuse of Dominance Provisions § 3.2.1(a) (2001) (5% for one year); Canada Merger Enforcement Guidelines § 3.4 (2004) (same); Chinese State Council Anti-monopoly Committee's Guidelines on Defining Relevant Markets Arts. 10 & 11(5%–10% for one year); Japan Business Combination Guidelines at 12 & n.2 (2010) (5–10% for about a year); New Zealand Mergers and Acquisitions Guidelines § 3.1 (2004) (5–10%); Singapore Guidelines on Market Definition § 2.8 (2007) (10%). *See also* Competition Commission of India, Abuse of Dominance Advocacy Booklet 3 (SSNIP test without specific percentage); South Korea Merger Guidelines VI (2009) (same); Competition Commission v. Patensie Beperk, 37/CR/JUN01, ¶ 47 (South Africa Competition Tribunal) (same).

79. *See* Australia Merger Guidelines § 5.44 n.38 (1999); Brazil CADE Resolution 20, Attachment II, § 2.1 (1999); Canada Abuse of Dominance Guidelines § 3.21(c) (2001); Singapore Guidelines on Market Definition §§ 5.5 and 5.6 (2007); Turkey Guidelines on the Definition of Relevant Market (2008).

80. Canada Merger Enforcement Guidelines §§ 4.1–4.10 (2004).

warranty period either through annual service contracts, which include all necessary parts, or on a per-call basis. It charges, through negotiations and bidding, different prices for equipment, service, and parts for different customers. Kodak provides 80% to 95% of the service for Kodak machines. . . .

In 1985 and 1986, Kodak implemented a policy of selling replacement parts for micrographic and copying machines only to buyers of Kodak equipment who use Kodak service or repair their own machines. . . . Kodak intended, through these policies, to make it more difficult for ISOs to sell service for Kodak machines. It succeeded. ISOs were unable to obtain parts from reliable sources, and many were forced out of business, while others lost substantial revenue. Customers were forced to switch to Kodak service even though they preferred ISO service. . . . [The Court concluded this constituted a tying agreement].

Having found sufficient evidence of a tying arrangement, we consider the other necessary feature of an illegal tying arrangement: appreciable economic power in the tying market. Market power is the power "to force a purchaser to do something that he would not do in a competitive market." *Jefferson Parish*. It has been defined as "the ability of a single seller to raise price and restrict output." *Fortner I*. The existence of such power ordinarily is inferred from the seller's possession of a predominant share of the market. *Jefferson Parish; Grinnell; Times–Picayune*.

Respondents contend that Kodak has more than sufficient power in the parts market to force unwanted purchases of the tied market, service. Respondents provide evidence that certain parts are available exclusively through Kodak. Respondents also assert that Kodak has control over the availability of parts it does not manufacture. According to respondents' evidence, Kodak has prohibited independent manufacturers from selling Kodak parts to ISOs, pressured Kodak equipment owners and independent parts distributors to deny ISOs the purchase of Kodak parts, and taken steps to restrict the availability of used machines.

Respondents also allege that Kodak's control over the parts market has excluded service competition, boosted service prices, and forced unwilling consumption of Kodak service. Respondents offer evidence that consumers have switched to Kodak service even though they preferred ISO service, that Kodak service was of higher price and lower quality than the preferred ISO service, and that ISOs were driven out of business by Kodak's policies. Under our prior precedents, this evidence would be sufficient to entitle respondents to a trial on their claim of market power.

Kodak counters that even if it concedes monopoly *share* of the relevant parts market, it cannot actually exercise the necessary market *power* for a Sherman Act violation. This is so, according to Kodak, because competition exists in the equipment market. Kodak argues that it could not have the ability to raise prices of service and parts above the level that would be charged in a competitive market because any increase in profits from a higher price in the aftermarkets at least would be offset by a corresponding loss in profits from lower equipment sales as consumers began purchasing equipment with more attractive service costs.

Kodak does not present any actual data on the equipment, service, or parts markets. Instead, it urges the adoption of a substantive legal rule that "equipment competition precludes any finding of monopoly power in derivative aftermarkets." . . . .

Legal presumptions that rest on formalistic distinctions rather than actual market realities are generally disfavored in antitrust law. This Court has preferred to resolve antitrust claims on a case-by-case basis, focusing on the "particular facts disclosed by the record." *Maple Flooring*. In determining the existence of market power, and specifically the "responsiveness of the sales of one product to price changes of the other," *du Pont*, this Court has examined closely the economic reality of the market at issue.

Kodak contends that there is no need to examine the facts when the issue is market power in the aftermarkets. A legal presumption against a finding of market power is warranted in this situation, according to Kodak, because the existence of market power in the service and parts markets absent power in the equipment market "simply makes no economic sense," and the absence of a legal presumption would deter procompetitive behavior . . . .

The extent to which one market prevents exploitation of another market depends on the extent to which consumers will change their consumption of one product in response to a price change in another, i.e., the "cross-elasticity of demand." Kodak's proposed rule rests on a factual assumption about the cross-elasticity of demand in the equipment and aftermarkets: "If Kodak raised its parts or service prices above competitive levels, potential customers would simply stop buying Kodak equipment. Perhaps Kodak would be able to increase short term profits through such a strategy, but at a devastating cost to its long term interests." Kodak argues that the Court should accept, as a matter of law, this "basic economic reality," that competition in the equipment market necessarily prevents market power in the aftermarkets.[17]

Even if Kodak could not raise the price of service and parts one cent without losing equipment sales, that fact would not disprove market power in the aftermarkets. The sales of even a monopolist are reduced when it sells goods at a monopoly price, but the higher price more than compensates for the loss in sales. Kodak's claim that charging more for service and parts would be a "short-run game," is based on the false dichotomy that there are only two prices that can be charged—a competitive price or a ruinous one. But there could easily be a middle, optimum price at which the increased revenues from the higher-priced sales of service and parts would more than compensate for the lower revenues from lost equipment sales. The fact that the equipment market imposes a restraint on prices in the aftermarkets by no means disproves the existence of power in those markets. See Areeda & Kaplow, at ¶ 340(b) ("The existence of significant substitution in the event of *further* price increases or even at the *current* price does not tell us whether the defendant *already* exercises significant

---

17. It is clearly true . . . that Kodak "cannot set service or parts prices without regard to the impact on the market for equipment." The fact that the cross-elasticity of demand is not zero proves nothing; the disputed issue is how much of an impact an increase in parts and service prices has on equipment sales and on Kodak's profits.

market power") (emphasis in original). Thus, contrary to Kodak's assertion, there is no immutable physical law—no "basic economic reality"—insisting that competition in the equipment market cannot coexist with market power in the aftermarkets.

We next consider the more narrowly drawn question: Does Kodak's theory describe actual market behavior so accurately that respondents' assertion of Kodak market power in the aftermarkets, if not impossible, is at least unreasonable?

To review Kodak's theory, it contends that higher service prices will lead to a disastrous drop in equipment sales. Presumably, the theory's corollary is to the effect that low service prices lead to a dramatic increase in equipment sales. According to the theory, one would have expected Kodak to take advantage of lower-priced ISO service as an opportunity to expand equipment sales. Instead, Kodak adopted a restrictive sales policy consciously designed to eliminate the lower-priced ISO service, an act that would be expected to devastate either Kodak's equipment sales or Kodak's faith in its theory. Yet, according to the record, it has done neither. Service prices have risen for Kodak customers, but there is no evidence or assertion that Kodak equipment sales have dropped.

Kodak and the United States attempt to reconcile Kodak's theory with the contrary actual results by describing a "marketing strategy of spreading over time the total cost to the buyer of Kodak equipment." In other words, Kodak could charge subcompetitive prices for equipment and make up the difference with supracompetitive prices for service, resulting in an overall competitive price. This pricing strategy would provide an explanation for the theory's descriptive failings—if Kodak in fact had adopted it. But Kodak never has asserted that it prices its equipment or parts subcompetitively and recoups its profits through service. Instead, it claims that it prices its equipment comparably to its competitors, and intends that both its equipment sales and service divisions be profitable. Moreover, this hypothetical pricing strategy is inconsistent with Kodak's policy toward its self-service customers. If Kodak were underpricing its equipment, hoping to lock in customers and recover its losses in the service market, it could not afford to sell customers parts without service. In sum, Kodak's theory does not explain the actual market behavior revealed in the record.

Respondents offer a forceful reason why Kodak's theory, although perhaps intuitively appealing, may not accurately explain the behavior of the primary and derivative markets for complex durable goods: the existence of significant information and switching costs. These costs could create a less responsive connection between service and parts prices and equipment sales.

For the service-market price to affect equipment demand, consumers must inform themselves of the total cost of the "package"—equipment, service and parts—at the time of purchase; that is, consumers must engage in accurate lifecycle pricing. Lifecycle pricing of complex, durable equipment is difficult and costly. In order to arrive at an accurate price, a consumer must acquire a substantial amount of raw data and undertake sophisticated analysis. The necessary information would include data on price, quality, and availability of products needed to operate, upgrade, or enhance the initial equipment, as well as service and repair costs, including estimates of breakdown frequency, nature of repairs, price of service and parts, length of "down-time" and losses incurred from down-time.

Much of this information is difficult—some of it impossible—to acquire at the time of purchase. During the life of a product, companies may change the service and parts prices, and develop products with more advanced features, a decreased need for repair, or new warranties. In addition, the information is likely to be customer-specific; lifecycle costs will vary from customer to customer with the type of equipment, degrees of equipment use, and costs of downtime.

Kodak acknowledges the cost of information, but suggests, again without evidentiary support, that customer information needs will be satisfied by competitors in the equipment markets. It is a question of fact, however, whether competitors would provide the necessary information. A competitor in the equipment market may not have reliable information about the lifecycle costs of complex equipment it does not service or the needs of customers it does not serve. Even if competitors had the relevant information, it is not clear that their interests would be advanced by providing such information to consumers.[21]

Moreover, even if consumers were capable of acquiring and processing the complex body of information, they may choose not to do so. Acquiring the information is expensive. If the costs of service are small relative to the equipment price, or if consumers are more concerned about equipment capabilities than service costs, they may not find it cost-efficient to compile the information. Similarly, some consumers, such as the Federal Government, have purchasing systems that make it difficult to consider the complete cost of the "package" at the time of purchase. State and local governments often treat service as an operating expense and equipment as a capital expense, delegating each to a different department. These governmental entities do not lifecycle price, but rather choose the lowest price in each market.

As Kodak notes, there likely will be some large-volume, sophisticated purchasers who will undertake the comparative studies and insist, in return for their patronage, that Kodak charge them competitive lifecycle prices. Kodak contends that these knowledgeable customers will hold down the package price for all other customers. There are reasons, however, to doubt that sophisticated purchasers will ensure that competitive prices are charged to unsophisticated purchasers, too. As an initial matter, if the

---

21. To inform consumers about Kodak, the competitor must be willing to forgo the opportunity to reap supracompetitive prices in its own service and parts markets. The competitor may anticipate that charging lower service and parts prices and informing consumers about Kodak in the hopes of gaining future equipment sales will cause Kodak to lower the price on its service and parts, cancelling any gains in equipment sales to the competitor and leaving both worse off. Thus, in an equipment market with relatively few sellers, competitors may find it more profitable to adopt Kodak's service and parts policy than to inform the consumers. See 2 P. Areeda & D. Turner, Antitrust Law ¶ 404b1 (1978); App. 177 (Kodak, Xerox, and IBM together have nearly 100% of relevant market). Even in a market with many sellers, any one competitor may not have sufficient incentive to inform consumers because the increased patronage attributable to the corrected consumer beliefs will be shared among other competitors.

number of sophisticated customers is relatively small, the amount of profits to be gained by supracompetitive pricing in the service market could make it profitable to let the knowledgeable consumers take their business elsewhere. More importantly, if a company is able to price-discriminate between sophisticated and unsophisticated consumers, the sophisticated will be unable to prevent the exploitation of the uninformed. A seller could easily price-discriminate by varying the equipment/parts/service package, developing different warranties, or offering price discounts on different components.

Given the potentially high cost of information and the possibility a seller may be able to price-discriminate between knowledgeable and unsophisticated consumers, it makes little sense to assume, in the absence of any evidentiary support, that equipment-purchasing decisions are based on an accurate assessment of the total cost of equipment, service, and parts over the lifetime of the machine.

Indeed, respondents have presented evidence that Kodak practices price-discrimination by selling parts to customers who service their own equipment, but refusing to sell parts to customers who hire third-party service companies. Companies that have their own service staff are likely to be high-volume users, the same companies for whom it is most likely to be economically worthwhile to acquire the complex information needed for comparative lifecycle pricing.

A second factor undermining Kodak's claim that supracompetitive prices in the service market lead to ruinous losses in equipment sales is the cost to current owners of switching to a different product. If the cost of switching is high, consumers who already have purchased the equipment, and are thus "locked-in," will tolerate some level of service-price increases before changing equipment brands. Under this scenario, a seller profitably could maintain supracompetitive prices in the aftermarket if the switching costs were high relative to the increase in service prices, and the number of locked-in customers were high relative to the number of new purchasers.

Moreover, if the seller can price-discriminate between its locked-in customers and potential new customers, this strategy is even more likely to prove profitable. The seller could simply charge new customers below-marginal cost on the equipment and recoup the charges in service, or offer packages with life-time warranties or long-term service agreements that are not available to locked-in customers.

Respondents have offered evidence that the heavy initial outlay for Kodak equipment, combined with the required support material that works only with Kodak equipment, makes switching costs very high for existing Kodak customers. And Kodak's own evidence confirms that it varies the package price of equipment/parts/service for different customers.

In sum, there is a question of fact whether information costs and switching costs foil the simple assumption that the equipment and service markets act as pure complements to one another.[24]

---

24. The dissent disagrees based on its hypothetical case of a tie between equipment and service. "The only thing lacking" to bring this case within the hypothetical case, states the dissent, "is concrete evidence that the restrictive parts policy was ... generally known." But

We conclude, then, that Kodak has failed to demonstrate that respondents' inference of market power in the service and parts markets is unreasonable, and that, consequently, Kodak is entitled to summary judgment. It is clearly reasonable to infer that Kodak has market power to raise prices and drive out competition in the aftermarkets, since respondents offer direct evidence that Kodak did so. It is also plausible, as discussed above, to infer that Kodak chose to gain immediate profits by exerting that market power where locked-in customers, high information costs, and discriminatory pricing limited and perhaps eliminated any long-term loss. Viewing the evidence in the light most favorable to respondents, their allegations of market power "make . . . economic sense." . . . .

Respondents also claim that they have presented genuine issues for trial as to whether Kodak has monopolized or attempted to monopolize the service and parts markets in violation of § 2 of the Sherman Act. . . . The existence of the first element, possession of monopoly power, is easily resolved. As has been noted, respondents have presented a triable claim that service and parts are separate markets, and that Kodak has the "power to control prices or exclude competition" in service and parts. *du Pont*. Monopoly power under § 2 requires, of course, something greater than market power under § 1. *See Fortner I*. Respondents' evidence that Kodak controls nearly 100% of the parts market and 80% to 95% of the service market, with no readily available substitutes, is, however, sufficient to survive summary judgment under the more stringent monopoly standard of § 2. *See NCAA. Cf. Grinnell* (87% of the market is a monopoly); *American Tobacco* (over 2/3 of the market is a monopoly).

Kodak also contends that, as a matter of law, a single brand of a product or service can never be a relevant market under the Sherman Act. We disagree. The relevant market for antitrust purposes is determined by the choices available to Kodak equipment owners. *See Jefferson Parish*. Because service and parts for Kodak equipment are not interchangeable with other manufacturers' service and parts, the relevant market from the Kodak-equipment owner's perspective is composed of only those companies that service Kodak machines. *See du Pont* (the "market is composed of products that have reasonable interchangeability").[30] . . .

■ JUSTICE SCALIA, with whom JUSTICES O'CONNOR and THOMAS join, dissenting. . . . In the absence of interbrand power, a seller's predominant or monopoly share of its single-brand derivative markets does not connote the power to raise derivative market prices *generally* by reducing quantity. . . . [A] rational consumer considering the purchase of Kodak equipment will inevitably factor into his purchasing decision the expected cost of aftermar-

---

the dissent's "only thing lacking" is the crucial thing lacking—evidence. Whether a tie between parts and service should be treated identically to a tie between equipment and service, as the dissent and Kodak argue, depends on whether the equipment market prevents the exertion of market power in the parts market. Far from being "anomalous," requiring Kodak to provide evidence on this factual question is completely consistent with our prior precedent.

30. Kodak erroneously contends that this Court in *du Pont* rejected the notion that a relevant market could be limited to one brand. The Court simply held in *du Pont* that one brand does not *necessarily* constitute a relevant market if substitutes are available. Here respondents contend there are no substitutes.

ket support. ... If Kodak set generally supracompetitive prices for either spare parts or repair services without making an offsetting reduction in the price of its machines, rational consumers would simply turn to Kodak's competitors for photocopying and micrographic systems. True, there are— as the Court notes—the occasional irrational consumers that consider only the hardware cost at the time of purchase (a category that regrettably includes the Federal Government, whose "purchasing system," we are told, assigns foremarket purchases and aftermarket purchases to different entities). But we have never before premised the application of antitrust doctrine on the lowest common denominator of consumer.

The Court attempts to counter this theoretical point with theory of its own. It says that there are "information costs"—the costs and inconvenience to the consumer of acquiring and processing life-cycle pricing data for Kodak machines—that "could create a less responsive connection between service and parts prices and equipment sales." But this truism about the functioning of markets for sophisticated equipment cannot create "market power" of concern to the antitrust laws where otherwise there is none. "Information costs," or, more accurately, gaps in the availability and quality of consumer information, pervade real-world markets; and because consumers generally make do with "rough cut" judgments about price in such circumstances, in virtually any market there are zones within which otherwise competitive suppliers may overprice their products without losing appreciable market share. We have never suggested that the principal players in a market with such commonplace informational deficiencies (and, thus, bands of apparent consumer pricing indifference) exercise market power in any sense relevant to the antitrust laws. ...

Respondents suggest that, even if the existence of interbrand competition prevents Kodak from raising prices *generally* in its single-brand aftermarkets, there remain certain consumers who are necessarily subject to abusive Kodak pricing behavior by reason of their being "locked in" to their investments in Kodak machines. ... But this "circumstantial" leverage created by consumer investment regularly crops up in smoothly functioning, even perfectly competitive, markets, and in most—if not all—of its manifestations, it is of no concern to the antitrust laws. The leverage held by the manufacturer of a malfunctioning refrigerator (which is measured by the consumer's reluctance to walk away from his initial investment in that device) is no different in kind or degree from the leverage held by the swimming pool contractor when he discovers a 5–ton boulder in his customer's backyard and demands an additional sum of money to remove it; or the leverage held by an airplane manufacturer over an airline that has "standardized" its fleet around the manufacturer's models; or the leverage held by a drill press manufacturer whose customers have built their production lines around the manufacturer's particular style of drill press; the leverage held by an insurance company over its independent sales force that has invested in company-specific paraphernalia; or the leverage held by a mobile home park owner over his tenants, who are unable to transfer their homes to a different park except at great expense. Leverage, in the form of *circumstantial* power, plays a role in each of these relationships; but in none of them is the leverage attributable to the dominant party's *market* power in any relevant sense. Though that power can plainly work to the injury of certain consumers, it produces only "a brief perturbation in competitive conditions—not the sort of thing the antitrust laws do or should worry about."

Questions on *Kodak*

1. Does *Kodak* overrule the *Cellophane* holding that a high cross-elasticity of demand at current prices negates a narrow market definition, when those current prices are alleged to be monopoly prices?

2. Did (and does) Kodak have any market power in parts at the time of equipment sales? Should that be the time for measuring market power rather than after the equipment is bought?

3. Would Kodak have been deemed to have relevant market power if it had: (1) sold Kodak equipment at a price that included lifetime parts & service, (2) required all purchasers of Kodak equipment to purchase Kodak parts & service, or (3) notified all new purchasers of Kodak equipment that they could not get Kodak parts without Kodak service? Does either (1) or (2) or (3) differ from the case at hand in an economically meaningful way? If so, how?

4. The Court held only that the plaintiff's case survived summary judgment. Are there evidentiary findings the trial court could still make on remand under which the defendant would prevail?

5. Suppose there are three mines in the world that can produce widgetium, a heavy raw ingredient that, given high transportation costs, must be transported to a local plant to transform into widgets. Each mine is owned by a different firm. Before a widget producer moves close to a particular mine, none of the firms that make widgetium have any market power over it. But once a widget producer moves close to a particular mine, then it cannot turn to any other mine for widgetium.

a. Would Justice Scalia conclude that no market power in a local widgetium market can exist because mining firms lack any market power on the worldwide market before producers enter a local market?

b. Does the fact that a widget producer decides to move into a particular local market mean that it has implicitly agreed to any subsequent anticompetitive conduct that the local mine might engage in? Or is it more reasonable to think each entrant entered the local market assuming that antitrust law would prevent any subsequent anticompetitive conduct?

c. What if all the widget producers in a particular local market knew when they entered that the local mine engaged in a practice X? Would the local mine have had any incentives to adopt practice X if it were truly anticompetitive? Should market power in this case thus be assessed pre-entry rather than post-entry? Should there be a coming to the nuisance rule that precludes suits by firms who enter into markets where anticompetitive practices are known to be used?

6. Consider the following argument. Purchasers of Kodak equipment could have asked for contractual terms protecting them against these post-purchase practices if they wanted such protection. Likewise, Kodak could have used contractual terms that explicitly authorized such post-purchase practices if it really wanted to engage in such practices. If the contract has not specified a result either way, then all we have is a midstream contract problem that should be resolved by whatever default rules might be provided by contract law or perhaps laws against consumer deception, rather than be resolved through antitrust actions. Is this persuasive? What about the contrary argument that everyone contracted under the default rule assumption that antitrust law would govern?

C.   SECOND ELEMENT: ANTICOMPETITIVE CONDUCT

The U.S. and EU approaches to monopolization/abuse of dominance share an important similarity in that both regimes require some form of anticompetitive conduct in addition to the requisite level of market power. Another similarity is that neither regime provides a definitive list of what conduct is deemed anticompetitive.

Both U.S. monopolization doctrine and EU abuse of a dominant position law cover various forms of agreements, like exclusionary vertical agreements or conditioned sale agreements whose terms or conditions may foreclose rivals in ways that enhance monopoly or dominant market power, such as exclusive dealing/single branding, tying, loyalty discounts, and bundled loyalty discounts. Those sorts of conditioned agreements are considered separately in Chapter 4, which also considers other bodies of law that bear on such agreements since they implicate a common body of economic analysis. This Chapter considers only unilateral conduct that does not require the agreement or compliance of others with any terms or conditions about how they will interact with other market actors.

1.   GENERAL STANDARDS

a.   THE CONDUCT ELEMENT FOR PROVING MONOPOLIZATION UNDER U.S. ANTITRUST LAW

We have seen above that the U.S. Supreme Court has held monopolization has two components: (1) the possession of monopoly power in the relevant market, and (2) "the willful acquisition or maintenance of that power as distinguished from growth or development as a consequence of a superior product, business acumen, or historic accident."[81] It is to this second element that we turn in this section.

The problem is that firms often willfully acquire or maintain monopoly power precisely through business acumen or developing a superior product. The two are not at all mutually exclusive concepts. And while cases of historic accident can be distinguished because they are not willful, it is hard to think of cases where a firm really has a monopoly thrust upon it

---

81. *Grinnell*, 384 U.S. at 570–571. This test has continued to be used in more recent Supreme Court cases. See *Trinko*, 540 U.S. at 407; *Kodak*, 504 U.S. at 481; *Aspen*, 472 U.S. at 596 n.19.

without the aid of any willful conduct. Further, this test never defines what it means by "business acumen." One would think such acumen might well include any business strategy that reaps supracompetitive profits that isn't prohibited by antitrust law. If so, then the term ultimately turns on the unarticulated criterion for prohibition. The definition of a "superior product" seems more inherently meaningful. But this test does not tell us what to do when the product is sold on terms that tend to exclude rivals—should those terms be deemed anticompetitive or to indicate superior product terms? Further, the Supreme Court has held on multiple occasions that sometimes a firm cannot deny its superior product to its rivals, meaning that there are some occasions where it is illegal to acquire or maintain a monopoly as a consequence of a superior product.[82]

Notwithstanding the use of the word "willful," it is clear that this second element does not require any proof about the subjective intent of the defendant. To the contrary, the Court has repeatedly stressed that "no monopolist monopolizes unconscious of what he is doing."[83] In other words, its references to intent do not refer to subjective intent but rather the *objective* intent that can be inferred from the firm's conduct. Courts do often examine proof of subjective intent in monopolization cases, but not because it is dispositive in its own right—rather they do so because evidence of a subjective intent can help the court to *interpret* otherwise ambiguous conduct and effects. But the ultimate question is an assessment of the conduct and its effects.

Inquiries into intent in any event cannot be divorced from assessments of conduct because an improper intent cannot simply be an intent to eliminate competition, which can underlie desirable acts like innovating to make a superior product that will drive one's rivals out of the market. Rather, an improper intent would be an intent to eliminate competition *improperly,* which again requires some normative assessment of conduct in question.

So what type of conduct is deemed improper? Much of the U.S. caselaw focuses on whether the conduct excludes rivals from the market.[84] The problem is that some conduct that tends to exclude rivals and eliminate competition, such as achieving greater efficiency, is highly desirable. Thus, we need some test to sort out which exclusionary conduct should be legal and which illegal.

One set of formulations stresses that conduct that excludes rivals does not constitute monopolization if the monopolist is motivated by "valid

---

82. *See Kodak,* 504 U.S. at 483 & n.32; *Aspen,* 472 U.S. at 600–11; Otter Tail Power Co. v. United States, 410 U.S. 366 (1973).

83. *See Aspen,* 472 U.S. at 602; United States v. Griffith, 334 U.S. 100, 105 (1948); *Am. Tobacco* 328 U.S. at 814; Times–Picayune Publishing Co. v. United States, 345 U.S. 594, 626 (1953).

84. *Kodak,* 504 U.S. at 482–83 (monopoly power used to "to foreclose competition, to gain a competitive advantage, or to destroy a competitor."); *Otter Tail,* 410 U.S. at 377 (same); *Griffith,* 334 U.S. at 107 (same); *Standard Oil,* 221 U.S. at 75 ("excluding others from the trade"); United States v. American Tobacco, 221 U.S. 106, 181 (1911) ("driving competitors out of business"); United States v. United Shoe Mach. Corp., 110 F.Supp. 295, 342 (D. Mass. 1953), aff'd per curiam, 347 U.S. 521 (1954) ("to exclude competition").

business reasons," a "normal business purpose," or "legitimate competitive reasons."[85] Again, the Court means not subjective intent but the objective purposes one can infer from the nature of the challenged conduct. But the problem is that these tests do not specify the criteria used to distinguish the invalid, abnormal, or illegitimate, so that each of these formulations turns on what content one gives to the key placeholder term—"valid," "normal," or "legitimate." The same is true for other formulations that try to distinguish between "improper conduct" and "honestly industrial" conduct,[86] and for attempted monopolization cases, which have defined the prohibited conduct as "conduct which *unfairly* tends to destroy competition" but neglected to define just what fairness means.[87]

Other U.S. caselaw more helpfully adds the word "anticompetitive" to the description of the illicit exclusionary conduct. *Aspen Skiing* described it as "the willful acquisition or maintenance of [monopoly] power by anticompetitive or exclusionary means," which the Court indicated was "conduct that '(1) tends to impair the opportunities of rivals, but also (2) either does not further competition on the merits or does so in an unnecessarily restrictive way.' "[88] And *Trinko* stated "the possession of monopoly power will not be found unlawful unless it is accompanied by an element of anticompetitive *conduct*."[89]

In short, under U.S. law, a monopolist's unilateral conduct is governed by the same rule of reason to judge whether it is anticompetitive as is concerted action by firms that lack monopoly power or any reasonable probability of acquiring it.[90] But as with concerted action, the term "anticompetitive" is not self-defining. Indeed, here the problem is somewhat worse because the doctrine by definition includes unilateral conduct, and thus cannot equate being anticompetitive with using means that reduce market rivalry by increasing coordination with rivals. Further, the Court has held that sometimes a monopolist is affirmatively obliged to diminish market rivalry through cooperation with rivals by giving them access to its product, thus indicating that at least sometimes vigorously competing with rivals by refusing to share its product can be characterized as "anticompetitive or exclusionary." Nor can "anticompetitive" conduct mean whatever conduct results in an outcome that diminishes market rivalry, for that would preclude the very possibility the Court is trying to distinguish—the possibility that desirable conduct can achieve or maintain a monopoly that extinguishes competition. Moreover, all we shall see, sometimes the very same conduct considered to be "competition on the merits" in the United States is not considered "normal competition" in Europe.

---

85. *Kodak*, 504 U.S. at 483 & n.32; *Aspen*, 472 U.S. at 605, 608.

86. *Aspen*, 472 U.S. at 596 (quoting jury instructions).

87. *Spectrum Sports*, 506 U.S. at 458 (emphasis added); *see also id.* at 459 (defining prohibited conduct as " 'unfair' or 'predatory' tactics").

88. *Aspen*, 472 U.S. at 595–96, 605 n.32.

89. *Trinko*, 540 U.S. at 407 (emphasis in original).

90. *Standard Oil*, 221 U.S. at 61–62.

b.   THE CONDUCT ELEMENT FOR PROVING ABUSE OF
DOMINANCE UNDER EU COMPETITION LAW

Guidance on the Commission's Enforcement Priorities in Applying Article 82 EC Treaty [now 102 TFEU] to Abusive Exclusionary Conduct by Dominant Undertakings

(Dec. 2008).

III. GENERAL APPROACH TO EXCLUSIONARY CONDUCT ...

B.   Foreclosure leading to consumer harm ("anticompetitive fore-closure")

19.   The aim of the Commission's enforcement activity in relation to exclusionary conduct is to ensure that dominant undertakings do not impair effective competition by foreclosing their rivals in an anticompetitive way and thus having an adverse impact on consumer welfare, whether in the form of higher price levels than would have otherwise prevailed or in some other form such as limiting quality or reducing consumer choice. In this document the term "anticompetitive foreclosure" is used to describe a situation where effective access of actual or potential competitors to supplies or markets is hampered or eliminated as a result of the conduct of the dominant undertaking whereby the dominant undertaking is likely to be in a position to profitably increase prices to the detriment of consumers. The identification of likely consumer harm can rely on qualitative and, where possible and appropriate, quantitative evidence. The Commission will moreover address such anticompetitive foreclosure both at the intermediate level and/or at the level of final consumers.

20.   The Commission will normally intervene under Article [102] where, on the basis of cogent and convincing evidence, the allegedly abusive conduct is likely to lead to anticompetitive foreclosure. The Commission considers the following factors to be generally relevant to such an assessment:

- the position of the dominant undertaking. In general, the stronger the dominant position, the higher the likelihood that conduct protecting that position leads to anticompetitive foreclosure;

- the conditions on the relevant market. This includes the conditions of entry and expansion, such as the existence of economies of scale and/or scope and network effects. Scale economies mean that competitors are less likely to enter or stay in the market if the dominant undertaking forecloses a significant part of the relevant market. Similarly, the conduct may allow the dominant undertaking to "tip" a market characterised by network effects in its favour or to further entrench its position on such a market. Likewise, if entry barriers in the upstream and/or downstream market are significant, this means that it may be costly for rivals to overcome possible foreclosure through vertical integration;

- the position of the dominant undertaking's competitors. This includes the importance of competitors for the maintenance of effective competition. A specific rival may play a significant competitive role even with only a small market share compared to other competitors: it may, for example be the closest competitor to the dominant firm, be a particularly innovative competitor, or have the reputation of systematically cutting prices. In its assessment, the Commission may also consider in appropriate cases, on the basis of information available, whether there are realistic, effective and timely counterstrategies that competitors would be likely to deploy;

- the position of the customers or input suppliers. This may include consideration of the possible selectivity of the conduct in question. The dominant undertaking may apply the practice only to selected customers or input suppliers who may be of particular importance for the entry or expansion of competitors, thereby enhancing the likelihood of anticompetitive foreclosure. They may, for example, be the ones most likely to respond to offers from alternative suppliers, they may represent a particular means of distributing the product that would be suitable for a new entrant, they may be situated in a geographic area well suited to new entry or they may be likely to influence the behaviour of other customers. In the case of input suppliers, those with whom the dominant firm has concluded exclusive supply arrangements may be the ones most likely to respond to requests by customers who are competitors of the dominant firm in a downstream market, or may produce a grade of the product—or produce at a location—particularly suitable for a new entrant. Any strategies at the disposal of the customers or input suppliers which could help to counter the conduct of the dominant undertaking will also be considered;

- the extent of the allegedly abusive conduct. In general, the higher the percentage of total sales in the relevant market affected by the conduct, the longer its duration, and the more regularly it has been applied, the greater is the likely foreclosure effect;

- possible evidence of actual foreclosure. If the conduct has been in place for a sufficient period of time, the market performance of the dominant firm and its competitors may provide direct evidence about anticompetitive foreclosure; for reasons attributable to the allegedly abusive conduct, the market share of the dominant firm may have risen or a decline in market share may have been slowed; for similar reasons, actual competitors may have been marginalised or may have exited, or potential competitors may have tried to enter and failed;

- direct evidence of any exclusionary strategy. This includes internal documents which contain direct evidence of a strategy to exclude competitors, such as a detailed plan to engage in certain conduct in order to exclude a rival, to prevent entry or to pre-empt the emergence of a market, or evidence of concrete threats of exclusionary action. Such direct evidence may be helpful to interpret the dominant undertaking's conduct.

21. When pursuing a case the Commission will develop the analysis of the above general factors, together with the more specific factors described below in the sections dealing with certain types of exclusionary conduct, and any other factors which it may consider to be appropriate. This

assessment will usually be made by comparing the actual or likely future situation in the relevant market (with the dominant undertaking's conduct in place) with an appropriate counterfactual, such as the simple absence of the conduct in question or with another realistic alternative scenario, having regard to established business practices.

22.   There may be circumstances where it may not be necessary for the Commission to carry out a detailed assessment before concluding that the conduct in question is likely to result in consumer harm. If it appears that the conduct can only raise obstacles to competition and that it creates no efficiencies, its anti-competitive effect may be inferred. This could be the case, for instance, if the dominant undertaking prevents its customers from testing the products of competitors or provides financial incentives to its customers on condition that they do not test such products, or pays a distributor or a customer to delay the introduction of a rival's product.

C.   Price-based exclusionary conduct

23.   The following considerations apply to price-based exclusionary conduct. Vigorous price competition is generally beneficial to consumers. With a view to preventing anticompetitive foreclosure, the Commission will normally only intervene where the conduct concerned has already been or is capable of hampering competition from competitors which are considered to be as efficient as the dominant undertaking.

24.   However, the Commission recognises that in certain circumstances a less efficient competitor may also exert a constraint which should be taken into account when considering whether a particular price-based conduct leads to anticompetitive foreclosure. The Commission will take a dynamic view of this constraint, given that in the absence of an abusive practice such a competitor may benefit from demand-related advantages, such as network and learning effects, which will tend to enhance its efficiency.

25.   In order to determine whether even a hypothetical competitor as efficient as the dominant undertaking would likely be foreclosed by the conduct in question, the Commission will examine economic data relating to cost and sales prices, and in particular whether the dominant undertaking is engaging in below-cost pricing. This will require that sufficiently reliable data are available. Where available, the Commission will use information on the costs of the dominant undertaking itself. If reliable information on those costs is not available, the Commission may decide to use the cost data of competitors or other comparable reliable data.

26.   The cost benchmarks that the Commission is likely to use are average avoidable cost (AAC) and long-run average incremental cost (LRAIC). Failure to cover AAC indicates that the dominant undertaking is sacrificing profits in the short term and that an as efficient competitor cannot serve the targeted customers without incurring a loss. LRAIC is usually above AAC because contrary to the latter (which only includes fixed costs if incurred during the period under examination), it includes product specific fixed costs made before the period in which allegedly abusive conduct took place. Failure to cover LRAIC indicates that the dominant undertaking is not recovering all the (attributable) fixed costs of producing

the good or service in question and that an as efficient competitor could be foreclosed from the market.

27.   If the data clearly suggest that an as efficient competitor can compete effectively with the pricing conduct of the dominant firm, the Commission will in principle infer that the dominant undertaking's pricing conduct is not likely to have an adverse impact on effective competition, and thus on consumers, and will be therefore unlikely to intervene. If, on the contrary, the data suggest that the price charged by the dominant undertaking has the potential to foreclose as efficient competitors, then the Commission will integrate this in the general assessment of anticompetitive foreclosure (see Section B above), taking into account other relevant quantitative and/or qualitative evidence.

D.   Objective necessity and efficiencies

28.   In the enforcement of Article [102], the Commission also intends to examine claims put forward by a dominant undertaking that its conduct is justified. A dominant undertaking may do so either by demonstrating that its conduct is objectively necessary or by demonstrating that its conduct produces substantial efficiencies which outweigh any anticompetitive effects on consumers. In this context, the Commission will assess whether the conduct in question is indispensable and proportionate to the goal allegedly pursued by the dominant undertaking.

29.   The question of whether conduct is objectively necessary and proportionate must be determined on the basis of factors external to the dominant undertaking. Exclusionary conduct may, for example, be considered objectively necessary for health or safety reasons related to the nature of the product in question. However, proof of whether conduct of this kind is objectively necessary must take into account that it is normally the task of public authorities to set and enforce public health and safety standards. It is not the task of a dominant undertaking to take steps on its own initiative to exclude products which it regards, rightly or wrongly, as dangerous or inferior to its own product.

30.   The Commission considers that a dominant undertaking may also justify conduct leading to foreclosure of competitors on the ground of efficiencies that are sufficient to guarantee that no net harm to consumers is likely to arise. In this context, the dominant undertaking will generally be expected to demonstrate, with a sufficient degree of probability, and on the basis of verifiable evidence, that the following cumulative conditions are fulfilled:

- the efficiencies have been, or are likely to be, realised as a result of the conduct. They may, for example, include technical improvements in the quality of goods, or a reduction in the cost of production or distribution;

- the conduct is indispensable to the realisation of these efficiencies: there must be no less anti-competitive alternatives to the conduct that are capable of producing the same efficiencies;

- the likely efficiencies brought about by the conduct concerned outweigh any likely negative effects on competition and consumer welfare in the affected markets;

- the conduct does not eliminate effective competition, by removing all or most existing sources of actual or potential competition. Rivalry between firms is an essential driver of economic efficiency, including dynamic efficiencies in the form of innovation. In its absence the dominant firm will lack adequate incentives to continue to create and pass on efficiency gains. Where there is no residual competition and no foreseeable threat of entry, the protection of rivalry and the competitive process outweighs possible efficiency gains. In the Commission's view, exclusionary conduct which maintains, creates or strengthens a market position approaching that of a monopoly can normally not be justified on the grounds that it also creates efficiency gains.

31. It is incumbent upon the dominant firm to provide all the evidence necessary to demonstrate that the conduct concerned is objectively justified. It then falls to the Commission to make the ultimate assessment of whether the conduct being examined is not objectively necessary and, based on a weighing-up of any apparent anti-competitive effects against any advanced and substantiated efficiencies, is likely to result in consumer harm.

Questions on the Article [102] Guidance Paper

1. The Guidance Paper states that "anticompetitive foreclosure" requires the presence of likely "consumer harm".

a. Why is it important to demonstrate consumer harm on top of anticompetitive foreclosure?

    i. Does foreclosure automatically translate in consumer harm?

    ii. Does the requirement to demonstrate consumer harm amount to an obligation to show recoupment in that the exclusionary conduct will subsequently allow the dominant firm to "exploit" its customers?

    iii. Or does this requirement simply signal that the potential efficiencies generated by the prima facie anticompetitive conduct will be taken into account?

b. How do you measure consumer harm? Is it only a matter of price increases or can consumers suffer in other ways?

2. The Guidance Paper suggests that the Commission will conduct a counterfactual analysis or a "but for" test. Is such a test easy to conduct? Doesn't it lead to mere speculation? Or can it achieve a useful purpose?

3. The Commission says that it "will normally only intervene where the conduct concerned has already been or is capable of hampering competition from competitors which are considered to be as efficient as the dominant undertaking", but it recognizes that "in certain circumstances a less efficient competitor may also exert a constraint which should be taken into account when considering whether a particular price-based conduct leads to anticompetitive foreclosure."

a. Does the above give clear guidance to dominant firms?

b. Does it make sense to protect less efficient competitors on the ground that they may subsequently become more efficient?

i.   Would this lead the Commission to engage in mere speculation? How can it be determined that a less efficient competitor may become more efficient tomorrow? Does the Guidance Paper offer guidance on this point?

ii.   Doesn't this approach amount to trading low prices today for potentially lower prices tomorrow?

c.   Does it make sense to protect competitors whose costs are higher than the dominant firm's costs but lower than the dominant firm's monopoly price? Couldn't such a less efficient competitor constrain the dominant firm from charging the full monopoly price by limiting the dominant firm to charging no more than the less efficient competitor's costs?

d.   If the dominant firm and a rival both have the same cost curve, which declines with output over the relevant range, but anticompetitive foreclosure has reduced rival output and relegated the rival to the high cost portion of the curve while the dominant firm is at the low cost portion of the curve, are the two firms equally efficient (because their cost curves are identical) or is the rival less efficient (because its costs are higher at current output levels)?

4.   How do the four conditions the Guidance Paper requires to prove an efficiency defense compare to Article 101(3)?

a.   Should defenses under Articles 101 and 102 be equated even though agreements are more avoidable than unilateral conducts?

b.   How easy will it be to establish that the efficiencies generated by a conduct outweigh its negative effects on competition and thus eliminate any harm to consumers?

c.   If the conduct meets the first three requirements, and thus makes consumers better off, why should it have to meet the fourth test that it does not eliminate effective competition by removing all or most existing sources of actual or potential competition?

i.   The Guidance Paper indicates that "[w]here there is no residual competition and no and no foreseeable threat of entry, the protection of rivalry and the competitive process outweighs possible efficiency gains." Does it make sense to prevent the realization of efficiencies leading for instance to lower prices or better products for the sake of "protecting rivalry"?

ii.   Is this approach inconsistent with the Guidance Paper's emphasis elsewhere on protecting consumer welfare rather than competitors? Or is it justified by the premise that such an elimination of competition will cause a long run harm to consumer welfare that exceeds any short term benefit? Is it clear that this premise is empirically accurate?[91]

----

91.   Generally gains from improvements in productive efficiency (such as reducing production costs) outweigh harms from the creation of allocative inefficiency (such as increasing market power) both in the short run and long run. Elhauge, *supra* note 29, at 779–81; Elhauge, *supra* note 33, at 274–75 & n.66. Further, efficiency may be most enhanced by competition to obtain dominance, and economic theory is highly divided on whether monopo-

c. THE CONDUCT ELEMENT IN OTHER NATIONS

With a few exceptions, most nations parallel the U.S. and EU in requiring some form of bad conduct in addition to the possession of the requisite market power.[92] Some nations define the requisite anticompetitive or exclusionary conduct in their law or regulation using general standards.[93] Many nations provide a non-exhaustive list of specific unilateral conducts that may be considered anticompetitive, generally encompassing predatory pricing, unilateral refusals to deal and price squeezes.[94] Some jurisdictions cover not only exclusionary behavior, but also exploitative conduct against consumers, especially unfair prices.[95]

2. PREDATORY PRICING

The concern about predatory pricing is that firms might strategically cut prices to unprofitable levels in the short term in order to eliminate or discipline rivals and then raise long run prices to supracompetitive levels, inflicting a net long term injury on consumers. The problem is that such harmful predatory pricing is often hard to distinguish from desirable competitive price-cutting, so that attempts to condemn the former may mistakenly condemn and deter the latter. The pervasive concern of predatory pricing doctrine is thus to fashion a rule that adequately deters harmful predatory pricing without overly deterring competitive price-cutting.

Such overdeterrence raises a serious problem both because competitive price-cutting is among the most desirable business activities and because rivals have a heavy anticompetitive incentive to stop it. The last thing one would want would be to enable firms to use antitrust law to discipline rival price cuts. This concern about overdeterrence plays out in many doctrinal

---

lists are more or less likely than a competitive market to invest in innovation and other efficiency improvements. *Id.* at 298–300.

92. *See supra* Chapter 3.A.3.

93. *See* Australia Trade Practices Act § 46 (conduct with a purpose to substantially damage rivals, entrants or deter competitive conduct); Mexico Competition Law Art. 10 (acts whose "which aim or effect is to improperly displace other agents from the market, substantially hinder their access thereto, or to establish exclusive advantages"); New Zealand Commerce Act § 36 (same); Russia Competition Law Arts. 10 ("Actions (lack of action) ... which result or can result in prevention, restriction or elimination of competition and (or) infringement of the interests of other persons ... "); South Africa Competition Act § 1(1)(x) ("an act that impedes or prevents a firm entering into, or expanding within, a market"); Venezuela Procompetition Act, Art. 6: ("Acts ... that willfully impede or obstruct the entry or exit of firms, goods or services into any or all areas of the market").

94. *See, e.g.,* Brazil Antitrust Law No. 8,884, Art. 21; Canadian Competition Act §§ 78–79; China Anti–Monopoly Law Art. 17; India Competition Act § 4(2); Israel Restrictive Trade Practices Law §§ 29, 29A(b); Mexico Competition Law Art. 10; Peru Competition Law Art. 10; Singapore Competition Act § 47(2); Singapore Guidelines on the Section 47 Prohibition Annex C (2007); Taiwan Fair Trade Act Art. 10; Thailand Trade Competition Act § 25; Turkey Competition Act, Art. 6; Saudi Arabia Competition Law, Art. 5; Venezuela Procompetition Act Art. 13. In contrast, Egypt provides for a list of potentially illegal unilateral conduct that does appear exhaustive. *See* Egypt Competition Law Art. 8.

95. *See infra* Chapter 3.C.3.

ways. It leads some courts to set high criteria for proving predatory pricing. The U.S. courts have done so by concluding that an intent to have such a predatory effect does not suffice and by requiring proof both of below-cost pricing and likely supra-competitive recoupment. It also leads some courts to impose higher standards of sufficient evidence for proving those elements, or to be less willing to infer a conspiracy to predatorily price.

The reciprocal problem is that all such efforts to reduce the overdeterrence of desirable competitive pricing by making predatory pricing harder to prove also necessarily increase the *under*deterrence of undesirable predatory pricing. The overarching question is thus what doctrine would achieve the optimal tradeoff that minimizes the total harm from the underdeterrence of predatory pricing and the overdeterrence of competitive price-cutting.

a.   BELOW–COST PREDATORY PRICING

Brooke Group Ltd. (Liggett) v. Brown & Williamson Tobacco Corp.

509 U.S. 209 (1993).

■ JUSTICE KENNEDY delivered the opinion of the Court . . .

I

. . . . Cigarette manufacturing has long been one of America's most concentrated industries, and for decades, production has been dominated by six firms: R.J. Reynolds, Philip Morris, American Brands, Lorillard, and the two litigants involved here, Liggett and Brown & Williamson. R.J. Reynolds and Philip Morris, the two industry leaders, enjoyed respective market shares of about 28% and 40% at the time of trial. Brown & Williamson ran a distant third, its market share never exceeding 12% at any time relevant to this dispute. Liggett's share of the market was even less, from a low of just over 2% in 1980 to a high of just over 5% in 1984.

The cigarette industry also has long been one of America's most profitable, in part because for many years there was no significant price competition among the rival firms. List prices for cigarettes increased in lock-step, twice a year, for a number of years, irrespective of the rate of inflation, changes in the costs of production, or shifts in consumer demand. Substantial evidence suggests that in recent decades, the industry reaped the benefits of prices above a competitive level . . .

[In 1980, Liggett decided to introduce a line of black and white generic cigarettes that were offered to consumers at list prices 30% below branded cigarettes and promoted to wholesalers with volume rebates. This hit Brown & Williamson especially hard because its brands were favored by price-sensitive consumers. Brown & Williamson responded by introducing its own line of generics with even larger volume rebates. Liggett alleged that Brown & Williamson's volume rebates violated the Robinson–Patman Act because they resulted in prices that were both discriminatory and below average variable costs, and were designed to pressure it to raise generic cigarette prices so they were closer to branded prices.]

... The jury awarded Liggett $49.6 million in damages, which the District Court trebled to $148.8 million. After reviewing the record, however, the District Court held that Brown & Williamson was entitled to judgment as a matter of law ... The United States Court of Appeals for the Fourth Circuit affirmed....

We ... affirm.

II. A

... By its terms, the Robinson–Patman Act condemns price discrimination only to the extent that it threatens to injure competition.... Thus, "the Robinson–Patman Act should be construed consistently with broader policies of the antitrust laws." ...

Liggett contends that Brown & Williamson's discriminatory volume rebates to wholesalers threatened substantial competitive injury by furthering a predatory pricing scheme designed to purge competition from the economy segment of the cigarette market. This type of injury, which harms direct competitors of the discriminating seller, is known as primary-line injury.....

... [P]rimary line competitive injury under the Robinson–Patman Act is of the same general character as the injury inflicted by predatory pricing schemes actionable under § 2 of the Sherman Act. There are, to be sure, differences between the two statutes. For example, we interpret § 2 of the Sherman Act to condemn predatory pricing when it poses "a dangerous probability of actual monopolization," *Spectrum Sports*, whereas the Robinson–Patman Act requires only that there be "a reasonable possibility" of substantial injury to competition before its protections are triggered. Falls City Industries, Inc. v. Vanco Beverage, Inc., 460 U. S. 428, 434 (1983). But whatever additional flexibility the Robinson–Patman Act standard may imply, the essence of the claim under either statute is the same: A business rival has priced its products in an unfair manner with an object to eliminate or retard competition and thereby gain and exercise control over prices in the relevant market.

Accordingly, whether the claim alleges predatory pricing under § 2 of the Sherman Act or primary-line price discrimination under the Robinson–Patman Act, two prerequisites to recovery remain the same. First, a plaintiff seeking to establish competitive injury resulting from a rival's low prices must prove that the prices complained of are below an appropriate measure of its rival's costs.[1] Although *Cargill* and *Matsushita* reserved as a formal matter the question " 'whether recovery should *ever* be available ... when the pricing in question is above some measure of incremental cost,' " *Cargill* (quoting *Matsushita*), the reasoning in both opinions suggests that only below-cost prices should suffice, and we have rejected elsewhere the notion that above-cost prices that are below general market levels or the

---

1. Because the parties in this case agree that the relevant measure of cost is average variable cost, however, we again decline to resolve the conflict among the lower courts over the appropriate measure of cost.

costs of a firm's competitors inflict injury to competition cognizable under the antitrust laws. *See* Atlantic Richfield Co. v. USA Petroleum Co., 495 U.S. 328, 340 (1990). "Low prices benefit consumers regardless of how those prices are set, and so long as they are above predatory levels, they do not threaten competition.... We have adhered to this principle regardless of the type of antitrust claim involved." Ibid. As a general rule, the exclusionary effect of prices above a relevant measure of cost either reflects the lower cost structure of the alleged predator, and so represents competition on the merits, or is beyond the practical ability of a judicial tribunal to control without courting intolerable risks of chilling legitimate price-cutting. "To hold that the antitrust laws protect competitors from the loss of profits due to such price competition would, in effect, render illegal any decision by a firm to cut prices in order to increase market share. The antitrust laws require no such perverse result." *Cargill*.

Even in an oligopolistic market, when a firm drops its prices to a competitive level to demonstrate to a maverick the unprofitability of straying from the group, it would be illogical to condemn the price cut: The antitrust laws then would be an obstacle to the chain of events most conducive to a breakdown of oligopoly pricing and the onset of competition. Even if the ultimate effect of the cut is to induce or reestablish supracompetitive pricing, discouraging a price cut and forcing firms to maintain supracompetitive prices, thus depriving consumers of the benefits of lower prices in the interim, does not constitute sound antitrust policy.

The second prerequisite to holding a competitor liable under the antitrust laws for charging low prices is a demonstration that the competitor had a reasonable prospect, or, under § 2 of the Sherman Act, a dangerous probability, of recouping its investment in below-cost prices. *See Matsushita; Cargill*. "For the investment to be rational, the [predator] must have a reasonable expectation of recovering, in the form of later monopoly profits, more than the losses suffered." *Matsushita*. Recoupment is the ultimate object of an unlawful predatory pricing scheme; it is the means by which a predator profits from predation. Without it, predatory pricing produces lower aggregate prices in the market, and consumer welfare is enhanced. Although unsuccessful predatory pricing may encourage some inefficient substitution toward the product being sold at less than its cost, unsuccessful predation is in general a boon to consumers.

That below-cost pricing may impose painful losses on its target is of no moment to the antitrust laws if competition is not injured: It is axiomatic that the antitrust laws were passed for "the protection of competition, not competitors." *Brown Shoe*.... Even an act of pure malice by one business competitor against another does not, without more, state a claim under the federal antitrust laws; those laws do not create a federal law of unfair competition or "purport to afford remedies for all torts committed by or against persons engaged in interstate commerce." Hunt v. Crumboch, 325 U.S. 821, 826 (1945).

For recoupment to occur, below-cost pricing must be capable, as a threshold matter, of producing the intended effects on the firm's rivals, whether driving them from the market, or, as was alleged to be the goal here, causing them to raise their prices to supracompetitive levels within a disciplined oligopoly. This requires an understanding of the extent and duration of the alleged predation, the relative financial strength of the predator and its intended victim, and their respective incentives and will. The inquiry is whether, given the aggregate losses caused by the below-cost pricing, the intended target would likely succumb.

If circumstances indicate that below-cost pricing could likely produce its intended effect on the target, there is still the further question whether it would likely injure competition in the relevant market. The plaintiff must demonstrate that there is a likelihood that the predatory scheme alleged would cause a rise in prices above a competitive level that would be sufficient to compensate for the amounts expended on the predation, including the time value of the money invested in it. . . .

Evidence of below-cost pricing is not alone sufficient to permit an inference of probable recoupment and injury to competition. Determining whether recoupment of predatory losses is likely requires an estimate of the cost of the alleged predation and a close analysis of both the scheme alleged by the plaintiff and the structure and conditions of the relevant market. If market circumstances or deficiencies in proof would bar a reasonable jury from finding that the scheme alleged would likely result in sustained supracompetitive pricing, the plaintiff's case has failed. In certain situations—for example, where the market is highly diffuse and competitive, or where new entry is easy, or the defendant lacks adequate excess capacity to absorb the market shares of his rivals and cannot quickly create or purchase new capacity—summary disposition of the case is appropriate. See, e.g., *Cargill.*

These prerequisites to recovery are not easy to establish, but they are not artificial obstacles to recovery; rather, they are essential components of real market injury. As we have said in the Sherman Act context, "predatory pricing schemes are rarely tried, and even more rarely successful," *Matsushita,* and the costs of an erroneous finding of liability are high. "[T]he mechanism by which a firm engages in predatory pricing—lowering prices—is the same mechanism by which a firm stimulates competition; because 'cutting prices in order to increase business often is the very essence of competition . . . [;] mistaken inferences . . . are especially costly, because they chill the very conduct the antitrust laws are designed to protect.'" *Cargill* (quoting *Matsushita*). It would be ironic indeed if the standards for predatory pricing liability were so low that antitrust suits themselves became a tool for keeping prices high.

B

Liggett does not allege that Brown & Williamson sought to drive it from the market but that Brown & Williamson sought to preserve supracompetitive profits on branded cigarettes by pressuring Liggett to raise its generic cigarette prices through a process of tacit collusion with the other cigarette companies. Tacit collusion, sometimes called oligopolistic price coordination or conscious parallelism, describes the process, not in itself unlawful, by which firms in a concentrated market might in effect share monopoly power, setting their prices at a profit-maximizing, supracompetitive level by recognizing their shared economic interests and their interdependence with respect to price and output decisions.

In *Matsushita*, we remarked upon the general implausibility of predatory pricing. Matsushita observed that such schemes are even more improbable when they require coordinated action among several firms. Matsushita involved an allegation of an express conspiracy to engage in predatory pricing. The Court noted that in addition to the usual difficulties that face a single firm attempting to recoup predatory losses, other problems render a conspiracy "incalculably more difficult to execute." In order to succeed, the conspirators must agree on how to allocate present losses and future gains among the firms involved, and each firm must resist powerful incentives to cheat on whatever agreement is reached.

However unlikely predatory pricing by multiple firms may be when they conspire, it is even less likely when, as here, there is no express coordination. Firms that seek to recoup predatory losses through the conscious parallelism of oligopoly must rely on uncertain and ambiguous signals to achieve concerted action. The signals are subject to misinterpretation and are a blunt and imprecise means of ensuring smooth cooperation, especially in the context of changing or unprecedented market circumstances. This anticompetitive minuet is most difficult to compose and to perform, even for a disciplined oligopoly.

From one standpoint, recoupment through oligopolistic price coordination could be thought more feasible than recoupment through monopoly: In the oligopoly setting, the victim itself has an economic incentive to acquiesce in the scheme. If forced to choose between cutting prices and sustaining losses, maintaining prices and losing market share, or raising prices and enjoying a share of supracompetitive profits, a firm may yield to the last alternative. Yet on the whole, tacit cooperation among oligopolists must be considered the least likely means of recouping predatory losses. In addition to the difficulty of achieving effective tacit coordination and the high likelihood that any attempt to discipline will produce an outbreak of competition, the predator's present losses in a case like this fall on it alone, while the later supracompetitive profits must be shared with every other oligopolist in proportion to its market share, including the intended victim. In this case, for example, Brown & Williamson, with its 11–12% share of the cigarette market, would have had to generate around $9 in supracompetitive profits for each $1 invested in predation; the remaining $8 would belong to its competitors, who had taken no risk. . . .

To the extent that the Court of Appeals may have held that the interdependent pricing of an oligopoly may never provide a means for achieving recoupment and so may not form the basis of a primary-line injury claim, we disagree. A predatory pricing scheme designed to preserve or create a stable oligopoly, if successful, can injure consumers in the same way, and to the same extent, as one designed to bring about a monopoly. However unlikely that possibility may be as a general matter, when the realities of the market and the record facts indicate that it has occurred and was likely to have succeeded, theory will not stand in the way of liability. See *Eastman Kodak*.

The Robinson–Patman Act ... suggests no exclusion from coverage when primary-line injury occurs in an oligopoly setting. Unlike the provisions of the Sherman Act, which speak only of various forms of express agreement and monopoly, the Robinson–Patman Act is phrased in broader, disjunctive terms, prohibiting price discrimination "where the effect of such discrimination may be substantially to lessen competition or tend to create a monopoly." For all the words of the Act to carry adequate meaning, competitive injury under the Act must extend beyond the monopoly setting. The language referring to a substantial lessening of competition was part of the original Clayton Act § 2, and the same phrasing appears in § 7 of that Act. In the § 7 context, it has long been settled that excessive concentration, and the oligopolistic price coordination it portends, may be the injury to competition the Act prohibits. See, e.g., *Philadelphia National Bank*. We adhere to "the normal rule of statutory construction that identical words used in different parts of the same act are intended to have the same meaning." We decline to create a per se rule of nonliability for predatory price discrimination when recoupment is alleged to take place through supracompetitive oligopoly pricing.

III

Although Liggett's theory of liability, as an abstract matter, is within the reach of the statute, ... Liggett [lacked sufficient evidence] to submit its case to the jury....

A

... [T]he record contains sufficient evidence from which a reasonable jury could conclude that Brown & Williamson envisioned or intended [to pressure Liggett to raise generic process.] There is also sufficient evidence in the record from which a reasonable jury could conclude that for a period of approximately 18 months, Brown & Williamson's prices on its generic cigarettes were below its costs, and that this below-cost pricing imposed losses on Liggett that Liggett was unwilling to sustain, given its corporate parent's effort to locate a buyer for the company. ... The evidence is inadequate to show that in pursuing this scheme, Brown & Williamson had a reasonable prospect of recovering its losses from below-cost pricing through slowing the growth of generics....

No inference of recoupment is sustainable on this record, because no evidence suggests that Brown & Williamson—whatever its intent in introducing black and whites may have been—was likely to obtain the power to raise the prices for generic cigarettes above a competitive level. Recoupment through supracompetitive pricing in the economy segment of the cigarette market is an indispensable aspect of Liggett's own proffered theory, because a slowing of growth in the economy segment, even if it results from an increase in generic prices, is not itself anticompetitive. Only if those higher prices are a product of nonmarket forces has competition suffered. If prices rise in response to an excess of demand over supply, or segment growth slows as patterns of consumer preference become stable, the market is functioning in a competitive manner. ... Because relying on tacit coordination among oligopolists as a means of recouping losses from predatory pricing is "highly speculative," competent evidence is necessary to allow a reasonable inference that it poses an authentic threat to competition. The evidence in this case is insufficient to demonstrate the danger of Brown & Williamson's alleged scheme.

B

Based on Liggett's theory of the case and the record it created, there are two means by which one might infer that Brown & Williamson had a reasonable prospect of producing sustained supracompetitive pricing in the generic segment adequate to recoup its predatory losses: first, if generic output or price information indicates that oligopolistic price coordination in fact produced supracompetitive prices in the generic segment; or second, if evidence about the market and Brown & Williamson's conduct indicate that the alleged scheme was likely to have brought about tacit coordination and oligopoly pricing in the generic segment, even if it did not actually do so.

1

In this case, the price and output data do not support a reasonable inference that Brown & Williamson and the other cigarette companies elevated prices above a competitive level for generic cigarettes. Supracompetitive pricing entails a restriction in output. In the present setting, in which output expanded at a rapid rate following Brown & Williamson's alleged predation, output in the generic segment can only have been restricted in the sense that it expanded at a slower rate than it would have absent Brown & Williamson's intervention. Such a counterfactual proposition is difficult to prove in the best of circumstances; here, the record evidence does not permit a reasonable inference that output would have been greater without Brown & Williamson's entry into the generic segment.

Following Brown & Williamson's entry, the rate at which generic cigarettes were capturing market share did not slow; indeed, the average rate of growth doubled. During the four years from 1980 to 1984 in which Liggett was alone in the generic segment, the segment gained market share at an average rate of 1% of the overall market per year, from .4% in 1980 to slightly more than 4% of the cigarette market in 1984. In the next five years, following the alleged predation, the generic segment expanded from 4% to more than 15% of the domestic cigarette market, or greater than 2% per year.

While this evidence tends to show that Brown & Williamson's participation in the economy segment did not restrict output, it is not dispositive. One could speculate, for example, that the rate of segment growth would have tripled, instead of doubled, without Brown & Williamson's alleged predation. But there is no concrete evidence of this. Indeed, the only industry projection in the record estimating what the segment's growth would have been without Brown & Williamson's entry supports the opposite inference. In 1984, Brown & Williamson forecast in an important planning document that the economy segment would account for 10% of the total cigarette market by 1988 if it did not enter the segment. In fact, in 1988, after what Liggett alleges was a sustained and dangerous anticompetitive campaign by Brown & Williamson, the generic segment accounted for over 12% of the total market. Thus the segment's output expanded more robustly than Brown & Williamson had estimated it would had Brown & Williamson never entered. . . .

Liggett places its principal reliance on direct evidence of price behavior. This evidence demonstrates that the list prices on all cigarettes, generic and branded alike, rose to a significant degree during the late 1980's. From 1986 to 1989, list prices on both generic and branded cigarettes increased twice a year by similar amounts. Liggett's economic expert testified that these price increases outpaced increases in costs, taxes, and promotional expenditures. The list prices of generics, moreover, rose at a faster rate than the prices of branded cigarettes, thus narrowing the list price differential between branded and generic products. Liggett argues that this would permit a reasonable jury to find that Brown & Williamson succeeded in bringing about oligopolistic price coordination and supracompetitive prices in the generic category sufficient to slow its growth, thereby preserving supracompetitive branded profits and recouping its predatory losses.

A reasonable jury, however, could not have drawn the inferences Liggett proposes. All of Liggett's data is based upon the list prices of various categories of cigarettes. Yet the jury had before it undisputed evidence that during the period in question, list prices were not the actual prices paid by consumers. As the market became unsettled in the mid–1980s, the cigarette companies invested substantial sums in promotional schemes, including coupons, stickers, and giveaways, that reduced the actual cost of cigarettes to consumers below list prices. This promotional activity accelerated as the decade progressed. Many wholesalers also passed portions of their volume rebates on to the consumer, which had the effect of further undermining the significance of the retail list prices. Especially in an oligopoly setting, in which price competition is most likely to take place through less observable and less regulable means than list prices, it would be unreasonable to draw conclusions about the existence of tacit coordination or supracompetitive pricing from data that reflects only list prices.

Even on its own terms, the list price data relied upon by Liggett to demonstrate a narrowing of the price differential between generic and full-priced branded cigarettes could not support the conclusion that supracompetitive pricing had been introduced into the generic segment. Liggett's gap data ignores the effect of "subgeneric" cigarettes, which were priced at discounts of 50% or more from the list prices of normal branded cigarettes. Liggett itself, while supposedly under the sway of oligopoly power, pioneered this development in 1988 with the introduction of its "Pyramid" brand. By the time of trial, five of the six major manufacturers offered a cigarette in this category at a discount from the full list price of at least 50%. Thus, the price difference between the highest priced branded cigarette and the lowest price cigarettes in the economy segment, instead of narrowing over the course of the period of alleged predation as Liggett would argue, grew to a substantial extent. . . .

It may be that a reasonable jury could conclude that the cumulative discounts attributable to subgenerics and the various consumer promotions did not cancel out the full effect of the increases in list prices, and that actual prices to the consumer did indeed rise, but rising prices do not themselves permit an inference of a collusive market dynamic. . . . Where, as here, output is expanding at the same time prices are increasing, rising prices are equally consistent with growing product demand. Under these conditions, a jury may not infer competitive injury from price and output data absent some evidence that tends to prove that output was restricted or prices were above a competitive level. *Cf. Monsanto.*

Quite apart from the absence of any evidence of that sort, an inference of supracompetitive pricing would be particularly anomalous in this case, as the very party alleged to have been coerced into pricing through oligopolistic coordination denied that such coordination existed: Liggett's own officers and directors consistently denied that they or other firms in the industry priced their cigarettes through tacit collusion or reaped supracompetitive profits. . . .

2

Not only does the evidence fail to show actual supracompetitive pricing in the generic segment, it also does not demonstrate its likelihood. At the time Brown & Williamson entered the generic segment, the cigarette industry as a whole faced declining demand and possessed substantial excess capacity. These circumstances tend to break down patterns of oligopoly pricing and produce price competition. . . . Tacit coordination is facilitated by a stable market environment, fungible products, and a small number of variables upon which the firms seeking to coordinate their pricing may focus. Uncertainty is an oligopoly's greatest enemy. By 1984, however, the cigarette market was in an obvious state of flux. The introduction of generic cigarettes in 1980 represented the first serious price competition in the cigarette market since the 1930's. This development was bound to unsettle previous expectations and patterns of market conduct and to reduce the cigarette firms' ability to predict each other's behavior.

The larger number of product types and pricing variables also decreased the probability of effective parallel pricing. When Brown & Williamson entered the economy segment in 1984, the segment included value–25s, black and whites, and branded generics. With respect to each product, the net price in the market was determined not only by list prices, but also by a wide variety of discounts and promotions to consumers, and by rebates to wholesalers. In order to coordinate in an effective manner and eliminate price competition, the cigarette companies would have been required, without communicating, to establish parallel practices with respect to each of these variables, many of which, like consumer stickers or coupons, were difficult to monitor. Liggett has not even alleged parallel behavior with respect to these other variables, and the inherent limitations of tacit collusion suggest that such multivariable coordination is improbable. . . .

Even if all the cigarette companies were willing to participate in a scheme to restrain the growth of the generic segment, they would not have been able to coordinate their actions and raise prices above a competitive level unless they understood that Brown & Williamson's entry into the segment was not a genuine effort to compete with Liggett. If even one other firm misinterpreted Brown & Williamson's entry as an effort to expand share, a chain reaction of competitive responses would almost certainly have resulted, and oligopoly discipline would have broken down, perhaps irretrievably. "[O]nce the trust among rivals breaks down, it is as hard to put back together again as was Humpty–Dumpty, and non-collusive behavior is likely to take over." . . .

Note and Questions About *Brooke*

Brooke holds that pricing is predatory only if it (1) disciplines or eliminates a competitor, (2) the price is below "an appropriate measure of costs" and (3) recoupment is likely. The last element requires evidence that there is a "reasonable prospect" (in a price discrimination case) or "dangerous probability" (in a straight predatory pricing case) that it will produce supracompetitive profits down the road that exceed the losses from the below-cost pricing. The first element is fairly standard. The second element is slightly more controversial, but let us leave discussion of it until the next section, which addresses whether above-cost pricing should ever be deemed predatory. It is the third element of recoupment that *Brooke* added and that raises the most significant questions.

1. Why shouldn't pricing below cost be enough?

a. Can't we infer from a below-cost price that the defendant must have intended to be predatory because otherwise such pricing is irrational?

    i. Is that inference valid given the possibility that

        a. the judge or jury might erroneously measure costs too high?

        b. the firm might have erroneously measured costs too low?

    ii. Are there other legitimate reasons why a firm with market power might price below cost, like meeting competition or offering a promotional price? Should those reasons provide a defense? If they should, why not just condemn below-cost pricing unless those defenses are established?

b. Should below-cost pricing suffice when coupled with evidence of anticompetitive intent?

    i. Will such evidence help resolve ambiguities about costs? About whether some other legitimate reason existed for a below cost price? Will it raise its own ambiguities and problems about proving intent?

    ii. If proof of anticompetitive intent were made a requirement, wouldn't it create a big underdeterrence problem because firms would just stop expressing their intent in their documents?

2. What does the recoupment element add?

a. Is harm to consumers possible without recoupment?

b. Doesn't the fact of below cost pricing or anticompetitive intent show the defendant itself must have thought recoupment likely? Why isn't the defendant best placed to decide this market issue? Should we infer likely recoupment from defendant intent? Or at least use intent to resolve ambiguities about likely recoupment?

c. Is proving a likelihood of recoupment easier than proving predatory intent and prices below cost? Less prone to error?

d. Why have multiple elements that go to the same issue?

e. If a defendant firm is in multiple markets, is it possible its recoupment would be in markets other than the one where below-cost pricing is occurring?

3. Which market structures make recoupment likely or implausible?

a. Isn't recoupment always likely or plausible if a firm really has monopoly power or enough market power to have a dangerous probability of acquiring it?

i. Does the recoupment element then really add anything to the market power element in a Sherman Act § 2 case?

ii. Is the use of the recoupment element here simply a result of the fact that this was not a section 2 case, but a Robinson–Patman Act case, where no proof of monopoly power was necessary? Does it effectively add a market power element to such Robinson–Patman Act cases?

b. Isn't recoupment always implausible on a competitive market?

c. Is recoupment plausible in an oligopoly?

i. Is *Brooke* correct that the oligopolies are unlikely to be markets where recoupment is likely? Why would oligopolists be any less likely to price predatorily and then recoup than a monopolist? Why isn't it easier to discipline rivals to acquiesce in high oligopoly prices than to drive rivals out of a monopoly market? Is the overdeterrence concern with deterring competitive price cutting bigger in oligopoly markets?

ii. Is recoupment sufficiently unlikely in oligopoly markets that they should be per se excluded from claims of predatory pricing?

4. *Brooke* indicated that, although unlikely, recoupment could still be proven in an oligopoly market by showing either (a) direct evidence that prices or output were adversely affected by oligopolistic coordination or (b) evidence that such oligopolistic coordination was likely to result from the conduct given the market structure. Do you agree with the Court that neither showing was made in this case?

a. Was there sufficient evidence of actual oligopoly pricing?

i. Why doesn't the evidence suffice that, after the alleged predatory pricing, generic list prices increased lock-step, twice a year, in ways unrelated to costs or demand? Even if list prices aren't actual prices given discounts, isn't this enough evidence for jury to conclude that prices rose? Is evidence of a rise in prices sufficient, or does the plaintiff have to show prices were uniform?

ii. Does the introduction of subgenerics at lower prices alter the conclusion?

iii. Does the fact that output increased disprove oligopoly pricing? Couldn't successful oligopolistic coordination prevent output from increasing as much as it otherwise would have given an increase in demand or reduction in cost?

iv. The Court concludes that the rate of growth increased because during the predatory period from 1980–84, generics went from .4% to 4% of the market, whereas afterward from 1984–89 they went from 4% to 14%. Thus a 1% yearly increase sped up to 2%. But couldn't one equally say that the generic market increased 10 fold for the first four years then slowed down to increasing less than four fold over the next five years? Which better corresponds to demonstrated supply elasticity?

v. The Court notes that the plaintiff denied any oligopolistic pricing going on—is that reliable evidence that it wasn't?

b. Was there sufficient evidence that the market structure indicated a likelihood of oligopoly pricing?

i. Is the market concentration consistent with oligopoly?

ii. Is declining demand or excess capacity inconsistent with oligopoly?

iii. Does the uncertainty created by new generics, varieties of cigarettes, and price discounts undermine the likelihood of oligopolistic coordination?

5. Isn't this case really about whether Brown & Williamson was protecting its low-price position on a differentiated rather than oligopolistic market? Wouldn't it have anticompetitive incentives to do that even without any prospect of oligopolistic coordination?

The U.S. Conflict on the Proper Cost Measure

Before *Brooke,* the lower U.S. appellate courts held that pricing below some measure of variable cost (like marginal, average variable, or average avoidable cost) was always or presumptively predatory, and pricing above such variable cost measures but below average total cost was presumptively non-predatory, but that the latter presumption could be rebutted by other evidence, such as proof of predatory intent or sacrificing short-term profits.[96] *Brooke* explicitly declined to take any view on the "appropriate" cost measure, and since *Brooke* appellate courts have split on whether *Brooke* thus precludes predation claims alleging prices above any variable cost

---

96. *See* Northeastern Telephone Co. v. AT&T, 651 F.2d 76, 88 (2d Cir.1981); O. Hommel Co. v. Ferro Corp., 659 F.2d 340, 347–50 (3d Cir.1981); Adjusters Replace–A–Car, Inc. v. Agency Rent–A–Car, Inc., 735 F.2d 884, 889–91 (5th Cir.1984); Arthur S. Langenderfer, Inc. v. S.E. Johnson Co., 729 F.2d 1050, 1056–57 (6th Cir. 1984); Chillicothe Sand & Gravel Co. v. Martin Marietta Corp., 615 F.2d 427, 432 (7th Cir.1980); MCI Communications v. AT&T, 708 F.2d 1081, 1114–23 (7th Cir. 1983) (stressing that long run incremental cost rather than fully distributed cost is the right way to measure average total cost); Morgan v. Ponder, 892 F.2d 1355, 1360 (8th Cir.1989); William Inglis & Sons Baking Co. v. ITT Continental Baking Co., 668 F.2d 1014, 1034–36 (9th Cir.1981); Instructional Sys. Dev. Corp. v. Aetna Casualty & Sur. Co., 817 F.2d 639, 648 (10th Cir.1987); McGahee v. Propane Gas Co., 858 F.2d 1487, 1503 (11th Cir.1988); Southern Pacific Communications Co. v. AT&T, 740 F.2d 980, 1005–07 (D.C.Cir.1984).

measure.[97] Plaintiffs often effectively concede the issue by basing their claims solely on the theory that the prices were below some measure of variable cost even in circuits that, before *Brooke,* embraced the latter sort of theory.[98]

The precise sort of variable cost measure to use also remains in doubt. Several circuits have stated that the correct measure is marginal cost, but that average variable cost can be used as a surrogate where marginal cost cannot be determined.[99] In contrast, the First Circuit, including in some opinions by now-Justice Breyer, instead refer to the "avoidable" or "incremental" cost of producing the "additional output" it can sell at the alleged predatory price, although it also allows usage of average variable costs when this measure is unavailable.[100] However, no circuit has really made a holding either way since no appellate case has yet raised the distinction between these incremental cost measures. The following analysis by Professor Elhauge provides theoretical support for Justice Breyer's test over one that focuses on marginal or average variable cost. (As we shall see, the EU Guidelines likewise seem to adopt the Breyer test for measuring costs in predatory pricing cases).

Elhauge, *Why Above–Cost Price Cuts to Drive out Entrants Do Not Signal Predation or Even Market Power—and the Implications for Defining Costs*

112 YALE L.J. 681 (2003).

. . . [T]he correct time period for judging whether costs are variable or avoidable is the time period of the alleged predatory pricing. . . . Until the alleged predatory price lasts long enough to be exceeded by those costs that were *variable for that period*, an equally efficient entrant cannot have suffered any loss it could have avoided by exit, and thus cannot have had any incentive to exit. . . . One implication of this is that, for purposes of predatory pricing law, one should thus not distinguish between sunk, fixed, avoidable, and variable costs with general definitions about whether they are escapable in a limited period, or need to be incurred to produce any

---

97. *Compare* Stearns Airport Equip. Co. v. FMC Corp., 170 F.3d 518, 532 (5th Cir.1999) (*Brooke* requires overruling prior cases holding that prices above incremental cost could sometimes be predatory if below average total cost); Advo, Inc. v. Philadelphia Newspapers, Inc., 51 F.3d 1191, 1198 (3d Cir.1995) (relying only on incremental costs despite pre-*Brooke* authority to the contrary); United States v. AMR Corp., 335 F.3d 1109, 1116–17 (10th Cir.2003) (relying only on incremental costs despite pre-*Brooke* authority to the contrary), *with* Spirit Airlines v. Northwest Airlines, 431 F.3d 917, 937–38 (6th Cir.2005) (sticking with pre-*Brooke* precedent that prices above average variable costs could be predatory if a contrary presumption were rebutted); Concord Boat Corp. v. Brunswick Corp., 207 F.3d 1039, 1061 (8th Cir.2000) (same).

98. *See* Vollrath Co. v. Sammi Corp., 9 F.3d 1455, 1461 (9th Cir.1993); Rebel Oil Co., Inc. v. Atlantic Richfield Co., 146 F.3d 1088, 1094 (9th Cir.1998).

99. *AMR*, 335 F.3d at 1116–17; *Stearns*, 170 F.3d at 532; *Advo*, 51 F.3d at 1198; *Northeastern Telephone*, 651 F.2d at 88 (2d Cir.1981).

100. *See* Clamp–All Corp. v. Cast Iron Soil Pipe Inst., 851 F.2d 478, 483 (1st Cir.1988) (Breyer, J.); Barry Wright Corp. v. ITT Grinnell Corp., 724 F.2d 227, 232 (1st Cir.1983) (Breyer, J.).

output or to produce anything beyond the first unit of output. Rather, the question of whether (and what) costs to consider should depend *solely* on whether they could be varied during the time period of the alleged predation....

What is the concern of those who favor using long-term costs even when the predatory pricing period is short? One theory is that predatory pricing at the "rival's variable costs" can induce their exit because "[t]he rival, who also incurs fixed costs, exhausts its financial resources and leaves the market." But this is wrong. As long as the price exceeds the costs a rival could vary during the relevant time period, the rival would lose money from leaving the market....

What do we do with software whose marginal or variable cost of production is near zero? The usual answer is that the "new economy" has to be treated differently because marginal or variable costs are so low. But this creation of an ad hoc exception is hardly satisfactory. In the old economy, marginal or variable costs are also often below average or long-term costs. Indeed, the distinction between these cost measures only matters because they sometimes diverge. If this divergence presents a big problem when it is large, it must present at least a small problem when it is small. Our theory for how to deal with that divergence should be able to address the full range of possible magnitudes rather than having ad hoc exceptions, especially since those exceptions create ambiguity about just what the vague dividing line might be.

The better answer is, instead, that it all depends on how long the pricing lasts. If pricing at a near-zero level occurs for a short time, it cannot persuade any equally efficient software rivals to exit, since they also will have near-zero marginal costs and thus retain a profit from operating during that period. If instead such pricing lasts for years, then it could be predatory because it would not allow an equally efficient software rival to recoup the software development costs of updating that software to stay in the market. The latter costs become variable to the rival if the predatory pricing is lengthy, but not if it is brief. Paradox solved....

Another common concern is that equally efficient firms might have different ratios of fixed and variable costs. For example, Williamson observes that more capital-intensive firms can have lower variable costs even when they are less efficient than more labor-intensive firms. He thus advocates using average total costs as a better means of sorting out the efficiencies of firms.

This is a reasonable concern with using the average variable costs of making the predator's *entire* output because that measure is by definition lower than average total costs. Thus, if allowed to price at this measure of average variable costs, even a firm exceeding its optimal capacity could price at a level that is lower than its marginal or average total costs, and thus lower than the costs of an equally efficient firm at providing that incremental output. An average variable cost test can thus offer inadequate protection to an equally efficient rival *if* it is based on an average of the costs that are variable for the predator's entire output.

But this. . . . simply means one must be more precise in defining the relevant output whose costs can be varied. Since our purpose is to determine what cost measure would prevent a firm from excluding an equally efficient rival, the relevant costs that are variable are not the costs of producing the predator's entire output. They are rather the variable costs of the alleged predatory *increase* in output that displaces the *rival's* output. This is because the concern is rival exit (or nonentry), and thus the question is which firm is more efficient at producing the rival's output. . . . This measure of variable costs, in effect, is the sum of the marginal costs for the predatory increase in output, but can be measured more simply by comparing the costs at the higher output to the costs at the lower output, rather than by trying to calculate the marginal costs of producing the last item at each output level. Assuming marginal costs are increasing, this total variable cost figure (when divided by the increased output to give a per-unit figure) will give an average variable cost that is lower than the marginal cost of producing the *last* item that the alleged predator makes, but will still protect a rival that is equally efficient at making the relevant increment of output.

Accordingly, if the capital-intensive firm has increased output to displace its rival's output, we should look only to the higher variable costs of the allegedly predatory increase in output, not to the lower variable costs of producing the predator's entire output. Prices at or above those higher average variable costs cannot drive out a rival that is equally efficient at making that increment of output. If the capital-intensive firm's variable costs of increasing its output enough to displace the rival are lower than the rival's own variable costs of producing that output, then the rival is in fact not equally efficient at making its output. Rather, the rival output can more efficiently be supplied by an increase in the capital-intensive firm's output, even though it may be exceeding its optimal capacity. . . .

[T]his analysis . . . greatly simplifies the cost inquiry. Courts need not determine marginal costs or make complex judgment calls about which costs should be considered variable and which fixed and when to use one cost measure over another. . . . Instead, the relevant incremental costs are simply the difference between the actual total costs the incumbent incurred during the period of alleged predation and the total costs it would have incurred without the alleged predatory increase in output. Unless there has been some exogenous increase in input costs, this can often be determined by simply comparing total costs before and after the alleged predatory behavior. Dividing this by the alleged predatory increase in output converts this into a per-unit incremental cost, which then simply can be compared to the per-unit price the predator charged during the alleged period of predation. . . .

C–62/86, AKZO Chemie BV v. Commission

[1991] E.C.R. I–3359.

[Benzoyl peroxide is a substance used in two different applications: as an additive in flour milling in the United Kingdom and Ireland and in plastics manufacture. ECS supplied benzoyl peroxide as a flour additive, whereas AKZO supplied the substance for plastics application. ECS complained to the Commission that AKZO had used threats to drive ECS out of the flour additives market unless ECS refrained from selling benzoyl peroxide for plastics applications. ECS alleged that, in order to achieve its objective, AKZO had introduced discriminatory and predatory price cutting directed at ECS's customers for benzoyl peroxide as a flour additive with the view of excluding it of that market. The Commission found that AKZO sold between average variable costs and average total costs and condemned it for abuse of its dominant position. AKZO appealed the matter before the ECJ.]

... [A]s the Court held in ... *Hoffman–La Roche*, the concept of abuse is an objective concept relating to the behaviour of an undertaking in a dominant position which is such as to influence the structure of a market where, as a result of the very presence of the undertaking in question, the degree of competition is weakened and through recourse to methods which, different from those which condition normal competition in products or services on the basis of the transactions of commercial operators, has the effect of hindering the maintenance of the degree of competition still existing in the market or the growth of that competition.

It follows that Article [102] prohibits a dominant undertaking from eliminating a competitor and thereby strengthening its position by using methods other than those which come within the scope of competition on the basis of quality. From that point of view, however, not all competition by means of price can be regarded as legitimate.

Prices below average variable costs (that is to say, those which vary depending on the quantities produced) by means of which a dominant undertaking seeks to eliminate a competitor must be regarded as abusive. A dominant undertaking has no interest in applying such prices except that of eliminating competitors so as to enable it subsequently to raise its prices by taking advantage of its monopolistic position, since each sale generates a loss, namely the total amount of the fixed costs (that is to say, those which remain constant regardless of the quantities produced) and, at least, part of the variable costs relating to the unit produced.

Moreover, prices below average total costs, that is to say, fixed costs plus variable costs, but above average variable costs, must be regarded as abusive if they are determined as part of a plan for eliminating a competitor. Such prices can drive from the market undertakings which are perhaps as efficient as the dominant undertaking but which, because of their smaller financial resources, are incapable of withstanding the competition waged against them. These are the criteria that must be applied to the situation in the present case....

Note and Questions on AKZO

1. The ECJ indicates that it will condemn prices between average variable cost (AVC) and average total cost (ATC) when there is evidence of predatory intent, which is similar to the position taken by some U.S. lower appellate courts. Is this a sound policy?

    a. Could prices above AVC ever drive out an equally efficient rival?

    b. Shouldn't firms price above AVC but below ATC when. . . .

    i. the market has invested large capital costs to make a product and then is surprised by a drop in demand that creates a lot of excess capacity? Wouldn't pricing to try to cover those sunk capital costs harm consumer welfare and inefficiently encourage entry?

    ii. a dominant firm has economies of scale so that the costs of producing additional output are lower than the average costs of producing all its output?

    c. If there is some risk that intent will erroneously be adjudicated, won't this test sometimes deter firms from engaging in desirable pricing below ATC?

    2. Is it always easy to distinguish between fixed and variable costs?

    3. Should the test consider the effects of the price cuts and the possibility of recoupment?

Note and Questions on Recoupment Under EU Law

    In the *Tetra Pak II* case, the Commission found that Tetra Pak, which had a 90% market share of the aseptic cartons market, had engaged in predatory pricing in the market for non-aseptic cartons.[101] On appeal before the ECJ, Tetra Pak argued that the possibility of recouping the losses after the competitor's exit was a "constitutive element in the notion of predatory pricing."[102] Since the sales below cost took place in the non-aseptic cartons market, on which it did not have a dominant position, it had no realistic chance of recouping its losses later. The ECJ, however, rejected that argument and upheld the finding of predatory pricing, stating:

> "it would not be appropriate, *in the circumstances of the present case*, to require in addition proof that Tetra Pak had a realistic chance of recouping its losses. It must be possible to penalize predatory pricing whenever there is a risk that competitors will be eliminated".[103]

The italicized language suggests the ECJ position may be different in other sorts of cases.

    1. Do you agree with the position adopted by ECJ in *Tetra Pak II* that, unlike in the U.S., recoupment should not be required for below-cost predatory pricing?

    2. What does this suggest about how the ECJ views the ratio of overdeterrence to underdeterrence risks compared to the U.S. Supreme Court?

---

101. Case C–333/94P, Tetra Pak International SA v. Commission, [1996] E.C.R. I–5951.

102. *Id.* at ¶ 40.

103. *Id.* at ¶ 44 (emphasis added).

3. Might overdeterrence concerns be less in the EU given that market power and costs are determined by the European Commission rather than by lay juries, and that treble damages cannot be awarded for a violation?

Commission Decision 2001/354/EC of 20 March 2001, Deutsche Post AG

O.J. 2001, L 125/27.

United Parcel Service ("UPS") is a privately owned American corporation with its head office in Atlanta, Georgia. It is one of Deutsche Post AG's main competitors in respect of "business-to-business" or "B-to-B" parcel services. UPS states that it also provides some mail-order parcel services, the "business-to-consumer" or "B-to-C" parcel services. . . .

Deutsche Post AG (DPAG) [was formerly a state-owned postal service company that was privatized in 2000 but in which a German government-owned development bank continued to hold a controlling block of shares.] DPAG's main activity is the delivery of letter post. DPAG has a statutory exclusive right to the "reserved area", that is to say the conveyance of letters weighing less than 200 g. . . .

In [its] application . . ., UPS alleged that DPAG was using revenue from its profitable letter-post monopoly to finance a strategy of below-cost selling in parcel services, which are open to competition. Without the cross-subsidies from the reserved area, DPAG would not have been able to finance below-cost selling there for any length of time. The applicant therefore calls for a prohibition of sales below cost and the structural separation of the reserved area and the parcel services open to competition. Otherwise, UPS contends, an efficient firm would not be able to compete and at the same time cover the cost of providing parcel services, which are open to competition. . . . This Decision is concerned with DPAG's rebates and prices for mail-order parcel services in Germany. Parcel services, including mail-order parcel services, are not the subject of exclusive rights in Germany. Since about 1976 there have been competitors in Germany who have been supplying parcel services, mainly B-to-B services. Within commercial parcel services as a whole, easily the most important segment from DPAG's point of view is that of mail-order parcel services.

The applicant's main allegation is that DPAG offers its commercial parcel service at below-cost prices with the aim of ousting competitors from the market. DPAG covers the resultant losses with the aid of the profits made in the reserved area. This means that DPAG hinders competition by cross-subsidising commercial parcel services through the reserved letter-post services.

The relevant cost concepts. From an economic point of view cross-subsidisation occurs where the earnings from a given service do not suffice to cover the incremental costs of providing that service and where there is another service or bundle of services the earnings from which exceed the stand-alone costs. The service for which revenue exceeds stand-alone cost is the source of the cross subsidy and the service in which revenue does not cover the incremental costs is its destination. . . .

This means that, when establishing whether the incremental costs incurred in providing mail-order parcel services are covered, the additional costs of producing that service, incurred solely as a result of providing the service, must be distinguished from the common fixed costs, which are not incurred solely as a result of this service.

The impact of DPAG's public service obligation. When calculating the share of the common fixed costs it must be borne in mind that DPAG is required by law to maintain a capacity reserve large enough to cover any peak demands that may arise in over-the-counter parcel services while meeting statutory service-quality standards for those services. Even if DPAG were no longer to offer mail-order parcel services, it would still be obliged vis-a-vis every mail-order customer to provide catalogues and parcels over the counter within a specified delivery target. This follows from the universal service obligation whereby every potential postal user is entitled to receive from DPAG over-the-counter parcel services of the prescribed quality at uniform prices. If DPAG were to stop offering a specific parcel service, it could not, unlike a private firm such as UPS, cut back on staff and equipment in perfect proportion to the reduction in volume. Even if the specific parcel service were stopped, staff and equipment could not be reduced to the full extent of the cut in service, as some staff and equipment are also needed to provide over-the-counter services that meet statutory quality standards.... This obligation to maintain a reserve capacity is known in economic terms as the carrier of last resort.

Where DPAG maintains an infrastructure to fulfil its public service mission, a distinction must be made between the cost of maintaining capacity and the specific incremental costs of producing individual services:

—The costs of maintaining capacity arise independently of the services provided and the volume of parcels processed only as a consequence of maintaining capacity to allow everyone the standard option of having their parcels sent over-the-counter in the normal way. The legal obligation to remain ready to offer a standard parcel delivery service at a uniform tariff increases the proportion of common fixed costs that a carrier of last resort bears in comparison with companies who do not have this obligation. Costs arising from the legal obligation to maintain an option for everyone to have parcels carried at a geographically averaged tariff also arise even if commercial parcels not dealt with at the postal counter are discontinued. This means that these capacity costs are not attributable to a specific service and must be treated as DPAG's common fixed costs. Common fixed costs cease to exist only where the statutory obligation no longer applies,

—On the other hand costs that are attributable to a specific service arise only where services other than over-the-counter parcel services are provided. These costs, which are dependent on the volume posted and arise solely as a function of the specific service, cease to exist if the service at issue is stopped.

To avoid subsidising mail-order parcel services by using revenue from the reserved area, DPAG must earn revenue on this parcel service which at least covers the costs attributable to or incremental to producing the specific service. Emphasising the coverage of costs attributable to a particular service also makes it possible to take account of the additional burden incurred by DPAG as a result of fulfilling its statutory obligation of maintaining network reserve capacity. As this emphasis is expressly intended to take account of network capacity costs as an additional burden. DPAG is required only to cover the costs attributable to the provision of mail-order parcel services. This means that these operations are not burdened with the common fixed cost of providing network capacity that DPAG incurs as a result of its statutory universal service obligation.

The calculation of service-specific costs for mail-order parcel services. DPAG currently provides mail-order parcel services via its 33 outward and inward freight centres and 476 delivery points. DPAG refers to this infrastructure as its "freight branch".... DPAG uses the same infrastructure for its other commercial parcel services, including the B-to-B service. It also uses that infrastructure for parcels sent from one private person to another—"P-to-P" services, parcels handed in at post office counters and for mail-order returns—"P-to-B" services. Mail-order parcel services, however, account for 71% of the total volume of commercial parcel services every year. Its reserved letter-post services, on the other hand, operate largely through a separate infrastructure. The only exception is the joint delivery service. Mail-order parcels are processed in the following stages.

Collection: in the case of large mail-order customers, parcels are not processed at the post-office branches or agencies to be taken to the outward freight centre. Instead, they are collected by DPAG from the customer's premises and transported direct to the centre. If the mail-order parcel service is discontinued, all the costs of collection are fully attributable to the mail order service and would be saved.

Sorting: at the outward freight centre the sorting stage comprises the coding and sorting of parcels for transport to the inward freight centre. At the inward freight centre it comprises the sorting of incoming items for onward transport to the delivery points. Large mail-order customers carry out several of the steps involved in the sorting process themselves, such as, for example calculating the appropriate charge or attaching the barcode label. The capital costs of setting up the 33 freight centres and 476 delivery points cannot be attributed to a particular service. These costs will be incurred as long as the statutory obligation to meet demand to legally required service-quality standards applies. The staffing and equipment costs of sorting, on the other hand, are entirely dependent on the actual volume of parcels to be conveyed. Thus the staffing and equipment costs of activities dependent on the volume processed can be attributed in direct proportion to the mail order parcel service.

Long-distance transport consists of transport between the 33 inward and outward freight centres. Even if the volume is small, a certain amount of long-distance transport between the centres must continue in order to maintain the service-quality standards for counter parcels as laid down by law. Thus the costs of long-distance transport, in terms of staffing, equipment and capital, are not attributable to a particular service and can be eliminated only if the statutory obligation to serve no longer applies.

Regional and local transport between the 33 freight centres and the 476 delivery points. As regards regional and local transport between freight centres and delivery points, a fall in volume would allow some delivery points to be amalgamated. If mail order parcel services were discontinued, regional and local transport costs would be reduced by approximately half, because this percentage is attributable to mail order parcel services.

Delivery: after distribution to DPAG's 476 delivery points, mail-order parcels are delivered. Delivery consists essentially of driving and delivery proper. Half of the operation is taken up with driving, and half with delivery itself. Driving is not attributable to a specific service to the same extent as the delivery proper. The costs of handing over a parcel, on the other hand, are mostly attributable to a specific service. If a large-volume service where as a rule only one parcel is delivered when the delivery vehicle stops (as in the case of mail-order services) is discontinued, the cost of delivery can be attributed to the specific service and saved in its entirety if the particular stop is no longer necessary.

On the basis of the above analysis of the distribution between common fixed costs and costs that are attributable to a particular service, the average incremental costs per item for mail-order parcel services (AIC–MO) have been covered by revenue as of the year 1996. . . .

Predatory pricing. Predatory pricing occurs where a dominant firm sells a service below cost with the intention of eliminating competitors or deterring entry, enabling it to further increase its market power. Such unjustifiably low prices infringe Article [102]. According to the case-law of the European Court of Justice, pricing below average variable costs must be regarded as abusive. This principle was established in AKZO, where the Court defined average variable costs as "costs which vary depending on the quantities produced". In determining which costs vary depending on the quantities produced, the division between common fixed costs and costs attributable to a specific service set forth earlier must be borne in mind in DPAG's favour. Given the public universal service obligation, only the additional costs of providing a particular service vary with volume produced.

On the basis of relationship between the costs of maintaining capacity and the incremental costs of providing a particular service, the following may be said about DPAG's activities other than its over-the-counter business: In the period 1990 to 1995 DPAG's revenue from mail-order parcels was below the incremental costs of providing this specific service. This means that in the period 1990 to 1995 every sale by DPAG in the mail-order parcel services business represented a loss which comprises all the capacity-maintenance costs and at least part of the additional costs of providing the service. In such circumstances, every additional sale not only entailed the loss of at least part of these additional costs, but made no contribution towards covering the carrier's capacity-maintenance costs. In the medium term, such a pricing policy is not in the carrier's own economic interest. This being so, DPAG had no economic interest in offering such a service in the medium term. DPAG could increase its overall result by either raising prices to cover the additional costs of providing the service or—where there is no demand for this service at a higher price—to discontinue providing the service, because revenue gained from its provision is below the additional costs incurred in providing it. However, DPAG, by remaining in this market without any foreseeable improvement in revenue restricted the activities of competitors which are in a position to offer this service at a price that covers their costs.

Questions on *Deutsche Post*

The main feature of *Deutsche Post* is that the Commission relied on the long-run average incremental cost (LRAIC) of providing a service to determine the dominant firm in question engaged in predatory pricing in the provision of such service.

1. How did the Commission proceed to determine the LRAIC of DPAG's provision of parcel services?

2. Why didn't the Commission rely on the traditional *AKZO* test? Should some adjustment be made where, as here, a defendant could subsidize losses in the target market with profits earned on a market where it enjoys a government-protected monopoly? Is changing the cost test to LRAIC the right adjustment?

3. Some commentators have suggested that the AKZO test is under-inclusive in industries where variable costs tend to represent a small fraction of total costs. Should an exception to the AKZO test also be allowed in such industries? In such case, would the *Deutsche Post* LRAIC test represent a good alternative to AKZO?

Case T–340/03, France Télécom/Commission

In the context of the development of high-speed internet access, the Commission decided, in July 1999, to launch a sectoral inquiry within the European Union . . . which focused in particular on the provision of local loop access services and use of the residential local loop. Against this background, in the light of the information gathered the Commission decided to take a close look at the prices which Wanadoo Interactive SA ("WIN") charged its residential customers in France for high-speed internet access. To this end, it launched proceedings of its own initiative in September 2001 . . .

By decision of 16 July 2003 relating to a proceeding under Article [102 TFEU] (Case COMP/38.233—Wanadoo Interactive) ("the decision"), the Commission found that "[WIN] infringed Article [102] by charging for its eXtense and Wanadoo ADSL services predatory prices that did not enable it to cover its variable costs until August 2001 or to cover its full costs from August 2001 onwards, as part of a plan to pre-empt the market in high-speed internet access during a key phase in its development" (Article 1). The Commission ordered it to bring the infringement to an end (Article 2) and imposed a fine on it of EUR 10.35 million (Article 4). . . .

That decision was notified to WIN on 23 July 2003 and, by document lodged at the Registry of the [General Court] on 2 October 2003, WIN sought annulment of the decision. . . .

Following a merger on 1 September 2004, France Télécom succeeded to the rights of WIN. . . .

I—The claim for annulment of the decision

In support of its claim for annulment, the applicant puts forward a number of procedural pleas, breach of the principle that penalties must be specific to the offender and breach of Article [102 TFEU] . . .

2.   The abuse of a dominant position. . . .

(b) The complaints relating to the test of predation

According to WIN, the Commission's error of law and manifest errors of assessment in applying the test of predation should result in the annulment of the decision finding a breach of Article 102 TFEU. WIN argues that it had a right to align its prices on those of its competitors, that there was no plan of predation and reduction of competition, and it was necessary to show that its costs were recovered.

WIN's right to align its prices on its competitors' prices

— Arguments of the parties

According to WIN, the right of any operator to align its prices in good faith on those previously charged by a competitor is at the very heart of the competitive process. That right is recognised by the Commission itself in its previous decisions, in the case-law of the Court and in the unanimous teachings of academic literature and economic analysis. The fact that the prices charged by competitors correspond to prices which are below cost for the undertaking concerned is of no relevance in this respect. . . .

— Findings of the Court

. . . In the present case, the Commission takes the view that a dominant undertaking should not be permitted to align its prices where the costs of the service in question would not be recovered by the dominant undertaking.

It is therefore appropriate to examine whether that restriction is compatible with Community law.

It should be recalled that, according to established case-law, although the fact that an undertaking is in a dominant position cannot deprive it of the right to protect its own commercial interests if they are attacked and such an undertaking must be allowed the right to take such reasonable steps as it deems appropriate to protect those interests, such behaviour cannot be countenanced if its actual purpose is to strengthen this dominant position and abuse it.

The specific obligations imposed on undertakings in a dominant position have been confirmed by the case-law on a number of occasions. The Court stated in Case T–111/96 ITT Promedia v Commission [1998] ECR II–2937, paragraph 139, that it follows from the nature of the obligations imposed by Article 102 TFEU that, in specific circumstances, undertakings in a dominant position may be deprived of the right to adopt a course of conduct or take measures which are not in themselves abuses and which would even be unobjectionable if adopted or taken by non-dominant undertakings.

WIN cannot therefore rely on an absolute right to align its prices on those of its competitors in order to justify its conduct. Even if alignment of prices by a dominant undertaking on those of its competitors is not in itself abusive or objectionable, it might become so where it is aimed not only at protecting its interests but also at strengthening and abusing its dominant position.

Absence of a plan of predation and reduction in competition

— Arguments of the parties

According to WIN, predation presupposes a significant reduction in competition. In its view, if there is no possibility of ousting competitors, or, at the very least, of hindering or restraining their conduct, a strategy of predation can in no way be considered to be rational. Therefore, by sanctioning WIN even though it recognised that its market share fell significantly during the period of the alleged infringement and that competition at the end of the period covered was healthy, the Commission committed a serious infringement of Article 102 TFEU. WIN could not possibly drive its competitors out of the market by maintaining prices that were too low. In addition, since the barriers to entry in this sector are low, it is particularly irrational to seek to oust competitors in a market segment of this type, as this would mean, even if there was foreclosure, having to face possible entry at every moment, which would remove any possible interest in ousting competitors. . . .

— Findings of the Court

As regards the conditions for the application of Article [102 TFEU] and the distinction between the object and effect of the abuse, it should be pointed out that, for the purposes of applying that article, showing an anti-competitive object and an anti-competitive effect may, in some cases, be one and the same thing. If it is shown that the object pursued by the conduct of an undertaking in a dominant position is to restrict competition, that conduct will also be liable to have such an effect. Thus, with regard to the practices concerning prices, the Court of Justice held in AKZO v Commission that prices below average variable costs applied by an undertaking in a dominant position are regarded as abusive in themselves because the only interest which the undertaking may have in applying such prices is that of eliminating competitors, and that prices below average total costs but above average variable costs are abusive if they are determined as part of a plan for eliminating a competitor. In that case, the Court did not require any demonstration of the actual effects of the practices in question. *Michelin*.

Furthermore, it should be added that, where an undertaking in a dominant position actually implements a practice whose object is to oust a competitor, the fact that the result hoped for is not achieved is not sufficient to prevent that being an abuse of a dominant position within the meaning of Article 102 TFEU. *Compagnie maritime belge*; *Irish Sugar*.

[The judgment of the General Court was confirmed by the Court of Justice in Case C–202/07 P, Judgement of 2 April 2009.]

Questions on *France Télécom v. Commission*

1. The Court says that "WIN cannot . . . rely on an absolute right to align its prices on those of its competitors in order to justify its conduct."

a. Why shouldn't firms, whether dominant or non-dominant, be authorized as a matter of principle to match their competitors' prices?

b. Wouldn't this principle stimulate price competition? Or would it, on the contrary, impede it?

c. Absent the possibility to match its competitors' prices, isn't a dominant firm condemned to wait until it loses sufficient market shares to no longer be dominant before being again able to engage in price competition? Or does this perhaps give the firm incentives to reduce its costs and become more efficient?

2. The Court claims that "As regards the conditions for the application of Article [102 TFEU] and the distinction between the object and effect of the abuse, it should be pointed out that, for the purposes of applying that article, showing an anti-competitive object and an anti-competitive effect may, in some cases, be one and the same thing. If it is shown that the object pursued by the conduct of an undertaking in a dominant position is to restrict competition, that conduct will also be liable to have such an effect" and that "where an undertaking in a dominant position actually implements a practice whose object is to oust a competitor, the fact that the result hoped for is not achieved is not sufficient to prevent that being an abuse of a dominant position within the meaning of Article 102 TFEU."

a. Are these statements compatible with the "effects-based" approach put forward by the Commission in its Guidance Paper?

b. Should a dominant firm be found as abusing its dominant position when its market share fell significantly during the period of the alleged infringement?

Guidance on the Commission's Enforcement Priorities in Applying Article 82 EC Treaty [now 102 TFEU] to Abusive Exclusionary Conduct by Dominant Undertakings

(Dec. 2008).

. . . C. Predation

In line with its enforcement priorities, the Commission will generally intervene where there is evidence showing that a dominant undertaking engages in predatory conduct by deliberately incurring losses or foregoing profits in the short term (referred to hereafter as "sacrifice"), so as to foreclose or be likely to foreclose one or more of its actual or potential competitors with a view to strengthening or maintaining its market power, thereby causing consumer harm.

a) Sacrifice

Conduct will be viewed by the Commission as entailing a sacrifice if the dominant undertaking, by charging a lower price for all or a particular part of its output over the relevant time period, or by expanding its output over the relevant time period, incurred or is incurring losses that could have been avoided. The Commission will take AAC as the appropriate starting point for assessing whether the dominant firm incurs or incurred avoidable losses. If a dominant undertaking charges a price below AAC for all or part of its output, it is not recovering the costs that could have been avoided by not producing that output: it is incurring a loss that could have been avoided. Pricing below AAC will thus in most cases be viewed by the Commission as a clear indication of sacrifice.

However, the concept of sacrifice includes not just pricing below AAC. In order to show a predatory strategy, the Commission may also investigate whether the allegedly predatory conduct led in the short term to net revenues lower than could have been expected from a reasonable alternative conduct, i.e. whether the dominant undertaking incurred a loss that it could have avoided. The Commission will not compare the actual conduct with hypothetical or theoretical alternatives that might have been more profitable. Only economically rational and practicable alternatives will be considered which, taking into account the market conditions and business realities facing the dominant undertaking, can realistically be expected to be more profitable.

In some cases it will be possible to rely upon direct evidence consisting of documents from the dominant undertaking showing clearly a predatory strategy, such as a detailed plan to sacrifice in order to exclude a rival, to prevent entry or to pre-empt the emergence of a market, or evidence of concrete threats of predatory action

b) Anticompetitive foreclosure

If sufficient reliable data are available, the Commission will apply the as efficient competitor analysis, described in paragraphs 24–26, to determine whether the conduct is capable of harming consumers. Normally only pricing below LRAIC is capable of foreclosing as efficient competitors from the market.

In addition to the factors already mentioned in paragraph 20, the Commission will generally investigate whether and how the suspected conduct reduces the likelihood that rivals will compete. For instance, if the dominant firm is better informed about cost or other market conditions, or can distort market signals about profitability, it may predate so as to influence the expectations of potential entrants and thereby deter entry. If the conduct and its likely effects are felt on multiple markets and/or in successive periods of possible entry, the dominant firm may be shown to be seeking a reputation for predatory conduct. If the targeted competitor is dependent on external financing, substantial price decreases or other predatory conduct by the dominant firm could adversely affect the competitor's performance so that its access to further financing may be seriously undermined.

The Commission does not consider that it is necessary to show that competitors have exited the market in order to show that there has been anticompetitive foreclosure. It cannot be excluded that the dominant undertaking may prefer to prevent the competitor from competing vigorously and have it follow the dominant firm's pricing, rather than eliminate it from the market altogether. Such disciplining avoids the risk inherent in eliminating competitors, in particular the risk that the assets of the competitor are sold at a low price and stay in the market, creating a new low cost entrant.

Generally speaking, consumers are likely to be harmed if the dominant undertaking can reasonably expect its market power after the predatory conduct comes to an end to be greater than it would have been had the firm not engaged in that conduct in the first place, i.e. if the firm is likely to be in a position to benefit from the sacrifice.

This does not mean that the Commission will only intervene if the dominant firm would be likely to be able to increase its prices above the level persisting in the market before the conduct. It is sufficient, for instance, that the conduct would be likely to prevent or delay a decline in prices that would otherwise have occurred. Identifying consumer harm is not a mechanical calculation of profits and losses, and proof of overall profits is not required. Likely consumer harm may be demonstrated by assessing the likely foreclosure effect of the conduct, combined with consideration of other factors, such as entry barriers. In this context, the Commission will also consider possibilities of re-entry.

It may be easier for the dominant undertaking to predate if it selectively targets specific customers with low prices, as this will limit the losses incurred by the dominant undertaking.

It is less likely that the dominant undertaking predates if the conduct concerns a low price applied generally for a long period of time.

c) Efficiencies

In general it is considered unlikely that predation will create efficiencies. However, provided that the conditions mentioned in Section III D above are fulfilled, the Commission will consider claims by dominant undertakings that the low pricing enables it to achieve economies of scale or efficiencies related to expanding the market.

Questions on the Commission's Guidance Paper

1. The Guidance Paper indicates that it will intervene in the presence of profit sacrifice leading to foreclosure of competitors. As to profit sacrifice, the Guidance Paper adopts average avoidable costs (AAC) as its presumptive benchmark, but defines it in a way similar to the tests of Justice Breyer and Professor Elhauge, "the average of the costs that could have been avoided if the company had not produced a discrete amount of (extra) output, in this case usually the amount allegedly subject to abusive conduct."

a. Is this benchmark in line with the average variable cost (AVC) benchmark adopted by the ECJ in *AKZO*?

i. Did ECJ there ever consider possible issues about the time period or portion of output to consider in assessing average variable costs? Doesn't the AAC test effectively just specify the time period and output over which costs must be variable?

ii. If one uses an AVC test, how does one determine the relevant time period and output to consider? If not linked to the period or output that is allegedly predatory, won't any such test be over- or underinclusive in particular cases?

b. Could there be benign explanations for prices below AAC, such as (i) promotional discounts on new products or services that the dominant firm wants consumers to try; (ii) situations where learning curve economies mean that production costs will be lower as the supplier gains experience in producing the product, so that it is worth pricing initially low in order to get the production; and (iii) situations of loss-leading or two-sided markets where the making of one sale at below cost is commercially justified by the follow-on or related market sales that are anticipated as a result?

i. Do cases (i) or (ii) really involve predatory pricing on any market in which the firm is dominant? Is such short-term pricing likely to have the requisite foreclosing effect on rivals?

ii. Does case (iii) really just mean the related market sales should be coupled in a way that shows the combined pricing is not below the combined costs?

iii. Is the Guidance Paper willing to consider these situations as justifications for prices below AAC?

c. Couldn't below-AAC prices simply reflect commercial misjudgment on the part of a dominant firm? If so, would this be a valid justification?

2. The Guidance Paper indicates that the concept of sacrifice can include pricing above AAC and that to show predatory pricing "the Commission may also investigate whether the allegedly predatory conduct led in the short term to net revenues lower than could have been expected from a reasonable alternative conduct, i.e. whether the dominant undertaking incurred a loss that it could have avoided."

a. Is this test supported by the case law of the ECJ?

b. Isn't it completely open ended?

i. Can't it always be argued that an alternative conduct would have been more profitable than the one adopted by the dominant firm?

ii. In any event, are antitrust law officials well placed to make these kinds of calls?

3. The Guidance Paper indicates that "consumers are likely to be harmed if the dominant undertaking can reasonably expect its market power after the predatory conduct comes to an end to be greater than it would have been had the firm not engaged in that conduct in the first place, i.e. if the firm is likely to be in a position to benefit from the sacrifice."

a. Does this mean that the Commission has introduced a recoupment test?

b. Do you think that proof of recoupment is necessary/desirable in predatory pricing cases?

4. Is the Guidance Paper right that there is hardly ever an efficiency defense to predatory pricing? Where the pricing is above AAC, should the increased allocative efficiency be deemed an efficiency defense? Or does only an increase in productive efficiency count as an efficiency defense?

Below–Cost Predatory Pricing in Other Nations

Other nations vary in the tests they use to define below-cost predatory pricing. Brazil, Egypt and India use marginal or average variable cost as the cost measure.[104] Canada uses average avoidable cost.[105] One Japanese statute uses average avoidable costs while another covers pricing between average avoidable costs and average total costs when other factors suggest the pricing would harm the fair competition order.[106] Mexico prohibits pricing "systematically" below average total cost as well as pricing "occasionally" below average variable cost.[107] Singapore and Turkey presume pricing below average variable cost is predatory and that pricing between average variable cost and average total cost may be predatory depending on whether the pricing had an anticompetitive purpose.[108] South Africa presumes that pricing below marginal or average variable costs is anticompetitive, but that pricing below another "appropriate measure of costs" for a "sustained period" can also be predatory if shown to be anticompetitive.[109] Australia, China, Colombia, Russia, and Saudi Arabia define predatory pricing as pricing below "cost" or "the relevant cost" without defining those costs.[110] Israel, Indonesia, South Korea, and Taiwan define predatory pricing more vaguely as pricing that is "unfair," "unreasonable," "very low," "much lower than cost," or "excessively" below cost, although some

---

104. *See* Brazil CADE Resolution 20, Attachment I, § 4 (1999) (average variable cost); Competition Commission of India (Determination of Cost of Production) Regulations § 3 (2009) (generally average variable cost, as a proxy for marginal cost); Egypt Competition Law Art 8(h) ("Selling products below their marginal cost or average variable cost.")

105. *See* Canada Competition Bureau, Predatory Pricing Enforcement Guidelines §§ 4.1–4.3 (2008) (pricing below average avoidable cost is predatory absent a legitimate business justification).

106. Japan Antimonopoly Law § 2(9)(iii) (2009), condemns unjustified pricing "excessively below the costs required for the supply" that impairs rivals, while Japan General Designations of Unfair Trade Practices § 6 (2009) states that it also covers "unjustly supplying goods or services for a low consideration" when that impairs rivals. Japanese Guidelines interpret the first to mean pricing below average avoidable costs and the latter to also cover pricing between those costs and average total costs if the price cutting harms the fair competition order considering the purpose, effects, and other factors. *See* Japan Guidelines Concerning Unjust Low Price Sales under the Antimonopoly Act at 5–6, 10–11 (2009).

107. Mexico Federal Economic Competition Law, Art. 10 (VII).

108. Singapore Guidelines on the Section 47 Prohibition § 11.4 (2007); Habas Decision, No. 06–66/887–256 (Turkey Competition Authority 2006).

109. South Africa Competition Act § 8(d)(iv); Nationwide Airlines v. South Africa Airways, 92/IR/OCT00, at 13 (South Africa Competition Tribunal) (interpreting § 8(c)).

110. *See* Australia Trade Practices Act § 46(1AA) (pricing at "less than the relevant cost" for an anticompetitive purpose); China Anti–Monopoly Law Art. 17 (pricing "below cost without any justifiable cause"); Colombia Decree 2153/92, Art. 50 (pricing below cost for purpose of excluding rivals); Russia Competition Law Art. 7(1) ("price is below the sum of the necessary production and distribution costs of the goods and profit, and is below the price formed under competitive conditions in the goods market"); Saudi Arabia Competition Law, Art. 5(1) ("price below cost, with the intention of forcing competitors out of the market").

of those terms may be interpreted to incorporate some cost measure, just as similar terms were interpreted in Japan.[111] Which cost measure seems best?

On recoupment, there is a international conflict that parallels the US–EC conflict. Canada, Mexico, New Zealand, Switzerland, and Taiwan have adopted a recoupment requirement.[112] Australia and South Africa have rejected it.[113] Most nations have not yet taken a position on this issue. Which approach seems right? Should the answer depend on the extent to which the nation's remedies raise overdeterrence concerns?

b.   ABOVE–COST PREDATORY PRICING

Although it might seem intuitive that predatory prices must be below-cost, in fact some lawmakers and scholars have concluded that certain above-cost price cuts should also be unlawful, whether or not we call them "predatory." Usually, the concern arises in markets where an incumbent dominant firm sells at a price well above its costs. Periodically, a new firm enters the market at a lower price. The incumbent dominant firm then lowers its price to beat (or match) the entrant. The incumbent never prices

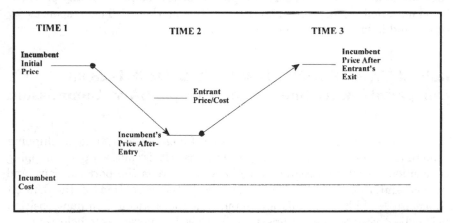

below its own costs. But because the entrant has higher costs (or lower quality), it cannot compete at the new price and is driven out of the market. Once the less efficient entrant is safely gone, the incumbent reestablishes the old price.

---

111. *See* Israel Restrictive Trade Practices Law § 29A ("unfair" pricing that might reduce competition or injure the public.); Indonesia Competition Law Art. 20 ("selling without making any profits" or "setting a very low price with the intention to eliminate or end their competitors' business"); Annex I.3.A. of the Enforcement Decree of the South Korea Fair Trade Act (pricing "excessively" below cost "without proper justification" when that could threaten to "exclude" competitors); OECD, Predatory Foreclosure 243 (2005) (Taiwan defines a predatory price as a price "much lower than cost").

112. *See* Canada Competition Bureau, Predatory Pricing Enforcement Guidelines at i–iii, § 5.1 (2008); OECD, Predatory Foreclosure 172, 188, 209, 243–44 (2005) (Mexico, New Zealand, Switzerland, and Taiwan).

113. Australia Trade Practices Act § 46(1AAA); OECD, Predatory Foreclosure 166 (2005) (South Korea); Nationwide Airlines v. South Africa Airways, 92/IR/OCT00, at 13 (South Africa Competition Tribunal).

The concern is that such reactive temporary price cuts will not only drive out entrants, but deter similar entry in the future, and thus allow the more efficient incumbent to perpetuate monopoly prices that exceed the price the next most efficient firm would charge. If so, the supposedly certain gains from short-run post-entry price competition never arrive because the entry never occurs, and the long-term loss is experienced with certainty every day. This concern can exist in any industry where incumbent firms are more efficient than potential entrants and exploit their market power (when entrants are not present) to charge prices well above incumbent costs. Indeed, if valid, this concern would overturn a general current skepticism based on the presumption that predatory pricing is rare because it requires the incumbent to sustain losses on a large number of sales. If harmful predation involved profitable above-cost pricing, it would be far more plausible and prevalent.

In academic scholarship, this has led to proposals by prominent economists to either (1) prevent monopolists from cutting price or raising output in response to entry at all, (2) ban such price cuts or output increases when they would not maximize short run profits, or (3) require that any price cut be maintained even after entrants left the market.[114] The responses by courts and lawmakers include the following.

Joined Cases T–24/93, T–25/93, T–26/93 & T–28/93, Compagnie Maritime Belge Transps. SA v. Commission

1996 E.C.R. II (CFI).

... Associated Central West Africa Lines ("Cewal") is a shipping conference whose secretariat is in Antwerp. It is made up of shipping companies operating a regular liner service between the ports of Zaïre and Angola and those of the North Sea, with the exception of the United Kingdom.... [T]he Commission found that there was a dominant position held collectively by the members of the Cewal conference. It held that ... the conference [violated Article 102 by] ... altering the conference's freight rates with respect to the rates in force so as to obtain rates identical to or lower than those charged by the main independent competitor for ships sailing on the same or similar dates (a practice known as "fighting ships")....

The Court observes that the Commission identified three factors constituting the practice of fighting ships used by members of Cewal to drive out its competitor G & C, namely: designating as fighting ships those Cewal vessels whose sailing dates were closest to the sailings of G & C ships without altering its scheduled timetables; jointly fixing fighting rates different from the rates normally charged by Cewal members so that they were the same or lower than G & C's advertised prices; and the resulting decrease in earnings, which was borne by Cewal's members.... The

---

114. Elhauge, *supra* note 33, at 684–85 (collecting sources).

applicants complain that the ... practice in question was different from that of predatory pricing.

... [T]he applicants do not contest that the three criteria constituting the test for the practice of fighting ships, as adopted by the Commission, were satisfied. ... [They argue] that the practice, as so defined, does not constitute an abuse of a dominant position within the meaning of Article [102 TFEU].

In the first place, they assert ... that the practice of which the Commission accuses them does not correspond with the definition which, in their view, is generally employed when the practice in question is penalized as anti-competitive. That argument cannot be accepted. The Court considers that it is not necessary to decide whether or not the definition employed by the Commission corresponds with other definitions put forward by the applicants. The only question is whether the practice as the Commission defined it in its decision, without being contradicted by the citations of learned writings and legislation embodied in the Decision, constitutes an abuse of a dominant position within the meaning of Article [102 TFEU].

Secondly, the applicants maintain that the Commission has failed to prove that they exceeded what is normal in competition in implementing the practice complained of.

As has already been pointed out, it has been consistently held that whilst the fact that an undertaking is in a dominant position cannot deprive it of entitlement to protect its own commercial interests if they are attacked; and whilst such an undertaking must be allowed the right to take such reasonable steps as it deems appropriate to protect those interests, such behaviour cannot be allowed if its real purpose is to strengthen this dominant position and thereby abuse it. . . .

In this regard, the Court considers, having regard in particular to the minutes of the Special Fighting Committee ... which refer to "getting rid" of the independent shipping operation, that the Commission has established to a sufficient legal standard that that practice was carried out with a view to removing Cewal's only competitor on the relevant market. In addition, the Court considers that whilst the mere name given to the practice used by the members of Cewal is not sufficient to characterize it as an infringement of Article [102], the Commission was entitled to regard the use by professionals in the international maritime transport sector of a well-known description in that sector of activity and the establishment of a Special Fighting Committee within the conference as disclosing an intention to implement a practice designed to affect the operation of competition.

Since the purpose of the practice was to remove their only competitor, the Court considers that the applicants cannot effectively argue that they merely reacted to an infringement by G & C of the monopoly legally granted to Cewal, compensated for discrimination which they suffered at the hands of Ogefrem, entered into a price war started by the competitor or even responded to expectations of their customers. Even assuming them to be proven, those circumstances could not render the response put into effect by the members of Cewal reasonable and proportionate.

Thirdly, the applicants rely on the increase in G & C's market share in order to maintain that the practice complained of had no effect and hence that there was no abuse of a dominant position. The Court however considers that, where one or more undertakings in a dominant position actually implement a practice whose aim is to remove a competitor, the fact that the result sought is not achieved is not enough to avoid the practice being characterized as an abuse of a dominant position within the meaning of Article [102] of the Treaty. Besides, contrary to the applicants' assertions, the fact that G & C's market share increased does not mean that the practice was without any effect, given that, if the practice had not been implemented, G & C's share might have increased more significantly. . . .

In the light of all those factors, the Court considers that the Commission was lawfully entitled to conclude that the practice of fighting ships, as defined in the Decision, constituted an abuse of a dominant position within the meaning of Article [102] of the Treaty.

Joined Cases C–395/96 P & C–396/96 P, Compagnie Maritime Belge Transps. SA v. Commission

2000 E.C.R. I–1365 (E.C.J.).

. . . The maritime transport market is a very specialised sector. It is because of the specificity of that market that the Council established, in Regulation No 4056/86, a set of competition rules different from that which applies to other economic sectors. The authorisation granted for an unlimited period to liner conferences to cooperate in fixing rates for maritime transport is exceptional in light of the relevant regulations and competition policy.

It is clear from the eighth recital in the preamble to Regulation No 4056/86 that the authorisation to fix rates was granted to liner conferences because of their stabilising effect and their contribution to providing adequate efficient scheduled maritime transport services. The result may be that, where a single liner conference has a dominant position on a particular market, the user of those services would have little interest in resorting to an independent competitor, unless the competitor were able to offer prices lower than those of the liner conference.

It follows that, where a liner conference in a dominant position selectively cuts its prices in order deliberately to match those of a competitor, it derives a dual benefit. First, it eliminates the principal, and possibly the only, means of competition open to the competing undertaking. Second, it can continue to require its users to pay higher prices for the services which are not threatened by that competition.

It is not necessary, in the present case, to rule generally on the circumstances in which a liner conference may legitimately, on a case by case basis, adopt lower prices than those of its advertised tariff in order to compete with a competitor who quotes lower prices . . .

It is sufficient to recall that the conduct at issue here is that of a conference having a share of over 90% of the market in question and only one competitor. The appellants have, moreover, never seriously disputed, and indeed admitted at the hearing, that the purpose of the conduct complained of was to eliminate G & C from the market.

The [General Court] did not, therefore, err in law, in holding that the Commission's objections to the effect that the practice known as fighting ships, as applied against G & C, constituted an abuse of a dominant position were justified. . . .

Note and Questions on *Compagnie Maritime*

The Commission's test relied on three factors: (1) the price cuts were reactive and selective, having been adopted in response to entry and only for those ships whose sailing dates directly competed with the entrant; (2) the reduced prices met (and once beat) the entrant; and (3) the price cuts reduced defendant profits compared to what they would have been with higher prices. The Commission got around *AKZO* by saying that, although this practice was not "predatory" pricing, it was nonetheless abusive. The General Court affirmed this theory, but also suggested the alternative theory that any above-cost price cut whose "real purpose" was to strengthen a dominant position by eliminating a competitor was illegal. The European Court of Justice declined to rule generally on when it was illegal for a dominant firm to make selective above-cost price cuts to meet a entrant, but held that at a minimum such selective price cuts were illegal when the firm had over 90% market share and had the avowed purpose of eliminating the entrant. As this suggests, there is a large range of doctrinal possibilities for defining which above-cost price cuts to prohibit.

1. Can an above-cost price cut ever eliminate an equally-efficient rival? If not, why should it ever be illegal?

a. Could a legal restriction on reactive above-cost price cuts encourage incumbent monopolists to charge everyday prices that are no greater than the costs of the next-most efficient firm?

b. Could a restriction on reactive above-cost price cuts also encourage entry that might eventually produce a rival as efficient as the incumbent?

2. Won't post-entry prices be raised by a legal restriction on above-cost price cuts in response to entry?

a. If the entrant would have entered anyway isn't this effect affirmatively harmful?

b. If the entrant would not have entered unless above-cost price cuts are restricted, is this post-entry effect relevant?

c. What proportion of entry do you think would be influenced by the existence of a legal restriction on above-cost price cuts?

i. Would such a restriction affect entry by entrants that are equally or more efficient than the incumbent?

ii. Would such a restriction affect entry by less-efficient entrants if the costs of entry are low enough that they would be exceeded by profits in the post-entry period before the incumbent can expand output enough to take away the entrants' sales?

3. If the law does restrict reactive above-cost price cuts, how long should it prevent the incumbent monopolist from cutting prices in response to entry?

a. If the restriction were indefinite, what would happen? Would that be desirable?

b. If the restriction expired at some point, wouldn't the incumbent then be able to drive out any less-efficient entrant?

i. If so, doesn't the fact that the restriction provides only temporary protection reduce the proportion of less-efficient firms whose entry would be induced by such a restriction? Won't the restriction cause additional entry only for those less-efficient entrants whose entry costs are in an intermediate range that is (a) high enough that they could not have been recouped in the short period before the incumbent could expand without a restriction but (b) low enough that they could be recouped in the somewhat longer period provided by the restriction?

ii. If the entrant would become more efficient over time, why wouldn't it be able to raise the initial capital to overcome its learning curve costs?

4. All the cases and scholarly proposals on restricting above-cost predation are limited to price or output changes made in response to entry.

a. Suppose entry is foreseeable before it actually occurs because it takes planning. Couldn't an incumbent monopolist evade the restriction by simply lowering prices before actual entry? If one tried to avoid this problem by defining "the moment of entry" as the moment when entry was first foreseeable, what problems might that create?

b. What if a monopolist responds to entry by increasing quality? Should that be restricted too? What problems would arise if quality changes were restricted? What problems would arise if quality changes were not restricted but price and output changes were?

c. If restricting above-cost price cuts in response to entry is desirable, why isn't it equally desirable to restrict "limit prices," which are intentionally designed to exclude rivals by setting prices below the costs of entrants even though that price is lower than the incumbent monopolist's short-term profit-maximizing price? Isn't the exclusionary purpose and effect on entrants the same? Is the effect on consumers the same?

5. What would any legal restrictions on above-cost price cuts do to incentives to create a dominant firm that is so much more efficient than other market options that it enjoys monopoly power? Without a restriction, might the incentives to create such a dominant firm be excessive?

6. Why should the selectiveness of a reactive above-cost price cut matter?

a. Couldn't a uniform above-cost price cut have the same anticompetitive effect of driving out entrants?

b. If a selective price cut really does not alter prices elsewhere, doesn't that mean the selected area must be its own market?

c. Doesn't the selectivity of an above-cost price cut show that prices in other markets must be further above costs, and thus excessive under EU law? Could we understand the EU doctrine against selective price cuts as an indirect way to get an excessive pricing in a world where it is administratively difficult to administer direct price regulation through antitrust authorities and easier to determine when price cuts are selective?

d. Even if not independently important, is the selectivity of the price cut important as an evidentiary matter because it:

    i. helps provide an objective benchmark as to what price level does maximize short-run profits? Doesn't the short-term profit-maximizing price in a market with an entrant differ from that price in other areas where there is no competitor?

    ii. helps dismiss the possibility that the price cut was prompted by some cost reduction rather than by entry? But should that suffice if entry has changed the profit-maximizing price?

7. Should proof of an intent to drive out the entrant matter? Don't all dominant firms have such a desire? Should such an intent by a dominant firm suffice to make a reactive above-cost price cut illegal without proving the price cut was selective? What if a monopolist cut prices both because doing so was profit-maximizing given the entry and because it desired to drive out the entrant?

8. The opinion of Advocate General Fenelly on this case stated that proof of recoupment should be a necessary element. Is there good reason to make recoupment necessary to prove above-cost predation even though *Tetra Pak II* held it inapplicable to a below-cost predation claim?

Case T–228/97, Irish Sugar PLC v. Commission

1999 E.C.R. II–2969 (CFI).

This action challenges [a] Commission Decision . . . in which the applicant, the sole processor of sugarbeet in Ireland and the principal supplier of sugar in that Member State, was fined for infringing Article [102 TFEU]. The product forming the subject-matter of the contested decision is white granulated sugar, on both the industrial sugar market and the retail sugar market. . . .

. . . The Commission [found] . . . that, in order to meet competition from imports of sugar from Northern Ireland or from its own reimported sugar . . . the applicant . . . granted rebates to retailers established along the border [between Ireland and North Ireland]. . . . The Commission . . . concludes . . . that:

"... Moreover, this rebate was intended to and did deter imports of sugar from Northern Ireland, ... thus limiting markets to the prejudice of customers. The border rebate therefore forms part of a policy of dividing markets and excluding competitors. The rebate was not based on an objective economic justification, such as the quantities purchased by the customer, marketing and transport costs or any promotional, warehousing, servicing or other functions which the relevant customer might have performed. It was granted on the sole basis of the retailer's place of business, in particular whether or not the relevant customer is established in the border area with Northern Ireland. Such a practice of selective or discriminatory pricing has been condemned by the Commission and the Court of Justice in earlier cases." . . .

. . . [B]etween 1985 and 1995 [the applicant] held a dominant position on the retail sugar market, on which it carried out more than 88% of sales throughout the whole of that period . . . In the particular circumstances of the case, the applicant cannot rely . . . either on the pricing policy of operators on the British market, or on its financial situation, or on the defensive nature of its conduct . . .

First of all, the influence of the pricing policy of operators active principally on a neighbouring market, in this case the British and Northern Ireland market, on that of operators active on another national market is of the very essence of a common market. Anything which restricts that influence must therefore be regarded as an obstacle to the achievement of that common market and prejudicial to the outcome of effective and undistorted competition, especially with regard to the interests of consumers. Therefore, where such obstacles are brought about by an undertaking holding a dominant position as extensive as that enjoyed by the applicant, that is an abuse incompatible with Article [102]. The applicant has, moreover, nowhere argued that the prices charged by its competitors along the border with Northern Ireland were below the cost price of the product, or supplied any evidence to that effect.

Secondly, the applicant cannot rely on the insufficiency of the financial resources at its disposal at the time to justify the selective and discriminatory granting of those border rebates and thereby escape the application of Article [102], without making a dead letter of the prohibition contained in that article. The circumstances in which an undertaking in a dominant position may be led to react to the limited competition which exists on the market, especially where that undertaking holds more than 88% of the market as in this case, form part of the competitive process which Article [102] is precisely designed to protect. Moreover, the applicant has several times underlined the high level of retail sale prices in Ireland, explaining it by the influence of the high level of the guaranteed intervention price in the context of the common organisation of the market in sugar.

Finally, the defensive nature of the practice complained of in this case cannot alter the fact that it constitutes an abuse for the purposes of Article [102(c)]. In this case, the applicant has been unable to establish an objective economic justification for the rebates. They were given to certain customers in the retail sugar market by reference solely to their exposure to competition resulting from cheap imports from another Member State and, in this case, by reference to their being established along the border with Northern Ireland. It also appears, according to the applicant's own statements, that it was able to practise such price rebates owing to the particular position it held on the Irish market. Thus it states that it was unable to practice such rebates over the whole of Irish territory owing to the financial losses it was making at the time. It follows that, by the applicant's own admission, its economic capacity to offer rebates in the region along the border with Northern Ireland depended on the stability of its prices in other regions, which amounts to recognition that it financed those rebates by means of its sales in the rest of Irish territory. By conducting itself in that way, the applicant abused its dominant position in the retail sugar market in Ireland, by preventing the development of free competition on that market and distorting its structures, in relation to both purchasers and consumers. The latter were not able to benefit, outside the region along the border with Northern Ireland, from the price reductions caused by the imports of sugar from Northern Ireland. . . .

It should be added that, contrary to what the applicant suggests, the Commission did not rely on the mere withdrawal of a competitor from the market as proof of the abusive nature of the border rebates. Moreover, where an undertaking in a dominant position actually implements a practice aimed at ousting a competitor, the fact that the result hoped for is not achieved is not sufficient to prevent that being an abuse of a dominant position within the meaning of Article [102] (*Compagnie Maritime*). In so far as the border rebates were aimed at securing the loyalty of purchasers exposed to offers from competitors, without enabling all the applicant's customers to benefit from the impact of competition on the sale prices of its products, the removal of a competitor following such a practice illustrates all the better the fact that it was an abuse within the meaning of Article [102]. . . .

Questions on *Irish Sugar*

1. Should it be a defense to a claim of selective price above-cost cuts that are intended to drive out an entrant that . . .

   a.   the price cut just matched the entrant's price?

   i.   Won't meeting be like undercutting if the incumbent product's quality or brand is better?

   ii.   If the law allowed a defense of meeting competition, wouldn't it have to allow the incumbent to price below the entrant when the entrant quality was higher? Could adjudication effectively monitor over time whether any price gap equals the value consumers put on any quality gap?

   b.   the price cut was justified by lower costs in that area?

   c.   the entrant was pricing below its own costs?

   d.   the incumbent kept the lower price in place after the entrant left the market?

2. Would your answers to any of the above defenses be the same if the price cut were below cost?

3. *Compagnie Maritime Belge* and *Irish Sugar* seem to suggest that firms with very high market shares (sometimes referred to as "superdominant") should be held to higher standards than firms that have merely sufficiently high market shares to be considered as dominant (e.g., 50%).

   i.   Does such a difference of treatment seem desirable?

ii.   Even if such a difference was desirable, how would you distinguish between dominant firms and superdominant firms?

4.   One factor taken into account by the ECJ in *Irish Sugar* was that Irish Sugar's pricing policy sought to restrict the possible imports of sugar from neighboring markets (Britain and Northern Ireland). Thus, the rebates in question were not only abusive, but they also prevented trade between Member States.

a.   Would that type of consideration (i.e., the risk of market partitioning along state lines) be considered relevant by a U.S. federal court in an antitrust case?

b.   Does your response to the last question suggest a difference in the objectives of EU competition law and U.S. antitrust law?

Enforcement Policy Regarding Unfair Exclusionary Conduct in the Air Transportation Industry

63 Fed. Reg. 17,919 (proposed Apr. 10, 1998).

. . . Following Congress's deregulation of the air transportation industry in 1978, all of the major air carriers restructured their route systems into "hub-and-spoke" networks. Major carriers have long charged considerably higher fares in most of their "spoke" city-pairs, or the "local hub markets," than in other city-pairs of comparable distance and density. In recent years, when small, new-entrant carriers have instituted new low-fare service in major carriers' local hub markets, the major carriers have increasingly responded with strategies of price reductions and capacity increases designed not to maximize their own profits but rather to deprive the new entrants of vital traffic and revenues. Once a new entrant has ceased its service, the major carrier will typically retrench its capacity in the market or raise its fares to at least their pre-entry levels, or both. The major carrier thus accepts lower profits in the short run in order to secure higher profits in the long run. This strategy can benefit the major carrier prospectively as well, in that it dissuades other carriers from attempting low-fare entry. It can hurt consumers in the long run by depriving them of the benefits of competition. In those instances where the major carrier's strategy amounts to unfair competition, we must take enforcement action in order to preserve the competitive process.

We hereby put all air carriers on notice, therefore, that as a matter of policy, we propose to consider that a major carrier is engaging in unfair exclusionary practices in violation of 49 U.S.C. 41712 if, in response to new entry into one or more of its local hub markets, it pursues a strategy of price cuts or capacity increases, or both, that either (1) causes it to forego more revenue than all of the new entrant's capacity could have diverted from it or (2) results in substantially lower operating profits—or greater operating losses—in the short run than would a reasonable alternative strategy for competing with the new entrant. Any strategy this costly to the major carrier in the short term is economically rational only if it eventually forces the new entrant to exit the market, after which the major carrier can readily recoup the revenues it has sacrificed to achieve this end. . . .

The Department's Mandate

Our mandate under 49 U.S.C. 41712 to prohibit unfair methods of competition authorizes us to stop air carriers from engaging in conduct that can be characterized as anticompetitive under antitrust principles even if it does not amount to a violation of the antitrust laws. The unfair exclusionary behavior we address here is analogous to (and may amount to) predation within the meaning of the federal antitrust laws.

Although the Supreme Court has said that predation rarely occurs and is even more rarely successful, our informal investigations suggest that the nature of the air transportation industry can at a minimum allow unfair exclusionary practices to succeed. Compared to firms in other industries, a major air carrier can price-discriminate to a much greater extent, adjust prices much faster, and shift resources between markets much more readily. Through booking and other data generated by computer reservations systems and other sources, air carriers have access to comprehensive, "real time" information on their competitors' activities and can thus respond to competitive initiatives more precisely and swiftly than firms in other industries. In addition, a major carrier's ability to shift assets quickly between markets allows it to increase service frequency and capture a disproportionate share of traffic, thereby reaping the competitive advantage of the S–Curve effect. These characteristics of the air transportation industry allow the major carrier to drive a new entrant from a local hub market. Having observed this behavior, other potential new entrants refrain from entering, leaving the major carrier free to reap greater profits indefinitely.

Enforcement Action

We will determine whether major carriers have engaged in unfair exclusionary practices on a case-by-case basis ... We anticipate that in the absence of strong reasons to believe that a major carrier's response to competition from a new entrant does not violate 49 U.S.C. 41712, we will institute enforcement proceedings to determine whether the carrier has engaged in unfair exclusionary practices when one or more of the following occurs:

(1) The major carrier adds capacity and sells such a large number of seats at very low fares that the ensuing self-diversion of revenue results in lower local revenue than would a reasonable alternative response,

(2) The number of local passengers that the major carrier carries at the new entrant's low fares (or at similar fares that are substantially below the major carrier's previous fares) exceeds the new entrant's total seat capacity, resulting, through self-diversion, in lower local revenue than would a reasonable alternative response, or

(3) The number of local passengers that the major carrier carries at the new entrant's low fares (or at similar fares that are substantially below the major carrier's previous fares) exceeds the number of low-fare passengers carried by the new entrant, resulting, through self-

diversion, in lower local revenue than would a reasonable alternative response.

As the term "reasonable alternative response" suggests, we by no means intend to discourage major carriers from competing aggressively against new entrants in their hub markets. A major carrier can minimize or even avoid self-diversion of local revenues, for example, by matching the new entrant's low fares on a restricted basis (and without significantly increasing capacity) and relying on its own service advantages to retain high-fare traffic. We have seen that major carriers can operate profitably in the same markets as low-fare carriers. As noted, major carriers are competing with Southwest, the most successful low-fare carrier, on a broad scale and are nevertheless reporting record or near-record earnings. We will consider whether a major carrier's response to new entry is consistent with its behavior in markets where it competes with other new-entrant carriers or with Southwest. Conceivably, a major carrier could both lower its fares and add capacity in response to competition from a new entrant without any inordinate sacrifice in local revenues. If the new entrant remained in the market, consumers would reap great benefits from the resulting competition, and we would not intercede. Conceivably, too, a new entrant's service might fail for legitimate competitive reasons: our enforcement policy will not guarantee new entrants success or even survival. Optimally, it will give them a level playing field. . . .

Note and Questions on the Proposed U.S. Department of Transportation Enforced Policy

In the final days of the Clinton Administration, the Department of Transportation decided not to adopt the above proposed enforcement guidelines but to develop standards by proceeding on a case-by-case basis with enforcement actions. The Bush Administration named as its Transportation Secretary Norman Mineta, who had filed comments opposing the proposed enforcement policy, and the proposed policy appears not to have been pursued.

1. Who was right on this issue, the Clinton Administration or the Bush Administration?

2. The proposed U.S. Department of Transportation enforcement policy, like the European Commission decision in *Compagnie Maritime*, would have prohibited reactive above-cost price cuts only if they failed to maximize short-run profits.

a. Is that a very administrable test? How likely is it that courts can ascertain the profit-maximizing level as market conditions change? Are administrability problems averted by requiring evidence that prices are "substantially" below the profit-maximizing level?

b. Couldn't price cuts that do maximize short-run profits still have the same adverse effect of driving out entrants and allowing the incumbent to restore monopoly prices that are higher than the costs of the next-most efficient firm? Should the law instead ban any price cut or output increase in response to entry? Might that create inefficiencies as market conditions change?

c. If a firm decision would sacrifice profits unless it drove out the entrant, couldn't we infer that its price cut must have been intended to drive out the entrant? Does the profit-sacrifice test thus simply provide an objective basis for assessing intent? Should one require evidence of such profit-sacrificing even if alternative reliable evidence of intent exists?

3. Are there features of the airline industry that make it particularly appropriate for a rule against reactive above-cost price cuts? If not, should the proposed rule be extended to all antitrust cases? If yes, should our rules on above-cost predation be promulgated industry by industry to take account of any variation in such features?

United States v. AMR Corp.

335 F.3d 1109 (10th Cir. 2003).

This case involves the nature of permissible competitive practices in the airline industry under the antitrust laws of this country, centered around the hub-and-spoke system of American Airlines. The United States brought this suit against ... American Airlines ..., alleging monopolization and attempted monopolization through predatory pricing in violation of § 2 of the Sherman Act. In essence, the government alleges that American engaged in multiple episodes of price predation in four city-pair airline markets, all connected to American's hub at Dallas/Fort Worth International Airport ("DFW"), with the ultimate purpose of using the reputation for predatory pricing it earned in those four markets to defend a monopoly at its DFW hub. At its root, the government's complaint alleges that American: (1) priced its product on the routes in question below cost; and (2) intended to recoup these losses by charging supracompetitive prices either on the four core routes themselves, or on those routes where it stands to exclude competition by means of its "reputation for predation." Finding that the government failed to demonstrate the existence of a genuine issue of material fact as to either of these allegations, the district court granted summary judgment in favor of American, ... [W]e ... affirm....

Airlines are predominantly organized in a hub-and-spoke system, with traffic routed such that passengers leave their origin city for an intermediate hub airport. Passengers traveling to a concentrated hub tend to pay higher average fares than those traveling on comparable routes that do not include a concentrated hub as an endpoint. This is known as the "hub premium" and a major airline's hub is often an important profit center. Entry of low cost carriers ("LCCs") into a hub market tends to drive down the fares charged by major carriers. Consequently, major carriers generally enjoy higher margins on routes where they do not face LCC competition.

Both American and Delta ... maintain hubs at DFW, though Delta's presence is considerably smaller than American's. As of May 2000, American's share of passengers boarded at DFW was 70.2%, Delta's share was roughly 18%, and LCC share was 2.4% ....

LCCs generally enjoy the advantage of having lower costs than major carriers, allowing them to offer lower fares than their major-airline competitors.[3] During the period between 1995 and 1997, a number of LCCs, including Vanguard, Western Pacific, and Sunjet, began to take advantage of these lower costs by entering certain city-pair routes serving DFW and charging lower fares than American. The instant case primarily involves DFW–Kansas City, DFW–Wichita, DFW–Colorado Springs, and DFW–Long Beach.

American responded to lower LCC fares on these routes with changes in: (1) pricing (matching LCC prices); (2) capacity (adding flights or switching to larger planes); and (3) yield management (making more seats available at the new, lower prices). By increasing capacity, American overrode its own internal capacity-planning models for each route, which had previously indicated that such increases would be unprofitable. In each instance, American's response produced the same result: the competing LCC failed to establish a presence, moved its operations, or ceased its separate existence entirely. Once the LCC ceased or moved its operations, American generally resumed its prior marketing strategy, reducing flights and raising prices to levels roughly comparable to those prior to the period of low-fare competition. Capacity was reduced after LCC exit, but usually remained higher than prior to the alleged episode of predatory activity.

. . . In the instant case, the anticompetitive conduct at issue is predatory pricing. The crux of the government's argument is that the "incremental" revenues and costs specifically associated with American's capacity additions show a loss. Because American spent more to add capacity than the revenues generated by the capacity additions, such capacity additions made no economic sense unless American intended to drive LCCs out of the market. Under the government's theory, American attempted to monopolize the four city-pair routes in question in order to develop a reputation as an exceedingly aggressive competitor and set an example to all potential competitors. Fearing American's predatory response, the theory goes, future potential competitors will decline to enter other DFW market routes and compete. If American succeeds in preventing or at least forestalling the formation of an LCC hub at DFW, it will then be able to charge higher prices on other DFW routes and thereby recoup the losses it incurred from its "capacity dumping" on the four core routes . . .

"Predatory pricing means pricing below some appropriate measure of cost." *Matsushita*.[6] Despite a great deal of debate on the subject, no consensus has emerged as to what the most "appropriate" measure of cost is in predatory pricing cases. Costs can generally be divided into those that

---

3. For example, in 1994, American calculated ValuJet's stage-length adjusted cost per available seat mile to be 4.32 cents, and American's to be 8.54 cents. Southwest has costs that are 30% lower than American's.

6. The government notes in its brief that the "gravamen of the complaint is not limited to American's pricing." Rather, the complained of behavior includes American's capacity additions. However, as the district court correctly noted, prices and productive output are "two sides of the same coin." While the specific behavior complained of in the instant case is an increase in output or frequency, these actions must be analyzed in terms of their effect on price and cost. Thus, in order to succeed in the present action, the government must meet the standards of proof for predatory pricing cases established in *Brooke Group*.

are "fixed" and do not vary with the level of output (management expenses, interest on bonded debt, property taxes, depreciation, and other irreducible overhead) and those that are "variable" and do vary with the level of output (materials, fuel, labor used to produce the product). Marginal cost, the cost that results from producing an additional increment of output, is primarily a function of variable cost because fixed costs, as the name would imply, are largely unaffected by changes in output. For predatory pricing cases, especially those involving allegedly predatory production increases, the ideal measure of cost would be marginal cost because "[a]s long as a firm's prices exceed its marginal cost, each additional sale decreases losses or increases profits." However, marginal cost, an economic abstraction, is notoriously difficult to measure and "cannot be determined from conventional accounting methods." Economists, therefore, must resort to proxies for marginal cost. A commonly accepted proxy for marginal cost in predatory pricing cases is Average Variable Cost ("AVC"), the average of those costs that vary with the level of output.

The Supreme Court has declined to state which of the various cost measures is definitive.... Because there may be times when courts need the flexibility to examine both AVC as well as other proxies for marginal cost in order to evaluate an alleged predatory pricing scheme, we again decline to dictate a definitive cost measure for all cases....

Conceding that AVC is a good proxy for marginal cost in most cases, the government nevertheless argues that there may be times when looking only to a market-wide AVC test will disguise the nature of the predatory conduct at issue. Where there is a challenge to well-defined incremental conduct, and where incremental costs may be directly and confidently measured utilizing alternative proxies to AVC, argues the government, the market-wide AVC test is inappropriate.

Considering this to be the situation in the instant case, the government proffers four tests that purport to measure reliably incremental costs—the precise costs associated with the capacity additions at issue.... Because Tests Two and Three rely on fully allocated costs and include many fixed costs, the district court held that utilizing these cost measures would be the equivalent of applying an average total cost test, implicitly ruled out by *Brooke Group*'s mention of incremental costs only. ... We agree with this conclusion. While we will accept alternative proxies to marginal cost beyond AVC, Tests Two and Three are simply not proxies for marginal or incremental cost....

[R]ather than determining whether the added capacity itself was priced below an appropriate measure of cost, Test One effectively treats forgone or "sacrificed" profits as costs, and condemns activity that may have been profitable as predatory.[13] Rather than isolating the costs actually associated

---

13. For example, if an airline earned $20.6 million on a route that cost $18 million to operate, it would have $2.6 million in profit. If the airline then added a flight to the route that would cost $500,000 to operate, but brought in an additional $1 million in revenue from passengers, the airline would make $500,000 profit. If adding this extra capacity to the route reduced the profitability of other flights on that route, reducing revenue for the rest of the route by $600,000 down to $20 million, under Test One, this conduct would be considered predatory because rather than comparing the additional flight's $1 million in revenue to its

with the capacity additions the government purports to measure directly, Test One simply performs a "before-and-after" comparison of the route as a whole, looking to whether profits on the route as a whole decline after capacity was added, not to whether the challenged capacity additions were done below cost. In the end, Test One indicates only that a company has failed to maximize short-run profits on the route as a whole. Such a pricing standard could lead to a strangling of competition, as it would condemn nearly all output expansions, and harm to consumers. We conclude that Test One is invalid as a matter of law....

Test Four attempts to reveal American's predatory conduct by measuring and comparing the incremental costs incurred by American when it added capacity to the city-pair routes in question to the incremental revenue it received from the additional capacity.... The costs included in [Test Four] include variable costs American incurs with respect to all of its operations at DFW. Because some of those variable costs do not vary proportionately with the level of flight activity, they are allocated arbitrarily to a flight or route.... American identifies these variable, non-proportional common costs as: (1) airport ticket agents, (2) arrival agents, (3) ramp workers, and (4) security. ... Because the cost component of Test Four includes arbitrarily allocated variable costs, it does not compare incremental revenue to average avoidable cost. Instead, it compares incremental revenue to a measure of both average variable cost and average avoidable cost. Therefore, Test Four does not measure only the avoidable or incremental cost of the capacity additions and cannot be used to satisfy the government's burden in this case.

We conclude that all four proxies are invalid as a matter of law.... Because it is uncontested that American did not price below AVC for any route as a whole, ... the government has not succeeded in establishing the first element of *Brooke Group,* pricing below an appropriate measure of cost.[15] ...

Questions on *American Airlines*

1. Should the incremental costs of adding capacity include the loss of revenue from lower prices on the nonincremental flights? Economists often define costs to include opportunity costs like lost profits from alternative uses. Would defining incremental costs to include foregone profits effectively convert a cost-based test into a profit-sacrifice test?

$500,000 in costs, Test One looks only to the reduction in profits on the route as a whole from $2.6 million to $2.5 million. Thus, this conduct would be labeled predatory because the profits for the route as a whole declined, even though the capacity additions themselves were profitable and the route as a whole was still profitable. *See* Einer Elhauge, *Why Above–Cost Price Cuts to Drive Out Entrants Are Not Predatory—and the Implications for Defining Costs and Market Power,* 112 Yale L.J. 681, 694 (2003).

15. The district court also stated that even if American had priced below an appropriate measure of cost, it was nevertheless entitled to summary judgment because "American's prices only matched, and never undercut, the fares of the new entrant, low cost carriers on the four core routes." ... However, unlike in the Robinson–Patman Act, such a defense is not expressly provided for by the terms of the Sherman Act. The Supreme Court has never mentioned the possibility of such a defense under the Sherman Act. We therefore decline to rule that the "meeting competition" defense applies in the § 2 context.

2. If above-cost pricing cannot be called predatory under U.S. law, should the same sort of concerns that animate proposals to ban reactive above-cost price cuts nonetheless influence decisions about what cost measure to use? Do they provide a reason to use average total cost rather than variable or marginal costs as the measure?

Other Nations' Treatment of Above-Cost Predatory Pricing Claims

The EC–US split on above-cost predatory pricing is paralleled by a split among other nations. South Korea, Switzerland, and maybe New Zealand allow claims of above-cost predatory pricing.[115] But most nations, including Brazil, Canada, Egypt, Japan, Saudi Arabia, South Africa, Taiwan, and Turkey preclude claims that above-cost pricing is predatory or exclusionary, although some of these nations do allow claims of straight excessive pricing.[116] Which approach is best and does the answer depend on the nation's remedial system?

3. PREDATORY OVERPAYING BY A MONOPSONIST

Weyerhaeuser Co. v. Ross–Simmons Hardwood Lumber

549 U.S. 312 (2007).

■ MR. JUSTICE THOMAS delivered the opinion of the Court.

Respondent Ross–Simmons, a sawmill, sued petitioner Weyerhaeuser, alleging that Weyerhaeuser drove it out of business by bidding up the price of sawlogs to a level that prevented Ross–Simmons from being profitable. A jury returned a verdict in favor of Ross–Simmons on its monopolization claim, and the Ninth Circuit affirmed. We granted certiorari to decide whether the test we applied to claims of predatory pricing in *Brooke*, also applies to claims of predatory bidding. We hold that it does. Accordingly, we vacate the judgment of the Court of Appeals.

I

This antitrust case concerns the acquisition of red alder sawlogs by the mills that process those logs in the Pacific Northwest. ... By 2001, Weyerhaeuser's mills were acquiring approximately 65 percent of the alder logs available for sale in the region.... From 1990 to 2000, Weyerhaeuser made more than $75 million in capital investments in its hardwood mills in the Pacific Northwest [to improve their efficiency]. By contrast, Ross–Simmons appears to have engaged in little efficiency-enhancing investment.

---

115. *See* OECD, Predatory Foreclosure at 8, 165, 189–90, 209 (2005).

116. *See* Brazil CADE Resolution 20, Attachment I, § 4 (1999); Canada Competition Bureau, Predatory Pricing Enforcement Guidelines § 2.1 (2008); Egypt Competition Law Art 8(h); Saudi Arabia Competition Law, Art. 5(1); Nationwide Airlines v. South Africa Airways, 92/IR/OCT00, at 13 (South Africa Competition Tribunal); OECD, Predatory Foreclosure 8, 158, 214, 243, 246 (2005) (Japan, Turkey, Taiwan).

Logs represent up to 75 percent of a sawmill's total costs. And from 1998 to 2001, the price of alder sawlogs increased while prices for finished hardwood lumber fell. These divergent trends in input and output prices cut into the mills' profit margins, and Ross–Simmons suffered heavy losses during this time. Saddled with several million dollars in debt, Ross–Simmons shut down its mill completely in May 2001. . . .

The District Court . . . instructed the jury that Ross–Simmons could prove that Weyerhaeuser's bidding practices were anticompetitive acts if the jury concluded that Weyerhaeuser "purchased more logs than it needed, or paid a higher price for logs than necessary, in order to prevent [Ross–Simmons] from obtaining the logs they needed at a fair price." . . .

III

Predatory bidding, which Ross–Simmons alleges in this case, involves the exercise of market power on the buy side or input side of a market. In a predatory-bidding scheme, a purchaser of inputs "bids up the market price of a critical input to such high levels that rival buyers cannot survive (or compete as vigorously) and, as a result, the predating buyer acquires (or maintains or increases its) monopsony power." Kirkwood, Buyer Power and Exclusionary Conduct, 72 Antitrust L.J. 625, 652 (2005) (hereinafter Kirkwood). Monopsony power is market power on the buy side of the market. As such, a monopsony is to the buy side of the market what a monopoly is to the sell side and is sometimes colloquially called a "buyer's monopoly."

A predatory bidder ultimately aims to exercise the monopsony power gained from bidding up input prices. To that end, once the predatory bidder has caused competing buyers to exit the market for purchasing inputs, it will seek to "restrict its input purchases below the competitive level," thus "reduc[ing] the unit price for the remaining input[s] it purchases." Salop, Anticompetitive Overbuying by Power Buyers, 72 Antitrust L.J. 669, 672 (2005) (hereinafter Salop). The reduction in input prices will lead to "a significant cost saving that more than offsets the profit[s] that would have been earned on the output." If all goes as planned, the predatory bidder will reap monopsonistic profits that will offset any losses suffered in bidding up input prices.[2] (In this case, the plaintiff was the defendant's competitor in the input-purchasing market. Thus, this case does not present a situation of suppliers suing a monopsonist buyer under § 2 of the Sherman Act, nor does it present a risk of significantly increased concentration in the market in which the monopsonist sells, *i.e.*, the market for finished lumber.)

IV

A

Predatory-pricing and predatory-bidding claims are analytically similar. This similarity results from the close theoretical connection between

---

2. If the predatory firm's competitors in the input market and the output market are the same, then predatory bidding can also lead to the bidder's acquisition of monopoly power in the output market. In that case, which does not appear to be present here, the monopsonist could, under certain market conditions, also recoup its losses by raising output prices to monopolistic levels.

monopoly and monopsony. See Kirkwood 653 (describing monopsony as the "mirror image" of monopoly); *Khan v. State Oil Co.,* 93 F.3d 1358, 1361 (C.A.7 1996) ("[M]onopsony pricing . . . is analytically the same as monopoly or cartel pricing and [is] so treated by the law"), vacated and remanded on other grounds, 522 U.S. 3 (1997); *Vogel v. American Soc. of Appraisers,* 744 F.2d 598, 601 (C.A.7 1984) ("[M]onopoly and monopsony are symmetrical distortions of competition from an economic standpoint"); see also Hearing on Monopsony Issues in Agriculture: Buying Power of Processors in Our Nation's Agricultural Markets before the Senate Committee on the Judiciary, 108th Cong., 1st Sess., 3 (2004). The kinship between monopoly and monopsony suggests that similar legal standards should apply to claims of monopolization and to claims of monopsonization. Cf. Noll, "Buyer Power" and Economic Policy, 72 Antitrust L.J. 589, 591 (2005) ("[A]symmetric treatment of monopoly and monopsony has no basis in economic analysis").

Tracking the economic similarity between monopoly and monopsony, predatory-pricing plaintiffs and predatory-bidding plaintiffs make strikingly similar allegations. A predatory-pricing plaintiff alleges that a predator cut prices to drive the plaintiff out of business and, thereby, to reap monopoly profits from the output market. In parallel fashion, a predatory-bidding plaintiff alleges that a predator raised prices for a key input to drive the plaintiff out of business and, thereby, to reap monopsony profits in the input market. Both claims involve the deliberate use of unilateral pricing measures for anticompetitive purposes.[3] And both claims logically require firms to incur short-term losses on the chance that they might reap supracompetitive profits in the future.

B

More importantly, predatory bidding mirrors predatory pricing in respects that we deemed significant to our analysis in *Brooke Group.* In *Brooke Group,* we noted that " 'predatory pricing schemes are rarely tried, and even more rarely successful.' " Predatory pricing requires a firm to suffer certain losses in the short term on the chance of reaping supracompetitive profits in the future. A rational business will rarely make this sacrifice. The same reasoning applies to predatory bidding. A predatory-bidding scheme requires a buyer of inputs to suffer losses today on the chance that it will reap supracompetitive profits in the future. For this reason, "[s]uccessful monopsony predation is probably as unlikely as successful monopoly predation." R. Blair & J. Harrison, Monopsony 66 (1993).

And like the predatory conduct alleged in *Brooke Group,* actions taken in a predatory-bidding scheme are often " ' "the very essence of competi-

---

3. Predatory bidding on inputs is not analytically different from predatory overbuying of inputs. Both practices fall under the rubric of monopsony predation and involve an input purchaser's use of input prices in an attempt to exclude rival input purchasers. The economic effect of the practices is identical: input prices rise. In a predatory-bidding scheme, the purchaser causes prices to rise by offering to pay more for inputs. In a predatory-overbuying scheme, the purchaser causes prices to rise by demanding more of the input. Either way, input prices increase. Our use of the term "predatory bidding" is not meant to suggest that different legal treatment is appropriate for the economically identical practice of "predatory overbuying."

tion." ' " Just as sellers use output prices to compete for purchasers, buyers use bid prices to compete for scarce inputs. There are myriad legitimate reasons—ranging from benign to affirmatively procompetitive—why a buyer might bid up input prices. A firm might bid up inputs as a result of miscalculation of its input needs or as a response to increased consumer demand for its outputs. A more efficient firm might bid up input prices to acquire more inputs as a part of a procompetitive strategy to gain market share in the output market. A firm that has adopted an input-intensive production process might bid up inputs to acquire the inputs necessary for its process. Or a firm might bid up input prices to acquire excess inputs as a hedge against the risk of future rises in input costs or future input shortages. There is nothing illicit about these bidding decisions. Indeed, this sort of high bidding is essential to competition and innovation on the buy side of the market.[4]

Brooke Group also noted that a failed predatory-pricing scheme may benefit consumers. The potential benefit results from the difficulty an aspiring predator faces in recouping losses suffered from below-cost pricing. Without successful recoupment, "predatory pricing produces lower aggregate prices in the market, and consumer welfare is enhanced." Failed predatory-bidding schemes can also, but will not necessarily, benefit consumers. See Salop 677–678. In the first stage of a predatory-bidding scheme, the predator's high bidding will likely lead to its acquisition of more inputs. Usually, the acquisition of more inputs leads to the manufacture of more outputs. And increases in output generally result in lower prices to consumers.[5] *Id.,* at 677; R. Blair & J. Harrison, *supra,* at 66–67. Thus, a failed predatory-bidding scheme can be a "boon to consumers" in the same way that we considered a predatory-pricing scheme to be.

In addition, predatory bidding presents less of a direct threat of consumer harm than predatory pricing. A predatory-pricing scheme ultimately achieves success by charging higher prices to consumers. By contrast, a predatory-bidding scheme could succeed with little or no effect on consumer prices because a predatory bidder does not necessarily rely on raising prices in the output market to recoup its losses. Salop 676. Even if output prices remain constant, a predatory bidder can use its power as the predominant buyer of inputs to force down input prices and capture monopsony profits. *Ibid.*

C

The general theoretical similarities of monopoly and monopsony combined with the theoretical and practical similarities of predatory pricing and predatory bidding convince us that our two-pronged *Brooke Group* test should apply to predatory-bidding claims.

---

4. Higher prices for inputs obviously benefit existing sellers of inputs and encourage new firms to enter the market for input sales as well.

5. Consumer benefit does not necessarily result at the first stage because the predator might not use its excess inputs to manufacture additional outputs. It might instead destroy the excess inputs. See Salop 677, n. 22. Also, if the same firms compete in the input and output markets, any increase in outputs by the predator could be offset by decreases in outputs from the predator's struggling competitors.

The first prong of *Brooke Group's* test requires little adaptation for the predatory-bidding context. A plaintiff must prove that the alleged predatory bidding led to below-cost pricing of the predator's outputs. That is, the predator's bidding on the buy side must have caused the cost of the relevant output to rise above the revenues generated in the sale of those outputs. As with predatory pricing, the exclusionary effect of higher bidding that does not result in below-cost output pricing "is beyond the practical ability of a judicial tribunal to control without courting intolerable risks of chilling legitimate" procompetitive conduct. Given the multitude of procompetitive ends served by higher bidding for inputs, the risk of chilling procompetitive behavior with too lax a liability standard is as serious here as it was in *Brooke Group*. Consequently, only higher bidding that leads to below-cost pricing in the relevant output market will suffice as a basis for liability for predatory bidding.

A predatory-bidding plaintiff also must prove that the defendant has a dangerous probability of recouping the losses incurred in bidding up input prices through the exercise of monopsony power. Absent proof of likely recoupment, a strategy of predatory bidding makes no economic sense because it would involve short-term losses with no likelihood of offsetting long-term gains. As with predatory pricing, making a showing on the recoupment prong will require "a close analysis of both the scheme alleged by the plaintiff and the structure and conditions of the relevant market."

Ross–Simmons has conceded that it has not satisfied the *Brooke Group* standard. Therefore, its predatory-bidding theory of liability cannot support the jury's verdict. . . .

Note and Questions on Weyerhaeuser

1. If the complaint is that the defendant has paid too much for inputs, how can a below-cost test be applied? The Court's answer was to look at whether the price of the predator's *output* was below cost given its overpaying for inputs.

2. Does this holding eliminate any distinctive claim for predatory overbidding because any claim for below-cost pricing of output was already covered by straight predatory pricing claim? Not quite because in a straight predatory pricing claim the issue would be whether the defendant has monopoly power in the output market, lowered prices in the output market, and could recoup lost profits in the output market. In contrast, in a predatory overbidding case, the defendant must have monopsony power in the input market, have raised prices in the input market, and be able to recoup profits in that input market.

For example, here the input market for logs was regional, whereas the output market for finished lumber seems to have been national. Weyerhaeuser may not have had any monopoly power in the output market, may not have affected national output prices at all, and eliminating one small rival like Ross–Simmons may not have enabled it to recoup any lost profits in the national output market. In the regional input market for Northwestern logs, in contrast, Weyerhaeuser had a 65% buyer share and plausible monopsony power, it had allegedly raised prices on that input market, and driving rivals out of that regional input market might allow it to recoup lost profits by paying the regional mills a low monopsony price in the future.

Predatory Over–Paying by a Dominant Firm in Other Nations

Japan prohibits impeding fair competition by "Unjustly purchasing goods or services for a high price, thereby tending to cause difficulties to the business activities of other entrepreneurs."[117] South Korea prohibits a dominant firm from "purchasing goods or services at unreasonably high prices compared to the normal transaction price," when there is "a possibility of excluding a competitor."[118] South Africa may mean something similar by its prohibition on anticompetitively "buying-up a scarce supply of intermediate goods or resources required by a competitor."[119] It is not yet clear in these nations what the criteria are for determining when a price is too high. Other nations (including the EU) have little law on the topic.

4.   EXCESSIVE PRICING

U.S. and EU law differ on excessive pricing, with the U.S. courts taking the position that merely charging profit-maximizing monopoly prices is not an antitrust violation, and the EU courts taking the position that a firm with a dominant position has a legal obligation not to charge excessive prices.

Verizon Communications v. Law Offices of Curtis V. Trinko

540 U.S. 398 (2004).

The mere possession of monopoly power, and the concomitant charging of monopoly prices, is not only not unlawful; it is an important element of the free-market system. The opportunity to charge monopoly prices—at least for a short period—is what attracts "business acumen" in the first place; it induces risk taking that produces innovation and economic growth. To safeguard the incentive to innovate, the possession of monopoly power will not be found unlawful unless it is accompanied by an element of anticompetitive *conduct*.

---

117.   Japan Designations of Unfair Trade Practices § 7 (2009).

118.   Enforcement Decree of the South Korea Fair Trade Act Art. 5(5)(i) & Annex I.3.B.

119.   South Africa Competition Act § 8(d)(v).

Case 27/76, United Brands Company and United Brands Continental B.V. v. Commission of the European Communities

[1978] E.C.R. 207.

[United Brands Company (UBC) was the largest seller of bananas in the world through its well-known Chiquita brand.]

... The Commission is of the Opinion that UBC has ... abused its dominant position by charging its customers in Germany ..., Denmark, the Netherlands, [Luxembourg and Belgium] unfair prices, which in the circumstances it considers are "excessive in relation to the economic value of the product supplied." ...

The prices charged by UBC to its customers in Germany ..., Denmark, the Netherlands, [Luxembourg and Belgium] are considerably higher, sometimes by as much as 100%, than the prices charged to customers in Ireland and produce for it a substantial and excessive profit in relation to the economic value of the product supplied.

The significance of these observations is accentuated by the fact that there is a 20 to 40% difference between the price of Chiquita and unbranded bananas, even though the quality of the latter is only slightly lower than that of labelled bananas and by the fact that the price of unbranded bananas of similar quality sold by its principal competitors is lower even though their undertakings are running at a profit.

Having regard to this situation the Commission considers a reduction by UBC of its price levels to prices at least 15% below the prices it charges its customers in the relevant market, except in Ireland, to be appropriate, since the unfair prices charged currently are an abuse by UBC of its dominant position.

The applicant, ... [argues that the Commission mistakenly relied on a] letter of 10 December 1974 pointing out "that UBC sold bananas to Irish ripeners at prices allowing it a considerably smaller margin than in some other Member States", the wording of which, settled before 31 December 1974, the date of the end of the financial year, has been retracted on two different occasions by the applicant and it appears from a document annexed to the application that the prices charged in Ireland produced a loss for UBC. . . .

The applicant takes the view that the difference in the price of branded and unlabelled bananas is justified, because the precautions taken between cutting and sale to the consumer fully explain this difference.

It endeavours to prove by another way that there are genuine differences in the quality of Chiquita bananas and those bearing other brand names and that the price difference—averaging 7.4% between 1970 and 1974—is justified.

It submits that the order to reduce its prices by 15% is unintelligible, since the prices in question vary each week on the whole of the relevant market, and unworkable, because a reduction of this size would cause it to sell a banana of a higher quality than its competitors below the prices which they charge for theirs.

The imposition by an undertaking in a dominant position directly or indirectly of unfair purchase or selling prices is an abuse to which exception can be taken under Article [102] of the Treaty. It is advisable therefore to ascertain whether the dominant undertaking has made use of the opportunities arising out of its dominant position in such a way as to reap trading benefits which it would not have reaped if there had been normal and sufficiently effective competition.In this case charging a price which is excessive because it has no reasonable relation to the economic value of the product supplied would be such an abuse.

This excess could, inter alia, be determined objectively if it were possible for it to be calculated by making a comparison between the selling price of the product in question and its cost of production, which would disclose the amount of the profit margin. However the Commission has not done this since it has not analysed UBC's costs structure. The questions therefore to be determined are whether the difference between the costs actually incurred and the price actually charged is excessive, and, if the answer to this question is in the affirmative, whether a price has been imposed which is either unfair in itself or when compared to competing products. Other ways may be devised—and economic theorists have not failed to think up several—of selecting the rules for determining whether the price of a product is unfair.

While appreciating the considerable and at times very great difficulties in working out production costs which may sometimes include a discretionary apportionment of indirect costs and general expenditure and which may vary significantly according to the size of the undertaking, its object, the complex nature of its set up, its territorial area of operations, whether it manufactures one or several products, the number of its subsidiaries and their relationship with each other, the production costs of the banana do not seem to present any insuperable problems. In this case it emerges from a study by the United Nations conference on trade and development of 10 February 1975 that the pattern of the production, packaging, transportation, marketing and distribution of bananas could have made it possible to compute the approximate production cost of this fruit and accordingly to calculate whether its selling price to ripener/distributors was excessive.

The Commission was at least under a duty to require UBC to produce particulars of all the constituent elements of its production costs. The accuracy of the contents of the documents produced by UBC could have been challenged but that would have been a question of proof.

The Commission bases its view that prices are excessive on an analysis of the differences—in its view excessive—between the prices charged in the different Member States and on the policy of discriminatory prices which has been considered above.... Having found that the prices charged to ripeners of the other Member states were considerably higher, sometimes by as much as 100%, than the prices charged to customers in Ireland, it concluded that UBC was making a very substantial profit.

Nevertheless the Commission has not taken into account in its reasoning several of UBC's letters in which were enclosed a confidential document retracting what is said in its letter of 10 December 1974 and pointing out that the prices charged in Ireland had produced a loss. The applicant also states that the prices charged on the relevant market did not allow it to make any profits during the last five years, except in 1975.

These assertions by the applicant are not supported by any accounting documents which prove the consolidated accounts of the UBC group or even by the consolidated accounts for the relevant market. However unreliable the particulars supplied by UBC may be ... the fact remains that it is for the Commission to prove that the applicant charged unfair prices.

UBC's retraction, which the Commission has not effectively refuted, establishes beyond doubt that the basis for the calculation adopted by the latter to prove that UBC's prices are excessive is open to criticism and on this particular point there is doubt which must benefit the applicant, especially as for nearly 20 years banana prices, in real terms, have not risen on the relevant market.

Although it is also true that the price of Chiquita bananas and those of its principal competitors is different, that difference is about 7%, a percentage which has not been challenged and which cannot automatically be regarded as excessive and consequently unfair.

In these circumstances it appears that the Commission has not adduced adequate legal proof of the facts and evaluations which formed the foundation of its finding that UBC had infringed Article [102] of the Treaty by directly and indirectly imposing unfair selling prices for bananas.

Note and Questions on *Trinko* and *United Brands*

U.S. antitrust law does not restrict the prices charged by a firm that lawfully acquired market power. Such prices may be prospectively regulated by industry-specific rate regulation, but such regulation is usually reserved for natural monopolies like utilities. In contrast, as *United Brands* illustrates, general EU competition law does prohibit a dominant firm from charging "excessive" prices. However, the claim was rejected on the facts of *United Brands* and such claims have rarely been pursued by European enforcement agencies.

1. Why shouldn't excessive pricing be illegal in the United States and vigorously prosecuted in Europe? Isn't a high price more harmful to consumer welfare than low predatory ones?

2. Can high supracompetitive prices ever be beneficial? Do they encourage investment to make better or cheaper products? Do they encourage entry or expansion to meet changing market needs?

3. How are courts supposed to determine whether prices are excessive under *United Brands*?

a. Doesn't any dominant firm necessarily charge prices that are excessively above cost? Does *United Brands* thus collapse the distinction between the separate elements of possessing dominant market power and abusing it?

b. The ECJ's test to determine whether a price is excessive is "whether the difference between the costs actually incurred and the price actually charged is excessive, and, if the answer to this question is in the affirmative, whether a price has been imposed which is either unfair in itself or when compared to competing products".

i. Is this test sufficiently objective to allow dominant firms to make sure their prices will not be "excessive"?

ii. Could the ECJ elaborate administrable standards for determining what the right nonexcessive price is and monitoring day-to-day prices for compliance? If so, what would they be?

c. Rather than comparing prices to costs, why not conclude that the price differences between nations show excessive pricing unless the defendant can show they are justified by cost differences?

i. Doesn't such price discrimination between nations generally indicate market power? And doesn't the price in the low-priced nations provide a nice competitive baseline that is better than making direct inquiries into costs?

ii. On the other hand, can't you argue that prices may vary across Member States due to a variety of reasons (differences in taxes, wages, incomes, or demand elasticities, etc.) and that therefore price comparisons across Member States may lead to misleading results?

iii. Here the Court concluded that the price differences were not sufficient because the defendant said it was losing money in Ireland and the Commission did not examine the cost data. But isn't it implausible the defendant was charging prices below marginal cost in Ireland since that would mean it was deliberately losing money? Couldn't one conclude that the national price differences should suffice to at least shift the burden to the defendant to show that they were justified by cost differences?

d. Should the price difference between UBC and unbranded bananas suffice? Does the answer depend on whether, as defendant claimed, there was a quality difference between them? Even if they are the same, should it suffice that the defendant invested in developing a brand reputation that lowers buyer information costs and causes them to buy the defendant's product?

4. Won't charging less than the profit-maximizing monopoly price tend to exclude entrants? Is any price charged by a dominant firm in Europe thus vulnerable to attack on the theory that it is either (a) excessive or (b) sacrifices profits to keep out rivals?

The Economics of Price Discrimination

Price discrimination is simply charging different prices for the same item. While this may sound bad, it is not always illegal and can sometimes efficiently expand output. If a firm with market power charges a *uniform* price, it has to take into account that any price reduction it makes to get a marginal customer will lose it profits from the inframarginal customers who are willing to pay a higher rate. Thus, a firm with market power that can charge only a uniform price maximizes profits by charging a price that many marginal customers will not pay even though they value the product more than the incremental cost of producing it. This is why such firms produce a subcompetitive level of output and allocative inefficiency.

In contrast, suppose a firm with market power engages in *perfect* price discrimination, lowering prices to marginal buyers while charging higher prices to inframarginal buyers, and charging each buyer precisely the amount that that buyer values the product. (In economic theory, such perfect price discrimination is called first-degree price discrimination.) With perfect price discrimination, the firm will produce the perfectly competitive level of output because it has incentives to sell to the marginal buyer at any price that exceeds its incremental cost. This will eliminate any allocative inefficiency. However, perfect price discrimination will also eliminate the consumer surplus that otherwise would result under any uniform price from the fact that inframarginal buyers value the product more than the price they pay. In short, compared to uniform pricing, perfect price discrimination lowers consumer welfare but raises efficiency and total welfare ex post.[120] U.S. and EU antitrust law appear to embrace a consumer welfare standard, although some argue that antitrust law should embrace an efficiency/total welfare standard.[121]

---

120. "Total welfare" is the sum of consumer welfare (the difference between consumer valuations and prices charged) and producer welfare (which is the difference between prices and costs, i.e., producer profits). "Total welfare" is thus equivalent to efficiency (the total difference between value and cost) and equal to the sum of consumer welfare and producer profits. If price discrimination increases producer profits by more than it decreases in consumer welfare, then it increases total welfare. This is why price discrimination can increase total welfare but reduce consumer welfare. In contrast, if price discrimination reduces total welfare, then it necessarily also reduces consumer welfare, which equals total welfare minus the profits the firm reaped from price discrimination. (Those profits must be positive or the firm would not price discriminate).

"Ex post" means that the welfare measures are comparing welfare after the price discrimination to welfare right before the price discrimination. Ex post total welfare thus does not take into account that an ability to engage in price discrimination may (because it increases the producer profits anticipated from gaining market power) have ex ante effects on the extent to which firms invest to obtain that market power. If the total welfare measure considers such ex ante effects (on top of the ex post effects), then it is called ex ante total welfare.

121. *See* Chapter 2.A; John B. Kirkwood & Robert H. Lande, *The Fundamental Goal of Antitrust: Protecting Consumers, Not Increasing Efficiency*, 84 NOTRE DAME L. REV. 191 (2008); Elhauge, *Tying, Bundled Discounts, and the Death of the Single Monopoly Profit Theory*, 123 HARVARD LAW REVIEW 397, 436–442 (2009) (summarizing case law and arguments favoring a consumer welfare standard); Elhauge, *The Failed Resurrection of the Single Monopoly Profit Theory*, 6(1) COMPETITION POLICY INTERNATIONAL 155, 167–172 (Spring 2010) (same).

However, truly perfect price discrimination is usually not possible. Suppose instead the firm can only engage in *imperfect* price discrimination. Such imperfect price discrimination usually involves charging different categories of buyers different prices that roughly correlate to the value that buyers in each category put on the product. (This is called third-degree price discrimination). Or imperfect price discrimination can involve offering a menu of product options and prices that causes buyers to self-select in ways that imperfectly correlate with their willingness to pay. (This called second-degree price discrimination).

Compared to the alternative of uniform pricing, such imperfect price discrimination can conceivably increase *or* decrease output, efficiency, consumer welfare, and total welfare ex post. However, it has been proven that, *unless* imperfect price discrimination increases total output, imperfect price discrimination *always reduces* efficiency, consumer welfare, and total welfare ex post.[122] The reason is that imperfect price discrimination reallocates some output from buyers who valued the product more to buyers who valued the product less, which harms consumer and total welfare unless the adverse welfare effects of this reallocation are offset by an output increase. Further, increasing output is necessary, but not sufficient, for price discrimination to increase ex post total welfare. Even if it increases output, price discrimination will increase ex post total welfare *only* if the welfare gains from the output increase (among categories of buyers who would not buy absent price discrimination) are large enough to exceed the welfare loss from the output misallocation (among categories of buyers who would buy whether prices were uniform or discriminatory).

Further, because perfect price discrimination decreases consumer welfare and increases total welfare ex post, imperfect price discrimination seems likely to do the same more often that not because it moves us closer to perfect price discrimination.[123] Consistent with this conclusion, linear demand models with equally distributed consumer valuations find that imperfect price discrimination among those consumer groups *usually* decreases consumer welfare and increases total welfare ex post.[124] But usually

122. Hal R. Varian, Price Discrimination, in 1 HANDBOOK OF INDUSTRIAL ORGANIZATION 597, 622–623 (Richard Schmalensee & Robert D. Willig eds., 1989); Richard Schmalensee, Output and Welfare Implications of Monopolistic Third–Degree Price Discrimination, 71 AM. ECON. REV. 242, 242 & n.1 (1981); Elhauge, *Tying, supra* note 121, at 431–32 (summarizing literature).

123. Elhauge, *Failed Resurrection, supra* note 121, at 166–67.

124. Elhauge, *Tying, supra* note 121, at 433, 479–481; Elhauge, *Failed Resurrection, supra* note 121, at 166; Barry Nalebuff, *Price Discrimination and Welfare,* 5(2) COMPETITION POL'Y INT'L 221, 227, 236 (2009). Imperfect price discrimination will also predictably redistribute consumer welfare away from the low-elasticity (price insensitive) consumers toward the high-elasticity (price sensitive) consumers. *See* JEAN TIROLE, THE THEORY OF INDUSTRIAL ORGANIZATION 137–40. To the extent that consumers who are more price sensitive are poorer, one might conclude that the redistributive benefits of reallocating consumer welfare from rich to poor consumers makes price discrimination desirable even though some consumer welfare is lost in the transfer and overall consumer welfare decreases. However, antitrust law generally focuses on overall consumer welfare rather than on the distribution of welfare among consumers of different income. *See* Elhauge, *Failed Resurrection, supra* note 121, at 198 (also arguing that focusing on the distribution of welfare among consumers given their

is not always, and imperfect price discrimination among consumers can sometimes increase consumer welfare or decrease total welfare.

If the buyers are not final consumers, but instead are intermediaries who resell to consumers, then imperfect price discrimination reduces output and total welfare, other than in cases where the price discrimination discourages inefficient integration.[125] The reason is that the disfavored intermediary paying a higher price will resell at a higher downstream price that tends to drive consumers to the favored intermediary, which will tend to drive up the profits of the favored intermediary and allow the price-discriminating supplier to increase prices to it as well. This effect will harm output and total welfare unless the efficiency and welfare benefits of avoiding inefficient integration are sufficiently large to offset those harms.

Ex ante effects also matter. Because price discrimination increases the profits a producer can anticipate reaping from market power, allowing price discrimination increases ex ante incentives to invest in activities that might garner market power. Where those activities involve obtaining anticompetitive regulations that hamper rival competition, such investments would be undesirable. When the activities involve innovating to create some product or production process that is sufficiently better or cheaper than rival options to enjoy market power, the innovation is desirable but the investments may not be if their costs are excessive compared to the innovation gain. Such investments can be excessive because firms competing for a market power position have incentives to incur costs that dissipate the monopoly profits they expect to earn from that market power. Judge Posner has argued that firms will dissipate all the monopoly profits ex ante (assuming that the long run costs to seeking market power are constant), whereas Professor Fisher has argued that they will only dissipate some of those monopoly profits (assuming instead that that obtaining market power has rising marginal costs).[126] Under Judge Posner's assumption, all ex post producer profits wash out ex ante, so that the ex ante total welfare effects are equal to the consumer welfare effects, which means perfect price discrimination reduces ex ante total welfare and imperfect price discrimination does too in the usual case where it reduces consumer welfare. Under Professor Fisher's assumption, the dissipated share will be less than 100%, but this still means that price discrimination that increases ex post total welfare might decrease ex ante total welfare.

Further, the patent race literature proves that, if firms anticipate obtaining 100% of the total surplus created by their innovations, they will invest excessively in innovation, creating an inefficient decrease in ex ante total welfare.[127] Because perfect price discrimination does give a firm 100%

incomes would be judicially inadministrable and less efficient than redistribution through taxation).

125. Michael L. Katz, *The Welfare Effects of Third–Degree Price Discrimination in Intermediate Goods Markets,* 77 Amer. Econ. Rev. 154, 161–165 (1987).

126. Richard A. Posner, *The Social Costs of Monopoly and Regulation,* 83 J. POL. ECON. 807, 807–09, 812, 822 (1975); Franklin M. Fisher, *The Social Costs of Monopoly and Regulation: Posner Reconsidered,* 93 J. POL. ECON. 410 (1985); Elhauge, *Tying, supra* note 121, at 441–42 (summarizing the debate).

127. See SUZANNE SCOTCHMER, INNOVATION AND INCENTIVES 100–03 (2004); Partha Dasgupta & Joseph Stiglitz, *Uncertainty, Industrial Structure, and the Speed of R&D,*

of total surplus, this literature proves that perfect price discrimination reduces ex ante total welfare even though it increases ex post total welfare. More generally, this patent race literature proves that investments will be excessive whenever firms obtain more than a certain fraction of the total surplus created by their innovation. This means that maintaining the rest of the fraction as consumer surplus is necessary to assure optimal investment. If we assume that patent law has already been designed to try to award innovators the optimal fraction of total surplus by allowing patent holders a normal monopoly profit during their patent term, then any price discrimination that allows innovators to extract more than that normal patent award will induce excessive investment and reduce ex ante total welfare.[128]

Another complication is that price discrimination is also ubiquitous in many markets where firms have no market power in the antitrust sense, including hotels, movie theaters, airlines, computers, automobiles, books, clothing, groceries, and a vast array of other products that offer various discounts, rebates and coupons.[129] Such firms may be engaged in monopolistic competition because of fixed costs or brand differentiation, and thus have downward sloping demand curves that permit price discrimination.[130] Yet because others would enter their market or product space if they earned supracompetitive profits, they will at best be able to use the profits from such price discrimination to cover their fixed costs and the common costs of producing goods for buyers who place different values on that good.[131] Because each firm is disciplined by competition from charging a price-discrimination schedule whose total revenue exceeds its total costs, such price discrimination should permit firms to incur greater fixed and common costs, and thus increase market output and efficiency.[132]

A recurring obstacle to price discrimination is that the seller must not only be able to identify which buyers are willing to pay more for the product, but also must prevent resales from the buyers who are buying at low prices to the buyers whom the seller wishes to charge high prices. Identifying buyer types can sometimes be accomplished by charging buyers according to the intensity of their use. If buyers value a copying machine more the more copies they make, a seller might price discriminate by charging buyers a base rate for the machine plus a metered rate per copy.

---

11 BELL J. ECON. 1, 18 (1980); Pankaj Tandon, *Rivalry and the Excessive Allocation of Resources to Research*, 14 BELL J. ECON. 152, 152, 156–57 (1983); Elhauge, *Tying, supra* note 121, at 440.

128. Elhauge, *Tying, supra* note 121, at 440; Elhauge, *Failed Resurrection, supra* note 121, at 170–72.

129. Elhauge, *Why Above–Cost Price Cuts, supra* note 33, at 732–33; Illinois Tool Works Inc. v. Independent Ink, Inc., 547 U.S. 28, 44–45 (2006).

130. *See* Chapter 3.a. Price discrimination without market power may also be possible if there is some demand discontinuity and buyers who are willing to pay a higher price select sellers either at random (because they are uninformed or price insensitive) or in proportion to the common costs incurred (such as when more flights or retail outlets offer greater convenience). *See* Elhauge, *Why Above–Cost Price Cuts, supra* note 33, at 736–43. Both types of price discrimination should be output-expanding. *Id.*

131. Elhauge, *Why Above–Cost Price Cuts, supra* note 33, at 732–54.

132. *Id.*

Other techniques include advertising price discounts in ways more likely to reach only less wealthy customers, or requiring effort to obtain the discounts that high income buyers who value their time more highly are less likely to exert. Preventing resales may sometimes require contractual restrictions, whose enforceability itself may raise antitrust issues. But in some industries, preventing resales is easy because the product does not lend itself to resale, such as personal services or serving hot perishable food.

In the United States, the Robinson–Patman Act regulates price discrimination in goods. The statute does not cover price discrimination that simply reaps higher profits from buyers but rather prohibits price discrimination only if it is reasonably likely to harm competition. *See* Chapters 3.a & 5.c. In Europe, Article 102(c) offers parallel protection, prohibiting dominant firms from "applying dissimilar conditions to equivalent transactions with other trading parties, thereby placing them at a competitive disadvantage." Both the U.S. and European provisions have been interpreted to cover two sorts of price discrimination.

Primary-line price discrimination is price discrimination that adversely affects *competition at the seller's level*. Here the concern is that the seller might use high prices in one area to fund predatory prices in another area. This sort of price discrimination has been subsumed by predatory pricing doctrine, with the main effect being (as discussed above) that U.S. and European courts are willing to apply more aggressive tests of predatory pricing when pricing is discriminatory or selective.

Secondary-line price discrimination is price discrimination that adversely affects *competition at the buyers' level*. Here the concern is that the buyers who bought at the higher price will be at a competitive disadvantage in their downstream markets. This topic will be covered in Chapter 5, which addresses conduct or agreements that arguably distort downstream competition. The ubiquitous issue there, as we shall see, is that sellers generally would seem to have little incentive to distort downstream competition because sellers benefit from a competitive downstream market for distributing their goods.

In Europe, Article 102(a) also prohibits a dominant firm from "directly or indirectly imposing unfair purchase or selling prices or other unfair trading conditions." Even if it were unwise to interpret this provision to prohibit uniformly excessive pricing, should it be interpreted to prohibit a dominant firm from engaging in price discrimination that reduces output or takes consumer surplus away from consumers? Would that be a more administrable test because there would be other prices to use as a benchmark? Is that the sort of limited excessive pricing claim the Commission in *United Brands* really meant to authorize?

Excessive Pricing in Other Nations

The US–EU split on excessive pricing also exists across other nations. Although many other nations do not prohibit exploitative abuses like excessive pricing, many other nations do, including: Brazil, Chile, China, India, Israel, Russia, Singapore, South Africa, South Korea, Taiwan, Thailand, and Turkey.[133] Chile, China, India, Israel, and Thailand make clear that they ban not only excessively high selling prices, but also excessively low buying prices.[134] Should nations prohibit dominant firms from selling at excessively high prices and/or buying at excessively low prices?

Some nations define what they mean by excessive prices. South Africa and Turkey parallel EU law in defining an "excessive price" as a price for a good or service which bears no reasonable relation to the economic value of that good or service.[135] South Korea prohibits "a sharp increase or insignificant decrease, without justifiable reason, in the price/cost of goods or services relative to changes in the supply and demand or in supply cost."[136] The South Korean test thus uses a past baseline and inquires into whether changes or lack of changes from that baseline were reasonable given other market changes. Russia prohibits a dominant firm from setting a price that "exceeds the sum of the necessary production and distribution costs of the goods and profit, and exceeds the price formed under competitive conditions in the goods market, with comparable composition of goods buyers or sellers, conditions of goods circulation, market entry conditions, government regulation, including taxation and customs-and-tariffs regulation (further on referred to a comparable goods market), if such a market exists in the Russian Federation or abroad."[137] The Russian test thus uses a competitive baseline that could be in the past or present and in the same or other markets. Brazil provides that the following should be considered for the purpose of determining the existence of unfair prices: "(I) the price of a product or service, or any increase therein, vis-à-vis any changes in the cost of their respective input or with quality improvements; (II) the price of a product previously manufactured, as compared to its market replacement without substantial changes; (III) the price for a similar product or service,

---

133. *See* Brazil Antitrust Law No. 8,884, Arts. 20(III), 21(XXIV) (illegal to act in ways intended or able to increase profits on a "discretionary basis" such as "to impose abusive prices"); Chile Competition Law, Art. 3(b) (prohibiting exploitative abuse of a dominant position when setting prices for sale or purchase); China Anti–Monopoly Law Art. 17(1) (banning a firm in dominant market position from "selling at unfairly high prices or buying at unfairly low prices"); India Competition Act § 4(2)(a)(ii) (banning dominant firm from imposing an unfair or discriminatory price for purchase or sale); Israel Restrictive Trade Practices Law § 29A (banning a monopolist from injuring the public by charging "unfair" buying or selling price or unfairly reducing output); Russia Competition Law Art. 6(1) (defining the prohibition on a "monopolistically high price"); Singapore Competition Act § 47(2) (banning a dominant firm from "limiting production, markets or technical development to the prejudice of consumers."); South Africa Competition Act § 8(a) (banning a dominant firm from charging an "excessive" price); Enforcement Decree of the South Korea Fair Trade Act Art. 5(1) (defining the prohibition on "unreasonable" pricing); OECD, Predatory Foreclosure 247 (2005) (Taiwan); Thailand Trade Competition Act § 25(1) (banning a dominant firm from "unreasonably" setting purchase or sale prices); Belko Decision, No. 01–17/150–39 (Turkey Competition Commission 2001) (banning excessive pricing by a dominant firm).

134. China Anti–Monopoly Law Art. 17(1); Chile Competition Law, Art. 3(b); India Competition Act § 4(2)(a)(ii); Israel Restrictive Trade Practices Law § 29A; Thailand Trade Competition Act § 25(1).

135. *See* South Africa Competition Act § 1(1)(ix); Belko Decision, No. 01–17/150–39 (Turkey Competition Commission 2001).

136. *See* Enforcement Decree of the South Korea Fair Trade Act Art. 5(1).

137. Russia Competition Law Art. 6(1).

or any improvement thereof, in competitive markets; and (IV) the existence of agreements or arrangements in any way, which cause an increase in the prices of a product or service, or in their respective costs."[138] The first three Brazilian factors basically use past or contemporaneous baselines to determine the reasonableness of price; the fourth factor really requires some anticompetitive conduct separate from the pricing. Should the EU adopt an approach similar to South Korea, Russia or Brazil to further refine what excessive pricing means?

5. EXCLUSIONS FROM OWNED PROPERTY–UNILATERAL REFUSALS TO DEAL

A firm that lacks dominant market power may be unable to agree with other firms to engage in a concerted refusal to deal, but can unilaterally choose with whom they deal without fear of antitrust liability. For a firm that has monopoly or dominant market power, the law is more complicated. Such a firm has no general duty to cooperate with its rivals. But it also has no privilege not to deal. The doctrinal question this raises is: just when is such a firm's unilateral refusal to deal illegal? The underlying policy issue this raises is: to what extent should antitrust law restrict rights to exclude created by various types of property law?

The general legal standards applicable to monopolization and abuse of dominance indicate that exclusions by a monopolist or dominant firm that hamper rival competition are exclusionary if they are not "competition on the merits" or "normal competition." The problem with this and similar tests is that they fail to explain which of the exclusions that hamper rival competition to allow and which to condemn.

At least one U.S. Supreme Court case indicated that the underlying norm is economic efficiency, equating "Improper exclusion" with "exclusion not the result of superior efficiency" and stating that "If a firm has been 'attempting to exclude rivals on some basis other than efficiency,' it is fair to characterize its behavior as predatory."[139] However, this seeming identification of efficiency as the relevant norm has not been repeated in other Supreme Court monopolization cases, including the ones that followed,[140] and even this decision never makes clear that efficiency is the sole normative standard rather than just one factor in determining whether a justification is "valid" or not.

---

138. *See* Brazil Antitrust Law No. 8,884, Art. 21(XXIV).

139. *Aspen*, 472 U.S. at 602–03, 605 (quoting R. Bork, The Antitrust Paradox 138, 160 (1978)); *see also id.* at 608, 610–11 (indicating that an absence of normal business purposes was proven by the defendant's "failure to offer any efficiency justification" for its conduct, and the conclusion that it "was not motivated by efficiency concerns.")

140. *Kodak*, 504 U.S. at 483 & n.32 (stating that "Liability turns ... on whether 'valid business reasons' can explain Kodak's actions," or whether it has "valid business justifications" or "legitimate competitive reasons," without ever identifying efficiency as the norm by which validity and legitimacy is judged); *Trinko*, 540 U.S. at 407 (using the *Grinnell* and anticompetitive conduct test, without defining them to turn on efficiency).

But even if the underlying test were clearly defined as efficiency, a larger conceptual problem would remain. *All* unilateral refusals to deal that matter must be based on the superior efficiency of the defendant's facilities, otherwise the denial could not harm rival competition. All such refusals also have the efficiency justification that enforcing a power to exclude rivals encourages ex ante investment to make those facilities so valuable that they enjoy monopoly or dominant market power. On the other hand, exclusions that further or maintain monopoly or dominant power tend to be inefficient ex post (i.e., after the creation of the facility) in that they increase allocative inefficiency. Clearly the U.S. Supreme Court does not mean to indicate that refusals to give rivals access to defendant facilities are either always efficient or never efficient, for the Court doctrine allows some refusals but not others. The question is how to weigh such ex ante and ex post efficiency arguments.

Otter Tail Power Company v. United States

410 U.S. 366 (1973).

■ MR. JUSTICE DOUGLAS delivered the opinion of the Court. . . .

[T]he District Court found that Otter Tail had attempted to monopolize and had monopolized the retail distribution of electric power in its service area in violation of § 2 of the Sherman Act. The District Court found that Otter Tail had attempted to prevent communities in which its retail distribution franchise had expired from replacing it with a municipal distribution system. The principal means employed were (1) refusals to sell power at wholesale to proposed municipal systems in the communities where it had been retailing power; (2) refusals to "wheel" power to such systems, that is to say, to transfer by direct transmission or displacement electric power from one utility to another over the facilities of an intermediate utility. . . .[141]

Otter Tail sells electric power at retail in 465 towns in Minnesota, North Dakota, and South Dakota. . . . In towns where Otter Tail distributes at retail, it operates under municipally granted franchises which are limited from 10 to 20 years. Each town in Otter Tail's service area generally can accommodate only one distribution system, making each town a natural monopoly market for the distribution and sale of electric power at retail. The aggregate of towns in Otter Tail's service area is the geographic market in which Otter Tail competes for the right to serve the towns at retail. That competition is generally for the right to serve the entire retail market within the composite limits of a town, and that competition is generally between Otter Tail and a prospective or existing municipal system. These towns number 510 and of those Otter Tail serves 91%, or 465.

. . . Between 1945 and 1970, there were contests in 12 towns served by Otter Tail over proposals to replace it with municipal systems. In only

---

141. [Editor's Note: Otter Tail did wholesale and wheel electric power to electric systems that it had not previously served at retail. *See* United States v. Otter Tail Power Co., 331 F. Supp. 54, 57–58 (D. Minn. 1971).]

three ... municipal systems actually established. Proposed municipal systems have great obstacles; they must purchase the electric power at wholesale. To do so they must have access to existing transmission lines. The only ones available [to the relevant towns] belong to Otter Tail.... Otter Tail refused to sell the new systems energy at wholesale and refused to agree to wheel power from other suppliers of wholesale energy.

... As respects Elbow Lake and Hankinson, Otter Tail simply refused to deal, although according to the findings it had the ability to do so. Elbow Lake, cut off from all sources of wholesale power, constructed its own generating plant. Both Elbow Lake and Hankinson requested the Bureau of Reclamation and various cooperatives to furnish them with wholesale power; they were willing to supply it if Otter Tail would wheel it. But Otter Tail refused, relying on provisions in its contracts which barred the use of its lines for wheeling power to towns which it had served at retail. Elbow Lake after completing its plant asked the Federal Power Commission, under § 202(b) of the Federal Power Act, to require Otter Tail to interconnect with the town and sell it power at wholesale.[142] The Federal Power Commission ordered first a temporary and then a permanent connection. Hankinson tried unsuccessfully to get relief from the North Dakota Commission and then filed a complaint with the federal commission seeking an order to compel Otter Tail to wheel. While the application was pending, the town council voted to withdraw it and subsequently renewed Otter Tail's franchise....

I

Otter Tail contends that by reason of the Federal Power Act it is not subject to antitrust regulation with respect to its refusal to deal. We disagree with that position.

"Repeals of the antitrust laws by implication from a regulatory statute are strongly disfavored, and have only been found in cases of plain repugnancy between the antitrust and regulatory provisions." Activities which come under the jurisdiction of a regulatory agency nevertheless may be subject to scrutiny under the antitrust laws....

The District Court determined that Otter Tail's consistent refusals to wholesale or wheel power to its municipal customers constituted illegal monopolization. Otter Tail maintains here that its refusals to deal should be immune from antitrust prosecution because the Federal Power Commission has the authority to compel involuntary interconnections of power pursuant to § 202(b) of the Federal Power Act. The essential thrust of § 202, however, is to encourage voluntary interconnections of power. Only if a power company refuses to interconnect voluntarily may the Federal Power Commission, subject to limitations unrelated to antitrust considerations, order the interconnection. The standard which governs its decision

---

142. [Editor's Note: This request was for standby power to supplement Elbow Lake's new generating plant. 331 F. Supp. at 60. The Court below found that it was economically unfeasible for anyone to build new transmission facilities to wheel electricity to Elbow Lake or Hankinson. *Id.* at 60–61. Further, the area's major generator of electricity, the Bureau of Reclamation, was forbidden to construct new transmission facilities to serve towns where wheeling arrangements could be negotiated. *See* Brief for the United States at 13.]

is whether such action is "necessary or appropriate in the public interest." Although antitrust considerations may be relevant, they are not determinative.

There is nothing in the legislative history which reveals a purpose to insulate electric power companies from the operation of the antitrust laws. To the contrary, the history of Part II of the Federal Power Act indicates an overriding policy of maintaining competition to the maximum extent possible consistent with the public interest. As originally conceived, Part II would have included a "common carrier" provision making it "the duty of every public utility to ... transmit energy for any person upon reasonable request ..." In addition, it would have empowered the Federal Power Commission to order wheeling if it found such action to be "necessary or desirable in the public interest." H.R. 5423, 74th Cong., 1st Sess.; S. 1725, 74th Cong., 1st Sess. These provisions were eliminated to preserve "the voluntary action of the utilities." S.Rep.No.621, 74th Cong., 1st Sess., 19.

It is clear, then, that Congress rejected a pervasive regulatory scheme for controlling the interstate distribution of power in favor of voluntary commercial relationships.[143] When these relationships are governed in the first instance by business judgment and not regulatory coercion, courts must be hesitant to conclude that Congress intended to override the fundamental national policies embodied in the antitrust laws....

Thus, there is no basis for concluding that the limited authority of the Federal Power Commission to order interconnections was intended to be a substitute for, or to immunize Otter Tail from, antitrust regulation for refusing to deal with municipal corporations.

II

The decree of the District Court enjoins Otter Tail from "(r)efusing to sell electric power at wholesale to existing or proposed municipal electric power systems in cities and towns located in (its service area)" and from refusing to wheel electric power over its transmission lines from other electric power lines to such cities and towns. But the decree goes on to provide:

> "The defendant shall not be compelled by the Judgment in this case to furnish wholesale electric service or wheeling service to a municipality except at rates which are compensatory and under terms and conditions which are filed with and subject to approval by the Federal Power Commission."

So far as wheeling is concerned, there is no authority granted the Commission under Part II of the Federal Power Act to order it, for the bills originally introduced contained common carrier provisions which were deleted. The Act as passed contained only the interconnection provision set forth in § 202(b). The common carrier provision in the original bill and the

---

143.   [Editor's Note: In addition to the powers noted in the text, the Federal Power Commission (FPC) had the power to regulate the rates charged for wheeling or for wholesale electricity. *See* Brief for the United States at 15–16. Retail rates were not subject to FPC regulation, and the states and municipalities in which Otter Tail operated tended not to regulate them either. *Id.* at 15.]

power to direct wheeling were left to the "voluntary coordination of electric facilities." Insofar as the District Court ordered wheeling to correct anticompetitive and monopolistic practices of Otter Tail, there is no conflict with the authority of the Federal Power Commission.

As respects the ordering of interconnections, there is no conflict on the present record. Elbow Lake applied to the Federal Power Commission for an interconnection with Otter Tail and, as we have said, obtained it. Hankinson renewed Otter Tail's franchise. So the decree of the District Court, as far as the present record is concerned, presents no actual conflict between the federal judicial decree and an order of the Federal Power Commission.... It will be time enough to consider whether the antitrust remedy may override the power of the Commission under § 202(b) as, if, and when the Commission denies the interconnection and the District Court nevertheless undertakes to direct it. At present, there is only a potential conflict, not a present concrete case or controversy concerning it.

III

The record makes abundantly clear that Otter Tail used its monopoly power in the towns in its service area to foreclose competition or gain a competitive advantage, or to destroy a competitor, all in violation of the antitrust laws. See *Griffith*. The District Court determined that Otter Tail has "a strategic dominance in the transmission of power in most of its service area" and that it used this dominance to foreclose potential entrants into the retail area from obtaining electric power from outside sources of supply. Use of monopoly power "to destroy threatened competition" is a violation of the "attempt to monopolize" clause of § 2 of the Sherman Act. *Lorain Journal*....

When a community serviced by Otter Tail decides not to renew Otter Tail's retail franchise when it expires, it may generate, transmit, and distribute its own electric power. We recently described the difficulties and problems of those isolated electric power systems. Interconnection with other utilities is frequently the only solution. That is what Elbow Lake in the present case did. There were no engineering factors that prevented Otter Tail from selling power at wholesale to those towns that wanted municipal plants or wheeling the power. The District Court found—and its findings are supported—that Otter Tail's refusals to sell at wholesale or to wheel were solely to prevent municipal power systems from eroding its monopolistic position....

V

Otter Tail argues that, without the weapons which it used, more and more municipalities will turn to public power and Otter Tail will go downhill.... "The promotion of self-interest alone does not invoke the rule of reason to immunize otherwise illegal conduct." The ... Sherman Act ... assumes that an enterprise will protect itself against loss by operating with superior service, lower costs, and improved efficiency. Otter Tail's theory collided with the Sherman Act as it sought to substitute for competition anticompetitive uses of its dominant economic power.

The fact that three municipalities which Otter Tail opposed finally got their municipal systems does not excuse Otter Tail's conduct. That fact does not condone the antitrust tactics which Otter Tail sought to impose. . . . The proclivity for predatory practices has always been a consideration for the District Court in fashioning its antitrust decree.

We do not suggest, however, that the District Court, concluding that Otter Tail violated the antitrust laws, should be impervious to Otter Tail's assertion that compulsory interconnection or wheeling will erode its integrated system and threaten its capacity to serve adequately the public. As the dissent properly notes, the Commission may not order interconnection if to do so "would impair (the utility's) ability to render adequate service to its customers." 16 U.S.C. s 824a(b). The District Court in this case found that the "pessimistic view" advanced in Otter Tail's "erosion study" "is not supported by the record." . . . Affirmed.

■ MR. JUSTICE STEWART, with whom THE CHIEF JUSTICE and MR. JUSTICE REHNQUIST join, concurring in part and dissenting in part. . . . [1] In the face of natural monopolies at retail and similar economies of scale in the subtransmission of power, Congress was forced to address the very problem raised by this case—use of the lines of one company by another. One obvious solution would have been to impose the obligations of a common carrier upon power companies owning lines capable of the wholesale transmission of electricity. Such provision was originally included in the bill. . . . Yet, after substantial debate, the Congress declined to follow this path. . . .

This legislative history, especially when viewed in the light of repeated subsequent congressional refusals to impose common carrier obligations in this area, indicates a clear congressional purpose to allow electric utilities to decide for themselves whether to wheel or sell at wholesale as they see fit. This freedom is qualified by a grant of authority to the Commission to order interconnection (but not wheeling) in certain circumstances. But the exercise of even that power is limited by a consideration of the ability of the regulated utility to function. . . .

As the District Court found, Otter Tail is a vertically integrated power company. But the bulk of its business—some 90% of its income—derives from sales of power at retail. . . . As a retailer of power, Otter Tail asserted a legitimate business interest in keeping its lines free for its own power sales and in refusing to lend a hand in its own demise by wheeling cheaper power from the Bureau of Reclamation to municipal consumers which might otherwise purchase power at retail from Otter Tail itself. . . .

Here, . . . a monopoly is sure to result either way. If the consumers of Elbow Lake receive their electric power from a municipally owned company or from Otter Tail, there will be a monopoly at the retail level, for there

---

1. The District Court looked to Otter Tail's service area, and measured market dominance in terms of the number of towns within that area served by Otter Tail. Computed this way, Otter Tail provides 91% of the retail market. As the appellant points out, however, these towns vary in size from more than 29,000 to 20 inhabitants. If Otter Tail's size were measured by actual retail sales, its market share would be only 28.9% of the electricity sold at retail within its geographic market area. It is important to note that another reasonable geographical market unit might be each individual municipality. Viewed this way, whichever power company sells electricity at retail in a town has a complete monopoly.

will in any event be only one supplier. The very reason for the regulation of private utility rates—by state bodies and by the Commission—is the inevitability of a monopoly that requires price control to take the place of price competition. . . .

Questions on *Otter Tail*

1. *Property Rights and Ex Ante Investment Incentives.* Why shouldn't Otter Tail be able to refuse municipalities access to its electricity or its ability to transmit electricity from other suppliers? Isn't that right to exclude others part and parcel of its property rights over its electricity and transmission lines?

a. If this has an adverse effect on rival electricity retailers, isn't that just a consequence of the fact that Otter Tail's wholesale electricity and transmission services are a superior product? If they weren't superior to other market alternatives, how could denying them hurt the rival electricity retailers?

b. If Otter Tail has to share its electricity and transmission wires with rivals, won't that decrease:

    i.   Otter Tail's incentives to invest in creating facilities that make or transmit (wheel) electricity?

    ii.   the incentives of other firms to invest in creating competitive facilities that make or transmit electricity? Is it unlikely any other firm would have invested in entering either market anyway because Otter Tail is the retailer in 91% of the towns that would buy wholesale electricity or transmission services, or is what matters more that (as the dissent pointed out) those towns only account for 28.9% of the electricity sales in the area?

c. Does it alter your view if Otter Tail's wholesale or wheeling monopoly power was the result of regulations that impeded others from entering either market? Should any antitrust duty to deal turn on the source of the monopoly power over the facility for which sharing is sought?

2. *Ex Post Efficiencies.* Is it clear that sharing Otter Tail's wholesale electricity or transmission wires with rivals would be efficient, even if we assume no *ex ante* effect on the incentives to create the facilities?

a. Is it possible there are productive efficiencies to having the wheeling, wholesaling and retailing of electricity done by one firm?

b. Might there also be pricing inefficiencies to having successive monopolies, one upstream at wholesale and the other downstream at retail? Which will result in higher prices to consumers? Which would be more profitable to the upstream monopolist?

The Successive Monopolies Problem

Assuming no price regulation, an integrated monopolist would charge a monopoly price based on the total true marginal costs of getting electricity to the town and then distributing it to retail customers. But if there are successive monopolies—one at wholesale and the other at retail—then the wholesaler would charge a monopoly price based on the true marginal cost of bringing the electricity to the city, and then the retailer would charge a monopoly price based on an inflated marginal cost that includes the wholesale monopoly profits. For example, suppose wholesaling electricity to retailers has a constant marginal cost of 5 cents/kilowatt hour (kwh), that retailing electricity has a constant marginal cost of 2 cents/kwh and that both markets have a constant demand elasticity of 2, so that a monopolist (not subject to price regulation) would price at double its marginal cost. See Chapter 3.a. Then an integrated monopolist would have a total marginal cost of 7 cents/kwh and charge a price of 14 cents/kwh. If they are separate, however, a wholesale monopolist would charge its monopoly price of 10 cents, and a retail monopolist would have marginal costs of 12 cents (10 cents for the wholesale electricity plus 2 cents of retailing costs) and charge 24 cents. Allowing the wholesale monopolist to integrate downstream would thus both lower prices to consumers and raise the integrated firm's profits because output would increase at lower prices and because it would now earn profits of 7 (rather than 5) cents/kwh.

---

3.   *Monopolist Incentives.* Electricity customers have to pay the sum of wholesale costs and retail markup. If Otter Tail has monopoly power over the sale and transmission of wholesale electricity, and we ignore any price regulation, wouldn't it maximize profits by fostering the most efficient means of retailing electricity with the lowest markup so it could charge a higher monopoly price for the sale or transmission of wholesale electricity?

a.   Absent price regulation, would Otter Tail have any incentives to vertically integrate across the upstream and downstream markets if doing so were inefficient?

b.   Might Otter Tail have concerns that, if allowed to exist, rival electricity retailers could in the long run enter its wholesale or transmission markets or provide a source of sales that might encourage other firms to enter those markets, thus diminishing Otter Tail's monopoly power in wholesaling and transmitting electricity?

c.   Might not the denial of wholesale electricity instead lead:

i.   rival electricity retailers to enter into the wholesale electricity market in the short run? Isn't that what in fact happened in Elbow Lake, which built its own generating plant?

ii.   other firms to create wheeling facilities to transmit wholesale electricity to the rival retailers?

iii.   Would the above results be procompetitive or anticompetitive? Would Otter Tail be likely to refuse to deal if it thought such entry would be the likely results?

4.   *Administrative Problems with Setting the Terms of a Duty to Deal.* Suppose there were no government price regulation. If Otter Tail had an antitrust duty to give rival retailers access to its wholesale electricity and transmission wires, how would it know what terms it had to offer?

a.   Could it offer to sell at $1 billion/kilowatt? A monopoly price? Nothing above its marginal cost? What would the last price do to incentives to create the facilities that are valuable enough to have monopoly power?

b. How are courts and juries supposed to retroactively set the right access price and myriad other contract terms?

i. Wouldn't the correct price vary depending on technical issues beyond the expertise of judges and juries and on market conditions that will continually change with time?

ii. And how can monopolists know what the court or jury they eventually draw will say were the terms they had to offer? Aren't varying courts and juries likely to arrive at varying conclusions?

5. *The Relevance of Agency Regulation.* Should any of our legal conclusions about the best antitrust doctrine on duties to deal be altered by the existence of government electricity regulation?

a. Does the fact that the Federal Power Commission has authority to order wholesale interconnections and regulate wholesale rates mean that:

i. courts should be more ready to impose an antitrust duty to deal because:

(1) the duty would be more administrable given that an expert agency would be able to prospectively and consistently set terms of dealing, monitor compliance, and adjust the terms with changing market conditions?

(2) either the agency sets rates well, and thus preserves sufficient ex ante incentives to invest in creation of the facilities valuable enough to enjoy monopoly power, or sets those prices badly, in which case the antitrust duty at those rates can hardly worsen matters?

ii. an antitrust duty should not be imposed because the Federal Power Commission can already impose a duty if doing so is in the public interest and any court decision might conflict with agency decisions about whether to impose a duty or what terms to adopt? Does the resulting antitrust decision on wholesale interconnections really result in anything different from Federal Power Commission regulation?

b. Does the fact that the Federal Power Commission has no authority to order firms to wheel and thus transmit electricity from another wholesaler to a retailer, but does have authority to set the rates charged for any wheeling that is done, mean that:

i. courts should be more ready to impose an antitrust duty to deal because:

(1) doing so would fill a gap in the regulatory scheme, or at least would not be redundant or raise conflicts with the regulatory scheme?

(2) courts could solve the administrability problem by relying on an expert agency to prospectively and consistently set terms of dealing, monitor compliance, and adjust the terms with changing market conditions?

(3) the reality of agency rate regulation means that an antitrust duty to deal at those rates cannot worsen ex ante incentives to create valuable facilities that enjoy monopoly power?

ii.   courts should not impose any antitrust duty to wheel because Congress rejected giving the Federal Power Commission authority to impose a duty to transmit electricity? Does this rejection indicate a legislative desire (a) to allow firms to refuse to deal or (b) to leave such refusals to deal subject to regulation by other sources of law like antitrust?

c.   Does the fact that wholesale and wheeling rates were regulated more effectively than retail rates help explain why a firm like Otter Tail might want to extend a wholesale and wheeling monopoly to retail monopolies?

i.   Is the possibility that this strategy might be used to evade price regulation of wholesaling and wheeling electricity a reason to impose an antitrust duty to deal?

ii.   Or is it a reason to leave it to the government regulators for them to decide whether this constitutes an evasion of their price regulation and, if so, how they want to remedy it?

6.   *The Relevance of Discrimination Among Buyers Based on Rivalry.* What relevance does it have that Otter Tail did wheel and wholesale electric power to electric systems that did *not* compete with it in retailing electricity?

a.   Does it help provide prices and other terms to use to enforce a duty to deal with systems that do compete with it at retail?

b.   Does it help assure us that those prices and terms are sufficient to create ex ante incentives to build the facilities valuable enough to enjoy monopoly power?

c.   Does it help indicate that there are no insuperable inefficiencies in splitting retailing from wheeling and wholesaling?

d.   Does the fact that Otter Tail is discriminating among buyers based on whether they are its rivals tend to support the conclusion that it does not have a legitimate purpose for the denial to deal with rivals but rather an anticompetitive one?

Should Natural Monopolies Be Immune From Monopolization Liability?

The *Otter Tail* Court implicitly rejected the dissent argument that, given that retailing electricity is a natural monopoly, the anticompetitive conduct could not constitute monopolization because it could not lead to the acquisition or maintenance of monopoly power that would not otherwise exist. One might argue that this argument is economically irrelevant because the real concern was not the retail monopoly against consumers, but rather that the defendant's conduct would mean all the towns would be controlled by the same entity, and thus foreclosed to a possible rival in the upstream market for wholesaling and wheeling electricity, which was not a natural monopoly. But the legal claim was monopolization of the retail market, so the court did implicitly reject the argument that there should be a natural-monopoly defense to a monopolization claim. Three major reasons support such a conclusion.[144] First, even if the market is a natural monopoly, anticompetitive conduct might adversely affect *which firm* acquires or maintains that monopoly power. It is thus desirable to maintain unimpeded competition to help assure the most efficient firm becomes the natural monopolist. Second, whether a market is a natural monopoly is often uncertain, and unimpeded competition helps provide a market test that the market really is a natural monopoly. Such unimpeded competition seems likely to be more accurate than antitrust courts and juries at determining whether the market is a natural monopoly and who should be the natural monopolist. Third, changing technologies, market conditions, or firm efficiencies may alter whether the market is a natural monopoly and/or which firm would be the best natural monopolist. A process of unimpeded market competition seems better suited than litigation to adjust either sort of conclusion with such changing conditions.

Aspen Skiing Co. v. Aspen Highlands Skiing Corp.

472 U.S. 585 (1985).

■ JUSTICE STEVENS delivered the opinion of the Court. . . .

[Aspen is a destination ski resort with four mountains. Defendant Ski Co. owned 3 of those 4 mountains, having developed one mountain, bought another in 1964 after it was already developed, and purchased and developed a third in 1967 after others obtained the land and permits. Plaintiff Highlands owned the fourth mountain. Developing another ski mountain in Aspen was difficult because it generally required approval both by the U.S. Forest Service, which was contingent on environmental concerns, and by the county, which had an anti-growth policy.]

[Starting in 1962, the competing Aspen ski mountains jointly offered all-Aspen six-day passes that were useable by skiers on any Aspen mountain, usually sold at a discount from the price for six daily lift ticket prices, with the revenue from the pass distributed to the firms in proportion to the number of skiers who used its mountains. This] provided convenience to the vast majority of skiers who visited the resort for weekly periods, but preferred to remain flexible about what mountain they might ski each day during the visit. . . .

Highlands' share of the revenues from the [all-Aspen] ticket was 17.5% in 1973–1974, 18.5% in 1974–1975, 16.8% in 1975–1976, and 13.2% in 1976–1977.[8] During these four seasons, Ski Co. did not offer its own 3–area, multi-day ticket in competition with the all-Aspen ticket.[9] By 1977, multiar-

---

144. *See* Elhauge, supra note 33, at, 325–26.

8. Highlands' share of the total market during those seasons, as measured in skier visits was 15.8% in 1973–1974, 17.1% in 1974–1975, 17.4% in 1975–1976, and 20.5% in 1976–1977.

9. In 1975, the Colorado Attorney General filed a complaint against Ski Co. and Highlands alleging, in part, that the negotiations over the 4–area ticket had provided them with a forum for price fixing in violation of § 1 of the Sherman Act. . . . In 1977, the case was

ea tickets accounted for nearly 35% of the total market. Holders of multiarea passes also accounted for additional daily ticket sales to persons skiing with them.

. . . [F]or the 1977–1978 season, Ski Co. offered to continue the all-Aspen ticket only if Highlands would accept a 13.2% fixed share of the ticket's revenues. [Highlands resisted on the grounds that the 1976–77 share was an outlier because of weather conditions that year, but when Ski company continued to refuse to divide revenue based on actual usage] Highlands eventually accepted a fixed percentage of 15% for the 1977–1978 season. No survey was made during that season of actual usage of the 4–area ticket at the two competitors' mountains.

In the 1970's the management of Ski Co. increasingly expressed their dislike for the all-Aspen ticket. They complained that a coupon method of monitoring usage was administratively cumbersome. They doubted the accuracy of the survey and decried the "appearance, deportment, [and] attitude" of the college students who were conducting it. In addition, Ski Co.'s president had expressed the view that the 4–area ticket was siphoning off revenues that could be recaptured by Ski Co. if the ticket was discontinued. In fact, Ski Co. had reinstated its 3–area, 6–day ticket during the 1977–1978 season, but that ticket had been outsold by the 4–area, 6–day ticket nearly two to one.

In March 1978, the Ski Co. management recommended to the board of directors that the 4–area ticket be discontinued for the 1978–1979 season. The board decided to offer Highlands a 4–area ticket provided that Highlands would agree to receive a 12.5% fixed percentage of the revenue— considerably below Highlands' historical average based on usage. Later in the 1978–1979 season, a member of Ski Co.'s board of directors candidly informed a Highlands official that he had advocated making Highlands "an offer that [it] could not accept."

Finding the proposal unacceptable, Highlands suggested a distribution of the revenues based on usage to be monitored by coupons, electronic counting, or random sample surveys. If Ski Co. was concerned about who was to conduct the survey, Highlands proposed to hire disinterested ticket counters at its own expense—"somebody like Price Waterhouse"—to count or survey usage of the 4–area ticket at Highlands. Ski Co. refused to consider any counterproposals, and Highlands finally rejected the offer of the fixed percentage. . . .

Ski Co. took additional actions that made it extremely difficult for Highlands to market its own multiarea package to replace the joint offering. Ski Co. discontinued the 3–day, 3–area pass for the 1978–1979 season,[13] and also refused to sell Highlands any lift tickets, either at the tour operator's discount or at retail. Highlands finally developed an alternative

---

settled by a consent decree that permitted the parties to continue to offer the 4–area ticket provided that they set their own ticket prices unilaterally before negotiating its terms.

13. . . . "with the three day ticket, a person could ski on the . . . Aspen Skiing Corporation mountains for three days and then there would be three days in which he could ski on our mountain; but with the six-day ticket, we are absolutely locked out of those people." As a result of "tremendous consumer demand" for a 3–day ticket, Ski Co. reinstated it late in the 1978–1979 season, but without publicity or a discount off the daily rate.

product, the "Adventure Pack," which consisted of a 3–day pass at Highlands and three vouchers, each equal to the price of a daily lift ticket at a Ski Co. mountain. The vouchers were guaranteed by funds on deposit in an Aspen bank, and were redeemed by Aspen merchants at full value. Ski Co., however, refused to accept them.

Later, Highlands redesigned the Adventure Pack to contain American Express Traveler's Checks or money orders instead of vouchers. Ski Co. eventually accepted these negotiable instruments in exchange for daily lift tickets.[15] Despite some strengths of the product, the Adventure Pack met considerable resistance from tour operators and consumers who had grown accustomed to the convenience and flexibility provided by the all-Aspen ticket.

Without a convenient all-Aspen ticket, Highlands basically "becomes a day ski area in a destination resort." Highlands' share of the market for downhill skiing services in Aspen declined steadily after the 4–area ticket based on usage was abolished in 1977: from 20.5% in 1976–1977, to 15.7% in 1977–1978, to 13.1% in 1978–1979, to 12.5% in 1979–1980, to 11% in 1980–1981. . . .

. . . . In her instructions to the jury, the District Judge explained that the offense of monopolization under § 2 of the Sherman Act has two elements: (1) the possession of monopoly power in a relevant market, and (2) the willful acquisition, maintenance, or use of that power by anticompetitive or exclusionary means or for anticompetitive or exclusionary purposes.[19] Although the first element was vigorously disputed at the trial and in the Court of Appeals, in this Court Ski Co. does not challenge the jury's special verdict finding that it possessed monopoly power. Nor does Ski Co. criticize the trial court's instructions to the jury concerning the second element of the § 2 offense. . . .

Ski Co. filed a motion for judgment notwithstanding the verdict, contending that the evidence was insufficient to support a § 2 violation as a matter of law. . . .[22] . . . The District Court denied Ski Co.'s motion and entered a judgment awarding Highlands treble damages of $7,500,000, costs and attorney's fees.[23]

---

15. Of course, there was nothing to identify Highlands as the source of these instruments, unless someone saw the skier "taking it out of an Adventure Pack envelope." For the 1981–1982 season, Ski Co. set its single ticket price at $22 and discounted the 3–area, 6–day ticket to $114. According to Highlands, this price structure made the Adventure Pack unprofitable.

19. In *Grinnell* we explained: "The offense of monopoly under § 2 of the Sherman Act has two elements: (1) the possession of monopoly power in the relevant market and (2) the willful acquisition or maintenance of that power as distinguished from growth or development as a consequence of a superior product, business acumen, or historic accident."

22. Counsel also appears to have argued that Ski Co. was under a legal obligation to refuse to participate in any joint marketing arrangement with Highlands . . . In this Court, Ski Co. does not question the validity of the joint marketing arrangement under § 1 of the Sherman Act. Thus, we have no occasion to consider the circumstances that might permit such combinations in the skiing industry. See generally *NCAA*; *BMI*; *GTE Sylvania*.

23. The District Court also entered an injunction requiring the parties to offer jointly a 4–area, 6–out–of–7–day coupon booklet substantially identical to the "Ski the Summit" booklet accepted by Ski Co. at its Breckenridge resort in Summit County, Colorado. The

The Court of Appeals affirmed in all respects. . . .

III

. . . . "The central message of the Sherman Act is that a business entity must find new customers and higher profits through internal expansion— that is, by competing successfully rather than by arranging treaties with its competitors." Ski Co., therefore, is surely correct in submitting that even a firm with monopoly power has no general duty to engage in a joint marketing program with a competitor. . . .

The absence of an unqualified duty to cooperate does not mean that every time a firm declines to participate in a particular cooperative venture, that decision may not have evidentiary significance, or that it may not give rise to liability in certain circumstances. The absence of a duty to transact business with another firm is, in some respects, merely the counterpart of the independent businessman's cherished right to select his customers and his associates. The high value that we have placed on the right to refuse to deal with other firms does not mean that the right is unqualified.

In *Lorain Journal,* we squarely held that this right was not unquali- fied. Between 1933 and 1948 the publisher of the Lorain Journal, a newspaper, was the only local business disseminating news and advertising in that Ohio town. In 1948, a small radio station was established in a nearby community. In an effort to destroy its small competitor, . . . the Journal refused to sell advertising to persons that patronized the radio station.

In holding that this conduct violated § 2 of the Sherman Act, the Court dispatched the same argument raised by the monopolist here:

> "The publisher claims a right as a private business concern to select its customers and to refuse to accept advertisements from whomever it pleases. We do not dispute that general right. 'But the word "right" is one of the most deceptive of pitfalls; it is so easy to slip from a qualified meaning in the premise to an unqualified one in the conclusion. Most rights are qualified.' The right claimed by the publisher is neither absolute nor exempt from regulation. Its exercise as a purposeful means of monopolizing interstate commerce is prohibited by the Sherman Act. . . .

In *Lorain Journal,* the violation of § 2 was an "attempt to monopo- lize," rather than monopolization, but the question of intent is relevant to both offenses. In the former case it is necessary to prove a "specific intent" to accomplish the forbidden objective—as Judge Hand explained, "an intent which goes beyond the mere intent to do the act." *United States v. Aluminum Co. of America,* 148 F.2d 416, 432 (CA2 1945). In the latter case evidence of intent is merely relevant to the question whether the chal- lenged conduct is fairly characterized as "exclusionary" or "anticompeti- tive"—to use the words in the trial court's instructions—or "predatory," to

---

injunction was initially for a 3–year period, but was later extended through the 1984–1985 season by stipulation of the parties. Highlands represents that "it will not seek an extension of the injunction." No question is raised concerning the character of the injunctive relief ordered by the District Court.

use a word that scholars seem to favor. Whichever label is used, there is agreement on the proposition that "no monopolist monopolizes unconscious of what he is doing." As Judge Bork stated more recently: "Improper exclusion (exclusion not the result of superior efficiency) is always deliberately intended."

The qualification on the right of a monopolist to deal with whom he pleases is not so narrow that it encompasses no more than the circumstances of *Lorain Journal.* In the actual case that we must decide, the monopolist did not merely reject a novel offer to participate in a cooperative venture that had been proposed by a competitor. Rather, the monopolist elected to make an important change in a pattern of distribution that had originated in a competitive market and had persisted for several years. The all-Aspen, 6–day ticket with revenues allocated on the basis of usage was first developed when three independent companies operated three different ski mountains in the Aspen area. It continued to provide a desirable option for skiers when the market was enlarged to include four mountains, and when the character of the market was changed by Ski Co.'s acquisition of monopoly power. Moreover, since the record discloses that interchangeable tickets are used in other multimountain areas which apparently are competitive,[30] it seems appropriate to infer that such tickets satisfy consumer demand in free competitive markets.

Ski Co.'s decision to terminate the all-Aspen ticket was thus a decision by a monopolist to make an important change in the character of the market.[31] Such a decision is not necessarily anticompetitive, and Ski Co. contends that neither its decision, nor the conduct in which it engaged to implement that decision, can fairly be characterized as exclusionary in this case. . . .

[W]e must assume that the jury followed the court's instructions. The jury must, therefore, have drawn a distinction "between practices which tend to exclude or restrict competition on the one hand, and the success of a business which reflects only a superior product, a well-run business, or luck, on the other." Since the jury was unambiguously instructed that Ski Co.'s refusal to deal with Highlands "does not violate Section 2 if valid business reasons exist for that refusal," we must assume that the jury concluded that there were no valid business reasons for the refusal. The question then is whether that conclusion finds support in the record.

---

30. Ski Co. itself participates in interchangeable ticket programs in at least two other markets. . . . Interchangeable lift tickets apparently are also available in some European skiing areas.

31. "In any business, patterns of distribution develop over time; these may reasonably be thought to be more efficient than alternative patterns of distribution that do not develop. The patterns that do develop and persist we may call the optimal patterns. By disturbing optimal distribution patterns one rival can impose costs upon another, that is, force the other to accept higher costs." Bork 156. In § 1 cases where this Court has applied the *per se* approach to invalidity to concerted refusals to deal, "the boycott often cut off access to a supply, facility or market necessary to enable the boycotted firm to compete, . . . and frequently the boycotting firms possessed a dominant position in the relevant market." *Northwest Stationers.*

IV

The question whether Ski Co.'s conduct may properly be characterized as exclusionary cannot be answered by simply considering its effect on Highlands. In addition, it is relevant to consider its impact on consumers and whether it has impaired competition in an unnecessarily restrictive way.[32] If a firm has been "attempting to exclude rivals on some basis other than efficiency," it is fair to characterize its behavior as predatory. It is, accordingly, appropriate to examine the effect of the challenged pattern of conduct on consumers, on Ski Co.'s smaller rival, and on Ski Co. itself.

Superior Quality of the All–Aspen Ticket ...

Over 80% of the skiers visiting the resort each year have been there before—40% of these repeat visitors have skied Aspen at least five times. Over the years, they developed a strong demand for the 6–day, all-Aspen ticket in its various refinements. Most experienced skiers quite logically prefer to purchase their tickets at once for the whole period that they will spend at the resort; they can then spend more time on the slopes and enjoying après-ski amenities and less time standing in ticket lines. The 4–area attribute of the ticket allowed the skier to purchase his 6–day ticket in advance while reserving the right to decide in his own time and for his own reasons which mountain he would ski on each day. It provided convenience and flexibility, and expanded the vistas and the number of challenging runs available to him during the week's vacation.

While the 3–area, 6–day ticket offered by Ski Co. possessed some of these attributes, the evidence supports a conclusion that consumers were adversely affected by the elimination of the 4–area ticket. In the first place, the actual record of competition between a 3–area ticket and the all-Aspen ticket in the years after 1967 indicated that skiers demonstrably preferred four mountains to three.... A consumer survey undertaken in the 1979–1980 season indicated that 53.7% of the respondents wanted to ski Highlands, but would not; 39.9% said that they would not be skiing at the mountain of their choice because their ticket would not permit it.... A major wholesale tour operator asserted that he would not even consider marketing a 3–area ticket if a 4–area ticket were available....

Highlands' Ability to Compete

The adverse impact of Ski Co.'s pattern of conduct on Highlands is not disputed in this Court.... The evidence concerning its attempt to develop a substitute product either by buying Ski Co.'s daily tickets in bulk, or by marketing its own Adventure Pack, demonstrates that it tried to protect itself from the loss of its share of the patrons of the all-Aspen ticket. The development of a new distribution system for providing the experience that skiers had learned to expect in Aspen proved to be prohibitively expensive. As a result, Highlands' share of the relevant market steadily declined after the 4–area ticket was terminated. The size of the damages award also

---

32. "Thus, 'exclusionary' comprehends at the most behavior that not only (1) tends to impair the opportunities of rivals, but also (2) either does not further competition on the merits or does so in an unnecessarily restrictive way." 3 P. Areeda & D. Turner, Antitrust Law 78 (1978).

confirms the substantial character of the effect of Ski Co.'s conduct upon Highlands.[38]

Ski Co.'s Business Justification

Perhaps most significant, however, is the evidence relating to Ski Co. itself, for Ski Co. did not persuade the jury that its conduct was justified by any normal business purpose. Ski Co. was apparently willing to forgo daily ticket sales both to skiers who sought to exchange the coupons contained in Highlands' Adventure Pack, and to those who would have purchased Ski Co. daily lift tickets from Highlands if Highlands had been permitted to purchase them in bulk. The jury may well have concluded that Ski Co. elected to forgo these short-run benefits because it was more interested in reducing competition in the Aspen market over the long run by harming its smaller competitor.

That conclusion is strongly supported by Ski Co.'s failure to offer any efficiency justification whatever for its pattern of conduct.[39] In defending the decision to terminate the jointly offered ticket, Ski Co. claimed that usage could not be properly monitored. The evidence, however, established that Ski Co. itself monitored the use of the 3–area passes based on a count taken by lift operators, and distributed the revenues among its mountains on that basis. Ski Co. contended that coupons were administratively cumbersome, and that the survey takers had been disruptive and their work inaccurate. Coupons, however, were no more burdensome than the credit cards accepted at Ski Co. ticket windows. Moreover, in other markets Ski Co. itself participated in interchangeable lift tickets using coupons. As for the survey, its own manager testified that the problems were much overemphasized by Ski Co. officials, and were mostly resolved as they arose. Ski Co.'s explanation for the rejection of Highlands' offer to hire—at its own expense—a reputable national accounting firm to audit usage of the 4–area tickets at Highlands' mountain, was that there was no way to "control" the audit.

In the end, Ski Co. was pressed to justify its pattern of conduct on a desire to disassociate itself from—what it considered—the inferior skiing services offered at Highlands. The all-Aspen ticket based on usage, however, allowed consumers to make their own choice on these matters of quality. Ski Co.'s purported concern for the relative quality of Highlands' product was supported in the record by little more than vague insinuations, and was sharply contested by numerous witnesses. Moreover, Ski Co.

---

38. In considering the competitive effect of Ski Co.'s refusal to deal or cooperate with Highlands, it is not irrelevant to note that similar conduct carried out by the concerted action of three independent rivals with a similar share of the market would constitute a *per se* violation of § 1 of the Sherman Act. See *Northwest Stationers*; Cf. *Lorain Journal*.

39. "The law can usefully attack this form of predation only when there is evidence of specific intent to drive others from the market by means other than superior efficiency and when the predator has overwhelming market size, perhaps 80 or 90 percent. Proof of specific intent to engage in predation may be in the form of statements made by the officers or agents of the company, evidence that the conduct was used threateningly and did not continue when a rival capitulated, or *evidence that the conduct was not related to any apparent efficiency.* These matters are not so difficult of proof as to render the test overly hard to meet." Bork 157 (emphasis added).

admitted that it was willing to associate with what it considered to be inferior products in other markets.

Although Ski Co.'s pattern of conduct may not have been as " 'bold, relentless, and predatory' " as the publisher's actions in *Lorain Journal,* the record in this case comfortably supports an inference that the monopolist made a deliberate effort to discourage its customers from doing business with its smaller rival. The sale of its 3–area, 6–day ticket, particularly when it was discounted below the daily ticket price, deterred the ticket holders from skiing at Highlands. The refusal to accept the Adventure Pack coupons in exchange for daily tickets was apparently motivated entirely by a decision to avoid providing any benefit to Highlands even though accepting the coupons would have entailed no cost to Ski Co. itself, would have provided it with immediate benefits, and would have satisfied its potential customers. Thus the evidence supports an inference that Ski Co. was not motivated by efficiency concerns and that it was willing to sacrifice short-run benefits and consumer goodwill in exchange for a perceived long-run impact on its smaller rival.

Because we are satisfied that the evidence in the record,[44] construed most favorably in support of Highlands' position, is adequate to support the verdict under the instructions given by the trial court, the judgment of the Court of Appeals is *Affirmed.*

Questions on *Aspen Skiing*

1. Is the Court right that *Lorain Journal* supports some antitrust duty to deal with rivals? Can't *Lorain Journal* be distinguished as a case where the defendant was dealing with buyers on the condition that those buyers not buy from its rivals? Isn't prohibiting such conditioned sales different from requiring a firm to sell to its rival? Doesn't it leave a firm free to make unconditioned sales to whomever it chooses?

2. How can one tell that this refusal to deal was illegal?

a. Doesn't the fact that Highlands wants to force Ski Co to deal with it rather than vice versa show that Ski Co's mountains offer a superior product?

    i. If so, then why isn't it innocent of monopolization because any exclusion resulted from that superior product?

    ii. Isn't it always true a rival would only want to impose a duty on a monopolist to offer its facility to the rival when the monopolist's facility is a superior product to what the rival can muster? Otherwise what harm would come from denying the facility to the rival?

b. How can one tell whether the business purpose for denying access is valid or not?

---

44. Given our conclusion that the evidence amply supports the verdict under the instructions as given by the trial court, we find it unnecessary to consider the possible relevance of the "essential facilities" doctrine, or the somewhat hypothetical question whether nonexclusionary conduct could ever constitute an abuse of monopoly power if motivated by an anticompetitive purpose. If, as we have assumed, no monopolist monopolizes unconscious of what he is doing, that case is unlikely to arise.

i. Why is the Court convinced that Ski Co's refusal to deal was not justified by administrative problems, the difficulties of monitoring, or a desire not to be associated with inferior mountains?

ii. Why shouldn't it be up to the owner of the mountains to determine the extent to which these are serious concerns? Are courts and juries likely to be well placed to decide technical issues about whether sharing access is feasible and how it should be done? Are varying courts and juries likely to reach consistent decisions on such issues?

c. Why isn't excluding rivals from the fruits of one's property rights always a valid business purpose?

i. Isn't it true that such an exclusion must be more profitable or the monopolist wouldn't do it? Ski Co did lose some profitable sales by declining to participate, but didn't its market share and thus profits increase the very first year when it stopped cooperating on the joint pass?

ii. Won't those increased profits increase ex ante incentives to invest in creating and maintaining property valuable enough to enjoy monopoly power? How does the strength of this argument turn on the extent to which one thinks such ski mountains (a) are endowed by nature versus (b) require significant investment to develop and maintain?

d. Does the decision here mean that monopolists always have to deal with rivals whenever it is feasible and consumers would want it and be willing to pay for it? Does the Court rely on any evidence other than this?

e. Why isn't offering a joint pass an illegal horizontal agreement? Isn't avoiding the risk of such antitrust violation itself a valid business justification?

f. Was there a refusal to deal here at all or just a disagreement on price? Didn't Ski Co in fact offer to continue cooperating on a joint pass if its rival would take less of the revenue?

i. Why isn't it fair for Ski Co to take a disproportionate share of the revenue given that it has 3 of the 4 mountains that contribute to the special convenience of a joint pass?

ii. What standards do courts or juries have to determine that the offered terms were not adequate?

g. Did Ski Co's decision drive its rival out of the market? Was it likely to? If not, why isn't it more anticompetitive to impose the shared monopoly of a joint pass rather than to have the firms compete by offering only separate passes?

3. What are the possible limits on the *Apsen* antitrust duty to deal?

a. Should any such antitrust duty to deal be limited to cases where the monopoly power over the facility for which sharing is sought was not created by investment, but was the result of some unearned advantage like government regulation or creations of nature like mountains?

i. If a facility with monopoly power was the result of unearned advantage, how would that affect:

(1) the fear that a duty to share will discourage the initial investment to create the facility?

(2) the fear that a duty to share will discourage rivals from engaging in competitive duplication, and thus will produce a shared monopoly instead of competition?

ii. What concerns might be raised if the source of the facility with monopoly power were part of the legal test?

(1) How would one handle mixed cases where the monopoly power resulted from a combination of investment and unearned advantages?

(2) Would such a test discourage investments to maintain or enhance the value of the facility?

(3) Would such a test encourage inefficient investments in the initial creation to get an exemption?

b. Should any *Aspen* duty to deal be limited to cases where, like here, the defendant had in the past dealt with its rival?

i. Is the fact of past dealing relevant to any functional considerations?

(1) Is the fact of past dealing relevant to whether a valid business justification might exist for not dealing now, especially if the practice were established in a competitive market?

(2) Does the fact of past dealing provide a ready benchmark to set the *terms* of mandated dealing? Won't such a benchmark become outmoded as market conditions change over time? Does this help explain why the plaintiff did not seek any extension of the injunction beyond four years?

ii. What concerns might be raised if termination of an existing relationship were a necessary element for an antitrust duty to deal?

(1) Do we want business dealings to give businesses tenure like law professors? Might this freeze inefficient relationships into place?

(2) Won't such an element discourage firms from initially doing any business that might help their rivals enter their market? Which is more anticompetitive, preventing a rival from entering a market or trying to cut it off after they have already entered?

iii. Can such a limitation be justified doctrinally? Didn't *Otter Tail* impose a duty to deal with new entrants into the electricity retail business to whom it had never before supplied or wheeled wholesale electricity?

c. If Ski Co. did not offer lift tickets to consumers, would it have to offer them to its rival? Should discrimination against rivals be a necessary condition to any *Aspen* antitrust duty to deal?[145]

    i.   Would a requirement that Ski Co just sell lift tickets to its rival at the same retail rate it charges other buyers and treat those with a resulting joint pass the same as its other customers: (a) make it easier to determine the price and other terms of any duty to deal?, (b) make it easier to vary those prices and terms with changing market conditions?, and (c) provide greater assurances of uniformity across different judges and juries?

    ii.   Would such a requirement maintain efficient incentives for ex ante investment by allowing the monopolist property owner to set the rate necessary to compensate its investment?

    iii.   If a monopolist property owner were subject only to a such a nondiscrimination duty and thus free to charge rivals the same monopoly rate it charged everyone else, would the duty unduly diminish rival incentives to duplicate the valuable facility?

    iv.   Unless a firm were in the business of selling what the rival wants to buy, would courts be well positioned to determine when it would be efficient (ex post of the creation of the facility) for the firm to sell that access to its facility separately?

    v.   Suppose a firm has monopoly power over some input and can also make a finished product that requires that essential input. Might a nondiscrimination duty give that firm inefficient incentives to never sell the input to anyone but instead use all the input to make the finished product? Was this a likely concern on the facts of *Aspen*? Of *Otter Tail*?

Eastman Kodak v. Image Technical Servs.

504 U.S. 451 (1992).

■ Justice Blackmun delivered the opinion of the Court.

[Portions of the opinion relating to market and monopoly power were excerpted Chapter 3.A, and portions relating to tying agreements are excerpted in Chapter 4.]

    ... Petitioner Eastman Kodak Company manufactures and sells photocopiers and micrographic equipment. Kodak also sells service and replacement parts for its equipment. Respondents are 18 independent service organizations (ISO's) that in the early 1980's began servicing Kodak copying and micrographic equipment. Kodak subsequently adopted policies to limit the availability of parts to ISO's and to make it more difficult for ISO's to compete with Kodak in servicing Kodak equipment....

    "The offense of monopoly under § 2 of the Sherman Act has two elements: (1) the possession of monopoly power in the relevant market and (2) the willful acquisition or maintenance of that power as distinguished from growth or development as a consequence of a superior product, business acumen, or historic accident." *Grinnell*.... The existence of the

---

145.   See Elhauge, *supra* note 37 at 305–14 (arguing that it should).

first element, possession of monopoly power, is easily resolved [for reasons excerpted above]. . . .

The second element of a § 2 claim is the use of monopoly power "to foreclose competition, to gain a competitive advantage, or to destroy a competitor." *Griffith*. If Kodak adopted its parts and service policies as part of a scheme of willful acquisition or maintenance of monopoly power, it will have violated § 2. *Grinnell*; *Aspen Skiing*.[32]

. . . [R]espondents have presented evidence that Kodak took exclusionary action to maintain its parts monopoly and used its control over parts to strengthen its monopoly share of the Kodak service market. Liability turns, then, on whether "valid business reasons" can explain Kodak's actions. *Aspen Skiing; Alcoa*. Kodak contends that it has three valid business justifications for its actions . . .

Kodak first asserts that by preventing customers from using ISOs, "it [can] best maintain high quality service for its sophisticated equipment" and avoid being "blamed for an equipment malfunction, even if the problem is the result of improper diagnosis, maintenance or repair by an ISO." Respondents have offered evidence that ISOs provide quality service and are preferred by some Kodak equipment owners. This is sufficient to raise a genuine issue of fact. . . .

Moreover, there are other reasons to question Kodak's proffered motive of commitment to quality service; its quality justification appears inconsistent with its thesis that consumers are knowledgeable enough to lifecycle price, and its self-service policy. Kodak claims the exclusive-service contract is warranted because customers would otherwise blame Kodak equipment for breakdowns resulting from inferior ISO service. Thus, Kodak simultaneously claims that its customers are sophisticated enough to make complex and subtle lifecycle-pricing decisions, and yet too obtuse to distinguish which breakdowns are due to bad equipment and which are due to bad service. Kodak has failed to offer any reason why informational sophistication should be present in one circumstance and absent in the other. In addition, because self-service customers are just as likely as others to blame Kodak equipment for breakdowns resulting from (their own) inferior service, Kodak's willingness to allow self-service casts doubt on its quality claim. In sum, we agree with the Court of Appeals that respondents "have presented evidence from which a reasonable trier of fact could conclude that Kodak's first reason is pretextual."

There is also a triable issue of fact on Kodak's second justification—controlling inventory costs. As respondents argue, Kodak's actions appear inconsistent with any need to control inventory costs. Presumably, the inventory of parts needed to repair Kodak machines turns only on breakdown rates, and those rates should be the same whether Kodak or ISOs perform the repair. More importantly, the justification fails to explain respondents' evidence that Kodak forced OEMs, equipment owners, and

---

32.   It is true that as a general matter a firm can refuse to deal with its competitors. But such a right is not absolute; it exists only if there are legitimate competitive reasons for the refusal. *See Aspen Skiing*.

parts brokers not to sell parts to ISOs, actions that would have no effect on Kodak's inventory costs.

Nor does Kodak's final justification entitle it to summary judgment on respondents' § 2 claim. Kodak claims that its policies prevent ISOs from "exploiting the investment Kodak has made in product development, manufacturing and equipment sales in order to take away Kodak's service revenues." Kodak does not dispute that respondents invest substantially in the service market, with training of repair workers and investment in parts inventory. Instead, according to Kodak, the ISOs are free-riding because they have failed to enter the equipment and parts markets. This understanding of free-riding has no support in our caselaw.[33] To the contrary, as the Court of Appeals noted, one of the evils proscribed by the antitrust laws is the creation of entry barriers to potential competitors by requiring them to enter two markets simultaneously. *Jefferson Parish; Fortner.*

None of Kodak's asserted business justifications, then, are sufficient to prove that Kodak is "entitled to a judgment as a matter of law" on respondents' § 2 claim. . . .

Questions on the *Kodak* Duty to Deal With Rivals

1. What reasons did Kodak offer for its refusal to supply parts to its service rivals? Why does the Court reject them as invalid?

2. Why can't rivals just duplicate Kodak's parts?

a. If they can, shouldn't any duty to deal be denied so that rivals enter the parts market and thus create competition in both parts and service?

b. If they can't because of Kodak's intellectual property rights in its parts, why isn't it valid justification that Kodak's intellectual property rights give it the legal right to exclude rivals from access to its parts in order to maximize its profits from them and give Kodak sufficient incentives to invest in innovation to create those intellectual property rights?

3. What, if any, anticompetitive effects did the refusal to deal have that Kodak could not have achieved simply by increasing its price on parts? Does every firm with unique parts for its equipment now have to sell those parts to rival service providers unless it can show that such provision would produce some inefficiency?

4. If Kodak were held to have a duty to deal after trial, how would a court set the prices and other terms at which it must sell parts to service rivals?

---

33. Kodak claims that both *GTE Sylvania* and *Monsanto* support its free-rider argument. Neither is applicable. In both [cases] the Court accepted free-riding as a justification because without restrictions a manufacturer would not be able to induce competent and aggressive retailers to make the kind of investment of capital and labor necessary to distribute the product. In *GTE Sylvania* the relevant market level was retail sale of televisions and in *Monsanto* retail sales of herbicides. Some retailers were investing in those markets; others were not, relying, instead, on the investment of the other retailers. To be applicable to this case, the ISOs would have to be relying on Kodak's investment in the service market; that, however, is not Kodak's argument.

5. Would Kodak have still lost the case if it had not previously sold parts to rival service providers? If it did not sell parts separately to buyers who did not compete with Kodak in selling service? Absent such termination of prior dealing or discrimination against rivals, would there be:

a. any market basis for concluding that separate provision of parts was efficient?

b. any consistent and reliable basis for the Court to set the terms at which Kodak had to sell parts to its service rivals? A basis that is continually updated with changing market conditions?

c. any assurance that the terms set for parts did not undermine ex ante incentives to create valuable parts?

Verizon Commun. v. Law Offices of Curtis V. Trinko

540 U.S. 398 (2004).

■ Justice Scalia delivered the opinion of the Court.

The Telecommunications Act of 1996 imposes certain duties upon incumbent local telephone companies in order to facilitate market entry by competitors, and establishes a complex regime for monitoring and enforcement. In this case we consider whether a complaint alleging breach of the incumbent's duty under the 1996 Act to share its network with competitors states a claim under § 2 of the Sherman Act.

I

Petitioner Verizon Communications Inc. is the incumbent local exchange carrier (LEC) serving New York State. Before the 1996 Act, Verizon, like other incumbent LECs, enjoyed an exclusive franchise within its local service area. The 1996 Act sought to "uproo[t]" the incumbent LECs' monopoly and to introduce competition in its place. Central to the scheme of the Act is the incumbent LEC's obligation under 47 U.S.C. § 251(c) to share its network with competitors, including provision of access to individual elements of the network on an "unbundled" basis. New entrants, so-called competitive LECs, resell these unbundled network elements (UNEs), recombined with each other or with elements belonging to the LECs.

Verizon . . . has signed interconnection agreements with rivals such as AT&T, as it is obliged to do under § 252, detailing the terms on which it will make its network elements available. (Because Verizon and AT&T could not agree upon terms, the open issues were subjected to compulsory arbitration under §§ 252(b) and (c).) . . . Part of Verizon's UNE obligation under § 251(c)(3) is the provision of access to operations support systems (OSS), a set of systems used by incumbent LECs to provide services to customers and ensure quality. Verizon's interconnection agreement and long-distance authorization each specified the mechanics by which its OSS obligation would be met. As relevant here, a competitive LEC sends orders for service through an electronic interface with Verizon's ordering system, and as Verizon completes certain steps in filling the order, it sends confirmation back through the same interface. Without OSS access a rival cannot fill its customers' orders.

In late 1999, competitive LECs complained to regulators that many orders were going unfilled, in violation of Verizon's obligation to provide access to OSS functions. The PSC and FCC opened parallel investigations, which led to a series of orders by the PSC and a consent decree with the FCC. Under the FCC consent decree, Verizon undertook to make a "voluntary contribution" to the U. S. Treasury in the amount of $3 million; under the PSC orders, Verizon incurred liability to the competitive LECs in the amount of $10 million. Under the consent decree and orders, Verizon was subjected to new performance measurements and new reporting requirements to the FCC and PSC, with additional penalties for continued noncompliance. In June 2000, the FCC terminated the consent decree. The next month the PSC relieved Verizon of the heightened reporting requirement.

Respondent Law Offices of Curtis V. Trinko, LLP, a New York City law firm, was a local telephone service customer of AT&T. The day after Verizon entered its consent decree with the FCC, respondent filed a complaint ... on behalf of itself and a class of similarly situated customers. The complaint ... alleged that Verizon had filled rivals' orders on a discriminatory basis as part of an anticompetitive scheme to discourage customers from becoming or remaining customers of competitive LECs, thus impeding the competitive LECs' ability to enter and compete in the market for local telephone service.... The complaint sought damages and injunctive relief for violation of § 2 of the Sherman Act.... We granted certiorari, limited to the question whether the Court of Appeals erred in reversing the District Court's dismissal of respondent's antitrust claims.

II

To decide this case, we must first determine what effect (if any) the 1996 Act has upon the application of traditional antitrust principles.... Under the sharing duties of § 251(c), incumbent LECs are required to offer three kinds of access.... [P]erhaps most intrusive, is the duty to offer access to UNEs on "just, reasonable, and nondiscriminatory" terms, a phrase that the FCC has interpreted to mean a price reflecting long-run incremental cost. A rival can interconnect its own facilities with those of the incumbent LEC, or it can simply purchase services at wholesale from the incumbent and resell them to consumers. The Act also imposes upon incumbents the duty to allow physical "collocation"—that is, to permit a competitor to locate and install its equipment on the incumbent's premises—which makes feasible interconnection and access to UNEs.

That Congress created these duties, however, does not automatically lead to the conclusion that they can be enforced by means of an antitrust claim. Indeed, a detailed regulatory scheme such as that created by the 1996 Act ordinarily raises the question whether the regulated entities are not shielded from antitrust scrutiny altogether by the doctrine of implied immunity. In some respects the enforcement scheme set up by the 1996 Act is a good candidate for implication of antitrust immunity, to avoid the real possibility of judgments conflicting with the agency's regulatory scheme "that might be voiced by courts exercising jurisdiction under the antitrust laws."

Congress, however, precluded that interpretation. Section 601(b)(1) of the 1996 Act is an antitrust-specific saving clause providing that "nothing in this Act or the amendments made by this Act shall be construed to modify, impair, or supersede the applicability of any of the antitrust laws." This bars a finding of implied immunity. As the FCC has put the point, the saving clause preserves those "claims that satisfy established antitrust standards."

But just as the 1996 Act preserves claims that satisfy existing antitrust standards, it does not create new claims that go beyond existing antitrust standards; that would be equally inconsistent with the saving clause's mandate that nothing in the Act "modify, impair, or supersede the applicability" of the antitrust laws. We turn, then, to whether the activity of which respondent complains violates preexisting antitrust standards.

III

The complaint alleges that Verizon denied interconnection services to rivals in order to limit entry. If that allegation states an antitrust claim at all, it does so under § 2 of the Sherman Act, which declares that a firm shall not "monopolize" or "attempt to monopolize." It is settled law that this offense requires, in addition to the possession of monopoly power in the relevant market, "the willful acquisition or maintenance of that power as distinguished from growth or development as a consequence of a superior product, business acumen, or historic accident." *Grinnell*. The mere possession of monopoly power, and the concomitant charging of monopoly prices, is not only not unlawful; it is an important element of the free-market system. The opportunity to charge monopoly prices—at least for a short period—is what attracts "business acumen" in the first place; it induces risk taking that produces innovation and economic growth. To safeguard the incentive to innovate, the possession of monopoly power will not be found unlawful unless it is accompanied by an element of anticompetitive *conduct*.

Firms may acquire monopoly power by establishing an infrastructure that renders them uniquely suited to serve their customers. Compelling such firms to share the source of their advantage is in some tension with the underlying purpose of antitrust law, since it may lessen the incentive for the monopolist, the rival, or both to invest in those economically beneficial facilities. Enforced sharing also requires antitrust courts to act as central planners, identifying the proper price, quantity, and other terms of dealing—a role for which they are ill-suited. Moreover, compelling negotiation between competitors may facilitate the supreme evil of antitrust: collusion. Thus, as a general matter, the Sherman Act "does not restrict the long recognized right of [a] trader or manufacturer engaged in an entirely private business, freely to exercise his own independent discretion as to parties with whom he will deal." United States v. Colgate & Co., 250 U.S. 300, 307 (1919).

However, "[t]he high value that we have placed on the right to refuse to deal with other firms does not mean that the right is unqualified." *Aspen*

Skiing. Under certain circumstances, a refusal to cooperate with rivals can constitute anticompetitive conduct and violate § 2. We have been very cautious in recognizing such exceptions, because of the uncertain virtue of forced sharing and the difficulty of identifying and remedying anticompetitive conduct by a single firm. The question before us today is whether the allegations of respondent's complaint fit within existing exceptions or provide a basis, under traditional antitrust principles, for recognizing a new one.

The leading case for § 2 liability based on refusal to cooperate with a rival, and the case upon which respondent understandably places greatest reliance, is *Aspen Skiing*.... *Aspen Skiing* is at or near the outer boundary of § 2 liability. The Court there found significance in the defendant's decision to cease participation in a cooperative venture. The unilateral termination of a voluntary (*and thus presumably profitable*) course of dealing suggested a willingness to forsake short-term profits to achieve an anticompetitive end. Similarly, the defendant's unwillingness to renew the ticket *even if compensated at retail price* revealed a distinctly anticompetitive bent.

The refusal to deal alleged in the present case does not fit within the limited exception recognized in Aspen Skiing. The complaint does not allege that Verizon voluntarily engaged in a course of dealing with its rivals, or would ever have done so absent statutory compulsion. Here, therefore, the defendant's prior conduct sheds no light upon the motivation of its refusal to deal—upon whether its regulatory lapses were prompted not by competitive zeal but by anticompetitive malice. The contrast between the cases is heightened by the difference in pricing behavior. In *Aspen Skiing*, the defendant turned down a proposal to sell at its own retail price, suggesting a calculation that its future monopoly retail price would be higher. Verizon's reluctance to interconnect at the cost-based rate of compensation available under § 251(c)(3) tells us nothing about dreams of monopoly.

The specific nature of what the 1996 Act compels makes this case different from *Aspen Skiing* in a more fundamental way. In *Aspen Skiing*, what the defendant refused to provide to its competitor was a product that it already sold at retail—to oversimplify slightly, lift tickets representing a bundle of services to skiers. Similarly, in *Otter Tail*, another case relied upon by respondent, the defendant was already in the business of providing a service to certain customers (power transmission over its network), and refused to provide the same service to certain other customers. In the present case, by contrast, the services allegedly withheld are not otherwise marketed or available to the public. The sharing obligation imposed by the 1996 Act created "something brand new"—"the wholesale market for leasing network elements." The unbundled elements offered pursuant to § 251(c)(3) exist only deep within the bowels of Verizon; they are brought out on compulsion of the 1996 Act and offered not to consumers but to rivals, and at considerable expense and effort. New systems must be designed and implemented simply to make that access possible—indeed, it is the failure of one of those systems that prompted the present complaint.[3]

---

3. Respondent also relies upon *Terminal Railroad* and *Associated Press*. These cases involved *concerted* action, which presents greater anticompetitive concerns and is amenable to

We conclude that Verizon's alleged insufficient assistance in the provision of service to rivals is not a recognized antitrust claim under this Court's existing refusal-to-deal precedents. This conclusion would be unchanged even if we considered to be established law the "essential facilities" doctrine crafted by some lower courts, under which the Court of Appeals concluded respondent's allegations might state a claim. We have never recognized such a doctrine, see *Aspen Skiing*; and we find no need either to recognize it or to repudiate it here. It suffices for present purposes to note that the indispensable requirement for invoking the doctrine is the unavailability of access to the "essential facilities"; where access exists, the doctrine serves no purpose. Thus, it is said that "essential facility claims should ... be denied where a state or federal agency has effective power to compel sharing and to regulate its scope and terms." P. Areeda & H. Hovenkamp, Antitrust Law, p. 150, ¶ 773e (2003 Supp.). Respondent believes that the existence of sharing duties under the 1996 Act supports its case. We think the opposite: The 1996 Act's extensive provision for access makes it unnecessary to impose a judicial doctrine of forced access. To the extent respondent's "essential facilities" argument is distinct from its general § 2 argument, we reject it.

IV

Finally, we do not believe that traditional antitrust principles justify adding the present case to the few existing exceptions from the proposition that there is no duty to aid competitors....

One factor of particular importance is the existence of a regulatory structure designed to deter and remedy anticompetitive harm. Where such a structure exists, the additional benefit to competition provided by antitrust enforcement will tend to be small, and it will be less plausible that the antitrust laws contemplate such additional scrutiny.... The regulatory framework that exists in this case demonstrates how, in certain circumstances, "regulation significantly diminishes the likelihood of major antitrust harm." *Town of Concord*. Consider, for example, the statutory restrictions upon Verizon's entry into the potentially lucrative market for long-distance service. To be allowed to enter the long-distance market in the first place, an incumbent LEC must be on good behavior in its local market. Authorization by the FCC requires state-by-state satisfaction of § 271's competitive checklist, which as we have noted includes the nondiscriminatory provision of access to UNEs.... The FCC's § 271 authorization order for Verizon to provide long-distance service in New York discussed at great length Verizon's commitments to provide access to UNEs, including the provision of OSS. Those commitments are enforceable by the FCC through continuing oversight; a failure to meet an authorization condition can result in an order that the deficiency be corrected, in the imposition of penalties, or in the suspension or revocation of long-distance approval....

The regulatory response to the OSS failure complained of in respondent's suit provides a vivid example of how the regulatory regime operates. When several competitive LECs complained about deficiencies in Verizon's

---

a remedy that does not require judicial estimation of free-market forces: simply requiring that the outsider be granted nondiscriminatory admission to the club.

servicing of orders, the FCC and PSC responded. The FCC soon concluded that Verizon was in breach of its sharing duties under § 251(c), imposed a substantial fine, and set up sophisticated measurements to gauge remediation, with weekly reporting requirements and specific penalties for failure. The PSC found Verizon in violation of the PAP even earlier, and imposed additional financial penalties and measurements with daily reporting requirements. In short, the regime was an effective steward of the antitrust function.

Against the slight benefits of antitrust intervention here, we must weigh a realistic assessment of its costs. Under the best of circumstances, applying the requirements of § 2 "can be difficult" because "the means of illicit exclusion, like the means of legitimate competition, are myriad." United States v. Microsoft Corp., 253 F. 3d 34, 58 (CADC 2001) (en banc) (per curiam). Mistaken inferences and the resulting false condemnations "are especially costly, because they chill the very conduct the antitrust laws are designed to protect." *Matsushita*. The cost of false positives counsels against an undue expansion of § 2 liability. One false-positive risk is that an incumbent LEC's failure to provide a service with sufficient alacrity might have nothing to do with exclusion. Allegations of violations of § 251(c)(3) duties are difficult for antitrust courts to evaluate, not only because they are highly technical, but also because they are likely to be extremely numerous, given the incessant, complex, and constantly changing interaction of competitive and incumbent LECs implementing the sharing and interconnection obligations. Amici States have filed a brief asserting that competitive LECs are threatened with "death by a thousand cuts"—the identification of which would surely be a daunting task for a generalist antitrust court. Judicial oversight under the Sherman Act would seem destined to distort investment and lead to a new layer of interminable litigation, atop the variety of litigation routes already available to and actively pursued by competitive LECs.

Even if the problem of false positives did not exist, conduct consisting of anticompetitive violations of § 251 may be, as we have concluded with respect to above-cost predatory pricing schemes, "beyond the practical ability of a judicial tribunal to control." *Brooke Group*. Effective remediation of violations of regulatory sharing requirements will ordinarily require continuing supervision of a highly detailed decree. We think that Professor Areeda got it exactly right: "No court should impose a duty to deal that it cannot explain or adequately and reasonably supervise. The problem should be deemed irremedia[ble] by antitrust law when compulsory access requires the court to assume the day-to-day controls characteristic of a regulatory agency." Areeda, 58 Antitrust L. J., at 853. In this case, respondent has requested an equitable decree to "[p]reliminarily and permanently enjoi[n] [Verizon] from providing access to the local loop market . . . to [rivals] on terms and conditions that are not as favorable" as those that Verizon enjoys. An antitrust court is unlikely to be an effective day-to-day enforcer of these detailed sharing obligations . . .

Accordingly, the judgment of the Court of Appeals is reversed . . .

Questions on *Verizon v. Trinko*

1. Does this case resolve when a monopolist does have an antitrust duty to deal? Does it resolve when a monopolist doesn't?

2. If *Aspen* is "at or near the outer boundary" what element was present in *Aspen* but missing here?

a. Is it that the *Aspen* defendant discriminated against its rival because it was not willing to sell to it even at the retail price it sold to others?

    i. But didn't the plaintiff allege here that Verizon discriminated against rival orders by treating them worse than orders for Verizion service?

    ii. Was there any evidence that Verizon provided more favorable wholesale leases of its telephone network to nonrival outsiders than the rivals? In favor of whom did Verizon allegedly discriminate? Is that the sort of discrimination among outsiders on the basis of rivalry that was present in *Aspen*?

b. Is it that the *Aspen* defendant terminated prior dealing?

    i. But isn't the allegation here that the defendant had altered a prior system of filling rival orders promptly? Is the difference that in *Aspen* the terminated prior dealing was voluntarily engaged in by the defendant? Why should that matter?

        (1) Is the voluntariness of prior dealing relevant to the ex post efficiency of sharing access or to the ex ante effect on incentives to create the facility?

        (2) Why shouldn't the fact that Congress and an expert agency imposed the duty and set the terms give an antitrust court sufficient confidence that sharing access is efficient and that the terms will provide adequate incentives to build facilities?

    ii. Didn't *Otter Tail* involve the element of discrimination against rivals but not the element of termination of prior dealing? How then does this factor distinguish *Otter Tail*?

c. Is it that the *Aspen* defendant sacrificed short-run profits by being unwilling to sell to its rival?

    i. But didn't the *Aspen* defendant's market share increase even in the short run? Was there any evidence there that its short run profits actually declined?

    ii. Didn't the defendant here also forego profitable sales at a regulatory rate that was supposed to fully compensate it?

    iii. Is sacrificing profits in the short run in order to exclude one's rivals necessarily bad? Isn't that often why firms invest in innovation or charge below the monopoly price?

3. Why is this a refusal to deal case at all? Wasn't access provided? If the *Aspen* elements were otherwise met, would it provide an antitrust duty to process rival requests for access quickly, or as quickly as the firm's own needs for access?

4. The Court begins by holding that the Telecommunication Act's antitrust savings clause means the regulatory statute can neither add nor subtract from baseline antitrust standards.

a. But doesn't its analysis in the end hold that the regulatory duty to deal (1) precludes application of the essential facility doctrine and (2) cuts against any other antitrust duty to deal because the regulatory authorities can always impose one when it is desirable? Doesn't that effectively reverse its earlier holding that the regulatory statute cannot narrow antitrust standards? Or is it that the antitrust standard always remains the same—weighing anticompetitive and procompetitive effects—and the regulation simply alters what those effects are likely to be?

b. Why doesn't the existence of government regulation cut *for* an antitrust duty to deal because it means a unitary expert agency stands ready to consistently set, monitor and update the terms of dealing?

    i. If, like in *Otter Tail*, the antitrust court simply piggybacks on this regulatory scheme, doesn't that reduce the risk of mistaken judicial decisions?

    ii. If the antitrust duty does simply piggyback, then what does it add to the regulatory scheme at all other than treble damages and possible class actions? Would adding those features just enhance enforcement of the regulatory duties? Or would they disrupt the regulatory tradeoff struck about the right duties and remedies?

    iii. Does *Verizon* overrule *Otter Tail*? Limit it to cases where the antitrust duty fills some regulatory gap?

5. Should *all* duties to deal be left to industry-specific government regulation and thus never be imposed as antitrust duties?

Einer Elhauge, *Defining Better Monopolization Standards*

56 STANFORD LAW REVIEW 253 (2003).

Current proposals by academics and enforcement officials . . . focus on redefining monopolization in terms of whether the defendant sacrificed short-term profits in order to reap long-run monopoly returns by excluding rivals. But . . . whether or not short-run profits were sacrificed in this way turns out to have no logical connection to whether the conduct was undesirable. To the contrary, sacrificing short-run profits to exclude rivals typically reflects socially desirable investments, and undesirable conduct that excludes rivals normally requires no sacrifice of short-run profits. Nor does a profit-sacrifice test explain the pattern of cases that have been held illegal by current precedent. Delayed gratification is not an antitrust offense, nor is it necessary for committing one. One can attempt to salvage these proposals by focusing not on the timing of actual profits, but on whether the activity would ever be profitable once undesirable profits are excluded. But then the test begs the key question, which is defining when profiting from the exclusion of rivals is desirable. . . .

Any monopolist maximizes its short-run profits by setting a monopoly price well above its costs—indeed, that is what makes monopolies allocatively inefficient. It follows then that a monopolist who sets its prices anywhere between its monopoly price and its costs must be sacrificing short-run profits, even though it is not pricing below cost. A monopolist who engages in such pricing thus cannot be in violation of U.S. predatory pricing doctrine under *Brooke*. But such a monopolist would be in violation of the proposed predation standard because it would be sacrificing short-run profits, and the only rational reason to do so would be to either keep out or drive out rivals and thus earn greater profits in the long run....

Investments in innovation that create monopoly power typically would be unprofitable but for the prospect of the monopoly returns reaped by excluding rivals. Normal competitive returns are available by just investing in bonds or the stock market. It is only the prospect of supracompetitive returns that could induce a firm to make risky investments in research that might not pan out. Further, even sure-thing investments in innovation involve sunk costs that would never be incurred but for the prospect that they could be recouped in the long run by supracompetitive above-cost pricing.

Thus, read literally, the proposed predation test would prohibit investments in innovation, subjecting them to treble damages....

One might be tempted to respond that "of course, we would not be stupid enough to apply the profit-sacrifice test to that sort of case," and that this is thus an attack on a straw man. But then one has to ask what precisely are the normative criteria that determine when the profit-sacrifice test would apply and when it wouldn't. If we have nothing to go on other than "we know it when we see it," then the resulting test is no better than a conclusory standard and a good deal worse since it does not even provide a placeholder term to remind us to undertake the normative analysis. If we would use implicit normative criteria for determining what sorts of conduct that exclude rivals is desirable even when it sacrifices profits, then those implicit criteria are what really does the work, and we should focus on defining them explicitly rather than hiding normative judgments in ad hoc decisions about when to apply the profit-sacrifice test....

The U.S. Essential Facilities Doctrine

Based largely on *Otter Tail*, all the U.S. federal circuit courts of appeals have recognized an essential facility doctrine that requires a monopolist to deal with rivals upon a showing that: (1) it is a monopolist in control of a facility essential for its rivals to compete; (2) it has denied use of that facility to a rival; (3) the facility cannot practicably be duplicated; and (4) sharing the facility is feasible.[146] This essential facility doctrine has been

---

146. See Interface Group v. Massachusetts Port Authority, 816 F.2d 9, 12 (1st Cir. 1987); Twin Labs. v. Weider Health & Fitness, 900 F.2d 566, 568–69 (2d Cir.1990); Ideal Dairy Farms v. John Labatt, 90 F.3d 737, 748 (3d Cir.1996); Laurel Sand v. CSX Transp., 924 F.2d 539, 544 (4th Cir. 1991); Mid–Texas Communications Sys. v. AT & T, 615 F.2d 1372, 1387 n.12 (5th Cir.), cert. denied, 449 U.S. 912 (1980); Directory Sales Mgmt. v. Ohio Bell Tel., 833 F.2d 606, 612 (6th Cir.1987); MCI Communications Corp. v. AT&T, 708 F.2d 1081, 1132–33

critiqued by many scholars,[147] and the Supreme Court in *Aspen* and *Trinko* made a point of emphasizing that it has never adopted the essential facilities doctrine. Much of the critique appears to reflect the misimpression that the essential facilities doctrine imposes a duty to deal even when refusing to do so would be more efficient and justified by legitimate business reasons. But in fact lower courts applying the essential facility doctrine have interpreted the feasibility element to serve the same function, holding that sharing a facility is not feasible if denying access serves legitimate business reasons like efficiency, customer satisfaction, cost reduction, service quality, avoiding free riding, or maintaining the defendant's capacity to serve its own customers.[148] Both the essential facilities doctrine and *Aspen* duty thus seem to require the absence of any sound *ex post* efficiency justification for the refusal to deal.

Indeed, the *Aspen* duty to deal appears to be broader in that it requires sharing even in cases where the denied facility, while helpful, was clearly not essential for the rival to compete, since the rival in *Aspen* in fact remained in the market without it. Nor did *Aspen* require evidence that the facilities in question were not practically duplicable (though it may have assumed nonduplicability given its statement of the facts) or that the facility was denied outright rather than offered at an unfavorable price (though those alternatives may be hard to distinguish).

Nonetheless, the lower court's version of the essential facility doctrine might justifiably be criticized as too broad because it does not require the sort of discrimination among outsiders on the basis of rivalry that was present in *Otter Tail* itself (which also involved true essentiality) and in *Aspen* and *Kodak* (which did not involve such true essentiality). The lower court doctrine thus (a) requires courts to undertake the administrative burden of determining what the terms of dealing should be and to update those terms as market conditions change and (b) creates the risk that the duty might deter rivals from creating a similar facility and deter firms from investing to create facilities that are so societally valuable that they are essential for a downstream market to exist at all. A reading that would have instead reconciled the Supreme Court caselaw would have been to say that a refusal to deal (which helps maintain or obtain monopoly power) violates antitrust law only when:

1. The defendants offer no *ex post* efficiency justification for their refusal to deal, as was true in *Otter Tail*, *Aspen* and *Kodak*;

(7th Cir.1983); Willman v. Heartland Hospital, 34 F.3d 605, 613 (8th Cir.1994); Ferguson v. Greater Pocatello Chamber of Commerce, 848 F.2d 976, 983 (9th Cir.1988); McKenzie v. Mercy Hospital, 854 F.2d 365, 369 (10th Cir.1988); Covad Commun. v. BellSouth, 299 F.3d 1272, 1286–88 (11th Cir.2002), vacated on other grounds, 540 U.S. 1147 (2004); Caribbean Broadcasting v. Cable & Wireless, 148 F.3d 1080, 1088 (D.C.Cir.1998); Intergraph Corporation v. Intel Corporation, 195 F.3d 1346, 1356–57 (Fed. Cir. 1999).

147. *See, e.g.,* IIIA AREEDA & HOVENKAMP, ANTITRUST LAW ¶¶ 770e, 771b–c, 773a (2002).

148. See Illinois v. Panhandle Eastern Pipe Line, 935 F.2d 1469, 1483 (7th Cir. 1991); Abcor Corp. v. AM Int'l, 916 F.2d 924 (4th Cir. 1990); Oahu Gas v. Pacific Resources, 838 F.2d 360, 368–70 (9th Cir. 1988); *MCI*, 708 F.2d at 1132, 1137–38; *Laurel Sand*, 924 F.2d at 545; *Willman*, 34 F.3d at 613; Southern Pacific v. AT&T, 740 F.2d 980, 1009 (D.C. Cir. 1984).

2. The defendant discriminates against its rivals by refusing to deal with them on the same terms it is willing to deal with nonrivals, as was true in *Otter Tail*, *Aspen* and *Kodak*; and

3. The facility is either

a. truly essential for rivals to compete, as in *Otter Tail*, or

b. something that the defendant formerly supplied to the rival voluntarily, as in *Aspen* and *Kodak*.

But the lower court essential facility doctrine does not require the second element, which may explain why the U.S. Supreme Court has always been so reluctant to embrace it. Nor is it clear why, if the second element were met by present day discrimination, it should matter whether the third element is met. Moreover, some fear that if present day discrimination were required as an element, it might lead a monopolist to inefficiently refuse to deal with anyone (through inefficient vertical integration) to avoid a duty to deal. If so, then one might favor a doctrine that required element 1 and *either* element 2 or 3.

EC duty to deal law, as we shall see next, resembles the essential facilities doctrine of the U.S. lower courts, in that it has not been limited to cases that involve discrimination among outsiders on the basis of rivalry.

The Application of U.S. Antitrust Duties to Deal to Intellectual Property

Two U.S. appellate circuits hold that antitrust duties to deal can apply to intellectual property as long as the plaintiff establishes the same elements that are necessary to rebut the presumption that any property owner is justified in excluding others.[149] In contrast, the Federal Circuit rejected case-by-case inquiry into the justification for exclusion, finding that absent proof of fraud, sham litigation or illegal tying, antitrust duties to deal are inapplicable "so long as that anticompetitive effect is not illegally extended beyond the statutory patent grant".[150] However, the Federal Circuit test is consistent with narrow versions of the antitrust duty, which would limit it to cases where the defendant discriminates among outsiders in a way that indicates a desire to reap a reward beyond the scope of its property (here patent) right, generally to monopolize some other market that uses that property as an input. Nor does there seem to be any categorical reason to treat intellectual property differently than other property rights to exclude, which raise similar issues about administrability and tradeoffs between ex ante incentives to make the property valuable and ex post efficiencies in sharing valuable property.[151] However,

---

149. *See* Image Technical Servs., Inc. v. Eastman Kodak Co., 125 F.3d 1195, 1218–20 (9th Cir. 1997) (owners of patents and copyrights must provide access to them if the plaintiff can rebut the presumption that they have a valid business justification for denying access); Data Gen. Corp. v. Grumman Sys. Support Corp., 36 F.3d 1147, 1184–87 & n.64 (1st Cir. 1994) (same for copyrights).

150. *See* In re Independent Service Organizations Antitrust Litigation, 203 F.3d 1322, 1325–30 (Fed. Cir. 2000).

151. See Chapter 2.G; Elhauge, supra note 33, at 304–05. This conclusion is consistent with 35 U.S.C. § 271(d)(4), which bars treating a refusal to license as a patent misuse (which

the U.S. Supreme Court has yet to adjudicate the extent to which U.S. antitrust duties to deal apply to intellectual property.

Cases 6 and 7/73, Commercial Solvents and Others v. Commission

[1974] E.C.R. 223.

[Aminobutanol is chemical essential for making ethambutol and other drugs. Commercial Solvents was the only supplier of aminobutanol in the EU. It had supplied aminobutanol to Zoja, which made drugs based on aminobutanol. But Commercial Solvents decided to change to a policy of making drugs based aminobutanol itself, and told Zoja it was reserving aminobutanol for its own use and would no longer be supplying it to Zoja.]

. . . [A]n undertaking being in a dominant position as regards the production of raw material and therefore able to control the supply to manufacturers of derivatives, cannot, just because it decides to start manufacturing these derivatives (in competition with its former customers) act in such a way as to eliminate their competition which in the case in question, would amount to eliminating one of the principal manufacturers of ethambutol in the Common Market. Since such conduct is contrary to the objectives expressed in Article 3(f) of the Treaty [now repealed] and set out in greater detail in Articles [101 and 102], it follows that an undertaking which has a dominant position in the market in raw materials and which, with the object of reserving such raw material for manufacturing its own derivatives, refuses to supply a customer, which is itself a manufacturer of these derivatives, and therefore risks eliminating all competition on the part of this customer, is abusing its dominant position within the meaning of Article [102]. . . .

Questions on Commercial Solvents

1. Does this case involve a termination of prior dealing similar to *Aspen* and *Kodak*?

2. Did this case involve any discrimination among outsiders against rivals and against nonrivals? Or did it just involve discrimination in favor of itself against all outsiders?

3. Did this case involve a product truly essential to rival competition like in *Otter Tail*?

4. Did this case involve a monopoly power over an upstream product that appeared to be largely unearned?

---

can invalidate the patent and effectively impose a business death penalty) but does not bar treating it as an antitrust violation (which can lead only to damages or perhaps compulsory licensing rather than invalidation because the patent would not be a fruit of any antitrust violation, *see* Chapter 1.). *See also Image Technical Servs.*, 125 F.3d at 1214 n.7 (legislative history does not indicate any intent to eliminate antitrust duty); Grid Systems Corp. v. Texas Instruments Inc., 771 F.Supp. 1033, 1037 n.2 (N.D. Cal. 1991) (§ 271(d) only relates to patent misuse not antitrust violations).

5. Did the Commission require proof that there was no *ex post* efficiency justification for not dealing with Zoja? Or did it view that implicitly established by the finding that Commercial Solvents's purpose was just to supply itself over its rivals, at least absent affirmative evidence that the efficiencies had changed since the period of prior dealing?

6. What are the pros and cons of mandating Commercial Solvents to supply Zoja with the input it needed to produce ethambutol?

a. Doesn't Commercial Solvents's refusal to supply Zoja risk eliminating competition on the downstream ethambutol market? Why would Commercial Solvents have incentives to eliminate more efficient downstream competition rather than just allow it and earn a greater share of consumer prices with higher upstream prices? If Zoja had market power in the downstream market, couldn't eliminating it actually improve efficiency by ending a successive monopolies problem? Could Zoja's elimination increase Commercial Solvents's upstream market power by reducing the odds Zoja would enter its upstream market?

b. How might a duty to deal affect the incentives of CSC and other chemical companies' incentives to invest into new substances? The incentives of Zoja to enter into the upstream market? To avoid adversely affecting those incentives, might one want to add further elements to the test used in *Commercial Solvents*? Which one(s)?

Joined Cases C–241/91P & C–242/91P, RADIO TELEFIS EIREANN (RTE) v. COMMISSION OF THE EUROPEAN COMMUNITIES (MAGILL)

[1995] E.C.R. I–743 (ECJ).

[The television companies in Britain and Ireland each published weekly TV magazines listing only their own programs. They refused to give lists of their TV programs for the following week to an independent weekly TV magazine called Magill, which wanted to publish all the programs of all the TV channels for the whole week, a product for which there was unsatisfied consumer demand. Intellectual Property Owners Inc. (IPO) was an organization that supported the TV channels against Magill. The Commission found in favor of Magill, and its decision was subsequently confirmed by the [General Court], whose judgment was then appealed to the ECJ.]

With regard to the issue of abuse, the arguments of the appellants and IPO wrongly presuppose that where the conduct of an undertaking in a dominant position consists of the exercise of a right classified by national law as "copyright", such conduct can never be reviewed in relation to Article [102] of the Treaty.

Admittedly, in the absence of Community standardization or harmonization of laws, determination of the conditions and procedures for granting protection of an intellectual property right is a matter for national rules. Further, the exclusive right of reproduction forms part of the author's rights, so that refusal to grant a licence, even if it is the act of an undertaking holding a dominant position, cannot in itself constitute abuse of a dominant position. *Volvo.*

However, it is also clear from that judgment that the exercise of an exclusive right by the proprietor may, in exceptional circumstances, involve abusive conduct.

In the present case, the conduct objected to is the appellants' reliance on copyright conferred by national legislation so as to prevent Magill or any other undertaking having the same intention from publishing on a weekly basis information (channel, day, time and title of programmes) together with commentaries and pictures obtained independently of the appellants.

Among the circumstances taken into account by the [General Court] in concluding that such conduct was abusive was, first, the fact that there was, according to the findings of the [General Court], no actual or potential substitute for a weekly television guide offering information on the programmes for the week ahead. On this point, the [General Court] confirmed the Commission's finding that the complete lists of programmes for a 24–hour period and for a 48–hour period at weekends and before public holidays published in certain daily and Sunday newspapers, and the television sections of certain magazines covering, in addition, "highlights" of the week's programmes, were only to a limited extent substitutable for advance information to viewers on all the week's programmes. Only weekly television guides containing comprehensive listings for the week ahead would enable users to decide in advance which programmes they wished to follow and arrange their leisure activities for the week accordingly. The [General Court] also established that there was a specific, constant and regular potential demand on the part of consumers.

Thus the appellants who were, by force of circumstance, the only sources of the basic information on programme scheduling which is the indispensable raw material for compiling a weekly television guide gave viewers wishing to obtain information on the choice of programmes for the week ahead no choice but to buy the weekly guides for each station and draw from each of them the information they needed to make comparisons.

The appellants' refusal to provide basic information by relying on national copyright provisions thus prevented the appearance of a new product, a comprehensive weekly guide to television programmes, which the appellants did not offer and for which there was a potential consumer demand. Such refusal constitutes an abuse under heading (b) of the second paragraph of Article [102] of the Treaty.

Second, there was no justification for such refusal either in the activity of television broadcasting or in that of publishing television magazines.

Third, and finally, as the [General Court] also held, the appellants, by their conduct, reserved to themselves the secondary market of weekly television guides by excluding all competition on that market (see the judgment in *Commercial Solvents*, since they denied access to the basic information which is the raw material indispensable for the compilation of such a guide).

In the light of all those circumstances, the [General Court] did not err in law in holding that the appellants' conduct was an abuse of a dominant position within the meaning of Article [102] of the Treaty.

Note and Questions on *Magill*

In *Magill*, the ECJ ruled that a dominant firm's refusal to licence intellectual property could involve abusive conduct if: (1) the refusal concerned a product that was indispensable for the production of a "new product" for which there was clear and unsatisfied consumer demand; (2) refusing to provide this essential information monopolized the separate (downstream) market; and (3) there was no objective justification for the refusal. As we will see, the "new product" condition appears to be limited to cases involving intellectual property.

1.   Do you see any valid reason to treat an input protected by an intellectual property right differently from one not protected by such a right?

2.   Does the requirement that the input be necessary to create a "new product" make sense? Will such a condition be easy to administer?

3.   Should it be relevant that the monopoly over the information contained in the TV listings was largely unearned and required no investment or innovation to create? Is a test that relies on such a factor administrable? Would it amount to a conclusion that the intellectual property right was erroneously granted? Should the EU be using competition law to second-guess the intellectual property rights created by member states?

4.   Might the fact that the monopoly power was unearned explain why the *Magill* court did not feel inclined to articulate its test in a way that required either:

a.   the termination of past dealing as existed in *Commercial Solvents*, *Aspen* and *Kodak*?

b.   discrimination among outsiders on the basis of rivalry such as existed in *Aspen* and *Kodak*?

5.   Need we be concerned here that the duty to deal would discourage rival efforts to create competition upstream given the nature of the facility here, that is the information about each TV station's broadcast schedule?

6.   Assuming a duty to deal should be imposed, at what price should the television companies have to license their TV listings?

a.   Is the right price zero because they did nothing to earn those listings? Even if the degree to which the monopoly power was earned should not be a condition of the duty, should it affect the price at which a defendant with such a duty must deal?

b.   Is the right answer zero even though the TV stations did charge for the single-station listings they distributed to viewers?

7.   Why do you think the television stations didn't license their TV listings to Magill?

a.   Is it likely that they want to monopolize the downstream market for TV listing magazines with their own single-station listing magazines? Wouldn't the television stations be better off with multi-station listing magazines that were more likely to be used by viewers and charging a price for their listings that give them a share of the efficiency gain created by multi-station magazines?

b. Would each television station have the right incentives to charge a price for its listings that gives them only a fair share of the efficiency gains created by multi-station magazines? Or would there be holdout problems because each station would have an incentive to try to expropriate a disproportionate share of those efficiency gains by charging a higher price for its listings? Might such holdout problems justify an antitrust duty to deal at a price (perhaps zero) set by antitrust adjudicators?

Case 7/97, OSCAR BRONNER GMBH & CO. KG v. MEDIAPRINT ZEITUNGS UND ZEITSCHRITENVERLAG GMBH & CO., KG

1998 E.C.R. I–7791.

The objects of Oscar Bronner are the editing, publishing, manufacture and distribution of the daily newspaper *Der Standard*. In 1994, that newspaper's share of the Austrian daily newspaper market was 3.6% of circulation and 6% of advertising revenues.

Mediaprint ... publishes the daily newspapers *Neue Kronen Zeitung* and *Kurier*.... In 1994, the combined market share of *Neue Kronen Zeitung* and *Kurier* was 46.8% of the Austrian daily newspaper market in terms of circulation and 42% in terms of advertising revenues. They reached 53.3% of the population from the age of 14 in private households and 71% of all newspaper readers.

For the distribution of its newspapers, Mediaprint has established a nationwide home-delivery scheme, ... The scheme consists of delivering the newspapers directly to subscribers in the early hours of the morning.

In its action under [Austrian competition law], Oscar Bronner seeks an order requiring Mediaprint to cease abusing its alleged dominant position on the market by including *Der Standard* in its home-delivery service against payment of reasonable remuneration. In support of its claim, Oscar Bronner argues that postal delivery, which generally does not take place until the late morning, does not represent an equivalent alternative to home-delivery, and that, in view of its small number of subscribers, it would be entirely unprofitable for it to organise its own home-delivery service. Oscar Bronner further argues that Mediaprint has discriminated against it by including another daily newspaper, *Wirtschaftsblatt*, in its home-delivery scheme, even though it is not published by Mediaprint.

In reply to those arguments, Mediaprint contends that the establishment of its home-delivery service required a great administrative and financial investment, and that making the system available to all Austrian newspaper publishers would exceed the natural capacity of its system. It also maintains that the fact that it holds a dominant position does not oblige it to subsidise competition by assisting competing companies. It adds that the position of *Wirtschaftsblatt* is not comparable to that of *Der Standard*, since the publisher of the former also entrusted the Mediaprint group with printing and the whole of distribution, including sale in kiosks, so that home-delivery constituted only part of a package of services.

Taking the view that, if the conduct of a market participant falls within the terms of Article [102] of the TFEU it must logically constitute an abuse of the market within the meaning of [an Austrian Provision that] is analogous in content, since under the principle of the primacy of Community law conduct which is incompatible with the latter cannot be tolerated under national law either, the [Austrian national court] decided that it first needed to resolve the question whether the conduct of Mediaprint infringed Article [102] of the Treaty. . . .

[T]he national court effectively asks whether the refusal by a press undertaking which holds a very large share of the daily newspaper market in a Member State and operates the only nationwide newspaper home-delivery scheme in that Member State to allow the publisher of a rival newspaper, which by reason of its small circulation is unable either alone or in cooperation with other publishers to set up and operate its own home-delivery scheme in economically reasonable conditions, to have access to that scheme for appropriate remuneration constitutes the abuse of a dominant position within the meaning of Article [102 TFEU].

. . . Emphasising that in this case the order for reference shows that a third undertaking was admitted to Mediaprint's home-delivery scheme, the Commission states that such an abuse, within the meaning of Article [102 TFEU], might consist, in the wording of subparagraph (c) of that provision, in applying dissimilar conditions to equivalent transactions with other trading parties. The Commission does not, however, consider that to be the case in the main proceedings, since the service sought by Oscar Bronner was not made subject to conditions other than those applicable to other trading parties, but was not offered at all if other services were not entrusted to Mediaprint at the same time. . . .

In examining whether an undertaking holds a dominant position within the meaning of Article [102 TFEU], it is of fundamental importance . . . to define the market in question . . . [I]t is therefore for the national court to determine, inter alia, whether home-delivery schemes constitute a separate market, or whether other methods of distributing daily newspapers, such as sale in shops or at kiosks or delivery by post, are sufficiently interchangeable with them to have to be taken into account also. In deciding whether there is a dominant position the court must also take account, as the Commission has emphasised, of the possible existence of regional home-delivery schemes.

If that examination leads the national court to conclude that a separate market in home-delivery schemes does exist, and that there is an insufficient degree of interchangeability between Mediaprint's nationwide scheme and other, regional, schemes, it must hold that Mediaprint, which according to the information in the order for reference operates the only nationwide home-delivery service in Austria, is de facto in a monopoly situation in the market thus defined, and thus holds a dominant position in it. . . .

Finally, it would need to be determined whether the refusal by the owner of the only nationwide home-delivery scheme in the territory of a Member State, which uses that scheme to distribute its own daily newspapers, to allow the publisher of a rival daily newspaper access to it constitutes an abuse of a dominant position within the meaning of Article [102

TFEU], on the ground that such refusal deprives that competitor of a means of distribution judged essential for the sale of its newspaper.

Although in *Commercial Solvents* and *CBEM* ... the Court of Justice held the refusal by an undertaking holding a dominant position in a given market to supply an undertaking with which it was in competition in a neighbouring market with raw materials (*Commercial Solvents v. Commission*) and services (*CBEM*) respectively, which were indispensable to carrying on the rival's business, to constitute an abuse, it should be noted, first, that the Court did so to the extent that the conduct in question was likely to eliminate all competition on the part of that undertaking.

Secondly, in *Magill*, ... the Court held that refusal by the owner of an intellectual property right to grant a licence, even if it is the act of an undertaking holding a dominant position, cannot in itself constitute abuse of a dominant position, but that the exercise of an exclusive right by the proprietor may, in exceptional circumstances, involve an abuse.

In *Magill*, the Court found such exceptional circumstances in the fact that the refusal in question concerned a product (information on the weekly schedules of certain television channels) the supply of which was indispensable for carrying on the business in question (the publishing of a general television guide), in that, without that information, the person wishing to produce such a guide would find it impossible to publish it and offer it for sale, the fact that such refusal prevented the appearance of a new product for which there was a potential consumer demand, the fact that it was not justified by objective considerations, and that it was likely to exclude all competition in the secondary market of television guides.

Therefore, even if that case-law on the exercise of an intellectual property right were applicable to the exercise of any property right whatever, it would still be necessary, for the *Magill* judgment to be effectively relied upon ..., not only that the refusal of the service comprised in home delivery be likely to eliminate all competition in the daily newspaper market on the part of the person requesting the service and that such refusal be incapable of being objectively justified, but also that the service in itself be indispensable to carrying on that person's business, inasmuch as there is no actual or potential substitute in existence for that home-delivery scheme.

That is certainly not the case even if, as in the case which is the subject of the main proceedings, there is only one nationwide home-delivery scheme in the territory of a Member State and, moreover, the owner of that scheme holds a dominant position in the market for services constituted by that scheme or of which it forms part.

In the first place, it is undisputed that other methods of distributing daily newspapers, such as by post and through sale in shops and at kiosks, even though they may be less advantageous for the distribution of certain newspapers, exist and are used by the publishers of those daily newspapers.

Moreover, it does not appear that there are any technical, legal or even economic obstacles capable of making it impossible, or even unreasonably difficult, for any other publisher of daily newspapers to establish, alone or in cooperation with other publishers, its own nationwide home-delivery scheme and use it to distribute its own daily newspapers.

It should be emphasised in that respect that, in order to demonstrate that the creation of such a system is not a realistic potential alternative and that access to the existing system is therefore indispensable, it is not enough to argue that it is not economically viable by reason of the small circulation of the daily newspaper or newspapers to be distributed.

For such access to be capable of being regarded as indispensable, it would be necessary at the very least to establish ... that it is not economically viable to create a second home-delivery scheme for the distribution of daily newspapers with a circulation comparable to that of the daily newspapers distributed by the existing scheme.

In the light of the foregoing considerations, the answer to the first question must be that the refusal by a press undertaking which holds a very large share of the daily newspaper market in a Member State and operates the only nationwide newspaper home-delivery scheme in that Member State to allow the publisher of a rival newspaper, which by reason of its small circulation is unable either alone or in cooperation with other publishers to set up and operate its own home-delivery scheme in economically reasonable conditions, to have access to that scheme for appropriate remuneration does not constitute abuse of a dominant position within the meaning of Article [102 TFEU]. . . .

Questions on *Bronner*

Like the U.S. essential facilities doctrine and *Magill*, this case requires that (1) the facility is truly essential in that it was nonduplicable and its denial would eliminate all competition on the downstream daily newspaper market and (2) the denial lacks any objective justification.

1. Which element was missing here?

2. Do you agree with the ECJ that it was not sufficient for Bronner to show that a small circulation paper like itself cannot create a nationwide distribution system, but rather it has to show that a second nationwide distribution system could not be created even for a newspaper that had the same circulation as defendants? Wouldn't the first showing simply establish that Bronner lacks sufficient economies of scale? Wouldn't the second show that the facility was truly nonduplicable? If a number of small circulation newspapers existed that, in aggregate, would support a second nationwide distribution system, might one expect a new firm to enter and offer such a system? Would that result be preferable to requiring all newspapers to share in the first nationwide distribution system?

3. Unlike *Magill*, this case did not require any evidence that the denied facility was necessary to the creation of a "new product." Is that element any less justified when the facility is not protected by intellectual property rights than when it is? Why? Doesn't the creation of facilities like a nationwide distribution system require investments under conditions of risk just like the creation of intellectual property rights?

4. Unlike in *Magill*, the monopoly power here appeared to be earned by the development of a nationwide distribution system.

a. Should this suffice to reject any duty to deal?

i. Why isn't such a distribution system a legitimate competitive advantage, access to which should not be provided to competitors?

ii. Should a vertically-integrated dominant firm have to give rivals access to every competitive advantage it develops when it is feasible and the advantage is great enough to drive rivals out of business? If it does, what does that do to the dominant firm's incentives to invest to create such competitive advantages? To the incentives of rivals to create their own nationwide distribution system?

b. Should other elements be added to the *Bronner* test to address the incentive problem? Should the test require discrimination on the basis of rivalry or termination of prior dealing, neither of which is a stated element of the *Bronner* test?

Case C–418/01, IMS Health GmbH & Co. OHG v. NDC Health GmbH & Co. KG

[2004] 4 CMLR 28.

... IMS and NDC are engaged in tracking sales of pharmaceutical and healthcare products. IMS provides data on regional sales of pharmaceutical products in Germany to pharmaceutical laboratories formatted according to the brick structure. Since January 2000 it has provided studies based on a brick structure consisting of 1860 bricks, or a derived structure consisting of 2847 bricks, each corresponding to a designated geographic area. According to the order for reference, those bricks were created by taking account of various criteria, such as the boundaries of municipalities, post codes, population density, transport connections and the geographical distribution of pharmacies and doctors' surgeries.

Several years ago IMS set up a working group in which undertakings in the pharmaceutical industry, which are clients of IMS, participated. That working group makes suggestions for improving and optimising market segmentation. The extent of the working group's contribution to the determination of market segmentation is a subject of dispute between IMS and NDC.

The national court found that IMS not only marketed its brick structures, but also distributed them free of charge to pharmacies and doctors' surgeries. According to the national court, that practice helped those structures to become the normal industry standard to which its clients adapted their information and distribution systems.

After leaving his post in 1998, a former manager of IMS created Pharma Intranet Information AG ('PII'), whose activity also consisted in marketing regional data on pharmaceutical products in Germany formatted on the basis of brick structures. At first, PII tried to market structures consisting of 2201 bricks. On account of reticence manifested by potential clients, who were accustomed to structures consisting of 1860 or 2847 bricks, it decided to use structures of 1860 or 3000 bricks, very similar to those used by IMS.

PII was acquired by NDC. . . .

[The German national courts found the brick structure used by IMS was a database that may be protected by German Copyright law, and referred] to the Court the following questions for a preliminary ruling:

> "1) Is Article [102 TFEU] to be interpreted as meaning that there is abusive conduct by an undertaking with a dominant position on the market where it refuses to grant a licence agreement for the use of a data bank protected by copyright to an undertaking which seeks access to the same geographical and actual market if the participants on the other side of the market, that is to say potential clients, reject any product which does not make use of the data bank protected by copyright because their set-up relies on products manufactured on the basis of that data bank?

> 2) Is the extent to which an undertaking with a dominant position on the market has involved persons from the other side of the market in the development of the data bank protected by copyright relevant to the question of abusive conduct by that undertaking

> 3) Is the material outlay (in particular with regard to costs) in which clients who have hitherto been supplied with the product of the undertaking having a dominant market position would be involved if they were in future to go over to purchasing the product of a competing undertaking which does not make use of the data bank protected by copyright relevant to the question of abusive conduct by an undertaking with a dominant position on the market?" . . .

The second and third questions . . . It is clear from . . . *Bronner* that, in order to determine whether a product or service is indispensable for enabling an undertaking to carry on business in a particular market, it must be determined whether there are products or services which constitute alternative solutions, even if they are less advantageous, and whether there are technical, legal or economic obstacles capable of making it impossible or at least unreasonably difficult for any undertaking seeking to operate in the market to create, possibly in cooperation with other operators, the alternative products or services. According to . . . *Bronner*, in order to accept the existence of economic obstacles, it must be established, at the very least, that the creation of those products or services is not economically viable for production on a scale comparable to that of the undertaking which controls the existing product or service.

It is for the national court to determine, in the light of the evidence submitted to it, whether such is the case in the dispute in the main proceedings. In that regard, . . . account must be taken of the fact that a high level of participation by the pharmaceutical laboratories in the improvement of the 1860 brick structure protected by copyright, on the supposition that it is proven, has created a dependency by users in regard to that structure, particularly at a technical level. In such circumstances, it is likely that those laboratories would have to make exceptional organisational and financial efforts in order to acquire the studies on regional sales of pharmaceutical products presented on the basis of a structure other than that protected by copyright. The supplier of that alternative structure might therefore be obliged to offer terms which are such as to rule out any economic viability of business on a scale comparable to that of the undertaking which controls the protected structure.

The answer to the second and third questions must, therefore, be that, for the purposes of determining the potentially abusive character of the refusal of an undertaking in a dominant position to grant a licence to use a brick structure protected by a copyright owned by it, the degree of participation by the users in the development of that structure and the outlay, particularly in terms of cost, on the part of potential users in order to purchase regional sales studies for pharmaceutical products presented on the basis of an alternative structure, are factors which must be taken into consideration in determining whether the protected structure is indispensable for the marketing of studies of that kind.

The first question ... It is clear from that case-law that, in order for the refusal by an undertaking which owns a copyright to give access to a product or service indispensable for carrying on a particular business to be treated as abusive, it is sufficient that three cumulative conditions be satisfied, namely, that that refusal is preventing the emergence of a new product for which there is a potential consumers demand, that it is unjustified and such as to exclude any competition on a secondary market....

[The *Bronner*] Court held that it was relevant, in order to assess whether the refusal to grant access to a product or a service indispensable for carrying on a particular business activity was an abuse, to distinguish an upstream market, constituted by the product or service, in that case the market for home delivery of daily newspapers, and a (secondary) downstream market, on which the product or service in question is used for the production of another product or the supply of another service, in that case the market for daily newspapers themselves.

The fact that the delivery service was not marketed separately was not regarded as precluding, from the outset, the possibility of identifying a separate market.

It appears, therefore ... that, for the purposes of the application of the earlier case-law, it is sufficient that a potential market or even hypothetical market can be identified. Such is the case where the products or services are indispensable in order to carry on a particular business and where there is an actual demand for them on the part of undertakings which seek to carry on the business for which they are indispensable.

Accordingly, it is determinative that two different stages of production may be identified and that they are interconnected, the upstream product is indispensable in as much as for supply of the downstream product.

Transposed to the facts of the case in the main proceedings, that approach prompts consideration as to whether the 1860 brick structure constitutes, upstream, an indispensable factor in the downstream supply of German regional sales data for pharmaceutical products.

It is for the national court to establish whether that is in fact the position, and, if so be the case, to examine whether the refusal by IMS to grant a licence to use the structure at issue is capable of excluding all competition on the market for the supply of German regional sales data on pharmaceutical products.

The first condition, relating to the emergence of a new product. . . . [The first] condition relates to the consideration that, in the balancing of the interest in protection of copyright and the economic freedom of its owner, against the interest in protection of free competition the latter can prevail only where refusal to grant a licence prevents the development of the secondary market to the detriment of consumers.

Therefore, the refusal by an undertaking in a dominant position to allow access to a product protected by copyright, where that product is indispensable for operating on a secondary market, may be regarded as abusive only where the undertaking which requested the licence does not intend to limit itself essentially to duplicating the goods or services already offered on the secondary market by the owner of the copyright, but intends to produce new goods or services not offered by the owner of the right and for which there is a potential consumer demand

It is for the national court to determine whether such is the case in the dispute in the main proceedings.

The second condition, relating to whether the refusal was unjustified. As to that condition, on whose interpretation no specific observations have been made, it is for the national court to examine, if appropriate, in light of the facts before it, whether the refusal of the request for a licence is justified by objective considerations.

Accordingly, the answer to the first question must be that the refusal by an undertaking which holds a dominant position and is the owner of an intellectual property right over a brick structure which is indispensable for the presentation of data on regional sales of pharmaceutical products in a Member State, to grant a licence to use that structure to another undertaking which also wishes to supply such data in the same Member State, constitutes an abuse of a dominant position within the meaning of [Article 102 TFEU] where the following conditions are fulfilled:

—the undertaking which requested the licence intends to offer, on the market for the supply of the data in question, new products or services not offered by the copyright owner and for which there is a potential consumer demand;

—the refusal is not justified by objective considerations;

—the refusal is such as to reserve to the copyright owner the market for the supply of data on sales of pharmaceutical products in the Member State concerned by eliminating all competition on that market.

Questions on *IMS*

1. Like *Bronner, Magill* and U.S. essential facilities doctrine, *IMS* requires evidence that the facility is truly essential and that denying it is objectively unjustified. Is the ECJ right that the degree of participation by the users in the development of the brick structure and the cost to them of using another structure should be relevant to whether the brick structure is sufficiently indispensible to give the defendant a duty to share it with rivals?

a. Do you see why it might be problematic in an information-provision market to allow a firm to get customers to tell them what breakdown of information they need and then copyright that breakdown to prevent rivals from offering information in a similar breakdown? Wouldn't this effectively allow the firm to eliminate competition in the provision of the information that its customers need? Isn't the breakdown that customers actually need nonduplicable, and if it offers a large cost advantage over other breakdowns, thus indispensible to rivals?

b. On the other hand, does taking this factor into account create a risk of discouraging firms from desirably involving customers in the development of improved products or services? Or do you think IMS would have done so to have a first mover advantage even if they could not prevent rivals from ever offering the same breakdown of information?

2. The ECJ rejected IMS' argument that, to prove the refusal excluded competition on a second market it was necessary to identify two markets: the market for the supply of the facility in question and the market for the goods or services for which access is needed. Instead, the ECJ stated, "it is sufficient that a potential market or even a hypothetical market can be identified."

a. Couldn't any intellectual property right "hypothetically" be marketed as a stand-alone item? If so, under this test couldn't the holder of any intellectual property right be forced to grant a license to any competitor that could prove that such a license is necessary to allow it to compete on a downstream market and that sharing the license would not create any *ex post* inefficiency?

b. If so, wouldn't this test create a huge disincentive for dominant firms to invest in innovation that would allow them to gain a competitive advantage vis-à-vis competitors?

3. As in *Magill*, this case narrows the doctrine by also requiring that the denied facility be necessary to offer "new products or services not offered by the copyright owner and for which there is a potential consumer demand," and making clear that this additional element is only imposed in cases where the essential facility is protected by intellectual property right.

a. Is it clear what a "new product" means? Does it have to be entirely different from the product already offered by the copyright holder or can it constitute a mere improvement over the product already sold on the market by the copyright holder? Does the consumer-demand standard eliminate the uncertainty?

b. Does the "new product" condition solve the problem of discouraging investments that create intellectual property rights? Doesn't it still discourage innovations that are so valuable that they also create the potential for derivative products?

c. Doesn't the "new product" condition at least eliminate the possibility that the refusal to deal actually improves efficiency by eliminating a problem of successive monopolies?

4. Might the Court have been influenced by the impression that the intellectual property here did not really require significant investment or innovation, but merely involved surveying buyers about what they wanted?

a. Is it likely that IMS would be discouraged from surveying its buyers because of the prospect that it might later have to allow rivals to supply the same consumer needs? Would you want to base antitrust liability on such judgments?

b. In a case where its test would otherwise impose a duty that would create strong ex ante disincentives to create the facility in question, do you think the ECJ would add an element requiring the termination of prior dealing and/or discrimination among outsiders on the basis of rivalry?

5. If on remand the national court did decide a duty to deal should be imposed, how should it set the price at which IMS must license the brick structure to its rivals?

Case T–201/04 Microsoft v. Commission

[2007] ECR II–3601.

. . . According to the contested decision, Microsoft abused its dominant position on the client PC operating systems market by refusing, first, to supply Sun and other competitors with the specifications for protocols implemented in Windows work group server operating systems and used by the servers running those systems to deliver file and print services and group and user administration services to Windows work group networks and, second, to allow those various undertakings to use those specifications in order to develop and market work group server operating systems. . . .

Microsoft's actual reasoning in the first part of this plea may be set out as follows:

— the present case must be appraised in the light of the various circumstances recognised by the Court of Justice in Magill, paragraph 107 above, and approved in IMS Health, paragraph 107 above;

— the circumstances in which a refusal by an undertaking in a dominant position to grant third parties a licence covering intellectual property rights may be characterised as abusive are, first, where the product or service concerned is indispensable for carrying on a particular business; second, where the refusal is liable to exclude all competition on a secondary market; third, where the refusal prevents the emergence of a new product for which there is potential consumer demand; and, fourth, where the refusal is not objectively justified;

— none of those four circumstances is present in this case; . . .

The central issue to be resolved . . . therefore is whether, as the Commission claims and Microsoft denies, the conditions on which an undertaking in a dominant position may be required to grant a licence covering its intellectual property rights are satisfied in the present case. . . .

It follows from the case-law cited above that the refusal by an undertaking holding a dominant position to license a third party to use a product covered by an intellectual property right cannot in itself constitute an abuse of a dominant position within the meaning of Article [102 TFEU]. It is only in exceptional circumstances that the exercise of the exclusive right by the owner of the intellectual property right may give rise to such an abuse.

It also follows from that case-law that the following circumstances, in particular, must be considered to be exceptional:

— in the first place, the refusal relates to a product or service indispensable to the exercise of a particular activity on a neighbouring market;

— in the second place, the refusal is of such a kind as to exclude any effective competition on that neighbouring market;

— in the third place, the refusal prevents the appearance of a new product for which there is potential consumer demand.

Once it is established that such circumstances are present, the refusal by the holder of a dominant position to grant a licence may infringe Article [102 TFEU] unless the refusal is objectively justified.

The Court notes that the circumstance that the refusal prevents the appearance of a new product for which there is potential consumer demand is found only in the case-law on the exercise of an intellectual property right.

[Note: The CFI then engaged in a heavy technical discussion rejecting Microsoft's arguments that the first two conditions—indispensability and elimination of competition were not met in this case. It then focused on the third condition—whether the interoperability information would be used to produce a "new product."]

The new product

... It must be emphasised that the fact that the applicant's conduct prevents the appearance of a new product on the market falls to be considered under Article [102(b)] EC, which prohibits abusive practices which consist in "limiting production, markets or technical developments to the ... prejudice of consumers".

Thus, at paragraph 54 of Magill ... the Court of Justice held that the refusal by the broadcasting companies concerned had to be characterised as abusive within the meaning of that provision because it prevented the appearance of a new product which the broadcasting companies did not offer and for which there was a potential consumer demand....

In IMS Health ... the Court of Justice, when assessing the circumstance relating to the appearance of a new product, also placed that circumstance in the context of the damage to the interests of consumers. Thus, at paragraph 48 of that judgment, the Court emphasized ... that that circumstance related to the consideration that, in the balancing of the interest in protection of the intellectual property right and the economic freedom of its owner against the interest in protection of free competition, the latter can prevail only where refusal to grant a licence prevents the development of the secondary market, to the detriment of consumers.

The circumstance relating to the appearance of a new product, as envisaged in Magill and IMS Health ... cannot be the only parameter which determines whether a refusal to license an intellectual property right is capable of causing prejudice to consumers within the meaning of Article 102(b) TFEU. As that provision states, such prejudice may arise where there is a limitation not only of production or markets, but also of technical development.

It was on that last hypothesis that the Commission based its finding in the contested decision. Thus, the Commission considered that Microsoft's refusal to supply the relevant information limited technical development to the prejudice of consumers within the meaning of [Article 102(b) TFEU] ... and it rejected Microsoft's assertion that it had not been demonstrated that its refusal caused prejudice to consumers....

The Court finds that the Commission's findings at the recitals referred to in the preceding paragraph are not manifestly incorrect.

Thus, in the first place, the Commission was correct to observe ... that "[owing] to the lack of interoperability that competing work group server operating system products can achieve with the Windows domain architecture, an increasing number of consumers are locked into a homogeneous Windows solution at the level of work group server operating systems".

It must be borne in mind that it has already been stated ... above that Microsoft's refusal prevented its competitors from developing work group server operating systems capable of attaining a sufficient degree of interoperability with the Windows domain architecture, with the consequence that consumers' purchasing decisions in respect of work group server operating systems were channelled towards Microsoft's products....

The limitation thus placed on consumer choice is all the more damaging to consumers because ... they consider that non-Microsoft work group server operating systems are better than Windows work group server operating systems with respect to a series of features to which they attach great importance, such as "reliability/availability of the ... system" and "security included with the server operating system".

In the second place, the Commission was correct to consider that the artificial advantage in terms of interoperability that Microsoft retained by its refusal discouraged its competitors from developing and marketing work group server operating systems with innovative features, to the prejudice, notably, of consumers ... That refusal has the consequence that those competitors are placed at a disadvantage by comparison with Microsoft so far as the merits of their products are concerned, particularly with regard to parameters such as security, reliability, ease of use or operating performance speed ...

The Commission's finding that "[i]f Microsoft's competitors had access to the interoperability information that Microsoft refuses to supply, they could use the disclosures to make the advanced features of their own products available in the framework of the web of interoperability relationships that underpin the Windows domain architecture" ... is corroborated by the conduct which those competitors had adopted in the past, when they had access to certain information concerning Microsoft's products. . . .

The Commission was careful to emphasise, in that context, that there was "ample scope for differentiation and innovation beyond the design of interface specifications" . . . In other words, the same specification can be implemented in numerous different and innovative ways by software designers.

Thus, the contested decision rests on the concept that, once the obstacle represented for Microsoft's competitors by the insufficient degree of interoperability with the Windows domain architecture has been removed, those competitors will be able to offer work group server operating systems which, far from merely reproducing the Windows systems already on the market, will be distinguished from those systems with respect to parameters which consumers consider important. . . .

It must be borne in mind, in that regard, that Microsoft's competitors would not be able to clone or reproduce its products solely by having access to the interoperability information covered by the contested decision. Apart from the fact that Microsoft itself acknowledges in its pleadings that the remedy prescribed by Article 5 of the contested decision would not allow such a result to be achieved . . ., it is appropriate to repeat that the information at issue does not extend to implementation details or to other features of Microsoft's source code . . . The Court also notes that the protocols whose specifications Microsoft is required to disclose in application of the contested decision represent only a minimum part of the entire set of protocols implemented in Windows work group server operating systems.

Nor would Microsoft's competitors have any interest in merely reproducing Windows work group server operating systems. Once they are able to use the information communicated to them to develop systems that are sufficiently interoperable with the Windows domain architecture, they will have no other choice, if they wish to take advantage of a competitive advantage over Microsoft and maintain a profitable presence on the market, than to differentiate their products from Microsoft's products with respect to certain parameters and certain features. It must be borne in mind that . . . the implementation of specifications is a difficult task which requires significant investment in money and time.

Last, Microsoft's argument that it will have less incentive to develop a given technology if it is required to make that technology available to its competitors . . . is of no relevance to the examination of the circumstance relating to the new product, where the issue to be decided is the impact of the refusal to supply on the incentive for Microsoft's competitors to innovate and not on Microsoft's incentives to innovate. That is an issue which will be decided when the Court examines the circumstance relating to the absence of objective justification.

The absence of objective justification

. . . The Court notes, as a preliminary point, that although the burden of proof of the existence of the circumstances that constitute an infringement of Article [102 TFEU] is borne by the Commission, it is for the dominant undertaking concerned, and not for the Commission, before the end of the administrative procedure, to raise any plea of objective justification and to support it with arguments and evidence. It then falls to the Commission, where it proposes to make a finding of an abuse of a dominant position, to show that the arguments and evidence relied on by the undertaking cannot prevail and, accordingly, that the justification put forward cannot be accepted.

In the present case . . . Microsoft relied as justification for its conduct solely on the fact that the technology concerned was covered by intellectual property rights. It made clear that if it were required to grant third parties access to that technology, that "would . . . eliminate future incentives to invest in the creation of more intellectual property" . . . In the reply, the applicant also relied on that fact that the technology was secret and valuable and that it contained important innovations.

The Court considers that, even on the assumption that it is correct, the fact that the communication protocols covered by the contested decision, or the specifications for those protocols, are covered by intellectual property rights cannot constitute objective justification within the meaning of Magill and IMS Health . . . Microsoft's argument is inconsistent with the raison d'être of the exception which that case-law thus recognises in favour of free competition, since if the mere fact of holding intellectual property rights could in itself constitute objective justification for the refusal to grant a licence, the exception established by the case-law could never apply. In other words, a refusal to license an intellectual property right could never be considered to constitute an infringement of Article [102 TFEU] even though in Magill and IMS Health . . . the Court of Justice specifically stated the contrary.

It must be borne in mind that . . . the Community judicature considers that the fact that the holder of an intellectual property right can exploit that right solely for his own benefit constitutes the very substance of his exclusive right. Accordingly, a simple refusal, even on the part of an undertaking in a dominant position, to grant a licence to a third party cannot in itself constitute an abuse of a dominant position within the meaning of Article [102 TFEU]. It is only when it is accompanied by exceptional circumstances such as those hitherto envisaged in the case-law that such a refusal can be characterised as abusive and that, accordingly, it is permissible, in the public interest in maintaining effective competition on the market, to encroach upon the exclusive right of the holder of the intellectual property right by requiring him to grant licences to third parties seeking to enter or remain on that market. It must be borne in mind that it has been established above that such exceptional circumstances were present in this case.

The argument which Microsoft puts forward in the reply, namely that the technology concerned is secret and of great value to the licensees and contains important innovations, cannot succeed either.

First, the fact that the technology concerned is secret is the consequence of a unilateral business decision on Microsoft's part. Furthermore, Microsoft cannot rely on the argument that the interoperability information is secret as a ground for not being required to disclose it unless the exceptional circumstances identified by the Court of Justice in Magill and IMS Health ... are present, and at the same time justify its refusal by what it alleges to be the secret nature of the information. Last, there is no reason why secret technology should enjoy a higher level of protection than, for example, technology which has necessarily been disclosed to the public by its inventor in a patent-application procedure.

Second, from the moment at which it is established that—as in this case—the interoperability information is indispensable, that information is necessarily of great value to the competitors who wish to have access to it.

Third, it is inherent in the fact that the undertaking concerned holds an intellectual property right that the subject-matter of that right is innovative or original. There can be no patent without an invention and no copyright without an original work.

The Court further observes that in the contested decision the Commission did not simply reject Microsoft's assertion that the fact that the technology concerned was covered by intellectual property rights justified its refusal to disclose the relevant information. The Commission also examined the applicant's argument that if it were required to give third parties access to that technology there would be a negative impact on its incentives to innovate....

The Court finds that, as the Commission correctly submits, Microsoft, which bore the initial burden of proof ..., did not sufficiently establish that if it were required to disclose the interoperability information that would have a significant negative impact on its incentives to innovate.

Microsoft merely put forward vague, general and theoretical arguments on that point. Thus, ... in its response of 17 October 2003 to the third statement of objections Microsoft merely stated that "[d]isclosure would ... eliminate future incentives to invest in the creation of more intellectual property", without specifying the technologies or products to which it thus referred.

In certain passages in the response referred to in the preceding paragraph, Microsoft envisages a negative impact on its incentives to innovate by reference to its operating systems in general, namely both those for client PCs and those for servers.

In that regard, it is sufficient to note that ... the Commission quite correctly refuted Microsoft's arguments relating to the fear that its products would be cloned. It must be borne in mind, in particular, that the remedy prescribed in Article 5 of the contested decision does not, and is not designed to, allows Microsoft's competitors to copy its products....

It follows that it has not been demonstrated that the disclosure of the information to which that remedy relates will significantly reduce—still less eliminate—Microsoft's incentives to innovate.

In that context, the Court observes that, as the Commission correctly finds at recitals 730 to 734 to the contested decision, it is normal practice for operators in the industry to disclose to third parties the information which will facilitate interoperability with their products and Microsoft itself had followed that practice until it was sufficiently established on the work group server operating systems market. Such disclosure allows the operators concerned to make their own products more attractive and therefore more valuable. In fact, none of the parties has claimed in the present case that such disclosure had had any negative impact on those operators' incentives to innovate.

The Court further considers that if the disclosures made under the United States settlement and the MCPP as regards server-to-client protocols had no negative impact on Microsoft's incentives to innovate (recital 728 to the contested decision), there is no obvious reason to believe that the consequences should be any different in the case of disclosure relating to server/server protocols. Last, the Court finds that Microsoft's assertion that in the contested decision the Commission applied a new evaluation test when rejecting the objective justification which Microsoft had submitted is based on a misreading of that decision.

That assertion is based on a single sentence in recital 783 to the contested decision, which is in a part of that decision containing the findings of the Commission's analysis . . . of the refusal at issue.

That sentence reads as follows:

"[A] detailed examination of the scope of the disclosure at stake leads to the conclusion that, on balance, the possible negative impact of an order to supply on Microsoft's incentives to innovate is outweighed by its positive impact on the level of innovation of the whole industry (including Microsoft)".

However, that sentence must be read in conjunction with the one coming immediately afterwards in the same recital, which states that " . . . the need to protect Microsoft's incentives to innovate cannot constitute an objective justification that would offset the exceptional circumstances identified".

It must also be compared with recital 712 to the contested decision, where the Commission sets out the following considerations:

"It has been established above . . . that Microsoft's refusal to supply [creates a risk of elimination of] competition in the relevant market for work group server operating systems, that this is due to the fact that the refused input is indispensable to carry on business in that market and that Microsoft's refusal has a negative impact on technical development to the prejudice of consumers. In view of these exceptional circumstances, Microsoft's refusal cannot be objectively justified merely by the fact that it constitutes a refusal to license intellectual property. It is therefore necessary to assess whether Microsoft's arguments regarding its incentives to innovate outweigh these exceptional circumstances."

In other words, in accordance with the principles laid down in the case-law . . ., the Commission, after establishing that the exceptional circumstances identified by the Court of Justice in Magill and IMS Health . . . were present in this case, then proceeded to consider whether the justification put forward by Microsoft, on the basis of the alleged impact on its incentives to innovate, might prevail over those exceptional circumstances, including the circumstance that the refusal at issue limited technical development to the prejudice of consumers within the meaning of Article [102 TFEU].

The Commission came to a negative conclusion but not by balancing the negative impact which the imposition of a requirement to supply the information at issue might have on Microsoft's incentives to innovate against the positive impact of that obligation on innovation in the industry as a whole, but after refuting Microsoft's arguments relating to the fear that its products might be cloned ..., establishing that the disclosure of interoperability was widespread in the industry concerned ... and showing that IBM's commitment to the Commission in 1984 was not substantially different from what Microsoft was ordered to do in the contested decision ... and that its approach was consistent with Directive 91/250 ...

It follows from all of the foregoing considerations that Microsoft has not demonstrated the existence of any objective justification for its refusal to disclose the interoperability at issue.

Questions on Microsoft

1. The General Court states that the "circumstance relating to the appearance of a new product, as envisaged in Magill and IMS Health ... cannot be the only parameter which determines whether a refusal to license an intellectual property right is capable of causing prejudice to consumers within the meaning of Article 102(b) TFEU. As that provision states, such prejudice may arise where there is a limitation not only of production or markets, but also of technical development."

a. Isn't this a significant extension of the "exceptional circumstances" test adopted in *Magill* and *IMS Health*?

b. Is this extension justified considering that an input/access seeker will always be in a position to claim that a refusal to supply will harm "technical development" whatever this concept means?

2. When addressing Microsoft's argument that, if it were required to give third parties access to its interoperability technology, there would be a negative impact on its incentives to innovate, the General Court finds that "as the Commission correctly submits, Microsoft, which bore the initial burden of proof ..., did not sufficiently establish that if it were required to disclose the interoperability information that would have a significant negative impact on its incentives to innovate"

a. Is it fair to place the burden on the firm holding technologies that are protected by intellectual property rights of demonstrating that mandatory licensing would hurt its incentives to innovate? How could that burden of proof be met?

b. Is there a better approach?

Guidance on the Commission's Enforcement Priorities in Applying Article 82 EC Treaty [now 102 TFEU] to Abusive Exclusionary Conduct by Dominant Undertakings

(Dec. 2008).

... D. Refusal to supply and margin squeeze

When setting its enforcement priorities, the Commission starts from the position that, generally speaking, any undertaking, whether dominant or not, should have the right to choose its trading partners and to dispose freely of its property. The Commission therefore considers that intervention on competition law grounds requires careful consideration where the application of Article [102] would lead to imposing an obligation to supply on the dominant firm. The existence of such an obligation—even for a fair remuneration—may undermine firms' incentives to invest and innovate and, thereby, possibly harm consumers. The knowledge that they may have a duty to supply against their will may lead dominant undertakings—or undertakings who foresee that they may become dominant—not to invest, or to invest less, in the activity in question. Also, competitors may be tempted to free ride on investments made by the dominant undertaking instead of investing themselves. Neither of these consequences would in the long run be in the interest of consumers.

Typically competition problems arise when the dominant undertaking competes on the "downstream" market with the buyer whom it refuses to supply. The term "downstream market" is used to refer to the market for which the refused input is needed in order to manufacture a product or provide a service. The present section deals only with this type of refusals.

Other types of possibly unlawful refusal to supply, in which the supply is made conditional upon the purchaser accepting limitations on its conduct, are not dealt with in this section. For instance, halting supplies in order to punish customers for dealing with competitors or refusing to supply customers that do not agree to tying arrangements, will be examined by the Commission in line with the principles set out in the sections on exclusive dealing and tying and bundling. Similarly, refusals to supply aimed at preventing the purchaser from engaging in parallel trade or from lowering its resale price are also not dealt with in this section.

The concept of refusal to supply covers a broad range of practices, such as a refusal to supply products to existing or new customers, to license intellectual property rights, including when this is necessary to provide interface information, or to grant access to an essential facility or a network.

The Commission does not regard it as necessary for the refused product to have been already traded: it is sufficient that there is demand from potential purchasers and that a potential market for the input at stake can be identified. Likewise, it is not necessary that there is actual refusal on the part of a dominant undertaking; "constructive refusal" is sufficient. Constructive refusal could, for example, take the form of unduly delaying or otherwise degrading the supply of the product or involve the imposition of unreasonable conditions in return for the supply.

Finally, instead of refusing to supply, a dominant undertaking may charge a price for the product on the upstream market which, compared to the price it charges downstream market,[54] does not allow even an equally efficient competitor to trade profitably in the downstream market on a lasting basis (a so-called "margin squeeze"). In margin squeeze cases the benchmark which the Commission will generally rely on to determine the costs of an equally efficient competitor are the LRAIC of the downstream division of the integrated dominant undertaking.[55]

---

54. Including a situation in which an integrated undertaking that sells a "system" of complementary products refuses to sell one of the complementary products on an unbundled basis to a competitor that produces the other complementary product.

55. In some cases, however, the LRAIC of a non-integrated competitor downstream might be used as the benchmark, for example when it is not possible to clearly allocate the dominant undertaking's costs to downstream and upstream operations.

The Commission will consider these practices as an enforcement priority if the following cumulative circumstances are present:

- the refusal relates to a product or service that is objectively necessary to be able to compete effectively on a downstream market;
- the refusal is likely to lead to the elimination of effective competition on the downstream market; and
- the refusal is likely to lead to consumer harm.

In certain specific cases, it may be clear that imposing an obligation to supply is manifestly not capable of having negative effects on the input owner's and/or other operators' incentives to invest and innovate upstream, whether ex ante or ex post. The Commission considers that this is particularly likely to be the case where regulation compatible with Community law already imposes an obligation to supply on the dominant undertaking and it is clear, from the considerations underlying such regulation, that the necessary balancing of incentives has already been made by the public authority when imposing such an obligation to supply. This could also be the case where the upstream market position of the dominant undertaking has been developed under the protection of special or exclusive rights or has been financed by state resources. In such specific cases there is no reason for the Commission to deviate from its general enforcement standard and it may show likely anticompetitive foreclosure without considering whether the above three cumulative circumstances are present.

a) Objective necessity of the input

In examining whether a refusal to supply deserves its priority attention, he Commission will consider whether the supply of the refused input is objectively needed for operators to be able to compete effectively on the market. This does not mean that, without the refused input, no competitor could ever enter or survive on the downstream market. Rather, an input is indispensable where there is no actual or potential substitute on which competitors in the downstream market could rely so as to counter—at least in the long term—the negative consequences of the refusal. In this regard, the Commission will normally make an assessment of whether competitors could effectively duplicate the input produced by the dominant undertaking in the foreseeable future. The notion of duplication means the creation of an alternative source of efficient supply that is capable of allowing competitors to exert a competitive constraint on the dominant undertaking in the downstream market.

The criteria set out in paragraph 80 apply both to cases of disruption of previous supply, and to refusals to supply a good or service which the dominant company has not previously supplied to others (de novo refusals to supply). However, it is more likely that the termination of an existing supply arrangement is found to be abusive than a de novo refusal to supply. For example, if the dominant undertaking had previously been supplying the requesting undertaking, and the latter had made relationship-specific investments in order to use the subsequently refused input, the Commission may be more likely to regard the input in question as indispensable. Similarly, the fact that the owner of the essential input in the past has found it in its interest to supply is an indication that supplying the input does not imply any risk that the owner receives inadequate compensation for the original investment. It would therefore be up to the dominant company to demonstrate why circumstances have actually changed in such a way that the continuation of its existing supply relationship would put in danger its adequate compensation.

b) Elimination of effective competition

If the requirements set out in paragraphs 82 to 83 are fulfilled, the Commission considers that a dominant undertaking's refusal to supply is generally liable to eliminate, immediately or over time, effective competition in the downstream market. The likelihood of effective competition being eliminated is generally greater the higher the market share of the dominant firm in the downstream market; the less capacity-constrained the dominant firm is relative to competitors in the downstream market; the closer the substitutability between the dominant firm's output and that of its competitors in the downstream market; the greater the proportion of competitors in the downstream market that are affected, and; the more likely it is that the demand that could be served by the foreclosed competitors would be diverted away from them to the advantage of the dominant undertaking.

c) Consumer harm

In examining the likely impact of a refusal to supply on consumer welfare, the Commission will examine whether for the consumers, the likely negative consequences of the refusal to supply in the relevant market outweigh over time the negative consequences of imposing an obligation to supply. If they do, the Commission will normally pursue the case.

The Commission considers that consumer harm may, for instance, arise where the competitors that the dominant undertaking forecloses are, as a result of the refusal, prevented from bringing to market innovative goods or services and/or where follow-on innovation is likely to be stifled. This may be particularly the case if the undertaking which requests supply does not intend to limit itself essentially to duplicating the goods or services already offered by the dominant undertaking on the downstream market, but intends to produce new or improved goods or services for which there is a potential consumer demand or is likely to contribute to technical development.

The Commission also considers that a refusal to supply may lead to consumer harm where the price in the upstream input market is regulated, the price in the downstream market is not regulated and the dominant undertaking, by excluding competitors on the downstream market through a refusal to supply, is able to extract more profits in the unregulated downstream market than it would otherwise do.

d) Efficiencies

The Commission will consider claims by the dominant undertaking that a refusal to supply is necessary to allow the dominant undertaking to realise an adequate return on the investments required to develop its input business, thus generating incentives to continue to invest in the future, taking the risk of failed projects into account. The Commission will also consider claims by the dominant undertaking that its own innovation will be negatively affected by the obligation to supply, or by the structural changes in the market conditions that imposing such an obligation will bring about, including the development of follow-on innovation by competitors.

However, when considering such claims, the Commission will ensure that the conditions set out in Section III D above are fulfilled. In particular, it falls on the dominant undertaking to demonstrate any negative impact which an obligation to supply is likely to have on its own level of innovation, and if a dominant undertaking has previously supplied the input in question, this can be relevant for the assessment of any claim that the refusal to supply is justified on efficiency grounds. . . .

Questions on the Commission's Guidance Paper

1. The Guidance Paper states that it will consider refusal to supply practices as an enforcement priority if the cumulative conditions set by the European Court of Justice in *Bronner* are present. It, however, adds the caveat that these conditions do not need to be satisfied, where imposing an obligation to supply is manifestly not capable of having negative effects on the input owner's and/or other operators' incentives to invest and innovate upstream, whether ex ante or ex post. This is likely to be the case in the following circumstances: (i) regulation compatible with EU law already imposes an obligation to supply on the dominant undertaking and it is clear, from the considerations underlying such regulation, that the necessary balancing of incentives has already been made by the public authority when imposing such an obligation to supply; or (ii) the upstream market position of the dominant undertaking has been developed under the protection of special or exclusive rights or has been financed by state resources.

a. Do you think these exceptions are justified?

b. Do you think that when an obligation to supply has been imposed by a Member State sector-specific regulator (e.g., a telecommunications agency), it is no longer necessary to verify whether the conditions set in *Bronner* are present?

    i. Don't EU competition law and Member State laws have different objectives? For instance, musn't regulation and regulators balance a broader set of objectives including not only the protection of competition but also the creation of competitive market structures, the promotion of investments in the telecommunications sector, and the maintenance and improvement of universal service?

    ii. In this respect, is it relevant that a national regulator may be required to balance incentives to invest and/or innovate before imposing regulatory obligations on a given operator? Since regulatory authorities and competition authorities pursue different objectives, isn't their balancing of a firm's incentives to innovate with the benefits of an obligation to deal likely to be different?

c. Similarly, do you think that a general exception whereby there would be no need for the Commission to satisfy the normal conditions for imposing an obligation to deal when the "firm's upstream market position has been developed under the protection of special or exclusive rights or has been financed by state resources" is justified?

    i. Would this exception be easy to apply? Do you think that the issue of whether or not the "firm's upstream market position has been developed under the protection of special or exclusive rights or has been financed by state resources" will always be clear cut?

ii.   Moreover, isn't there a risk that this exception may negatively affect incentives to invest? When the conditions of *Bronner* are satisfied this is not a relevant issue as it is not viable for competitors to build their own infrastructure. However, when these conditions are not satisfied can't this exception simply induce competitors to rely on the dominant firm's infrastructure instead of building its own?

2.   The Commission states that it "will consider claims by the dominant undertaking that a refusal to supply is necessary to allow the dominant undertaking to realise an adequate return on the investments required to develop its input business, thus generating incentives to continue to invest in the future, taking the risk of failed projects into account." It, however, indicates that "it falls on the dominant undertaking to demonstrate any negative impact which an obligation to supply is likely to have on its own level of innovation, and if a dominant undertaking has previously supplied the input in question, this can be relevant for the assessment of any claim that the refusal to supply is justified on efficiency grounds."

a.   Is it fair to impose on the dominant firm the burden of showing the negative impact that an obligation to supply would have on its own level of innovation?

b.   Doesn't this turn on its head the principle that "any undertaking, whether dominant or not, should have the right to choose its trading partners and to dispose freely of its property", which is recognized elsewhere in the Guidance Paper?

c.   Will the burden of proving that an obligation to deal will hurt the dominant firm's level of innovation be easier in practice?

d.   Wouldn't it be preferable to take as a starting point that an obligation to supply a particular input or share a technology will always hurt a dominant firm's to invest?

Unilateral Refusals to Deal in Other Nations

Many other nations also prohibit some unilateral refusals to deal. Canada makes a unilateral refusal to deal illegal under the same circumstances as a concerted refusal to deal, that is when it (1) substantially injures a business that (2) cannot obtain the product elsewhere on usual market terms because of a lack of competition among suppliers and (3) is willing to pay the supplier's usual trade terms, (4) the defendant has an ample supply of the product, and (5) the refusal will likely cause an anticompetitive effect.[152] Although a dominant position is not required, the second and fourth elements would seem to be true only when market power existed. The third element also seems to embrace a nondiscrimination test similar to the one that is consistent with U.S. Supreme Court caselaw. Mexico likewise applies the same rule of reason to unilateral refusals to deal that it applies to concerted refusals to deal, requiring market power,

---

152.   *See* Canada Competition Act § 75.

an exclusionary purpose, and a lack of efficiencies that offset any anticompetitive effects.[153] Japan makes a unilateral refusal to deal with rivals or those who deal with rivals illegal if the refusal is unjust and tends to impede competition and exclude competitors.[154]

South Korea has the most intricate regime. South Korea law makes it an unfair trade practice for a firm whose market share is 10% or higher to refuse to initiate or to end or restrict dealing with particular firms if either (1) the purpose was to make it difficult for the buyer to operate or to coerce the buyer into conduct prohibited by law or (2) the refusal had the effect of making it difficult for the buyer to operate because the denied product is essential to business operations and the buyer cannot easily find a substitute trader, and (3) the refusal was not justified by seller inability, buyer lack of creditworthiness, offsetting procompetitive effects, or other reasonable justifications.[155] South Korea law also makes it an abuse of a dominant position for a firm with dominant market power to refuse to deal when that either (1) has the purpose of maintaining or strengthening its dominant market power and that such anticompetitive effects were objectively possible or (2) that the refusal actually had anticompetitive market effects (from which the same purpose would be inferred).[156] Thus, while South Korea unfair trade practice law focuses on whether the denial was intended to harm or did harm the buyer, this provision in South Korea abuse of dominance law focuses on whether the denial had anticompetitive effects.[157]

Australia and New Zealand make unilateral refusals to deal that take advantage of market power illegal when they have an exclusionary purpose.[158] China prohibits a dominant firm from refusing to deal "without a justifiable reason."[159] Venezuela and Peru likewise prohibit 'unjustified' refusals to deal.[160] Saudi Arabia prohibits a dominant firm from "Refusing to deal with another firm without justification in order to restrict . . . its entry into the market."[161] South Africa makes it illegal for a dominant firm

---

153. *See* Mexico Competition Law Arts. 10(V), 11.

154. *See* Japan Antimonopoly Act § 2(9); Japan Designations of Unfair Trade Practices § 2 (2009); Japan Distribution Guidelines at 9–10.

155. South Korea Fair Trade Act Art 23(1)(i) (2010); Enforcement Decree of the South Korea Fair Trade Act Appendix 1.B (2010); Case No. 2004 Du 8514, Korean Supreme Court Judgment, March 30, 2007; South Korea Guidelines for Review of Unfair Trade Practices V.1.B (2009).

156. South Korea Fair Trade Art. 3–2(1) (2010); South Korea Guidelines on Reviewing Abuses of Market Dominance IV.3.D (2002); Case No. 2002 Du 8626, Korean Supreme Court En Banc Judgment, November 22, 2007.

157. Other provisions of South Korea abuse of dominance do focus on whether the denied product or facility was essential for the buyer to operate. Enforcement Decree of the South Korea Fair Trade Act Art. 5(3)(iii) & 5(4)(iii); South Korea Guidelines on Reviewing Abuses of Market Dominance IV.3.C & 4.C (2009) (also requiring a lack of justification).

158. *See* Melway Publishing v. Robert Hicks Pty., Ltd., 205 C.L.R. 1, 27 (Australian High Court 2001); OECD, Predatory Foreclosure 185 (2005) (New Zealand).

159. China Anti–Monopoly Law Art. 17(3).

160. Venezuela Procompetition Act, Art. 13(3); Peru Competition Law, Art. 10(2)(a). In Peru offsetting efficiencies are accepted as a valid justification for refusals to deal.

161. Saudi Arabia Competition Law Art. 5(4). Further, Saudi Implementing Regulation Art. 6(1)(i) prohibits dominant firms from refusing to deal with any clients under customary business practices if the refusal has no justification and limits competition.

to "refuse to give a competitor access to an essential facility when it is economically feasible to do so," or to refuse to supply "scarce goods" when economically feasible unless the firm can show that procompetitive gains offset the anticompetitive effects.[162] Turkey and Singapore also embrace the essential facilities doctrine.[163] Brazil and Israel assess unilateral refusals to deal under a rule of reason.[164] Russia makes a refusal to deal by dominant firm illegal if they result or can result in anticompetitive effects.[165] Egypt makes a refusal to deal by a dominant firm illegal if it restricts the buyers' freedom to access or exit the market.[166]

6.   PRICE SQUEEZES

Suppose a dominant firm both controls an input its rival needs and competes downstream with that rival. Rather than refusing to supply that input to its rival, it sets the price for that input relatively high and sets its competing downstream price relatively low, so that the difference between the input price and the downstream price is not large enough to support the costs of its rival, thus driving the rival out of business. Suppose, for example, an upstream monopolist in wholesale electricity sets the wholesale price at 6 cents/kwh and offers a retail price of 7 cents/kwh, and its rival's cost of retailing electricity is 2 cents/kwh so that a rival that depends on its wholesale electricity cannot offer a retail price lower than 8 cents/kwh. The rival will then be driven from the market even though the defendant's retail price exceeds its combined wholesale/retail costs. Such cases are said to involve price squeezes.

Price squeezes can exclude an equally efficient rival only if the upstream-downstream price differential is lower than the defendants' own downstream costs. The same sort of analysis that applies to predatory pricing thus suggest a necessary element for proving an illegal price squeeze should be proving that the price differential is below the defendant's own costs. Thus, in the above example, if the defendant's own cost of retailing electricity is 2 cent/kwh, then the price squeeze can exclude an equally efficient rival because the wholesale-retail price differential is only 1 cent/kwh. But if the defendant's cost of retailing electricity were 1 cent/kwh, then the price differential would not be lower than the defendant's downstream cost and the price squeeze should not be actionable. The price squeeze would still eliminate a rival with retailing costs of 2 cents/kwh, but that is because the rival is simply less efficient at retailing than the defendant.

---

162.   South Africa Competition Act § 8(b), (d)(ii).

163.   Turkey Competition Board Decision No. 07–13/101–30, at line 2430ff (2007); Singapore Guidelines on the Section 47 Prohibition Annex C §§ 11.28 to 11.31 (2007).

164.   Brazil Antitrust Law No. 8,884, Art.21(VI); Brazil CADE Resolution 20, Attachment I, § B.4 (1999); Israel Restrictive Trade Practices Law § 29.

165.   Russia Competition Law Art. 10(1)(5). This law does not apply to refusals to provide intellectual property rights. *Id.* Art. 10(4).

166.   Egypt Competition Law Art. 8(b).

Although price squeezes thus share a cost-test in common with predatory pricing, the problem is not with the low downstream price, which by hypothesis is above the combined upstream-downstream cost,[167] but with an excessive upstream price. After all, if the defendant resolved the price squeeze by raising the downstream price, that would clearly harm consumer welfare and allocative efficiency. The concern is thus not that the defendant set the downstream price too low, but that it has arbitrarily raised the upstream price to make it impossible for an equally efficient downstream rival to profitably deal with it. In short, the underlying concern is that the excessive upstream price amounts to a constructive refusal to deal.

Consistent with this characterization, although a below-cost price differential is necessary to exclude equally efficient downstream rivals, it is not sufficient to impose such an exclusion nor to show any exclusion is anticompetitive. As with outright refusals to deal, one must ask whether the rival has economically feasible alternative sources of the input. After all, the below-cost price differential created by a price squeeze is something the rival must endure only to the extent it buys the defendant's input; if it can buy the input elsewhere, then it faces only a nonpredatory downstream price. Nor is a refusal to supply the input at a reasonable price necessarily anticompetitive even if it does exclude the rival. As with any refusal to deal, one must be attentive to the extent to which a dominant upstream firm has efficient versus anticompetitive incentives to displace a downstream rival, and whether any duty to provide inputs at lower prices is administrable and will adversely affect ex ante investment incentives.

Indeed, it would be odd to treat a price squeeze, which at least offers the upstream product at some price, more harshly than an absolute refusal to deal, which effectively sets an infinite upstream price. If the law did, any firm worried about being charged with a price squeeze could simply take the even more onerous step of refusing to supply the downstream firm at all. Thus, although proving a price-differential below the defendant's downstream costs should substitute for showing a refusal to deal, the other elements of a refusal to deal should still have to be proven to make a price squeeze illegal.

Pacific Bell Telephone v. Linkline Communications

129 S.Ct. 1109 (2009).

■ CHIEF JUSTICE ROBERTS delivered the opinion of the Court.

The plaintiffs in this case, respondents here, allege that a competitor subjected them to a "price squeeze" in violation of § 2 of the Sherman Act. They assert that such a claim can arise when a vertically integrated firm sells inputs at wholesale and also sells finished goods or services at retail. If that firm has power in the wholesale market, it can simultaneously raise the wholesale price of inputs and cut the retail price of the finished good.

---

167. If the downstream price is below the defendant's combined upstream-downstream cost, then one can simply rely on predatory pricing doctrine without need to resort to any doctrine on price squeezes.

This will have the effect of "squeezing" the profit margins of any competitors in the retail market. Those firms will have to pay more for the inputs they need; at the same time, they will have to cut their retail prices to match the other firm's prices. The question before us is whether such a price-squeeze claim may be brought under § 2 of the Sherman Act when the defendant is under no antitrust obligation to sell the inputs to the plaintiff in the first place. We hold that no such claim may be brought.

I

This case involves the market for digital subscriber line (DSL) service, which is a method of connecting to the Internet at high speeds over telephone lines. AT&T owns much of the infrastructure and facilities needed to provide DSL service in California. In particular, AT&T controls most of what is known as the "last mile"—the lines that connect homes and businesses to the telephone network. Competing DSL providers must generally obtain access to AT&T's facilities in order to serve their customers.

Until recently, the Federal Communications Commission (FCC) required incumbent phone companies such as AT&T to sell transmission service to independent DSL providers, under the theory that this would spur competition. In 2005, the Commission largely abandoned this forced-sharing requirement in light of the emergence of a competitive market beyond DSL for high-speed Internet service; DSL now faces robust competition from cable companies and wireless and satellite services. As a condition for a recent merger, however, AT&T remains bound by the mandatory interconnection requirements, and is obligated to provide wholesale "DSL transport" service to independent firms at a price no greater than the retail price of AT&T's DSL service.

The plaintiffs are four independent Internet service providers (ISPs) that compete with AT&T in the retail DSL market. Plaintiffs do not own all the facilities needed to supply their customers with this service. They instead lease DSL transport service from AT&T pursuant to the merger conditions described above. AT&T thus participates in the DSL market at both the wholesale and retail levels; it provides plaintiffs and other independent ISPs with wholesale DSL transport service, and it also sells DSL service directly to consumers at retail.

In July 2003, the plaintiffs brought suit in District Court, alleging that AT&T violated § 2 of the Sherman Act by monopolizing the DSL market in California. The complaint alleges that AT&T refused to deal with the plaintiffs, denied the plaintiffs access to essential facilities, and engaged in a "price squeeze." Specifically, plaintiffs contend that AT&T squeezed their profit margins by setting a high wholesale price for DSL transport and a low retail price for DSL Internet service.... The District Court held that AT&T had no antitrust duty to deal with the plaintiffs, but it denied the motion to dismiss with respect to the price-squeeze claims ... On interlocutory appeal, the Court of Appeals for the Ninth Circuit affirmed the District Court's denial of AT&T's motion for judgment on the pleadings on the price-squeeze claims ...

We granted certiorari, to resolve a conflict over whether a plaintiff can bring price-squeeze claims under § 2 of the Sherman Act when the defendant has no antitrust duty to deal with the plaintiff. See Covad Communications Co. v. Bell Atlantic Corp., 398 F.3d 666, 673–674 (C.A.D.C.2005) (holding that *Trinko* bars such claims). We reverse.

III

A

. . . As a general rule, businesses are free to choose the parties with whom they will deal, as well as the prices, terms, and conditions of that dealing. See United States v. Colgate & Co., 250 U.S. 300, 307 (1919). But there are rare instances in which a dominant firm may incur antitrust liability for purely unilateral conduct. For example, we have ruled that firms may not charge "predatory" prices-below-cost prices that drive rivals out of the market and allow the monopolist to raise its prices later and recoup its losses. *Brooke Group.* Here, however, the complaint at issue does not contain allegations meeting those requirements.

There are also limited circumstances in which a firm's unilateral refusal to deal with its rivals can give rise to antitrust liability. See *Aspen.* Here, however, the District Court held that AT&T had no such antitrust duty to deal with its competitors, and this holding was not challenged on appeal.[2]

The challenge here focuses on retail prices—where there is no predatory pricing—and the terms of dealing—where there is no duty to deal. Plaintiffs' price-squeeze claims challenge a different type of unilateral conduct in which a firm "squeezes" the profit margins of its competitors. This requires the defendant to be operating in two markets, a wholesale ("upstream") market and a retail ("downstream") market. A firm with market power in the upstream market can squeeze its downstream competitors by raising the wholesale price of inputs while cutting its own retail prices. This will raise competitors' costs (because they will have to pay more for their inputs) and lower their revenues (because they will have to match the dominant firm's low retail price). Price-squeeze plaintiffs assert that defendants must leave them a "fair" or "adequate" margin between the wholesale price and the retail price. In this case, we consider whether a plaintiff can state a price-squeeze claim when the defendant has no obligation under the antitrust laws to deal with the plaintiff at wholesale.

B

1. A straightforward application of our recent decision in *Trinko* forecloses any challenge to AT&T's wholesale prices. In *Trinko*, Verizon was required by statute to lease its network elements to competing firms at wholesale rates. The plaintiff—a customer of one of Verizon's rivals—

---

2.   The Court of Appeals assumed that any duty to deal arose only from FCC regulations, and the question on which we granted certiorari made the same assumption. Even aside from the District Court's reasoning, it seems quite unlikely that AT&T would have an antitrust duty to deal with the plaintiffs. Such a duty requires a showing of monopoly power, but—as the FCC has recognized—the market for high-speed Internet service is now quite competitive; DSL providers face stiff competition from cable companies and wireless and satellite providers.

asserted that Verizon denied its competitors access to interconnection support services, making it difficult for those competitors to fill their customers' orders . . .

We held that the plaintiff's claims were not actionable under § 2. Given that Verizon had no antitrust duty to deal with its rivals at all, we concluded that "Verizon's alleged insufficient assistance in the provision of service to rivals" did not violate the Sherman Act. *Trinko* thus makes clear that if a firm has no antitrust duty to deal with its competitors at wholesale, it certainly has no duty to deal under terms and conditions that the rivals find commercially advantageous.

In this case, as in *Trinko*, the defendant has no antitrust duty to deal with its rivals at wholesale; any such duty arises only from FCC regulations, not from the Sherman Act. There is no meaningful distinction between the "insufficient assistance" claims we rejected in *Trinko* and the plaintiffs' price-squeeze claims in the instant case. The *Trinko* plaintiffs challenged the quality of Verizon's interconnection service, while this case involves a challenge to AT&T's pricing structure. But for antitrust purposes, there is no reason to distinguish between price and nonprice components of a transaction. See, e.g., American Telephone & Telegraph Co. v. Central Office Telephone, Inc., 524 U.S. 214, 223 (1998) ("Any claim for excessive rates can be couched as a claim for inadequate services and vice versa"). The nub of the complaint in both *Trinko* and this case is identical—the plaintiffs alleged that the defendants (upstream monopolists) abused their power in the wholesale market to prevent rival firms from competing effectively in the retail market. *Trinko* holds that such claims are not cognizable under the Sherman Act in the absence of an antitrust duty to deal.

The District Court and the Court of Appeals did not regard *Trinko* as controlling because that case did not directly address price-squeeze claims. This is technically true, but the reasoning of *Trinko* applies with equal force to price-squeeze claims. AT&T could have squeezed its competitors' profits just as effectively by providing poor-quality interconnection service to the plaintiffs, as Verizon allegedly did in *Trinko*. But a firm with no duty to deal in the wholesale market has no obligation to deal under terms and conditions favorable to its competitors. If AT&T had simply stopped providing DSL transport service to the plaintiffs, it would not have run afoul of the Sherman Act. Under these circumstances, AT&T was not required to offer this service at the wholesale prices the plaintiffs would have preferred.

2.   The other component of a price-squeeze claim is the assertion that the defendant's retail prices are "too low." Here too plaintiffs' claims find no support in our existing antitrust doctrine.

"[C]utting prices in order to increase business often is the very essence of competition." *Matsushita*. In cases seeking to impose antitrust liability for prices that are too low, mistaken inferences are "especially costly, because they chill the very conduct the antitrust laws are designed to protect." *Ibid.*; see also *Brooke Group*. To avoid chilling aggressive price competition, we have carefully limited the circumstances under which plaintiffs can state a Sherman Act claim by alleging that prices are too low. Specifically, to prevail on a predatory pricing claim, a plaintiff must demonstrate that: (1) "the prices complained of are below an appropriate measure of its rival's costs"; and (2) there is a "dangerous probability" that the defendant will be able to recoup its "investment" in below-cost prices. *Brooke Group*. "Low prices benefit consumers regardless of how those prices are set, and so long as they are above predatory levels, they do not threaten competition." Atlantic Richfield Co. v. USA Petroleum Co., 495 U.S. 328, 340 (1990).

In the complaint at issue in this interlocutory appeal, there is no allegation that AT&T's conduct met either of the Brooke Group requirements. Recognizing a price-squeeze claim where the defendant's retail price remains above cost would invite the precise harm we sought to avoid in *Brooke Group*: Firms might raise their retail prices or refrain from aggressive price competition to avoid potential antitrust liability.

3. Plaintiffs' price-squeeze claim, looking to the relation between retail and wholesale prices, is thus nothing more than an amalgamation of a meritless claim at the retail level and a meritless claim at the wholesale level. If there is no duty to deal at the wholesale level and no predatory pricing at the retail level, then a firm is certainly not required to price both of these services in a manner that preserves its rivals' profit margins.

C

1. Institutional concerns also counsel against recognition of such claims. We have repeatedly emphasized the importance of clear rules in antitrust law. Courts are ill suited "to act as central planners, identifying the proper price, quantity, and other terms of dealing." *Trinko.* " 'No court should impose a duty to deal that it cannot explain or adequately and reasonably supervise. The problem should be deemed irremedia[ble] by antitrust law when compulsory access requires the court to assume the day-to-day controls characteristic of a regulatory agency.' " *Id.;* see also Town of Concord v. Boston Edison Co., 915 F.2d 17, 25 (C.A.1 1990) (Breyer, C.J.) ("[A]ntitrust courts normally avoid direct price administration, relying on rules and remedies . . . that are easier to administer").

It is difficult enough for courts to identify and remedy an alleged anticompetitive practice at one level, such as predatory pricing in retail markets or a violation of the duty-to-deal doctrine at the wholesale level. Recognizing price-squeeze claims would require courts simultaneously to police both the wholesale and retail prices to ensure that rival firms are not being squeezed. And courts would be aiming at a moving target, since it is the interaction between these two prices that may result in a squeeze.

Perhaps most troubling, firms that seek to avoid price-squeeze liability will have no safe harbor for their pricing practices. See *Town of Concord* (antitrust rules "must be clear enough for lawyers to explain them to clients"). At least in the predatory pricing context, firms know they will not incur liability as long as their retail prices are above cost. No such guidance is available for price-squeeze claims.

The most commonly articulated standard for price squeezes is that the defendant must leave its rivals a "fair" or "adequate" margin between the wholesale price and the retail price. One of our colleagues has highlighted the flaws of this test in Socratic fashion:

> "[H]ow is a judge or jury to determine a 'fair price?' Is it the price charged by other suppliers of the primary product? None exist. Is it the price that competition 'would have set' were the primary level not monopolized? How can the court determine this price without examining costs and demands, indeed without acting like a rate-setting regulatory agency, the rate-setting proceedings of which often last for several years? Further, how is the court to decide the proper size of the price 'gap?' Must it be large enough for all independent competing firms to make a 'living profit,' no matter how inefficient they may be? ... And how should the court respond when costs or demands change over time, as they inevitably will?" *Town of Concord.*

Some amici respond to these concerns by proposing a "transfer price test" for identifying an unlawful price squeeze: A price squeeze should be presumed if the upstream monopolist could not have made a profit by selling at its retail rates if it purchased inputs at its own wholesale rates. Whether or not that test is administrable, it lacks any grounding in our antitrust jurisprudence. An upstream monopolist with no duty to deal is free to charge whatever wholesale price it would like; antitrust law does not forbid lawfully obtained monopolies from charging monopoly prices. Similarly, the Sherman Act does not forbid—indeed, it encourages—aggressive price competition at the retail level, as long as the prices being charged are not predatory. If both the wholesale price and the retail price are independently lawful, there is no basis for imposing antitrust liability simply because a vertically integrated firm's wholesale price happens to be greater than or equal to its retail price.

2. Amici assert that there are circumstances in which price squeezes may harm competition. For example, they assert that price squeezes may raise entry barriers that fortify the upstream monopolist's position; they also contend that price squeezes may impair nonprice competition and innovation in the downstream market by driving independent firms out of business.

The problem, however, is that amici have not identified any independent competitive harm caused by price squeezes above and beyond the harm that would result from a duty-to-deal violation at the wholesale level or predatory pricing at the retail level. To the extent a monopolist violates one of these doctrines, the plaintiffs have a remedy under existing law. We do not need to endorse a new theory of liability to prevent such harm.

IV

... Plaintiffs have also filed an amended complaint, and the District Court concluded that this complaint, generously construed, could be read as alleging conduct that met the *Brooke Group* requirements for predatory pricing.[168] That order, however, applied the "no set of facts" pleading

---

168. [Editor's Note: The District Court held that the amended complaint could be interpreted to allege that the defendant charged rivals and the defendant's retail affiliates a

standard that we have since rejected as too lenient. See Bell Atlantic Corp. v. Twombly, 550 U.S. 544, 561–563 (2007). It is for the District Court on remand to consider whether the amended complaint states a claim upon which relief may be granted in light of the new pleading standard we articulated in *Twombly*, whether plaintiffs should be given leave to amend their complaint to bring a claim under *Brooke Group*, and such other matters properly before it. Even if the amended complaint is further amended to add a *Brooke Group* claim, it may not survive a motion to dismiss. For if AT&T can bankrupt the plaintiffs by refusing to deal altogether, the plaintiffs must demonstrate why the law prevents AT&T from putting them out of business by pricing them out of the market. Nevertheless, such questions are for the District Court to decide in the first instance. We do not address these issues here, as they are outside the scope of the question presented and were not addressed by the Court of Appeals in the decision below.

* * *

Trinko holds that a defendant with no antitrust duty to deal with its rivals has no duty to deal under the terms and conditions preferred by those rivals. *Brooke Group* holds that low prices are only actionable under the Sherman Act when the prices are below cost and there is a dangerous probability that the predator will be able to recoup the profits it loses from the low prices. In this case, plaintiffs have not stated a duty-to-deal claim under *Trinko* and have not stated a predatory pricing claim under *Brooke Group*. They have nonetheless tried to join a wholesale claim that cannot succeed with a retail claim that cannot succeed, and alchemize them into a new form of antitrust liability never before recognized by this Court. We decline the invitation to recognize such claims. Two wrong claims do not make one that is right . . .

Questions on *Linkline*

1. If the upstream-downstream price differential is lower than the defendant's own costs of operating downstream, why should the elements of a duty to deal have to be proven? On the one hand, such a low differential could drive out equally efficient downstream rivals even if all the duty to deal elements were not met. On the other hand, a doctrine based solely on the price differential would encourage a defendant to refuse to sell to its rival at all in any case where the duty to deal elements were not met. Further, if the other elements limiting a duty to deal make sense in the case of outright refusals, they would seem to make equal or more sense in a

---

wholesale price that was high enough that its affiliates' retail prices were below the combination of those affiliates' wholesale and retail costs. App. to Pet. for Cert. 48a–50a. It concluded that this allegation satisfied the *Brooke Group* standard as interpreted in *Covad*. *Id*. 39a–40a, 47a–48a. *Covad* held that an "appropriate measure" of costs under *Brooke Group* could include a combination of the upstream price that the defendant charged downstream firms and the defendant's own costs of operating downstream. *See* Covad Communications v. BellSouth, 374 F.3d 1044, 1050–51 (11th Cir. 2004). This standard effectively compares the upstream-downstream price differential to the defendant's costs of operating downstream, rather than comparing the downstream price to the defendant's combined upstream-downstream costs.]

case where an unduly high price allegedly amounts to a constructive refusal.

2.   If the duty to deal elements are proven, what else should be required to prove that the price squeeze was illegal? Should the second prong require proof that:

(a) the downstream price is lower than the defendant's combined upstream-downstream costs?

(b) the upstream price is higher than the defendant charged nonrivals or voluntarily offered previously to the rival?

(c) the upstream-downstream price differential is lower than the defendant's costs of operating downstream?

(d) the upstream-downstream price differential is lower than the rival's costs of operating downstream?

Requiring (a) would have various problems. It would make any price squeeze claim superfluous because it would add nothing to a straight predatory pricing claim. It would eviscerate any duty to deal because a defendant could always effectively refuse to deal by setting an arbitrarily high price on the upstream product. It would also be inconsistent with other cases holding that offering unfavorable upstream terms can amount to a constructive refusal to deal if the other elements for an illegal refusal to deal were met. *See Aspen; Trinko; see also Associated Press* (same for concerted refusal to deal); *Terminal R.R.* (same).

Choosing (b) would be consistent with this last set of cases and the *Linkine* opinion's implicit recognition that an unduly high upstream price can be a constructive refusal to deal. But (b) would again make a price squeeze claim superfluous because it would add nothing to a straight claim that discriminatory or terminated dealings amount to an illegal constructive refusal to deal. It would also make examination of the downstream price largely irrelevant and create liability in cases where the pricing could not eliminate an equally efficient downstream rival.

Choosing (c) would provide some distinctive meaning to a price squeeze claim. It could also provide a test for determining when the constructive refusal to deal was likely to eliminate equally efficient downstream rivals. It would also be consistent with the Eleventh Circuit decision in *Covad* and would make U.S. doctrine parallel EU doctrine on price squeezes.[169]

Choosing (d) would provide some distinctive meaning to a price squeeze claim. However, it would ban conduct that could not eliminate an equally efficient rival. It would also make U.S. price squeeze doctrine broader than E.C. doctrine. Finally, it would create administrative problems when the rival uses a downstream process that incurs higher costs to improve product quality. In such a case, requiring that the defendant maintain a price differential that equaled its rival's downstream costs would mean that the defendant would either have to: (a) charge the same

---

169.   *See Covad*, 374 F.3d at 1050–51. Guidance on the Commission's Enforcement Priorities in Applying Article 82 EC Treaty [now 102 TFEU] to Abusive Exclusionary Conduct by Dominant Undertakings ¶¶ 79–80 (Feb. 9, 2009); Case T–5/97, Industries Des Poudres Sph'eriques SA v. Commission, [2000] E.C.R. II–3755.

downstream price for a lower quality product, in which case the defendant could not survive downstream, or (b) switch to the downstream process that incurs higher costs, thus depriving customers of the option of choosing a product with a lower price and quality that some of them might find preferable. The alternative of adjusting the price difference for the quality difference would be very difficult for courts to administer. In contrast, using the defendant's own downstream costs as the test provides a market test of whether the rival's downstream process provides a quality improvement that exceeds its additional cost for some customers and reveals how many customers prefer that quality-cost tradeoff.

Case T–271/03, *Deutsche Telekom v. Commission*, 2008 ECR II 477

The applicant, Deutsche Telekom AG, is the incumbent telecommunications operator in Germany.... The applicant operates the German fixed telephone network. Before the full liberalisation of telecommunications markets, it enjoyed a legal monopoly in the retail provision of fixed-line telecommunications services. The German markets in the provision of infrastructure and in the provision of telephone services have been liberalised since 1 August 1996 Since then, the applicant has faced varying degrees of competition from alternative operators on the two markets....

The applicant offers access to its local networks to other telecommunications operators and to subscribers. As regards the applicant's access services and charges, it is therefore necessary to distinguish between the local network access services which the applicant offers its competitors ("wholesale access") and the local network access services which the applicant offers its subscribers ("retail access").

I—Wholesale access

By Decision No 223a of the Federal Ministry of Post and Telecommunications ('BMPT'') of 28 May 1997, the applicant was required to offer its competitors fully unbundled access to the local loop with effect from June 1997.... The applicant's charges for wholesale access are made up of two components: a monthly subscription charge, and a one-off charge.... Under Paragraph 29(1) of the TKG, the applicant is required to apply the charges authorised by RegTP [i.e., the German regulator] throughout the period of validity of RegTP's authorization....

II   Retail access

As regards retail access, the applicant offers two basic variants: the traditional analogue connection (... "T–Net") and the digital narrowband connection (... "T–ISDN"). Both these variants of end-user access can be provided over the applicant's existing copper pair network. The applicant also offers end-users a broadband [ADSL] connection ("T–DSL"), for which it had to upgrade the existing T–Net and T–ISDN networks so as to be able to offer broadband services such as faster Internet access.

The applicant's charges for retail access ... for analogue and ISDN lines are regulated by a price cap system. By contrast, the applicant sets its retail prices for ADSL at its own discretion, but these may be reviewed subsequently.... The applicant's retail prices are made up of two components: a basic monthly charge, which depends on the quality of the line and services supplied, and a one-off charge for a new connection or takeover of a line, depending on the work needed at the two ends of the line. The applicant does not charge its end-users the cost of discontinuance....

On 21 May 2003, the Commission adopted Decision 2003/707/EC relating to a proceeding under Article [102 TFEU].... According to the Commission, the relevant product or service markets are the upstream market in local network access for the applicant's competitors at the wholesale level and the downstream market in access to narrowband connections (analogue and ISDN lines) and broadband connections (ADSL lines) at the retail level.... Geographically, those markets cover the territory of Germany....

The Commission finds that the applicant holds a dominant position on all the relevant product and service markets. According to the Commission, the applicant has infringed Article [102 TFEU] by operating abusive pricing in the form of a "margin squeeze" by charging its competitors prices for wholesale access that are higher than its prices for retail access to the local network.... As regards the margin squeeze, recitals 102 to 105 to the contested decision state:

"102   A margin squeeze exists if the charges to be paid to [the applicant] for wholesale access, taking monthly charges and one-off charges together, are so expensive that competitors are forced to charge their end-users prices higher than the prices [the applicant] charges its own end-users for similar services. If wholesale charges are higher than retail charges, [the applicant's] competitors, even if they are at least as efficient as [the applicant], can never make a profit, because on top of the wholesale charges they pay to [the applicant] they also have other costs such as marketing, billing, debt collection, etc....

104   [The applicant] takes the view that there cannot be abusive pricing in the form of a margin squeeze in the present case, because wholesale charges are imposed by the regulatory authority....

105 Contrary to [the applicant's] view, however, the margin squeeze is a form of abuse that is relevant to this case. On related markets on which competitors buy wholesale services from the established operator, and depend on the established operator in order to compete on a downstream product or service market, there can very well be a margin squeeze between regulated wholesale and retail prices. To show that there is a margin squeeze it is sufficient that there should be a disproportion between the two charges such that competition is restricted. Of course it has also to be shown that the undertaking subject to price regulation has the commercial discretion to avoid or end the margin squeeze on its own initiative. If it has that discretion, as it has in the present case ..., the question which prices the undertaking can change without the intervention of the State is

relevant only for purposes of the choice of remedies to bring the margin squeeze to an end." ...

According to the Commission, "there is an abusive margin squeeze if the difference between the retail prices charged by a dominant undertaking and the wholesale prices it charges its competitors for comparable services is negative, or insufficient to cover the product-specific costs to the dominant operator of providing its own retail services on the downstream market" ...

Absence of an abuse as the applicant did not have sufficient scope to avoid a margin squeeze

(a) Arguments of the parties

The applicant submits that it did not have sufficient scope to avoid the margin squeeze alleged in the contested decision. First, it notes that the Commission itself found that the applicant did not have scope to fix charges for wholesale access. Charges for wholesale access, which are fixed by RegTP, ought to correspond to the cost of efficient service provision. Therefore, they do not necessarily correspond to the applicant's costs.

Second, the applicant did not have scope to fix its charges for retail access either. As regards the period from 1998 to 2001, any abuse by the applicant is precluded by the fact that RegTP alone—and previously the BMPT—is responsible for the applicant's charges for narrowband connections ...

(b) Findings of the Court

It follows from the case-law that Articles [101 TFEU] and [102 TFEU] apply only to anti-competitive conduct engaged in by undertakings on their own initiative. If anti-competitive conduct is required of undertakings by national legislation or if the latter creates a legal framework which itself eliminates any possibility of competitive activity on their part, Articles [101 TFEU] and [102 TFEU] do not apply. In such a situation, the restriction of competition is not attributable, as those provisions implicitly require, to the autonomous conduct of the undertakings ...

In that regard it must nevertheless be observed that the possibility of excluding particular anti-competitive conduct from the scope of Articles [101 TFEU] and [102 TFEU], on the ground that it has been required of the undertakings in question by existing national legislation or that the legislation has eliminated any possibility of competitive conduct on their part, has been only partially accepted by the Court of Justice ...

For the national legal framework to have the effect of making [101 TFEU] and [102 TFEU] inapplicable to the anti-competitive activities of undertakings, the restrictive effects on competition must originate solely in the national law ...

Articles [101 TFEU] and [102 TFEU] may apply, however, if it is found that the national legislation leaves open the possibility of competition which may be prevented, restricted or distorted by the autonomous conduct of undertakings ...

[The decision of the GC was confirmed by the ECJ in C–280/08 P in its judgment of October 10, 2010.]

Questions on Deutsche Telekom

The decision of the CFI in Deutsche Telekom illustrates the tension that may occur between sector-specific rules and authorities and antitrust rules and authorities. In this case, the German telecommunications regulator had approved the rates proposed by Deutsche Telekom, but Deutsche Telekom's competitors complained to the European Commission that these rates amounted to a margin squeeze. In its defence, DT contended that if there was any infringement of Community law, the Commission should not be acting against an undertaking whose charges were regulated, but against Germany (under Article 258 TFEU). The Commission, however, rejected that argumentation on the ground that, pursuant to a constant case-law, "competition rules may apply where the sector-specific legislation does not preclude the undertakings it governs from engaging in autonomous conduct that prevents, restricts or distorts competition". The Commission considered that, despite the intervention of the RegTP, DT retained a commercial discretion, which would have allowed it to restructure its tariffs further so as to reduce or indeed to put an end to the margin squeeze. In its judgment, the CFI supported the decision of the Commission.

1. How does the approach taken by the CFI in this case differ from the position of the US Supreme Court in *Trinko*?

    a. Is the Supreme Court approach preferable to the one of the European Commission?

    b. Can the different approaches be partly explained by the differences in the enforcement structure between EC competition law and US antitrust law?

        i.   Is the fact that private antitrust actions can lead to treble damages a factor to take into consideration?

        ii. Did the fact that Trinko was a class action launched by a law firm, which was less interested in the protection of a competitive telecommunications market structure than by the prospect of earning a large financial compensation, play a role?

    c. Isn't also the hierarchy of norms different in the US and in the EC? Is, for instance the fact that EC competition rules are for the most part written in the Treaty relevant?

    d. Finally, is the fact that while in Trinko the US regulators (FCC and PSC) had taken an appropriate remedy to put an end to the abusive practices of Verizon, while in the latter case the RegTP had failed to deal with the margin squeeze problem that was faced by DT's competitors relevant?

        i.   In this respect, should the Commission intervene when there is a sector-specific remedy that protects a competitive market structure in a given industry, which has been correctly enforced by a national regulator, and which does not violate EC competition rules (i.e., there is an "effective" regulatory remedy)?

ii. Should the Commission intervene when there is a sector-specific regime designed to protect a competitive market structure, but when such regime has not been applied by the regulator (sleepy regulator).

Case C–52/09, *TeliaSonera*, not reported yet

[This case originated in a reference for a preliminary ruling made by Stockholm District Court in which it asked the ECJ a series questions on the interpretation of Article 102 TFEU concerning an alleged abuse of a dominant position in the form of a margin squeeze. The reference was made in the course of proceedings between TeliaSonera Sverige AB and the Konkurrensverket (the Swedish Competition Authority). TeliaSonera is the incumbent operator of the fixed telephone network in Sweden. Apart from providing broadband services to the benefit of end-users (retail market), TeliaSonera offered access to its metallic access network to other operators (wholesale market), which were also active on the end-user market. The Swedish Competition Authority alleges that TeliaSonera abused its dominant position on the wholesale market by applying a margin—between the wholesale price for ADSL products and the retail price for ADSL services it offers to consumers—which would not have been sufficient to cover TeliaSonera's incremental costs on the retail market. Against that background, the Stockholm District Court decided to stay the proceedings in the case and to refer questions to the ECJ.]

Consideration of the questions referred for a preliminary ruling

... [T]he referring court, in essence, asks the Court to clarify in what circumstances the spread, between, on the one hand, the wholesale prices for ADSL input services supplied to operators and, on the other hand, the retail prices for broadband connection services supplied to end users, resulting from the pricing practice applied by a vertically integrated telecommunications undertaking, may constitute an abuse, within the meaning of Article 102 TFEU, by that undertaking of its dominant position.

In particular, after ascertaining whether the other conditions for the applicability of Article 102 TFEU are satisfied in the present case—including whether TeliaSonera holds a dominant position and whether trade between Member States was affected by its conduct—it is for the referring court to examine, in essence, whether the pricing practice introduced by TeliaSonera is unfair in so far as it squeezes the margins of its competitors on the retail market for broadband connection services to end users....

The absence of any regulatory obligation to supply

... The special responsibility which a dominant undertaking has not to allow its conduct to impair genuine undistorted competition in the internal market concerns specifically the conduct, by commission or omission, which that undertaking decides on its own initiative to adopt (see, to that effect, the order in *Unilever Bestfoods v Commission*).

... TeliaSonera maintains, in that regard, that, in order specifically to protect the economic initiative of dominant undertakings, they should remain free to fix their terms of trade, unless those terms are so disadvantageous for those entering into contracts with them that those terms may be regarded, in the light of the relevant criteria set out in *Bronner* ...., as entailing a refusal to supply.

Such an interpretation is based on a misunderstanding of that judgment. In particular, it cannot be inferred from ... that judgment that the conditions to be met in order to establish that a refusal to supply is abusive must necessarily also apply when assessing the abusive nature of conduct which consists in supplying services or selling goods on conditions which are disadvantageous or on which there might be no purchaser.

Such conduct may, in itself, constitute an independent form of abuse distinct from that of refusal to supply....

Whether an anti-competitive effect is required and whether the product offered by the undertaking must be indispensable

The referring court seeks to ascertain ... whether the abusive nature of the pricing practice in question depends on whether there actually is an anti-competitive effect and, if so, how that effect can be determined. Moreover, it seeks to ascertain whether the product offered by TeliaSonera on the wholesale market must be indispensable for entry onto the retail market.

It must be observed in that regard that, bearing in mind the concept of abuse of a dominant position ..., the Court has ruled out the possibility that the very existence of a pricing practice of a dominant undertaking which leads to the margin squeeze of its equally efficient competitors can constitute an abuse within the meaning of Article 102 TFEU without it being necessary to demonstrate an anti-competitive effect (see, to that effect, *Deutsche Telekom v Commission*).

The case-law has furthermore made clear that the anti-competitive effect must relate to the possible barriers which such a pricing practice may create to the growth on the retail market of the services offered to end users and, therefore, on the degree of competition in that market (Deutsche Telekom v Commission).

Accordingly, the practice in question, adopted by a dominant undertaking, constitutes an abuse within the meaning of Article 102 TFEU, where, given its effect of excluding competitors who are at least as efficient as itself by squeezing their margins, it is capable of making more difficult, or impossible, the entry of those competitors onto the market concerned (see, to that effect, *Deutsche Telekom v Commission*).

It follows that, in order to establish whether such a practice is abusive, that practice must have an anti-competitive effect on the market, but the effect does not necessarily have to be concrete, and it is sufficient to demonstrate that there is an anti-competitive effect which may potentially exclude competitors who are at least as efficient as the dominant undertaking.

Where a dominant undertaking actually implements a pricing practice resulting in a margin squeeze on its equally efficient competitors, with the purpose of driving them from the relevant market, the fact that the desired result, namely the exclusion of those competitors, is not ultimately achieved does not alter its categorisation as abuse within the meaning of Article 102 TFEU.

However, in the absence of any effect on the competitive situation of competitors, a pricing practice such as that at issue in the main proceedings cannot be classified as an exclusionary practice where the penetration of those competitors in the market concerned is not made any more difficult by that practice (see, to that effect, *Deutsche Telekom v Commission*, paragraph 254).

In the present case, it is for the referring court to examine whether the effect of TeliaSonera's pricing practice was likely to hinder the ability of competitors at least as efficient as itself to trade on the retail market for broadband connection services to end users.

In that examination that court must take into consideration all the specific circumstances of the case.

In particular, the first matter to be analysed must be the functional relationship of the wholesale products to the retail products. Accordingly, when assessing the effects of the margin squeeze, the question whether the wholesale product is indispensable may be relevant.

Where access to the supply of the wholesale product is indispensable for the sale of the retail product, competitors who are at least as efficient as the undertaking which dominates the wholesale market and who are unable to operate on the retail market other than at a loss or, in any event, with reduced profitability suffer a competitive disadvantage on that market which is such as to prevent or restrict their access to it or the growth of their activities on it (see, to that effect, *Deutsche Telekom v Commission*).

In such circumstances, the at least potentially anti-competitive effect of a margin squeeze is probable.

However, taking into account the dominant position of the undertaking concerned in the wholesale market, the possibility cannot be ruled out that, by reason simply of the fact that the wholesale product is not indispensable for the supply of the retail product, a pricing practice which causes margin squeeze may not be able to produce any anti-competitive effect, even potentially. Accordingly, it is again for the referring court to satisfy itself that, even where the wholesale product is not indispensable, the practice may be capable of having anti-competitive effects on the markets concerned.

Secondly, it is necessary to determine the level of margin squeeze of competitors at least as efficient as the dominant undertaking. If the margin is negative, in other words if, in the present case, the wholesale price for the ADSL input services is higher than the retail price for services to end users, an effect which is at least potentially exclusionary is probable, taking into account the fact that, in such a situation, the competitors of the dominant undertaking, even if they are as efficient, or even more efficient, compared with it, would be compelled to sell at a loss.

If, on the other hand, such a margin remains positive, it must then be demonstrated that the application of that pricing practice was, by reason, for example, of reduced profitability, likely to have the consequence that it would be at least more difficult for the operators concerned to trade on the market concerned.

That said, it must be borne in mind that an undertaking remains at liberty to demonstrate that its pricing practice, albeit producing an exclusionary effect, is economically justified (see, to that effect, Case C–95/04 P *British Airways v Commission* [2007] ECR I–2331, paragraph 69, and *France Télécom v Commission*, paragraph 111).

The assessment of the economic justification for a pricing practice established by an undertaking in a dominant position which is capable of producing an exclusionary effect is to be made on the basis of all the circumstances of the case (see, to that effect, *Nederlandsche Banden-Industrie-Michelin v Commission*). In that regard, it has to be determined whether the exclusionary effect arising from such a practice, which is disadvantageous for competition, may be counterbalanced, or outweighed, by advantages in terms of efficiency which also benefit the consumer. If the exclusionary effect of that practice bears no relation to advantages for the market and consumers, or if it goes beyond what is necessary in order to attain those advantages, that practice must be regarded as an abuse (*British Airways v Commission*).

It must then be concluded that, in order to establish that a pricing practice resulting in margin squeeze is abusive, it is necessary to demonstrate that, taking into account, in particular, the fact that the wholesale product is indispensable, that practice produces, at least potentially, an anti-competitive effect on the retail market which is not in any way economically justified.

Questions on TeliaSonera

1. The ECJ states that "it cannot be inferred from [*Bronner*] that the conditions to be met in order to establish that a refusal to supply is abusive must necessarily also apply when assessing the abusive nature of conduct which consists in supplying services or selling goods on conditions which are disadvantageous or on which there might be no purchaser."

a. In *Bronner*, the ECJ made it clear that a refusal by a dominant firm to give access to an input infringed Article 102 TFEU only provided that certain conditions were met, such as for instance that the input in question is *necessary* for the dominant firm's rivals to compete on a downstream market.

   i. Should the conditions imposed by the ECJ in *Bronner* also apply in the case of a margin squeeze? Should, for instance, the Commission be entitled to find that a dominant firm has committed a margin squeeze abuse although the input in question is not indispensable?

ii. Wouldn't the relaxation of the *Bronner* test in case of margin squeeze abuse lead to the perverse result that dominant firms would be better off refusing to give access to a non-indispensable input rather exposing themselves to claims that the price at which this input is sold creates margin squeeze?

b. The ECJ states that margin squeeze 'may, in itself, constitute an independent form of abuse distinct from that of refusal to supply.' But aren't refusal to supply and margin squeeze abuses different means of achieving the same end, margin squeeze being a constructive refusal to supply? Shouldn't therefore both require the showing that the *Bronner* conditions are met?

2. The ECJ provides that to establish a margin squeeze abuse, it is necessary to show that the conduct in question creates an anti-competitive effect and that in the case at stake, the Swedish Court had to "take into consideration all the specific circumstances of the case" to assess the presence of such an effect. The ECJ then states that "taking into account the dominant position of the undertaking concerned in the wholesale market, the possibility cannot be ruled out that, by reason simply of the fact that the wholesale product is not indispensable for the supply of the retail product, a pricing practice which causes margin squeeze may not be able to produce any anti-competitive effect, even potentially." Hence, the ECJ turns the condition of "indispensability" that, pursuant to the Bronner case, is a pre-condition to a finding of a refusal to supply abuse into one of the elements that need to be considered by courts (or competition authorities) when they seek to determine the presence of an anti-competitive effect.

a. Does this difference of approach makes sense?

b. From the point of view of judicial economy, would it not be better to make indispensability a pre-condition of a finding an abuse in a margin squeeze case?

Price Squeezes in Other Nations

Canada law expressly bans price squeezes by a dominant firm if they have the purpose of impeding the expansion or entry of an unintegrated rival and are likely to substantially lessen competition.[171] Canada does yet appear to have defined the conditions necessary to prove the price squeeze has anticompetitive effects. Singapore tests for price squeezes by determining whether the dominant firm's downstream business would make (at least) a normal profit if it paid the same input price that it charged its competitors, given the firm's revenues at the time.[172] This seems similar to the EU test and one possible interpretation of the U.S. test in *Linkline*. Other nations have little law on the topic.

---

171. Canada Competition Act §§ 78(1), 79.

172. 3 Singapore Guidelines on the Section 47 Prohibition §§ 11.18 and 11.19 (2007).

D.   CAUSAL CONNECTION BETWEEN FIRST AND SECOND ELEMENTS REQUIRED?

Einer Elhauge, *Defining Better Monopolization Standards*

56 STANFORD LAW REVIEW 253 (2003).

. . . U.S. antitrust law does not merely require "monopoly power" in the abstract, but a causal connection between the challenged exclusionary conduct and the acquisition or maintenance of that power. Such a causal connection is implicit in the language of § 2, which makes it illegal to "monopolize," "attempt to monopolize," or "conspire . . . to monopolize." The "-ize" suffix proves crucial, for it indicates that the gravamen of the offense is the illicit creation or maintenance of a monopoly power that otherwise would not exist, at least not to the same degree. Thus, the statutory language calls for proof of some causal connection between the illicit conduct and the extent of monopoly power, or in the case of attempted monopolization, at least a dangerous threat of such a causal connection.

Of course, it will often be unclear just how the market would have developed but for the defendant's misconduct, especially when a monopolist is squelching the development of a new firm or technology. Courts have resolved that problem by holding that, because the wrongdoer appropriately bears the burden of any uncertainty caused by its misconduct, a plaintiff need only prove the exclusionary conduct was reasonably capable of making a significant causal contribution to the acquisition or maintenance of monopoly power. But the underlying basis for liability remains the reasonable likelihood of some causal link between the exclusionary conduct and the extent of the defendant's monopoly power.

The significance of this causal link can be highlighted by the contrast with EU law, which does not require it. EU competition law instead makes the illegal act the "abuse . . . of a dominant position," and thus focuses on whether any dominant market power that already exists was improperly used. This provision thus does not on its face cover conduct that improperly creates (or even less, attempts to create) dominant market power, but does prohibit a firm that uses even properly acquired market power to charge "unfair . . . prices." United States antitrust law, in contrast, focuses solely on illicit conduct that bears some reasonable causal connection to monopoly power, leaving completely unregulated the prices charged by a firm that properly acquired or maintained such power.

Although this doctrinal difference may have resulted from the happenstance of the verb chosen for drafting, the U.S. approach reflects a much sounder policy. Illicit conduct that creates dominant market power leads to higher prices that are both avoidable and socially undesirable. It is thus important to condemn such conduct, and the failure of EU competition law to do so leaves an unsound gap in its regulation of anticompetitive behavior. In contrast, when a firm uses proper conduct to create something sufficiently more valuable than existing market options to enjoy dominant market power, then any high prices it earns are the proper social reward for that creation, and the denial of that reward by EU law seems equally unsound. . . .

This need [under U.S. law] to prove a causal connection between the exclusionary conduct and the acquisition or maintenance of monopoly power might seem inconsistent with language in *Kodak* that resurrected a sentence from *Griffith* defining monopolization as "the use of monopoly power 'to foreclose competition, to gain a competitive advantage', or to destroy a competitor.' " Literally read, this language seems to condemn the use of monopoly power to gain a competitive advantage or to disadvantage rivals in some other market in which the defendant never had monopoly power. But this language in *Kodak* was dicta. Indeed, the *Kodak* Court immediately followed this language with a sentence indicating that *Kodak* would be liable only "[i]f Kodak adopted its parts and service policies as part of a scheme of willful acquisition or maintenance of monopoly power." This sentence appears to reverse any implication that the first language eliminated the need to prove a causal connection to the initial or continued existence of monopoly power. Further reversing any such implication was the later statement in *Spectrum Sports* that § 2 condemns unilateral conduct "only when it actually monopolizes or dangerously threatens to do so."

. . . A causal link between exclusionary conduct and monopoly power is not at all disproved by evidence that the alleged monopolist's prices, profits, or market share declined during the period of exclusionary conduct. Monopolizing activities are frequently undertaken not to create monopoly power but rather to maintain and slow down the erosion of existing monopoly power. In fact, it is precisely when a monopolist sees its monopoly power waning because of a new market threat or technology that it is most desperate to cling to that power, and thus most tempted to use anticompetitive conduct to slow down that erosion and maintain some degree of monopoly power for as long as possible. Thus, there is no reason to assume exclusionary conduct will typically increase monopoly prices, profits, or shares. Rather its anticompetitive effect may typically be to prevent monopoly prices, profits, or shares from dropping further and faster, often by slowing down a market shift to a better or cheaper rival or new product. This is why the Court's monopolization test correctly condemns not just the acquisition but also the "maintenance" of monopoly power with exclusionary conduct, which includes conduct that simply slows down the erosion of monopoly power. . . .

Monopoly Leveraging

The *Griffith* language noted above had led some U.S. lower courts to approve a theory of monopoly leveraging that covered the use of monopoly power to gain a *non-monopoly* competitive advantage in another market.[174]

---

174. *See* Berkey Photo, Inc. v. Eastman Kodak Co., 603 F.2d 263 (2d Cir. 1979); Covad Commun. v. BellSouth, 299 F.3d 1272, 1284–85 (11th Cir.2002); Kerasotes Michigan Theatres v. National Amusements, 854 F.2d 135, 136–38 (6th Cir.1988).

But other lower courts had rejected any monopoly leveraging theory that claims to find monopolization without any proof that defendant's conduct helped it obtain or maintain a monopoly in some market.[175] Subsequent to the Elhauge article above, the U.S. Supreme Court has squarely resolved this split in lower court authority in favor of the latter position.[176] This does not mean no monopoly-leveraging cases can be brought under U.S. law, just that a monopolization case utilizing such a theory would have to prove the monopoly power was leveraged to gain or maintain monopoly power in the other market. In other words, under current U.S. law, monopoly leveraging may explain the source of the power to engage in anticompetitive conduct in another market, but does not dispense with the requirement to prove the causal connection between that anticompetitive conduct and the degree of market power in that other market required by the relevant antitrust statute.

Which side does EU law take on monopoly leveraging? Consider the following.

Case C–333/94 P, Tetra Pak v. Commission

[1996] E.C.R. I–5951.

... In the judgment under appeal ... the [General Court] found that:

—Tetra Pak, whose registered office is in Switzerland, coordinates the policy of a group of companies, originally Swedish, which has acquired a global dimension. The Tetra Pak group specializes in equipment for the packaging of liquid or semi-liquid food products in cartons. Its activities cover both the aseptic and the non-aseptic packaging sectors. They consist essentially in manufacturing cartons and carton-filling machines.

—In 1983, 90% of cartons were used for the packaging of milk and other liquid dairy products. In 1987 that share was approximately 79%. Approximately 16% of cartons were at that time used for packaging fruit juice. Other products (wine, mineral water, tomato-based products, soups, sauces and baby food) accounted for the remaining 5%.

—In the aseptic sector, Tetra Pak manufactures the "Tetra Brik" system, designed for packaging UHT milk. In that sector, only one competitor of Tetra Pak, PKL, also manufactures a comparable system of aseptic packaging. Possession of an aseptic-filling technique is the key to market entry both for machines and for aseptic cartons.

—In contrast, non-aseptic packaging calls for less sophisticated equipment. The "Tetra Rex" carton, used by Tetra Pak on the market for non-aseptic cartons, is in direct competition with the "Pure–Pak" carton produced by the Norwegian group Elopak. ...

---

175. *See* Fineman v. Armstrong World Indus., 980 F.2d 171, 206 (3d Cir. 1992); Alaska Airlines v. United Airlines, 948 F.2d 536, 548 (9th Cir. 1991); Virgin Atl. Airways v. British Airways PLC, 257 F.3d 256, 272 (2d Cir. 2001).

176. *See* Verizon Communications v. Law Offices of Curtis V. Trinko, 540 U.S. 398, 415 n.4 (2004).

—The structure of supply in the aseptic sector was, according to the contested decision, quasi-monopolistic, with Tetra Pak holding 90 to 95% of the market. Its only real competitor, PKL, held almost all of the remaining market share of 5 to 10%.

—The structure of the non-aseptic sector was oligopolistic. At the time when the contested decision was adopted, Tetra Pak held 50 to 55% of the market in the Community. In 1985, Elopak held some 27% of the market in non-aseptic machines and cartons, followed by PKL which had approximately 11% of that market. The remainder of the market in cartons was divided between three companies, and the remainder of the market in non-aseptic machines between ten or so small manufacturers.

—On 27 September 1983, Elopak Italia filed a complaint with the Commission against Tetra Pak Italiana and its associate companies in Italy, accusing it of having engaged in trading practices amounting to an abuse within the meaning of Article [102 of the TFEU]. Those practices essentially involved, according to Elopak, the sale of cartons at predatory prices, the imposition of unfair conditions on the supply of machines for filling those cartons and, in certain cases, the sale of that equipment at prices which were also predatory.

—On 16 December 1988, the Commission decided to initiate proceedings in this matter. In the contested decision, those infringements were summarized as follows:

"1. the pursuit of a marketing policy aimed at severely restricting supply and compartmentalizing the national markets within the Community;

2. the imposition on users of Tetra Pak products in all Member States of numerous contractual clauses . . . having the essential object of unduly binding them to Tetra Pak and of artificially eliminating potential competition;

3. the charging of prices for cartons which have been shown to discriminate between users in different Member States and, at least in Italy, eliminate competitors;

4. the charging of prices for machines which have been shown to

—discriminate between users in different Member States,

—discriminate, at least in Italy, between users within the same country, and

—eliminate competitors, at least in Italy and the United Kingdom;

5. various specific practices aimed, at least in Italy, at eliminating competitors and/or their technology from certain markets."

—The Commission ordered Tetra Pak to adopt certain measures to put an end to the infringements found, and imposed a fine of [Euro] 75 million. . . . Tetra Pak sought annulment of the contested decision and an order that the Commission pay costs. The [General Court] dismissed Tetra Pak's application and ordered it to pay costs. . . .

In its second plea, Tetra Pak principally casts doubt on the reasoning followed by the [General Court] . . . which reads:

"It follows from all the above considerations that, in the circumstances of this case, Tetra Pak's practices on the non-aseptic markets are liable to be caught by Article [102] of the Treaty without its being necessary to establish the existence of a dominant position on those markets taken in isolation, since that undertaking's leading position on the non-aseptic markets, combined with the close associative links between those markets and the aseptic markets, gave Tetra Pak freedom of conduct compared with the other economic operators on the non-aseptic markets, such as to impose on it a special responsibility under Article [102] to maintain genuine undistorted competition on those markets."

In Tetra Pak's submission, the case-law cited by the [General Court] . . . does not justify the conclusion that conduct on a market other than the dominated market, which is not intended to reinforce the position on the dominated market, is covered by Article [102]. Tetra Pak maintains that such a conclusion cannot even be justified by the associative links between the various markets found by the Commission and the [General Court].

In developing its argument, Tetra Pak refers particularly to the fact that in its previous case-law the Court of Justice has always examined either abuses which took place on the dominated market and whose effects were felt on another market or abuses which were committed on a market on which the undertaking did not hold a dominant position but which strengthened its position on the dominated market.

It must first be stressed that there can be no question of challenging the [General Court]'s assessment . . . that Article [102] gives no explicit guidance as to the requirements relating to where on the product market the abuse took place. That Court was therefore correct in stating . . . that the actual scope of the special responsibility imposed on a dominant undertaking must be considered in the light of the specific circumstances of each case which show a weakened competitive situation.

In that regard, the case-law cited by the [General Court] is relevant. *Commercial Solvents* and *CBEM v. CLT and IPB* provide examples of abuses having effects on markets other than the dominated markets. In *AKZO* and *BPB Industries and British Gypsum v. Commission*, the Community judicature found certain conduct on markets other than the dominated markets and having effects on the dominated markets to be abusive. The [General Court] was therefore right in concluding from that case-law . . . that it must reject the applicant's arguments to the effect that the Community judicature had ruled out any possibility of Article [102] applying to an act committed by an undertaking in a dominant position on a market distinct from the dominated market. . . .

It is true that application of Article [102] presupposes a link between the dominant position and the alleged abusive conduct, which is normally not present where conduct on a market distinct from the dominated market produces effects on that distinct market. In the case of distinct, but associated, markets, as in the present case, application of Article [82] to conduct found on the associated, non-dominated, market and having effects on that associated market can only be justified by special circumstances.

In that regard, the [General Court] first considered ... that it was relevant that Tetra Pak held 78% of the overall market in packaging in both aseptic and non-aseptic cartons, that is to say seven times more than its closest competitor.... [I]t stressed Tetra Pak's leading position in the non-aseptic sector. Then ... it found that Tetra Pak's position on the aseptic markets, of which it held nearly a 90% share, was quasi-monopolistic. It noted that that position also made Tetra Pak a favoured supplier of non-aseptic systems. Finally, ... it concluded that, in the circumstances of the case, application of Article [102] was justified by the situation on the different markets and the close associative links between them.

The relevance of the associative links which the [General Court] thus took into account cannot be denied. The fact that the various materials involved are used for packaging the same basic liquid products shows that Tetra Pak's customers in one sector are also potential customers in the other. That possibility is borne out by statistics showing that in 1987 approximately 35% of Tetra Pak's customers bought both aseptic and non-aseptic systems. It is also relevant to note that Tetra Pak and its most important competitor, PKL, were present on all four markets. Given its almost complete domination of the aseptic markets, Tetra Pak could also count on a favoured status on the non-aseptic markets. Thanks to its position on the former markets, it could concentrate its efforts on the latter by acting independently of the other economic operators.

The circumstances thus described, taken together and not separately, justified the [General Court], without any need to show that the undertaking was dominant on the non-aseptic markets, in finding that Tetra Pak enjoyed freedom of conduct compared with the other economic operators on those markets.

Accordingly, the [General Court] was right to accept the application of Article [102 TFEU] in this case, given that the quasi-monopoly enjoyed by Tetra Pak on the aseptic markets and its leading position on the distinct, though closely associated, non-aseptic markets placed it in a situation comparable to that of holding a dominant position on the markets in question as a whole.

An undertaking in such a situation must necessarily be able to foresee that its conduct may be caught by Article [102 TFEU]. Thus, contrary to the appellant's argument, the requirements of legal certainty are observed.

Questions on *Tetra Pak*

1. Does *Tetra Pak* condemn conduct that does not create or enhance market power in any market? Or does it rather require a showing that some market power was created or enhanced in the non-aseptic markets here?

a. If the former, does that make any sense? Could conduct that does not create or enhance market power in any market have any anticompetitive effect? Doesn't the language stating that "Tetra Pak enjoyed freedom of conduct" in the non-aseptic markets indicate that it had market power in those markets?

b. If the latter, why doesn't the Court just conclude that Tetra Pak abused a dominant position in the non-aseptic markets? Is it holding that the market power that existed on the non-aseptic market was short of dominant power, and if so does such a distinction between market power and dominant power make sense?

c. If the conduct did create dominant market power in the non-aseptic markets that did not exist beforehand, could such conduct be covered as an abuse of a dominant position in those markets? Does the reference to the pre-existing dominant position in the aseptic market thus allow the Court to fill the gap otherwise left by the fact that EU law does not otherwise cover anticompetitive conduct that creates market power?

2. Tetra Pak argued that the prior cases all involved either acts on the dominant market that affected other markets, or effects in other markets that strengthened the dominance in the first market. Is the ECJ's response persuasive that these prior cases "found certain conduct on markets other than the dominated markets and having effects on the dominated markets to be abusive"? Isn't that just Tetra Pak's second category? Do these cases justify extending the doctrine to conduct by a dominant firm in a nondominated market that does not enhance its power in the dominant market?

3. The Court stated that "relevance of the associative links . . . cannot be denied" but what precisely is the economic relevance of such association? If conduct had the same anticompetitive effect without the same association, would it then be legal? What is the test of whether markets are sufficiently associated? What should it be?

4. Why would such an association mean that having a dominant position in some markets and a leading position in others is "comparable to that of holding a dominant position on the markets in question as a whole"? How can one determine when this is so?

E. ATTEMPTED MONOPOLIZATION

The text of Article 102 does not appear to embrace the concept of "attempted monopolization," but rather seems to prohibit only abuses of an existing dominant position. This concept covers attempts by companies that hold an existing dominant position to extend this position through anti-competitive conduct. But it does not appear to cover abusive conduct that tries to create a dominant position, even if it succeeds in doing so, let alone if it attempts and fails.

In contrast, U.S. antitrust law explicitly covers not only anticompetitive conduct that successfully leads to the initial acquisition of monopoly power as monopolization, but also anticompetitive conduct that attempted such an acquisition but was unsuccessful at it, as long as the effort had a dangerous probability of success. Which approach is better? Consider the following.

Lorain Journal v. United States

342 U.S. 143 (1951).

■ JUSTICE BURTON delivered the opinion of the Court.

The principal question here is whether a newspaper publisher's conduct constituted an attempt to monopolize ..., justifying the injunction issued against it [by the district court]. ...

The [Lorain Journal,] here called the publisher ... enjoyed a substantial monopoly in Lorain of the mass dissemination of news and advertising, both of a local and national character.

However, in 1948 ... a corporation independent of the publisher, was licensed ... to establish and operate in Elyria, Ohio, eight miles south of Lorain, a radio station ... [with the] call letters, WEOL.... Since then it has operated its principal studio in Elyria and a branch studio in Lorain. Lorain has about twice the population of Elyria and is by far the largest community in the station's immediate area.... Substantially all of the station's income is derived from its broadcasts of advertisements of goods or services. About 16% of its income comes from national advertising under contracts with advertisers outside of Ohio....

The court below found that appellants knew that a substantial number of Journal advertisers wished to use the facilities of the radio station as well. For some of them it found that advertising in the Journal was essential for the promotion of their sales in Lorain County. It found that at all times since WEOL commenced broadcasting, appellants had executed a plan conceived to eliminate the threat of competition from the station. Under this plan the publisher refused to accept local advertisements in the Journal from any Lorain County advertiser who advertised or who appellants believed to be about to advertise over WEOL. The court found expressly that the purpose and intent of this procedure was to destroy the broadcasting company.

... To carry out appellants' plan, the publisher monitored WEOL programs to determine the identity of the station's local Lorain advertisers. Those using the station's facilities had their contracts with the publisher terminated and were able to renew them only after ceasing to advertise through WEOL. The program was effective. Numerous Lorain County merchants testified that, as a result of the publisher's policy, they either ceased or abandoned their plans to advertise over WEOL....

Because of the Journal's complete daily newspaper monopoly of local advertising in Lorain and its practically indispensable coverage of 99% of the Lorain families, this practice forced numerous advertisers to refrain from using WEOL for local advertising. That result not only reduced the number of customers available to WEOL in the field of local Lorain advertising and strengthened the Journal's monopoly in that field, but more significantly tended to destroy and eliminate WEOL altogether. Attainment of that sought-for elimination would automatically restore to the publisher of the Journal its substantial monopoly in Lorain of the mass dissemination of all news and advertising, interstate and national, as well as local. It would deprive not merely Lorain but Elyria and all surrounding communities of their only nearby radio station.... Numerous Lorain advertisers wished to supplement their local newspaper advertising with local radio advertising but could not afford to discontinue their newspaper advertising in order to use the radio.

WEOL's greatest potential source of income was local Lorain advertising. Loss of that was a major threat to its existence. The court below found unequivocally that appellants' conduct amounted to an attempt by the publisher to destroy WEOL and, at the same time, to regain the publisher's pre–1948 substantial monopoly over the mass dissemination of all news and advertising.

To establish this violation of § 2 as charged, it was not necessary to show that success rewarded appellants' attempt to monopolize. The injunctive relief ... sought to forestall that success. While appellants' attempt to monopolize did succeed insofar as it deprived WEOL of income, WEOL has not yet been eliminated. The injunction may save it. "[W]hen that intent [to monopolize] and the consequent dangerous probability exist, this statute [the Sherman Act], like many others and like the common law in some cases, directs itself against that dangerous probability as well as against the completed result." Swift & Co. v. United States, 196 U.S. 375, 396.

... [I]t seems clear that if all the newspapers in a city, in order to monopolize the dissemination of news and advertising by eliminating a competing radio station, conspired to accept no advertisements from anyone who advertised over that station, they would violate §§ 1 and 2 of the Sherman Act. *Cf. Fashion Originators'*. It is consistent with that result to hold here that a single newspaper, already enjoying a substantial monopoly in its area, violates the "attempt to monopolize" clause of § 2 when it uses its monopoly to destroy threatened competition.

The publisher claims a right as a private business concern to select its customers and to refuse to accept advertisements from whomever it pleases. We do not dispute that general right. "But the word 'right' is one of the most deceptive of pitfalls; it is so easy to slip from a qualified meaning in the premise to an unqualified one in the conclusion. Most rights are qualified." The right claimed by the publisher is neither absolute nor exempt from regulation. Its exercise as a purposeful means of monopolizing interstate commerce is prohibited by the Sherman Act. The operator of the radio station, equally with the publisher of the newspaper, is entitled to the protection of that Act. *"In the absence of any purpose to create or maintain a monopoly*, the act does not restrict the long recognized right of trader or manufacturer engaged in an entirely private business, freely to exercise his own independent discretion as to parties with whom he will deal." (Emphasis supplied.) United States v. Colgate & Co., 250 U.S. 300, 307. See *Associated Press* ...

The judgment accordingly is Affirmed.

Questions on *Lorain Journal*

1. Is there any procompetitive justification the conduct in this case might have?

2. If this conduct is anticompetitive and thus harmful to advertisers, why would they agree to buy from Lorain Journal under such an anticompetitive condition?

3. Would it be better for the law to wait until the conduct actually restored Lorain Journal's monopoly power in the local advertising market to make sure the anticompetitive effect materialized?

a. Might there be an interim anticompetitive harm before Lorain Journal's monopoly was restored?

b. Is anything possibly desirable lost by prohibiting the conduct in the meantime?

4. Would EU law prohibit this conduct? If so, would it be because:

a. Newspapers and radio would be viewed as associated markets under *Tetra–Pak*?

b. EU law has a weaker market power requirement than monopolization doctrine, so that the market power element would have been met?

i. Does a weaker market power requirement support having antitrust law omit any attempt claim?

ii. Or should anticompetitive conduct that attempts to gain even that weaker market power be condemned? Does your answer turn on just how clear it is the conduct is anticompetitive?

United States v. American Airlines

743 F.2d 1114 (5th Cir. 1984).

■ W. EUGENE DAVIS, CIRCUIT JUDGE:

The question presented in this antitrust case is whether the government's complaint states a claim of attempted monopolization under section 2 of the Sherman Act against the defendants, American Airlines, and its president Robert L. Crandall, for Crandall's proposal to the president of Braniff Airlines that the two airlines control the market and set prices. The district court dismissed the complaint for failure to state a claim ... We disagree and reverse. . . .

In February 1982, American and Braniff together enjoyed a market share of more than ninety percent of the passengers on non-stop flights between DFW and eight major cities, and more than sixty percent of the passengers on flights between DFW and seven other cities. The two airlines had more than ninety percent of the passengers on many flights connecting at DFW, when no non-stop service was available between the cities in question. Overall, American and Braniff accounted for seventy-six percent of monthly enplanements at DFW.

For some time before February 1982, American and Braniff were competing fiercely for passengers flying to, from and through DFW, by offering lower fares and better service. During a telephone conversation between Robert Crandall, American's president, and Howard Putnam, Braniff's president, the following exchange occurred:

> Crandall: I think it's dumb as hell for Christ's sake, all right, to sit here and pound the * * * out of each other and neither one of us making a * * * * * * dime.
>
> Putnam: Well—
>
> Crandall: I mean, you know, goddamn, what the * * * * is the point of it? . . .
>
> Putnam: Do you have a suggestion for me?
>
> Crandall: Yes. I have a suggestion for you. Raise your goddamn fares twenty percent. I'll raise mine the next morning.
>
> Putnam: Robert, we—
>
> Crandall: You'll make more money and I will too.
>
> Putnam: We can't talk about pricing.
>
> Crandall: Oh bull * * *, Howard. We can talk about any goddamn thing we want to talk about.

Putnam did not raise Braniff's fares in response to Crandall's proposal; instead he presented the government with a tape recording of the conversation.

The United States subsequently sought an injunction . . . against American Airlines and Crandall based on . . . attempted monopolization.[177] On a motion by the defendants, the district court dismissed the government's complaint for failure to state a claim . . .

Our first step in the analysis of the requisites of attempted monopolization is a consideration of the elements of the completed offense of monopolization.

To establish illegal monopolization two elements must be shown: (1) the possession of monopoly power in the relevant market, and (2) "the willful acquisition or maintenance of that power as distinguished from growth or development as a consequence of a superior product, business acumen, or historic accident." *Grinnell*. Monopoly power is "the power to control price or exclude competition." *du Pont*. If these two elements are shown, the offense of actual monopolization is complete; it is well established that there is no additional requirement that the power actually be exercised. *United States v. Griffith*, 334 U.S. 100, 107 1243 (1948); *American Tobacco Co. v. United States*, 328 U.S. 781, 810–13 (1946). . . .

Applying these principles to the case at hand, we conclude that if Putnam had accepted Crandall's offer, the two airlines, at the moment of acceptance, would have acquired monopoly power. At that same moment, the offense of joint monopolization would have been complete. . . .

Both Crandall and Putnam were the chief executive officers of their airlines; each arguably had the power to implement Crandall's plan. The airlines jointly had a high market share in a market with high barriers to

---

177. [Editor's Note: "The Government [sought] as relief to enjoin American from employing Crandall for a period of twenty-four months and to enjoin American from communicating any price information with a competitor for a period of ten years." United States v. American Airlines, Inc., 570 F.Supp. 654, 657 (N.D.Tex.1983).]

entry. American and Braniff, at the moment of Putnam's acceptance, would have monopolized the market. Under the facts alleged, it follows that Crandall's proposal was an act that was the most proximate to the commission of the completed offense that Crandall was capable of committing. Considering the alleged market share of American and Braniff, the barriers to entry by other airlines, and the authority of Crandall and Putnam, the complaint sufficiently alleged that Crandall's proposal had a dangerous probability of success. . . . In sum, our decision that the government has stated a claim does not add attempt to violations of Section 1 of the Sherman Act or lower the incipiency gate of Section 2.

Finally, we note one final consequence of our reasoning. If a defendant had the requisite intent and capacity, and his plan if executed would have had the prohibited market result, it is no defense that the plan proved to be impossible to execute. As applied here, if Putnam from the beginning never intended to agree such fact would be of no aid to Crandall and American. . . .

Our decision that the government's complaint states a claim of attempted monopolization is consistent with the Act's language and purpose. The application of section 2 principles to defendants' conduct will deter the formation of monopolies at their outset when the unlawful schemes are proposed, and thus, will strengthen the Act.

Under appellees' construction of the Act, an individual is given a strong incentive to propose the formation of cartels. If the proposal is accepted, monopoly power is achieved; if the proposal is declined, no antitrust liability attaches. If section 2 liability attaches to conduct such as that alleged against Crandall, naked proposals for the formation of cartels are discouraged and competition is promoted.[15]

Appellees argue that price fixing is an offense under section 1 of the Sherman Act and since the government charges that Crandall sought to have American and Braniff fix prices, the government's complaint in reality seeks to have us write an attempt provision into section 1. This argument is meritless. Appellees confuse the section 1 offense of price fixing with the power to control price following acquisition of monopoly power under section 2. Under the facts alleged in the complaint, Crandall wanted both to obtain joint monopoly power and to engage in price fixing. That he was not able to price fix and thus, has no liability under section 1, has no effect on whether his unsuccessful efforts to monopolize constitute attempted monopolization. . . .

---

15. We disagree with the appellees' contention that our application of § 2 would discourage discussion among potential partners in mergers and joint ventures. Parties who wish to engage in substantial mergers or joint ventures, under the pre-screening procedures of the Hart–Scott–Rodino . . . Act, must notify the Justice Department's Antitrust Division and the Federal Trade Commission before consummating the transaction. The government may have no objection to the transaction, or it may sue to block the transaction . . . Chances that such a transaction would raise a dangerous probability of successful monopolization, are extremely remote.

Transactions that are too small to be subject to the Hart–Scott–Rodino Act will rarely pose a dangerous probability of successful monopolization. If there are such cases, however, and if in such cases the firm proposing the transaction acts with a specific intent to monopolize, then we see no reason why § 2 liability should not attach.

We hold that an agreement is not an absolute prerequisite for the offense of attempted joint monopolization and that the government's complaint sufficiently alleged facts that if proved would permit a finding of attempted monopolization by defendants. We therefore vacate the dismissal of the complaint and remand for further proceedings consistent with this opinion.

Questions on *American Airlines* Attempted Cartel Case

1. Why didn't the government bring this case under Sherman Act § 1? Is an attempted price-fixing agreement covered by § 1? Isn't that what occurred here?

2. Is an attempted conspiracy to monopolize covered by § 2? Isn't that what occurred here?

3. Does it evade the limited language of § 2 to classify this case as an attempted monopolization case?

4. Does it alter your conclusion that agreements or combinations to form a monopoly cartel had long been held to constitute monopolization as well as a violation of § 1?[178]

5. Is there anything procompetitive one could say about the conduct in this case?

6. Until another firm accepts an offer to form a price-fixing cartel, could there be any anticompetitive effect? Why not wait until that effect materializes before one condemns the conduct in question?

7. If there were three equally sized firms in a market, would a call from one of them to a second offering to fix prices constitute attempted monopolization? If there were four such firms in the market? Five? At what point does the dangerous probability of success run out?

8. The government in this case sought an injunction rather than a criminal penalty.

a. Was the conduct it sought to enjoin itself anticompetitive? If not, what would be the basis for enjoining it? If the injunction merely prohibited offering to enter into a price-fixing agreement, would it add anything to the statutory prohibition that already exists?

b. Would a criminal penalty also have been appropriate?

c. Is an injunction requiring that a CEO be fired likely to be an especially strong deterrent for a corporation run by a CEO?

d. Could damage remedies ever be awarded for a rejected offer to enter into a price-fixing cartel?

9. Would the conduct in this case violate EU law? If so, how? If not, should EU law be changed to prohibit such conduct?

---

178. See, e.g., United States v. Grinnell Corp., 384 U.S. 563, 576 (1966); American Tobacco Co. v. United States, 328 U.S. 781, 783–84, 808–09, 813–14 (1946) (noting that this constitutes monopolization as well as a conspiracy to monopolize); Standard Oil Co. v. United States, 221 U.S. 1, 70–75 (1911) (same); *Lorain Journal* (same in dicta).

Spectrum Sports v. McQuillan

506 U.S. 447 (1993).

■ JUSTICE WHITE delivered the opinion of the Court.

[The sole manufacturer of Sorbothane, a shock-absorbing polymer useful in medical, athletic, and equestrian products, had five regional distributors in 1981, one of which was McQuillan and another of which was Spectrum Sports. In 1982, the manufacturer decided to shift medical products to one national distributor, and informed McQuillan that it must give up its athletic shoe distributorship if it wanted to retain its right to distribute equestrian products. When McQuillan refused to stop distributing athletic shoe products, the manufacturer terminated McQuillan as a distributor of all sorbothane products, appointed another company national distributor of equestrian products, and appointed Spectrum Sports national distributor of athletic shoe products. McQuillan sued, alleging among other things attempted monopolization, and won $1 million in attorney fees and $1.7 million in compensatory damages, which were trebled.]

On the § 2 issue that petitioners present here, the Court of Appeals. . . . rejected petitioners' argument that attempted monopolization had not been established because respondents had failed to prove that petitioners had a specific intent to monopolize a relevant market. The court also held that in order to show that respondents' attempt to monopolize was likely to succeed it was not necessary to present evidence of the relevant market or of the defendants' market power. In so doing, the Ninth Circuit relied on *Lessig v. Tidewater Oil Co.*, 327 F.2d 459 (9th Cir. 1964), and its progeny. The Court of Appeals noted that these cases, in dealing with attempt to monopolize claims, had ruled that "if evidence of unfair or predatory conduct is presented, it may satisfy both the specific intent and dangerous probability elements of the offense, without any proof of relevant market or the defendant's market power." If, however, there is insufficient evidence of unfair or predatory conduct, there must be a showing of "relevant market or the defendant's marketpower." . . . .

This Court first addressed the meaning of attempt to monopolize under § 2 in *Swift*. The Court's opinion, written by Justice Holmes, contained the following passage:

> "Where acts are not sufficient in themselves to produce a result which the law seeks to prevent—for instance, the monopoly—but require further acts in addition to the mere forces of nature to bring that result to pass, an intent to bring it to pass is necessary in order to produce a dangerous probability that it will happen. But when that intent and the consequent dangerous probability exist, this statute, like many others and like the common law in some cases, directs itself against that dangerous probability as well as against the completed result.

The Court went on to explain, however, that not every act done with intent to produce an unlawful result constitutes an attempt. "It is a question of proximity and degree." *Swift* thus indicated that intent is necessary, but alone is not sufficient, to establish the dangerous probability of success that is the object of § 2's prohibition of attempts.

The Court's decisions since *Swift* have reflected the view that the plaintiff charging attempted monopolization must prove a dangerous probability of actual monopolization, which has generally required a definition of the relevant market and examination of market power. In *Walker Process*, we found that enforcement of a fraudulently obtained patent claim could violate the Sherman Act. We stated that, to establish monopolization or attempt to monopolize under § 2 of the Sherman Act, it would be necessary to appraise the exclusionary power of the illegal patent claim in terms of the relevant market for the product involved. The reason was that "[w]ithout a definition of that market there is no way to measure [the defendant's] ability to lessen or destroy competition."

Similarly, this Court reaffirmed in *Copperweld* that "Congress authorized Sherman Act scrutiny of single firms only when they pose a danger of monopolization. Judging unilateral conduct in this manner reduces the risk that the antitrust laws will dampen the competitive zeal of a single aggressive entrepreneur." Thus, the conduct of a single firm, governed by § 2, "is unlawful only when it threatens actual monopolization." *Id. See also Lorain Journal; Griffith; American Tobacco.*

The Courts of Appeals other than the Ninth Circuit have followed this approach. Consistent with our cases, it is generally required that to demonstrate attempted monopolization a plaintiff must prove (1) that the defendant has engaged in predatory or anticompetitive conduct with (2) a specific intent to monopolize and (3) a dangerous probability of achieving monopoly power. In order to determine whether there is a dangerous probability of monopolization, courts have found it necessary to consider the relevant market and the defendant's ability to lessen or destroy competition in that market.

. . . . We are not at all inclined . . . to embrace *Lessig*'s interpretation of § 2, for there is little if any support for it in the statute or the case law, and the notion that proof of unfair or predatory conduct alone is sufficient to make out the offense of attempted monopolization is contrary to the purpose and policy of the Sherman Act . . . The purpose of the Act is not to protect businesses from the working of the market; it is to protect the public from the failure of the market. The law directs itself not against conduct which is competitive, even severely so, but against conduct which unfairly tends to destroy competition itself. It does so not out of solicitude for private concerns but out of concern for the public interest. Thus, this Court and other courts have been careful to avoid constructions of § 2 which might chill competition, rather than foster it. It is sometimes difficult to distinguish robust competition from conduct with long-term anticompetitive effects; moreover, single-firm activity is unlike concerted activity covered by § 1, which "inherently is fraught with anticompetitive risk." *Copperweld.* For these reasons, § 2 makes the conduct of a single firm unlawful only when it actually monopolizes or dangerously threatens to do so. The concern that § 2 might be applied so as to further anticompetitive ends is plainly not met by inquiring only whether the defendant has engaged in "unfair" or "predatory" tactics. Such conduct may be sufficient to prove the necessary intent to monopolize, which is something more than an intent to compete vigorously, but demonstrating the dangerous probability of monopolization in an attempt case also requires inquiry into the relevant product and geographic market and the defendant's economic power in that market.

We hold that petitioners may not be liable for attempted monopolization under § 2 of the Sherman Act absent proof of a dangerous probability that they would monopolize a particular market and specific intent to monopolize. In this case, the trial instructions allowed the jury to infer specific intent and dangerous probability of success from the defendants' predatory conduct, without any proof of the relevant market or of a realistic probability that the defendants could achieve monopoly power in that market. In this respect, the instructions misconstrued § 2, as did the Court of Appeals in affirming the judgment of the District Court . . .

Note and Questions on *Spectrum Sports*

Spectrum Sports holds that the elements of attempted monopolization are: (1) anticompetitive conduct; (2) a specific intent to monopolize; and (3) a dangerous probability of achieving monopoly power. It further holds that: (a) a court cannot infer last two elements from first; and (b) proof of dangerous probability requires some definition of the market and proof that defendants have or could obtain monopoly power in that market.

1.   Why shouldn't one infer an intent to monopolize and a dangerous probability of success from anticompetitive conduct?

a.   Isn't that a rational inference, especially if the defendant offers no other explanation for its conduct? Why would a defendant engage in anticompetitive conduct unless it wanted to gain market power and believed it had a dangerous probability of succeeding? Wouldn't anticompetitive conduct otherwise cause the defendant to lose sales given the inefficiency of such conduct?

b.   What is the court worried might happen if it does not add the last two elements?

   i.   If courts often have difficulty distinguishing anticompetitive conduct from procompetitive conduct, might there be an overdeterrence problem from basing the entire test on proof of anticompetitive conduct? Why does the Court think this problem is bigger than in § 1 agreement cases? Does adding the last two elements help reduce this overdeterrence problem?

   ii.   What if courts sometimes make mistakes in defining markets or assessing whether monopoly power is a dangerous probability, or the sheer expense or uncertainty of proving those elements sometimes deters litigants from bringing otherwise meritorious cases? Wouldn't requiring this additional element then increase underdeterrence?

   iii.   Has the Court struck the optimal tradeoff of overdeterrence and underdeterrence? How could it tell?

c.   Why not instead allow the last two elements to be inferred from anticompetitive conduct when that conduct is unambiguous or egregious? Would it be easy for the Court to police lower courts under such a theory?

2. How much market power is needed to show a dangerous probability of success? Is it the same as monopoly power or less? If it were the same as monopoly power, then wouldn't the attempted monopolization claim be superfluous?

3. What does the intent element add?

a. Is it enough to show an intent to get a monopoly? Would an intent to get a monopoly by making the best product on the market suffice, or must an intent to get a monopoly through anticompetitive conduct be shown? If the latter, then what does the intent requirement add to the other two elements?

b. Doesn't any firm that engages in anticompetitive conduct necessarily intend the conduct it engaged in? Does any firm that intentionally engages in anticompetitive conduct that has a dangerous probability of bringing it monopoly power attempt to monopolize unconscious of what it is doing?

c. Would it make sense to read the intent element as requiring that the anticompetitive conduct either be obviously anticompetitive on its face or designed by the defendant to be anticompetitive?

i. Wouldn't this basically exclude conduct that had a procompetitive purpose and had anticompetitive effects that outweighed them, or require a sufficiently large imbalance to make it obvious the conduct was mainly anticompetitive or designed to be so?

ii. Wouldn't this basically amount to requiring worse anticompetitive conduct for an attempted monopolization case than for a monopolization case?

iii. Would doing so help address an increased overdeterrence problem that otherwise would result from the lower market power requirement under attempted monopolization doctrine?

4. If every firm intends its conduct, and the conduct deemed anticompetitive were the same for an attempted monopolization claim as for a monopolization claim, then wouldn't the monopolization claim be superfluous since attempted monopolization would cover the same conduct with a weaker market power requirement? If the specific intent element basically requires worse anticompetitive conduct for attempted monopolization than for monopolization, would the two claims then be distinctive and offer varying ways of optimizing the tradeoff between overdeterrence and underdeterrence?

5. Should courts instead adopt a full sliding-scale, requiring stronger proof of anticompetitive conduct the weaker the market power, and vice versa? Could EU law be interpreted to provide such a test?

Attempted Monopolization in Other Nations

Some nations, including Japan and Brazil, follow the U.S. in covering attempts to create the requisite market power.[179] Unlike the United States,

---

179.   *See* Japan Antimonopoly Act § 89(2); Brazil Antitrust Law No. 8,884, Art. 20.

the attempt provisions in these nations also explicitly cover attempted restraints of trade, and would thus directly cover the *American Airlines* sort of case. Other nations, including China, follow the EU in prohibiting only abuses of an existing dominant position.[180] Should the law prohibit attempts to anticompetitively acquire market power or enter into anticompetitive agreements? Wouldn't it harm markets to have to wait until such attempts succeed to bring suit? Wouldn't it lessen deterrence if such attempts are immune when unsuccessful?

---

180. *See* Argentina Competition Law Art. 1; China Anti–Monopoly Law Chapter 3; Egypt Competition Law, Art. 8; Saudi Arabia Competition Law, Art. 5; Singapore Guidelines on the Section 47 Prohibition ¶ 2.1 (2007); Turkey Competition Act Art. 6.

CHAPTER 4

VERTICAL AGREEMENTS THAT RESTRICT DEALING WITH RIVALS

A. INTRODUCTION

This chapter concerns exclusionary agreements. Most are downstream agreements between a defendant and its buyers that restrict the ability of those buyers to buy from the defendant's rivals. But the analysis applies equally to upstream agreements between a defendant and its suppliers that restrict the ability of those suppliers to supply the defendant's rivals. Indeed, to some extent, the distinction collapses because any agreement between a manufacturer and the distributors who buy and resell their products could equally be thought of as an agreement for the supply of distribution services. The incidence of payment and formality of title transfers generally does not affect the relevant antitrust inquiry. For simplicity, the following discussion will refer to exclusionary agreements between defendants and their buyers, but throughout it should be understood that it could equally apply to their upstream variant. The dominant concern is that such agreements will foreclose a sufficient share of the downstream (or upstream) market to impede the competitiveness of the defendant's rivals.

Some exclusionary agreements sell a product on the condition that buyers not buy that same product from the defendant's rivals. Such agreements are called exclusive dealing, and they are the topic of Section B.

Other exclusionary agreements involve tying, whereby a seller agrees to sell one product only on the condition that the buyer also take a second product from the seller. This is the topic of Section C. Sometimes tying restricts the buyer from buying the other product from rivals; sometimes it just requires purchasing a certain amount of that product from the defendant and thus has the practical effect of reducing sales by rivals.

Both exclusive dealing and tying agreements also exist in less absolute forms. Loyalty discount or rebates are like exclusive dealing agreements that are less absolute in form. Rather than imposing an absolute obligation not to deal with rivals, they can condition discounts or rebates on buyers buying all or a high percentage of their purchases from the defendant. Likewise, tying can take the less absolute form of bundled discounts or rebates, which make discounts or rebates conditional on the buyer purchasing both product A and product B from the defendant. Loyalty and bundled discounts are considered in Section D.

Legally, such vertical exclusionary agreements can be challenged under multiple statutes. In the United States, they can be challenged under

Sherman Act § 1 because they involve agreements that constitute restraints of trade if they are on balance anticompetitive. But they can also be challenged under Sherman Act § 2 if the defendant has monopoly power (or a dangerous probability of acquiring it) and the exclusionary agreements anticompetitively help obtain or maintain such monopoly power. Or the FTC can challenge them under FTC Act § 5 if they are anticompetitive. Finally, they can be challenged under another statute that we have not yet introduced:

Clayton Act § 3, 15 U.S.C. § 14

It shall be unlawful for any person . . . to lease or make a sale . . . of goods . . ., whether patented or unpatented, . . . or fix a price charged therefor, or discount from, or rebate upon, such price, on the condition, agreement, or understanding that the lessee or purchaser thereof shall not use or deal in the goods . . . of a competitor or competitors of the lessor or seller, where the effect . . . may be to substantially lessen competition or tend to create a monopoly in any line of commerce.

This statute effectively requires two elements: (1) sales or discounts of goods that are conditioned on the purchaser not dealing with rivals; and (2) proof that their effect may be to substantially lessen competition. The latter may be proven in a case-by-case manner or, as we shall see in the case of tying, inferred from the nature of the agreement.

Whichever U.S. statute is invoked, the underlying economics of the relevant agreement is the same, and each statute effectively imposes the same requirement of proving the agreement is anticompetitive. Thus, it is fruitful to analyze them together when considering their application to exclusionary agreements. Further, limitations specific to one of the statutes may not matter much as a practical matter given the existence of the others. For example, the fact that Clayton Act § 3 is limited to goods means that it does not govern similar agreements that involve sales or discounts on services or land, and the fact that it is limited to sales or leases means it does not cover upstream exclusive dealing that forecloses inputs. But neither limitation matters much because such agreements would remain covered by Sherman Act § 1.[1] Likewise, the fact that Sherman Act § 2 is limited to defendants with monopoly or near-monopoly power may not matter much because Sherman Act § 1 remains available to

---

1. Because Congress enacted Clayton Act § 3 in 1914, twenty-four years after the Sherman Act, one might be tempted by the argument that it must have been intended to extend more broadly or there would have been no point in enacting it. But the statute was largely a reaction to Congressional fears that the courts were interpreting (or might interpret) the Sherman Act unduly narrowly in 1914. Thus, while Congress must have intended Clayton Act § 3 to be broader than the 1914 interpretation it feared courts were giving (or might give) the Sherman Act, it did not necessarily intend Clayton Act § 3 to extend beyond the broader interpretation given by modern courts to the Sherman Act. A stronger argument for finding Clayton Act § 3 broader might rest simply on its text, which requires proof only that the agreement "may" substantially lessen competition, whereas the Sherman Act generally requires evidence that anticompetitive effects are likely. Courts have not tended to hold that the § 3 language relieves a plaintiff of its obligation to show that anticompetitive effects were more likely than not. Still, some modern courts appear to treat Clayton Act § 3 claims more generously at the margins.

cover cases where defendants have some lesser amount of market power. The degree of market power, or of market foreclosure, may well be relevant to assessing the likelihood or size of anticompetitive effects, but that is equally true under any of the statutes.

Under EU law, vertical exclusionary restrictions can be examined under TFEU Articles 101 and 102. Although the EU cases discussed in this Chapter were generally brought under Article 102 because they involved dominant firms, the applicability of Article 101 to vertical agreements was made clear in *Consten Grundig*.[2]

The current block exemption regulation provides that, with certain exceptions, a vertical agreement is presumed procompetitive under Article 101 if the market share of the seller (or in the case of exclusive dealing, the market share of the foreclosed buyers) is less than 30%.

Commission Regulation (EU) No 330/2010 of 20 April 2010 on the Application of Article 101(3) of the Treaty on the Functioning of the European Union to Categories of Vertical Agreements and Concerted Practices

O.J. 2010, L 102/1.

The category of agreements which can be regarded as normally satisfying the conditions laid down in Article 101(3) of the Treaty includes vertical agreements for the purchase or sale of goods or services where those agreements are concluded between non-competing undertakings, between certain competitors or by certain associations of retailers of goods. It also includes vertical agreements containing ancillary provisions on the assignment or use of intellectual property rights. The term "vertical agreements" should include the corresponding concerted practices.

For the application of Article 101(3) of the Treaty by regulation, it is not necessary to define those vertical agreements which are capable of falling within Article 101(1) of the Treaty. In the individual assessment of agreements under Article 101(1) of the Treaty, account has to be taken of several factors, and in particular the market structure on the supply and purchase side.

The benefit of the block exemption established by this Regulation should be limited to vertical agreements for which it can be assumed with sufficient certainty that they satisfy the conditions of Article 101(3) of the Treaty.

Certain types of vertical agreements can improve economic efficiency within a chain of production or distribution by facilitating better coordination between the participating undertakings. In particular, they can lead to a reduction in the transaction and distribution costs of the parties and to an optimisation of their sales and investment levels.

---

2.   Case 56 & 58/64, Consten and Grundig v. Commission, [1966] E.C.R. 299.

The likelihood that such efficiency-enhancing effects will outweigh any anti-competitive effects due to restrictions contained in vertical agreements depends on the degree of market power of the parties to the agreement and, therefore, on the extent to which those undertakings face competition from other suppliers of goods or services regarded by their customers as interchangeable or substitutable for one another, by reason of the products' characteristics, their prices and their intended use.

It can be presumed that, where the market share held by each of the undertakings party to the agreement on the relevant market does not exceed 30%, vertical agreements which do not contain certain types of severe restrictions of competition generally lead to an improvement in production or distribution and allow consumers a fair share of the resulting benefits.

Above the market share threshold of 30 %, there can be no presumption that vertical agreements falling within the scope of Article 101(1) of the Treaty will usually give rise to objective advantages of such a character and size as to compensate for the disadvantages which they create for competition. At the same time, there is no presumption that those vertical agreements are either caught by Article 101(1) of the Treaty or that they fail to satisfy the conditions of Article 101(3) of the Treaty.

This Regulation should not exempt vertical agreements containing restrictions which are likely to restrict competition and harm consumers or which are not indispensable to the attainment of the efficiency-enhancing effects. In particular, vertical agreements containing certain types of severe restrictions of competition such as minimum and fixed resale-prices, as well as certain types of territorial protection, should be excluded from the benefit of the block exemption established by this Regulation irrespective of the market share of the undertakings concerned.

In order to ensure access to or to prevent collusion on the relevant market, certain conditions should be attached to the block exemption. To this end, the exemption of non-compete obligations should be limited to obligations which do not exceed a defined duration. For the same reasons, any direct or indirect obligation causing the members of a selective distribution system not to sell the brands of particular competing suppliers should be excluded from the benefit of this Regulation.

The market-share limitation, the non-exemption of certain vertical agreements and the conditions provided for in this Regulation normally ensure that the agreements to which the block exemption applies do not enable the participating undertakings to eliminate competition in respect of a substantial part of the products in question.

The Commission may withdraw the benefit of this Regulation, pursuant to Article 29(1) of Council Regulation (EC) No 1/2003 of 16 December 2002 on the implementation of the rules on competition laid down in Articles 81 and 82 of the Treaty [4], where it finds in a particular case that an agreement to which the exemption provided for in this Regulation applies nevertheless has effects which are incompatible with Article 101(3) of the Treaty.

The competition authority of a Member State may withdraw the benefit of this Regulation pursuant to Article 29(2) of Regulation (EC) No 1/2003 in respect of the territory of that Member State, or a part thereof where, in a particular case, an agreement to which the exemption provided for in this Regulation applies nevertheless has effects which are incompatible with Article 101(3) of the Treaty in the territory of that Member State, or in a part thereof, and where such territory has all the characteristics of a distinct geographic market.

In determining whether the benefit of this Regulation should be withdrawn pursuant to Article 29 of Regulation (EC) No 1/2003, the anti-competitive effects that may derive from the existence of parallel networks of vertical agreements that have similar effects which significantly restrict access to a relevant market or competition therein are of particular importance. Such cumulative effects may for example arise in the case of selective distribution or non compete obligations.

In order to strengthen supervision of parallel networks of vertical agreements which have similar anti-competitive effects and which cover more than 50% of a given market, the Commission may by regulation declare this Regulation inapplicable to vertical agreements containing specific restraints relating to the market concerned, thereby restoring the full application of Article 101 of the Treaty to such agreements.

B. EXCLUSIVE DEALING

Exclusive dealing agreements are an agreement to sell a product on the condition that the buyer takes all (or effectively all) of its requirements of that product from the seller. Such agreements have possible anticompetitive effects, but may also have possible redeeming efficiencies.

Possible Anticompetitive Effects. The major anticompetitive concern is that such agreements might foreclosure enough of the market to rival competition to impair competition. Such foreclosure might impede rival efficiency, entry, existence, or expandability, any of which can anti-competitively increase the market power of the foreclosing firm.

In most industries, there are economies of scale, so that firms can lower their costs by expanding until they reach the output level that minimizes their costs, which is called the minimum efficient scale. If foreclosure prevents a competitive number of rivals from maintaining this scale, or from expanding their operations to reach it, then it impairs their efficiency.[3] Foreclosure can similarly deprive rivals of economies of scope if, without the foreclosure, rival expansion would have enabled them to offer a variety of products that can be more efficiently produced or sold together than separately. Further, even if rivals are able to achieve their minimum

---

3. Note that this anticompetitive effect is not necessarily eliminated if the unforeclosed market can sustain merely one rival, for if one rival exists it would be less likely to undercut monopoly pricing since it knows it will make less profit in the long run if it did. Rather, to avoid this anticompetitive effect, the unforeclosed market must be large enough to sustain the number of rivals at their minimum efficient scale that is sufficient to prevent such coordination.

efficient scale and scope of production, foreclosure that bars rivals from the most efficient suppliers[4] or means of distribution[5] can also impair rival efficiency by increasing their costs. Most industries are also characterized by a learning curve,[6] so that substantial foreclosure of the market can impair rival efficiency by simply slowing down rival expansion even though it does not outright prevent that expansion.

If rival efficiency is impaired in any of these ways, then rivals will have to cover their now-higher costs by charging higher prices than they otherwise would have. In the extreme case, these higher prices will be unsustainable, and thus rival entry will be deterred and existing rivals will be eliminated. But even if foreclosure reduced rival efficiency without outright eliminating them, it will worsen the market options available to consumers, and mean that these rivals will impose less of a constraint on the defendant's market power than they otherwise would have. This can thus enhance or maintain that market power even if it does not eliminate rivals or bar their entry.

Many modern industries are also characterized by network effects, which means that one seller's product is more valuable to buyers the more that other buyers have purchased the same good from that seller. Where network effects exist, foreclosure can impair rival efficiency by denying rivals access to the number of buyers they need to make their products more valuable to all buyers. Rather than raising rivals' costs, this strategy succeeds by lowering the value of rivals' products. This also worsens the market options available to consumers and lessens the ability of rivals to constrain the monopolist's market power.

In markets where competition by innovation is important, foreclosure can deny rivals economies of scale in recouping investments in research. If firms are foreclosed from a significant share of the market, then successful innovations will have a smaller payoff than they otherwise would have, which will discourage efficient investments in research and innovation.

Foreclosure might also enhance defendant market power by impairing rival expandability even if it does not affect rival efficiency. Standard economic models calculate market power to be directly proportional to defendant market share and inversely proportional to the market share and elasticity of supply of rivals, with the latter measured by the percentage increase in rival supply that will be made in response to a certain percentage increase in price. These standard models effectively assume rivals' ability to expand depends in part on how large they already are. Thus, if a

---

4. *See* Krattenmaker & Salop, Anticompetitive Exclusion, 96 Yale L.J., 234–45 (1986); Stephen C. Salop & David T. Scheffman, *Raising Rivals' Costs*, 73 AM. ECON. REV. 267 (1983) (Special Issue).

5. *See* LePage's v. 3M, 324 F.3d 141, 159–60 & n.14 (3d Cir. 2003) (en banc); Microsoft v. United States, 253 F.3d 34, 70–71 (D.C. Cir. 2001) (en banc); HOVENKAMP, FEDERAL ANTITRUST POLICY 431 (2d ed. 1999). Although such distributors are nominally buyers, one can conceptualize their foreclosure as effectively a foreclosure of the most efficient suppliers of a necessary input called distribution services.

6. See, e.g., James E. Hodder & Yael A. Ilan, *Declining Prices and Optimality When Costs Follow an Experience Curve*, 7 MANAGERIAL & DECISION ECON. 229 (1986); A. Michael Spence, *The Learning Curve and Competition*, 12 BELL J. ECON. 49 (1981).

firm can through foreclosure obtain a high share of the market and relegate its rivals to a small share, it can lessen the ability of rivals to constrain its prices given a constant elasticity of supply and thus increase its prices even if it has not lessened the efficiency of rivals.[7]

When exclusive dealing agreements are obtained by seller commitments to give exclusive buyers a discount from the price available to nonexclusive buyers, then exclusive dealing agreements can also discourage price competition for nonexclusive buyers.[8] The reason is that any price reduction to win sales to nonexclusive buyers would, given the exclusivity discount, require lowering prices to captive exclusive buyers. The discouragement to price competition for nonexclusive buyers is greater the higher the foreclosure share and discount level, and the more that rivals also use exclusive dealing agreements that exacerbate the aggregate foreclosure. It does not depend on rival efficiency being impaired.

Similarly, in an oligopolistic market, exclusive dealing agreements might aid oligopolistic coordination by effectively allocating the market among oligopolists, making it difficult to increase market share by decreasing prices.

Finally, foreclosure can take the form of seller-buyer collaboration to exploit downstream buyers by precluding rival competition. Suppose, for example, that a seller of widgets on a national market pays the only ten retailers in a regional market $1 million each to agree to exclusively sell the seller's product, thus foreclosing competition from rival widget makers. With a regional monopoly, the seller can now raise prices on its widgets to supracompetitive levels to retailers in that market, which those retailers will pass on without fear that the higher prices will cause them to lose market share to other retailers because they all have the same agreement. In effect, the exclusionary agreements here allow the seller to serve as a regional cartel ringmaster, splitting the resulting supracompetitive profits with the retailers.[9] This anticompetitive effect does not require that the foreclosure impair rival efficiency in any of the other ways indicated above. It suffices that the foreclosure precludes competition that would otherwise have constrained market power in a downstream regional market.

---

7. To put the point mathematically, if ϵ_{def} is the firm-specific demand elasticity of the defendant, then under standard economic measures the degree of its market power is determined by the equation $(P-MC)/P = -1/\epsilon_{def}$. See Chapter 3. Further, if we call ϵ_{mkt} the marketwide demand elasticity, call $\epsilon_{rivsupp}$ the supply elasticity of rivals, and call S the share of the defendant (which of course means $1-S$ is the share of all the other firms), then it can be shown that $\epsilon_{def} = \epsilon_{mkt}/S + \epsilon_{rivsupp}(1-S)/S$. See Chapter 3. The result is that enhancing defendant market share in ways unrelated to product merits (such as through foreclosure) is anticompetitive even if it does not lower rival efficiency because it lowers the defendant's firm-specific demand elasticity ϵ_{def}, and thus increases its market power, given a constant rival supply elasticity and market demand elasticity.

8. Elhauge, *How Loyalty Discounts Can Perversely Discourage Discounting*, 5 JOURNAL OF COMPETITION LAW & ECONOMICS 189 (2009).

9. *See generally* Krattenmaker & Salop, *supra* note 4, at 238–40; Elizabeth Granitz & Benjamin Klein, *Monopolization by Raising Rivals' Costs: The Standard Oil Case*, 39 J.L. & ECON. 1 (1996); Hovenkamp, *Mergers & Buyers*, 77 VA. L. REV. 1369 (1991); IV AREEDA, HOVENKAMP & SOLOW, ANTITRUST LAW ¶ 943b, 204–06 & n.4 (1998).

All the above theories require not only substantial foreclosure of some properly defined market, but some significant barriers to entry and expansion in the foreclosed market. For example, suppose the foreclosed buyers are dealers who merely resell the product to ultimate consumers, entry barriers to being a dealer are zero, and any entrant can immediately and costlessly expand sales to any extent necessary. In that case, foreclosure of dealers cannot effectively foreclose rivals because they can simply create a new entrant who can immediately access the entire consumer market. Or, if the foreclosure covered say 50% of the retail market, the retailers covering the other 50% could instantly expand their purchases of any superior rival product and then resell that increased amount to the consumers, assuming they can easily switch from one type of retailer to another. But foreclosure can limit rival sales if barriers to dealer entry and expandability are significant. Nor are the above factors likely to be an issue if the foreclosed buyers do not merely resell the product, but use it in some fashion. This is clearest when buyers are the ultimate consumers of the product, for then a rival could not possibly overcome foreclosure by creating new buyers and having them expand to make all market purchases.

Possible Redeeming Efficiencies. Although exclusive dealing agreements can have many possible anticompetitive effects, they also have many possible redeeming efficiencies that help explain why they are often used even by firms without market power who are not foreclosing a substantial share of any market. They might reduce uncertainty about whether future sales will occur at the contractually set price. This can lower risk-bearing costs or inventory costs, or give firms the contractual commitments they need to invest in expanding their capacity in a way that achieves economies of scale. One might wonder why sellers could not achieve even greater certainty by specifying not just the contractual price but the future volume of sales. The problem is that where the buyer is a firm that either distributes the product or uses it as an input in some downstream market, specifying future volume might impose excessive risks on the buyer that market demand for the product will collapse, costs that grow greater the longer the term of the contractual relationship. Exclusivity avoids this risk while still providing the seller with at least the assurance that the buyer will take all it can profitably use.

Exclusive dealing might also encourage relation-specific investments between the seller and buyer that increase their efficiency only with each other. For example, suppose sellers *A*, *B*, and *C* all have plants in a central location equidistant from buyers *X*, *Y* and *Z*, who are located in various directions away from that central location. The sellers can supply all the buyers equally well, but in addition to manufacturing costs of $100 per unit, must incur transportation costs of $20 per unit to supply any of the buyers, bringing the total cost to $120. Suppose, further, that it is efficient for the seller *A* to build its new plant next to buyer *X* in order to eliminate those transportation costs, but if it did so, *A* would have to charge $110 per unit in order to cover the costs of the plant move. If *A* did not secure an exclusive dealing agreement with *X* at a price over $110, then *A* might fear

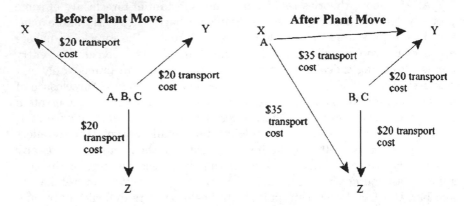

that X would expropriate A's investment in the plant move by insisting on a price of $100 after A made the move. After the plant move, A could not respond by threatening to instead supply Y and Z because now its costs of supplying Y and Z are $135 and it cannot compete with B and C who can sell to them at $120. To avoid this problem, A and X might then agree on an exclusive dealing agreement at a price of $115, which splits the joint surplus of $10 created by the plant move. This is better for both A and X because A gets $5 more per unit, and X saves $5 per unit. But if exclusive dealing were not possible, that might deter A from ever moving the plant, which would be inefficient because the saved transportation costs exceed the costs of moving the plant.

In this example, the plant move is a relationship-specific investment because it creates additional value only if A stays related to X. This is only one of a myriad relationship-specific investments that might be made, such as tailoring product characteristics or marketing to particular buyers, or training employees to develop special knowledge in the needs of a particular buyer or the product of particular seller. Any of these sorts of relationship-specific investments might be efficiently encouraged by exclusive dealing arrangements. For example, when the buyers are distributors, exclusive dealing might encourage manufacturers to spend on things like advertising that will increases foot traffic to its distributors without fear that customers will be diverted to other brands.[10] In this example, the advertising is a relationship-specific investment encouraged by exclusive dealing.

Another possible efficiency justification might reflect the economics of contracting. Modern economic theory on contracts emphasizes that often the optimal performance that contracting parties want to specify is not verifiable in the sense that parties cannot have high confidence that deviations will be detected and proven in a court of law.[11] In such cases, the most efficient contract will not be one that just tries to specify the desired performance but will instead be one that structures incentives or contractual powers in a way that minimizes the likelihood the contracting parties

10.   *See* Howard P. Marvel, *Exclusive Dealing*, 25 J.L. & Econ. 1 (1982).

11.   *See generally* Patrick Bolton & Mathias Dewatripont, Contract Theory (2005).

will want to deviate from optimal performance or that puts the power in the hands of the party with the least incentive to do so. And sometimes the most efficient way to structure incentives or powers might be to adopt an exclusive dealing term.

For example, suppose a manufacturer wants to contract to get a distributor to expend efforts marketing the manufacturer's brand in a given territory. The contract could specify the desired marketing efforts, but it might be difficult to specify precisely what is desired (especially given constantly changing market conditions) or to verify whether the specified performance was given. How, for example, could one verify whether the distributor's sales pitches for the manufacturer were sufficiently enthusiastic? To avoid this problem, one might want to define a more verifiable benchmark, such as a requirement to resell a minimum volume. But that not only might impose excessive risk on the distributor that market demand for the product will collapse, but it will also create insufficient incentives to sell more than the minimum when market demand exceeds expectations. Thus, the parties may instead want to rely on an exclusive dealing term that prohibits the distributor from carrying other brands because that naturally gives the dealer incentives to want to market the manufacturers' brands (because it cannot make money on another brand) and because deviations from such an exclusive dealing term are much easier to verify than insufficiently enthusiastic marketing efforts.

In short, exclusive dealing can have procompetitive efficiencies. Thus, the general modern view in antitrust economics is that exclusive dealing arrangements have sufficient mixed effects that they should be neither per se illegal nor per se legal. Instead, they should be judged under a rule of reason that weighs the likely or actual anticompetitive effects against any efficiency justifications.

United States v. Griffith

334 U.S. 100 (1948).

■ Mr. Justice Douglas delivered the opinion of the Court. . . .

[The appellees were a chain of affiliated movie theaters that in April 1939 operated in 85 towns across Oklahoma, Texas, and New Mexico.] Fifty-three of the towns (62 percent) were closed towns, i.e., towns in which there were no competing theatres. Five years earlier the . . . appellees had theatres in approximately 37 towns, 18 of which were competitive and 19 of which (51 per cent) were closed. It was during that five-year period that the acts and practices occurred which, according to the allegations of the complaint, constitute violations of §§ 1 and 2 of the Sherman Act.

[The chain negotiated agreements with each distributor that generally licensed first-run exhibitions of all that distributor's films that season in all the chain's towns, with the rental specified often a fixed minimum paid by the chain as a whole.[12]] . . . . The complaint charged that certain exclusive privileges which these agreement granted the appellee exhibitors over their

---

12. [Editor's Note: Although the Court did not mention it, sometimes the film rental charged was a percentage of theater revenues. *See* 68 F. Supp. at 186.]

competitors unreasonably restrained competition by preventing their competitors from obtaining enough first-or second-run films from the distributors[6] to operate successfully. . . .

The District Court . . . found that . . . appellees did not condition the
licensing of films in any competitive situation on the licensing of such films
in a non-competitive situation, or vice versa. . . .

In United States v. Crescent Amusement Co., 323 U.S. 173, a group of
affiliated exhibitors, such as we have in the present case, were found to
have violated §§ 1 and 2 of the Sherman Act by the pooling of their buying
power and the negotiation of master agreements similar to those we have
here. A difference between that case and the present one, which the
District Court deemed to be vital, was that in the former the buying power
was used for the avowed purpose of eliminating competition and of acquiring a monopoly of theatres in the several towns, while no such purpose was
found to exist here. To be more specific, the defendants in the former case
through the pooling of their buying power increased their leverage over
their competitive situations by insisting that they be given monopoly rights
in towns where they had competition, else they would give a distributor no
business in their closed towns.

It is, however, not always necessary to find a specific intent to restrain
trade or to build a monopoly in order to find that the anti-trust laws have
been violated. It is sufficient that a restraint of trade or monopoly results
as the consequence of a defendant's conduct or business arrangements. To
require a greater showing would cripple the Act. As stated in *Alcoa*, "no
monopolist monopolizes unconscious of what he is doing." Specific intent in
the sense in which the common law used the term is necessary only where
the acts fall short of the results condemned by the Act. . . . And so, even if
we accept the District Court's findings that appellees had no intent or
purpose unreasonably to restrain trade or to monopolize, we are left with
the question whether a necessary and direct result of the master agreements was the restraining or monopolizing of trade within the meaning of
the Sherman Act.

Anyone who owns and operates the single theatre in a town, or who
acquires the exclusive right to exhibit a film, has a monopoly in the popular
sense. But he usually does not violate § 2 of the Sherman Act unless he has
acquired or maintained his strategic position, or sought to expand his
monopoly, or expanded it by means of those restraints of trade which are
cognizable under § 1. . . . [T]he existence of power "to exclude competition
when it is desired to do so" is itself a violation of § 2, provided it is coupled
with the purpose or intent to exercise that power. *American Tobacco*. It is
indeed "unreasonable, per se, to foreclose competitors from any substantial
market." *International Salt*. The anti-trust laws are as much violated by
the prevention of competition as by its destruction. It follows a fortiori that
the use of monopoly power, however lawfully acquired, to foreclose compe-

---

6.   . . . The charge that these distributors conspired with each other was eliminated from
the complaint . . . But the charge that each of the distributors had conspired with the appellee
exhibitors was retained.

tition, to gain a competitive advantage, or to destroy a competitor, is unlawful.

A man with a monopoly of theatres in any one town commands the entrance for all films into that area. If he uses that strategic position to acquire exclusive privileges in a city where he has competitors, he is employing his monopoly power as a trade weapon against his competitors. It may be a feeble, ineffective weapon where he has only one closed or monopoly town. But as those towns increase in number throughout a region, his monopoly power in them may be used with crushing effect on competitors in other places. He need not be as crass as the exhibitors in *Crescent*, in order to make his monopoly power effective in his competitive situations. Though he makes no threat to withhold the business of his closed or monopoly towns unless the distributors give him the exclusive film rights in the towns where he has competitors, the effect is likely to be the same where the two are joined. When the buying power of the entire circuit is used to negotiate films for his competitive as well as his closed towns, he is using monopoly power to expand his empire. And even if we assume that a specific intent to accomplish that result is absent, he is chargeable in legal contemplation with that purpose since the end result is the necessary and direct consequence of what he did.

The consequence of such a use of monopoly power is that films are licensed on a non-competitive basis in what would otherwise be competitive situations. That is the effect whether one exhibitor makes the bargain with the distributor or whether two or more exhibitors lump together their buying power, as appellees did here. It is in either case a misuse of monopoly power under the Sherman Act. If monopoly power can be used to beget monopoly, the Act becomes a feeble instrument indeed. Large-scale buying is not, of course, unlawful per se. It may yield price or other lawful advantages to the buyer. It may not, however, be used to monopolize or to attempt to monopolize interstate trade or commerce. Nor, as we hold in United States v. Paramount Pictures, Inc., 334 U.S. 131, may it be used to stifle competition by denying competitors less favorably situated access to the market.

Appellees were concededly using their circuit buying power to obtain films. Their closed towns were linked with their competitive towns. No effort of concealment was made as evidenced by the fact that the rental specified was at times the total minimum amount required to be paid by the circuit as a whole. Monopoly rights in the form of certain exclusive privileges were bargained for and obtained. These exclusive privileges, being acquired by the use of monopoly power, were unlawfully acquired. The appellees, having combined with each other and with the distributors to obtain those monopoly rights, formed a conspiracy in violation of §§ 1 and 2 of the Act. . . .

What effect these practices actually had on the competitors of appellee exhibitors or on the growth of the Griffith circuit we do not know. The District Court, having started with the assumption that the use of circuit buying power was wholly lawful, naturally attributed no evil to it and thus treated the master agreements as legitimate weapons of competition. Since it found that no competitors were driven out of business, or acquired by appellees, or impeded in their business by threats or coercion, it concluded that appellees had not violated the Sherman Act in any of the ways charged in the complaint. These findings are plainly inadequate if we start, as we must, from the premise that the circuit buying power was unlawfully employed. On the record as we read it, it cannot be doubted that the monopoly power of appellees had some effect on their competitors and on the growth of the Griffith circuit. Its extent must be determined on a remand of the cause. We remit to the District Court not only that problem but also the fashioning of a decree which will undo as near as may be the wrongs that were done and prevent their recurrence in the future.... Reversed.

Note and Questions on *Griffith* and *Lorain Journal*

Three years after *Griffith*, the *Lorain Journal* case was decided. See Chapter 3. Although *Lorain Journal* is often thought of as a refusal to deal case, the case might more properly be thought of as an exclusive dealing case because the claim there was that the defendant newspapers refused to sell advertising to buyers who bought advertising from the defendant's radio rival. Further, it was the compliance by many advertisers with that exclusive condition that threatened to injure the ability of that rival to compete and to restore the defendant's monopoly in local advertising. *Griffith* and *Lorain Journal* thus both stand for the proposition that exclusive dealing can constitute monopolization or attempted monopolization, as well as an agreement in restraint of trade.

1. If these exclusionary agreements did have an anticompetitive effect, why would the advertisers in *Lorain Journal* and the distributors in *Griffith* agree to them? Are the answers necessarily the same?

a. Does the *Griffith* theater chain likely have monopoly power against national distributors of movies? Does the fact that it provides the only means to reach consumers in some towns suffice to give it monopoly power over distributors, or does the fact that distributors can market their films in other towns protect them?

b. Would an anticompetitive increase in the monopoly power that the *Griffith* theater chain exercises against consumers in southwestern towns necessarily harm distributors? Couldn't the supracompetitive profits that the theater chain earns be split with the distributors in the form of higher rental fees?[13] Isn't this the direct result to the extent rental fees were a percentage of theater revenue?

c. Even if all the distributors would be harmed if enough distributors agreed to exclusionary agreements that create a theater monopoly, might distributors have collective action problems that cause them to agree in exchange for a small increase in their rental fees in the short run?[14]

---

13. *See* Elhauge, Defining Better Monopolization Standards, 56 Stanford L.Rev. 253, 288–292 (2003) (explaining how intermediate buyers can profit from joining an exclusionary scheme that creates supracompetitive profits against downstream buyers).

14. *See* id. at 284–88 (explaining how collective action problems can give each buyer incentives to agree an exclusionary scheme whose marketwide effect harms them all).

i.   If one of many distributors thought the other distributors were going to agree to the exclusionary conditions, wouldn't the distributor conclude that the harmful monopoly will result regardless of what it decides, so it might as well agree and get the offsetting short run benefit of higher rental fees?

ii.   If one of many distributors thought the other distributors would refuse to agree to the exclusionary conditions, wouldn't the distributor conclude that it will avoid the harmful monopoly regardless of what it decides, so it still might as well agree and get the short run benefit of higher rental fees?

iii.   Do you see how the underlying problem is that the benefits of avoiding a theater monopoly are enjoyed by all distributors, but the costs of resisting it are incurred only by those who hold out, and individual distributor decisions make little difference to whether a theater monopoly results, but definitely determine whether they forgo a short run benefit?

2.   The *Griffith* Court held that an antitrust violation was shown even though there was no evidence the theater chain ever threatened to withhold business in monopoly towns to get exclusive rights in other towns. Should proof be required that the monopolist demanded the exclusionary condition?

a.   Without any demand by the theater chain, do individual distributors have incentives to offer exclusionary conditions that have marketwide anticompetitive effects in exchange for individual benefits? Should the case turn on who initiated the exclusionary agreement?

b.   What can Griffith do to avoid liability in the future?

Standard Fashion v. Magrane–Houston

258 U.S. 346 (1922).

■ MR. JUSTICE DAY delivered the opinion of the Court. . . .

Petitioner is a New York corporation engaged in the manufacture and distribution of [clothing] patterns. [Respondent was a retailer who agreed to sell petitioner's patterns.] Petitioner agreed to sell to respondent standard patterns at a discount of 50 per cent. from retail prices . . . Respondent agreed . . . not to sell or permit to be sold on its premises during the term of the contract any other make of patterns . . . [The contract term was two years, and automatically renewed for another two year term unless terminated.] Either party desiring to terminate the agreement was required to give the other party 3 months' notice in writing within 30 days after the expiration of any contract period . . . [Respondent violated the contract by switching to the patterns of one of petitioner's rivals. Petitioner sued to enforce the contract, and the courts below held the contract unenforceable because it violated Clayton Act § 3].

Section 3 condemns sales or agreement where the effect of such sale or contract of sale "may" be to substantially lessen competition or tend to create monopoly. It thus deals with consequences to follow the making of the restrictive covenant limiting the right of the purchaser to deal in the goods of the seller only. But we do not think that the purpose in using the word "may" was to prohibit the mere possibility of the consequences described. It was intended to prevent such agreements as would under the circumstances disclosed probably lessen competition, or create an actual tendency to monopoly. That it was not intended to reach every remote lessening of competition is shown in the requirement that such lessening must be substantial.

Both courts below found that the contract . . . substantially lessened competition and tended to create monopoly. These courts put special stress upon the fact found that of 52,000 so-called pattern agencies in the entire country, the petitioner . . . approximately controlled two-fifths of such agencies. As the Circuit Court of Appeals . . . pertinently observed:

> "The restriction of each merchant to one pattern manufacturer must in hundreds, perhaps in thousands, of small communities amount to giving such single pattern manufacturer a monopoly of the business in such community. Even in the larger cities, to limit to a single pattern maker the pattern business of dealers most resorted to by customers whose purchases tend to give fashions their vogue, may tend to facilitate further combinations; so that the plaintiff, or some other aggressive concern, instead of controlling two-fifths, will shortly have almost, if not quite, all the pattern business."

We agree with these conclusions, . . . Affirmed.

Questions on *Standard Fashion*

1. Why does the Court interpret the word "may" in Clayton Act § 3 to mean "probably will"? Is this just a rewriting of the Act? Given this interpretation, what does Clayton Act § 3 add to Sherman Act § 1?

2. How does the Court know that 40% foreclosure of 52,000 retailers would probably cause anticompetitive effects in that case? Does it seem likely that these agreements impaired the competitiveness of rival pattern manufacturers? That entry barriers to creating new retail premises are high? Does it matter that in smaller cities the defendant's exclusive agreements probably cover all the retailers?

3. Should it have been a defense that retailers must have been better off because they got a 50% discount from retail prices and voluntarily agreed to the arrangement?

Standard Oil and Standard Stations v. United States

337 U.S. 293 (1949).

■ Mr. Justice Frankfurter delivered the opinion of the Court. . . .

Standard Oil . . . sells through its own service stations, to the operators of independent service stations, and to industrial users. It is the largest seller of gasoline in [Western U.S.]. In 1946 its combined sales amounted to

23% of the total taxable gallonage sold there in that year: sales by company-owned service stations constituted 6.8% of the total, sales under exclusive dealing contracts with independent service stations, 6.7% of the total; the remainder were sales to industrial users. Retail service-station sales by Standard's six leading competitors absorbed 42.5% of the total taxable gallonage; the remaining retail sales were divided between more than seventy small companies. It is undisputed that Standard's major competitors employ similar exclusive dealing arrangements. In 1948 only 1.6% of retail outlets were what is known as "split-pump" stations, that is, sold the gasoline of more than one supplier.

Exclusive supply contracts with Standard had been entered ... by the operators of 5,937 independent stations, or 16% of the retail gasoline outlets in the Western area ... It was also found that independent dealers had entered 742 oral contracts by which they agreed to sell only Standard's gasoline.... Of the written agreements, 2,712 were for varying specified terms; the rest were effective from year to year but terminable "at the end of the first 6 months of any contract year, or at the end of any such year, by giving to the other at least 30 days prior thereto written notice...."

Since § 3 of the Clayton Act was directed to prohibiting specific practices even though not covered by the broad terms of the Sherman Act,[4] it is appropriate to consider first whether the enjoined contracts fall within the prohibition of the narrower Act.... The District Court held that the requirement of showing an actual or potential lessening of competition ... was adequately met by proof that the contracts covered "a substantial number of outlets and a substantial amount of products, whether considered comparatively or not." Given such quantitative substantiality, the substantial lessening of competition—so the court reasoned—is an automatic result, for the very existence of such contracts denies dealers opportunity to deal in the products of competing suppliers and excludes suppliers from access to the outlets controlled by those dealers. Having adopted this standard of proof, the court excluded as immaterial testimony bearing on "the commercial merits or demerits of the present system as contrasted with a system which prevailed prior to its establishment and which would prevail if the court declared the present arrangement (invalid)." The court likewise deemed it unnecessary to make findings, on the basis of evidence that was admitted, whether the number of Standard's competitors had increased or decreased since the inauguration of the requirements-contract system, whether the number of their dealers had increased or decreased, and as to other matters which would have shed light on the comparative status of Standard and its competitors before and after the adoption of that system....

---

4. After the Clayton Bill, H.R. 15657, had passed the House, the Senate struck § 4, [the equivalent of what became § 3 in the Act], on the ground that such practices were subject to condemnation by the Federal Trade Commission under the then pending Trade Commission Bill. In support of a motion to reconsider this vote, Senator Reed of Missouri argued that the Trade Commission would be unlikely to outlaw agreements of a type held by this Court, in Henry v. A. B. Dick Co., 224 U.S. 1, not to be in violation of the Sherman Act. See 51 Cong.Rec. 14088, 14090–92. The motion was agreed to. Id. at 14223.

The issue before us, therefore, is whether the requirement of showing that the effect of the agreements "may be to substantially lessen competition" may be met simply by proof that a substantial portion of commerce is affected or whether it must also be demonstrated that competitive activity has actually diminished or probably will diminish.

The *Standard Fashion* case ... settled one question of interpretation of § 3. The Court said: "... we do not think that the purpose in using the word 'may' was to prohibit the mere possibility of the consequences described. It was intended to prevent such agreements as would under the circumstances disclosed probably lessen competition, or create an actual tendency to monopoly." The Court went on to add that the fact that the Section "was not intended to reach every remote lessening of competition is shown in the requirement that such lessening must be substantial", but because it deemed the finding of two lower courts that the contracts in question did substantially lessen competition and tend to create monopoly amply supported by evidence that the defendant controlled two-fifths of the nation's pattern agencies, it did not pause to indicate where the line between a "remote" and a "substantial" lessening should be drawn.

... *International Salt*, at least as to contracts tying the sale of a nonpatented to a patented product, rejected the necessity of demonstrating economic consequences once it has been established that "the volume of business affected" is not "insignificant or insubstantial" and that the effect of the contracts is to "foreclose competitors from (a) substantial market." ... It is clear, therefore, that unless a distinction is to be drawn for purposes of the applicability of § 3 between requirements contracts and contracts tying the sale of a nonpatented to a patented product, the showing that Standard's requirements contracts affected a gross business of $58,000,000 comprising 6.7% of the total in the area goes far toward supporting the inference that competition has been or probably will be substantially lessened.

In favor of confining the standard laid down by the *International Salt* case to tying agreements, important economic differences may be noted. Tying agreements serve hardly any purpose beyond the suppression of competition. The justification most often advanced in their defense—the protection of the good will of the manufacturer of the tying device—fails in the usual situation because specification of the type and quality of the product to be used in connection with the tying device is protection enough. If the manufacturer's brand of the tied product is in fact superior to that of competitors, the buyer will presumably choose it anyway. The only situation, indeed, in which the protection of good will may necessitate the use of tying clauses is where specifications for a substitute would be so detailed that they could not practicably be supplied. In the usual case only the prospect of reducing competition would persuade a seller to adopt such a contract and only his control of the supply of the tying device, whether conferred by patent monopoly or otherwise obtained, could induce a buyer to enter one. The existence of market control of the tying device, therefore, affords a strong foundation for the presumption that it has been or probably will be used to limit competition in the tied product also.

Requirements contracts, on the other hand, may well be of economic advantage to buyers as well as to sellers, and thus indirectly of advantage to the consuming public. In the case of the buyer, they may assure supply, afford protection against rises in price, enable long-term planning on the basis of known costs,[9] and obviate the expense and risk of storage in the quantity necessary for a commodity having a fluctuating demand. From the seller's point of view, requirements contracts may make possible the substantial reduction of selling expenses, give protection against price fluctuations, and—of particular advantage to a newcomer to the field to whom it is important to know what capital expenditures are justified—offer the possibility of a predictable market. They may be useful, moreover, to a seller trying to establish a foothold against the counterattacks of entrenched competitors. Since these advantages of requirements contracts may often be sufficient to account for their use, the coverage by such contracts of a substantial amount of business affords a weaker basis for the inference that competition may be lessened than would similar coverage by tying clauses, especially where use of the latter is combined with market control of the tying device. . . .

Thus, even though the qualifying clause of § 3 is appended without distinction of terms equally to the prohibition of tying clauses and of requirements contracts, pertinent considerations support, certainly as a matter of economic reasoning, varying standards as to each for the proof necessary to fulfill the conditions of that clause. If this distinction were accepted, various tests of the economic usefulness or restrictive effect of requirements contracts would become relevant. Among them would be evidence that competition has flourished despite use of the contracts, and under this test much of the evidence tendered by appellant in this case would be important. Likewise bearing on whether or not the contracts were being used to suppress competition, would be the conformity of the length of their term to the reasonable requirements of the field of commerce in which they were used. Still another test would be the status of the defendant as a struggling newcomer or an established competitor. Perhaps most important, however, would be the defendant's degree of market control, for the greater the dominance of his position, the stronger the inference that an important factor in attaining and maintaining that position has been the use of requirements contracts to stifle competition rather than to serve legitimate economic needs.

Yet serious difficulties would attend the attempt to apply these tests. We may assume, as did the court below, that no improvement of Standard's competitive position has coincided with the period during which the requirements-contract system of distribution has been in effect. We may assume further that the duration of the contracts is not excessive and that Standard does not by itself dominate the market. But Standard was a major competitor when the present system was adopted, and it is possible that its position would have deteriorated but for the adoption of that system. When it is remembered that all the other major suppliers have also been using

---

9. This advantage is not conferred by Standard's contracts, each of which provides that the price to be paid by the dealer is to be the "Company's posted price to its dealers generally at time and place of delivery."

requirements contracts, and when it is noted that the relative share of the business which fell to each has remained about the same during the period of their use, it would not be farfetched to infer that their effect has been to enable the established suppliers individually to maintain their own standing and at the same time collectively, even though not collusively, to prevent a late arrival from wresting away more than an insignificant portion of the market. If, indeed, this were a result of the system, it would seem unimportant that a short-run by-product of stability may have been greater efficiency and lower costs, for it is the theory of the antitrust laws that the long-run advantage of the community depends upon the removal of restraints upon competition.

Moreover, to demand that bare inference be supported by evidence as to what would have happened but for the adoption of the practice that was in fact adopted or to require firm prediction of an increase of competition as a probable result of ordering the abandonment of the practice, would be a standard of proof if not virtually impossible to meet, at least most ill-suited for ascertainment by courts.[13] Before the system of requirements contracts was instituted, Standard sold gasoline through independent service-station operators as its agents, and it might revert to this system if the judgment below were sustained. Or it might, as opportunity presented itself, add service stations now operated independently to the number managed by its subsidiary, Standard Stations, Inc. From the point of view of maintaining or extending competitive advantage, either of these alternatives would be just as effective as the use of requirements contracts, although of course insofar as they resulted in a tendency to monopoly they might encounter the anti-monopoly provisions of the Sherman Act. As appellant points out, dealers might order petroleum products in quantities sufficient to meet their estimated needs for the period during which requirements contracts are now effective, and even that would foreclose competition to some degree. So long as these diverse ways of restricting competition remain open, therefore, there can be no conclusive proof that the use of requirements contracts has actually reduced competition below the level which it would otherwise have reached or maintained.

We are dealing here with a particular form of agreement specified by § 3 and not with different arrangements, by way of integration or otherwise, that may tend to lessen competition. To interpret that section as requiring proof that competition has actually diminished would make its very explicitness a means of conferring immunity upon the practices which it singles out. Congress has authoritatively determined that those practices are detrimental where their effect may be to lessen competition. It has not left at large for determination in each case the ultimate demands of the "public interest" ... Though it may be that such an alternative to the present system as buying out independent dealers and making them dependent employees of Standard Stations, Inc., would be a greater detri-

---

13. The dual system of enforcement provided for by the Clayton Act must have contemplated standards of proof capable of administration by the courts as well as by the Federal Trade Commission and other designated agencies. Our interpretation of the Act, therefore, should recognize that an appraisal of economic data which might be practicable if only the latter were faced with the task may be quite otherwise for judges unequipped for it either by experience or by the availability of skilled assistance.

ment to the public interest than perpetuation of the system, this is an issue, like the choice between greater efficiency and freer competition, that has not been submitted to our decision. We are faced, not with a broadly phrased expression of general policy, but merely a broadly phrased qualification of an otherwise narrowly directed statutory provision.

In this connection it is significant that the qualifying language was not added until after the House and Senate bills reached Conference. The conferees responsible for adding that language were at pains, in answering protestations that the qualifying clause seriously weakened the Section, to disclaim any intention seriously to augment the burden of proof to be sustained in establishing violation of it.[15] It seems hardly likely that, having with one hand set up an express prohibition against a practice thought to be beyond the reach of the Sherman Act, Congress meant, with the other hand, to reestablish the necessity of meeting the same tests of detriment to the public interest as that Act had been interpreted as requiring. Yet the economic investigation which appellant would have us require is of the same broad scope as was adumbrated with reference to unreasonable restraints of trade.... To insist upon such an investigation would be to stultify the force of Congress' declaration that requirements contracts are to be prohibited wherever their effect "may be" to substantially lessen competition. If in fact it is economically desirable for service stations to confine themselves to the sale of the petroleum products of a single supplier, they will continue to do so though not bound by contract, and if in fact it is important to retail dealers to assure the supply of their requirements by obtaining the commitment of a single supplier to fulfill them, competition for their patronage should enable them to insist upon such an arrangement without binding them to refrain from looking elsewhere.

We conclude, therefore, that the qualifying clause of § 3 is satisfied by proof that competition has been foreclosed in a substantial share of the line of commerce affected. It cannot be gainsaid that observance by a dealer of his requirements contract with Standard does effectively foreclose whatever opportunity there might be for competing suppliers to attract his patronage, and it is clear that the affected proportion of retail sales of petroleum products is substantial. In view of the widespread adoption of such contracts by Standard's competitors and the availability of alternative ways of obtaining an assured market, evidence that competitive activity has not actually declined is inconclusive. Standard's use of the contracts creates just such a potential clog on competition as it was the purpose of § 3 to

---

15. Representative Floyd of Arkansas, one of the managers on the part of the House, explained the use of the word "substantially" as deriving from the opinion of this Court in Addyston Pipe & Steel Co. v. United States, 175 U.S. 211, and quoted the passage ... in which it is said that "the power of Congress to regulate interstate commerce comprises the right to enact a law prohibiting a citizen from entering into these private contracts which directly and substantially, and not merely indirectly, remotely, incidentally and collaterally, regulate to a greater or less degree commerce among the States." 51 Cong.Rec. 16317–18. Senator Chilton, one of the managers on the part of the Senate, denying that the clause weakened the bill, stated that the words "where the effect may be" mean "where it is possible for the effect to be." Id. at 16002. Senator Overman, also a Senate conferee, argued that even the elimination of competition in a single town would substantially lessen competition. Id. at 15935.

remove wherever, were it to become actual, it would impede a substantial amount of competitive activity.

Since the decree below is sustained by our interpretation of § 3 of the Clayton Act, we need not go on to consider whether it might also be sustained by § 1 of the Sherman Act. . . . Affirmed.

Questions on *Standard Stations*

The Court's conclusion appears to be that Clayton Act § 3 is violated whenever a substantial *share* of the relevant market is foreclosed, even if anticompetitive effects have not been directly shown and even if there are redeeming efficiencies.

1. Does it make sense to infer likely anticompetitive effects from the foreclosure of a substantial share of the market without requiring direct proof of anticompetitive effects? Isn't that like *Indiana Dentists'* holding that anticompetitive effects can be proven directly or inferred from market power?

2. Does it make sense not to infer likely anticompetitive effects from foreclosure of a substantial *amount* of sales, which the Court did when considering tying cases under Clayton Act § 3?

3. Does it make sense to exclude evidence of procompetitive efficiencies for exclusive dealing when the Court itself acknowledges that they exist?

a. Is refusing to look at procompetitive justifications in exclusive dealing cases inconsistent with the Court's willingness to examine them in tying cases, especially given that the Court concludes they are stronger in exclusive dealing cases? Why should that difference lead the Court to adopt an easier rule on anticompetitive effects in tying cases?

b. Is the Court right that this conclusion is compelled for exclusive dealing by the statutory language and legislative history? Isn't that language and history equally applicable to tying cases? Doesn't the language and history instead justify overruling *Standard Fashion*'s probability standard and requiring only that the restraint "may" have a net anticompetitive effect, rather than using a standard that ignores demonstrated efficiencies?

c. Is the Court right that firms will voluntarily stick to exclusive dealing arrangements if they are efficient? Doesn't that ignore the possibility of relationship-specific investments or other post-contract changes that might make it profitable to deviate from an efficient agreement that was mutually beneficial ex ante but not ex post?

d. Won't this decision just encourage excessive vertical integration or mergers because efficiencies can be introduced to defend those?

  i. Wouldn't those alternatives leave even less room for competition than does exclusive dealing?

  ii. Doesn't the resulting doctrine at the margin induce some integration or mergers even when it would be more efficient to solve the underlying economic issue with a contractual restriction?

4. Does the fact that other leading firms use the same type of exclusive dealing arrangement:

a. Increase the anticompetitive effect on other rivals? Increase the likelihood of an efficiency justification? Both?

b. Should evidence have been admissible to prove whether the pro- or anticompetitive effect turned out to be greater in fact, such as examining whether exclusive dealing increased or decreased: (a) prices to consumers, (b) market output or (c) the number of rivals or dealers? Will it be easy to determine whether those are true given that the correct baseline is the "but for" world without exclusive dealing, which is not necessarily the same as the world before exclusive dealing because other factors may have changed over time?

5. Would evidence on whether the defendant's market share increased with exclusive dealing indicate the net effects were more anticompetitive or procompetitive? Isn't an increased defendant market share consistent with either conclusion because its market share might have increased either from lowering rival efficiency or from improving its own? If all the leading firms that engaged in exclusive dealing had constant market shares, could that be consistent both with oligopolistic coordination that excluded rivals and with equal increases in their efficiencies?

FTC v. Motion Picture Advertising Service
344 U.S. 392 (1953).

■ MR. JUSTICE DOUGLAS delivered the opinion of the Court.

Respondent is a producer and distributor of advertising motion pictures which depict and describe commodities offered for sale by commercial establishments. Respondent contracts with theatre owners for the display of these advertising films ... These contracts run for terms up to five years, the majority being for one or two years. A substantial number of them contains a provision that the theatre owner will display only advertising films furnished by respondent, with the exception of films for charities or for governmental organizations, or announcements of coming attractions. Respondent and three other companies in the same business (against which proceedings were also brought) together had exclusive arrangements for advertising films with approximately three-fourths of the total number of theatres in the United States which display advertising films for compensation. Respondent had exclusive contracts with almost 40 percent of the theatres in the area where it operates.

The Federal Trade Commission, the petitioner, filed a complaint charging respondent with the use of "Unfair methods of competition" in violation of § 5 of the Federal Trade Commission Act. The Commission found that ... [the] exclusive contracts have limited the outlets for films of competitors and has forced some competitors out of business because of their inability to obtain outlets for their advertising films.... The Court of Appeals reversed....

The Commission found in the present case that respondent's exclusive contracts unreasonably restrain competition and tend to monopoly. Those findings are supported by substantial evidence. This is not a situation where by the nature of the market there is room for newcomers, irrespective of the existing restrictive practices. The number of outlets for the films is quite limited. And due to the exclusive contracts, respondent and the three other major companies have foreclosed to competitors 75 percent of all available outlets for this business throughout the United States. It is, we think, plain from the Commission's findings that a device which has sewed up a market so tightly for the benefit of a few falls within the prohibitions of the Sherman Act and is therefore an "unfair method of competition" within the meaning of § 5(a) of the Federal Trade Commission Act.

An attack is made on that part of the order which restricts the exclusive contracts to one-year terms. It is argued that one-year contracts will not be practicable. It is said that the expenses of securing these screening contracts do not warrant one-year agreements, that investment of capital in the business would not be justified without assurance of a market for more than one year, that theatres frequently demand guarantees for more than a year or otherwise refuse to exhibit advertising films.... The Commission considered this argument and concluded that, although the exclusive contracts were beneficial to the distributor and preferred by the theatre owners, their use should be restricted in the public interest. The Commission found that the term of one year had become a standard practice and that the continuance of exclusive contracts so limited would not be an undue restraint upon competition, in view of the compelling business reasons for some exclusive arrangement.[2] The precise impact of a particular practice on the trade is for the Commission, not the courts, to determine. The point where a method of competition becomes "unfair" within the meaning of the Act will often turn on the exigencies of a particular situation, trade practices, or the practical requirements of the business in question. Certainly we cannot say that exclusive contracts in this field should have been banned in their entirety or not at all, that the Commission exceeded the limits of its allowable judgment.... Reversed.

■ MR. JUSTICE FRANKFURTER, Whom MR. JUSTICE BURTON JOINS, dissenting.... Although we are told that respondent and three other companies have exclusive exhibition contracts with three-quarters of the theaters in the country that accept advertising, there are no findings indicating how many of these contracts extend beyond the one-year period which the Commission finds not unduly restrictive. We do have an indication from the record that more than half of respondent's exclusive contracts run for only one year; if that is so, that part of respondent's hold on the market found unreasonable by the Commission boils down to exclusion of other competitors from something like 1,250 theaters, or about 6%, of the some 20,000 theaters in the country. The hold is on about 10% of the theaters that accept advertising.

The Court's opinion ... states without discussion that such exclusion from a market without more "falls within the prohibitions of the Sherman

---

2. ... "In contacting the theater it is necessary for the respondent to estimate the amount of space it will be able to sell to advertisers. Since film advertising space in theaters is limited to four, five, or six advertisements, it is not unreasonable for respondent to contract for all space available in such theaters, particularly in territories canvassed by its salesmen at regular and frequent intervals. It is therefore the conclusion of the Commission in the circumstances here that an exclusive screening agreement for a period of one year is not an undue restraint upon competition." 47 F.T.C. 389.

Act" because, taken with exclusive contracts of other competitors, 75% of the market is shut off. But there is no reliance here on conspiracy or concerted action to foreclose the market, a charge that would of course warrant action under the Sherman Law. Indeed, we must assume that respondent and the other three companies are complying with an earlier order of the Commission directed at concerted action. While the existence of the other exclusive contracts is, of course, not irrelevant in a market analysis, see *Standard Stations*, this Court has never decided that they may, in the absence of conspiracy, be aggregated to support a charge of Sherman Law violation.... And although we are not told in this case whether the pressure for exclusive contracts comes mainly from the distributor or the theater, there are indications that theaters often insist on exclusive provisions.... I would have the Court of Appeals remand this case to the Commission.

Cumulative Foreclosure

Motion Picture Advertising holds that, in an exclusive dealing case under Sherman Act § 1 and FTC Act § 5, the foreclosure share should be measured by aggregating the foreclosure produced by the leading sellers: here aggregating the four leading firms to get a foreclosure of 75%. This proposition also seemed suggested by the language in *Standard Stations* finding Clayton Act § 3 met in part because the exclusive dealing agreements were used not only by the defendant but by the seven leading firms.[15] Neither case required any evidence that the sellers conspired with each other to impose exclusive dealing. Any conspiracy requirement would in any event be met by the vertical agreements between sellers and buyers.

---

15. Subsequent cases have confirmed the understanding that aggregating foreclosure is appropriate. Tampa Electric v. Nashville Coal, 365 U.S. 320, 334 (1961) (describing and distinguishing *Standard Stations* as a case where there was an "industry-wide practice of relying upon exclusive contracts"); United States v. Philadelphia Nat'l Bank, 374 U.S. 321, 365–66 (1963) ("In [Standard Stations], this Court held violative of § 3 of the Clayton Act exclusive contracts whereby the defendant company, which accounted for 23% of the sales in the relevant market and, together with six other firms, accounted for 65% of such sales, maintained control over outlets through which approximately 7% of the sales were made. In [Motion Picture] we held unlawful, under § 1 of the Sherman Act and § 5 of the Federal Trade Commission Act, rather than under § 3 of the Clayton Act, exclusive arrangements whereby the four major firms in the industry had foreclosed 75% of the relevant market"); Jefferson Parish v. Hyde, 466 U.S. 2, 30 n.51 (1984) (favorably citing both *Standard Stations* and *Tampa Electric* on the appropriate foreclosure measure under exclusive dealing doctrine). *See also* IX AREEDA, ANTITRUST LAW 94, 103–04 (1991) ("the relevant foreclosure aggregates those of the defendant and of his rivals."); XI HOVENKAMP, ANTITRUST LAW 160 (1998) ("When exclusive dealing is used to facilitate collusion ... the relevant foreclosure becomes the *aggregate* foreclosure imposed by the upstream firms in the collusive group.")

A contrary conclusion was reached in Paddock Publ'ns. v. Chicago Tribune, 103 F.3d 42 (7th Cir. 1996), but that decision was based on the erroneous premise that the *Motion Picture* decision rested on a distinction between the Sherman and FTC Act's requirements on concerted action. Further, *Paddock* also ignored all the other Supreme Court precedent noted above and the fact that vertical agreements can also satisfy the concerted action requirement. Even more clearly in conflict with binding Supreme Court precedent is the odd decision in Dickson v. Microsoft Corp., 309 F.3d 193, 212 (4th Cir. 2002), which holds that even a single seller's exclusionary agreements with multiple buyers cannot be aggregated, and that substantial foreclosure can thus be proven only if a single seller's exclusionary agreement with an

But does aggregating the foreclosure of nonconspiring sellers to assess anticompetitive effects make sense as an economic matter? The answer largely turns on whether the cumulative foreclosure has deprived the market of a competitive number of efficient rivals by barring some firms from achieving their minimum efficient size. If a market had twenty equal-sized firms, all of whom had exclusionary agreements, then the aggregate foreclosure would be 100%, but the agreements would not deprive the market of a competitive number of firms (assuming twenty firms suffices to achieve full competitiveness) and thus would have no anticompetitive effect. But suppose instead two manufacturers use exclusive agreements that, in aggregate, foreclose enough of the market to preclude rivals from achieving their minimum efficient size, but that neither firm's agreements alone would result in sufficient foreclosure to do so. If the market is large enough to sustain more than two firms at their minimum efficient size, then the cumulative foreclosure is the relevant measure of whether the exclusionary agreements have an anticompetitive effect. Such cumulative foreclosure creates an effective duopoly where consumers would have otherwise enjoyed a more competitive market with more firms.

Likewise, exclusive dealing agreements by four sellers that foreclose a fifth seller would be anticompetitive if the market could sustain five sellers at their minimum efficient size and a market with five firms would behave more competitively than market with four firms. Further, even if the relevant market could sustain only four firms at their minimum efficient size, such foreclosure can anticompetitively keep out a firm that would have been more efficient if it had been allowed to compete openly and achieve its own economies of size. In short, foreclosure can anticompetitively affect the identity of firms in the market as well as the number of them.

What is the minimum number of firms is that assures competitive behavior rather than oligopolistic coordination? That depends on the particulars of each market and how conducive it is to such coordination. *See* Chapters 6–7. The U.S. and EU merger guidelines suggest that the normal presumption is that oligopolistic coordination is unlikely if there are more than five to six major firms in a market. *See* Chapter 7. Professor Areeda concludes that the test of whether foreclosure is "substantial" should be "that foreclosure be presumed unreasonable when it reaches 20 percent for an individual seller or a total of 50 percent for five or fewer sellers."[16]

individual buyer alone forecloses a substantial share of the market. This holding is contrary to *Standard Fashion*, which aggregated the manufacturer's exclusive contracts with 20,800 different merchants to conclude 40% of the market was foreclosed. *Standard Stations* and *Motion Picture* likewise aggregated not only foreclosure by different sellers, but exclusionary agreements those sellers had with thousands of different buyers. Further, in many monopolization cases, the Supreme Court found it illegal when a monopolist agrees to do business with many different firms—none of whom alone forecloses a significant share of the market—on the condition that they not deal with the monopolist's rivals. *See Kodak; Lorain Journal; Griffith; United Shoe.* In all these cases, the Supreme Court has aggregated the monopolist's exclusionary agreements with many different firms to ascertain their exclusionary effect on the monopolists' rivals.

16. *See* AREEDA, *supra* note 14, at 375, 377, 387. *See also* HOVENKAMP, *supra* note 14, at 152, 160 (single firm foreclosure of 20% and evidence that the selling market concentration has an HHI of at least 1800.)

Because the anticompetitive concern is foreclosing other firms from reaching their minimum efficient size, the aggregation should include only exclusive dealing agreements by large manufacturers that reduce the number of firms below the competitive level (or preclude more efficient firms from the market) by preventing rivals from achieving their minimum efficient size. One should not include in any aggregation exclusive dealing agreements entered into by minor firms whose market share is well below the minimum efficient size. Such agreements cannot contribute to preventing a greater number of firms from operating at the minimum efficient size in the market, and are likely to have the procompetitive effect of helping those minor firms achieve their own economies of size.

Even if one did not simply aggregate the foreclosure produced by different manufacturers, the existence of other factors foreclosing the rest of the market to rivals would remain highly relevant to determining the anticompetitive effect of any single firm's exclusionary agreements. For example, if one firm had an exclusionary agreement foreclosing 60% of the market, and the other 40% could be shown to be unavailable due to regulation, then that regulation would be taken into account by a proper economic analysis, and would indicate that the single exclusionary agreement had foreclosed all the market that would otherwise be available to rivals and thus would produce the various anticompetitive effects outlined above. The same follows if the other 40% is instead foreclosed by another firm's exclusionary agreements. This fact would still mean that the single firm's exclusionary agreement under consideration had foreclosed all of the market that would otherwise be left available to rivals, and thus would impair rival efficiency. In short, even if not simply aggregated, the anticompetitive effect of one firm's exclusionary agreements can depend on whether other firms have similar exclusionary agreements.[17] Indeed, even the Frankfurter dissent in *Motion Picture Advertising* to aggregating foreclosure acknowledged that "the existence of the other exclusive contracts is, of course, not irrelevant in a market analysis."

Given cumulative foreclosure, the anticompetitive effect (and thus legality) of an exclusionary agreement can change over time as other firms adopt similar agreements. Suppose a market has five major firms with 19% of the market each. The first major firm to adopt an exclusive dealing agreement may not foreclose a substantial share of the market. But if the other four major firms follow suit, then the aggregate foreclosure of 95% will be substantial, which would turn all the agreements invalid assuming that redeeming efficiencies did not exist or were inadmissible. This is not as odd as it seems because antitrust "legality usually depends upon market circumstances as they exist from time to time; a reasonable restraint in today's environment can become unreasonable when market conditions change. [Thus], if cumulative foreclosure affects the competitive threat, we must weigh it when judging the legality of a restraint."[18]

---

17. See United States v. General Dynamics, 415 U.S. 486 (1974) (in assessing the competitive significance of a merger a court should exclude production that has already been committed by contract).

18. IX Areeda, Antitrust Law 388 (1991).

But the fact that other firms adopt the same exclusive dealing arrangements may also suggest those arrangements are efficient. Are such efficiencies rendered admissible by the next case?

Tampa Electric v. Nashville Coal

365 U.S. 320 (1961).

■ MR. JUSTICE CLARK delivered the opinion of the Court.

We granted certiorari to review a declaratory judgment holding illegal under § 3 of the Clayton Act a requirements contract between the parties providing for the purchase by petitioner of all the coal it would require as boiler fuel at its Gannon Station in Tampa, Florida, over a 20–year period. Both the District court and the Court of Appeals ... agreed with respondents that the contract fell within the proscription of § 3 and therefore was illegal and unenforceable. We cannot agree that the contract suffers the claimed anti-trust illegality ...

The Facts

Petitioner Tampa Electric Company is a public utility located in Tampa, Florida. It produces and sells electric energy to a service area, including the city, extending from Tampa Bay eastward 60 miles to the center of the State, and some 30 miles in width. As of 1954 petitioner operated two electrical generating plants comprising a total of 11 individual generating units, all of which consumed oil in their burners. In 1955 Tampa Electric decided to expand its facilities by the construction of an additional generating plant to be comprised ultimately of six generating units, and to be known as the "Francis J. Gannon Station." Although every electrical generating plant in peninsular Florida burned oil at that time, Tampa Electric decided to try coal as boiler fuel in the first two units constructed at the Gannon Station. Accordingly, it contracted with the respondents to furnish the expected coal requirements for the units. The agreement, dated May 23, 1955, embraced Tampa Electric's "total requirements of fuel ... for the operation of its first two units to be installed at the Gannon Station ... not less than 225,000 tons of coal per unit per year," for a period of 20 years. The contract further provided that "if during the first 10 years of the term ... the Buyer constructs additional units (at Gannon) in which coal is used as the fuel, it shall give the Seller notice thereof two years prior to the completion of such unit or units and upon completion of same the fuel requirements thereof shall be added to this contract." It was understood and agreed, however, that "the Buyer has the option to be exercised two years prior to completion of said unit or units of determining whether coal or some other fuel shall be used in same." Tampa Electric had the further option of reducing, up to 15%, the amount of its coal purchases covered by the contract after giving six months' notice of an intention to use as fuel a by-product of any of its local customers. The minimum price was set at $6.40 per ton delivered, subject to an escalation clause based on labor cost and other factors. Deliveries were originally expected to begin in March 1957, for the first unit, and for the second unit at the completion of its construction.

In April 1957, soon before the first coal was actually to be delivered and after Tampa Electric, in order to equip its first two Gannon units for the use of coal, had expended some $3,000,000 more than the cost of constructing oil-burning units, and after respondents had expended approximately $7,500,000 readying themselves to perform the contract, the latter advised petitioner that the contract was illegal under the antitrust laws, would therefore not be performed, and no coal would be delivered.... [Tampa Electric then had to buy the coal from other coal producers at prices of up to $8.80 per ton.]

Application of § 3 of the Clayton Act

... United Shoe Machinery Corp. v. United States, 1922, 258 U.S. 451, ... held that even though a contract does "not contain specific agreements not to use the (goods) of a competitor," if "the practical effect * * * is to prevent such use," it comes within the condition of the section as to exclusivity. The Court also held, as it had in *Standard Fashion*, that a finding of domination of the relevant market by the lessor or seller was sufficient to support the inference that competition had or would be substantially lessened by the contracts involved there.... *Standard Stations* ... again considered § 3 and its application to exclusive supply or, as they are commonly known, requirements contracts. It held that such contracts are proscribed by § 3 if their practical effect is to prevent lessees or purchasers from using or dealing in the goods, etc., of a competitor or competitors of the lessor or seller and thereby "competition has been foreclosed in a substantial share of the line of commerce affected."

In practical application, even though a contract is found to be an exclusive-dealing arrangement, it does not violate the section unless the court believes it probable that performance of the contract will foreclose competition in a substantial share of the line of commerce affected. Following the guidelines of earlier decisions, certain considerations must be taken. First, the line of commerce, i.e., the type of goods, wares, or merchandise, etc., involved must be determined, where it is in controversy, on the basis of the facts peculiar to the case. Second, the area of effective competition in the known line of commerce must be charted by careful selection of the market area in which the seller operates, and to which the purchaser can practicably turn for supplies. In short, the threatened foreclosure of competition must be in relation to the market affected....

Third, and last, the competition foreclosed by the contract must be found to constitute a substantial share of the relevant market. That is to say, the opportunities for other traders to enter into or remain in that market must be significantly limited....

To determine substantiality in a given case, it is necessary to weigh the probable effect of the contract on the relevant area of effective competition, taking into account the relative strength of the parties, the proportionate volume of commerce involved in relation to the total volume of commerce in the relevant market area, and the probable immediate and future effects which pre-emption of that share of the market might have on effective competition therein. It follows that a mere showing that the contract itself involves a substantial number of dollars is ordinarily of little consequence.

The Application of § 3 Here

... We ..., for the purposes of this case, assume, but do not decide, that the contract is an exclusive-dealing arrangement within the compass of § 3, and that the line of commerce is bituminous coal.

Relevant Market of Effective Competition

Neither the Court of Appeals nor the District Court considered in detail the question of the relevant market. They do seem, however, to have been satisfied with inquiring only as to competition within "Peninsular Florida." ... Respondents contend that the coal tonnage covered by the contract must be weighed against either the total consumption of coal in peninsular Florida, or all of Florida, ... or, at most, all of Florida and Georgia. If the latter area were considered the relevant market, Tampa Electric's proposed requirements would be 18% of the tonnage sold therein....

We are persuaded that ... neither peninsular Florida, nor the entire State of Florida, nor Florida and Georgia combined constituted the relevant market of effective competition.... By far the bulk of the overwhelming tonnage marketed from the same producing area as serves Tampa is sold outside of Georgia and Florida, and the producers were "eager" to sell more coal in those States. While the relevant competitive market is not ordinarily susceptible to a "metes and bounds" definition, it is of course the area in which respondents and the other 700 producers effectively compete. The record shows that, like the respondents, they sold bituminous coal "suitable for (Tampa's) requirements," mined in parts of Pennsylvania, Virginia, West Virginia, Kentucky, Tennessee, Alabama, Ohio and Illinois. We take notice of the fact that the approximate total bituminous coal (and lignite) product in the year 1954 from the districts in which these 700 producers are located was 359,289,000 tons, of which some 290,567,000 tons were sold on the open market.... [The coal consumed in Florida and Georgia came from seven states.] From these statistics it clearly appears that the proportionate volume of the total relevant coal product as to which the challenged contract pre-empted competition, less than 1%, is, conservatively speaking, quite insubstantial. A more accurate figure, even assuming pre-emption to the extent of the maximum anticipated total requirements, 2,250,000 tons a year, would be .77%.

Effect on Competition in the Relevant Market

It may well be that in the context of antitrust legislation protracted requirements contracts are suspect, but they have not been declared illegal per se. Even though a single contract between single traders may fall within the initial broad proscription of the section, it must also suffer the qualifying disability, tendency to work a substantial—not remote—lessening of competition in the relevant competitive market. It is urged that the present contract pre-empts competition to the extent of purchases worth perhaps $128,000,000, and that this "is, of course, not insignificant or insubstantial." While $128,000,000 is a considerable sum of money, even in these days, the dollar volume, by itself, is not the test, as we have already pointed out.

The remaining determination, therefore, is whether the pre-emption of competition to the extent of the tonnage involved tends to substantially foreclose competition in the relevant coal market. We think not. That market sees an annual trade in excess of 250,000,000 tons of coal and over a billion dollars—multiplied by 20 years it runs into astronomical figures. There is here neither a seller with a dominant position in the market as in *Standard Fashions*; nor myriad outlets with substantial sales volume, coupled with an industry-wide practice of relying upon exclusive contracts, as in *Standard Stations*, nor a plainly restrictive tying arrangement as in *International Salt*. On the contrary, we seem to have only that type of contract which "may well be of economic advantage to buyers as well as to sellers." *Standard Stations*. In the case of the buyer it "may assure supply," while on the part of the seller it "may make possible the substantial reduction of selling expenses, give protection against price fluctuations, and ... offer the possibility of a predictable market." *Id.* The 20–year period of the contract is singled out as the principal vice, but at least in the case of public utilities the assurance of a steady and ample supply of fuel is necessary in the public interest. Otherwise consumers are left unprotected against service failures owing to shutdowns; and increasingly unjustified costs might result in more burdensome rate structures eventually to be reflected in the consumer's bill.... This is not to say that utilities are immunized from Clayton Act proscriptions, but merely that, in judging the term of a requirements contract in relation to the substantiality of the foreclosure of competition, particularized considerations of the parties' operations are not irrelevant. In weighing the various factors, we have decided that in the competitive bituminous coal marketing area involved here the contract sued upon does not tend to foreclose a substantial volume of competition.

We need not discuss the respondents' further contention that the contract also violates § 1 and § 2 of the Sherman Act, for if it does not fall within the broader proscription of § 3 of the Clayton Act it follows that it is not forbidden by those of the former.

The judgment is reversed and the case remanded to the District Court for further proceedings not inconsistent with this opinion.

Note and Questions on *Tampa Electric*

Standard Stations and *Motion Picture Advertising* seemed to have adopted a quasi-per se rule, condemning exclusive dealing agreements that in aggregate foreclosed a substantial market share, without regard to any redeeming efficiencies. Modern courts generally take *Tampa Electric* to have overruled that quasi-per se rule, and to hold that substantiality turns on what amounts to a general rule of reason analysis that includes examination of procompetitive efficiencies. It is not at all clear that this is what *Tampa Electric* intended given that it cites *Standard Stations* favorably. *Tampa Electric* may have simply meant that if the cumulative foreclosure share is too small to trigger the quasi-per se rule of *Standard Stations*, then rule of reason analysis applies. That is how the Supreme Court itself seemed to interpret its holding the next year.[19] Indeed, on this

---

19. *See* Brown Shoe v. United States, 370 U.S. 294, 330 (1962) (describing *Tampa Electric* as holding that "a requirement contract may escape censure if only a small share of

view, the remarkable thing is that the Court was willing to require evidence of some procompetitive justification even when the foreclosure share was only 0.77%. But modern appellate courts, including four justices in 1984, and one appellate judge who has become a Supreme Court justice, instead read *Tampa Electric* to adopt a general rule of reason for exclusive dealing agreements.[20] Although perhaps not justified by a literal parsing of the precedent, this conclusion makes sense as part of a more general policy judgment being made by the courts after the 1960s that antitrust economics did not support the categorical hostility of various legal rules on vertical agreements, including this one.

1. Do you think it is appropriate for subsequent courts to have adopted a general rule of reason approach based on this case? Doesn't that eliminate any distinction between Clayton Act § 3 and Sherman Act § 1 on exclusive dealing agreements? Is this consistent with the statutory text and legislative history?

2. Why did the Court decide the relevant market was broader than Florida and Georgia? Was the Court correct in light of the anticompetitive concerns raised by exclusive dealing agreements?

3. Was the exclusive dealing agreement here justified by relationship-specific investments? If similar relationship-specific investments caused enough sellers and buyers to adopt enough exclusive dealing agreements to foreclose a substantial share of the market, should they be condemned?

4. Why do you think the seller here wanted to void the exclusive dealing contract? Should a seller be able to void such contracts when the exclusivity term favors them?

United States v. Microsoft

253 F.3d 34 (D.C. Cir. 2001) (en banc).

■ PER CURIAM. . . .

. . . The District Court determined that Microsoft had maintained a monopoly in the market for Intel-compatible PC operating systems in violation of § 2. . . . Defining the market as Intel-compatible PC operating systems, the District Court found that Microsoft has a greater than 95% share. It also found the company's market position protected by a substantial entry barrier. . . .

Operating systems perform many functions, including allocating computer memory and controlling peripherals such as printers and keyboards. Operating systems also function as platforms for software applications. They do this by "exposing"—*i.e.*, making available to software developers— routines or protocols that perform certain widely-used functions. These are

---

the market is involved, if the purpose of the agreement is to insure to the customer a sufficient supply of a commodity vital to the customer's trade or to insure to the supplier a market for his output and if there is no trend toward concentration in the industry").

20. *See Jefferson Parish*, 466 U.S. at 44–45 (O'Connor, J, concurring in the judgment, joined by Burger, C.J., and Powell & Rehnquist J.J.); Barry Wright v. ITT Grinnell Corp., 724 F.2d 227, 236 (1st Cir. 1983) (Breyer, J.).

known as Application Programming Interfaces, or "APIs." For example, Windows contains an API that enables users to draw a box on the screen. Software developers wishing to include that function in an application need not duplicate it in their own code. Instead, they can "call"—*i.e.*, use—the Windows API. Windows contains thousands of APIs, controlling everything from data storage to font display.

Every operating system has different APIs. Accordingly, a developer who writes an application for one operating system and wishes to sell the application to users of another must modify, or "port," the application to the second operating system. This process is both time-consuming and expensive.

"Middleware" refers to software products that expose their own APIs. Because of this, a middleware product written for Windows could take over some or all of Windows's valuable platform functions—that is, developers might begin to rely upon APIs exposed by the middleware for basic routines rather than relying upon the API set included in Windows. If middleware were written for multiple operating systems, its impact could be even greater. The more developers could rely upon APIs exposed by such middleware, the less expensive porting to different operating systems would be. Ultimately, if developers could write applications relying exclusively on APIs exposed by middleware, their applications would run on any operating system on which the middleware was also present. Netscape Navigator and Java—both at issue in this case—are middleware products written for multiple operating systems.

... Microsoft argues that ... [a] contradiction lies between plaintiffs' § 2 theory, under which Microsoft preserved its monopoly against middleware technologies that threatened to become viable substitutes for Windows, and its theory of the relevant market, under which middleware is not presently a viable substitute for Windows. Because middleware's threat is only nascent, however, no contradiction exists. Nothing in § 2 of the Sherman Act limits its prohibition to actions taken against threats that are already well-developed enough to serve as present substitutes. Because market definition is meant to identify products "reasonably interchangeable by consumers," and because middleware is not now interchangeable with Windows, the District Court had good reason for excluding middleware from the relevant market.

... [A]fter concluding that Microsoft had monopoly power, the District Court held that Microsoft had violated § 2 by engaging in a variety of exclusionary acts (not including predatory pricing), to maintain its monopoly by preventing the effective distribution and use of products that might threaten that monopoly. Specifically, the District Court held Microsoft liable for: (1) the way in which it integrated IE into Windows; (2) its various dealings with Original Equipment Manufacturers ("OEMs"), Internet Access Providers ("IAPs"), Internet Content Providers ("ICPs"), Independent Software Vendors ("ISVs"), and Apple Computer; (3) its efforts to contain and to subvert Java technologies; and (4) its course of conduct as a whole. Upon appeal, Microsoft argues that it did not engage in any exclusionary conduct....

From a century of case law on monopolization under § 2 ... several principles do emerge. First, to be condemned as exclusionary, a monopolist's act must have an "anticompetitive effect." That is, it must harm the competitive *process* and thereby harm consumers. In contrast, harm to one or more *competitors* will not suffice....

Second, the plaintiff, on whom the burden of proof of course rests, must demonstrate that the monopolist's conduct indeed has the requisite anticompetitive effect....

Third, if a plaintiff successfully establishes a *prima facie* case under § 2 by demonstrating anticompetitive effect, then the monopolist may proffer a "procompetitive justification" for its conduct. If the monopolist asserts a procompetitive justification—a nonpretextual claim that its conduct is indeed a form of competition on the merits because it involves, for example, greater efficiency or enhanced consumer appeal—then the burden shifts back to the plaintiff to rebut that claim.

Fourth, if the monopolist's procompetitive justification stands unrebutted, then the plaintiff must demonstrate that the anticompetitive harm of the conduct outweighs the procompetitive benefit. In cases arising under § 1 of the Sherman Act, the courts routinely apply a similar balancing approach under the rubric of the "rule of reason." The source of the rule of reason is *Standard Oil Co. v. United States,* 221 U.S. 1 (1911), in which the Supreme Court used that term to describe the proper inquiry under both sections of the Act....

Finally, in considering whether the monopolist's conduct on balance harms competition and is therefore condemned as exclusionary for purposes of § 2, our focus is upon the effect of that conduct, not upon the intent behind it. Evidence of the intent behind the conduct of a monopolist is relevant only to the extent it helps us understand the likely effect of the monopolist's conduct....

[The court concluded that various bundles foreclosed OEMs (original equipment manufacturers), which it described as one of the two most efficient methods of distribution (the second being IAPs). The portions of the opinion dealing with such bundling are excerpted in Chapter 4.B].

3. Agreements With Internet Access Providers [IAPs]. The District Court ... condemned as exclusionary Microsoft's agreements with various IAPs ... to provide easy access to IAPs' services from the Windows desktop in return for the IAPs' agreement to promote IE exclusively and to keep shipments of internet access software using Navigator under a specific percentage, typically 25%.... Microsoft concluded these exclusive agreements with all "the leading IAPs," including the major OLSs [Online Services]. The most significant of the OLS deals is with AOL, which, when the deal was reached, "accounted for a substantial portion of all existing Internet access subscriptions and ... attracted a very large percentage of new IAP subscribers." Under that agreement Microsoft puts the AOL icon in the OLS folder on the Windows desktop and AOL does not promote any non-Microsoft browser, nor provide software using any non-Microsoft browser except at the customer's request, and even then AOL will not supply more than 15% of its subscribers with a browser other than IE....

Following *Tampa Electric,* courts considering antitrust challenges to exclusive contracts have taken care to identify the share of the market foreclosed. Some courts have indicated that § 3 of the Clayton Act and § 1 of the Sherman Act require an equal degree of foreclosure before prohibiting exclusive contracts. *See, e.g., Roland Mach. Co. v. Dresser Indus., Inc.,* 749 F.2d 380, 393 (7th Cir.1984) (Posner, J.). Other courts, however, have held that a higher market share must be foreclosed in order to establish a violation of the Sherman Act as compared to the Clayton Act. *See, e.g., Barr Labs. v. Abbott Labs.,* 978 F.2d 98, 110 (3d Cir.1992); 11 HERBERT HOVENKAMP, ANTITRUST LAW ¶ 1800c4 (1998) ("'[T]he cases are divided, with a likely majority stating that the Clayton Act requires a smaller showing of anticompetitive effects."). . . .

In this case, plaintiffs challenged Microsoft's exclusive dealing arrangements with the IAPs under both §§ 1 and 2 of the Sherman Act. The District Court, in analyzing the § 1 claim, stated, "unless the evidence demonstrates that Microsoft's agreements excluded Netscape altogether from access to roughly forty percent of the browser market, the Court should decline to find such agreements in violation of § 1." The court recognized that Microsoft had substantially excluded Netscape from "the most efficient channels for Navigator to achieve browser usage share," and had relegated it to more costly and less effective methods (such as mass mailing its browser on a disk or offering it for download over the internet); but because Microsoft has not "completely excluded Netscape" from reaching any potential user by some means of distribution, however ineffective, the court concluded the agreements do not violate § 1. Plaintiffs did not cross-appeal this holding.

Turning to § 2, the court stated: "the fact that Microsoft's arrangements with various [IAPs and other] firms did not foreclose enough of the relevant market to constitute a § 1 violation in no way detracts from the Court's assignment of liability for the same arrangements under § 2. . . . [A]ll of Microsoft's agreements, including the non-exclusive ones, severely restricted Netscape's access to those distribution channels leading most efficiently to the acquisition of browser usage share."

On appeal Microsoft argues that "courts have applied the same standard to alleged exclusive dealing agreements under both Section 1 *and* Section 2," and it argues that the District Court's holding of no liability under § 1 necessarily precludes holding it liable under § 2. The District Court appears to have based its holding with respect to § 1 upon a "total exclusion test" rather than the 40% standard drawn from the caselaw. Even assuming the holding is correct, however, we nonetheless reject Microsoft's contention.

The basic prudential concerns relevant to §§ 1 and 2 are admittedly the same: exclusive contracts are commonplace—particularly in the field of distribution—in our competitive, market economy, and imposing upon a firm with market power the risk of an antitrust suit every time it enters into such a contract, no matter how small the effect, would create an unacceptable and unjustified burden upon any such firm. At the same time, however, we agree with plaintiffs that a monopolist's use of exclusive contracts, in certain circumstances, may give rise to a § 2 violation even though the contracts foreclose less than the roughly 40% or 50% share usually required in order to establish a § 1 violation.

In this case, plaintiffs allege that, by closing to rivals a substantial percentage of the available opportunities for browser distribution, Microsoft managed to preserve its monopoly in the market for operating systems. The IAPs constitute one of the two major channels by which browsers can be distributed. Microsoft has exclusive deals with "fourteen of the top fifteen access providers in North America[, which] account for a large majority of all Internet access subscriptions in this part of the world." By ensuring that the "majority" of all IAP subscribers are offered IE either as the default browser or as the only browser, Microsoft's deals with the IAPs clearly have a significant effect in preserving its monopoly; they help keep usage of Navigator below the critical level necessary for Navigator or any other rival to pose a real threat to Microsoft's monopoly.

Plaintiffs having demonstrated a harm to competition, the burden falls upon Microsoft to defend its exclusive dealing contracts with IAPs by providing a procompetitive justification for them. Significantly, Microsoft's only explanation for its exclusive dealing is that it wants to keep developers focused upon its APIs—which is to say, it wants to preserve its power in the operating system market. That is not an unlawful end, but neither is it a procompetitive justification for the specific means here in question, namely exclusive dealing contracts with IAPs. Accordingly, we affirm the District Court's decision holding that Microsoft's exclusive contracts with IAPs are exclusionary devices, in violation of § 2 of the Sherman Act.

4. Dealings with Internet Content Providers [ICPs], Independent Software Vendors [ISVs], and Apple Computer ... The District Court described Microsoft's deals with ISVs as follows:

> ... Microsoft has promised to give preferential support, in the form of early Windows 98 and Windows NT betas, other technical information, and the right to use certain Microsoft seals of approval, to important ISVs that agree to certain conditions. One of these conditions is that the ISVs use Internet Explorer as the default browsing software for any software they develop with a hypertext-based user interface. Another condition is that the ISVs use Microsoft's "HTML Help," which is accessible only with Internet Explorer, to implement their applications' help systems.

The District Court further found that the effect of these deals is to "ensure [ ] that many of the most popular Web-centric applications will rely on browsing technologies found only in Windows," and that Microsoft's deals with ISVs therefore "increase[ ] the likelihood that the millions of consumers using [applications designed by ISVs that entered into agreements with Microsoft] will use Internet Explorer rather than Navigator."

The District Court did not specifically identify what share of the market for browser distribution the exclusive deals with the ISVs foreclose. Although the ISVs are a relatively small channel for browser distribution, they take on greater significance because, as discussed above, Microsoft had largely foreclosed the two primary channels to its rivals. In that light, one can tell from the record that by affecting the applications used by "millions" of consumers, Microsoft's exclusive deals with the ISVs had a substantial effect in further foreclosing rival browsers from the market.... Because, by keeping rival browsers from gaining widespread distribution (and potentially attracting the attention of developers away from the APIs in Windows), the deals have a substantial effect in preserving Microsoft's monopoly, we hold that plaintiffs have made a *prima facie* showing that the deals have an anticompetitive effect.

Of course, that Microsoft's exclusive deals have the anticompetitive effect of preserving Microsoft's monopoly does not, in itself, make them unlawful. A monopolist, like a competitive firm, may have a perfectly legitimate reason for wanting an exclusive arrangement with its distributors. Accordingly, Microsoft had an opportunity to, but did not, present the District Court with evidence demonstrating that the exclusivity provisions have some such procompetitive justification. On appeal Microsoft likewise does not claim that the exclusivity required by the deals serves any legitimate purpose; instead, it states only that its ISV agreements reflect an attempt "to persuade ISVs to utilize Internet-related system services in Windows rather than Navigator." As we explained before, however, keeping developers focused upon Windows—that is, preserving the Windows monopoly—is a competitively neutral goal. Microsoft having offered no procompetitive justification for its exclusive dealing arrangements with the ISVs, we hold that those arrangements violate § 2 of the Sherman Act.

Finally, the District Court held that Microsoft's dealings with Apple violated the Sherman Act. ... The District Court found that "ninety percent of [Apple's] Mac OS users running a suite of office productivity applications [use] Microsoft's Mac Office." Further, the District Court found that:

> In 1997, Apple's business was in steep decline, and many doubted that the company would survive much longer.... [M]any ISVs questioned the wisdom of continuing to spend time and money developing applications for the Mac OS. Had Microsoft announced in the midst of this atmosphere that it was ceasing to develop new versions of Mac Office, a great number of ISVs, customers, developers, and investors would have interpreted the announcement as Apple's death notice.

Microsoft recognized the importance to Apple of its continued support of Mac Office. In June 1997 Microsoft Chairman Bill Gates determined that the company's negotiations with Apple " 'have not been going well at all.... Apple let us down on the browser by making Netscape the standard install.' Gates then reported that he had already called Apple's CEO ... to ask 'how we should announce the cancellation of Mac Office....' " The District Court further found that, within a month of Gates' call, Apple and Microsoft had reached an agreement pursuant to which

> Microsoft's primary obligation is to continue releasing up-to-date versions of Mac Office for at least five years.... [and] Apple has agreed ... to "bundle the most current version of [IE] ... with [Mac OS]" ... [and to] "make [IE] the default [browser]"....
> Navigator is not installed on the computer hard drive during the default installation, which is the type of installation most users

elect to employ.... [The] Agreement further provides that ... Apple may not position icons for nonMicrosoft browsing software on the desktop of new Macintosh PC systems or Mac OS upgrades.

The agreement also prohibits Apple from encouraging users to substitute another browser for IE, and states that Apple will "encourage its employees to use [IE]."

This exclusive deal between Microsoft and Apple has a substantial effect upon the distribution of rival browsers. If a browser developer ports its product to a second operating system, such as the Mac OS, it can continue to display a common set of APIs. Thus, usage share, not the underlying operating system, is the primary determinant of the platform challenge a browser may pose. Pre-installation of a browser (which can be accomplished either by including the browser with the operating system or by the OEM installing the browser) is one of the two most important methods of browser distribution, and Apple had a not insignificant share of worldwide sales of operating systems. Because Microsoft's exclusive contract with Apple has a substantial effect in restricting distribution of rival browsers, and because (as we have described several times above) reducing usage share of rival browsers serves to protect Microsoft's monopoly, its deal with Apple must be regarded as anticompetitive.

Microsoft offers no procompetitive justification for the exclusive dealing arrangement. It makes only the irrelevant claim that the IE-for-Mac Office deal is part of a multifaceted set of agreements between itself and Apple, that does not mean it has any procompetitive justification. Accordingly, we hold that the exclusive deal with Apple is exclusionary, in violation of § 2 of the Sherman Act....

The U.S. Lower Court Splits on Foreclosure Thresholds and Terminability Relevance

Although the *Microsoft* district court held that 40% foreclosure had to be shown to prove substantial foreclosure, in fact the lower courts are split on the minimum foreclosure that must be shown to infer an anticompetitive effect. Some courts have held that 24% suffices.[21] Others have indicated that 30–40% is usually necessary.[22] Moreover, as the *Microsoft* court indicates, courts require a significantly lower foreclosure share in Sherman Act § 2 cases than in Sherman Act § 1 cases (thus suggesting that liability turns on some sort of sliding scale of market power and foreclosure) and some courts also require a somewhat lower foreclosure share in Clayton § 3 cases than in Sherman Act § 1 cases.

Although the relevant Supreme Court cases clearly condemn exclusionary agreements even when they are terminable,[23] there has not been a

---

21. Twin City Sportservice, Inc. v. Charles O. Finley & Co., Inc., 676 F.2d 1291, 1298, 1304 (9th Cir. 1982).

22. Stop & Shop Supermarket Co. v. Blue Cross & Blue Shield of R.I., 373 F.3d 57, 68 (1st Cir. 2004) (generally need at least 30–40%).

23. *See* FTC v. Brown Shoe, 384 U.S. 316, 318–19 & n.13 (1966) (condemning agreement even though buyers could "voluntarily withdraw" at any time), *rev'g* 339 F.2d 45, 53 (8th Cir.

Supreme Court case on the topic since 1966, and lower courts have since split on this issue as well. Some lower courts continue to adhere to the older Supreme Court cases by holding that terminability does not undermine the foreclosing effect of an exclusionary agreement.[24] Other lower courts have instead suggested that an ability to terminate (or not renew) exclusionary agreements in less than one year indicates that those agreements presumptively or probably lack any substantial foreclosing effect.[25] The latter cases do not typically explain their deviation from Supreme Court precedent, nor how such a presumption could be consistent with buyer incentives to enter into those exclusionary agreements.[26]

Questions on *Microsoft*'s Exclusive Dealing Holdings

1. Is exclusive dealing here intended to create market power in the foreclosed market (browsers) or in the operating system market?

2. Should the tests for substantial foreclosure differ for Sherman Act § 1 and § 2? Given that the particular anticompetitive effect on the operating system market alleged here was that agreements prevented rival browsers from being sufficiently *ubiquitous* to compete with Windows as a rival platform for running applications, wouldn't any significant foreclosure percentage suffice? Wouldn't this anticompetitive effect exist even if Netscape were foreclosed from, say, a 20% share of the browser market?

3. Is requiring a number like 30–40% in more typical cases consistent with the Supreme Court rulings above? Didn't *Tampa Electric* require further inquiry into procompetitive justifications even at less than 1%? Should the test differ for Sherman Act § 1 and Clayton Act § 3? By that much?

4. Should the test for substantial foreclosure turn on whether some fixed numerical percentage is met in all cases, or rather on the significance of that percentage given:

a. the relevant economies of scale, etc., in that industry that affect what sort of foreclosure share is likely to produce anticompetitive effects?

1964) (sustaining agreement in part because "[r]etailers were free to abandon the arrangement at any time they saw it to their advantage so to do"); Standard Oil Co. v. United States, 337 U.S. 293, 296 (1949) (invalidating exclusive dealing agreements that lasted only one year and were terminable upon thirty days notice); Standard Fashion Co. v. Magrane–Houston Co., 258 U.S. 346, 352 (1922) (invalidating exclusive dealing agreements that were terminable upon three months notice).

24. *See* United States v. Dentsply, Intl., 399 F.3d 181, 193 (3d Cir. 2005); *LePage's*, 324 F.3d at 157 n.11; Minnesota Mining & Manuf. Co. v. Appleton Papers, Inc., 35 F. Supp. 2d 1138 (D. Minn.1999); American Express Travel v. Visa, 2005 WL 1515399, at *6–7 (S.D.N.Y.); Masimo Corp. v. Tyco Health Care, 2006 WL 1236666 (C.D.Cal.).

25. *See* Omega Envtl. v. Gilbarco, Inc., 127 F.3d 1157, 1163–64 (9th Cir. 1997); Thompson Everett, Inc. v. National Cable Adver., 57 F.3d 1317, 1326 (4th Cir. 1995); U.S. Healthcare, Inc. v. Healthsource, Inc., 986 F.2d 589, 596 (1st Cir. 1993); Roland Mach. Co. v. Dresser Indus., Inc., 749 F.2d 380, 395 (7th Cir. 1984).

26. *See* Elhauge, supra note 13, at 340–342 (explaining the economic error in any presumption favoring exclusive agreements shorter than one year).

b.   the existence and strength of any offsetting procompetitive justifications? Given Microsoft's failure to even assert a procompetitive justification, shouldn't any significant foreclosure have sufficed to conclude that any effect must on balance be anticompetitive?

5.   If the test were 40%, should it (as the district court thought) require evidence that rivals were totally foreclosed from all distributors who could reach 40% of buyers, or should it (as the court of appeals held) suffice that rivals were foreclosed from the most efficient means of distribution? If some methods of distribution are significantly more efficient than others, doesn't that mean they are in a different market for distribution services?

6.   Should it count as substantial foreclosure where, as here:

a.   the foreclosed internet access providers promised only not to "promote" rival browsers and to supply no more than 15–25% of their customers with a rival browser? Should such 75–85% foreclosure count as "exclusive" dealing, and does it matter whether it is instead exclusionary dealing?

b.   the 75–85% foreclosed internet access providers are only "one of the two major channels by which browsers can be distributed" and enough of them were foreclosed that a " 'majority' of all IAP subscribers are offered IE either as the default browser or as the only browser"?

c.   Independent Software Vendors and Apple agreed to use Microsoft browser as their default browser?

EU Guidelines on Vertical Restraints

O.J. 2010, C 130/1.

1.   The framework of analysis

Outside the scope of the block exemption, it is relevant to examine whether in the individual case the agreement falls within the scope of Article 101(1) and if so whether the conditions of Article 101(3) are satisfied. Provided that they do not contain restrictions of competition by object and in particular hardcore restrictions of competition, there is no presumption that vertical agreements falling outside the block exemption because the market share threshold is exceeded fall within the scope of Article 101(1) or fail to satisfy the conditions of Article 101(3). Individual assessment of the likely effects of the agreement is required. Companies are encouraged to do their own assessment. Agreements that either do not restrict competition within the meaning of Article 101(1) or which fulfil the conditions of Article 101(3) are valid and enforceable. . . .

The assessment of whether a vertical agreement has the effect of restricting competition will be made by comparing the actual or likely future situation on the relevant market with the vertical restraints in place with the situation that would prevail in the absence of the vertical restraints in the agreement. In the assessment of individual cases, the Commission will take, as appropriate, both actual and likely effects into account. . . .

Vertical restraints are generally less harmful than horizontal restraints. The main reason for the greater focus on horizontal restraints is that such restraints may concern an agreement between competitors producing identical or substitutable goods or services. In such horizontal relationships, the exercise of market power by one company (higher price of its product) may benefit its competitors. This may provide an incentive to competitors to induce each other to behave anti-competitively. In vertical relationships, the product of the one is the input for the other-, in other words, the activities of the parties to the agreement are complementary to each other. The exercise of market power by either the upstream or downstream company would therefore normally hurt the demand for the product of the other. The companies involved in the agreement therefore usually have an incentive to prevent the exercise of market power by the other.

Such self-restraining character should not, however, be over-estimated. When a company has no market power, it can only try to increase its profits by optimising its manufacturing and distribution processes, with or without the help of vertical restraints. More generally, because of the complementary role of the parties to a vertical agreement in getting a product on the market, vertical restraints may provide substantial scope for efficiencies. However, when an undertaking does have market power it can also try to increase its profits at the expense of its direct competitors by raising their costs and at the expense of its buyers and ultimately consumers by trying to appropriate some of their surplus. This can happen when the upstream and downstream company share the extra profits or when one of the two uses vertical restraints to appropriate all the extra profits.

2.   Analysis of specific vertical restraints...

2.1.   Single branding.

Under the heading of "single branding" fall those agreements which have as their main element the fact that the buyer is obliged or induced to concentrate its orders for a particular type of product with one supplier. That component can be found amongst others in non-compete and quantity-forcing on the buyer. A non-compete arrangement is based on an obligation or incentive scheme which makes the buyer purchase more than 80% of its requirements on a particular market from only one supplier. It does not mean that the buyer can only buy directly from the supplier, but that the buyer will not buy and resell or incorporate competing goods or services. Quantity-forcing on the buyer is a weaker form of non-compete, where incentives or obligations agreed between the supplier and the buyer make the latter concentrate its purchases to a large extent with one supplier. Quantity-forcing may for example take the form of minimum purchase requirements, stocking requirements or non-linear pricing, such as conditional rebate schemes or a two-part tariff (fixed fee plus a price per unit). A so-called "English clause", requiring the buyer to report any better offer and allowing him only to accept such an offer when the supplier does not match it, can be expected to have the same effect as a single branding obligation, especially when the buyer has to reveal who makes the better offer.

The possible competition risks of single branding are foreclosure of the market to competing suppliers and potential suppliers, softening of competition and facilitation of collusion between suppliers in case of cumulative use and, where the buyer is a retailer selling to final consumers, a loss of in-store inter-brand competition. Such restrictive effects have a direct impact on inter-brand competition.

Single branding is exempted by the Block Exemption Regulation where the supplier's and buyer's market share each do not exceed 30% and are subject to a limitation in time of five years for the non-compete obligation. The remainder of this section provides guidance for the assessment of individual cases above the market share threshold or beyond the time limit of five years.

The capacity for single branding obligations of one specific supplier to result in anticompetitive foreclosure arises in particular where, without the obligations, an important competitive constraint is exercised by competitors that either are not yet present on the market at the time the obligations are concluded, or that are not in a position to compete for the full supply of the customers. Competitors may not be able to compete for an individual customer's entire demand because the supplier in question is an unavoidable trading partner at least for part of the demand on the market, for instance because its brand is a "must stock item" preferred by many final consumers or because the capacity constraints on the other suppliers are such that a part of demand can only be provided for by the supplier in question. The market position of the supplier is thus of main importance to assess possible anti-competitive effects of single branding obligations.

If competitors can compete on equal terms for each individual customer's entire demand, single branding obligations of one specific supplier are generally unlikely to hamper effective competition unless the switching of supplier by customers is rendered difficult due to the duration and market coverage of the single branding obligations. The higher its tied market share, that is, the part of its market share sold under a single branding obligation, the more significant foreclosure is likely to be. Similarly, the longer the duration of the single branding obligations, the more significant foreclosure is likely to be. Single branding obligations shorter than one year entered into by non-dominant companies are generally not considered to give rise to appreciable anti-competitive effects or net negative effects. Single branding obligations between one and five years entered into by non-dominant companies usually require a proper balancing of pro- and anti-competitive effects, while single branding obligations exceeding five years are for most types of investments not considered necessary to achieve the claimed efficiencies or the efficiencies are not sufficient to outweigh their foreclosure effect. Single branding obligations are more likely to result in anti-competitive foreclosure when entered into by dominant companies.

When assessing the supplier's market power, the market position of its competitors is important. As long as the competitors are sufficiently numerous and strong, no appreciable anti-competitive effects can be expected. Foreclosure of competitors is not very likely where they have similar market positions and can offer similarly attractive products. In such a case, foreclosure may, however, occur for potential entrants when a number of major suppliers enter into single branding contracts with a significant number of buyers on the relevant market (cumulative effect situation). This is also a situation where single branding agreements may facilitate collusion between competing suppliers. If, individually, those suppliers are covered by the Block Exemption Regulation, a withdrawal of the block exemption may be necessary to deal with such a negative cumulative effect. A tied market share of less than 5% is not considered in general to contribute significantly to a cumulative foreclosure effect.

In cases where the market share of the largest supplier is below 30% and the market share of the five largest suppliers is below 50%, there is unlikely to be a single or a cumulative anti-competitive effect situation. Where a potential entrant cannot penetrate the market profitably, it is likely to be due to factors other than single branding obligations, such as consumer preferences.

Entry barriers are important to establish whether there is anticompetitive foreclosure. Wherever it is relatively easy for competing suppliers to create new buyers or find alternative buyers for their product, foreclosure is unlikely to be a real problem. However, there are often entry barriers, both at the manufacturing and at the distribution level.

Countervailing power is relevant, as powerful buyers will not easily allow themselves to be cut off from the supply of competing goods or services. More generally, in order to convince customers to accept single branding, the supplier may have to compensate them, in whole or in part, for the loss in competition resulting from the exclusivity. Where such compensation is given, it may be in the individual interest of a customer to enter into a single branding obligation with the supplier. But it would be wrong to conclude automatically from this that all single branding obligations, taken together, are overall beneficial for customers on that market and for the final consumers. It is in particular unlikely that consumers as a whole will benefit if there are many customers and the single branding obligations, taken together, have the effect of preventing the entry or expansion of competing undertakings.

Lastly, "the level of trade" is relevant. Anticompetitive foreclosure is less likely in case of an intermediate product. When the supplier of an intermediate product is not dominant, the competing suppliers still have a substantial part of demand that is free. Below the level of dominance an anticompetitive foreclosure effect may however arise in a cumulative effect situation. A cumulative anticompetitive effect is unlikely to arise as long as less than 50% of the market is tied.

Where the agreement concerns the supply of a final product at the wholesale level, the question whether a competition problem is likely to arise depends in large part on the type of wholesaling and the entry barriers at the wholesale level. There is no real risk of anticompetitive foreclosure if competing manufacturers can easily establish their own wholesaling operation. Whether entry barriers are low depends in part on the type of wholesaling, that is, whether or not wholesalers can operate efficiently with only the product concerned by the agreement (for example ice cream) or whether it is more efficient to trade in a whole range of products (for example frozen foodstuffs). In the latter case, it is not efficient for a manufacturer selling only one product to set up its own wholesaling operation. In that case, anti-competitive effects may arise. In addition, cumulative effect problems may arise if several suppliers tie most of the available wholesalers.

For final products, foreclosure is in general more likely to occur at the retail level, given the significant entry barriers for most manufacturers to start retail outlets just for their own products. In addition, it is at the retail level that single branding agreements may lead to reduced in-store inter-brand competition. It is for these reasons that for final products at the retail level, significant anti-competitive effects may start to arise, taking into account all other relevant factors, if a non-dominant supplier ties 30% or more of the relevant market. For a dominant company, even a modest tied market share may already lead to significant anti-competitive effects.

At the retail level, a cumulative foreclosure effect may also arise. Where all suppliers have market shares below 30%, a cumulative anticompetitive foreclosure effect is unlikely if the total tied market share is less than 40% and withdrawal of the block exemption is therefore unlikely. That figure may be higher when other factors like the number of competitors, entry barriers etc. are taken into account. Where not all companies have market shares below the threshold of the Block Exemption Regulation but none is dominant, a cumulative anticompetitive foreclosure effect is unlikely if the total tied market share is below 30%.

Where the buyer operates from premises and land owned by the supplier or leased by the supplier from a third party not connected with the buyer, the possibility of imposing effective remedies for a possible foreclosure effect will be limited. In that case, intervention by the Commission below the level of dominance is unlikely.

In certain sectors, the selling of more than one brand from a single site may be difficult, in which case a foreclosure problem can better be remedied by limiting the effective duration of contracts.

Where appreciable anti-competitive effects are established, the question of a possible exemption under Article 101(3) arises. For non-compete obligations, the efficiencies described in points (a) (free riding between suppliers), (d), (e) (hold-up problems) and (h) (capital market imperfections) of paragraph (107), may be particularly relevant.

[Paragraph 107: While trying to give a fair overview of the various justifications for vertical restraints, these Guidelines do not claim to be complete or exhaustive. The following reasons may justify the application of certain vertical restraints:

(a) To solve a "free-rider" problem. One distributor may free-ride on the promotion efforts of another distributor. That type of problem is most common at the wholesale and retail level. Exclusive distribution or similar restrictions may be helpful in avoiding such free-riding. Free-riding can also occur between suppliers, for instance where one invests in promotion at the buyer's premises, in general at the retail level, that may also attract customers for its competitors. Non-compete type restraints can help to overcome free-riding.

For there to be a problem, there needs to be a real free-rider issue. Free-riding between buyers can only occur on pre-sales services and other promotional activities, but not on after-sales services for which the distributor can charge its customers individually. The product will usually need to be relatively new or technically complex or the reputation of the product must be a major determinant of its demand, as the customer may otherwise very well know what it wants, based on past purchases. And the product must be of a reasonably high value as it is otherwise not attractive for a customer to go to one shop for information and to another to buy. Lastly, it must not be practical for the supplier to impose on all buyers, by contract, effective promotion or service requirements.

Free-riding between suppliers is also restricted to specific situations, namely to cases where the promotion takes place at the buyer's premises and is generic, not brand specific.

(b) To "open up or enter new markets". Where a manufacturer wants to enter a new geographic market, for instance by exporting to another country for the first time, this may involve special "first time investments" by the distributor to establish the brand on the market. In order to persuade a local distributor to make these investments, it may be necessary to provide territorial protection to the distributor so that it can recoup these investments by temporarily charging a higher price. Distributors based in other markets should then be restrained for a limited period from selling on the new market (see also paragraph (61) in Section III.4). This is a special case of the free-rider problem described under point (a).

(c) The "certification free-rider issue". In some sectors, certain retailers have a reputation for stocking only "quality" products. In such a case, selling through those retailers may be vital for the introduction of a new product. If the manufacturer cannot initially limit its sales to the premium stores, it runs the risk of being de-listed and the product introduction may fail. There may, therefore, be a reason for allowing for a limited duration a restriction such as exclusive distribution or selective distribution. It must be enough to guarantee introduction of the new product but not so long as to hinder large-scale dissemination. Such benefits are more likely with "experience" goods or complex goods that represent a relatively large purchase for the final consumer.

(d) The so-called "hold-up problem". Sometimes there are client-specific investments to be made by either the supplier or the buyer, such as in special equipment or training. For instance, a component manufacturer that has to build new machines and tools in order to satisfy a particular requirement of one of its customers. The investor may not commit the necessary investments before particular supply arrangements are fixed.

However, as in the other free-riding examples, there are a number of conditions that have to be met before the risk of under-investment is real or significant. Firstly, the investment must be relationship-specific. An investment made by the supplier is considered to be relationship-specific when, after termination of the contract, it cannot be used by the supplier to supply other customers and can only be sold at a significant loss. An investment made by the buyer is considered to be relationship-specific when, after termination of the contract, it cannot be used by the buyer to purchase and/or use products supplied by other suppliers and can only be sold at a significant loss. An investment is thus relationship-specific because it can only, for instance, be used to produce a brand-specific component or to store a particular brand and thus cannot be used profitably to produce or resell alternatives. Secondly, it must be a long-term investment that is not recouped in the short run. And thirdly, the investment must be asymmetric, that is, one party to the contract invests more than the other party. Where these conditions are met, there is usually a good reason to have a vertical restraint for the duration it takes to depreciate the investment. The appropriate vertical restraint will be of the non-compete type or quantity-forcing type when the investment is made by the supplier and of the exclusive distribution, exclusive customer allocation or exclusive supply type when the investment is made by the buyer.

(e) The "specific hold-up problem that may arise in the case of transfer of substantial know-how". The know-how, once provided, cannot be taken back and the provider of the know-how may not want it to be used for or by its competitors. In as far as the know-how was not readily available to the buyer, is substantial and indispensable for the operation of the agreement, such a transfer may justify a non-compete type of restriction, which would normally fall outside Article 101(1).

(f) The "vertical externality issue". A retailer may not gain all the benefits of its action taken to improve sales; some may go to the manufacturer. For every extra unit a retailer sells by lowering its resale price or by increasing its sales effort, the manufacturer benefits if its wholesale price exceeds its marginal production costs. Thus, there may be a positive externality bestowed on the manufacturer by such retailer's actions and from the manufacturer's perspective the retailer may be pricing too high and/or making too little sales efforts. The negative externality of too high pricing by the retailer is sometimes called the "double marginalisation problem" and it can be avoided by imposing a maximum resale price on the retailer. To increase the retailer's sales efforts selective distribution, exclusive distribution or similar restrictions may be helpful.

(g) "Economies of scale in distribution". In order to have scale economies exploited and thereby see a lower retail price for its product, the manufacturer may want to concentrate the resale of its products on a limited number of distributors. To do so, it could use exclusive distribution, quantity forcing in the form of a minimum purchasing requirement, selective distribution containing such a requirement or exclusive sourcing.

(h) "Capital market imperfections". The usual providers of capital (banks, equity markets) may provide capital sub-optimally when they have imperfect information on the quality of the borrower or there is an inadequate basis to secure the loan. The buyer or supplier may have better information and be able, through an exclusive relationship, to obtain extra security for its investment. Where the supplier provides the loan to the buyer, this may lead to non-compete or quantity forcing on the buyer. Where the buyer provides the loan to the supplier, this may be the reason for having exclusive supply or quantity forcing on the supplier.

(i) "Uniformity and quality standardisation". A vertical restraint may help to create a brand image by imposing a certain measure of uniformity and quality standardisation on the distributors, thereby increasing the attractiveness of the product to the final consumer and increasing its sales. This can for instance be found in selective distribution and franchising.]

In the case of an efficiency as described in paragraph (107)(a), (107)(d) and (107)(h), quantity forcing on the buyer could possibly be a less restrictive alternative. A non-compete obligation may be the only viable way to achieve an efficiency as described in paragraph (107)(e), (hold-up problem related to the transfer of know-how).

In the case of a relationship-specific investment made by the supplier (see paragraph (107)(d)), a non-compete or quantity forcing agreement for the period of depreciation of the investment will in general fulfil the conditions of Article 101(3). In the case of high relationship-specific investments, a non-compete obligation exceeding five years may be justified. A relationship-specific investment could, for instance, be the installation or adaptation of equipment by the supplier when this equipment can be used afterwards only to produce components for a particular buyer. General or market-specific investments in (extra) capacity are normally not relationship-specific investments. However, where a supplier creates new capacity specifically linked to the operations of a particular buyer, for instance a company producing metal cans which creates new capacity to produce cans on the premises of or next to the canning facility of a food producer, this new capacity may only be economically viable when producing for this particular customer, in which case the investment would be considered to be relationship-specific.

Where the supplier provides the buyer with a loan or provides the buyer with equipment which is not relationship-specific, this in itself is normally not sufficient to justify the exemption of an anticompetitive foreclosure effect on the market. In case of capital market imperfection, it may be more efficient for the supplier of a product than for a bank to provide a loan (see paragraph (107)(h)). However, in such a case the loan should be provided in the least restrictive way and the buyer should thus in general not be prevented from terminating the obligation and repaying the outstanding part of the loan at any point in time and without payment of any penalty.

The transfer of substantial know-how (paragraph (107)(e)) usually justifies a non-compete obligation for the whole duration of the supply agreement, as for example in the context of franchising.

Example of non-compete obligation

The market leader in a national market for an impulse consumer product, with a market share of 40%, sells most of its products (90%) through tied retailers (tied market share 36%). The agreements oblige the retailers to purchase only from the market leader for at least four years. The market leader is especially strongly represented in the more densely populated areas like the capital. Its competitors, 10 in number, of which some are only locally available, all have much smaller market shares, the biggest having 12%. Those 10 competitors together supply another 10% of the market via tied outlets. There is strong brand and product differentiation in the market. The market leader has the strongest brands. It is the only one with regular national advertising campaigns. It provides its tied retailers with special stocking cabinets for its product.

The result on the market is that in total 46% (36% + 10%) of the market is foreclosed to potential entrants and to incumbents not having tied outlets. Potential entrants find entry even more difficult in the densely populated areas where foreclosure is even higher, although it is there that they would prefer to enter the market. In addition, owing to the strong brand and product differentiation and the high search costs relative to the price of the product, the absence of in-store inter-brand competition leads to an extra welfare loss for consumers. The possible efficiencies of the outlet exclusivity, which the market leader claims result from reduced transport costs and a possible hold-up problem concerning the stocking cabinets, are limited and do not outweigh the negative effects on competition. The efficiencies are limited, as the transport costs are linked to quantity and not exclusivity and the stocking cabinets do not contain special know-how and are not brand specific. Accordingly, it is unlikely that the conditions of Article 101(3) are fulfilled.

Example of quantity forcing

A producer X with a 40% market share sells 80% of its products through contracts which specify that the reseller is required to purchase at least 75% of its requirements for that type of product from X. In return X is offering financing and equipment at favourable rates. The contracts have a duration of five years in which repayment of the loan is foreseen in equal instalments. However, after the first two years buyers have the possibility to terminate the contract with a six-month notice period if they repay the outstanding loan and take over the equipment at its market asset value. At the end of the five-year period the equipment becomes the property of the buyer. Most of the competing producers are small, twelve in total with the biggest having a market share of 20%, and engage in similar contracts with different durations. The producers with market shares below 10% often have contracts with longer durations and with less generous termination clauses. The contracts of producer X leave 25% of requirements free to be supplied by competitors. In the last three years, two new producers have entered the market and gained a combined market share of around 8%, partly by taking over the loans of a number of resellers in return for contracts with these resellers.

Producer X's tied market share is 24% (0,75 × 0,80 × 40%). The other producers' tied market share is around 25%. Therefore, in total around 49% of the market is foreclosed to potential entrants and to incumbents not having tied outlets for at least the first two years of the supply contracts. The market shows that the resellers often have difficulty in obtaining loans from banks and are too small in general to obtain capital through other means like the issuing of shares. In addition, producer X is able to demonstrate that concentrating its sales on a limited number of resellers allows him to plan its sales better and to save transport costs. In the light of the efficiencies on the one hand and the 25% non-tied part in the contracts of producer X, the real possibility for early termination of the contract, the recent entry of new producers and the fact that around half the resellers are not tied on the other hand, the quantity forcing of 75% applied by producer X is likely to fulfil the conditions of Article 101(3).

Note and Questions on the EU Guidelines on Vertical Restraints

The EU guidelines use the same sort of rule of reason approach for exclusive dealing as U.S. law, considering both efficiency justifications and the anticompetitive effects that might result from cumulative foreclosure. They also indicate a presumption that cumulative foreclosure must be over 30% (if some sellers have a market share over 30%) or over 40% (if none do), which resembles the 30–40% threshold used by some U.S. lower appellate courts. They also indicate that single branding can be pursued not only through non-compete obligations (which the U.S. calls exclusive dealing) but also tying or quantity-forcing obligations. Quantity-forcing obligations include not only minimum volume requirements but also discounts based on the volume or share of purchases from the defendant. The relevant foreclosure is what is produced by the combination of any exclusionary agreements.

1. Do the standards on cumulative foreclosure make economic sense? Shouldn't the threshold depend not on numerology but on what degree of foreclosure is necessary to produce anticompetitive effects given the particular economics of the market in question?

2. Are the guidelines right to treat foreclosure produced by quantity-forcing agreements the same as non-compete obligations? Are the likely anticompetitive effects from foreclosing 48% of a market any different if a firm does so with 100% exclusive dealing obligations with 48% of buyers as opposed to with 80% obligations with 60% of buyers?

3. The guidelines treat English clauses (i.e., rights of first refusal) the same as non-compete obligations, which we shall see is the same stance the U.S. courts have taken toward tying agreements with such rights of first refusal. Are the anticompetitive effects really the same? Even if the anticompetitive effect is not the same, do such clauses deter rivals from offering lower prices at all? Do they help oligopolists coordinate prices?

Guidance on the Commission's Enforcement Priorities in Applying Article 82 EC Treaty [now 102 TFEU] to Abusive Exclusionary Conduct by Dominant Undertakings

(Dec. 2008).

A. Exclusive dealing

32. A dominant undertaking may try to foreclose its competitors by hindering them from selling to customers through use of exclusive purchasing obligations or rebates, together referred to as exclusive dealing.[23] This

---

23. The notion of exclusive dealing also includes exclusive supply obligations or incentives with the same effect, whereby the dominant undertaking tries to foreclose its competitors by hindering them from purchasing from suppliers. The Commission considers that such input

section sets out the circumstances which are most likely to prompt an intervention by the Commission in respect of exclusive dealing arrangements entered into by dominant undertakings.

a) Exclusive Purchasing

33.   An exclusive purchasing obligation requires a customer on a particular market to purchase exclusively or to a large extent only from the dominant undertaking. Certain other obligations, such as stocking requirements, which appear to fall short of requiring exclusive purchasing, may in practice lead to the same effect.

34.   In order to convince customers to accept exclusive purchasing, the dominant undertaking may have to compensate them, in whole or in part, for the loss in competition resulting from the exclusivity. Where such compensation is given, it may be in the individual interest of a customer to enter into an exclusive purchasing obligation with the dominant undertaking. But it would be wrong to conclude automatically from this that all exclusive purchasing obligations, taken together, are beneficial for customers overall, including those currently not purchasing from the dominant undertaking, and the final consumers. The Commission will focus its attention on those cases where it is likely that consumers as a whole will not benefit. This will, in particular, be the case if there are many customers and the exclusive purchasing obligations of the dominant undertaking, taken together, have the effect of preventing the entry or expansion of competing undertakings.

35.   In addition to the factors mentioned in paragraph 20, the following factors will generally be of particular relevance in determining whether the Commission will intervene against exclusive purchasing arrangements.

36.   The capacity for exclusive purchasing obligations to result in anticompetitive foreclosure arises in particular where, without the obligations, an important competitive constraint is exercised by competitors who either are not yet present in the market at the time the obligations are concluded, or who are not in a position to compete for the full supply of the customers. Competitors may not be able to compete for an individual customer's entire demand because the dominant undertaking is an unavoidable trading partner at least for part of the demand on the market, for instance because its brand is a "must stock item" preferred by many final consumers or because the capacity constraints on the other suppliers are such that a part of demand can only be provided for by the dominant supplier. If competitors can compete on equal terms for each individual customer's entire demand, exclusive purchasing obligations are generally unlikely to hamper effective competition unless the switching of supplier by customers is rendered difficult due to the duration of the exclusive purchasing obligation. In general, the longer the duration of the obligation, the greater the likely foreclosure effect. However, if the dominant undertaking is an unavoidable trading partner for all or most customers, even an exclusive

foreclosure is in principle liable to result in anticompetitive foreclosure if the exclusive supply obligation or incentive ties most of the efficient input suppliers and customers competing with the dominant undertaking are unable to find alternative efficient sources of input supply.

purchasing obligation of short duration can lead to anticompetitive foreclosure. . . .

(c) Efficiencies

46. Provided that the conditions set out in Section III D are fulfilled, . . . the Commission will consider evidence demonstrating that exclusive dealing arrangements result in advantages to particular customers if those arrangements are necessary for the dominant undertaking to make certain relationship-specific investments in order to be able to supply those customers.

Exclusive Dealing in Other Nations

Canada has a provision similar to Clayton Act § 3 that condemns exclusive dealing that substantially lessens competition, except that the Canada statute is explicit that its coverage includes requirements to deal "primarily" in the supplier's products and that it infers possible anticompetitive effects based either on the supplier being "major" or the exclusive dealing being "widespread," thus specifically including cumulative foreclosure.[27] Australia likewise condemns exclusive dealing that substantially lessens competition, and explicitly defines exclusive dealing to include requirements that a buyer will not "except to a limited extent" deal with the supplier's rivals, and in addition extends the concept to include exclusive dealing in "goods or services" or upstream exclusive dealing that forecloses suppliers.[28]

Japan deems "unjustly trading with another party on condition that the said party shall not trade with a competitor" to be an unfair trade practice if it "tends to impede fair competition."[29] Its guidelines provide that this is the case when a firm whose market share exceeds 10% (or is one of the three largest market shares) engages in exclusive dealing that lacks a proper justification and may make it hard for rivals to easily find alternative trading partners.[30] The last element embodies a form of substantial foreclosure and includes the cumulative foreclosure principle that exclusive dealing by multiple sellers increases the anticompetitive effect. Argentina, Brazil, India, Mexico, South Africa, Taiwan, and Turkey likewise apply some form of rule of reason review, with South Africa requiring a dominant position and Turkey requiring a 40% market share.[31]

---

27. Canada Competition Act § 77.

28. Australia Trade Practices Act § 47. The exception to this rule of reason is that Australia per se prohibits third-line forcing (conditioning a sale or discount on the buyer purchasing from a third party) unless the condition was notified to the Commission. *See* Australia Trade Practices Act § 47(6)–(7), (10A).

29. Japan Antimonopoly Law § 2(9); Japan General Designations of Unfair Trade Practices § 11 (2009).

30. *See* Japan Distribution Guidelines at 10–12.

31. *See* Argentina Competition Law Arts. 1, 2 (j); Brazil Antitrust Law No. 8,884, Arts. 20, 21(IV–VI); Brazil CADE Resolution 20, Attachment I, § B. 3 (1999); India Competition Act § 3(4)(b) (defining exclusive dealing to include any agreement to restrict supplying or purchasing from others); Mexico Competition Law Arts. 10(IV) & 11; South Africa Competition Act § 8(d)(i): Taiwan Fair Trade Act Art. 19(6); Taiwan Enforcement Rules to the Fair

South Korea condemns "wrongfully" transacting on exclusive terms, which probably involves some form of rule of reason review, although the term could also be interpreted to merely inquire into the defendant's purpose.[32] Egypt prohibits a dominant firm from upstream exclusive dealing with suppliers when it drives out rivals or deters entry, and Saudi Arabia prohibits a dominant firm from downstream exclusive dealing with buyers when that limits competition.[33] These laws probably mean some form of rule of reason review, but could be interpreted to require inquiry only into anticompetitive effects and not into procompetitive justifications. China makes it unlawful for a dominant firm to engage in exclusive dealing "without any justifiable cause."[34] This provision probably also implies rule of reason review, but if taken literally, the China provision could be interpreted to (1) condemn unjustified exclusive dealing without any proof of anticompetitive effects and (2) allow exclusive dealing that has some justification even if the anticompetitive effects outweigh the procompetitive effects.

C. TYING

Tying is a refusal to sell one product unless the buyer also takes another product. The product that will not be sold without the other is called the tying product, and generally it is the product in which the defendant has the greatest market power. The tied product is the one that buyers have to take to get the tying product.

Possible Anticompetitive Effects. The claim that tying can be anticompetitive has been strongly critiqued by the single monopoly profit theory, which argued that (as with the upstream firm who vertically integrates into downstream markets) there was only a single monopoly profit that could not be increased by tying.[35] Their classic example was a monopolist in nuts who tried to tie nuts to bolts. Suppose nuts and bolts each cost 10 cents to make and thus would be priced at 10 cents each if the market for both was competitive. Suppose further that the profit-maximizing price for a combined monopolist in both nuts and bolts would be 40 cents for the nut-bolt set that consumers need. If we have a nut monopolist and a competitive market in bolts, then the nut monopolist would simply charge 30 cents for nuts, with the customers paying 10 cents for bolts on a competitive market to arrive at 40 cents for the nut-bolt set. The nut monopolist would earn monopoly profits of 20 cents per set used. It would

---

Trade Act Art. 27; Turkey Communiqué on Block Exemptions regarding Vertical Agreements (No.2002/2) Art. 2 (amended in 2007).

32.   Enforcement Decree of the South Korea Fair Trade Act Appendix I, Art. 7.A.

33.   Egypt Competition Law Art. 8(i); Egypt Executive Regulation Art. 13(i); Saudi Implementing Regulations, Art. 6(1)(g).

34.   China Anti–Monopoly Law Art. 17(4).

35.   *See* Ward S. Bowman, Jr., *Tying Arrangements and the Leverage Problem*, 67 YALE L.J. 19, 21–23 (1957); Aaron Director & Edward H. Levi, *Law and the Future: Trade Regulation*, 51 NW. U. L. REV. 281, 290, 292–94 (1956); Robert Bork, The Antitrust Paradox (1978); Richard Posner, Antitrust Law: An Economic Perspective (2001).

earn no additional monopoly profits by tying its sale of nuts to bolts because if it did so the monopoly price would be 40 cents and the cost 20 cents, leaving it with profits of 20 cents a set. In fact, if a competitive market were more efficient and would lower the price of bolts down to 5 cents, the monopolist in nuts would prefer that, because then it could sell nuts for 35 cents and earn 25 cents a set. Thus, the single monopoly profit theory suggested a firm would use tying only if there were some efficiency to doing so.

However, the models indicating a single monopoly profit depended on five key assumptions: (1) buyers do not use varying amounts of the tied product with the tying product; (2) buyer demand for the two products has a strong positive correlation; (3) buyers do not use varying amounts of the tying product; (4) the competitiveness of the tied market is fixed; *and* (5) the competitiveness of the tying market is fixed.[36] Modern antitrust economics scholarship proves that relaxing any *one* of these assumptions invalidates the single monopoly profit theory, and that each relaxed assumption makes possible a distinctive anticompetitive result.

(1) Intraproduct Price Discrimination. If buyers use varying amount of the tied product with the tying product, then tying may allow a form of price discrimination on the tying product that increases monopoly profits.[37] Suppose that a monopolist sells some capital product that is used with a consumable product: for example, printers that are used with paper. Suppose further that usage of the consumable varies for different buyers in a way that correlates to the value of the capital product to each buyer. Buyers who use more paper are using their printers more often and thus presumably derive more value out from their printers. If so, the monopolist could lower the price for its printer down to marginal cost, contingent on buyers taking all their paper from the seller, with the paper price set well above marginal cost. Then buyers who use more paper will pay more, allowing the monopolist to price discriminate among buyers of printers. This may be the most effective means of price discrimination if the monopolist could not otherwise tell which buyer is more likely to use its printer, and if the monopolist could not otherwise meter usage of its machine in an easy to monitor way.[38] If so, this form of tying would increase monopoly profits even if it results in no substantial foreclosure share in the tied paper market. However, it does require market power in the tying product.

Tying that produces intra-product price discrimination also decreases both consumer welfare and ex post total welfare unless it produces some output-increasing efficiency.[39] Moreover, if we put aside possible productive

---

36. Elhauge, *Tying, Bundled Discounts, and the Death of the Single Monopoly Profit Theory*, 123 HARVARD LAW REVIEW 397, 400, 404–420 (2009).

37. *Jefferson Parish*, 466 U.S. at 15 & n.23 (collecting academic literature and treating such intraproduct price discrimination as an anticompetitive effect).

38. Difficulties in monitoring which paper a buyer uses might cause a seller to instead engage in technological tying that does not require monitoring. For example, it might design its printer so it can only work with its printer cartridges, which it sells at far above marginal costs.

39. Elhauge, *Tying, supra* note 36, at 405, 430–434, 439–442 (summarizing the economic literature).

efficiencies or inefficiencies, tying that produces intraproduct price discrimination among consumers will (assuming equally distributed consumer valuations) usually decrease consumer welfare, increase ex post total welfare, and decrease ex ante total welfare.[40] But such tying can also increase or decrease all forms of welfare. Further, if the buyers are not final consumers, but instead are intermediaries who resell to consumers, then tying that produces intraproduct price discrimination reduces output and total welfare, other than in cases where the price discrimination discourages inefficient integration.[41]

(2) Interproduct Price Discrimination. If buyer demand for two products does not have a strong positive correlation, then tying can also profitably permit price discrimination across buyers of both products.[42] This is true even if the products are used or bundled in a fixed ratio. Suppose, for example, a firm is a monopolist in products A and B, both of which cost $10 to make. Suppose there are 1000 buyers who value product A at $20 and product B at $25, but the other 1000 buyers value product B at $20 and product A at $25. If the monopolist has to price the products separately, and cannot distinguish which buyers value A or B more highly or prevent resale between them, it would sell A at $20 and B at $20, thus making $40,000 in profits because if it prices them each at $25 it will make less, just $30,000 in profits. If instead, the monopolist can sell the bundle at a price of $45, then all the buyers would take the bundle, and the monopolist would make $50,000 in profits. More generally, bundling can allow a defendant to profitably price discriminate when buyers preferences between product A and B do not have a strong positive correlation.[43] This form of tying can increase profits without any substantial tied foreclosure share, but it does require some degree of market power in both products.[44]

Tying that produces inter-product price discrimination decreases both consumer welfare and ex post total welfare unless it produces some output-

---

40. *Id.* at 430–34, 479–81; Elhauge, *The Failed Resurrection of the Single Monopoly Profit Theory*, 6(1) Competition Policy Int'l 155, 166–167 (Spring 2010); Barry Nalebuff, *Price Discrimination and Welfare*, 5(2) Competition Policy Int'l 221, 227, 236 (2009). Productive efficiencies concern the possibility that tying might decrease costs or increase product value, and productive inefficiencies concern the opposite possibility (such as when tying requires incurring additional monitoring costs or altering product design for the worse).

41. Michael L. Katz, *The Welfare Effects of Third–Degree Price Discrimination in Intermediate Goods Markets*, 77 Amer. Econ. Rev. 154, 161–165 (1987).

42. Elhauge, *Tying, supra* note 36, at 405–407; George J. Stigler, *United States v. Loew's Inc.: A Note on Block–Booking*, 1963 SUP. CT. REV. 152; *Jefferson Parish*, 466 U.S. at 15 & n.23 (citing Stigler's article and treating such interproduct price discrimination as an anticompetitive effect).

43. See William James Adams & Janet L. Yellen, *Commodity Bundling and the Burden of Monopoly*, 90 Q.J. ECON. 475, 485 (1976); R. Preston McAfee et al., *Multiproduct Monopoly, Commodity Bundling, and Correlation of Values*, 104 Q.J. ECON. 371, 372–73, 377 (1989); Richard Schmalensee, *Gaussian Demand and Commodity Bundling*, 57 J. BUS. S211, S220 (1984). If the strength of demand relative to cost is high enough, then bundling can increase monopoly profits for anything other than a perfect positive correlation. Id. at S215, S220. For lower demand-to-cost ratios, strong but imperfect positive correlations may defeat this strategy.

44. See Richard Schmalensee, *Commodity Bundling by Single–Product Monopolies*, 25 J.L. & ECON. 67, 67–69 (1982).

increasing efficiency.[45] Further, if we put aside possible productive efficiencies or inefficiencies, tying that produces inter-product price discrimination will (assuming a normal distribution of buyer valuations) always decrease consumer welfare absent perfect positive demand correlation.[46] In contrast, such tying has conflicting effects on ex post total welfare. It decreases ex post total welfare if the strength of demand relative to cost is not high, but increases it otherwise.[47] The negative effects on consumer welfare coupled with mixed effects on ex post total welfare mean that such tying is likely to reduce ex ante total welfare.[48]

(3) Extracting Individual Consumer Surplus. If buyers use varying amounts units of the tying product, then tying can extract individual consumer surplus. The basic reason is that, even at a monopoly price for the tying product, each multi-unit buyer enjoys some consumer surplus because it values the last unit it purchases at the monopoly price and values the prior (or inframarginal) units at something more, given that any buyer rationally uses its initial units to meet its greatest needs first. The difference between each buyer's valuation of those inframarginal units and the monopoly price will be the consumer surplus enjoyed by each buyer at the monopoly price. A tying firm can expropriate that consumer surplus by allowing buyers to purchase the tying product at the monopoly price only if buyers agree to purchase their needs of some tied product at supracompetitive prices. Each buyer will accept the tie as long as the burden of paying supracompetitive prices on the tied product is less than the consumer surplus they would lose by being unable to buy the tying product at the monopoly price.[49] This form of tying can increase profits without a substantial tied foreclosure share, but does require tying market power.[50]

Tying that extracts individual consumer welfare always reduces consumer welfare if the tying firm chooses profit-maximizing prices.[51] The ex post total welfare effects can vary. However, if (as typical in most tying cases) spending or valuation is significantly higher for the tying product than the tied product (for buyers subject to the tie), then tying will reduce

---

45. Adams & Yellen, *supra* note 43, at 482–83, 491–92; Elhauge, *Tying*, *supra* note 36, at 406–07.

46. Schmalensee, *Gaussian Demand and Commodity Bundling,* supra note 43, at S221–22, S229.

47. *Id.*

48. Elhauge, *Tying*, *supra* note 36, at 439–442.

49. *See* M. L. Burstein, *The Economics of Tie–In Sales*, 42 REVIEW OF ECONOMICS & STATISTICS 68, 68–69 (1960); M.L. Burstein, *A Theory of Full–Line Forcing*, 55 NORTHWESTERN LAW REVIEW 62, 73–91 (1960); Elhauge, *Tying*, *supra* note 36, at 407–413. Burstein's theory that tying could be used to squeeze out consumer surplus on the tying product was distinguished from price discrimination and cited favorably in Fortner Enter. v. United States Steel, 394 U.S. 495, 513–514 & n.8 (1969) (White, J., dissenting) ("they may be used to force a full line of products on the customer so as to extract more easily from him a monopoly return on one unique product in the line") (citing Burstein), which was in turn cited favorably as an explanation for the quasi-per se rule against tying both in *Jefferson Parish*, 466 U.S. at 13 n.19 (same), and in the dissenting opinion in Eastman Kodak v. Image Technical Servs., 504 U.S. 451, 487 (1992) (Scalia, J., joined by O'Connor & Thomas, JJ., dissenting) (same).

50. Elhauge, *Tying*, *supra* note 36, at 412–13.

51. *Id.* at 412.

ex post total welfare.[52] Further, the negative effects on consumer welfare coupled with at best mixed effects on ex post total welfare mean that such tying is likely to reduce ex ante total welfare.[53]

(4) Increased Tied Market Power. If the tied market is not perfectly competitive, then tying that forecloses a substantial share of the tied market can reduce rival competitiveness by impairing rival efficiency, entry, existence, aggressiveness, or expandability.[54] Any one of these adverse effects on rival competitiveness can in turn anticompetitively increase the tying firm's market power in the tied market, thus raising prices and harming consumers.

Consider first situations where tying can reduce tied rival efficiency. If there are costs to entering the tied market, tying can profitably deter entry by an equally efficient rival by foreclosing enough of the tied market to make entry profits lower than entry costs.[55] Likewise, if there are fixed costs to operating in the tied market, tying can cause equally efficient rivals in the tied market to exit (or deter their entry) and thus enable the tying firm to obtain a monopoly in the tied market.[56] More generally, for the same reasons discussed in Section B for exclusive dealing, foreclosing the tied market can create anticompetitive effects by depriving tied market rivals of economies of scale, scope, distribution, supply, research, learning, and/or network effects. If tied market foreclosure decreases rival efficiency in any of those ways, it will worsen the market options available to buyers and lessen the constraint on the tying firm's market power in the tied market, thus enabling it to raise prices in the tied market even though rivals are not completely eliminated.

Even if tying does not impair rival efficiency, foreclosure can also impair rival competitiveness by decreasing rival aggressiveness or expandability. Tying can decrease rival aggressiveness in at least two scenarios. First, if firms in the tied market engage in Cournot competition, which means each firm sets output in response to the output choices of others, then tying can encourage tied product rivals to reduce output and charge higher prices.[57] Second, if the tied market is concentrated, but (absent tying) would be undifferentiated and result in Bertrand competition that drives prices down to cost, tying can effectively differentiate the tied market (because buyer valuations for the tying product vary) and induce the rival to charge higher tied product prices.[58] Tying in both scenarios will

---

52.   *Id.* at 412, 435.

53.   Elhauge, *Tying, supra* note 36, at 439–442.

54.   Elhauge, *Tying, supra* note 36, at 413–417.

55.   *See* Barry Nalebuff, *Bundling as an Entry Barrier*, 119 Q.J. ECON. 159, 160–61, 168–70 (2004).

56.   *See* Michael D. Whinston, *Tying Foreclosure, and Exclusion,* 80 AM. ECON. REV. 837, 840, 846 (1990).

57.   See José Carbajo et al., *A Strategic Motivation for Commodity Bundling*, 38 J. INDUS. ECON. 283, 285–86, 290–92 (1990). The reason is that tying effectively commits the tying firm to increase its share of tied product output, which makes it profitable for rivals to lower output and increase prices, reducing total output of the tied product. *Id.*

58.   *See id.* at 285, 287–89. Without tying, the tied market would be undifferentiated because, even though buyer valuations of the tied product vary, buyers consider the tied

increase profits for the tying firm if, absent tying, tying product revenue would exceed tied product revenue, which is typical in tying cases. Tying in both scenarios will also harm consumer welfare.[59]

Tying can also decrease rival expandability and increase tied prices if the tying firm has market power in the tied market. Standard economic models calculate market power to be directly proportional to a firm's market share and inversely proportional to its rivals' supply elasticity, which is the percentage increase in rival supply that would result from a one percent increase in market price.[60] These standard models reasonably assume rivals' ability to expand depends on how large they already are. Thus, if a tying firm can through foreclosure obtain a higher share of the tied market for reasons unrelated to product merits, it will lower rivals' share of the tied market and thus lessen rival expandability and the constraint on tied product prices.

However, tying that impairs tied rival competitiveness *without* increasing the degree of tying market power cannot increase monopoly profits if (1) the products are used or bundled in a fixed ratio *and* (2) the tied product has no utility without the tying product.[61] The reason is that buyers of the tying product would interpret any premium on the tied product as a per-unit price increase on the tying product. Thus, a firm using a tie cannot reap any additional profits from those buyers that the firm could not have achieved without a tie by simply exercising its power to increase the tying product price, a tying market power which by hypothesis was not increased.

However, even without affecting tying market power, tying to impair tied market rivals can increase monopoly profits if only one of the above two conditions holds. If the products are used or bundled in a fixed ratio, but the tied product also has separate utility when not used with the tying product, then the firm can reap additional profits because it can (given diminished rival competitiveness) charge higher than but-for prices on purchases of the tied product that are not used with the tying product. Likewise, if the products are always used together, but in varying ratios, then tying that impairs tied market rival competitiveness can increase monopoly profits because the tie reduces the consumer surplus that buyers can get by rejecting the tie. Each buyer will accept the tie if the consumer surplus they would get by rejecting the tie and buying only the tied product is lower than the consumer surplus they would get from buying both the tying product at monopoly prices and the tied product at elevated prices.

---

products of the firm and its rival to be fungible. With tying, however, the fact that buyer valuations of the tying and tied products vary will differentiate buyers in their willingness to shift from the rival tied product to the tied bundle in response to a rival price increase.

59. *Id.* at 289, 292.

60. Define P as price, C as marginal cost, S as the firm's market share, ϵ_{rs} as the rival supply elasticity, and ϵ_m as the market demand elasticity (the percentage reduction in market output that would result from a one percent increase in market price). Then the firm's degree of market power (as measured its ability to raise prices above cost) is determined by the equation $(P\text{-}C)/P = S/[\epsilon_m + \epsilon_{rs}(1\text{--}S)]$. *See* William M. Landes & Richard A. Posner, *Market Power in Antitrust Cases*, 94 HARV. L. REV. 937, 945 (1981).

61. *See* Whinston, *supra* note 56, at 840, 850; Elhauge, *Tying*, *supra* note 36, at 416.

The tie that impairs tied market rivals will lower the former consumer surplus and thus allow the tying firm to extract more consumer surplus with a tie.

(5) Increased Tying Market Power. If one relaxes the assumption that the degree of tying market power is fixed, then tying can create additional anticompetitive effects by making the degree of tying market power higher than it would have been without tying.[62] Tying can increase tying power above but-for levels by either (1) foreclosing enough of the tied market to deter or delay later entry into the tying market, (2) raising the costs of a partial substitute that constrains tying market power, or (3) transferring market power from a waning technology to the next-generation technology. Let's take each scenario in turn.

First, suppose that a firm's tying market power is vulnerable to an increased threat of future entry if successful rival producers exist in the tied market. If so, then the firm has incentives to engage in defensive leveraging, foreclosing the tied market in order to deter or delay later entry into the tying market, thus maintaining its tying market power for a longer time or at a higher degree than it would have without tying. For example, recent literature shows that successful tied product makers are often more likely to evolve into tying product makers in future periods, in which case a firm has incentives to foreclose rivals in the tied market in order to prevent or reduce the erosion of its tying market power over time.[63] Alternatively, a firm's tying market power might be vulnerable to future entry or expansion by a single-market rival. Such a rival is often more likely to enter the tying market if buyers have attractive rival options in the tied market, especially if both products are essential inputs into some larger operation.[64]

Second, defensive leveraging has even stronger—and more immediate—anticompetitive effects if a firm's tying market power is otherwise constrained by the fact that the tied product is a partial substitute for the tying product. Foreclosing the market for the tied partial substitute can immediately protect or enhance the firm's tying market power, even if such foreclosure does not deter or delay entry into the tying market.[65]

Third, defensive leveraging also has even stronger—and more permanent—anticompetitive effects if the technological trend is from the market where the firm has market power to the market where the foreclosure is occurring. In such a case, a firm can use foreclosure not just to delay the erosion of its current market power over a waning technology, but to

---

62.   Elhauge, *Tying*, *supra* note 36, at 417–419.

63.   *See, e.g.*, Dennis W. Carlton & Michael Waldman, *The Strategic Use of Tying to Preserve and Create Market Power in Evolving Industries*, 33 RAND J. ECON. 194, 194–96, 198–212 (2002); Dennis W. Carlton, *A General Analysis of Exclusionary Conduct and Refusal to Deal*, 68 ANTITRUST L.J. 659, 668–70 (2001); Feldman, *Defensive Leveraging in Antitrust*, 87 GEO. L.J. 2079 (1999).

64.   *See* Choi & Stefanandis, *Bundling, Entry Deterrence, and Specialist Innovators*, 79 J. BUSINESS 2575 (2006); Choi & Stefanandis, *Tying, Investment, and the Dynamic Leverage Theory*, 32 RAND J. Econ. 52 (2001); Barry Nalebuff, *Exclusionary Bundling*, 50 ANTITRUST BULLETIN 321, 324–327 (2005).

65.   *See* Ordover & Willing, *An Economic Definition of Predation*, 91 YALE L.J. 8, 38–41 (1981); Whinston, *supra* note 56, at 852–54.

develop new market power over the technology of the future.[66] Such tying can have long-lasting adverse effects by creating market power in the new technology that otherwise might not have existed or by preventing the most efficient firm from winning the new market.

Conditions Necessary for the Possible Anticompetitive Effects. The first three possible anticompetitive effects require tying market power, but do not require a substantial foreclosure share in the tied market. Tying agreements producing any of those three effects—intraproduct price discrimination, interproduct price discrimination, and extracting individual consumer surplus—all reduce consumer and total welfare absent some output-increasing efficiency. However, tying agreements having only such effects do not increase the degree of market power in the tied or tying market, and thus might not fit within monopolization doctrine to the extent that enhancing market power is a legal element.

The last two possible anticompetitive effects—increasing tied or tying market power—do require a substantial tied foreclosure share.[67] These two effects are also reinforced by the first three anticompetitive effects, which prove that a foreclosing tie need not require any short-term profit sacrifice by the tying firm.[68] Likewise, any anticompetitive profits from the last two anticompetitive effects makes the first three effects all the more attractive to tying firms and exacerbates the anticompetitive effects.

When the tied products are used in a fixed ratio, buyers cannot use varying amounts of the tied or tying products, which knocks out the possibility of intraproduct price discrimination or individual consumer surplus extraction. When the products cannot be used separately, demand for them will generally have a strong positive correlation that knocks out interproduct price discrimination. Further, if the products both (1) have a fixed ratio and (2) lack separate utility, that also knocks out the possibility of increasing profits by increasing tied market power. Thus, the combination of (1) a fixed ratio and (2) no separate utility precludes any of the first four possible anticompetitive effects, leaving only the possibility that a substantial tied foreclosure share might increase the degree of tying market power. The combination of (1) a fixed ratio, (2) no separate utility, and (3) no substantial tied foreclosure share precludes all five of the possible anticompetitive effects. When those three conditions are met, the single monopoly profit theory holds.[69]

Possible Redeeming Efficiencies. Tying also has possible redeeming efficiencies. For the first three anticompetitive effects, tying can sometimes create output-increasing efficiencies by cutting the price for the tying product and allowing sales to categories of buyers who otherwise would not buy the tying product. When it does so, tying is likely to increase ex post total welfare, although such ties are also likely to reduce consumer welfare

---

66. *See* Carlton & Waldman, *supra* note 63, at 194, 196–97, 212–15; Carlton, *supra* note 63, at 670–71.

67. The foreclosure produced by a tie should be aggregated with any foreclosure produced by other exclusionary agreements like exclusive dealing.

68. Elhauge, *Tying, supra* note 36, at 404, 415–16.

69. *Id.* at 400–02.

and ex ante total welfare, although the opposite welfare effects might obtain in particular cases. In addition, tying can have the following productive efficiencies, which might be large enough to offset any anticompetitive effects. Indeed, when there is neither tying market power nor substantial tied market foreclosure, then some productive efficiency must explain the tie.

(1) When Bundling Lowers Costs or Increases Value. Two products may be cheaper to make or distribute together, or they may be more valuable to the buyer if the seller bundles them than if the buyer does. For example, it is presumably more efficient to sell cars with the tires on than to sell them without tires and have consumers buy and install the tires separately. As this example suggests, such efficiency arguments can often instead be framed as arguments that the two items are really components of a single product rather than separate products at all. When package cost-savings are asserted as a justification, often plaintiffs respond that a less restrictive alternative would be to offer the products separately and then at a package discount that is no greater than the cost-savings. But this test may be difficult for courts to administer and the possibility of court error may discourage price cutting down to the full amount of the cost-savings. Likewise, when the bundle is justified as more valuable, the less restrictive alternative might be to offer them both separately and then together. But it may sometimes be too costly to make separate offerings for which there is little consumer demand. For example, while shoe manufacturers could be required to carry shoes both in pairs and separately, that may not be worth the inventory costs because consumers generally only want shoes in pairs, leaving aside the few consumers who have one foot, lost one shoe, or have two feet that are significantly different in size.

(2) When Bundling Improves Quality. Sometimes the seller of the tying product might require that buyers use its tied product with it because they worry that buyers will otherwise use an inferior substitute that will make the tying product work less well and lower its brand reputation. A less restrictive alternative might be simply informing the buyer about the quality issue. But buyers may have free rider problems if they do not bear the full cost of the loss in brand reputation. For example, a fast food franchisor might sell its franchise (the tying product) to the franchisees who own the individual fast food restaurants on the condition that the franchisees buy their chicken (the tied product) only from the franchisor. The franchisor might worry that simply informing the buyer of the quality issue would not suffice because franchisees might free ride off of the brand's reputation to get walk-in traffic and skimp on costs by buying inferior chicken. If all the franchisees do this, the value of the franchise will be diminished for all of them, but each may figure that it alone will have little impact on the overall brand reputation. Thus each may have incentives to underweigh quality relative to costs. Another less restrictive alternative might be to specify the relevant quality of the associated product that buyers can use. But it may be difficult to specify that quality (what is tasty chicken?) or hard to monitor compliance with a general quality standard (it may be easier to see who is delivering chicken to the restaurant than to determine the quality of the chicken that others are delivering).

(3) Metering to Shift Financing or Risk–Bearing Costs to the Firm that Can Minimize Them. Sometimes tying might allow a form of price metering that could be understood not as price discrimination, but as an efficient way of shifting financing or risk-bearing costs from buyers to a seller that can bear them more cheaply. Suppose, for example, that it would be more costly for small buyers to finance the costs of capital equipment than for the seller. Then it might be efficient for the seller to effectively provide financing to buyers by selling the capital equipment below cost, with the buyer repaying the seller with supracompetitive payments on the associated consumable. The seller might accomplish the same by leasing the equipment, but the transaction costs of leasing might be higher.

Or suppose the problem is that the buyers are small businesses who do not vary *ex ante* in the value they attach to the capital equipment but who face the risk that some of them will do badly (and end up not needing the equipment) whereas others will do well (and end up using them a lot). Then it might make sense for the seller to sell the capital equipment very cheaply and make its profits in supracompetitive prices on the consumable. This will reduce the business risks to the buyers because those who will pay less will be those who have done badly in business. It will shift those risks to the seller, who may well face lower risk-bearing costs because it has many buyers, giving it a diversified portfolio that protects it against buyer-specific business declines. Again, leasing the equipment with payments dependent on usage might well be a less restrictive alternative, but perhaps transaction costs would impede that result.

U.S. Law on Tying. Under U.S. antitrust law, a so-called "quasi-per se" rule applies to tying under Sherman Act § 1 and Clayton Act § 3. The rule is "per se" in the sense that it condemns tying without requiring a showing that any substantial share of the tied market has been foreclosed. Rather, it suffices that the tie covers a nontrivial dollar amount of tied product.[70] But it is only a "quasi-per se" rule because it requires proof that the defendant has market power in the tying product.[71] In short, the "quasi-per se" rule against tying requires proof of tying market power but not substantial tied market foreclosure, and thus apparently reflects the policy judgment that the first three anticompetitive effects described above deserve antitrust condemnation.[72]

Efficiency justifications are also probably admissible under the quasi-per se rule. This is unclear because the U.S. Supreme Court has so far rejected every efficiency justification that has been offered for tying, and often has done so using language indicating that it believes that generally no justification for tying exists that does not have a less restrictive alternative.[73] However, the Supreme Court has also consistently considered

---

70. *See International Salt*; Northern Pacific Railway v. United States, 356 U.S. 1 (1958); *Loew's.*

71. *See Jefferson Parish.*

72. Elhauge, *Tying, supra* note 36, at 420–26.

73. *See International Salt*, 332 U.S. at 397–98; *Standard Stations*, 337 U.S. at 305–06; Times–Picayune Publishing v. United States, 345 U.S. 594, 605 (1953); *Northern Pacific*, 356 U.S. at 5–6 & n.5; *Loew's*, 371 U.S. at 44; *Jefferson Parish*, 466 U.S. at 9–10 & n.14, 25 n.42; IBM v. United States, 298 U.S. 131, 138–39 (1936)

justifications before rejecting them.[74] Further, its most recent tying case states that the "view that tying arrangements may well be procompetitive ultimately prevailed" in its caselaw, which it categorized as rejecting the prior view that ties have no "legitimate business purpose" or "serve hardly any purpose beyond the suppression of competition."[75] This was dicta because the case concerned when market power existed, and the language could be read to mean only that ties have sufficient procompetitive virtues to require some showing of market power, but it probably signals a willingness to consider a defense of procompetitive justifications even when market power exists. Moreover, efficiencies play a role in determining what counts as separate products that are capable of being tied together at all. However, unless the combination is a new product,[76] the Court seems to prefer to infer such efficiencies from competitive market practices rather than having them proven directly.[77] For example, competitive markets at one time sold cars without bumpers or wipers but later sold cars with bumpers and wipers included, thus indicating there were efficiencies to selling them together that changed them from separate products to a single car product.

In short, calling current U.S. tying doctrine a "quasi-per se" rule is really a misnomer. Rather, the doctrine provides for a form of rule of reason review that requires proving either tying market power or a substantial tied foreclosure share and then weighs any anticompetitive effects against any offered efficiency justifications.[78] Proving tying market power allows one to infer one of the three first anticompetitive effects absent any efficiency justification, and proving a substantial tied foreclosure share allows one to infer one of the last two anticompetitive effects absent an efficiency justification. The fact that the court condemns ties based on market power absent an efficiency justification simply confirms that the Court views the first three anticompetitive effects as sufficient to condemn ties under Sherman Act § 1 and Clayton Act § 3.[79]

Whether we call it a quasi-per se rule or simply a specific form of rule of reason analysis, current U.S. tying doctrine has five elements:

(1) Separate Tying and Tied Products. The allegedly tied items cannot be mere components of a single product, like pens and pen caps. As noted, courts normally infer a single product from competitive market practices.[80] However, courts will also find a single product where the bundle combines

---

74.   *See* sources cited in last note; *Kodak*, 504 U.S. at 479–80 & n.27, 485–86; *Fortner I*, 394 U.S. at 506. *See also NCAA*, 468 U.S. at 104 n.26 (although the Court "has spoken of a 'per se' rule against tying arrangements, it has also recognized that tying may have procompetitive justifications that make it inappropriate to condemn without considerable market analysis.")

75.   Illinois Tool Works v. Independent Ink, 547 U.S. 28, 36 (2006).

76.   *See* United States v. Jerrold Electronics, 187 F.Supp. 545 (E.D. Pa. 1960), *aff'd per curiam*, 365 U.S. 567 (1961).

77.   *See Jefferson Parish*, 466 U.S. at 19–24; *Kodak*, 504 U.S. at 462.

78.   Elhauge, *Tying, supra* note 36, at 425–26.

79.   *Id.* at 420–26. Those three anticompetitive effects would presumably not suffice under Sherman Act § 2, because they would not show a causal connection between the tie and the degree of market power. *See id.* at 439 n.112; Chapter 3.D.

80.   *See* X AREEDA, ELHAUGE & HOVENKAMP, ANTITRUST LAW ¶ 1744–45 (1996).

components into a new product that operates better when bundled together by the defendant than when bundled together by the end user.[81] Two items (like aluminum ingot and manufacturing services) are also deemed parts of a single product if the buyers to whom the defendant sells only want them as a single finished product (say as aluminum tubes).[82] In such a case, a rival who seeks to have the defendant unbundle one of the items (say aluminum ingot) so the rival can make the same finished product as the defendant really is asserting not a tie but an antitrust duty to deal, which is subject to the limitations on that duty noted in Chapter 3. Two items might also be deemed parts of a single product if intellectual property law encourages bundling them together.[83] Finally, rather than being components of a single product, two items might fail to be separate because they are really the same product.[84] Selling a product on the condition that the buyer purchase more of the same product is addressed not by tying doctrine but rather by doctrines involving exclusionary agreements on single products, like exclusive dealing.

(2) Tying Condition. The defendant must have sold the tying product on the condition that the purchaser take the seller's tied product. Such a condition might take the form of altering the tying product technologically to make rival products operate worse with it, when the technological alternation does not improve performance.[85] It might also take the form of coercive pricing, which charges buyers a higher price for the tying product unless the buyer accepts the tie. Such pricing is often called a bundled "discount," but can more aptly be described as an unbundled "penalty" whenever the unbundled price exceeds the but-for price that would have been charged without bundled pricing. Such an unbundled penalty can have the same first three anticompetitive effects as a tie and thus should be condemnable based on tying market power and the absence of offsetting efficiencies, just as the quasi-per se rule does for ties.[86] Indeed, tying is really just a special case of unbundled penalty, where the unbundled price on the tying product is set at infinity. But, as Section 4.D will show, U.S. law on bundled pricing remains quite unclear.

(3) Non–Trivial Tied Sales. There must be a non-trivial dollar amount of sales in the tied product. A plaintiff need not show that a substantial share of the tied product is foreclosed, although four justices were ready to add that requirement in 1984.[87]

---

81. *See id.* ¶ 1746.

82. *Id.* ¶ 1748.

83. *See id.* ¶ 1749.

84. *See id.* ¶ 1747; *Times–Picayune*, 345 U.S. at 613–14.

85. *See id.* ¶ 1757 (but concluding this is true only for rule of reason review, and requires in addition proof of substantial foreclosure of the tied market and evidence that less than 10–25% of the complementary product used with the defendant's primary product comes from its rivals).

86. Elhauge, *Tying, supra* note 36, at 402–03, 450–455, 468–69. If the unbundled price does not exceed the but-for price, then the bundled discount cannot be anticompetitive unless a substantial foreclosure share exists and thus should not be treated the same as a tie. *Id.* at 403, 451, 469–70.

87. *See Jefferson Parish*, 466 U.S. 2 (O'Connor, J. joined by Burger, C.J., Powell and Rehnquist, JJ., concurring in the judgment).

(4) Tying Market Power. The defendant must have market power in the tying product. Although past cases inferred this on thin grounds, more recent cases emphasize the need for real economic market power, with one recent U.S. Supreme Court case holding that a market share of 30% standing alone was not enough and another declining to infer such power from the mere existence of a patent.[88]

(5) No Offsetting Efficiencies. When the first four elements are proven, then a tie can probably still escape condemnation in cases where the defendant can prove the tie was the least restrictive means of producing offsetting efficiencies that were passed on to consumers to an extent large enough to eliminate any harm to consumer welfare.

If quasi-per se illegal tying cannot be proven, bundling can generally still be challenged under the general rule of reason that operates as a backstop.[89] This might be true if the tying and tied products are not deemed separate, the condition is not deemed sufficiently absolute to constitute a tie, or the defendant lacks market power. The first and last of these possibilities would, however, seem to require either proof of substantial foreclosure of some market or direct proof of the sort of anticompetitive effects that likely reflect substantial foreclosure.

EU Law on Tying. Tying is referred to in both Articles 101(1) and Article 102 of the TFEU. Article 101(1) includes, as agreements that

> "... shall be prohibited as incompatible with the common market: all agreements ... which: ... make the conclusion of contracts subject to acceptance by the other parties of supplementary obligations which, by their nature or according to commercial usage, have no connection with the subject of such contracts."

Similarly, Article 102 includes tying in its (non-exhaustive) list of categories of abuses, with a definition similar to Article 101(1).

Tying can thus fall under Article 101(1) when it is part of an agreement concluded by a non-dominant supplier and a buyer. However, Regulation 330/2010 on vertical restraints provides for a safe harbor system whereby vertical agreements involving tying will be presumed compatible with Article 101 if the market share of the supplier is below 30% on the relevant market. A similar position has been followed by the Commission in Regulation 772/2004 for technology transfer agreements.

Thus, EU tying law effectively requires not only a tying condition between two separate products but at least a 30% market share in the tying product, which is similar to U.S. law. EU caselaw traditionally did not require any showing that a substantial share of the tied market was foreclosed, although the recent Commission *Microsoft* decision and Discussion Paper signal that the Commission may be ready to begin requiring a foreclosure share. Although a tie by firm with a market share over 30% falls within Article 101(1)'s presumptive prohibition, justifications are admissible under Article 101(3) and parallel doctrines in a dominance case.

---

88.   *See Jefferson Parish,* 466 U.S. 2; *Illinois Tool Works,* 126 S.Ct. 1281.

89.   *See* Areeda, Elhauge & Hovenkamp, Antitrust Law ¶ 1742 (1996); *Times–Picayune,* 345 U.S. at 614–15; *Fortner I,* 394 U.S. at 499–500; *Jefferson Parish,* 466 U.S. at 18, 29–30.

Thus, in its traditional form, EU tying law comes quite close to the elements of U.S. tying doctrine. The EU caselaw has, however, generally focused on tying as an abuse of dominance under Article 102.

Jefferson Parish Hospital v. Hyde

466 U.S. 2 (1984).

■ JUSTICE STEVENS delivered the opinion of the Court. . . .

In July 1977, respondent Edwin G. Hyde, a board certified anesthesiologist, applied for admission to the medical staff of East Jefferson Hospital. The credentials committee and the medical staff executive committee recommended approval, but the hospital board denied the application because the hospital was a party to a contract providing that all anesthesiological services required by the hospital's patients would be performed by Roux & Associates . . . Respondent then commenced this action seeking a declaratory judgment that the contract is unlawful and an injunction ordering petitioners to appoint him to the hospital staff . . .[4]. . . .

The Court of Appeals held that the case involves a "tying arrangement" because the "users of the hospital's operating rooms (the tying product) are also compelled to purchase the hospital's chosen anesthesia service (the tied product)." Having defined the relevant geographic market for the tying product as the East Bank of Jefferson Parish, the court held that the hospital possessed "sufficient market power in the tying market to coerce purchasers of the tied product." Since the purchase of the tied product constituted a "not insubstantial amount of interstate commerce," . . . the tying arrangement was therefore illegal "per se."

II

. . . It is far too late in the history of our antitrust jurisprudence to question the proposition that certain tying arrangements pose an unacceptable risk of stifling competition and therefore are unreasonable "per se." The rule was first enunciated in *International Salt*, and has been endorsed by this Court many times since. The rule also reflects congressional policies underlying the antitrust laws. In enacting § 3 of the Clayton Act, Congress expressed great concern about the anticompetitive character of tying arrangements. While this case does not arise under the Clayton Act, the congressional finding made therein concerning the competitive consequences of tying is illuminating, and must be respected.

It is clear, however, that every refusal to sell two products separately cannot be said to restrain competition. If each of the products may be purchased separately in a competitive market, one seller's decision to sell the two in a single package imposes no unreasonable restraint on either market, particularly if competing suppliers are free to sell either the entire

---

4. . . . The fees for anesthesiological services are billed separately to the patients by the hospital. They cover the hospital's costs and the professional services provided by Roux. After a deduction of eight percent to provide a reserve for uncollectible accounts, the fees are divided equally between Roux and the hospital.

package or its several parts.[17] For example, we have written that "if one of a dozen food stores in a community were to refuse to sell flour unless the buyer also took sugar it would hardly tend to restrain competition if its competitors were ready and able to sell flour by itself." *Northern Pac.* Buyers often find package sales attractive; a seller's decision to offer such packages can merely be an attempt to compete effectively—conduct that is entirely consistent with the Sherman Act.

Our cases have concluded that the essential characteristic of an invalid tying arrangement lies in the seller's exploitation of its control over the tying product to force the buyer into the purchase of a tied product that the buyer either did not want at all, or might have preferred to purchase elsewhere on different terms. When such "forcing" is present, competition on the merits in the market for the tied item is restrained and the Sherman Act is violated.

> "... By conditioning his sale of one commodity on the purchase of another, a seller coerces the abdication of buyers' independent judgment as to the 'tied' product's merits and insulates it from the competitive stresses of the open market. But any intrinsic superiority of the 'tied' product would convince freely choosing buyers to select it over others anyway." *Times–Picayune.*[19]

Accordingly, we have condemned tying arrangements when the seller has some special ability—usually called "market power"—to force a purchaser to do something that he would not do in a competitive market.[20]

----

17.   "Of course where the buyer is free to take either product by itself there is no tying problem even though the seller may also offer the two items as a unit at a single price." *Northern Pac.*.

19.   ... For example, Justice WHITE has written: "There is general agreement in the cases and among the commentators that the fundamental restraint against which the tying proscription is meant to guard is the use of power over one product to attain power over another, or otherwise to distort freedom of trade and competition in the second product. This distortion injures the buyers of the second product, who because of their preference for the seller's brand of the first are artificially forced to make a less than optimal choice in the second. And even if the customer is indifferent among brands of the second product and therefore loses nothing by agreeing to use the seller's brand of the second in order to get his brand of the first, such tying agreements may work significant restraints on competition in the tied product. The tying seller may be working toward a monopoly position in the tied product and, even if he is not, the practice of tying forecloses other sellers of the tied product and makes it more difficult for new firms to enter that market. They must be prepared not only to match existing sellers of the tied product in price and quality, but to offset the attraction of the tying product itself. Even if this is possible through simultaneous entry into production of the tying product, entry into both markets is significantly more expensive than simple entry into the tied market, and shifting buying habits in the tied product is considerably more cumbersome and less responsive to variations in competitive offers. In addition to these anticompetitive effects in the tied product, tying arrangements may be used to evade price control in the tying product through clandestine transfer of the profit to the tied product; they may be used as a counting device to effect price discrimination; and they may be used to force a full line of products on the customer so as to extract more easily from him a monopoly return on one unique product in the line." *Fortner I*, 394 U.S. at 512–514 (dissenting opinion) (footnotes omitted).

20.   This type of market power has sometimes been referred to as "leverage." Professors Areeda and Turner provide a definition that suits present purposes. " 'Leverage' is loosely defined here as a supplier's ability to induce his customer for one product to buy a second

When "forcing" occurs, our cases have found the tying arrangement to be unlawful.

Thus, the law draws a distinction between the exploitation of market power by merely enhancing the price of the tying product, on the one hand, and by attempting to impose restraints on competition in the market for a tied product, on the other. When the seller's power is just used to maximize its return in the tying product market, where presumably its product enjoys some justifiable advantage over its competitors, the competitive ideal of the Sherman Act is not necessarily compromised. But if that power is used to impair competition on the merits in another market, a potentially inferior product may be insulated from competitive pressures. This impairment could either harm existing competitors or create barriers to entry of new competitors in the market for the tied product, and can increase the social costs of market power by facilitating price discrimination, thereby increasing monopoly profits over what they would be absent the tie.[23] And from the standpoint of the consumer—whose interests the statute was especially intended to serve—the freedom to select the best bargain in the second market is impaired by his need to purchase the tying product, and perhaps by an inability to evaluate the true cost of either product when they are available only as a package. . . .

Per se condemnation—condemnation without inquiry into actual market conditions—is only appropriate if the existence of forcing is probable. Thus, application of the per se rule focuses on the probability of anticompetitive consequences. Of course, as a threshold matter there must be a substantial potential for impact on competition in order to justify per se condemnation. If only a single purchaser were "forced" with respect to the purchase of a tied item, the resultant impact on competition would not be sufficient to warrant the concern of antitrust law. It is for this reason that we have refused to condemn tying arrangements unless a substantial volume of commerce is foreclosed thereby. Similarly, when a purchaser is "forced" to buy a product he would not have otherwise bought even from another seller in the tied product market, there can be no adverse impact on competition because no portion of the market which would otherwise have been available to other sellers has been foreclosed.

Once this threshold is surmounted, per se prohibition is appropriate if anticompetitive forcing is likely. For example, if the government has granted the seller a patent or similar monopoly over a product, it is fair to presume that the inability to buy the product elsewhere gives the seller market power. Any effort to enlarge the scope of the patent monopoly by using the market power it confers to restrain competition in the market for a second product will undermine competition on the merits in that second market. Thus, the sale or lease of a patented item on condition that the buyer make all his purchases of a separate tied product from the patentee is unlawful.

---

product from him that would not otherwise be purchased solely on the merit of that second product." V. P. Areeda & D. Turner, Antitrust Law ¶ 1134a at 202 (1980).

23. Sales of the tied item can be used to measure demand for the tying item; purchasers with greater needs for the tied item make larger purchases and in effect must pay a higher price to obtain the tying item.

The same strict rule is appropriate in other situations in which the existence of market power is probable. When the seller's share of the market is high, or when the seller offers a unique product that competitors are not able to offer, the Court has held that the likelihood that market power exists and is being used to restrain competition in a separate market is sufficient to make per se condemnation appropriate. Thus, in *Northern Pac.*, we held that the railroad's control over vast tracts of western real estate, although not itself unlawful, gave the railroad a unique kind of bargaining power that enabled it to tie the sales of that land to exclusive, long term commitments that fenced out competition in the transportation market over a protracted period. When, however, the seller does not have either the degree or the kind of market power that enables him to force customers to purchase a second, unwanted product in order to obtain the tying product, an antitrust violation can be established only by evidence of an unreasonable restraint on competition in the relevant market.

In sum, any inquiry into the validity of a tying arrangement must focus on the market or markets in which the two products are sold, for that is where the anticompetitive forcing has its impact. Thus, in this case our analysis of the tying issue must focus on the hospital's sale of services to its patients, rather than its contractual arrangements with the providers of anesthesiological services. In making that analysis, we must consider whether petitioners are selling two separate products that may be tied together, and, if so, whether they have used their market power to force their patients to accept the tying arrangement.

III

The hospital has provided its patients with a package that includes the range of facilities and services required for a variety of surgical operations. At East Jefferson Hospital the package includes the services of the anesthesiologist.[28] Petitioners argue that the package does not involve a tying arrangement at all—that they are merely providing a functionally integrated package of services. . . .

Our cases indicate, however, that the answer to the question whether one or two products are involved turns not on the functional relation between them, but rather on the character of the demand for the two items.[29] In *Times–Picayune,* the Court held that a tying arrangement was

---

28. It is essential to differentiate between the Roux contract and the legality of the contract between the hospital and its patients. The Roux contract is nothing more than an arrangement whereby Roux supplies all of the hospital's needs for anesthesiological services. That contract raises only an exclusive dealing question. The issue here is whether the hospital's insistence that its patients purchase anesthesiological services from Roux creates a tying arrangement.

29. The fact that anesthesiological services are functionally linked to the other services provided by the hospital is not in itself sufficient to remove the Roux contract from the realm of tying arrangements. We have often found arrangements involving functionally linked products at least one of which is useless without the other to be prohibited tying devices. See *Mercoid Corp. v. Mid–Continent Co.,* 320 U.S. 661 (1944) (heating system and stoker switch); *Morton Salt Co. v. Suppiger Co.,* 314 U.S. 488 (1942) (salt machine and salt); *International Salt, supra* (same); *Leitch Mfg. Co. v. Barber Co.,* 302 U.S. 458 (1938) (process patent and material used in the patented process); *IBM v. United States,* 298 U.S. 131 (1936) (computer and computer punch cards); *Carbice Corp. v. American Patents Corp.,* 283 U.S. 27 (1931) (ice

not present because the arrangement did not link two distinct markets for products that were distinguishable in the eyes of buyers. . . .

The requirement that two distinguishable product markets be involved follows from the underlying rationale of the rule against tying. The definitional question depends on whether the arrangement may have the type of competitive consequences addressed by the rule. The answer to the question whether petitioners have utilized a tying arrangement must be based on whether there is a possibility that the economic effect of the arrangement is that condemned by the rule against tying—that petitioners have foreclosed competition on the merits in a product market distinct from the market for the tying item.[34] Thus, in this case no tying arrangement can exist unless there is a sufficient demand for the purchase of anesthesiological services separate from hospital services to identify a distinct product market in which it is efficient to offer anesthesiological services separately from hospital services.

Unquestionably, the anesthesiological component of the package offered by the hospital could be provided separately and could be selected either by the individual patient or by one of the patient's doctors if the hospital did not insist on including anesthesiological services in the package it offers to its customers. As a matter of actual practice, anesthesiological services are billed separately from the hospital services petitioners provide. There was ample and uncontroverted testimony that patients or surgeons often request specific anesthesiologists to come to a hospital and provide anesthesia, and that the choice of an individual anesthesiologist separate from the choice of a hospital is particularly frequent in respondent's specialty, obstetric anesthesiology.[36] . . . The record amply supports the conclusion that consumers differentiate between anesthesiological services and the other hospital services provided by petitioners.[39]

---

cream transportation package and coolant); *FTC v. Sinclair Refining Co.,* 261 U.S. 463 (1923) (gasoline and underground tanks and pumps); *United Shoe Mach. Co. v. United States,* 258 U.S. 451 (1921) (shoe machinery and supplies, maintenance, and peripheral machinery); *United States v. Jerrold Electronics Corp.,* 187 F.Supp. 545, 558–560 (E.D. Pa.1960) (components of television antennas), aff'd, 365 U.S. 567 (1961) (*per curiam*). In fact, in some situations the functional link between the two items may enable the seller to maximize its monopoly return on the tying item as a means of charging a higher rent or purchase price to a larger user of the tying item. See n. 23, *supra.*

34. Of course, the Sherman Act does not prohibit "tying," it prohibits "contracts . . . in restraint of trade." Thus, in a sense the question whether this case involves "tying" is beside the point. The legality of petitioners' conduct depends on its competitive consequences, not whether it can be labeled "tying." If the competitive consequences of this arrangement are not those to which the per se rule is addressed, then it should not be condemned irrespective of its label.

36. . . . As a statistical matter, only 27 per cent of anesthesiologists have financial relationships with hospitals. . . .

39. One of the most frequently cited statements on this subject was made by Judge Van Dusen in *United States v. Jerrold Electronics Corp.,* 187 F.Supp. 545 (E.D. Pa.1960), aff'd, 365 U.S. 567 (1961) (*per curiam*). While this statement was specifically made with respect to § 3 of the Clayton Act, its analysis is also applicable to § 1 of the Sherman Act, since with respect to the definition of tying the standards used by the two statutes are the same. See *Times–Picayune.*

Thus, the hospital's requirement that its patients obtain necessary anesthesiological services from Roux combined the purchase of two distinguishable services in a single transaction. Nevertheless, the fact that this case involves a required purchase of two services that would otherwise be purchased separately does not make the Roux contract illegal. As noted above, there is nothing inherently anticompetitive about packaged sales. Only if patients are forced to purchase Roux's services as a result of the hospital's market power would the arrangement have anticompetitive consequences. If no forcing is present, patients are free to enter a competing hospital and to use another anesthesiologist instead of Roux.[41] The fact that petitioners' patients are required to purchase two separate items is only the beginning of the appropriate inquiry.[42]

"There are several facts presented in this record which tend to show that a community television antenna system cannot properly be characterized as a single product. Others who entered the community antenna field offered all the equipment necessary for a complete system, but none of them sold their gear exclusively as a single package as did Jerrold. The record also establishes that the number of pieces in each system varied considerably so that hardly any two versions of the alleged product were the same. Furthermore, the customer was charged for each item of equipment and not a lump sum for total payment. Finally, while Jerrold had cable and antennas to sell which were manufactured by other concerns, it required that the electronic equipment in the system be bought from it." 187 F.Supp., at 559.

The record here shows that other hospitals often permit anesthesiological services to be purchased separately, that anesthesiologists are not fungible in that the services provided by each are not precisely the same, that anesthesiological services are billed separately, and that the hospital required purchases from Roux even though other anesthesiologists were available and Roux had no objection to their receiving staff privileges at East Jefferson. Therefore, the *Jerrold* analysis indicates that there was a tying arrangement here. *Jerrold* also indicates that tying may be permissible when necessary to enable a new business to break into the market. See *id.*, at 555–558. Assuming this defense exists, and assuming it justified the 1971 Roux contract in order to give Roux an incentive to go to work at a new hospital with an uncertain future, that justification is inapplicable to the 1976 contract, since by then Roux was willing to continue to service the hospital without a tying arrangement.

41. An examination of the reason or reasons why petitioners denied respondent staff privileges will not provide the answer to the question whether the package of services they offered to their patients is an illegal tying arrangement. As a matter of antitrust law, petitioners may give their anesthesiology business to Roux because he is the best doctor available, because he is willing to work long hours, or because he is the son-in-law of the hospital administrator without violating the per se rule against tying. Without evidence that petitioners are using market power to force Roux upon patients there is no basis to view the arrangement as unreasonably restraining competition whatever the reasons for its creation. Conversely, with such evidence, the per se rule against tying may apply. Thus, we reject the view of the District Court that the legality of an arrangement of this kind turns on whether it was adopted for the purpose of improving patient care.

42. Petitioners argue and the District Court found that the exclusive contract had what it characterized as procompetitive justifications in that an exclusive contract ensures 24–hour anesthesiology coverage, enables flexible scheduling, and facilitates work routine, professional standards and maintenance of equipment. The Court of Appeals held these findings to be clearly erroneous since the exclusive contract was not necessary to achieve these ends. Roux was willing to provide 24–hour coverage even without an exclusive contract and the credentials committee of the hospital could impose standards for staff privileges that would ensure staff would comply with the demands of scheduling, maintenance, and professional standards. In the past, we have refused to tolerate manifestly anticompetitive conduct simply because the health care industry is involved. See *Maricopa.*. Petitioners seek no special solicitude. We have also uniformly rejected similar "goodwill" defenses for tying arrangements, finding that the use of contractual quality specifications are generally sufficient to protect quality without the use of a tying arrangement. See *Standard Stations; International Salt; IBM v. United States,*

IV

The question remains whether this arrangement involves the use of market power to force patients to buy services they would not otherwise purchase. Respondent's only basis for invoking the per se rule against tying and thereby avoiding analysis of actual market conditions is by relying on the preference of persons residing in Jefferson Parish to go to East Jefferson, the closest hospital. A preference of this kind, however, is not necessarily probative of significant market power.

Seventy per cent of the patients residing in Jefferson Parish enter hospitals other than East Jefferson. Thus East Jefferson's "dominance" over persons residing in Jefferson Parish is far from overwhelming.[43] The fact that a substantial majority of the parish's residents elect not to enter East Jefferson means that the geographic data does not establish the kind of dominant market position that obviates the need for further inquiry into actual competitive conditions. The Court of Appeals acknowledged as much; it recognized that East Jefferson's market share alone was insufficient as a basis to infer market power, and buttressed its conclusion by relying on "market imperfections" that permit petitioners to charge noncompetitive prices for hospital services: the prevalence of third party payment for health care costs reduces price competition, and a lack of adequate information renders consumers unable to evaluate the quality of the medical care provided by competing hospitals. While these factors may generate "market power" in some abstract sense,[44] they do not generate the kind of market power that justifies condemnation of tying.

Tying arrangements need only be condemned if they restrain competition on the merits by forcing purchases that would not otherwise be made. A lack of price or quality competition does not create this type of forcing. If consumers lack price consciousness, that fact will not force them to take an anesthesiologist whose services they do not want—their indifference to price will have no impact on their willingness or ability to go to another hospital where they can utilize the services of the anesthesiologist of their choice. Similarly, if consumers cannot evaluate the quality of anesthesiological services, it follows that they are indifferent between certified anesthesioligists even in the absence of a tying arrangement—such an arrangement cannot be said to have foreclosed a choice that would have otherwise been made "on the merits." ...[47] ...

---

298 U.S. 131, 138–140 (1936). Since the District Court made no finding as to why contractual quality specifications would not protect the hospital, there is no basis for departing from our prior cases here.

43. In fact its position in this market is not dissimilar from the market share at issue in *Times–Picayune,* which the Court found insufficient as a basis for inferring market power. Moreover, in other antitrust contexts this Court has found that market shares comparable to that present here do not create an unacceptable likelihood of anticompetitive conduct. See *United States v. Connecticut National Bank,* 418 U.S. 656 (1974); *du Pont.*

44. As an economic matter, market power exists whenever prices can be raised above the levels that would be charged in a competitive market. See *Fortner II,* 429 U.S., at 620; *Fortner I,* 394 U.S., at 503–504.

47. Nor is there an indication in the record that respondents' practices have increased the social costs of its market power. Since patients' anesthesiological needs are fixed by medical judgment, respondent does not argue that the tying arrangement facilitates price

V

In order to prevail in the absence of per se liability, respondent has the burden of proving that the Roux contract violated the Sherman Act because it unreasonably restrained competition. That burden necessarily involves an inquiry into the actual effect of the exclusive contract on competition among anesthesiologists. This competition takes place in a market that has not been defined. The market is not necessarily the same as the market in which hospitals compete in offering services to patients; it may encompass competition among anesthesiologists for exclusive contracts such as the Roux contract and might be statewide or merely local.[48] There is, however, insufficient evidence in this record to provide a basis for finding that the Roux contract, as it actually operates in the market, has unreasonably restrained competition. The record sheds little light on how this arrangement affected consumer demand for separate arrangements with a specific anesthesiologist. The evidence indicates that some surgeons and patients preferred respondent's services to those of Roux, but there is no evidence that any patient who was sophisticated enough to know the difference between two anesthesiologists was not also able to go to a hospital that would provide him with the anesthesiologist of his choice.[50]

In sum, all that the record establishes is that the choice of anesthesiologists at East Jefferson has been limited to one of the four doctors who are

---

discrimination. Where variable-quantity purchasing is unavailable as a means to enable price discrimination, commentators have seen less justification for condemning tying. While tying arrangements like the one at issue here are unlikely to be used to facilitate price discrimination, they could have the similar effect of enabling hospitals "to evade price control in the tying product through clandestine transfer of the profit to the tied product...." *Fortner I,* 394 U.S., at 513 (WHITE, J., dissenting). Insurance companies are the principal source of price restraint in the hospital industry; they place some limitations on the ability of hospitals to exploit their market power. Through this arrangement, petitioners may be able to evade that restraint by obtaining a portion of the anesthesiologists' fees and therefore realize a greater return than they could in the absence of the arrangement. This could also have an adverse effect on the anesthesiology market since it is possible that only less able anesthesiologists would be willing to give up part of their fees in return for the security of an exclusive contract. However, there are no findings of either the District Court or the Court of Appeals which indicate that this type of exploitation of market power has occurred here. The Court of Appeals found only that Roux's use of nurse anesthetists increased its and the hospital's profits, but there was no finding that nurse anesthetists might not be used with equal frequency absent the exclusive contract. Indeed, the District Court found that nurse anesthetists are utilized in all hospitals in the area. Moreover, there is nothing in the record which details whether this arrangement has enhanced the value of East Jefferson's market power or harmed quality competition in the anesthesiology market.

48.   While there was some rather impressionistic testimony that the prevalence of exclusive contracts tended to discourage young doctors from entering the market, the evidence was equivocal and neither the District Court nor the Court of Appeals made any findings concerning the contract's effect on entry barriers. Respondent does not press the point before this Court. It is possible that under some circumstances an exclusive contract could raise entry barriers since anesthesiologists could not compete for the contract without raising the capital necessary to run a hospital-wide operation. However, since the hospital has provided most of the capital for the exclusive contractor in this case, that problem does not appear to be present.

50.   If, as is likely, it is the patient's doctor and not the patient who selects an anesthesiologist, the doctor can simply take the patient elsewhere if he is dissatisfied with Roux. The District Court found that most doctors in the area have staff privileges at more than one hospital.

associated with Roux and therefore have staff privileges.[51] Even if Roux did not have an exclusive contract, the range of alternatives open to the patient would be severely limited by the nature of the transaction and the hospital's unquestioned right to exercise some control over the identity and the number of doctors to whom it accords staff privileges. If respondent is admitted to the staff of East Jefferson, the range of choice will be enlarged from four to five doctors, but the most significant restraints on the patient's freedom to select a specific anesthesiologist will nevertheless remain.[52] Without a showing of actual adverse effect on competition, respondent cannot make out a case under the antitrust laws, and no such showing has been made.... [R]eversed.

■ JUSTICE BRENNAN, with Whom JUSTICE MARSHALL Joins, Concurring. As the opinion for the Court demonstrates, we have long held that tying arrangements are subject to evaluation for *per se* illegality under § 1 of the Sherman Act. Whatever merit the policy arguments against this longstanding construction of the Act might have, Congress, presumably aware of our decisions, has never changed the rule by amending the Act. In such circumstances, our practice usually has been to stand by a settled statutory interpretation and leave the task of modifying the statute's reach to Congress. I see no reason to depart from that principle in this case and therefore join the opinion and judgment of the Court.

■ JUSTICE O'CONNOR, with Whom CHIEF JUSTICE BURGER, JUSTICE POWELL, and JUSTICE REHNQUIST Join, Concurring in the Judgment.... I concur in the Court's decision to reverse but write separately to explain why I believe the Hospital–Roux contract, whether treated as effecting a tie between services provided to patients, or as an exclusive dealing arrangement between the Hospital and certain anesthesiologists, is properly analyzed under the Rule of Reason.

... The Court has on occasion applied a *per se* rule of illegality in actions alleging tying in violation of § 1 of the Sherman Act. Under the usual logic of the *per se* rule, a restraint on trade that rarely serves any purposes other than to restrain competition is illegal without proof of market power or anti-competitive effect.... Some of our earlier cases did indeed declare that tying arrangements serve "hardly any purpose beyond the suppression of competition." *Standard Stations.* However, this declaration was not taken literally even by the cases that purported to rely upon it. In practice, a tie has been illegal only if the seller is shown to have

---

51. The effect of the contract has, of course, been to remove the East Jefferson Hospital from the market open to Roux's competitors. Like any exclusive requirements contract, this contract could be unlawful if it foreclosed so much of the market from penetration by Roux's competitors as to unreasonably restrain competition in the affected market, the market for anesthesiological services. See generally *Tampa Electric*; *Standard Stations.* However, respondent has not attempted to make this showing.

52. The record simply tells us little if anything about the effect of this arrangement on price or quality of anesthesiological services. As to price, the arrangement did not lead to an increase in the price charged to the patient. As to quality, the record indicates little more than that there have never been any complaints about the quality of Roux's services, and no contention that his services are in any respect inferior to those of respondent. Moreover, the self interest of the hospital, as well as the ethical and professional norms under which it operates, presumably protect the quality of anesthesiological services.

"sufficient economic power with respect to the tying product to appreciably restrain free competition in the market for the tied product...." *Northern Pacific,....* The Court has never been willing to say of tying arrangements, as it has of price-fixing, division of markets and other agreements subject to *per se* analysis, that they are always illegal, without proof of market power or anticompetitive effect.

The *"per se"* doctrine in tying cases has thus always required an elaborate inquiry into the economic effects of the tying arrangement.[1] As a result, tying doctrine incurs the costs of a rule of reason approach without achieving its benefits: the doctrine calls for the extensive and time-consuming economic analysis characteristic of the rule of reason, but then may be interpreted to prohibit arrangements that economic analysis would show to be beneficial.... The time has therefore come to abandon the *"per se"* label and refocus the inquiry on the adverse economic effects, and the potential economic benefits, that the tie may have....

For products to be treated as distinct, the tied product must, at a minimum, be one that some consumers might wish to purchase separately *without also purchasing the tying product.* When the tied product has no use other than in conjunction with the tying product, a seller of the tying product can acquire no *additional* market power by selling the two products together.... [T]here is no sound economic reason for treating surgery and anesthesia as separate services. Patients are interested in purchasing anesthesia only in conjunction with hospital services, so the Hospital can acquire no *additional* market power by selling the two services together. Accordingly, the link between the Hospital's services and anesthesia administered by Roux will affect neither the amount of anesthesia provided nor the combined price of anesthesia and surgery for those who choose to become the Hospital's patients. In these circumstances, anesthesia and surgical services should probably not be characterized as distinct products for tying purposes.

Even if they are, the tying should not be considered a violation of § 1 of the Sherman Act because tying here cannot increase the seller's already absolute power over the volume of production of the tied product, which is an inevitable consequence of the fact that very few patients will choose to undergo surgery without receiving anesthesia. The Hospital–Roux contract therefore has little potential to harm the patients. On the other side of the balance, the District Court found, and the Court of Appeals did not dispute, that the tie-in conferred significant benefits upon the hospital and the patients that it served....

Whether or not the Hospital–Roux contract is characterized as a tie between distinct products, the contract unquestionably does constitute exclusive dealing. Exclusive dealing arrangements are independently subject to scrutiny under § 1 of the Sherman Act, and are also analyzed under the Rule of Reason. *Tampa Electric....* At issue here is an exclusive

---

1. This inquiry has been required in analyzing both the prima facie case and affirmative defenses. Most notably, *Jerrold Electronics Corp.*, upheld a requirement that buyers of television systems purchase the complete system, as well as installation and repair service, on the grounds that the tie assured that the systems would operate and thereby protected the seller's business reputation.

dealing arrangement between a firm of four anesthesiologists and one relatively small hospital.... Plainly ... the arrangement forecloses only a small fraction of the markets in which anesthesiologists may sell their services, and a still smaller fraction of the market in which hospitals may secure anesthesiological services. The contract therefore survives scrutiny under the Rule of Reason....

Questions on *Jefferson Parish*

1. Is the Court correct that it is too late to question the per se rule against tying, or is the dissent correct that it should be overruled?

a. Hasn't the Court all along been adding and subtracting elements to tying in a common law fashion? Hasn't it overruled or narrowed other per se rules? Is this tying doctrine much of a per se rule anyway?

b. Should the legislative history showing that the Congress that enacted Clayton Act § 3 was opposed to tying affect the interpretation of Sherman Act § 1 in this nongoods case? Does that legislative history dictate the result here given that the text of Clayton Act § 3 requires a showing that "the effect ... may be to substantially lessen competition"?

c. If it were a matter of first impression, should the quasi-per se rule of tying be changed to require proof that a substantial *share* of the tied market was foreclosed? Wouldn't a firm with tying market power that imposes a tie that affects a substantial dollar amount of commerce still be able to harm consumer welfare by increasing intraproduct or interproduct price discrimination or by extracting individual consumer surplus?

d. Does the hospital here have any motive to impose such anticompetitive effects?

i. Does footnote 4 indicate the hospital would profit from increased profits for its exclusive anesthesiologists?

ii. Are hospital services and anesthesiology likely to have a strong positive demand correlation and always used in fixed proportions? Or might the proportion of each vary enough to make it plausible that tying might further intraproduct price discrimination or help extract individual consumer surplus for hospital services?[90]

2. What does the Court require to show the necessary "forcing" for a tying agreement?

a. Is it anything other than market power in the tying product and the existence of a linkage to a tied product that might distort the choices a buyer otherwise might make about which tied product to buy or what price to pay for it?

b. In United Shoe Machinery v. United States, 258 U.S. 451 (1922), the Court held that it is irrelevant (a) whether the tie was frequently unenforced and (b) whether buyers would in fact have bought the defen-

---

90. Elhauge, *Tying, supra* note 36, at 443 & n.124 (noting that justices seemed to assume fixed proportions, but that this empirical premise was factually debatable).

dant's tied product without the tie. Does the Court purport to overrule these *United Shoe* holdings?

3.   Is the Court correct that tying law should not apply to . . .

a.   any tie that applies to "only a single purchaser"?

i.   Couldn't such a tie affect a substantial share of the market, such as if the market only had a few buyers? If a substantial share were foreclosed, couldn't all the anticompetitive effects of tying still occur? Would a single buyer with a dominant market share necessarily have incentives to resist an anticompetitive tie?

ii.   Couldn't such a tie easily affect a substantial volume of commerce, thus satisfying the quasi-per se rule? If it did, couldn't it easily result in increased intraproduct or interproduct price discrimination or extracting individual consumer surplus?

b.   any tie that causes the purchaser "to buy a product he would not have otherwise bought even from another seller in the tied product market"?

i.   Could such a tie cause the anticompetitive effects that depend on substantial foreclosure of rivals?

ii.   Couldn't such a tie increase intraproduct or interproduct price discrimination or extract individual consumer surplus?

4.   The Court's separate products test is whether there is "sufficient demand for the purchase of [the tied product] separate from [the tying product] to identify a distinct product market in which it is efficient to offer [the tied product] separately from [the tying product]."

a.   Does the Court directly examine the extent of such demand and existence of such efficiencies? Or does it infer them from actual market practices?

i.   If the defendant were an absolute monopolist that was able to prevent any separate sale of the tied product, would any inference from market practices be warranted? Or is it warranted here only because the market practice of unbundling existed on other competitive markets?

ii.   Does the fact that components are separately billed indicate separate provision is efficient? Is that true for factory-installed car options that are priced separately but not sold separately? Might such separate billing sometimes just indicate that customers want the product customized without necessarily indicating that it is efficient to provide the products separately?

b.   Even though the focus on the efficiency of separate provision makes sense, isn't this test a little imprecisely stated? If a firm sells its cars with carburetors installed, is that a tie of separate products because markets do support the separate sale of carburetors? Don't we also need to ask whether there is enough demand for the tying product to allow it to efficiently be sold separately? Thus, in the car example, isn't the key fact that there is no general market practice of selling cars without carburetors?

Is such an additional inquiry necessarily precluded by the Court's language that no tie can exist unless its test is met?

c. Is the Court right to reject the concurring opinion's test that products cannot be separate if the tied product cannot function without the tying product?

    i. Would such a test be consistent with precedent?

    ii. Would such a test accurately identify cases where no anticompetitive effect were possible? While such a test would identify cases where the tie could not increase the defendant's ability to exploit tied market customers not otherwise reached by its tying market power, couldn't tying in such a case still increase price discrimination, extract consumer surplus, and increase tying market power by requiring two-level entry?

    iii. Wouldn't such a test:

        (1) exclude the cases where a tie by a tying market monopolist is most likely to foreclose the entire tied market?

        (2) focus the per se rule on cases where the tie is most likely to produce insubstantial foreclosure (because the tied product has many other uses)?

5. Is the Court right that there was insufficient evidence of market power in this case?

a. Does the Court offer any argument for rejecting the Court of Appeal's definition narrowing the geographic market to the East Bank of Jefferson Parish because consumers tend to go to the closest hospital?

b. Assuming the geographic market extends to all of Jefferson Parish, why isn't 30% enough market share to indicate market power?

c. Why doesn't the fact that consumers are price insensitive because of insurance and lack of information indicate market power? What does the Court mean by saying this may indicate an economic power to raise prices above competitive levels but not the sort of market power that raises tying concerns?

6. On justifications:

a. is the Court rejecting them on principle for tying agreements or because the facts of this case do not support them?

b. the tie was said to be justified because it "ensures 24–hour anesthesiology coverage, enables flexible scheduling, and facilitates work routine, professional standards and maintenance of equipment." See n.42. Is it likely to be true that those justifications could be equally advanced through "contractual quality specifications"? Doesn't granting exclusivity to one team of anesthesiologists minimize incentive and monitoring problems that might be raised by specifications?

7. If viewed as an exclusive dealing case, all the justices agreed that the correct market to look at would be the market for selling anesthesiologist services to hospitals rather than the market for selling hospital services to consumers.

a. Why should the relevant market for the exclusive dealing claim differ from the relevant market for the tying claim? Isn't the consumer market relevant to tying only under the anticompetitive theories that focus on price discrimination or extracting individual consumer surplus, rather than those that focus on foreclosure?

b. Why did the Court think the geographic market for anesthesiologist services to hospitals was much larger than the one for hospital services? If foreclosed from working at the East Jefferson Parish hospital, is it likely that the marginal anesthesiologists would switch to working out of Jefferson Parish? More likely than that a consumer would switch to a hospital outside Jefferson Parish if unable to use another anesthesiologist for his medical procedure?

Eastman Kodak v. Image Technical Servs.

504 U.S. 451 (1992).

■ JUSTICE BLACKMUN delivered the opinion of the Court.

[Portions of the opinion relating to market and monopoly power and duties to deal were excerpted in Chapter 3.] . . .

In 1985 and 1986, Kodak implemented a policy of selling replacement parts for micrographic and copying machines only to buyers of Kodak equipment who use Kodak service or repair their own machines. . . . Customers were forced to switch to Kodak service even though they preferred ISO service. . . . In 1987, the ISO's filed the present action in the District Court, alleging, *inter alia,* that Kodak had unlawfully tied the sale of service for Kodak machines to the sale of parts, in violation of § 1 of the Sherman Act . . .

A tying arrangement is "an agreement by a party to sell one product but only on the condition that the buyer also purchases a different (or tied) product, or at least agrees that he will not purchase that product from any other supplier." *Northern Pacific.* Such an arrangement violates § 1 of the Sherman Act if the seller has "appreciable economic power" in the tying product market and if the arrangement affects a substantial volume of commerce in the tied market. . . .

For service and parts to be considered two distinct products, there must be sufficient consumer demand so that it is efficient for a firm to provide service separately from parts. *Jefferson Parish.* Evidence in the record indicates that service and parts have been sold separately in the past and still are sold separately to self-service equipment owners. Indeed, the development of the entire high-technology service industry is evidence of the efficiency of a separate market for service.

Kodak insists that because there is no demand for parts separate from service, there cannot be separate markets for service and parts. By that logic, we would be forced to conclude that there can never be separate markets, for example, for cameras and film, computers and software, or automobiles and tires. That is an assumption we are unwilling to make. "We have often found arrangements involving functionally linked products at least one of which is useless without the other to be prohibited tying devices." *Jefferson Parish*.

Kodak's assertion also appears to be incorrect as a factual matter. At least some consumers would purchase service without parts, because some service does not require parts, and some consumers, those who self-service for example, would purchase parts without service. Enough doubt is cast on Kodak's claim of a unified market that it should be resolved by the trier of fact.

Finally, respondents have presented sufficient evidence of a tie between service and parts. The record indicates that Kodak would sell parts to third parties only if they agreed not to buy service from ISO's.[8]

Having found sufficient evidence of a tying arrangement, we consider the other necessary feature of an illegal tying arrangement: appreciable economic power in the tying market.... [The Court found such market power in the portions excerpted in Chapter 3.A.]

Nor are we persuaded by Kodak's contention that it is entitled to a legal presumption on the lack of market power because ... there is a significant risk of deterring procompetitive conduct.... The alleged conduct—higher service prices and market foreclosure—is facially anticompetitive and exactly the harm that antitrust laws aim to prevent.... Kodak contends that, despite the appearance of anti-competitiveness, its behavior actually favors competition because its ability to pursue innovative marketing plans will allow it to compete more effectively in the equipment market. A pricing strategy based on lower equipment prices and higher aftermarket prices could enhance equipment sales by making it easier for the buyer to finance the initial purchase.[26] It is undisputed that competition is enhanced when a firm is able to offer various marketing options, including bundling of support and maintenance service with the sale of equipment. Nor do such actions run afoul of the antitrust laws.[27] But the procompetitive effect of the specific conduct challenged here, eliminating all consumer parts and service options, is far less clear.[28]

We need not decide whether Kodak's behavior has any procompetitive effects and, if so, whether they outweigh the anticompetitive effects. We note only that Kodak's service and parts policy is simply not one that appears always or almost always to enhance competition, and therefore to

---

8. In a footnote, Kodak contends that this practice is only a unilateral refusal to deal, which does not violate the antitrust laws. Assuming, *arguendo,* that Kodak's refusal to sell parts to any company providing service can be characterized as a unilateral refusal to deal, its alleged sale of parts to third parties on condition that they buy service from Kodak is not.

26. It bears repeating that in this case Kodak has never claimed that it is in fact pursuing such a pricing strategy.

27. See *Jefferson Parish* ("Buyers often find package sales attractive; a seller's decision to offer such packages can merely be an attempt to compete effectively—conduct that is entirely consistent with the Sherman Act"). See also Yates & DiResta, Software Support and Hardware Maintenance Practices: Tying Considerations, The Computer Lawyer, Vol. 8, No. 6, p. 17 (1991) (describing various service and parts policies that enhance quality and sales but do not violate the antitrust laws).

28. Two of the largest consumers of service and parts contend that they are worse off when the equipment manufacturer also controls service and parts.

warrant a legal presumption without any evidence of its actual economic impact. In this case, when we weigh the risk of deterring procompetitive behavior by proceeding to trial against the risk that illegal behavior will go unpunished, the balance tips against summary judgment.

For the foregoing reasons, we ... affirm the denial of summary judgment on respondents' § 1 claim.[29]

■ JUSTICE SCALIA, with Whom JUSTICE O'CONNOR and JUSTICE THOMAS Join, dissenting.... *Per se* rules of antitrust illegality are reserved for those situations where logic and experience show that the risk of injury to competition from the defendant's behavior is so pronounced that it is needless and wasteful to conduct the usual judicial inquiry into the balance between the behavior's procompetitive benefits and its anticompetitive costs.... The *per se* rule against tying is just such a rule: Where the conditions precedent to application of the rule are met, *i.e.,* where the tying arrangement is backed up by the defendant's market power in the "tying" product, the arrangement is adjudged in violation of § 1 of the Sherman Act, without *any* inquiry into the practice's actual effect on competition and consumer welfare. But see *Jerrold* (accepting affirmative defense to *per se* tying allegation).

Despite intense criticism of the tying doctrine in academic circles, the stated rationale for our *per se* rule has varied little over the years. When

---

29. The dissent urges a radical departure in this Court's antitrust law. It argues that because Kodak has only an "inherent" monopoly in parts for its equipment, the antitrust laws do not apply to its efforts to expand that power into other markets. The dissent's proposal to grant *per se* immunity to manufacturers competing in the service market would exempt a vast and growing sector of the economy from antitrust laws. Leaving aside the question whether the Court has the authority to make such a policy decision, there is no support for it in our jurisprudence or the evidence in this case.

Even assuming, despite the absence of any proof from the dissent, that all manufacturers possess some inherent market power in the parts market, it is not clear why that should immunize them from the antitrust laws in another market. The Court has held many times that power gained through some natural and legal advantage such as a patent, copyright, or business acumen can give rise to liability if "a seller exploits his dominant position in one market to expand his empire into the next." *Times–Picayune.* Moreover, on the occasions when the Court has considered tying in derivative aftermarkets by manufacturers, it has not adopted any exception to the usual antitrust analysis, treating derivative aftermarkets as it has every other separate market. See *International Salt*; *IBM v. United States*, 298 U.S. 131 (1936); *United Shoe Machinery Corp. v. United States*, 258 U.S. 451 (1922)....

Nor does the record in this case support the dissent's proposed exemption for aftermarkets. The dissent urges its exemption because the tie here "does not permit the manufacturer to project power over a class of consumers distinct from that which it is already able to exploit (and fully) without the inconvenience of the tie." Beyond the dissent's obvious difficulty in explaining why Kodak would adopt this expensive tying policy if it could achieve the same profits more conveniently through some other means, respondents offer an alternative theory, supported by the record, that suggests Kodak *is* able to exploit some customers who in the absence of the tie would be protected from increases in parts prices by knowledgeable customers.

At bottom, whatever the ultimate merits of the dissent's theory, at this point it is mere conjecture. Neither Kodak nor the dissent have provided any evidence refuting respondents' theory of forced unwanted purchases at higher prices and price discrimination. While it may be, as the dissent predicts, that the equipment market will prevent any harms to consumers in the aftermarkets, the dissent never makes plain why the Court should accept that theory on faith rather than requiring the usual evidence needed to win a summary judgment motion.

the defendant has genuine "market power" in the tying product—the power to raise price by reducing output—the tie potentially enables him to extend that power into a second distinct market, enhancing barriers to entry in each. In addition:

> "[T]ying arrangements may be used to evade price control in the tying product through clandestine transfer of the profit to the tied product; they may be used as a counting device to effect price discrimination; and they may be used to force a full line of products on the customer so as to extract more easily from him a monopoly return on one unique product in the line." *Fortner I* (WHITE, J., dissenting. . . .)

[W]ith respect to tying, we have recognized that bundling arrangements not coerced by the heavy hand of market power can serve the procompetitive functions of facilitating new entry into certain markets, see, *e.g.,* *Brown Shoe Co. v. United States,* 370 U.S. 294, 330 (1962), permitting "clandestine price cutting in products which otherwise would have no price competition at all because of fear of retaliation from the few other producers dealing in the market," *Fortner I* (WHITE, J., dissenting), assuring quality control, see, *e.g.,* *Standard Stations,* and, where "the tied and tying products are functionally related, . . . reduc[ing] costs through economies of joint production and distribution." *Fortner I* (WHITE, J., dissenting). "Accordingly, we have [only] condemned tying arrangements [under the *per se* rule] when the seller has some special ability—usually called 'market power'—to force a purchaser to do something that he would not do in a competitive market." *Jefferson Parish.* . . .

It is quite simply anomalous that a manufacturer functioning in a competitive equipment market should be exempt from the *per se* rule when it bundles equipment with parts and service, but not when it bundles parts with service. . . . Under the Court's analysis, the *per se* rule may now be applied to single-brand ties effected by the most insignificant players in fully competitive interbrand markets, as long as the arrangement forecloses aftermarket competitors from more than a *de minimis* amount of business. This seems to me quite wrong. A tying arrangement "forced" through the exercise of such power no more implicates the leveraging and price discrimination concerns behind the *per se* tying prohibition than does a tie of the foremarket brand to its aftermarket derivatives, which . . . would not be subject to *per se* condemnation [because of the lack of interbrand market power in equipment].[2] . . .

---

2. Even *with* interbrand power, I may observe, it is unlikely that Kodak could have incrementally exploited its position through the tie of parts to service alleged here. Most of the "service" at issue is inherently associated with the parts, *i.e.,* that service involved in incorporating the parts into Kodak equipment, and the two items tend to be demanded by customers in fixed proportions (one part with one unit of service necessary to install the part). When that situation obtains, " 'no revenue can be derived from setting a higher price for the tied product which could not have been made by setting the optimum price for the tying product.' " P. Areeda & L. Kaplow, Antitrust Analysis ¶ 426(a), p. 706 (4th ed. 1988) (quoting Bowman, Tying Arrangements and the Leverage Problem, 67 Yale L.J. 19 (1957)). These observations strongly suggest that Kodak parts and the service involved in installing them should not be treated as distinct products for antitrust tying purposes.

The Court ... says that there are "information costs"—the costs and inconvenience to the consumer of acquiring and processing life-cycle pricing data for Kodak machines—that "could create a less responsive connection between service and parts prices and equipment sales." But this truism about the functioning of markets for sophisticated equipment cannot create "market power" of concern to the antitrust laws where otherwise there is none. "Information costs," or, more accurately, gaps in the availability and quality of consumer information, pervade real-world markets; and because consumers generally make do with "rough cut" judgments about price in such circumstances, in virtually any market there are zones within which otherwise competitive suppliers may overprice their products without losing appreciable market share. We have never suggested that the principal players in a market with such commonplace informational deficiencies (and, thus, bands of apparent consumer pricing indifference) exercise market power in any sense relevant to the antitrust laws. "While [such] factors may generate 'market power' in some abstract sense, they do not generate the kind of market power that justifies condemnation of tying." *Jefferson Parish.*

... [W]hen a manufacturer uses its control over single-branded parts to acquire influence in single-branded service, the monopoly "leverage" is almost invariably of no practical consequence, because of perfect identity between the consumers in each of the subject aftermarkets (those who need replacement parts for Kodak equipment and those who need servicing of Kodak equipment). When that condition exists, the tie does not permit the manufacturer to project power over a class of consumers distinct from that which it is already able to exploit (and fully) without the inconvenience of the tie. Cf., *e.g.,* Bowman, Tying Arrangements and the Leverage Problem, 67 Yale L.J. 19, 21–27 (1957).

We have never before accepted the thesis the Court today embraces: that a seller's inherent control over the unique parts for its own brand amounts to "market power" of a character sufficient to permit invocation of the *per se* rule against tying. As the Court observes, we have applied the *per se* rule to manufacturer ties of *foremarket* equipment to aftermarket derivatives—but only when the manufacturer's monopoly power in the equipment, coupled with the use of derivative sales as "counting devices" to measure the intensity of customer equipment usage, enabled the manufacturer to engage in price discrimination, and thereby more fully exploit its interbrand power. See *International Salt*; *IBM v. United States,* 298 U.S. 131 (1936); *United Shoe Machinery Corp. v. United States,* 258 U.S. 451 (1922). That sort of enduring opportunity to engage in price discrimination is unavailable to a manufacturer—like Kodak—that lacks power at the interbrand level. A tie between two aftermarket derivatives does next to nothing to improve a competitive manufacturer's ability to extract monopoly rents from its consumers.[3] ...

---

3. The Court insists that the record in this case suggests otherwise, *i.e.,* that a tie between parts and service somehow *does* enable Kodak to increase overall monopoly profits. Although the Court does not identify the record evidence on which it relies, the suggestion, apparently, is that such a tie facilitates price discrimination between sophisticated, "high-volume" users of Kodak equipment and their unsophisticated counterparts. The sophisticated

We have recognized in closely related contexts that the deterrent effect of *inter*brand competition on the exploitation of *intra*brand market power should make courts exceedingly reluctant to apply rules of *per se* illegality to intrabrand restraints. For instance, we have refused to apply a rule of *per se* illegality to vertical nonprice restraints "because of their potential for a simultaneous reduction of intrabrand competition and stimulation of interbrand competition," *GTE Sylvania*, the latter of which we described as "the primary concern of antitrust law,".... In the absence of interbrand power, a manufacturer's bundling of aftermarket products may serve a multitude of legitimate purposes: It may facilitate manufacturer efforts to ensure that the equipment remains operable and thus protect the seller's business reputation, see *Jerrold*; it may create the conditions for implicit consumer financing of the acquisition cost of the tying equipment through supracompetitively-priced aftermarket purchases, see, *e.g.*, A. Oxenfeldt, Industrial Pricing and Market Practices 378 (1951); and it may, through the resultant manufacturer control of aftermarket activity, "yield valuable information about component or design weaknesses that will materially contribute to product improvement," 3 Areeda & Turner ¶ 733c, at 258–259; see also *id.*, ¶ 829d, at 331–332. Because the interbrand market will generally punish intrabrand restraints that consumers do not find in their interest, we should not—under the guise of a *per se* rule—condemn such

---

users (who, the Court presumes, invariably self-service their equipment) are permitted to buy Kodak parts without also purchasing supracompetitively priced Kodak service, while the unsophisticated are—through the imposition of the tie—compelled to buy both.

While superficially appealing, at bottom this explanation lacks coherence. Whether they self-service their equipment or not, rational foremarket consumers (those consumers who are not yet "locked in" to Kodak hardware) will be driven to Kodak's competitors if the price of Kodak equipment, together with the expected cost of aftermarket support, exceeds competitive levels. This will be true no matter how Kodak distributes the total system price among equipment, parts, and service. Thus, as to these consumers, Kodak's lack of interbrand power wholly prevents it from employing a tie between parts and service as a vehicle for price discrimination. Nor does a tie between parts and service offer Kodak incremental exploitative power over those consumers—sophisticated or not—who have the supposed misfortune of being "locked in" to Kodak equipment. If Kodak desired to exploit its circumstantial power over this wretched class by pressing them up to the point where the cost to each consumer of switching equipment brands barely exceeded the cost of retaining Kodak equipment and remaining subject to Kodak's abusive practices, it could plainly do so without the inconvenience of a tie, through supracompetitive parts pricing alone. Since the locked-in *sophisticated* parts purchaser is as helpless as the locked-in *unsophisticated* one, I see nothing to be gained by price discrimination in favor of the former. If such price discrimination were desired, however, it would not have to be accomplished indirectly, through a tie of parts to service. Section 2(a) of the Robinson–Patman Act would prevent giving lower parts prices to the sophisticated customers only "where the effect of such discrimination may be substantially to lessen competition or tend to create a monopoly in any line of commerce, or to injure, destroy, or prevent competition with any person who either grants or knowingly receives the benefit of such discrimination, or with customers of either of them...." *Ibid.*; see, *e.g.*, *Falls City Industries, Inc. v. Vanco Beverage, Inc.*, 460 U.S. 428, 434–435 (1983). That prohibited effect often occurs when price-discriminated goods are sold for resale (*i.e.*, to purchasers who are necessarily in competition with one another). *E.g.*, *FTC v. Morton Salt Co.*, 334 U.S. 37, 47 (1948); see P. Areeda & L. Kaplow, Antitrust Analysis ¶ 600, p. 923 (1988) ("Secondary-line injury arises [under the Robinson–Patman Act] when a powerful firm buying supplies at favorable prices thereby gains a decisive advantage over its competitors that are forced to pay higher prices for their supplies"). It rarely occurs where, as would be the case here, the price-discriminated goods are sold to various businesses for consumption.

potentially procompetitive arrangements simply because of the antitrust defendant's inherent power over the unique parts for its own brand.

I would instead evaluate the aftermarket tie alleged in this case under the rule of reason, where the tie's *actual* anticompetitive effect in the tied product market, together with its potential economic benefits, can be fully captured in the analysis, Disposition of this case does not require such an examination, however, as respondents apparently waived any rule-of-reason claim they may have had in the District Court. I would thus reverse the Ninth Circuit's judgment on the tying claim outright. . . .

Questions on *Kodak*

1. Does this case effectively end the possibility that the quasi-per se rule against tying might be overruled? Do even the dissenters sign on to it and the basic rationales for not requiring evidence of substantial foreclosure in the tied market?

2. The Court adopts the same separate products test as *Jefferson Parish*, again inferring the efficiency of separate provision from actual market practices, and again rejecting the alternative test that there must be some demand to use the tied product without the tying product.

a. Suppose the dissent were right that service is not only useless without parts, but also that service and parts are used only in fixed proportions. Is the dissent right that those factors would eliminate all anticompetitive effects? Those two factors would eliminate anticompetitive concerns that any market profits in parts might be increased by intraproduct or interproduct price discrimination among those subject to the tie or by extracting individual consumer surplus.[91] Those two factors would also eliminate the possibility that foreclosing a substantial share of the tied service market could create tied market power that the defendant could exploit against tied product purchases that otherwise would not have been subject to its tying market power in parts.[92] Those two factors thus (if true) knock out four of the five possible anticompetitive effects from tying.

However, those two factors would not eliminate the fifth possibility: that tied market foreclosure might enhance tying market power. Suppose, though, we add a third premise, which the dissent probably assumed: that Kodak had patents over parts for its own machines, which presumably is how Kodak prevented others from making those parts. If so, the patents probably would bar rivals from entering the parts market even without any tie, so that the tie was unlikely to reduce rival entry into the parts market, and thus unlikely to increase tying market power.[93] True, even without affecting parts entry, foreclosing rival service providers might enhance tying market power if service were a partial substitute for parts. But partial substitutability would be inconsistent with the Kodak dissenters' factual premise that parts and services are used in fixed ratios: partial substitutes by definition can be used in varying ratios.

---

91. Elhauge, *supra* note, at 444–445.

92. *Id.* at 445.

93. *Id.* at 445.

Moreover, *Kodak* had the unusual feature that one of the alleged anticompetitive effects flowed not from the tie itself, but from alleged discrimination between buyers who were and were not subject to the tie. A fixed ratio and lack of separate utility failed to eliminate the possibility that the fact that the tie was *not* used with self-service buyers created harmful price discrimination between self-service buyers and service-purchasing buyers.[94]

b. Is the dissent right about its factual assumptions that the tie here involved fixed ratios and no separate utility? As the Court pointed out, service is sometimes purchased without parts, and those who self-service buy parts without buying service. Thus, the ratio of usage varies. This variability reintroduces all the possible anticompetitive effects.[95] It also seems quite likely that service is a partial substitute for parts. After all, firms that use more service to maintain their machines tend to have them break down less often, and thus need fewer parts. Further, firms can sometimes use additional service to repair existing parts without replacing them. This partial substitutability means that foreclosing service could increase tying power over parts.

3. Is the dissent right that, even if Kodak technically has economic market power in the sense of an ability to price above cost, it does not have the sort of market power that implicates the tying doctrine? How are the information costs here different from those in *Jefferson Parish*?

a. Is one difference that here the information costs are used to rebut the claim that the market power in parts will be constrained by the lack of market power in equipment, whereas in *Jefferson Parish* the claim was that information costs were the source of market power itself?

b. Is another difference that in *Jefferson Parish* the lack of information was alleged to operate when decisions to buy the tied product were made, and thus meant the tie could not distort buyer choices on the merits about from whom to purchase the tied product, whereas here the information costs were claimed to operate only at the equipment purchase stage, and thus were not inconsistent with the proposition that without the tie buyers could have made informed choices to buy service from someone else?

4. Does the Court's opinion suggest that procompetitive justifications are admissible notwithstanding the quasi-per se rule against tying? Does it seem plausible here that the tie efficiently made it easier for buyers to finance equipment purchases? Does that theory have to depend on the premise that the tie between parts and service permitted higher aftermarket prices?

Illinois Tool Works Inc. v. Independent Ink, Inc.

547 U.S. 28 (2006).

■ JUSTICE STEVENS delivered the opinion of the Court.

In *Jefferson Parish*, we repeated the well-settled proposition that "if the Government has granted the seller a patent or similar monopoly over a

---

94. *Id.* at 446.

95. *Id.* at 445.

product, it is fair to presume that the inability to buy the product elsewhere gives the seller market power." This presumption of market power, applicable in the antitrust context when a seller conditions its sale of a patented product (the "tying" product) on the purchase of a second product (the "tied" product), has its foundation in the judicially created patent misuse doctrine. In 1988, Congress substantially undermined that foundation, amending the Patent Act to eliminate the market power presumption in patent misuse cases. See 35 U.S.C. § 271(d). The question presented to us today is whether the presumption of market power in a patented product should survive as a matter of antitrust law despite its demise in patent law. We conclude that the mere fact that a tying product is patented does not support such a presumption. . . .

American courts first encountered tying arrangements in the course of patent infringement litigation. . . . In the years since . . . , four different rules of law have supported challenges to tying arrangements. They have been condemned as improper extensions of the patent monopoly under the patent misuse doctrine, as unfair methods of competition under § 5 of the Federal Trade Commission Act, as contracts tending to create a monopoly under § 3 of the Clayton Act, and as contracts in restraint of trade under § 1 of the Sherman Act. . . .

Over the years, however, this Court's strong disapproval of tying arrangements has substantially diminished. Rather than relying on assumptions, in its more recent opinions the Court has required a showing of market power in the tying product. Our early opinions consistently assumed that "[t]ying arrangements serve hardly any purpose beyond the suppression of competition." *Standard Stations*. In 1962, in *Loew's*, the Court relied on this assumption despite evidence of significant competition in the market for the tying product. . . .

The assumption that "[t]ying arrangements serve hardly any purpose beyond the suppression of competition," rejected in *Fortner II*, has not been endorsed in any opinion since. Instead, it was again rejected just seven years later in *Jefferson Parish*, where, as in *Fortner II*, we unanimously reversed a Court of Appeals judgment holding that an alleged tying arrangement constituted a per se violation of § 1 of the Sherman Act. Like the product at issue in the Fortner cases, the tying product in Jefferson Parish-hospital services—was unpatented, and our holding again rested on the conclusion that the plaintiff had failed to prove sufficient power in the tying product market to restrain competition in the market for the tied product-services of anesthesiologists. . . .

. . . [T]he presumption that a patent confers market power arose outside the antitrust context as part of the patent misuse doctrine . . . , [which provides] a patent misuse defense to infringement claims when a patentee uses its patent "as the effective means of restraining competition with its sale of an unpatented article." . . . The presumption that a patent confers market power migrated from patent law to antitrust law in *International Salt*. . . .

Although the patent misuse doctrine and our antitrust jurisprudence became intertwined in *International Salt*, subsequent events initiated their untwining.... Three years before we decided *International Salt*, this Court had expanded the scope of the patent misuse doctrine to include not only supplies or materials used by a patented device, but also tying arrangements involving a combination patent and "unpatented material or [a] device [that] is itself an integral part of the structure embodying the patent." *Mercoid*, 320 U.S. at 665; *see also* Dawson Chemical Co. v. Rohm & Haas Co., 448 U.S. 176, 188–198 (1980) (describing in detail *Mercoid* and the cases leading up to it). In reaching this conclusion, the Court explained that it could see "no difference in principle" between cases involving elements essential to the inventive character of the patent and elements peripheral to it; both, in the Court's view, were attempts to "expan[d] the patent beyond the legitimate scope of its monopoly."

Shortly thereafter, Congress codified the patent laws for the first time. At least partly in response to our *Mercoid* decision, Congress included a provision in its codification that excluded some conduct, such as a tying arrangement involving the sale of a patented product tied to an "essential" or "nonstaple" product that has no use except as part of the patented product or method, from the scope of the patent misuse doctrine. § 271(d); see also *Dawson*, 448 U.S., at 214. Thus, at the same time that our antitrust jurisprudence continued to rely on the assumption that "tying arrangements generally serve no legitimate business purpose," *Fortner I*, Congress began chipping away at the assumption in the patent misuse context from whence it came.

It is Congress' most recent narrowing of the patent misuse defense, however, that is directly relevant to this case. Four years after our decision in *Jefferson Parish* repeated the patent-equals-market-power presumption, Congress amended the Patent Code to eliminate that presumption in the patent misuse context. The relevant provision reads:

> "(d) No patent owner otherwise entitled to relief for infringement or contributory infringement of a patent shall be denied relief or deemed guilty of misuse or illegal extension of the patent right by reason of his having done one or more of the following: ... (5) conditioned the license of any rights to the patent or the sale of the patented product on the acquisition of a license to rights in another patent or purchase of a separate product, *unless, in view of the circumstances, the patent owner has market power in the relevant market for the patent or patented product on which the license or sale is conditioned.*" 35 U.S.C. § 271(d)(5) (emphasis added).

The italicized clause makes it clear that Congress did not intend the mere existence of a patent to constitute the requisite "market power." Indeed, fairly read, it provides that without proof that [the patent holder] had market power in the relevant market, its conduct at issue in this case was neither "misuse" nor an "illegal extension of the patent right."

While the 1988 amendment does not expressly refer to the antitrust laws, it certainly invites a reappraisal of the per se rule announced in *International Salt*. A rule denying a patentee the right to enjoin an infringer is significantly less severe than a rule that makes the conduct at issue a federal crime punishable by up to 10 years in prison. See 15 U.S.C. § 1. It would be absurd to assume that Congress intended to provide that the use of a patent that merited punishment as a felony would not constitute "misuse." Moreover, given the fact that the patent misuse doctrine provided the basis for the market power presumption, it would be anomalous to preserve the presumption in antitrust after Congress has eliminated its foundation. Cf. 10 P. AREEDA, H. HOVENKAMP, & E. ELHAUGE, ANTITRUST LAW ¶ 1737c (2d ed.2004) (hereinafter Areeda).

After considering the congressional judgment reflected in the 1988 amendment, we conclude that tying arrangements involving patented products should be evaluated under the standards applied in cases like *Fortner II* and *Jefferson Parish* rather than under the per se rule applied in [old patent misuse cases]. While some such arrangements are still unlawful, such as those that are the product of a true monopoly or a marketwide conspiracy, see, e.g., United States v. Paramount Pictures, Inc., 334 U.S. 131, 145–146 (1948), that conclusion must be supported by proof of power in the relevant market rather than by a mere presumption thereof....

Rather than arguing that we should retain the rule of per se illegality, respondent contends that we should endorse a rebuttable presumption that patentees possess market power when they condition the purchase of the patented product on an agreement to buy unpatented goods exclusively from the patentee. Respondent recognizes that a large number of valid patents have little, if any, commercial significance, but submits that those that are used to impose tying arrangements on unwilling purchasers likely do exert significant market power. Hence, in respondent's view, the presumption would have no impact on patents of only slight value and would be justified, subject to being rebutted by evidence offered by the patentee, in cases in which the patent has sufficient value to enable the patentee to insist on acceptance of the tie.

Respondent also offers a narrower alternative, suggesting that we differentiate between tying arrangements involving the simultaneous purchase of two products that are arguably two components of a single product—such as the provision of surgical services and anesthesiology in the same operation, *Jefferson Parish*, or the licensing of one copyrighted film on condition that the licensee take a package of several films in the same transaction, *Loew's*—and a tying arrangement involving the purchase of unpatented goods over a period of time, a so-called "requirements tie." According to respondent, we should recognize a presumption of market power when faced with the latter type of arrangements because they provide a means for charging large volume purchasers a higher royalty for use of the patent than small purchasers must pay, a form of discrimination that "is strong evidence of market power."

The opinion that imported the "patent equals market power" presumption into our antitrust jurisprudence, however, provides no support for respondent's proposed alternative. In *International Salt*, it was the existence of the patent on the tying product, rather than the use of a requirements tie, that led the Court to presume market power. Moreover, the requirements tie in that case did not involve any price discrimination between large volume and small volume purchasers or evidence of noncompetitive pricing. Instead, the leases at issue provided that if any competitor offered salt, the tied product, at a lower price, "the lessee should be free to buy in the open market, unless appellant would furnish the salt at an equal price."

. . . [T]he vast majority of academic literature recognizes that a patent does not necessarily confer market power. Similarly, while price discrimination may provide evidence of market power, particularly if buttressed by evidence that the patentee has charged an above-market price for the tied package, see, e.g., 10 Areeda ¶ 1769c, it is generally recognized that it also occurs in fully competitive markets, see, e.g., Baumol & Swanson, The New Economy and Ubiquitous Competitive Price Discrimination: Identifying Defensible Criteria of Market Power, 70 Antitrust L.J. 661, 666 (2003); 9 Areeda ¶ 1711; Landes & Posner 374–375. We are not persuaded that the combination of these two factors should give rise to a presumption of market power when neither is sufficient to do so standing alone. Rather, the lesson to be learned from *International Salt* and the academic commentary is the same: Many tying arrangements, even those involving patents and requirements ties, are fully consistent with a free, competitive market. For this reason, we reject both respondent's proposed rebuttable presumption and their narrower alternative.

It is no doubt the virtual consensus among economists that has persuaded the enforcement agencies to reject the position that the Government took when it supported the per se rule that the Court adopted in the 1940's. In antitrust guidelines issued jointly by the Department of Justice and the Federal Trade Commission in 1995, the enforcement agencies stated that in the exercise of their prosecutorial discretion they "will not presume that a patent, copyright, or trade secret necessarily confers market power upon its owner." U.S. Dept. of Justice and FTC, Antitrust Guidelines for the Licensing of Intellectual Property § 2.2 (Apr. 6, 1995). While that choice is not binding on the Court, it would be unusual for the Judiciary to replace the normal rule of lenity that is applied in criminal cases with a rule of severity for a special category of antitrust cases.

Congress, the antitrust enforcement agencies, and most economists have all reached the conclusion that a patent does not necessarily confer market power upon the patentee. Today, we reach the same conclusion, and therefore hold that, in all cases involving a tying arrangement, the plaintiff must prove that the defendant has market power in the tying product. . . .

Questions on *Illinois Tool Works*

1. Is it so clear that, if market power has to be proven in a patent misuse tying case, it should also have to be proven in an antitrust tying case? A finding of patent misuse means that others can infringe the patent, which is tantamount to invalidating it, and thus can be a business "death penalty." A finding of antitrust tying generally just leads to damages and injunctions, and although the Court raises the specter of criminal antitrust liability, no one has been criminally prosecuted for tying for a long time (if ever) and the DOJ, which has the sole power to criminally prosecute antitrust violations, itself indicates that it requires market power even when the tying product is patented.

2. Did the presumption that a patent confers market power ever make sense?

a. Although patents confer a legal monopoly over an idea, does that necessarily mean that the idea enjoys economic market power over competing ideas? Any more than a legal monopoly over the use of a particular plant necessarily confers economic market power when other plants can provide the same functionality? *See* Chapter 2.G.

b. Even if it is wrong to assume patentees always have market power, are they likely enough to do so that it makes sense to presume they do and allow the defendant to rebut by showing their patent confers no market power? Who is likely to have more access to evidence about the market power enjoyed by the defendant's patents, the plaintiff or the defendant?

3. Does a presumption of market power at least make sense in a case where . . .

a. the patent is tied to another product, thus indicating enough power to impose the tie?

i. Doesn't presuming power from the tie in this way only make sense if there are no procompetitive efficiencies to tying? If there are such efficiencies, then couldn't a seller in a highly competitive market succeed through such efficient tying?

ii. If one could presume power from the tie, would there be any reason to limit this doctrine to cases where the tying product was patented?

b. the patent is tied to a requirements contract for some consumable in a way that suggests price discrimination?

i. Doesn't price discrimination always indicate some economic market power? Does it necessarily indicate market power in the antitrust sense given that it often exists on markets that antitrust would regard as competitive?

ii. Does usage of a requirements contract necessarily mean the tie is being used as a vehicle for price discrimination? Couldn't there be some other reason, like quality control given difficulties of specifying and monitoring quality, or metering in order to shift financing and risk-bearing costs to the party that can best minimize them?

iii. If a presumption of market power in such a case did make sense, wouldn't it make equal sense in *any* case where the sale of one product is tied to a requirements contract on a consumable, whether or not the tying product was patented?

4. Where market power is shown, does this case indicate that procompetitive justifications are admissible? Or does it indicate only that procompetitive justifications are sufficiently likely that the law should require demonstrable proof of market power?

United States v. Microsoft

253 F.3d 34 (D.C. Cir. 2001) (en banc).

■ Opinion for the Court filed PER CURIAM. . . .

The District Court determined that Microsoft had maintained a monopoly in the market for Intel-compatible PC operating systems in violation of § 2 . . . and illegally tied two purportedly separate products, Windows and Internet Explorer ("IE"), in violation of § 1. . . .

II. MONOPOLIZATION

[Portions addressing monopoly power and framing the inquiry into exclusionary conduct are excerpted above.] . . .

1. Licenses Issued to Original Equipment Manufacturers [OEMs]

The District Court condemned a number of provisions in Microsoft's agreements licensing Windows to OEMs, because it found that Microsoft's imposition of those provisions (like many of Microsoft's other actions at issue in this case) serves to reduce usage share of Netscape's browser and, hence, protect Microsoft's operating system monopoly. . . . Browser usage share is important because . . . a browser (or any middleware product, for that matter) must have a critical mass of users in order to attract software developers to write applications relying upon the APIs it exposes, and away from the APIs exposed by Windows. Applications written to a particular browser's APIs, however, would run on any computer with that browser, regardless of the underlying operating system. . . . If a consumer could have access to the applications he desired—regardless of the operating system he uses—simply by installing a particular browser on his computer, then he would no longer feel compelled to select Windows in order to have access to those applications; he could select an operating system other than Windows based solely upon its quality and price. In other words, the market for operating systems would be competitive. Therefore, Microsoft's efforts to gain market share in one market (browsers) served to meet the threat to Microsoft's monopoly in another market (operating systems) by keeping rival browsers from gaining the critical mass of users necessary to attract developer attention away from Windows as the platform for software development. . . .

a. *Anticompetitive effect of the license restrictions* . . .

The District Court concluded that the first license restriction—the prohibition upon the removal of desktop icons, folders, and Start menu entries—thwarts the distribution of a rival browser by preventing OEMs from removing visible means of user access to IE. The OEMs cannot practically install a second browser in addition to IE, the court found, in part because . . . a certain number of novice computer users, seeing two browser icons, will wonder which to use when and will call the OEM's support line. Support calls are extremely expensive and, in the highly competitive original equipment market, firms have a strong incentive to minimize costs. . . .

[T]he OEM channel is one of the two primary channels for distribution of browsers. By preventing OEMs from removing visible means of user access to IE, the license restriction prevents many OEMs from pre-installing a rival browser and, therefore, protects Microsoft's monopoly from the competition that middleware might otherwise present. Therefore, we conclude that the license restriction at issue is anticompetitive. . . .

The second license provision at issue prohibits OEMs from modifying the initial boot sequence—the process that occurs the first time a consumer turns on the computer. . . . Microsoft's prohibition on any alteration of the boot sequence . . . prevents OEMs from using that process to promote the services of IAPs, many of which—at least at the time Microsoft imposed the restriction—used Navigator rather than IE in their internet access software. . . . Because this prohibition has a substantial effect in protecting Microsoft's market power, and does so through a means other than competition on the merits, it is anticompetitive. . . .

Finally, . . . Microsoft prohibits OEMs from causing any user interface other than the Windows desktop to launch automatically, from adding icons or folders different in size or shape from those supplied by Microsoft, and from using the "Active Desktop" feature to promote third-party brands. These restrictions impose significant costs upon the OEMs; prior to Microsoft's prohibiting the practice, many OEMs would change the appearance of the desktop in ways they found beneficial.

The dissatisfaction of the OEM customers does not, of course, mean the restrictions are anticompetitive. The anticompetitive effect of the license restrictions is, as Microsoft itself recognizes, that OEMs are not able to promote rival browsers, which keeps developers focused upon the APIs in Windows. This kind of promotion is not a zero-sum game; but for the restrictions in their licenses to use Windows, OEMs could promote multiple IAPs and browsers. By preventing the OEMs from doing so, this type of license restriction, like the first two restrictions, is anticompetitive: Microsoft reduced rival browsers' usage share not by improving its own product but, rather, by preventing OEMs from taking actions that could increase rivals' share of usage.

b. *Microsoft's justifications for the license restrictions* . . .

Microsoft's primary copyright argument borders upon the frivolous. The company claims an absolute and unfettered right to use its intellectual property as it wishes: "[I]f intellectual property rights have been lawfully acquired," it says, then "their subsequent exercise cannot give rise to antitrust liability." That is no more correct than the proposition that use of one's personal property, such as a baseball bat, cannot give rise to tort liability. As the Federal Circuit succinctly stated: "Intellectual property rights do not confer a privilege to violate the antitrust laws." *In re Indep. Serv. Orgs. Antitrust Litig.,* 203 F.3d 1322, 1325 (Fed.Cir.2000).

Although Microsoft never overtly retreats from its bold and incorrect position on the law, it also makes two arguments to the effect that it is not exercising its copyright in an unreasonable manner, despite the anticompetitive consequences of the license restrictions discussed above. In the first variation upon its unqualified copyright defense, Microsoft cites two cases indicating that a copyright holder may limit a licensee's ability to engage in significant and deleterious alterations of a copyrighted work. . . . The only license restriction Microsoft seriously defends as necessary to prevent a "substantial alteration" of its copyrighted work is the prohibition on OEMs automatically launching a substitute user interface upon completion of the boot process. We agree that a shell that automatically prevents the Windows desktop from ever being seen by the user is a drastic alteration of Microsoft's copyrighted work, and outweighs the marginal anticompetitive effect of prohibiting the OEMs from substituting a different interface automatically upon completion of the initial boot process. We therefore hold that this particular restriction is not an exclusionary practice that violates § 2 of the Sherman Act.

In a second variation upon its copyright defense, Microsoft argues that the license restrictions merely prevent OEMs from taking actions that would reduce substantially the value of Microsoft's copyrighted work: that is, Microsoft claims each license restriction in question is necessary to prevent OEMs from so altering Windows as to undermine "the principal value of Windows as a stable and consistent platform that supports a broad range of applications and that is familiar to users." Microsoft, however, never substantiates this claim, and, because an OEM's altering the appearance of the desktop or promoting programs in the boot sequence does not affect the code already in the product, the practice does not self-evidently affect either the "stability" or the "consistency" of the platform.... Therefore, we conclude Microsoft has not shown that the OEMs' liberality reduces the value of Windows except in the sense that their promotion of rival browsers undermines Microsoft's monopoly—and that is not a permissible justification for the license restrictions.

Apart from copyright, Microsoft raises one other defense of the OEM license agreements: It argues that, despite the restrictions in the OEM license, Netscape is not completely blocked from distributing its product. That claim is insufficient to shield Microsoft from liability for those restrictions because, although Microsoft did not bar its rivals from all means of distribution, it did bar them from the cost-efficient ones.

In sum, we hold that with the exception of the one restriction prohibiting automatically launched alternative interfaces, all the OEM license restrictions at issue represent uses of Microsoft's market power to protect its monopoly, unredeemed by any legitimate justification. The restrictions therefore violate § 2 of the Sherman Act.

2. Integration of IE and Windows ...

a. *Anticompetitive effect of integration*

As a general rule, courts are properly very skeptical about claims that competition has been harmed by a dominant firm's product design changes. *See, e.g., Foremost Pro Color, Inc. v. Eastman Kodak Co.,* 703 F.2d 534, 544–45 (9th Cir.1983). In a competitive market, firms routinely innovate in the hope of appealing to consumers, sometimes in the process making their products incompatible with those of rivals; the imposition of liability when a monopolist does the same thing will inevitably deter a certain amount of innovation. This is all the more true in a market, such as this one, in which the product itself is rapidly changing. Judicial deference to product innovation, however, does not mean that a monopolist's product design decisions are per se lawful. *See Foremost Pro Color,* 703 F.2d at 545; *see also Cal. Computer Prods.,* 613 F.2d at 739, 744; *In re IBM Peripheral EDP Devices Antitrust Litig.,* 481 F.Supp. 965, 1007–08 (N.D.Cal.1979).

The District Court first condemned as anticompetitive Microsoft's decision to exclude IE from the "Add/Remove Programs" utility in Windows 98.... This change reduces the usage share of rival browsers not by making Microsoft's own browser more attractive to consumers but, rather, by discouraging OEMs from distributing rival products. Because Microsoft's conduct, through something other than competition on the merits, has the effect of significantly reducing usage of rivals' products and hence protecting its own operating system monopoly, it is anticompetitive ...

Second, the District Court found that Microsoft designed Windows 98 [to sometimes override] ... the user's choice of a browser other than IE as his or her default browser.... Because the override reduces rivals' usage share and protects Microsoft's monopoly, it too is anticompetitive.

Finally, the District Court condemned Microsoft's decision to bind IE to Windows 98 "by placing code specific to Web browsing in the same files as code that provided operating system functions." Putting code supplying browsing functionality into a file with code supplying operating system functionality "ensure[s] that the deletion of any file containing browsing-specific routines would also delete vital operating system routines and thus cripple Windows...." As noted above, preventing an OEM from removing IE deters it from installing a second browser because doing so increases the OEM's product testing and support costs; by contrast, had OEMs been able to remove IE, they might have chosen to pre-install Navigator alone.... [S]uch commingling has an anticompetitive effect ...

b. *Microsoft's justifications for integration*

Microsoft proffers no justification for two of the three challenged actions that it took in integrating IE into Windows—excluding IE from the Add/Remove Programs utility and commingling browser and operating system code.... Accordingly, we hold that Microsoft's exclusion of IE from the Add/Remove Programs utility and its commingling of browser and operating system code constitute exclusionary conduct, in violation of § 2.

... Microsoft claims that it was necessary to design Windows to override the user's preferences when he or she invokes one of "a few" out "of the nearly 30 means of accessing the Internet." According to Microsoft:

> The Windows 98 Help system and Windows Update feature depend on ActiveX controls not supported by Navigator, and the now-discontinued Channel Bar utilized Microsoft's Channel Definition Format, which Navigator also did not support. Lastly, Windows 98 does not invoke Navigator if a user accesses the Internet through "My Computer" or "Windows Explorer" because doing so would defeat one of the purposes of those features—enabling users to move seamlessly from local storage devices to the Web *in the same browsing window.*

The ... plaintiffs offer no rebuttal whatsoever. Accordingly, Microsoft may not be held liable for this aspect of its product design....

IV. TYING

Microsoft also contests the District Court's determination of liability under § 1 of the Sherman Act. The District Court concluded that Microsoft's contractual and technological bundling of the IE web browser (the "tied" product) with its Windows operating system ("OS") (the "tying" product) resulted in a tying arrangement that was per se unlawful. . . .

There is no doubt that "[i]t is far too late in the history of our antitrust jurisprudence to question the proposition that *certain* tying arrangements pose an unacceptable risk of stifling competition and therefore are unreasonable '*per se.*' " *Jefferson Parish* (emphasis added). But there are strong reasons to doubt that the integration of additional software functionality into an OS falls among these arrangements. Applying per se analysis to such an amalgamation creates undue risks of error and of deterring welfare-enhancing innovation.

The Supreme Court has warned that " '[i]t is only after considerable experience with certain business relationships that courts classify them as *per se* violations. . . .' " *BMI*. Yet the sort of tying arrangement attacked here is unlike any the Supreme Court has considered. The early Supreme Court cases on tying dealt with arrangements whereby the sale or lease of a patented product was conditioned on the purchase of certain unpatented products from the patentee. Later Supreme Court tying cases did not involve market power derived from patents, but continued to involve contractual ties.

In none of these cases was the tied good physically and technologically integrated with the tying good. Nor did the defendants ever argue that their tie improved the value of the tying product to users *and* to makers of complementary goods. In those cases where the defendant claimed that use of the tied good made the tying good more valuable to users, the Court ruled that the same result could be achieved via quality standards for substitutes of the tied good. Here Microsoft argues that IE and Windows are an integrated physical product and that the bundling of IE APIs with Windows makes the latter a better applications platform for third-party software. It is unclear how the benefits from IE APIs could be achieved by quality standards for different browser manufacturers. We do not pass judgment on Microsoft's claims regarding the benefits from integration of its APIs. We merely note that these and other novel, purported efficiencies suggest that judicial "experience" provides little basis for believing that, "because of their pernicious effect on competition and lack of *any* redeeming virtue," a software firm's decisions to sell multiple functionalities as a package should be "conclusively presumed to be unreasonable and therefore illegal without elaborate inquiry as to the precise harm they have caused or the business excuse for their use." *N. Pac. Ry.*, 356 U.S. at 5 (emphasis added).

Nor have we found much insight into software integration among the decisions of lower federal courts. . . . While the paucity of cases examining software bundling suggests a high risk that per se analysis may produce inaccurate results, the nature of the platform software market affirmatively suggests that per se rules might stunt valuable innovation. We have in mind two reasons.

First, . . . the separate-products test is a poor proxy for net efficiency from newly integrated products. Under per se analysis the first firm to merge previously distinct functionalities (*e.g.,* the inclusion of starter motors in automobiles) or to eliminate entirely the need for a second function (*e.g.,* the invention of the stain-resistant carpet) risks being condemned as having tied two separate products because at the moment of integration there will appear to be a robust "distinct" market for the tied product. *See* 10 AREEDA, ELHAUGE & HOVENKAMP, ANTITRUST LAW ¶ 1746, at 224. Rule of reason analysis, however, affords the first mover an opportunity to demonstrate that an efficiency gain from its "tie" adequately offsets any distortion of consumer choice.

The failure of the separate-products test to screen out certain cases of productive integration is particularly troubling in platform software markets such as that in which the defendant competes. Not only is integration common in such markets, but it is common among firms without market power. We have already reviewed evidence that nearly all competitive OS vendors also bundle browsers. Moreover, plaintiffs do not dispute that OS vendors can and do incorporate basic internet plumbing and other useful functionality into their OSs. Firms without market power have no incentive to package different pieces of software together unless there are efficiency gains from doing so. The ubiquity of bundling in competitive platform software markets should give courts reason to pause before condemning such behavior in less competitive markets.

Second, because of the pervasively innovative character of platform software markets, tying in such markets may produce efficiencies that courts have not previously encountered and thus the Supreme Court had not factored into the per se rule as originally conceived. For example, the bundling of a browser with OSs enables an independent software developer to count on the presence of the browser's APIs, if any, on consumers' machines and thus to omit them from its own package. . . . Of course, these arguments may not justify Microsoft's decision to bundle APIs in this case, particularly because Microsoft did not merely bundle with Windows the APIs from IE, but an entire browser application (sometimes even without APIs). . . . Furthermore, the interest in efficient API diffusion obviously supplies a far stronger justification for simple price-bundling than for Microsoft's contractual or technological bars to subsequent *removal* of functionality. But our qualms about redefining the boundaries of a defendant's product and the possibility of consumer gains from simplifying the work of applications developers makes us question any hard and fast approach to tying in OS software markets.

There may also be a number of efficiencies that, although very real, have been ignored in the calculations underlying the adoption of a per se rule for tying. We fear that these efficiencies are common in technologically dynamic markets where product development is especially unlikely to follow an easily foreseen linear pattern. . . .

These arguments all point to one conclusion: we cannot comfortably say that bundling in platform software markets has so little "redeeming virtue," and that there would be so "very little loss to society" from its ban, that "an inquiry into its costs in the individual case [can be] considered [ ] unnecessary." We ... [thus] vacate the District Court's finding of per se tying liability under Sherman Act § 1. We remand the case for evaluation of Microsoft's tying arrangements under the rule of reason....

Our judgment regarding the comparative merits of the per se rule and the rule of reason is confined to the tying arrangement before us, where the tying product is software whose major purpose is to serve as a platform for third-party applications and the tied product is complementary software functionality....

[T]he fact that we have already considered some of the behavior plaintiffs allege to constitute tying violations in the monopoly maintenance section does not resolve the § 1 inquiry.... In order for the District Court to conclude these practices also constitute § 1 tying violations, plaintiffs must demonstrate that their benefits—if any—are outweighed by the harms in the *tied product* market....

Questions on *U.S. Microsoft* Case Holdings on Tying

1. Should any of the conduct be deemed a tie or foreclosing given that OEMs could install a second browser as long as they were willing to incur customer technical support calls?

2. Is the court correct that being barred from the most efficient means of distribution suffices to create an anticompetitive effect even if other means of distribution remain open so that rivals are not completely foreclosed from reaching any users?

3. Of the various theories for why tying might be anticompetitive, which seems most applicable here?

4. Should the lack of any articulated legitimate justifications for most of the restraints have led the court to simply condemn them as naked restraints, thus avoiding any elaborate inquiry into their anticompetitive effects?

a. Why can't Microsoft justify all its restrictions as preventing alterations to its copyrighted software?

b. What is wrong with Microsoft's claim that OEM alterations might produce quality problems?

5. Is the court's decision that the tie here should be subject to rule of reason review consistent with Supreme Court precedent?

a. Does this case involve a different sort of agreement than the court had previously considered, or just a different industry?

   i. Don't many other industries also involve innovation and histories of integrating elements into products over time?

   ii. Even if the only difference from prior cases is the industry at issue here, does the great plasticity of software—which makes it easy to bundle or unbundle countless functionalities—suggest that a per se tying rule might be inappropriate?

b. Does this seem like a weaker case for per se scrutiny than *Kodak*?

   c. Is the court right that a separate products test based on market practices is a poor screen when the claim is that innovation produced a new desirable way of integrating what used to be separate products? Why couldn't the court just call it a tie and deem that an admissible justification that could be a defense?

   6. If the various procompetitive justifications the court cites in the tying section are valid, such as the notion that integration increases the value of third-party software developers that can rely on all computers having the same browser APIs, why aren't they equally valid for the monopolization inquiry?

   7. Is the Court right that the tying inquiry is different under § 1 because it must focus on whether procompetitive justifications offset anti-competitive effects in the tied market? Couldn't a § 1 claim also be made on the theory that tying creates anticompetitive effects in the tying market? Would that add anything to the monopolization claim?

EU Guidelines on Vertical Restraints

O.J. 2010, C 130/1.

   Tying refers to situations where customers that purchase one product (the tying product) are required also to purchase another distinct product (the tied product) from the same supplier or someone designated by the latter. Tying may constitute an abuse within the meaning of Article 102. Tying may also constitute a vertical restraint falling under Article 101 where it results in a single branding type of obligation for the tied product. Only the latter situation is dealt with in these Guidelines.

   Whether products will be considered as distinct depends on customer demand. Two products are distinct where, in the absence of the tying, a substantial number of customers would purchase or would have purchased the tying product without also buying the tied product from the same supplier, thereby allowing stand-alone production for both the tying and the tied product. Evidence that two products are distinct could include direct evidence that, when given a choice, customers purchase the tying and the tied products separately from different sources of supply, or indirect evidence, such as the presence on the market of undertakings specialised in the manufacture or sale of the tied product without the tying product, or evidence indicating that undertakings with little market power, particularly on competitive markets, tend not to tie or not to bundle such products. For instance, since customers want to buy shoes with laces and it is not practicable for distributors to lace new shoes with the laces of their choice, it has become commercial usage for shoe manufacturers to supply shoes with laces. Therefore, the sale of shoes with laces is not a tying practice.

   Tying may lead to anticompetitive foreclosure effects on the tied market, the tying market, or both at the same time. The foreclosure effect depends on the tied percentage of total sales on the market of the tied product. On the question of what can be considered appreciable foreclosure under Article 101(1), the analysis for single branding can be applied. Tying means that there is at least a form of quantity-forcing on the buyer in respect of the tied product. Where in addition a non-compete obligation is agreed in respect of the tied product, this increases the possible foreclosure effect on the market of the tied product. The tying may lead to less competition for customers interested in buying the tied product, but not the tying product. If there is not a sufficient number of customers that will buy the tied product alone to sustain competitors of the supplier on the tied market, the tying can lead to those customers facing higher prices. If the tied product is an important complementary product for customers of the tying product, a reduction of alternative suppliers of the tied product and hence a reduced availability of that product can make entry onto the tying market alone more difficult.

Tying may also directly lead to prices that are above the competitive level, especially in three situations. Firstly, if the tying and the tied product can be used in variable proportions as inputs to a production process, customers may react to an increase in price for the tying product by increasing their demand for the tied product while decreasing their demand for the tying product. By tying the two products the supplier may seek to avoid this substitution and as a result be able to raise its prices. Secondly, when the tying allows price discrimination according to the use the customer makes of the tying product, for example the tying of ink cartridges to the sale of photocopying machines (metering). Thirdly, when in the case of long-term contracts or in the case of after-markets with original equipment with a long replacement time, it becomes difficult for the customers to calculate the consequences of the tying.

Tying is exempted under the Block Exemption Regulation when the market share of the supplier, on both the market of the tied product and the market of the tying product, and the market share of the buyer, on the relevant upstream markets, do not exceed 30%. It may be combined with other vertical restraints, which are not hardcore restrictions under that Regulation, such as non-compete obligations or quantity forcing in respect of the tying product, or exclusive sourcing. The remainder of this section provides guidance for the assessment of tying in individual cases above the market share threshold.

The market position of the supplier on the market of the tying product is obviously of central importance to assess possible anti-competitive effects. In general, this type of agreement is imposed by the supplier. The importance of the supplier on the market of the tying product is the main reason why a buyer may find it difficult to refuse a tying obligation.

The market position of the supplier's competitors on the market of the tying product is important in assessing the supplier's market power. As long as its competitors are sufficiently numerous and strong, no anti-competitive effects can be expected, as buyers have sufficient alternatives to purchase the tying product without the tied product, unless other suppliers are applying similar tying. In addition, entry barriers on the market of the tying product are relevant to establish the market position of the supplier. When tying is combined with a non-compete obligation in respect of the tying product, this considerably strengthens the position of the supplier.

Buying power is relevant, as important buyers will not easily be forced to accept tying without obtaining at least part of the possible efficiencies. Tying not based on efficiency is therefore mainly a risk where buyers do not have significant buying power.

Where appreciable anti-competitive effects are established, the question whether the conditions of Article 101(3) are fulfilled arises. Tying obligations may help to produce efficiencies arising from joint production or joint distribution. Where the tied product is not produced by the supplier, an efficiency may also arise from the supplier buying large quantities of the tied product. For tying to fulfil the conditions of Article 101(3), it must, however, be shown that at least part of these cost reductions are passed on to the consumer, which is normally not the case when the retailer is able to obtain, on a regular basis, supplies of the same or equivalent products on the same or better conditions than those offered by the supplier which applies the tying practice. Another efficiency may exist where tying helps to ensure a certain uniformity and quality standardisation. However, it needs to be demonstrated that the positive effects cannot be realised equally efficiently by requiring the buyer to use or resell products satisfying minimum quality standards, without requiring the buyer to purchase these from the supplier or someone designated by the latter. The requirements concerning minimum quality standards would not normally fall within the scope of Article 101(1). Where the supplier of the tying product imposes on the buyer the suppliers from which the buyer must purchase the tied product, for instance because the formulation of minimum quality standards is not possible, this may also fall outside the scope of Article 101(1), especially where the supplier of the tying product does not derive a direct (financial) benefit from designating the suppliers of the tied product.

Introduction to EU Cases on Tying as an Abuse of Dominance

As noted above, the ECJ case-law on tying has involved firms holding a dominant position on a relevant market. They thus triggered the application of Article 102. These cases are discussed hereafter.

Commission Decision 88/138/EEC, Eurofix–Bauco v. Hilti

O.J. 1988, L65/19.

[Hilti was the largest European producer of nail guns, nails and cartridge strips. Eurofix and Bauco complained that Hilti was excluding them from the market in nails compatible with Hilti products by refusing to sell Hilti-cartridges without Hilti nails to distributors, and by cutting off the supply of Hilti-cartridges to rival nail makers.] Further, ... Hilti has abused its dominant position in the EEC in the relevant market for nail guns and most importantly the markets for Hilti-compatible cartridge strips and nails. It has done this principally through its attempts to prevent or limit the entry of independent producers of Hilti-compatible consumables into these markets. Hilti's attempts to block or limit such entry went beyond the means legitimately available to a dominant company. The different aspects of Hilti's commercial behaviour were designed to this effect and were aimed at preventing Hilti-compatible cartridge strips from being freely available. Without such availability of Hilti-compatible cartridge strips, for which in the EEC Hilti until recently enjoyed protection afforded by patents, independent producers of Hilti-compatible nails have been severely restricted in their penetration of the market. Furthermore, customers have been obliged to rely on Hilti for both cartridges and nails for their Hilti nail guns. By limiting the effective competition from new entrants Hilti has been able to preserve its dominant position. The ability to carry out its illegal policies stems from its power on the markets for Hilti-compatible cartridge strips and nail guns (where its market position is strongest and the barriers to entry are highest) and aims at reinforcing its dominance on the Hilti-compatible nail market (where it is potentially more vulnerable to new competition). The individual aspects of this overall policy of hindering new entrants in the market for Hilti-compatible nails by preventing the free availability of cartridge strips are set out below....

(i) *Tying, reduced discounts and other discriminatory policies on cartridge-only orders*. Making the sale of patented cartridge strips conditional upon taking a corresponding complement of nails constitutes an abuse of a dominant position, as do reduced discounts and other discriminatory policies ... on cartridge-only orders. These policies leave the consumer with no choice over the source of his nails and as such abusively exploit him. In addition, these policies all have the object or effect of excluding independent nail makers who may threaten the dominant position Hilti holds. The tying and reduction of discounts were not isolated incidents but a generally applied policy.

(ii) *Inducing independent distributors not to fulfil certain orders for export*. Because of these policies the independent nail makers, if they were to sell their nails, had to provide their own supplies of Hilti-compatible cartridge strips. Both complainants attempted to import Hilti cartridge strips from the Netherlands. Therefore, in an attempt to reinforce its tying policy in the UK where it was under attack from independent nail makers, Hilti, once it realised their source, induced its Dutch distributor to stop the supply of cartridge strips. This action foreclosed that source of supply to customers and further had the effect of partitioning the common market....

(iii) *Refusal to fulfil the complete orders for cartridge strips made by established customers or dealers who might resell them*. Hilti further refused supplies of cartridges to its long-standing customers because it objected to their possible resale to independent nail makers. This veto over the rights of a purchaser to dispose of products constitutes an abuse of a dominant position, all the more so when it is designed to prevent the free availability of Hilti-compatible cartridge strips, with the aim of blocking entry into the market for Hilti-compatible nails.

(iv) *Frustrating or delaying legitimately available licences of right under Hilti's patents*. In view of the above policies and refusal to supply by Hilti, nail makers were obliged to obtain non-Hilti cartridge strips which necessitated a patent licence. In the UK this was available as a licence of right. Despite its legal availability Hilti still tried to prevent any such licence coming into existence by the size of the royalty demanded.... Hilti's behaviour in deliberately demanding an unreasonably high level of royalty with the sole objective of blocking the grant of a licence constitutes an abuse of a dominant position....

(v) *Refusal without objective reason to honour guarantees.* Hilti's policy of attempting to block the sale of independents' nails took another course in that it was made known that guarantees on nail guns would not be honoured if non-Hilti nails were used....

Objective justification

... Hilti maintains that nails made by certain independent nail makers, and in particular those made by the complainants Eurofix and Bauco are substandard in that they are not fit for the purpose for which they are intended. Furthermore it is alleged that they are dangerous in that they are not capable of penetrating certain base materials sufficiently such that reliable and secure fixings cannot be made in these base materials....

Hilti itself accepts that the above concerns relating to the safety, reliability and operation of its [nail guns] are not sufficient to justify the commercial behaviour which is the object of this Decision since it does not constitute the least restrictive action necessary to attain the objective of safety. Hilti considers its proposed distribution system is the least restrictive way this can be done. It does however maintain that all its actions have been motivated by a desire to ensure the safe and reliable operation of its products, and not by any commercial advantage it may have derived from such action....

As regards Hilti's claim that its behaviour even if not the least restrictive possible to attain its objectives was motivated purely by safety considerations, the Commission would make the following points:

... Hilti did not take any action, legal or otherwise, that would normally be expected of a company that was purely motivated by considerations of safety and reliability. Confronted with the use of what it alleges are the substandard and potentially dangerous nails of the complainants:

—Hilti rarely put into writing to its customers the alleged dangers of, and unfitness for use of, the complainants' nails....

—Hilti never wrote to or communicated with the complainants to express its concern about the reliability, fitness, safety or otherwise of their nails.

—As far as the Commission is aware Hilti never took the normal course of action of reporting the complainants to the United Kingdom Trading Standards Department for what on the basis of its own arguments would constitute false advertising or misrepresentation in the United Kingdom....

—As far as the Commission is aware Hilti never took the appropriate step of making complaints to national or Government bodies in the United Kingdom such as the Health and Safety Executive which could have acted under the Health and Safety at Work Act 1974 or the

Trading Standards Department which could have acted under the Consumer Safety Act 1978. . . .

The Commission considers that in view of the above the behaviour by Hilti cannot be described as being motivated solely by a concern over the safety and reliability of its [nail guns] and use of substandard consumables. Hilti's actions described as abusive in this Decision reflect a commercial interest in stopping the penetration of the market of non-Hilti consumables since the main profit from [nail guns] originates from the sale of consumables, not from the sale of nail guns. This is without prejudice to the possibility that Hilti had a genuine concern about safety and reliability. However, Hilti did not take the actions that would be normally expected had this been its only concern. A company faced with safety worries may not resort to behaviour which is an abuse under Article [102]; it should rather explore the other legitimate and normally more efficient ways of dealing with its concerns. . . .

Hilti purports to have decided unilaterally that the independents' nails were unsafe or unfit for use. On this basis Hilti attempts to justify the policies which are described in this decision and the general thrust of which have the object or effect of preventing the entry into the market of the independent nail producers. Hilti, a dominant company, therefore attempted to impose its own allegedly justified safety requirements without regard to the safety and product liability requirements that already exist in the different Member States. . . .

In view of those apparently adequate safety controls or standards existing in the EEC the Commission does not consider Hilti's argument concerning safety to be an objective justification for the behaviour which is the object of the present proceedings. . . .

[Hilti appealed the Commission's decision finding that it abused its dominant position before the GC for its tying practices. The GC confirmed the decision of the Commission.]

Commission Decision 92/163/EEC, Tetra Pak II

O.J. 1992, L 72/1.

Tetra Pak allegedly tied the sales of carton packaging materials to the sale of its filling machines. The obligation that only Tetra Pak cartons be used on machines and the obligation to obtain supplies exclusively [from Tetra Pak] are complementary and make the system airtight: not only is it not possible for the purchaser of a machine to use packaging other than that bearing the Tetra Pak mark, but moreover he may not obtain supplies of packaging from any source other than Tetra Pak itself (or a company designated by Tetra Pak). . . .

Such a system of tied sales, which again limits outlets and makes contracts subject to acceptance of conditions (the purchase of cartons) which have no connection with their purpose (the sale of machines), constitutes a serious infringement of Article [102] and a practice which has been denounced on many occasions by the Commission and the Court of Justice.

... Tetra Pak's position may be summarized more or less as follows.

Tetra Pak does not consider itself to be a supplier of packaging equipment and containers but rather of "integrated distribution systems for liquid and semi-liquid foods intended for human consumption". These systems comprise know-how, equipment, containers, servicing and training.

In addition to the economies of scale and cost savings at the level of raw materials and distribution which may result from stable relations with customers over a long period, the exclusive purchasing obligation is, in Tetra Pak's view, justified for technical reasons, considerations of product liability and health, and by the need to protect its reputation.

At a technical level, Tetra Pak considers that the high technology of its machines demands the use of cartons specifically designed for them, which in turn requires a thorough knowledge of the machines and their peculiarities, of the products to be packaged, and of the possible interactions between those machines and products. The obligation to obtain supplies exclusively from Tetra Pak, by means of the link it establishes between the equipment and type of packaging, leads to synergistic effects at the level of research and development and after-sales service. There is therefore a "natural link" between the machine and the type of packaging it uses, which ... excludes—according to Tetra Pak—the possibility of an infringement of Article [102 TFEU].

Tetra Pak takes the view that the system of tied sales also benefits the user if products are defective, since it enables Tetra Pak to offer the consumer a comprehensive performance guarantee and eliminates the difficult question of dividing responsibility between the supplier of machines and the supplier of containers (single source of responsibilities).

On the question of health, Tetra Pak considers that, in view of the specific interactions between the machines and the packaging intended for them, only the use of Tetra Pak cartons can prevent the emergence of public health problems which might prove extremely detrimental to the consumer, above all in the aseptic sector.

Finally, Tetra Pak believes that it has a legitimate interest, for the defence of its reputation and in view of the technical and public-health aspects referred to above, in seeking to ensure that only packaging coming from its own sources is used on its machines.

Tetra Pak also refers to "commercial usage" and the absence of effective competition for the cartons which may be used on Tetra Pak machines.

It is a priori very difficult to conceive of the existence between products having totally distinct physical characteristics and resulting from completely different production processes of "natural links" which ... rule out any possibility of an infringement of Article [102]. There therefore remains only the hypothesis of functional, reciprocal and exclusive links relating to the use of machines and cartons in the packaging process. The Commission wonders why, if the claim that only Tetra Pak cartons may, for technical reasons, be used on Tetra Pak machines is true, this group sees the need to make such use the subject of a contractual obligation. If there is genuinely no technical alternative, such an obligation is unnecessary. However, if such an alternative does exist, the choice should be left to the user, and any obligation to purchase solely from an undertaking which is in a position such as that occupied by Tetra Pak should be prohibited.

Moreover, there is a degree of competition in the non-aseptic market, where there are, and always have been, manufacturers or distributors of cartons usable on different makes of machine; this fact alone contradicts Tetra Pak's thesis and invalidates its arguments. If such competition has not existed for cartons used on Tetra Pak's machines (aseptic or non-aseptic), the reason is to be found precisely in the tied-sales system and the patent policy pursued by Tetra Pak which, by denying all prospects of an outlet, discourage any potential producer or distributor.

But, by its very conduct, Tetra Pak itself contradicts its assertion that the technical and other reasons invoked imply that only cartons manufactured by the manufacturer of a given machine may be correctly used on that machine. This is because Tetra Pak sells, and indeed imposes on its clients, its own cartons for machines of other manufacturers ... which have perhaps been adapted slightly but were certainly not designed for Tetra Pak cartons. Furthermore, since Tetra Pak is not—as it has itself stated—an agent for these manufacturers but merely an occasional intermediary, it can only have a passive and superficial knowledge of this equipment, which moreover rules out in this case the synergistic effects referred to above.

In any case, if the "synergies" which, according to Tetra Pak, result at an economic and technical level from the combination within one and the same undertaking of equipment and container sales operations are of benefit solely to the producer, and if real advantages exist for the user in an integrated supply system, they will be apparent without it being necessary to make recourse to contractual obligations: it is up to the user, and not the producer, to compare such advantages with those offered by open systems, and to make his choice freely.

Moreover, the Commission is well aware of the technical and, perhaps, public-health problems which might result from packaging not meeting the particular specifications of Tetra Pak machines and the related problems of determining reciprocal responsibilities and protecting the good name of the undertakings in question. However, these are problems which arise with any production process which uses equipment and accessories of various origins, and which have repercussions for public health whenever products intended for human consumption or, more generally, products which may directly or indirectly affect public health are involved. For such problems, which are commonplace and familiar to users, there are adequate technical solutions (publication of standards and specifications to be complied with) and a legal framework (general legal liability) intended specifically to solve the problems which arise from the failure on the part of the parties concerned to implement these technical solutions. The proportionality rule excludes the use of restrictive practices where these are not indispensable. This rule is all the more vital in the case in hand since the restrictions of competition involved are particularly serious and are brought to bear on markets on which—even without them—competition is already extremely limited.

Finally, it is difficult to invoke commercial usage when, in the non-aseptic sector, this tied products clause is not the general rule and when, in the aseptic sector, there are only two producers. It is also odd to mention the absence of effective competition for cartons usable on Tetra Pak machines when operating a system of tied sales which specifically prevents the emergence of any competition.

Tetra Pak's particular attachment to the tied products clauses is due to the fact that, more than any other conventional tied sales practice, this system has proved to be one of the essential components of the group's trading policy. As we have seen, it enables competition to be limited to the sale (or leasing) of machines since such operations guarantee, through the application of [the tying obligations], that Tetra Pak can sell cartons to the user during the entire life of machines or the term of the lease relating to them. Tetra Pak thereby limits competition to the area which is most favourable to it, i.e. that of machines, where the technological entry barriers are very high, especially on the aseptic market, where it enjoys a virtual monopoly. By the same token, these same contractual clauses prevent the emergence of any competition in the cartons sector, where the technological barriers are much lower.

Because of the income from the sale of cartons ... which this system guarantees, it also makes it financially easier, as we have seen, to place Tetra Pak machines because it enables the group to sell at a loss if necessary, even to the extent of placing them at the disposal of dairies free of charge in some cases. It thus allows a trading policy to be pursued which no longer respects the economic reality of prices. . . .

[This decision was confirmed by the General Court. Tetra Pak appealed the General Court judgment before the ECJ, which in turn confirmed the decision of the General Court.]

Note and Questions on *Hilti* and *Tetra Pak II*

Hilti and *Tetra Pak II* suggest that the following elements must be met for a tying practice to fall under the prohibition contained in Article 102: (i) the tying and tied goods are two separate products; (ii) the firm is dominant in the tying product market; (iii) the firm does not allow customers to obtain the tying product without the tied product; (iv) the tie forecloses competition to some extent; and (v) the tie is not the least restrictive way to further a procompetitive justification that would offset the anticompetitive effects. This resembles the elements under Article 101 or U.S. tying law other than the heightened market power requirement.

1. Which criteria were used by the Commission in *Tetra Pak II* to demonstrate that the filling machines and the packaging cartons were separate products? Is such a conclusion justified by the fact that: (a) the machines and cartons are physically different; (b) Tetra Pak thought a tying agreement was necessary to guarantee its cartons would be used on its machines; (c) in other markets, buyers get machines and cartons from different suppliers?

2. Although *Hilti* and *Tetra Pak II* require dominance in the tying product market, they do not require evidence of dominance in the tied market. Should they have?

3. Did defendants Hilti and Tetra Pak allow their customers to obtain the tying product without buying the tied product? Would it make any difference if customers were allowed to buy the tying and the tied products separately, but were given financial incentives to buy the two together?

4. Do *Hilti* and *Tetra Pak II* require any showing that the foreclosure produced by the tie was substantial or produced anticompetitive effects? Did the cases assume the foreclosure was substantial and anticompetitive or implicitly hold that no evidence on those points was required?

5. Do *Hilti* and *Tetra Pak II* allow the undertakings in question to show that tying is justified by an objective reason? What would constitute an objective reason? Why weren't the offered justifications successful?

Case T–201/04, Microsoft v. Commission, [2004] ECR II 4463

C—The bundling of Windows Media Player with the Windows client PC operating system

In this second issue, Microsoft relies on two pleas: first, infringement of Article [102 TFEU] and, second, breach of the principle of proportionality. The first plea concerns the Commission's finding that Microsoft's conduct in making the availability of the Windows client PC operating system conditional on the simultaneous acquisition of Windows Media Player constitutes an abusive tied sale (Article 2(b) of the contested decision). The second plea relates to the remedy prescribed in Article 6 of the contested decision. . . .

2. First plea, alleging infringement of Article [102 TFEU] . . .

a) The necessary conditions for a finding of abusive tying . . .

Findings of the Court

The arguments which Microsoft puts forward in relation to the first three parts of the first plea . . . will be examined in conjunction with the four other conditions which must be satisfied to substantiate the finding of abusive tying. In carrying out that examination, the Court will proceed as follows. First, it will examine the condition relating to the existence of two separate products in the light of the arguments advanced by Microsoft on the second and third parts of the plea. Second, it will examine the condition to the effect that the conclusion of contracts is made subject to supplementary obligations, in the light of the arguments which Microsoft puts forward in support of the third part of the plea. Third, the Court will analyse the condition relating to the restriction of competition on the market in the light of the submissions made by Microsoft in connection with the first part of the plea. Fourth, it will examine the objective justifications on which the applicant relies, taking into account the arguments which it puts forward in connection with the second part of the plea.

b) The existence of two separate products

. . . Microsoft contends, in substance, that media functionality is not a separate product from the Windows client PC operating system but forms an integral part of that system. As a result, what is at issue is a single product, namely the Windows client PC operating system, which is constantly evolving. In Microsoft's submission, customers expect that any client PC operating system will have the functionalities which they perceive as essential, including audio and video functionalities, and that those functionalities will be constantly updated. . . .

First of all, it must be observed that, as the Commission correctly states at recital 803 to the contested decision, the distinctness of products for the purpose of an analysis under Article [102 TFEU] has to be assessed by reference to customer demand. Furthermore, Microsoft clearly shares that opinion (see paragraph 890 above).

The Commission was also correct to state, at the same recital, that in the absence of independent demand for the allegedly tied product, there can be no question of separate products and no abusive tying.

Microsoft's argument that the Commission thus applied the wrong test and that it ought in reality to have ascertained whether what was alleged to be the tying product was regularly offered without the tied product or whether customers "want[ed] Windows without media functionality" cannot be accepted.

In the first place, the Commission's argument finds support in the case-law. . . .

In the second place, as the Commission correctly observes in its pleadings, Microsoft's argument, based on the concept that there is no demand for a Windows client PC operating system without a streaming media player, amounts to contending that complementary products cannot constitute separate products for the purposes of Article [102 TFEU], which is contrary to the Community case-law on bundling. To take Hilti, for example, it may be assumed that there was no demand for a nail gun magazine without nails, since a magazine without nails is useless. However, that did not prevent the Community Courts from concluding that those two products belonged to separate markets.

In the case of complementary products, such as client PC operating systems and application software, it is quite possible that customers will wish to obtain the products together, but from different sources. For example, the fact that most client PC users want their client PC operating system to come with word-processing software does not transform those separate products into a single product for the purposes of Article [102 TFEU]. . . .

In the third place, and in any event, Microsoft's argument cannot succeed because, as the Commission observes at recital 807 to the contested decision, there exists a demand for client PC operating systems without streaming media players, for example by companies afraid that their staff might use them for non-work-related purposes. That fact is not disputed by Microsoft.

Next, the Court finds that a series of factors based on the nature and technical features of the products concerned, the facts observed on the market, the history of the development of the products concerned and also Microsoft's commercial practice demonstrate the existence of separate consumer demand for streaming media players....

In the fourth place, Windows Media Player can be downloaded, independently of the Windows client PC operating system, from Microsoft's Internet site. Likewise, Microsoft releases upgrades of Windows Media Player, independently of releases or upgrades of its Windows client PC operating system.

In the fifth place, Microsoft engages in promotions specifically dedicated to Windows Media Player ...

In the sixth place, as the Commission pertinently observes at recital 813 to the contested decision, Microsoft offers SDK licences which differ according to whether they relate to the Windows client PC operating system or to Windows Media technologies. There is thus a specific SDK licence for Windows Media Player.

Last, and in the seventh place, in spite of the bundling applied by Microsoft, a not insignificant number of customers continue to acquire media players from Microsoft's competitors, separately from their client PC operating system, which shows that they regard the two products as separate.

The foregoing facts demonstrate to the requisite legal standard that the Commission was correct to conclude that client PC operating systems and streaming media players constituted two separate products for the purposes of Article [102 TFEU]....

c) Consumers are unable to choose to obtain the tying product without the
     tied product

... Microsoft contends, in essence, that the fact that it integrated Windows Media Player in the Windows client PC operating system does not entail any coercion or supplementary obligation within the meaning of Article [102(d) TFEU]. In support of its argument, it emphasises, in the first place, that customers pay nothing extra for the media functionality of Windows; in the second place, that they are not obliged to use that functionality; and, in the third place, that they are not prevented from installing and using competitors' media players.

The Court observes that it cannot be disputed that, in consequence of the impugned conduct, consumers are unable to acquire the Windows client PC operating system without simultaneously acquiring Windows Media Player, which means that the condition that the conclusion of contracts is made subject to acceptance of supplementary obligations must be considered to be satisfied. As the Commission correctly states at recital 827 to the contested decision, in most cases that coercion is applied primarily to OEMs, and is then passed on to consumers. OEMs, who assemble client PCs, install on those PCs a client PC operating system provided by a software producer or developed by themselves. OEMs who wish to install a Windows operating system on the client PCs which they assemble must obtain a licence from Microsoft in order to do so. Under Microsoft's licensing system, it is not possible to obtain a licence on the Windows operating system without Windows Media Player....

The coercion thus applied to OEMs is not just contractual in nature, but also technical. In effect, it is common ground that it was not technically possible to uninstall Windows Media Player. The Court considers that the arguments which Microsoft puts forward must be rejected.

Thus, in the first place, Microsoft cannot rely on the fact that customers are not required to pay anything extra for Windows Media Player.

First, while it is true that Microsoft does not charge a separate price for Windows Media Player, it cannot be inferred that the media player is provided free of charge....

Second, and in any event, it does not follow from either Article [102(d) TFEU] or the case-law on bundling that consumers must necessarily pay a certain price for the tied product in order for it to be concluded that they are subject to supplementary obligations within the meaning of that provision.

Nor, in the second place, is it relevant for the purposes of the examination of the present condition that, as Microsoft claims, consumers are not obliged to use the Windows Media Player which they find pre-installed on their client PC and that they can install and use other undertakings' media players on their PCs. Again, neither Article [102(d) TFEU] nor the case-law on bundling requires that consumers must be forced to use the tied product or prevented from using the same product supplied by a competitor of the dominant undertaking in order for the condition that the conclusion of contracts is made subject to acceptance of supplementary obligations to be capable of being regarded as satisfied. For example, as the Commission correctly observes ... in Hilti users were not forced to use the Hilti branded nails which they obtained with the Hilti branded nail gun.

It follows from all of the foregoing considerations that the Commission was correct to find that the condition relating to the imposition of supplementary obligations was satisfied in the present case.

d) The foreclosure of competition

Microsoft claims, in substance, that the Commission has failed to prove that the integration of Windows Media Player in the Windows client PC operating system involved foreclosure of competition, so that the fourth constituent element of abusive tying ... is not fulfilled in this case. In particular, Microsoft contends that the Commission, recognising that it was not dealing with a classical tying case, had to apply a new and highly speculative theory, relying on a prospective analysis of the possible reactions of third parties, in order to reach the conclusion that the tying at issue was likely to foreclose competition.

The Court considers that Microsoft's arguments are unfounded and that they are based on a selective and inaccurate reading of the contested decision. Those arguments essentially focus on the second of the three stages of the Commission's reasoning set out at recitals 835 to 954 to the contested decision....

The Commission's analysis of the foreclosure condition begins at recital 841 to the contested decision, where the Commission states that in the present case there are good reasons not to assume without further analysis that the bundling of Windows and Windows Media Player constitutes conduct which by its very nature is liable to foreclose competition. ... In substance, the conclusion which the Commission reached is based on the finding that the bundling of Windows Media Player with the Windows client PC operating system—the operating system pre-installed on the great majority of client PCs sold throughout the world—without the possibility of removing that media player from the operating system, allows Windows Media Player to benefit from the ubiquity of that operating system on client PCs, which cannot be counterbalanced by the other methods of distributing media players.

The Court considers that that finding, which is the subject-matter of the first stage of the Commission's reasoning ... is entirely well founded.

Thus, in the first place, it is clear that owing to the bundling, Windows Media Player enjoyed an unparalleled presence on client PCs throughout the world, because it thereby automatically achieved a level of market penetration corresponding to that of the Windows client PC operating system and did so without having to compete on the merits with competing products....

As will be explained in greater detail below, no third-party media player could achieve such a level of market penetration without having the advantage in terms of distribution that Windows Media Player enjoys as a result of Microsoft's use of its Windows client PC operating system....

In the second place, it is clear that, as the Commission correctly states at recital 845 to the contested decision, "[u]sers who find [Windows Media Player] pre-installed on their client PCs are indeed in general less likely to use alternative media players as they already have an application which delivers media streaming and playback functionality". The Court therefore considers that, in the absence of the bundling, consumers wishing to have a streaming media player would be induced to choose one from among those available on the market....

In the third place, the Court considers that the Commission was correct to state ... that the impugned conduct created disincentives for OEMs to ship third-party media players on their client PCs....

In the fourth place, the Court finds that the Commission was also correct to find that methods of distributing media players other than pre-installation by OEMs could not offset Windows Media Player's ubiquity....

First, while it is true that downloading via the Internet enables suppliers to reach a large number of users, it is less effective than pre-installation by OEMs. First, downloading does not guarantee competing media players distribution equivalent to Windows Media Player's. ... Second, downloading, unlike using a pre-installed product, is seen as complicated by a significant number of users. Third, as the Commission observes at recital 866 to the contested decision, a significant number of download attempts—more than 50%, according to tests carried out by RealNetworks in 2003—are not successfully concluded. While it is true that broadband makes downloading faster and less complex, it must be borne in mind that in 2002 only one in six households in Europe with Internet access had a broadband connection. . . . Fourth, users will probably tend to consider that a media player integrated in the client PC which they have bought will work better than a product which they install themselves. . . . Fifth and last, in most undertakings employees cannot download software from the Internet as that complicates the work of the network administrators. . . .

It follows from the foregoing that in the analysis set out at recitals 843 to 878 to the contested decision, which is the first stage of its reasoning, the Commission demonstrated to the requisite legal standard that the bundling of Windows and Windows Media Player from May 1999 inevitably had significant consequences for the structure of competition. That practice allowed Microsoft to obtain an unparalleled advantage with respect to the distribution of its product and to ensure the ubiquity of Windows Media Player on client PCs throughout the world, thus providing a disincentive for users to make use of third-party media players and for OEMs to pre-install such players on client PCs. . . .

In the light of all the foregoing considerations, the Court concludes that the Commission's findings in the first stage of its reasoning are in themselves sufficient to establish that the fourth constituent element of abusive bundling is present in this case. Those findings are not based on any new or speculative theory, but on the nature of the impugned conduct, on the conditions of the market and on the essential features of the relevant products. They are based on accurate, reliable and consistent evidence which Microsoft, by merely contending that it is pure conjecture, has not succeeded in showing to be incorrect.

It follows from the foregoing that it is not necessary to examine the arguments which Microsoft puts forward against the findings made by the Commission in the other two stages of its reasoning. None the less, the Court considers that it should examine them briefly.

In the second stage of its reasoning, the Commission seeks to establish that the ubiquity of Windows Media Player as a result of its bundling with Windows is capable of having an appreciable impact on content providers and software designers.

The Commission's theory is based on the fact that the market for streaming media players is characterised by significant indirect network effects or, to use the expression employed by Mr Gates, on the existence of a "positive feedback loop". That expression describes the phenomenon where, the greater the number of users of a given software platform, the more there will be invested in developing products compatible with that platform, which, in turn reinforces the popularity of that platform with users.

The Court considers that the Commission was correct to find that such a phenomenon existed in the present case and to find that it was on the basis of the percentages of installation and use of media players that content providers and software developers chose the technology for which they would develop their own products. . . .

First, as to the effects of the bundling on content providers, the Court considers that the Commission's assessment of that issue . . . is well founded.

More particularly, the Commission was quite correct to find that the provision of several different technologies gave rise to additional development, infrastructure and administrative costs for content providers, who were therefore inclined to use only one technology for their products if that allowed them to reach a wide audience. . . .

In the second place, the Court considers that the Commission . . . correctly assessed the effects of the bundling on software developers.

More particularly, the Commission was correct to observe . . . that software developers were inclined to create applications for a single platform if that enabled them to reach virtually all potential users of their products, whereas porting, marketing and supporting other platforms gave rise to additional costs. . . .

In the third place, the Court recalls that, at recitals 897 to 899 to the contested decision, the Commission states that the ubiquity which Windows Media Player enjoys by virtue of the bundling also has effects on adjacent markets, such as media players on wireless information devices, set-top boxes, DRM solutions and on-line music delivery. On that point, it is sufficient to state that Microsoft has put forward no argument capable of vitiating that assessment.

In light of the foregoing considerations, the Court concludes that the second stage of the Commission's reasoning is well founded. . . .

It follows from the foregoing considerations that the final conclusion which the Commission sets out at recitals 978 to 984 to the contested decision concerning the anti-competitive effects of the bundling is well founded. The Commission is correct to make the following findings:

— Microsoft uses Windows as a distribution channel to ensure for itself a significant competitive advantage on the media players market . . . ;

— because of the bundling, Microsoft's competitors are a priori at a disadvantage even if their products are inherently better than Windows Media Player . . . ;

— Microsoft interferes with the normal competitive process which would benefit users by ensuring quicker cycles of innovation as a consequence of unfettered competition on the merits . . . ;

— the bundling increases the content and applications barriers to entry, which protect Windows, and facilitates the erection of such barriers for Windows Media Player . . . ;

— Microsoft shields itself from effective competition from vendors of potentially more efficient media players who could challenge its position, and thus reduces the talent and capital invested in innovation of media players . . . ;

— by means of the bundling, Microsoft may expand its position in adjacent media-related software markets and weaken effective competition, to the detriment of consumers . . . ;

— by means of the bundling, Microsoft sends signals which deter innovation in any technologies in which it might conceivably take an interest and which it might tie with Windows in the future. . . .

The Commission therefore had ground to state . . . that there was a reasonable likelihood that tying Windows and Windows Media Player would lead to a lessening of competition so that the maintenance of an effective competition structure would not be ensured in the foreseeable future. It must be made clear that the Commission did not state that the tying would lead to the elimination of all competition on the market for streaming media players. Microsoft's argument that, several years after the beginning of the abuse at issue, a number of third-party media players are still present on the market therefore does not invalidate the Commission's argument.

It follows from all of the foregoing considerations that Microsoft has put forward no argument capable of vitiating the merits of the findings made by the Commission in the contested decision concerning the condition relating to the foreclosure of competition. The Court must therefore conclude that the Commission has demonstrated to the requisite legal standard that the condition was satisfied in the present case.

Questions on EU *Microsoft* Case

1.   *Separate Products.* Does it make sense for the General Court to allow the Commission to find separate products based on the facts that there is "separate consumer demand for streaming media players."

a.   Doesn't this test lead to absurd results?

(i) Doesn't this mean that every time there is an after market of spare parts for a given product, the product and its parts are separate products? For instance, does the fact that a market exists for shoe laces mean that shoes and laces are separate products?

(ii) Does the General Court's separate products test force dominant firms to offer "à la carte" versions of their products? For instance, if given a choice, some consumers may prefer to buy a Dell PC with an HP keyboard, does this test force Dell to supply PCs and keyboards separately unless bundling them together has a procompetitive justification?

b.   What would be a better test?

(i) To the question of whether there is separate demand for the tied product, shouldn't one add a second question, which is whether there is separate demand for the tying product without the tied product?

(ii) Wouldn't a test requiring that, for two products to be considered separate, there should be separate demand for both the tying *and* the tied product avoid absurd results? Going back to the above example, while there might be separate demand for shoes laces, there is surely no separate demand for shoes without laces.

2. *The Tying Condition.* In support of its argument that the fact that it integrated Windows Media Player (WMP) with Windows does not entail a supplementary obligation within the meaning of Article 102(d) TFEU, Microsoft "emphasizes ... that customers pay nothing extra for the media functionality of Windows ..."

a. Does the fact that Microsoft offers WMP for free mean it has not committed a tie?

(i) How can we know that Microsoft doesn't charge for WMP since there is no version of Windows without WMP? Couldn't the price of WMP be included in the price of Windows?

(ii) Couldn't any tie to sell an *A–B* bundle for *X* euros be reframed as giving *B* for free to anyone who bought *A* for *X* euros? Thus, wouldn't failing to apply tying doctrine to the free redistribution of the tied product create a huge loophole that would eviscerate tying doctrine?

(iii) If WMP were thought to be sold for free, couldn't there be a separate claim that Microsoft has engaged in predatory pricing by selling WMP below variable costs even if such costs are very small? Would that require showing dominance in the media player market?

b. In rejecting Microsoft's second and third arguments that "that they are not obliged to use that functionality; and ... that they are not prevented from installing and using competitors' media players", the General Court accepts the Commission's observation that "in *Hilti* users were not forced to use the Hilti branded nails which they obtained with the Hilti branded nail gun". But aren't the circumstances of the *Hilti* and *Microsoft* cases entirely different?

(i) In Hilti, weren't nails for Hilti cartridge strips "rival goods"? In other words, wasn't the use of Hilti nails necessarily excluding the use of third party nails, hence foreclosing competition?

(ii) By contrast, does anything prevent consumers from purchasing a new PC with Windows from acquiring, installing and using several media players on their PC (multi-homing)? In other words, can one seriously claim that coercion exist when the tied product is non-rival? Are buyers likely to incur the labor costs installing another media player?

3. *The Foreclosure Effect.* In its assessment of foreclosure, the General Court states that the presence of WMP on all Windows PCs and the resulting ubiquity that this presence "allowed Microsoft to obtain an unparalleled advantage with respect to the distribution of its product and to ensure the ubiquity of Windows Media Player on client PCs throughout the world, thus providing a disincentive for users to make use of third-party media players and for OEMs to pre-install such players on client PCs." It then concludes that these findings, which are based "on the nature of the impugned conduct, on the conditions of the market and on the essential features of the relevant products" were "in themselves sufficient to establish that the fourth constituent element of abusive bundling is present in this case.''

a. Is this position in line with the effects-based approach provided in the Guidance Paper whereby ''the aim of the Commission's enforcement activity in relation to exclusionary conduct is to ensure that dominant undertakings do not impair effective competition by foreclosing their rivals in an anticompetitive way and thus having an adverse impact on consumer welfare, whether in the form of higher price levels than would have otherwise prevailed or in some other form such as limiting quality or reducing consumer choice''?

b. Isn't the proper test whether competitors have equal access to distribution channels or whether competitors are foreclosed from a substantial share of the market or from the most efficient methods of distribution? In a case concerning access to distribution (e.g., *Bronner*), should the Commission have to show that the foreclosure significantly impeded the ability of rivals to penetrate the market?

Guidance on the Commission's Enforcement Priorities in Applying Article 82 EC Treaty [now 102 TFEU] to Abusive Exclusionary Conduct by Dominant Undertakings

(Dec. 2008).

48. ''Tying'' usually refers to situations where customers that purchase one product (the tying product) are required also to purchase another product from the dominant undertaking (the tied product). Tying can take place on a technical or contractual basis.[33] ''Bundling'' usually refers to the way products are offered and priced by the dominant undertaking. In the case of pure bundling the products are only sold jointly in fixed proportions. In the case of mixed bundling, often referred to as a multiproduct rebate, the products are also made available separately, but the sum of the prices when sold separately is higher than the bundled price.

49. Tying and bundling are common practices intended to provide customers with better products or offerings in more cost effective ways. However, an undertaking which is dominant in one product market (or more) of a tie or bundle (referred to as the tying market) can harm consumers through tying or bundling by foreclosing the market for the other products that are part of the tie or bundle (referred to as the tied market) and, indirectly, the tying market.

50. The Commission will normally take action under Article [102] where an undertaking is dominant in the tying market[34] and where, in

---

33. Technical tying occurs when the tying product is designed in such a way that it only works properly with the tied product (and not with the alternatives offered by competitors). Contractual tying occurs when the customer who purchases the tying product undertakes also to purchase the tied product (and not the alternatives offered by competitors).

34. The undertaking should be dominant in the tying market, though not necessarily in the tied market. In bundling cases, the undertaking needs to be dominant in one of the

addition, the following conditions are fulfilled: (i) the tying and tied products are distinct products, and (ii) the tying practice is likely to lead to anticompetitive foreclosure.[35]

(a) Distinct products.

51.   Whether the products will be considered by the Commission to be distinct depends on customer demand. Two products are distinct if, in the absence of tying or bundling, a substantial number of customers would purchase or would have purchased the tying product without also buying the tied product from the same supplier, thereby allowing stand-alone production for both the tying and the tied product.[36] Evidence that two products are distinct could include direct evidence that, when given a choice, customers purchase the tying and the tied products separately from different sources of supply, or indirect evidence, such as the presence on the market of undertakings specialised in the manufacture or sale of the tied product without the tying product[37] or of each of the products bundled by the dominant undertaking, or evidence indicating that undertakings with little market power, particularly in competitive markets, tend not to tie or not to bundle such products.

(b) Anticompetitive foreclosure in the tied and/or tying market

52.   Tying or bundling may lead to anticompetitive effects in the tied market, the tying market, or both at the same time. However, even when the aim of the tying or bundling is to protect the dominant undertaking's position in the tying market, this is done indirectly through foreclosing the tied market. In addition to the factors already mentioned in paragraph 20, the Commission considers that the following factors are generally of particular importance for identifying cases of likely or actual anticompetitive foreclosure.

53.   The risk of anticompetitive foreclosure is expected to be greater where the dominant undertaking makes its tying or bundling strategy a lasting one, for example through technical tying which is costly to reverse. Technical tying also reduces the opportunities for resale of individual components.

54.   In the case of bundling, the undertaking may have a dominant position for more than one of the products in the bundle. The greater the number of such products in the bundle, the stronger the likely anticompetitive foreclosure. This is particularly true if the bundle is difficult for a competitor to replicate, either on its own or in combination with others.

55.   The tying may lead to less competition for customers interested in buying the tied product, but not the tying product. If there is not a sufficient number of customers who will buy the tied product alone to

---

bundled markets. In the special case of tying in after-markets, the condition is that the undertaking is dominant in the tying market and/or the tied after-market.

35.   Case T–201/04 Microsoft v Commission [2007] ECR II–3601, in particular paragraphs 842, 859 to 862, 867 and 869.

36.   Case T–201/04 Microsoft v Commission [2007] ECR II–3601, paragraphs 917, 921 and 922.

37.   Case T–30/89 Hilti v Commission [1991] ECR II–1439, paragraph 67.

sustain competitors of the dominant undertaking in the tied market, the tying can lead to those customers facing higher prices.

56. If the tying and the tied product can be used in variable proportions as inputs to a production process, customers may react to an increase in price for the tying product by increasing their demand for the tied product while decreasing their demand for the tying product. By tying the two products the dominant undertaking may seek to avoid this substitution and as a result be able to raise its prices.

57. If the prices the dominant undertaking can charge in the tying market are regulated, tying may allow the dominant undertaking to raise prices in the tied market in order to compensate for the loss of revenue caused by the regulation in the tying market.

58. If the tied product is an important complementary product for customers of the tying product, a reduction of alternative suppliers of the tied product and hence a reduced availability of that product can make entry to the tying market alone more difficult....

(d) Efficiencies

62. Provided that the conditions set out in Section III D are fulfilled, the Commission will look into claims by dominant undertakings that their tying and bundling practices may lead to savings in production or distribution that would benefit customers. The Commission may also consider whether such practices reduce transaction costs for customers, who would otherwise be forced to buy the components separately, and enable substantial savings on packaging and distribution costs for suppliers. It may also examine whether combining two independent products into a new, single product might enhance the ability to bring such a product to the market to the benefit of consumers. The Commission may also consider whether tying and bundling practices allow the supplier to pass on efficiencies arising from its production or purchase of large quantities of the tied product.

Tying Doctrine in Other Nations

Indonesia has a per se rule against tying that seems to neither require proof of market power nor consider offsetting efficiencies.[96] Other nations generally judge tying under some form of a rule of reason. Argentina bans ties that restrict competition or abuse a dominant position.[97] Brazil, Peru, and Russia weigh the anticompetitive effects of a tie against any procompetitive efficiencies.[98] Canada's parallel to Clayton Act § 3 covers "tied selling" explicitly rather than just implicitly, but also focuses on exclusionary effects in a way that suggests some significant individual or cumulative foreclosure in the tied market is required.[99] China prohibits tying by a

---

96. Indonesia Competition Law Art. 15(2).

97. Argentina Competition Law Arts. 1, 2 (i).

98. Brazil Antitrust Law No. 8,884, Arts. 20, 21(XIII); Brazil CADE Resolution 20, Attachment I, § 5 (1999); Peru Competition Law Art. 10(c) and 9; Russia Competition Law Arts. 11(5) & 13.

99. Canada Competition Act § 77.

dominant firm "without any justifiable cause."[100] India bans tying when it has an "appreciable adverse effect on competition."[101] A firm that has a dominant position in Egypt and Venezuela or monopoly power in Israel cannot impose conditions "unrelated" to the subject matter of the contract, which in a tying case probably turns on whether the tie advances a procompetitive purpose related to the transactions.[102] Japan bans "unjustly" tying as an unfair trade practice when it "tends to impede fair competition."[103] Mexico bans tying when the defendant has market power, the purpose is exclusionary, and efficiencies do not offset the anticompetitive effects.[104] Saudi Arabia bans tying by a dominant firm that has anticompetitive effects.[105] South Africa bans tying by a dominant firm unless it can prove that procompetitive efficiencies offset the anticompetitive effects.[106] South Korea condemns "wrongfully" requiring a tie when doing so violates "normal business practices."[107] Taiwan judges when ties are illegal based on the totality of market factors.[108] Turkey bans ties based on proof of tying market power and anticompetitive effects, which can be inferred from a substantial foreclosure share.[109]

D. LOYALTY AND BUNDLED DISCOUNTS

Loyalty Discounts and Their Similarities to Exclusive Dealing. Loyalty discounts are agreements whereby a seller gives buyers a price discount if buyers remain loyal to the seller by buying all, or some high percentage, of the relevant product from the seller. Loyalty rebates are the same, except that a rebate check is sent later to compliant buyers rather than having the discount taken off the price the buyer pays for the product. Loyalty programs may also provide other benefits that are not given on a per unit basis but are conditional on the buyer maintaining loyalty.

The terminology of "discount" or "rebates" can be misleading because it suggests that these agreements reflect lower prices, which may not be true when they are anticompetitive. All we know from the mere fact of a loyalty "discount" or "rebate" is that there is a price difference between

---

100. China Anti–Monopoly Law Art. 17(5).

101. India Competition Act § 3(4)(a).

102. Egypt Competition Law, Art. 8(d); Israel Restrictive Trade Practices Law § 29A(b)(4); Venezuela Procompetition Act Art. 13(5).

103. Japan Antimonopoly Law § 2(9); Japan General Designations of Unfair Trade Practices § 10 (2009).

104. Mexico Competition Law Arts. 10(III) & 11.

105. Saudi Implementing Regulations, Art. 8(j).

106. South Africa Competition Act § 8(d)(iii).

107. Enforcement Decree of the South Korea Fair Trade Act Appendix I, Art. 5.A. Ties by a dominant firm can also be an abuse of dominance. KFTC Decision, 2002 Kyungchok 0453 (February 24, 2006).

108. Taiwan Fair Trade Act Art. 19(6); Taiwan Enforcement Rules to the Fair Trade Act Art. 27.

109. Turkey Competition Act Arts 4 (f), 6 (c); Turkey Competition Board Decision No. 09–34/786–191 (2009).

the noncompliant price charged to buyers who decline to comply with the loyalty condition and the lower price charged to those who do. Often, perhaps usually, such a price difference will reflect a real discount from but-for price that would have been paid without any loyalty program. However, if the defendant has raised that noncompliant price above the but-for price it would have charged without any loyalty program, or if its prices have generally been inflated by the foreclosure effects generated by the loyalty program, then the "discounted" price paid by loyal buyers may well be higher than the but-for price. Without some comparison to but-for prices, any loyalty discount or rebate could equally be called a disloyalty penalty imposed on buyers who refuse to restrict purchases from the seller's rivals. Rather than call them either loyalty discounts or disloyalty penalties, it would be more neutral to call them price differences conditioned on loyalty, because an important question is precisely whether the prices charged to those who refuse to abide by those conditions are above but-for prices (in which case they are really penalties) or below but-for prices (in which case they are really discounts). Because the terminology of loyalty discounts and rebates is so prevalent, we shall use it to refer to all price differences conditioned on loyalty, but it should not be understood to indicate that they reflect prices lower than but-for prices.

Loyalty discounts and rebates can differ in form from traditional exclusive dealing agreements in two ways. First, many loyalty discounts or rebates do not impose an absolute obligation to avoid dealing with rivals, but rather may condition the receipt of discounts or rebates on buyers restricting their purchases from rivals. When loyalty discounts and rebates do not require an affirmative buyer commitment, they are less absolute in form than exclusive dealing because they permit buyers a continual choice between complying with the loyalty condition and forgoing the discounts or rebates.

But this distinction may be more formal than real. Although exclusive dealing agreements are absolute in form, in fact under contract law any contractual obligation is a promise to either comply with the obligation or pay expectation damages, so that really such agreements continue to leave buyers with an ongoing choice. Obtaining expectation damages for violating an exclusive dealing agreement may also be difficult because it requires bringing a successful lawsuit and the amount of damages is often hard to establish. Moreover, because any exclusive dealing agreement that violates antitrust law is unenforceable under contract law, an absolute contractual obligation that violated antitrust law would not actually enjoy any contractual penalties for noncompliance. Thus, often the only real penalty suppliers impose on buyers (or suppliers) who do not comply with an absolute exclusive dealing contract is refusing to deal with that buyer in the future. And the main penalty termination may impose is the loss of discounts that were given in exchange for the buyer agreement to the exclusivity term.

Similarly, even without buyer commitments, loyalty discounts or rebates could be understood as an absolute obligation that sets the financial penalty at the amount of the forgone discounts or rebates. Indeed, one can understand loyalty discounts or rebates as a way of making loyalty agreements more enforceable because it is easy for a seller to self-enforce such an agreement by withholding discounts or rebates, whereas an absolute obligation would generally require litigation and more uncertain proof of damages. Further, the amount of discounts and rebates can be set well above expectation damages, which would be impermissible under the standard contracts rule against penalty clauses.[110] In any event, under U.S. law, Clayton Act § 3 expressly treats discounts conditioned on not dealing with a rival as equivalent to agreements not to deal with a rival, and EU law treats loyalty discounts as similar to exclusive dealing under Article 102.

Second, loyalty discounts or rebates are often less than 100% exclusive. They may, for example, make the receipt of discounts or rebates conditional on buyers making 80% or 90% of their purchases from the defendant, thus restricting rivals to 10–20% of sales to those buyers. Because the anticompetitive effects generally turn on the total share of the market foreclosed, such agreements raise very similar issues to exclusive dealing.[111] For example, if the loyalty agreements foreclose 90% of sales to buyers who make 80% of purchases, then they achieve 72% marketwide foreclosure. This is likely to be even more anticompetitive than 100% exclusive dealing agreements with buyers who make 70% of purchases, which forecloses only 70% of the market.

Because they are based on the share of purchases made from the defendant, loyalty discounts also differ from volume-based discounts, which provide buyers with financial inducements if they purchase a given volume of product from the defendant. Compared to share-based discounts, volume-based discounts are generally less restrictive because they do not restrain the buyer from buying any volume they wish from the defendant's rivals, and they are more closely related to possible volume-based efficiencies. But where the volume is set in a way that covers all or most of each buyer's needs, their practical effect can be much the same. As we shall see, EU law treats certain volume-based discounts as "loyalty-inducing," and thus subject to the same restrictions as loyalty discounts, when they are deemed likely to have similar effects.

Loyalty discounts can raise the same anticompetitive concerns as exclusive dealing. The main concern remains that they will foreclose a sufficient market share to impede the competitiveness of rivals, and thus increase the seller's market power in the foreclosed market. Further, while loyalty discounts may often, perhaps usually, involve real discounts, there may also be cases where the noncompliant price exceeds the but-for price that would be charged without any loyalty program, in which case the loyalty discount is really a disloyalty penalty, which makes the coercive effect quite similar to the coercive threat under exclusive dealing. Indeed,

---

110. Although standard contract law forbids imposing financial penalties for breach that exceed a reasonable estimate of the harm caused by that breach, the same result can generally be obtained by reframing penalties as a bonus for performance because contract law generally refuses to second-guess the adequacy of consideration, which is the value the parties were willing to pay for performance. Loyalty discounts and rebates basically exploit this distinction to convert contractually unenforceable penalties for failing to perform a loyalty condition into enforceable bonuses for performing them.

111. Indeed, in Microsoft v. United States, 253 F.3d 34, 70–71 (D.C. Cir. 2001) (en banc), the court treated an agreement that foreclosed 75–85% of the covered distributors as exclusive dealing agreements.

one can think of exclusive dealing as simply a special case of loyalty discounts where the disloyal price is set at infinity. But a disloyal price of less than infinity can have the same economic effect. For example, suppose a firm with market power, which sells a product for $100 without any loyalty condition, decides to raise the noncompliant price to $150 with a "discount" of $50, bringing the price back to $100, for any buyer who agrees to take 100% of the product from the firm. For buyers who do not value any units of the product more than $150, such a loyalty "discount" has precisely the same economic impact as absolute exclusive dealing because the threat is to deprive them of all the consumer surplus they would enjoy from buying that firm's product for $100 unless they agree to loyalty condition. Such examples do not mean all loyalty discounts reflect disloyalty penalties, but they mean that some could. Whether actual loyalty discounts reflect disloyalty penalties depends on whether the actual prices charged to disloyal buyers exceed but-for levels.

In those cases where loyalty discounts are really disloyalty penalties, the coercive effect can be smaller in degree than exclusive dealing for some buyers, but is similar in kind. In the above example, for buyers who value at least some units of the product more than $150, the threatened loss of consumer surplus is somewhat less with the loyalty discount than with exclusive dealing because such buyers could retain *some* of that consumer surplus by rejecting the loyalty discount and buying some units at $150, whereas they would get none of it if they rejected exclusive dealing. However, the threatened loss of consumer surplus is similar in kind, and can create the same externality problem. To avoid such an individual penalty, each buyer can have incentives to agree to a loyalty condition that (when many buyers agree) impairs rival competitiveness and raises prices because most of the harm of each individual agreement is externalized onto the rest of the market (other than for an individual buyer that has more than a 50% market share).

Further, even if the loyalty discount (or exclusive dealing) offers a real short-term discount from but-for prices to compliant buyers, the buyers can all be harmed by accepting such a loyalty discount when the long-term effects of impairing rival competitiveness are higher prices. Indeed, an interesting body of economic literature finds that, because of externality problems, each buyer in a market with many buyers (who do not coordinate with each other) would have incentives to agree to anticompetitive loyalty discounts for a trivial short-term discount, even though the collective effect of all of them doing so is to create a substantial foreclosure share that impairs rival competitiveness in a way that greatly increases long-term prices above but-for levels.[112] Their analysis indicates that if, for example, there are 10,000 buyers of a product, any individual buyer's agreement to a

112. MICHAEL D. WHINSTON, LECTURES ON ANTITRUST ECONOMICS 144–47, 166 (2006); Elhauge, *Defining Better*, supra note 13, at 284–92; Elhauge, *How Loyalty Discounts, supra* note 8, at 190, 217–19; Joseph Farrell, *Deconstructing Chicago on Exclusive Dealing*, 50 ANTITRUST BULL. 465, 476 (2005); Louis Kaplow & Carl Shapiro, *Antitrust*, in 2 HANDBOOK OF LAW & ECONOMICS 1073, 1203–10 (A.Mitchell Polinsky & Steven Shavell eds., 2007); Eric B. Rasmusen, J. Mark Ramseyer & John S. Wiley, Jr., *Naked Exclusion,* 81 AM. ECON. REV. 1137 (1991); Ilya R. Segal & Michael D. Whinston, Comment, *Naked Exclusion*, 90 AM. ECON. REV. 296 (2000).

loyalty commitment that contributes to a marketwide price increase externalizes 99.99% of the harm caused by that buyer's contribution to the market price increase. Such an externality would mean each buyer has incentives to agree to a loyalty commitment in exchange for any individual discount (or avoided price penalty) that exceeded 0.01% of that buyer's contribution to the marketwide price increase.

In a market with only one buyer, that buyer could not externalize any of the anticompetitive costs onto other buyers in the same market. Likewise, the externality problem across buyers in the same market could be defeated if a market has only a few concentrated buyers who can coordinate on a policy of rejecting anticompetitive loyalty discounts. However, externality problems can be worsened when the relevant buyers are not consumers, but intermediaries who resell to others. Such intermediate buyers might be able to externalize an even higher percentage of the harm by passing much or all of the price increase on to downstream buyers. Thus, some economic literature indicates that intermediate buyers are even more likely to agree to loyalty commitments that lead to a substantial foreclosure share that has anticompetitive effects on rival competitiveness.[113]

One often observes sophisticated buyers initiating requests for loyalty discounts. Some might conclude that such sophisticated buyer initiation likely indicates that the loyalty discounts benefit buyers. Sometimes this will be true, especially in cases where the loyalty discount reflects a real discount and forecloses only a small market share or in other cases where there is no externality problem. However, in cases where buyer decisions are driven by the above externality problem, then even the most sophisticated individual buyer has incentives to initiate a request for an anticompetitive loyalty discount, because each buyer individually benefits from receiving one given that most of the costs of their individual loyalty commitment is externalized onto others, even though the collective effect of all of them initiating a request for loyalty discounts is that all buyers are harmed. Where buyer decisions are driven by the externality problem, the fact that buyers initiate a request for loyalty discounts is similar to the fact that (before laws that banned littering) individuals often initiated littering even though the collective result of all of them doing so was to harm everyone. Moreover, sophisticated intermediate buyers might have incentives to request loyalty rebates that give them a share of supracompetitive upstream profits or loyalty discounts that give them a special discount unavailable to rivals in order to gain a competitive advantage in the downstream market.[114]

None of this means that all loyalty discounts have such anticompetitive effects or that any per se rule is appropriate. Many loyalty discounts involve true discounts and small foreclosure shares that are unlikely to

---

113. Jose Miguel Abito & Julian Wright, *Exclusive Dealing with Imperfect Downstream Competition*, 26 INT'L J. INDUS. ORG. 227 (2008); Elhauge, *Defining Better, supra* note 13, at 288–92; Farrell, *supra* note 165, at 475–77; John Simpson & Abraham L. Wickelgren, *Naked Exclusion, Efficient Breach, and Downstream Competition*, 97 AM. ECON. REV. 1305, 1306 (2007); Christodoulos Stefanadis, *Selective Contracts, Foreclosure, and the Chicago School View*, 41 J.L. & ECON. 429 (1998).

114. Elhauge, *Defining Better, supra* note 13, at 288–92;

create anticompetititve effects, and as we shall see below, loyalty discounts can have efficiencies that offset their anticompetitive effects. Rule of reason analysis is thus appropriate, as with exclusive dealing, to determine which loyalty discounts have net anticompetitive effects and which do not.

Where market conditions create the above sort of externality problems, loyalty discounts that create a substantial foreclosure share that impairs rival competitiveness can produce anticompetitive harm even though all the prices are above cost, as prices are with exclusive dealing. For example, suppose a monopolist charges $200 for a product that costs $100 to make, which it sells to thousands of buyers. Other firms stand poised to enter the market, or to expand until they achieve sufficient scale to reduce their costs to $100, in which case competition will drive prices down to $100. To prevent this competitive outcome, the monopolist announces a loyalty program under which its price is $210 unless buyers agree to be loyal and buy 90% of their needs from the monopolist, in which case buyers get a nominal "discount" of $10. Then the externality theory predicts that all the buyers have incentives to agree because each individual decision to agree gets each buyer all of the nominal $10 "discount" but externalizes the vast bulk of each buyer agreement's marginal contribution to market-wide foreclosure onto the rest of the market. The result can thus be a 90% foreclosure share that prevents rivals from entering or expanding enough to achieve economies of scale, so that the buyers all continue to pay the monopoly price of $200, which is double the $100 price they would have paid but for the loyalty program.

The above example assumed a disloyalty penalty, but similar results could follow with a real loyalty discount. To illustrate, take the hypothetical above, but now instead assume the firm maintains the noncompliant price at $200, giving a true $10 discount (to $190) to buyers who agree to the loyalty condition. Then the externality theory predicts that all buyers still have individual incentives to agree to get the $10 discount, even though the collective result is to create a 90% foreclosure share that prevents rivals from entering and lowering long-term prices to $100. The buyers here get the short-term benefit of a $10 price reduction, but suffer a long-term price increase of $90 over but-for levels (continuing to pay the loyalty discount price of $190 rather than the $100 they would have paid without a loyalty program). However, in other cases, rule of reason analysis might reveal that the short-term price cut exceeded the long-term price increase.

Loyalty discounts can also perversely discourage discounting even when they have no effect on rival efficiency. The essential reason is that firms using loyalty discounts have less incentive to compete for free buyers, because any price reduction to win sales to free buyers will, given the loyalty discount, also lower prices to the buyers that agreed to the loyalty condition.[115] This in turn can reduce the incentive of rivals to cut prices, because there will exist an above-cost price that rivals can charge to free

---

115. See Elhauge, *How Loyalty Discounts, supra* note 8. This effect does not require 100% exclusion nor any contractual commitment to the loyalty condition. The article proves the textual proposition for loyalty discounts that promise the buyers who agree to them a price lower than the price paid by free buyers. The same point would seem to also extend to bundled discounts that promise buyers who agree to the bundle better prices than buyers who do not.

buyers without being undercut by the firm using loyalty discounts. The discouragement to price competition is stronger the greater the discount level and the greater the cumulative share of the market covered by loyalty discounts, but can persist in smaller degrees even at low discount and foreclosure levels.

Bundled Discounts and Their Similarities to Tying. Bundled discounts are agreements to charge a buyer less if he takes both product *A* and *B* from the seller than if the buyer were to buy *A* and *B* separately. The product over which the firm has market power is the "linking" product and the other product is the "linked" product. When the buyer has to buy a high percentage of their linked product purchases from the seller to get the bundled discount, the bundled discount is a bundled loyalty discount. Bundled discounts can have all the same anticompetitive effects as tying whenever the unbundled price for the linking product (the product over which the firm has market power) exceeds the but-for price for that product (the price the firm would charge "but for" the bundling).[116] In other words, bundled "discounts" have all the same effects as tying whenever the price difference really reflects an unbundled penalty. Indeed, one can think of absolute tying as simply a special case of a bundled discount where the unbundled price for *A* is set at infinity.

Suppose, for example, a seller has market power in *A*, which sells independently for $100, and no market power in *B*, which sells at a competitive price of $50. He then raises the unbundled price for *A* to $140 but offers to sell the *A–B* bundle for a price of $160. The penalty for rejecting the bundle is that the buyer has to pay $40 extra for *A*, which may be less than the penalty for rejecting a classic tie if the buyer values some units of *A* at more than $140. But in either case rejection would entail a loss of consumer surplus on product A that can cause buyers to accept the bundle/tie if that loss exceeds the consumer surplus they lose from buying *B* for $10 over competitive market rates.

If the unbundled price does not exceed the but-for price, then bundled discounts cannot have three of the possible anticompetitive effects created by tying: increasing intraproduct or interproduct price discrimination or extracting individual consumer surplus.[117] However, such bundled discounts can still have the other two anticompetitive effects of increasing the degree of tied or tying market power when they create a substantial foreclosure share.[118] Further, the same externality problems that exist for loyalty discounts also apply to bundled discounts, and thus give buyers incentives to accept trivial discounts for agreeing to anticompetitive bundled discounts that create a substantial foreclosure share that creates a marketwide harm that is mainly externalized onto others.[119]

None of these anticompetitive effects depends on any price being below cost. However, the ability of bundled discounts to produce anticompetitive effects depends on the same conditions that limit the ability of ties to do so.

---

116. Elhauge, *Tying, supra* note 36, at 402–03, 450–55.

117. *Id.*

118. *Id.* at 456–59.

119. *Id.*

A fixed product ratio (such as is true for unit-to-unit bundled discounts) means bundled discounts, like ties, cannot increase intraproduct price discrimination or extract individual consumer surplus. A strong positive demand correlation (usually present when the products lack separate utility) knocks out the possibility of increasing interproduct price discrimination. The absence of a substantial foreclosure share means ties cannot increase the degree of tied or tying market power. Thus, the possibility of any anticompetitive effect is precluded by a combination of (1) a fixed ratio, (2) no separate utility, and (3) no substantial foreclosure share.

Cost–Based Tests of Possible Predatory Pricing Impact. For reasons noted above, the ability of loyalty and bundled discounts to achieve anticompetitive effects similar to exclusive dealing and tying does not depend on the discounted prices being below cost, any more than they did for exclusive dealing or tying. However, cost-based tests can tell us when loyalty and bundled discounts can achieve the same anticompetitive effects as predatory pricing.

For bundled discounts, the appropriate cost-based test defines the incremental price for the linked product as the bundled price minus the unbundled price for the linking product. If this incremental price for the linked product is below the defendant's cost of producing the linked product, then the cost test is flunked. (The same results can be obtained by applying the whole bundled discount to the linked product price).

For loyalty discounts, the cost-based inquiry turns on the extent to which buyers preferences would allow switching 100% to the rival. If buyer demand for the defendant's product is entirely contestable, then the inquiry would simply be whether the loyalty discount results in prices that are below the defendant's costs. However, suppose instead buyer demand for the defendant's product is partly contestable but partly incontestable. This might be true if some amount of the product must be bought to use with an installed base of capital or if the buyer is a distributor who has some downstream customers with an inelastic preference for the defendant's product. If so, loyalty discounts that cover both the contestable and incontestable portion of buyer demand amount to intraproduct bundled discounts. The appropriate cost-based test would then define the incremental price on the contestable portion as the total discounted price on the amount needed to meet the loyalty condition minus the undiscounted price on the incontestable portion of that amount. If this incremental price is below the defendant's cost of serving the contestable portion of demand, then the cost test is flunked.

The proper cost measure used in a cost-based test must take account of the fact that bundled and loyalty discounts can often last a long period because, unlike predatory pricing, they are profitable for the defendant. Because the relevant measure of cost includes all costs that are variable over the period of the alleged violation, *see* Chapter 3.C.2.a, if that period lasts a long time that may include something close to what is typically considered average total costs.

Some people think that in practice most bundled or loyalty discounts are procompetitive and thus worry more about overdeterrence than underdeterrence and prefer a cost-based test that lessens overdeterrence by offering a clearer safe harbor. Others think that a cost-based test is a poor choice to optimize the balance between overdeterrence and underdeterrence because it perversely exempts the most anticompetitive bundled and loyalty discounts—those that raises price well above costs—and because they believe a cost-based test has the following defects.

First, if the anticompetitive concern is that loyalty or bundled discounts will create marketwide foreclosure that impairs rival efficiency, then such a cost-based foreclosure test assumes away the very anticompetitive concern being tested. Rivals that are equally efficient (in the sense of having a long run cost curve that is as low as the defendant) might be unable to achieve a price as low as the defendant's costs precisely because the foreclosure has relegated them to the high cost portion of their cost curve. It would seem to be bootstrapping to allow a dominant seller to use loyalty or bundled discounts that impair the efficiency of its rivals, and then cite the rivals' lower efficiency as proof that those agreements cannot have an anticompetitive effect.[120]

Second, unlike in a straight case of low pricing, an equally efficient rival may have very little incentive to lower its price to its costs to try to overcome a bundled discount or a loyalty discount. To the contrary, loyalty discounts can perversely discourage rivals from cutting prices to free buyers. This effect persists even though rival prices exceed costs, and indeed the problem is that the loyalty discount can affirmatively give rivals incentives to set prices further above costs than they otherwise would.[121] In addition, in the bundled discount case, the rival will know that no matter how much it lowers its price down to costs, an equally efficient defendant with market power over another product can always exceed it with a bundled discount. Likewise, for loyalty discounts, a rival for the contestable portion of demand will know that no matter how much the rival lowers its prices down to costs, the defendant can always offset it with discounts on the incontestable portion of demand. To legally require price reductions down to cost in such cases can thus amount to requiring economically irrational behavior we are unlikely to see.

Third, it is not clear why antitrust concerns should be limited to equally efficient rivals, because impairing or excluding less efficient rivals can also have anticompetitive effects by removing a constraint on the defendant's market power. Suppose, for example, a monopolist has costs of $100 and could charge a monopoly price of $200 but for the existence of a less efficient rival that has costs of $150. Then driving out that less efficient rival with loyalty or bundled discounts will harm consumer welfare. While there are special reasons to limit predatory pricing doctrine to prices that are below cost, those reasons are not nearly as powerful when

---

120. In a bundled discount case, one might thus want to instead compare the incremental price for the tied product in the bundle to the rival's prices for that product, or to the rival's costs (including a fair rate of return). See X Areeda, Elhauge & Hovenkamp, Antitrust Law ¶ 1758e, at 350 (1996). The problem is that the products might differ in features or quality a way that makes the price comparison difficult. Further, this sort of approach rewards inefficiency by giving less efficient rivals greater rights, and makes it difficult for firms to gauge when their bundled discounts are illegal.

121. *See* Elhauge, Loyalty Discounts, *supra* note 8.

the issue is attaching to those prices conditions requiring loyalty or bundled purchases.[122]

Fourth, a cost-based test bears no relationship to whether the bundled discounts are producing the same anticompetitive effects as tying can without a substantial foreclosure share. Because antitrust doctrine condemns ties that increase interproduct and intraproduct price discrimination and extract individual consumer surplus, bundled discounts that create the same effects would seem equally subject to condemnation. A cost-based test fails to pick up these effects because it assumes the only relevant effects flow from foreclosing rivals in a way that impairs rival competitiveness.

Fifth, a cost-based test would not capture the concern that foreclosure might impair rival expandability or aid oligopolistic coordination.

Sixth, a cost-based test also fails to capture the concern that intermediate buyers might collude with sellers to create a foreclosure that helps exploit downstream buyers, and then divide up the supracompetitive profits.[123] In such cases, it may not be possible for rivals to offset the benefits to buyers by just offering prices at the seller's costs, because rivals would also have to offer a share of supracompetitive profits that are unavailable to them.

Seventh, cost-based tests are notoriously difficult to administer. Cost data is very hard to assess, and it is often very hard to get reliable cost data at all.

Finally, unlike with predatory pricing, what requires justification in the case of loyalty and bundled discounts is not the pricing, but the loyalty or bundled condition attached to the pricing. Such conditions create anticompetitive problems that are not raised by mere low pricing. They discourage discounting to unconditioned buyers. Loyalty conditions attached to low prices also prevent rivals from winning sales by matching prices one purchase at a time, but instead require the rival to be able to replace all the units a purchaser has, which may be difficult, especially if some of the purchases are hard to contest, such as when some are used with some installed base of capital equipment. Bundled discounts in addition require rivals to overcome discounts on other products.

Possible Efficiencies. Loyalty and bundled discounts raise some, but not all, of the same possible efficiencies as exclusive dealing and tying agreements. It is generally hard to argue that loyalty and bundled discounts are designed to improve quality because they do not guarantee 100% usage of the allegedly higher quality product. It is also generally hard to argue that they increase value to the buyer, because that would make it be unnecessary to give a discount to get buyers to comply. Further, to the extent the justification is to provide certainty that lowers the sellers' risk-bearing or inventory costs or that encourages relationship-specific investment by the seller, the problem is that loyalty and bundled discounts often lack commitments that prohibit the buyer from changing its purchases, and

---

122.   *See* Elhauge, *Tying, supra* note 36, at 464 n.198, 474.

123.   *See* Chapter 4.B.

thus do not create the requisite seller certainty in the way that exclusive dealing obligations might.

Loyalty and bundled discounts might be justified by cost savings, but this raises two issues. First, if the discount amount exceeds any cost savings, then such discounts go beyond this justification and suggest a foreclosing purpose. Perhaps such discounts can be justified as an effective cut in a supracompetitive price (if the discounted price remains above cost), but what requires justification is linking the discount to a loyalty or bundled condition. On the other hand, if firms fear tribunals will later erroneously decide costs are higher than they really are, a prohibition on discounts that exceed the cost savings might deter desirable price-cutting.

Second, if cost-savings are related to volume-based efficiencies, volume-based discounts would generally be an alternative that is not only less restrictive but more effective, thus suggesting share-based discounts must be meant to achieve some nonefficiency goal. After all, a share-based discount gives a greater discount to a compliant small buyer than to a noncompliant large buyer even if the latter purchases a greater total volume and generates more efficiencies. At least presumptively, then, volume-based efficiencies support only volume-based discounts that are uniform in the sense that every buyer can get the same discount if it buys the same volume.

Perhaps one explanation for using share-based discounts to achieve volume-based efficiencies is that, in volatile industries, it may be too risky for the buyer to make volume-based commitments. This is especially likely to be the case when the buyer is distributing a product whose local demand fluctuates; the seller might be able to assess that risk more accurately than the buyer and to spread the localized risk among multiple distributors. If so, share-based commitments might be the best alternative to accomplish similar efficiencies with lower risk-bearing costs. True, volume-based discounts do not require any contractual commitment to buy a fixed volume. But to the extent buyers have to make effective commitments (such as to market the seller's product or design their own product to use the seller's product as an input) they may be unwilling to make it unless they know they can get a low price no matter how well the product does. Still, this efficiency seems unlikely in industries where purchase requirements are relatively stable, such as hospitals buying medical devices whose volume is determined by patient need.

Another possibility is that loyalty and bundled discounts efficiently resolve problems with verifiability of effort that are raised by the economics of contracting.[124] One could, for example, imagine them incentivizing marketing efforts in a way that other legal duties could not. And they might do so in a way that is less anticompetitive, and less risky for the distributor, than an exclusive dealing obligation. For example, suppose a seller wants to pay for $1 million in marketing effort by a distributor. However, it knows that if it just hands over the cash, it will have a hard time verifying the effectiveness of that marketing effort. It also knows that specifying marketing duties might not be efficient, because the type of marketing effort that

---

124. See Chapter 4.B.

will be the most effective will turn on local and future conditions that the distributor is best placed to judge. One way to avoid such problems might be to use share-based or volume-based discounts or rebates, so that the distributor earns the $1 million (in the form of discounts or rebates) only if their efforts actually effectively moved enough of the product. This gives the distributor natural incentives to engage in marketing efforts and exercise its best judgment to make those efforts effective. And share-based discounts might be more efficient than volume-based discounts where the latter seem too risky for the distributor.

Conclusion. In short, loyalty and bundled discounts seem to have enough possible efficiencies and anticompetitive potential to be judged under some form of rule of reason review rather than being deemed per se legal or illegal.

United States v. Loew's Inc.

371 U.S. 38 (1962).

■ Mr. Justice Goldberg delivered the opinion of the Court.

These consolidated appeals present as a key question the validity under § 1 of the Sherman Act of block booking of copyrighted feature motion pictures for television exhibition. We hold that the tying agreements here are illegal and in violation of the Act.

The United States brought separate civil antitrust actions ... against six major distributors ... alleging that each defendant ... had, in selling to television stations, conditioned the license or sale of one or more feature films upon the acceptance by the station of a package or block containing one or more unwanted or inferior films....

The court entered separate final judgments against the defendants, wherein each was enjoined from [(a) conditioning the sale of a film on the purchase of another or (b) offering package discounts that had the effect of imposing such a condition.]

... The requisite economic power is presumed when the tying product is patented or copyrighted ... The district judge found that each copyrighted film block booked by appellants for television use "was in itself a unique product"; that feature films "varied in theme, in artistic performance, in stars, in audience appeal, etc.," and were not fungible; and that since each defendant by reason of its copyright had a "monopolistic" position as to each tying product, "sufficient economic power" to impose an appreciable restraint on free competition in the tied product was present....[6] We agree. These findings of the district judge, supported by the record, confirm the presumption of uniqueness resulting from the existence of the copyright itself.

---

6. To use the trial court's apt example, forcing a television station which wants "Gone With The Wind" to take "Getting Gertie's Garter" as well is taking undue advantage of the fact that to television as well as motion picture viewers there is but one "Gone With The Wind."

Moreover, there can be no question in this case of the adverse effects on free competition resulting from appellants' illegal block booking contracts. Television stations forced by appellants to take unwanted films were denied access to films marketed by other distributors who, in turn, were foreclosed from selling to the stations. Nor can there be any question as to the substantiality of the commerce involved. The 25 contracts found to have been illegally block booked involved payments to appellants ranging from $60,800 in the case of Screen Gems to over $2,500,000 in the case of Associated Artists. A substantial portion of the licensing fees represented the cost of the inferior films which the stations were required to accept. These anticompetitive consequences are an apt illustration of the reasons underlying our recognition that the mere presence of competing substitutes for the tying product, here taking the form of other programming material as well as other feature films, is insufficient to destroy the legal, and indeed the economic, distinctiveness of the copyrighted product. By the same token, the distinctiveness of the copyrighted tied product is not inconsistent with the fact of competition, in the form of other programming material and other films, which is suppressed by the tying arrangements. . . .

Appellants (other than C & C) make the additional argument that each of them was found to have entered into such a small number of illegal contracts as to make it improper to enter injunctive relief. Appellants urge that their over-all sales policies were to allow selective purchasing of films, and that in light of this, the fact that a few contracts were found to be illegal does not justify the entering of injunctive relief. We disagree. Illegality having been properly found, appellants cannot now complain that its incidence was too scattered to warrant injunctive relief. . . . There is no reason to disturb the judge's legal conclusions and decree merely because he did not find more illegal agreements when, as here, the illegal behavior of each defendant had substantial anticompetitive effects. . . .

The United States contends that the relief afforded by the final judgments is inadequate and that to be adequate it must also: (1) require the defendants to price the films individually and offer them on a picture-by-picture basis; (2) prohibit noncost-justified differentials in price between a film when sold individually and when sold as part of a package . . . Some of the practices which the Government seeks to have enjoined with its requested modifications are acts which may be entirely proper when viewed alone. To ensure, however, that relief is effectual, otherwise permissible practices connected with the acts found to be illegal must sometimes be enjoined. . . .

The final judgments as entered only prohibit a price differential between a film offered individually and as part of a package which "has the effect of conditioning the sale or license of such film upon the sale or license of one or more other films." The Government contends that this provision appearing by itself is too vague and will lead to unnecessary litigation. Differentials unjustified by cost savings may already be prohibited under the decree as it now appears. Nevertheless, the addition of a specific provision to prevent such differentials will prevent uncertainty in the operation of the decree. To ensure that litigation over the scope and application of the decrees is not left until a contempt proceeding is brought, the second requested modification should be added. The Government, however, seeks to make distribution costs the only saving which can legitimately be the basis of a discount. We would not so limit the relevant cost justifications. To prevent definitional arguments, and to ensure that all proper bases of quantity discount may be used, the modification should be worded in terms of allowing all legitimate cost justifications. . . .

Questions on *Loew's*

1. Does it seem possible that the tying agreements here foreclosed a substantial enough share of any market to impair the competitiveness of rival film distributors? Do you think any of the films had the market power necessary to impose that sort of anticompetitive effect?

2. Is it possible that the tying agreements here helped facilitate price discrimination? Suppose there are two sorts of television stations. Some value "Gone With The Wind" at $200,000 and "Getting Gertie's Garter" at $50,000. Others value "Gone With The Wind" at $180,000 and "Getting Gertie's Garter" at $70,000.

a. If a distributor with both films charged separate prices that were low enough to sell both films, what would it have to charge for each? How much would it make?

b. If the distributor instead sold both films as a package, what package price could it set to sell both films to both television stations? Would the distributor make more or less money? Would market output be reduced or enhanced? Consumer welfare?

c. Do copyrights give the distributors enough market power to create that effect? Would competition among distributors prevent such block-booking and price discrimination from occurring?

d. Suppose the distributor instead sold "Gone With The Wind" at an unbundled price of $200,000, "Getting Gertie's Garter" at an unbundled price of "$70,000" and a package of both for $249,000. Would it effectively achieve the same result?

3. Do the Court's rulings on the decrees:

a. necessarily condemn package discounts that are not cost-justified?

b. do they allow package discounts that are cost-justified even if they induce buyers to accept the bundle?

4. Wouldn't a doctrine that condemns package discounts that exceed package cost savings deter lower prices?

a. If the amount of the cost savings were uncertain, what effect might such a doctrine have on the prices a bundler would set?

b. Should package discounts that exceed package cost savings always be allowed if the resulting package price exceeds the cost of producing the package? Is this any different from above-cost price cutting?

c. What if the defendant artificially raises its unbundled price for the tying product well above the separate price it would otherwise charge for it, and then adopts a package discount? Can't that be the equivalent of absolute tying even though the resulting package price exceeds the package cost?

FTC v. Brown Shoe

384 U.S. 316 (1966).

■ MR. JUSTICE BLACK delivered the opinion of the Court.

. . . Proceeding under the authority of [FTC Act] § 5, the Federal Trade Commission filed a complaint against the Brown Shoe Co., Inc., one of the world's largest manufacturers of shoes . . . The unfair practices charged against Brown revolve around the "Brown Franchise Stores' Program" through which Brown sells its shoes to some 650 retail stores. The complaint alleged that under this plan Brown . . . had "entered into contracts or franchises with a substantial number of its independent retail shoe store operator customers which require said customers to restrict their purchases of shoes for resale to the Brown lines and which prohibit them from purchasing, stocking or reselling shoes manufactured by competitors of Brown." Brown's customers who entered into these restrictive franchise agreements, so the complaint charged, were given in return special treatment and valuable benefits which were not granted to Brown's customers who did not enter into the agreements. In its answer to the Commission's complaint Brown admitted that approximately 259 of its retail customers had executed written franchise agreements and that over 400 others had entered into its franchise program without execution of the franchise agreement. Also in its answer Brown attached as an exhibit an unexecuted copy of the "Franchise Agreement" which, when executed by Brown's representative and a retail shoe dealer, obligates Brown to give to the dealer but not to other customers certain valuable services, including among others architectural plans, costly merchandising records, services of a Brown field representative, and a right to participate in group insurance at lower rates than the dealer could obtain individually. In return, according to the franchise agreement set out in Brown's answer, the retailer must make this promise:

> "In return I will: '1. Concentrate my business within the grades and price lines of shoes representing Brown Shoe Company Franchises of the Brown Division and will have no lines conflicting with Brown Division Brands of the Brown Shoe Company.' "

Brown's answer further admitted that the operators of "such Brown Franchise Stores in individually varying degrees accept the benefits and perform the obligations contained in such franchise agreements or implicit in such Program," and that Brown refuses to grant these benefits "to dealers who are dropped or voluntarily withdraw from the Brown Franchise Program . . ."[125] The foregoing admissions of Brown as to the existence and operation of the franchise program were buttressed by many

---

125. [Editor's Note: The lower court had sustained the agreements in part because "[r]etailers were free to abandon the arrangement at any time they saw it to their advantage so to do." Brown Shoe v. FTC, 339 F.2d 45, 53 (8th Cir. 1964).]

separate detailed fact findings of a trial examiner, one of which findings was that the franchise program effectively foreclosed Brown's competitors from selling to a substantial number of retail shoe dealers.[2] Based on these findings and on Brown's admissions the Commission concluded that the restrictive contract program was an unfair method of competition within the meaning of § 5 and ordered Brown to cease and desist from its use.

On review the Court of Appeals set aside the Commission's order.... Thus the question we have for decision is whether the Federal Trade Commission can declare it to be an unfair practice for Brown, the second largest manufacturer of shoes in the Nation, to pay a valuable consideration to hundreds of retail shoe purchasers in order to secure a contractual promise from them that they will deal primarily with Brown and will not purchase conflicting lines of shoes from Brown's competitors. We hold that the Commission has power to find, on the record here, such an anticompetitive practice unfair, subject of course to judicial review....

[T]he Commission has broad powers to declare trade practices unfair. This broad power of the Commission is particularly well established with regard to trade practices which conflict with the basic policies of the Sherman and Clayton Acts even though such practices may not actually violate these laws. The record in this case shows beyond doubt that Brown, the country's second largest manufacturer of shoes, has a program, which requires shoe retailers, unless faithless to their contractual obligations with Brown, substantially to limit their trade with Brown's competitors. This program obviously conflicts with the central policy of both § 1 of the Sherman Act and § 3 of the Clayton Act against contracts which take away freedom of purchasers to buy in an open market. Brown nevertheless contends that the Commission had no power to declare the franchise program unfair without proof that its effect "may be to substantially lessen competition or tend to create a monopoly" which of course would have to be proved if the Government were proceeding against Brown under § 3 of the Clayton Act rather than § 5 of the Federal Trade Commission Act. We reject the argument that proof of this § 3 element must be made for ... the Commission has power under § 5 to arrest trade restraints in their incipiency without proof that they amount to an outright violation of § 3 of the Clayton Act or other provisions of the antitrust laws.... Reversed.

Questions on *FTC v. Brown Shoe*

The Court here holds that the FTC can condemn exclusive dealing or loyalty discounts without proof that a substantial share of the market was

---

2. In its opinion the Commission found that the services provided by Brown in its franchise program were the "prime motivation" for dealers to join and remain in the program; that the program resulted in franchised stores purchasing 75% of their total shoe requirements from Brown—the remainder being for the most part shoes which were not "conflicting" lines, as provided by the agreement; that the effect of the plan was to foreclose retail outlets to Brown's competitors, particularly small manufacturers; and that enforcement of the plan was effected by teams of field men who called upon the shoe stores, urged the elimination of other manufacturers' conflicting lines and reported deviations to Brown who then cancelled under a provision of the agreement.

foreclosed if those agreements would violate Clayton Act § 3 and Sherman Act § 1 if substantial market foreclosure were shown.

1. Does it make sense to allow the FTC to condemn exclusive dealing or loyalty discount agreements without proof of substantial market foreclosure or direct proof of anticompetitive effect? What anticompetitive effect could such agreements have without such substantial foreclosure?

2. Should antitrust law condemn loyalty agreements like this when the buyer can terminate the loyalty condition at any time if it is willing to forgo benefits the seller provides to loyal buyers?

a. In a market with many buyers, does any individual buyer have any incentive to forgo such benefits in order to try to prevent marketwide foreclosure?

b. Doesn't Clayton Act § 3 specifically cover loyalty discounts?

Concord Boat v. Brunswick Corp.

207 F.3d 1039 (8th Cir. 2000).

■ DIANA E. MURPHY, CIRCUIT JUDGE.

A number of boat builders brought this antitrust action against stern drive engine manufacturer Brunswick Corporation (Brunswick) for violations of Sections 1 and 2 of the Sherman Act.... The case was tried to a jury for ten weeks, and a verdict was returned in favor of the boat builders ... The district court ... denied [Brunswick's] motions for a new trial and for judgment as a matter of law on the boat builders' claims.... [W]e reverse....

Neither side contests the finding of the jury that the relevant market is the market for inboard and stern drive marine engines.... Stern drive engines are used primarily in recreational power boats known as runabouts, which are typical water skiing boats, and in cruising boats, which are larger and more expensive boats and usually have cabins....

Brunswick has been the market leader in stern drive engine manufacturing for many years, and by 1983 it had earned a 75% market share.... From 1984 to 1994, Brunswick offered a 3% discount to boat builders who bought 80% of their engines from the company, a 2% discount for 70% of all purchases, and a 1% discount for those who took 60% of their needs from Brunswick. For the 1995 to 1997 model year program, the market share requirements were reduced so that the maximum 3% discount could be earned by buying 70% from Brunswick; customers could receive a 2% discount for 65% market share and 1% for 60% market share. Another feature was added to the program in 1989 to offer long term discounts of an additional 1 or 2% to anyone who signed a market share agreement for two to three years.[3] Boat builders also could receive a volume discount of up to 5% based on the quantity of engines purchased....

---

3. Four financially troubled boatbuilders—Baja, Porter, Pro–Line, and Fountain—entered into long term contracts with Brunswick in exchange for financial assistance.... The Baja and Fountain contracts required those companies to purchase 100% of their engines from Brunswick. Porter was required to purchase 99%, and Pro–Line's contract contained a 50%

Neither the regular market share discount program, the long term program, nor the volume discount program obligated boat builders and dealers to purchase engines from Brunswick, and none of the programs restricted the ability of builders and dealers to purchase engines from other engine manufacturers. Builders and dealers were able to buy up to 40% of their engines from other manufacturers and still obtain a discount from Brunswick. Several boat builders chose to take a higher percentage of their engines from Brunswick than necessary to qualify for its largest market share discount; some purchased 95 or 100% of their engines from Brunswick. . . .

It is undisputed that the market share discounts were not exclusive contracts. At most the programs were de facto exclusive dealing arrangements. Dr. Hall testified at trial that the discount programs were "voluntary contracts. Nobody forced the boatmakers individually to accept these. They accepted these contracts because they individually got a deal from it. They got their discounts if they bought a lot of Brunswick engines."

Section 1 claims that allege only de facto exclusive dealing may be viable. The principle criteria used to evaluate the reasonableness of a contractual arrangement include the extent to which competition has been foreclosed in a substantial share of the relevant market, the duration of any exclusive arrangement, and the height of entry barriers.

The boat builders failed to produce sufficient evidence to demonstrate that Brunswick had foreclosed a substantial share of the stern drive engine market through anticompetitive conduct. They also did not demonstrate that Brunswick's discount program was in any way exclusive. The programs did not require the boat builders to commit to Brunswick for any specified period of time. They were free to walk away from the discounts at any time, and they in fact switched to OMC engines at various points when that manufacturer offered superior discounts. . . .

The boat builders also did not show that significant barriers to entry existed in the stern drive engine market. If entry barriers to new firms are not significant, it may be difficult for even a monopoly company to control prices through some type of exclusive dealing arrangement because a new firm or firms easily can enter the market to challenge it. . . .

In sum, the boat builders failed to establish Section 1 violations or a sufficient causal connection between the alleged violations and their injuries. In order to make out their case they had to produce evidence to show that Brunswick's market share discount programs were an unreasonable contractual arrangement, based on the amount of market foreclosure, exclusivity, and the erection of entry barriers. . . .

To establish a Section 2 violation, plaintiffs must show that 1) the defendant possessed monopoly power in the relevant market and 2) the defendant willfully acquired or maintained this monopoly power by anticompetitive conduct as opposed to gaining that power as a result "of a superior product, business acumen, or historical accident." . . .

---

market share threshold. The boat builders' expert testified that these companies made up about 5% of the stern drive engine market.

The boat builders argue that the discount programs and acquisitions were part of a deliberate plan to exclude competitors from the stern drive engine market, and that this exclusion enabled Brunswick to charge supracompetitive high prices for its engines.... Because cutting prices in order to increase business often is the very essence of competition, which antitrust laws were designed to encourage, it "is beyond the practical ability of a judicial tribunal to control [above cost discounting] without courting intolerable risks of chilling legitimate price cutting." *Brooke*.... If a firm has discounted prices to a level that remains above the firm's average variable cost, "the plaintiff must overcome a strong presumption of legality by showing other factors indicating that the price charged is anticompetitive." *Morgan*, 892 F.2d at 1360. This is because a firm's ability to offer above cost discounts is attributable to "the lower cost structure of the alleged predator, and so represents competition on the merits...." *Brooke*....

No one argues in this case that Brunswick's discounts drove the engine price below cost, and Brunswick contends that its discounts were therefore per se lawful. The district court questioned Brunswick's per se legality theory, since the boat builders' claim was that Brunswick's conduct as a whole ... enabled it to "charge [ ] anticompetitive *high* prices for its engines." The court examined several cases that had "rejected the argument that *any* pricing practice that leads to above costs prices is *per se* lawful under the antitrust laws." *See LePage's.* The cases examined by the district court all involve bundling or tying, however, which "cannot exist unless two separate product markets have been linked." Because only one product, stern drive engines, is at issue here and there are no allegations of tying or bundling with another product, we do not find these cases persuasive.

The boat builders also have not shown that Brunswick's superior market share was achieved or maintained "by means other than the competition on the merits...." A Section 2 defendant's proffered business justification is the most important factor in determining whether its challenged conduct is not competition on the merits....

Brunswick's business justification in this case is that it was trying to sell its product. Cutting prices is the "very essence of competition." Brunswick's competitors also cut prices in order to attract additional business, confirming that such a practice was a normal competitive tool within the stern drive manufacturing industry. In addition, Brunswick's discount programs were not exclusive dealing contracts and its customers were not required either to purchase 100% from Brunswick or to refrain from purchasing from competitors in order to receive the discount (and in fact could purchase up to 40% of requirements from other sellers without forgoing the discount). Boat builders and dealers were free to walk away from Brunswick's discounts at any time, and the evidence showed that they did so when Brunswick's competitors offered better discounts, thus discrediting the boat builders' theory that the discounts created "golden handcuffs" and entry barriers for other engine manufacturers....

Questions on *Concord Boat*

1. Did the defendants offer any efficiency justification for the conditions restricting buyers from buying more than 20–40% of their purchases from the defendant's rivals? Is a justification for lowering prices the same as a justification for conditioning lower prices on compliance with an condition restricting purchases from rivals?

2. Did the plaintiffs show foreclosure of a substantial share of the market? Even if they had, would that suffice to show likely anticompetitive effects without proof of significant entry barriers?

3. Should the case turn on the fact that the conditions required that buyers make 60–80% of their purchases from the defendant rather than 100%? If 100% of buyers commit to buying 60% from the defendant, would the foreclosure and likely anticompetitive effect be smaller than if 50% of buyers commit to buying 100% from the defendant?

4. Should the case turn on the fact that the discounts were only 1–3%? Is it implausible that buyers would accept an anticompetitive condition for such a small discount? Does the size of the discount affect the ability of rivals to match it?

5. Should loyalty discounts be illegal only if the discounted price is below cost? If so, should that also be the rule for all exclusive dealing agreements since they generally require some sort of discount from a monopoly price to induce acceptance? Wouldn't this convert all exclusive dealing cases into predatory pricing cases?

6. Does it matter that buyers voluntarily agreed to the loyalty discounts? Aren't all buyer agreements to exclusionary agreements voluntary? Does this mean all such agreements are procompetitive?

7. Does it matter that the loyalty conditions were terminable to buyers who were willing to forgo the discounts? Do buyers have any different incentives to terminate than they have to enter into exclusionary agreements that give them discounts in exchange for abiding by loyalty conditions?

8. Are the anticompetitive effects increased or lessened by the fact that (a) other sellers also used loyalty discounts and (b) buyers sometimes switched from loyalty discounts with one seller to loyalty discounts with the other?

LePage's Inc. v. 3M

324 F.3d 141 (3d Cir. 2003) (en banc).

■ SLOVITER, CIRCUIT JUDGE, with whom BECKER, CHIEF JUDGE, NYGAARD, McKEE, AMBRO, FUENTES, and SMITH, CIRCUIT JUDGES, join:

Minnesota Mining and Manufacturing Company ("3M") appeals from the District Court's order ... declining to overturn the jury's verdict for LePage's in its suit against 3M under Section 2 of the Sherman Act ("§ 2"). 3M raises various objections to the trial court's decision but essentially its position is a legal one: it contends that a plaintiff cannot succeed in a § 2 monopolization case unless it shows that the conceded monopolist sold its product below cost. Because we conclude that exclusionary conduct, such as the exclusive dealing and bundled rebates proven here, can sustain a verdict under § 2 against a monopolist and because we find no other reversible error, we will affirm.

I. Factual Background

3M, which manufactures Scotch tape for home and office use, dominated the United States transparent tape market with a market share above 90% until the early 1990s. It has conceded that it has a monopoly in that market. LePage's ... around 1980, decided to sell "second brand" and private label transparent tape, *i.e.*, tape sold under the retailer's name rather than under the name of the manufacturer. By 1992, LePage's sold 88% of private label tape sales in the United States, which represented but a small portion of the transparent tape market. Private label tape sold at a lower price to the retailer and the customer than branded tape.

Distribution patterns and consumer acceptance accounted for a shift of some tape sales from branded tape to private label tape. With the rapid growth of office superstores, such as Staples and Office Depot, and mass merchandisers, such as Wal–Mart and Kmart, distribution patterns for second brand and private label tape changed as many of the large retailers wanted to use their "brand names" to sell stationery products, including transparent tape. 3M also entered the private label business during the early 1990s and sold its own second brand under the name "Highland."

LePage's claims that, in response to the growth of this competitive market, 3M engaged in a series of related, anticompetitive acts aimed at restricting the availability of lower-priced transparent tape to consumers. It also claims that 3M devised programs that prevented LePage's and the other domestic company in the business, Tesa Tuck, Inc., from gaining or maintaining large volume sales and that 3M maintained its monopoly by stifling growth of private label tape and by coordinating efforts aimed at large distributors to keep retail prices for Scotch tape high. LePage's claims that it barely was surviving at the time of trial and that it suffered large operating losses from 1996 through 1999.

LePage's brought this antitrust action asserting that 3M used its monopoly over its Scotch tape brand to gain a competitive advantage in the private label tape portion of the transparent tape market in the United States through the use of 3M's multi-tiered "bundled rebate" structure, which offered higher rebates when customers purchased products in a number of 3M's different product lines. LePage's also alleges that 3M offered to some of LePage's customers large lump-sum cash payments, promotional allowances and other cash incentives to encourage them to enter into exclusive dealing arrangements with 3M....

[T]he jury returned its verdict for LePage's on ... its monopolization ... clai[m]....

III. Monopolization—Applicable Legal Principles ...

In this case, the parties agreed that the relevant product market is transparent tape and the relevant geographic market is the United States.... LePage's argues that 3M willfully maintained its monopoly in the transparent tape market through exclusionary conduct, primarily by bundling its rebates and entering into contracts that expressly or effectively required dealing virtually exclusively with 3M, which LePage's characterizes as *de facto* exclusive. 3M does not argue that it did not engage in this conduct. It agrees that it offered bundled rebates and entered into some exclusive dealing contracts, although it argues that only the few contracts that are expressly exclusive may be considered as such. Instead, 3M argues that its conduct was legal as a matter of law because it never priced its transparent tape below its cost.... For this proposition it relies on the Supreme Court's decision in *Brooke Group*....

It is therefore necessary for us, at the outset, to examine whether we must accept 3M's legal theory that after *Brooke Group,* no conduct by a monopolist who sells its product above cost—no matter how exclusionary the conduct—can constitute monopolization in violation of § 2 of the Sherman Act.... LePage's, unlike the plaintiff in *Brooke Group,* does not make a predatory pricing claim.... Nothing in any of the Supreme Court's opinions in the decade since the *Brooke Group* decision suggested that the opinion overturned decades of Supreme Court precedent that evaluated a monopolist's liability under § 2 by examining its exclusionary, i.e., predatory, conduct.... Thus, nothing that the Supreme Court has written since *Brooke Group* dilutes the Court's consistent holdings that a monopolist will be found to violate § 2 of the Sherman Act if it engages in exclusionary or predatory conduct without a valid business justification.

IV.   Monopolization—Exclusionary Conduct ...

B. *Bundled Rebates*

... 3M offered many of LePage's major customers substantial rebates to induce them to eliminate or reduce their purchases of tape from LePage's. Rather than competing by offering volume discounts which are concededly legal and often reflect cost savings, 3M's rebate programs offered discounts to certain customers conditioned on purchases spanning six of 3M's diverse product lines. The product lines covered by the rebate program were: Health Care Products, Home Care Products, Home Improvement Products, Stationery Products (including transparent tape), Retail Auto Products, and Leisure Time. In addition to bundling the rebates, both of 3M's rebate programs set customer-specific target growth rates in each product line. The size of the rebate was linked to the number of product lines in which targets were met, and the number of targets met by the buyer determined the rebate it would receive on all of its purchases. If a customer failed to meet the target for any one product, its failure would cause it to lose the rebate across the line. This created a substantial incentive for each customer to meet the targets across all product lines to maximize its rebates.

The rebates were considerable, not "modest" as 3M states. For example, Kmart, which had constituted 10% of LePage's business, received $926,287 in 1997, and in 1996 Wal–Mart received more than $1.5 million, Sam's Club received $666,620, and Target received $482,001. Just as significant as the amounts received is the powerful incentive they provided to customers to purchase 3M tape rather than LePage's in order not to forego the maximum rebate 3M offered. The penalty would have been

$264,000 for Sam's Club, $450,000 for Kmart, and $200,000 to $310,000 for American Stores....

[O]ne of the leading treatises notes that "the great majority of bundled rebate programs yield aggregate prices above cost. Rather than analogizing them to predatory pricing, they are best compared with tying, whose foreclosure effects are similar. Indeed, the 'package discount' is often a close analogy." Phillip E. Areeda & Herbert Hovenkamp, Antitrust Law ¶ 794, at 83 (Supp.2002). The treatise then discusses the anticompetitive effect as follows:

> The anticompetitive feature of package discounting is the strong incentive it gives buyers to take increasing amounts or even all of a product in order to take advantage of a discount aggregated across multiple products. In the anticompetitive case, which we presume is in the minority, the defendant rewards the customer for buying its product *B* rather than the plaintiff's *B*, not because defendant's *B* is better or even cheaper. Rather, the customer buys the defendant's *B* in order to receive a greater discount on *A*, which the plaintiff does not produce. In that case the rival can compete in *B* only by giving the customer a price that compensates it for the foregone *A* discount.

Id. The authors then conclude: "Depending on the number of products that are aggregated and the customer's relative purchases of each, even an equally efficient rival may find it impossible to compensate for lost discounts on products that it does not produce." *Id.* at 83–84.

The principal anticompetitive effect of bundled rebates as offered by 3M is that when offered by a monopolist they may foreclose portions of the market to a potential competitor who does not manufacture an equally diverse group of products and who therefore cannot make a comparable offer..... LePage's private-label and second-tier tapes are ... less expensive but otherwise of similar quality to Scotch-brand tape. Indeed, before 3M instituted its rebate program, LePage's had begun to enjoy a small but rapidly expanding toehold in the transparent tape market. 3M's incentive was thus ... to preserve the market position of Scotch-brand tape by discouraging widespread acceptance of the cheaper, but substantially similar, tape produced by LePage's.... [T]he bundled rebates reflected an exploitation of the seller's monopoly power. ... [T]he evidence in this case shows that Scotch-brand tape is indispensable to any retailer in the transparent tape market.... 3M's rebates required purchases bridging 3M's extensive product lines. In some cases, these magnified rebates to a particular customer were as much as half of LePage's entire prior tape sales to that customer....

C. *Exclusive Dealing*

The second prong of LePage's claim of exclusionary conduct by 3M was its actions in entering into exclusive dealing contracts with large customers. 3M acknowledges only the expressly exclusive dealing contracts with Venture and Pamida which conditioned discounts on exclusivity. It minimizes these because they represent only a small portion of the market.

However, LePage's claims that 3M made payments to many of the larger customers that were designed to achieve sole-source supplier status. . . .

3M also disclaims as exclusive dealing any arrangement that contained no express exclusivity requirement. . . . [T]he law is to the contrary. No less an authority than the United States Supreme Court has so stated. In *Tampa Elec.*, . . . the Court took cognizance of arrangements which, albeit not expressly exclusive, effectively foreclosed the business of competitors.

LePage's introduced powerful evidence that could have led the jury to believe that rebates and discounts to Kmart, Staples, Sam's Club, National Office Buyers and "UDI" were designed to induce them to award business to 3M to the exclusion of LePage's. Many of LePage's former customers refused even to meet with LePage's sales representatives. A buyer for Kmart, LePage's largest customer which accounted for 10% of its business, told LePage's: "I can't talk to you about tape products for the next three years" and "don't bring me anything 3M makes." Kmart switched to 3M following 3M's offer of a $1 million "growth" reward which the jury could have understood to require that 3M be its sole supplier. Similarly, Staples was offered an extra 1% bonus rebate if it gave LePage's business to 3M. . . .

The foreclosure of markets through exclusive dealing contracts is of concern under the antitrust laws. As one of the leading treatises states:

> unilaterally imposed quantity discounts can foreclose the opportu-
> nities of rivals when a dealer can obtain its best discount only by
> dealing exclusively with the dominant firm. For example, discounts
> might be cumulated over lengthy periods of time, such as a
> calendar year, when no obvious economies result.

3A Phillip E. Areeda & Herbert Hovenkamp, *Antitrust Law* ¶ 768b2, at 148 (2d Ed.2002); *see also* 11 Herbert Hovenkamp, *Antitrust Law* ¶ 1807a, at 115–16 (1998) (quantity discounts may foreclose a substantial portion of the market). Discounts conditioned on exclusivity are "problematic" "when the defendant is a dominant firm in a position to force manufacturers to make an all-or-nothing choice." *Id.* at 117 n. 7. . . .

LePage's produced evidence that the foreclosure caused by exclusive dealing practices was magnified by 3M's discount practices, as some of 3M's rebates were "all-or-nothing" discounts, leading customers to maximize their discounts by dealing exclusively with the dominant market player, 3M, to avoid being severely penalized financially for failing to meet their quota in a single product line. Only by dealing exclusively with 3M in as many product lines as possible could customers enjoy the substantial discounts. Accordingly, the jury could reasonably find that 3M's exclusion-ary conduct violated § 2.

V.   Anticompetitive Effect

It has been LePage's position in pursuing its § 2 claim that 3M's exclusionary "tactics foreclosed the competitive process by preventing rivals from competing to gain (or maintain) a presence in the market." When a monopolist's actions are designed to prevent one or more new or potential competitors from gaining a foothold in the market by exclusion-ary, i.e. predatory, conduct, its success in that goal is not only injurious to the potential competitor but also to competition in general. It has been recognized, albeit in a somewhat different context, that even the foreclosure of "one significant competitor" from the market may lead to higher prices and reduced output. *Roland Mach. Co. v. Dresser Indus., Inc.,* 749 F.2d 380, 394 (7th Cir.1984)....

[I]n this case, the jury could have reasonably found that 3M's exclusionary conduct cut LePage's off from key retail pipelines necessary to permit it to compete profitably.[14] It was only after LePage's entry into the market that 3M introduced the bundled rebates programs. If 3M were successful in eliminating competition from LePage's second-tier or private-label tape, 3M could exercise its monopoly power unchallenged, as Tesa Tuck was no longer in the market.... "Plaintiff introduced evidence that ... 3M's bundled rebate programs caused distributors to displace Le Page's entirely, or in some cases, drastically reduce purchases from Le Page's." ... [These were often customized for particular buyers to cause them to drop LePage's and Tesa in favor of 3M.]

... [T]he District Court found that "[LePage's] introduced substantial evidence that the anticompetitive effects of 3M's rebate programs caused Le Page's losses." The jury was capable of calculating from the evidence the amount of rebate a customer of 3M would lose if it failed to meet 3M's quota of sales in even one of the bundled products. The discount that LePage's would have had to provide to match the discounts offered by 3M through its bundled rebates can be measured by the discounts 3M gave or offered. For example, LePage's points out that in 1993 Sam's Club would have stood to lose $264,900, and Kmart $450,000 for failure to meet one of 3M's growth targets in a single product line. Moreover, the effect of 3M's rebates on LePage's earnings, if LePage's had attempted to match 3M's discounts, can be calculated by comparing the discount that LePage's would have been required to provide. That amount would represent the impact of 3M's bundled rebates on LePage's ability to compete, and that is what is relevant under § 2 of the Sherman Act.

The impact of 3M's discounts was apparent from the chart introduced by LePage's showing that LePage's earnings as a percentage of sales plummeted to below zero—to negative 10%—during 3M's rebate program. Demand for LePage's tape, especially its private-label tape, decreased significantly following the introduction of 3M's rebates.... Prior to the introduction of 3M's rebate program, LePage's sales had been skyrocketing. Its sales to Staples increased by 440% from 1990 to 1993. Following the introduction of 3M's rebate program which bundled its private-label tape with its other products, 3M's private-label tape sales increased 478% from 1992 to 1997. LePage's in turn lost a proportional amount of sales. It lost key large volume customers, such as Kmart, Staples, American Drugstores, Office Max, and Sam's Club. Other large customers, like Wal–Mart, drastically cut back their purchases.

---

14. In the transparent tape market, superstores like Kmart and Wal–Mart provide a crucial facility to any manufacturer—they supply high volume sales with the concomitant substantially reduced distribution costs. By wielding its monopoly power in transparent tape and its vast array of product lines, 3M foreclosed LePage's from that critical bridge to consumers that superstores provide, namely, cheap, high volume supply lines.

As a result, LePage's manufacturing process became less efficient and its profit margins declined. In transparent tape manufacturing, large volume customers are essential to achieving efficiencies of scale. As 3M concedes, " 'large customers were extremely important to [LePage's], to everyone.' ... Large volumes ... permitted 'long runs,' making the manufacturing process more economical and predictable."

There was a comparable effect on LePage's share of the transparent tape market. In the agreed upon relevant market for transparent tape in the United States, LePage's market share dropped 35% from 1992 to 1997. In 1992, LePage's net sales constituted 14.44% of the total transparent tape market. By 1997, LePage's sales had fallen to 9.35%. Finally, in March of 1997, LePage's was forced to close one of its two plants. That same year, the only other domestic transparent tape manufacturer, Tesa Tuck, Inc., bowed out of the transparent tape business entirely in the United States. Had 3M continued with its program it could have eventually forced LePage's out of the market.

The relevant inquiry is the anticompetitive effect of 3M's exclusionary practices considered together. [See] *Cont'l Ore Co. v. Union Carbide & Carbon Corp.*, 370 U.S. 690, 699 (1962).... The anticompetitive effect of 3M's exclusive dealing arrangements, whether explicit or inferred, cannot be separated from the effect of its bundled rebates. 3M's bundling of its products via its rebate programs reinforced the exclusionary effect of those programs.

3M's exclusionary conduct not only impeded LePage's ability to compete, but also it harmed competition itself, a *sine qua non* for a § 2 violation. LePage's presented powerful evidence that competition itself was harmed by 3M's actions. The District Court recognized this in its opinion, when it said:

> The jury could reasonably infer that 3M's planned elimination of the lower priced private label tape, as well as the lower priced Highland brand, would channel consumer selection to the higher priced Scotch brand and lead to higher profits for 3M. Indeed, Defendant concedes that "3M could later recoup the profits it has forsaken on Scotch tape and private label tape by selling more higher priced Scotch tape ... if there would be no competition by others in the private label tape segment when 3M abandoned that part of the market to sell only higher-priced Scotch tape."

3M could effectuate such a plan because there was no ease of entry. The District Court found that there was "substantial evidence at trial that significant entry barriers prevent competitors from entering the ... tape market in the United States...."

There was evidence from which the jury could have determined that 3M intended to force LePage's from the market, and then cease or severely curtail its own private-label and second-tier tape lines.... LePage's expert testified that the price of Scotch-brand tape increased since 1994, after 3M instituted its rebate program. In its opinion, the District Court cited the deposition testimony of a 3M employee acknowledging that the payment of the rebates after the end of the year discouraged passing the rebate on to the ultimate customers. The District Court thus observed, "the record amply reflects that 3M's rebate programs did not benefit the ultimate consumer."

As the foregoing review of the evidence makes clear, there was sufficient evidence for the jury to conclude the long-term effects of 3M's conduct were anticompetitive. We must therefore uphold its verdict on liability unless 3M has shown adequate business justification for its practices.

VI. Business Reasons Justification

... The defendant bears the burden of "persuad[ing] the jury that its conduct was justified by any normal business purpose." *Aspen Skiing*. Although 3M alludes to its customers' desire to have single invoices and single shipments in defense of its bundled rebates, 3M cites to no testimony or evidence ... that would support any actual economic efficiencies in having single invoices and/or single shipments. It is highly unlikely that 3M shipped transparent tape along with retail auto products or home improvement products to customers such as Staples or that, if it did, the savings stemming from the joint shipment approaches the millions of dollars 3M returned to customers in bundled rebates.

There is considerable evidence in the record that 3M entered the private-label market only to "kill it." That is precisely what § 2 of the Sherman Act prohibits by covering conduct that maintains a monopoly. Maintaining a monopoly is not the type of valid business reason that will excuse exclusionary conduct....

Questions on *LePage's*

1. Was the court right to reject the test that bundled discounts are legal if the bundled price is above the cost of making the bundle?

2. What is the court's test for determining when bundled discounts are anticompetitive? Is the court just applying the rule of reason test that bundled discounts are unlawful when direct evidence of anticompetitive effects exists (here harm to rival efficiency) unless some efficiency justification exists for the bundling? Is that a better test than the cost-based test?

3. What is the court's test for determining when loyalty discounts given for exclusivity are anticompetitive?

a. Did the court inquire into whether an equally efficient firm could match the loyalty discount?

b. Did the court calculate a foreclosure percentage?

i. Should it have to when the defendant is a monopolist and can cite no procompetitive justification for the exclusivity condition?

ii. Should it have to when the exclusive condition covers the most efficient means of distribution like K–Mart and Wal–Mart?

iii. Should it have to when there is direct evidence of anticompetitive effects on rival economies of scale?

4. Which of the possible anticompetitive concerns seems most plausible on these facts? Is it more likely 3M aimed to gain market power in private label tape or to increase its market power in brand name tape?

Cascade Health Solutions v. PeaceHealth

502 F.3d 895 (9th Cir. 2007).

■ GOULD, CIRCUIT JUDGE: . . .

McKenzie and PeaceHealth are the only two providers of hospital care in Lane County, Oregon. The . . . relevant market in this case is the market for primary and secondary acute care hospital services in Lane County. Primary and secondary acute care hospital services are common medical services like setting a broken bone and performing a tonsillectomy. Some hospitals also provide what the parties call "tertiary care," which includes more complex services like invasive cardiovascular surgery and intensive neonatal care. . . . In Lane County, PeaceHealth operates three hospitals while McKenzie operates one. McKenzie's . . . hospital . . . offers primary and secondary acute care . . . [but] does not provide tertiary care. . . . In Lane County, PeaceHealth has a 90% market share of tertiary neonatal services, a 93% market share of tertiary cardiovascular services, and a roughly 75% market share of primary and secondary care services. . . . PeaceHealth offered bundled discounts to Regence and other insurers in this case. Specifically, PeaceHealth offered insurers discounts if the insurers made PeaceHealth their exclusive preferred provider for primary, secondary, and tertiary care.

Bundled discounts are pervasive, and examples abound. Season tickets, fast food value meals, all-in-one home theater systems—all are bundled discounts. Like individual consumers, institutional purchasers seek and obtain bundled discounts, too. . . . Bundled discounts generally benefit buyers because the discounts allow the buyer to get more for less. Bundling can also result in savings to the seller because it usually costs a firm less to sell multiple products to one customer at the same time than it does to sell the products individually. . . .

However, it is possible, at least in theory, for a firm to use a bundled discount to exclude an equally or more efficient competitor and thereby reduce consumer welfare in the long run. For example, a competitor who sells only a single product in the bundle (and who produces that single product at a lower cost than the defendant) might not be able to match profitably the price created by the multi-product bundled discount. This is true even if the post-discount prices for both the entire bundle and each product in the bundle are above the seller's cost. Judge Kaplan's opinion in *Ortho* provides an example of such a situation:

> Assume for the sake of simplicity that the case involved the sale of two hair products, shampoo and conditioner, the latter made only by A and the former by both A and B. Assume as well that both must be used to wash one's hair. Assume further that A's average variable cost for conditioner is $2.50, that its average variable cost for shampoo is $1.50, and that B's average variable cost for shampoo is $1.25. B therefore is

the more efficient producer of shampoo. Finally, assume that A prices conditioner and shampoo at $5 and $3, respectively, if bought separately but at $3 and $2.25 if bought as part of a package. Absent the package pricing, A's price for both products is $8. B therefore must price its shampoo at or below $3 in order to compete effectively with A, given that the customer will be paying A $5 for conditioner irrespective of which shampoo supplier it chooses. With the package pricing, the customer can purchase both products from A for $5.25, a price above the sum of A's average variable cost for both products. In order for B to compete, however, it must persuade the customer to buy B's shampoo while purchasing its conditioner from A for $5. In order to do that, B cannot charge more than $0.25 for shampoo, as the customer otherwise will find A's package cheaper than buying conditioner from A and shampoo from B. On these assumptions, A would force B out of the shampoo market, notwithstanding that B is the more efficient producer of shampoo, without pricing either of A's products below average variable cost.

It is worth reiterating that, as the example above shows, a bundled discounter can exclude rivals who do not sell as great a number of product lines without pricing its products below its cost to produce them. Thus, a bundled discounter can achieve exclusion without sacrificing any short-run profits.

In this case, McKenzie asserts it could provide primary and secondary services at a lower cost than PeaceHealth. Thus, the principal anticompetitive danger of the bundled discounts offered by PeaceHealth is that the discounts could freeze McKenzie out of the market for primary and secondary services because McKenzie, like seller B in Judge Kaplan's example, does not provide the same array of services as PeaceHealth and therefore could possibly not be able to match the discount PeaceHealth offers insurers.

. . . [T]he district court based its jury instruction regarding the anti-competitive effect of bundled discounting on the Third Circuit's en banc decision in *LePage's*. . . . As the bipartisan Antitrust Modernization Commission ("AMC") recently noted, the . . . *LePage's* standard . . . asks the jury to consider whether the plaintiff has been excluded from the market, but does not require the jury to consider whether the plaintiff was at least as efficient of a producer as the defendant. Thus, the *LePage's* standard could protect a less efficient competitor at the expense of consumer welfare. . . . The AMC also lamented that *LePage's* "offers no clear standards by which firms can assess whether their bundled rebates are likely to pass antitrust muster." The Commission noted that efficiencies, and not schemes to acquire or maintain monopoly power, likely explain the use of bundled discounts because many firms without market power offer them. . . . The AMC proposed that:

> Courts should adopt a three-part test to determine whether bundled discounts or rebates violate Section 2 of the Sherman Act. To prove a violation of Section 2, a plaintiff should be required to show each one of the following elements (as well as other elements of a Section 2 claim): (1) after allocating all discounts and rebates attributable to the

entire bundle of products to the competitive product, the defendant sold the competitive product below its incremental cost for the competitive product; (2) the defendant is likely to recoup these short-term losses; and (3) the bundled discount or rebate program has had or is likely to have an adverse effect on competition.

The AMC reasoned that the first element would (1) subject bundled discounts to antitrust scrutiny only if they could exclude a hypothetical equally efficient competitor and (2) provide sufficient clarity for businesses to determine whether their bundled discounting practices run afoul of § 2. . . .

. . . [I]n neither *Brooke Group* nor *Weyerhaeuser* did the Court go so far as to hold that in every case in which a plaintiff challenges low prices as exclusionary conduct the plaintiff must prove that those prices were below cost. But the Court's opinions strongly suggest that, in the normal case, above-cost pricing will not be considered exclusionary conduct for antitrust purposes, and the Court's reasoning poses a strong caution against condemning bundled discounts that result in prices above a relevant measure of costs.

. . . [W]e hold that the exclusionary conduct element of a claim arising under § 2 of the Sherman Act cannot be satisfied by reference to bundled discounts unless the discounts result in prices that are below an appropriate measure of the defendant's costs. . . . The next question we must address is how we define the appropriate measure of the defendant's costs in bundled discounting cases and how we determine whether discounted prices fall below that mark. . . .

PeaceHealth and some amici urge us to adopt a rule they term the "aggregate discount" rule. This rule condemns bundled discounts as anticompetitive only in the narrow cases in which the discounted price of the entire bundle does not exceed the bundling firm's incremental cost to produce the entire bundle. PeaceHealth and amici argue that support for such a rule can be found in the Supreme Court's single product predation cases-*Brooke Group* and *Weyerhaeuser*.

We are not persuaded that those cases require us to adopt an aggregate discount rule in multi-product discounting cases. As we discussed above, bundled discounts present one potential threat to consumer welfare that single product discounts do not: A competitor who produces fewer products than the defendant but produces the competitive product at or below the defendant's cost to produce that product may nevertheless be excluded from the market because the competitor cannot match the discount the defendant offers over its numerous product lines. This possibility exists even when the defendant's prices are above cost for each individual product and for the bundle as a whole. Under a discount aggregation rule, anticompetitive bundled discounting schemes that harm competition may too easily escape liability.

Additionally, as commentators have pointed out, *Brooke Group*'s safe harbor for above-cost discounting in the single product discount context is not based on a theory that above-cost pricing strategies can never be anticompetitive, but rather on a cost-benefit rejection of a more nuanced rule. That is, the safe harbor rests on the premise that "any consumer benefit created by a rule that permits inquiry into above-cost, single-product discounts, but allows judicial condemnation of those deemed legitimately exclusionary, would likely be outweighed by the consumer harm occasioned by overdeterring nonexclusionary discounts." Lambert, 89 Minn. L.Rev. at 1705. So, in adopting an appropriate cost-based test for bundled discounting cases, we should not adopt an aggregate discount rule without inquiring whether a rule exists that is more likely to identify anticompetitive bundled discounting practices while at the same time resulting in little harm to competition.

The first potential alternative cost-based standard we consider derives from the district court's opinion in *Ortho*. This standard deems a bundled discount exclusionary if the plaintiff can show that it was an equally efficient producer of the competitive product, but the defendant's bundled discount made it impossible for the plaintiff to continue to produce profitably the competitive product. As the district court in Ortho phrased the standard: a plaintiff basing a § 2 claim on an anticompetitive bundled discount "must allege and prove either that (a) the monopolist has priced below its average variable cost or (b) the plaintiff is at least as efficient a producer of the competitive product as the defendant, but that the defendant's pricing makes it unprofitable for the plaintiff to continue to produce." . . .

However, one downside of *Ortho*'s standard is that it does not provide adequate guidance to sellers who wish to offer procompetitive bundled discounts because the standard looks to the costs of the actual plaintiff. A potential defendant who is considering offering a bundled discount will likely not have access to information about its competitors' costs, thus making it hard for that potential discounter, under the *Ortho* standard, to determine whether the discount it wishes to offer complies with the antitrust laws. Also, the *Ortho* standard, which asks whether the actual plaintiff is as efficient a producer as the defendant, could require multiple suits to determine the legality of a single bundled discount. While it might turn out that the plaintiff in one particular case is not as efficient a producer of the competitive product as the defendant, another rival might be. This second rival would have to bring another suit under the *Ortho* approach. We decline to adopt a rule that might encourage more antitrust litigation than is reasonably necessary to ferret out anticompetitive practices. Accordingly, we do not adopt *Ortho*'s approach, which we believe would be unduly cumbersome for sellers to assess and thus might chill procompetitive bundled discounting.

Instead, as our cost-based rule, we adopt what amici refer to as a "discount attribution" standard. Under this standard, the full amount of the discounts given by the defendant on the bundle are allocated to the competitive product or products. If the resulting price of the competitive product or products is below the defendant's incremental cost to produce them, the trier of fact may find that the bundled discount is exclusionary for the purpose of § 2. This standard makes the defendant's bundled discounts legal unless the discounts have the potential to exclude a hypothetical equally efficient producer of the competitive product. . . . .

The discount attribution standard provides clear guidance for sellers that engage in bundled discounting practices. A seller can easily ascertain its own prices and costs of production and calculate whether its discounting practices run afoul of the rule we have outlined. Unlike under the *Ortho* standard, under the discount attribution standard a bundled discounter need not fret over and predict or determine its rivals' cost structure ...

The next issue before us is the appropriate measure of incremental costs in a bundled discounting case.... We have ... held that a plaintiff can establish a prima facie case of predatory pricing by proving that the defendant's prices were below average variable cost. We see no reason to depart from these principles in the bundled discounting context, and we hold that the appropriate measure of costs for our cost-based standard is average variable cost....

In summary, we hold the following: To prove that a bundled discount was exclusionary or predatory for the purposes of a monopolization or attempted monopolization claim under § 2 of the Sherman Act, the plaintiff must establish that, after allocating the discount given by the defendant on the entire bundle of products to the competitive product or products, the defendant sold the competitive product or products below its average variable cost of producing them....[21] ...

Before trial, the district court granted PeaceHealth summary judgment on McKenzie's claim that PeaceHealth illegally tied primary and secondary services to its provision of tertiary services in violation of § 1 of the Sherman Act, ... because McKenzie presented no evidence that the insurers were coerced into taking the tied product ... As evidence that no

---

21. ... [T]he AMC's proposed standard in bundled discounting cases, in addition to requiring below-cost pricing, also contains two further proposed elements.

The second element proposed by the AMC is that there is a dangerous probability that the defendant will recoup its investment in the bundled discounting program. This requirement ... is imported from the single product predatory pricing context, but we think imported incorrectly. We do not believe that the recoupment requirement from single product cases translates to multi-product discounting cases. Single-product predatory pricing, unlike bundling, necessarily involves a loss for the defendant. For a period of time, the defendant must sell below its cost, with the intent to eliminate its competitors so that, when its competition is eliminated, the defendant can charge supracompetitive prices, recouping its losses and potentially more. By contrast, as discussed above, exclusionary bundling does not necessarily involve any loss of profits for the bundled discounter. As the example from *Ortho* illustrates, a bundled discounter can exclude its rivals who do not sell as many product lines even when the bundle as a whole, and the individual products within it, are priced above the discounter's incremental cost to produce them. The trier of fact can identify cases that present this possibility for anticompetitive exclusion by applying the discount attribution standard outlined above. Under that standard, the ultimate question is whether the bundled discount would exclude an equally efficient rival. But because discounts on all products in the bundle have been allocated to the competitive product in issue, a conclusion of below-cost sales under the discount attribution standard may occur in some cases even where there is not an actual loss because the bundle is sold at a price exceeding incremental cost. In such a case, we do not think it is analytically helpful to think in terms of recoupment of a loss that did not occur.

The third element proposed by the AMC is that "the bundled discount or rebate program has had or is likely to have an adverse effect on competition." We view this final element as redundant because it is no different than the general requirement of "antitrust injury" that a plaintiff must prove in any private antitrust action.

For these reasons, while adopting the AMC's proposal to require below-cost sales to prove exclusionary conduct, we do not adopt the element of recoupment, which we think may be inapplicable in some cases, and we do not adopt the element of "adverse effect on competition" as we think that is superfluous in light of the general and pre-existing requirement of antitrust injury ...

coercion was present in this case, the district court, in granting summary judgment to PeaceHealth, relied heavily on the deposition testimony of Farzenah Whyte, Regence's contract negotiator, who testified that Regence voluntarily entered into its contracts with PeaceHealth. PeaceHealth also points out that some insurers contracted to purchase PeaceHealth's services without exclusivity, indicating that PeaceHealth did not force those who wanted tertiary services to purchase primary and secondary services from PeaceHealth also. However, when all justifiable factual inferences are drawn in McKenzie's favor, there is no doubt that PeaceHealth's practice of giving a larger discount to insurers who dealt with it as an exclusive preferred provider may have coerced some insurers to purchase primary and secondary services from PeaceHealth rather than from McKenzie. We conclude that, as a whole, the evidence shows genuine factual disputes about whether PeaceHealth forced insurers either as an implied condition of dealing or as a matter of economic imperative through its bundled discounting, to take its primary and secondary services if the insurers wanted tertiary services.

First, while Whyte testified that Regence was not explicitly forced to deal exclusively with PeaceHealth, Whyte also testified that the higher prices PeaceHealth would have charged Regence had McKenzie been admitted to Regence's PPP would have had a "large impact" on Regence. Also, Whyte stated that she had been "held hostage" by PeaceHealth's pricing practices.

Standing alone, the fact that a customer would end up paying higher prices to purchase the tied products separately does not necessarily create a fact issue on coercion. However, the record contains additional evidence of economic coercion. For example, while PeaceHealth emphasizes that four insurers in Lane County purchased PeaceHealth's services separately, "a trivial proportion of separate sales shows that the package discount is as effective as an outright refusal to sell [the tying product] separately." 10 Areeda & Hovenkamp, supra, ¶ 1758b at 327 (2d ed.2004). In this case, there are twenty-eight insurers operating in Lane County. The fact that only four of them, or about 14% percent, made a separate purchase may indicate some degree of coercion, placing this issue in the realm of disputed facts that must be tendered to a jury. See id. at 328 (suggesting that a less than 10% proportion of separate sales indicates an illegal tie). Additionally, McKenzie provided some evidence that its prices on primary and secondary services were lower than PeaceHealth's prices on those services. Again, while not dispositive evidence of an illegal tie, it is a permissible inference that a rational customer would not purchase PeaceHealth's allegedly overpriced product in the absence of a tie. McKenzie also offered expert testimony that Regence's exclusive relationship with PeaceHealth made no economic sense, evidencing coercion . . .

Questions on *Cascade Health*

1. Is the court right to reject the "aggregate discount" test, which would require showing that the bundled price exceeded the costs of making the bundle?

2. Is the court right to adopt a "discount attribution" test that asks whether, if the whole bundled discount is attributed to the competitive product, the effective price for that product is below the defendant's cost of making that product?

    a. Won't this test allow bundled discounts that drive out less-efficient rivals even though the bundling has no efficiency justification? Is there any good reason to allow that?

    b. Isn't there a risk that the test could allow the defendant to immunize itself from antitrust liability by foreclosing enough of the market to raise its rivals' costs and above its own?

    c. Isn't the complaint not with the low prices but with the condition linked to those prices? If lower prices was the aim, couldn't PeaceHealth have just cut prices without bundling?

    3. Is the court right to reject the *Ortho* test that instead asks whether, after discount attribution, the price is below the costs of an actual rival that is at least as efficient? Even if it were easy to figure out which rivals were in fact less efficient, isn't a problem with the *Ortho* test that there is no reason to allow a defendant be able to use bundled discounts that result in an effective price below its own costs just because the existing rivals are less-efficient?

    4. Was the court right to reject the AMC elements requiring recoupment (because bundled discounts require no short term loss) and anticompetitive effect (because duplicative of antitrust injury)?

    5. Should the cost standard be based on variable or total costs? Does the answer turn on how long the bundled discounts last? Should a firm be able to use bundled discounts to deprive rivals of their normal rate of return?

    6. Should the test for when a bundled discount is sufficiently coercive to constitute a tie be: (a) a low proportion of separate sales, (b) whether the unbundled price exceeds the but-for price, (c) whether the effective price is lower than cost, or (d) whether the bundle's nominal price for the competitive product exceeds the rival's price?

The U.S. Lower Court Splits on Loyalty and Bundled Discounts

    Clayton Act § 3 explicitly makes it unlawful to substantially lessen competition by selling goods with a "discount" that is conditioned on the buyer not buying from rivals, which has been read to cover bundled or unbundled agreements of this sort whenever they have the practical effect of inducing such loyalty. Supreme Court cases have also established that it is not an antitrust defense that buyers were not 100% precluded by the loyalty condition,[126] could have avoided a loyalty or bundling condition by paying more,[127] or could have terminated a loyalty condition at will by

---

    126. *See* FTC v. Brown Shoe, 384 U.S. 316, 318 (1966) (condemning discounts conditioned on obligation to "concentrate" dealer business on the defendant's shoes, which in practice meant 75% of purchases).

    127. *See* Standard Fashion v. Magrane–Houston, 258 U.S. 346, 351–52 (1922) (loyalty condition); United Shoe Machinery v. United States, 258 U.S. 451, 464 (1922) (bundling condition).

foregoing such benefits.[128] Nor has any Supreme Court antitrust case finding loyalty discounts illegal required a below-cost price. But these cases all were before 1967, and the lack of recent Supreme Court cases has led to splits by modern lower courts on various key issues, in addition to the splits on foreclosure thresholds and terminability relevance noted in Section 4.B.

First, lower courts are split on whether loyalty discounts must result in prices that are below cost to give rise to antitrust liability.[129]

Second, lower courts are split on whether a loyalty condition must be at or near 100% to be actionable under antitrust law. Some suggest they must be.[130] Others have held they need not be.[131]

Third, lower courts are split on the tests applicable to bundled discounts. Some courts in bundled discount cases have concluded that the issue is whether the tied product is below the defendants' cost once all the discounts on the tying product are attributed to it.[132] Others have condemned bundled loyalty discounts unless "the components are separately available to the customer on a basis as favorable as the tie-in arrangement."[133] And yet others have condemned bundled discounts whenever they helped maintain monopoly power by making rebates on a monopoly product contingent on taking a non-monopoly product.[134]

Fourth, courts are split on whether to apply a form of abbreviated rule of reason review to loyalty or bundled discounts when the defendant fails to articulate any procompetitive efficiencies.[135] *LePage's* focused on the defendant's failure to offer a procompetitive justifications in finding the defendant liable even though the foreclosure share was never established,[136] thus implicitly adopting abbreviated rule of reason review. In contrast, *Concord Boat* found no liability even though the defendant failed to proffer any plausible procompetitive justifications,[137] thus implicitly rejecting abbreviated rule of reason review.

---

128. *See* FTC v. Brown Shoe, 384 U.S. 316 (1966).

129. *Compare* Concord Boat v. Brunswick Corp., 207 F.3d 1039, 1061–62 (8th Cir. 2000) (holding they must be below cost), *with* LePage's v. 3M, 324 F.3d 141, 147–52 (3d Cir. 2003) (en banc) (holding they need not be below cost).

130. *Concord Boat,* 207 F.3d at 1056, 1062–63 (seeming to require 100% obligation).

131. *See* United States v. Dentsply Int'l, Inc., 399 F.3d 181 (3d Cir. 2005) (condemning agreements that did not require 100% exclusivity but only that dealers not add new rival product lines); Microsoft v. United States, 253 F.3d 34, 68 (D.C. Cir. 2001) (en banc) (condemning agreements that conditioned favorable terms on 75% commitment).

132. *See* Cascade Health Solutions v. PeaceHealth, 502 F.3d 895 (9th Cir. 2007).

133. *See* Advance Business Systems v. SCM Corp., 415 F.2d 55, 62 (4th Cir. 1969).

134. *See* SmithKline Corp. v. Eli Lilly & Co., 575 F.2d 1056 (3d Cir. 1978).

135. FTC v. Indiana Federation of Dentists, 476 U.S. 447, 459–60 (1986) (holding abbreviated rule of reason appropriate where the defendant fails to articulate any procompetitive justification for a restraint).

136. *LePage's,* 324 F.3d at 152, 163–64.

137. *Concord Boat,* 207 F.3d at 1062. The only "justification" the defendant proffered to defend its conduct is that it was trying to sell its products, which is not a procompetitive justification because many anticompetitive arrangements have the goal of increasing the defendant's sales. *See Microsoft,* 253 F.3d at 71.

In your view, which side is right on these legal splits? Which way do you predict they will be resolved?

Case 85–76, Hoffmann–La Roche v. Commission

1979 E.C.R. 461.

[Hoffman–La Roche had entered into "fidelity agreements" with 22 large purchasers of vitamins which had the following main features. Roche paid a rebate to those customers who had obtained all or most of their requirements from Roche calculated on vitamin total purchases. The amount of the rebate differed from customer to customer and typically varied between 1% and 5%, although one customer received rebates of 12.5% to 20%.]

An undertaking which is in a dominant position on a market and ties purchasers—even if it does so at their request—by an obligation or promise on their part to obtain all or most of their requirements exclusively from the said undertaking abuses its dominant position within the meaning of article [102] of the Treaty, whether the obligation in question is stipulated without further qualification or whether it is undertaken in consideration of the grant of a rebate.

The same applies if the said undertaking, without tying the purchasers by a formal obligation, applies, either under the terms of agreements concluded with these purchasers or unilaterally, a system of fidelity rebates, that is to say discounts conditional on the customer's obtaining all or most of its requirements—whether the quantity of its purchases be large or small—from the undertaking in a dominant position.

Obligations of this kind to obtain supplies exclusively from a particular undertaking, whether or not they are in consideration of rebates or of the granting of fidelity rebates intended to give the purchaser an incentive to obtain his supplies exclusively from the undertaking in a dominant position, are incompatible with the objective of undistorted competition within the common market, because—unless there are exceptional circumstances which may make an agreement between undertakings in the context of article [101] and in particular of paragraph (3) of that article, permissible—they are not based on an economic transaction which justifies this burden or benefit but are designed to deprive the purchaser of or restrict his possible choices of sources of supply and to deny other producers access to the market.

The fidelity rebate, unlike quantity rebates exclusively linked with the volume of purchases from the producer concerned, is designed through the grant of a financial advantage to prevent customers from obtaining their supplies from competing producers.

Furthermore the effect of fidelity rebates is to apply dissimilar conditions to equivalent transactions with other trading parties in that two purchasers pay a different price for the same quantity of the same product depending on whether they obtain their supplies exclusively from the undertaking in a dominant position or have several sources of supply.

Finally these practices by an undertaking in a dominant position and especially on an expanding market tend to consolidate this position by means of a form of competition which is not based on the transactions effected and is therefore distorted. . . .

The applicant nevertheless submits that the agreed rebates are quantity and not fidelity rebates or that they correspond to an economic transaction with the customer justifying consideration of this kind.

In considering this submission it is necessary to distinguish between those contracts which provide for rebates at a fixed rate and those in which rebates at progressive rates are provided for.

(a) Contracts which provide for rebates at a fixed rate. First the applicant's argument cannot be accepted in the case of those contracts which provide for a rebate at a fixed rate.

In fact—and without prejudice to the observation that where exclusivity has been formally accepted the granting or not of a rebate is in the final analysis irrelevant—none of the said contracts includes any undertaking relating to fixed or only estimated quantities or linked to the volume of purchases but they all refer to "requirements" or a proportion of the said requirements.

Moreover in most of them the parties have themselves described the clause as a fidelity rebate clause . . . or used terms which strongly underline the link between the exclusivity and the rebates allowed. . . .

(b) Contracts which provide for rebates at progressive rates. A number of the contracts at issue . . . contain, on the one hand, an undertaking relating to "the major part" of the purchaser's requirements and, on the other hand, a rebate clause providing for a discount, the percentage whereof increases—in general from 1% to 2%, and then to 3%— depending on whether during the period of one year a greater or lesser percentage of the purchaser's estimated requirements has been met, each of the contracts containing a value estimate (in pounds sterling) of the total requirements and, in addition, in the case of two of the contracts . . . a quantitative estimate of each of the types of vitamins referred to in the contract.

By way of example reference may be made to the Beecham contract . . . whereby, since the annual requirements were estimated at a maximum of pounds 300,000, the rebate provided for was 1% if the turnover reached 60%, namely pounds 180,000, 1.5% if it reached 70%, namely pounds 210,000, and 2% if it reached 80%, namely pounds 240,000. There are similar formulae in the other contracts, the estimate of requirements differing from contract to contract and from year to year, obviously to allow for the customer's capacity of absorption.

Although the contracts at issue contain elements which appear at first sight to be of a quantitative nature as far as concerns their connexion with the granting of a rebate on aggregate purchases, an examination of them however shows that they are in fact a specially worked out form of fidelity rebate. . . .

This method of calculating the rebates differs from the granting of quantitative rebates, linked solely to the volume of purchases from the producers concerned in that the rebates at issue are not dependent on quantities fixed objectively and applicable to all possible purchasers but on estimates made, from case to case, for each customer according to the latter's presumed capacity of absorption, the objective which it is sought to attain being not the maximum quantity but the maximum requirements.

Consequently the Commission was also right to regard the said contracts containing fidelity rebates as an abuse of a dominant position. . . .

Questions on *Hoffmann–La Roche*

1. Why does the ECJ regard fidelity rebates as more anticompetitive than quantity rebates?

2. Does this case condemn fidelity rebates under a per se rule?

a. Doesn't a dominant position also have to be shown? Would the same legal standards apply under Article 101 if the firm had some level of market power below dominance? Should it?

b. Does this decision allow even a dominant firm to show that loyalty discounts may have the sort of procompetitive justifications listed in Article 101(3)?

i. Did the defendant in this case offer any such justification? Isn't the absence of such a redeeming virtue in fact the strongest basis for concluding that the object must have been anticompetitive? Does this case effectively apply abbreviated rule-of-reason review?

ii. Is the offering of a discount itself a procompetitive justification? Isn't what requires justification the loyalty condition, not the lower price, which could be offered without any condition restricting purchases from rivals? Could any "discount" offered to compliant buyers be equally characterized as a price "penalty" inflicted on noncompliant buyers? Do we have to know what but-for prices would have been without the scheme before we can determine whether the price offered to compliant buyers reflects any true discount or whether the price charged to noncompliant buyers reflects a true price penalty?

c. Does the case hold that substantial foreclosure need not be shown? Or did it simply assume such substantial foreclosure existed because the loyalty discounts covered 22 large purchasers? Should some proof of substantial foreclosure or anticompetitive effect be required before loyalty discounts are condemned?

3. Should loyalty discounts be deemed per se *legal* whenever the discounted price is above cost? Wouldn't such a standard convert all exclusionary agreement cases into predatory pricing cases? Would that be desirable?

Case 322/101, Nederlandsche Banden–Industrie Michelin v. Commission (Michelin I)

[1983] E.C.R. 346.

[Michelin offered its dealers an annual variable discount based on the dealer's turnover in Michelin heavy vehicle, van and car tyres in the previous year. The dealer received the discount, or the full rate thereof, only if he achieved an annual sales target set by Michelin. Neither the discount as a whole nor the scale of discounts was published by Michelin. The Commission concluded that this discount scheme violated Article 102.]

... [T]he Court has held in *Hoffman–La Roche* that in contrast to a quantity discount, which is linked solely to the volume of purchases from the manufacturer concerned, a loyalty rebate, which by offering customers financial advantages tends to prevent them from obtaining their supplies from competing manufacturers, amounts to an abuse within the meaning of Article [102 TFEU].

As regards the system at issue in this case, which is characterized by the use of sales targets, it must be observed that this system does not amount to a mere quantity discount linked solely to the volume of goods purchased since the progressive scale of the previous year's turnover indicates only the limits within which the system applies.... On the other hand the system in question did not require dealers to enter into any exclusive dealing agreements or to obtain a specific proportion of their supplies from Michelin, ... [which] distinguishes it from loyalty rebates of the type which the Court had to consider in ... *Hoffmann–La Roche.*

In deciding whether Michelin abused its dominant position in applying its discount system it is therefore necessary to consider all the circumstances, particularly the criteria and rules for the grant of the discount, and to investigate whether, in providing an advantage not based on any economic service justifying it, the discount tends to remove or restrict the buyer's freedom to choose his sources of supply, to bar competitors from access to the market, to apply dissimilar conditions to equivalent transactions with other trading parties or to strengthen the dominant position by distorting competition....

The discount system in question was based on an annual reference period. However, any system under which discounts are granted according to the quantities sold during a relatively long reference period has the inherent effect, at the end of that period, of increasing pressure on the buyer to reach the purchase figure needed to obtain the discount or to avoid suffering the expected loss for the entire period. In this case the variations in the rate of discount over a year as a result of one last order, even a small one, affected the dealer's margin of profit on the whole year's sales of Michelin heavy-vehicle tyres. In such circumstances, even quite slight variations might put dealers under appreciable pressure.

That effect was accentuated still further by the wide divergence between Michelin's market share and those of its main competitors. If a competitor wished to offer a dealer a competitive inducement for placing an order, especially at the end of the year, it had to take into account the absolute value of Michelin's annual target discount and fix its own discount at a percentage which, when related to the dealer's lesser quantity of purchases from that competitor, was very high. Despite the apparently low percentage of Michelin's discount, it was therefore very difficult for its competitors to offset the benefits or losses resulting for dealers from attaining or failing to attain Michelin's targets, as the case might be.

Furthermore, the lack of transparency of Michelin's entire discount system, whose rules moreover changed on several occasions during the relevant period, together with the fact that neither the scale of discounts nor the sales targets or discounts relating to them were communicated in writing to dealers meant that they were left in uncertainty and on the whole could not predict with any confidence the effect of attaining their targets or failing to do so.

All those factors were instrumental in creating for dealers a situation in which they were under considerable pressure, especially towards the end of a year, to attain Michelin's sales targets if they did not wish to run the risk of losses which its competitors could not easily make good by means of the discounts which they themselves were able to offer. Its network of commercial representatives enabled Michelin to remind dealers of this situation at any time so as to induce them to place orders with it.

Such a situation is calculated to prevent dealers from being able to select freely at any time in the light of the market situation the most favourable of the offers made by the various competitors and to change supplier without suffering any appreciable economic disadvantage. It thus limits the dealers' choice of supplier and makes access to the market more difficult for competitors. Neither the wish to sell more nor the wish to spread production more evenly can justify such a restriction of the customer's freedom of choice and independence. The position of dependence in which dealers find themselves and which is created by the discount system in question is not therefore based on any countervailing advantage which may be economically justified.

It must therefore be concluded that by binding dealers in the Netherlands to itself by means of the discount system described above Michelin committed an abuse, within the meaning of article [102] of the Treaty, of its dominant position in the market for new replacement tyres for heavy vehicles. . . .

Questions on *Michelin I*

1. Although this case involved volume-based discounts rather than share-based loyalty discounts, the ECJ nonetheless condemned them in part because the target volume was set differently for each dealer and varied with the prior year's purchases.

a. Why should it matter whether volume-based discounts vary for different firms? If tailored to the volume of each dealer, could volume-based discounts effectively amount to the same thing as a share-based loyalty discount?

b. Does a lack of transparency affect the likelihood that tailored volume-based discounts could really reflect share-based loyalty discounts?

c. Is the Court holding that the scheme here really amounted to share-based loyalty discounts? That they should be treated similarly because the defendant's conduct made it too difficult to ascertain whether they were or not? Or was the Court just concerned that different dealers were treated differently?

2. The ECJ was also concerned that year long volume-based discounts would create a lot of pressure on dealers at the end of the year if they were below their target. Is this a sensible ground to conclude the discounts were more likely to be anticompetitive? Couldn't one equally say that such volume-based discounts would create less pressure earlier in the year, and no pressure at all at the end of the year for dealers who had exceeded their target? Are year-long agreements of this sort categorically likely to be more anticompetitive than shorter ones?

3. Another factor the ECJ considered was the wide divergence between Michelin's market share and the shares of its main competitors?

a. Why should that matter? Isn't that generally likely to be true if the defendant has a dominant position triggering Article 102 scrutiny?

b. Suppose the ECJ meant the following: given Michelin's high market share, every dealer had to carry some Michelin tires to satisfy its customers. Thus, a dealer could not simply switch its business next year to a Michelin rival that offered a better loyalty discount. Would this effectively bundle a discount on the Michelin tires that have to be offered with a discount on the tires for which dealers have discretion? Does this suggest a greater anticompetitive concern?

4. As in *Hoffmann–La Roche,* the defendant here failed to offer a procompetitive justification. Given this, should any volume-based discount be deemed illegal under abbreviated-rule-of-reason review without any need to show the special factors that made the ECJ particularly concerned about these volume-based discounts?

Case T–203/01, Manufacture française des pneumatiques Michelin v. Commission (Michelin II)

[2003] ECR II–4071.

. . . [Michelin paid rebates to its dealers based on the quantity of tires they purchased the year before.] The quantity rebates system provided for an annual refund expressed as a percentage of the turnover achieved by the dealer with the applicant, the rate increasing gradually according to the quantities purchased. In that regard, the general conditions provided for three scales, depending on the tyres in question (all types, heavy plant tyre and retreads). In 1995, for example, the all types scale consisted of 47 steps. The rebate percentages ranged from 7.5% on a turnover of FRF 9,000 to 13% on a turnover of over FRF 22 million. The heavy plant tyre and retreads categories each had their own scale. In 1995 for example, the rebates ranged, in the case of retreads, from 2% on a turnover of over FRF 7,000 to 6% on a turnover in excess of FRF 3.92 million. . . .

[Michelin also paid a service bonus based on its assessment of whether the dealer had earned various service points. The bonus] ranged from 0% to 1.5% during the period 1980 to 1991 and from 0% to 2.25% for the period 1992 to 1996. The maximum score was 35 points and the maximum bonus was earned for a score of at least 31 out of 35 points. . . . [Michelin also offered other bonuses, including: (1) a progress bonus based on increased purchases from the prior year, (2) a PRO bonus based on a combination of progress, quantity of tires returned for retreading, and total output, and (3) a Michelin Friends Club bonus for promotion of Michelin tires.]

[The Commission deemed the above an abuse of a dominant position, fining Michelin 19.76 million euros and prohibiting it from engaging in the conduct again. Michelin appealed.]

First plea: the Commission infringed Article [102 TFEU] by holding that the quantity rebates constituted an abuse within the meaning of that provision ... [I]t is apparent from a consistent line of decisions that a loyalty rebate, which is granted in return for an undertaking by the customer to obtain his stock exclusively or almost exclusively from an undertaking in a dominant position, is contrary to Article [102 TFEU]. Such a rebate is designed through the grant of financial advantage, to prevent customers from obtaining their supplies from competing producers. *Hoffmann–La Roche*; *Michelin I*.

More generally, ... a rebate system which has a foreclosure effect on the market will be regarded as contrary to Article [102 TFEU] if it is applied by an undertaking in a dominant position. For that reason, the Court has held that a rebate which depended on a purchasing target being achieved also infringed Article [102 TFEU]. *Michelin I*.

Quantity rebate systems linked solely to the volume of purchases made from an undertaking occupying a dominant position are generally considered not to have the foreclosure effect prohibited by Article [102 TFEU]. *Michelin I*; *Portugal v Commission*. If increasing the quantity supplied results in lower costs for the supplier, the latter is entitled to pass on that reduction to the customer in the form of a more favourable tariff. Quantity rebates are therefore deemed to reflect gains in efficiency and economies of scale made by the undertaking in a dominant position.

It follows that a rebate system in which the rate of the discount increases according to the volume purchased will not infringe Article [102 TFEU] unless the criteria and rules for granting the rebate reveal that the system is not based on an economically justified countervailing advantage but tends, following the example of a loyalty and target rebate, to prevent customers from obtaining their supplies from competitors. *Hoffmann–La Roche*; *Michelin I*; *Irish Sugar*; *Portugal v. Commission*.

In determining whether a quantity rebate system is abusive, it will therefore be necessary to consider all the circumstances, particularly the criteria and rules governing the grant of the rebate, and to investigate whether, in providing an advantage not based on any economic service justifying it, the rebates tend to remove or restrict the buyer's freedom to choose his sources of supply, to bar competitors from access to the market, to apply dissimilar conditions to equivalent transactions with other trading parties or to strengthen the dominant position by distorting competition. *Hoffmann–La Roche*; *Michelin I*; and *Irish Sugar*.

The abusive nature of the quantity rebate system applied by the applicant ... This Court considers that it is necessary, first, to consider whether the Commission had good reason to conclude, in the contested decision, that the quantity rebate system was loyalty-inducing or, in other words, that it sought to tie dealers to the applicant and to prevent them from obtaining supplies from the applicant's competitors....

The loyalty-inducing nature of the quantity rebates ... In the present case, the Commission infers that the quantity rebates are loyalty-inducing from the following evidence: the fact that the discount is calculated on the dealer's entire turnover with Michelin and the fact that the reference period applied for the purpose of the discount is one year ... [T]he Court of Justice held in *Michelin I* that any system under which discounts are granted according to the quantities sold during a relatively long reference period has the inherent effect, at the end of that period, of increasing pressure on the buyer to reach the purchase figure needed to obtain the discount or to avoid suffering the expected loss for the entire period ... [I]t cannot be denied that the loyalty-inducing nature of a system of discounts calculated on total turnover achieved increases in proportion to the length of the reference period. A quantity rebate system has no loyalty-inducing effect if discounts are granted on invoice according to the size of the order. If a discount is granted for purchases made during a reference period, the loyalty-inducing effect is less significant where the additional discount applies only to the quantities exceeding a certain threshold than where the discount applies to total turnover achieved during the reference period. In the latter case, the saving which may be made by reaching a higher scale applies to total turnover achieved whereas, in the former case, it applies only to the additional amount purchased.

However, the applicant claims that the question whether the discount is calculated on total turnover or only on the additional amount purchased is merely a question of presentation. It states, in that regard, that a discount of a specific amount may always be expressed either as a percentage of the additional volume purchased or as a percentage of the total volume, although the percentage will be higher when the basis of the discount is the additional volume rather than the total volume.

That argument must be rejected. When the discount is granted by tranche, the discount obtained for the purchase of an additional unit never exceeds the percentage for the tranche in question. If the [program here] comprised a quantity rebate system in which the discount was calculated by tranche, the consequence, for example, of reaching the FRF 30,000 threshold in turnover would be that, for purchasing units exceeding that turnover threshold, a dealer would obtain a discount of 9.25% instead of 9%. In other words, by increasing his turnover with the applicant from FRF 29,999 to FRF 30,000, the dealer would obtain, in a discount system calculated by tranche, an additional discount of 0.25% or FRF 0.0025 (0.25% additional discount on the amount of FRF 1). A dealer's interest in reaching such a threshold is relatively limited. On the other hand, if, as in the present case, the discount applies to the total volume purchased, an increase in turnover with the applicant from FRF 29,999 to FRF 30,000 brings the dealer an additional discount of FRF 75 (0.25% additional discount on the amount of FRF 30 000), which is 7,500% of the additional turnover achieved (FRF 75 additional discount on an additional turnover of FRF 1). A dealer has a genuine interest in reaching a further threshold as regards both the thresholds at the lower end of the scale, as the above example shows, and those at the upper end of the scale. For example, by increasing his turnover from FRF 16,384,999 to FRF 16,387,000, a dealer would earn an additional discount of FRF 1 in a by tranche discount system (0.05% additional discount on the amount of FRF 2,001). In the system applied by the applicant, the additional discount was FRF 8,193.5 (0.05% additional discount on an amount of FRF 16 387 000), or an additional discount of approximately 410% of the additional turnover achieved (FRF 8,193.5 additional discount on an additional turnover of FRF 2,001).

It follows from all of the foregoing that a quantity rebate system in which there is a significant variation in the discount rates between the lower and higher steps, which has a reference period of one year and in which the discount is fixed on the basis of total turnover achieved during the reference period, has the characteristics of a loyalty-inducing discount system.

Admittedly, as the applicant points out, the aim of any competition on price and any discount system is to encourage the customer to purchase more from the same supplier.

However, an undertaking in a dominant position has a special responsibility not to allow its conduct to impair genuine undistorted competition on the common market. *Michelin I*. Not all competition on price can be regarded as legitimate. *AKZO*; *Irish Sugar*. An undertaking in a dominant position cannot have recourse to means other than those within the scope of competition on the merits.

In those circumstances, it is necessary to consider whether, in spite of appearances, the quantity rebate system applied by the applicant is based on a countervailing advantage which may be economically justified. *Michelin I*; *Irish Sugar*; *Portugal v. Commission* or, in other words, if it rewards an economy of scale made by the applicant because of orders for large quantities. If increasing the quantity supplied results in lower costs for the supplier, the latter is entitled to pass on that reduction to the customer in the form of a more favourable tariff. . . .

[T]he applicant provides no specific information in that regard. . . . Far from establishing that the quantity rebates were based on actual cost savings, the applicant merely states generally that the quantity rebates were justified by "economies of scale in the areas of production costs and distribution". However, such a line of argument is too general and is insufficient to provide economic reasons to explain specifically the discount rates chosen for the various steps in the rebate system in question. *Portugal v. Commission*.

It follows from all of the foregoing that the Commission was entitled to conclude, in the contested decision, that the quantity rebate system at issue was designed to tie truck tyre dealers in France to the applicant by granting advantages which were not based on any economic justification. Because it was loyalty-inducing, the quantity rebate system tended to prevent dealers from being able to select freely at any time, in the light of the market situation, the most advantageous of the offers made by various competitors and to change supplier without suffering any appreciable economic disadvantage. The rebate system thus limited the dealers' choice of supplier and made access to the market more difficult for competitors, while the position of dependence in which the dealers found themselves, and which was created by the discount system in question, was not therefore based on any countervailing advantage which might be economically justified. *Michelin I.*

The applicant cannot find support in the transparent nature of the quantity rebate system. A loyalty-inducing rebate system is contrary to Article [102 TFEU], whether it is transparent or not. Furthermore, the quantity rebates formed part of a complex system of discounts, some of which on the applicant's own admission constituted an abuse. The simultaneous application of various discount systems—namely, the quantity rebates, the service bonus, the progress bonus, and the bonuses linked to the PRO Agreement and the Michelin Friends Club—which were not obtained on invoice, made it impossible for the dealer to calculate the exact purchase price of Michelin tyres at the time of purchase. That situation inevitably put dealers in a position of uncertainty and dependence on the applicant.

The applicant's argument alleging that the Directorate–General for Competition, Consumer Affairs and Fraud Prevention (the DGCCRF) approved the quantity rebate system must also be rejected. Firstly, the documents referred to by the applicant provide no proof of the DGCCRF's approval. Secondly, it is in any event immaterial whether granting the discounts was compatible with French law or was approved by the DGCCRF, given the primacy of Community law on the matter and the direct effectiveness of Article [102 TFEU]. The alleged conformity of the quantity rebate system with United States competition law is likewise irrelevant in the present case.

It follows that the first plea must be rejected in its entirety.

Second plea: the Commission infringed Article [102 TFEU] by finding that the service bonus system constituted an abuse within the meaning of that provision ... [The Commission stated]: "The granting of the points was somewhat subjective and gave Michelin a margin of discretion in its assessment...." The Commission adds ...: Some of the headings were by their very nature subjective in their assessment and/or the number of points granted could vary depending on the quality of the service provided. However, the tally of the points scored was calculated by Michelin's representative, who also set the targets and the corresponding points for the current year. Michelin's ability to unilaterally decrease the bonus during the year if the targets were not met is yet another factor which enabled Michelin to make the conditions granted to dealers dependent on its subjective assessment. Michelin's argument that use was made of this possibility only in exceptional cases does not alter the fact that it was an abuse....

[T]he fact that the service bonus remunerates services rendered by the dealer has no relevance for the purpose of determining whether the bonus in question infringes Article [102 TFEU].... The granting of a discount by an undertaking in a dominant position to a dealer must be based on an objective economic justification. *Irish Sugar.* It cannot depend on a subjective assessment by the undertaking in a dominant position of the extent to which the dealer has met his commitments and is thus entitled to a discount. As the Commission points out in the contested decision, such an assessment of the extent to which the dealer has met his commitments enables the undertaking in a dominant position "to put strong pressure on the dealer ... and allow[s] it, if necessary, to use the arrangement in a discriminatory manner."

It follows that a discount system which is applied by an undertaking in a dominant position and which leaves that undertaking a considerable margin of discretion as to whether the dealer may obtain the discount must be considered unfair and constitutes an abuse by an undertaking of its dominant position on the market within the meaning of Article [102 TFEU]. *Hoffmann–La Roche*. Because of the subjective assessment of the criteria giving entitlement to the service bonus, dealers were left in uncertainty and on the whole could not predict with any confidence the rate of discount which they would receive by way of service bonus. *Michelin I*. ...

It is therefore clear from all of the foregoing that the Commission was correct to find ... that the service bonus was unfair, because of the subjectivity of the assessment of the criteria giving entitlement to the bonus, and that it must be regarded as an abuse within the meaning of Article [102 TFEU]. ...

Fifth plea: the Commission should have carried out a detailed analysis of the effects of the practices called in question. ... In support of its argument, the applicant refers to the consistent line of decisions which show that an "abuse" is an objective concept referring to the behaviour of an undertaking in a dominant position which is such as to influence the structure of a market where, as a result of the very presence of the undertaking in question, the degree of competition is already weakened and which, through recourse to methods different from those governing normal competition in products or services on the basis of the transactions of commercial operators, has the effect of hindering the maintenance of the degree of competition still existing in the market or the growth of that competition. *Hoffmann–La Roche*; *AKZO*; *Irish Sugar*.

The "effect" referred to in the case-law cited in the preceding paragraph does not necessarily relate to the actual effect of the abusive conduct complained of. For the purposes of establishing an infringement of Article [102 TFEU], it is sufficient to show that the abusive conduct of the undertaking in a dominant position tends to restrict competition or, in other words, that the conduct is capable of having that effect.

Thus, in *Michelin I*, the Court of Justice ... concluded that Michelin had infringed Article 102 TFEU, since its discount system "[was] calculated to prevent dealers from being able to select freely at any time in the light of the market situation the most favourable of the offers made by the various competitors and to change supplier without suffering any appreciable economic disadvantage".

It follows that, for the purposes of applying Article [102 TFEU], establishing the anti-competitive object and the anti-competitive effect are one and the same thing. *Irish Sugar*. If it is shown that the object pursued by the conduct of an undertaking in a dominant position is to limit competition, that conduct will also be liable to have such an effect.

Thus, with regard to the practices concerning prices, the Court held in AKZO. v. Commission ... that prices below average variable costs applied by an undertaking in a dominant position are regarded as abusive in themselves because the only interest which the undertaking may have in applying such prices is that of eliminating competitors ... and that prices below average total costs but above average variable costs are abusive if they are determined as part of a plan for eliminating a competitor ... In that case, the Court did not require any demonstration of the actual effects of the practices in question.

In the same sense, the Community judicature has held that whilst the fact that an undertaking is in a dominant position cannot deprive it of its entitlement to protect its own commercial interests when they are attacked, and whilst such an undertaking must be allowed the right to take such reasonable steps as it deems appropriate to protect those interests, such behaviour cannot be allowed if its purpose is to strengthen that dominant position and thereby abuse it. *United Brands*; *British Gypsum*; *Compagnie Maritime Belge*; *Irish Sugar*.

In the contested decision, the Commission demonstrated that the purpose of the discount systems applied by the applicant was to tie the dealers to the applicant. Those practices tended to restrict competition because they sought, in particular, to make it more difficult for the applicant's competitors to enter the relevant market.

The applicant cannot base an argument on the fact that its market shares and prices fell during the period in question. When an undertaking actually implements practices with the aim of restricting competition, the fact that the result sought is not achieved is not enough to avoid the application of Article 102 TFEU. *Compagnie Maritime Belge*. In any event, it is very probable that the fall in the applicant's market shares ... and in its sales prices ... would have been greater if the practices criticised in the contested decision had not been applied.

The fifth plea ... must therefore also be rejected.

Questions on *Michelin II*

1. Does this case reinterpret *Hoffman–La Roche* to hold that a loyalty discount by a dominant firm is illegal even if an objective justification exists? Or does it merely recognize that *Hoffman–La Roche* condemned unjustified loyalty discounts by a dominant firm without requiring any proof of substantial foreclosure?

2. This case states that a volume-based discount is legal unless it lacks an economic justification. What, then, is the difference in treatment of loyalty and quantity discounts? Aren't both just governed by abbreviated rule of reason scrutiny when no procompetitive justification exists?

3. This case holds that even a transparent volume-based discount is "loyalty inducing" if the discounts are significant and based on the total volume purchases over one year.

    a. What is the effect of characterizing a volume-based discount as "loyalty-inducing"? Does it render the discounts per se illegal? Or does it simply shift the burden on justifications so that the justification has to be proven rather being presumed? If the latter, does that support the conclusion that an explicit loyalty discount is illegal only if a justification is not proven?

    b. Is the only real difference thus that for loyalty discounts the defendant always bears the burden on procompetitive justifications whereas for volume-based discounts the defendant bears the burden only when they are deemed loyalty inducing because of special circumstances?

    c. Does the fact that a volume-based discount is significant and based on the total volume purchases over one year really make it tantamount to a loyalty discount? Does it justify shifting the burden on procompetitive justifications for other reasons?

    4. The case also holds that a quantity discount can be deemed loyalty-inducing if the amount of the discount depends on the subjective assessment of the dominant firm, as with the service bonus. Why should that matter? Even if such subjectivity affects who bears the burden on justification, why isn't the argument that the service bonuses increase service quality enough? Is it because the service quality is too subjective to constitute an "objective" justification?

    5. The only procompetitive justification the ECJ mentions involves economies of scale. Should this language be read to exclude the possibility that other procompetitive justifications are admissible to validate a loyalty discount or loyalty-inducing quantity discount? Would it be sensible to make the only admissible procompetitive justification that the discount reflected seller cost-saving because of economies of scale?

    6. Even if a procompetitive justification cannot be shown, should proof of anticompetitive effects be required?

    a. Did evidence that market shares and prices fell from past levels prove the absence of anticompetitive effects? Or is the issue whether market shares and prices were above or below but-for levels? Is the latter very easy to assess?

    b. Might these difficulties explain why the case does not require evidence of anticompetitive effects when the conduct could have anticompetitive effects and no procompetitive justification has been articulated? If negative effects are possible, and positive effects are not, does the underdeterrence-overdeterrence tradeoff favor condemnation?

    7. If a defendant can show a procompetitive justification for a loyalty-inducing discount, the court in dicta suggests the agreement would be deemed to have no foreclosing effect, which would make it effectively per se legal. Does this make sense? If a procompetitive justification exists, shouldn't an adjudicator assess the magnitude of any anticompetitive effects and determine whether they are larger?

    8. Should any volume-based discount be per se legal as long as the discounted price is above cost? Does current EU law prevent dominant firms from responding to competition by lowering prices to above cost levels as long as no conditions are attached to those prices?

British Airways Case

In March 2007 the European Court of Justice issued an important new judgment on loyalty rebates in the *British Airways* case. To make sense of it, we shall have to first examine the GC decision that it reviewed.

Case T–219/99 British Airways PLC v. Commission

[2003] ECR II–5917.

... British Airways PLC (BA) is the largest British airline company ...

BA concluded agreements with travel agents established in the United Kingdom and accredited by the International Air Transport Association (IATA) entitling them to a basic standard commission on their sales of BA air tickets. Between 1976 and 1997, that commission amounted to 9% on sales of international tickets and 7.5% for ticket sales on domestic flights.

In addition to that basic commission system, BA concluded agreements with IATA travel agents comprising three distinct systems of financial incentives: marketing agreements, global agreements and, finally, a performance reward scheme.

Marketing agreements and global agreements. The first system of incentives established by BA consisted of marketing agreements, which enabled certain IATA travel agents established in the United Kingdom to receive payments in addition to their basic commission, namely:

— a performance reward, plus certain special bonuses, based on the volume of sectors flown on BA;

— cash sums from a fund for travel agents to use for staff training;

— cash sums from a business development fund established by BA with a view to increasing its revenue and the resources of which were to be used by each agent for financing promotional projects in favour of BA....

Those marketing agreements, concluded for one year at a time, were in principle reserved for United Kingdom IATA travel agents with more than GBP 500 000 annual sales of BA tickets (flown revenue). Travel agents with annual flown revenue exceeding GBP 500 000 but below GBP 10 million were offered a standard marketing agreement. Those with a flown revenue exceeding GBP 10 million entered into a marketing agreement individually negotiated with BA.

The performance reward was calculated on a sliding scale, based on the extent to which a travel agent increased the value of its sales of BA tickets. In addition to the general performance reward, certain routes qualified for a special performance bonus. Payment of the performance reward or the special bonus was subject to travel agents increasing their sales of BA tickets from one year to the next....

In addition to the marketing agreements, BA concluded a second type of incentive agreement (global agreements) with three IATA travel agents. For the 1992/1993 winter season, BA set up global incentive programmes with three travel agents, entitling them to receive additional commissions calculated by reference to the growth of BA's share in their worldwide sales.

New system of performance rewards.... BA [also added] ... a third type of incentive agreements, consisting of a new system of performance rewards ... In addition to the new basic flat commission rate of 7% to be applied thenceforth to all tickets sold in the United Kingdom, each travel agent could earn an additional commission of up to 3% for international tickets and up to 1% for domestic tickets. The size of the additional variable element for domestic and international tickets depended on the travel agents' performance in selling BA tickets. The agents' performance was measured by comparing the total flown revenue arising from the sales of BA tickets issued by an agent in a particular calendar month with that achieved during the corresponding month in the previous year.

Under the new system of performance rewards, every percentage point of improvement in performance level over a benchmark of 95% earned the travel agent an additional variable element of 0.1% by way of extra commission on the sale of international tickets and in addition to the basic commission of 7%. For sales of domestic tickets, the variable element was 0.1% for every 3% increase in sales over the 95% benchmark. The maximum variable element payable to travel agents under the new performance rewards system was 3% for international tickets and 1% for domestic tickets for a performance level of 125% or above in both cases....

The Commission [concluded] that BA is a purchaser in a dominant position on the United Kingdom market for air travel agency services.... [T]he Commission [described the above commission schemes as follows]:

"The commission schemes for travel agents described above all have one notable feature in common. In each case meeting the targets for sales growth leads to an increase in the commission paid on all tickets sold by the agent, not just on the tickets sold after the target is reached. In the [marketing agreement] schemes the cash bonus per ticket paid to the travel agent increases for all tickets sold. In the [performance reward scheme] the percentage commission paid increases for all ticket sales by the travel agent. This means that when a travel agent is close to one of the thresholds for an increase in commission rate selling relatively few extra BA tickets can have a large effect on his commission income. Conversely a competitor of BA who wishes to give a travel agent an incentive to divert some sales from BA to the competing airline will have to pay a much higher rate of commission than BA on all of the tickets sold by it to overcome this effect.

"An example will illustrate this effect of the BA commission schemes. Assume a travel agent's sales of international air tickets amounted to [GBP] 100,000 a month in the benchmark year. If the travel agent sells [GBP] 100,000 worth of BA international air tickets a month it will earn the basic commission of 7% and a performance reward of 0.5% [(100 − 95)(0.1%)], giving a total commission income on international air ticket sales of [GBP] 7,500 [100,000(7% + 0.5%)]. If the travel agent diverted 1% of its international ticket sales to a competitor of BA, its performance reward would decrease to 0.4% [(99 − 95)(0.1%)] and this reduced rate would be applied to all of the agent's sales of BA tickets. The agent's commission income from the sale of international BA tickets would drop to [GBP] 7,326 [99,000(7% + 0.4%)]. A reduction of [GBP] 1,000 in sales of international BA tickets leads to a drop of [GBP] 174 in commission income. The marginal commission rate can be said to be 17.4%. In practical terms, this means that a competitor to BA that could offer flights that would replace [GBP] 1,000 of the travel agent's sales of BA tickets would have to offer a commission of 17.4% on these tickets to compensate the travel agent for its loss of BA commission revenue. Although BA also has to offer this high marginal rate of commission to increase its sales of tickets, it is at an advantage over the new entrant which must offer this high rate of commission on all of its sales ... This effect increases if the number of tickets in question is a smaller percentage of the travel agent's benchmark sales of BA tickets. This effect is also increased if the travel agent in question is not only earning extra commissions under the performance reward system but can also earn bonuses under a marketing agreement.

... The [Commission concluded that this commission scheme] constitutes an abuse of a dominant position in that, first, it has the effect of encouraging those agents to maintain or increase their sales of BA tickets rather than selling their services to BA's competitors, those financial incentives not depending on the volume of BA tickets sold by those agents in absolute terms, and, secondly, it has the effect of imposing on the agents in question dissimilar conditions to equivalent transactions.... [The Commission thus fined BA 6.8 million euros.]

... BA challenges the Commission's assertion that its performance reward schemes ... produced an exclusionary effect in relation to competing airlines....

The exclusionary effect on airlines competing with BA arising from the "fidelity-building" nature of BA's performance reward schemes ...

Findings of the Court—In order to determine whether BA abused its dominant position by applying its performance reward schemes to travel agents established in the United Kingdom, it is necessary to consider the criteria and rules governing the granting of those rewards, and to investigate whether, in providing an advantage not based on any economic service justifying it, they tended to remove or restrict the agents' freedom to sell their services to the airlines of their choice and thereby hinder the access of BA's competitor airlines to the United Kingdom market for air travel agency services. *Hoffmann–La Roche*; *Michelin*; *Irish Sugar*.

It needs to be determined in this case whether the marketing agreements and the new performance reward scheme had a fidelity-building effect in relation to travel agents established in the United Kingdom and, if they did, whether those schemes were based on an economically justified consideration. *Michelin*; *Portugal v Commission*; *Irish Sugar*.

Concerning, first, the fidelity-building character of the schemes in question, the Court finds that, by reason of their progressive nature with a very noticeable effect at the margin, the increased commission rates were capable of rising exponentially from one reference period to another, as the number of BA tickets sold by agents during successive reference periods progressed.

Conversely, the higher revenues from BA ticket sales were, the stronger was the penalty suffered by the persons concerned in the form of a disproportionate reduction in the rates of performance rewards, even in the case of a slight decrease in sales of BA tickets compared with the previous reference period. BA cannot therefore deny the fidelity-building character of the schemes in question.

Nor, in order to deny the fidelity-building effect of its performance reward schemes on travel agents, can BA successfully rely on the argument that those agents have only a slight influence on travellers' choice of airlines. BA has itself argued that those agents provide a useful service filtering information communicated to passengers who are faced with the proliferation of different air transport fare structures.

Moreover, even if, as BA maintains, the advantages granted to travel agents depended on the level of the target thresholds and the rate of success obtained in relation to those thresholds, the fidelity-building effect on travel agents arising from the performance rewards must nevertheless be regarded as established.

Furthermore, BA's objection that its "fidelity agreements" did not prevent its competitors from concluding similar agreements with travel agents established in the United Kingdom does not carry conviction. BA's five main competitors on the United Kingdom market for air travel agency services cannot be regarded as having been in a position to grant the same advantages to travel agents.

It should be remembered in that respect that, during the whole of the period during which the disputed performance reward schemes were applied, the number of BA tickets sold by travel agents established in the United Kingdom in respect of air routes to and from United Kingdom airports invariably represented a multiple both of the ticket sales achieved by each of those five main competitors and of the cumulative total of those sales.

In those circumstances, it has been demonstrated to the requisite legal standard that the rival undertakings were not in a position to attain in the United Kingdom a level of revenue capable of constituting a sufficiently broad financial base to allow them effectively to establish a reward scheme similar to BA's in order to counteract the exclusionary effect of that scheme against them on the United Kingdom market for air travel agency services.

Concerning, secondly, the question whether the performance reward schemes applied by BA were based on an economically justified consideration, it is true that the fact that an undertaking is in a dominant position cannot deprive it of its entitlement, within reason, to perform the actions which it considers appropriate in order to protect its own commercial interests when they are threatened. Irish Sugar.

However, the protection of the competitive position of an undertaking which, like BA, occupies a dominant position must, at the very least, in order to be lawful, be based on criteria of economic efficiency. *Irish Sugar*.

In this case, BA does not appear to have demonstrated that the fidelity-building character of its performance reward schemes was based on an economically justified consideration.

The achievement of sales growth targets for BA tickets by travel agents established in the United Kingdom resulted in the application of a higher rate of commission not just on the BA tickets sold once those sales targets had been met but on all BA tickets handled during the reference period in question.

The additional remuneration of the agents thus appears to bear no objective relation to the consideration arising for BA from the sale of the additional air tickets.

To that extent, BA's performance reward schemes cannot be regarded as constituting the consideration for efficiency gains or cost savings resulting from the sale of BA tickets after attainment of the said objectives. On the contrary, that retrospective application of increased commission rates to all BA tickets sold by a travel agent during the reference period in question must even be regarded as likely to entail the sale of certain BA tickets at a price disproportionate to the productivity gain obtained by BA from the sale of those extra tickets.

Even if, as BA maintains, any airline has an interest in selling extra seats on its flights rather than leaving them unoccupied, the advantage represented by a better rate of occupancy of the aircraft must, in a case such as the present, normally be considerably reduced by reason of the extra cost incurred by BA through the increase in the remuneration of the agent arising from that retrospective application of the increased commission.

Being thus devoid of any economically justified consideration, the disputed performance reward schemes must be regarded as tending essentially to remunerate sales growth of BA tickets from one reference period to another and thus reinforce the fidelity to BA of travel agents established in the territory of the United Kingdom.

Agents were thereby deterred from offering their travel agency services to airlines in competition with BA, whose entry into or progress in the United Kingdom market for travel agency services was thereby necessarily hindered.

BA can have had no interest in applying its reward schemes other than ousting rival airlines and thereby hindering maintenance of the existing level of competition or the development of that competition on the United Kingdom market for air travel agency services.

In particular, BA cannot validly argue that, above a certain aircraft occupancy rate, additional ticket sales necessarily generate profits. As has just been mentioned, the consideration for ticket sales carried out by an agent once the latter's sales growth target had been reached represented an additional cost, in the form of retrospective application of the increased commission to all BA tickets sold during the reference period in question, which was liable to be equal to, or greater than, that profit.

Moreover, BA itself acknowledged at the hearing that there was no precise relationship between, on the one hand, any economies of scale achieved by virtue of extra BA tickets being sold after the attainment of the sales objectives and, on the other, the increases in the rates of remuneration paid by way of consideration to travel agents established in the United Kingdom.

Contrary to what BA maintains, its performance reward schemes could not therefore constitute a mode of exercise of the normal operation of competition or allow it to reduce its costs. The opposite arguments by BA in that regard are not capable of demonstrating that its performance reward schemes had an objective economic justification.

The Commission was therefore right to hold that BA abused its dominant position on the United Kingdom market for air travel agency services by restricting, through the application of performance reward schemes not based on a justified economic consideration, the freedom of those agents to supply their services to the airlines of their choice and, in consequence, restricting the access of those airlines to the United Kingdom market for air travel agency services.

Finally, BA cannot accuse the Commission of failing to demonstrate that its practices produced an exclusionary effect. In the first place, for the purposes of establishing an infringement of Article 102 EC, it is not necessary to demonstrate that the abuse in question had a concrete effect on the markets concerned. It is sufficient in that respect to demonstrate that the abusive conduct of the undertaking in a dominant position tends to restrict competition, or, in other words, that the conduct is capable of having, or likely to have, such an effect.

Moreover, it appears not only that the disputed practices were indeed likely to have a restrictive effect on the United Kingdom markets for air travel agency services and air transport, but also that such an effect has been demonstrated in a concrete way by the Commission.

Since, at the time of the conduct complained of, travel agents established in the United Kingdom carried out 85% of all air ticket sales in the territory of the United Kingdom, BA's abusive conduct on the United Kingdom market for air travel agency services cannot fail to have had the effect of excluding competing airlines (to their detriment) from the United Kingdom air transport markets, by reason of the close nexus existing between the markets in question, as has been established in the examination of the fourth plea.

By reason of that effect produced by the reward schemes applied by BA on the United Kingdom air transport markets, the Court cannot accept BA's argument that the contested decision contains no analysis of the air transport markets or empirical proof of the damage which its financial incentive schemes caused to competitor airlines or to travellers.

Furthermore, where an undertaking in a dominant position actually puts into operation a practice generating the effect of ousting its competitors, the fact that the hoped-for result is not achieved is not sufficient to prevent a finding of abuse of a dominant position within the meaning of Article [102 TFEU].

Moreover, the growth in the market shares of some of BA's airline competitors, which was modest in absolute value having regard to the small size of their original market shares, does not mean that BA's practices had no effect. In the absence of those practices, it may legitimately be considered that the market shares of those competitors would have been able to grow more significantly. *Compagnie Maritime Belge Transports.*

The Commission did not therefore make any errors of assessment in holding that BA contravened Article [102 TFEU] by applying to air travel agents in the United Kingdom performance reward schemes that ... had as their object and effect, without any economically justified consideration, the reward of the loyalty of those agents to BA and thereby the ousting of rival airlines both from the United Kingdom market for air travel agency services and, as a necessary consequence, from the United Kingdom air travel markets. . . .

Questions on the CFI judgment in *British Airways*

1.   Why were these rebates considered loyalty-inducing? Is it for the same reasons as in *Michelin I & II*? Or did the Court rely on something different?

2.   The Court concluded that the evidence it recounted demonstrated rivals could not match the discount. Did the evidence so demonstrate? Does the fact that British Airways sells a multiple of the sales by rivals suffice to so demonstrate?

3.   Do you agree with the Court's conclusion that these rebates were devoid of economic justification?

a.   Why does the Court reject British Airways' argument that these rebates are related to its economic interest in selling extra seats on its flights rather than leaving them unoccupied? Shouldn't the fact that the airline industry is a sector with high fixed costs and low variable costs be taken into account by the GC in its reasoning? Isn't BA's desire to recover its fixed costs through additional sales a legitimate economic justification?

b.   Does the fact that the rebates are on all seats sold, and not just on the marginal increase in sales, suffice to show that the rebates were not reasonably related to this efficiency justification?

c.   Isn't it a question of fact whether profit gained by a higher occupancy rate is higher or lower than the cost incurred by the granting of rebates? Does the GC ever recount facts establishing this? Does the Court offer any facts to support its probabilistic conclusion that the costs of rebates are "liable" to exceed the increased profits? Or is it enough that there was no necessary or precise relationship?

    d. Why isn't it a less anticompetitive alternative for British Airways to just lower prices on marginal seats? Don't airlines price discriminate all the time to fill planes?

    4. The Court also holds that it is unnecessary to prove actual anti-competitive effects because it was shown that the rebates were likely to have such an effect. But is the likelihood of such an effect sufficiently demonstrated by the facts that the dominant firm had 85% market share and utilized such rebates? Is this likelihood rebutted by the evidence that rival market shares increased after the rebates?

Judgment of the Court of Justice in Case C–95/04 P British Airways v. Commission

15 March 2007.

The first plea, alleging error of law in the Court's assessment of the exclusionary effect of the bonus schemes at issue

    In this plea, BA criticises the findings in ... the judgment under appeal, according to which the bonuses granted by BA both had a "fidelity-building" and thus an exclusionary effect, and lacked justification from an economic point of view.

The first part of the first plea, concerning the criterion for assessing the possible exclusionary effect of the bonus schemes at issue

Arguments of the parties

    BA argues, first, that the Court of First Instance erred in law by applying an incorrect test for assessing the bonus schemes at issue, namely the test concerning the fidelity-building effect of those schemes....

    The approach thus adopted by the Court of First Instance is, BA submits, incompatible with the case-law of the Court of Justice. In its submission, the judgments in *Hoffmann–La Roche* and in *Michelin* ... demonstrate that the granting by an undertaking occupying a dominant position of higher commissions may be abusive only if it is subject to the condition that the co-contractor is obliged, de jure or de facto, to deal solely or mainly with that undertaking or if it limits the capacity of the co-contractor to choose freely the undertaking with which it wishes to deal. By contrast, those judgments did not condemn the granting of higher commissions on all sales above a threshold, since, even if a higher commission does give the co-contractor a strong incentive to sell more products of the dominant undertaking, it does not imply that that co-contractor accepts anything anti-competitive and does not prevent rival undertakings from granting all types of commission that they consider appropriate.

    BA regards that distinction as fundamental. Unless it is made subject to the condition that the other party deal exclusively (or mainly) with the dominant undertaking or limits the markets of competitors in some other way, a generous commission is merely a form of competition on price....

    BA submits that such limitation of competitors' markets by the dominant undertaking requires more than the mere granting of generous bonuses. It can be envisaged only in two situations, neither of which is present in this case, namely:

— where the granting of bonuses is made subject to the condition that the recipient deals exclusively or mainly with the undertaking in a dominant position; or

— where the recipient of the bonuses cannot choose freely between the undertaking occupying a dominant position and its competitors. That would be the case if the recipient could expect to make profits only by dealing exclusively or mainly with the dominant undertaking or where that undertaking practises unfair competition through pricing ("predatory prices") and its competitors cannot resist that pressure. . . .

Findings of the Court

In order to determine whether the undertaking in a dominant position has abused such a position by applying a system of discounts such as that described [above], the Court has held that it is necessary to consider all the circumstances, particularly the criteria and rules governing the grant of the discount, and to investigate whether, in providing an advantage not based on any economic service justifying it, the discount tends to remove or restrict the buyer's freedom to choose his sources of supply, to bar competitors from access to the market, to apply dissimilar conditions to equivalent transactions with other trading parties or to strengthen the dominant position by distorting competition. *Michelin*.

It follows that in determining whether, on the part of an undertaking in a dominant position, a system of discounts or bonuses which constitute neither quantity discounts or bonuses nor fidelity discounts or bonuses within the meaning of the judgment in *Hoffmann–La Roche* constitutes an abuse, it first has to be determined whether those discounts or bonuses can produce an exclusionary effect, that is to say whether they are capable, first, of making market entry very difficult or impossible for competitors of the undertaking in a dominant position and, secondly, of making it more difficult or impossible for its co-contractors to choose between various sources of supply or commercial partners.

It then needs to be examined whether there is an objective economic justification for the discounts and bonuses granted. . . . [A]n undertaking is at liberty to demonstrate that its bonus system producing an exclusionary effect is economically justified.

With regard to the first aspect, the case-law gives indications as to the cases in which discount or bonus schemes of an undertaking in a dominant position are not merely the expression of a particularly favourable offer on the market, but give rise to an exclusionary effect.

First, an exclusionary effect may arise from goal-related discounts or bonuses, that is to say those the granting of which is linked to the attainment of sales objectives defined individually. *Michelin*.

It is clear from the findings of the Court of First Instance . . . that the bonus schemes at issue were drawn up by reference to individual sales objectives, since the rate of the bonuses depended on the evolution of the turnover arising from BA ticket sales by each travel agent during a given period.

It is also apparent from the case-law that the commitment of co-contractors towards the undertaking in a dominant position and the pressure exerted upon them may be particularly strong where a discount or bonus does not relate solely to the growth in turnover in relation to purchases or sales of products of that undertaking made by those co-contractors during the period under consideration, but extends also to the whole of the turnover relating to those purchases or sales. In that way, relatively modest variations—whether upwards or downwards—in the turn-over figures relating to the products of the dominant undertaking have disproportionate effects on co-contractors. *Michelin.*

The Court of First Instance found that the bonus schemes at issue gave rise to a similar situation. Attainment of the sales progression objectives gave rise to an increase in the commission paid on all BA tickets sold by the travel agent concerned, and not just on those sold after those objectives had been attained ... It could therefore be of decisive impor-tance for the commission income of a travel agent as a whole whether or not he sold a few extra BA tickets after achieving a certain turnover ... The Court of First Instance ... states that the progressive nature of the increased commission rates had a "very noticeable effect at the margin" and emphasises the radical effects which a small reduction in sales of BA tickets could have on the rates of performance-related bonus.

Finally, the Court took the view that the pressure exerted on resellers by an undertaking in a dominant position which granted bonuses with those characteristics is further strengthened where that undertaking holds a very much larger market share than its competitors. *Michelin.* It held that, in those circumstances, it is particularly difficult for competitors of that undertaking to outbid it in the face of discounts or bonuses based on overall sales volume. By reason of its significantly higher market share, the undertaking in a dominant position generally constitutes an unavoidable business partner in the market. Most often, discounts or bonuses granted by such an undertaking on the basis of overall turnover largely take precedence in absolute terms, even over more generous offers of its compet-itors. In order to attract the co-contractors of the undertaking in a dominant position, or to receive a sufficient volume of orders from them, those competitors would have to offer them significantly higher rates of discount or bonus.

In the present case, the Court of First Instance held ... that BA's market share was significantly higher than that of its five main competitors in the United Kingdom. It concluded ... that the rival airlines were not in a position to grant travel agents the same advantages as BA, since they were not capable of attaining in the United Kingdom a level of revenue capable of constituting a sufficiently broad financial base to allow them effectively to establish a reward scheme similar to BA's.

Therefore, the Court of First Instance was right to examine ... whether the bonus schemes at issue had a fidelity-building effect capable of producing an exclusionary effect ...

It follows from the whole of the above considerations that the first part of the first plea is in part inadmissible and in part unfounded.

The second part of the first plea, concerning the assessment by the Court of First Instance of the relevance of the objective economic justification for the bonus schemes at issue

Arguments of the parties

BA challenges as erroneous the finding by the Court of First Instance ... that BA's commissions were not based on an economically justified consideration. BA argues that it is economically justified for an airline to reward travel agents which allow it to increase its sales and help it to cover its high fixed costs by bringing additional passengers....

Findings of the Court

Discounts or bonuses granted to its co-contractors by an undertaking in a dominant position are not necessarily an abuse and therefore prohibited by Article [102 TFEU]. According to consistent case-law, only discounts or bonuses which are not based on any economic counterpart to justify them must be regarded as an abuse. *Hoffmann–La Roche*; *Michelin*.

[T]he Court of First Instance was right, after holding that the bonus schemes at issue produced an exclusionary effect, to examine whether those schemes had an objective economic justification.

Assessment of the economic justification for a system of discounts or bonuses established by an undertaking in a dominant position is to be made on the basis of the whole of the circumstances of the case. *Michelin*. It has to be determined whether the exclusionary effect arising from such a system, which is disadvantageous for competition, may be counterbalanced, or outweighed, by advantages in terms of efficiency which also benefit the consumer. If the exclusionary effect of that system bears no relation to advantages for the market and consumers, or if it goes beyond what is necessary in order to attain those advantages, that system must be regarded as an abuse.

In this case, correctly basing its examination upon the criteria thus inferred from the case-law, the Court of First Instance examined whether there was an economic justification for the bonus schemes at issue. [I]t adopted a position in relation to the arguments submitted by BA, which concerned, in particular, the high level of fixed costs in air transport and the importance of aircraft occupancy rates. On the basis of its assessment of the circumstances of the case, the Court of First Instance came to the conclusion that those systems were not based on any objective economic justification ...

Therefore, the second part of the first plea must be dismissed as inadmissible.

The second plea, alleging error of law in that the Court of First Instance did not examine the probable effects of the commissions granted by BA, or take account of the evidence that they had no material effect on competing airlines

Arguments of the parties

By its second plea, BA effectively accuses the Court of First Instance of not examining the probable effects of the bonus schemes at issue, namely the existence or otherwise of an exclusionary effect, whereas Article [102 TFEU] requires that, in each case, the actual or probable effects of the practices complained of should be examined, rather than conclusions being reached on the basis of their form, or of presumptions of such an effect . . .

Findings of the Court

Concerning BA's argument that the Court of First Instance did not examine the probable effects of the bonus schemes at issue, it is sufficient to note that, in . . . the judgment under appeal, the Court of First Instance explained the mechanism of those schemes.

Having emphasised the very noticeable effect at the margin, linked to the progressive nature of the increased commission rates, it described the exponential effect on those rates of an increase in the number of BA tickets sold during successive periods, and, conversely, the disproportionate reduction in those rates in the event of even a slight decrease in sales of BA tickets in comparison with the previous period.

On that basis, the Court of First Instance was able to conclude, without committing any error of law, that the bonus schemes at issue had a fidelity-building effect. It follows that BA's plea accusing the Court of not examining the probable effects of those schemes is unfounded. . . . .

The second plea must therefore be dismissed as in part inadmissible and in part unfounded.

The third plea, alleging an error of law in that the Court of First Instance did not examine whether BA's conduct involved a "prejudice [to] consumers" within the meaning of subparagraph (b) of the second paragraph of Article [102 TFEU]

Arguments of the parties

In its third plea, BA considers that the Court of First Instance erred in law by failing to examine whether the bonus schemes at issue caused prejudice to consumers, as required by subparagraph (b) of the second paragraph of Article [102 TFEU], as interpreted by the Court of Justice in *Suiker Unie*. Without making any analysis of that condition, the Court of First Instance confined itself . . . to examining the impact of BA's conduct on its competitors in United Kingdom air transport markets.

Referring to the judgment in *Europemballage* and *Continental Can*, the Commission and Virgin argue that that plea is unfounded, since Article [102 TFEU] covers not only practices likely to cause immediate damage to consumers but also those which cause them damage by undermining an effective structure of competition.

Findings of the Court

It should be noted first that, as explained [above], discounts or bonuses granted by an undertaking in a dominant position may be contrary to

Article [102 TFEU] even where they do not correspond to any of the examples mentioned in the second paragraph of that article.

Moreover, as the Court has already held ... in *Europemballage* and *Continental Can*, Article [102 TFEU] is aimed not only at practices which may cause prejudice to consumers directly, but also at those which are detrimental to them through their impact on an effective competition structure ...

The Court of First Instance was therefore entitled, without committing any error of law, not to examine whether BA's conduct had caused prejudice to consumers within the meaning of subparagraph (b) of the second paragraph of Article [102 TFEU], but to examine ... whether the bonus schemes at issue had a restrictive effect on competition and to conclude that the existence of such an effect had been demonstrated by the Commission in the contested decision.

Having regard to those considerations, the third plea must be dismissed as unfounded.

Questions on the ECJ judgment in *British Airways*

1. Many legal commentators criticized the EU courts harshly for allegedly holding that fidelity rebates imposed by dominant firms were quasi per se illegal, because it seemed that the only possible justification for dominant firms was to demonstrate that the amount of the rebates in question was equal to the savings of production costs from the economies of scale generated by increased sales. In this case, however, the ECJ states that "[i]t has to be determined whether the exclusionary effect arising from a [rebate] system [such as the one in question], which is disadvantageous for competition, may be counterbalanced, or outweighed, by advantages in terms of efficiency which also benefit the consumer."

a. Does the ECJ allow dominant firms applying rebates to offer a pro-competitive justification? Is this justification limited to the realization of economies of scale?

b. Does this clearly signal that the ECJ is willing to follow a rule of reason approach in its assessment of rebate schemes?

c. If dominant firms are allowed to outline the pro-competitive advantages of their rebates, why weren't the explanations offered by British Airways sufficient to justify the rebates in question?

2. Does the ECJ impose on the Commission (or, when a decision is appealed, on the GC) a duty to show the precise market effects of the alleged anti-competitive rebates? Should they impose such an obligation?

3. The ECJ states that "Article [102 TFEU] is aimed not only at practices which may cause prejudice to consumers directly, but also at those which are detrimental to them through their impact on an effective competition structure ..." However, should the Commission have to prove that any alteration to the competition structure (caused by the challenged rebates) actually had an anticompetitive impact on consumers?

Guidance on the Commission's Enforcement Priorities in Applying Article 82 EC Treaty [now 102 TFEU] to Abusive Exclusionary Conduct by Dominant Undertakings

(Dec. 2008).

A.   Exclusive dealing.... *(b) Conditional rebates*

37.   Conditional rebates are rebates granted to customers to reward them for a particular form of purchasing behaviour. The usual nature of a conditional rebate is that the customer is given a rebate if its purchases over a defined reference period exceed a certain threshold, the rebate being granted either on all purchases (retroactive rebates) or only on those made in excess of those required to achieve the threshold (incremental rebates). Conditional rebates are not an uncommon practice. Undertakings may offer such rebates in order to attract more demand, and as such they may stimulate demand and benefit consumers. However, such rebates—when granted by a dominant undertaking—can also have actual or potential foreclosure effects similar to exclusive purchasing obligations. Conditional rebates can have such effects without necessarily entailing a sacrifice for the dominant undertaking.[26]

38.   In addition to the factors already mentioned in paragraph 20, the following factors are of particular importance to the Commission in determining whether a given system of conditional rebates is liable to result in anticompetitive foreclosure and, consequently, will be part of the Commission's enforcement priorities.

39.   As with exclusive purchasing obligations, the likelihood of anticompetitive foreclosure is higher where competitors are not able to compete on equal terms for the entire demand of each individual customer. A conditional rebate granted by a dominant undertaking may enable it to use the "non contestable" portion of the demand of each customer (that is to say, the amount that would be purchased by the customer from the dominant undertaking in any event) as leverage to decrease the price to be paid for the "contestable" portion of demand (that is to say, the amount for which the customer may prefer and be able to find substitutes).[27]

40.   In general terms, retroactive rebates may foreclose the market significantly, as they may make it less attractive for customers to switch small amounts of demand to an alternative supplier, if this would lead to loss of the retroactive rebates.[28] The potential foreclosing effect of retroactive rebates is in principle strongest on the last purchased unit of the product before the threshold is exceeded. However, what is in the Commission's view relevant for an assessment of the loyalty enhancing effect of a

---

26.   In this regard, the assessment of conditional rebates differs from that of predation, which always entails a sacrifice.

27.   See Case T–203/01 Michelin v Commission (Michelin II) [2003] ECR II–4071, paragraphs 162 and 163. See also Case T–219/99 British Airways v Commission [2003] ECR II–5917, paragraphs 277 and 278.

28.   Case 322/81 Nederlandsche Banden Industrie Michelin v Commission (Michelin I) [1983] ECR 3461, paragraphs 70 to 73.

rebate is not simply the effect on competition to provide the last individual unit, but the foreclosing effect of the rebate system on (actual or potential) competitors of the dominant supplier. The higher the rebate as a percentage of the total price and the higher the threshold, the greater the inducement below the threshold and, therefore, the stronger the likely foreclosure of actual or potential competitors.

41. When applying the methodology explained in paragraphs 23 to 27, the Commission intends to investigate, to the extent that the data are available and reliable, whether the rebate system is capable of hindering expansion or entry even by competitors that are equally efficient by making it more difficult for them to supply part of the requirements of individual customers. In this context the Commission will estimate what price a competitor would have to offer in order to compensate the customer for the loss of the conditional rebate if the latter would switch part of its demand ("the relevant range") away from the dominant undertaking. The effective price that the competitor will have to match is not the average price of the dominant undertaking, but the normal (list) price less the rebate the customer loses by switching, calculated over the relevant range of sales and in the relevant period of time. The Commission will take into account the margin of error that may be caused by the uncertainties inherent in this kind of analysis.

42. The relevant range over which to calculate the effective price in a particular case depends on the specific facts of each case and on whether the rebate is incremental or retroactive. For incremental rebates, the relevant range is normally the incremental purchases that are being considered. For retroactive rebates, it will generally be relevant to assess in the specific market context how much of a customer's purchase requirements can realistically be switched to a competitor (the "contestable share" or "contestable portion"). If it is likely that customers would be willing and able to switch large amounts of demand to a (potential) competitor relatively quickly, the relevant range is likely to be relatively large. If, on the other hand, it is likely that customers would only be willing or able to switch small amounts incrementally, then the relevant range will be relatively small. For existing competitors their capacity to expand sales to customers and the fluctations in those sales over time may also provide an indication of the relevant range. For potential competitors, an assessment of the scale at which a new entrant would realistically be able to enter may be undertaken, where possible. It may be possible to take the historical growth pattern of new entrants in the same or in similar markets as an indication of a realistic market share of a new entrant.[29]

---

29. The relevant range will be estimated on the basis of data which may have varying degrees of precision. The Commission will take this into account in drawing any conclusions regarding the dominant undertaking's ability to foreclose equally efficient competitors. It may also be useful to calculate how big a share of customers' requirements on average the entrant should capture as a minimum so that the effective price is at least as high as the LRAIC of the dominant company. In a number of cases the size of this share, when compared with the actual market shares of competitors and their shares of the customers' requirements, may make it clear whether the rebate scheme is capable to have an anticompetitive foreclosure effect.

43. The lower the estimated effective price over the relevant range is compared to the average price of the dominant supplier, the stronger the loyalty-enhancing effect. However, as long as the effective price remains consistently above the LRAIC of the dominant undertaking, this would normally allow an equally efficient competitor to compete profitably not-withstanding the rebate. In those circumstances the rebate is normally not capable of foreclosing in an anti-competitive way.

44. Where the effective price is below AAC, as a general rule the rebate scheme is capable of foreclosing even equally efficient competitors. Where the effective price is between AAC and LRAIC, the Commission will investigate whether other factors point to the conclusion that entry or expansion even by equally efficient competitors is likely to be affected. In this context, the Commission will investigate whether and to what extent competitors have realistic and effective counterstrategies at their disposal, for instance their capacity to also use a "non contestable' portion of their buyers" demand as leverage to decrease the price for the relevant range. Where competitors do not have such counterstrategies at their disposal, the Commission will consider that the rebate scheme is capable of foreclosing equally efficient competitors.

45. As indicated in paragraph 27, this analysis will be integrated in the general assessment, taking into account other relevant quantitative or qualitative evidence. It is normally important to consider whether the rebate system is applied with an individualised or a standardised threshold. An individualised threshold—one based on a percentage of the total re-quirements of the customer or an individualised volume target—allows the dominant supplier to set the threshold at such a level as to make it difficult for customers to switch suppliers, thereby creating a maximum loyalty enhancing effect.[30] By contrast, a standardised volume threshold—where the threshold is the same for all or a group of customers—may be too high for some smaller customers and/or too low for larger customers to have a loyalty enhancing effect. If, however, it can be established that a standar-dised volume threshold approximates the requirements of an appreciable proportion of customers, the produce anticompetitive foreclosure effects.

(c) Efficiencies

46. Provided that the conditions set out in Section III D are fulfilled, the Commission will consider claims by dominant undertakings that rebate systems achieve cost or other advantages which are passed on to custom-ers.[31] Transaction-related cost advantages are often more likely to be achieved with standardised volume targets than with individualised volume targets. Similarly, incremental rebate schemes are in general more likely to give resellers an incentive to produce and resell a higher volume than retroactive rebate schemes.[32] . . .

---

30. See Case 85/76 Hoffmann–La Roche & Co. v Commission [1979] ECR 461, para-graphs 89 and 90; Case T–288/97 Irish Sugar v Commission [1999] ECR II–2969, paragraph 213; Case T–219/99 British Airways v Commission [2003] ECR II–5917, paragraphs 7 to 11 and 270 to 273.

31. For instance, for rebates see Case C–95/04 P British Airways v Commission [2007] ECR I–2331, paragraph 86.

32. See, to that effect, Case T–203/01 Michelin v Commission (Michelin II) [2003] ECR II–4071, paragraphs 56 to 60, 74 and 75.

B. Tying and bundling ... *(c) Multi-product rebates*

59. A multi-product rebate may be anticompetitive on the tied or the tying market if it is so large that equally efficient competitors offering only some of the components cannot compete against the discounted bundle.

60. In theory, it would be ideal if the effect of the rebate could be assessed by examining whether the incremental revenue covers the incremental costs for each product in the dominant undertaking's bundle. However, in practice assessing the incremental revenue is complex. Therefore, in its enforcement practice the Commission will in most situations use the incremental price as a good proxy. If the incremental price that customers pay for each of the dominant undertaking's products in the bundle remains above the LRAIC of the dominant undertaking from including that product in the bundle, the Commission will normally not intervene since an equally efficient competitor with only one product should in principle be able to compete profitably against the bundle. Enforcement action may, however, be warranted if the incremental price is below the LRAIC, because in such a case even an equally efficient competitor may be prevented from expanding or entering.[38]

61. If the evidence suggests that competitors of the dominant undertaking are selling identical bundles, or could do so in a timely way without being deterred by possible additional costs, the Commission will generally regard this as a bundle competing against a bundle, in which case the relevant question is not whether the incremental revenue covers the incremental costs for each product in the bundle, but rather whether the price of the bundle as a whole is predatory.

(d) Efficiencies

62. Provided that the conditions set out in Section III D are fulfilled, the Commission will look into claims by dominant undertakings that their tying and bundling practices may lead to savings in production or distribution that would benefit customers ...

Loyalty and Bundled Discounts in Other Nations

Australia, Canada, and South Africa have statutes that, like Clayton Act § 3, define exclusive dealing and tying in a way that makes clear that they cover cases where a seller simply conditions discounts or other favorable terms on the buyer primarily dealing with the seller or buying a second product from it.[138] Japan deems loyalty rebates subject to the same standards as exclusive dealing if they have "the function of restricting the handling of competing products."[139] Mexico bans loyalty discounts when

---

38. In principle, the LRAIC cost benchmark is relevant here as long as competitors are not able to also sell bundles (see paragraphs 23 to 27 and paragraph 61).

138. *See* Canada Competition Act § 77; Australia Trade Practices Act § 47. South Africa probably also does this under its prohibition against anticompetitively "inducing" a firm not to deal with rivals. South Africa Competition Act § 8(d)(i).

139. *See* Japan Distribution Guidelines at 31–32. Other applicable provisions make it an unfair trade practice to tend to impede fair competition by "unjustly inducing or coercing customers of a competitor to deal with oneself," Japan Antimonopoly Law § 2(9), "inducing

the defendant has market power, the purpose is exclusionary, and they cannot be justified on efficiency grounds.[140] Brazil bans loyalty discounts that have the purpose or capacity of harming competition or increasing supracompetitive profits.[141] Saudi Arabia bans loyalty or bundled discounts if they are unjustifiable and might lead to granting a favorable or negative position.[142]

In other nations, it is understood that pricing conditioned on such exclusion is governed by the general rules applicable to anticompetitive agreements or unilateral conduct. In South Korea, loyalty discounts can be condemned as an abuse of dominance or unfair trade practice.[143] Some nations require both dominant market power and substantial foreclosure to condemn loyalty discounts.[144]

---

customers of a competitor to deal with oneself by offering unjust benefits in the light of normal business practices," or "dealing with the other party on conditions which unjustly restrict any transaction between the said party and his other transacting party," Japan Designations of Unfair Trade Practices §§ 9, 14 (2009).

140. *See* Mexico Competition Law Arts. 10–11.

141. Brazil Antitrust Law No. 8,884, Arts. 20, 21(IV–VI, XI); Brazil CADE Resolution 20, Attachment I, § B.6 (1999).

142. Saudi Implementing Regulations, Art. 6(2)(f).

143. KFTC Decision, 2007 Dokgam 1790, November 5, 2008.

144. See Singapore Guidelines on the Section 47 Prohibition §§ 11.11 to 11.13 (2007).

CHAPTER 5

AGREEMENTS AND CONDUCT THAT ARGUABLY DISTORT DOWNSTREAM COMPETITION IN DISTRIBUTING A SUPPLIER'S PRODUCTS

A. INTRODUCTION

Like Chapter 4, this chapter addresses vertical agreements and conduct, but the concern is at a different level of competition. Chapter 4 addressed the concern that such vertical agreements and conduct might restrict competition from the rivals of a powerful upstream firm in a way that creates anticompetitive effects on the upstream market that benefit the powerful firm. This chapter instead addresses the concern that vertical agreements and conduct might distort downstream competition in distributing a supplier's products.

With vertical distributional agreements that restrain the prices at which dealers can resell the upstream firm's product, or restrain where or to whom they can sell it, the concern is generally that price or nonprice competition among the downstream dealers might be lessened. With vertical conduct like secondary-line price discrimination, the concern is that supplying some input at different prices to different downstream firms might provide the firm getting the input at the lower price with an unfair competitive advantage in the downstream market.

In either sort of situation, legal doctrines designed to address such concerns have confronted the following sort of critique. The upstream firm that is engaging in the vertical agreement or conduct has no financial incentive to lessen downstream competition in the distribution of its products. Quite the opposite: a manufacturer's interest is normally in decreasing the retail margin. Suppose, for example, that a manufacturer has a product that it wholesales for $80 to retailers who sell it for $100, thus reaping a $20 markup. If the manufacturer can reduce the retail margin to $10 through increased retail competition, then the manufacturer can increase its wholesale price to $90 and still sell the same quantity because retail consumers will still be paying $100. Or the manufacturer might increase its wholesale price to $85, resulting in a retail price of $95 and increased sales because consumers will be paying less. Standing alone, a decreased retail margin should benefit a manufacturer with some combination of increased wholesale prices and sales.

Thus, the critique continues, if the upstream firm has agreed to restrain downstream competition in the distribution of its products, then it must believe that any increased retail margin is offset by some improvement in the efficiency of distribution, such as reducing free riding in service or advertising among dealers. The manufacturer's own incentives thus indicate that any vertical distributional restraint that has some anticompetitive effect on the downstream market must have an offsetting procompetitive justification.[1] Accordingly, we should deem such conduct per se legal or at least presumptively reasonable.

The responses to this critique are usually of four sorts. First, it may be that the restraint indirectly does have some anticompetitive effect upstream. Vertical agreements that fix resale prices might, for example, facilitate oligopolistic coordination among upstream manufacturers because retail prices are easier for each other to monitor than wholesale prices. However, such a theory would seem to require proof that in fact the relevant market was oligopolistic, that all the oligopolists used similar agreements, and that those agreements facilitated their oligopolistic coordination. It might thus be thought better covered by the law on agreements or conduct alleged to facilitate oligopolistic coordination, which is addressed in Chapter 6.

Second, it may be that the vertical restraint reflects the market power of a downstream cartel or firm, and is thus imposed on the upstream firms against their interests. For example, if the dealers agree among themselves that they will distribute products only if the manufacturers fix their resale prices at a certain level or divide their territories in a certain way, that is effectively the same thing as a buyer cartel or horizontal market division that may force manufacturers to agree contrary to their interests. Likewise, if a downstream firm with buyer market power insists on being the only outlet for a supplier in a given area, that is effectively a form of exclusive dealing that forecloses rival downstream firms from access to that supplier.[2] If the foreclosure of suppliers is extensive enough to impair the ability of downstream firms to compete, then there is no reason to treat this form of upstream exclusive dealing differently than the downstream variant. However, these sorts of theories would seem to require evidence that there was either a downstream horizontal agreement or a downstream firm with

---

1. The situation would be different if, instead of just restraining the distribution of its own goods, the manufacturer restrained the terms on which all competing goods were distributed as well. Suppose, for example, a widget manufacturer entered into vertical agreements with every retailer providing that each would not sell anyone's widgets for less than $100. Then the manufacturer would essentially be organizing a horizontal cartel through these vertical agreements that would create a supracompetitive surplus, and could reach some mutually beneficial agreement with retailers that would split that surplus in a way that benefited both the manufacturers and retailers but harmed downstream consumers. Such a case could be addressed as monopolization/dominance or an implicit horizontal agreement. See *Griffith* (holding that an upstream version of such cartel ringmastering constituted monopolization); *Interstate Circuit* (holding that an upstream version of such cartel ringmastering constituted a horizontal agreement). In this chapter, however, we deal only with vertical restraints limited to the distribution of the manufacturer's own goods; that is, we address intrabrand restraints and not interbrand restraints.

2. *See, e.g., Griffith.*

market power. And if such proof were available, then a case could instead proceed under the doctrines discussed respectively in Chapters 2 and 4.

Third, vertical restraints may be designed to get dealers to push the manufacturer's brand irrespective of its merits. For example, a manufacturer might impose high resale prices on all its dealers so that its brand enjoys a high profit margin that makes it more profitable for dealers to push its brand over the brands of other manufacturers. Pushing might take overt forms like outright recommendations to buyers or more subtle forms like placing the favored brand on shelves that are at eye-level or the end of aisles that customers notice most. If only some manufacturers use vertical price-fixing to encourage dealers to push their brands, then the effect will be to distort dealer recommendations to consumers and thus harm consumer welfare. *See* VIII Areeda, Antiturst Law ¶ 1614, at 194–198 (1989). Alternatively, other manufacturers might feel obliged to do the same thing to avoid disfavorable treatment, with the result that none of them gains any advantage but all of them suffer the costs of excessive retail margins and unresponsive retail prices. *Id.* at 197–98. One might think manufacturers could achieve the same sort of brand-pushing by simply paying dealers a bonus for increased sales. However, doing that would effectively be the same as reducing the wholesale price, which if intrabrand retail competition is high, would lower retail prices and bring retailer profit margins back to competitive levels, eliminating the incentive to push. *Id.* at 195. However, the brand-pushing theory would apply only to multibrand dealers, and only if the dealers are likely to be able to influence consumer choice. Moreover, others would argue that brand-pushing is not an illegitimate effort to distort dealer advice, but instead desirable competition for promotional services. *See* Benjamin Klein, *Assessing Resale Price Maintenance After* Leegin, forthcoming in Handbook of Antitrust Economics (ed. Einer Elhauge). The critics respond that, although bidding for promotional services is involved, such bidding is not procompetitive when the promotional service consists of retailer efforts to mislead consumers. Areeda, *supra*, at 197.

Fourth, vertical restraints might be designed to facilitate downstream price discrimination against consumers. For example, a supplier might sell at a higher wholesale price in geographic markets where consumers are richer and willing to pay more than in poorer markets. If retailers in the poorer markets can buy at the low wholesale price and resell the product in the richer markets, they will undercut the supplier's higher price in the latter. To stop this, a manufacturer might impose vertical territorial restraints to prevent retailers in the poorer markets from reselling to the richer markets. Or it might impose vertical price restrictions that prevent anyone from selling in the richer markets below some minimum price.

A ban on such vertical restraints can thus reduce price discrimination. But if this is the theory, one might think liability should turn on proof that the vertical restraints actually did support price discrimination. Further, although price discrimination usually reduces consumer welfare, it can increase it, and it usually increases ex post total welfare and efficiency, which matters to the extent one prefers the latter as the antitrust standard. *See* Chapter 3. Even if price discrimination reduces *total* consumer welfare, adverse distributive effects may result if ending price discrimination raises prices in poorer markets (reducing consumer welfare there) and lowers prices in richer markets (increasing consumer welfare there). In the US, there is no ban on consumer price discrimination, just on discrimination that distorts competition between those selling downstream in the same market. However, agreements that facilitate consumer price discrimination have been condemned under tying doctrine and may have been at issue in the *Dr. Miles* case that originally made vertical price-fixing per se illegal. In the EC, price discrimination has been viewed as a very important harm, especially when the price discrimination is between different national markets, both because EU law is more concerned generally with excessive pricing and consumer price discrimination, *see* Chapter 3, and more importantly because EU competition law has stressed the trade policy of creating a common market that transcends national boundaries.

Even to the extent anticompetitive effects exist, one might think they are offset by possible procompetitive justifications. For example, restricting resale prices might encourage retailers to provide important services in explaining complicated products without fear that customers will first go to the full service retailer to figure out what they want to buy and then buy the product from a discount retailer who can sell at a cut rate because it provides no services. Such free riding might discourage all retailers from providing a valuable service to consumers.

However, some commentators argue that the alleged procompetitive purposes for some forms of vertical restraints, like agreements fixing resale prices, are not really advanced by those agreements, at least not in any way that a less restrictive alternative could not equally achieve.[3] For example, some argue that free riding on services is often inapplicable either because the retailers do not offer the type of services on which others could free ride or because the terminated retailers provide the same services as other retailers. Further, some argue that, when free-riding does occur, the manufacturer could simply require those services, pay separately for them, or provide it itself. If one were confident in this conclusion, one might conclude that the absence of any real procompetitive justification means that some anticompetitive theory must in fact explain the conduct.

In the United States, vertical agreements that restrain the distribution of a supplier's goods are governed by the same Sherman Act § 1 that governs horizontal agreements, but the caselaw that elaborates when such vertical agreements are judged under the rule of reason or per se rule differs considerably from the caselaw described in Chapter 2. Price discrimination in commodities that may distort downstream competition is instead governed by the Robinson–Patman Act, which as detailed below has exceptions when the price discrimination is justified by cost differences, changing market conditions, or good faith efforts to meet competition. 15 U.S.C. § 13.

Vertical agreements that restrain distribution of a supplier's goods have been the subject of a number of decisions of the Commission and

---

3. *See, e.g.,* Robert Pitofsky, *In Defense of Discounters: The No–Frills Case for a Per Se Rule Against Vertical Price Fixing,* 71 GEORGETOWN L J 1487 (1983).

judgments of the EU courts, the first major case being *Consten Grundig* adopted by the ECJ in 1966, which will be discussed below. Because vertical agreements are a common commercial practice, the Commission decided to adopt several block exemption regulations, which have been replaced by Commission Regulation 330/2010 of 20 April 2010 on the application of Article 101(3) TFEU to categories of vertical agreements and concerted practices (see Chapter 4). On price discrimination, the main relevant provision is Article 102(c)'s prohibition on dominant firms "applying dissimilar conditions to equivalent transactions with other trading parties, thereby placing them at a competitive disadvantage."

B.   Intrabrand Distributional Restraints on Resale

A vertical minimum price-fixing agreement is an agreement between a manufacturer and dealer that fixes the minimum prices at which the dealer can resell the manufacturer's brand. A vertical maximum price-fixing agreement instead fixes the maximum price of dealer resale of that brand. A vertical nonprice agreement restrains distribution of a manufacturer's brand in some way other than price, usually by limiting where or to whom the dealer can resell that brand.

All three types of vertical agreements were once per se illegal in the United States. Then the Supreme Court in succession overruled the per se rules against vertical nonprice restraints (in 1977), vertical maximum price-fixing (in 1997), and vertical minimum price-fixing (in 2007). The following covers that evolution, which in part reflects the growing influence of antitrust economics on U.S. antitrust law.

The EU judges both vertical territorial restraints and vertical minimum price-fixing under an abbreviated rule of reason, where the agreements are presumptively condemned under Article 101(1) without need to prove anticompetitive effects, but can be justified under Article 101(3), although such justifications rarely succeed in practice. The EU uses a rule of per se legality for vertical maximum price-fixing if the seller's market share is below 30%, with a rule of reason governing cases where the share exceeds 30%.

1.   Vertical Nonprice Restraints on Distribution

Vertical agreements to restrain distribution of a manufacturer's brand in ways other than price have a lot of similarities with vertical restraints that set minimum prices, but have many significant differences as well. The most important type of vertical nonprice agreements are those that limit to whom a dealer can resell the manufacturer's product. Sometimes these take the form of vertical territorial restraints, limiting dealers to a particular geographic area. Other times they reflect customer limitations, such as limiting one dealer to reselling to commercial users and another to reselling to consumers. Either should be distinguished from exclusive dealing or other similar exclusionary agreements, which limit the manufacturers the dealer can carry, and thus have possible foreclosing effects that may impede interbrand competition between manufacturers. See Chapter 4.[4]

Such vertical nonprice restraints are similar to vertical minimum price-fixing in that either might procompetitively curb free riding in services. Likewise, either might anticompetitively reflect coercion by a dealer cartel or a dealer with market power, a manufacturer desire for brand pushing by multibrand dealers, or the pursuit of a price discrimination scheme that usually decreases consumer welfare but could increase it. Both types of agreements are likely to have, and be intended to have, similar effects on retail prices, though resale price maintenance is more likely to totally preclude the possibility of a low price, high-volume dealer. More important, for either sort of agreement, manufacturers may have incentives to efficiently trade off the procompetitive benefits of increasing retailing efforts against the anticompetitive effects of reducing retail competition.

The differences in possible anticompetitive effects are various. Unlike vertical minimum price-fixing, vertical nonprice restraints don't have a possible adverse effect on *inter*brand price competition by impeding the ability of retailers to adjust prices in response to competition from other brands. Vertical limits on territories and customers also don't facilitate oligopolistic coordination between manufacturers, although a nonprice agreement on something like standard delivery terms might. On the other hand, especially when dealers are made the sole outlets in an area, such agreements impose a more severe restraint on *intra*brand competition because they curb price *and* nonprice competition between retailers in distributing that brand. Further, vertical territorial restraints that coincide with national boundaries raise particular concerns in the EU about impeding free trade on a common market.

Vertical nonprice restraints that limit the number of retailers that can sell a given manufacturer's products to certain customers also have possible additional procompetitive benefits compared to vertical price fixing. First, they might encourage dealer investments to develop demand for that manufacturer's goods in that area, a special case of which is that they might be necessary to encourage dealers to enter the market at all. A price restraint could not accomplish the same thing because the manufacturer

---

4. This can lead to somewhat confusing terminology because an agreement that makes a dealer the "exclusive dealer" in a territory for a particular manufacturer is generally considered a vertical nonprice restraint on distribution rather than "exclusive dealing" within the meaning of Chapter 4. The reason is that such an agreement does not bar that dealer from carrying other manufacturers and thus has intrabrand effects but not interbrand effects, where the manufacturers are the relevant competing "brands." To minimize confusion, we will call such dealers "sole outlets" rather than "exclusive dealers."

However, if the relevant anticompetitive concern is that the sole outlet dealer is using its market power to foreclose a substantial share of vital suppliers in a way that impairs the competitiveness of rival supplier-dealers, then that would raise a claim of upstream exclusive dealing under the methodology of Chapter 4. *See Griffith.* In the latter sort of case, the dealer would not have incentives to trade off procompetitive and anticompetitive effects, but it must be shown that the dealer has the requisite market power to set terms and that it has procured a substantial foreclosure of suppliers that indicates likely anticompetitive effects on the retail market. In a traditional vertical distributional restraint case, dealer market power and substantial supplier foreclosure are not elements.

could later add extra dealers who could free ride on the investment and erode it with nonprice competition or the manufacturer might adjust (or fail to adjust) future prices. Second, vertical nonprice restraints might be designed to assure that dealers resell only to those qualified to carry or use the product. A wholesaler might thus be limited to reselling to dealers who are qualified to handle the product; a retailer might be limited to reselling to customers who have the knowledge to use that version of the product safely. Third, vertical nonprice restraints might usefully encourage specialization. One might want each dealer to specialize in a particular type of customer because that makes them more effective in assessing and serving their needs.

Again, all these procompetitive justifications resonate as persuasive with courts only because the manufacturer's incentives give us more confidence they are actually being pursued. After all, one could in theory offer all the same justifications in a horizontal case involving market division among retailers—the difference is that there the retailers would be affirmatively motivated by the additional profits they would reap if the agreement did have anticompetitive effects at retail, whereas a manufacturer is harmed by such anticompetitive effects and thus should not voluntarily incur them unless they are offset by improved manufacturer distribution, which may be procompetitive.

Vertical nonprice restraints might also help aid price discrimination. If each dealer's customer set conforms to a different level of willingness to pay for the product, then each can charge a different price and be charged a different wholesale price, so as to maximize the manufacturer's profits. Barring the dealers from selling to each other's customers can prevent them from undermining this price discrimination. Such price discrimination might increase or decrease efficiency, total welfare, and consumer welfare, though it usually decreases consumer welfare and increases total welfare. Where price discrimination benefits buyers in some nations but harms those in others, it raises special EU concerns about free trade.

Continental T.V. v. GTE Sylvania

433 U.S. 36 (1977).

■ MR. JUSTICE POWELL delivered the opinion of the Court. . . .

Respondent GTE Sylvania Inc. (Sylvania) manufactures and sells television sets. . . . Prompted by a decline in its market share to a relatively insignificant 1% to 2% of national television sales,[1] Sylvania conducted an intensive reassessment of its marketing strategy, and in 1962 adopted the franchise plan challenged here. Sylvania phased out its wholesale distributors and began to sell its televisions directly to a smaller and more select group of franchised retailers. An acknowledged purpose of the change was to decrease the number of competing Sylvania retailers in the hope of attracting the more aggressive and competent retailers thought necessary

---

1. RCA at that time was the dominant firm with as much as 60% to 70% of national television sales in an industry with more than 100 manufacturers.

to the improvement of the company's market position.[2] To this end, Sylvania limited the number of franchises granted for any given area and required each franchisee to sell his Sylvania products only from the location or locations at which he was franchised.[3] A franchise did not constitute an exclusive territory, and Sylvania retained sole discretion to increase the number of retailers in an area in light of the success or failure of existing retailers in developing their market. The revised marketing strategy appears to have been successful during the period at issue here, for by 1965 Sylvania's share of national television sales had increased to approximately 5%, and the company ranked as the Nation's eighth largest manufacturer of color television sets.

[Because Sylvania's share of San Francisco sales were half its national average, Sylvania added another retailer in San Francisco close to its existing retailer, Continental TV. Continental responded by asking to open a store in Sacramento. Sylvania denied this request because its existing retailers there already had its share of Sacramento sales at triple its national average. Continental TV opened a store in Sacramento anyway, and Sylvania enforced its locational agreement by terminating Continental's franchise to sell Sylvania televisions. The District Court instructed the jury that a vertical agreement restricting the location of a dealer was illegal per se under United States v. Arnold, Schwinn & Co., 388 U.S. 365 (1967), and the jury found Sylvania liable for trebled damages of $1,774,515. The Court of Appeals reversed.]

II

[*Schwinn* held that vertical restraints on the customers a dealer can sell to are per se violation of Sherman § 1 if title to the goods has passed from the manufacturer to the dealer, but are governed by the rule of reason if title, dominion and risk have not passed so that the dealer is acting as an agent of the manufacturer.] . . . In the present case, it is undisputed that title to the television sets passed from Sylvania to Continental. Thus, the *Schwinn* per se rule applies unless Sylvania's restriction on locations falls outside *Schwinn*'s prohibition against a manufacturer's attempting to restrict a "retailer's freedom as to where and to whom it will resell the products." . . . In intent and competitive impact, the retail-customer restriction in *Schwinn* is indistinguishable from the location restriction in the present case. In both cases the restrictions limited the freedom of the retailer to dispose of the purchased products as he desired. The fact that one restriction was addressed to territory and the other to customers is irrelevant to functional anti-trust analysis, and indeed, to the language and broad thrust of the opinion in *Schwinn* . . .

III

Sylvania argues that if *Schwinn* cannot be distinguished, it should be reconsidered. Although *Schwinn* is supported by the principle of stare

---

2. The number of retailers selling Sylvania products declined significantly as a result of the change, but in 1965 there were at least two franchised Sylvania retailers in each metropolitan center of more than 100,000 population.

3. Sylvania imposed no restrictions on the right of the franchisee to sell the products of competing manufacturers.

decisis, we are convinced that the need for clarification of the law in this area justifies reconsideration. *Schwinn* itself was an abrupt and largely unexplained departure from White Motor Co. v. United States, 372 U.S. 253 (1963), where only four years earlier the Court had refused to endorse a per se rule for vertical restrictions. Since its announcement, *Schwinn* has been the subject of continuing controversy and confusion, both in the scholarly journals and in the federal courts. The great weight of scholarly opinion has been critical of the decision, and a number of the federal courts confronted with analogous vertical restrictions have sought to limit its reach. In our view, the experience of the past 10 years should be brought to bear on this subject of considerable commercial importance.

... Per se rules of illegality are appropriate only when they relate to conduct that is manifestly anticompetitive. As the Court explained in Northern Pacific R. Co. v. United States, 356 U.S. 1, 5 (1958), "there are certain agreements or practices which because of their pernicious effect on competition and lack of any redeeming virtue are conclusively presumed to be unreasonable and therefore illegal without elaborate inquiry as to the precise harm they have caused or the business excuse for their use."[16] In essence, the issue before us is whether *Schwinn*'s per se rule can be justified under the demanding standards of *Northern Pacific*....

The market impact of vertical restrictions[18] is complex because of their potential for a simultaneous reduction of intrabrand competition and stimulation of interbrand competition.[19] Significantly, the Court in

---

16. Per se rules thus require the Court to make broad generalizations about the social utility of particular commercial practices. The probability that anticompetitive consequences will result from a practice and the severity of those consequences must be balanced against its pro-competitive consequences. Cases that do not fit the generalization may arise, but a per se rule reflects the judgment that such cases are not sufficiently common or important to justify the time and expense necessary to identify them. Once established, per se rules tend to provide guidance to the business community and to minimize the burdens on litigants and the judicial system of the more complex rule-of-reason trials, but those advantages are not sufficient in themselves to justify the creation of per se rules. If it were otherwise, all of antitrust law would be reduced to per se rules, thus introducing an unintended and undesirable rigidity in the law.

18. As in *Schwinn*, we are concerned here only with nonprice vertical restrictions. The per se illegality of price restrictions has been established firmly for many years and involves significantly different questions of analysis and policy. As Mr. Justice White notes, some commentators have argued that the manufacturer's motivation for imposing vertical price restrictions may be the same as for nonprice restrictions. There are, however, significant differences that could easily justify different treatment. In his concurring opinion in *White Motor*, Mr. Justice Brennan noted that, unlike nonprice restrictions, "[r]esale price maintenance is not only designed to, but almost invariably does in fact, reduce price competition not only *among* sellers of the affected product, but quite as much *between* that product and competing brands." Professor Posner also recognized that "industry-wide resale price maintenance might facilitate cartelizing." Furthermore, Congress recently has expressed its approval of a per se analysis of vertical price restrictions by repealing those provisions of the Miller–Tydings and McGuire Acts allowing fair trade pricing at the option of the individual States. Consumer Goods Pricing Act of 1975, 89 Stat. 801, amending 15 U.S.C. §§ 1, 45(a). No similar expression of congressional intent exists for nonprice restrictions.

19. Interbrand competition is the competition among the manufacturers of the same generic product television sets in this case and is the primary concern of antitrust law. The extreme example of a deficiency of interbrand competition is monopoly, where there is only

Schwinn did not distinguish among the challenged restrictions on the basis of their individual potential for intrabrand harm or interbrand benefit. Restrictions that completely eliminated intrabrand competition among Schwinn distributors were analyzed no differently from those that merely moderated intrabrand competition among retailers. The pivotal factor was the passage of title: All restrictions were held to be per se illegal where title had passed, and all were evaluated and sustained under the rule of reason where it had not. The location restriction at issue here would be subject to the same pattern of analysis under *Schwinn*.

It appears that this distinction between sale and nonsale transactions resulted from the Court's effort to accommodate the perceived intrabrand harm and interbrand benefit of vertical restrictions. The per se rule for sale transactions reflected the view that vertical restrictions are "so obviously destructive" of intrabrand competition that their use would "open the door to exclusivity of outlets and limitation of territory further than prudence permits."[21] Conversely, the continued adherence to the traditional rule of reason for nonsale transactions reflected the view that the restrictions have too great a potential for the promotion of interbrand competition to justify complete prohibition. The Court's opinion provides no analytical support for these contrasting positions. Nor is there even an assertion in the opinion that the competitive impact of vertical restrictions is significantly affected by the form of the transaction. Non-sale transactions appear to be excluded from the per se rule, not because of a greater danger of intrabrand harm or a greater promise of interbrand benefit, but rather because of the Court's unexplained belief that a complete per se prohibition would be too "inflexibl[e]."

---

one manufacturer. In contrast, intrabrand competition is the competition between the distributors wholesale or retail of the product of a particular manufacturer.

The degree of intrabrand competition is wholly independent of the level of interbrand competition confronting the manufacturer. Thus, there may be fierce intrabrand competition among the distributors of a product produced by a monopolist and no intrabrand competition among the distributors of a product produced by a firm in a highly competitive industry. But when interbrand competition exists, as it does among television manufacturers, it provides a significant check on the exploitation of intrabrand market power because of the ability of consumers to substitute a different brand of the same product.

21.   The Court also stated that to impose vertical restrictions in sale transactions would "violate the ancient rule against restraints on alienation." The isolated reference has provoked sharp criticism from virtually all of the commentators on the decision, most of whom have regarded the Court's apparent reliance on the "ancient rule" as both a misreading of legal history and a perversion of antitrust analysis. We quite agree with Mr. Justice Stewart's dissenting comment in *Schwinn* that "the state of the common law 400 or even 100 years ago is irrelevant to the issue before us: the effect of the antitrust laws upon vertical distributional restraints in the American economy today." We are similarly unable to accept Judge Browning's interpretation of *Schwinn*. In this dissent below he argued that the decision reflects the view that the Sherman Act was intended to prohibit restrictions on the autonomy of independent businessmen even though they have no impact on "price, quality, and quantity of goods and services." This view is certainly not explicit in *Schwinn*, which purports to be based on an examination of the "impact (of the restrictions) upon the marketplace." Competitive economies have social and political as well as economic advantages, but an antitrust policy divorced from market considerations would lack any objective benchmarks. As Mr. Justice Brandeis reminded us: "Every agreement concerning trade, every regulation of trade, restrains. To bind, to restrain, is of their very essence." *Chicago Board of Trade....*

Vertical restrictions reduce intrabrand competition by limiting the number of sellers of a particular product competing for the business of a given group of buyers. Location restrictions have this effect because of practical constraints on the effective marketing area of retail outlets. Although intrabrand competition may be reduced, the ability of retailers to exploit the resulting market may be limited both by the ability of consumers to travel to other franchised locations and, perhaps more importantly, to purchase the competing products of other manufacturers. None of these key variables, however, is affected by the form of the transaction by which a manufacturer conveys his products to the retailers.

Vertical restrictions promote interbrand competition by allowing the manufacturer to achieve certain efficiencies in the distribution of his products. These "redeeming virtues" are implicit in every decision sustaining vertical restrictions under the rule of reason. Economists have identified a number of ways in which manufacturers can use such restrictions to compete more effectively against other manufacturers. See, e.g., Preston, Restrictive Distribution Arrangements: Economic Analysis and Public Policy Standards, 30 Law & Contemp.Prob. 506, 511 (1965).[22] For example, new manufacturers and manufacturers entering new markets can use the restrictions in order to induce competent and aggressive retailers to make the kind of investment of capital and labor that is often required in the distribution of products unknown to the consumer. Established manufacturers can use them to induce retailers to engage in promotional activities or to provide service and repair facilities necessary to the efficient marketing of their products. Service and repair are vital for many products, such as automobiles and major household appliances. The availability and quality of such services affect a manufacturer's goodwill and the competitiveness of his product. Because of market imperfections such as the so-called "free rider" effect, these services might not be provided by retailers in a purely competitive situation, despite the fact that each retailer's benefit would be greater if all provided the services than if none did.

Economists also have argued that manufacturers have an economic interest in maintaining as much intrabrand competition as is consistent with the efficient distribution of their products. Bork, The Rule of Reason and the Per Se Concept: Price Fixing and the Market Division (II), 75 Yale L.J. 373, 403 (1966); Posner, supra, n. 13, at 283, 287–288.[24] Although the

---

22. Marketing efficiency is not the only legitimate reason for a manufacturer's desire to exert control over the manner in which his products are sold and serviced. As a result of statutory and common-law developments, society increasingly demands that manufacturers assume direct responsibility for the safety and quality of their products. For example, at the federal level, apart from more specialized requirements, manufacturers of consumer products have safety responsibilities under the Consumer Product Safety Act, and obligations for warranties under the Consumer Product Warranties Act. Similar obligations are imposed by state law. The legitimacy of these concerns has been recognized in cases involving vertical restrictions. See, e.g., Tripoli Co. v. Wella Corp., 425 F.2d 932 (CA3 1970).

24. "Generally a manufacturer would prefer the lowest retail price possible, once its price to dealers has been set, because a lower retail price means increased sales and higher manufacturer revenues." Note, 88 Harv.L.Rev. 636, 641 (1975). In this context, a manufacturer is likely to view the difference between the price at which it sells to its retailers and their price to the consumer as his "cost of distribution," which it would prefer to minimize. Posner, *supra*, n. 13, at 283.

view that the manufacturer's interest necessarily corresponds with that of the public is not universally shared, even the leading critic of vertical restrictions concedes that *Schwinn*'s distinction between sale and nonsale transactions is essentially unrelated to any relevant economic impact. Comanor, Vertical Territorial and Customer Restrictions: White Motor and Its Aftermath, 81 Harv.L.Rev. 1419, 1422 (1968).[25] Indeed, to the extent that the form of the transaction is related to interbrand benefits, the Court's distinction is inconsistent with its articulated concern for the ability of smaller firms to compete effectively with larger ones. Capital requirements and administrative expenses may prevent smaller firms from using the exception for nonsale transactions.[26]

We conclude that the distinction drawn in *Schwinn* between sale and nonsale transactions is not sufficient to justify the application of a per se rule in one situation and a rule of reason in the other. The question remains whether the per se rule stated in *Schwinn* should be expanded to include non-sale transactions or abandoned in favor of a return to the rule of reason. We have found no persuasive support for expanding the per se rule. As noted above, the *Schwinn* Court recognized the undesirability of "prohibit[ing] all vertical restrictions of territory and all franchising...."[27] And even Continental does not urge us to hold that all such restrictions are per se illegal.

We revert to the standard articulated in *Northern Pacific* ... for determining whether vertical restrictions must be "conclusively presumed to be unreasonable and therefore illegal without elaborate inquiry as to the precise harm they have caused or the business excuse for their use." Such restrictions, in varying forms, are widely used in our free market economy. As indicated above, there is substantial scholarly and judicial authority supporting their economic utility. There is relatively little authority to the contrary.[28] Certainly, there has been no showing in this case, either generally or with respect to Sylvania's agreements, that vertical restrictions have or are likely to have a "pernicious effect on competition" or that they

---

25. Professor Comanor argues that the promotional activities encouraged by vertical restrictions result in product differentiation and, therefore, a decrease in interbrand competition. This argument is flawed by its necessary assumption that a large part of the promotional efforts resulting from vertical restrictions will not convey socially desirable information about product availability, price, quality, and services. Nor is it clear that a per se rule would result in anything more than a shift to less efficient methods of obtaining the same promotional effects.

26. We also note that per se rules in this area may work to the ultimate detriment of the small businessmen who operate as franchisees. To the extent that a per se rule prevents a firm from using the franchise system to achieve efficiencies that it perceives as important to its successful operation, the rule creates an incentive for vertical integration into the distribution system, thereby eliminating to that extent the role of independent businessmen.

27. Continental's contention that balancing intrabrand and interbrand competitive effects of vertical restrictions is not a "proper part of the judicial function," is refuted by *Schwinn* itself. *Topco* is not to the contrary, for it involved a horizontal restriction among ostensible competitors.

28. There may be occasional problems in differentiating vertical restrictions from horizontal restrictions originating in agreements among the retailers. There is no doubt that restrictions in the latter category would be illegal per se, see, e.g., *General Motors*; *Topco*, but we do not regard the problems of proof as sufficiently great to justify a per se rule.

"lack . . . any redeeming virtue." Accordingly, we conclude that the per se rule stated in *Schwinn* must be overruled.[30] In so holding we do not foreclose the possibility that particular applications of vertical restrictions might justify per se prohibition under *Northern Pacific*. But we do make clear that departure from the rule-of-reason standard must be based upon demonstrable economic effect rather than as in *Schwinn* upon formalistic line drawing.

In sum, we conclude that the appropriate decision is to return to the rule of reason that governed vertical restrictions prior to *Schwinn*. When anticompetitive effects are shown to result from particular vertical restrictions they can be adequately policed under the rule of reason, the standard traditionally applied for the majority of anticompetitive practices challenged under § 1 of the Act. Accordingly, the decision of the Court of Appeals is *Affirmed*.

■ MR. JUSTICE WHITE, Concurring in the Judgment. . . . It is common ground among the leading advocates of a purely economic approach to the question of distribution restraints that the economic arguments in favor of allowing vertical nonprice restraints generally apply to vertical price restraints as well. Although the majority asserts that "the per se illegality of price restrictions . . . involves significantly different questions of analysis and policy," I suspect this purported distinction may be as difficult to justify as that of *Schwinn* under the terms of the majority's analysis. . . . The effect, if not the intention, of the Court's opinion is necessarily to call into question the firmly established per se rule against price restraints. . . .

Questions on *Sylvania*

1. Did *Schwinn*'s sale/nonsale distinction make sense? Does it relate more to whether there is an agreement with a separate actor or to whether that agreement is anticompetitive?

2. Do you agree with *Sylvania*'s decision to apply the rule of reason?

a. Is it correct under the *Northern Pacific* test that per se rules should govern only when a restraint has no redeeming virtue and almost always has pernicious effect on competition?

b. Is the decision correct if the appropriate test is instead whether a per se rule would reduce the aggregate harm from over-and underdeterrence? Won't adopting a rule of reason increase underdeterrence? Can courts accurately assess justifications and whether they offset any anticompetitive effects?

c. Could one reduce the aggregate harm from over-and underdeterrence by having this per se rule (like the one against tying) limited to cases where the manufacturer has market power? Would that really be a per se rule? Does manufacturer market power increase or decrease the likelihood

---

30. The importance of stare decisis is, of course, unquestioned, but as Mr. Justice Frankfurter stated in Helvering v. Hallock, 309 U.S. 106, 119 (1940), "stare decisis is a principle of policy and not a mechanical formula of adherence to the latest decision, however recent and questionable, when such adherence involves collision with a prior doctrine more embracing in its scope, intrinsically sounder, and verified by experience."

of the anticompetitive effects that might be caused by vertical nonprice restraints?

3. Even if *Schwinn* was wrongly decided, should the Court overrule statutory precedent that Congress has let stand or let Congress do it?

4. Do you agree with Justice White that this ruling implies that the per se rule against vertical minimum price-fixing should be overruled too?

a. Doesn't it also flunk the *Northern Pacific* test?

b. Is the mix of over-and underdeterrence significantly different for the per se rule against vertical price-fixing than for vertical nonprice restraints?

5. Should the rule on vertical nonprice restraints be per se *legality*?

6. Couldn't a horizontal agreement dividing territories among dealers have precisely the same procompetitive justifications as this scheme of vertical agreements? Should the Court thus overrule the per se rule against horizontal market divisions among dealers? What is the difference?

EU Law on Vertical Territorial Restraints

Since the first days of EU competition policy, the Commission and the EU courts have been opposed to the presence in vertical agreements of territorial restrictions designed to prevent parallel trade between Member States. Parallel trade concerns a significant amount of goods and services in certain economic sectors (drugs, motor vehicles, etc.). It is stimulated by the price differences existing between Member States. Such differences are due to a variety of factors, such as taxation, labor costs, regulatory regimes, and currency fluctuations (though such fluctuations have now disappeared between the Member States that belong to the Euro zone).

The main reason why the Commission and the EU courts seek to protect parallel trade is that, unlike US antitrust law, the purposes of EU competition law include not only economic efficiency but also promoting the creation of an integrated market where goods and services would flow across Member States without being impeded by State or private measures. Protecting parallel trade is thus seen as a helpful contribution to the creation of a single market.

Joined Cases 56 and 58–64, Consten and Grundig v. Commission

English Special Edition 1966 page 299.

[Grundig, a German firm, decided to start marketing some of its products in France. It persuaded Consten, a wholesaler, to promote its brand in that country. The distribution agreement provided that Grundig would not supply the contract products in France to other distributors than Consten and it would protect Consten's exclusivity by restraining its wholesalers in Germany and distributors elsewhere from exporting to France. Parallel importers, however, started to buy products in Germany to resell them in France at prices that were 25% lower than those of the

Consten network. Consten and Grunding sued the parallel importers in the French courts. The Court of Appeals of Paris adjourned the proceedings to enable the parties to notify the agreement to the Commission. Following the notification made by the parties, the Commission adopted a decision concluding that the exclusive territory allocated to Consten and the export bans imposed on the other dealers were contrary to [Article 101(1) TFEU]. Consten and Grunding appealed this decision before the ECJ.]

The contested decision states that the principal reason for the refusal of exemption lies in the fact that the requirement contained in Article [101(3)(a)] is not satisfied. ... The applicants maintain that the admission of parallel imports would mean that the sole representative would no longer be in a position to engage in advance planning. A certain degree of uncertainty is inherent in all forecasts of future sales possibilities. Such forecasting must in fact be based on a series of variable and uncertain factors. The admission of parallel imports may indeed involve increased risks for the concessionnaire who gives firm orders in advance for the quantities of goods which he considers he will be able to sell. However, such a risk is inherent in all commercial activity and thus cannot justify special protection on this point.

The applicants complain that the Commission did not consider on the basis of concrete facts whether it is possible to provide guarantee and after-sales services without absolute territorial protection. They emphasize in particular the importance for the reputation of the Grundig name of the proper provision of these services for all the Grundig machines put on the market. The freeing of parallel imports would compel Consten to refuse these services for machines imported by its competitors who did not themselves carry out these services satisfactorily. Such a refusal would also be contrary to the interests of consumers. As regards the free guarantee service, the decision states that a purchaser can normally enforce his right to such a guarantee only against his supplier and subject to conditions agreed with him. The applicant parties do not seriously dispute that statement.

The fears concerning the damage which might result for the reputation of Grundig products from an inadequate service do not, in the circumstances, appear justified. In fact, UNEF, the main competitor of Consten, although it began selling Grundig products in France later than Consten and while having had to bear not inconsiderable risks, nevertheless supplies a free guarantee and after-sales services against remuneration upon conditions which, taken as a whole, do not seem to have harmed the reputation of the Grundig name. Moreover, nothing prevents the applicants from informing consumers, through adequate publicity, of the nature of the services and any other advantages which may be offered by the official distribution network for Grundig products. It is thus not correct that the publicity carried out by Consten must benefit parallel importers to the same extent. Consequently, the complaints raised by the applicants are unfounded.

The applicants complain that the Commission did not consider whether absolute territorial protection was still indispensable to enable the risk costs borne by Consten in launching the Grundig products on the French market to be amortized. The defendant objects that before the adoption of the contested decision it had at no time became aware of any market introduction costs which had not been amortized. This statement by the defendant has not been disputed. The Commission cannot be expected of its own motion to make inquiries on this point. Further, the argument of the applicants amounts in substance to saying that the concessionnaire would not have accepted the agreed conditions without absolute territorial protection. However, that fact has no connexion with the improvements in distribution referred to in article [101(3)]. Consequently this complaint cannot be upheld.

The applicant Grundig maintains, further, that without absolute territorial protection the sole distributor would not be inclined to bear the costs necessary for market observation since the result of his efforts might benefit parallel importers. The defendant objects that such market observation, which in particular allows the application to the products intended for export to France of technical improvements desired by the French consumer, can be of benefit only to Consten. In fact, Consten, in its capacity as sole concessionnaire which is not threatened by the contested decision, would be the only one to receive the machines equipped with the features adapted especially to the French market. Consequently this complaint is unfounded.

Questions on *Consten Grunding*

1. Why are the Commission and the ECJ so keen to protect parallel traders?

a. Does parallel trading between US states occur to a great extent?

i. Why are price differences often more significant between EU Member States than among US states?

ii. Does the adoption of a common currency (the Euro) increase or decrease the level of parallel trade across Member States?

iii. Do US courts seek to protect parallel trading?

b. Should the protection of parallel traders be a concern when there is a significant degree of interbrand competition?

c. Does the prohibition of territorial restrictions, such as those in *Consten Grundig*, necessarily lead to more competition and an integrated common market? Won't it give incentives to suppliers to integrate vertically, thereby reducing the number of distributors in the Member States?

2. In this case, why didn't the ECJ accept any of the reasons advanced by Consten and Grunding to justify their efforts to prevent parallel trade?

a. Did the ECJ give more importance to the protection of interbrand or intrabrand competition?

b. Some authors have criticized this judgment as failing to pay sufficient attention to the need to protect the ex ante incentives of Consten to invest into the promotion of a new brand. Do you agree with this view?

c. Did the ECJ compare the situation after the agreement was made with the situation that would have occurred without the agreement? Would this not have been a better test?

Commission Regulation (EU) No 330/2010 of 20 April 2010 on the Application of Article 101(3) of the Treaty on the Functioning of the European Union to Categories of Vertical Agreements and Concerted Practices

O.J. 2010, L 102/1.

Article 4. Restrictions that remove the benefit of the block exemption—hardcore restrictions

The exemption provided for in Article 2 shall not apply to vertical agreements which, directly or indirectly, in isolation or in combination with other factors under the control of the parties, have as their object: ...

(b) the restriction of the territory into which, or of the customers to whom, a buyer party to the agreement, without prejudice to a restriction on its place of establishment, may sell the contract goods or services, except:

(i) the restriction of active sales into the exclusive territory or to an exclusive customer group reserved to the supplier or allocated by the supplier to another buyer, where such a restriction does not limit sales by the customers of the buyer,

(ii) the restriction of sales to end users by a buyer operating at the wholesale level of trade,

(iii) the restriction of sales by the members of a selective distribution system to unauthorised distributors within the territory reserved by the supplier to operate that system, and

(iv) the restriction of the buyer's ability to sell components, supplied for the purposes of incorporation, to customers who would use them to manufacture the same type of goods as those produced by the supplier.

EU Guidelines on Vertical Restraints

O.J. 2010, C 130/1.

The hardcore restriction set out in Article 4(b) of the Block Exemption Regulation concerns agreements or concerted practices that have as their direct or indirect object the restriction of sales by a buyer party to the agreement or its customers, in as far as those restrictions relate to the territory into which or the customers to whom the buyer or its customers may sell the contract goods or services. This hardcore restriction relates to market partitioning by territory or by customer group. That may be the result of direct obligations, such as the obligation not to sell to certain customers or to customers in certain territories or the obligation to refer orders from these customers to other distributors. It may also result from indirect measures aimed at inducing the distributor not to sell to such customers, such as refusal or reduction of bonuses or discounts, termination of supply, reduction of supplied volumes or limitation of supplied volumes to the demand within the allocated territory or customer group, threat of contract termination, requiring a higher price for products to be exported, limiting the proportion of sales that can be exported or profit pass-over obligations. It may further result from the supplier not providing a Union-wide guarantee service under which normally all distributors are obliged to provide the guarantee service and are reimbursed for this service by the supplier, even in relation to products sold by other distributors into their territory. Such practices are even more likely to be viewed as a restriction of the buyer's sales when used in conjunction with the implementation by the supplier of a monitoring system aimed at verifying the effective destination of the supplied goods, such as the use of differentiated labels or serial numbers. However, obligations on the reseller relating to the display of the supplier's brand name are not classified as hardcore. As Article 4(b) only concerns restrictions of sales by the buyer or its customers, this implies that restrictions of the supplier's sales are also not a hardcore restriction ... Article 4(b) applies without prejudice to a restriction on the buyer's place of establishment. Thus, the benefit of the Block Exemption Regulation is not lost if it is agreed that the buyer will restrict its distribution outlet(s) and warehouse(s) to a particular address, place or territory.

There are four exceptions to the hardcore restriction in Article 4(b) of the Block Exemption Regulation. The first exception in Article 4(b)(i) allows a supplier to restrict active sales by a buyer party to the agreement to a territory or a customer group which has been allocated exclusively to another buyer or which the supplier has reserved to itself. A territory or customer group is exclusively allocated when the supplier agrees to sell its product only to one distributor for distribution in a particular territory or to a particular customer group and the exclusive distributor is protected against active selling into its territory or to its customer group by all the other buyers of the supplier within the Union, irrespective of sales by the supplier. The supplier is allowed to combine the allocation of an exclusive territory and an exclusive customer group by for instance appointing an exclusive distributor for a particular customer group in a certain territory. Such protection of exclusively allocated territories or customer groups must, however, permit passive sales to such territories or customer groups. For the application of Article 4(b) of the Block Exemption Regulation, the Commission interprets "active" and "passive" sales as follows:

— "Active" sales mean actively approaching individual customers by for instance direct mail, including the sending of unsolicited e-mails, or visits; or actively approaching a specific customer group or customers in a specific territory through advertisement in media, on the internet or other promotions specifically targeted at that customer group or targeted at customers in that territory. Advertisement or promotion that is only attractive for the buyer if it (also) reaches a specific group of customers or customers in a specific territory, is considered active selling to that customer group or customers in that territory.

— "Passive" sales mean responding to unsolicited requests from individual customers including delivery of goods or services to such customers. General advertising or promotion that reaches customers in other distributors' (exclusive) territories or customer groups but which is a reasonable way to reach customers outside those territories or customer groups, for instance to reach customers in one's own territory, are considered passive selling. General advertising or promotion is considered a reasonable way to reach such customers if it would be attractive for the buyer to undertake these investments also if they would not reach customers in other distributors' (exclusive) territories or customer groups.

The internet is a powerful tool to reach a greater number and variety of customers than by more traditional sales methods, which explains why certain restrictions on the use of the internet are dealt with as (re)sales restrictions. In principle, every distributor must be allowed to use the internet to sell products. In general, where a distributor uses a website to sell products that is considered a form of passive selling, since it is a reasonable way to allow customers to reach the distributor. The use of a website may have effects that extend beyond the distributor's own territory and customer group; however, such effects result from the technology allowing easy access from everywhere. If a customer visits the web site of a distributor and contacts the distributor and if such contact leads to a sale, including delivery, then that is considered passive selling. The same is true if a customer opts to be kept (automatically) informed by the distributor and it leads to a sale. Offering different language options on the website does not, of itself, change the passive character of such selling. The Commission thus regards the following as examples of hardcore restrictions of passive selling given the capability of these restrictions to limit the distributor's access to a greater number and variety of customers:

(a) an agreement that the (exclusive) distributor shall prevent customers located in another (exclusive) territory from viewing its website or shall automatically re-rout its customers to the manufacturer's or other (exclusive) distributors' websites. This does not exclude an agreement that the distributor's website shall also offer a number of links to websites of other distributors and/or the supplier;

(b) an agreement that the (exclusive) distributor shall terminate consumers' transactions over the internet once their credit card data reveal an address that is not within the distributor's (exclusive) territory;

(c) an agreement that the distributor shall limit its proportion of overall sales made over the internet. This does not exclude the supplier requiring, without limiting the online sales of the distributor, that the buyer sells at least a certain absolute amount (in value or volume) of the products offline to ensure an efficient operation of its brick and mortar shop (physical point of sales), nor does it preclude the supplier from making sure that the online activity of the distributor remains consistent with the supplier's distribution model. This absolute amount of required offline sales can be the same for all buyers, or determined individually for each buyer on the basis of objective criteria, such as the buyer's size in the network or its geographic location;

(d) an agreement that the distributor shall pay a higher price for products intended to be resold by the distributor online than for products intended to be resold offline. This does not exclude the supplier agreeing with the buyer a fixed fee (that is, not a variable fee where the sum increases with the realised offline turnover as this would amount indirectly to dual pricing) to support the latter's offline or online sales efforts.

A restriction on the use of the internet by distributors that are party to the agreement is compatible with the Block Exemption Regulation to the extent that promotion on the internet or use of the internet would lead to active selling into, for instance, other distributors' exclusive territories or customer groups. The Commission considers online advertisement specifically addressed to certain customers as a form of active selling to those customers. For instance, territory-based banners on third party websites are a form of active sales into the territory where these banners are shown. In general, efforts to be found specifically in a certain territory or by a certain customer group is active selling into that territory or to that customer group. For instance, paying a search engine or online advertisement provider to have advertisements displayed specifically to users in a particular territory is active selling into that territory.

However, under the Block Exemption the supplier may require quality standards for the use of the internet site to resell its goods, just as the supplier may require quality standards for a shop or for selling by catalogue or for advertising and promotion in general. This may be relevant in particular for selective distribution. Under the Block Exemption, the supplier may, for example, require that its distributors have one or more brick and mortar shops or showrooms as a condition for becoming a member of its distribution system. Subsequent changes to such a condition are also possible under the Block Exemption, except where those changes have as their object to directly or indirectly limit the online sales by the distributors. Similarly, a supplier may require that its distributors use third party platforms to distribute the contract products only in accordance with the standards and conditions agreed between the supplier and its distributors for the distributors' use of the internet. For instance, where the distributor's website is hosted by a third party platform, the supplier may require that customers do not visit the distributor's website through a site carrying the name or logo of the third party platform.

There are three further exceptions to the hardcore restriction set out in Article 4(b) of the Block Exemption Regulation. All three exceptions allow for the restriction of both active and passive sales. Under the first exception, it is permissible to restrict a wholesaler from selling to end users, which allows a supplier to keep the wholesale and retail level of trade separate. However, that exception does not exclude the possibility that the wholesaler can sell to certain end users, such as bigger end users, while not allowing sales to (all) other end users. The second exception allows a supplier to restrict an appointed distributor in a selective distribution system from selling, at any level of trade, to unauthorised distributors located in any territory where the system is currently operated or where the supplier does not yet sell the contract products (referred to as "the territory reserved by the supplier to operate that system" in Article

4(b)(iii)). The third exception allows a supplier to restrict a buyer of components, to whom the components are supplied for incorporation, from reselling them to competitors of the supplier. The term "component" includes any intermediate goods and the term "incorporation" refers to the use of any input to produce goods.

Questions on the Commission Guidelines

1. Why do the guidelines introduce a distinction in the treatment of active and passive sales? Is it to prevent suppliers from granting absolute territorial protection to exclusive distributors, thereby preventing all intra-brand competition with the exclusive territory in question?

2. Is it always easy to distinguish between active and passive sales? If a distributor knowingly sells large quantities to an arbitrageur who actively resells its product in other nations, is that a passive sale if the distributor did not solicit the business of the arbitrageur? Does that distinction make any sense?

3. Won't allowing passive sales undermine the effectiveness of a vertical territorial restraint without eliminating it?

a. If the vertical territorial restraint is on balance anticompetitive, shouldn't the law also ban agreements restricting active sales?

b. If the vertical territorial restraint is on balance procompetitive, shouldn't the law also allow agreements restricting passive sales?

c. Is there any reason to think that the ratio of anticompetitive and procompetitive effects differs for active and passive sales?

d. Doesn't this active-passive distinction just (i) channel distribution into the hands of arbitrageurs that may be a less efficient means of distribution and that must be supported with an additional set of profits and (ii) force manufacturers to adopt possibly less efficient means of enforcing their territorial restraints?

Direct v. Indirect Market Partitioning

The Commission guidelines explain that market partitioning by territory may be the result of direct obligations, such as the obligation not to sell to certain customers or to customers in certain territories, or indirect measures aimed at inducing the distributor not to sell to such customers, such as refusal or reduction of bonuses or discounts, refusal to supply, etc. Hereafter, we review two Commission decisions, one relating to a case of a direct market partitioning measure (i.e., an export ban) and the other relating to a case of an indirect market partitioning measure (i.e., a system of dual pricing).

Commission Decision 98/273/EC, VW
O.J. 1998, L 124/60.

. . . . [T]he Commission received a growing number of letters from German and Austrian consumers complaining of difficulties encountered with the purchase in Italy of new motor vehicles of the Volkswagen and Audi makes for re-export to Germany or Austria. . . . Volkswagen and Audi distribute their vehicles in the Community through selective delivery networks. Volkswagen and Audi have appointed Autogerma as sole importer in Italy for their vehicles. Autogerma concludes distribution agreements with the dealers in the network on the basis of a standard dealership agreement covering sales of both VW and Audi vehicles. . . .

A.   Article [101(1)]

An examination of the agreements and concerted practices entered into by Volkswagen, Audi and Autogerma . . . demonstrates that within the framework provided by the exclusive and selective distribution network they and their Italian dealers have agreed a policy for partitioning the market. That market-partitioning policy takes the form of an export ban/restriction imposed on Italian dealers.

The export ban/restriction derives from a system of measures consisting of preventive measures, monitoring measures and penalties. . . . The export ban/restriction incorporates a prohibition of cross-deliveries, that is deliveries within the distribution network. Italian authorised dealers are prohibited from supplying to VW and Audi authorised dealers in other Member States. . . .

The system for identifying authorised dealers engaging in exporting and the penalties associated with it, have as their object the restriction of intra-brand competition. The intention is to prevent Italian authorised dealers from exploiting competitive advantages they enjoy over authorised dealers from other Member States, as a result of currency fluctuations for example, by selling vehicles to customers who are not resident in their contract territory or in Italy. The only distinction drawn is whether the customer is resident or non-resident in the contract territory or in Italy; no distinction is made between final consumers, intermediaries acting on their behalf, other authorised dealers belonging to the distribution network, or independent dealers outside the network. Markets are thus being partitioned. That the object is to restrict competition is apparent both from the combination of measures and from the individual measures in isolation. . . .

The effect of the measures is to restrict cross-border sales of vehicles. Authorised dealers were repeatedly told that they were free to sell vehicles only within their contract territories. If they failed to comply, they were told to expect penalties. Dealers complied with Autogerma's instructions and refrained from sales to customers resident outside their contract territory. . . . Authorised dealers have frequently refused to make sales to consumers on the ground that if they sold for export, there would be reprisals on the part of the main importer, and indeed that their dealership contract might be terminated. Authorised dealers responded to enquiries from outside their contract territory by a standard letter, even when the enquiries obviously came from final consumers; in that letter, they advised the customer not to purchase from them because of the long delivery time. . . .

Volkswagen and Audi, through Autogerma, have agreed with the Italian authorised dealers an export ban/restriction under which those dealers are required to refrain from selling VW and Audi vehicles outside their contract territories. . . . These are appreciable restrictions of competition with an appreciable effect on trade between Member States. There is therefore an infringement of the prohibition in Article [101(1)].

B. Article [101(3)] . . .

Pursuant to Article [101(3)], the Commission may, under certain conditions, grant an individual exemption from the ban in Article [101(1)]. . . . But since Volkswagen, Audi and Autogerma have not notified any of the agreements concluded with the authorised dealers under their market-partitioning policy . . . an individual exemption cannot be granted.

If the agreements had indeed been notified, they would not have qualified for exemption in any event. Even if it could be assumed that such an export ban/restriction helped to improve the distribution of goods, there would still be the fact that consumers do not share in the resulting benefit. Consumers are prevented from taking advantage of the single market and of differences in the price of motor vehicles between the Member States. The right of consumers to buy goods of their choice anywhere they want in the single market is restricted. The restriction is plain when one considers the content of the written undertaking. The export ban/restriction is in serious contradiction with the objective of consumer protection which Article [101(3)] makes an integral part of the Community's competition rules.[5]

Commission Decision 2001/791 Glaxo Wellcome,

O.J. 2001, L 302/1.

This decision concerns the compatibility with Article [101 TFEU] of Glaxo Wellcome SA's sales conditions regarding pharmaceutical products supplied to Spanish wholesalers. Pursuant to clause 4 of these sales conditions, Glaxo Wellcome SA [GW] operates a distinction between, on the one hand, the prices charged to wholesalers reselling its products to Spanish pharmacies or hospitals for (reimbursable) end-use in Spain and, on the other hand, prices charged to wholesalers exporting the products. The latter prices are higher than those applied in case of domestic re-sales. . . .

A. ARTICLE [101(1) TFEU]

The Commission considers that Clause 4 of the new sales conditions constitutes an agreement between GW (and its subsidiaries) and all Spanish wholesalers who have subscribed to these conditions after having received a copy thereof. . . .

(a) Clause 4 is tantamount to an export ban or a dual-pricing system

Objective to impede parallel trade. Although GW contends that the new sales conditions do not block and are not intended to block exports by

---

5. [Editor's Note: The Commission imposed on VW the largest fine ever imposed for a vertical agreement, 100 million Euros, which was reduced to 90 million Euros in appeals to the General Court and ECJ, but otherwise its judgment was generally upheld.].

Spanish wholesalers where these have an advantage due to superior efficiency or differences in exchange rates, it admits ... that the agreement is "intended to reduce the incentive for Spanish traders to engage in parallel trade of prescription medicines purchased at the low prices set by the Spanish Government". It follows that GW's objective is clearly to impede parallel trade by obliging Spanish wholesalers to purchase the drugs at prices which are higher than the maximum industrial price for domestic sales.

Effective exclusion or restriction of parallel trade. ... [For] GW's eight leading products which GW considers to be most subject to parallel trade, the Clause 4B prices either exclude or restrict parallel trade in a large majority of cases. The Clause 4B prices exclude such trade by making it economically uninteresting for wholesalers in more than 40% of the cases: 66 out of 161 cases if no account is taken of the wholesalers' own costs. This percentage increases slightly if a 5% wholesale cost margin is added to domestic and export prices (68 cases) and even more in a 15% cost margin scenario (74 cases). In around 35% of the cases, the Clause 4B prices impede parallel trade by making it economically less interesting for the wholesalers (57 cases). Admittedly, that percentage decreases when one adds a 5% wholesale cost (45 cases) or a 15% cost (24 cases). I follows that Clause 4 produces an effect tantamount to that of an export ban in a considerable number of cases while impeding parallel trade in other cases in very much the same way as a system of dual pricing.

Analogy with export bans. The Commission has already imposed a fine on a pharmaceutical company for a policy aimed at banning parallel trade. In *Sandoz*, it prohibited a practice whereby the company had displayed the words "export prohibited" over a number of years on its sales invoices. The Court of Justice upheld the Commission's decision. A pricing policy which makes it economically uninteresting for wholesalers to indulge in parallel trade must be considered to be at least as effective as an outright contractual export ban in excluding such trade because it involves in principle no cost of monitoring compliance. ...

Analogy with dual pricing. To the extent that the Clause 4B prices render parallel trade more costly and thus economically less interesting, GW's policy can be equated with systems of dual pricing of the kind prohibited in *Moï Chandon* or *Distillers* and *Gosme/Martell*. In the first case, the Commission qualified a clause which reserved list prices for champagne to products for consumption in the United Kingdom as a restriction by object. Since it was not allowed to export products at these list prices, the system was classified as tantamount to a ban on export of champagne "on the said terms". This resembles the present situation, where the wholesalers are not allowed to export at the Clause 4A price. Exports are only possible at the higher Clause 4B price and therefore not on the terms which prevail in Spain. Likewise in *Distillers*, UK customers were charged different prices depending on whether they resold inside or outside the United Kingdom. The Commission declared that the price terms amounted to an indirect export prohibition because they rendered sales to other Member States at the very least more difficult. In *Gosme/Martell*, the Commission held that *Martell*'s discount system which made exports more expensive and less profitable, was contrary to Article [101(1)] since its object and effect was to protect a higher price level in France resulting from government intervention in the form of price freezes and price controls. . . .

The Court of Justice (and the [General Court]) have always qualified agreements containing export bans, dual-pricing systems or other limitations of parallel trade as restricting competition "by object". That is to say, prohibited by Article [101(1)] without there being any need for an assessment of their actual effects. In principle they are not eligible for exemption pursuant to Article [101(3)]. Reference can be made to the judgments in *NV IAZ International Belgium v. Commission, Sandoz v. Commission* and more recently to *Volkswagen v. Commission*. In the latter case, the Court of First Instance upheld the Commission's decision which had classified various measures making parallel imports more difficult (without excluding them altogether) as restrictions "by object." These included measures reducing the bonus granted to retailers in the cases of exports thereby reducing the incentives to engage in parallel trade.

GW's new sales conditions entail restrictions of competition "by object" within the meaning of Article [101(1)]. It is settled case-law that for the purpose of the application of Article [101(1)] there is no need to take account of the actual effects of an agreement when it has as its object the prevention, restriction or distortion of competition within the common market. Consequently, the Commission is not required to show actual anti-competitive effects where the anti-competitive object of the conduct in question is proved. . . .

B.   ARTICLE [101(3) TFEU] . . .

It is important to note that it is for the notifying party to justify the restrictions of competition resulting from the notified agreement by demonstrating that these restrictions fulfil all four conditions of Article [101(3) TFEU]. It is not for the Commission to prove that its intervention against these restrictions of competition produces a benefit for consumer welfare. Furthermore, the restriction at issue in this case constitutes a particularly serious attempt to partition the common market. Although there is in principle no restriction which cannot be exempted under Article [101(3)], GW has failed to provide sufficient evidence that the restriction of competition resulting from the new sales conditions should benefit from an exemption.

(a) First condition (technical progress)

GW argues that parallel trade has caused losses for R&D since the revenue lost due to parallel trade is revenue that would have been spent on the development of innovative products in the absence of such trade. According to GW, Clause 4 of its new sales conditions aims at remedying this situation by restricting parallel trade. By combatting parallel trade, the new sales conditions create extra financial resources for R&D and thus promote technical progress. . . .

Impact of parallel trade on R&D: no causal link. The Commission does not dispute that R&D is an important parameter of competition in the pharmaceutical sector and needs appropriate financing. However, there is no evidence that parallel trade has caused reductions in GW's R&D budget or that it has prevented that budget from growing. In this respect, the Commission offers the following observations.

Parallel trade and profits: it is a matter of discretion for pharmaceutical companies to decide how much they wish to invest in R&D. Any savings they might hypothetically make by preventing parallel trade would therefore not automatically lead to higher R&D investments. It is conceivable that these savings might merely be added to the companies' profits. Obviously, the generation of extra profits alone cannot justify an exemption. In this regard, GW's argument would mean that the first condition for exemption would be fulfilled for every agreement that could be said to contribute to an increase in the revenues of a firm engaged in R&D. The condition would in any case be meaningless, since it is in the nature of any agreement restricting competition to be likely to increase a firm's earnings.

Parallel trade and costs: GW itself admits "that parallel trade is not the key driver for decisions on R&D". A whole series of factors influence decisions on R&D expenditure, including—as GW admits—the general level of current profits, the expected profitability of the products in the R&D pipelines as well as interest rates, exchange-rate volatility, uncertainty about future demand, etc. Parallel trade may have some impact on revenue and profits. However, there is no reason why a pharmaceutical company should react to losses of revenue resulting from parallel trade by cutting the R&D budget rather than any other budgetary item. . . .

(b) First condition (improving distribution)

GW puts forward several arguments to demonstrate that parallel trade is detrimental to the distribution of its pharmaceutical products. Firstly parallel trade causes a disruption of its distribution system. Secondly, it prevents the manufacturer from planning its distribution rationally since parallel trade leads to a situation of undersupply in the source country and of oversupply in the target country. Thirdly, parallel trade enhances the risk of late introduction of innovative products in low price countries. The new sales conditions should remedy this situation and ensure that GW will not cease commercialising particular products in Spain.

Parallel trade does not disrupt GW's distribution system: although GW argues that parallel trade removes the incentive and the means for wholesalers located outside Spain to provide the level of services for which they are remunerated by GW, it does not provide any examples of such services. Nor does it elaborate on the extent—if any—to which it, as producer, is required to pay for these services; As outlined above, the GW's products are distributed by independent wholesalers. Wholesalers set their own resale price taking into account the level of service they wish to provide.

Parallel trade does not disrupt GW's ability to plan distribution rationally: GW argues that parallel trade leads to oversupply in the target countries of parallel trade, for example, the United Kingdom, and product shortages in the source country, for example, Spain. . . . GW has failed to give examples of product shortages in Spain or examples where it had not introduced a product to the Spanish market, presumably because despite a lower price the sales in Spain still make a positive contribution to GW's profits.... Parallel trade does not cause delays for product launches in Spain: GW refers to the London Economics study which reports average introduction delays for countries such as the United Kingdom, Germany and the Netherlands of one to two months, whereas in Spain and France these delays range from five to six months (Spain) to nine to twelve months (France). It also submits IMS data suggesting that product delays in Spain extend to six quarters compared to three quarters in the United Kingdom. The question is, however, whether parallel trade has anything to do with this and, as a consequence, whether measures limiting such trade will contribute to reducing these market delays.

The Commission sees no causal link. Product launches depend on a number of factors, not least on the outcome of price discussions between the pharmaceutical company and the national authorities. In fact, GW itself cites this as the main reason for the late introduction of some of its products in Spain. Incidentally, this illustrates that it is the company itself that has full discretion to decide whether it is profitable enough to introduce a particular product on the market....

GW insists that for pharmaceutical products parallel trade cannot achieve any benefits for the consumer. From a consumer welfare perspective, according to GW, the consumer is in a better position with GW's system than with parallel trade. GW asserts more specifically that parallel trade in pharmaceutical products is different from that in other commodities (such as cars or hi-fi equipment) because the patient does not derive any benefit from parallel trade in the form of lower prices. This is so, according to GW, because patients are reimbursed by the national health organisations. These organisations are the real consumers, because in economic terms, they purchase the drugs. As far as the United Kingdom is concerned, GW's new sales conditions for Spain allegedly even benefits the NHS as they enable it to maintain a policy which promotes R&D....

In this respect, it should be recalled once more that it is for the notifying party to justify its restriction of competition by showing that its agreement fulfils the conditions of Article [101(3)]. It is not for the Commission to prove that its intervention against this restriction increases consumer welfare. It is therefore only for the sake of completeness that the Commission addresses a number of arguments by which GW contests that its intervention as a competition authority will serve general consumer welfare interests.

Since the new sales conditions cover exports to all other Member States, not just to the United Kingdom, the beneficial effects of parallel trade will be illustrated on this broader basis. First, parallel-traded products offer a second source of supply. This is especially important from a consumer's point of view when branded and patented products are involved. Patented medicines enjoy protection for at least 20 years. In cases where only a few alternatives are available, parallel trade will offer the only source of competition.

Second, GW's unqualified assertion that the nature of reimbursement systems precludes any benefit for patients from parallel trade is incorrect. Patients benefit directly from parallel trade either when they have to pay the full amount of the purchase price themselves or when reimbursement is only partial and is expressed as a percentage of the actual purchase price (in contrast with a flat fee). ... Furthermore, partial reimbursement and co-payment exists in many Member States. When patients receive reimbursement calculated as a percentage of the actual purchase price (for example, Belgium an France) parallel trade may benefit them directly.

Finally, it can be observed that some high price countries (for example, the Netherlands) de facto provide incentives to parallel trade without any cost-saving effects for the health care budget. Where reimbursement is in the form of a flat fee, pharmacists and other intermediaries benefit from purchasing cheaper parallel-traded products because such purchases yield higher profits. The notion of the consumer is not restricted to the final consumer, that is, the patient. Therefore, the interests of wholesalers, pharmacies, national health budgets, insurance schemes can also be taken into account. Furthermore, the possibility of these pharmacies passing on part of their savings to their clients, for example via annual bonuses where authorised by national legislation, should also not be ruled out. Ultimately, all patients pay for the national health system. Public health systems are financed via contributions or by general taxes. Any savings made by these schemes via the purchase of cheaper parallel-traded drugs indirectly benefit the schemes' members. . . .

Case T–168/01, Glaxosmithkline Services v. Commission
(September 27, 2006).

[Glaxosmithkline challenged the Decision of the Commission before the General Court.]

The existence of an anticompetitive object

It follows from the case-law that agreements which ultimately seek to prohibit parallel trade must in principle be regarded as having as their object the restriction of competition . . .

It also follows from the case-law that agreements that clearly intend to treat parallel trade unfavourably must in principle be regarded as having as their object the restriction of competition . . .

However, GSK is correct to maintain that, having regard to the legal and economic context, the Commission could not rely on the mere fact that Clause 4 of the General Sales Conditions established a system of differentiated price intended to limit parallel trade as the basis for its conclusion that that provision had as its object the restriction of competition.

In effect, the objective assigned to Article [101(1) TFEU], which constitutes a fundamental provision indispensable for the achievement of the missions entrusted to the Community, in particular for the functioning of the internal market ... is to prevent undertakings, by restricting competition between themselves or with third parties, from reducing the welfare of the final consumer of the products in question ...

Consequently, the application of Article [101(1) TFEU] to the present case cannot depend solely on the fact that the agreement in question is intended to limit parallel trade in medicines or to partition the common market, which leads to the conclusion that it affects trade between Member States, but also requires an analysis designed to determine whether it has as its object or effect the prevention, restriction or distortion of competition on the relevant market, to the detriment of the final consumer ...

[I]f account is taken of the legal and economic context in which GSK's General Sales Conditions are applied, it cannot be presumed that those conditions deprive the final consumers of medicines of such advantages. In effect, the wholesalers, whose function, as the Court of Justice has held, is to ensure that the retail trade receives supplies with the benefit of competition between producers ... are economic agents operating at an intermediate stage of the value chain and may keep the advantage in terms of price which parallel trade may entail, in which case that advantage will not be passed on to the final consumers....

At no point, however, does the Commission examine the specific and essential characteristic of the sector, which relates to the fact that the prices of the products in question, which are subject to control by the Member States, which fix them directly or indirectly at what they deem to be the appropriate level, are determined at structurally different levels in the Community and, unlike the prices of other consumer goods to which the Commission referred in its written submissions and at the hearing, such as sports items or motor cycles, are in any event to a significant extent shielded from the free play of supply and demand.

That circumstance means that it cannot be presumed that parallel trade has an impact on the prices charged to the final consumers of medicines reimbursed by the national sickness insurance scheme and thus confers on them an appreciable advantage analogous to that which it would confer if those prices were determined by the play of supply and demand.

Accordingly, it cannot be considered that examination of Clause 4 of the General Sales Conditions, which according to GSK is designed to ensure that the wholesale price set by the Kingdom of Spain is actually charged only for the medicines to which it was intended by law to apply, reveals in itself that competition is prevented, restricted or distorted.

— *The existence of an anti-competitive effect* ...

In order to examine the effect of an agreement on competition, it is necessary, first of all, to define the relevant market or markets, from both a material and a geographic point of view. *Delimitis* ...

It is necessary, in the second place, to examine the actual or potential effects of the agreement on competition. That examination entails a comparison of the competitive situation resulting from the agreement and the situation that would exist in its absence. *Société technique minière; John Deere v Commission* ...

GSK maintains, in substance, that the Commission has not shown ... that Clause 4 of the General Sales Conditions had the effect of restricting competition.

That is not the case, however. On the contrary, the Commission concluded, following a relatively brief examination ... that Clause 4 also had the effect of reducing the welfare of final consumers by preventing them from taking advantage, in the form of a reduction in prices and costs, of the participation of the Spanish wholesalers in intrabrand competition on the markets of destination of the parallel trade originating in Spain.

Thus, the Commission found ... that Clause 4 of the General Sales Conditions required the Spanish wholesalers who bought the medicines sold in Spain by GW to pay a higher price (the Clause 4B price) than the price set by the Spanish authorities, which they would have paid in the absence of the General Sales Conditions (the Clause 4A price). Clause 4 thus has the effect of reducing or cancelling, in numerous cases, the differential hitherto existing between the prices applicable in Spain and those applicable in other Member States of the Community. The number of cases concerned is significant, whether the costs incurred by the Spanish wholesalers when they engage in parallel trade (transport, repackaging, etc.) are disregarded or whether they are taken into consideration. GSK does not dispute those findings of fact.

Next, the Commission found ... that in some Member States an admittedly small part of the price of medicines covered by the General Sales Conditions was borne by the patient, who in that sense constituted a final consumer, within the economic sense of that term, of the products in question. The Commission also found ... that the remainder of the price of those medicines was reimbursed by the national sickness insurance scheme, which also constituted a final consumer of the products in question, in that it spread the economic risks borne for their health by those covered by the insurance schemes. The Court of Justice has already referred to the special nature, in that respect, of the trade in pharmaceutical products, namely the fact that social security institutions are substituted for consumers as regards responsibility for the payment of medical expenses. *Duphar and Others*.

Even accepting that competition between the Spanish wholesalers who engage in parallel trade, or between those wholesalers and the distributors established on the market of the Member State of destination of the parallel trade, is limited to the point of allowing them to apply resale prices which are lower than the prices applied by those distributors only to the extent strictly necessary to attract retailers, as convincingly explained in some of the documents produced by GSK, the Commission was entitled to infer ... from the findings of fact set out in the preceding paragraphs that Clause 4 of the General Sales Conditions impeded that competition and, in substance, the pressure which in its absence would have existed on the unit price of the medicines in question, to the detriment of the final consumer, taken to mean both the patient and the national sickness insurance scheme acting on behalf of claimants.

It is true that.... considered at the individual level of one of the national markets affected by Clause 4 of the General Sales Conditions, such as the United Kingdom market, may be marginal. However, the Commission also observed ... that the fact of impeding this pressure, by means of an agreement concluded with a significant number of Spanish wholesalers and affecting a significant number of products and national markets in the Community, contributed or could contribute, by a network effect, to reinforcing the pre-existing price rigidity on the market. Such reinforcement infringes Article [101(1) TFEU] (see, to that effect, *Metro I* and *Van Landewyck and Others v Commission*).

GSK has not adduced evidence of an error on that point. On the contrary, it acknowledged at the hearing that Clause 4 of the General Sales Conditions, although mainly intended to prevent the transfer of surplus to the wholesalers, might have the effect of reducing the admittedly restricted benefit which their participation in competition provides for the final consumer on the markets of destination of the parallel trade....

Accordingly, it must be concluded that the Commission was entitled to find, in the light of elements whose relevance has not been validly called in question by GSK, that Clause 4 of the General Sales Conditions had the effect of reducing the welfare of final consumers by preventing them from taking advantage, in the form of a reduction in prices and costs, of the participation of the Spanish wholesalers in intrabrand competition on the national markets of destination of the parallel trade originating in Spain . . .

It follows from the foregoing that GSK has not succeeded in calling in question the Commission's conclusion that the General Sales Conditions constituted an agreement within the meaning of Article [101(1) TFEU] . . .

B—The plea alleging infringement of Article [101(3) TFEU]

. . . b) Evidence of a gain in efficiency

. . . In order to be capable of being exempted under Article [101(3) TFEU], an agreement must contribute to improving the production or distribution of goods or to promoting technical or economic progress. That contribution is not identified with all the advantages which the undertakings participating in the agreement derive from it as regards their activities, but with appreciable objective advantages, of such a kind as to offset the resulting disadvantages for competition....

It is therefore for the Commission, in the first place, to examine whether the factual arguments and the evidence submitted to it show, in a convincing manner, that the agreement in question must enable appreciable objective advantages to be obtained . . .

That approach may entail a prospective analysis, in which case it is appropriate to ascertain whether, in the light of the factual arguments and the evidence provided, it seems more likely either that the agreement in question must make it possible to obtain appreciable advantages or that it will not . . .

In the affirmative, it is for the Commission, in the second place, to evaluate whether those appreciable objective advantages are of such a kind as to offset the disadvantages identified for competition in the context of the examination carried out under Article [101(3) TFEU] . . .

In the present case, GSK claimed that Clause 4 of the General Sales Conditions would make it possible to secure advantages both upstream of the relevant market, by encouraging innovation, and on the market itself, by optimising the distribution of medicines. As those markets correspond to different stages of the value chain, the final consumer likely to benefit from those advantages is the same.

The Court must therefore determine, first of all, whether the Commission was entitled to conclude that GSK's factual arguments and evidence, examination of which entailed a prospective analysis, did not demonstrate, with a sufficient degree of probability, that Clause 4 of the General Sales Conditions would make it possible to obtain an appreciable advantage of such a kind as to offset the disadvantage which it entailed for competition, by encouraging innovation.

The existence of an appreciable objective advantage

Having regard to the nature of GSK's criticisms, it is appropriate, in the first place, to present the factual arguments and the evidence in support of its request for an exemption on this point and then, in the second place, to review the way in which the Commission examined them . . .

[T]hose arguments centre on two axes, which are closely linked yet distinct. First, . . . parallel trade in medicines marketed by GW in Spain leads to a loss in efficiency for interbrand competition, in so far as it reduces GSK's capacity for innovation. Second, Clause 4 of the General Sales Conditions will lead to a gain in efficiency for interbrand competition in so far as it will enable GSK's capacity for innovation to be increased. . . .

GSK's arguments . . . are essentially as follows.

First, according to the documents produced by GSK, parallel trade in medicines marketed in Spain by GW entails a loss in efficiency. In effect:

— the sector for patented medicines reimbursed by a national sickness insurance scheme is characterised by the fact that innovation constitutes the determining parameter of interbrand competition;

— innovation in ensured by a level of R&D expenditure which is both substantial and higher than that which characterises most other industries; in GSK's case, that expenditure represents approximately 14% of its turnover, or approximately GBP 1.3 billion;

— as investment in R&D is costly, high-risk and long-term, it is mainly financed from the undertaking's own funds rather than by borrowing; in GSK's case it is financed exclusively from its own funds;

— R&D financing is dependent on current returns and also on anticipated returns; in GSK's case, the fact that its capacity for financing increased by 230 times in the 1980s and 1990s was made possible by the existence of very successful medicines, in particular Zantac, which accounted for 40% of its world-wide revenues until 1994;

— parallel trade has the effect of reducing the returns of the pharmaceutical company concerned (schematically, for each unit sold at a price of 100 in the country of origin there is a corresponding unsold unit at a price of 100 + n in the country of destination) and, thus, of impeding the possibility of applying, for all sales made in each national market, an optimum price, that is to say, a price set by reference to the preferences peculiar to each Member States;

— that impact is concentrated on certain products and on certain geographic markets; in GSK's case, the losses mainly affect certain medicines consumed in the United Kingdom;

— that impact is significant, owing to the significant differential existing between the prices in force in the various Member States of the Community; in particular, the differential between the Spanish price and the United Kingdom price was, in 1998, for the eight medicines principally concerned (paragraph 11 above), between a minimum of 21% and a maximum of 132%;

— in that regard, GSK provides estimates, containing confidential figures, of the loss of revenue caused by parallel trade from all Member States to the United Kingdom and concerning all of its medicines, and also relating to the loss of revenue caused by parallel trade from Spain to the United Kingdom and relating to the eight medicines principally concerned, for 1996, 1997 and 1998;

— parallel trade also has the effect of reducing the amount which GSK is authorised to deduct, by way of investment in R&D, from the amount of its profits taken into account for the purpose of determining whether it exceeds the maximum rate of return on investment set by National Health Service; in that regard, GSK provides estimates, containing confidential figures, of the amount of the reduction caused by parallel trade from all origins and parallel trade from Spain, in 1998;

— the fact that the pharmaceutical company continues to make what are apparently significant profits does not deprive those arguments of relevance, in so far as it is necessary to take account of the method of accounting for investments in R&D, the way in which they are spread over time, their average cost and the degree of risk which they entail;

— last, parallel trade has the effect of reducing the capacities for financing R&D; in that regard, GSK provides estimates, containing confidential figures, relating to the percentage of its pre-tax profits which it reinvests in R&D and to the reduction in its R&D budget to which the loss in revenue caused by parallel trade from Spain to the United Kingdom and relating to the eight medicines principally concerned correspond, for the years 1996 to 1998;

— the fact that that reduction is quantitatively limited does not deprive that argument of relevance, in so far as it concerns the impact of parallel trade from Spain to the United Kingdom and relating to the eight medicines principally concerned between 1996 and 1998 and in so far as a quantitatively limited reduction may in any event have significant qualitative effects, in particular by leading to less profitable or more risky projects being abandoned; GSK provides a list of nine projects abandoned for that reason;

— on the other hand, parallel trade has few positive effects, as parallel traders do not compete on price to any significant extent and keep for themselves a substantial part of the differential between the price in force in the Member State of origin and that applied in the Member State of destination, so that the downward pressure on prices is reduced and the final consumer ultimately derives only a limited benefit.

Second, according to the documents produced by GSK, Clause 4 of the General Sales Conditions will lead to a gain in efficiency. In effect:

— the cost of R&D is global and joint in that it corresponds to an activity carried out on a world-wide scale and that, for a significant proportion, it is not attributable to a specific production site or a specific product;

— the pharmaceutical companies do not control their prices in most Member States; they agree to serve a national market on condition that the price set by the public authorities allows them to cover their marginal costs, but they must still succeed, where they can, in covering their entire global and joint R&D costs;

— the differentiated pricing system provided for in Clause 4 of the General Sales Conditions will make it possible to cover the cost of R&D by ensuring that the prices are set, on each national market, at the level corresponding to the preferences of the final consumer, that is to say, ultimately of the Member State concerned; in particular, it will make it possible to prevent the price fixed by the Kingdom of Spain from being exported to the United Kingdom;

— the strong competitive pressure by innovation which prevails in the sector ensures that GSK will act as a rational economic operator by transforming, in so far as necessary, those additional profits into investment in R&D.

Having regard to the relevance of the factual arguments and the evidence submitted by GSK, the Commission's examination of the loss in efficiency associated with parallel trade, of the extent of that loss of efficiency and of the gain in efficiency associated with Clause 4 of the General Sales Conditions cannot be accepted as sufficient to support the conclusions which the Commission reached on those points . . .

— *The loss of efficiency associated with parallel trade*

The Court notes that the conclusion that it has not been shown that parallel trade leads to a loss in efficiency by altering GSK's capacity for innovation is based on an examination . . . which does not take into consideration all the factual arguments and evidence pertinently submitted by GSK, contrary to what the Commission maintained in its written submissions, and is not supported by convincing evidence. While the Commission is clearly not required to examine all the arguments submitted to it, it must, on the other hand, . . . examine all the evidence which is relevant and, so far as necessary, refute it by means of evidence capable of substantiating its conclusion.

Taken as a whole, those arguments revealed that the competitive problem faced by GSK and the solution which it had sought to apply were, according to GSK, as follows.

First, the medicines sector is characterised by the importance of competition by innovation. R&D is costly and risky. Its cost is simultaneously a fixed cost (it is not connected with the number of medicines sold), a joint cost (it is incurred upstream from production and distribution and, in part, is not linked with a particular medicine) and a global cost (it is not connected with a particular country). It is most frequently financed from an undertaking's own funds rather than from borrowing. It therefore requires an optimum flow of income. The optimisation of income may be ensured by adapting the prices of medicines to the preferences of final consumers, where those preferences differ. Price differentiation thus allows the cost of R&D to be recovered from the final consumers who are prepared to pay for it. That practice of differentiated prices, which is presented here in a simplified form, is known to economists as "Ramsey Pricing".

Second, the implementation of that practice in the medicines sector is characterised by certain particular traits. When medicines are protected by patents, their price may be maintained, in the particular interest of the producer, at a higher level than the marginal cost throughout the life of the patent. However, when those medicines are reimbursed by the national sickness insurance schemes, their price must, in the general interest, be maintained directly (price control) or indirectly (control of benefits) at a level which is not excessively higher than the marginal cost. The extent of that excess reflects the preference of the final consumer, that is to say, essentially, the national sickness insurance scheme. If the latter is relatively sensitive to the price of the medicine, the excess will tend to be small; if it is relatively insensitive to that price, the excess will tend to be significant. In practice, that degree of sensitivity depends on various parameters, such as the standard of living or the state of public finances. The fraction of the cost of R&D recovered by producers of medicines therefore varies from one Member State to another, according to the income which the applicable price makes available. In the present case, it is in the United Kingdom that GSK could, owing to the regulations applicable, recuperate the global and joint part of its R&D costs.

Third, parallel trade has the effect of reducing that income, to an uncertain but real degree. That practice, which economists know as "free riding", is characterised by the fact that the intermediary leaves the role which he traditionally plays in the value chain and becomes an arbitrageur and thus obtains a greater part of the profit. The legitimacy of that transfer of wealth from producer to intermediary is not in itself of interest to competition law, which is concerned only with its impact on the welfare of the final consumer. In so far as the intermediary participates in intrabrand competition, parallel trade may have a pro-competitive effect. In the medicines sector, however, that activity is also seen in a special light, since it does not bring any significant added value for the final consumer.

Fourth, Clause 4 of the General Sales Conditions seeks to optimise income and to neutralise parallel trade. It limits the possibilities previously afforded to GW's wholesalers to sell, outside Spain, medicines bought at the price set with a view to reimbursement by the Spanish sickness insurance scheme. It therefore allows sales in other Member States to be made at the price determined with a view to reimbursement by their respective national sickness insurance schemes. The fact that the profit is retained by the producer will in all likelihood give rise to a gain in efficiency by comparison with the situation in which the profit is shared with the intermediary, because a rational producer which is able to ensure the profitability of its innovations and which operates in a sector characterised by healthy competition on innovation has every interest in reinvesting at least a part of its surplus profit in innovation.

However, . . . the Commission, after acknowledging the importance of competition by innovation in the relevant sector, failed to undertake a rigorous examination of the factual arguments and the evidence submitted by GSK concerning the nature of the investments in R&D, the characteristics of the financing of R&D, the impact of parallel trade on R&D and the applicable regulations, but confined itself . . . to observations which, to say the least, are fragmentary and, as GSK rightly claims, of limited relevance or value.

Such an omission is particularly serious where the Commission is required to determine whether the conditions for the application of Article [101(3) TFEU] are satisfied in a legal and economic context, such as that characteristic of the pharmaceutical sector, where competition is distorted by the presence of national regulations. That circumstance obliges the Commission to examine with particular attention the arguments and evidence submitted to it by the person relying on Article [101(3) TFEU] . . .

— The extent of the loss in efficiency associated with parallel trade

The subsidiary conclusion that it is not in any event demonstrated that parallel trade leads to an appreciable loss in efficiency by altering GSK's capacity to innovate is not convincingly supported and the examination on which its is based . . . does not take into account all the relevant elements put forward in that regard.

— *The gain in efficiency associated with Clause 4 of the General Sales Conditions*

It must be observed that, as GSK correctly maintains, the Commission carried out no serious examination of its factual arguments and its evidence relating, not to the disadvantages of parallel trade, but to the advantages of Clause 4 of the General Sales Conditions . . .

The balancing exercise

After concluding its examination of the factual arguments and the evidence submitted by GSK and finding that they did not demonstrate the existence of an appreciable objective advantage, the Commission did not carry out the complex assessment . . . which would have been involved by the exercise seeking to balance that advantage against the disadvantage for competition identified in the part of the Decision devoted to the application of Article [101(1) TFEU], as it stated on a number of occasions at the hearing . . .

Consequently, the Commission's conclusion that there is no need to carry out a balancing exercise, which would show in any event that the advantage associated with Clause 4 does not offset the disadvantage which it represents for competition, cannot be upheld. The Commission was required, first, to conduct an appropriate examination of GSK's factual arguments and evidence, in order to be in a position to carry out, second, the complex assessment necessary in order to weigh up the disadvantage and the advantage associated with Clause 4 of the General Sales Conditions.

Conclusion

It follows from the foregoing that the Commission could not lawfully conclude that, as regards the existence of a contribution to the promotion of technical progress, GSK had not demonstrated that the first condition for the application of Article [101(3) TFEU] was satisfied. . . .

Questions on *VW* and *Glaxo–Wellcome*

1. In both *VW* and *Glaxo–Wellcome*, the parties attempted to limit parallel trade.

a. Did they rely on the same methods to achieve that purpose?

b. Compared to dual pricing, are export bans more, less, or equally restrictive of competition?

2. VW's attempts to restrict parallel trade were initiated as a response to increased parallel trading between Italy and Germany due to price fluctuations. Were these circumstances present in *Consten Grundig*? In other words, should the moment at which export restrictions are imposed (at the time of the conclusion of a distribution agreement or later on in response to price fluctuations resulting in increased parallel trade) play a role in the assessment of such practices under EU competition law?

3. Pharmaceutical products generally have low marginal costs of production but high fixed costs of research and development. Don't the vertical restraints here help enable Glaxo to engage in price discrimination, charging buyers in richer nations (like the UK) prices well-above marginal cost and charging buyers in poorer nations (like Spain) prices closer to marginal cost?

a. Won't a legal rule that undermines such price discrimination make it harder for Glaxo to spread the common costs of research and development across the widest group of buyers?[6] Won't that likely decrease research and development and decrease output?

b. If such price discrimination were undermined, won't the likely upshot be to lower prices in the UK but raise them in Spain, and maybe even not to introduce new products in Spain? Is that likely to be distributionally attractive?

c. Why does the General Court strike down the Glaxo Decision of the Commission?

(i) Does the General Court conclude that pharmaceutical corporations should have the right to block parallel trade to achieve efficiencies?

(ii) Or does it more narrowly suggest the Commission should have done a better job at taking into consideration the efficiencies invoked

---

6. *See generally* Elhauge, *Why Above–Cost Price Cuts to Drive out Entrants Do Not Signal Predation or Even Market Power—and the Implications for Defining Costs,* 112 Yale L.J. 681, 726–54 (2003) (arguing that even without market power firms often engage in price discrimination to spread their common costs over the greatest number of buyers and that this efficiently allows them to expand total output).

by Glaxo and balanced them against the anti-competitive effects generated by its dual-pricing scheme?

(iii) Besides the requirement for a more rigorous Article 101(3) analysis, isn't the main effect of this judgement the fact that measures designed to restrict parallel trade will not be automatically considered as restrictions by "object" under Article 101(1)?

(iv) Why is this so significant? Does this judgment qualify the overarching notion that EU competition law should be an element of market integration?

d.   In the US, a major issue has arisen about consumers who go to Canada to buy drugs more inexpensively at the lower prices fixed by Canada's government health insurance plan. Should this be allowed or prohibited by the US government? Should the US government itself import drugs from Canada for Medicare or Medicaid?

e.   Drug manufacturers are often reluctant to sell drugs at low prices in undeveloped nations even when those prices are above marginal cost because they fear reimportation will undermine the higher prices in developed nations that they need to maximize profits from their patents and cover research and development costs. The result is that drugs are often unavailable in undeveloped nations at any price that their consumers or governments can afford, resulting in unmet health needs. Should drug manufacturers be allowed to price discriminate between developed and undeveloped nations? Should governments help to enforce such price discrimination?

4.   When price differences between Member States are due to public policy choices made by the governments of the Member States in question, isn't there a risk that allowing parallel pricing might interfere with these choices?

a.   What do you think, for instance, of a situation whereby a Member State decides to voluntarily keep the prices of certain drugs high in order to avoid excessive consumption or assure adequate research and development? Could such a policy objective be undermined by parallel trading?

b.   If so, would it be the role of a private corporation to protect public policy objectives through restrictions of competition?

Cases C 501/06 P, C–513/06 P, C–515/06 P and C 519/06 P, GlaxoSmithKline v. Commission

(October 2009).

[The Commission went on to appeal the Judgment of the General Court to the ECJ.]

GSK's ground of appeal relating to Article [101(1) TFEU]

First of all, it must be borne in mind that the anti-competitive object and effect of an agreement are not cumulative but alternative conditions for assessing whether such an agreement comes within the scope of the prohibition laid down in Article [101(1) TFEU]. According to settled case-law since the judgment in Case 56/65 LTM [1966] ECR 235, the alternative nature of that condition, indicated by the conjunction "or", leads first to the need to consider the precise purpose of the agreement, in the economic context in which it is to be applied. Where, however, the analysis of the content of the agreement does not reveal a sufficient degree of harm to competition, the consequences of the agreement should then be considered and for it to be caught by the prohibition it is necessary to find that those factors are present which show that competition has in fact been prevented, restricted or distorted to an appreciable extent. It is also apparent from the case-law that it is not necessary to examine the effects of an agreement once its anti-competitive object has been established. . . .

Secondly, to examine the anti-competitive object of the agreement before its anti-competitive effect is all the more justified because, if the error of law alleged by the Commission, Aseprofar and EAEPC turns out to be substantiated, GSK's appeal directed at the grounds of the judgment under appeal relating to the anti-competitive effect of the agreement will fall to be dismissed.

Consequently, it is appropriate to ascertain whether the [General Court]'s assessment as to whether the agreement has an anti-competitive object . . . is in accordance with the principles extracted from the relevant case-law.

According to settled case-law, in order to assess the anti-competitive nature of an agreement, regard must be had inter alia to the content of its provisions, the objectives it seeks to attain and the economic and legal context of which it forms a part. . . . In addition, although the parties' intention is not a necessary factor in determining whether an agreement is restrictive, there is nothing prohibiting the Commission or the Community judicature from taking that aspect into account. . . . With respect to parallel trade, the Court has already held that, in principle, agreements aimed at prohibiting or limiting parallel trade have as their object the prevention of competition. . . .

As observed by the Advocate General in point 155 of her Opinion, that principle, according to which an agreement aimed at limiting parallel trade is a "restriction of competition by object", applies to the pharmaceuticals sector.

The Court has, moreover, held in that regard, in relation to the application of Article [101TFEU] and in a case involving the pharmaceuticals sector, that an agreement between producer and distributor which might tend to restore the national divisions in trade between Member States might be such as to frustrate the Treaty's objective of achieving the integration of national markets through the establishment of a single market. Thus on a number of occasions the Court has held agreements aimed at partitioning national markets according to national borders or making the interpenetration of national markets more difficult, in particular those aimed at preventing or restricting parallel exports, to be agreements whose object is to restrict competition within the meaning of that article of the Treaty. . . .

With respect to the [General Court's] statement that, while it is accepted that an agreement intended to limit parallel trade must in principle be considered to have as its object the restriction of competition, that applies in so far as it may be presumed to deprive final consumers of the advantages of effective competition in terms of supply or price, the Court notes that neither the wording of Article [101(1) TFEU] nor the case-law lend support to such a position.

First of all, there is nothing in that provision to indicate that only those agreements which deprive consumers of certain advantages may have an anti-competitive object. Secondly, it must be borne in mind that the Court has held that, like other competition rules laid down in the Treaty, Article [101 TFEU] aims to protect not only the interests of competitors or of consumers, but also the structure of the market and, in so doing, competition as such. Consequently, for a finding that an agreement has an anti-competitive object, it is not necessary that final consumers be deprived of the advantages of effective competition in terms of supply or price. . . .

It follows that, by requiring proof that the agreement entails disadvantages for final consumers as a prerequisite for a finding of anti-competitive object and by not finding that that agreement had such an object, the Court of First Instance committed an error of law. . . .

The grounds of appeal relating to Article [101(3) TFEU] . . .

[In the rest of its judgment, the Court of Justice rejected the arguments raised by the Commission and the other appellants regarding the Court of First Instance treatment of Article [101(3) TFEU].]

Questions on GlaxoSmithKline v. Commission

As observed above, one of the main effects of the judgement of the General Court in this case was that measures designed to restrict parallel trade were no longer to be automatically considered as restrictions by "object" under Article 101(1).

1. Why doesn't the ECJ support the position taken by the General Court ?

2. Do you think that prohibiting agreements that restrict parallel trade between Member States under an abbreviated rule of reason makes sense? Does it make sense to treat these agreements like naked horizontal restraints?

3. What do you think of the following statement made by the ECJ: "it must be borne in mind that the Court has held that, like other competition rules laid down in the Treaty, Article [101TFEU] aims to protect not only the interests of competitors or of consumers, but also the structure of the market and, in so doing, competition as such."

a. Do you think that competition rules should seek to protect "the interests of competitors"?

b. Similarly, should competition authorities aim at protecting the "structure of the market"?

Other Nations' Treatment of Vertical Non-Price Restraints on Distribution

Canada deems vertical territorial restraints a "market restriction" that the Tribunal may prohibit if it is likely to substantially lessen competition because the seller is a major supplier or it is widespread.[7] Japan's antitrust statute deems a vertical territorial restraint as unlawful if it "tends to impede fair competition" by "restrict[ing] unjustly the business activities of" the buyer.[8] Japanese guidelines clarify that this does not ban assigning areas of primary responsibility for the purpose of developing an effective distribution or service network, but does ban the creation of strict territories if the seller's market share exceeds 10% (or is one of the three largest market shares) and the vertical territorial restraint is likely to maintain price levels given the levels of interbrand and intrabrand competition.[9] Most nations apply some form of rule of reason to vertical non-price agreements that restrain intrabrand distribution.[10] However, Egypt makes vertical non-price restraints by a dominant firm per se illegal.[11]

2. VERTICAL MAXIMUM PRICE-FIXING

With other vertical distributional restraints, the manufacturer's interest in minimizing retailer profit margin is normally invoked to support the claim that the manufacturer must believe that distributional efficiencies (like reducing free riding in services) offset any anticompetitive effects generated by the restraints. In contrast, vertical maximum price-fixing cannot further the reduction of free riding in dealer services. Instead, it seems to reflect quite directly the manufacturer's procompetitive interest in minimizing the retail profit margin. Vertical agreements that fix maximum prices also don't raise the same anticompetitive concerns as agreements that set minimum prices because they can't induce dealers to engage in brand pushing and are unlikely to reflect dealer market power or to help facilitate oligopolistic coordination by manufacturers. The only exception would seem to be the case where the maximum is really a minimum.

Why wouldn't retail competition be a better way of determining the optimal retail profit margin than having the supplier set it? Generally two sorts of reasons are invoked. First, a supplier might develop a brand reputation for low or fair prices that helps bring in customers, but be worried that individual dealers will have incentives to free ride on that brand reputation by charging higher prices. For example, consider a Mc-

---

7. *See* Canadian Competition Act § 77(1), (3).

8. Japan Antimonopoly Law § 2(9).

9. *See* Japan Distribution Guidelines 28–29 (1991).

10. *See* Australia Trade Practices Act § 47(2)(f), (3)(f), (10); Brazil CADE Resolution 20, Attachment I, § 2 (1999); India Competition Act § 3(4)(c); Mexico Competition Law Arts. 10(I) & 11; Peru Competition Law, Art. 12(4); South Africa Competition Act § 5(1); South Korea Guidelines on Reviewing Unfair Trade Practices V.7.B. (2009); Venezuela Regulation No. 1 of the Procompetition Act, Art. 4(1).

11. Egypt Competition Law, Art. 8(c).

Donald's restaurant on a highway. Many people will pull off the highway to eat there because the McDonald's brand reputation causes them to expect low prices. If the franchisee who owns that store charges prices that are somewhat higher than normal McDonald's prices, those people will probably just go ahead and buy rather than bother leaving and stopping at another place. But they will leave the restaurant expecting higher prices from the brand than they did before. Because any loss of brand reputation for low prices will mostly be externalized onto the other McDonald's restaurants at which these people will be less likely to stop in the future, each restaurant has incentives to free ride on the brand reputation by charging higher prices. This can harm all the restaurants in the end because they will be unable to offer the brand reputation that maximizes their clientele and profitability. An agreement imposed by the supplier (here franchisor) that fixes maximum prices can curb such free riding. One can generalize this beyond the McDonald's sort of case: all brands have some reputational position and need to get customers to overcome the transaction costs of going to a store or looking at their brand within a store. They may thus need to set maximum prices to avoid free riding on their reputation for a particular price level because such free-riding will diminish customer willingness to go to their stores or examine their brand.

Second, the most efficient means of distribution may be for a supplier to just have one dealer in a given area, such as having one newspaper delivery firm to cover a certain city. Or it might simply be that the local market is too thin to efficiently support a large enough number of dealers to produce retail competition. If the supplier's product enjoys any market power, this will give that dealer a certain degree of local market power, which was effectively created by the manufacturer. This creates a successive market power problem that will lead the retailer to mark up the prices to levels that are inefficiently high and decrease supplier profits. *See* Chapter 3. The supplier might thus try to curb this by fixing maximum resale prices.

One might wonder why the latter problem could not be solved by simply charging the retailer the optimal price plus a lump sum franchise fee per year that equals the expected monopoly profits.[12] This would effectively auction off the rights to this local market power. But this strategy raises various problems. (1) The manufacturer may have difficulty accurately projecting expected monopoly profits that vary over time with changing local retailing costs and demand. (2) The risk-bearing costs of entering into such an arrangement may be higher for retailers because if local retailing costs are higher (or demand lower) than expected, then the retailer loses out. (3) Exploiting local market power may diminish brand traffic by lessening the brand reputation for low or at least nonexploitative prices. For all these reasons, a manufacturer may find it more attractive to fix maximum resale prices and alter them with changing market conditions.

Alternatively, a manufacturer could accomplish the same control over dealer market power by simply engaging in vertical integration. But such

---

12. *See, e.g.,* JEAN TIROLE, THE THEORY OF INDUSTRIAL ORGANIZATION 176 (1988).

vertical integration may be inefficient compared to using separate dealers. Further, vertical integration would be a more (rather than less) restrictive alternative to having independent dealers with discretion over how they do their business as long as they do not exceed maximum prices.

State Oil Co. v. Khan

522 U.S. 3 (1997).

■ O'CONNOR, J., delivered the opinion for a unanimous Court.

... In *Albrecht v. Herald*, 390 U.S. 145 (1968), this Court held that vertical maximum price fixing is a per se violation of [Sherman Act § 1]. In this case, we are asked to reconsider that decision in light of subsequent decisions of this Court. We conclude that *Albrecht* should be overruled....

A review of this Court's decisions leading up to and beyond *Albrecht* is relevant to our assessment of the continuing validity of the per se rule established in Albrecht. Beginning with *Dr. Miles,* the Court recognized the illegality of agreements under which manufacturers or suppliers set the minimum resale prices to be charged by their distributors. By 1940, the Court broadly declared all business combinations "formed for the purpose and with the effect of raising, depressing, fixing, pegging, or stabilizing the price of a commodity in interstate or foreign commerce" illegal per se. *Socony*. Accordingly, the Court condemned an agreement between two affiliated liquor distillers to limit the maximum price charged by retailers in Kiefer–Stewart Co. v. Joseph E. Seagram & Sons, 340 U.S. 211 (1951), noting that agreements to fix maximum prices, "no less than those to fix minimum prices, cripple the freedom of traders and thereby restrain their ability to sell in accordance with their own judgment." Id. at 213.

In subsequent cases, the Court's attention turned to arrangements through which suppliers imposed restrictions on dealers with respect to matters other than resale price. In ... *Schwinn*, the Court ... held that, upon the transfer of title to goods to a distributor, a supplier's imposition of territorial restrictions on the distributor was "so obviously destructive of competition" as to constitute a per se violation of the Sherman Act....

Albrecht, decided the following Term, involved a newspaper publisher who had granted exclusive territories to independent carriers subject to their adherence to a maximum price on resale of the newspapers to the public. Influenced by its decisions in *Socony, Kiefer–Stewart*, and *Schwinn*, the Court concluded that it was per se unlawful for the publisher to fix the maximum resale price of its newspapers. The Court acknowledged that "[m]aximum and minimum price fixing may have different consequences in many situations," but nonetheless condemned maximum price fixing for "substituting the perhaps erroneous judgment of a seller for the forces of the competitive market."

Albrecht was animated in part by the fear that vertical maximum price fixing could allow suppliers to discriminate against certain dealers, restrict the services that dealers could afford to offer customers, or disguise minimum price fixing schemes. The Court rejected the notion (both on the record of that case and in the abstract) that, because the newspaper publisher "granted exclusive territories, a price ceiling was necessary to protect the public from price gouging by dealers who had monopoly power in their own territories."

In a vigorous dissent, Justice Harlan asserted that the majority had erred in equating the effects of maximum and minimum price fixing. Justice Harlan pointed out that, because the majority was establishing a per se rule, the proper inquiry was "not whether dictation of maximum prices is ever illegal, but whether it is always illegal." He also faulted the majority for conclusively listing "certain unfortunate consequences that maximum price dictation might have in other cases," even as it rejected evidence that the publisher's practice of fixing maximum prices counteracted potentially anticompetitive actions by its distributors. Justice Stewart also dissented, asserting that the publisher's maximum price fixing scheme should be properly viewed as promoting competition, because it protected consumers from dealers such as Albrecht, who, as "the only person who could sell for home delivery the city's only daily morning newspaper," was "a monopolist within his own territory."

Nine years later, in *Sylvania*, the Court overruled *Schwinn*, thereby rejecting application of a per se rule in the context of vertical nonprice restrictions. . . .

In *Sylvania*, the Court declined to comment on *Albrecht*'s per se treatment of vertical maximum price restrictions, noting that the issue "involve[d] significantly different questions of analysis and policy." Subsequent decisions of the Court, however, have hinted that the analytical underpinnings of *Albrecht* were substantially weakened by *Sylvania*. . . .

Most recently, in *ARCO*, although *Albrecht*'s continuing validity was not squarely before the Court, some disfavor with that decision was signaled by our statement that we would "assume, arguendo, that *Albrecht* correctly held that vertical, maximum price fixing is subject to the per se rule." More significantly, we specifically acknowledged that vertical maximum price fixing "may have procompetitive interbrand effects," and pointed out that, in the wake of *Sylvania*, "[t]he procompetitive potential of a vertical maximum price restraint is more evident . . . than it was when *Albrecht* was decided, because exclusive territorial arrangements and other nonprice restrictions were unlawful per se in 1968."

Thus, our reconsideration of *Albrecht*'s continuing validity is informed by several of our decisions, as well as a considerable body of scholarship discussing the effects of vertical restraints. Our analysis is also guided by our general view that the primary purpose of the antitrust laws is to protect interbrand competition. See, e.g., *Business Electronics*. "Low prices," we have explained, "benefit consumers regardless of how those prices are set, and so long as they are above predatory levels, they do not threaten competition." *ARCO*. Our interpretation of the Sherman Act also incorporates the notion that condemnation of practices resulting in lower prices to consumers is "especially costly" because "cutting prices in order to increase business often is the very essence of competition." *Matsushita*.

So informed, we find it difficult to maintain that vertically-imposed maximum prices could harm consumers or competition to the extent necessary to justify their per se invalidation. As Chief Judge Posner wrote for the Court of Appeals in this case:

"As for maximum resale price fixing, unless the supplier is a monopolist he cannot squeeze his dealers' margins below a competitive level; the attempt to do so would just drive the dealers into the arms of a competing supplier. A supplier might, however, fix a maximum resale price in order to prevent his dealers from exploiting a monopoly position.... [S]uppose that State Oil, perhaps to encourage ... dealer services ... has spaced its dealers sufficiently far apart to limit competition among them (or even given each of them an exclusive territory); and suppose further that Union 76 is a sufficiently distinctive and popular brand to give the dealers in it at least a modicum of monopoly power. Then State Oil might want to place a ceiling on the dealers' resale prices in order to prevent them from exploiting that monopoly power fully. It would do this not out of disinterested malice, but in its commercial self-interest. The higher the price at which gasoline is resold, the smaller the volume sold, and so the lower the profit to the supplier if the higher profit per gallon at the higher price is being snared by the dealer." 93 F.3d, at 1362.

See also R. BORK, THE ANTITRUST PARADOX 281–282 (1978) ("There could, of course, be no anticonsumer effect from [the type of price fixing considered in *Albrecht*], and one suspects that the paper has a legitimate interest in keeping subscriber prices down in order to increase circulation and maximize revenues from advertising").

We recognize that the *Albrecht* decision presented a number of theoretical justifications for a per se rule against vertical maximum price fixing. But criticism of those premises abounds. The *Albrecht* decision was grounded in the fear that maximum price fixing by suppliers could interfere with dealer freedom. In response, as one commentator has pointed out, "the ban on maximum resale price limitations declared in *Albrecht* in the name of 'dealer freedom' has actually prompted many suppliers to integrate forward into distribution, thus eliminating the very independent trader for whom *Albrecht* professed solicitude." 7 P. AREEDA, ANTITRUST LAW ¶ 1635, p. 395 (1989). For example, integration in the newspaper industry since *Albrecht* has given rise to litigation between independent distributors and publishers.

The *Albrecht* Court also expressed the concern that maximum prices may be set too low for dealers to offer consumers essential or desired services. But such conduct, by driving away customers, would seem likely to harm manufacturers as well as dealers and consumers, making it unlikely that a supplier would set such a price as a matter of business judgment. In addition, *Albrecht* noted that vertical maximum price fixing could effectively channel distribution through large or specially-advantaged dealers. It is unclear, however, that a supplier would profit from limiting its market by excluding potential dealers. Further, although vertical maximum price fixing might limit the viability of inefficient dealers, that consequence is not necessarily harmful to competition and consumers.

Finally, *Albrecht* reflected the Court's fear that maximum price fixing could be used to disguise arrangements to fix minimum prices, which remain illegal per se. Although we have acknowledged the possibility that maximum pricing might mask minimum pricing, see *Maricopa County*, we believe that such conduct as with the other concerns articulated in *Albrecht* can be appropriately recognized and punished under the rule of reason.

Not only are the potential injuries cited in *Albrecht* less serious than the Court imagined, the per se rule established therein could in fact exacerbate problems related to the unrestrained exercise of market power by monopolist-dealers. Indeed, both courts and antitrust scholars have noted that *Albrecht*'s rule may actually harm consumers and manufacturers. Other commentators have also explained that *Albrecht*'s per se rule has even more potential for deleterious effect on competition after our decision in *Sylvania*, because, now that vertical nonprice restrictions are not unlawful per se, the likelihood of dealer monopoly power is increased. We do not intend to suggest that dealers generally possess sufficient market power to exploit a monopoly situation. Such retail market power may in fact be uncommon. See, e.g., *Business Electronics*; *Sylvania*. Nor do we hold that a ban on vertical maximum price fixing inevitably has anticompetitive consequences in the exclusive dealer context.

After reconsidering *Albrecht*'s rationale and the substantial criticism the decision has received, however, we conclude that there is insufficient economic justification for per se invalidation of vertical maximum price fixing. That is so not only because it is difficult to accept the assumptions underlying *Albrecht*, but also because *Albrecht* has little or no relevance to ongoing enforcement of the Sherman Act. See *Copperweld*. Moreover, neither the parties nor any of the amici curiae have called our attention to any cases in which enforcement efforts have been directed solely against the conduct encompassed by *Albrecht*'s per se rule.

Respondents argue that reconsideration of *Albrecht* should require "persuasive, expert testimony establishing that the per se rule has distorted the market." Their reasoning ignores the fact that *Albrecht* itself relied solely upon hypothetical effects of vertical maximum price fixing. Further, *Albrecht*'s dire predictions have not been borne out, even though manufacturers and suppliers appear to have fashioned schemes to get around the per se rule against vertical maximum price fixing. In these circumstances, it is the retention of the rule of *Albrecht*, and not, as respondents would have it, the rule's elimination, that lacks adequate justification. See, e.g., *Sylvania*.

. . . In the context of this case, we infer little meaning from the fact that Congress has not reacted legislatively to *Albrecht*. In any event, the history of various legislative proposals regarding price fixing seems neither clearly to support nor to denounce the per se rule of *Albrecht*. Respondents are of course free to seek legislative protection from gasoline suppliers of the sort embodied in the Petroleum Marketing Practices Act, 92 Stat. 322, 15 U.S.C. § 2801 et seq. For the reasons we have noted, however, the remedy for respondents' dispute with State Oil should not come in the form of a per se rule affecting the conduct of the entire marketplace.

Despite what Chief Judge Posner aptly described as *Albrecht*'s "infir-mities, [and] its increasingly wobbly, moth-eaten foundations," 93 F.3d at 1363, there remains the question whether *Albrecht* deserves continuing respect under the doctrine of stare decisis. The Court of Appeals was correct in applying that principle despite disagreement with *Albrecht*, for it is this Court's prerogative alone to overrule one of its precedents.

We approach the reconsideration of decisions of this Court with the utmost caution. Stare decisis reflects "a policy judgment that 'in most matters it is more important that the applicable rule of law be settled than that it be settled right.' " *Agostini v. Felton*, 117 S.Ct. 1997, 2016 (1997). It "is the preferred course because it promotes the evenhanded, predictable, and consistent development of legal principles, fosters reliance on judicial decisions, and contributes to the actual and perceived integrity of the judicial process." *Payne v. Tennessee*, 501 U.S. 808, 827 (1991). . . .

But "[s]tare decisis is not an inexorable command." *Ibid.* In the area of antitrust law, there is a competing interest, well-represented in this Court's decisions, in recognizing and adapting to changed circumstances and the lessons of accumulated experience. Thus, the general presumption that legislative changes should be left to Congress has less force with respect to the Sherman Act in light of the accepted view that Congress "expected the courts to give shape to the statute's broad mandate by drawing on com-mon-law tradition." *Professional Engineers*. As we have explained, the term "restraint of trade," as used in § 1, also "invokes the common law itself, and not merely the static content that the common law had assigned to the term in 1890." *Business Electronics*; see also *Sylvania*. Accordingly, this Court has reconsidered its decisions construing the Sherman Act when the theoretical underpinnings of those decisions are called into serious ques-tion. See, e.g., *Copperweld; Sylvania*.

Although we do not "lightly assume that the economic realities under-lying earlier decisions have changed, or that earlier judicial perceptions of those realities were in error," we have noted that "different sorts of agreements" may amount to restraints of trade "in varying times and circumstances," and "[i]t would make no sense to create out of the single term 'restraint of trade' a chronologically schizoid statute, in which a 'rule of reason' evolves with new circumstances and new wisdom, but a line of per se illegality remains forever fixed where it was." *Business Electronics*. Just as *Schwinn* was "the subject of continuing controversy and confusion" under the "great weight" of scholarly criticism, *Sylvania*, *Albrecht* has been widely criticized since its inception. With the views underlying *Albrecht* eroded by this Court's precedent, there is not much of that decision to salvage.

Although the rule of *Albrecht* has been in effect for some time, the inquiry we must undertake requires considering " 'the effect of the anti-trust laws upon vertical distributional restraints in the American economy today.' " *Sylvania*. As the Court noted in *ARCO*, there has not been another case since *Albrecht* in which this Court has "confronted an unadul-terated vertical, maximum-price-fixing arrangement." Now that we con-front *Albrecht* directly, we find its conceptual foundations gravely weak-ened.

In overruling *Albrecht*, we of course do not hold that all vertical maximum price fixing is per se lawful. Instead, vertical maximum price fixing, like the majority of commercial arrangements subject to the antitrust laws, should be evaluated under the rule of reason. In our view, rule-of-reason analysis will effectively identify those situations in which vertical maximum price fixing amounts to anticompetitive conduct. . . .

Questions on *State Oil v. Khan*

1. Was the case correctly decided?

2. Is there any more reason to differentiate maximum and minimum price-fixing in the vertical context than in the horizontal context? Are the justifications any different? The anticompetitive effects? The incentives of the decisionmakers?

3. Should vertical maximum price-fixing be per se *legal*? Why not?

a. Even if there are some odd cases where it might have anticompetitive effects, are judges and juries likely to be better than manufacturers at weighing those anticompetitive effects against the procompetitive effects?

b. Should we at least limit any review of vertical maximum price-fixing to cases where there was affirmative proof that the maximum really operated as a minimum and the agreement was procured by dealers with market power?

4. Assuming *Albrecht*'s foundation had been so eroded that it should have been overruled, should the Supreme Court have done so or Congress? If the Supreme Court could do so, why couldn't a lower court? Consider the following argument: "The main reason the Supreme Court should ever overrule statutory precedent is that Congress is too busy to rectify every interpretive mistake the Supreme Court makes. Thus, the Supreme Court itself should correct misinterpretations where the Court is confident Congress would agree if Congress were to consider the issue. But it is also true that the Supreme Court is too busy to rectify every interpretive mistake it makes. Thus, where a lower court feels confident that the Supreme Court would overrule a precedent if it were to consider it, then it should no longer feel itself bound by that precedent."

Commission Regulation (EU) No 330/2010 of 20 April 2010 on the Application of Article 101(3) of the Treaty on the Functioning of the European Union to Categories of Vertical Agreements and Concerted Practices

O.J. 2010, L 102/1.

Article 4. Restrictions that remove the benefit of the block exemption—hardcore restrictions

The exemption provided for in Article 2 shall not apply to vertical agreements which, directly or indirectly, in isolation or in combination with other factors under the control of the parties, have as their object:

(a) the restriction of the buyer's ability to determine its sale price, without prejudice to the possibility of the supplier to impose a maximum sale price or recommend a sale price, provided that they do not amount to a fixed or minimum sale price as a result of pressure from, or incentives offered by, any of the parties . . .

EU Guidelines on Vertical Restraints

O.J. 2010, C 130/1.

The hardcore restriction set out in Article 4(a) of the Block Exemption Regulation concerns resale price maintenance (RPM), that is, agreements or concerted practices having as their direct or indirect object the establishment of a fixed or minimum resale price or a fixed or minimum price level to be observed by the buyer. In the case of contractual provisions or concerted practices that directly establish the resale price, the restriction is clear cut. . . .

However, the use of . . . a list of recommended prices or maximum prices by the supplier to the buyer is not considered in itself as leading to RPM.

Other Nations' Treatment of Vertical Maximum Price–Fixing

Taiwan continues to make vertical maximum price-fixing per se illegal.[13] But most nations do not. Brazil, Egypt, Mexico, Peru, South Africa, and Venezuela, apply a rule of reason to vertical maximum price-fixing.[14] Others, like South Korea, allow vertical maximum price-fixing if it is justified.[15] Finally, some nations, including Canada, China, Japan, and New Zealand cover resale price maintenance using terms that do not cover vertical maximum price-fixing and may thus make it per se legal.[16] Which approach would you adopt?

3. Vertical Agreements Fixing Minimum Resale Prices

In the United States, vertical minimum price-fixing agreements were regarded as per se illegal from 1911 until the 2007 decision that is excerpted next. Under EU competition law, the Commission has concluded that the imposition by a supplier of minimum retail prices on its distributors has the object of restricting competition. This position has been

---

13. Taiwan Fair Trade Law Art. 18.

14. *See* Brazil Antitrust Law No. 8,884, Art.21(XI); Brazil CADE Resolution 20, Attachment I, § 1 (1999); Egypt Competition Law Art. 7; Mexico Competition Law Arts. 10(II) & 11; Peru Competition Law, Art. 12(4); South African Competition Act § 5(1); Venezuela Regulation No. 1 of the Procompetition Act, Art 4 (1).

15. South Korea Fair Trade Act Art. 29.

16. *See* Canada Competition Act § 76; China Anti–Monopoly Law Arts. 14; Japan Designations of Unfair Trade Practices § 12 (2009); New Zealand Commerce Act § 37.

confirmed by the ECJ in a series of judgments.[17] Regulation 330/2010 provides for a block exemption of certain categories of vertical agreements when the supplier has less than a 30% market share. However, even when this threshold is not exceeded, a vertical agreement cannot be exempted when it contains "hard-core restrictions". Pursuant to Article 4(a) of Regulation 330/2010, a vertical agreement providing for resale price maintenance is deemed such a hard-core restriction.

Leegin Creative Leather Products v. PSKS, Inc.

551 U.S. 877 (2007).

■ JUSTICE KENNEDY delivered the opinion of the Court.

In *Dr. Miles Medical Co.* v. *John D. Park & Sons Co.*, 220 U. S. 373 (1911), the Court established the rule that it is *per se* illegal under § 1 of the Sherman Act for a manufacturer to agree with its distributor to set the minimum price the distributor can charge for the manufacturer's goods. The question presented by the instant case is whether the Court should overrule the *per se* rule and allow resale price maintenance agreements to be judged by the rule of reason, the usual standard applied to determine if there is a violation of § 1. The Court has abandoned the rule of *per se* illegality for other vertical restraints a manufacturer imposes on its distributors. Respected economic analysts, furthermore, conclude that vertical price restraints can have procompetitive effects. We now hold that *Dr. Miles* should be overruled and that vertical price restraints are to be judged by the rule of reason.

I

[Leegin made Brighton brand leather goods and accessories. The jury found that Leegin had entered into agreements with its retailers that fixed the minimum prices they could charge, a finding that Leegin did not dispute on appeal. On the ground that such agreements are *per se* illegal, the District Court excluded expert defense testimony describing the pro-competitive effects of Leegin's pricing policy. The jury awarded $1.2 million in damages to PSKS, a retailer terminated for undercutting Leegin's minimum retail prices, which after trebling and attorney fees came to almost $4 million. The Fifth Circuit affirmed.]

II

. . . The rule of reason is the accepted standard for testing whether a practice restrains trade in violation of § 1. . . . Resort to *per se* rules is confined to restraints . . . "that would always or almost always tend to restrict competition and decrease output." *Business Electronics Corp.* v. *Sharp Electronics Corp.*, 485 U. S. 717, 723. To justify a *per se* prohibition a restraint must have "manifestly anticompetitive" effects, *GTE Sylvania*, and "lack . . . any redeeming virtue," *Northwest Stationers*.

---

17. See, e.g., Case 161/84, Pronuptia de Paris GmbH v Pronuptia de Paris Irmgard Schillgallis, 1986 E.C.R. 353.

As a consequence, the *per se* rule is appropriate only after courts have had considerable experience with the type of restraint at issue, see *BMI*, and only if courts can predict with confidence that it would be invalidated in all or almost all instances under the rule of reason, see *Maricopa*. It should come as no surprise, then, that "we have expressed reluctance to adopt *per se* rules with regard to restraints imposed in the context of business relationships where the economic impact of certain practices is not immediately obvious." *Khan*. And, as we have stated, a "departure from the rule-of-reason standard must be based upon demonstrable economic effect rather than ... upon formalistic line drawing." *GTE Sylvania*.

III

... The reasoning of the Court's more recent jurisprudence has rejected the rationales on which *Dr. Miles* was based. By relying on the common-law rule against restraints on alienation, the Court justified its decision based on "formalistic" legal doctrine rather than "demonstrable economic effect," *GTE Sylvania*. The Court in *Dr. Miles* relied on a treatise published in 1628, but failed to discuss in detail the business reasons that would motivate a manufacturer situated in 1911 to make use of vertical price restraints. Yet the Sherman Act's use of "restraint of trade" "invokes the common law itself, ... not merely the static content that the common law had assigned to the term in 1890." *Business Electronics*. The general restraint on alienation, especially in the age when then-Justice Hughes used the term, tended to evoke policy concerns extraneous to the question that controls here. Usually associated with land, not chattels, the rule arose from restrictions removing real property from the stream of commerce for generations. The Court should be cautious about putting dispositive weight on doctrines from antiquity but of slight relevance. We reaffirm that "the state of the common law 400 or even 100 years ago is irrelevant to the issue before us: the effect of the antitrust laws upon vertical distributional restraints in the American economy today." *GTE Sylvania*.

Dr. Miles, furthermore, treated vertical agreements a manufacturer makes with its distributors as analogous to a horizontal combination among competing distributors. In later cases, however, the Court rejected the approach of reliance on rules governing horizontal restraints when defining rules applicable to vertical ones. See, *e.g., Business Electronics* (disclaiming the "notion of equivalence between the scope of horizontal *per se* illegality and that of vertical *per se* illegality"); *Maricopa* (noting that "horizontal restraints are generally less defensible than vertical restraints"). Our recent cases formulate antitrust principles in accordance with the appreciated differences in economic effect between vertical and horizontal agreements, differences the *Dr. Miles* Court failed to consider.

The reasons upon which *Dr. Miles* relied do not justify a *per se* rule. As a consequence, it is necessary to examine, in the first instance, the economic effects of vertical agreements to fix minimum resale prices, and to determine whether the *per se* rule is nonetheless appropriate.

A

Though each side of the debate can find sources to support its position, it suffices to say here that economics literature is replete with procompetitive justifications for a manufacturer's use of resale price maintenance. Even those more skeptical of resale price maintenance acknowledge it can have procompetitive effects. The few recent studies documenting the competitive effects of resale price maintenance also cast doubt on the conclusion that the practice meets the criteria for a *per se* rule. See T. Overstreet, Resale Price Maintenance: Economic Theories and Empirical Evidence 170 (1983) (hereinafter Overstreet) (noting that "[e]fficient uses of [resale price maintenance] are evidently not unusual or rare"); see also Ippolito, Resale Price Maintenance: Empirical Evidence From Litigation, 34 J. Law & Econ. 263, 292–293 (1991) (hereinafter Ippolito).

The justifications for vertical price restraints are similar to those for other vertical restraints. See *GTE Sylvania*. Minimum resale price maintenance can stimulate interbrand competition—the competition among manufacturers selling different brands of the same type of product—by reducing intrabrand competition—the competition among retailers selling the same brand. The promotion of interbrand competition is important because "the primary purpose of the antitrust laws is to protect [this type of] competition." *Khan*. A single manufacturer's use of vertical price restraints tends to eliminate intrabrand price competition; this in turn encourages retailers to invest in tangible or intangible services or promotional efforts that aid the manufacturer's position as against rival manufacturers. Resale price maintenance also has the potential to give consumers more options so that they can choose among low-price, low-service brands; high-price, high-service brands; and brands that fall in between.

Absent vertical price restraints, the retail services that enhance interbrand competition might be underprovided. This is because discounting retailers can free ride on retailers who furnish services and then capture some of the increased demand those services generate. *GTE Sylvania*. Consumers might learn, for example, about the benefits of a manufacturer's product from a retailer that invests in fine showrooms, offers product demonstrations, or hires and trains knowledgeable employees. Or consumers might decide to buy the product because they see it in a retail establishment that has a reputation for selling high-quality merchandise. Marvel & McCafferty, Resale Price Maintenance and Quality Certification, 15 Rand J. Econ. 346, 347–349 (1984) (hereinafter Marvel & McCafferty). If the consumer can then buy the product from a retailer that discounts because it has not spent capital providing services or developing a quality reputation, the high-service retailer will lose sales to the discounter, forcing it to cut back its services to a level lower than consumers would otherwise prefer. Minimum resale price maintenance alleviates the problem because it prevents the discounter from undercutting the service provider. With price competition decreased, the manufacturer's retailers compete among themselves over services.

Resale price maintenance, in addition, can increase interbrand competition by facilitating market entry for new firms and brands. "[N]ew manufacturers and manufacturers entering new markets can use the restrictions in order to induce competent and aggressive retailers to make the kind of investment of capital and labor that is often required in the distribution of products unknown to the consumer." *GTE Sylvania*; see

Marvel & McCafferty 349 (noting that reliance on a retailer's reputation "will decline as the manufacturer's brand becomes better known, so that [resale price maintenance] may be particularly important as a competitive device for new entrants"). New products and new brands are essential to a dynamic economy, and if markets can be penetrated by using resale price maintenance there is a procompetitive effect.

Resale price maintenance can also increase interbrand competition by encouraging retailer services that would not be provided even absent free riding. It may be difficult and inefficient for a manufacturer to make and enforce a contract with a retailer specifying the different services the retailer must perform. Offering the retailer a guaranteed margin and threatening termination if it does not live up to expectations may be the most efficient way to expand the manufacturer's market share by inducing the retailer's performance and allowing it to use its own initiative and experience in providing valuable services. See Mathewson & Winter, The Law and Economics of Resale Price Maintenance, 13 Rev. Indus. Org. 57, 74–75 (1998) (hereinafter Mathewson & Winter); Klein & Murphy, Vertical Restraints as Contract Enforcement Mechanisms, 31 J. Law & Econ. 265, 295 (1988); see also Deneckere, Marvel, & Peck, Demand Uncertainty, Inventories, and Resale Price Maintenance, 111 Q. J. Econ. 885, 911 (1996) (noting that resale price maintenance may be beneficial to motivate retailers to stock adequate inventories of a manufacturer's goods in the face of uncertain consumer demand).

B

While vertical agreements setting minimum resale prices can have procompetitive justifications, they may have anticompetitive effects in other cases; and unlawful price fixing, designed solely to obtain monopoly profits, is an ever present temptation. Resale price maintenance may, for example, facilitate a manufacturer cartel. See *Business Electronics*. An unlawful cartel will seek to discover if some manufacturers are undercutting the cartel's fixed prices. Resale price maintenance could assist the cartel in identifying price-cutting manufacturers who benefit from the lower prices they offer. Resale price maintenance, furthermore, could discourage a manufacturer from cutting prices to retailers with the concomitant benefit of cheaper prices to consumers.

Vertical price restraints also "might be used to organize cartels at the retailer level." *Business Electronics*. A group of retailers might collude to fix prices to consumers and then compel a manufacturer to aid the unlawful arrangement with resale price maintenance. In that instance the manufacturer does not establish the practice to stimulate services or to promote its brand but to give inefficient retailers higher profits. Retailers with better distribution systems and lower cost structures would be prevented from charging lower prices by the agreement. Historical examples suggest this possibility is a legitimate concern. See, *e.g.,* Marvel & McCafferty, The Welfare Effects of Resale Price Maintenance, 28 J. Law & Econ. 363, 373 (1985) (hereinafter Marvel) (providing an example of the power of the National Association of Retail Druggists to compel manufacturers to use resale price maintenance); Hovenkamp 186 (suggesting that the retail druggists in *Dr. Miles* formed a cartel and used manufacturers to enforce it).

A horizontal cartel among competing manufacturers or competing retailers that decreases output or reduces competition in order to increase price is, and ought to be, *per se* unlawful. See *Texaco*; *GTE Sylvania*. To the extent a vertical agreement setting minimum resale prices is entered upon to facilitate either type of cartel, it, too, would need to be held unlawful under the rule of reason. This type of agreement may also be useful evidence for a plaintiff attempting to prove the existence of a horizontal cartel.

Resale price maintenance, furthermore, can be abused by a powerful manufacturer or retailer. A dominant retailer, for example, might request resale price maintenance to forestall innovation in distribution that decreases costs. A manufacturer might consider it has little choice but to accommodate the retailer's demands for vertical price restraints if the manufacturer believes it needs access to the retailer's distribution network. A manufacturer with market power, by comparison, might use resale price maintenance to give retailers an incentive not to sell the products of smaller rivals or new entrants. See, *e.g.,* Marvel 366–368. As should be evident, the potential anticompetitive consequences of vertical price restraints must not be ignored or underestimated.

C

Notwithstanding the risks of unlawful conduct, it cannot be stated with any degree of confidence that resale price maintenance "always or almost always tend[s] to restrict competition and decrease output." *Business Electronics*. Vertical agreements establishing minimum resale prices can have either procompetitive or anticompetitive effects, depending upon the circumstances in which they are formed. And although the empirical evidence on the topic is limited, it does not suggest efficient uses of the agreements are infrequent or hypothetical. See Overstreet 170; see also *id.,* at 80 (noting that for the majority of enforcement actions brought by the Federal Trade Commission between 1965 and 1982, "the use of [resale price maintenance] was not likely motivated by collusive dealers who had successfully coerced their suppliers"); Ippolito 292 (reaching a similar conclusion). As the rule would proscribe a significant amount of procompetitive conduct, these agreements appear ill suited for *per se* condemnation.

Respondent [PSKS] contends, nonetheless, that vertical price restraints should be *per se* unlawful because of the administrative convenience of *per se* rules. See, *e.g., GTE Sylvania* (noting "*per se* rules tend to provide guidance to the business community and to minimize the burdens on litigants and the judicial system"). That argument suggests *per se* illegality is the rule rather than the exception. This misinterprets our antitrust law. *Per se* rules may decrease administrative costs, but that is only part of the equation. Those rules can be counterproductive. They can increase the total cost of the antitrust system by prohibiting procompetitive conduct the antitrust laws should encourage. They also may increase litigation costs by promoting frivolous suits against legitimate practices. The Court has thus explained that administrative "advantages are not sufficient in themselves to justify the creation of *per se* rules," *GTE Sylvania*, and has relegated their use to restraints that are "manifestly anticompetitive," *id.*. Were the Court now to conclude that vertical price restraints should be *per se* illegal based on administrative costs, we would undermine, if not overrule, the traditional "demanding standards" for adopting *per se* rules. Any possible reduction in administrative costs cannot alone justify the *Dr. Miles* rule.

Respondent also argues the *per se* rule is justified because a vertical price restraint can lead to higher prices for the manufacturer's goods. See also Overstreet 160 (noting that "price surveys indicate that [resale price maintenance] in most cases increased the prices of products sold"). Respondent is mistaken in relying on pricing effects absent a further showing of anticompetitive conduct. Cf. *id.*, at 106 (explaining that price surveys "do not necessarily tell us anything conclusive about the welfare effects of [resale price maintenance] because the results are generally consistent with both procompetitive and anticompetitive theories"). For, as has been indicated already, the antitrust laws are designed primarily to protect interbrand competition, from which lower prices can later result. See *Khan*. The Court, moreover, has evaluated other vertical restraints under the rule of reason even though prices can be increased in the course of promoting procompetitive effects. See, *e.g.*, *Business Electronics*. And resale price maintenance may reduce prices if manufacturers have resorted to costlier alternatives of controlling resale prices that are not *per se* unlawful. See *infra*; see also Marvel 371.

Respondent's argument, furthermore, overlooks that, in general, the interests of manufacturers and consumers are aligned with respect to retailer profit margins. The difference between the price a manufacturer charges retailers and the price retailers charge consumers represents part of the manufacturer's cost of distribution, which, like any other cost, the manufacturer usually desires to minimize. See *GTE Sylvania* ("Economists . . . have argued that manufacturers have an economic interest in maintaining as much intrabrand competition as is consistent with the efficient distribution of their products"). A manufacturer has no incentive to overcompensate retailers with unjustified margins. The retailers, not the manufacturer, gain from higher retail prices. The manufacturer often loses; interbrand competition reduces its competitiveness and market share because consumers will "substitute a different brand of the same product." *Id.*; see *Business Electronics*. As a general matter, therefore, a single manufacturer will desire to set minimum resale prices only if the "increase in demand resulting from enhanced service . . . will more than offset a negative impact on demand of a higher retail price." Mathewson & Winter 67.

The implications of respondent's position are far reaching. Many decisions a manufacturer makes and carries out through concerted action can lead to higher prices. A manufacturer might, for example, contract with different suppliers to obtain better inputs that improve product quality. Or it might hire an advertising agency to promote awareness of its goods. Yet no one would think these actions violate the Sherman Act because they lead to higher prices. The antitrust laws do not require manufacturers to produce generic goods that consumers do not know about or want. The manufacturer strives to improve its product quality or to promote its brand because it believes this conduct will lead to increased demand despite higher prices. The same can hold true for resale price maintenance.

Resale price maintenance, it is true, does have economic dangers. If the rule of reason were to apply to vertical price restraints, courts would have to be diligent in eliminating their anticompetitive uses from the market. This is a realistic objective, and certain factors are relevant to the inquiry. For example, the number of manufacturers that make use of the practice in a given industry can provide important instruction. When only a few manufacturers lacking market power adopt the practice, there is little likelihood it is facilitating a manufacturer cartel, for a cartel then can be undercut by rival manufacturers. Likewise, a retailer cartel is unlikely when only a single manufacturer in a competitive market uses resale price maintenance. Interbrand competition would divert consumers to lower priced substitutes and eliminate any gains to retailers from their price-fixing agreement over a single brand. Resale price maintenance should be subject to more careful scrutiny, by contrast, if many competing manufacturers adopt the practice. Cf. F.M. Scherer & D. Ross, Industrial Market Structure and Economic Performance 558 (3d ed. 1990) (noting that "except when [resale price maintenance] spreads to cover the bulk of an industry's output, depriving consumers of a meaningful choice between high-service and low-price outlets, most [resale price maintenance arrangements] are probably innocuous"); Easterbrook, Vertical Arrangements and the Rule of Reason, 53 Antitrust L.J. 135, 162 (1984) (suggesting that "every one of the potentially-anticompetitive outcomes of vertical arrangements depends on the uniformity of the practice").

The source of the restraint may also be an important consideration. If there is evidence retailers were the impetus for a vertical price restraint, there is a greater likelihood that the restraint facilitates a retailer cartel or supports a dominant, inefficient retailer. If, by contrast, a manufacturer adopted the policy independent of retailer pressure, the restraint is less likely to promote anticompetitive conduct. A manufacturer also has an incentive to protest inefficient retailer-induced price restraints because they can harm its competitive position.

As a final matter, that a dominant manufacturer or retailer can abuse resale price maintenance for anticompetitive purposes may not be a serious concern unless the relevant entity has market power. If a retailer lacks market power, manufacturers likely can sell their goods through rival retailers. See also *Business Electronics* (noting "[r]etail market power is rare, because of the usual presence of interbrand competition and other dealers"). And if a manufacturer lacks market power, there is less likelihood it can use the practice to keep competitors away from distribution outlets.

The rule of reason is designed and used to eliminate anticompetitive transactions from the market. This standard principle applies to vertical price restraints. A party alleging injury from a vertical agreement setting minimum resale prices will have, as a general matter, the information and resources available to show the existence of the agreement and its scope of operation. As courts gain experience considering the effects of these restraints by applying the rule of reason over the course of decisions, they can establish the litigation structure to ensure the rule operates to eliminate anticompetitive restraints from the market and to provide more guidance to businesses. Courts can, for example, devise rules over time for offering proof, or even presumptions where justified, to make the rule of reason a fair and efficient way to prohibit anticompetitive restraints and to promote procompetitive ones.

For all of the foregoing reasons, we think that were the Court considering the issue as an original matter, the rule of reason, not a *per se* rule of unlawfulness, would be the appropriate standard to judge vertical price restraints.

IV

We do not write on a clean slate, for the decision in *Dr. Miles* is almost a century old. So there is an argument for its retention on the basis of *stare decisis* alone. Even if *Dr. Miles* established an erroneous rule, *"[s]tare decisis* reflects a policy judgment that in most matters it is more important that the applicable rule of law be settled than that it be settled right." *Khan.* And concerns about maintaining settled law are strong when the question is one of statutory interpretation. See, *e.g., Hohn* v. *United States*, 524 U. S. 236, 251 (1998).

Stare decisis is not as significant in this case, however, because the issue before us is the scope of the Sherman Act. *Khan* ("[T]he general presumption that legislative changes should be left to Congress has less force with respect to the Sherman Act"). From the beginning the Court has treated the Sherman Act as a common-law statute. See *Professional Engineers.* Just as the common law adapts to modern understanding and greater experience, so too does the Sherman Act's prohibition on "restraint[s] of trade" evolve to meet the dynamics of present economic conditions. The case-by-case adjudication contemplated by the rule of reason has implemented this common-law approach. Likewise, the boundaries of the doctrine of *per se* illegality should not be immovable. For "[i]t would make no sense to create out of the single term 'restraint of trade' a chronologically schizoid statute, in which a 'rule of reason' evolves with new circumstance and new wisdom, but a line of *per se* illegality remains forever fixed where it was." *Business Electronics*

A

Stare decisis, we conclude, does not compel our continued adherence to the *per se* rule against vertical price restraints. As discussed earlier, respected authorities in the economics literature suggest the *per se* rule is inappropriate, and there is now widespread agreement that resale price maintenance can have procompetitive effects. It is also significant that both the Department of Justice and the Federal Trade Commission—the antitrust enforcement agencies with the ability to assess the long-term impacts of resale price maintenance—have recommended that this Court replace the *per se* rule with the traditional rule of reason. In the antitrust context the fact that a decision has been "called into serious question" justifies our reevaluation of it. *Khan*.

Other considerations reinforce the conclusion that *Dr. Miles* should be overturned. Of most relevance, "we have overruled our precedents when subsequent cases have undermined their doctrinal underpinnings." *Dickerson* v. *United States*, 530 U. S. 428, 443 (2000). The Court's treatment of vertical restraints has progressed away from *Dr. Miles'* strict approach. We have distanced ourselves from the opinion's rationales. This is unsurprising, for the case was decided not long after enactment of the Sherman Act when the Court had little experience with antitrust analysis. Only eight years after *Dr. Miles*, moreover, the Court reined in the decision by holding that a manufacturer can announce suggested resale prices and refuse to deal with distributors who do not follow them. *Colgate*.

In more recent cases the Court, following a common-law approach, has continued to temper, limit, or overrule once strict prohibitions on vertical restraints. In 1977, the Court overturned the *per se* rule for vertical nonprice restraints, adopting the rule of reason in its stead. *GTE Sylvania*. While the Court in a footnote in *GTE Sylvania* suggested that differences between vertical price and nonprice restraints could support different legal treatment, the central part of the opinion relied on authorities and arguments that find unequal treatment "difficult to justify," *id*. (White, J., concurring in judgment).

Continuing in this direction, in two cases in the 1980's the Court defined legal rules to limit the reach of *Dr. Miles* and to accommodate the doctrines enunciated in *GTE Sylvania* and *Colgate*. In *Monsanto*, the Court required that antitrust plaintiffs alleging a § 1 price-fixing conspiracy must present evidence tending to exclude the possibility a manufacturer and its distributors acted in an independent manner. Unlike Justice Brennan's concurrence, which rejected arguments that *Dr. Miles* should be overruled, the Court "decline[d] to reach the question" whether vertical agreements fixing resale prices always should be unlawful because neither party suggested otherwise. In *Business Electronics* the Court further narrowed the scope of *Dr. Miles*. It held that the *per se* rule applied only to specific agreements over price levels and not to an agreement between a manufacturer and a distributor to terminate a price-cutting distributor.

Most recently, in 1997, after examining the issue of vertical maximum price-fixing agreements in light of commentary and real experience, the Court overruled a 29–year–old precedent treating those agreements as *per se* illegal. *Khan* . . . . . Our continued limiting of the reach of the decision in *Dr. Miles* and our recent treatment of other vertical restraints justify the conclusion that *Dr. Miles* should not be retained.

The *Dr. Miles* rule is also inconsistent with a principled framework, for it makes little economic sense when analyzed with our other cases on vertical restraints. If we were to decide the procompetitive effects of resale price maintenance were insufficient to overrule *Dr. Miles*, then cases such as *Colgate* and *GTE Sylvania* themselves would be called into question. These later decisions, while they may result in less intrabrand competition, can be justified because they permit manufacturers to secure the procompetitive benefits associated with vertical price restraints through other methods. The other methods, however, could be less efficient for a particular manufacturer to establish and sustain. The end result hinders competition and consumer welfare because manufacturers are forced to engage in second-best alternatives and because consumers are required to shoulder the increased expense of the inferior practices.

The manufacturer has a number of legitimate options to achieve benefits similar to those provided by vertical price restraints. A manufacturer can exercise its *Colgate* right to refuse to deal with retailers that do not follow its suggested prices. The economic effects of unilateral and concerted price setting are in general the same. See, *e.g., Monsanto.* The problem for the manufacturer is that a jury might conclude its unilateral policy was really a vertical agreement, subjecting it to treble damages and potential criminal liability. *Ibid.; Business Electronics.* Even with the stringent standards in *Monsanto* and *Business Electronics*, this danger can lead, and has led, rational manufacturers to take wasteful measures. A manufacturer might refuse to discuss its pricing policy with its distributors except through counsel knowledgeable of the subtle intricacies of the law. Or it might terminate longstanding distributors for minor violations without seeking an explanation. The increased costs these burdensome measures generate flow to consumers in the form of higher prices.

Furthermore, depending on the type of product it sells, a manufacturer might be able to achieve the procompetitive benefits of resale price maintenance by integrating downstream and selling its products directly to consumers. *Dr. Miles* tilts the relative costs of vertical integration and vertical agreement by making the former more attractive based on the *per se* rule, not on real market conditions. See *Business Electronics*; see generally Coase, The Nature of the Firm, 4 Economica, New Series 386 (1937). This distortion might lead to inefficient integration that would not otherwise take place, so that consumers must again suffer the consequences of the suboptimal distribution strategy. And integration, unlike vertical price restraints, eliminates all intrabrand competition. See, *e.g., GTE Sylvania.*

There is yet another consideration. A manufacturer can impose territorial restrictions on distributors and allow only one distributor to sell its goods in a given region. Our cases have recognized, and the economics literature confirms, that these vertical nonprice restraints have impacts similar to those of vertical price restraints; both reduce intrabrand competition and can stimulate retailer services. See, *e.g., Business Electronics*; *Monsanto.* Cf. Scherer & Ross 560 (noting that vertical nonprice restraints "can engender inefficiencies at least as serious as those imposed upon the consumer by resale price maintenance"); Steiner, How Manufacturers Deal with the Price–Cutting Retailer: When Are Vertical Restraints Efficient?, 65 Antitrust L. J. 407, 446–447 (1997) (indicating that "antitrust law should recognize that the consumer interest is often better served by [resale price maintenance]—contrary to its per se illegality and the rule-of-reason status of vertical nonprice restraints"). The same legal standard (*per se* unlawfulness) applies to horizontal market division and horizontal price fixing because both have similar economic effect. There is likewise little economic justification for the current differential treatment of vertical price and nonprice restraints. Furthermore, vertical nonprice restraints may prove less efficient for inducing desired services, and they reduce intrabrand competition more than vertical price restraints by eliminating both price and service competition.

In sum, it is a flawed antitrust doctrine that serves the interests of lawyers—by creating legal distinctions that operate as traps for the unwary—more than the interests of consumers—by requiring manufacturers to choose second-best options to achieve sound business objectives.

B

Respondent's arguments for reaffirming *Dr. Miles* on the basis of *stare decisis* do not require a different result. Respondent looks to congressional action concerning vertical price restraints. In 1937, Congress passed the Miller–Tydings Fair Trade Act, 50 Stat. 693, which made vertical price restraints legal if authorized by a fair trade law enacted by a State. Fifteen years later, Congress expanded the exemption to permit vertical price-setting agreements between a manufacturer and a distributor to be enforced against other distributors not involved in the agreement. McGuire Act, 66 Stat. 632. In 1975, however, Congress repealed both Acts. Consumer Goods Pricing Act, 89 Stat. 801. That the *Dr. Miles* rule applied to vertical price restraints in 1975, according to respondent, shows Congress ratified the rule.

This is not so. The text of the Consumer Goods Pricing Act did not codify the rule of *per se* illegality for vertical price restraints. It rescinded statutory provisions that made them *per se* legal. Congress once again placed these restraints within the ambit of § 1 of the Sherman Act. And, as has been discussed, Congress intended § 1 to give courts the ability "to develop governing principles of law" in the common-law tradition. *Texas Industries, Inc. v. Radcliff Materials, Inc.*, 451 U. S. 630, 643 (1981); see *Business Electronics* ("The changing content of the term 'restraint of trade' was well recognized at the time the Sherman Act was enacted"). Congress could have set the *Dr. Miles* rule in stone, but it chose a more flexible option. We respect its decision by analyzing vertical price restraints, like all restraints, in conformance with traditional § 1 principles, including the principle that our antitrust doctrines "evolv[e] with new circumstances and new wisdom." *Business Electronics*.

The rule of reason, furthermore, is not inconsistent with the Consumer Goods Pricing Act. Unlike the earlier congressional exemption, it does not treat vertical price restraints as *per se* legal. In this respect, the justifications for the prior exemption are illuminating. Its goal "was to allow the States to protect small retail establishments that Congress thought might otherwise be driven from the marketplace by large-volume discounters." *California Retail Liquor Dealers Assn. v. Midcal Aluminum, Inc.*, 445 U. S. 97, 102 (1980). The state fair trade laws also appear to have been justified on similar grounds. The rationales for these provisions are foreign to the Sherman Act. Divorced from competition and consumer welfare, they were designed to save inefficient small retailers from their inability to compete. The purpose of the antitrust laws, by contrast, is "the protection of *competition*, not *competitors*." *Atlantic Richfield Co. v. USA Petroleum Co.*,

495 U. S. 328, 338 (1990) (internal quotation marks omitted). To the extent Congress repealed the exemption for some vertical price restraints to end its prior practice of encouraging anticompetitive conduct, the rule of reason promotes the same objective.

Respondent also relies on several congressional appropriations in the mid–1980's in which Congress did not permit the Department of Justice or the Federal Trade Commission to use funds to advocate overturning *Dr. Miles*. See, *e.g.*, 97 Stat. 1071. We need not pause long in addressing this argument. The conditions on funding are no longer in place, and they were ambiguous at best. As much as they might show congressional approval for *Dr. Miles*, they might demonstrate a different proposition: that Congress could not pass legislation codifying the rule and reached a short-term compromise instead.

Reliance interests do not require us to reaffirm *Dr. Miles*. To be sure, reliance on a judicial opinion is a significant reason to adhere to it, *Payne* v. *Tennessee*, 501 U. S. 808, 828 (1991), especially "in cases involving property and contract rights," *Khan*. The reliance interests here, however, like the reliance interests in *Khan*, cannot justify an inefficient rule, especially because the narrowness of the rule has allowed manufacturers to set minimum resale prices in other ways. And while the *Dr. Miles* rule is longstanding, resale price maintenance was legal under fair trade laws in a majority of States for a large part of the past century up until 1975.

It is also of note that during this time "when the legal environment in the [United States] was most favorable for [resale price maintenance], no more than a tiny fraction of manufacturers ever employed [resale price maintenance] contracts." Overstreet 6; see also *id.*, at 169 (noting that "no more than one percent of manufacturers, accounting for no more than ten percent of consumer goods purchases, ever employed [resale price maintenance] in any single year in the [United States]"); Scherer & Ross 549 (noting that "[t]he fraction of U.S. retail sales covered by [resale price maintenance] in its heyday has been variously estimated at from 4 to 10 percent"). To the extent consumers demand cheap goods, judging vertical price restraints under the rule of reason will not prevent the market from providing them. Cf. Easterbrook 152–153 (noting that "S.S. Kresge (the old K–Mart) flourished during the days of manufacturers' greatest freedom" because "discount stores offer a combination of price and service that many customers value" and that "[n]othing in restricted dealing threatens the ability of consumers to find low prices"); Scherer & Ross 557 (noting that "for the most part, the effects of the [Consumer Goods Pricing Act] were imperceptible because the forces of competition had already repealed the [previous antitrust exemption] in their own quiet way").

For these reasons the Court's decision in *Dr. Miles* is now overruled. Vertical price restraints are to be judged according to the rule of reason.

V

Noting that Leegin's president has an ownership interest in retail stores that sell Brighton, respondent claims Leegin participated in an unlawful horizontal cartel with competing retailers. Respondent did not make this allegation in the lower courts, and we do not consider it here.

The judgment of the Court of Appeals is reversed, and the case is remanded for proceedings consistent with this opinion. . . .

■ JUSTICE BREYER, with whom JUSTICE STEVENS, JUSTICE SOUTER, and JUSTICE GINSBURG join, dissenting.

. . . The Court justifies its departure from ordinary considerations of *stare decisis* by pointing to a set of arguments well known in the antitrust literature for close to half a century. Congress has repeatedly found in these arguments insufficient grounds for overturning the *per se* rule. And, in my view, they do not warrant the Court's now overturning so well-established a legal precedent.

I

. . . The case before us asks which kind of approach the courts should follow where minimum resale price maintenance is at issue. Should they apply a *per se* rule (or a variation) that would make minimum resale price maintenance always (or *almost* always) unlawful? Should they apply a "rule of reason"? Were the Court writing on a blank slate, I would find these questions difficult. But, of course, the Court is not writing on a blank slate, and that fact makes a considerable legal difference.

To best explain why the question would be difficult were we deciding it afresh, I briefly summarize several classical arguments for and against the use of a *per se* rule. The arguments focus on three sets of considerations, those involving: (1) potential anticompetitive effects, (2) potential benefits, and (3) administration. The difficulty arises out of the fact that the different sets of considerations point in different directions.

On the one hand, agreements setting minimum resale prices may have serious anticompetitive consequences. *In respect to dealers:* Resale price maintenance agreements, rather like horizontal price agreements, can diminish or eliminate price competition among dealers of a single brand or (if practiced generally by manufacturers) among multibrand dealers. In doing so, they can prevent dealers from offering customers the lower prices that many customers prefer; they can prevent dealers from responding to changes in demand, say falling demand, by cutting prices; they can encourage dealers to substitute service, for price, competition, thereby threatening wastefully to attract too many resources into that portion of the industry; they can inhibit expansion by more efficient dealers whose lower prices might otherwise attract more customers, stifling the development of new, more efficient modes of retailing; and so forth.

In respect to producers: Resale price maintenance agreements can help to reinforce the competition-inhibiting behavior of firms in concentrated industries. In such industries firms may tacitly collude, *i.e.*, observe each other's pricing behavior, each understanding that price cutting by one firm is likely to trigger price competition by all. Where that is so, resale price maintenance can make it easier for each producer to identify (by observing retail markets) when a competitor has begun to cut prices. And a producer who cuts wholesale prices *without* lowering the minimum resale price will stand to gain little, if anything, in increased profits, because the dealer will be unable to stimulate increased consumer demand by passing along the producer's price cut to consumers. In either case, resale price maintenance agreements will tend to prevent price competition from "breaking out"; and they will thereby tend to stabilize producer prices.

Those who express concern about the potential anticompetitive effects find empirical support in the behavior of prices before, and then after, Congress in 1975 repealed the Miller–Tydings Fair Trade Act, and the McGuire Act. Those Acts had permitted (but not required) individual States to enact "fair trade" laws authorizing minimum resale price maintenance. At the time of repeal minimum resale price maintenance was lawful in 36 States; it was unlawful in 14 States. Comparing prices in the former States with prices in the latter States, the Department of Justice argued that minimum resale price maintenance had raised prices by 19% to 27%.

After repeal, minimum resale price maintenance agreements were unlawful *per se* in every State. The Federal Trade Commission (FTC) staff, after studying numerous price surveys, wrote that collectively the surveys "indicate[d] that [resale price maintenance] in most cases increased the prices of products sold with [resale price maintenance]." Bureau of Economics Staff Report to the FTC, T. Overstreet, Resale Price Maintenance: Economic Theories and Empirical Evidence, 160 (1983) (hereinafter Overstreet). Most economists today agree that, in the words of a prominent antitrust treatise, "resale price maintenance tends to produce higher consumer prices than would otherwise be the case." 8 Areeda & Hovenkamp P1604b, at 40 (finding "[t]he evidence . . . persuasive on this point"). See also Brief for William S. Comanor and Frederic M. Scherer as *Amici Curiae* 4 ("It is uniformly acknowledged that [resale price maintenance] and other vertical restraints lead to higher consumer prices").

On the other hand, those favoring resale price maintenance have long argued that resale price maintenance agreements can provide important consumer benefits. The majority lists two: First, such agreements can facilitate new entry. For example, a newly entering producer wishing to build a product name might be able to convince dealers to help it do so—if, but only if, the producer can assure those dealers that they will later recoup their investment. Without resale price maintenance, late-entering dealers might take advantage of the earlier investment and, through price competition, drive prices down to the point where the early dealers cannot recover what they spent. By assuring the initial dealers that such later price competition will not occur, resale price maintenance can encourage them to carry the new product, thereby helping the new producer succeed. The result might be increased competition at the producer level, *i.e.*, greater *inter*-brand competition, that brings with it net consumer benefits.

Second, without resale price maintenance a producer might find its efforts to sell a product undermined by what resale price maintenance advocates call "free riding." Suppose a producer concludes that it can succeed only if dealers provide certain services, say, product demonstrations, high quality shops, advertising that creates a certain product image, and so forth. Without resale price maintenance, some dealers might take a "free ride" on the investment that others make in providing those services. Such a dealer would save money by not paying for those services and could consequently cut its own price and increase its own sales. Under these circumstances, dealers might prove unwilling to invest in the provision of necessary services.

Moreover, where a producer and not a group of dealers seeks a resale price maintenance agreement, there is a special reason to believe some such benefits exist. That is because, other things being equal, producers should want to encourage price competition among their dealers. By doing so they will often increase profits by selling more of their product. And that is so, even if the producer possesses sufficient market power to earn a super-normal profit. That is to say, other things being equal, the producer will benefit by charging his dealers a competitive (or even a higher-than-competitive) wholesale price while encouraging price competition among them. Hence, if the producer is the moving force, the producer must have some special reason for wanting resale price maintenance; and in the absence of, say, concentrated producer markets (where that special reason might consist of a desire to stabilize wholesale prices), that special reason may well reflect the special circumstances just described: new entry, "free riding," or variations on those themes.

The upshot is, as many economists suggest, sometimes resale price maintenance can prove harmful; sometimes it can bring benefits. But before concluding that courts should consequently apply a rule of reason, I would ask such questions as, how often are harms or benefits likely to occur? How easy is it to separate the beneficial sheep from the antitrust goats?

Economic discussion, such as the studies the Court relies upon, can *help* provide answers to these questions, and in doing so, economics can, and should, inform antitrust law. But antitrust law cannot, and should not, precisely replicate economists' (sometimes conflicting) views. That is because law, unlike economics, is an administrative system the effects of which depend upon the content of rules and precedents only as they are applied by judges and juries in courts and by lawyers advising their clients. And that fact means that courts will often bring their own administrative judgment to bear, sometimes applying rules of *per se* unlawfulness to business practices even when those practices sometimes produce benefits.

I have already described studies and analyses that suggest (though they cannot prove) that resale price maintenance can cause harms with some regularity—and certainly when dealers are the driving force. But what about benefits? How often, for example, will the benefits to which the Court points occur in practice? I can find no economic consensus on this point. There is a consensus in the literature that "free riding" takes place. But "free riding" often takes place in the economy without any legal effort to stop it. Many visitors to California take free rides on the Pacific Coast Highway. We all benefit freely from ideas, such as that of creating the first supermarket. Dealers often take a "free ride" on investments that others have made in building a product's name and reputation. The question is how often the "free riding" problem is serious enough significantly to deter dealer investment.

To be more specific, one can easily *imagine* a dealer who refuses to provide important presale services, say a detailed explanation of how a product works (or who fails to provide a proper atmosphere in which to sell expensive perfume or alligator billfolds), lest customers use that "free" service (or enjoy the psychological benefit arising when a high-priced retailer stocks a particular brand of billfold or handbag) and then buy from another dealer at a lower price. Sometimes this must happen in reality. But does it happen often? We do, after all, live in an economy where firms, despite *Dr. Miles' per se* rule, still sell complex technical equipment (as well as expensive perfume and alligator billfolds) to consumers.

All this is to say that the ultimate question is not whether, but *how much,* "free riding" of this sort takes place. And, after reading the briefs, I must answer that question with an uncertain "sometimes." See, *e.g.,* Brief for William S. Comanor and Frederic M. Scherer as *Amici Curiae* 6–7 (noting "skepticism in the economic literature about how often [free riding] actually occurs").

How easily can courts identify instances in which the benefits are likely to outweigh potential harms? My own answer is, *not very easily.* For one thing, it is often difficult to identify *who*—producer or dealer—is the moving force behind any given resale price maintenance agreement. Suppose, for example, several large multibrand retailers all sell resale-price-maintained products. Suppose further that small producers set retail prices because they fear that, otherwise, the large retailers will favor (say, by allocating better shelf-space) the goods of other producers who practice resale price maintenance. Who "initiated" this practice, the retailers hoping for considerable insulation from retail competition, or the producers, who simply seek to deal best with the circumstances they find? For another thing, as I just said, it is difficult to determine just when, and where, the "free riding" problem is serious enough to warrant legal protection.

I recognize that scholars have sought to develop check lists and sets of questions that will help courts separate instances where anticompetitive harms are more likely from instances where only benefits are likely to be found. But applying these criteria in court is often easier said than done. The Court's invitation to consider the existence of "market power," for example, invites lengthy time-consuming argument among competing experts, as they seek to apply abstract, highly technical, criteria to often ill-defined markets. And resale price maintenance cases, unlike a major merger or monopoly case, are likely to prove numerous and involve only private parties. One cannot fairly expect judges and juries in such cases to apply complex economic criteria without making a considerable number of mistakes, which themselves may impose serious costs.

Are there special advantages to a bright-line rule? Without such a rule, it is often unfair, and consequently impractical, for enforcement officials to bring criminal proceedings. And since enforcement resources are limited, that loss may tempt some producers or dealers to enter into agreements that are, on balance, anticompetitive.

Given the uncertainties that surround key items in the overall balance sheet, particularly in respect to the "administrative" questions, I can concede to the majority that the problem is difficult. And, if forced to decide now, at most I might agree that the *per se* rule should be slightly modified to allow an exception for the more easily identifiable and temporary condition of "new entry." But I am not now forced to decide this question.

The question before us is not what should be the rule, starting from scratch. We here must decide whether to change a clear and simple price-related antitrust rule that the courts have applied for nearly a century.

II

We write, not on a blank slate, but on a slate that begins with *Dr. Miles* and goes on to list a century's worth of similar cases, massive amounts of advice that lawyers have provided their clients, and untold numbers of business decisions those clients have taken in reliance upon that advice. Indeed a Westlaw search shows that *Dr. Miles* itself has been cited dozens of times in this Court and hundreds of times in lower courts. Those who wish this Court to change so well-established a legal precedent bear a heavy burden of proof. I am not aware of any case in which this Court has overturned so well-established a statutory precedent. Regardless, I do not see how the Court can claim that ordinary criteria for over-ruling an earlier case have been met.

A

I can find no change in circumstances in the past several decades that helps the majority's position. In fact, there has been one important change that argues strongly to the contrary. In 1975, Congress repealed the McGuire and Miller–Tydings Acts. And it thereby consciously *extended Dr. Miles' per se* rule. Indeed, at that time the Department of Justice and the FTC, then urging application of the *per se* rule, discussed virtually every argument presented now to this Court as well as others not here presented. And they explained to Congress why Congress should reject them. Congress fully understood, and consequently intended, that the result of its repeal of McGuire and Miller–Tydings would be to make minimum resale price maintenance *per se* unlawful. See, *e.g.*, S. Rep. No. 94–466, pp. 1–3 (1975) ("Without [the exemptions authorized by the Miller–Tydings and McGuire Acts,] the agreements they authorize would violate the antitrust laws. . . . [R]epeal of the fair trade laws generally will prohibit manufacturers from enforcing resale prices").

Congress did not prohibit this Court from reconsidering the *per se* rule. But enacting major legislation premised upon the existence of that rule constitutes important public reliance upon that rule. And doing so aware of the relevant arguments constitutes even stronger reliance upon the Court's keeping the rule, at least in the absence of some significant change in respect to those arguments.

Have there been any such changes? There have been a few economic studies, described in some of the briefs, that argue, contrary to the testimony of the Justice Department and FTC to Congress in 1975, that resale price maintenance is not harmful. One study, relying on an analysis of litigated resale price maintenance cases from 1975 to 1982, concludes that resale price maintenance does not ordinarily involve producer or dealer collusion. See Ippolito, Resale Price Maintenance: Empirical Evidence from Litigation, 34 J. Law & Econ. 263, 281–282, 292 (1991). But this study equates the failure of plaintiffs to *allege* collusion with the *absence* of collusion—an equation that overlooks the superfluous nature of allegations of horizontal collusion in a resale price maintenance case and the tacit form that such collusion might take.

The other study provides a theoretical basis for concluding that resale price maintenance "need not lead to higher retail prices." Marvel & McCafferty, The Political Economy of Resale Price Maintenance, 94 J. Pol. Econ. 1074, 1075 (1986). But this study develops a theoretical model "under the assumption that [resale price maintenance] is efficiency-enhancing." Its only empirical support is a 1940 study that the authors acknowledge is much criticized. And many other economists take a different view. See Brief for William S. Comanor and Frederic M. Scherer as *Amici Curiae* 4.

Regardless, taken together, these studies at most may offer some mild support for the majority's position. But they cannot constitute a major change in circumstances.

Petitioner [Leegin] and some *amici* have also presented us with newer studies that show that resale price maintenance sometimes brings consumer benefits. Overstreet 119–129 (describing numerous case studies). But the proponents of a *per se* rule have always conceded as much. What is remarkable about the majority's arguments is that *nothing* in this respect *is new*. The only new feature of these arguments lies in the fact that the most current advocates of overruling *Dr. Miles* have abandoned a host of other not-very-persuasive arguments upon which prior resale price maintenance proponents used to rely.

The one arguable exception consists of the majority's claim that "even absent free riding," resale price maintenance "may be the most efficient way to expand the manufacturer's market share by inducing the retailer's performance and allowing it to use its own initiative and experience in providing valuable services." I cannot count this as an exception, however, because I do not understand how, in the absence of free-riding (and assuming competitiveness), an established producer would need resale price maintenance. Why, on these assumptions, would a dealer not "expand" its "market share" as best that dealer sees fit, obtaining appropriate payment from consumers in the process? There may be an answer to this question. But I have not seen it. And I do not think that we should place significant weight upon justifications that the parties do not explain with sufficient clarity for a generalist judge to understand.

No one claims that the American economy has changed in ways that might support the majority. Concentration in retailing has increased. That change, other things being equal, may enable (and motivate) more retailers, accounting for a greater percentage of total retail sales volume, to seek resale price maintenance, thereby making it more difficult for price-cutting competitors (perhaps internet retailers) to obtain market share.

Nor has anyone argued that concentration among manufacturers that might use resale price maintenance has diminished significantly. And as far as I can tell, it has not.... At the very least, the majority has not explained how these, or other changes in the economy could help support its position.

In sum, there is no relevant change. And without some such change, there is no ground for abandoning a well-established antitrust rule.

B

With the preceding discussion in mind, I would consult the list of factors that our case law indicates are relevant when we consider overruling an earlier case. . . .

First, the Court applies *stare decisis* more "rigidly" in statutory than in constitutional cases. This is a statutory case.

Second, the Court does sometimes overrule cases that it decided wrongly only a reasonably short time ago. . . . We here overrule one *statutory* case, *Dr. Miles*, decided 100 years ago, and we overrule the cases that reaffirmed its *per se* rule in the intervening years.

Third, the fact that a decision creates an "unworkable" legal regime argues in favor of overruling. Implementation of the *per se* rule, even with the complications attendant the exception allowed for in *Colgate*, has proved practical over the course of the last century, particularly when compared with the many complexities of litigating a case under the "rule of reason" regime. No one has shown how moving from the *Dr. Miles* regime to "rule of reason" analysis would make the legal regime governing minimum resale price maintenance more "administrable," particularly since *Colgate* would remain good law with respect to *unreasonable* price maintenance.

Fourth, the fact that a decision "unsettles" the law may argue in favor of overruling. The *per se* rule is well-settled law, as the Court itself has previously recognized. *Sylvania.* It is the majority's change here that will unsettle the law.

Fifth, the fact that a case involves property rights or contract rights, where reliance interests are involved, argues against overruling. This case involves contract rights and perhaps property rights (consider shopping malls). And there has been considerable reliance upon the *per se* rule. As I have said, Congress relied upon the continued vitality of *Dr. Miles* when it repealed Miller–Tydings and McGuire. The Executive Branch argued for repeal on the assumption that *Dr. Miles* stated the law. Moreover, whole sectors of the economy have come to rely upon the *per se* rule. A factory outlet store tells us that the rule "form[s] an essential part of the regulatory background against which [that firm] and many other discount retailers have financed, structured, and operated their businesses." Brief for Burlington Coat Factory Warehouse Corp. as *Amicus Curiae* 5. The Consumer Federation of America tells us that large low-price retailers would not exist without *Dr. Miles*; minimum resale price maintenance, "by stabilizing price levels and preventing low-price competition, erects a potentially insurmountable barrier to entry for such low-price innovators." Brief for Consumer Federation of America as *Amicus Curiae* 5, 7–9 (discussing, *inter alia*, comments by Wal–Mart's founder 25 years ago that relaxation of the *per se* ban on minimum resale price maintenance would be a " 'great danger' " to Wal–Mart's then-relatively-nascent business). New distributors, including internet distributors, have similarly invested time, money, and labor in an effort to bring yet lower cost goods to Americans.

This Court's overruling of the *per se* rule jeopardizes this reliance, and more. What about malls built on the assumption that a discount distributor will remain an anchor tenant? What about home buyers who have taken a home's distance from such a mall into account? What about Americans, producers, distributors, and consumers, who have understandably assumed, at least for the last 30 years, that price competition is a legally guaranteed way of life? The majority denies none of this. It simply says that these "reliance interests . . . , like the reliance interests in *Khan*, cannot justify an inefficient rule."

The Court minimizes the importance of this reliance, adding that it "is also of note" that at the time resale price maintenance contracts were lawful " 'no more than a tiny fraction of manufacturers ever employed' " the practice. By "tiny" the Court means manufacturers that accounted for up to " 'ten percent of consumer goods purchases' " annually. That figure in today's economy equals just over $300 billion. Putting the Court's estimate together with the Justice Department's early 1970's study translates a legal regime that permits all resale price maintenance into retail bills that are higher by an average of roughly $750 to $1000 annually for an American family of four. Just how much higher retail bills will be after the Court's decision today, of course, depends upon what is now unknown, namely how courts will decide future cases under a "rule of reason." But these figures indicate that the amounts involved are important to American families and cannot be dismissed as "tiny."

Sixth, the fact that a rule of law has become "embedded" in our "national culture" argues strongly against overruling. The *per se* rule forbidding minimum resale price maintenance agreements has long been "embedded" in the law of antitrust. It involves price, the economy's " 'central nervous system.' " It reflects a basic antitrust assumption (that consumers often prefer lower prices to more service). It embodies a basic antitrust objective (providing consumers with a free choice about such matters). And it creates an easily administered and enforceable bright line, "Do not agree about price," that businesses as well as lawyers have long understood.

The only contrary *stare decisis* factor that the majority mentions consists of its claim that this Court has "[f]rom the beginning . . . treated the Sherman Act as a common-law statute," and has previously overruled antitrust precedent. It points in support to *Khan*, . . . and to *Sylvania* . . . The Court decided *Khan*, however, 29 years after *Albrecht*—still a significant period, but nowhere close to the century *Dr. Miles* has stood. The Court specifically noted the *lack* of any significant reliance upon *Albrecht*. *Khan* (*Albrecht* has had "little or no relevance to ongoing enforcement of the Sherman Act"). *Albrecht* had far less support in traditional antitrust principles than did *Dr. Miles*. And Congress had nowhere expressed support for *Albrecht*'s rule.

In *Sylvania*, the Court, in overruling *Schwinn*, explicitly distinguished *Dr. Miles* on the ground that while Congress had "recently . . . expressed its approval of a *per se* analysis of vertical price restrictions" by repealing the Miller–Tydings and McGuire Acts, "[n]o similar expression of congressional intent exists for nonprice restrictions." Moreover, the Court decided *Sylvania* only a decade after *Schwinn*. And it based its overruling on a generally perceived need to avoid "confusion" in the law, a factor totally absent here.

The Court suggests that it is following "the common-law tradition." But the common law would not have permitted overruling *Dr. Miles* in these circumstances. Common-law courts rarely overruled well-established earlier rules outright. Rather, they would over time issue decisions that gradually eroded the scope and effect of the rule in question, which might eventually lead the courts to put the rule to rest. One can argue that modifying the *per se* rule to make an exception, say, for new entry, could prove consistent with this approach. To swallow up a century-old precedent, potentially affecting many billions of dollars of sales, is not. . . .

Moreover, a Court that rests its decision upon economists' views of the economic merits should also take account of legal scholars' views about common-law overruling. Professors Hart and Sacks list 12 factors (similar to those I have mentioned) that support judicial "adherence to prior holdings." They all support adherence to *Dr. Miles* here. See H. Hart & A. Sacks, The Legal Process 568–569 (W. Eskridge & P. Frickey eds. 1994). Karl Llewellyn has written that the common-law judge's "conscious reshaping" of prior law "must so move as to hold the degree of movement down to the degree to which need truly presses." The Bramble Bush 156 (1960). Where here is the pressing need? The Court notes that the FTC argues here in favor of a rule of reason. But both Congress and the FTC, unlike courts, are well-equipped to gather empirical evidence outside the context of a single case. As neither has done so, we cannot conclude with confidence that the gains from eliminating the *per se* rule will outweigh the costs. . . .

* * *

The only safe predictions to make about today's decision are that it will likely raise the price of goods at retail and that it will create considerable legal turbulence as lower courts seek to develop workable principles. I do not believe that the majority has shown new or changed conditions sufficient to warrant overruling a decision of such long standing. All ordinary *stare decisis* considerations indicate the contrary. For these reasons, with respect, I dissent.

Notes and Questions on *Leegin*

1. Both the majority and dissent essentially conceded that economic theory was mixed on vertical minimum price-fixing, with both pro-and anticompetitive effects. The majority stressed that given this mixed theory, the traditional standard for a per se rule was not met. The dissent stressed that, given this mixed theory, one should go with stare decisis. Which side has the better of this argument?

2. Is the traditional standard for adopting a per se rule right? It asks whether conduct almost always has anticompetitive effects and hardly ever has procompetitive ones, which is to say whether a per se rule would hardly ever make errors. But isn't the real question whether the per se rule creates fewer errors than application of the rule of reason: that is, which approach would minimize total over- and underdeterrence? The dissent seems to have implicitly adopted the latter standard, noting the high risk of error in applying the rule of reason.

3. The Court recognized at least four theories as to why manufacturers might agree to anticompetitive vertical price-fixing despite ordinary manufacturer incentives to minimize retail markups. Namely, vertical price-fixing might: (1) reflect a cartel among retailers; (2) facilitate oligopolistic coordination among manufacturers; (3) be imposed by a powerful retailer to impede competition by an efficient retail rival; (4) be used by a powerful manufacturer "to give retailers an incentive not to sell the products of smaller rivals or new entrants" (i.e., for brand pushing). What sort of other evidence would you require to establish these theories? Isn't the brand pushing problem possible even when no manufacturer has market power?

4. Given the mixed theory, is the issue easily resolved by the empirical evidence stressed by the dissent, that during the period of the Fair Trade Acts, retail prices were higher in states that had passed statutes allowing and enforcing minimum retail prices fixed by manufacturers than in other states, and lower after repeal of those acts than before? The majority responded by stressing that higher prices might be procompetitive if they were coupled with more services that consumers wanted. But isn't the simpler problem with this empirical evidence that it compares a rule of per se illegality to a rule of per se *legality*? A rule of per se legality is likely to have more anticompetitive effects than a rule of reason that remains available to redress anticompetitive forms of the conduct, and thus the comparative effects are not the same as switching from a rule of per se illegality to a rule of reason. Further here, the repealed statute went beyond a rule of per se legality to make vertical minimum resale prices enforceable against nonagreeing retailers too.

5. Do the standard rules on stare decisis really apply in antitrust? As a matter of practice, the Court seems to overrule antitrust decisions in common law fashion all the time. And the text of the Sherman Act incorporates capacious common law language that might be thought to effectively delegate antitrust issues to the Courts for ongoing resolution.

6. Even if generally the Court exercises common law power over antitrust doctrine, should vertical minimum price-fixing be treated differently because here Congress passed a specific statute repealing the Fair Trade Acts? Do you agree with the dissent that this repeal indicated a legislative preference for bringing back the per se rule, or with the majority that it instead indicated a preference for returning the issue to federal courts for common law resolution?

7. In terms of common law fit with other antitrust doctrines, the majority stressed how anomalous the rule against vertical minimum price-fixing was given that the Court had already overruled the per se rules against vertical nonprice and maximum price-fixing. The dissent stressed that vertical minimum price-fixing was somewhat more likely to be anticompetitive than either of those practices and that any implications from the Fair Trade Act repeal applied only to vertical minimum price-fixing. But isn't the bigger problem of fit that, given *BMI*, the per se rule against *horizontal* price-fixing no longer applies in cases where it advances a procompetitive justification that is ancillary to a productive relationship? Given *BMI*, adhering to *Dr. Miles* would have meant having antitrust law treat vertical minimum price-fixing that is ancillary to a productive business relation between a supplier and distributor *worse* than the law treats horizontal price-fixing that is ancillary to productive business relations like joint ventures between rivals.

8. The dissent suggests that this decision will create a sea change in legal practice. But many factors limited the actual enforcement of *Dr. Miles*. First, under the *Business Electronics* case discussed by the Court, ambiguous agreements (including even a vertical agreement to terminate a retailer because of price-fixing) were interpreted to constitute a vertical nonprice agreement subject to rule of reason scrutiny rather than per se scrutiny. Second, under *Colgate* and *Monsanto,* if a supplier "unilaterally" demanded that its dealers adhere to minimum resale prices and those dealers acquiesced by complying with the minimum resale prices, it was not deemed a vertical agreement at all, thus meaning it was effectively per se legal. *See* Chapter 6. Third, U.S. enforcement agencies rarely, if ever, brought actions against vertical minimum price fixing because they were persuaded by the economic critique of *Dr. Miles*. Fourth, rival manufacturers or retailers usually cannot bring suit against vertical minimum price-fixing because they cannot show antitrust injury given that they would only benefit if such an agreement caused other manufacturers or retailers to charge anticompetitively high prices. *See* Chapter 1. Fifth, while consumers do have antitrust standing, to prove injury and damages they must prove a net anticompetitive effect, which requires satisfying an effective rule of reason that negated the practical advantage of any per se rule on liability. And in fact they hardly ever brought suit. The upshot was that the per se rule against vertical minimum price-fixing was generally invoked only, as in *Leegin*, by retailers subject to the vertical price-fixing agreement, either in a suit brought to challenge their termination for noncompliance or defensively to avoid enforcement of such an agreement. The per se rule thus provided little incremental enforcement whenever retailers were willing participants. Is ending such suits a big change?

9. The dissent also stressed reliance on the old per se rule.

a. Given the above, was there really likely to have been much reliance on it?

b. Does that reliance really differ depending on whether the overruled doctrine was around for 96 years, as here, or for 10 or 29 years as in *GTE Sylvania* and *Khan*. Isn't any meaningful current reliance likely to have been incurred within the last ten years?

c. Reliance is an important reason not to change the law when reliance increases the costs or reduces the benefits of a change, as when a technological investment makes a shift to new pollution controls more costly or less beneficial. But when reliance does not alter the costs or benefits of the legal change, then the more efficient doctrine would seem to be requiring parties to bear the risk of legal change rather than making their reliance a reason to avoid that change.[18] Does it seem likely that any

---

18.   *See* ELHAUGE, STATUTORY DEFAULT RULES Chapter 306–308 (Harvard Univ. Press 2008).

reliance that might have been made here alters the desirability of overruling *Dr. Miles*?

10. *Leegin* suggests various things about how to conduct rule of reason analysis in future vertical minimum price-fixing cases.

a. One is to dismiss cases where "only a few manufacturers lacking market power adopt the practice," but to use more careful scrutiny "if many competing manufacturers adopt the practice." Does this suggest aggregating the shares of the manufacturers on concentrated markets, the way the Court doctrine does on exclusive dealing agreements?

b. Another is to assume it is more likely that a restraint is anticompetitive if initiated by a dealer than if initiated by a manufacturer. But even if a dealer initiated the restraint, don't dealers have incentives to offer terms they think manufacturers would find efficient and profitable? Even if a manufacturer initiated the restraint, doesn't any individual manufacturer have incentives to get dealers to carry its products by offering terms it knows a powerful dealer or dealer cartel will find profitable, even if those profits come at the expense of consumer welfare? Don't manufacturers also have incentives to initiate restraints that encourage pushing their brands or that facilitate oligopolistic coordination among manufacturers?

Commission Regulation (EU) No 330/2010 of 20 April 2010 on the Application of Article 101(3) of the Treaty on the Functioning of the European Union to Categories of Vertical Agreements and Concerted Practices

O.J. 2010, L 102/1.

Article 4. Restrictions that remove the benefit of the block exemption—hardcore restrictions

The exemption provided for in Article 2 shall not apply to vertical agreements which, directly or indirectly, in isolation or in combination with other factors under the control of the parties, have as their object:

(a) the restriction of the buyer's ability to determine its sale price, without prejudice to the possibility of the supplier to impose a maximum sale price or recommend a sale price, provided that they do not amount to a fixed or minimum sale price as a result of pressure from, or incentives offered by, any of the parties . . .

EU Guidelines on Vertical Restraints

O.J. 2010, C 130/1.

[R]esale price maintenance (RPM), that is, agreements or concerted practices having as their direct or indirect object the establishment of a fixed or minimum resale price or a fixed or minimum price level to be observed by the buyer, are treated as a hardcore restriction. Where an agreement includes RPM, that agreement is presumed to restrict competition and thus to fall within Article 101(1). It also gives rise to the presumption that the agreement is unlikely to fulfil the conditions of Article 101(3), for which reason the block exemption does not apply. However, undertakings have the possibility to plead an efficiency defence under Article 101(3) in an individual case. It is incumbent on the parties to substantiate that likely efficiencies result from including RPM in their agreement and demonstrate that all the conditions of Article 101(3) are fulfilled. It then falls to the Commission to effectively assess the likely negative effects on competition and consumers before deciding whether the conditions of Article 101(3) are fulfilled.

RPM may restrict competition in a number of ways. Firstly, RPM may facilitate collusion between suppliers by enhancing price transparency on the market, thereby making it easier to detect whether a supplier deviates from the collusive equilibrium by cutting its price. RPM also undermines the incentive for the supplier to cut its price to its distributors, as the fixed resale price will prevent it from benefiting from expanded sales. Such a negative effect is particularly plausible where the market is prone to collusive outcomes, for instance if the manufacturers form a tight oligopoly, and a significant part of the market is covered by RPM agreements. Second, by eliminating intra-brand price competition, RPM may also facilitate collusion between the buyers, that is, at the distribution level. Strong or well organised distributors may be able to force or convince one or more suppliers to fix their resale price above the competitive level and thereby help them to reach or stabilise a collusive equilibrium. The resulting loss of price competition seems especially problematic when the RPM is inspired by the buyers, whose collective horizontal interests can be expected to work out negatively for consumers. Third, RPM may more generally soften competition between manufacturers and/or between retailers, in particular when manufacturers use the same distributors to distribute their products and RPM is applied by all or many of them. Fourth, the immediate effect of RPM will be that all or certain distributors are prevented from lowering their sales price for that particular brand. In other words, the direct effect of RPM is a price increase. Fifth, RPM may lower the pressure on the margin of the manufacturer, in particular where the manufacturer has a commitment problem, that is, where it has an interest in lowering the price charged to subsequent distributors. In such a situation, the manufacturer may prefer to agree to RPM, so as to help it to commit not to lower the price for subsequent distributors and to reduce the pressure on its own margin. Sixth, RPM may be implemented by a manufacturer with market power to foreclose smaller rivals. The increased margin that RPM may offer distributors, may entice the latter to favour the particular brand over rival brands when advising customers, even where such advice is not in the interest of these customers, or not to sell these rival brands at all. Lastly, RPM may reduce dynamism and innovation at the distribution level. By preventing price competition between different distributors, RPM may prevent more efficient retailers from entering the market or acquiring sufficient scale with low prices. It also may prevent or hinder the entry and expansion of distribution formats based on low prices, such as price discounters.

However, RPM may not only restrict competition but may also, in particular where it is supplier driven, lead to efficiencies, which will be assessed under Article 101(3). Most notably, where a manufacturer introduces a new product, RPM may be helpful during the introductory period of expanding demand to induce distributors to better take into account the manufacturer's interest to promote the product. RPM may provide the distributors with the means to increase sales efforts and if the distributors on this market are under competitive pressure this may induce them to expand overall demand for the product and make the launch of the product a success, also for the benefit of consumers. Similarly, fixed resale prices, and not just maximum resale prices, may be necessary to organise in a franchise system or similar distribution system applying a uniform distribution format a coordinated short term low price campaign (2 to 6 weeks in most cases) which will also benefit the consumers. In some situations, the extra margin provided by RPM may allow retailers to provide (additional) pre-sales services, in particular in case of experience or complex products. If enough customers take advantage from such services to make their choice but then purchase at a lower price with retailers that do not provide such services (and hence do not incur these costs), high-service retailers may reduce or eliminate these services that enhance the demand for the supplier's product. RPM may help to prevent such free-riding at the distribution level. The parties will have to convincingly demonstrate that the RPM agreement can be expected to not only provide the means but also the incentive to overcome possible free riding between retailers on these services and that the pre-sales services overall benefit consumers as part of the demonstration that all the conditions of Article 101(3) are fulfilled.

The practice of recommending a resale price to a reseller or requiring the reseller to respect a maximum resale price is covered by the Block Exemption Regulation when the market share of each of the parties to the agreement does not exceed the 30% threshold, provided it does not amount to a minimum or fixed sale price as a result of pressure from, or incentives offered by, any of the parties. The remainder of this section provides guidance for the assessment of maximum or recommended prices above the market share threshold and for cases of withdrawal of the block exemption.

The possible competition risk of maximum and recommended prices is that they will work as a focal point for the resellers and might be followed by most or all of them and/or that maximum or recommended prices may soften competition or facilitate collusion between suppliers.

An important factor for assessing possible anti-competitive effects of maximum or recommended resale prices is the market position of the supplier. The stronger the market position of the supplier, the higher the risk that a maximum resale price or a recommended resale price leads to a more or less uniform application of that price level by the resellers, because they may use it as a focal point. They may find it difficult to deviate from what they perceive to be the preferred resale price proposed by such an important supplier on the market.

Where appreciable anti-competitive effects are established for maximum or recommended resale prices, the question of a possible exemption under Article 101(3) arises. For maximum resale prices, the efficiency described in paragraph (107)(f) (avoiding double marginalisation), may be particularly relevant. A maximum resale price may also help to ensure that the brand in question competes more forcefully with other brands, including own label products, distributed by the same distributor.

Questions on the EU Guidelines on Vertical Restraints

1. Why does the Commission, supported by the EU courts, deem resale price maintenance a hard-core restriction?

a. Can it be a tool to facilitate collusion between competing suppliers or to partition markets across national lines?

b. Does it restrict intrabrand competition, interbrand competition, or both?

2. Does resale price maintenance always restrict competition? Can't resale price maintenance be used to correct some market failures, like preventing the negative effects free-riding may create on investments in distribution facilities?

3. Should resale price maintenance be a concern when there is strong interbrand competition?

4. Is an agreement, which does not fall under a block exemption, automatically in breach of Article 101?

a. Can't it still be exempted under Article 101(3)?

b. Given that Article 101(3) allows a balancing of the pro-and anti-competitive effects of a given agreement, isn't it the ideal instrument to assess resale price maintenance?

5. Considering that Article 101(3) analysis may be a source of uncertainty, as the parties have to self-assess whether their agreement meets the conditions contained in that provision, won't the parties decide to rely on alternative instruments to correct market failures, such as free riding?

a. Are there alternatives to resale price maintenance to prevent other distributors from free riding on the pre-sales efforts of the distributor in question?

b. Won't the supplier reach the conclusion that, to escape the limitations imposed by Regulation 330/2010 on its freedom to opt for certain distribution strategies, it is better off integrating vertically?

c. What are the effects of vertical integration on intrabrand competition?

d. What are its effects, if any, on interbrand competition?

Case 243/83, SA Binon & Cie v. SA Agence et Messageries de la Presse

1985 E.C.R. 2015.

[SA Binon & Cie (Binon) brought an action in a Belgian court seeking an order directing SA Agence et Messageries de la Presse (AMP) to cease refusing to supply Binon the newspapers and periodicals that Binon wanted to retail in Belgium. AMP was a distributor that supplied Belgian retailers with virtually all foreign papers and periodicals and close to 70% of Belgian papers and periodicals. AMP and the newspaper and periodical publishers operated a selective distribution system[30] whereby every retail outlet was subject to the approval of a regional consultative committee. The President of the Commercial Court of Brussels submitted to the ECJ the question whether Article 101 was compatible with a provision within the framework of the selective distribution system whereby the distributor reserved the right to fix the prices retailers could charge.]

AMP contends ... that the prices of newspapers and periodicals are fixed by the publishers and not, as the national court seems to think, by the distribution agency. Observance by retailers of the prices fixed by publishers arises from the ... special characteristics of the distribution of newspapers and periodicals.

The government of the Federal Republic of Germany, which [submitted observations on this question] considers that the freedom of the press, as a fundamental right protected by the constitutional law of the Member States and by the Court's case-law, entails the freedom to contribute to the formation of public opinion. For that reason newspapers and periodicals as well as their distribution have special characteristics. The nature of newspapers and periodicals requires an extremely rapid system for their distribution in view of the very limited period during which they can be sold before they are out of date; at the end of that period, the length of which varies according to the specific publication in question, newspapers and periodicals have practically no value. To those factors must be added the heterogeneity of newspapers and periodicals and the lack of elasticity in demand since each newspaper or periodical has more or less its own body of customers.

The German government concludes that, from the point of view of competition, the position of the market in newspapers and periodicals is so special that it is not possible to apply to it without modification principles which have been developed in completely different contexts. If the possibility of fixing prices for newspapers and periodicals is not accepted any effective distribution system for such products would be incompatible with the rules on competition and the effect on the diversity and freedom of the press would be disastrous. From that point of view it is not unimportant to note that systems of fixed prices in relation to the distribution of newspapers and periodicals are accepted under the legislation of most Member States or are operated without encountering any difficulties....

It should be observed in the first place that provisions which fix the prices to be observed in contracts with third parties constitute, of themselves, a restriction on competition within the meaning of article [101(1)] which refers to agreements which fix selling prices as an example of an agreement prohibited by the Treaty.

---

30. Article 1(d) of Regulation 2790/1999 provides that " 'Selective distribution system' means a distribution system where the supplier undertakes to sell the contract goods or services, either directly or indirectly, only to distributors selected on the basis of specified criteria and where these distributors undertake not to sell such goods or services to unauthorised distributors".

In those circumstances, where an agreement which establishes a selective distribution system and which affects trade between Member States includes such a provision, an exemption from the prohibition contained in Article [101(1) TFEU] may only be granted by means of a decision adopted by the Commission in the conditions laid down by Article [101(3)].

If, in so far as the distribution of newspapers and periodicals is concerned, the fixing of the retail price by publishers constitutes the sole means of supporting the financial burden resulting from the taking back of unsold copies and if the latter practice constitutes the sole method by which a wide selection of newspapers and periodicals can be made available to readers, the Commission must take account of those factors when examining an agreement for the purposes of article [101(3)].

Consequently, the answer to the third question must be that the requirement, in the framework of a selective distribution system for newspapers and periodicals which affects trade between Member States, that fixed prices must be respected renders that system incompatible with Article 101(1) TFEU. However, the Commission may, in considering an application for exemption under Article [101(3)], examine whether, in a particular case, such an element of a distribution system may be justified.

Questions on *Binon*

1. Is the German government correct that resale price maintenance prohibitions should be less applicable to newspapers and magazines? Why?

a. Does the fact that newspapers are quickly perishable make special treatment appropriate? Isn't that also true of fresh fruits and vegetables?

b. Should high prices be maintained to allow newspapers and periodicals to survive? Would this be a legitimate reason to restrict competition?

2. The Court allows submission of the justification that "the fixing of the retail price by publishers constitutes the sole means of supporting the financial burden resulting from the taking back of unsold copies."

a. Why would this ever be the case? Aren't there less restrictive alternatives to address the burden of taking back unsold copies?

b. Couldn't it be argued that allowing retailers to lower the prices of newspapers by reducing their margin would in fact allow them to sell more newspapers and thus return fewer unsold copies?

Other Nations' Treatment of Vertical Minimum Price–Fixing

Many nations, including Australia, Indonesia, New Zealand, Saudi Arabia, South Africa, Taiwan, and Turkey, have per se rules against vertical minimum price-fixing.[19] Several other nations apply a rule of

---

19. Australia Trade Practices Act § 48; Indonesia Competition Law Art. 8; New Zealand Commerce Act § 37; Saudi Arabia Implementing Regulations Art. 6(2)(e); South Africa Competition Act § 5(2); Taiwan Fair Trade Law, Article 18; Turkey Competition Act, Art. 4(a) and Communiqué on Block Exemptions regarding Vertical Agreements (No.2002/2), Art. 4(a).

reason, including Brazil, Canada, China, Egypt, India, Mexico, Peru, and South Korea.[20] Japan law bans vertical minimum-price-fixing as an unfair trade practice if it "tends to impede fair competition" and lacks a "proper justification," unless it has been exempted by the Japan Fair Trade Commission.[21] Although this seems to state a rule of reason, JFTC guidelines and caselaw indicate more of a per se approach.[22] Which approach would you choose?

4. How to Characterize Agreements

a. ARE DUAL DISTRIBUTION AGREEMENTS VERTICAL OR HORIZONTAL?

Often a manufacturer chooses to use independent distributors in some locations, but to distribute on its own in other locations. This is generally called a dual distribution arrangement. For example, the *Leegin* manufacturer also operated at retail, but the Court declined to address whether this meant the agreement restraining retail prices should be deemed horizontal, rather than vertical. The same issue would be raised in *Sylvania*, if *Sylvania* operated its own retailer in Sacramento. Should its agreement restricting the locations of its retailers then be deemed vertical (because Sylvania supplies the retailer as a manufacturer) or horizontal (because Sylvania is a competing retailer)? As a practical matter, the issue has been most relevant for vertical nonprice restraints because there the distinction in legal treatment between vertical and horizontal agreements has existed the longest.

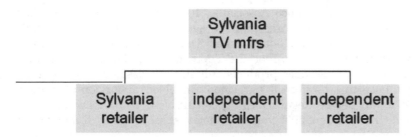

20. *See* Brazil Antitrust Law No. 8,884, Art.21(XI); Brazil CADE Resolution 20, Attachment I, § 1 (1999); Canada Competition Act § 76; China Anti–Monopoly Law Arts. 14(2) & 15; Egypt Competition Law, Art. 7; India Competition Act § 3(4)(e); Mexico Competition Law Arts. 10(II) & 11; Peru Competition Law, Art. 12(4). The South Korean Supreme Court recently departed from that nation's prior per se rule by allowing defendants to offer justifications, but it put the burden of proof on defendants. *See* Case No. 2009 Du 9543, Korean Supreme Court Judgment, November 25, 2010.

21. *See* Japan Antimonopoly Act §§ 2(9), 19; Japan Designations of Unfair Trade Practices § 12 (2009); MITSUO MATSUSHITA, THE ANTIMONOPOLY LAW OF JAPAN 191 (Institute for International Economics) (exemptions so far for pharmaceuticals and cosmetics).

22. Japan Distribution Guidelines 22–23 (1991); ABA, II COMPETITION LAWS OUTSIDE THE UNITED STATES at Japan–37 (2001).

The U.S. Supreme Court has not yet addressed this question post-*Sylvania*, and its pre-*Sylvania* decisions were in conflict on this issue.[23] Most circuit courts have held that dual distribution restraints on territories are categorically vertical and governed by ordinary rule-of-reason scrutiny.[24] But several circuit courts classify dual distribution restraints as vertical when they serve manufacturer interests, but horizontal when they serve retailer interests.[25] Which position is correct?

1.   Does the fact that the manufacturer rather than an independent retailer has one of the retail locations . . .

a.   make the restraint any less competitive? Any less justifiable?

b.   alter or attenuate the manufacturer's incentive to the minimize retail profit margin?

c.   increase or decrease the likelihood that the restraint was coerced by a dealer cartel or dealer market power?

2.   If an inquiry into whether the restraint is primarily in the interests of dealers or manufacturers makes sense in a dual distribution case, does it make equal sense in a purely vertical case?

a.   Can that inquiry be resolved by evidence of who initiated the restraint?

b.   If not, does it turn on whether the restraint primarily has anticompetitive effects on retail margins or procompetitive effects on distribution, in which case it just replicates the rule of reason inquiry?

c.   Or should the inquiry into whose interests are being served be interpreted as asking whether a procompetitive justification exists? Does a dual distribution situation at least indicate that abbreviated rule of reason review should apply if the defendant has no procompetitive justification?

3.   United States v. Topco Associates, 405 U.S. 596 (1972), concerned a case where various small stores that averaged a 6% market share in their regional markets created an entity called Topco to buy, transport, warehouse, and distribute goods under the Topco label to the member stores, which agreed to sell the Topco products only in their designated territories. The Court held this territorial agreement involved a horizontal market division that was per se illegal. Does *Topco* survive *Sylvania*? Didn't *Topco* also involve the creation of a vertical relationship? Does it differ from a

---

23.   *Compare* United States v. McKesson & Robbins, Inc., 351 U.S. 305, 312–13 (1956) (horizontal); Schwegmann Bros. v. Calvert Corp., 341 U.S. 384, 389 (1951) (same), *with* White Motor Co. v. United States, 372 U.S. 253, 261 (1963) (vertical); United States v. Arnold Schwinn & Co., 388 U.S. 365, 370, 372 (1967) (vertical).

24.   Electronics Communications v. Toshiba America, 129 F.3d 240, 243 (2d Cir. 1997); AT & T v. JMC Telecom, 470 F.3d 525, 531 (3d Cir. 2006); PSKS, Inc. v. Leegin Creative Leather Prods., Inc., 615 F.3d 412, 420–21 (5th Cir. 2010); International Logistics v. Chrysler, 884 F.2d 904, 906 (6th Cir. 1989); Illinois Corporate Travel v. American Airlines, 889 F.2d 751, 753 (7th Cir. 1989); Smalley & Co. v. Emerson & Cuming, 13 F.3d 366, 368 (10th Cir. 1993).

25.   Donald B. Rice Tire v. Michelin Tire, 638 F.2d 15, 16 (4th Cir. 1981); Hampton Audio Electronics v. Contel Cellular, 1992 WL 131169, at *3 (4th Cir. 1992); Ryko Manufacturing v. Eden Services, 823 F.2d 1215, 1231 (8th Cir. 1987); Krehl v. Baskin–Robbins, 664 F.2d 1348, 1356–57 (9th Cir. 1982); Midwestern Waffles v. Waffle House, 734 F.2d 705, 711, 720 (11th Cir. 1984).

dual distribution agreement in the likely incentives of the supplier? In whether it is likely to have interbrand effects?

4. Was *Palmer v. BRG* effectively just a dual distribution case since Harcourt Brace supplied materials for BRG to use in Georgia and used the materials itself outside of Georgia? Does it differ in likely incentives or probability of interbrand effects?

Commission Regulation (EU) No 330/2010 of 20 April 2010 on the Application of Article 101(3) of the Treaty on the Functioning of the European Union to Categories of Vertical Agreements and Concerted Practices

O.J. 2010, L 102/1.

Article 2. Exemption

1. Pursuant to Article 101(3) of the Treaty and subject to the provisions of this Regulation, it is hereby declared that Article 101(1) of the Treaty shall not apply to vertical agreements.

This exemption shall apply to the extent that such agreements contain vertical restraints.

2. The exemption provided for in paragraph 1 shall apply to vertical agreements entered into between an association of undertakings and its members, or between such an association and its suppliers, only if all its members are retailers of goods and if no individual member of the association, together with its connected undertakings, has a total annual turnover exceeding EUR 50 million. Vertical agreements entered into by such associations shall be covered by this Regulation without prejudice to the application of Article 101 of the Treaty to horizontal agreements concluded between the members of the association or decisions adopted by the association. . . .

4. The exemption provided for in paragraph 1 shall not apply to vertical agreements entered into between competing undertakings. However, it shall apply where competing undertakings enter into a non-reciprocal vertical agreement and:

(a) the supplier is a manufacturer and a distributor of goods, while the buyer is a distributor and not a competing undertaking at the manufacturing level; or

(b) the supplier is a provider of services at several levels of trade, while the buyer provides its goods or services at the retail level and is not a competing undertaking at the level of trade where it purchases the contract services.

5. This Regulation shall not apply to vertical agreements the subject matter of which falls within the scope of any other block exemption regulation, unless otherwise provided for in such a regulation.

EU Guidelines on Vertical Restraints

O.J. 2010, C 130/1.

Article 2(4) of the Block Exemption Regulation explicitly excludes "vertical agreements entered into between competing undertakings" from its application. Vertical agreements between competitors are dealt with, as regards possible collusion effects, in the Commission Guidelines on the applicability of Article 81 of the EC Treaty [now 101 TFEU] to horizontal cooperation agreements. However, the vertical aspects of such agreements need to be assessed under these Guidelines. Article 1(1)(c) of the Block Exemption Regulation defines a competing undertaking as "an actual or potential competitor". Two companies are treated as actual competitors if they are active on the same relevant market. A company is treated as a potential competitor of another company if, absent the agreement, in case of a small but permanent increase in relative prices it is likely that this first company, within a short period of time normally not longer than one year, would undertake the necessary additional investments or other necessary switching costs to enter the relevant market on which the other company is active. That assessment must be based on realistic grounds; the mere theoretical possibility of entering a market is not sufficient. A distributor that provides specifications to a manufacturer to produce particular goods under the distributor's brand name is not to be considered a manufacturer of such own-brand goods.

Article 2(4) of the Block Exemption Regulation contains two exceptions to the general exclusion of vertical agreements between competitors. These exceptions concern non-reciprocal agreements. Non-reciprocal agreements between competitors are covered by the Block Exemption Regulation where (a) the supplier is a manufacturer and distributor of goods, while the buyer is only a distributor and not also a competing undertaking at the manufacturing level, or (b) the supplier is a provider of services operating at several levels of trade, while the buyer operates at the retail level and is not a competing undertaking at the level of trade where it purchases the contract services. The first exception covers situations of dual distribution, that is, the manufacturer of particular goods also acts as a distributor of the goods in competition with independent distributors of its goods. In case of dual distribution it is considered that in general any potential impact on the competitive relationship between the manufacturer and retailer at the retail level is of lesser importance than the potential impact of the vertical supply agreement on competition in general at the manufacturing or retail level. The second exception covers similar situations of dual distribution, but in this case for services, when the supplier is also a provider of products at the retail level where the buyer operates.

b.   VERTICAL AGREEMENTS TO "BOYCOTT" THE RIVAL OF A DEALER WITHOUT ANY PROCOMPETITIVE JUSTIFICATION

NYNEX v. Discon

525 U.S. 128 (1998).

■ JUSTICE BREYER delivered the opinion of the Court.

In this case we ask whether the antitrust rule that group boycotts are illegal per se as set forth in *Klor's*, applies to a buyer's decision to buy from one seller rather than another, when that decision cannot be justified in terms of ordinary competitive objectives. We hold that the per se group boycott rule does not apply. . . .

This case involves the business of removing . . . obsolete telephone equipment . . .—a business called "removal services." Discon, Inc., the respondent, sold removal services used by New York Telephone . . . a subsidiary of NYNEX Corporation. NYNEX also owns Materiel Enterprises Company, a purchasing entity that bought removal services for New York Telephone. . . . [Discon] claims . . . that Materiel Enterprises had switched its purchases from Discon to Discon's competitor, AT & T Technologies, as part of an attempt to defraud local telephone service customers by hood-winking regulators. According to Discon, Materiel Enterprises would pay AT & T Technologies more than Discon would have charged for similar removal services. It did so because it could pass the higher prices on to New York Telephone, which in turn could pass those prices on to telephone consumers in the form of higher regulatory-agency-approved telephone service charges. At the end of the year, Materiel Enterprises would receive a special rebate from AT & T Technologies, which Materiel Enterprises would share with its parent, NYNEX. Discon added that it refused to participate in this fraudulent scheme, with the result that Materiel Enterprises would not buy from Discon, and Discon went out of business.

. . . The case before us involves *Klor's*. The Second Circuit did not forbid the defendants to introduce evidence of "justification." To the contrary, it invited the defendants to do so, for it said that the "per se rule" would apply only if no "pro-competitive justification" were to be found. Thus, the specific legal question before us is whether an antitrust court considering an agreement by a buyer to purchase goods or services from one supplier rather than another should (after examining the buyer's reasons or justifications) apply the per se rule if it finds no legitimate business reason for that purchasing decision. We conclude no boycott-related per se rule applies and that the plaintiff here must allege and prove harm, not just to a single competitor, but to the competitive process, i.e., to competition itself.

Our conclusion rests in large part upon precedent, for precedent limits the per se rule in the boycott context to cases involving horizontal agreements among direct competitors. . . . Although *Klor's* involved a threat made by a single powerful firm, it also involved a horizontal agreement among those threatened, namely, the appliance suppliers, to hurt a competitor of the retailer who made the threat. This Court emphasized in *Klor's* that the agreement at issue was

"not a case of a single trader refusing to deal with another, nor even of a manufacturer and a dealer agreeing to an exclusive distributorship. Alleged in this complaint is a wide combination consisting of manufacturers, distributors and a retailer." *Klor's*.

This Court subsequently pointed out specifically that *Klor's* was a case involving not simply a "vertical" agreement between supplier and customer, but a case that also involved a "horizontal" agreement among competitors. See *Business Electronics*. And in doing so, the Court held that a "vertical restraint is not illegal per se unless it includes some agreement on price or price levels." This precedent makes the per se rule inapplicable, for the case before us concerns only a vertical agreement and a vertical restraint, a restraint that takes the form of depriving a supplier of a potential customer.

Nor have we found any special feature of this case that could distinguish it from the precedent we have just discussed. We concede Discon's claim that the petitioners' behavior hurt consumers by raising telephone service rates. But that consumer injury naturally flowed not so much from a less competitive market for removal services, as from the exercise of market power that is lawfully in the hands of a monopolist, namely, New York Telephone, combined with a deception worked upon the regulatory agency that prevented the agency from controlling New York Telephone's exercise of its monopoly power.

To apply the per se rule here—where the buyer's decision, though not made for competitive reasons, composes part of a regulatory fraud—would transform cases involving business behavior that is improper for various reasons, say, cases involving nepotism or personal pique, into treble-damages antitrust cases. And that per se rule would discourage firms from changing suppliers—even where the competitive process itself does not suffer harm.

The freedom to switch suppliers lies close to the heart of the competitive process that the antitrust laws seek to encourage. At the same time, other laws, for example, "unfair competition" laws, business tort laws, or regulatory laws, provide remedies for various "competitive practices thought to be offensive to proper standards of business morality." Thus, this Court has refused to apply per se reasoning in cases involving that kind of activity.

Discon points to another special feature of its complaint, namely, its claim that Materiel Enterprises hoped to drive Discon from the market lest Discon reveal its behavior to New York Telephone or to the relevant regulatory agency. That hope, says Discon, amounts to a special anticompetitive motive.

We do not see how the presence of this special motive, however, could make a significant difference. That motive does not turn Materiel Enterprises' actions into a "boycott" within the meaning of this Court's precedents. Nor, for that matter, do we understand how Discon believes the motive affected Materiel Enterprises' behavior. Why would Discon's demise have made Discon's employees less likely, rather than more likely, to report the overcharge/rebate scheme to telephone regulators? Regardless, a per se rule that would turn upon a showing that a defendant not only knew about but also hoped for a firm's demise would create a legal distinction—between corporate knowledge and corporate motive—that does not necessarily correspond to behavioral differences and which would be difficult to prove, making the resolution of already complex antitrust cases yet more difficult. We cannot find a convincing reason why the presence of this special motive should lead to the application of the per se rule.

Finally, we shall consider an argument that is related tangentially to Discon's per se claims. The complaint alleges that New York Telephone (through Materiel Enterprises) was the largest buyer of removal services in New York State, and that only AT & T Technologies competed for New York Telephone's business. One might ask whether these accompanying allegations are sufficient to warrant application of a *Klor's*-type presumption of consequent harm to the competitive process itself.

We believe that these allegations do not do so, for, as we have said, antitrust law does not permit the application of the per se rule in the boycott context in the absence of a horizontal agreement. (Though in other contexts, say, vertical price fixing, conduct may fall within the scope of a per se rule not at issue here.) The complaint itself explains why any such presumption would be particularly inappropriate here, for it suggests the presence of other potential or actual competitors, which fact, in the circumstances, could argue against the likelihood of anticompetitive harm. The complaint says, for example, that New York Telephone itself was a potential competitor in that New York Telephone considered removing its equipment by itself, and in fact did perform a few jobs itself. The complaint also suggests that other nearby small local telephone companies needing removal services must have worked out some way to supply them. The complaint's description of the removal business suggests that entry was easy, perhaps to the point where other firms, employing workers who knew how to remove a switch and sell it for scrap, might have entered that business almost at will. To that extent, the complaint suggests other actual or potential competitors might have provided roughly similar checks upon "equipment removal" prices and services with or without Discon. At the least, the complaint provides no sound basis for assuming the contrary. Its simple allegation of harm to Discon does not automatically show injury to competition. . . .

Questions on *NYNEX v. Discon*

1. Why should this vertical boycott be treated any differently than the horizontal boycott organized by a dealer in *Klor's*, where the court held that any proof of harm to competition was unnecessary?

a. Do the overdeterrence or underdeterrence concerns differ? Which sort of agreements not to deal with others are more avoidable and less likely to have procompetitive purposes and require antitrust review of ubiquitous business conduct?

b. How does rule of reason review help with overdeterrence or underdeterrence problems?

2. Why shouldn't this alleged vertical agreement be illegal under the rule of reason?

a. Why doesn't the complaint indicate a naked restraint given the alleged absence of any procompetitive justification? What problems might be created if such an allegation sufficed to trigger inquiry into the merit of justifications before addressing whether anticompetitive effects were likely?

b. Why isn't a requisite anticompetitive effect alleged by the allegations that consumers were harmed? Were those consumers hurt by the creation of market power or by the deception of regulators? Is the latter a concern of competition law?

3. Does this ruling mean that *no* vertical agreement can ever constitute a boycott or a naked restraint? Suppose a seller pays a buyer not to buy from a rival but never sells to that buyer itself. Can that be condemned without proof of anticompetitive effect? Does condemning that sort of agreement without proof of anticompetitive effects raise fewer overdeterrence concerns and more underdeterrence concerns? What could a seller in such a case possibly gain unless harming its rival has anticompetitive effects in the seller's market?

C.   PRICE DISCRIMINATION THAT ARGUABLY DISTORTS DOWNSTREAM COMPETITION

Primary-line price discrimination involves cases where the concern is that the lower price is targeted at customers of the seller's rivals and will discipline the rivals or drive them out of the market. Such cases were addressed in Chapter 3. Secondary-line price discrimination instead involves cases where the concern is that the businesses that buy at the higher price will be at a competitive disadvantage, thus distorting competition on the downstream market where those businesses compete. Secondary-line price discrimination thus differs from what one might call "pure" price discrimination against consumers, which is designed to maximize the seller's profits but cannot impede competition among buyers because consumers do not compete on any market that is further downstream. Tertiary-line price discrimination raises the same concern as secondary-line price discrimination one level further downstream; that customers of favored buyers might have an unfair competitive advantage over customers of disfavored buyers.

Prohibitions on the above forms of price discrimination do not prevent sellers from charging different prices to different types of ultimate consumers, such as the movie theater that charges different prices for adults and children, because those consumers do not compete in a downstream market. Of course, different retailers might have different sets of customers, so that a supplier might want to achieve such consumer price discrimination by charging different prices to retailers with different sets of customers. But prohibitions on primary, secondary, or tertiary price discrimination are unlikely to impede such price discrimination because they require a showing that the buyers charged different prices compete downstream in the same market, which suggests they are reselling to the same set of consumers. However, EU law may restrict consumer price discrimination when a firm is dominant. See Chapter 3.

Robinson–Patman Act § 2, 15 U.S.C. § 13[26]

(a) Price; selection of customers. It shall be unlawful for any person . . . either directly or indirectly, to discriminate in price between different purchasers of commodities of like grade and quality . . . where the effect of such discrimination may be substantially to lessen competition or tend to create a monopoly in any line of commerce, or to injure, destroy, or prevent competition with any person who either grants or knowingly receives the benefit of such discrimination, or with customers of either of them: *Provided,* That nothing herein contained shall prevent differentials which make only due allowance for differences in the cost of manufacture, sale, or delivery resulting from the differing methods or quantities in which such commodities are to such purchasers sold or delivered: *Provided, however,* That the Federal Trade Commission may fix and establish quantity limits, and revise the same as it finds necessary, as to particular commodities or classes of commodities, where it finds that available purchasers in greater quantities are so few as to render differentials on account thereof unjustly discriminatory or promotive of monopoly in any line of commerce; and the foregoing shall then not be construed to permit differentials based on differences in quantities greater than those so fixed and established: *And provided further,* That nothing herein contained shall prevent persons engaged in selling goods, wares, or merchandise in commerce from selecting their own customers in bona fide transactions and not in restraint of trade: *And provided further,* That nothing herein contained shall prevent price changes from time to time where in response to changing conditions affecting the market for or the marketability of the goods concerned, such as but not limited to actual or imminent deterioration of perishable goods, obsolescence of seasonal goods, distress sales under court process, or sales in good faith in discontinuance of business in the goods concerned.

(b) Burden of rebutting prima-facie case of discrimination. Upon proof being made . . . that there has been discrimination in price or services or facilities furnished, the burden of rebutting the prima-facie case thus made by showing justification shall be upon the person charged with a violation of this section, and unless justification shall be affirmatively shown, the Commission is authorized to issue an order terminating the discrimination: *Provided, however,* That nothing herein contained shall prevent a seller rebutting the prima-facie case thus made by showing that his lower price or the furnishing of services or facilities to any purchaser or purchasers was made in good faith to meet an equally low price of a competitor, or the services or facilities furnished by a competitor.

FTC v. Morton Salt Co.

334 U.S. 37 (1948).

■ Mr. Justice Black delivered the opinion of the Court. . . .

[The Court of Appeals set aside an FTC decision finding that Respondent had violated the Robinson–Patman Act.] . . . Respondent sells its

---

26. The Robinson–Patman Act was a 1936 amendment of former Clayton Act § 2, which had previously prohibited anticompetitive price discrimination but exempted price differences based on quantity and arguably had an narrower definition of the requisite anticompetitive effects.

finest brand of table salt, known as Blue Label, on what it terms a standard quantity discount system available to all customers. Under this system the purchasers pay a delivered price and the cost to both wholesale and retail purchasers of this brand differs according to the quantities bought. These prices are as follows, after making allowance for rebates and discounts:

	Per case
Less-than-carload purchases	$1.60
Carload purchases	1.50
5,000-case purchases in any consecutive 12 months	1.40
50,000-case purchases in any consecutive 12 months	1.35

Only five companies have ever bought sufficient quantities of respondent's salt to obtain the $1.35 per case price. These companies could buy in such quantities because they operate large chains of retail stores in various parts of the country. As a result of this low price these five companies have been able to sell Blue Label salt at retail cheaper than wholesale purchasers from respondent could reasonably sell the same brand of salt to independently operated retail stores, many of whom competed with the local outlets of the five chain stores ...

First. Respondent's basic contention ... is that its "standard quantity discounts, available to all on equal terms, as contrasted for example, to hidden or special rebates, allowances, prices or discounts, are not discriminatory, within the meaning of the Robinson–Patman Act." Theoretically, these discounts are equally available to all, but functionally they are not. For as the record indicates ... no single independent retail grocery store, and probably no single wholesaler, bought as many as 50,000 cases or as much as $50,000 worth of table salt in one year. Furthermore, the record shows that, while certain purchasers were enjoying one or more of respondent's standard quantity discounts, some of their competitors made purchases in such small quantities that they could not qualify for any of respondent's discounts, even those based on carload shipments. The legislative history of the Robinson–Patman Act makes it abundantly clear that Congress considered it to be an evil that a large buyer could secure a competitive advantage over a small buyer solely because of the large buyer's quantity purchasing ability. The Robinson–Patman Act was passed to deprive a large buyer of such advantages except to the extent that a lower price could be justified by reason of a seller's diminished costs due to quantity manufacture, delivery or sale, or by reason of the seller's good faith effort to meet a competitor's equally low price.

Section 2 of the original Clayton Act had included a proviso that nothing contained in it should prevent "discrimination in price * * * on account of differences in the grade, quality, or quantity of the commodity sold, or that makes only due allowance for difference in the cost of selling or transportation * * *." That section has been construed as permitting quantity discounts, such as those here, without regard to the amount of the seller's actual savings in cost attributable to quantity sales or quantity deliveries. The House Committee Report on the Robinson–Patman Act considered that the Clayton Act's proviso allowing quantity discounts so weakened § 2 "as to render it inadequate, if not almost a nullity." The Committee considered the present Robinson–Patman amendment to § 2 "of great importance." Its purpose was to limit "the use of quantity price differentials to the sphere of actual cost differences. Otherwise," the report continued, "such differentials would become instruments of favor and privilege and weapons of competitive oppression." The Senate Committee reporting the bill emphasized the same purpose, as did the Congressman in charge of the Conference Report when explaining it to the House just before final passage. And it was in furtherance of this avowed purpose—to protect competition from all price differentials except those based in full on cost savings—that § 2(a) of the amendment provided "That nothing herein contained shall prevent differentials which make only due allowance for differences in the cost of manufacture, sale, or delivery resulting from the differing methods or quantities in which such commodities are to such purchasers sold or delivered."

The foregoing references, without regard to others which could be mentioned, establish that respondent's standard quantity discounts are discriminatory within the meaning of the Act, and are prohibited by it whenever they have the defined effect on competition.

Second. [The respondent had the burden of proving that cost savings justified its quantity discount differentials.] First, the general rule of statutory construction that the burden of proving justification or exemption under a special exception to the prohibitions of a statute generally rests on one who claims its benefits, requires that respondent undertake this proof under the proviso of § 2(a). Secondly, § 2(b) of the Act specifically imposes the burden of showing justification upon one who is shown to have discriminated in prices. And the Senate committee report on the bill explained that the provisos of § 2(a) throw "upon any who claims the benefit of those exceptions the burden of showing that their case falls within them." We think that the language of the Act, and the legislative history just cited, show that Congress meant by using the words "discrimination in price" in § 2 that in a case involving competitive injury between a seller's customers the Commission need only prove that a seller had charged one purchaser a higher price for like goods than he had charged one or more of the purchaser's competitors....

Third. . . . [T]he statute does not require the Commission to find that injury has actually resulted. The statute requires no more than that the effect of the prohibited price discriminations "may be substantially to lessen competition . . . or to injure, destroy, or prevent competition." After a careful consideration of this provision of the Robinson–Patman Act, we have said that "the statute does not require that the discriminations must in fact have harmed competition, but only that there is a reasonable possibility that they 'may' have such an effect." Corn Products v. FTC, 324 U.S. 726, 742.[14] Here the Commission found what would appear to be

---

14. This language is to be read also in the light of the following statement in the same case. ". . . But as was held in the *Standard Fashion* case, with respect to the like provisions of § 3 of the Clayton Act . . . the use of the word 'may' was not to prohibit discriminations

obvious, that the competitive opportunities of certain merchants were injured when they had to pay respondent substantially more for their goods than their competitors had to pay. The findings are adequate.

Fourth. It is urged that the evidence is inadequate to support the Commission's findings of injury to competition. As we have pointed out, however, the Commission is authorized by the Act to bar discriminatory prices upon the "reasonable possibility" that different prices for like goods to competing purchasers may have the defined effect on competition. That respondent's quantity discounts did result in price differentials between competing purchasers sufficient in amount to influence their resale price of salt was shown by evidence. This showing in itself is adequate to support the Commission's appropriate findings that the effect of such price discriminations "may be substantially to lessen competition . . . and to injure, destroy and prevent competition." . . .

It is also argued that respondent's less-than-carload sales are very small in comparison with the total volume of its business and for that reason we should reject the Commission's finding that the effect of the carload discrimination may substantially lessen competition and may injure competition between purchasers who are granted and those who are denied this discriminatory discount. To support this argument, reference is made to the fact that salt is a small item in most wholesale and retail businesses and in consumers' budgets. For several reasons we cannot accept this contention.

There are many articles in a grocery store that, considered separately, are comparatively small parts of a merchant's stock. Congress intended to protect a merchant from competitive injury attributable to discriminatory prices on any or all goods sold in interstate commerce, whether the particular goods constituted a major or minor portion of his stock. Since a grocery store consists of many comparatively small articles, there is no possible way effectively to protect a grocer from discriminatory prices except by applying the prohibitions of the Act to each individual article in the store.

Furthermore, in enacting the Robinson–Patman Act Congress was especially concerned with protecting small businesses which were unable to buy in quantities, such as the merchants here who purchased in less-than-carload lots. To this end it undertook to strengthen this very phase of the old Clayton Act. The committee reports on the Robinson–Patman Act emphasized a belief that § 2 of the Clayton Act had "been too restrictive in requiring a showing of general injury to competitive conditions. . . ." The new provision, here controlling, was intended to justify a finding of injury to competition by a showing of "injury to the competitor victimized by the discrimination."[18] Since there was evidence sufficient to show that the less-

---

having 'the mere possibility' of those consequences, but to reach those which would probably have the defined effect on competition."

324 U.S. at page 738. The Committee Reports and Congressional debate on this provision of the Robinson–Patman Act indicate that it was intended to have a broader scope than the corresponding provision of the old Clayton Act. *See* note 18 *infra.*

18. In explaining this clause of the proposed Robinson–Patman Act, the Senate Judiciary Committee said:

than-carload purchasers might have been handicapped in competing with the more favored carload purchasers by the differential in price established by respondent, the Commission was justified in finding that competition might have thereby been substantially lessened or have been injured within the meaning of the Act.

Apprehension is expressed in this Court that enforcement of the Commission's order against respondent's continued violations of the Robinson–Patman Act might lead respondent to raise table salt prices to its carload purchasers. Such a conceivable, though, we think, highly improbable contingency, could afford us no reason for upsetting the Commission's findings and declining to direct compliance with a statute passed by Congress.

... It would greatly handicap effective enforcement of the Act to require testimony to show that which we believe to be self-evident, namely, that there is a "reasonable possibility" that competition may be adversely affected by a practice under which manufacturers and producers sell their goods to some customers substantially cheaper than they sell like goods to the competitors of these customers. This showing in itself is sufficient to justify our conclusion that the Commission's findings of injury to competition were adequately supported by evidence....

The judgment of the Circuit Court of Appeals is reversed ...

Questions on *Morton Salt*

1. Should a quantity discount that is available to all buyers who buy that quantity be deemed price discrimination? Does the statutory language or legislative history dictate such an interpretation?

2. Although the Court is certainly right that the statute puts the burden of proving cost justifications on a firm that has engaged in price discrimination, does that necessarily indicate the defendant should have the burden of proof on whether it has engaged in price discrimination at all by giving a quantity discount that is equally available to all buyers?

3. Does Morton Salt have any incentive to diminish competition among its wholesalers and retailers? Any incentive to harm smaller ones?

a. Was there any evidence Morton Salt had foreclosed enough of the downstream market to impair rival efficiency?

b. Any evidence that the individual wholesalers and retailers buying larger quantities bought enough to give them buyer market power?

c. Given the above, why would Morton Salt give a quantity discount unless it were cost justified? Should this suffice to merit a presumption that

---

"This clause ... tends to exclude from the bill otherwise harmless violations of its letter, but accomplishes a substantial broadening of a similar clause now contained in section 2 of the Clayton Act. The latter has in practice been too restrictive, in requiring a showing of general injury to competitive conditions in the line of commerce concerned; whereas the more immediately important concern is in injury to the competitor victimized by the discrimination. Only through such injuries, in fact, can the larger general injury result, and to catch the weed in the seed will keep it from coming to flower." S.Rep. No.1502, 74th Cong., 2d Sess. 4. See also H.Rep.No.2287, 74th Cong., 2d Sess. 8; 80 Cong.Rec. 9417.

the quantity discount was cost justified, and thus to shift the burden of proof on that question back to the plaintiff?

4. Does this decision effectively invalidate all quantity discounts that cannot be proven to be cost justified? All such quantity discounts that larger buyers get but some competing buyers are too small to get?

5. Given the language quoted in footnote 14, did *Corn Products* really dictate the adoption of a "reasonable possibility" test of harm rather than a "probable" test?

6. Doesn't the Court effectively read the last element out of the statute with its conclusion that the existence of substantial price differences itself suffices to infer the element of a reasonable likelihood of anticompetitive effects?

7. Does this decision require proof of injury to competition, or to individual competitors?

a. Does the statutory language support or require the latter reading? Should the legislative history be read to support or require it even if the text doesn't?

b. If the legislative purpose were simply to protect small businesses that couldn't buy in big quantities, then why does the statute allow a cost justification defense? Given that a manufacturer in a competitive market would only be offering the quantity discount if it were cost justified, doesn't the Court's interpretation effectively protect small businesses only in cases where a cost justification exists but can't be proven?

8. Was there much proof of a reasonable likelihood of injury to individual competitors given the evidence that salt was a small share of their costs? Was the Court right to rule that such an injury was established by evidence of "price differentials between competing purchasers sufficient in amount to influence their resale price of salt"?

9. If price discrimination is a concern, is there any reason to limit that concern to price discrimination about commodities, as the Robinson–Patman Act does?

Texaco v. Hasbrouck

496 U.S. 543 (1990).

■ JUSTICE STEVENS delivered the opinion of the Court.

Petitioner (Texaco) sold gasoline directly to respondents and several other retailers in Spokane, Washington, at its retail tank wagon prices (RTW) while it granted substantial discounts to two distributors. [The two distributors, Gull and Dompier, acted both as wholesalers, reselling some gas to independent stations, and as retailers, selling some gas in their own stations. Neither maintained any significant storage facilities and Dompier was reimbursed for hauling the gas to its stations.] ... [T]he stations supplied by the two distributors increased their sales volume dramatically, while respondents' sales suffered a corresponding decline. Respondents filed an action against Texaco ... alleging that the distributor discounts violated § 2(a) of the [Robinson–Patman] Act. Respondents recovered treble damages, and the Court of Appeals for the Ninth Circuit affirmed the judgment. We granted certiorari to consider Texaco's contention that legitimate functional discounts do not violate the Act because a seller is not responsible for its customers' independent resale pricing decisions. While we agree with the basic thrust of Texaco's argument, we conclude that in this case it is foreclosed by the facts of record. . . .

It is appropriate to begin our consideration of the legal status of functional discounts[11] by examining the language of the Act. . . . The Act contains no express reference to functional discounts. It does contain two affirmative defenses that provide protection for two categories of discounts—those that are justified by savings in the seller's cost of manufacture, delivery or sale, and those that represent a good faith response to the equally low prices of a competitor. As the case comes to us, neither of those defenses is available to Texaco.

In order to establish a violation of the Act, respondents had the burden of proving four facts: (1) that Texaco's sales to Gull and Dompier were made in interstate commerce; (2) that the gasoline sold to them was of the same grade and quality as that sold to respondents; (3) that Texaco discriminated in price as between Gull and Dompier on the one hand and respondents on the other; and (4) that the discrimination had a prohibited effect on competition. Moreover, for each respondent to recover damages, he had the burden of proving the extent of his actual injuries. J. Truett Payne Co. v. Chrysler Motors Corp., 451 U.S. 557 (1981).

The first two elements of respondents' case are not disputed in this Court,[14] and we do not understand Texaco to be challenging the sufficiency of respondents' proof of damages. Texaco does argue, however, that although it charged different prices, it did not "discriminate in price" within the meaning of the Act, and that, at least to the extent that Gull and Dompier acted as wholesalers, the price differentials did not injure competition. We consider the two arguments separately.

Texaco's first argument would create a blanket exemption for all functional discounts. Indeed carried to its logical conclusion, it would exempt all price differentials except those given to competing purchasers. . . . Although [some legislative history] does support Texaco's argument, we remain persuaded that the argument is foreclosed by the text of the Act itself. In the context of a statute that plainly reveals a concern with competitive consequences at different levels of distribution, and carefully defines specific affirmative defenses, it would be anomalous to assume that the Congress intended the term "discriminate" to have such a limited meaning. . . . The reasons we gave for our decision in *Anheuser–Busch* apply here as well. . . .

---

11. . . . "A functional discount is one given to a purchaser based on its role in the supplier's distributive system, reflecting, at least in a generalized sense, the services performed by the purchaser for the supplier."

14. Texaco has not contested here the proposition that branded gas and unbranded gas are of like grade and quality. See FTC v. Borden Co., 383 U.S. 637, 645–646 (1966) ("the economic factors inherent in brand names and national advertising should not be considered in the jurisdictional inquiry under the statutory 'like grade and quality' test").

"the statute itself spells out the conditions which make a price difference illegal or legal, and we would derange this integrated statutory scheme were we to read other conditions into the law by means of the nondirective phrase, 'discriminate in price.' Not only would such action be contrary to what we conceive to be the meaning of the statute, but, perhaps because of this, it would be thoroughly undesirable. As one commentator has succinctly put it, 'Inevitably every legal controversy over any price difference would shift from the detailed governing provisions—"injury," ' cost justification, 'meeting competition,' etc.—over into the 'discrimination' concept of ad hoc resolution divorced from specifically pertinent statutory text."

Since we have already decided that a price discrimination within the meaning of § 2(a) "is merely a price difference," we must reject Texaco's first argument. . . .

In *Morton Salt*, we held that a injury to competition may be inferred from evidence that some purchasers had to pay their supplier "substantially more for their goods than their competitors had to pay." *See also* Falls City Industries, Inc. v. Vanco Beverage, Inc., 460 U.S. 428, 435–436 (1983). Texaco, supported by the United States and the Federal Trade Commission as amici curiae, (the Government), argues that this presumption should not apply to differences between prices charged to wholesalers and these charged to retailers. Moreover, they argue that it would be inconsistent with fundamental antitrust policies to construe the Act as requiring a seller to control his customers' resale prices. The seller should not be held liable for the independent pricing decisions of his customers. As the Government correctly notes, this argument endorses the position advocated 35 years ago in the Report of the Attorney General's National Committee to Study the Antitrust Laws (1955).

After observing that suppliers ought not to be held liable for the independent pricing decisions of their buyers,[16] and that without functional discounts distributors might go uncompensated for services they performed,[17] the Committee wrote:

"The Committee recommends, therefore, that suppliers granting functional discounts either to single-function or to integrated

---

16. "In the Committee's view, imposing on any dual supplier a legal responsibility for the resale policies and prices of his independent distributors contradicts basic antitrust policies. Resale-price fixing is incompatible with the tenets of a free and competitive economy. . . . And even short of such arrangements, a conscious adherence in a supplier's sales to retail customers to the price quotations by independent competing distributors is hardly feasible as a matter of business operation, or safe as a matter of law."

17. "In our view, to relate discounts or prices solely to the purchaser's resale activities without recognition of his buying functions thwarts competition and efficiency in marketing. It compels affirmative discrimination against a substantial class of distributors, and hence serves as a penalty on integration. If a businessman actually fulfills the wholesale function by relieving his suppliers of risk, storage, transportation, administration, etc., his performance, his capital investment, and the saving to his suppliers, are unaffected by whether he also performs the retailing function, or any number of other functions. A legal rule disqualifying him from discounts recognizing wholesaling functions actually performed compels him to render these functions free of charge."

buyers should not be held responsible for any consequences of their customers' pricing tactics. Price cutting at the resale level is not in fact, and should not be held in law, "the effect of" a differential that merely accords due recognition and reimbursement for actual marketing functions. The price cutting of a customer who receives this type of differential results from his own independent decision to lower price and operate at a lower profit margin per unit. The legality or illegality of this price cutting must be judged by the usual legal tests. In any event, consequent injury or lack of injury should not be the supplier's legal concern.

"On the other hand, the law should tolerate no subterfuge. For instance, where a wholesaler-retailer buys only part of his goods as a wholesaler, he must not claim a functional discount on all. Only to the extent that a buyer actually performs certain functions, assuming all the risk, investment, and costs involved, should he legally qualify for a functional discount. Hence a distributor should be eligible for a discount corresponding to any part of the function he actually performs on that part of the goods for which he performs it."

We generally agree with this description of the legal status of functional discounts. A supplier need not satisfy the rigorous requirements of the cost justification defense in order to prove that a particular functional discount is reasonable and accordingly did not cause any substantial lessening of competition between a wholesaler's customers and the supplier's direct customers.[18] The record in this case, however, adequately supports the finding that Texaco violated the Act.

The hypothetical predicate for the Committee's entire discussion of functional discounts is a price differential "that merely accords due recog-

---

18. In theory, a supplier could try to defend a functional discount by invoking the Act's cost justification defense, but the burden of proof with respect to the defense is upon the supplier, and interposing the defense "has proven difficult, expensive, and often unsuccessful." 3 E. Kintner & J. Bauer, Federal Antitrust Law, § 23.19, pp. 366–367 (1983). Moreover, to establish the defense a "seller must show that the price reductions given did not exceed the actual cost savings," id., § 23.10, p. 345, and this requirement of exactitude is ill-suited to the defense of discounts set by reference to legitimate, but less precisely measured, market factors.

Discounters will therefore likely find it more useful to defend against claims under the Act by negating the causation element in the case against them: a legitimate functional discount will not cause any substantial lessening of competition. The concept of substantiality permits the causation inquiry to accommodate a notion of economic reasonableness with respect to the pass-through effects of functional discounts, and so provides a latitude denied by the cost-justification defense. We thus find ourselves in substantial agreement with the view that:

"Conceived as a vehicle for allowing differential pricing to reward distributive efficiencies among customers operating at the same level, the cost justification defense focuses on narrowly defined savings to the seller derived from the different method or quantities in which goods are sold or delivered to different buyers.... Moreover, the burden of proof as to the cost justification defense is on the seller charged with violating the Act, whereas the burden of proof remains with the enforcement agency or plaintiff in circumstances involving functional discounts since functional pricing negates the probability of competitive injury, an element of a prima facie case of violation."

Rill, Availability and Functional Discounts Justifying Discriminatory Pricing, 53 Antitrust L. J. 929, 935 (1985).

nition and reimbursement for actual marketing functions." Such a discount is not illegal. In this case, however, ... there was no substantial evidence indicating that the discounts to Gull and Dompier constituted a reasonable reimbursement for the value to Texaco of their actual marketing functions. Indeed, Dompier was separately compensated for its hauling function, and neither Gull and Dompier maintained any significant storage facilities. ...

As we have already observed, the "due recognition and reimbursement" concept endorsed in the Attorney General's Committee's study would not countenance a functional discount completely untethered to either the supplier's savings or the wholesaler's costs. The longstanding principle that functional discounts provide no safe harbor from the Act is likewise evident from the practice of the Federal Trade Commission, which has, while permitting legitimate functional discounts, proceeded against those discounts which appeared to be subterfuges to avoid the Act's restrictions....[21]....

Both Gull and Dompier received the full discount on all their purchases even though most of their volume was resold directly to consumers. The extra margin on those sales obviously enabled them to price aggressively in both their retail and their wholesale marketing. To the extent that Dompier and Gull competed with respondents in the retail market, the presumption of adverse effect on competition recognized in the *Morton Salt* case becomes all the more appropriate. Their competitive advantage in that market also constitutes evidence tending to rebut any presumption of legality that would otherwise apply to their wholesale sales.

The evidence indicates, moreover, that Texaco affirmatively encouraged Dompier to expand its retail business and that Texaco was fully informed about the persistent and marketwide consequences of its own pricing policies. Indeed, its own executives recognized that the dramatic impact on the market was almost entirely attributable to the magnitude of the distributor discount and the hauling allowance. Yet at the same time that Texaco was encouraging Dompier to integrate downward, and supplying Dompier with a generous discount useful to such integration, Texaco was inhibiting upward integration by the respondents: two of the respondents sought permission from Texaco to haul their own fuel using their own tankwagons, but Texaco refused. The special facts of this case thus

---

21. See also In re Mueller Co., 60 F.T.C. 120, 127–128 (1962) (refusing to make allowance for functional discounts in any way that would "add a defense to a prima facie violation of Section 2(a) which is not included in either Section 2(a) or Section 2(b)"). The FTC in *Mueller* expressly disavowed dicta from Doubleday and Co., 52 F.T.C. 169 (1955) suggesting that functional discounts are per se legal if justified by the buyer's costs. *Mueller* held that the discounts were controlled instead by the reasoning propounded in In re General Foods Corp., 52 F.T.C. 798 (1956), which refers to the value of the services to the supplier giving the discount.

We need not address the relative merits of *Mueller* and *Doubleday* in order to resolve the case before us. We do, however, reject the requirement of exactitude which might be inferred from *Doubleday's* dictum that a functional discount offered to a buyer "should not exceed the cost of that part of the function he actually performs on that part of the goods for which he performs it." As already noted, a causation defense in a functional discount case does not demand the rigorous accounting associated with a cost justification defense.

make it peculiarly difficult for Texaco to claim that it is being held liable for the independent pricing decisions of Gull or Dompier. . . .

Such indirect competitive effects surely may not be presumed automatically in every functional discount setting, and, indeed, one would expect that most functional discounts will be legitimate discounts which do not cause harm to competition. At the least, a functional discount that constitutes a reasonable reimbursement for the purchasers' actual marketing functions will not violate the Act. When a functional discount is legitimate, the inference of injury to competition recognized in the Morton Salt case will simply not arise. Yet it is also true that not every functional discount is entitled to a judgment of legitimacy, and that it will sometimes be possible to produce evidence showing that a particular functional discount caused a price discrimination of the sort the Act prohibits. When such anti-competitive effects are proved—as we believe they were in this case—they are covered by the Act.[30] . . .

The judgment is affirmed.

■ Justice White, concurring in the result. . . . [T]he Court not only declares that a price differential that merely accords due recognition and reimbursement for actual marketing functions does not trigger the presumption of an injury to competition, but also announces that "[s]uch a discount is not illegal." There is nothing in the Act to suggest such a defense . . .

■ Justice Scalia, with whom Justice Kennedy joins, concurring in the judgment. . . . [P]etitioner argues at length that even if petitioner's discounts to Gull and Dompier cannot be shown to be cost based they should be exempted, because the "functional discount" is an efficient and legitimate commercial practice that is ordinarily cost based, though it is all but impossible to establish cost justification in a particular case. The short answer to this argument is that it should be addressed to Congress.

The Court does not, however, provide that response, but accepts this last argument in somewhat modified form. . . . Relying on a mass of extratextual materials, the Court concludes that the Act permits such "reasonable" functional discounts even if the supplier cannot satisfy the "rigorous requirements of the cost justification defense." I find this conclusion quite puzzling. The language of the Act is straightforward: Any price discrimination whose effect "may be substantially . . . to injure, destroy, or prevent competition" is prohibited, unless it is immunized by the "cost justification" defense, i.e., unless it "make[s] only due allowance for differences in the cost of manufacture, sale, or delivery resulting from the differing methods or quantities in which [the] commodities are . . . sold or delivered." 15 U.S.C. § 13(a). There is no exception for "reasonable" functional discounts that do not meet this requirement. Indeed, I am at a loss to understand what *makes* a functional discount "reasonable" *unless* it meets this requirement. It does not have to meet it penny for penny, of course: The "rigorous requirements of the cost justification defense" to which the Court refers, are not the rigors of mathematical precision, but

---

30. The parties do not raise, and we therefore need not address, the question whether the inference of injury to competition might also be negated by evidence that disfavored buyers could make purchases at a reasonable discount from favored buyers.

the rigors of *proof* that the amount of the discount and the amount of the cost saving are close enough that the difference cannot produce any *substantial* lessening of competition. How is one to determine that a functional discount is "reasonable" except by proving (through the normally, alas, "rigorous" means) that it meets this test? Shall we use a nationwide average?

I suppose a functional discount can be "reasonable" (in the relevant sense of being unlikely to subvert the purposes of the Act) if it is not commensurate with the supplier's costs *saved* (as the cost justification defense requires), but is commensurate with the wholesaler's costs *incurred* in performing services for the supplier. Such a discount would not produce the proscribed effect upon competition, since if it constitutes only reimbursement for the wholesaler one would not expect him to pass it on. The relevant measure of the discount in order to determine "reasonableness" on that basis, however, is not the measure the Court applies to Texaco ("value to [the supplier] of [the distributor's] actual marketing functions"), but rather "cost to the distributor of the distributor's actual marketing functions"—which is of course not necessarily the same thing. I am therefore quite unable to understand what the Court has in mind by its "reasonable" functional discount that is not cost justified.

To my mind, there is one plausible argument for the proposition that a functional basis for differential pricing *ipso facto*—cost justification or not—negates the probability of competitive injury, thus destroying an element of the plaintiff's prima facie case: In a market that is really functionally divided, retailers are in competition with one another, not with wholesalers. That competition among retailers cannot be injured by the supplier's giving lower prices to wholesalers—because if the price differential is passed on, all retailers will simply purchase from wholesalers instead of from the supplier. Or, to put it differently, when the market is functionally divided all competing retailers have the opportunity of obtaining the same price from wholesalers, and the supplier's functional price discrimination alone does not cause any injury to competition. Therefore (the argument goes), if functional division of the market is established, it should be up to the complaining retailer to show that some special factor (*e.g.*, an agreement between the supplier and the wholesaler that the latter will not sell to the former's retailer-customers) prevents this normal market mechanism from operating. As the Court notes, this argument was not raised by the parties here or below, and it calls forth a number of issues that would benefit from briefing and factual development. I agree that we should not decide the merit of this argument in the first instance.

Questions on *Texaco v. Hasbrouck*

1. Should charging different prices to wholesalers than to retailers ever count as price discrimination? Always count as price discrimination? What is the answer under this case?

2. If charging different prices to wholesalers than to retailers is price discrimination, what criteria should be used to determine when it is illegal?

a. Why does the Court adopt a reasonable relation to reimbursement for marketing services test? Is part of the reason that firms often have mixed wholesale-retail functions?

b. Why shouldn't the test just be whether the price difference is cost justified under the statute?

    i. Is the problem that the statutory test is just based on whether the price difference is justified by a difference in the *supplier*'s costs, rather than by a difference in the costs or value of wholesaling versus retailing? If the supplier could supply retailers at the same cost as it supplies wholesalers, why would it ever deal with wholesalers?

    ii. Is the difference that the Court is allowing the cost difference to be established more loosely than it normally needs to be established to prove a cost-justification?

        (a) Is that reading consistent with the statutory text? Would it have been more consistent to say a difference loosely justified by different functions is not really a discriminatory price at all?

        (b) Just how much looser is the proof under the Court's test?

        (c) How easy do you suppose it is to prove the cost-savings associated with using a wholesaler? Can courts accurately allocate costs across products and determine marginal cost with changing market conditions?

        (d) Would strictly requiring that every discount be cost justified discourage price discounts that come close to the actual cost savings, given the fear that a court might mistakenly find the discount exceeded the cost difference? Is discouraging this sort of discounting procompetitive or anticompetitive?

c. If a supplier does sell to wholesalers at a lower price but one that reflects the value or cost of their services, then are the retailers supplied by those wholesalers likely to do any better than the retailers supplied directly? Wouldn't any injury be the result of those wholesalers' greater efficiency?

3. Would a better doctrine provide that, unless something prevents the favored wholesaler from reselling to certain retailers, then any injury to those retailers results in their inability to compete for the business of that wholesaler rather than any pricing decision of the supplier?

4. Does Texaco have any anticompetitive incentive to favor Dompier and Gull over other distributors? Doesn't Texaco have incentives to offer the latter greater discounts only when those discounts are functionally justified?

5. Footnote 14 cites the *Borden* rule that a branded and unbranded product are "of like grade and quality" if they are physically the same. Do you agree with this rule? Does it ignore the economic reality that brand names can have as much impact on consumer willingness to pay as physical features?

Volvo Trucks N.A. v. Reeder–Simco GMC

546 U.S. 164 (2006).

■ Justice Ginsburg delivered the opinion of the Court.

This case concerns specially ordered products—heavy-duty trucks supplied by Volvo . . . and sold by franchised dealers through a competitive bidding process. In this process, the retail customer states its specifications and invites bids, generally from dealers franchised by different manufacturers. Only when a Volvo dealer's bid proves successful does the dealer arrange to purchase the trucks, which Volvo then builds to meet the customer's specifications.

Reeder . . ., a Volvo dealer located in Fort Smith, Arkansas, commenced suit against Volvo alleging that Reeder's sales and profits declined because Volvo offered other dealers more favorable price concessions than those offered to Reeder. Reeder sought redress for its alleged losses under . . . the . . . Robinson–Patman Act . . . Reeder prevailed at trial and on appeal . . .

We granted review on the federal claim to resolve the question whether a manufacturer offering its dealers different wholesale prices may be held liable for price discrimination proscribed by Robinson–Patman, absent a showing that the manufacturer discriminated between dealers contemporaneously competing to resell to the same retail customer. . . . [T]he Robinson–Patman Act, we hold, does not reach the case Reeder presents. The Act centrally addresses price discrimination in cases involving competition between different purchasers for resale of the purchased product. Competition of that character ordinarily is not involved when a product subject to special order is sold through a customer-specific competitive bidding process.

I

. . . It is common practice in the industry for manufacturers to offer customer-specific discounts to their dealers. Volvo decides on a case-by-case basis whether to offer a discount and, if so, what the discount rate will be, taking account of such factors as industry-wide demand and whether the retail customer has, historically, purchased a different brand of trucks. The dealer then uses the discount offered by Volvo in preparing its bid; it purchases trucks from Volvo only if and when the retail customer accepts its bid.

Reeder was one of many Volvo dealers, each assigned by Volvo to a geographic territory. Reeder's territory encompassed ten counties in Arkansas and two in Oklahoma. Although nothing prohibits a Volvo dealer from bidding outside its territory, Reeder rarely bid against another Volvo dealer. In the atypical event that the same retail customer solicited a bid from more than one Volvo dealer, Volvo's stated policy was to provide the same price concession to each dealer competing head to head for the same sale . . . .

Reeder dominantly relied on comparisons between concessions Volvo offered when Reeder bid against non-Volvo dealers, with concessions accorded to other Volvo dealers similarly bidding against non-Volvo dealers for other sales. Reeder's evidence compared concessions Reeder received on four occasions when it bid successfully against non-Volvo dealers (and thus purchased Volvo trucks), with more favorable concessions other successful Volvo dealers received in connection with bidding processes in which Reeder did not participate. Reeder also compared concessions offered by Volvo on several occasions when Reeder bid unsuccessfully against non-Volvo dealers (and therefore did not purchase Volvo trucks), with more favorable concessions received by other Volvo dealers who gained contracts on which Reeder did not bid.

Reeder's vice-president, Heck, testified that Reeder did not look for instances in which it received a *larger* concession than another Volvo dealer, although he acknowledged it was "quite possible" that such instances occurred. Nor did Reeder endeavor to determine by any statistical analysis whether Reeder was disfavored on average as compared to another dealer or set of dealers. . . .

II . . .

To establish the secondary-line injury of which it complains, Reeder had to show that (1) the relevant Volvo truck sales were made in interstate commerce; (2) the trucks were of "like grade and quality"; (3) Volvo "discriminate[d] in price between" Reeder and another purchaser of Volvo trucks; and (4) "the effect of such discrimination may be . . . to injure, destroy, or prevent competition" to the advantage of a favored purchaser, *i.e.,* one who "receive[d] the benefit of such discrimination." 15 U.S.C. § 13(a). It is undisputed that Reeder has satisfied the first and second requirements. Volvo and the United States, as *amicus curiae,* maintain that Reeder cannot satisfy the third and fourth requirements, because Reeder has not identified any differentially-priced transaction in which it was both a "purchaser" under the Act and "in actual competition" with a favored purchaser for the same customer.

A hallmark of the requisite competitive injury, our decisions indicate, is the diversion of sales or profits from a disfavored purchaser to a favored purchaser. We have also recognized that a permissible inference of competitive injury may arise from evidence that a favored competitor received a significant price reduction over a substantial period of time. See *Morton Salt; Falls City Industries,* 460 U.S. at 435. Absent actual competition with a favored Volvo dealer, however, Reeder cannot establish the competitive injury required under the Act.

III

The evidence Reeder offered at trial falls into three categories: (1) comparisons of concessions Reeder received for four successful bids against *non-Volvo* dealers, with larger concessions other successful Volvo dealers received for *different sales* on which Reeder did not bid (purchase-to-purchase comparisons); (2) comparisons of concessions offered to Reeder in connection with several unsuccessful bids against *non-Volvo* dealers, with greater concessions accorded other Volvo dealers who competed successfully for *different sales* on which Reeder did not bid (offer-to-purchase comparisons); and (3) evidence of two occasions on which Reeder bid against another Volvo dealer (head-to-head comparisons). The Court of Appeals concluded that Reeder demonstrated competitive injury under the Act because Reeder competed with favored purchasers "at the same functional level . . . and within the same geographic market." As we see it, however, selective comparisons of the kind Reeder presented do not show the injury to competition targeted by the Robinson–Patman Act. . . .

Both the purchase-to-purchase and the offer-to-purchase comparisons fall short, for in none of the discrete instances on which Reeder relied did Reeder compete with beneficiaries of the alleged discrimination *for the same customer*. Nor did Reeder even attempt to show that the compared dealers were consistently favored vis-à-vis Reeder. Reeder simply paired occasions on which it competed with *non-Volvo* dealers for a sale to Customer A with instances in which other Volvo dealers competed with *non-Volvo* dealers for a sale to Customer B. The compared incidents were tied to no systematic study and were separated in time by as many as seven months.

We decline to permit an inference of competitive injury from evidence of such a mix-and-match, manipulable quality. No similar risk of manipulation occurs in cases kin to the chain-store paradigm. Here, there is no discrete "favored" dealer comparable to a chain store or a large independent department store—at least, Reeder's evidence is insufficient to support an inference of such a dealer or set of dealers. For all we know, Reeder, on occasion, might have gotten a better deal vis-à-vis one or more of the dealers in its comparisons.

Reeder may have competed with other Volvo dealers for the opportunity to bid on potential sales in a broad geographic area. At that initial stage, however, competition is not affected by differential pricing; a dealer in the competitive bidding process here at issue approaches Volvo for a price concession only after it has been selected by a retail customer to submit a bid. Competition for an opportunity to bid . . . is based on a variety of factors, including the existence *vel non* of a relationship between the potential bidder and the customer, geography, and reputation.[3] . . . That Volvo dealers may bid for sales in the same geographic area does not import that they in fact competed for the same customer-tailored sales. In sum, the purchase-to-purchase and offer-to-purchase comparisons fail to show that Volvo sold at a lower price to Reeder's "competitors," hence those comparisons do not support an inference of competitive injury. . . .

Reeder did offer evidence of two instances in which it competed head to head with another Volvo dealer. When multiple dealers bid for the business of the *same* customer, only one dealer will win the business and thereafter purchase the supplier's product to fulfill its contractual commitment. Because Robinson–Patman "prohibits only discrimination 'between different *purchasers*,'" Volvo and the United States argue, the Act does not reach markets characterized by competitive bidding and special-order sales, as opposed to sales from inventory. We need not decide that question today.

---

3. A dealer's reputation for securing favorable concessions, we recognize, may influence the customer's bidding invitations. We do not pursue that point here, however, because Reeder did not present-or even look for-evidence that Volvo consistently disfavored Reeder while it consistently favored certain other dealers.

Assuming the Act applies to the head-to-head transactions, Reeder did not establish that it was *disfavored* vis-à-vis other Volvo dealers in the rare instances in which they competed for the same sale—let alone that the alleged discrimination was substantial. See 1 ABA Section of Antitrust Law, Antitrust Law Developments 478–479 (5th ed. 2002) ("No inference of injury to competition is permitted when the discrimination is not substantial." (collecting cases)).

Reeder's evidence showed loss of only one sale to another Volvo dealer, a sale of 12 trucks that would have generated $30,000 in gross profits for Reeder. Per its policy, Volvo initially offered Reeder and the other dealer the same concession. Volvo ultimately granted a larger concession to the other dealer, but only after it had won the bid. In the only other instance of head-to-head competition Reeder identified, Volvo increased Reeder's initial 17% discount to 18.9%, to match the discount offered to the other competing Volvo dealer; neither dealer won the bid. In short, if price discrimination between two purchasers existed at all, it was not of such magnitude as to affect substantially competition between Reeder and the "favored" Volvo dealer.

IV

Interbrand competition, our opinions affirm, is the "primary concern of antitrust law." *GTE Sylvania.* The Robinson–Patman Act signals no large departure from that main concern. Even if the Act's text could be construed in the manner urged by Reeder and embraced by the Court of Appeals, we would resist interpretation geared more to the protection of existing *competitors* than to the stimulation of *competition.* In the case before us, there is no evidence that any favored purchaser possesses market power, the allegedly favored purchasers are dealers with little resemblance to large independent department stores or chain operations, and the supplier's selective price discounting fosters competition among suppliers of different brands. By declining to extend Robinson–Patman's governance to such cases, we continue to construe the Act "consistently with broader policies of the antitrust laws." *Brooke Group*; see *Automatic Canteen Co. of America v. FTC,* 346 U.S. 61, 63 (1953) (cautioning against Robinson–Patman constructions that "extend beyond the prohibitions of the Act and, in doing so, help give rise to a price uniformity and rigidity in open conflict with the purposes of other antitrust legislation").

[T]he judgment of the Court of Appeals for the Eighth Circuit is reversed . . .

■ Justice Stevens, with whom Justice Thomas joins, dissenting. . . . For decades, juries have routinely inferred the requisite injury to competition under the Robinson–Patman Act from the fact that a manufacturer sells goods to one retailer at a higher price than to its competitors. This rule dates back to . . . *Morton Salt* . . . We have treated as competitors those who sell "in a single, interstate retail market." *Falls City* Under this approach—uncontroversial until today—Reeder would readily prevail. There is ample evidence that Volvo charged Reeder higher prices than it charged to competing dealers in the same market over a period of many months. . . .

Volvo nonetheless argues that no competitive injury could have occurred because it never discriminated against Reeder when Reeder and another Volvo dealer were seeking concessions with regard to the same ultimate customer. In Volvo's view, each transaction was a separate market, one defined by the customer and those dealers whom it had asked for bids. For each specific customer who has solicited bids, Reeder's only "competitors" were the other dealers making bids. Accordingly, if none of these other dealers were Volvo dealers, then Reeder suffered no competitive harm (relative to other Volvo dealers) when Volvo gave it a discriminatorily high price.

... Nothing in the statute or in our precedent suggests that "competition" is evaluated by a transaction-specific inquiry, and such an approach makes little sense. It requires us to ignore the fact that competition among truck dealers is a continuing war waged over time rather than a series of wholly discrete events. Each time Reeder managed to resell trucks it had purchased at discriminatorily high prices, it was forced either to accept lower profit margins than were available to favored Volvo dealers or to pass on the higher costs to its customers (who then might well go to a different dealer the next time). And we have long indicated that lost profits relative to a competitor are a proper basis for permitting the *Morton Salt* inference. . . .

The Court appears to hold that, absent head-to-head bidding with a favored dealer, a dealer in a competitive bidding market can suffer no competitive injury.[4] It is unclear whether that holding is limited to franchised dealers who do not maintain inventories, or excludes virtually all franchisees from the effective protection of the Act. In either event, it is not faithful to the statutory text. . . .

Questions on *Volvo*

1. The Court stressed that the Robinson–Patman Act covers secondary-line price discrimination only between purchasing dealers who compete in the same downstream market.

a. Do you agree with the Court that in the case of competitive bidding for specialty customer orders, each customer order is ordinarily a separate market, so that purchasing dealers are not in downstream competition unless they are both bidding for the same customer's order?

b. Should it instead suffice, as the dissent opined, that the purchasing dealers generally competed in the same geographic market for sales even though they were not charged different prices when they were both competing for the same customer orders?

---

4. Indeed, if Volvo's argument about the meaning of "purchaser" ultimately meets with this Court's approval, then the Robinson–Patman Act will simply not apply in the special-order context. Any time a special-order dealer fails to complete a transaction because the high price drives away its ultimate customer, there will be no Robinson–Patman violation because the dealer will not meet the "purchaser" requirement, and any time the dealer completes the transaction but at a discriminatorily high price, there will be no violation because the dealer has no "competition" (as the majority sees it) for that specific transaction at the moment of purchase.

c. Does this case suggest that *Texaco v. Hasbrouck* could have been resolved on the simple ground that the Robinson–Patman Act does not cover discrimination between wholesalers and retailers because they do not compete for the same customers? Or does it suffice that a disfavored retailer has difficulty competing with rival retailers who are supplied by a favored wholesaler that cannot or will not supply the disfavored retailer?

2. Suppose that whenever they are not bidding for the same customer, Volvo offers other purchasing dealers Volvos at lower prices than Reeder. Won't Reeder tend to make worse bids than other Volvo dealers with the result that:

a. customers are less likely to invite future bids from Reeder than other Volvo dealers? Did the plaintiff establish this was true? Did the Court leave open the possibility such a claim might be valid? See footnote 3.

b. Reeder will lose more customers to non-Volvo dealers, with the result that Reeder does less well in the market generally?

3. Suppose Reeder and another Volvo dealer are bidding for the same customer order, and Volvo offers the other Volvo dealer a lower price.

a. Won't this still fail to satisfy the Court's test because only one of the dealers will win the bid and purchase the Volvo trucks for resale, so that Volvo's conduct cannot constitute price discrimination between different "purchasers" under the Act?

b. If so, won't the effective result be that selling to dealers who engage in competitive bidding for specialty orders can *never* be subject to the Robinson–Patman Act?

    i. If so, is that a bad thing? Why would we want Robinson–Patman Act rules extended to such cases? Why not limit it to cases of price discrimination among dealers who resell from inventory?

    ii. Should the Act be changed to cover discriminatory *offers*? If it were, isn't the problem that, with the market defined as one customer order, any single discriminatory offer that causes one dealer to win would necessarily eliminate all competition in that market?

c. Did Reeder actually show any discriminatory offers in cases where it and another dealer were bidding for the same customer?

4. If there were some covered price discrimination, the Court seems to require evidence that the price discrimination (a) systematically disfavored the plaintiff and (b) occurred in a substantial number of cases.

a. Do these requirements seem sensible? Which of the elements of a Robinson–Patman Act case are they necessary to prove: the existence of price discrimination or the impact on competition?

b. Given that these requirements were not met, was there any need to reach the other issues in this case?

5. The Court states in the end that it interprets the Robinson–Patman Act according to the general antitrust principle of protecting interbrand competition rather than intrabrand competition and individual competitors.

a. But doesn't its interpretation protect Reeder *only* against intra-brand competition with other Volvo dealers and not at all against discriminatory prices that hurt Reeder's ability to engage in interbrand competition with non-Volvo dealers?

b. Couldn't all the complications in this case have been avoided if the Act were interpreted to require proof of a probable effect on "competition" on the broader geographic market rather than inferring such an effect from substantial price discrimination involving one dealer on the market? Although this would require overruling *Morton Salt*, wouldn't such an interpretation adhere better to the statutory text, which requires separate proof of price discrimination and a probable effect on competition? Is the Court hinting it might be ready to engage in such an overruling?

Other Robinson–Patman Act Provisions

The Robinson–Patman Act also contains a variety of other provisions designed to prevent sellers from evading the basic restriction on unjustified commodity price discrimination by paying brokerage or commission fees for nonexistent services, § 2(c), or giving discriminatory access to allowances or services, § 2(d)–(e). These clauses go beyond the basic restriction in that they require no proof of effects nor permit the defense of cost-justification. § 2(c) also allows no defense of meeting competition, and may not even require discrimination. Finally, § 2(f) makes a buyer liable if it knowingly induces or receives a prohibited price discrimination. All these are codified at 15 U.S.C. § 13(c)–(f). In addition, although rarely enforced, Robinson–Patman Act § 3 does impose criminal penalties for knowing price discrimination with an anticompetitive purpose. *See* 15 U.S.C. § 13a.

Damien Geradin and Nicolas Petit, *Price Discrimination under EC Law: The Need for a Case-by-Case Approach*

2 JOURNAL OF COMPETITION LAW AND ECONOMICS 479 (2006).

Article [102(c)] considers the fact for one or several firms holding a dominant position of "applying dissimilar conditions to equivalent transactions with other trading parties, thereby placing them at a competitive disadvantage" an abuse of a dominant position. As noted above, the ECJ also considers as an abuse the application of similar conditions to unequal transactions. The ECJ case-law indicates that "dissimilar conditions" also include "dissimilar prices". Price discrimination thus clearly falls within the scope of Article [102(c)].

The language of this provision triggers the following remarks. First, among the conditions which need to be met for applying Article [102(c)] is a requirement that the measure under investigation applies dissimilar prices to "equivalent transactions". The evaluation of the equivalence of two transactions is not an easy matter as there are a myriad of factors that can be invoked to justify the lack of equivalence between two transactions. The most obvious reason for stating that two transactions are not equivalent is that the sales involve different costs for the seller. The problem is of course to determine how significant cost differences should be for two transactions to be considered non-equivalent. Indeed, if all cost differences, however small, were to be taken into consideration very few transactions should be considered as equivalent. It could also be argued that differences regarding the moment at which sales are made render two transactions non-equivalent. For many products or services (airline tickets, package holidays, etc.), the moment at which a sale is made has a major impact on the price imposed by the sellers. When the cost of providing the product or service in question does not differ depending on the time of sale, it is subject to question whether a time of sale difference could justify a finding that two transactions are not equivalent. Finally, there is some uncertainty as to whether differences relating to the situation of the buyers can be taken into consideration when assessing the equivalence or lack of equivalence of two transactions. For instance, applying prices inversely related to the elasticity of buyers is a strategy frequently used by firms to expand output. But when the cost of supplying consumers sorted on the basis of their elasticity does not differ, it is not clear whether differences in elasticity of demand can render transactions non equivalent under the terms of Article [102(c)]. Unfortunately, the decisional practice of the Commission and the case-law of the Community courts fail to provide any clear guidance on the above issues. In fact, the Commission and the courts generally assume that two transactions are equivalent without much analysis.

The application of Article [102(c)] also requires that dissimilarly treated equivalent transactions should place some of the dominant firm's trading parties at a competitive disadvantage against others. This condition clearly indicates that Article [102(c)] essentially seeks to prevent "secondary line" injury. Scholarly discussions regarding price discrimination often draw a distinction between "primary line" injury, which is occasioned by the dominant firm to its competitors by applying different prices to its own customers, and "secondary line" injury, which is imposed on one of several customers of the dominant firm as against one or several other customers. The reference to the placing of the dominant firm's "trading parties at a competitive disadvantage" clearly indicates that the parties Article [102(c)] seeks to protect are the customers of the dominant player and not its competitors. Literally all legal scholars seem to agree on this point. The need for a competitive disadvantage to occur also suggests that for Article [102(c)] to apply, the dominant firm's customers should be in competition with each other. This requirement makes the finding of a discriminatory abuse dependent on the finding a downstream market on which these firms compete.

The Commission and the Community courts have largely ignored the above condition with the result that they have applied Article [102(c)] to dominant firms' pricing practices, which have little to do with putting their trading parties at a competitive disadvantage. For instance, Article [102(c)] has been applied to pricing practices, such as fidelity rebates or selective price cuts, which were allegedly designed to harm the dominant firms' competitors. These practices are classic examples of primary line discrimination which should not be covered by Article [102(c)]. As pointed out by several authors, they should instead be treated under Article [102(c)], which is the proper legal basis for dominant firms' practices which produce exclusionary effects. Similarly, Article [102(c)] has been used to condemn practices which essentially sought to partition markets along national lines. Here again, such practices have little to do with the secondary line injury scenarios which Article [102(c)] is designed to prevent. . . .

Under certain circumstances, there is an incentive for firms to discriminate between their customers. This might be, for instance, the case for firms facing fixed-costs recovery problems or producing a range of differentiated products, firms engaging in product versioning, deriving costs savings from discriminating, etc. However, Article [102(c)] deals with price discrimination placing trading partners at a competitive disadvantage. The question thus turns on whether rational non vertically-integrated operators have an incentive to price discriminate so as to place one of their trading parties at a competitive disadvantage. This is unlikely to be the case for several reasons. First, upstream firms benefit from a competitive downstream market for distributing their goods. The possibility to grant a competitive price advantage to a distributor may certainly, in the short run, give the latter a strong incentive to distribute the goods efficiently. But in the long run, the insulation of the distributor from competitive pressures may affect its efficiency in distributing the product. Second, an upstream firm granting a competitive price advantage to a purchaser may send a risky signal to the market. Purchasers will be reluctant to order products from the seller in the future, if they face the risk of being discriminated against subsequently. Third, the grant of a competitive advantage may lead to the exclusion of the discriminated purchasers and in turn to increased concentration on the purchasing market. This would increase the countervailing buying power of the seller's downstream distributors and accordingly limits its own market power.

This is not to say, however, that no situation of secondary line injury price discrimination may arise. A first scenario could, for instance, take place in a situation (close to the one envisioned in the Robinson Patman Act) where a supplier facing two different kinds of customers according to their purchasing power (e.g., large supermarkets and small retail outlets), would discriminate in favour of the former and, as a result, give them a competitive advantage. This would distort downstream competition as the powerful buyer would end up paying a sub-competitive price on its purchases whereas rival buyers would pay a supra-competitive price for their purchases. In addition, both sub-competitive and supra-competitive prices would lead to lower output than the competitive price. Indeed, the sub-competitive prices will lower output by making sellers less willing to produce for the powerful buyer; the supra-competitive prices will lower output by making rival buyers less willing to purchase the products or services covered. The question whether, as a matter of policy, competition rules should be solicited to sanction the seller for price discrimination calls a negative answer. Indeed, it would be nonsensical as, in a situation of this kind, it is the purchaser, not the seller, that exploits its market power to place its competitors at a competitive disadvantage. The appropriate target for enforcement authorities should thus not be the price discriminator, but the firm benefiting from the price discrimination. So far, Commission and the Community courts have rightly refrained from using Article102(c) in such settings.

A second scenario where the upstream firm could have an incentive to grant a competitive advantage to a purchaser could appear where the downstream market is composed of purchasers forming a dominant oligopoly that tacitly colludes both upstream (so as to be charged uniform subcompetitive prices for the input) and downstream (charging supra-competitive prices to customers). In this situation, the upstream firm could have an interest in granting a competitive advantage to one of the oligopolists. A reduction of the input price to one of the oligopolists would indeed likely trigger a deviation from the collusive equilibrium downstream and hence induce the necessity for all operators to increase output at the retail level. As output would rise, the orders addressed to the seller would increase. In these cases, again, sanctioning the secondary line price discrimination would be nonsensical, but for different reasons. The price discrimination would most likely result in a rise of output at the retail level and thus enhance consumer welfare by reintroducing price competition downstream.

The two latter scenarios are, however, only likely to occur in very specific circumstances. Thus, it can be safely considered that non vertically-integrated firms would price discriminate to grant a competitive advantage to some buyers at the expense of others only in limited circumstances.

British Airways PLC v. Commission

17 December 2003, Case T-219/99.

Subparagraph (c) of the second paragraph of Article [102 TFEU] provides that abuse of a dominant position may consist in applying dissimilar conditions to equivalent transactions with other trading parties, thereby placing them at a competitive disadvantage.

It is undisputed that ... attainment by United Kingdom travel agents of their BA tickets sales growth targets led to an increase in the rate of commission paid to them by BA not only on BA tickets sold after the target was reached but also on all BA tickets handled by the agents during the reference period in question. To that extent, the performance reward schemes at issue could result in different rates of commission being applied to an identical amount of revenue generated by the sale of BA tickets by two travel agents, since their respective sales figures, and hence their rates of growth, would have been different during the previous reference period. By remunerating at different levels services that were nevertheless identical and supplied during the same reference period, those performance reward schemes distorted the level of remuneration which the parties concerned received in the form of commissions paid by BA.

As BA has stated itself, United Kingdom travel agents compete intensely with each other, and this ability to compete depends on their ability to provide seats on flights suited to travellers' wishes, at a reasonable cost. Being dependent on the financial resources of each agent, that ability of agents to compete in supplying air travel agency services to travellers and to stimulate the demand of airlines for such services was naturally affected by the discriminatory conditions of remuneration inherent in BA's performance reward schemes.

BA's arguments based on the importance of the size of the travel agents established in the United Kingdom are irrelevant. The performance reward schemes in dispute were, in themselves, based on a parameter unrelated to the criterion of the size of the undertakings, since they were based on the extent to which travel agents increased their sales of BA tickets in relation to the threshold constituted by the number of BA tickets sold during the previous reference period.

In those circumstances, the Commission was right to hold that BA's performance reward schemes constituted an abuse of BA's dominant position on the United Kingdom market for air travel agency services, in that they produced discriminatory effects within the network of travel agents established in the United Kingdom, thereby inflicting on some of them a competitive disadvantage within the meaning of subparagraph (c) of the second paragraph of Article [102 TFEU]. . . .

Questions on *British Airways*

1.   Why did BA discriminate between travel agents?

a.   Don't all volume or growth-based rebate schemes necessary discriminate between distributors, thereby placing some of them at a "competitive disadvantage"?

b.   Does this case thus mean that all such rebates violate Article 102(c)? If not, how can we distinguish between volume or growth-based rebates that are compatible with Article 102(c) and those that are incompatible?

c.   If discrimination between distributors is an issue, do quantity rebates fare any better than fidelity rebates? While quantity rebates probably give a commercial advantage to large distributors because they typically buy large quantities, fidelity rebates place large and small distributors on an equal footing, since what matters to get a rebate is not the volume of quantity purchased but the percentage of a distributor's requirement purchased from the dominant firm.

2.   In light of the above, should the fact that rebates introduce discrimination between customers be a factor in the competition analysis or should that analysis only focus on the risks that such rebates generate foreclosure effects? In other words, once a foreclosure effect has been identified, should discrimination within the meaning of Article 102(c) be examined as a separate violation of competition law?

3.   Placed in a US context, would BA's rebate scheme violate the Robinson–Patman Act? More generally, would such a scheme be a violation of U.S. antitrust law?

Other Nations' Treatment of Price Discrimination

Some nations have quite broad prohibitions of price discrimination. Indonesia bans any firm from using contracts that price discriminate.[27]

---

27.   Indonesia Competition Law Art. 6.

Japan deems "unjustly discriminating against other business entities" in a way that "tends to impede fair competition" to be an unfair trade practice.[28] India bans price discrimination by a dominant firm unless necessary to meet competition.[29] Israel bans price discrimination by a monopolist that gives some buyers an "unfair" competitive advantage over others.[30] Venezuela makes price discrimination by a dominant firm illegal if it gives some buyers a competitive disadvantage.[31] Egypt prohibits a dominant firm from price discriminating between similar transactors.[32] Turkey makes price discrimination among buyers with equal status illegal if the seller is dominant or if it has the purpose or likely effect of restricting competition.[33]

Other nations have much more narrow rules about when price discrimination is unlawful. Canada recently replaced its prior per se ban on price discrimination with a more flexible rule that requires evidence of "likely substantial anti-competitive effect."[34] South Africa and Singapore prohibit price discrimination only when the seller has dominant market power, substantial anticompetitive effects are likely, and the price difference cannot be explained by cost differences, changing market conditions, or good faith efforts to meet competition.[35] Mexico bans price discrimination by a firm with market power among "different purchasers situated in equality of conditions" (thus perhaps implicitly allowing the same defenses) if any anticompetitive effects are not offset by procompetitive efficiencies.[36] China similarly prohibits a dominant firm from discriminating among "trading parties with equal standing without any justifiable cause."[37] Russia bans price discrimination by a dominant firm that creates a competitive disadvantage unless it has procompetitive justifications.[38] Brazil bans price discrimination when it has the purpose or capacity to injure competition or increase supracompetitive profits, which regulations clarify is the case when it is used to exclude rivals (in ways similar to predatory pricing, price squeezes, or loyalty or bundled discounts) or when it otherwise harms consumer welfare.[39] Peru prohibits a dominant firm from price discriminating among equivalent transactions without justification if it creates a competitive disadvantage, unless the price discrimination reflects common

---

28. *See* Japan Antimonopoly Law § 2(9).

29. India Competition Act § 4(2)(a)(ii).

30. Israel Restrictive Trade Practices Law § 29A(b)(3).

31. Venezuela Procompetition Act, Art. 13(4).

32. Egypt Competition Law, Art. 8(e).

33. Turkey Competition Act, Arts. 4(e) & 6(b).

34. Canada Competition Bureau, A Guide to Amendments to the Competition Act 2 (2009).

35. *See, e.g.,* South Africa Competition Act § 9; Singapore Guidelines on the Section 47 Prohibition §§ 11.14 to 11.17 (2007).

36. *See* Mexico Competition Law Arts. 10–11.

37. China Anti–Monopoly Law Art. 17(6).

38. Russia Competition Law Arts. 4(8), 10(1)(8), 13(1).

39. *See* Brazil Antitrust Law No. 8,884, Arts. 20, 21(XII); Brazil CADE Resolution 20, Attachment I, § 6 (1999).

commercial practices like discounts for volume or advance payment.[40] Taiwan bans price discrimination when it lacks justification and is likely to lessen competition.[41]

In 1995, Australia repealed its price discrimination provision altogether.[42] Should other nations follow suit? If not, should all nations at least narrow their price discrimination laws in ways similar to those of the nations in the preceding paragraph?

---

40. Peru Competition Law, Art. 10.2(b).

41. Taiwan Fair Trade Act Art. 19.

42. *See* Australia Competition Policy Reform Act 1995.

CHAPTER 6

PROVING AN AGREEMENT OR CONCERTED ACTION

Sherman Act § 1 and Article 101 TFEU both condemn anticompetitive agreements or concerted action even when firms do not have the monopoly or dominant market power necessary to trigger Sherman Act § 2 or Article 102 TFEU. This chapter addresses the standards for proving such an agreement or concerted action. We first address the foundational issue of how to determine whether the defendants are separate entities capable of having an agreement or instead a single actor whose unilateral conduct can generally be challenged only under the more demanding standards of Sherman Act § 2 or Article 102. We then address standards for proving a vertical and horizontal agreement or concerted action, and the extent to which oligopolistic coordination itself can be covered. We leave until the next chapter a particular class of agreements—mergers that unite what were separate entities into one.

A. ARE THE DEFENDANTS SEPARATE ENTITIES?

Copperweld Corp. v. Independence Tube Corp.

467 U.S. 752 (1984).

■ CHIEF JUSTICE BURGER delivered the opinion of the Court....

Review of this case calls directly into question whether the coordinated acts of a parent and its wholly owned subsidiary can, in the legal sense contemplated by § 1 of the Sherman Act, constitute a combination or conspiracy. The so-called "intra-enterprise conspiracy" doctrine provides that § 1 liability is not foreclosed merely because a parent and its subsidiary are subject to common ownership.... In no case has the Court considered the merits of the intra-enterprise conspiracy doctrine in depth ... Although the Court has expressed approval of the doctrine on a number of occasions, a finding of intra-enterprise conspiracy was in all but perhaps one instance unnecessary to the result....

Petitioners, joined by the United States as amicus curiae, urge us to repudiate the intra-enterprise conspiracy doctrine. The central criticism is that the doctrine gives undue significance to the fact that a subsidiary is separately incorporated and thereby treats as the concerted activity of two entities what is really unilateral behavior flowing from decisions of a single enterprise.

807

We limit our inquiry to the narrow issue squarely presented: whether a parent and its wholly owned subsidiary are capable of conspiring in violation of § 1 of the Sherman Act. We do not consider under what circumstances, if any, a parent may be liable for conspiring with an affiliated corporation it does not completely own. . . .

The Sherman Act contains a "basic distinction between concerted and independent action." *Monsanto.* The conduct of a single firm is governed by § 2 alone and is unlawful only when it threatens actual monopolization. It is not enough that a single firm appears to "restrain trade" unreasonably, for even a vigorous competitor may leave that impression. . . . In part because it is sometimes difficult to distinguish robust competition from conduct with long-run anti-competitive effects, Congress authorized Sherman Act scrutiny of single firms only when they pose a danger of monopolization. Judging unilateral conduct in this manner reduces the risk that the antitrust laws will dampen the competitive zeal of a single aggressive entrepreneur.

Section 1 of the Sherman Act, in contrast, reaches unreasonable restraints of trade effected by a "contract, combination . . . or conspiracy" between *separate* entities. It does not reach conduct that is "wholly unilateral." Concerted activity subject to § 1 is judged more sternly than unilateral activity under § 2. Certain agreements, such as horizontal price fixing and market allocation, are thought so inherently anticompetitive that each is illegal per se without inquiry into the harm it has actually caused. Other combinations, such as mergers, joint ventures, and various vertical agreements, hold the promise of increasing a firm's efficiency and enabling it to compete more effectively. Accordingly, such combinations are judged under a rule of reason, an inquiry into market power and market structure designed to assess the combination's actual effect. Whatever form the inquiry takes, however, it is not necessary to prove that concerted activity threatens monopolization.

The reason Congress treated concerted behavior more strictly than unilateral behavior is readily appreciated. Concerted activity inherently is fraught with anticompetitive risk. It deprives the marketplace of the independent centers of decisionmaking that competition assumes and demands. In any conspiracy, two or more entities that previously pursued their own interests separately are combining to act as one for their common benefit. This not only reduces the diverse directions in which economic power is aimed but suddenly increases the economic power moving in one particular direction. Of course, such mergings of resources may well lead to efficiencies that benefit consumers, but their anticompetitive potential is sufficient to warrant scrutiny even in the absence of incipient monopoly. . . .

The distinction between unilateral and concerted conduct is necessary for a proper understanding of the terms "contract, combination . . . or conspiracy" in § 1. Nothing in the literal meaning of those terms excludes coordinated conduct among officers or employees of the same company. But it is perfectly plain that an internal "agreement" to implement a single, unitary firm's policies does not raise the antitrust dangers that § 1 was designed to police. The officers of a single firm are not separate economic actors pursuing separate economic interests, so agreements among them do not suddenly bring together economic power that was previously pursuing divergent goals. Coordination within a firm is as likely to result from an effort to compete as from an effort to stifle competition. In the marketplace, such coordination may be necessary if a business enterprise is to compete effectively. For these reasons, officers or employees of the same firm do not provide the plurality of actors imperative for a § 1 conspiracy.

There is also general agreement that § 1 is not violated by the internally coordinated conduct of a corporation and one of its unincorporated divisions. Although this Court has not previously addressed the question, there can be little doubt that the operations of a corporate enterprise organized into divisions must be judged as the conduct of a single actor. The existence of an unincorporated division reflects no more than a firm's decision to adopt an organizational division of labor. A division within a corporate structure pursues the common interests of the whole rather than interests separate from those of the corporation itself; a business enterprise establishes divisions to further its own interests in the most efficient manner. Because coordination between a corporation and its division does not represent a sudden joining of two independent sources of economic power previously pursuing separate interests, it is not an activity that warrants § 1 scrutiny.

Indeed, a rule that punished coordinated conduct simply because a corporation delegated certain responsibilities to autonomous units might well discourage corporations from creating divisions with their presumed benefits. This would serve no useful antitrust purpose but could well deprive consumers of the efficiencies that decentralized management may bring. . . .

For similar reasons, the coordinated activity of a parent and its wholly owned subsidiary must be viewed as that of a single enterprise for purposes of § 1 of the Sherman Act. A parent and its wholly owned subsidiary have a complete unity of interest. Their objectives are common, not disparate; their general corporate actions are guided or determined not by two separate corporate consciousnesses, but one. They are not unlike a multiple team of horses drawing a vehicle under the control of a single driver. With or without a formal "agreement," the subsidiary acts for the benefit of the parent, its sole shareholder. If a parent and a wholly owned subsidiary do "agree" to a course of action, there is no sudden joining of economic resources that had previously served different interests, and there is no justification for § 1 scrutiny.

Indeed, the very notion of an "agreement" in Sherman Act terms between a parent and a wholly owned subsidiary lacks meaning. A § 1 agreement may be found when "the conspirators had a unity of purpose or a common design and understanding, or a meeting of minds in an unlawful arrangement." But in reality a parent and a wholly owned subsidiary always have a "unity of purpose or a common design." They share a common purpose whether or not the parent keeps a tight rein over the subsidiary; the parent may assert full control at any moment if the subsidiary fails to act in the parent's best interests.[18]

The intra-enterprise conspiracy doctrine looks to the form of an enterprise's structure and ignores the reality. Antitrust liability should not depend on whether a corporate subunit is organized as an unincorporated division or a wholly owned subsidiary. A corporation has complete power to maintain a wholly owned subsidiary in either form. The economic, legal, or other considerations that lead corporate management to choose one structure over the other are not relevant to whether the enterprise's conduct seriously threatens competition. Rather, a corporation may adopt the subsidiary form of organization for valid management and related purposes. Separate incorporation may improve management, avoid special tax problems arising from multistate operations, or serve other legitimate interests. Especially in view of the increasing complexity of corporate operations, a business enterprise should be free to structure itself in ways that serve efficiency of control, economy of operations, and other factors dictated by business judgment without increasing its exposure to antitrust liability. Because there is nothing inherently anticompetitive about a corporation's decision to create a subsidiary, the intra-enterprise conspiracy doctrine "impose[s] grave legal consequences upon organizational distinctions that are of de minimis meaning and effect."

If antitrust liability turned on the garb in which a corporate subunit was clothed, parent corporations would be encouraged to convert subsidiaries into unincorporated divisions.... Such an incentive serves no valid antitrust goals but merely deprives consumers and producers of the benefits that the subsidiary form may yield....

Any reading of the Sherman Act that remains true to the Act's distinction between unilateral and concerted conduct will necessarily disappoint those who find that distinction arbitrary. It cannot be denied that § 1's focus on concerted behavior leaves a "gap" in the Act's proscription against unreasonable restraints of trade. An unreasonable restraint of trade may be effected not only by two independent firms acting in concert; a single firm may restrain trade to precisely the same extent if it alone possesses the combined market power of those same two firms. Because the Sherman Act does not prohibit unreasonable restraints of trade as such— but only restraints effected by a contract, combination, or conspiracy—it leaves untouched a single firm's anticompetitive conduct (short of threatened monopolization) that may be indistinguishable in economic effect from the conduct of two firms subject to § 1 liability.

We have already noted that Congress left this "gap" for eminently sound reasons. Subjecting a single firm's every action to judicial scrutiny for reasonableness would threaten to discourage the competitive enthusi-

---

18. [Some] ... Courts of Appeals [have used] ... criteria [that] measure the "separateness" of the subsidiary: whether it has separate control of its day-to-day operations, separate officers, separate corporate headquarters, and so forth. At least when a subsidiary is wholly owned, however, these factors are not sufficient to describe a separate economic entity for purposes of the Sherman Act. The factors simply describe the manner in which the parent chooses to structure a subunit of itself. They cannot overcome the basic fact that the ultimate interests of the subsidiary and the parent are identical, so the parent and the subsidiary must be viewed as a single economic unit.

asm that the antitrust laws seek to promote. Moreover, whatever the wisdom of the distinction, the Act's plain language leaves no doubt that Congress made a purposeful choice to accord different treatment to unilateral and concerted conduct. Had Congress intended to outlaw unreasonable restraints of trade as such, § 1's requirement of a contract, combination, or conspiracy would be superfluous, as would the entirety of § 2. . . .

The appropriate inquiry in this case, therefore, is not whether the coordinated conduct of a parent and its wholly owned subsidiary may ever have anticompetitive effects, as the dissent suggests. Nor is it whether the term "conspiracy" will bear a literal construction that includes parent corporations and their wholly owned subsidiaries. For if these were the proper inquiries, a single firm's conduct would be subject to § 1 scrutiny whenever the coordination of two employees was involved. Such a rule would obliterate the Act's distinction between unilateral and concerted conduct, contrary to the clear intent of Congress as interpreted by the weight of judicial authority. Rather, the appropriate inquiry requires us to explain the logic underlying Congress' decision to exempt unilateral conduct from § 1 scrutiny, and to assess whether that logic similarly excludes the conduct of a parent and its wholly owned subsidiary. Unless we second-guess the judgment of Congress to limit § 1 to concerted conduct, we can only conclude that the coordinated behavior of a parent and its wholly owned subsidiary falls outside the reach of that provision.

Although we recognize that any "gap" the Sherman Act leaves is the sensible result of a purposeful policy decision by Congress, we also note that the size of any such gap is open to serious question. Any anticompetitive activities of corporations and their wholly owned subsidiaries meriting antitrust remedies may be policed adequately without resort to an intra-enterprise conspiracy doctrine. A corporation's initial acquisition of control will always be subject to scrutiny under § 1 of the Sherman Act and § 7 of the Clayton Act. Thereafter, the enterprise is fully subject to § 2 of the Sherman Act and § 5 of the Federal Trade Commission Act. That these statutes are adequate to control dangerous anticompetitive conduct is suggested by the fact that not a single holding of antitrust liability by this Court would today be different in the absence of an intra-enterprise conspiracy doctrine. It is further suggested by the fact that the Federal Government, in its administration of the antitrust laws, no longer accepts the concept that a corporation and its wholly owned subsidiaries can "combine" or "conspire" under § 1. Elimination of the intra-enterprise conspiracy doctrine with respect to corporations and their wholly owned subsidiaries will therefore not cripple antitrust enforcement. It will simply eliminate treble damages from private state tort suits masquerading as antitrust actions. . . .

We hold that Copperweld and its wholly owned subsidiary Regal are incapable of conspiring with each other for purposes of § 1 of the Sherman Act. To the extent that prior decisions of this Court are to the contrary, they are disapproved and overruled. . . .

Questions on *Copperweld*

1. Why shouldn't Sherman Act § 1 cover conspiracies between a parent and wholly owned subsidiary?

a. The court stresses that the effect of such a conspiracy would be the same as if they were divisions of a single corporation, but isn't it also the same as if they had been separately owned?

b. Even if the end result is the same, which is more likely to worsen market performance: a conspiracy between jointly owned firms or between separately owned firms? Absent a conspiracy, which would have had more financial incentive to compete with each other?

c. Which is more likely to have a procompetitive justification: an agreement between jointly owned firms or one between separately owned firms?

2. Could jointly owned firms that share profits and decisionmakers ever avoid having "a unity of purpose or a common design and understanding"?

3. The Court notes that this decision leaves a possible gap: unilateral restraints by firms with less than monopoly power.

a. Would we want every unilateral decision by such a firm to be reviewable under the rule of reason? Given litigation costs and the risk of adjudication error, might this lead to an overdeterrence of desirable conduct that exceeds any reduction in underdeterrence of undesirable conduct?

b. Could we maintain per se rules for activities like price-fixing if all unilateral activities were covered?

c. If we limited any such doctrine to firms that were separately incorporated, wouldn't that just cause such firms to operate as divisions instead? Would that advance any procompetitive interest?

4. Most but not all cases hold that under *Copperweld* two subsidiaries that are wholly owned by a common parent or set of shareholders cannot conspire with each other.[1] Which position is correct?

5. Should Sherman Act § 1 cover conspiracies between a parent and a 51%-owned subsidiary? Does the legal ability to elect the board of the subsidiary suffice if the financial incentives are not completely aligned the way they would be with a wholly-owned subsidiary?[2]

---

1. For cases holding they cannot conspire, see Siegel Transfer v. Carrier Express, 54 F.3d 1125 (3d Cir. 1995); Advanced Health–Care Servs. v. Radford Cmty. Hosp., 910 F.2d 139, 146 (4th Cir. 1990); Hood v. Tenneco Texas Life Ins., 739 F.2d 1012 (5th Cir. 1984); Century Oil Tool v. Prod. Specialties, 737 F.2d 1316, 1317 (5th Cir. 1984); Guzowski v. Hartman, 969 F.2d 211, 214 (6th Cir. 1992); Freeman v. San Diego Ass'n of Realtors, 322 F.3d 1133, 1147 (9th Cir. 2003). In contrast, Mitchael v. Intracorp., 179 F.3d 847, 857 (10th Cir. 1999), applied a "complete unity of interest" test and declined to hold that it always meant that two wholly owned subsidiaries cannot conspire with each other.

2. The cases are somewhat divided. Some hold that firms with such an ownership structure cannot conspire, though these decisions may depend on the ownership share being high or at least over 50%. See Total Benefit Services v. Group Ins. Admin., Inc., 1993–1 Trade Cas. (CCH) ¶ 70,148 (E.D. La. 1993) (85%); Bell Atlantic Business Systems Services v. Hitachi Data Systems, 849 F.Supp. 702, 706 (N.D. Cal. 1994) (parent owned 80% but dicta suggested anything over 50% would suffice); Novatel Communications v. Cellular Telephone, 1986 WL 15507 (N.D. Ga.) (51%). Some indicate those with a majority stake can conspire with the corporation, though some have an exception when the stake is close to 100%. See Tunis Brothers Co. v. Ford Motor, 763 F.2d 1482, 1495 n. 20 (3d Cir. 1985) (finding conspiracy even though firm owned 79% of equity and 100% of voting stock), vacated on other grounds, 475

6. What if the parent has a 30% stake that is enough to give it working control over the subsidiary?[3] Should it matter that this does not give it the legal ability to elect the corporate board if it gives it the practical ability to do so? Should the test turn on whether the stake is high enough that its acquisition would be deemed a combination subject to review as an antitrust merger?[4]

Case C–73/95 P, Viho Europe BV v. Commission

1996 E.C.R. I–5457.

[Viho Europe lodged a complaint against Parker Pen's vertical territorial agreements with its subsidiaries. The Commission and the General Court found Parker Pen and its subsidiaries constituted a single economic unit incapable of concerted action within Article 101(1).]

The appellant claims that the fact that the conduct in question occurs within a group of companies does not preclude the application of Article [101(1)], since the division of responsibilities between the companies in the Parker group aims to maintain and partition national markets by means of absolute territorial protection. The evaluation of such conduct, which has harmful effects on competition, should not therefore depend on whether it takes place within a group or between Parker and its independent distributors. The appellant points out that such territorial protection prevents third parties such as itself from obtaining supplies freely within the Community from the subsidiary which offers the best commercial terms, so as to be able to pass such benefits on to the consumer. . . .

It should be noted, first of all, that it is established that Parker holds 100% of the shares of its subsidiaries in Germany, Belgium, Spain, France and the Netherlands and that the sales and marketing activities of its subsidiaries are directed by an area team appointed by the parent company and which controls, in particular, sales targets, gross margins, sales costs, cash flow and stocks. The area team also lays down the range of products to

U.S. 1105 (1986); Fishman v. Estate of Wirtz, 807 F.2d 520, 541 n.19 (7th Cir. 1986) (rejecting single entity claim when the common investors were not identical and it was not clear the common investors had majority control over one firm); American Vision Centers v. Cohen, 711 F.Supp. 721 (E.D.N.Y. 1989) (conspiracy where stake was 54%); Aspen Title & Escrow v. Jeld–Wen, Inc., 677 F.Supp. 1477, 1486 (D. Or. 1987) (conspiracy where stake was 60–75% but not where it was a de minimis amount below 100%, like 97.5%); Leaco Enterprises v. General Electric, 737 F.Supp. 605, 609 (D. Or. 1990) (concluding that 91.9% was de minimis amount less than 100%); *Siegel Transfer*, 54 F.3d at 1134 & n.7 (affirming single entity finding under de minimus standard where parent owned 99.92% and suggesting in dicta it would find a single entity for any share above 80%). Other cases leave it to the factfinder to decide case by case whether the related firms acted as a single entity. See Computer Identics v. Southern Pacific Co., 756 F.2d 200, 204–05 (1st Cir. 1985); Coast Cities Truck Sales v. Navistar International Transportation, 912 F.Supp. 747, 765–66 (D. N.J. 1995).

3. The cases are scarce. See Sonitrol of Fresno, Inc. v. American Telephone and Telegraph, 1986 WL 953 (D.D.C.) (even if parent had de facto control it was not a single entity with a subsidiary where its stake was below 50% and thus did not confer legal control.).

4. Acquiring a minority share of another corporation constitutes a merger under U.S. antitrust law if it confers working control or even if the investor influences business decisions. *See* Chapter 7.

be sold, monitors advertising and issues directives concerning prices and discounts.

Parker and its subsidiaries thus form a single economic unit within which the subsidiaries do not enjoy real autonomy in determining their course of action in the market, but carry out the instructions issued to them by the parent company controlling them.

In those circumstances, the fact that Parker's policy of referral, which consists essentially in dividing various national markets between its subsidiaries, might produce effects outside the ambit of the Parker group which are capable of affecting the competitive position of third parties cannot make Article [101(1)] applicable.... On the other hand, such unilateral conduct could fall under Article [102] of the Treaty if the conditions for its application, as laid down in that article, were fulfilled. . . .

Questions on *Viho*

1.   *Viho* is an important case as it establishes that there cannot be an agreement within the meaning of Article 101 TFEU between firms belonging to a single economic unit. Will it always be easy to determine whether different firms belong to a single economic unit?

a.   In *Viho*, this test was not difficult to apply as Parker held 100% of the shares of its subsidiaries in Germany, Belgium, Spain, France and the Netherlands, but what would have happened if Parker had only held 50% of the shares of its distributors in these different Member States?

b.   Besides market shares, should other elements be taken into account to determine whether distinct entities belong to a single economic unit?

2.   What are the consequences of a finding that several distinct entities belong to a single economic unit?

a.   Does it mean that this "economic unit" will escape antitrust scrutiny?

b.   Does it mean that a firm (mother company) could be held responsible for competition law infringements of other firms that are part of that unit (subsidiaries)? Could this have significant implications in the case of international cartels?

c.   Could this also have implications for the calculations of the thresholds (in terms of market shares, etc.) that are found in EU competition secondary legislation (e.g., block exemption regulations) or guidelines?

The Relevance of Agency Relations

Copperweld states that "corporations cannot conspire with their own officers" and its logic suggests that a firm cannot conspire with agents that share its economic interest.[5] But the answer can be different under U.S.

---

5.   *See Siegel Transfer*, 54 F.3d 1125; Mann v. Princeton Community Hospital Assn., 1992–1 Trade Cas. (CCH) ¶ 69,738 (4th Cir. 1992); R. Ernest Cohn D.C., D.A.B.C.O. v. Bond, 953 F.2d 154 (4th Cir. 1991); Surgical Care Center v. Hospital Service District No. 1, 309 F.3d

law if agents have a personal motive to conspire that is independent of the firm's objectives.[6] More generally, the single entity doctrine raises the question of when someone, including another firm, should be considered an "agent" rather than a separate person capable of conspiring. Categorization difficulties come up most often when a firm sells through a dealer using a "consignment contract" where the supplier retains title and gives a fee or commission to the dealer upon sale. If all those arrangements were an agreement between separate entities, then antitrust law on vertical agreements would apply every time a firm used a salesperson on commission or had a delivery person collect the sales price. If all such arrangements were deemed to involve an agency relationship that could not be a conspiracy, then it would be easy to evade scrutiny of any vertical agreement with independent dealers by simply having the manufacturer retain title and pay the dealer a "commission" equal to the difference between the wholesale price and the distributor's resale price.

The basic answer U.S. antitrust law gives is to treat such arrangements as agency relations only when the actors lack the sort of independent economic stake that, without the restraint, would make them efficient independent decisionmakers. Thus, in United States v. General Electric, 272 U.S. 476 (1926), the Court found an agency relation rather than a vertical price-fixing agreement where the supplier retained not only title but the risk of loss from fire, and dealers received a fixed commission per sale. In contrast, in Simpson v. Union Oil Co., 377 U.S. 13 (1964), the Court found a vertical price-fixing agreement rather than an agency relation where the supplier retained title but its dealers were responsible for the risk of loss from fire and received a commission that was somewhat dependent on the resale price. This pattern of results makes sense. In *General Electric,* allowing the dealers to set the sales price would have led to economic disaster because, with a fixed commission/sale, the dealers would have incentives to set the sales price at $0 to maximize the number of sales. In contrast, in *Simpson,* the dealer was responsible for losses and received a commission that depended somewhat on the sales price. Thus, absent a vertical price-fixing agreement, the *Simpson* dealer would, if considering a decision to cut retail prices, have had economic incentives to consider both the upside (increased sales) and downside (decreased revenue per sale).[7]

836, 841 (5th Cir. 2002); Ozark Heartland Electronics v. Radio Shack, 278 F.3d 759, 763–64 (8th Cir. 2002); Tiftarea Shopper v. Georgia Shopper, 786 F.2d 1115, 1118 (11th Cir. 1986).

   6. See Victorian House v. Fisher Camuto Corp., 769 F.2d 466, 469 (8th Cir. 1985); Motive Parts Warehouse v. Facet Enters., 774 F.2d 380, 387 (10th Cir. 1985). But see Nurse Midwifery Ass'n v. Hibbett, 927 F.2d 904 (6th Cir. 1991) (rejecting such a test). The courts are divided on whether a hospital can conspire with its medical staff. See Willman v. Heartland Hosp. E., 34 F.3d 605, 610 (8th Cir. 1994) (collecting sources on both sides).

   7. *Simpson* distinguished *General Electric* on the quite different grounds that it involved a patented product, but *General Electric* itself made clear that, if the arrangement had involved independent purchasers rather than agents, it would have deemed it vertical price-fixing, and that its ruling on agents applied whether or not the product was patented. In *American Needle,* the Supreme Court adopted the functional distinction between *Simpson* and *General Electric* that is described in the text above.

In short, it makes sense to deem an actor selling on consignment a nonagent only if antitrust law would want to preserve their ability to make independent decisions. And preserving that ability is only desirable if they would have efficient economic incentives to consider both the benefits and costs of price cutting.

The EU guidelines on vertical restraints define an agent as when "a legal or physical person (the agent) is vested with the power to negotiate and/or conclude contracts on behalf of another person (the principal), either in the agent's own name or in the name of the principal, for the purchase of goods or services by the principal, or sale of goods or services supplied by the principal."[8] As far as the competition law consequences of the designation of a legal or physical person are concerned, the guidelines specify that:

> "For the purposes of applying Article 101(1), the agreement will be justified as an agency agreement if the agent does not bear any, or bears only insignificant, risks in relation to the contracts concluded and/or negotiated on behalf of the principal and in relation to market-specific investments for that field of activity, or in relation to other activities required by the principal to be undertaken on the same product market. However, risks that are related to the activity of providing agency services in general, such as the risk of the agent's income being dependent upon his success as an agent or general investments in for instance premises or personnel, are not material to this assessment."[9]

The Commission notes, however, that

> "Exclusive agency provisions will in general not lead to anti-competitive effects. However, single branding provisions and post-tenure non-compete provisions, which concern inter-brand competition, may infringe Article 101(1) if they lead to or contribute to a (cumulative) foreclosure effect on the relevant market where the contract goods or services are sold or purchased.

> An agency agreement may also fall within the scope of Article 101(1), even if the principal bears all the relevant financial and commercial risks, where it facilitates collusion. This could for instance be the case when a number of principals use the same agents while collectively excluding others from using these agents, or when they use the agents to collude on marketing strategy or to exchange sensitive market information between the principals."[10]

American Needle v. National Football League

130 S.Ct. 2201 (2010).

■ Justice Stevens delivered the opinion of the Court.

. . . The question whether an arrangement is a contract, combination, or conspiracy is different from and antecedent to the question whether it

---

8. Commission notice—Guidelines on Vertical Restraints, O.J. 2010, C 130/1, at § 12.

9. Id. at § 15.

10. Id. at §§ 19–20.

unreasonably restrains trade. This case raises that antecedent question about the business of the 32 teams in the National Football League (NFL) and a corporate entity that they formed to manage their intellectual property. We conclude that the NFL's licensing activities constitute concerted action that is not categorically beyond the coverage of [Sherman Act] § 1. The legality of that concerted action must be judged under the Rule of Reason.

I

Originally organized in 1920, the NFL is an unincorporated association that now includes 32 separately owned professional football teams. Each team has its own name, colors, and logo, and owns related intellectual property. Like each of the other teams in the league, the New Orleans Saints and the Indianapolis Colts, for example, have their own distinctive names, colors, and marks that are well known to millions of sports fans.

Prior to 1963, the teams made their own arrangements for licensing their intellectual property and marketing trademarked items such as caps and jerseys. In 1963, the teams formed National Football League Properties (NFLP) to develop, license, and market their intellectual property. Most, but not all, of the substantial revenues generated by NFLP have either been given to charity or shared equally among the teams. However, the teams are able to and have at times sought to withdraw from this arrangement.

Between 1963 and 2000, NFLP granted nonexclusive licenses to a number of vendors, permitting them to manufacture and sell apparel bearing team insignias. Petitioner, American Needle, Inc., was one of those licensees. In December 2000, the teams voted to authorize NFLP to grant exclusive licenses, and NFLP granted Reebok International Ltd. an exclusive 10-year license to manufacture and sell trademarked headwear for all 32 teams. It thereafter declined to renew American Needle's nonexclusive license.

American Needle [alleged] ... that the agreements between the NFL, its teams, NFLP, and Reebok violated ... the Sherman Act.... The Court of Appeals for the Seventh Circuit affirmed [a district court decision dismissing the § 1 claims.] The panel observed that "in some contexts, a league seems more aptly described as a single entity immune from antitrust scrutiny, while in others a league appears to be a joint venture between independently owned teams that is subject to review under § 1." Relying on Circuit precedent, the court limited its inquiry to the particular conduct at issue, licensing of teams' intellectual property. The panel agreed with petitioner that "when making a single-entity determination, courts must examine whether the conduct in question deprives the marketplace of the independent sources of economic control that competition assumes." The court, however, discounted the significance of potential competition among the teams regarding the use of their intellectual property because the teams "can function only as one source of economic power when collectively producing NFL football." The court noted that football itself can only be carried out jointly. Moreover, "NFL teams share a vital economic interest in collectively promoting NFL football . . . [to] compet[e] with other forms of entertainment." "It thus follows," the court found, "that only one source of economic power controls the promotion of NFL football," and "it makes little sense to assert that each individual team has the authority, if not the responsibility, to promote the jointly produced NFL football." Recognizing that NFL teams have "license[d] their intellectual property collectively" since 1963, the court held that § 1 did not apply. . . .

II

. . . The meaning of the term "contract, combination . . . or conspiracy" is informed by the " 'basic distinction' " in the Sherman Act " 'between concerted and independent action' " that distinguishes § 1 of the Sherman Act from § 2. *Copperweld*. . . . Congress used this distinction between concerted and independent action to deter anticompetitive conduct and compensate its victims, without chilling vigorous competition through ordinary business operations. The distinction also avoids judicial scrutiny of routine, internal business decisions.

Thus, in § 1 Congress "treated concerted behavior more strictly than unilateral behavior." *Id.* This is so because unlike independent action, "[c]oncerted activity inherently is fraught with anticompetitive risk" insofar as it "deprives the marketplace of independent centers of decisionmaking that competition assumes and demands." *Id.* And because concerted action is discrete and distinct, a limit on such activity leaves untouched a vast amount of business conduct. As a result, there is less risk of deterring a firm's necessary conduct; courts need only examine discrete agreements; and such conduct may be remedied simply through prohibition.[2] Concerted activity is thus "judged more sternly than unilateral activity under § 2," *Id.* For these reasons, § 1 prohibits any concerted action "in restraint of trade or commerce," even if the action does not "threate[n] monopolization," *Id.* And therefore, an arrangement must embody concerted action in order to be a "contract, combination . . . or conspiracy" under § 1.

III

We have long held that concerted action under § 1 does not turn simply on whether the parties involved are legally distinct entities. Instead, we have eschewed such formalistic distinctions in favor of a functional consideration of how the parties involved in the alleged anticompetitive conduct actually operate.

As a result, we have repeatedly found instances in which members of a legally single entity violated § 1 when the entity was controlled by a group of competitors and served, in essence, as a vehicle for ongoing concerted activity. In *United States v. Sealy, Inc.,* 388 U.S. 350 (1967), for example, a group of mattress manufacturers operated and controlled Sealy, Inc., a

---

2. If Congress prohibited independent action that merely restrains trade (even if it does not threaten monopolization), that prohibition could deter perfectly competitive conduct by firms that are fearful of litigation costs and judicial error. Moreover, if every unilateral action that restrained trade were subject to antitrust scrutiny, then courts would be forced to judge almost every internal business decision.

company that licensed the Sealy trademark to the manufacturers, and dictated that each operate within a specific geographic area. The Government alleged that the licensees and Sealy were conspiring in violation of § 1, and we agreed. We explained that "[w]e seek the central substance of the situation" and therefore "we are moved by the identity of the persons who act, rather than the label of their hats." *Id.* We thus held that Sealy was not a "separate entity, but ... an instrumentality of the individual manufacturers." *Id.* In similar circumstances, we have found other formally distinct business organizations covered by § 1. See, *e.g., Northwest Wholesale Stationers; NCAA; United States v. Topco Associates,* 405 U.S. 596, 609 (1972); *Associated Press; Terminal Railroad..* We have similarly looked past the form of a legally "single entity" when competitors were part of professional organizations[3] or trade groups.[4]

Conversely, there is not necessarily concerted action simply because more than one legally distinct entity is involved. Although, under a now-defunct doctrine known as the "intraenterprise conspiracy doctrine," we once treated cooperation between legally separate entities as necessarily covered by § 1, we now embark on a more functional analysis.... We finally reexamined the intraenterprise conspiracy doctrine in *Copperweld,* and concluded that it was inconsistent with the " 'basic distinction between concerted and independent action.' " *Id.* Considering it "perfectly plain that an internal agreement to implement a single, unitary firm's policies does not raise the antitrust dangers that § 1 was designed to police," *id.,* we held that a parent corporation and its wholly owned subsidiary "are incapable of conspiring with each other for purposes of § 1 of the Sherman Act," *id..* We explained that although a parent corporation and its wholly owned subsidiary are "separate" for the purposes of incorporation or formal title, they are controlled by a single center of decisionmaking and they control a single aggregation of economic power. Joint conduct by two such entities does not "depriv[e] the marketplace of independent centers of decisionmaking," *id.,* and as a result, an agreement between them does not constitute "a contract, combination ... or conspiracy" for the purposes of § 1.[5]

IV

As *Copperweld* exemplifies, "substance, not form, should determine whether a[n] ... entity is capable of conspiring under § 1." *Id.* This inquiry is sometimes described as asking whether the alleged conspirators

---

3. See, *e.g., Indiana Dentists; Maricopa; Professional Engineers; Goldfarb v. Virginia State Bar,* 421 U.S. 773 (1975).

4. See, *e.g., Allied Tube & Conduit Corp. v. Indian Head, Inc.,* 486 U.S. 492 (1988); *Radiant Burners v. Peoples Gas Light & Coke,* 364 U.S. 656 (1961) *(per curiam); Fashion Originators..*

5. This focus on "substance, not, form," *Copperweld,* can also be seen in our cases about whether a company and its agent are capable of conspiring under § 1. See, *e.g., Simpson v. Union Oil Co. of Cal.,* 377 U.S. 13, 20–21, 84 S.Ct. 1051, 12 L.Ed.2d 98 (1964); see also E. Elhauge & D. Geradin, Global Antitrust Law and Economics 787–788, and n. 7 (2007) (hereinafter Elhauge & Geradin) (explaining the functional difference between *Simpson* and *United States v. General Elec. Co.,* 272 U.S. 476 (1926), in which we treated a similar agreement as beyond the reach of § 1).

are a single entity. That is perhaps a misdescription, however, because the question is not whether the defendant is a legally single entity or has a single name; nor is the question whether the parties involved "seem" like one firm or multiple firms in any metaphysical sense. The key is whether the alleged "contract, combination . . ., or conspiracy" is concerted action— that is, whether it joins together separate decisionmakers. The relevant inquiry, therefore, is whether there is a contract, "combination . . . or conspiracy" amongst "separate economic actors pursuing separate economic interests," *id.*, such that the agreement "deprives the marketplace of independent centers of decisionmaking," *id.,* and therefore of "diversity of entrepreneurial interests," *Fraser v. Major League Soccer, L.L. C.,* 284 F.3d 47, 57 (C.A.1 2002) (Boudin, C. J.), and thus of actual or potential competition.

Thus, while the president and a vice president of a firm could (and regularly do) act in combination, their joint action generally is not the sort of "combination" that § 1 is intended to cover. Such agreements might be described "as really unilateral behavior flowing from decisions of a single enterprise." *Copperweld.* Nor, for this reason, does § 1 cover "internally coordinated conduct of a corporation and one of its unincorporated divisions," *id.*, because "[a] division within a corporate structure pursues the common interests of the whole," *id.,* and therefore "coordination between a corporation and its division does not represent a sudden joining of two independent sources of economic power previously pursuing separate interests," *id.* Nor, for the same reasons, is "the coordinated activity of a parent and its wholly owned subsidiary" covered. See *id.* They "have a complete unity of interest" and thus "[w]ith or without a formal 'agreement,' the subsidiary acts for the benefit of the parent, its sole shareholder." *Id.*

Because the inquiry is one of competitive reality, it is not determinative that two parties to an alleged § 1 violation are legally distinct entities. Nor, however, is it determinative that two legally distinct entities have organized themselves under a single umbrella or into a structured joint venture. The question is whether the agreement joins together "independent centers of decisionmaking." *Id.* If it does, the entities are capable of conspiring under § 1, and the court must decide whether the restraint of trade is an unreasonable and therefore illegal one.

V

The NFL teams do not possess either the unitary decisionmaking quality or the single aggregation of economic power characteristic of independent action. Each of the teams is a substantial, independently owned, and independently managed business. "[T]heir general corporate actions are guided or determined" by "separate corporate consciousnesses," and "[t]heir objectives are" not "common." *Copperweld*; see also *North American Soccer League v. NFL,* 670 F.2d 1249, 1252 (C.A.2 1982) (discussing ways that "the financial performance of each team, while related to that of the others, does not . . . necessarily rise and fall with that of the others"). The teams compete with one another, not only on the playing field, but to attract fans, for gate receipts and for contracts with managerial and playing personnel.

Directly relevant to this case, the teams compete in the market for intellectual property. To a firm making hats, the Saints and the Colts are two potentially competing suppliers of valuable trademarks. When each NFL team licenses its intellectual property, it is not pursuing the "common interests of the whole" league but is instead pursuing interests of each "corporation itself," *Copperweld*; teams are acting as "separate economic actors pursuing separate economic interests," and each team therefore is a potential "independent cente[r] of decisionmaking," *id.* Decisions by NFL teams to license their separately owned trademarks collectively and to only one vendor are decisions that "depriv[e] the marketplace of independent centers of decisionmaking," *id.,* and therefore of actual or potential competition. See *NCAA* (observing a possible § 1 violation if two separately owned companies sold their separate products through a "single selling agent"); cf. Areeda & Hovenkamp 1478a, at 318 ("Obviously, the most significant competitive threats arise when joint venture participants are actual or potential competitors").

In defense, respondents argue that by forming NFLP, they have formed a single entity, akin to a merger, and market their NFL brands through a single outlet. But it is not dispositive that the teams have organized and own a legally separate entity that centralizes the management of their intellectual property. An ongoing § 1 violation cannot evade § 1 scrutiny simply by giving the ongoing violation a name and label. "Perhaps every agreement and combination in restraint of trade could be so labeled." *Timken Roller Bearing v. United States,* 341 U.S. 593, 598 (1951).

The NFL respondents may be similar in some sense to a single enterprise that owns several pieces of intellectual property and licenses them jointly, but they are not similar in the relevant functional sense. Although NFL teams have common interests such as promoting the NFL brand, they are still separate, profit-maximizing entities, and their interests in licensing team trademarks are not necessarily aligned. Common interests in the NFL brand "*partially* unit[e] the economic interests of the parent firms," Broadley, Joint Ventures and Antitrust Policy, 95 Harv. L.Rev. 1521, 1526 (1982) (emphasis added), but the teams still have distinct, potentially competing interests.

It may be, as respondents argue, that NFLP "has served as the 'single driver' of the teams" "promotional vehicle," " 'pursu[ing] the common interests of the whole.' " Brief for NFL Respondents 28 (quoting *Copperweld*). But illegal restraints often are in the common interests of the parties to the restraint, at the expense of those who are not parties. It is true, as respondents describe, that they have for some time marketed their trademarks jointly. But a history of concerted activity does not immunize conduct from § 1 scrutiny. "Absence of actual competition may simply be a manifestation of the anticompetitive agreement itself." *Freeman,* 322 F.3d, at 1149.

Respondents argue that nonetheless, as the Court of Appeals held, they constitute a single entity because without their cooperation, there would be no NFL football. It is true that "the clubs that make up a professional sports league are not completely independent economic competitors, as they depend upon a degree of cooperation for economic survival." *Brown,* 518 U.S., at 248. But the Court of Appeals' reasoning is unpersuasive.

The justification for cooperation is not relevant to whether that cooperation is concerted or independent action.[6] A "contract, combination ... or conspiracy," § 1, that is necessary or useful to a joint venture is still a "contract, combination ... or conspiracy" if it "deprives the marketplace of independent centers of decisionmaking," *Copperweld.* See *NCAA* ("[J]oint ventures have no immunity from antitrust laws"). Any joint venture involves multiple sources of economic power cooperating to produce a product. And for many such ventures, the participation of others is necessary. But that does not mean that necessity of cooperation transforms concerted action into independent action; a nut and a bolt can only operate together, but an agreement between nut and bolt manufacturers is still subject to § 1 analysis. Nor does it mean that once a group of firms agree to produce a joint product, cooperation amongst those firms must be treated as independent conduct. The mere fact that the teams operate jointly in some sense does not mean that they are immune.[7]

The Court of Appeals carved out a zone of antitrust immunity for conduct arguably related to league operations by reasoning that coordinated team trademark sales are necessary to produce "NFL football," a single NFL brand that competes against other forms of entertainment. But defining the product as "NFL football" puts the cart before the horse: Of course the NFL produces NFL football; but that does not mean that cooperation amongst NFL teams is immune from § 1 scrutiny. Members of any cartel could insist that their cooperation is necessary to produce the "cartel product" and compete with other products.

The question whether NFLP decisions can constitute concerted activity covered by § 1 is closer than whether decisions made directly by the 32 teams are covered by § 1. This is so both because NFLP is a separate corporation with its own management and because the record indicates that most of the revenues generated by NFLP are shared by the teams on an equal basis. Nevertheless we think it clear that for the same reasons the 32 teams' conduct is covered by § 1, NFLP's actions also are subject to § 1, at least with regards to its marketing of property owned by the separate teams. NFLP's licensing decisions are made by the 32 potential competitors, and each of them actually owns its share of the jointly managed assets. Cf. *Sealy,* 388 U.S. at 352–354. Apart from their agreement to cooperate in exploiting those assets, including their decisions as the NFLP, there would be nothing to prevent each of the teams from making its own

---

6. As discussed *infra,* necessity of cooperation is a factor relevant to whether the agreement is subject to the Rule of Reason. See *NCAA* (holding that NCAA restrictions on televising college football games are subject to Rule of Reason analysis for the "critical" reason that "horizontal restraints on competition are essential if the product is to be available at all").

7. In any event, it simply is not apparent that the alleged conduct was necessary at all. Although two teams are needed to play a football game, not all aspects of elaborate interleague cooperation are necessary to produce a game. Moreover, even if leaguewide agreements are necessary to produce football, it does not follow that concerted activity in marketing intellectual property is necessary to produce football.

market decisions relating to purchases of apparel and headwear, to the sale of such items, and to the granting of licenses to use its trademarks.

We generally treat agreements within a single firm as independent action on the presumption that the components of the firm will act to maximize the firm's profits. But in rare cases, that presumption does not hold. Agreements made within a firm can constitute concerted action covered by § 1 when the parties to the agreement act on interests separate from those of the firm itself,[8] and the intrafirm agreements may simply be a formalistic shell for ongoing concerted action. See, *e.g., Topco Associates,* 405 U.S. at 609; *Sealy,* 388 U.S. at 352–354.

For that reason, decisions by the NFLP regarding the teams' separately owned intellectual property constitute concerted action. Thirty-two teams operating independently through the vehicle of the NFLP are not like the components of a single firm that act to maximize the firm's profits. The teams remain separately controlled, potential competitors with economic interests that are distinct from NFLP's financial well-being. Unlike typical decisions by corporate shareholders, NFLP licensing decisions effectively require the assent of more than a mere majority of shareholders. And each team's decision reflects not only an interest in NFLP's profits but also an interest in the team's individual profits. The 32 teams capture individual economic benefits separate and apart from NFLP profits as a result of the decisions they make for the NFLP. NFLP's decisions thus affect each team's profits from licensing its own intellectual property. "Although the business interests of" the teams "will *often* coincide with those of the" NFLP "as an entity in itself, that commonality of interest exists in every cartel." *Los Angeles Memorial Coliseum Comm'n v. NFL,* 726 F.2d 1381, 1389 (C.A.9 1984) (emphasis added). In making the relevant licensing decisions, NFLP is therefore "an instrumentality" of the teams. *Sealy,* 388 U.S. at 352–354; see also *Topco Associates,* 405 U.S. at 609.

If the fact that potential competitors shared in profits or losses from a venture meant that the venture was immune from § 1, then any cartel "could evade the antitrust law simply by creating a 'joint venture' to serve as the exclusive seller of their competing products." *Major League Baseball Properties, Inc. v. Salvino, Inc.,* 542 F.3d 290, 335 (C.A.2 2008) (Sotomayor, J., concurring in judgment). "So long as no agreement," other than one made by the cartelists sitting on the board of the joint venture, "explicitly listed the prices to be charged, the companies could act as monopolies through the 'joint venture.' " *Id.* (Indeed, a joint venture with a single management structure is generally a better way to operate a cartel because it decreases the risks of a party to an illegal agreement defecting from that agreement). However, competitors "cannot simply get around" antitrust

---

8. See Areeda & Hovenkamp 1471; Elhauge & Geradin 786–787, and n. 6; see also *Capital Imaging Assoc. v. Mohawk Valley Medical Assoc., Inc.,* 996 F.2d 537, 544 (C.A.2 1993); *Bolt v. Halifax Hospital Medical Center,* 891 F.2d 810, 819 (C.A.11 1990); *Oksanen v. Page Memorial Hospital,* 945 F.2d 696, 706 (C.A.4 1991); *Motive Parts Warehouse v. Facet Enterprises,* 774 F.2d 380, 387–388 (C.A.10 1985); *Victorian House, Inc. v. Fisher Camuto Corp.,* 769 F.2d 466, 469 (C.A.8 1985); *Weiss v. York Hospital,* 745 F.2d 786, 828 (C.A.3 1984).

liability by acting "through a third-party intermediary or 'joint venture.'" *Id.,* at 336.[9]

VI

Football teams that need to cooperate are not trapped by antitrust law. "[T]he special characteristics of this industry may provide a justification" for many kinds of agreements. *Brown,* 518 U.S. at 252 (STEVENS, J., dissenting). The fact that NFL teams share an interest in making the entire league successful and profitable, and that they must cooperate in the production and scheduling of games, provides a perfectly sensible justification for making a host of collective decisions. But the conduct at issue in this case is still concerted activity under the Sherman Act that is subject to § 1 analysis.

When "restraints on competition are essential if the product is to be available at all," *per se* rules of illegality are inapplicable, and instead the restraint must be judged according to the flexible Rule of Reason. *NCAA* ("Our decision not to apply a *per se* rule to this case rests in large part on our recognition that a certain degree of cooperation is necessary if the type of competition that petitioner and its member institutions seek to market is to be preserved"); see also *Dagher.* In such instances, the agreement is likely to survive the Rule of Reason. See *BMI* ("Joint ventures and other cooperative arrangements are also not usually unlawful ... where the agreement ... is necessary to market the product at all"). And depending upon the concerted activity in question, the Rule of Reason may not require a detailed analysis; it "can sometimes be applied in the twinkling of an eye." *NCAA.*

Other features of the NFL may also save agreements amongst the teams. We have recognized, for example, "that the interest in maintaining a competitive balance" among "athletic teams is legitimate and important," *NCAA.* While that same interest applies to the teams in the NFL, it does not justify treating them as a single entity for § 1 purposes when it comes to the marketing of the teams' individually owned intellectual property. It is, however, unquestionably an interest that may well justify a variety of collective decisions made by the teams. What role it properly plays in applying the Rule of Reason to the allegations in this case is a matter to be considered on remand....

---

9. For the purposes of resolving this case, there is no need to pass upon the Government's position that entities are incapable of conspiring under § 1 if they have "effectively merged the relevant aspect of their operations, thereby eliminating actual and potential competition ... in that operational sphere" and "the challenged restraint [does] not significantly affect actual or potential competition ... outside their merged operations." Brief for United States as *Amicus Curiae* 17. The Government urges that the choices to "offer only a blanket license" and "to have only a single headwear licensee" might not constitute concerted action under its test. *Id.,* at 32. However, because the teams still own their own trademarks and are free to market those trademarks as they see fit, even those two choices were agreements amongst potential competitors and would constitute concerted action under the Government's own standard. At any point, the teams could decide to license their own trademarks. It is significant, moreover, that the teams here control NFLP. The two choices that the Government might treat as independent action, although nominally made by NFLP, are for all functional purposes choices made by the 32 entities with potentially competing interests.

Accordingly, the judgment of the Court of Appeals is reversed, and the case is remanded for further proceedings consistent with this opinion.

Note and Questions on *American Needle*

Formalism v. Functionalism. The *American Needle* opinion makes clear that whether separate entities exist for antitrust agreement purposes turns not on formalisms but on whether functionally there exist independent economic decisionmakers that could be restricted by an antitrust agreement. If, without the alleged agreement, the actors would still act in the same way because of common control and an identical economic interest, then any "agreement" between them cannot meaningfully restrain their decisions and thus they are treated as a single entity incapable of conspiring. But if, without the alleged agreement, the actors have enough separate control and divergent economic interests that they could make independent economic decisions, then an agreement between them can restrain their decisions and thus they are treated as separate entities capable of conspiring. Actors are particularly likely to be treated as separate entities if they are actual or potential competitors in the market being restrained.

Consistent with its rejection of formalism, the Court makes clear that single entity status could not be established by the mere fact that the joint venture was a separate corporate entity with its own corporate management. Instead, the Court cited two functional factors to support its conclusion that NFLP decisions reflected a horizontal agreement among the NFL team members: (1) the joint venture was subject to ongoing control by team members that have their own independent management and economic interests, and (2) the ongoing ability of those decisionmakers to unilaterally compete in the relevant market, here because the team members were "potentially competing suppliers of valuable trademarks" given that "the teams still own their own trademarks and are free to market those trademarks as they see fit ... At any point, the teams could decide to license their own trademarks." The Court's holding thus makes it clear that joint venture decisions will receive separate entity treatment when both factors are met.

The Court also made clear that the first factor could not be disproven by showing the members of the joint venture had a *collective* economic interest. As the Court observed, such a collective economic interest generally exists for illegal horizontal agreements, as with the cartel that maximizes collective profits for it members. What matters is whether the members retained some separate control and economic interest so that, freed from the restraint of the alleged agreement, they might make independent economic decisions that could be contrary to that collective economic interest, like the cartel members who have independent incentives to undercut the cartel price. The Court further made clear that the second factor could not be disproven by showing that the members had a recent history of not actually competing in the relevant activity (here that they had for some time marketed trademarks only jointly) because that might simply reflect the results of a successful anticompetitive agreement. Instead, the second factor could be met by showing that the members potentially *could* compete by licensing their own trademarks.

When the Two Functional Factors Point in Opposing Directions. The Court's decision did not resolve what to do when the two functional factors point in opposing directions. As the Court noted in footnote 9, the Government effectively argued that the second factor should be deemed necessary for separate entity treatment, reasoning that, to the extent the joint venture eliminated actual and potential competition between the members, the joint venture constituted a merger of the members into a single entity. In such a case, the *formation* of the joint venture would itself be a horizontal agreement under the Government standard, and thus subject to antitrust scrutiny under both § 1 and the merger doctrines discussed in Chapter 7. But *subsequent* decisions by the joint venture would be treated as decisions by a single entity (rather than as an agreement among its members) to the extent they were within the scope of merged activities. The Court in footnote 9 declined to hold whether the Government standard was correct because it concluded that the second factor was met in the actual case, as well as in the Government's two hypotheticals. But the Court also emphasized the first factor in response to the government in footnote 9, stating: "It is significant, moreover, that the teams here control NFLP." Thus, the Court's decision left it unresolved whether the first factor might alone suffice for separate entity treatment. Should it?

The first factor would seem to hold for any joint venture, which by definition is an arrangement where firms engage in some joint business activity (the joint venture) but retain independent status and continue to operate separately to some extent (which is what distinguishes a joint venture from a merger). Thus, if meeting the first factor suffices for separate entity treatment, then all decisions by a joint venture involve an agreement between the members. In contrast, if the second factor is necessary for separate entity treatment, then most but not all joint venture decisions would be agreements among their members. Most would be because most joint ventures do not preclude actual or potential competition by their members with the joint venture on most joint venture activities. But not all would be because sometimes joint ventures preclude actual or potential competition by their members on at least some joint venture activities, which under the government approach would be treated as effectively merging those aspects of their business activities. Thus, under the Government's suggested standard, decisions by a joint venture would be decisions by a single entity only to the extent they involved merged business activities on which the members were not actual or potential competitors.

To see what is potentially at stake in the as-yet unresolved issue, suppose each of the NFL teams had instead irrevocably transferred all their trademark rights to NFLP. An irrevocable transfer of trademark rights would mean that the teams were no longer actual or potential competitors in the licensing market, unless NFLP decided to grant those rights back. The second factor thus would likely be deemed unmet. However, the first factor would still be met because the independent teams would have ongoing control over how NFLP licenses and over whether NFLP grants trademark rights back to the teams. Under the Government's suggested approach, the teams would be treated as having effectively merged their trademark licensing into the joint venture. Thus, while this merger would be a horizontal agreement, subsequent licensing decisions by NFLP would be treated as decisions by a single entity rather than as horizontal agreements among its members.[11] In contrast, if the first factor suffices for separate entity treatment, then not only would the combination of trademark rights into NFLP be a horizontal agreement, but also each licensing decision by NFLP would reflect a *separate* horizontal agreement that was subject to antitrust scrutiny.

How should such a hypothetical irrevocable transfer of trademark rights to NFLP be treated? The answer to this question does not really alter *whether* an antitrust agreement exists because under the Government approach the merger would still be an agreement. Instead, the answer alters the *timing* and *scope* of the agreement that is subject to antitrust scrutiny. An approach that made the first factor sufficient for separate entity treatment would be less vulnerable to statute of limitations problems and would focus more on specific licensing decisions. An approach (like the Government's) that made the second factor necessary for separate entity treatment means that the effective merger may be hard to challenge after the statute of limitations runs out and would not focus on those specific licensing decisions. The latter approach could be justified by the view that the horizontal combination that created any market power was the irrevocable transfer of rights and that condemning NFLP licensing decisions could not alter that irrevocable combination or create any additional horizontal competition among the members. A possible response is that, while an "irrevocable" rights transfer is irrevocable by an individual team, it is not irrevocable by the joint venture, which could always transfer those rights back. Thus, the choice between approaches may in part turn on whether one thinks that prohibiting particular licensing agreements by the NFLP might lead the independent teams to exercise their joint control over the NFLP to grant those trademark rights back to the teams. But even if the latter is true, it might seem odd to suggest that a horizontal agreement is invalid because it restrains competition that could not exist unless another horizontal agreement restored that competition. It might be simpler to treat the moment of horizontal combination as the key moment whenever individual firms can no longer unilaterally deviate from it, on the expectation that in the future the joint venture would exercise any collective rights in their collective interests.

Is the actual case that different from this irrevocable transfer hypothetical? As the Court describes the facts, in 2000 the teams authorized the NFLP to grant exclusive rights to the club trademarks and then had NFLP grant exclusive rights on headgear to Reebok. Further, the record indicates that the NFL team resolution authorizing the exclusive Reebok license provided that "the member clubs hereby approve the necessary grant of

---

11. Such licensing decisions might still be subject to review as unilateral conduct under the doctrines discussed in Chapter 3 (if the NFLP had monopoly power or a dangerous probability of acquiring it) or as vertical agreements between NFLP and its licenses under the doctrines discussed in Chapters 4–5.

licenses" and that "the member clubs agree to give their full cooperation as necessary to implement and further the" exclusive licence with Reebok.[12] Doesn't this language effectively transfer the team trademark rights to NFLP and then Reebok because the teams approved the necessary grants and an individual team decision to license its trademark would violate the exclusive NFLP license that the team authorized and pledged to support? If so, then the teams' agreement to authorize NFLP to grant this exclusive license would seem to make it a single entity when it did so under the Government approach, but the Court seemed to reject that conclusion in footnote 9. Perhaps the fact that the exclusive license to Reebok was only 10 years might suffice to make the teams potential future competitors under the government approach, and also might make it more realistic that the team members might exercise their joint control to decline to renew the exclusive license in the future, thus making it more sensible to focus on the first factor.

Justifications and the Limited Nature of the Functional Inquiry on Single Entity Status. Although the Court focused on a functional analysis, it made clear that this focus did *not* mean an inquiry into whether the cooperation furthered some functional goal. For purposes of ascertaining whether separate entities exist, the functional inquiry is simply into whether there exist independent economic decisionmakers whose decisions might be restrained by the alleged agreement. Thus, the Court stressed that the existence of a functional reason for cooperation is not relevant to whether an agreement exists; such a reason just goes to whether the agreement has a *justification* that helps it survive Rule of Reason scrutiny. As the Court stressed, when agreements on issues like the production and scheduling of games are necessary to provide a product at all, such a powerful justification makes the agreement likely to survive Rule of Reason review. Indeed, such a conclusion seems not only likely but inevitable, because if there could be no product without the agreement, then the agreement does not restrain any competition. But the Court observed that the need to cooperate to put on football games did not show that the teams needed to cooperate in marketing intellectual property. Another possible justification in sports leagues is that some restraints might improve product quality by increasing the competitive balance between teams. Whether this justification applied to the joint licensing was a matter the Court left to be determined on remand, but it made clear that, even if it applied, it would just be a factor to be considered under the Rule of Reason, and would not justify treating the joint venture as a single entity. How should this justification be treated on remand?

Relationship to **Texaco v. Dagher.** As discussed in Chapter 2, *Texaco v. Dagher* held that, because the formation of the joint venture there was not alleged to be anticompetitive, the joint venture's agreement to fix the price of its product could not violate the per se rule or abbreviated rule of reason. Because this holding was about the right standard to apply to the agreement, rather than to the existence of the agreement, it does not conflict with the holding in *American Needle*. But *American Needle* does seem to cut back on dicta in *Texaco v. Dagher* which stated:

---

12.   *See* Joint Appendix in American Needle v. NFL at 465–66.

Texaco and Shell Oil formed a joint venture, Equilon, to consolidate their operations in the western United States, thereby ending
competition between the two companies ... Texaco and Shell Oil
did not compete with one another in the relevant market—namely,
the sale of gasoline to service stations in the western United States
... In other words, the pricing policy challenged here amounts to
little more than price setting by a single entity—albeit within the
context of a joint venture—and not a pricing agreement between
competing entities with respect to their competing products....
When "persons who would otherwise be competitors pool their
capital and share the risks of loss as well as the opportunities for
profit ... such joint ventures [are] regarded as a single firm
competing with other sellers in the market."

In *American Needle*, under the joint venture the teams also withdrew from
the relevant trademark market, and thus did not compete with each other
in that relevant market but instead shared profits in that market through a
joint venture. Nonetheless, it sufficed in *American Needle* that the joint
venture members were *potential* competitors and had independent interests
and exercised joint control over the joint venture in which they shared
profits, which was also true in *Texaco v. Dagher* because Texaco and Shell
Oil could have re-entered the market for selling gasoline in the western
United States. Yet the Court deemed the NFLP joint venture not to be a
single entity. Hence, the apparent conflict between *American Needle* and
the dicta in *Texaco v. Dagher*. However, *Texaco v. Dagher* did not seem
fully committed to its single entity conclusion because it held that the
plaintiffs "should have challenged [the joint venture conduct] pursuant to
the rule of reason," which would have been impossible if the joint venture
were a single entity engaged in above-cost pricing. Perhaps the best
explanation for the overbroad dicta in *Texaco v. Dagher* was that there the
alleged conduct—fixing prices for the joint venture product—was unavoidable because those prices would also have been fixed if the joint venture set
different prices for the different brands, so that there was no way to
separate the legitimacy of price-setting by the joint venture from the
legitimacy of the joint venture itself. Do you find *Needle* consistent with
Dagher and, if so, how would you reconcile them?

Single Entity Theory in Other Nations

A Canada statute explicitly provides that, for antitrust purposes, no
agreement can exist between principals and agents or between affiliated
entities, with the latter defined to include any two firms controlled by the
same person.[13] Australia, Israel, and New Zealand deem a parent and
subsidiary to be one person incapable of entering into an antitrust agreement as long as the parent owns more than 50% of the subsidiary voting
stock; Israel also does so if the parent has the right to appoint more than
half the directors.[14] South Africa does the same if the subsidiary is 100%

---

13. *See* Canadian Competition Act §§ 45(6)(a), 76(40), 77(4), 90.1(7).

14. *See* Australia Trade Practices Act § 4A; Israel Restrictive Trade Practices Law § 1,
3(5); New Zealand Commerce Act §§ 2(7) and 44(1A) and Companies Act § 5(1)(a)(iii).

owned, but will infer an agreement from parallel conduct by firms with substantial shareholdings less than 100% absent some independent explanation.[15] South Korea exempts agreements between entities that are substantially and economically a "de facto single business" from the rules against price-fixing and other cartel activities, with the exception of bid-rigging.[16] Singapore and Turkey consider a parent and subsidiary to be a single economic unit when they lack economic independence.[17]

In other nations, single entity issues sometimes arise even for provisions that apply to unilateral conduct. Although Japanese law imposes no agreement requirement to deem vertical restraints an unfair trade practice, it provides that transactions between parents or subsidiaries cannot be an unfair trade practice if the parent owns 100% of the subsidiary, or owns between 50–100% and the transactions are equivalent to intracompany transactions given other factors affecting the relations between the firms.[18] In contrast, South Korea provides that the unfair trade practice of providing undue support to "other enterprises," which has no agreement requirement but does require help to some "other" firm, has no exception even if the parent owns 100% of the other firm or they otherwise constitute a single economic unit.[19]

B. STANDARDS FOR FINDING A VERTICAL AGREEMENT

Vertical agreements raise a distinctive set of tricky issues. The core problem is that because the firms are in some supply relationship, they must necessarily be in some sort of agreement. And because they can generally choose whom to supply, they can effectively reach understandings by simply refusing to deal with buyers who do not comply with announced conditions. When a supplier unilaterally demands compliance with an anticompetitive condition and buyers acquiesce in that demand, should it be regarded as an agreement? When the agreement involves some exclusionary condition, like tying or exclusive dealing, the usual answer is "yes" under U.S. law, on the ground that the sale agreement satisfies any agreement requirement and the announced condition of tying or exclusivity is what makes it a tying or exclusive agreement, a conclusion reinforced by the fact that Clayton Act § 3 simply covers sales that are conditioned on the buyer not dealing with rivals.[20] On the other hand, when the vertical agreement involves some intrabrand restraint on distribution, the usual answer under U.S. law is "no," on the ground that a nonmonopoly supplier

---

15. *See* South Africa Competition Act § 4(2), (3), (5).

16. South Korea Guidelines on Reviewing Cartel Activities V (2009).

17. Singapore Guidelines on the Section 34 Prohibition §§ 2.5 to 2.8 (2007); Turkey Competition Act Art.3 (definition of undertaking); Turkey Competition Board Decision No. 01–33/331–94 (2001) (no economic independence when parent owns more than 50% of the subsidiary's shares and dominates its board of directors).

18. *See* Japan Distribution Guidelines at 47.

19. South Korea Fair Trade Act Art. 23(1)(vii); Guidelines on Reviewing Undue Supportive Behavior (2009); Supreme Court Judgment, Case No. 2001Du2034, November 12, 2004.

20. *See* AREEDA, ELHAUGE & HOVENKAMP, X ANTITRUST LAW ¶¶ 1752f1, 1754 (1996).

is free to unilaterally choose with whom it wishes to deal. However, we shall see that the last answer can be "yes" under U.S. law when the supplier seeks and obtains assurances from dealers that they will comply or the supplier engages in individualized exhortation to induce noncomplying dealers back into line.

Monsanto Co. v. Spray–Rite Service Corp.

465 U.S. 752 (1984).

■ JUSTICE POWELL delivered the opinion of the Court.

This case presents a question as to the standard of proof required to find a vertical price-fixing conspiracy in violation of § 1 of the Sherman Act. . . .

Petitioner Monsanto Co. manufactures chemical products, including agricultural herbicides. . . . [I]ts sales accounted for approximately 15% of the corn herbicide market and 3% of the soybean herbicide market. In the corn herbicide market, the market leader commanded a 70% share. In the soybean herbicide market, two other competitors each had between 30% and 40% of the market. Respondent Spray–Rite Service Corp. was engaged in the wholesale distribution of agricultural chemicals from 1955 to 1972. . . . Spray–Rite was a discount operation, buying in large quantities and selling at a low margin. . . . Monsanto declined to renew Spray–Rite's distributorship. . . . Spray–Rite was the 10th largest out of approximately 100 distributors of Monsanto's primary corn herbicide. . . .

Spray–Rite brought this action under § 1 of the Sherman Act. . . . [T]he jury found that . . . the termination of Spray–Rite was pursuant to a conspiracy between Monsanto and one or more of its distributors to set resale prices. . . . The Court of Appeals . . . affirmed. . . . The court stated that "proof of termination following competitor complaints is sufficient to support an inference of concerted action." . . . We reject the statement by the Court of Appeals . . . of the standard of proof required to submit a case to the jury in distributor-termination litigation, but affirm the judgment under the standard we announce today. . . .

This Court has drawn two important distinctions that are at the center of this and any other distributor-termination case. First, there is the basic distinction between concerted and independent action—a distinction not always clearly drawn by parties and courts. Section 1 of the Sherman Act requires that there be a "contract, combination . . . or conspiracy" between the manufacturer and other distributors in order to establish a violation. Independent action is not proscribed. A manufacturer of course generally has a right to deal, or refuse to deal, with whomever it likes, as long as it does so independently. United States v. Colgate & Co., 250 U.S. 300, 307 (1919). Under *Colgate*, the manufacturer can announce its resale prices in advance and refuse to deal with those who fail to comply. And a distributor is free to acquiesce in the manufacturer's demand in order to avoid termination.

The second important distinction in distributor-termination cases is that between concerted action to set prices and concerted action on nonprice restrictions. The former have been *per se* illegal since the early years of national antitrust enforcement. See *Dr. Miles*. The latter are judged under the rule of reason. . . . See *Sylvania*.

While these distinctions in theory are reasonably clear, often they are difficult to apply in practice. . . . [T]he economic effect of all of the conduct described above—unilateral and concerted vertical price setting, agreements on price and nonprice restrictions—is in many, but not all, cases similar or identical. And judged from a distance, the conduct of the parties in the various situations can be indistinguishable. For example, the fact that a manufacturer and its distributors are in constant communication about prices and marketing strategy does not alone show that the distributors are not making independent pricing decisions. A manufacturer and its distributors have legitimate reasons to exchange information about the prices and the reception of their products in the market. Moreover, it is precisely in cases in which the manufacturer attempts to further a particular marketing strategy by means of agreements on often costly nonprice restrictions that it will have the most interest in the distributors' resale prices. The manufacturer often will want to ensure that its distributors earn sufficient profit to pay for programs such as hiring and training additional salesmen or demonstrating the technical features of the product, and will want to see that "free-riders" do not interfere. See *Sylvania*. Thus, the manufacturer's strongly felt concern about resale prices does not necessarily mean that it has done more than the *Colgate* doctrine allows.

Nevertheless, it is of considerable importance that independent action by the manufacturer, and concerted action on nonprice restrictions, be distinguished from price-fixing agreements, since under present law the latter are subject to *per se* treatment and treble damages. On a claim of concerted price fixing, the antitrust plaintiff must present evidence sufficient to carry its burden of proving that there was such an agreement. If an inference of such an agreement may be drawn from highly ambiguous evidence, there is a considerable danger that the doctrines enunciated in *Sylvania* and *Colgate* will be seriously eroded.

The flaw in the evidentiary standard adopted by the Court of Appeals in this case is that it disregards this danger. Permitting an agreement to be inferred merely from the existence of complaints, or even from the fact that termination came about "in response to" complaints, could deter or penalize perfectly legitimate conduct. As Monsanto points out, complaints about price cutters "are natural—and from the manufacturer's perspective, unavoidable—reactions by distributors to the activities of their rivals." Such complaints, particularly where the manufacturer has imposed a costly set of nonprice restrictions, "arise in the normal course of business and do not indicate illegal concerted action." Moreover, distributors are an important source of information for manufacturers. In order to assure an efficient distribution system, manufacturers and distributors constantly must coordinate their activities to assure that their product will reach the consumer persuasively and efficiently. To bar a manufacturer from acting solely because the information upon which it acts originated as a price complaint would create an irrational dislocation in the market.... [8]

Thus, something more than evidence of complaints is needed. There must be evidence that tends to exclude the possibility that the manufacturer and nonterminated distributors were acting independently. As Judge Aldisert has written, the antitrust plaintiff should present direct or circumstantial evidence that reasonably tends to prove that the manufacturer and others "had a conscious commitment to a common scheme designed to achieve an unlawful objective." Cf. American Tobacco Co. v. United States, 328 U.S. 781, 810 (1946) (circumstances must reveal "a unity of purpose or a common design and understanding, or a meeting of minds in an unlawful arrangement").[9] ...

Applying this standard to the facts of this case, we believe there was sufficient evidence for the jury reasonably to have concluded that Monsanto and some of its distributors were parties to an "agreement" or "conspiracy" to maintain resale prices and terminate price cutters. In fact there was substantial *direct* evidence of agreements to maintain prices. There was testimony from a Monsanto district manager, for example, that Monsanto on at least two occasions in early 1969, about five months after Spray–Rite was terminated, approached price-cutting distributors and advised that if they did not maintain the suggested resale price, they would not receive adequate supplies of Monsanto's new corn herbicide. When one of the distributors did not assent, this information was referred to the Monsanto regional office, and it complained to the distributor's parent company. There was evidence that the parent instructed its subsidiary to comply, and the distributor informed Monsanto that it would charge the suggested price. Evidence of this kind plainly is relevant and persuasive as to a meeting of minds.[10]

An arguably more ambiguous example is a newsletter from one of the distributors to his dealer-customers. The newsletter is dated October 1, 1968, just four weeks before Spray–Rite was terminated. It was written after a meeting between the author and several Monsanto officials, and discusses Monsanto's efforts to "[get] the 'market place in order.'" The newsletter reviews some of Monsanto's incentive and shipping policies, and then states that in addition "every effort will be made to maintain a minimum market price level." The newsletter relates these efforts as follows:

---

8. We do not suggest that evidence of complaints has no probative value at all, but only that the burden remains on the antitrust plaintiff to introduce additional evidence sufficient to support a finding of an unlawful contract, combination, or conspiracy.

9. The concept of "a meeting of the minds" or "a common scheme" in a distributor-termination case includes more than a showing that the distributor conformed to the suggested price. It means as well that evidence must be presented both that the distributor communicated its acquiescence or agreement, and that this was sought by the manufacturer.

10. In addition, there was circumstantial evidence that Monsanto sought agreement from the distributor to conform to the resale price. The threat to cut off the distributor's supply came during Monsanto's "shipping season" when herbicide was in short supply. The jury could have concluded that Monsanto sought this agreement at a time when it was able to use supply as a lever to force compliance.

"In other words, we are assured that Monsanto's company-owned outlets will not retail at less than their suggested retail price to the trade as a whole. Furthermore, those of us on the distributor level are not likely to deviate downward on price to anyone as the idea is implied that doing this possibly could discolor the outlook for continuity as one of the approved distributors during the future upcoming seasons. So, none interested in the retention of this arrangement is likely to risk being deleted from this customer service opportunity. Also, as far as the national accounts are concerned, they are sure to recognize the desirability of retaining Monsanto's favor on a continuing basis by respecting the wisdom of participating in the suggested program in a manner assuring order on the retail level 'playground' throughout the entire country. It is elementary that harmony can only come from following the rules of the game and that in case of dispute, the decision of the umpire is final."

It is reasonable to interpret this newsletter as referring to an agreement or understanding that distributors and retailers would maintain prices, and Monsanto would not undercut those prices on the retail level and would terminate competitors who sold at prices below those of complying distributors; these were "the rules of the game."[11] . . .

We conclude that the Court of Appeals applied an incorrect standard to the evidence in this case. The correct standard is that there must be evidence that tends to exclude the possibility of independent action by the manufacturer and distributor. That is, there must be direct or circumstantial evidence that reasonably tends to prove that the manufacturer and others had a conscious commitment to a common scheme designed to achieve an unlawful objective. Under this standard, the evidence in this case created a jury issue as to whether Spray–Rite was terminated pursuant to a price-fixing conspiracy between Monsanto and its distributors. The judgment of the court below is affirmed.

Questions on *Monsanto*

1. Should the law distinguish between agreements and a unilateral supplier demand followed by dealer acquiescence?

a. Is there any difference in their likely effect on dealer autonomy or resale decisions? Given that even a formal contract fixing resale prices would have been unenforceable at the time, wasn't the only enforceable sanction in both cases termination of future dealing?

---

11. The newsletter also is subject to the interpretation that the distributor was merely describing the likely reaction to unilateral Monsanto pronouncements. But Monsanto itself appears to have construed the flyer as reporting a price-fixing understanding. Six weeks after the newsletter was written, a Monsanto official wrote its author a letter urging him to "correct immediately any misconceptions about Monsanto's marketing policies." The letter disavowed any intent to enter into an agreement on resale prices. The interpretation of these documents and the testimony surrounding them properly was left to the jury.

b. Would making unilateral action illegal increase overdeterrence of supplier suggestions about resale prices or decisions about which dealers to select?

c. If supplier demand and dealer acquiescence are clear, is it likely the scheme reflects dealer power?

d. If supplier demand and dealer acquiescence are fuzzy, is it likely the scheme furthers oligopolistic coordination?

2. Was the Court right to hold that a supplier's decision to terminate a dealer in response to complaints by other dealers about that dealer's price-cutting was insufficient to prove an agreement or at least an agreement on price?

a. Do suppliers have independent incentives to curb price-cutting by dealers? If so, might not those incentives make them unilaterally decide to terminate a dealer in response to dealer complaints about its price-cutting even without any price-fixing agreements with dealers?

b. Aren't dealer complaints about other dealers' pricing inevitable? If so, wouldn't the right to select dealers be undermined if one need only allege a termination that followed complaints by other dealers?

3. The court's general standard was that the evidence cannot be equally consistent with conspiracy as not; rather it must at least tend to exclude possibility of independent action. Isn't that general standard met in cases where a supplier demanded conformance unilaterally and dealers acquiesced? Doesn't the supplier's view that such a demand is necessary and the evidence that the dealers acquiesced to it tend to exclude independent decisionmaking about resale prices?

4. The Court more specifically suggested in footnote 9 that distributor termination cases needed evidence that the dealer "communicated acquiescence ... and that this was sought by the manufacturer." Was evidence meeting this more specific test actually present in case?

a. Was the evidence that the supplier twice told price-cutting distributors they would not receive adequate supplies if they continued to deviate from suggested retail prices any different from demand-and-acquiescence?

b. Was this test satisfied by the evidence that the supplier made complaints to the parent of one noncomplying dealer, the parent told the dealer to comply, and the dealer informed the supplier it would charge the suggested retail price? While this evidence suggests the requisite assurance was obtained, was there any evidence that the supplier wanted that assurance communicated to it? Wouldn't the supplier have been just as happy (if not more) with actual compliance without hearing any assurances?

c. Was this test satisfied by the evidence that the supplier made the threat to cut off a noncomplying dealer during a time of shortage, thus suggesting the timing was designed to secure compliance? Isn't it true in all demand and acquiescence cases that the threat to terminate is designed to secure compliance?

d. Was this test satisfied by the evidence that a newsletter from a distributor to its dealer-customers stated that the distributor was assured that the supplier's company-owned stores would not retail for less than the suggested retail price and that no distributor was likely to deviate because deviation risked termination?

i.   Did anything in the newsletter indicate that the supplier had sought and obtained the distributors' assurances about resale prices? Didn't the newsletter merely note that such acquiescence was likely given the supplier's threat to terminate noncompliers?

ii.   Did the fact that the supplier immediately sent the author a letter disavowing any agreement and asking the author to correct any misimpression along those lines indicate, as the Court thought, that the supplier itself construed the newsletter as reporting a price-fixing understanding? Or does it just indicate that the supplier was (rightly) worried someone might mistakenly get that impression?

5.   Given that the Court found this evidence was actually sufficient, doesn't the case effectively hold that a unilaterally announced condition coupled with individualized exhortation to induce noncomplying dealers back into line suffices to prove an agreement even without any evidence that dealer assurances were sought and obtained? Can we justify such a doctrine on the grounds that:

a.   such individualized exhortation is more likely than unilateral demands to lead to the sort of precision that facilitates oligopolistic coordination?

b.   compared to a broader doctrine, prohibiting only such individualized exhortation is less likely to impede the desirable selection and substitution of better dealers by suppliers?

Cases C–2/01 P and C–3/01P, Bundesverband der Arzneimittel–Importeure eV and Commission v. Bayer AG

... Bayer AG ... manufactured and marketed under the trade name "Adalat" ... a range of medicinal preparations ... designed to treat cardio-vascular disease. In most Member States, the price of Adalat is directly or indirectly fixed by the national health authorities.... [T]he prices fixed by the Spanish and French health services were, on average, 40% lower than prices in the United Kingdom. Because of those price differences, wholesalers in Spain exported Adalat to the United Kingdom from 1989 onwards. French wholesalers followed suit as from 1991. According to Bayer, sales of Adalat by its British subsidiary, Bayer UK, fell by almost half between 1989 and 1993 on account of the parallel imports, entailing a loss in turnover of DEM 230 million for the British subsidiary, representing a loss of revenue to Bayer of DEM 100 million. Faced with that situation, the Bayer Group changed its delivery policy, and began to cease fulfilling all of the increasingly large orders placed by wholesalers in Spain and France with its Spanish and French subsidiaries....

According to the Commission, Bayer France and Bayer Spain infringed Article [101(1) TFEU] by imposing an export ban as part of their commercial relations with their respective wholesalers. ... [The] Commission has deduced the existence of that export ban from its analysis of Bayer's conduct, and especially from the existence of a system of identifying exporting wholesalers and applying successive reductions in the volumes delivered to them by Bayer France and Bayer Spain if the wholesalers concerned were exporting all or part of the medicinal products supplied to them. ... [T]he Commission concluded ... that Bayer France and Bayer Spain had subjected their wholesalers to a permanent threat of reducing the quantities supplied, a threat which was repeatedly carried out if they did not comply with the export ban.

The Commission held that the conduct of the wholesalers showed that they had not only understood that an export ban applied to the goods supplied, but also that they had aligned their conduct on that ban. They had thereby demonstrated, at least in appearance in relation to Bayer France and Bayer Spain, their acceptance of the export ban imposed by their supplier as part of the continuous commercial relations which the wholesalers had with that supplier....

[T]he General Court annulled the contested decision ... [, concluding there was insufficient evidence of an agreement covered by Article 101(1)] ...

The need for a system of monitoring and penalties as a precondition for finding an agreement concerning an export ban....

[A]ppellants argue that the [General Court] was wrong to hold that, as a necessary condition for there to be an agreement within the meaning of Article [101(1) TFEU], Bayer had to have implemented a system for monitoring the final destination of consignments of Adalat and penalising exporting wholesalers. However, it does not in any way appear from the judgment under appeal that the [General Court] did hold that there could not be an agreement on an export ban unless there were such a system of monitoring and penalties on wholesalers.

In examining the alleged intention of Bayer to impose an export ban, the [General Court] held, on the one hand, that the Commission has not proved to the requisite legal standard either that Bayer France and Bayer Spain imposed an export ban on their respective wholesalers, or that Bayer established a systematic monitoring of the actual final destination of the packets of Adalat supplied after the adoption of its new supply policy ... or that it made supplies of this product conditional on compliance with the alleged export ban.

... [The] [General Court] did not ... [conclude] that the absence of a system of subsequent monitoring and penalties in itself implied the absence of an agreement prohibited by Article [101(1) TFEU]. On the other hand, such an absence was regarded as one of the relevant factors in the analysis concerning Bayer's alleged intention to impose an export ban and, therefore, the existence of an agreement in this case. In that regard, although the existence of an agreement does not necessarily follow from the fact that there is a system of subsequent monitoring and penalties, the establishment of such a system may nevertheless constitute an indicator of the existence of an agreement....

The mere fact that the unilateral policy of quotas implemented by Bayer, combined with the national requirements on the wholesalers to offer a full product range, produces the same effect as an export ban does not mean either that the manufacturer imposed such a ban or that there was an agreement prohibited by Article [101(1) TFEU].

Therefore, in holding that the Commission had not established to the requisite legal standard the existence of a system of subsequent monitoring and penalties on wholesalers, the [General Court] has not erred in law ...

The plea in law concerning the need for the manufacturer to require a particular line of conduct from the wholesalers or to seek to obtain their adherence to its policy ...

It does not appear from the judgment under appeal that the [General Court] took the view that an agreement within the meaning of Article [101(1) TFEU] could not exist unless one business partner demands a particular line of conduct from the other. On the contrary, ... the [General Court] set out from the principle that the concept of an agreement within the meaning of Article [101(1) TFEU] centres around the existence of a concurrence of wills between at least two parties, the form in which it is manifested being unimportant so long as it constitutes the faithful expression of the parties' intention. The Court further recalled, ... that for there to be an agreement within the meaning of Article [101(1) TFEU] it is sufficient that the undertakings in question should have expressed their common intention to conduct themselves on the market in a specific way.

Since, however, the question arising in this case is whether a measure adopted or imposed apparently unilaterally by a manufacturer in the context of the continuous relations which it maintains with its wholesalers constitutes an agreement within the meaning of Article [101(1) TFEU], the [General Court] examined the Commission's arguments ... to the effect that Bayer infringed that article by imposing an export ban as part of the ... continuous commercial relations [of Bayer France and Bayer Spain] with their customers, and that the wholesalers' subsequent conduct reflected an implicit acquiescence in that ban ... [I]t is clear from the Court's analysis concerning the system for monitoring the distribution of the consignments of Adalat delivered that it did not in any way require proof of an express ban.

Concerning the appellants' arguments that the [General Court] should have acknowledged that the manifestation of Bayer's intention to restrict parallel imports could constitute the basis of an agreement prohibited by Article [101(1) TFEU], it is true that the existence of an agreement within the meaning of that provision can be deduced from the conduct of the parties concerned. However, such an agreement cannot be based on what is only the expression of a unilateral policy of one of the contracting parties, which can be put into effect without the assistance of others. To hold that an agreement prohibited by Article [101(1) TFEU] may be established simply on the basis of the expression of a unilateral policy aimed at preventing parallel imports would have the effect of confusing the scope of that provision with that of Article [102 TFEU].

For an agreement within the meaning of Article [101(1) TFEU] to be capable of being regarded as having been concluded by tacit acceptance, it is necessary that the manifestation of the wish of one of the contracting parties to achieve an anti-competitive goal constitute an invitation to the other party, whether express or implied, to fulfil that goal jointly, and that applies all the more where, as in this case, such an agreement is not at first sight in the interests of the other party, namely the wholesalers. Therefore, the [General Court] was right to examine whether Bayer's conduct supported the conclusion that the latter had required of the wholesalers, as a condition of their future contractual relations, that they should comply with its new commercial policy . . .

The plea in law that the [General Court] wrongly took the genuine wishes of the wholesalers into account . . .

[T]he [General Court] set out from the general principle that in order for there to be an agreement within the meaning of Article [101(1) TFEU] it is sufficient that the undertakings in question should have expressed their joint intention to conduct themselves on the market in a specific way. Having concluded, when examining the alleged intention of Bayer to impose an export ban, that the latter had not imposed such a ban, the [General Court] proceeded to make an analysis of the wholesalers' conduct in order to determine whether there was nevertheless an agreement prohibited by Article [101(1) TFEU]. In that context, it first rejected the argument that an agreement was established by reason of a tacit acceptance by the wholesalers of the alleged export ban, since, as it had just held, the Commission had not sufficiently established in law either that Bayer had imposed such a ban or that the supply of medicinal products was conditional on compliance with that alleged ban.

In those circumstances, the [General Court] went on to examine whether having regard to the actual conduct of the wholesalers following the adoption by the applicant of its new policy of restricting supplies, the Commission could legitimately conclude that they acquiesced in that policy. The [General Court] thus sought to determine whether, in the absence of an export ban, the wholesalers nevertheless shared the intention of Bayer to prevent parallel imports. In the context of that analysis, the [General Court] did not make any error of law by referring to the genuine wishes of the wholesalers to continue ordering medicinal products for export and for the needs of the national market. . . .

[T]he [General Court] held that the documents supplied by the Commission do not establish that the wholesalers wished to give Bayer the impression that, in response to its declared wish, they were proposing to reduce their orders to a given level. The wholesalers' strategy was, on the contrary, by distributing orders for export amongst the various branches, to make Bayer believe that the needs of the national markets had grown. Far from establishing the existence of a meeting of minds, that strategy merely constituted an attempt by the wholesalers to turn to their advantage the application of Bayer's unilateral policy, the implementation of which did not depend on their cooperation.

It follows that the Court must dismiss as unfounded the plea that the [General Court] was wrong to find a lack of concordance between the wishes of Bayer and the wishes of the wholesalers concerning Bayer's policy seeking to reduce parallel imports.

The need for subsequent acquiescence with measures forming part of contin-uous business relations governed by pre-established general agreements . . .

[I]t is important to note that this case raises the question of the existence of an agreement prohibited by Article [101(1) TFEU]. The mere concomitant existence of an agreement which is in itself neutral and a measure restricting competition that has been imposed unilaterally does not amount to an agreement prohibited by that provision. Thus, the mere fact that a measure adopted by a manufacturer, which has the object or effect of restricting competition, falls within the context of continuous business relations between the manufacturer and its wholesalers is not sufficient for a finding that such an agreement exists.

The case of *Sandoz* concerned an export ban imposed by a manufactur-er in the context of continuous business relations with wholesalers. The Court of Justice held that there was an agreement prohibited by Article [101(1) TFEU]. However, . . . that conclusion was based upon the existence of an export ban imposed by the manufacturer which had been tacitly accepted by the wholesalers . . . [T]he Court of Justice held that [t]he repeated orders of the products and the successive payments without protest by the customer of the prices indicated on the invoices, bearing the words export prohibited, constituted a tacit acquiescence on the part of the latter in the clauses stipulated in the invoice and the type of commercial relations underlying the business relations between Sandoz PF and its clientele. The existence of a prohibited agreement in that case therefore rested not on the simple fact that the wholesalers continued to obtain supplies from a manufacturer which had shown its intention to prevent exports, but on the fact that an export ban had been imposed by the manufacturer and tacitly accepted by the wholesalers. Therefore, the appel-lants cannot usefully rely on the *Sandoz* judgment in support of their plea that the [General Court] erred in law by requiring acquiescence of the wholesalers in the measures imposed by the manufacturer . . .

Since all the pleas in law . . . have been rejected . . . , the appeals must be dismissed.

Questions on *Bayer*

1.   Why was it so critical for the Commission to establish the presence of an agreement under Article 101(1)? Even if an agreement were absent, couldn't Bayer's conduct fall under Article 102? If Bayer's conduct fell neither under Article 101(1) nor under Article 102, does this mean that nondominant manufacturers can restrict parallel trade by unilaterally limiting sales to wholesalers?

2.   Under this decision, what is necessary to prove an agreement under Article 101(1)?

a.   Does the ECJ require that wholesalers expressly acquiesce to a supplier's declared intention to restrict export?

b.   If tacit acceptance is sufficient, how does the ECJ distinguish the case in question from its earlier judgment in *Sandoz?*

3.   Did the Commission bring any kind of direct evidence (exchange of letters, etc.) establishing the existence of an agreement between Bayer and the wholesalers? In the absence of such evidence, should courts err on the side of prudence as a matter of policy?

4.   Did the ECJ's holding that no agreement existed turn mainly on the evidence that: (a) the "agreement" was not in the interest of the wholesalers; (b) Bayer could carry out its commercial policy without the cooperation of the wholesalers; (c) Bayer did not have a system of monitoring compliance with its policy against exports; or (d) Bayer did not impose an express ban on exports?

5.   Suppose Bayer unilaterally announced a policy of terminating any dealer that sold outside its member state, and dealers decided to comply with this policy to avoid termination. Does that constitute an agreement under EU law or two unilateral decisions?

6.   Are U.S. and EU standards for inferring a vertical agreement the same or different?

Finding a Vertical Distributional Agreement in Other Nations

Other nations generally lack any equivalent to the *Colgate* doctrine permitting firms to announce they will refuse to deal with distributors who do not comply with distributional restraints. Brazil, Canada and Mexico treat unilaterally imposed vertical restraints on resale prices or territories the same as vertical agreements.[21] Even suggesting resale prices falls within the Canadian rule unless the producer makes clear that the distributor need not follow that suggestion and would in no way suffer in its business relations if it didn't.[22] Australia, Japan, South Africa and South Korea likewise treat the unilateral imposition of a minimum resale price or nonprice distribution restraints the same as an agreement, but deem it legal to make nonbinding suggestions of resale prices or other distribution policies.[23] Saudi Arabia and Turkey likewise treat the unilateral imposition of resale prices the same as vertical agreements fixing resale prices, with both condemning them when they set minimum prices and Turkey allowing them when they set maximum prices.[24] Should the U.S. and EU join these nations in abandoning the difficult distinction between vertical agreements and unilateral demands that are followed by acquiescence?

---

21.   *See* Brazil Antitrust Law No. 8,884, Art.21(XI); Canadian Competition Act §§ 76(1), 77(1), (3); Mexico Federal Economic Competition Law Art. 10.

22.   *See* Canadian Competition Act § 76(5).

23.   *See* Australia Trade Practices Act § 47(2)(f), (3)(f), (13), § 96–98; Japan General Designations of Unfair Trade Practices §§ 12, 14; Japan Distribution Guidelines at 22–23, 25–26; South African Competition Act § 5(3); South Korea Fair Trade Act Art. 2(vi), Guidelines on Reviewing Resale Price Maintenance 2.C (2009).

24.   Saudi Implementing Regulations, Art.6(2)(e); Turkey Communiqué on Block Exemptions Regarding Vertical Agreements (No. 2002/2) Art. 4.

C.   STANDARDS FOR FINDING A HORIZONTAL AGREEMENT OR CONCERTED ACTION

An explicit agreement is clearly covered under both U.S. and EU law even without parallel conduct. But because horizontal agreements restraining competition are generally illegal, explicit evidence of them is often hard to come by. Thus, the more usual and more difficult issue is when to infer an agreement or concerted action from circumstances given parallel conduct.

In U.S. caselaw, the terms "agreement" and "concerted action" are generally used interchangeably to refer to the sort of joint decision covered by Sherman Act § 1, as distinguished from the sort of separate decisions covered only by Sherman Act § 2. Article 101 TFEU similarly covers "agreements" and "concerted practices," with the latter designed to prevent firms from evading Article 101 by colluding in ways that may not involve an agreement per se, but nevertheless involve an element of anti-competitive cooperation.[25] The Commission need not distinguish between them but can simply find "an agreement and/or a concerted practice."[26] "[T]he importance of the concept of a concerted practice is not its distinction from an agreement but from parallel behaviour that does not infringe the competition rules."[27]

Thus, both U.S. and EU law focus on a distinction between (a) parallel separate action and (b) agreement/concerted action. However, on both sides of the Atlantic, the conclusions drawn about this distinction in the cases often seem obscure or conclusory. We can clarify the analysis by breaking down the problem into various sorts of situations, each of which will be illustrated by the excerpted cases that follow below.

(1) In some cases the parallel conduct is at least equally consistent with an independent motive that each firm would pursue regardless of what the other firms did. In such cases, we shall see there is no agreement or concerted action under both U.S. and EU law.

(2) In other cases, the parallel conduct would be unprofitable if other firms did not engage in the same conduct. These cases are tricky because firms might engage in such parallel conduct either because they have a hidden agreement or because they are in an oligopolistic market and recognize their price interdependence. We can break this set down into three further sets of cases. (a) Sometimes, such parallel conduct seems implausible without a hidden explicit agreement, in which case an agreement will be inferred under both U.S. and EU law. (b) Other times, the parallel conduct follows common invitations or secret meetings, in which case an agreement can again be inferred under both U.S. and EU law. (c)

---

25. Case 48/69, ICI v. Commission, [1972] E.C.R. 619.

26. Case C–49/92, Commission v. Anic, [1999] E.C.R. I–4125; Cases T–305/94, etc., NV Limburgse Vinyl Maatschappij v. Commission, [1999] E.C.R. II–931, paras. 695–99.

27. See Bellamy & Child, *European Community Law of Competition*, 5th Ed., P.M. Roth, Ed., Sweet & Maxwell, 2001, p. 61.

Finally, sometimes, such parallel conduct can be explained by separate decisions that take into account price interdependence on oligopolistic markets. Both U.S. and EU law hold that such oligopolistic coordination does not involve an agreement or concerted action. The basis for this conclusion probably lies less in the belief than such coordination does not involve a joint understanding than in the problem that firms on oligopolistic markets cannot avoid knowing their prices are interdependent when they set their prices, so that it would be hard to define any prohibition in a way that tells firms how to behave.

(3) On the other hand, both U.S. and EU law do ban agreements or concerted practices that facilitate oligopolistic coordination by making it easier for oligopolists to settle on common price and notice and respond to deviations, such as bans on secret discounts. U.S. and EU law may even ban interdependent adoption of such facilitating practices. The reason appears to be that such facilitating agreements or practices can be avoided, and thus condemned in a meaningful way.

Further, avoidable practices that facilitate oligopolistic coordination can be illegal even when purely unilateral under FTC Act § 5 and as an abuse of a collective dominant position under Article 102 TFEU.

1. PARALLEL CONDUCT EQUALLY CONSISTENT WITH AN INDEPENDENT MOTIVE

Theatre Enterprises v. Paramount Film Distributing
346 U.S. 537 (1954).

■ MR. JUSTICE CLARK delivered the opinion of the Court.

Petitioner brought this suit ... alleging that respondent motion picture producers and distributors had violated the antitrust laws by conspiring to restrict "first-run" pictures to downtown Baltimore theatres, thus confining its suburban theatre to subsequent runs and unreasonable "clearances."[5] After hearing the evidence a jury returned a general verdict for respondents. The Court of Appeals affirmed ... Petitioner ... urges ... that the trial judge should have directed a verdict in its favor ...

[P]etitioner owns and operates the Crest Theatre, located in a neighborhood shopping district some six miles from the downtown shopping center in Baltimore, Maryland. The Crest, possessing the most modern improvements and appointments, opened on February 26, 1949. Before and after the opening, petitioner, through its president, repeatedly sought to obtain first-run features for the theatre. Petitioner approached each respondent separately, initially requesting exclusive first-runs, later asking for first-runs [at the same time as a downtown theatre] ... But respondents uniformly rebuffed petitioner's efforts and adhered to an established policy of restricting first-runs in Baltimore to the eight downtown theatres.

---

5. "A clearance is the period of time, usually stipulated in license contracts, which must elapse between runs of the same feature within a particular area or in specified theatres."

Admittedly there is no direct evidence of illegal agreement between the respondents and no conspiracy is charged as to the independent exhibitors in Baltimore, who account for 63% of first-run exhibitions. The various respondents advanced much the same reasons for denying petitioner's offers. Among other reasons, they asserted that [simultaneous] first-runs are normally granted only to noncompeting theatres. Since the Crest is in "substantial competition" with the downtown theatres, a [simultaneous] arrangement would be economically unfeasible. And even if respondents wished to grant petitioner such a license, no downtown exhibitor would waive his clearance rights over the Crest and agree to a simultaneous showing. As a result, if petitioner were to receive first-runs, the license would have to be an exclusive one. However, an exclusive license would be economically unsound because the Crest is a suburban theatre, located in a small shopping center, and served by limited public transportation facilities; and, with a drawing area of less than one-tenth that of a downtown theatre, it cannot compare with those easily accessible theatres in the power to draw patrons. Hence the downtown theatres offer far greater opportunities for the widespread advertisement and exploitation of newly released features, which is thought necessary to maximize the over-all return from subsequent runs as well as first-runs. The respondents, in the light of these conditions, attacked the guaranteed offers of petitioner, one of which occurred during the trial, as not being made in good faith. Respondents Loew's and Warner refused petitioner an exclusive license because they owned the three downtown theatres receiving their first-run product.

The crucial question is whether respondents' conduct toward petitioner stemmed from independent decision or from an agreement, tacit or express. To be sure, business behavior is admissible circumstantial evidence from which the fact finder may infer agreement. But this Court has never held that proof of parallel business behavior conclusively establishes agreement or, phrased differently, that such behavior itself constitutes a Sherman Act offense. Circumstantial evidence of consciously parallel behavior may have made heavy inroads into the traditional judicial attitude toward conspiracy; but "conscious parallelism" has not yet read conspiracy out of the Sherman Act entirely. Realizing this, petitioner attempts to bolster its argument for a directed verdict by urging that the conscious unanimity of action by respondents should be "measured against the background and findings in the *Paramount* case." In other words, since the same respondents had conspired in the *Paramount* case to impose a uniform system of runs and clearances without adequate explanation to sustain them as reasonable restraints of trade, use of the same device in the present case should be legally equated to conspiracy. But the *Paramount* decrees, even if admissible, were only prima facie evidence of a conspiracy covering the area and existing during the period there involved. Alone or in conjunction with the other proof of the petitioner, they would form no basis for a directed verdict. Here each of the respondents had denied the existence of any collaboration and in addition had introduced evidence of the local conditions surrounding the Crest operation which, they contended, precluded it from being a successful first-run house. They also attacked the good faith of the guaranteed offers of the petitioner for first-run pictures and attributed uniform action to individual business judgment motivated by the desire for maximum revenue. This evidence, together with other testimony of an explanatory nature, raised fact issues requiring the trial judge to submit the issue of conspiracy to the jury ... *Affirmed*.

Questions on *Theatre Enterprises*

1. Was there an independent business reason that would explain the parallel conduct by the film producers and distributors here? Would an individual film distributor be happy or upset if other distributors exhibited movies with Crest rather than downtown theaters?

2. If this were deemed a horizontal agreement, how could a producer or distributor avoid entering into one? Would we want antitrust law to force them to exhibit their movies with Crest?

3. Should the defendants' denial of any agreement be determinative? Should the fact that they had entered into a prior conspiracy?

4. Was there any evidence suggesting that an agreement here was more likely than not?

5. Should the Court have affirmed if the jury verdict had gone the other way?

Matsushita Electric v. Zenith Radio

475 U.S. 574 (1986).

■ JUSTICE POWELL delivered the opinion of the Court ...

[Respondents Zenith Radio and Emerson Radio are U.S. television manufacturers. Petitioners are 21 corporations that made or sold Japanese television and other "consumer electronic products" (CEPs). Respondents claimed] that petitioners had illegally conspired to drive American firms from the American CEP market. According to respondents, the gist of this conspiracy was a " 'scheme to raise, fix and maintain artificially *high* prices for television receivers sold by [petitioners] in Japan and, at the same time, to fix and maintain *low* prices for television receivers exported to and sold in the United States.' " These "low prices" were allegedly at levels that produced substantial losses for petitioners. The conspiracy allegedly began as early as 1953, and according to respondents was in full operation by sometime in the late 1960's ... The District Court ... court found that the admissible evidence did not raise a genuine issue of material fact as to the existence of the alleged conspiracy ... The Court of Appeals ... reversed. . . .

We begin by emphasizing what respondents' claim is *not*. Respondents cannot recover antitrust damages based solely on an alleged cartelization of the Japanese market, because American antitrust laws do not regulate the competitive conditions of other nations' economies.[6] Nor can respondents recover damages for any conspiracy by petitioners to charge higher than

---

6. The Sherman Act does reach conduct outside our borders, but only when the conduct has an effect on American commerce.

competitive prices in the American market. Such conduct would indeed violate the Sherman Act, but it could not injure respondents: as petitioners' competitors, respondents stand to gain from any conspiracy to raise the market price in CEPs. Finally, for the same reason, respondents cannot recover for a conspiracy to impose nonprice restraints that have the effect of either raising market price or limiting output. Such restrictions, though harmful to competition, actually *benefit* competitors by making supra-competitive pricing more attractive . . .

Respondents nevertheless argue that these supposed conspiracies, if not themselves grounds for recovery of antitrust damages, are circumstantial evidence of another conspiracy that *is* cognizable: a conspiracy to monopolize the American market by means of pricing below the market level. The thrust of respondents' argument is that petitioners used their monopoly profits from the Japanese market to fund a concerted campaign to price predatorily and thereby drive respondents and other American manufacturers of CEPs out of business. Once successful, according to respondents, petitioners would cartelize the American CEP market, restricting output and raising prices above the level that fair competition would produce. The resulting monopoly profits, respondents contend, would more than compensate petitioners for the losses they incurred through years of pricing below market level.

The Court of Appeals found that respondents' allegation of a horizontal conspiracy to engage in predatory pricing, if proved, would be a *per se* violation of § 1 of the Sherman Act.[8] Petitioners did not appeal from that conclusion. . . .

To survive petitioners' motion for summary judgment, respondents must establish that there is a genuine issue of material fact as to whether petitioners entered into an illegal conspiracy that caused respondents to suffer a cognizable injury . . . [I]f the factual context renders respondents' claim implausible—if the claim is one that simply makes no economic sense—respondents must come forward with more persuasive evidence to support their claim than would otherwise be necessary. . . .

Respondents correctly note that "[on] summary judgment the inferences to be drawn from the underlying facts . . . must be viewed in the light most favorable to the party opposing the motion." But antitrust law limits the range of permissible inferences from ambiguous evidence in a § 1 case. Thus, in *Monsanto,* we held that conduct as consistent with permissible competition as with illegal conspiracy does not, standing alone, support an inference of antitrust conspiracy. To survive a motion for summary judgment or for a directed verdict, a plaintiff seeking damages for a violation of

---

8. . . . We need not resolve [the] debate [about the right cost measure in § 2 predatory pricing cases] here because unlike the cases cited above, this is a Sherman Act § 1 case. For purposes of this case, it is enough to note that respondents have not suffered an antitrust injury unless petitioners conspired to drive respondents out of the relevant markets by (i) pricing below the level necessary to sell their products, or (ii) pricing below some appropriate measure of cost. An agreement without these features would either leave respondents in the same position as would market forces or would actually benefit respondents by raising market prices. Respondents therefore may not complain of conspiracies that, for example, set maximum prices above market levels, or that set minimum prices at *any* level.

§ 1 must present evidence "that tends to exclude the possibility" that the alleged conspirators acted independently. *Monsanto*. Respondents in this case, in other words, must show that the inference of conspiracy is reasonable in light of the competing inferences of independent action or collusive action that could not have harmed respondents....

A predatory pricing conspiracy is by nature speculative. Any agreement to price below the competitive level requires the conspirators to forgo profits that free competition would offer them. The forgone profits may be considered an investment in the future. For the investment to be rational, the conspirators must have a reasonable expectation of recovering, in the form of later monopoly profits, more than the losses suffered ... [T]he success of such schemes is inherently uncertain: the short-run loss is definite, but the long-run gain depends on successfully neutralizing the competition. Moreover, it is not enough simply to achieve monopoly power, as monopoly pricing may breed quick entry by new competitors eager to share in the excess profits. The success of any predatory scheme depends on *maintaining* monopoly power for long enough both to recoup the predator's losses and to harvest some additional gain. Absent some assurance that the hoped-for monopoly will materialize, *and* that it can be sustained for a significant period of time, "[the] predator must make a substantial investment with no assurance that it will pay off." For this reason, there is a consensus among commentators that predatory pricing schemes are rarely tried, and even more rarely successful.

These observations apply even to predatory pricing by a *single firm* seeking monopoly power. In this case, respondents allege that a large number of firms have conspired over a period of many years to charge below-market prices in order to stifle competition. Such a conspiracy is incalculably more difficult to execute than an analogous plan undertaken by a single predator. The conspirators must allocate the losses to be sustained during the conspiracy's operation, and must also allocate any gains to be realized from its success. Precisely because success is speculative and depends on a willingness to endure losses for an indefinite period, each conspirator has a strong incentive to cheat, letting its partners suffer the losses necessary to destroy the competition while sharing in any gains if the conspiracy succeeds. The necessary allocation is therefore difficult to accomplish. Yet if conspirators cheat to any substantial extent, the conspiracy must fail, because its success depends on depressing the market price for *all* buyers of CEPs. If there are too few goods at the artificially low price to satisfy demand, the would-be victims of the conspiracy can continue to sell at the "real" market price, and the conspirators suffer losses to little purpose.

Finally, if predatory pricing conspiracies are generally unlikely to occur, they are especially so where, as here, the prospects of attaining monopoly power seem slight. In order to recoup their losses, petitioners must obtain enough market power to set higher than competitive prices, and then must sustain those prices long enough to earn in excess profits what they earlier gave up in below-cost prices. Two decades after their conspiracy is alleged to have commenced, petitioners appear to be far from achieving this goal: the two largest shares of the retail market in television sets are held by RCA and respondent Zenith, not by any of petitioners. Moreover, those shares, which together approximate 40% of sales, did not decline appreciably during the 1970's. Petitioners' collective share rose rapidly during this period, from one-fifth or less of the relevant markets to close to 50%. Neither the District Court nor the Court of Appeals found, however, that petitioners' share presently allows them to charge monopoly prices; to the contrary, respondents contend that the conspiracy is ongoing—that petitioners are still artificially *depressing* the market price in order to drive Zenith out of the market. The data in the record strongly suggest that that goal is yet far distant.[15]

The alleged conspiracy's failure to achieve its ends in the two decades of its asserted operation is strong evidence that the conspiracy does not in fact exist. Since the losses in such a conspiracy accrue before the gains, they must be "repaid" with interest. And because the alleged losses have accrued over the course of two decades, the conspirators could well require a correspondingly long time to recoup. Maintaining supracompetitive prices in turn depends on the continued cooperation of the conspirators, on the inability of other would-be competitors to enter the market, and (not incidentally) on the conspirators' ability to escape antitrust liability for their *minimum* price-fixing cartel. Each of these factors weighs more heavily as the time needed to recoup losses grows. If the losses have been substantial—as would likely be necessary in order to drive out the competition—petitioners would most likely have to sustain their cartel for years simply to break even.

Nor does the possibility that petitioners have obtained supracompetitive profits in the Japanese market change this calculation. Whether or not petitioners have the *means* to sustain substantial losses in this country over a long period of time, they have no *motive* to sustain such losses absent some strong likelihood that the alleged conspiracy in this country will eventually pay off. . . .

In *Monsanto*, we emphasized that courts should not permit factfinders to infer conspiracies when such inferences are implausible, because the effect of such practices is often to deter procompetitive conduct. Respondents, petitioners' competitors, seek to hold petitioners liable for damages caused by the alleged conspiracy to cut prices. Moreover, they seek to establish this conspiracy indirectly, through evidence of other combinations (such as the check-price agreements and the five company rule) whose natural tendency is to raise prices, and through evidence of rebates and other price-cutting activities that respondents argue tend to prove a combination to suppress prices. [The district court correctly found that an expert report finding below-cost pricing was unsupported by the evidence.] But cutting prices in order to increase business often is the very essence of competition. Thus, mistaken inferences in cases such as this one are especially costly, because they chill the very conduct the antitrust laws are designed to protect . . .

---

15. Respondents offer no reason to suppose that entry into the relevant market is especially difficult, yet without barriers to entry it would presumably be impossible to maintain supracompetitive prices for an extended time. . . .

In most cases, this concern must be balanced against the desire that illegal conspiracies be identified and punished. That balance is, however, unusually one-sided in cases such as this one. As we earlier explained, predatory pricing schemes require conspirators to suffer losses in order eventually to realize their illegal gains; moreover, the gains depend on a host of uncertainties, making such schemes more likely to fail than to succeed. These economic realities tend to make predatory pricing conspiracies self-deterring: unlike most other conduct that violates the antitrust laws, failed predatory pricing schemes are costly to the conspirators. Finally, unlike predatory pricing by a single firm, *successful* predatory pricing conspiracies involving a large number of firms can be identified and punished once they succeed, since some form of minimum price-fixing agreement would be necessary in order to reap the benefits of predation. Thus, there is little reason to be concerned that by granting summary judgment in cases where the evidence of conspiracy is speculative or ambiguous, courts will encourage such conspiracies. . . .

As our discussion . . . shows, petitioners had no motive to enter into the alleged conspiracy. To the contrary, as presumably rational businesses, petitioners had every incentive *not* to engage in the conduct with which they are charged, for its likely effect would be to generate losses for petitioners with no corresponding gains. . . . The Court of Appeals erred in two respects: (i) the "direct evidence" on which the court relied had little, if any, relevance to the alleged predatory pricing conspiracy; and (ii) the court failed to consider the absence of a plausible motive to engage in predatory pricing.

The "direct evidence" on which the court relied was evidence of *other* combinations, not of a predatory pricing conspiracy. Evidence that petitioners conspired to raise prices in Japan provides little, if any, support for respondents' claims: a conspiracy to increase profits in one market does not tend to show a conspiracy to sustain losses in another. Evidence that petitioners agreed to fix *minimum* prices (through the check-price agreements) for the American market actually works in petitioners' favor, because it suggests that petitioners were seeking to place a floor under prices rather than to lower them. The same is true of evidence that petitioners agreed to limit the number of distributors of their products in the American market—the so-called five company rule. That practice may have facilitated a horizontal territorial allocation, but its natural effect would be to raise market prices rather than reduce them. Evidence that tends to support any of these collateral conspiracies thus says little, if anything, about the existence of a conspiracy to charge below-market prices in the American market over a period of two decades.

That being the case, the absence of any plausible motive to engage in the conduct charged is highly relevant to whether a "genuine issue for trial" exists . . . Lack of motive bears on the range of permissible conclusions that might be drawn from ambiguous evidence: if petitioners had no rational economic motive to conspire, and if their conduct is consistent with other, equally plausible explanations, the conduct does not give rise to an inference of conspiracy. Here, the conduct in question consists largely of (i) pricing at levels that succeeded in taking business away from respondents, and (ii) arrangements that may have limited petitioners' ability to compete with each other (and thus kept prices from going even lower). This conduct suggests either that petitioners behaved competitively, or that petitioners conspired to *raise* prices. Neither possibility is consistent with an agreement among 21 companies to price below market levels. Moreover, the predatory pricing scheme that this conduct is said to prove is one that makes no practical sense: it calls for petitioners to destroy companies larger and better established than themselves, a goal that remains far distant more than two decades after the conspiracy's birth. Even had they succeeded in obtaining their monopoly, there is nothing in the record to suggest that they could recover the losses they would need to sustain along the way. In sum, in light of the absence of any rational motive to conspire, neither petitioners' pricing practices, nor their conduct in the Japanese market, nor their agreements respecting prices and distribution in the American market, suffice to create a "genuine issue for trial."[21]

On remand, the Court of Appeals is free to consider whether there is other evidence that is sufficiently unambiguous to permit a trier of fact to find that petitioners conspired to price predatorily for two decades despite the absence of any apparent motive to do so. The evidence must "[tend] to exclude the possibility" that petitioners underpriced respondents to compete for business rather than to implement an economically senseless conspiracy. *Monsanto*. In the absence of such evidence, there is no "genuine issue for trial" under Rule 56(e), and petitioners are entitled to have summary judgment reinstated . . .

The decision of the Court of Appeals is reversed, and the case is remanded for further proceedings consistent with this opinion. *It is so ordered*.

Questions on *Matsushita*

1. Was there any direct evidence of a conspiracy to charge predatory prices?

2. Was there even parallel conduct in this case given the lack of evidence that any prices were below cost? Would proving a conspiracy to engage in low but above-cost pricing suffice to establish (a) an antitrust violation or (b) that the plaintiffs suffered antitrust injury from that conspiracy?

3. If the evidence on cost were ambiguous, should courts infer a conspiracy to charge predatory prices from

    a. evidence of a conspiracy to raise prices in Japan?

    b. evidence of a conspiracy to fix minimum prices in the U.S.?

4. If the evidence on costs and a conspiracy to charge predatory prices were otherwise ambiguous, what can we infer from the likelihood that the

---

21. We do not imply that, if petitioners had had a plausible reason to conspire, ambiguous conduct could suffice to create a triable issue of conspiracy. Our decision in *Monsanto* establishes that conduct that is as consistent with permissible competition as with illegal conspiracy does not, without more, support even an inference of conspiracy.

Japanese firms had individual or collective financial incentives to engage in such a conspiracy?

5. When the court says the evidence must " 'ten[d] to exclude the possibility' that the alleged conspirators acted independently" does it mean the evidence: (a) must make the possibility of independent action 0%, or (b) just cannot be equally consistent with independent or concerted action?

Cement Manufacturers Protective Ass'n v. United States

268 U.S. 588 (1925).

■ MR. JUSTICE STONE, delivered the opinion of the Court.

[The Cement Manufacturers' Protective Association and its member cement makers collected and disseminated to each other information about: (a) whether buyers with requirements contracts for specific jobs were taking more cement than the job required and (b) when buyers were delinquent on obligations to pay for cement. The district court enjoined these activities as a violation of Sherman Act § 1.] ...

Specific Job Contracts ...

The specific job contract is a form of contract in common use by manufacturers of cement [whereby contractors had the option to take future deliveries of cement at the contract price up to the quantity required for a specific job.] ... It enables contractors to bid for future construction work with the assurance that the requisite cement will be available at a definitely ascertained maximum price.

In view of the option features of the contract referred to, the contractor is involved in no business risk if he enter into several specific job contracts with several manufacturers for the delivery of cement for a single specific job. The manufacturer, however, is under no moral or legal obligation to supply cement except such as is required for the specific job. If, therefore, the contractor takes advantage of his position and of the peculiar form of the specific job contract, as modified by the custom of the trade, to secure deliveries from each of several manufacturers of the full amount of cement required for the particular job, he in effect secures the future delivery of cement not required for the particular job, which he is not entitled to receive, which the manufacturer is under no legal or moral obligation to deliver, and which presumably he would not deliver if he had information that it was not to be used in accordance with his contract. The activities of the defendants complained of are directed toward securing this information and communicating it to members, and thus placing them in a position to prevent contractors from securing future deliveries of cement which they are not entitled to receive under their specific job contracts, and which experience shows they endeavor to procure especially in a rising market....

Exchange of Information Concerning Credits

Members of the association render monthly reports of all accounts of customers two months or more over due, giving the name and address of the delinquent debtor; the amount of the overdue account in ledger balance; [and] accounts in hands of attorneys for collection. . . . There were never any comments concerning names appearing on the list of delinquent debtors. The government neither charged nor proved that there was any agreement with respect to the use of this information or with respect to the persons to whom or conditions under which credit should be extended. The evidence falls far short of establishing any understanding on the basis of which credit was to be extended to customers, or that any co-operation resulted from the distribution of this information, or that there were any consequences from it other than such as would naturally ensue from the exercise of the individual judgment of manufacturers in determining, on the basis of available information, whether to extend credit or to require cash or security from any given customer . . .

Legal Consequence of Defendants' Activities

. . . That a consequence of the gathering and dissemination of information with respect to the specific job contracts was to afford, to manufacturers of cement, opportunity and grounds for refusing deliveries of cement which the contractors were not entitled to call for, an opportunity of which manufacturers were prompt to avail themselves, is . . . not open to dispute. We do not see, however, in the activity of the defendants with respect to specific job contracts any basis for the contention that they constitute an unlawful restraint of commerce. The government does not rely on any agreement or understanding among members of the association that members would either make use of the specific job contract, or that they would refuse to deliver "excess" cement under specific job contracts. Members were left free to use this type of contract and to make such deliveries or not as they chose and the evidence . . . shows that in 1920 padded specific job contracts were cut down something less than two-thirds of the total amount of the padding as a result of the of gathering and reporting this information. It may be assumed, however, if manufacturers take the precaution to draw their sales contracts in such form that they are not to be required to deliver cement not needed for the specific jobs described in these contracts, that they would, to a considerable extent, decline to make deliveries, upon receiving information showing that the deliveries claimed were not called for by the contracts.

Unless the provisions in the contract are waived by the manufacturer, demand for and receipt of such deliveries by the contractor would be a fraud on the manufacturer, and in our view the gathering and dissemination of information which will enable sellers to prevent the perpetration of fraud upon them, which information they are free to act upon or not as they choose, cannot be held to be an unlawful restraint upon commerce, even though in the ordinary course of business most sellers would act on the information and refuse to make deliveries for which they were not legally bound . . .

Distribution of information as to credit and responsibility of buyers undoubtedly prevents fraud and cuts down to some degree commercial transactions which would otherwise be induced by fraud. . . . [W]e cannot regard the procuring and dissemination of information which tends to prevent the procuring of fraudulent contracts or to prevent the fraudulent securing of deliveries of merchandise on the pretense that the seller is bound to deliver it by his contract, as an unlawful restraint of trade even though such information be gathered and disseminated by those who are engaged in the trade or business principally concerned . . .

The judgment of the District Court is reversed.

Questions on *Cement Manufacturers*

1. Why would buyers want to buy more cement than they needed on a requirements contract? Would they want to do so when market prices went above or below the contract price?

2. Would an agreement not to sell cement to buyers who had bad credit or overbought cement on requirements contracts be a Sherman Act § 1 violation?

3. Can we infer an agreement not to sell to those buyers from the fact that cement makers often cancelled contracts with such buyers after receiving information that those buyers had bad credit or overbought cement on requirements contracts?

a. If you were a cement maker who knew the buyer had bad credit or was taking more cement than it needed for a requirements contract, would you want to do business with that buyer?

b. Would your desire to cease doing business with that buyer depend on whether other cement makers ceased doing business with that buyer, or would you be even happier if your rivals continued to sell to buyers with bad credit who were defrauding sellers?

4. Is it efficient or procompetitive to give cement makers information about buyer credit and overpurchases on requirements contracts that each cement maker can use to make its own independent decisions?

Joined Cases 29/83 and 30/83, Compagnie Royale Asturienne Des Mines Sa and Rheinzink GmbH v. Commission

1984 E.C.R. 1679.

. . . The concerted action taken by Asturienne and Rheinzink which is the subject of Article 1(1) of the contested decision must, according to the preamble to the [contested] decision, be seen against the background of measures taken to protect markets by certain major producers of rolled zinc products. Those measures were prompted by the fact that, at that time, the prices charged by those producers for rolled zinc products were higher in Germany and in France than in certain other Member States, in particular Belgium, and in many non-member countries. Those price differences, which were sometimes considerable, favoured the activity of importers who bought rolled zinc products in a country where prices were low in order to resell them in a country where prices were higher, in particular

... Germany. The concerted action taken by Asturienne and Rheinzink was designed to prevent such parallel imports.

The two applicants maintain that the Commission has not proved that they took concerted action with a view to the protection of the German market.... It is not disputed that during 1976 Asturienne and Rheinzink delivered large quantities of rolled zinc products to Schiltz, in Belgium, for sale in Egypt, at prices close to those charged for sales intended for the Belgian market. The rolled zinc products sent to Belgium were relabelled by Schiltz and then loaded on to lorries bound for Germany, where they were resold at prices lower than those normally charged in that country. It is also agreed that this practice continued until the end of October 1976, that two employees of Rheinzink discovered, at that time, that the products delivered to Schiltz were being re-exported to Germany, and that both Rheinzink and Asturienne discontinued their deliveries to Schiltz between 21 and 29 October 1976.

According to the contested decision, the cessation of deliveries to Schiltz by the two undertakings could not be explained other than by an exchange of information between them with a view to taking parallel action against Schiltz as part of a concerted practice protecting the level of prices on the German market, in particular by preventing parallel imports or the reintroduction of rolled zinc products originating in Germany. In arriving at that conclusion, the decision relies on the following factors:

On 21 October 1976, the date on which Asturienne suspended its deliveries to Schiltz "for no apparent reason", Rheinzink accused Schiltz of not complying with the clause concerning exportation to Egypt. The commission maintains that it cannot be regarded as a coincidence that those events occurred on the same date.

On 26 October 1976, Rheinzink informed Asturienne by telex message that it intended to reduce its prices on the German market by about 3%, a communication which would have been "devoid of purpose as between competitors other than as part of a concerted effort to combat together parallel exports to that market";

On 29 October 1976, Rheinzink discontinued its deliveries to Schiltz after attempting unsuccessfully to induce the latter to put an end to its exports to the Federal Republic of Germany.

Not until 8 November 1976, that is to say, after the Rheinzink employees had completed their inquiries in regard to Schiltz and its German buyer, did Asturienne demand payment from Schiltz of the sums which were still owed to it.

The Commission's reasoning is based on the supposition that the facts established cannot be explained other than by concerted action by the two undertakings. Faced with such an argument, it is sufficient for the applicants to prove circumstances which cast the facts established by the Commission in a different light and which thus allow another explanation of the facts to be substituted for the one adopted by the contested decision.

The applicants have in fact proved the existence of such circumstances. The Commission was obliged to admit that, contrary to the findings in the decision, Asturienne had completely fulfilled an order from Schiltz for 240 tonnes of rolled zinc products at the time when it ceased deliveries to it on 21 October 1976. Asturienne has also proved, by producing invoices and telex messages, that it had already had difficulties with Schiltz regarding the payment of certain invoices relating to deliveries made in September, that it had demanded payment of those invoices by telex communications of 14 October and 2 November, and that problems of the same kind had arisen over payment of the invoices relating to the 240 tonnes delivered in October. . . . In those circumstances, the cessation of deliveries to Schiltz by Asturienne, and the moment at which that cessation took place, can be explained by considerations arising from the financial relations between Asturienne and Schiltz.

The fact that on 26 October 1976 Rheinzink sent a telex communication to Asturienne concerning the reduction of prices on the German market does not, in itself, constitute evidence establishing the existence of a concerted practice, not least because the Commission has not proved or even alleged that this had an effect on the prices charged by Asturienne.

It follows from the foregoing that the commission has not produced sufficiently precise and coherent proof to justify the view that the parallel behaviour of the two undertakings in question was the result of concerted action by them. Consequently, . . . Article [(1)] of the contested decision must be declared void.

Questions on *Companie Asturienne des Mines and Rheinzink v. Commission*

1. What are the main implications of this case for the Commission when it seeks to establish the presence of a concerted practice?

2. Did Rheinzink and Asturienne have independent motives to stop dealing with Schiltz? Did they also have interdependent motives? If Rheinzink had not stopped dealing with Schiltz, would it have altered whether it was advantageous to Asturienne to stop dealing with Schiltz?

3. Would this case come out the same way under U.S. standards? Would the U.S. cases come out the same way under this case?

4. Was the Court right to find insufficient the evidence that Rheinzink sent a telex communication to Asturienne concerning the reduction of prices on the German market?

a. Isn't the exchange of information over price a practice designed to facilitate coordination over price?

b. Are there other rational explanations for the exchange of such information between competitors?

c. Is the problem that (i) there was no evidence Asturienne ever communicated price information back in return or (ii) the Commission did not allege an agreement to fix prices or exchange price information but rather alleged an agreement not to deal with Schiltz?

2.   Parallel Conduct that Would Be Unprofitable If Not Engaged in by Other Firms

a.   WHERE PARALLEL CONDUCT IS IMPLAUSIBLE WITHOUT AN EXPLICIT AGREEMENT

Eastern States Retail Lumber Dealers' Ass'n v. United States

234 U.S. 600 (1914).

■ Mr. Justice Day delivered the opinion of the court . . .

The defendants are various lumber associations composed largely of retail lumber dealers in New York, New Jersey, Pennsylvania, Connecticut, Massachusetts, Rhode Island, Maryland and the District of Columbia . . . [They collected information from their retailer members about which wholesalers were competing with those retailers by selling directly to consumers and circulated the lists of such wholesalers to each retailer member. The District Court enjoined these activities as a violation of Sherman Act § 1.]

. . . When viewed in the light of the history of these associations and the conflict in which they were engaged to keep the retail trade to themselves and to prevent wholesalers from interfering with what they regarded as their rights in such trade there can be but one purpose in giving the information in this form to the members of the retail associations of the names of all wholesalers who by their attempt to invade the exclusive territory of the retailers, as they regard it, have been guilty of unfair competitive trade. These lists were quite commonly spoken of as blacklists, and when the attention of a retailer was brought to the name of a wholesaler who had acted in this wise it was with the evident purpose that he should know of such conduct and act accordingly. True it is that there is no agreement among the retailers to refrain from dealing with listed wholesalers, nor is there any penalty annexed for the failure so to do, but he is blind indeed who does not see the purpose in the predetermined and periodical circulation of this report to put the ban upon wholesale dealers whose names appear in the list of unfair dealers trying by methods obnoxious to the retail dealers to supply the trade which they regard as their own. Indeed this purpose is practically conceded in the brief of the learned counsel for the appellants:

> "It was and is conceded by defendants and the Court below found
> that the circulation of this information would have a natural
> tendency to cause retailers receiving these reports to withhold
> patronage from listed concerns. That was of course the very object
> of the defendants in circulating them."

In other words, the circulation of such information among the hundreds of retailers as to the alleged delinquency of a wholesaler with one of their number had and was intended to have the natural effect of causing such retailers to withhold their patronage from the concern listed.

. . . Here are wholesale dealers in large number engaged in interstate trade upon whom it is proposed to impose as a condition of carrying on that trade that they shall not sell in such manner that a local retail dealer may regard such sale as an infringement of his exclusive right to trade, upon pain of being reported as an unfair dealer to a large number of other retail dealers associated with the offended dealer, the purpose being to keep the wholesaler from dealing not only with the particular dealer who reports him but with all others of the class who may be informed of his delinquency . . . This record abounds in instances where the offending dealer was thus reported, the hoped for effect, unless he discontinued the offending practice, realized, and his trade directly and appreciably impaired.

But it is said that in order to show a combination or conspiracy within the Sherman Act some agreement must be shown under which the concerted action is taken. It is elementary, however, that conspiracies are seldom capable of proof by direct testimony and may be inferred from the things actually done, and when in this case by concerted action the names of wholesalers who were reported as having made sales to consumers were periodically reported to the other members of the associations, the conspiracy to accomplish that which was the natural consequence of such action may be readily inferred . . .

Questions on *Eastern States Lumber*

1. If one cannot infer a conspiracy to stop doing business with buyers who appeared on the lists of offending buyers circulated in *Cement Manufacturers*, why can one infer a conspiracy to stop doing business with wholesalers who appeared on the lists of offending wholesalers circulated in this case?

2. Assuming that there were hundreds of retailers, does an individual retailer who receives information that a wholesaler is competing at retail have a financial incentive to stop doing business with that wholesaler?

a. Would the decision of a single retailer out of hundreds to stop doing business with such a wholesaler likely stop that wholesaler from competing at retail?

b. Would a decision by many other retailers to stop doing business with such a wholesaler likely deter it from competing at retail regardless of what a single retailer decided?

c. Holding the decisions of other retailers constant, would it likely be profitable for an individual to cease doing business with such a wholesaler even if it offered the best price?

3. In addition to the mere fact that the associations circulated a list of wholesalers who competed at retail, the Court noted that the record abounded in evidence that such circulations did in fact lead many retailers to stop doing business with those wholesalers.

    a. Would such parallel conduct by retailers be plausible unless there were also a conspiracy to boycott wholesalers who appeared on the list?

    b. Can one thus infer a conspiracy to boycott wholesalers who competed at retail from the list circulation coupled with the parallel conduct?

    4. Would there have been any point in circulating a list of wholesalers who competed at retail unless the associations thought retailers would respond by ceasing to do business with such wholesalers?

    a. Was there any reason to think circulation of the list would lead retailers to cease doing business with wholesalers on the list unless there were some agreement to boycott them?

    b. Can one thus infer an agreement to boycott wholesalers on the list from the circulation of the list itself?

American Column & Lumber v. United States

257 U.S. 377 (1921).

■ MR. JUSTICE CLARKE delivered the opinion of the Court.

[The American Hardwood Manufacturers' Association had 400 members, 365 of which participated in the "Open Competition Plan" (the Plan), whereby each member gave the Association daily reports on the terms of each of its sales (including copies of the invoices), monthly reports on its output and inventory, and a list of its prices. The Association then disseminated to members weekly summaries of all sales, including price and purchaser, and monthly summaries of the production, inventory, and price lists of each member, coupled with a report analyzing current market conditions and projecting future market conditions. The Plan also provided for monthly meetings to "afford opportunity for the discussion of all subjects of interest to the members." The participants made 33% of the hardwood produced in the United States. The district court enjoined these activities as a violation of Sherman Act § 1.]

The record shows that the Plan was evolved by a committee, which, in recommending its adoption, said: "The purpose of the plan is to disseminate among members accurate knowledge of production and market conditions so that each member may gauge the market intelligently instead of guessing at it; to make competition open and above board instead of secret and concealed; to substitute, in estimating market conditions, frank and full statements of our competitors for the frequently misleading and colored statements of the buyer."

After stating that the purpose was not to restrict competition or to control prices but to "furnish information to enable each member to intelligently make prices and to intelligently govern his production," the committee continues: "The chief concern of the buyer, as we all know, is to see that the price he pays is no higher than that of his competitors, against whom he must sell his product in the market. The chief concern of the seller is to get as much as anybody else for his lumber; in other words to get what is termed the top of the market for the quality he offers. By making prices known to each other they will gradually tend toward a standard *in harmony with market conditions,* a situation advantageous to both buyer and seller."

. . . [A] further explanation of the objects and purposes of the Plan was made in an appeal to members to join it, in which it is said: "The theoretical proposition at the basis of the Open Competition Plan is that *Knowledge regarding prices actually made is all that is necessary to keep prices at reasonably stable and normal levels.* The Open Competition Plan is a central clearing house for information on prices, trade statistics and practices. By keeping all members fully and quickly informed of what the others have done, the work of the Plan results in *a certain uniformity of trade practice.* There is no agreement to follow the practice of others, *although members do follow their most intelligent competitors,* if they know what these competitors have been actually doing." . . .

And in another later and somewhat similar, appeal sent to all the members, this is found: "Competition, blind, vicious, unreasoning, may stimulate trade to abnormal activity, but such condition is no more sound than that medieval spirit some still cling to of taking a club and going out and knocking the other fellow and taking away his bone. The keynote to modern business success is mutual confidence and co-operation. *Co-operative competition, not cutthroat competition.* Co-operation is a matter of business, because it pays, because it enables you to get the best price for your product, because you come into closer *personal contact with the market.* Co-operation will only replace *undesirable competition* as you develop a co-operative spirit. For the first time in the history of the industry, the hardwood manufacturers are organized into one compact, comprehensive body, equipped to serve the whole trade in a thorough and efficient manner . . . More members mean more power to do more good for the industry. With co-operation of this kind we will very soon have enlisted in our efforts practically every producing interest, *and you know what that means.*"

Thus, the Plan proposed a system of cooperation among the members, consisting of the interchange of reports of sales, prices, production, and practices, and in meetings of the members for discussion, for the avowed purpose of substituting "co-operative competition" for cutthroat competition, of keeping "prices at reasonably stable and normal levels," and of improving the "human relations" among the members. But the purpose to agree upon prices or production was always disclaimed . . .

Plainly it would be very difficult to devise a more minute disclosure of everything connected with one's business than is here provided for by this Plan, and very certainly only the most attractive prospect could induce any man to make it to his rivals and competitors . . . This extensive interchange of reports, supplemented as it was by monthly meetings at which an opportunity was afforded for discussion "of all subjects of interest to the members," very certainly constituted an organization through which agreements, actual or implied, could readily be arrived at and maintained, if the members desired to make them.

[In fact, the conduct went beyond the Plan in that: (1) weekly regional meetings were held; (2) the weekly sales report included a forecast of future market conditions that ended up being discussed at practically every meeting; (3) before each meeting members were asked to the output they had last month and estimated they would have next month, and to state their general view of market conditions, which the Association used to provide estimates of actual and future market conditions to all members.]

The Plan on paper provided only for reports of past transactions and much is made of this in the record and in argument—that reporting to one another past transactions cannot fix prices for the future. But ... [the] questions [directed at members before the meetings] plainly invited an estimate and discussion of future market conditions by each member, and a co-ordination of them by an expert analyst could readily evolve an attractive basis for cooperative, even if unexpressed, "harmony" with respect to future prices ...

This elaborate plan for the interchange of reports does not simply supply to each member the amount of stock held, the sales made and the prices received, by every other member of the group, thereby furnishing the data for judging the market, on the basis of supply and demand and current prices. It goes much farther. It not only furnishes such information, with respect to stock, sales and prices, but also reports, giving the views of each member as to "market conditions for the next few months"; what the production of each will be for the next "two months"; frequent analyses of the reports by an expert, with, we shall see, significant suggestions as to both future prices and production; and opportunities for future meetings for the interchange of views, which the record shows were very important. It is plain that the only element lacking in this scheme to make it a familiar type of the competition suppressing organization is a definite agreement as to production and prices. But this is supplied: By the disposition of men "to follow their most intelligent competitors," especially when powerful; by the inherent disposition to make all the money possible, joined with the steady cultivation of the value of "harmony" of action; and by the system of reports, which makes the discovery of price reductions inevitable and immediate. The sanctions of the plan obviously are financial interest, intimate personal contact, and business honor, all operating under the restraint of exposure of what would be deemed bad faith and of trade punishment by powerful rivals ...

[In meetings and reports members were repeatedly advised that increasing production or overproduction would be bad business because there was not enough demand and that business would be good if members did not increase production. This] is sufficient to convincingly show that one of the prime purposes of the meetings ... and of the various reports, was to induce members to co-operate in restricting production, thereby keeping the supply low and the prices high, and that whenever there was any suggestion of running the mills to an extent which would bring up the supply to a point which might affect prices, the advice against operations which might lead to such result was put in the strongest possible terms. The co-operation is palpable and avowed, its purpose is clear, and we shall see that it was completely realized.

Next, the record shows clearly that the members ... assiduously cultivated, through the [association] letters ... speaking for them all, and through the discussions at the meetings, the general conviction that higher and higher price were obtainable and a disposition on the part of all to demand them. [Plan reports repeatedly advised that there was no reason to cut prices because, given the reduced amount of lumber stock on the market, market demand exceeded supply and was leading to increased prices.] To this we must add that constantly throughout the minutes of the various meetings there is shown discussion of the stock and production reports in which the shortage of supply was continually emphasized, with the implication, not disguised, that higher prices must result. Men in general are so easily persuaded to do that which will obviously prove profitable that this reiterated opinion from the analyst of their association, with all obtainable data before him, that higher prices were justified and could easily be obtained, must, inevitably have resulted, as it did result, in concert of action in demanding them.

But not only does the record thus show a persistent purpose to encourage members to unite in pressing for higher and higher prices, without regard to cost, but there are many admissions by members, not only that this was the purpose of the Plan, but that it was fully realized. [The court collected many quotes from members who stated the Plan had enabled them to raise prices.] ... These quotations are sufficient to show beyond discussion that the purpose of the organization, and especially of the frequent meetings, was to bring about a concerted effort to raise prices regardless of cost or merit, and so was unlawful, and that the members were soon entirely satisfied that the Plan was "carrying out the purpose for which it was intended."

As to the price conditions during the year: Without going into detail, the record shows that the prices of the grades of hardwood in most general use were increased to an unprecedented extent during the year. Thus, the increases in prices of varieties of oak, range from 33.3% to 296% during the year; of gum, 60% to 343%, and of ash, from 55% to 181%. While it is true that 1919 was a year of high and increasing prices generally, and that wet weather may have restricted production to some extent, we cannot but agree with the members of the Plan themselves, as we have quoted them, and with the District Court, in the conclusion that the united action of this large and influential membership of dealers contributed greatly to this extraordinary price increase.

Such close co-operation, between many persons, firms, and corporations controlling a large volume of interstate commerce, as is provided for in this Plan, is plainly in theory, as it proved to be in fact, inconsistent with that free and unrestricted trade which the statute contemplates shall be maintained, and that the persons conducting the association fully realized this is apparent from their protesting so often as they did ... that they sought only to supplant cutthroat competition with what in their own judgment would be "fair and reasonable competition," ... and by their repeated insistence that the Sherman Law, "designed to prevent the restraint of trade, is itself one of the greatest restrainers of trade, and should be repealed." ...

Genuine competitors do not make daily, weekly, and monthly reports of the minutest details of their business to their rivals, as the defendants did; they do not contract, as was done here, to submit their books to the discretionary audit, and their stocks to the discretionary inspection, of their rivals, for the purpose of successfully competing with them; and they do not submit the details of their business to the analysis of an expert, jointly employed, and obtain from him a "harmonized" estimate of the market as it is, and as, in his specially and confidentially informed judgment, it promises to be. This is not the conduct of competitors, but is so clearly that of men united in an agreement, express or implied, to act together and pursue a common purpose under a common guide that, if it did not stand confessed a combination to restrict production and increase prices in interstate commerce, and as, therefore, a direct restraint upon that commerce, as we have seen that it is, that conclusion must inevitably have been inferred from the facts which were proved. To pronounce such abnormal conduct on the part of 365 natural competitors, controlling one-third of the trade of the country in an article of prime necessity, a "new form of competition," and not an old form of combination in restraint of trade, as it so plainly is, would be for this court to confess itself blinded by words and forms to realities which men in general very plainly see, and understand and condemn, as an old evil in a new dress and with a new name.

The Plan is, essentially, simply an expansion of the gentleman's agreement of former days, skillfully devised to evade the law. To call it open competition, because the meetings were nominally open to the public, or because some voluminous reports were transmitted to the Department of Justice, or because no specific agreement to restrict trade or fix prices is proved, cannot conceal the fact that the fundamental purpose of the Plan was to procure "harmonious" individual action among a large number of naturally competing dealers with respect to the volume of production and prices, without having any specific agreement with respect to them, and to rely for maintenance of concerted action in both respects, not upon fines and forfeitures as in earlier days, but upon what experience has shown to be the more potent and dependable restraints, of business honor and social penalties—cautiously reinforced by many and elaborate reports, which would promptly expose to his associates any disposition in any member to deviate from the tacit understanding that all were to act together under the subtle direction of a single interpreter of their common purposes, as evidenced in the minute reports of what they had done and in their expressed purposes as to what they intended to do.

In the presence of this record it is futile to argue that the purpose of the Plan was simply to furnish those engaged in this industry, with widely scattered units, the equivalent of such information as is contained in the newspaper and government publications with respect to the market for commodities sold on Boards of Trade or Stock Exchanges. One distinguishing and sufficient difference is that the published reports go to both seller and buyer, but these reports go to the seller only; and another is that there is no skilled interpreter of the published reports, such as we have in this case, to insistently recommend harmony of action likely to prove profitable in proportion as it is unitedly pursued ... Affirmed ...

[Justices Holmes, Brandeis and McKenna dissented, concluding that any market effects that resulted from better-informed sellers was not anticompetitive. Brandeis and McKenna added that: (1) it was not anticompetitive to give sellers advice about the implications of market facts for decisions they should make about production and prices; (2) that sellers did not keep a uniform portion of their capacity unused, and in fact engaged in strenuous efforts to increase production in the face of difficult weather and labor conditions; and (3) that there was no uniformity in prices, and that the member expectation that the Plan would increase prices simply reflected the belief that better information would lead to that result.]

Questions on *American Column*

1. Although firms in a competitive market might have legitimate interests in data on *average* market prices, output, and inventory to make their own independent business plans, do they have any legitimate interest in *individuated* information about what particular rivals are charging and producing and what individual buyers are paying?

a. Would members of a cartel prefer to have average or individuated information on output and prices? Which better helps to spot those undercutting the cartel?

b. Can we infer the members must have had some sort of cartel agreement to be willing to exchange such sensitive individuated information?

2. Do competitive firms have a legitimate interest in meeting weekly to discuss each other's projections of future output and prices? To collectively send each other advice/exhortations not to expand output or lower prices? To impose social sanctions on those who do not follow that advice?

3. Does the evidence that prices in fact increased show that there must have been an agreement on prices?

a. Couldn't this simply be attributable to the end of World War I increasing demand and the wet weather decreasing supply?

b. Does the fact that the price increase was not uniform undermine any inference of cartel? Is such an inference undermined by the lack of evidence that the members left a uniform share of capacity unused or stopped adding capacity?

American Tobacco v. United States

328 U.S. 781 (1946).

■ MR. JUSTICE BURTON delivered the opinion of the Court.

The petitioners are The American Tobacco Company, Liggett & Myers Tobacco Company, R. J. Reynolds Tobacco Company, ... and certain officials of the respective companies who were convicted by a jury ... of violating §§ 1 and 2 of the Sherman Anti–Trust Act ... Each petitioner was fined $5,000 on each of the other counts, making $15,000 for each petitioner and a total of $255,000 ... The Circuit Court of Appeals ... affirmed each conviction.

... [A]lthough American, Liggett and Reynolds gradually dropped in their percentage of the national domestic cigarette production from 90.7% in 1931 to 73.3%, 71% and 68%, respectively, in 1937, 1938 and 1939, they have accounted at all times for more than 68%, and usually for more than 75%, of the national production. The balance of the cigarette production has come from six other companies. No one of those six ever has produced more than the 10.6% once reached by Brown & Williamson in 1939 ...

The verdicts show ... that the jury found that the petitioners conspired to fix prices ... in the distribution and sale of their principal products. The petitioners sold and distributed their products to jobbers and to selected dealers who bought at list prices, less discounts ... The list prices charged and the discounts allowed by petitioners have been practically identical since 1923 and absolutely identical since 1928. Since the latter date, only seven changes have been made by the three companies and those have been identical in amount. The increases were first announced by Reynolds. American and Liggett thereupon increased their list prices in identical amounts.

The following record of price changes is circumstantial evidence of the existence of a conspiracy and of a power and intent to exclude competition coming from cheaper grade cigarettes. During the two years preceding June, 1931, the petitioners produced 90% of the total cigarette production in the United States. In that month tobacco farmers were receiving the lowest prices for their crops since 1905. The costs to the petitioners for tobacco leaf, therefore, were lower than usual during the past 25 years, and their manufacturing costs had been declining. It was one of the worst years of financial and economic depression in the history of the country. On June 23, 1931, Reynolds, without previous notification or warning to the trade or public, raised the list price of Camel cigarettes, constituting its leading cigarette brand, from $6.40 to $6.85 a thousand. The same day, American increased the list price for Lucky Strike cigarettes, its leading brand, and Liggett the price for Chesterfield cigarettes, its leading brand, to the identical price of $6.85 a thousand. No economic justification for this raise was demonstrated. The president of Reynolds stated that it was "to express our own courage for the future and our own confidence in our industry." The president of American gave as his reason for the increase, "the opportunity of making some money." He further claimed that because Reynolds had raised its list price, Reynolds would therefore have additional funds for advertising and American had raised its price in order to have a similar amount for advertising. The officials of Liggett claimed that they thought the increase was a mistake as there did not seem to be any reason for making a price advance but they contended that unless they also raised their list price for Chesterfields, the other companies would have greater resources to spend in advertising and thus would put Chesterfield cigarettes at a competitive disadvantage. This general price increase soon resulted in higher retail prices and in a loss in volume of sales. Yet in 1932, in the midst of the national depression with the sales of the petitioners' cigarettes falling off greatly in number, the petitioners still were making tremendous profits as a result of the price increase. Their net profits in that year amounted to more than $100,000,000. This was one of the three biggest years in their history ...

There was evidence that when dealers received an announcement of the price increase from one of the petitioners and attempted to purchase some of the leading brands of cigarettes from the other petitioners at their unchanged prices before announcement of a similar change, the latter refused to fill such orders until their prices were also raised, thus bringing about the same result as if the changes had been precisely simultaneous ...

It is not the form of the combination or the particular means used but the result to be achieved that the statute condemns. It is not of importance whether the means used to accomplish the unlawful objective are in themselves lawful or unlawful. Acts done to give effect to the conspiracy may be in themselves wholly innocent acts. Yet, if they are part of the sum of the acts which are relied upon to effectuate the conspiracy which the statute forbids, they come within its prohibition. No formal agreement is necessary to constitute an unlawful conspiracy. Often crimes are a matter of inference deduced from the acts of the person accused and done in pursuance of a criminal purpose ... The essential combination or conspiracy in violation of the Sherman Act may be found in a course of dealings or other circumstances as well as in any exchange of words. Where the circumstances are such as to warrant a jury in finding that the conspirators had a unity of purpose or a common design and understanding, or a meeting of minds in an unlawful arrangement, the conclusion that a conspiracy is established is justified ...

Questions on *American Tobacco*

1. Suppose you are one of three oligopolists, and one firm announces it will raise prices by 10%. If you don't announce you will match that price increase, then it is predictable that the first firm would rescind its price increase. Suppose you take this prediction into account and thus decide to match the first firm's announced price increase without ever discussing anything with the first firm. Should that be deemed an antitrust conspiracy? Is there any way for you to set prices without taking into account the likely reaction of your rivals?

2. As we shall see, U.S. antitrust law holds that such oligopolistic coordination is not itself an antitrust conspiracy. But how is the evidence in *American Tobacco* any different?

3. Would we expect pure oligopolistic coordination to lead to precisely the same prices for decades, often on the same day? Is such precision implausible without an actual agreement on prices? Or would it be rational for American and Liggett to adopt a strategy of immediately matching any price increase by Reynolds?

4. If the evidence is equally consistent with *independent* or concerted action, then *Matsushita* and *Monsanto* teach that no agreement can be inferred under U.S. law. But suppose the evidence is equally consistent with *oligopolistic* or concerted action.

    a. Do the same factors that were recited in those cases counsel against inferring an agreement, or do concerns about underdeterring the concerted action dominate because there is no concern about overdeterring oligopolistic coordination?

    b. Does *American Tobacco* effectively hold that when the evidence is equally consistent with *oligopolistic* or concerted action, then a conspiracy should be inferred? If the courts did not adopt such a rule, wouldn't it be harder to infer a conspiracy in an oligopolistic industry because interdependence is typically a plausible alternative explanation? Would it make sense to have the standards of proving a conspiracy hardest to satisfy in the most concentrated industries? To make oligopolistic pricing a defense to a price-fixing claim?

Case 48/69, Imperial Chemical Indus. v. Commission (Dyestuffs)

1972 E.C.R. 619.

    . . . [T]hree general and uniform increases in the prices of dyestuffs took place in the Community. Between 7 and 20 January 1964, a uniform increase of 15 per cent in the prices of most dyes based on aniline, with the exception of certain categories, took place in Italy, the Netherlands, Belgium and Luxembourg and in certain third countries. On 1 January 1965 an identical increase took place in Germany. On the same day almost all producers in all the countries of the Common Market except France introduced a uniform increase of 10 per cent on the prices of dyes and pigments excluded from the increase of 1964. Since the ACNA undertaking did not take part in the increase of 1965 on the Italian market, the other undertakings did not maintain the announced increase of their prices on that market. Towards mid-October 1967, an increase for all dyes was introduced, except in Italy, by almost all producers, amounting to 8 per cent in Germany, the Netherlands, Belgium and Luxembourg, and 12 per cent in France.

    [T]he Commission found that the increases were the result of concerted practices, which infringed Article [101(1)] of the Treaty, between [various] undertakings . . . It therefore imposed a fine of 50,000 U.A on each of these undertakings, with the exception of ACNA, for which the fine was fixed at 40,000 U.A. . . .

The concept of a concerted practice

    Article [101] draws a distinction between the concept of "concerted practices" and that of "agreements between undertakings" or of "decisions by associations of undertakings"; the object is to bring within the prohibition of that article a form of coordination between undertakings which, without having reached the stage where an agreement properly so-called has been concluded, knowingly substitutes practical cooperation between them for the risks of competition. By its very nature, then, a concerted practice does not have all the elements of a contract but may inter alia arise out of coordination which becomes apparent from the behaviour of the participants.

Although parallel behaviour may not by itself be identified with a concerted practice, it may however amount to strong evidence of such a practice if it leads to conditions of competition which do not correspond to the normal conditions of the market, having regard to the nature of the products, the size and number of the undertakings, and the volume of the said market. This is especially the case if the parallel conduct is such as to enable those concerned to attempt to stabilize prices at a level different from that to which competition would have led, and to consolidate established positions to the detriment of effective freedom of movement of the products in the common market and of the freedom of consumers to choose their suppliers.

Therefore the question whether there was a concerted action in this case can only be correctly determined if the evidence upon which the contested decision is based is considered, not in isolation, but as a whole, account being taken of the specific features of the market in the products in question.

The characteristic features of the market in dyestuffs

The market in dyestuffs is characterized by the fact that 80 per cent of the market is supplied by about ten producers, very large ones in the main, which often manufacture these products together with other chemical products or pharmaceutical specialities. The production patterns and therefore the cost structures of these manufacturers are very different and this makes it difficult to ascertain competing manufacturers' costs.

The total number of dyestuffs is very high, each undertaking producing more than a thousand. The average extent to which these products can be replaced by others is considered relatively good for standard dyes, but it can be very low or even non-existent for speciality dyes. As regards speciality products, the market tends in certain cases towards an oligopolistic situation. Since the price of dyestuffs forms a relatively small part of the price of the final product of the user undertaking, there is little elasticity of demand for dyestuffs on the market as a whole and this encourages price increases in the short term.

Another factor is that the total demand for dyestuffs is constantly increasing, and this tends to induce producers to adopt a policy enabling them to take advantage of this increase. In the territory of the Community, the market in dyestuffs in fact consists of five separate national markets with different price levels which cannot be explained by differences in costs and charges affecting producers in those countries. Thus the establishment of the Common Market would not appear to have had any effect on this situation, since the differences between national price levels have scarcely decreased. On the contrary, it is clear that each of the national markets has the characteristics of an oligopoly and that in most of them price levels are established under the influence of a "priceleader", who in some cases is the largest producer in the country concerned, and in other cases is a producer in another Member State or a third State, acting through a subsidiary.

According to the experts this dividing-up of the market is due to the need to supply local technical assistance to users and to ensure immediate delivery, generally in small quantities, since, apart from exceptional cases, producers supply their subsidiaries established in the different Member States and maintain a network of agents and depots to ensure that user undertakings receive specific assistance and supplies. It appears from the data produced during the course of the proceedings that even in cases where a producer establishes direct contact with an important user in another Member State, prices are usually fixed in relation to the place where the user is established and tend to follow the level of prices on the national market. Although the foremost reason why producers have acted in this way is in order to adapt themselves to the special features of the market in dyestuffs and to the needs of their customers, the fact remains that the dividing-up of the market which results tends, by fragmenting the effects of competition, to isolate users in their national market, and to prevent a general confrontation between producers throughout the common market ...

The increases of 1964, 1965 and 1967

The increases of 1964, 1965 and 1967 covered by the contested decision are interconnected. The increase of 15 per cent in the prices of most aniline dyes in Germany on 1 January 1965 was in reality nothing more than the extension to another national market of the increase applied in January 1964 in Italy, the Netherlands, Belgium and Luxembourg. The increase in the prices of certain dyes and pigments introduced on 1 January 1965 in all the Member States, except France, applied to all the products which had been excluded from the first increase. The reason why the price increase of 8 per cent introduced in the autumn of 1967 was raised to 12 per cent for France was that there was a wish to make up for the increases of 1964 and 1965 in which that market had not taken part because of the price control system. Therefore the three increases cannot be isolated one from another, even though they did not take place under identical conditions.

In 1964 all the undertakings in question announced their increases and immediately put them into effect, the initiative coming from Ciba–Italy which, on 7 January 1964, following instructions from Ciba–Switzerland, announced and immediately introduced an increase of 15 per cent. This initiative was followed by the other producers on the Italian market within two or three days. On 9 January ICI Holland took the initiative in introducing the same increase in the Netherlands, whilst on the same day Bayer took the same initiative on the Belgo–Luxembourg market. With minor differences, particularly between the price increases by the German undertakings on the one hand and the Swiss and United Kingdom undertakings on the other, these increases concerned the same range of products for the various producers and markets, namely, most aniline dyes other than pigments, food colourings and cosmetics.

As regards the increase of 1965 certain undertakings announced in advance price increases amounting, for the German market, to an increase of 15 per cent for products whose prices had already been similarly increased on the other markets, and to 10 per cent for products whose prices had not yet been increased. These announcements were spread over the period between 14 October and 28 December 1964. The first announcement was made by BASF, on 14 October 1964, followed by an announcement by Bayer on 30 October and by Castella on 5 November. These increases were simultaneously applied on 1 January 1965 on all the markets except for the French market because of the price freeze in that State, and the Italian market where, as a result of the refusal by the principal Italian producer, ACNA, to increase its prices on the said market, the other producers also decided not to increase theirs. ACNA also refrained from putting its prices up by 10 per cent on the German market. Otherwise the increase was general, was simultaneously introduced by all the producers mentioned in the contested decision, and was applied without any differences concerning the range of products.

As regards the increase of 1967, during a meeting held at Basel on 19 August 1967, which was attended by all the producers mentioned in the contested decision except ACNA, the Geigy undertaking announced its intention to increase its selling prices by 8 per cent with effect from 16 October 1967. On that same occasion the representatives of Bayer and Francolor stated that their undertakings were also considering an increase. From mid-September all the undertakings mentioned in the contested decision announced a price increase of 8 per cent, raised to 12 per cent for France, to take effect on 16 October in all the countries except Italy, where ACNA again refused to increase its prices, although it was willing to follow the movement in prices on two other markets, albeit on dates other than 16 October.

Viewed as a whole, the three consecutive increases reveal progressive cooperation between the undertakings concerned. In fact, after the experience of 1964, when the announcement of the increases and their application coincided, although with minor differences as regards the range of products affected, the increases of 1965 and 1967 indicate a different mode of operation. Here, the undertakings taking the initiative, BASF and Geigy respectively, announced their intentions of making an increase some time in advance, which allowed the undertakings to observe each other's reactions on the different markets, and to adapt themselves accordingly. By means of these advance announcements the various undertakings eliminated all uncertainty between them as to their future conduct and, in doing so, also eliminated a large part of the risk usually inherent in any independent change of conduct on one or several markets. This was all the more the case since these announcements, which led to the fixing of general and equal increases in prices for the markets in dyestuffs, rendered the market transparent as regard the percentage rates of increase.

Therefore, by the way in which they acted, the undertakings in question temporarily eliminated with respect to prices some of the preconditions for competition on the market which stood in the way of the achievement of parallel uniformity of conduct. The fact that this conduct was not spontaneous is corroborated by an examination of other aspects of the market.

In fact, from the number of producers concerned it is not possible to say that the European market in dyestuffs is, in the strict sense, an oligopoly in which price competition could no longer play a substantial role. These producers are sufficiently powerful and numerous to create a considerable risk that in times of rising prices some of them might not follow the general movement but might instead try to increase their share of the market by behaving in an individual way.

Furthermore, the dividing-up of the Common Market into five national markets with different price levels and structures makes it improbable that a spontaneous and equal price increase would occur on all the national markets. Although a general, spontaneous increase on each of the national markets is just conceivable, these increases might be expected to differ according to the particular characteristics of the different national markets. Therefore, although parallel conduct in respect of prices may well have been an attractive and risk-free objective for the undertakings concerned, it is hardly conceivable that the same action could be taken spontaneously at the same time, on the same national markets and for the same range of products.

Nor is it any more plausible that the increases of January 1964, introduced on the Italian market and copied on the Netherlands and Belgo–Luxembourg markets which have little in common with each other either as regards the level of prices or the pattern of competition, could have been brought into effect within a period of two or three days without prior concertation. As regards the increases of 1965 and 1967 concertation took place openly, since all the announcements of the intention to increase prices with effect from a certain date and for a certain range of products made it possible for producers to decide on their conduct regarding the special cases of France and Italy. In proceeding in this way, the undertakings mutually eliminated in advance any uncertainties concerning their reciprocal behaviour on the different markets and thereby also eliminated a large part of the risk inherent in any independent change of conduct on those markets.

The general and uniform increase on those different markets can only be explained by a common intention on the part of those undertakings, first, to adjust the level of prices and the situation resulting from competition in the form of discounts, and secondly, to avoid the risk, which is inherent in any price increase, of changing the conditions of competition. The fact that the price increases announced were not introduced in Italy and that ACNA only partially adopted the 1967 increase in other markets, far from undermining this conclusion, tends to confirm it.

The function of price competition is to keep prices down to the lowest possible level and to encourage the movement of goods between the Member States, thereby permitting the most efficient possible distribution of activities in the matter of productivity and the capacity of undertakings to adapt themselves to change. Differences in rates encourage the pursuit of one of the basic objectives of the Treaty, namely the interpenetration of national markets and, as a result, direct access by consumers to the sources of production of the whole community.

By reason of the limited elasticity of the market in dyestuffs, resulting from factors such as the lack of transparency with regard to prices, the interdependence of the different dyestuffs of each producer for the purpose of building up the range of products used by each consumer, the relatively low proportion of the cost of the final product of the user undertaking represented by the prices of these products, the fact that it is useful for users to have a local supplier and the influence of transport costs, the need to avoid any action which might artificially reduce the opportunities for interpenetration of the various national markets at the consumer level becomes particularly important on the market in the products in question.

Although every producer is free to change his prices, taking into account in so doing the present or foreseeable conduct of his competitors, nevertheless it is contrary to the rules on competition contained in the Treaty for a producer to cooperate with his competitors, in any way whatsoever, in order to determine a coordinated course of action relating to a price increase and to ensure its success by prior elimination of all uncertainty as to each other's conduct regarding the essential elements of that action, such as the amount, subject-matter, date and place of the increases.

In these circumstances and taking into account the nature of the market in the products in question, the conduct of the applicant, in conjunction with other undertakings against which proceedings have been taken, was designed to replace the risks of competition and the hazards of competitors' spontaneous reactions by cooperation constituting a concerted practice prohibited by Article 101 TFEU.

Questions on *Dyestuffs*

1. Does the ECJ equate parallel behaviour with a concerted practice? What is the probative value of parallel behaviour when it comes to demonstrating a concerted practice?

2. Does it seem plausible that this pattern of parallel action could have resulted without a secret agreement? What did the Court think?

3. Why aren't the 1964 price increases explicable by separate decisions to follow the price leader in each nation? Is it implausible that the price leader would separately pick the same price increase of 15% in each nation? Is it implausible that the price followers would match the price increases within 2–3 days?

4. Why is the Court more concerned about the 1965 announcements of future increases than the 1964 immediate price increases that others met? If unilateral announcements of a future price increase lead other firms to announce the same, is that an agreement on price? When we get to the next section, consider whether advance price announcements should be illegal as a practice that facilitates oligopolistic coordination even if they do not constitute an agreement.

5. Why is the Court even more concerned about the 1967 meetings where producers announce future price increases and the others respond by announcing the same thing? Does that sort of discussion equal an agreement on price? Can the agreement to hold the meeting where advance price announcements are made be condemned even if it is not an agreement on price?

6. Some scholars criticized the judgment of the ECJ in *Dyestuffs* for its rather superficial analysis of market conditions. Do you agree?

b.   WHERE PARALLEL CONDUCT FOLLOWS COMMON
INVITATIONS OR SECRET MEETINGS

Interstate Circuit v. United States

306 U.S. 208 (1939).

■ MR. JUSTICE STONE delivered the opinion of the Court . . .

[The district court found that appellants agreed with each other to enter into and carry out the contracts that were unreasonable restraints of trade] . . . The [eight] distributor appellants are engaged in the business of distributing in interstate commerce motion picture films, copyrights on which they own or control, for exhibition in theatres throughout the United States. They distribute about 75% of all first-class feature films exhibited in the United States. They solicit from motion picture theatre owners and managers in Texas and other states applications for licenses to exhibit films, and forward the applications, when received from such exhibitors, to their respective New York offices, where they are accepted or rejected . . .

The exhibitor group of appellants consists of Interstate Circuit, Inc., and Texas Consolidated Theatres, Inc., and . . . are affiliated with each other and with Paramount Pictures Distributing Co., Inc., one of the distributor appellants. [Interstate and Texas Consolidated collectively had a monopoly on first-run theatres in many Texas cities, but in many (but not all) of these cities there were rival second-run theatres.]

On July 11, 1934, following a previous communication on the subject to the eight branch managers of the distributor appellants, O'Donnell, the manager of Interstate and Consolidated, sent to each of them a letter on the letterhead of Interstate, each letter naming all of them as addressees, in which he asked compliance with two demands as a condition of Interstate's continued exhibition of the distributors' films in its "A" or first-run theatres at a night admission of 40 cents or more. One demand was that the distributors "agree that in selling their product to subsequent runs, that this 'A' product will never be exhibited at any time or in any theatre at a smaller admission price than 25 cents for adults in the evening." The other was that "on 'A' pictures which are exhibited at a night admission of 40 cents or more—they shall never be exhibited in conjunction with another feature picture under the so-called policy of double features." The letter added that with respect to the "Rio Grande Valley situation," with which Consolidated alone was concerned, "We must insist that all pictures exhibited in our 'A' theatres at a maximum night admission price of 35 cents must also be restricted to subsequent runs in the Valley at 25 cents."

The admission price customarily charged for preferred seats at night in independently operated subsequent-run theatres in Texas at the time of these letters was less than 25 cents . . . In most of them the admission was 15 cents or less. It was also the general practice in those theatres to provide double bills either on certain days of the week or with any feature picture which was weak in drawing power. The distributor appellants had generally provided in their license contracts for a minimum admission price of 10 or 15 cents, and three of them had included provisions restricting double-billing. But none was at any time previously subject to contractual compulsion to continue the restrictions. The trial court found that the proposed restrictions constituted an important departure from prior practice.

The local representatives of the distributors, having no authority to enter into the proposed agreements, communicated the proposal to their home offices. Conferences followed between Hoblitzelle and O'Donnell, acting for Interstate and Consolidated, and the representatives of the various distributors. In these conferences each distributor was represented by its local branch manager and by one or more superior officials from outside the state of Texas. In the course of them each distributor agreed with Interstate for the 1934–35 season to impose both the demanded restrictions upon their subsequent-run licensees in the six Texas cities served by Interstate, except Austin and Galveston. . . . None of the distributors yielded to the demand that subsequent runs in towns in the Rio Grande Valley served by Consolidated should be restricted. One distributor, Paramount, which was affiliated with Consolidated, agreed to impose the restrictions in certain other Texas and New Mexico cities.

The trial court found that the distributor appellants agreed and conspired among themselves to take uniform action upon the proposals made by Interstate, . . . and that the restrictions operated to increase the income of the distributors and of Interstate and to deflect attendance from later-run exhibitors who yielded to the restrictions to the first-run theatres of Interstate. . . .

Although the films were copyrighted, appellants do not deny that the conspiracy charge is established if the distributors agreed among themselves to impose the restrictions upon subsequent-run exhibitors. As is usual in cases of alleged unlawful agreements to restrain commerce, the Government is without the aid of direct testimony that the distributors entered into any agreement with each other to impose the restrictions upon subsequent-run exhibitors. In order to establish agreement it is compelled to rely on inferences drawn from the course of conduct of the alleged conspirators.

The trial court drew the inference of agreement from the nature of the proposals made on behalf of Interstate and Consolidated; from the manner in which they were made; from the substantial unanimity of action taken upon them by the distributors; and from the fact that appellants did not call as witnesses any of the superior officials who negotiated the contracts with Interstate or any official who, in the normal course of business, would have had knowledge of the existence or non-existence of such an agreement among the distributors. This conclusion is challenged by appellants because not supported by subsidiary findings or by the evidence. We think this inference of the trial court was rightly drawn from the evidence . . .

The O'Donnell letter named on its face as addressees the eight local representatives of the distributors, and so from the beginning each of the distributors knew that the proposals were under consideration by the others. Each was aware that all were in active competition and that without substantially unanimous action with respect to the restrictions for any given territory there was risk of a substantial loss of the business and good will of the subsequent-run and independent exhibitors, but that with it there was the prospect of increased profits. There was, therefore, strong motive for concerted action, full advantage of which was taken by Interstate and Consolidated in presenting their demands to all in a single document.

There was risk, too, that without agreement diversity of action would follow. Compliance with the proposals involved a radical departure from the previous business practices of the industry and a drastic increase in admission prices of most of the subsequent-run theatres. Acceptance of the proposals was discouraged by at least three of the distributors' local managers. Independent exhibitors met and organized a futile protest which they presented to the representatives of Interstate and Consolidated. While as a result of independent negotiations either of the two restrictions without the other could have been put into effect by any one or more of the distributors and in any one or more of the Texas cities served by Interstate, the negotiations which ensued and which in fact did result in modifications of the proposals resulted in substantially unanimous action of the distributors, both as to the terms of the restrictions and in the selection of the four cities where they were to operate.

One distributor, it is true, did not agree to impose the restrictions in Houston, but this was evidently because it did not grant licenses to any subsequent-run exhibitor in that city, where its own affiliate operated a first-run theatre. The proposal was unanimously rejected as to Galveston and Austin, as was the request that the restrictions should be extended to the cities of the Rio Grande Valley served by Consolidated. We may infer that Galveston was omitted because in that city there were no subsequent-run theatres in competition with Interstate. But we are unable to find in the record any persuasive explanation, other than agreed concert of action, of the singular unanimity of action on the part of the distributors by which the proposals were carried into effect as written in four Texas cities but not in a fifth or in the Rio Grande Valley. Numerous variations in the form of the provisions in the distributors' license agreements and the fact that in later years two of them extended the restrictions into all six cities, do not weaken the significance or force of the nature of the response to the proposals made by all the distributor appellants. It taxes credulity to believe that the several distributors would, in the circumstances, have accepted and put into operation with substantial unanimity such far-reaching changes in their business methods without some understanding that all were to join, and we reject as beyond the range of probability that it was the result of mere chance ... [Defendants presented alternative reasons why they each might have independently rejected the proposal in Austin and the Rio Grande Valley, none of which the Court found persuasive.] In the face of this action and similar unanimity with respect to other features of the proposals, and the strong motive for such unanimity of action, we decline to speculate whether there may have been other and more legitimate reasons for such action not disclosed by the record, but which, if they existed, were known to appellants ... Taken together, the circumstances of the case which we have mentioned, when uncontradicted and with no more explanation than the record affords, justify the inference that the distributors acted in concert and in common agreement in imposing the restrictions upon their licensees in the four Texas cities.

This inference was supported and strengthened when the distributors, with like unanimity, failed to tender the testimony, at their command, of any officer or agent of a distributor who knew, or was in a position to know, whether in fact an agreement had been reached among them for concerted action. When the proof supported, as we think it did, the inference of such concert, the burden rested on appellants of going forward with the evidence to explain away or contradict it. They undertook to carry that burden by calling upon local managers of the distributors to testify that they had acted independently of the other distributors, and that they did not have conferences with or reach agreements with the other distributors or their representatives. The failure under the circumstances to call as witnesses those officers who did have authority to act for the distributors and who were in a position to know whether they had acted in pursuance of agreement is itself persuasive that their testimony, if given, would have been unfavorable to appellants. The production of weak evidence when strong is available can lead only to the conclusion that the strong would have been adverse. Silence then becomes evidence of the most convincing character.

While the District Court's finding of an agreement of the distributors among themselves is supported by the evidence, we think that in the circumstances of this case such agreement for the imposition of the restrictions upon subsequent-run exhibitors was not a prerequisite to an unlawful conspiracy. It was enough that, knowing that concerted action was contemplated and invited, the distributors gave their adherence to the scheme and participated in it. Each distributor was advised that the others were asked to participate; each knew that cooperation was essential to successful operation of the plan. They knew that the plan, if carried out, would result in a restraint of commerce, which, we will presently point out, was unreasonable within the meaning of the Sherman Act, and knowing it, all participated in the plan. The evidence is persuasive that each distributor early became aware that the others had joined. With that knowledge they renewed the arrangement and carried it into effect for the two successive years.

It is elementary that an unlawful conspiracy may be and often is formed without simultaneous action or agreement on the part of the conspirators. Acceptance by competitors, without previous agreement, of an invitation to participate in a plan, the necessary consequence of which, if carried out, is restraint of interstate commerce, is sufficient to establish an unlawful conspiracy under the Sherman Act.

[The Court also held that the vertical agreements between the distributors and Interstate Circuit and Consolidated were unreasonable restraints even where there was no horizontal agreement to enter into those vertical agreements, rejecting the argument that they were a proper exercise of the distributor's copyrights because the agreements were imposed to further

Interstate's monopoly power in exhibiting movies in major Texas cities.] *Affirmed*.

■ MR. JUSTICE ROBERTS, dissenting ... The Government stresses the fact that each of the distributors must have acted with knowledge that some or all of the others would grant or had granted Interstate's demand. But such knowledge was merely notice to each of them that if it was successfully to compete for the first run business in important Texas cities it must meet the terms of competing distributors or lose the business of Interstate ...

Questions on *Interstate Circuit*

1. Part of the opinion bases the inference of a horizontal agreement among the distributors on the grounds that the parallel action would have been implausible absent such an agreement.

a. Is it implausible that, without an actual agreement, the eight distributors would have simultaneously accepted the agreement as to the same cities and rejected it as to the same cities? Couldn't this parallel conduct just reflect variations in the market power of Interstate–Consolidated in those cities, which would be the same for each distributor?

b. Suppose the parallel conduct were equally consistent with (i) a horizontal agreement among the distributors and (ii) separate decisions to accept Interstate's demands as to some cities. Can one still infer an agreement from the distributors' refusal to supply witnesses to testify about whether they reached a horizontal agreement? Is this an exception to the *Matsushita* standard or is simply the case that the failure to supply witnesses in such a case itself makes an agreement more likely than independent action because the distributors would have incentives to supply the witnesses if they acted independently?

2. The more famous part of the opinion indicates that—even if there were no secret conversations among the distributors to reach a horizontal agreement—a conspiracy among the distributors could be inferred from the fact that (1) each received an invitation to common action; (2) each knew others were invited; (3) each knew that joint action was necessary for success; and (4) each accepted the invitation.

a. Could one, as the dissent did, view Interstate's decision to let each distributor know the same proposal had been made to all distributors not as an effort to get the distributors to collaborate with each other, but rather as an effort to play them off against each other by letting them know they had to compete for the business of Interstate? Does the answer turn on whether the distributors would only want to agree jointly rather than individually?

b. Why was joint action necessary for success?

i. Wouldn't any individual distributor be happy to be the only one to accept Interstate's demands and exhibit movies in the major Texas cities?

ii. Is it likely Interstate would have continued with the plan if it only got access to movies by one of the distributors? Wouldn't it have likely negotiated for access to movies by the other distributors on different terms? Would a distributor be happy to be the only one who agreed to have its movies exhibited in subsequent runs for no less than 25 cents if other distributors could undercut that price?

     iii. Is it likely the distributors collectively benefitted from agreeing to set their exhibition prices for second run movies at no less than 25 cents? If so, isn't this less a case of Interstate pressuring them with its monopoly power to act against their interests than of Interstate serving as a cartel ringmaster for the distributors?

    c. Wouldn't this *Interstate Circuit* test also condemn ordinary oligopoly price leadership? In such an oligopoly: (1) isn't the announcement of a price increase an invitation to common action; (2) doesn't each oligopolist know the others are invited to match that price increase; (3) doesn't each oligopolist know that joint action was necessary for success because if one doesn't match the increase it will be rescinded; and (4) doesn't each accept the invitation by raising its prices?

     i. Should this test be interpreted to condemn ordinary oligopoly price leadership? If so, how could one define the offense in a way that oligopolists could avoid behaving illegally? Is it practicable to ask them to ignore the reality of their price interdependence when making their pricing decisions? Could courts figure out whether they had done so other than by asking whether the prices were reasonable?

     ii. In contrast, where, as in this case, a conspiracy is inferred from secret meetings and a letter that invites common action, can't firms avoid liability by not engaging in such meetings or invitations? Can we square the *Interstate Circuit* test with the doctrine allowing pure oligopolistic price coordination by changing the first element to "(1) each received an *avoidable* invitation to common action"? Is it probable the *Interstate Circuit* Court was implicitly assuming avoidability?

    3. In the *Dyestuffs* case excerpted above, the Court held that the 1967 meeting where one producer announced future price increases and others followed suit constituted an agreement on price. Would that 1967 meeting constitute an agreement on price under the rule of *Interstate Circuit*? Would the facts of *Interstate Circuit* be deemed an agreement under *Dyestuffs*?

c. WHERE PARALLEL CONDUCT CAN BE EXPLAINED BY OLIGOPOLISTIC PRICE INTERDEPENDENCE

In *Twombly*, the U.S. Supreme Court made it clear that interdependent parallel conduct, or mere oligopolistic coordination, does not suffice to show an antitrust conspiracy under U.S. law.[28] This was widely understood before, but surprisingly never quite explicitly held by prior Supreme Court cases.[29] *Twombly* further held that a Sherman Act § 1 complaint should be

---

    28. Bell Atlantic v. Twombly, 550 U.S. 544, 553 (2007).

    29. *See* ELHAUGE & GERADIN, GLOBAL ANTITRUST LAW & ECONOMICS 837 (1st ed., Foundation Press 2007).

dismissed if all it alleged was parallel conduct coupled with a bare assertion that a conspiracy existed. Some specific fact additional to parallel conduct (often called a "plus factor") must not only be ultimately proven, but alleged in the complaint. This was the widespread practice of lower courts on pleading standards for antitrust conspiracies, but arguably conflicted with some older Supreme Court caselaw that stated a complaint should not be dismissed unless there was no doubt the plaintiff could prove no set of facts that would support his claim.

Twombly offered little guidance on what the necessary plus factors might be. Given the Supreme Court caselaw summarized above, it would seem that the requisite additional evidence could be provided not only by direct evidence of a conspiracy, but also by evidence that indicates the parallel conduct either was implausible without an explicit agreement or followed common invitations or secret meetings. The lower courts have sometimes gone further to suggest that the requisite plus factor could be shown by a "motivation for common action," that is, some indication that the firms would have a disincentive to engage in the conduct unless others did the same.[30] The problem is that this plus factor is true for cases of pure oligopolistic coordination, when no conspiracy is inferred. Another plus factor the lower courts have sometimes used is evidence of adverse economic performance, like excessive prices or profits. But again this is true in cases of pure oligopoly. Such plus factors thus now seem insufficient after *Twombly*.

One other interesting feature of *Twombly* is that it indicated that oligopolistic coordination might consist not only of coordination on price, but also coordination on a strategy of not moving into the areas where each other competed.[31] This is interesting because, as we shall see in Chapter 7, it is often incorrectly assumed that oligopolistic coordination and market differentiation are mutually exclusive. *Twombly* suggests that the Court has recognized that firms might coordinate on a strategy of maintaining their differentiated status. Thus, a merger on a differentiated market might be condemned on the ground that the merger makes it easier to coordinate on maintaining product or geographic differentiation.

Joined Cases C–89/85, C–104/85, C–114/85, C–116/85, C–117/85 and C–125/85 to C–129/85, A. Ahlström Osakeyhtiö and Others v. Commission ("Woodpulp II")

1993 E.C.R. I–1307.

[The market for the supply of wood pulp was characterized by long-term agreements between producers and buyers, as well as by a system of "quarterly announcements" whereby the producer would inform its customers of the maximum price that would prevail during the following quarter and would guarantee a quantity of pulp reserved for that customer. The customer could purchase higher or lower quantities of pulp and could negotiate discounts with the producers. The price actually paid by the

---

30.   *See* AREEDA, KAPLOW & EDLIN, ANTITRUST ANALYSIS 226–31 (6th ed. 2004).

31.   Bell Atlantic v. Twombly, 550 U.S. 544, 567 (2007).

customer for its supplies of pulp was referred to as the "transaction price". The Commission condemned forty of the fifty pulp producers that sold in the [EU] for concerting about both announced and transaction prices. It concluded that the producer's parallel pricing could not be explained as resulting from independently chosen pricing strategies in a narrow oligopolistic market.]

Since the Commission has no documents which directly establish the existence of concertation between the producers concerned, it is necessary to ascertain whether the system of quarterly price announcements, the simultaneity or near-simultaneity of the price announcements and the parallelism of price announcements as found during the period from 1975 to 1981 constitute a firm, precise and consistent body of evidence of prior concertation.

In determining the probative value of those different factors, it must be noted that parallel conduct cannot be regarded as furnishing proof of concertation unless concertation constitutes the only plausible explanation for such conduct. It is necessary to bear in mind that, although Article [101 TFEU] prohibits any form of collusion which distorts competition, it does not deprive economic operators of the right to adapt themselves intelligently to the existing and anticipated conduct of their competitors. Accordingly, it is necessary in this case to ascertain whether the parallel conduct alleged by the Commission cannot, taking account of the nature of the products, the size and the number of the undertakings and the volume of the market in question, be explained otherwise than by concertation.

The system of price announcements . . .

[T]he Commission regards the system of quarterly price announcements as evidence of concertation at an earlier stage. . . . [T]he applicants maintain that the system is ascribable to the particular commercial requirements of the pulp market.

The [court-appointed] experts observe first that the system of announcements at issue must be viewed in the context of the long-term relationships which existed between producers and their customers and which were a result both of the method of manufacturing the pulp and of the cyclical nature of the market. In view of the fact that each type of paper was the result of a particular mixture of pulps having their own characteristics and that the mixture was difficult to change, a relationship based on close cooperation was established between the pulp producers and the paper manufacturers. Such relations were all the closer since they also had the advantage of protecting both sides against the uncertainties inherent in the cyclical nature of the market: they guaranteed security of supply to buyers and at the same time security of demand to producers.

The experts point out that it is in the context of those long-term relationships that, after the Second World War, purchasers demanded the introduction of that system of announcements. Since pulp accounts for between 50% and 75% of the cost of paper, those purchasers wished to ascertain as soon as possible the prices which they might be charged in order to estimate their costs and to fix the prices of their own products. However, as those purchasers did not wish to be bound by a high fixed price in the event of the market weakening, the announced price was regarded as a ceiling price below which the transaction price could always be renegotiated.

The explanation given for the use of a quarterly cycle is that it is the result of a compromise between the paper manufacturers' desire for a degree of foreseeability as regards the price of pulp and the producers' desire not to miss any opportunities to make a profit in the event of a strengthening of the market ...

(b) The simultaneity or near-simultaneity of announcements

In ... its decision, the Commission claims that the close succession or even simultaneity of price announcements would not have been possible without a constant flow of information between the undertakings concerned. According to the applicants, the simultaneity or near-simultaneity of the announcements, even if it were established, must instead be regarded as a direct result of the very high degree of transparency of the market. Such transparency, far from being artificial, can be explained by the extremely well-developed network of relations which, in view of the nature and the structure of the market, have been established between the various traders.

The [court-appointed] experts have confirmed that analysis in their report and at the hearing which followed. First, they pointed out, a buyer was always in contact with several pulp producers. One reason for that was connected with the paper-making process, but another was that, in order to avoid becoming overdependent on one producer, pulp buyers took the precaution of diversifying their sources of supply. With a view to obtaining the lowest possible prices, they were in the habit, especially in times of falling prices, of disclosing to their suppliers the prices announced by their competitors.

Secondly, it should be noted that most of the pulp was sold to a relatively small number of large paper manufacturers. Those few buyers maintained very close links with each other and exchanged information on changes in prices of which they were aware.

Thirdly, several producers who made paper themselves purchased pulp from other producers and were thus informed, in times of both rising prices and falling prices, of the prices charged by their competitors. That information was also accessible to producers who did not themselves manufacture paper but were linked to groups that did.

Fourthly, that high degree of transparency in the pulp market resulting from the links between traders or groups of traders was further reinforced by the existence of agents established in the Community who worked for several producers and by the existence of a very dynamic trade press. In connection with the latter point, it should be noted that most of the applicants deny having communicated to the trade press any information on their prices and that the few producers who acknowledged having done so point out that such communications were sporadic and were made at the request of the press itself.

Finally, it is necessary to add that the use of rapid means of communication, such as the telephone and telex, and the very frequent recourse by the paper manufacturers to very well-informed trade buyers meant that, notwithstanding the number of stages involved, producer, agent, buyer, agent, producer, information on the level of the announced prices spreads within a matter of days, if not within a matter of hours on the pulp market.

Parallelism of announced prices

The parallelism of announced prices on which the Commission relies as evidence of concertation is ... that the prices announced by the Canadian and United States producers were the same from the first quarter of 1975 to the third quarter of 1977 and from the first quarter of 1978 to the third quarter of 1981, that the prices announced by the Swedish and Finnish producers were the same from the first quarter of 1975 to the second quarter of 1977 and from the third quarter of 1978 to the third quarter of 1981 and, finally, that the prices of all the producers were the same from the first quarter of 1976 to the second quarter of 1977 and from the third quarter of 1979 to the third quarter of 1981.

According to the Commission, the only explanation for such parallelism of prices is concertation between the producers. That contention is essentially based on the considerations that follow. In the first place, the single price charged by the producers during the period at issue cannot be regarded as an equilibrium price, that is to say a price resulting from the natural operation of the law of supply and demand. The Commission emphasizes that there was no testing of the market "by trial and error", as evidenced by the stability of prices established between the first quarter of 1975 and the fourth quarter of 1976, and the fact that, generally in the case of softwood from the third quarter of 1979 to the second quarter of 1980, the first higher price demanded was always followed by the other producers.

Nor can the argument concerning "price leadership" be accepted: the similarity of announced prices, and that of transaction prices moreover, cannot be explained by the existence of a market leader whose prices were adopted by its competitors. The order in which the announcements were made continued to change from quarter to quarter and no one producer held a strong enough position to act as leader.

Secondly, the Commission considers that, since economic conditions varied from one producer to another or from one group of producers to another, they should have charged different prices. Pulp manufacturers with low costs should have lowered their prices in order to increase their market shares to the detriment of their least efficient competitors ... So far as the size of orders is concerned, the Commission considers that since the sale of large quantities enabled producers to cut their costs substantially, the price records should have shown significant price differences between purchasers of large quantities and purchasers of small quantities. In practice, those differences rarely amounted to more than 3%.

Thirdly, the Commission claims that, at any rate for a time in 1976, 1977 and 1981, announced prices for pulp stood at an artificially high level which differed widely from that which might have been expected under normal competitive conditions . . .

The applicants disputed the view that parallelism of prices was attributable to concertation. In commissioning the second expert's report, the Court requested the experts to specify whether, in their opinion, the natural operation of the wood pulp market should lead to a differential price structure or to a uniform price structure. It is apparent from the expert's report, together with the ensuing discussion, that the experts regard the normal operation of the market as a more plausible explanation for the uniformity of prices than concertation. . . .

The experts describe the market as a group of oligopolies-oligopsonies consisting of certain producers and of certain buyers and each corresponding to a given kind of pulp. That market structure results largely from the method of manufacturing paper pulp: since paper is the result of a characteristic mixture of pulps, each paper manufacturer can deal only with a limited number of pulp producers and, conversely, each pulp producer can supply only a limited number of customers. Within the groupings so constituted, cooperation was further consolidated by the finding that it offered both buyers and sellers of pulp security against the uncertainties of the market.

That organization of the market, in conjunction with its very high degree of transparency, leads in the short-term to a situation where prices are slow to react. The producers know that, if they were to increase their prices, their competitors would no doubt refrain from following suit and thus lure their customers away. Similarly, they would be reluctant to reduce their prices in the knowledge that, if they did so, the other producers would follow suit, assuming that they had spare production capacity. Such a fall in prices would be all the less desirable in that it would be detrimental to the sector as a whole: since overall demand for pulp is inelastic, the loss of revenue resulting from the reduction in prices could not be offset by the profits made as a result of the increased sales and there would be a decline in the producers' overall profits.

In the long-term, the possibility for buyers to turn, at the price of some investment, to other types of pulp and the existence of substitute products, such as Brazilian pulp or pulp from recycled paper, have the effect of mitigating oligopolistic trends on the market. That explains why, over a period of several years, fluctuations in prices have been relatively contained.

Finally, the transparency of the market could be responsible for certain overall price increases recorded in the short-term: when demand exceeds supply, producers who are aware—as was the case on the pulp market— that the level of their competitors' stocks is low and that their production capacity utilization rate is high would not be afraid to increase their prices. There would then be a serious likelihood of their being followed by their competitors . . .

Conclusions

Following that analysis, it must be stated that, in this case, concertation is not the only plausible explanation for the parallel conduct. To begin with, the system of price announcements may be regarded as constituting a rational response to the fact that the pulp market constituted a long-term market and to the need felt by both buyers and sellers to limit commercial risks. Further, the similarity in the dates of price announcements may be regarded as a direct result of the high degree of market transparency, which does not have to be described as artificial. Finally, the parallelism of prices and the price trends may be satisfactorily explained by the oligopolistic tendencies of the market and by the specific circumstances prevailing in certain periods. Accordingly, the parallel conduct established by the Commission does not constitute evidence of concertation.

In the absence of a firm, precise and consistent body of evidence, it must be held that concertation regarding announced prices has not been established by the Commission.

Questions on *Woodpulp II*

1. Given this decision, when does parallel conduct suffice to prove a concerted practice?

a. Does the ECJ provide any clear guidance on this issue?

b. Can we at best say that parallel conduct will or will not be evidence of concertation depending on the characteristics of the market in question?

    i. Which market characteristics disproved concerted action here?

    ii. How did the experts characterize the market in question?

c. Read together, do *Dyestuffs* and *Woodpulp II* mean that parallel conduct will only escape being deemed a concerted practice in oligopolistic markets? Or is the difference that in *Dyestuffs* the pattern of price changes and future announcements were implausible without an actual agreement even if the *Dyestuffs* market is properly characterized as oligopolistic? Which case involved a more oligopolistic market?

2. In situations of parallelism of prices, who bears the burden of proof of the existence or non-existence of concertation? Does the Commission need to show that there is no plausible explanation for the parallel behaviour in question or is the burden on the parties to show that there is a plausible explanation for the parallelism in question?

3. As noted above, some scholars criticized the judgment of the ECJ in *Dyestuffs* for its rather superficial analysis of market conditions. Did the ECJ do better on this account in *Woodpulp II*?

Standards for Proving a Horizontal Agreement in Other Nations

In Canada, a court can infer a conspiracy from circumstantial evidence, but only if such evidence proves the conspiracy "beyond a reasonable doubt."[32] Mere oligopolistic coordination is not sufficient to find an agreement absent some plus factor.[33] Brazil, Japan, Russia and South Korea

---

32. Canada Competition Act § 45(3).

33. *See* Canada Competition Bureau, Competitor Collaboration Enforcement Guidelines § 2.2 (2009).

more generally provide that either an explicit or tacit agreement suffices, but not mere oligopolistic coordination.[34] South Korea presumes an agreement if it is likely based on market characteristics, economic incentives, and contacts among the firms.[35] China defines the covered "monopoly agreements" as horizontal "agreements, decisions or other concerted actions which eliminate or restrict competition."[36] Taiwan defines "concerted action" to be a horizontal "agreement" and "any other form of mutual understanding," including "a meeting of minds ... which would in effect lead to joint actions."[37] A recent Egyptian decision found a horizontal agreement based on evidence of secret meetings followed by parallel price increases and output restrictions and market divisions.[38]

Under Mexican law, pricing differently in Mexico from internationally, or pricing the same as rivals, constitutes circumstantial evidence of a price-fixing conspiracy.[39] In Turkey, a concerted practice is presumed from evidence of price changes, output restrictions, or parallel conduct unless the firms can provide another economically rational explanation.[40] Should other nations adopt this latter approach of inferring a conspiracy from supracompetitive pricing itself?

3.   AGREEMENTS OR PRACTICES THAT FACILITATE OLIGOPOLISTIC PRICE COORDINATION

For oligopolistic price coordination to work, oligopolists must collectively have market power and be able to do three things: (1) settle on cooperative price; (2) notice individual firm defections from that price; and (3) respond to such defections in a way that makes defection unprofitable. If an increase in prices would lead to rapid expansion by fringe firms or entry by other firms or products, then the oligopolists will not be able to raise prices no matter how well they coordinate. The existence of the three features that facilitate coordination will also largely turn on market conditions.

---

34. Roundtable on Prosecuting Cartels Without Direct Evidence of Agreement, Contribution from Brazil, 37 OECD, 4–5 (03 Feb 2006); Roundtable on Prosecuting Cartels Without Direct Evidence of Agreement, Contribution from Japan, 28 OECD, 1, 3–4 (24 Jan 2006); ABA, II COMPETITION LAWS OUTSIDE THE UNITED STATES at Japan–20–21 (2001); Roundtable on Prosecuting Cartels Without Direct Evidence of Agreement, Contribution from Korea, 38 OECD, 3–4 (08 Feb 2006); Roundtable on Prosecuting Cartels Without Direct Evidence of Agreement, Contribution from Russia, 10 OECD, 2 (15 Dec. 2005).

35. South Korea Fair Trade Act Art. 19(5) (2007).

36. China Anti–Monopoly Law Art. 13.

37. Taiwan Fair Trade Act Art. 7.

38. Egypt Decision no.2900/2008 (25/08/2008) affirmed on appeal.

39. *See* Mexico Competition Regulations Art. (I).

40. Roundtable on Prosecuting Cartels Without Direct Evidence of Agreement, Contribution from Turkey, 17 OECD, 2 (04 Jan. 2006). Turkey has invoked this presumption even absent evidence of deliberate parallel-pricing behavior, where additional factors such as exchange of commercial data pointed to collusion along with a general market analysis pointing to a distorted competition Turkey Competition Board Decision No. 07–64/794–291 (2007).

For example, if the firms make homogeneous products and have homogeneous production and delivery costs, then it will be relatively easy to settle on the same price, know when other firms have defected, and respond with a price cut that takes away any advantage from their price cut. But when firms make heterogenous products and have varying costs of production or delivery, then all three factors are more difficult. In such a case each firm will find that a different price is profit-maximizing and thus find it harder to agree on a common price. Varying product features or delivery costs may make it harder to determine whether firms are under-cutting the oligopoly price or are simply making the appropriate adjust-ment given the differences in product features or transportation costs. Such variation also makes it harder to respond because any deviating firm will have more attraction to a certain set of consumers who have product preferences or geographical locations closer to that firm. Finally, when products or associated services vary, then each firm will have incentives to engage in nonprice competition (by making its product or associated services better) in a way that can eat away the profits from oligopoly pricing.

Likewise, oligopolistic coordination will be easier if the market involves public pricing for incremental sales that can be adjusted daily in response to the prices of others. But suppose instead purchases in the market involve secret discounts and/or simultaneous bidding for large contracts. Then it will be harder for firms to notice each other's defections or respond to them in time. There will also be higher incentives to undermine the oligopoly price, both because defections are less likely to be noticed and because any penalty may be offset by the gain of locking in a large contract.

However, oligopolists sometimes do not simply accept intrinsic market conditions that impede coordination. Instead, they may enter into agree-ments that facilitate oligopolistic coordination by making it easier to settle on common price and to notice and respond to deviations. For example, they may agree to standardize their products or associated services, charge delivery costs from a common basing point rather than their actual loca-tions, eliminate secret discounting, or exchange price information with each other.

Even if the oligopolistic price coordination itself cannot be challenged as a price-fixing agreement, can an agreement that facilitates oligopolistic coordination be challenged as an agreement that unreasonably restrains trade? The general answer is "yes" because in these cases the facilitating agreement is itself an agreement that leads to more anticompetitive results. Indeed, even the interdependent adoption of such facilitating practices can be challenged as an antitrust violation because (unlike with oligopolistic price coordination itself) the illegal activity can be defined in a way that firms can avoid. Such interdependent adoption of facilitating practices is most clearly covered by statutes like FTC Act § 5 that require no agree-ment for a violation, but might also be deemed a tacit agreement that should (unlike oligopolistic price coordination) be deemed an antitrust conspiracy under Sherman Act § 1 because it defines conduct the firms can avoid. Thus, oligopolistic coordination on a facilitating practice can be an antitrust violation or conspiracy even though oligopolistic coordination on price cannot be.

Maple Flooring Manufacturers Ass'n. v. United States

268 U.S. 563 (1925).

■ MR. JUSTICE STONE delivered the opinion of the Court ...

[The Maple Flooring Manufacturers Association had 22 defendant members that made maple, beech, and birch flooring, generally in Michigan, Minnesota or Wisconsin.] ... [I]n the year 1922 the defendants produced 70% of the total production of these types of flooring, the percentage having been gradually diminished during the five years preceding, the average for the five years being 74.2% ... The activities ... of which the Government complains may be summarized as follows:

(1) The computation and distribution among the members of the association of the average cost to association members of all dimensions and grades of flooring.

(2) The compilation and distribution among members of a booklet showing freight rates on flooring from Cadillac, Michigan, to between five and six thousand points of shipment in the United States.

(3) The gathering of statistics which at frequent intervals are supplied by each member of the Association to the Secretary of the Association giving complete information as to the quantity and kind of flooring sold and prices received by the reporting members, and the amount of stock on hand, which information is summarized by the Secretary and transmitted to members without, however, revealing the identity of the members in connection with any specific information thus transmitted.

(4) Meetings at which the representatives of members congregate and discuss the industry and exchange views as to its problems.

Before considering these phases of the activities of the Association, it should be pointed out that it is neither alleged nor proved that there was any agreement among the members of the Association either affecting production, fixing prices or for price maintenance. Both by the articles of association and in actual practice, members have been left free to sell their product at any price they choose and to conduct their business as they please. Although the bill alleges that the activities of the defendants hereinbefore referred to resulted in the maintenance of practical uniformity of net delivered prices as between the several corporate defendants, the evidence fails to establish such uniformity and it was not seriously urged before this Court that any substantial uniformity in price had in fact resulted from the activities of the Association, although it was conceded by defendants that the dissemination of information as to cost of the product and as to production and prices would tend to bring about uniformity in prices through the operation of economic law. Nor was there any direct proof that the activities of the Association had affected prices adversely to consumers. On the contrary, the defendants offered a great volume of evidence tending to show that the trend of prices of the product of the defendants corresponded to the law of supply and demand and that it evidenced no abnormality when compared with the price of commodities generally. There is undisputed evidence that the prices of members were fair and reasonable and that they were usually lower than the prices of non-members and there is no claim that defendants were guilty of unfair or arbitrary trade practices.

[The Government alleged, and the district court found, that the Association's activities constituted an agreement that restrained trade in violation of Sherman Act § 1.] . . .

It cannot, we think, be questioned that data as to the average cost of flooring circulated among the members of the Association when combined with a calculated freight rate which is either exactly or approximately the freight rate from the point of shipment, plus an arbitrary percentage of profit, could be made the basis for fixing prices or for an agreement for price maintenance . . . But . . . the record is barren of evidence that the published list of costs and the freight-rate book have been so used by the present Association . . .

The names of purchasers were not reported and . . . the identifying number of the mill making the report was omitted. All reports of sales and prices dealt exclusively with past and closed transactions. The statistics gathered by the defendant Association are given wide publicity. They are published in trade journals which are read by from 90 to 95% of the persons who purchase the products of Association members. They are sent to the Department of Commerce which publishes a monthly survey of current business. They are forwarded to the Federal Reserve and other banks and are available to anyone at any time desiring to use them. It is to be noted that the statistics gathered and disseminated do not include current price quotations; information as to employment conditions; geographical distribution of shipments; the names of customers or distribution by classes of purchasers; the details with respect to new orders booked, such as names of customers, geographical origin of orders; or details with respect to unfilled orders, such as names of customers, their geographical location; the names of members having surplus stocks on hand; the amount of rough lumber on hand; or information as to cancellation of orders. Nor do they differ in any essential respect from trade or business statistics which are freely gathered and publicly disseminated in numerous branches of industry producing a standardized product such as grain, cotton, coal oil, and involving interstate commerce, whose statistics disclose volume and material elements affecting costs of production, sales price and stock on hand . . .

[M]eetings appear to have been held monthly . . . Trade conditions generally, as reflected by the statistical information disseminated among members, were discussed; the market prices of rough maple flooring were also discussed, as were also manufacturing and market conditions. . . . There was no occasion to discuss past prices, as those were fully detailed in the statistical reports, and the Association was advised by counsel that future prices were not a proper subject of discussion. It was admitted by several witnesses, however, that upon occasion the trend of prices and future prices became the subject of discussion outside the meeting among individual representatives of the defendants attending the meeting. The Government, however, does not charge, nor is it contended, that there was any understanding or agreement, either express or implied, at the meetings or elsewhere, with respect to prices. . . .

In *Eastern States Retail Lumber* . . . [it] was conceded by the defendants, and the court below found, that the circulation of this information would have a natural tendency to cause retailers receiving these reports to withhold patronage from listed concerns; that it therefore, necessarily, tended to restrain wholesalers from selling to the retail trade, which in itself was an undue and unreasonable restraint of commerce. Moreover, the court said: "This record abounds in instances where the offending dealer was thus reported, the hoped for effect, unless he discontinued the offending practice, realized, and his trade directly and appreciably impaired." There was thus presented a case in which the court could not only see that the combination would necessarily result in a restraint on commerce which was unreasonable, but where in fact such restraints had actually been effected by the concerted action of the defendants.

In *American Column* the . . . record disclosed a systematic effort, participated in by the members of the Association and led and directed by the secretary of the Association, to cut down production and increase prices. The court not only held that this concerted effort was in itself unlawful, but that it resulted in an actual excessive increase of price to which the court found the "united action of this large and influential membership of dealers contributed greatly." The opinion of the court in that case rests squarely on the ground that there was a combination on the part of the members to secure concerted action in curtailment of production and increase of price, which actually resulted in a restraint of commerce, producing increase of price . . .

It is not, we think, open to question that the dissemination of pertinent information concerning any trade or business tends to stabilize that trade or business and to produce uniformity of price and trade practice. Exchange of price quotations of market commodities tends to produce uniformity of prices in the markets of the world. Knowledge of the supplies of available merchandise tends to prevent over-production and to avoid the economic disturbances produced by business crises resulting from overproduction. But the natural effect of the acquisition of wider and more scientific knowledge of business conditions, on the minds of the individuals engaged in commerce, and its consequent effect in stabilizing production and price, can hardly be deemed a restraint of commerce or if so it cannot, we think, be said to be an unreasonable restraint, or in any respect unlawful.

It is the consensus of opinion of economists and of many of the most important agencies of Government that the public interest is served by the gathering and dissemination, in the widest possible manner, of information with respect to the production and distribution, cost and prices in actual sales, of market commodities, because the making available of such information tends to stabilize trade and industry, to produce fairer price levels and to avoid the waste which inevitably attends the unintelligent conduct of economic enterprise. Free competition means a free and open market among both buyers and sellers for the sale and distribution of commodities.

Competition does not become less free merely because the conduct of commercial operations becomes more intelligent through the free distribution of knowledge of all the essential factors entering into the commercial transaction. General knowledge that there is an accumulation of surplus of any market commodity would undoubtedly tend to diminish production, but the dissemination of that information cannot in itself be said to be restraint upon commerce in any legal sense. The manufacturer is free to produce, but prudence and business foresight based on that knowledge influence free choice in favor of more limited production. Restraint upon free competition begins when improper use is made of that information through any concerted action which operates to restrain the freedom of action of those who buy and sell.

It was not the purpose or the intent of the Sherman Anti–Trust Law to inhibit the intelligent conduct of business operations, nor do we conceive that its purpose was to suppress such influences as might affect the operations of interstate commerce through the application to them of the individual intelligence of those engaged in commerce, enlightened by accurate information as to the essential elements of the economics of a trade or business, however gathered or disseminated. Persons who unite in gathering and disseminating information in trade journals and statistical reports on industry; who gather and publish statistics as to the amount of production of commodities in interstate commerce, and who report market prices, are not engaged in unlawful conspiracies in restraint of trade merely because the ultimate result of their efforts may be to stabilize prices or limit production through a better understanding of economic laws and a more general ability to conform to them, for the simple reason that the Sherman Law neither repeals economic laws nor prohibits the gathering and dissemination of information. Sellers of any commodity who guide the daily conduct of their business on the basis of market reports would hardly be deemed to be conspirators engaged in restraint of interstate commerce. They would not be any the more so merely because they became stockholders in a corporation or joint owners of a trade journal, engaged in the business of compiling and publishing such reports.

[N]or do we think that the proper application of the principles of decision of *Eastern States Retail Lumber* or *American Column* ... leads to any such result. The court held that the defendants in those cases were engaged in conspiracies against interstate trade and commerce because it was found that the character of the information which had been gathered and the use which was made of it led irresistibly to the conclusion that they had resulted, or would necessarily result, in a concerted effort of the defendants to curtail production or raise prices of commodities shipped in interstate commerce. The unlawfulness of the combination arose not from the fact that the defendants had effected a combination to gather and disseminate information, but from the fact that the court inferred from the peculiar circumstances of each case that concerted action had resulted, or would necessarily result, in tending arbitrarily to lessen production or increase prices.

Viewed in this light, can it be said in the present case, that the character of the information gathered by the defendants, or the use which is being made of it, leads to any necessary inference that the defendants either have made or will make any different or other use of it than would normally be made if like statistics were published in a trade journal or were published by the Department of Commerce, to which all the gathered statistics are made available? The cost of production, prompt information as to the cost of transportation, are legitimate subjects of enquiry and knowledge in any industry. So likewise is the production of the commodity in that industry, the aggregate surplus stock, and the prices at which the commodity has actually been sold in the usual course of business.

We realize that such information, gathered and disseminated among the members of a trade or business, may be the basis of agreement or concerted action to lessen production arbitrarily or to raise prices beyond the levels of production and price which would prevail if no such agreement or concerted action ensued and those engaged in commerce were left free to base individual initiative on full information of the essential elements of their business. Such concerted action constitutes a restraint of commerce and is illegal and may be enjoined, as may any other combination or activity necessarily resulting in such concerted action as was the subject of consideration in *American Column.* . . . But in the absence of proof of such agreement or concerted action having been actually reached or actually attempted, under the present plan of operation of defendants we can find no basis in the gathering and dissemination of such information by them or in their activities under their present organization for the inference that such concerted action will necessarily result within the rule laid down in those cases.

We decide only that trade associations or combinations of persons or corporations which openly and fairly gather and disseminate information as to the cost of their product, the volume of production, the actual price which the product has brought in past transactions, stocks of merchandise on hand, approximate cost of transportation from the principal point of shipment to the points of consumption, as did these defendants, and who, as they did, meet and discuss such information and statistics without however reaching or attempting to reach any agreement or any concerted action with respect to prices or production or restraining competition, do not thereby engage in unlawful restraint of commerce . . . *[R]eversed* . . .

Questions on *Maple Flooring*

1. Unlike *American Column,* here the parties did not exchange individuated information or discuss future prices or output, but only exchanged aggregate or average information about past prices and output.

a. Which sort of information would be most useful to oligopolists?

b. Does this case hold that an agreement to exchange aggregated past information, standing alone, is per se legal even among oligopolists?[41] Or

---

41. When it does not stand alone, but is used to facilitate a price-fixing cartel, an agreement to exchange such aggregated information has been held per se illegal under EC law, thus making those who participate in such an exchange liable even if they did not participate

does this case apply a rule of reason that saves this agreement only because there was no evidence that it led to uniform or increased prices?

    i.   How is the Court's decision consistent with its admission that any information exchange tended to make prices uniform and stabilize prices and output? If such price effects come from the independent usage of accurate market information to make production decisions, is that the sort of price effect condemned by antitrust? Or is it procompetitive?

    ii.   If this is a rule of reason case, does that mean that firms that exchange aggregated past information are at risk if it does lead to price uniformity or increases?

    c.   Does this case turn on the fact that 22 firms were involved, which is probably too many for oligopolistic coordination?[42]

    2.   Should an agreement to hold a meeting to discuss future prices be per se illegal among oligopolists? Isn't such a meeting inherently dangerous and likely to lead to anticompetitive effects? If agreements to hold such meetings were condemned, is it hard for oligopolists to know how to avoid condemnation? Would condemnation raise much of an overdeterrence concern?

    3.   Suppose 5 oligopolists agree to hold a meeting to have an antitrust professor lecture to them about oligopoly pricing theory. Should the agreement to hold such an educational seminar itself be condemned as an agreement that facilitates oligopolistic coordination?

United States v. Container Corp.

393 U.S. 333 (1969).

■ MR. JUSTICE DOUGLAS delivered the opinion of the Court.

    This is a civil antitrust action charging a price-fixing agreement in violation of § 1 of the Sherman Act. The District Court dismissed the complaint [after conducting a bench trial].

    The case as proved is unlike any other price decisions we have rendered. There was here an exchange of price information but no agreement to adhere to a price schedule as in . . . *Socony*. There was here an exchange of information concerning specific sales to identified customers, not a statistical report on the average cost to all members, without identifying the parties to specific transactions, as in *Maple Flooring*. While there was present here, as in *Cement Mfrs.*, an exchange of prices to specific customers, there was absent the controlling circumstance, *viz.*, that

---

in the price-fixing cartel itself. *See* Commission Decision of 13 July 1994, Cartonboard, O.J. 1994, L 243/1.

    42.   Some empirical work indicates that oligopolistic coordination is unlikely to significantly increase prices after there are five firms in the market. *See* Bresnahan & Reiss, *Entry and Competition in Concentrated Markets,* 99 J. POL., ECON. 977 (1991). This figure relates to the concentration levels that U.S. and EC merger guidelines consider likely to lead to adverse price effects. See Chapter 7. However, at the time of *Maple Flooring,* the Court probably thought oligopolistic coordination was feasible with many more firms.

cement manufacturers, to protect themselves from delivering to contractors more cement than was needed for a specific job and thus receiving a lower price, exchanged price information as a means of protecting their legal rights from fraudulent inducements to deliver more cement than needed for a specific job.

Here all that was present was a request by each defendant of its competitor for information as to the most recent price charged or quoted, whenever it needed such information and whenever it was not available from another source. Each defendant on receiving that request usually furnished the data with the expectation that it would be furnished reciprocal information when it wanted it. That concerted action is of course sufficient to establish the combination or conspiracy, the initial ingredient of a violation of § 1 of the Sherman Act. There was of course freedom to withdraw from the agreement. But the fact remains that when a defendant requested and received price information, it was affirming its willingness to furnish such information in return.

There was to be sure an infrequency and irregularity of price exchanges between the defendants; and often the data were available from the records of the defendants or from the customers themselves. Yet the essence of the agreement was to furnish price information whenever requested. Moreover, although the most recent price charged or quoted was sometimes fragmentary, each defendant had the manuals with which it could compute the price charged by a competitor on a specific order to a specific customer. Further, the price quoted was the current price which a customer would need to pay in order to obtain products from the defendant furnishing the data.

The defendants account for about 90% of the shipment of corrugated containers from plants in the Southeastern United States. While containers vary as to dimensions, weight, color, and so on, they are substantially identical, no matter who produces them, when made to particular specifications. The prices paid depend on price alternatives. Suppliers when seeking new or additional business or keeping old customers, do not exceed a competitor's price. It is common for purchasers to buy from two or more suppliers concurrently. A defendant supplying a customer with containers would usually quote the same price on additional orders, unless costs had changed. Yet where a competitor was charging a particular price, a defendant would normally quote the same price or even a lower price.

The exchange of price information seemed to have the effect of keeping prices within a fairly narrow ambit. Capacity has exceeded the demand from 1955 to 1963, the period covered by the complaint, and the trend of corrugated container prices has been downward. Yet despite this excess capacity and the downward trend of prices, the industry has expanded in the Southeast from 30 manufacturers with 49 plants to 51 manufacturers with 98 plants. An abundance of raw materials and machinery makes entry into the industry easy with an investment of $50,000 to $75,000.

The result of this reciprocal exchange of prices was to stabilize prices though at a downward level. Knowledge of a competitor's price usually meant matching that price. The continuation of some price competition is not fatal to the Government's case. The limitation or reduction of price competition brings the case within the ban, for as we held in *Socony,* interference with the setting of price by free market forces is unlawful *per se.* Price information exchanged in some markets may have no effect on a truly competitive price. But the corrugated container industry is dominated by relatively few sellers. The product is fungible and the competition for sales is price. The demand is inelastic, as buyers place orders only for immediate, short-run needs. The exchange of price data tends toward price uniformity. For a lower price does not mean a larger share of the available business but a sharing of the existing business at a lower return. Stabilizing prices as well as raising them is within the ban of § 1 of the Sherman Act. As we said in *Socony,* "in terms of market operations stabilization is but one form of manipulation." The inferences are irresistible that the exchange of price information has had an anticompetitive effect in the industry, chilling the vigor of price competition. The agreement in the present case, though somewhat casual, is analogous to those in *American Column,* and *United States v. American Linseed Oil Co.,* 262 U.S. 371.

Price is too critical, too sensitive a control to allow it to be used even in an informal manner to restrain competition. *Reversed.*

■ Mr. Justice Fortas, concurring ... I join in the judgment and opinion of the Court. I do not understand the Court's opinion to hold that the exchange of specific information among sellers as to prices charged to individual customers, pursuant to mutual arrangement, is a *per se* violation of the Sherman Act.

Absent *per se* violation, proof is essential that the practice resulted in an unreasonable restraint of trade. There is no single test to determine when the record adequately shows an "unreasonable restraint of trade"; but a practice such as that here involved, which is adopted for the purpose of arriving at a determination of prices to be quoted to individual customers, inevitably suggests the probability that it so materially interfered with the operation of the price mechanism of the marketplace as to bring it within the condemnation of this Court's decisions.

Theoretical probability, however, is not enough unless we are to regard mere exchange of current price information as so akin to price-fixing by combination or conspiracy as to deserve the *per se* classification. I am not prepared to do this, nor is it necessary here. In this case, the probability that the exchange of specific price information led to an unlawful effect upon prices is adequately buttressed by evidence in the record. This evidence, although not overwhelming, is sufficient in the special circumstances of this case to show an actual effect on pricing and to compel us to hold that the court below erred in dismissing the Government's complaint.

In summary, the record shows that the defendants sought and obtained from competitors who were part of the arrangement information about the competitors' prices to specific customers. "In the majority of instances," the District Court found, that once a defendant had this information he quoted substantially the same price as the competitor, although a higher or lower price would "occasionally" be quoted. Thus the exchange of prices made it possible for individual defendants confidently to name a price equal to that which their competitors were asking. The obvious effect was to "stabilize" prices by joint arrangement—at least to limit any price cuts to the minimum necessary to meet competition. In addition, there was evidence that, in some instances, during periods when various defendants ceased exchanging prices exceptionally sharp and vigorous price reductions resulted.

On this record, taking into account the specially sensitive function of the price term in the antitrust equation, I cannot see that we would be justified in reaching any conclusion other than that defendants' tacit agreement to exchange information about current prices to specific customers did in fact substantially limit the amount of price competition in the industry. That being so, there is no need to consider the possibility of a *per se* violation.

■ MR. JUSTICE MARSHALL, with Whom MR. JUSTICE HARLAN and MR. JUSTICE STEWART Join, dissenting. I agree with the Court's holding that there existed an agreement among the defendants to exchange price information whenever requested. However, I cannot agree that that agreement should be condemned, either as illegal *per se*, or as having had the purpose or effect of restricting price competition in the corrugated container industry in the Southeastern United States . . .

I do not believe that the agreement in the present case is so devoid of potential benefit or so inherently harmful that we are justified in condemning it without proof that it was entered into for the purpose of restraining price competition or that it actually had that effect . . . Complete market knowledge is certainly not an evil in perfectly competitive markets. This is not, however, such a market, and there is admittedly some danger that price information will be used for anticompetitive purposes, particularly the maintenance of prices at a high level. If the danger that price information will be so used is particularly high in a given situation, then perhaps exchange of information should be condemned.

I do not think the danger is sufficiently high in the present case. Defendants are only 18 of the 51 producers of corrugated containers in the Southeastern United States. Together, they do make up 90% of the market and the six largest defendants do control 60% of the market. But entry is easy; an investment of $50,000 to $75,000 is ordinarily all that is necessary. In fact, the number of sellers has increased from 30 to the present 51 in the eight-year period covered by the complaint. The size of the market has almost doubled because of increased demand for corrugated containers. Nevertheless, some excess capacity is present. The products produced by defendants are undifferentiated. Industry demand is inelastic, so that price changes will not, up to a certain point, affect the total amount purchased. The only effect of price changes will be to reallocate market shares among sellers.

In a competitive situation, each seller will cut his price in order to increase his share of the market, and prices will ultimately stabilize at a competitive level—*i.e.*, price will equal cost, including a reasonable return on capital. Obviously, it would be to a seller's benefit to avoid such price competition and maintain prices at a higher level, with a corresponding increase in profit. In a market with very few sellers, and detailed knowledge of each other's price, such action is possible. However, I do not think it can be concluded that this particular market is sufficiently oligopolistic, especially in light of the ease of entry, to justify the inference that price information will necessarily be used to stabilize prices. Nor do I think that the danger of such a result is sufficiently high to justify imposing a *per se* rule without actual proof. . . .

The Court does not hold that the agreement in the present case was a deliberate attempt to stabilize prices. The evidence in the case, largely the result of stipulation, would not support such a holding . . . Nor do I believe that the Government has proved that the exchange of price information has in this case had the necessary effect of restraining price competition. . . . The record indicates that defendants have offered voluminous evidence concerning price trends and competitive behavior in the corrugated container market. Their exhibits indicate a downward trend in prices, with substantial price variations among defendants and among their different plants. There was also a great deal of shifting of accounts. The District Court specifically found that the corrugated container market was highly competitive and that each defendant engaged in active price competition. The Government would have us ignore this evidence and these findings, and assume that because we are dealing with an industry with overcapacity and yet continued entry, the new entrants must have been attracted by high profits. The Government then argues that high profits can only result from stabilization of prices at an unduly high level. Yet, the Government did not introduce any evidence about the level of profits in this industry, and no evidence about price levels . . . The Government admits that the price trend was down, but asks the Court to assume that the trend would have been accelerated with less informed, and hence more vigorous, price competition.[3] In the absence of any proof whatsoever, I cannot make such an assumption. It is just as likely that price competition was furthered by the exchange as it is that it was depressed.

Finally, the Government focuses on the finding of the District Court that in a majority of instances a defendant, when it received what it considered reliable price information, would quote or charge substantially the same price. The Court and my Brother FORTAS also focus on this finding. Such an approach ignores, however, the remainder of the District Court's findings. The trial judge found that price decisions were individual decisions, and that defendants frequently did cut prices in order to obtain a particular order. And, the absence of any price parallelism or price uniformity and the downward trend in the industry undercut the conclusion that price information was used to stabilize prices . . .

Questions on *Container*

1. Is it likely that firms exchanged individual price quotes in order to undercut each other's prices?

---

3. There was no effort to demonstrate that the price behavior of those manufacturers who did not exchange price information, if any, varied significantly from the price behavior of those who did. In fact, several of the District Court's findings indicate that when certain defendants stopped exchanging price information, their price behavior remained essentially the same, and, in some cases, prices actually increased.

a. If they did, would firms be willing to provide such information to each other?

b. What could they gain by exchanging individual price quotes other than avoiding decisions to undercut prices by mistake? Doesn't that purpose indicate supracompetitive pricing?

2. The one point on which all the justices agreed seems to be that this case involved an agreement to exchange individual price information.

a. Was there any direct evidence of such an agreement? Wasn't the "agreement" just inferred from a reciprocal practice of answering requests?

b. Does this case accordingly indicate that the interdependent adoption of a facilitating practice like exchanging individual price quotes can constitute an antitrust conspiracy? Are there any overdeterrence concerns about condemning such a facilitating practice? Any concerns that firms could not avoid such interdependent behavior?

3. Should an agreement to exchange individual price information be per se illegal?

a. Does it have anticompetitive potential? Any procompetitive virtue?

b. Did *American Column* indicate the answer must be yes since it so holds even in an unconcentrated market? Or does it merely hold that the agreement was unreasonable there because of evidence that prices increased?

c. Why would firms exchange such sensitive individuated information unless doing so facilitated either oligopolistic coordination or a secret agreement on price? If firms wouldn't, then should the per se rule apply whether or not the market is oligopolistic?

d. Does the dissent implicitly agree that an agreement to exchange price information should be illegal at least when the market is actually oligopolistic?

4. Was this market actually oligopolistic? Consider:

a. Product homogeneity

b. the number of competitors

c. the ease of entry

d. the trend of increasing entry and continued excess capacity.

   i.   Is entry consistent with supracompetitive prices?

   ii.   At a time when other firms find the market prices attractive enough to enter, why would incumbent firms maintain excess capacity unless they were trying to suppress output? Wouldn't the excess capacity have to be more costly than used capacity and new entry? Is the latter likely given that new entrants must face capital costs that are sunk for incumbents?

5. Were actual anticompetitive effects shown? Consider the evidence that:

a. most of the time a firm who received price information charged the same price as its rival *b.* when firms stopped exchanging prices, that sometimes produced sharp price reductions, sometimes produced no change, and sometimes produced a price increase

c. the trend of decreasing prices and increasing market output

6. If sellers cannot exchange price quotes, why don't the firms just ask the buyers? If the purpose of exchanging information between sellers is to prevent buyers from falsely claiming other sellers were giving them discounts, why doesn't this fall within the rule of *Cement Manufacturers*?

a. Is the difference that in *Cement Manufacturers* it was efficient to curb such buyer deception, whereas here buyer deception procompetitively undermines oligopolistic coordination?

b. Is the difference that here there would be no incentive to exchange the information unless there were also an agreement not to undercut prices, whereas in *Cement Manufacturers* the defendants might exchange the information even without an agreement about how to use it because they all had independent motives to use it to prevent buyers from shifting additional risks onto sellers?

7. What if sellers decided to pose as buyers and ask other sellers what they are quoting?

a. Could one infer an agreement in such a case?

b. Should it be condemned as a unilateral facilitating practice even absent an agreement?

United States v. United States Gypsum

438 U.S. 422 (1978).

■ Mr. Chief Justice Burger delivered the opinion of the Court.

... The gypsum board industry is highly concentrated, with the number of producers ranging from 9 to 15 in the period 1960–1973. The eight largest companies accounted for some 94% of the national sales with the seven "single-plant producers" accounting for the remaining 6%. Most of the major producers and a large number of the single-plant producers are members of the Gypsum Association which since 1930 has served as a trade association of gypsum board manufacturers ...

The focus of the Government's price-fixing case at trial was interseller price verification—that is, the practice allegedly followed by the gypsum board manufacturers of telephoning a competing producer to determine the price currently being offered on gypsum board to a specific customer ... [T]he question upon which the Court of Appeals focused [was] whether verification of price concessions with competitors for the sole purpose of taking advantage of the § 2(b) meeting-competition defense should ... preclud[e] liability under § 1 of the Sherman Act ...

Section 2(a) of the Clayton Act, as amended by the Robinson–Patman Act, embodies a general prohibition of price discrimination between buyers when an injury to competition is the consequence. The primary exception to the § 2(a) bar is the meeting-competition defense which is incorporated as a proviso to the burden-of-proof requirements set out in § 2(b) ... [I]n Standard Oil Co. v. FTC, 340 U.S. 231 (1951) ... we ... constru[ed] § 2(b) to provide an absolute defense to liability for price discrimination ...

In FTC v. A. E. Staley Mfg. Co., 324 U.S. 746 (1945), the Court provided the first and still the most complete explanation of the kind of showing which a seller must make in order to satisfy the good-faith requirement of the § 2(b) defense:

> "Section 2(b) does not require the seller to justify price discriminations by showing that in fact they met a competitor's price. But it does place on the seller the burden of showing that the price was made in good faith to meet a competitor's ... We agree with the Commission that the statute at least requires the seller, who has knowingly discriminated in price, to show the existence of facts which would lead a reasonable and prudent person to believe that the granting of a lower price would in fact meet the equally low price of a competitor." *Id.*, at 759–760.

Application of these standards to the facts in *Staley* led to the conclusion that the § 2(b) defense had not been made out. The record revealed that the lower price had been based simply on reports of salesmen, brokers, or purchasers with no efforts having been made by the seller "to investigate or verify" the reports or the character and reliability of the informants. Similarly, in Corn Products Co. v. FTC, 324 U.S. 726 (1945), decided the same day, the § 2(b) defense was not allowed because "[the] only evidence said to rebut the *prima facie* case ... of the price discriminations was given by witnesses who had no personal knowledge of the transactions, and was limited to statements of each witness's assumption or conclusion that the price discriminations were justified by competition."

Staley's "investigate or verify" language coupled with *Corn Products'* focus on "personal knowledge of the transactions" have apparently suggested to a number of courts that, at least in certain circumstances, direct verification of discounts between competitors may be necessary to meet the burden-of-proof requirements of the § 2(b) defense ...

A good-faith belief, rather than absolute certainty, that a price concession is being offered to meet an equally low price offered by a competitor is sufficient to satisfy the § 2(b) defense. While casual reliance on uncorroborated reports of buyers or sales representatives without further investigation may not, as we noted earlier, be sufficient to make the requisite showing of good faith, nothing in the language of § 2(b) or the gloss on that language in *Staley* and *Corn Products* indicates that direct discussions of price between competitors are required ... On the contrary, the § 2(b) defense has been successfully invoked in the absence of interseller verification on numerous occasions.....

The so-called problem of the untruthful buyer which concerned the Court of Appeals does not in our view call for a different approach to the § 2(b) defense. The good-faith standard remains the benchmark against which the seller's conduct is to be evaluated, and we agree with the Government and the FTC that this standard can be satisfied by efforts falling short of interseller verification in most circumstances where the seller has only vague, generalized doubts about the reliability of its commercial adversary—the buyer.[29] Given the fact-specific nature of the inquiry, it is difficult to predict all the factors the FTC or a court would consider in appraising a seller's good faith in matching a competing offer in these circumstances. Certainly, evidence that a seller had received reports of similar discounts from other customers, or was threatened with a termination of purchases if the discount were not met, would be relevant in this regard. Efforts to corroborate the reported discount by seeking documentary evidence or by appraising its reasonableness in terms of available market data would also be probative as would the seller's past experience with the particular buyer in question.

There remains the possibility that in a limited number of situations a seller may have substantial reasons to doubt the accuracy of reports of a competing offer and may be unable to corroborate such reports in any of the generally accepted ways ... As an abstract proposition, resort to interseller verification as a means of checking the buyer's reliability seems a possible solution to the seller's plight, but careful examination reveals serious problems with the practice.

Both economic theory and common human experience suggest that interseller verification—if undertaken on an isolated and infrequent basis with no provision for reciprocity or cooperation—will not serve its putative function of corroborating the representations of unreliable buyers regarding the existence of competing offers. Price concessions by oligopolists generally yield competitive advantages only if secrecy can be maintained; when the terms of the concession are made publicly known, other competitors are likely to follow and any advantage to the initiator is lost in the process. See also *Container*. Thus, if one seller offers a price concession for the purpose of winning over one of his competitor's customers, it is unlikely that the same seller will freely inform its competitor of the details of the concession so that it can be promptly matched and diffused. Instead, such a seller would appear to have at least as great an incentive to misrepresent the existence or size of the discount as would the buyer who received it. Thus verification, if undertaken on a one-shot basis for the sole purpose of complying with the § 2(b) defense, does not hold out much promise as a means of shoring up buyers' representations.

The other variety of interseller verification is, like the conduct charged in the instant case, undertaken pursuant to an agreement, either tacit or express, providing for reciprocity among competitors in the exchange of price information. Such an agreement would make little economic sense, in our view, if its sole purpose were to guarantee all participants the opportunity to match the secret price concessions of other participants under

---

29. "Although a seller may take advantage of the meeting competition defense only if it has a commercially reasonable belief that its price concession is necessary to meet an equally low price of a competitor, a seller may acquire this belief, and hence perfect its defense, by doing everything reasonably feasible—short of violating some other statute, such as the Sherman Act—to determine the veracity of a customer's statement that he has been offered a lower price. If, after making reasonable, lawful, inquiries, the seller cannot ascertain that the buyer is lying, the seller is entitled to make the sale ... There is no need for a seller to discuss price with his competitors to take advantage of the meeting competition defense." (Citations omitted.) Brief for United States 86–87, and n. 78.

§ 2(b). For in such circumstances, each seller would know that his price concession could not be kept from his competitors and no seller participating in the information-exchange arrangement would, therefore, have any incentive for deviating from the prevailing price level in the industry. See *Container*. Regardless of its putative purpose, the most likely consequence of any such agreement to exchange price information would be the stabilization of industry prices. Instead of facilitating use of the § 2(b) defense, such an agreement would have the effect of eliminating the very price concessions which provide the main element of competition in oligopolistic industries and the primary occasion for resort to the meeting-competition defense....

We are left, therefore, on the one hand, with doubts about both the need for and the efficacy of interseller verification as a means of facilitating compliance with § 2(b), and, on the other, with recognition of the tendency for price discussions between competitors to contribute to the stability of oligopolistic prices and open the way for the growth of prohibited anticompetitive activity. To recognize even a limited ... exception for interseller verification in such circumstances would be to remove from scrutiny under the Sherman Act conduct falling near its core with no assurance, and indeed with serious doubts, that competing antitrust policies would be served thereby. In Automatic Canteen Co. v. FTC, 346 U.S. 61, 74 (1953), the Court suggested that as a general rule the Robinson–Patman Act should be construed so as to insure its coherence with "the broader antitrust policies that have been laid down by Congress"; that observation buttresses our conclusion that exchanges of price information—even when putatively for purposes of Robinson–Patman Act compliance—must remain subject to close scrutiny under the Sherman Act.[32]

Questions on *Gypsum*

1. Is allowing selective price cuts only to meet competition (rather than to undercut it in advance or beat it in response) a desirable statutory policy? Doesn't this feature of the Robinson–Patman Act help enforce oligopolistic pricing?

2. If a buyer could get the same price discount from another seller, would a second seller offering the same discount harm the rival of that buyer? Could this explain the meeting competition defense?

---

32. That the § 2(b) defense may not be available in every situation where a competing offer has in fact been made is not, in our view, a meaningful objection to our holding. The good-faith requirement of the § 2(b) defense implicitly suggests a somewhat imperfect matching between competing offers actually made and those allowed to be met. Unless this requirement is to be abandoned, it seems clear that inadequate information will, in a limited number of cases, deny the defense to some who, if all the facts had been known, would have been entitled to invoke it. For reasons already discussed, interseller verification does not provide a satisfactory solution to this seemingly inevitable problem of inadequate information. Moreover, § 2(b) affords only a defense to liability and not an affirmative right under the Act. While sellers are, of course, entitled to take advantage of the defense when they can satisfy its requirements, efforts to increase its availability at the expense of broader, affirmative antitrust policies must be rejected.

3. Does the seller have to actually meet competition or just have a good faith belief it is meeting competition?

4. Do buyers have incentives to be truthful about whether a rival seller has offered a lower price? If the seller cannot ask rival sellers, how can it ever be sure whether the buyer is lying? What sort of investigation or verification of buyer veracity would suffice?

a. Can it just rely on what the buyer tells it? Does the fact that other buyers aren't reporting similar discounts disprove the possibility that a rival is providing a selective discount? Does the fact that the buyer threatens to buy elsewhere really provide verification?

b. If the buyer refuses to provide documentation, would the seller be acting in good faith to believe the buyer? Great Atlantic & Pacific Tea v. FTC, 440 U.S. 69 (1979), held that it did when coupled with a buyer threat to buy elsewhere because *Gypsum* prohibited the seller from asking the rival seller.

c. If the seller does obtain documentary proof of the rival offer, doesn't that accomplish much the same as interseller verification? Isn't the real rationale for the *Container* decision to prevent sellers from curbing buyer deceptions that can undermine cartel or oligopolistic pricing? Can that rationale really be squared with a legal requirement of thorough investigation before lowering prices to meet what a buyer says the rivals are offering?

5. Won't this test sometimes prevent a seller from meeting a rival price cut because it cannot determine that the buyer is not lying about the rival price quote and cannot ask the rival seller?

6. Does it seem likely that a practice of asking rival sellers is likely to lead to accurate answers that encourage price concessions to meet competition?

7. Robinson–Patman Act § 2(f) makes a buyer liable if it knowingly induces or receives a prohibited price discrimination. Can a buyer be held liable under § 2(f) when it knows the seller's price has beat the competition even though the seller is not liable because it in good faith thought it was just meeting competition? In *Great Atlantic,* the Court held no because: (1) the § 2(f) language requiring "a prohibited price discrimination" meant buyer liability depended on seller liability under § 2(a); and (2) interpreting § 2(f) to prohibit the knowing receipt of a price cut that did not meet competition would require buyers to inform sellers when they have beaten competition and thus lead to the equivalent of the exchange of price information prohibited in *Container.* The Court left open whether a buyer that affirmatively lied about a rival bid should be liable under § 2(f) where the seller relied in good faith on the buyer's representations. Should such a lying buyer be liable given the Court's reasoning?

FTC v. Cement Institute

333 U.S. 683 (1948).

■ Mr. Justice Black delivered the opinion of the Court.

. . . [The FTC charged that respondents, the Cement Institute and its 74 members that made or sold cement, committed an unfair method of competition in violation of FTC Act § 5.] ... The core of the charge was that the respondents had restrained and hindered competition in the sale and distribution of cement by means of a combination among themselves made effective through mutual understanding or agreement to employ a multiple basing point system of pricing. It was alleged that this system resulted in the quotation of identical terms of sale and identical prices for cement by the respondents at any given point in the United States. This system had worked so successfully, it was further charged, that for many years prior to the filing of the complaint, all cement buyers throughout the nation, with rare exceptions, had been unable to purchase cement for delivery in any given locality from any one of the respondents at a lower price or on more favorable terms than from any of the other respondents ...

The Commission has jurisdiction to declare that conduct tending to restrain trade is an unfair method of competition even though the selfsame conduct may also violate the Sherman Act ... [A]lthough all conduct violative of the Sherman Act may likewise come within the unfair trade practice prohibitions of the Trade Commission Act, the converse is not necessarily true. It has long been recognized that there are many unfair methods of competition that do not assume the proportions of Sherman Act violations. Hence a conclusion that respondents' conduct constituted an unfair method of competition does not necessarily mean that their same activities would also be found to violate § 1 of the Sherman Act ...

The Multiple Basing Point Delivered Price System.—... Goods may be sold and delivered to customers at the seller's mill or warehouse door or may be sold free on board (f.o.b.) trucks or railroad cars immediately adjacent to the seller's mill or warehouse. In either event the actual cost of the goods to the purchaser is, broadly speaking, the seller's "mill price" plus the purchaser's cost of transportation. However, if the seller fixes a price at which he undertakes to deliver goods to the purchaser where they are to be used, the cost to the purchaser is the "delivered price." A seller who makes the "mill price" identical for all purchasers of like amount and quality simply delivers his goods at the same place (his mill) and for the same price (price at the mill). He thus receives for all f.o.b. mill sales an identical net amount of money for like goods from all customers. But a "delivered price" system creates complications which may result in a seller's receiving different net returns from the sale of like goods. The cost of transporting 500 miles is almost always more than the cost of transporting 100 miles. Consequently if customers 100 and 500 miles away pay the same "delivered price," the seller's net return is less from the more distant customer ...

The best known early example of a basing point price system was called "Pittsburgh plus." It related to the price of steel. The Pittsburgh price was the base price, Pittsburgh being therefore called a price basing point. In order for the system to work, sales had to be made only at delivered prices. Under this system the delivered price of steel from anywhere in the United States to a point of delivery anywhere in the

United States was in general the Pittsburgh price plus the railroad freight rate from Pittsburgh to the point of delivery. Take Chicago, Illinois, as an illustration of the operation and consequences of the system. A Chicago steel producer was not free to sell his steel at cost plus a reasonable profit. He must sell it at the Pittsburgh price plus the railroad freight rate from Pittsburgh to the point of delivery. Chicago steel customers were by this pricing plan thus arbitrarily required to pay for Chicago produced steel the Pittsburgh base price plus what it would have cost to ship the steel by rail from Pittsburgh to Chicago had it been shipped. The theoretical cost of this fictitious shipment became known as "phantom freight." But had it been economically possible under this plan for a Chicago producer to ship his steel to Pittsburgh, his "delivered price" would have been merely the Pittsburgh price, although he actually would have been required to pay the freight from Chicago to Pittsburgh. Thus the "delivered price" under these latter circumstances required a Chicago (non-basing point) producer to "absorb" freight costs. That is, such a seller's net returns became smaller and smaller as his deliveries approached closer and closer to the basing point.

Several results obviously flow from use of a single basing point system such as "Pittsburgh plus" originally was. One is that the "delivered prices" of all producers in every locality where deliveries are made are always the same regardless of the producers' different freight costs. Another is that sales made by a non-base mill for delivery at different localities result in net receipts to the seller which vary in amounts equivalent to the "phantom freight" included in, or the "freight absorption" taken from the "delivered price."

As commonly employed by respondents, the basing point system is not single but multiple. That is, instead of one basing point, like that in "Pittsburgh plus," a number of basing point localities are used. In the multiple basing point system, just as in the single basing point system, freight absorption or phantom freight is an element of the delivered price on all sales not governed by a basing point actually located at the seller's mill. And all sellers quote identical delivered prices in any given locality regardless of their different costs of production and their different freight expenses. Thus the multiple and single systems function in the same general manner and produce the same consequences—identity of prices and diversity of net returns . . .

This Court's opinion in *Cement Mfrs.* . . . known as the *Old Cement* case, is relied on by the respondents in almost every contention they present. We think it has little relevance, if any at all, to the issues in this case . . . In the first place, unlike the *Old Cement* case, the Commission does here specifically charge a combination to utilize the basing point system as a means to bring about uniform prices and terms of sale . . . In the second place, individual conduct, or concerted conduct, which falls short of being a Sherman Act violation may as a matter of law constitute an "unfair method of competition" prohibited by the Trade Commission Act. A major purpose of that Act, as we have frequently said, was to enable the Commission to restrain practices as "unfair" which, although not yet having grown into Sherman Act dimensions would, most likely do so if left unrestrained. The Commission and the courts were to determine what conduct, even though it might then be short of a Sherman Act violation, was an "unfair method of competition." This general language was deliberately left to the "commission and the courts" for definition because it was thought that "There is no limit to human inventiveness in this field"; that consequently, a definition that fitted practices known to lead towards an unlawful restraint of trade today would not fit tomorrow's new inventions in the field; and that for Congress to try to keep its precise definitions abreast of this course of conduct would be an "endless task."

Findings and Evidence.—... [W]e think that the following facts ... are sufficient to warrant the Commission's finding of concerted action.

When the Commission rendered its decision there were about 80 cement manufacturing companies in the United States operating about 150 mills. Ten companies controlled more than half of the mills and there were substantial corporate affiliations among many of the others. This concentration of productive capacity made concerted action far less difficult than it would otherwise have been. The belief is prevalent in the industry that because of the standardized nature of cement, among other reasons, price competition is wholly unsuited to it. That belief is historic. It has resulted in concerted activities to devise means and measures to do away with competition in the industry. Out of those activities came the multiple basing point delivered price system. Evidence shows it to be a handy instrument to bring about elimination of any kind of price competition. The use of the multiple basing point delivered price system by the cement producers has been coincident with a situation whereby for many years, with rare exceptions, cement has been offered for sale in every given locality at identical prices and terms by all producers. Thousands of secret sealed bids have been received by public agencies which corresponded in prices of cement down to a fractional part of a penny. [The Court cited an example where 11 bidders each submitted identical sealed bids of $3.286854 per barrel with the identical discount of 10 cents per barrel for payment within 15 days.]

Occasionally foreign cement has been imported, and cement dealers have sold it below the delivered price of the domestic product. Dealers who persisted in selling foreign cement were boycotted by the domestic producers. Officers of the Institute took the lead in securing pledges by producers not to permit sales f.o.b. mill to purchasers who furnished their own trucks, a practice regarded as seriously disruptive of the entire delivered price structure of the industry.

During the depression in the 1930's, slow business prompted some producers to deviate from the prices fixed by the delivered price system. Meetings were held by other producers; an effective plan was devised to punish the recalcitrants and bring them into line. The plan was simple but successful. Other producers made the recalcitrant's plant an involuntary base point. The base price was driven down with relatively insignificant losses to the producers who imposed the punitive basing point, but with heavy losses to the recalcitrant who had to make all its sales on this basis. In one instance, where a producer had made a low public bid, a punitive base point price was put on its plant and cement was reduced 10 cents per barrel; further reductions quickly followed until the base price at which this recalcitrant had to sell its cement dropped to 75 cents per barrel, scarcely one-half of its former base price of $1.45. Within six weeks after the base price hit 75 cents capitulation occurred and the recalcitrant joined a Portland cement association. Cement in that locality then bounced back to $1.15, later to $1.35, and finally to $1.75.

The foregoing are but illustrations of the practices shown to have been utilized to maintain the basing point price system. Respondents offered testimony that cement is a standardized product, that "cement is cement," that no differences existed in quality or usefulness, and that purchasers demanded delivered price quotations because of the high cost of transportation from mill to dealer. There was evidence, however, that the Institute and its members had, in the interest of eliminating competition, suppressed information as to the variations in quality that sometimes exist in different cements. Respondents introduced the testimony of economists to the effect that competition alone could lead to the evolution of a multiple basing point system of uniform delivered prices and terms of sale for an industry with a standardized product and with relatively high freight costs. These economists testified that for the above reasons no inferences of collusion, agreement, or understanding could be drawn from the admitted fact that cement prices of all United States producers had for many years almost invariably been the same in every given locality in the country. There was also considerable testimony by other economic experts that the multiple basing point system of delivered prices as employed by respondents contravened accepted economic principles and could only have been maintained through collusion.

The Commission did not adopt the views of the economists produced by the respondents. It decided that even though competition might tend to drive the price of standardized products to a uniform level, such a tendency alone could not account for the almost perfect identity in prices, discounts, and cement containers which had prevailed for so long a time in the cement industry. The Commission held that the uniformity and absence of competition in the industry were the results of understandings or agreements entered into or carried out by concert of the Institute and the other respondents. It may possibly be true, as respondents' economists testified, that cement producers will, without agreement express or implied and without understanding explicit or tacit, always and at all times (for such has been substantially the case here) charge for their cement precisely, to the fractional part of a penny, the price their competitors charge. Certainly it runs counter to what many people have believed, namely, that without agreement, prices will vary—that the desire to sell will sometimes be so strong that a seller will be willing to lower his prices and take his chances. We therefore hold that the Commission was not compelled to accept the views of respondents' economist-witnesses that active competition was bound to produce uniform cement prices. The Commission was authorized to find understanding, express or implied, from evidence that the industry's Institute actively worked, in cooperation with various of its members, to maintain the multiple basing point delivered price system; that this pricing system is calculated to produce, and has produced, uniform prices and terms of sale throughout the country; and that all of the respondents have sold their cement substantially in accord with the pattern required by the multiple basing point system.

Unfair Methods of Competition.—We sustain the Commission's holding that concerted maintenance of the basing point delivered price system is an unfair method of competition prohibited by the Federal Trade Commission Act. In so doing we give great weight to the Commission's conclusion . . . [T]he express intention of Congress [was] to create an agency whose membership would at all times be experienced, so that its conclusions would be the result of an expertness coming from experience . . . The kind of specialized knowledge Congress wanted its agency to have was an expertness that would fit it to stop at the threshold every unfair trade practice—that kind of practice which, if left alone, "destroys competition and establishes monopoly."

We cannot say that the Commission is wrong in concluding that the delivered-price system as here used provides an effective instrument which, if left free for use of the respondents, would result in complete destruction of competition and the establishment of monopoly in the cement industry . . . We uphold the Commission's conclusion that the basing point delivered price system employed by respondents is an unfair trade practice which the Trade Commission may suppress.[19]

Questions on *Cement Institute*

1. Was there an agreement that would also violate Sherman Act § 1 here? What evidence was there that the members actually agreed on basing point pricing?

a. Do firms have any independent incentive to adhere to a basing point system that allows rivals to sell in the firm's own city? Wouldn't they do so only if there were some form of agreement or tacit coordination?

b. What other factors also negate independent action?

    i.   pledges not to charge f.o.b. mill?

    ii.   identical pricing?

    iii.   punishment of defectors by making them a basing point with a low base price?

    iv.   suppression of quality information?

c. Given the large number of firms, is it likely the firms were able to adhere to the basing point system and engage in all the above conduct just with tacit coordination?

d. If they did just use tacit coordination, should we still condemn the interdependent adoption of a basing point system as an agreement? Or should we only condemn such interdependent adoption as a unilateral unfair practice under FTC Act § 5?

---

19. While we hold that the Commission's findings of combination were supported by evidence, that does not mean that existence of a "combination" is an indispensable ingredient of an "unfair method of competition" under the Trade Commission Act.

e. Should the FTC Act be given broader scope than the Sherman Act on this issue because it is enforced by an expert agency that can only enjoin the prohibited conduct, rather than by criminal penalties or private parties seeking treble damages?

i. Would that same argument suggest that enforcement by the European Commission means Article 101 should be interpreted more broadly than Sherman Act § 1?

ii. Would this argument justify allowing the FTC or the European Commission to condemn oligopolist price coordination itself or just unilateral practices that might facilitate it?

2. Is an agreement to use basing point pricing likely to be anticompetitive in an oligopolistic market? Was this market oligopolistic given that it involved 74 firms? Is it likely that there are fewer firms that effectively compete for local cement sales?

3. Are anticompetitive effects proven by . . .

a. identical pricing? Couldn't competition produce identical pricing of a homogeneous product given a common basing point?

b. the importation of foreign cement despite high transportation costs?

4. Do actual anticompetitive effects have to be proven? Or is an agreement to adopt a common basing point sufficiently likely to have anticompetitive effects and sufficiently unlikely to have procompetitive effects that it should be condemned per se? Does the answer depend on whether the market is oligopolistic?

Commission Decision 92/157, UK Agricultural Tractor Registration Exchange (UK Tractors)

1992 O.J., L 68/19.

I. FACTS . . .

On 4 January 1988, the Agricultural Engineers Association Ltd (AEA), the United Kingdom trade association of manufacturers and importers of agricultural machinery, notified an information exchange agreement called the UK Agricultural Tractor Registration Exchange ("the Exchange"). That agreement concerns an exchange of information identifying the volume of retail sales and market shares of eight manufacturers and importers of agricultural tractors on the United Kingdom market. . . .

The United Kingdom market is dominated by four suppliers which together held some 76 to 77% of the market. These suppliers are Ford, Case, Massey–Ferguson and John Deere. Since the takeover of Ford New Holland by Fiat, these four suppliers now hold an approximate total market share of 80% of the United Kingdom market. These four major suppliers, which each hold market shares of between 15 and 25%, are followed by suppliers which hold between 2 and 3% of the United Kingdom market. This is the case for Renault, Deutz and Same–Lamborghini. The eight, now seven, members of the Exchange together hold some 87 to 88% of the

United Kingdom tractor market while the remaining 12% of the market is shared by several small manufacturers who are not members. . . .

The eight, now seven, main suppliers of the United Kingdom market have set up, with the help of the AEA . . ., an information exchange identifying the retail sales and market shares of each member of the United Kingdom market with detailed breakdowns by product, territory and time periods. . . . The information exchanged between the members of the Exchange through the AEA . . . is mainly taken from the V55 forms which are used for the registration of tractors with the United Kingdom Department of Transport. For tractors [that] need not be registered (e.g. those not to be used on a public road), the dealer must undertake to supply a copy of the V55 form . . . to be included in the database together with the data on the tractors which must be registered. . . .

II.   LEGAL ASSESSMENT . . .

The AEA and the eight, now seven, members of the Exchange are parties to an agreement within the meaning of Article [101(1)]. The . . . AEA are only allowed to release the information identifying the sales of each member on the basis of a mutual and reciprocal acceptance by each member of the release. . . .

The Exchange leads to restrictions of competition for two reasons:

(a) Prevention of hidden competition in a highly concentrated market

The Exchange restricts competition because it creates a degree of market transparency between the suppliers in a highly concentrated market which is likely to destroy what hidden competition there remains between the suppliers in that market on account of the risk and ease of exposure of independent competitive action. In this highly concentrated market, "hidden competition" is essentially that element of uncertainty and secrecy between the main suppliers regarding market conditions without which none of them has the necessary scope of action to compete efficiently. Uncertainty and secrecy between suppliers is a vital element of competition in this kind of market. Indeed active competition in these market conditions becomes possible only if each competitor can keep its actions secret or even succeeds in misleading its rivals.

This reasoning, however, in no way undermines the positive competitive benefits of transparency in a competitive market characterized by many buyers and sellers. Where there is a low degree of concentration, market transparency can increase competition in so far as consumers benefit from choices made in full knowledge of what is on offer. It is emphasized that the United Kingdom tractor market is neither a low concentration market nor is the transparency in question in any way directed towards, or of benefit to, consumers.

On the contrary, the high market transparency between suppliers on the United Kingdom tractor market which is created by the Exchange takes the surprise effect out of a competitor's action thus resulting in a shorter space of time for reactions with the effect that temporary advantages are greatly reduced. Because all competitive actions can immediately be noticed by an increase in sales, the consequences are that in the case of a price reduction or any other marketing incentives by one company the other can react immediately, thus eliminating any advantage of the initiator. This effect of neutralizing and thus stabilizing the market positions of the oligopolists is in this case likely to occur because there are no external competitive pressures on the members of the Exchange except parallel imports which are however also monitored as has been explained above.

The United Kingdom tractor market is clearly a highly concentrated market where competition is already weakened by the fact that:

—four firms dominate the market with a combined market share of approximately 80%,

—these four firms have created an information exchange with four, now three, other well-known suppliers capable of challenging their market position with the effect that the conditions of a narrow oligopoly have been artificially created between the eight, now seven, best established competitors on this market by giving them information on any change in volumes and market shares at manufacturer and dealer level,

—these eight, now seven, suppliers are active in all other Community markets and know the pattern of trade and products supplied on the United Kingdom market for a long period of time; in particular, there is no difficulty knowing the prices charged by each member because in this industry there are list prices and a simple telephone enquiry will readily reveal the general level of discounts applied by each manufacturer's dealer network; this information is also available from customers who inform the dealers of competitors' prices in a given territory,

—the market is protected from competition from outside the United Kingdom by the fact that there are high barriers to entry and that there are only insignificant imports from outside the Community.

In addition, demand is very dispersed. There are numerous buyers, the majority of whom do not have the possibility of purchasing tractors in other Member States (transport difficulties, import formalities, registration, service, trade-ins, etc.). Thus, demand transferability in this market is very low which weakens the competitive pressure from the demand side on the limited number of suppliers established within the United Kingdom and therefore reinforces their economic strength on that market.

On the United Kingdom tractor market, therefore, the only difficult, but very important, market data to obtain is the exact volume of sales of each manufacturer/dealer so as to be able to notice instantly changes in sales volumes and market shares of each member of the oligopoly and of each dealer at the level of dealer territories. This market knowledge allows each member and dealer to react immediately and thus to neutralize whatever initiative any one of the members/dealers of the oligopoly would take to increase its sales. However, the result in practice is that few such initiatives will be taken precisely because every supplier knows very well that the position of each of the others is and that, thanks to the transparency created by the system, any initiative on his part can be detected at once by the others.

The very detailed product and geographic market information on retail sales gives each manufacturer and dealer fully reliable market knowledge

... which is accessible on an instant or very short time basis (daily, monthly or quarterly). It allows them:

—to establish with accuracy the market positions and performances of their rivals and to follow constantly any changes of these market positions,

—to see at once whether there has been any increase in the retail sales of a rival, to see the territory in which such an increase takes place, to detect the models which contribute such an increase and finally to follow whether and to what extent any price or other marketing strategies of rivals are successful,

—to limit price competition as far as possible by allowing suppliers and dealers to react to any price-cutting or other market strategies selectively by limiting their response to the absolute minimum degree necessary in terms of product and territory and by being sure to hit the right target,

—to react more quickly if the market positions start changing.

The Exchange further helps the established firms and dealers with considerable market shares (i.e. the four biggest firms holding approximately 80% of the United Kingdom market) to defend their market positions more efficiently than they could do without the detailed information on retail sales of their rivals and any changes thereof. By their wider market coverage and sales volume, these firms and dealers already have the advantage of better market knowledge which is further strengthened by the fact that they can react more effectively to any increase in sales by the smaller competitors on the market. This is confirmed by the fact that, during their participation in the Exchange, the main four suppliers have essentially maintained their combined market share vis-à-vis the other members of the Exchange on the United Kingdom market.

In the absence of the Exchange, firms would have to compete in a market with some measure of uncertainty as to the exact place, degree and means of attack by rivals. This uncertainty is a normal competitive risk bringing about stronger competition because reaction and reduction of prices cannot be limited to the absolute minimum degree necessary to defend an established position. Uncertainty would lead the firms to compete more strongly than if they knew exactly how much of a response was necessary to meet competition. They would have to exceed a minimum response, for instance by offering more favourable discounts to move their stock or by offering discounts for more products and in more territories. The Exchange reduces uncertainty by revealing the actions and reactions of all participating competitors who represent 87 to 88% of the United Kingdom market. There is thus a prevention of hidden competition which results necessarily from the Exchange.

(b) Increase of barriers to entry for non-members

The Exchange not only lessens competition between members of the Exchange and between their dealers, it also restricts competition between members and non members of the Exchange even if the Exchange in principle admits any manufacturer or importer to the information Exchange.

If a supplier chooses not to become a member of the Exchange, he is disadvantaged by the fact that he does not have available the detailed and accurate market information about other suppliers which is available to members of the Exchange. Detailed knowledge of the sales pattern for tractors on the United Kingdom market improves the members' ability to defend their positions vis-à-vis non-members.

If a supplier chooses to become a member of the Exchange, he must reveal his exact retail sales by product and by every small geographic territory with the result that the Exchange then permits the established suppliers with considerable market shares and extensive dealer networks to become aware of the existence of new entry and to instantly detect the market penetration by any such new member. This market information on any new member will permit the established suppliers to defend their acquired positions by placing selective actions designed to contain the new member.

As a result, for a small supplier it is neither advantageous to become a member of the Exchange nor to stay outside the Exchange. In both cases the Exchange advantages the big suppliers who already belong to it. The presence of the smaller suppliers in the Exchange shows indeed that these suppliers have not been able to contest the position of the four biggest suppliers, i.e. Ford, Case, Massey–Ferguson and John Deere, and that market expansion is only possible through acquisition—such as the recent acquisition of Ford by Fiat. The presence of the four smaller suppliers can therefore only be explained by the fact that the UK Exchange is part of a network of similar Exchanges in other Community countries and that the eight suppliers participate in various exchanges on a reciprocal basis. These other exchanges are presently under investigation . . . .

Questions on *UK Tractors*

1. The European Commission concludes that the Exchange restricts competition because it creates a degree of market transparency between the suppliers in a highly concentrated market. This could destroy what remains of "hidden competition" in that market.

    a. What does the European Commission mean by "hidden competition"?

    b. Why is market transparency more of a problem in concentrated markets than in non-concentrated markets? Could we even say that transparency is welfare enhancing in non-concentrated markets?

    c. The European Commission also refers to the presence of barriers to entry and a dispersed demand. Are these relevant factors in the assessment of the exchange mechanism? Why?

2. The European Commission states that the exchange mechanism necessarily plays to the disadvantage of smaller competitors or new entrants.

    a. Are you convinced by its arguments?

b. Couldn't a very aggressive new entrant simply do away with this information and gain market share by cutting prices?

c. Does the agreement provide for retaliation mechanisms against firms that refuse to participate in data exchange?

3. Suppose that without any explicit words of agreement, European oligopolists all coordinated on a facilitating practice like making advance price announcements (see *Dyestuffs*), exchanging price information (see *Container*), or using the same basing point for pricing (see *Cement Institute*).

a. Would that be a concerted practice that violates Article 101?

b. Even if it constitutes unilateral conduct that cannot violate Article 101, would such facilitating practices constitute an abuse of their collective dominant position under Article 102? *See* Chapter 3.A.2, 3.B.2.

CHAPTER 7

MERGERS

Mergers (or "concentrations") are the combination of previously independent firms into one firm. For antitrust purposes, it does not matter whether the combination reflects a formal merger of two corporations into a single corporation or instead the acquisition of another firm's assets or stock. Nor does it matter whether, after the merger, the acquired business becomes a subsidiary that continues to be a separate legal entity. All that matters is that what used to be separate businesses pursuing independent profit motives have now been combined into one common ownership structure that gives the businesses a joint profit motive.

There are three kinds of mergers. (1) Horizontal mergers combine firms that used to compete in selling or buying in the same market. They raise similar issues to horizontal agreements, except that in addition they raise the concern that they might help create a market concentration that leads to oligopolistic coordination. (2) Vertical mergers combine firms that used to sell and buy on opposite sides of the same market. They raise issues similar to vertical agreements. (3) Conglomerate mergers include any business combination that is not horizontal or vertical. However, one of the concerns conglomerate mergers raise is that, but for the merger, one of the firms might have entered the market of the other, so that the conglomerate merger eliminates potential horizontal competition. Another concern is that a conglomerate merger might lead the merged entity to engage in anticompetitive vertical conduct or agreements. So conglomerate mergers can raise concerns that are horizontal or vertical in nature.

When a partial stock acquisition gives one firm effective control over another firm, it is generally treated as a merger. However, partial stock acquisitions might also be condemned as anticompetitive even when they do not confer enough control to constitute a merger. Such noncontrolling acquisitions might be condemned on the theories that they lessen competition by either: (1) giving the acquirer the ability to influence competitive conduct of the target firm; (2) giving the acquirer confidential information in the target firm; or (3) lessening financial incentives of the firms to compete with each other.

U.S. Merger Law. In the United States, mergers are covered by Sherman Act § 1 if they anticompetitively restrain trade because every merger involves an agreement. However, although a merger necessarily gives the combined firm a power to jointly fix prices, mergers are not per se illegal. This is because, as long as they involve some economic integration, mergers generally have some plausible efficiency justification to them. Thus, like joint ventures, mergers are judged under the rule of reason unless they are a sham. Mergers are likewise covered by FTC Act § 5, and a merger that created a firm with monopoly power would violate Sherman Act § 2.

Mergers are also covered by a statute this book has not yet examined:

Clayton Act § 7, 15 U.S.C. § 18

No person shall ... acquire ... the whole or any part of the assets of another person ... where in any line of commerce or in any section of the country, the effect of such acquisition may be substantially to lessen competition, or to tend to create a monopoly.

The term "person" includes not just natural persons but all legal entities like corporations. Mergers are normally challenged under Clayton Act § 7 rather than Sherman Act § 1 because historically the former was thought to have more lenient standards. The term "may be substantially to lessen" indeed suggests a purpose to block a merger as long as there is some risk of significant anticompetitive effects. However, the legislative history indicates an intent to require at least proof of some reasonable probability of anticompetitive effects, and the agencies and some courts often seem to read the language to require (like similar language in Clayton Act § 3) a showing that anticompetitive effects are more likely than not. The standards of proof under Clayton Act § 7 have become sufficiently tougher over time that it is no longer clear that there is much of a substantive difference between how Clayton Act § 7 and Sherman Act § 1 treat mergers. However, because almost all cases are brought under the former, the issue does not appear to have been adjudicated.

Whichever statute is used, antitrust merger regulation embodies a containment policy against allowing mergers that will create an anticompetitive market structure on the theory that it is easier to prevent such effects prophylactically rather than to undo the market structure or police monopoly or oligopoly pricing directly. Thus, the emphasis is on reviewing mergers before they are consummated and blocking the ones with predicted anticompetitive effects. This prophylactic approach means enforcement agencies and adjudicators must necessarily forecast the anticompetitive effects before they occur.

Under the Hart–Scott–Rodino Act, a filing about a proposed acquisition of "voting securities or assets" of another firm must presumptively be made if the dollar amounts involved exceed certain thresholds. See 15 USC § 18a(a). The filing requirement does not apply if the acquired voting securities both (1) are solely for investment purposes and (2) do not give the acquirer more than 10% of the target's voting securities. 15 USC § 18a(c)(9). The agencies have taken the position that the first prong cannot be satisfied if the firms are even considering a merger at the time of the transaction.[1] A filing is unnecessary for acquisitions of convertible

---

1. FTC & DOJ Annual Report to Congress 7 (2004). The FTC implementation regulation regarding Hart–Scott–Rodino filing requirements states that it treats a stock holding as solely for investment only "if the person holding or acquiring such voting securities has no intention of participating in the formulation, determination, or direction of the basic business decisions of the issuer." 16 C.F.R. § 801.1(i)(1). The FTC's report regarding the purpose of this provision states:

voting securities that do not presently entitle the holder to vote for directors, with the filing instead required before the conversion is made.[2]

In the initial filing, the merging parties provide the relevant agency with documents and analyses of the effects of the merger. (The DOJ and FTC have divided up merger work by specializing in different industries.) Unless the agencies make a "second request" for additional information within 30 days (15 days for cash tender offers), the parties may consummate their merger. In 95% of cases, the agencies decide no second request is necessary, generally because of low market share and concentration figures, though they may also rely on evidence from prior investigations, public data, and input from market participants, especially buyers.[3] In the 5% of cases where the agency makes a second request, it engages in a detailed analysis to decide whether the merger is likely to have anticompetitive effects. Parties opposed to the merger may also weigh in with their own facts and analyses. If the merger creates anticompetitive effects only in certain markets, like a merger between nationwide retailers that creates excessive market concentration in just a few local markets, then the merging parties often simply agree to divest assets in those local markets. Or firms may offer conduct remedies, like guarantees to refrain from raising prices or to charge the same price as in a competitive market, although the U.S. agencies strongly prefer structural remedies (like divestitures) over conduct remedies.[4]

If the merging parties and the agency cannot come to an agreement, then the agency must go to court to seek a preliminary injunction blocking the merger.[5] Likewise, even if the agency declines to pursue a case, a private litigant is free to go to court to enjoin a merger. Thus, ultimately the decision whether to approve the merger is up to the courts.

However, as a practical matter, many merging parties drop a proposed merger if the agency is opposed, both because it is often difficult to maintain merger financing for the long period that litigation would take and because the agencies enjoy favorable standards of proof on preliminary injunctions that require them to show only a reasonable likelihood of

---

merely voting the stock will not be considered evidence of an intent inconsistent with investment purpose. However, certain types of conduct could be so viewed. These include but are not limited to: (1) Nominating a candidate for the board of directors of the issuer; (2) proposing corporate action requiring shareholder approval; (3) soliciting proxies; (4) having a controlling shareholder, director, officer or employee simultaneously serving as an officer or director of the issuer; (5) being a competitor of the issuer; or (6) doing any of the foregoing with respect to any entity directly or indirectly controlling the issuer.

43 Fed. Reg. 33,450, 33,465 (1978). Factor (5) is particularly important because it indicates that voting shares in a competing firm can suffice to lose the solely-for-investment exception to the filing requirement.

2. 16 C.F.R. §§ 802.31, 801.1(f)(2), 801.32.

3. *See* U.S. DOJ/FTC, Commentary on the Horizontal Merger Guidelines (March 2006).

4. *See* DOJ, Antitrust Division Policy Guide to Merger Remedies at III.A (Oct. 2004).

5. If the FTC obtains such a preliminary injunction, it then itself adjudicates whether the merger violates antitrust law, though that determination is subject to appellate review. *See* Chapter 1. The DOJ would instead proceed to a trial at a district court for such a permanent adjudication. *Id.*

success. In addition, the enforcement agencies have had a narrower view of which mergers are anticompetitive than the available U.S. Supreme Court caselaw. Thus, for most of the last few decades, merging firms were wary of going to court when the Supreme Court precedent was more adverse than agency enforcement policy.

Further, other private parties rarely seek to challenge a merger that the agency has cleared. In part this is because agencies generally do a good job of identifying the anticompetitive mergers. But it also reflects the fact that private parties do not have the benefit of the extensive information collected by the government, and have difficulty conducting discovery quickly enough to block a merger before it occurs. In addition, competitors almost always lack standing to challenge a horizontal merger, and buyers generally have collective action problems in organizing to bring litigation and will not yet have suffered the sort of damages that might attract class action counsel. And after the merger, courts are reluctant to give an injunction to "unscramble the eggs" by undoing the merger, and it is often difficult to prove measurable damages if the claim is one like increased oligopoly pricing.

Thus, in practice, almost all substantive decisions about mergers are made by the enforcement agencies rather than by the courts. Further, when merger cases do get to court, they rarely last long enough to get to the U.S. Supreme Court. Indeed, the Supreme Court has not decided a case about the substantive standards that govern federal merger antitrust law since the 1976 enactment of the Hart–Scott–Rodino Act. The odd result is that we are left with many old Supreme Court cases that have never been overruled yet clearly do not reflect modern merger practice. For example, *Brown Shoe v. United States*, 370 U.S. 294 (1962), condemned a horizontal merger even where the market share of the combined firm was 5% and condemned a vertical merger that foreclosed all of 1.2% of the relevant market, and along the way suggested that efficiencies were grounds to condemn (not justify) the merger. Any effort to challenge such a merger today would not only fail but be laughed at by the agencies and probably most courts. Even *United States v. Philadelphia National Bank*, 374 U.S. 321 (1963), which held that a merger was presumptively unlawful if the merger would create a firm with a 30% market share and increase the market share of the two biggest firms from 44% to 59%, is broader and less rigorous than modern practice. And the latter case of *United States v. Von's Grocery*, 384 U.S. 270 (1966), held that this approach also presumptively condemned a merger that created a firm with 7.5% market share and increased the market share of the two largest firms by all of 1.4%, which again brings us back to a claim that would be deemed laughable in modern practice. *Brown Shoe* and *Philadelphia National Bank* also reflected a Goldilocks approach to market definition. That is, in both cases one market definition was too broad (because it would have made the market shares of the merging firms small) and another was too narrow (because it would have put the merging firms in separate markets and thus meant there was no horizontal merger that increased market concentration at all), and the Court responded by choosing a medium market definition that was "just right" (big enough to include both firms but not much larger). Modern practice takes a much more rigorous approach to market definition, as we saw in Chapter 3.

This leads to the rather unusual result that "the law in action" on mergers is mainly agency enforcement policy. The inconvenient fact that these old Supreme Court cases would condemn many mergers that are now routinely approved is politely ignored by the agencies and even by the lower courts in the few merger cases that reach them, which instead tend to rely more on the enforcement guidelines issued by the agencies. Further, these guidelines are actually broader than the actual enforcement practices of the agencies. Unfortunately, the U.S. agencies generally do not write opinions to explain their merger decisions, in part because they must render those decisions quickly and those decisions are just about whether to litigate, and the vast bulk of agency decisions are decisions not to bring litigation that under U.S. law are a matter of prosecutorial discretion that is unreviewable by the courts. Thus, to get a sense of what actual merger practice is like in the United States, we will supplement these guidelines with some empirical data on actual merger practice, and focus on a few lower court cases that (while not authoritative) more accurately reflect actual modern enforcement practice than does Supreme Court precedent.

The Exception for Passive Investments that Lack Anticompetitive Effects. Because Clayton Act § 7 prohibits acquiring "any part of the stock" of another firm—voting or nonvoting—when the effect "may be substantially to lessen competition," it can prohibit acquisitions of noncontrolling stakes in a corporation under the same legal standard applicable to mergers. 15 U.S.C. § 18. However, Clayton Act § 7 does "not apply to persons purchasing such stock solely for investment and not using the same by voting or otherwise to bring about, or in attempting to bring about, the substantial lessening of competition." 15 U.S.C. § 18. This exception has two prongs: the stock purchase (1) must be solely for investment and (2) must not be used to lessen competition substantially or to attempt to do so.[6]

The first prong requires that the investment be purely passive, which excludes not only investments that give working control, but also investments that give the acquirer influence over the target's business decisions or access to the target's sensitive business information.[7] The second prong imposes a more rigorous standard than ordinary Clayton Act § 7 review, which requires only that the stock acquisition would probably tend to substantially lessen competition.[8] Thus, whereas an active investment can be condemned if it may substantially lessen competition, a passive invest-

---

6. See United States v. Tracinda Inv. Corp., 477 F.Supp. 1093, 1098 (C.D. Cal. 1979); Anaconda Co. v. Crane Co., 411 F.Supp. 1210, 1219 (S.D.N.Y. 1975).

7. United States v. E.I. du Pont de Nemours & Co., 353 U.S. 586, 597–606 (1957) (even absent evidence that 23% stake conferred working control, passive investment exception did not apply where the investing firm tried to influence business decisions); *Tracinda*, 477 F.Supp. at 1098; *Anaconda*, 411 F.Supp. at 1218–19; United States v. Amax, Inc., 402 F.Supp. 956, 974 (D. Conn. 1975); United States v. Gillette Co., 55 Fed. Reg. 28,312 (July 10, 1990); U.S. DOJ/FTC Horizontal Merger Guidelines § 13 (2010) (agencies will consider whether partial stock acquisition lessens competition by giving the acquirer an ability to influence the target or access to the target's confidential business information).

8. *Tracinda*, 477 F.Supp. at 1098 & 1099 n.5; *Anaconda*, 411 F.Supp. at 1218–19.

ment can be condemned only if it actually does so, or was intended to do so. A purely passive investment might lessen competition if it lessens the incentives of the acquirer to compete with the target because the acquirer gets a share of profits from any lost sales that go to the target.[9]

EU Merger Law. The TFEU does not contain any provisions to deal with mergers. The Commission and the ECJ at first attempted to fill this lacuna by relying on Articles 101 and 102 of the TFEU to catch some mergers.[10] The inadequacy of these provisions to control mergers, however, became quickly clear and, in 1989, the Council of Ministers adopted Regulation 4064/89, also known as the EU Merger Control Regulation (EMCR).[11] Article 2 of this 1989 regulation provided that:

> A concentration which creates or strengthens a dominant position as a result of which effective competition would be significantly impeded in the common market or in a substantial part of it shall be declared incompatible with the common market.

By a "concentration," the EU means much the same as a merger under U.S. law, with the specifics detailed in Article 3 of the regulation. To have a sufficient Community dimension to trigger review under EU law (rather than under the competition law of a member state), the merger also must involve firms with a sufficiently large revenue, with the precise lines defined in Article 1 and turning on the distribution of firm revenue in the EU and its member states. The EMCR has also been supplemented by an implementing regulation and a number of Commission notices providing guidance on various aspects of EMCR enforcement.

The key substantive difference between the EU regulation and U.S. law was that the EU regulation prohibited only a merger that "creates or strengthens a dominant position" in a way that significantly impeded competition. On its face this regulation might seem to cover only mergers that created a single firm with a dominant position and thus leave mergers that created or strengthened oligopolies unregulated. However, this problem was largely addressed by decisions concluding that, when oligopolists coordinated with each other on price or output, they possessed "collective dominance." Thus, a merger that created or strengthened an oligopoly was deemed to have created or strengthened a collective dominant position. Nonetheless, concerns were expressed that the regulation failed to cover

---

9. U.S. DOJ/FTC Horizontal Merger Guidelines § 13 (2010); Daniel P. O'Brien & Steven C. Salop, *Competitive Effects of Partial Ownership: Financial Interest and Corporate Control,* 67 ANTITRUST L.J. 559 (2000); David Gilo, *The Anticompetitive Effect of Passive Investment,* 99 MICH. L. REV. 1, 8–28 (2000). Even if Clayton Act § 7 did not apply, a purely passive investment that lessened competitive incentives in a way that was likely to produce anticompetitive effects would be reviewable as an unreasonable restraint of trade or unfair trade practice (and maybe even as monopolization or attempted monopolization if the firms collectively have or threaten monopoly power), *see* Chapters 2–5, or as a facilitating agreement or practice if it seems likely to aid oligopolistic coordination by lessening incentives to defect, *see* Chapter 6.C.3.

10. On the application of Article 101 to mergers, see Cases 142 and 156/84, BAT and Reynolds v. Commission, [1987] E.C.R. 4487 and on the application of Article 82 to mergers, see Case 6/72, Europemballage Corp. & Continental Can Inc. v. Commission, [1973] E.C.R. 215.

11. Council Regulation 4064/89 on the control of concentrations between undertakings, O.J. 1989, L 395/1.

mergers in oligopolistic markets that were likely to create uncoordinated "unilateral" anticompetitive effects (which we explain below) without creating any single firm dominance or oligopolistic coordination. This was a special concern for mergers between two firms that were close to each other on a differentiated market. Even when these firms' combined market share was below the threshold of dominance, such a merger could nevertheless lead to price increases.

In part to remedy this problem, this regulation was replaced with Regulation 139/2004, which became effective on May 1, 2004. During the negotiations of the new EMCR, some delegations wanted to fill this "oligopoly gap" with the "significant lessening of competition" test, which was used in the U.S. Other delegations, however, wanted to retain the dominance test and, after lengthy negotiations, the Member States settled on a compromise between the dominance and the significantly lessening test. Article 2(3) of the new EMCR thus reads:

> A concentration which would significantly impede effective competition, in the common market or in a substantial part of it, in particular as a result of the creation or strengthening of a dominant position, shall be declared incompatible with the common market.

This test thus expands the scope of the prior test because it allows the prohibition of a merger that would significantly impede competition even if such a merger would not create or strengthen a dominant position. However, it keeps a reference to the old dominance test and thus preserves the decisional practice of the Commission and the Community courts case-law. The objectives of the new formulation are well expressed in recitals 25 and 26 of the EMCR:

> (25) ... [U]nder certain circumstances, concentrations involving the elimination of important competitive constraints that the merging parties had exerted upon each other, as well as a reduction of competitive pressure on the remaining competitors, may, even in the absence of a likelihood of coordination between the members of the oligopoly, result in a significant impediment to effective competition. The Community courts have, however, not to date expressly interpreted Regulation (EEC) No 4064/89 as requiring concentrations giving rise to such non-coordinated effects to be declared incompatible with the common market. Therefore, in the interests of legal certainty, it should be made clear that this Regulation permits effective control of all such concentrations by providing that any concentration which would significantly impede effective competition, in the common market or in a substantial part of it, should be declared incompatible with the common market. The notion of "significant impediment to effective competition" in Article 2(2) and (3) should be interpreted as extending, beyond the concept of dominance, only to the anticompetitive effects of a concentration resulting from the non-coordinated behaviour of undertakings which would not have a dominant position on the market concerned.

(26) A significant impediment to effective competition generally results from the creation or strengthening of a dominant position. With a view to preserving the guidance that may be drawn from past judgments of the European courts and Commission decisions pursuant to Regulation (EEC) No 4064/89, while at the same time maintaining consistency with the standards of competitive harm which have been applied by the Commission and the Community courts regarding the compatibility of a concentration with the common market, this Regulation should accordingly establish the principle that a concentration with a Community dimension which would significantly impede effective competition, in the common market or in a substantial part thereof, in particular as a result of the creation or strengthening of a dominant position, is to be declared incompatible with the common market.

The new EMCR also acknowledges the importance of taking efficiencies into account in the assessment of mergers. Its 29th recital provides:

In order to determine the impact of a concentration on competition in the common market, it is appropriate to take account of any substantiated and likely efficiencies put forward by the undertakings concerned. It is possible that the efficiencies brought about by the concentration counteract the effects on competition, and in particular the potential harm to consumers, that it might otherwise have and that, as a consequence, the concentration would not significantly impede effective competition, in the common market or in a substantial part of it, in particular as a result of the creation or strengthening of a dominant position.

This represents an important development because, under the old EMCR, the Commission was often reluctant to accept efficiency justifications when assessing mergers. This new provision eliminates any doubt that efficiencies should be taken into account when assessing mergers under EU law.

Other Nations. Over 80 nations, accounting for 80% of world output, have merger notification laws, but differ widely on their notification thresholds, and often change them over time.[12] Nations also differ on whether notification is mandatory. The nations that require require mandatory notification for mergers meeting the applicable thresholds include Argentina, Brazil, Canada, China, Colombia, Egypt, India, Japan, Israel, Mexico, Saudi Arabia, South Africa, South Korea, Taiwan, Thailand, and Turkey.[13] The nations that instead make notification voluntarily available to firms that wish to avoid the risk of having their merger challenged later include Australia, Chile, New Zealand, Singapore, and Venezuela.[14] Further, nations vary on whether a merger can be completed before the agency has an reviewed the merger. The nations that prohibit parties from closing the transaction until the waiting period has expired include Canada, China, Colombia, India, Israel, Japan, Mexico, Saudi Arabia, South Africa, South

---

12. *See* ABA, I COMPETITION LAWS OUTSIDE THE UNITED STATES 14 (2001).

13. *See, e.g.,* China Anti–Monopoly Law Arts. 21–24; Taiwan Fair Trade Act Art. 11.

14. Chile has an exception requiring mandatory review for media mergers.

Korea, Taiwan, and Turkey.[15] The nations that allow parties to close the merger pending review, subject to the risk it may be undone or penalized later, include Australia, Brazil, New Zealand, Singapore, and Venezuela.[16]

Nations also differ somewhat in their substantive standards. Argentina, Australia, Canada, Japan, Mexico, New Zealand, Singapore, and South Africa judge mergers under a "substantial lessening of competition" test.[17] Saudi Arabia and Turkey use the EU's former "dominant position" test,[18] while Brazil, South Korea, and Venezuela apply (like the EU) a hybrid test condemning mergers that fail either standard. Mergers are prohibited in China if they "will or may eliminate or restrict competition" and in India if the merger "is likely to cause an appreciable adverse effect on competition," which would seem to encompass any theory by which a merger might lessen competition.[19]

Australia, Brazil, Canada, China, South Africa, South Korea, and Taiwan also explicitly state that (as in the U.S. and EU) mergers can be approved if anticompetitive harms are offset by efficiency benefits, though some nations consider not only efficiency benefits that are passed on to consumers but also other public interest benefits like increasing employment or exports.[20] As we shall see, Canada also considers the distribution of effects if a merger harms some consumers but creates efficiency benefits for producers and their shareholders. The OECD has weighed in against the inclusion of broader public interest goals, concluding that: "The inclusion of multiple objectives ... increases the risks of conflicts and inconsistent application of competition policy. The interests of different stakeholders may severely constrain the independence of competition policy authorities, lead to political intervention and compromise, and adversely affect one of the major benefits of the competitive process, namely economic efficiency."[21]

A 2003 study estimated that the average multi-jurisdictional merger now requires eight filings, seven months, and millions in costs.[22] There are also costs associated with the risks of inconsistent decisions, especially on the merger remedies. There have thus been efforts for greater cooperation and procedural and substantive convergence in merger policy.

---

15.   *See, e.g.,* China Anti–Monopoly Law Arts. 25–26; Taiwan Fair Trade Act Art. 11.

16.   A pending bill in Brazil may, if adopted, change its law to require pre-merger approval. Argentina take an intermediate position, allowing parties to close a merger pending review only if they do not take effective control. Egypt requires post-merger notification, but does not appear to have any provision setting forth conditions under which the merger might be undone or penalized if proper notification is made.

17.   *See, e.g,* Australia Trade Practices Act § 50; Canada Competition Act § 92; Japan Antimonopoly Act §§ 10, 15–16; Mexico Federal Economic Competition Law Art. 16; South Africa Competition Act § 12A.

18.   *See, e.g.,* Saudi Arabia Executive Regulation Art. 7(a).

19.   China Anti–Monopoly Law Art. 28; India Competition Act §§ 6(1), 20(4).

20.   *See* Australia Trade Practices Act § 90(9A); Brazil Antitrust Law No. 8,884, Art.54 (considering wider benefits as long as consumers share in benefits or are not damaged); Brazil Horizontal Merger Guidelines § (2001); Canada Competition Act § 96; China Anti–Monopoly Law Art. 28 (merger permissible if "the favorable impact of the concentration on competition obviously exceeds the adverse impact, or that the concentration is in harmony with the public interests"); Saudi Arabia Implementing Regulations Arts.7(4) and 7(5); South Africa Competition § 12A, South Korea Fair Trade Act Art. 7(2)(i) (2009); Taiwan Fair Trade Act Art. 12.

21.   OECD Secretariat, The Objectives of Competition Law and Policy, CCNM/GF/COMP(2003)3, at 2.

A. HORIZONTAL MERGERS

Horizontal mergers raise two sorts of general anticompetitive concerns: unilateral effects and oligopolistic effects.

(1) Unilateral effects. A horizontal merger might allow the merged firm to exercise market power unilaterally. There are essentially two theories of how such unilateral effects might occur.

(a) *Merger Creates Unilateral Market Power Given Constraints on Rivals.* The merger might result in a single firm with significant market power, such as when the merged firm's market share is large and rivals' ability to expand is constrained by capacity or other factors.

(b) *Merged Brands Close to Each Other on Differentiated Market.* A merger between two firms whose brands are close to each other in a differentiated market might lead to adverse unilateral effects even though their share of the larger market is not great.

(2) Oligopoly Effects. A horizontal merger might create a more concentrated market structure that allows the leading firms in the market to engage in oligopolistic pricing, or to engage in it more effectively. In both the U.S. and the EU, the level of market concentration is generally measured by the Herfindal–Hirschman Index, which is the sum of the square of each firm's market shares. Thus, if a market had two firms with 50% market share, the HHI would be $50^2 + 50^2 = 5000$. If one firm had a 30% share and the other 70%, the HHI would be $30^2 + 70^2 = 5800$. One can express the HHI in decimals (.5000 and .5800 in the above cases), but like baseball batting averages, the decimal is generally dropped in discussion. There are essentially two theories about how multiple firms in concentrated markets might elevate prices to supra-competitive levels: Cournot interactions and oligopolistic coordination.

(a) Cournot v. Bertrand Interactions. The Cournot model assumes that each firm chooses whatever output level maximizes its profits, taking the output levels of the other firms as given. If so, and all firms have constant marginal costs and homogeneous products, then it can be shown that the marketwide Lerner Index (which measures the extent to which prices exceed marginal cost) equals the HHI (expressed in decimals) divided by the market demand elasticity.[23] Although the 2010 Merger Guidelines describe Cournot effects as one of the "coordinated" effects, Cournot effects require neither coordinating on common terms nor monitoring and retaliation to deter individually rational efforts to deviate from those terms.

---

22. PricewaterhouseCoopers, *A tax on mergers? Surveying the time and costs to business of multi-jurisdictional merger reviews*, a study commissioned by the International Bar Association and the American Bar Association (2003).

23. More precisely, if S_i is the market share of firm i (its quantity over the market quantity), and L_i equals the Lerner Index (P–MC)/P for firm i, then $\Sigma S_i L_i = HHI/\epsilon$ where ϵ equals the absolute value of the marketwide demand elasticity. *See* CARLTON & PERLOF, MODERN INDUSTRIAL ORGANIZATION 268 (3rd ed. 2000). A market with a 100% monopolist would have an

Instead, Cournot effects require only that each firm make individually rational decisions, which will reflect the individually rational responses of other firms. On the other hand, if the assumptions are the same but firms pick prices and not quantity and can instantaneously expand output to supply the whole market, then the Bertrand model shows that (even in a duopoly) firms that are not coordinating their behavior will find it profit-maximizing to choose a price that undercuts the price chosen by the other until the prices of each are driven down to marginal cost. Which model best describes uncoordinated market behavior in a concentrated market may depend on the nature of the industry. In some markets, where producing a given output requires serious advance planning, it may be more accurate to say that firms decide on their output, and then sell it at whatever price they can get for it. In other markets, it may be more accurate to say what firms really pick is their price, and then sell whatever output they can at that price.

(b) Coordinated Oligopoly Behavior. If they can engage in coordinated interaction, then firms in concentrated markets can elevate prices to supracompetitive levels whether they choose output, prices, or both. Suppose, for example, a market has two firms, each with 50% market share and costs of $20/unit. One firm announces that next month it will raise its prices from $20 to $25. The other firm knows that if it does not match the $25 price, then the first firm will rescind its price increase and they will each earn less profit. Thus, although in the short run it would be profit-maximizing for the other firm to undercut that price slightly, charging $24.99 and taking market share, it has incentives to instead coordinate with the other firm by matching its price increase.

Through such coordination, a few firms that collectively have market power can price supracompetitively without entering into an actual horizontal agreement that violates the antitrust laws. See Chapter 6. The ability of the firms to do so will depend on whether market conditions make it easy to: (1) settle on a cooperative price; (2) notice defection by other firms from that price; and (3) respond to such defection. The most significant factor is the number of firms. The greater the number of firms, the more difficult it will be to meet those conditions because other firms are less likely to notice defection by a particular firm or to respond to it, and it is harder to settle on a common price. Some empirical evidence indicates that after five firms, the addition of more firms makes little difference,[24] suggesting that five firms is normally sufficient to prevent oligopolistic coordination. A market with five equally sized firms would have an HHI of 2000.

Other market factors may also impede oligopolistic coordination. If the product is not homogeneous, but instead firms offer products with varying quality or characteristics, it will be difficult to settle on a common schedule of prices reflecting those variations and to notice and respond to defection by others, which may take the form of nonprice competition. If pricing is not public but privately negotiated, or if secret discounts are made from public pricing, then it will be harder to notice or respond to defection by

---

HHI of 1.0000 and thus its Lerner Index = $1/\epsilon$ as noted in Chapter 3. See also Chapter 1 on NEIO models.

24. *See* Bresnahan & Reiss, *Entry and Competition in Concentrated Markets,* 99 J. POL., ECON. 977 (1991).

others. If the costs of firms vary, it will be difficult to settle on a common price. If the market consists of infrequent bids for large projects, then the incentives to defect to get the bid will be large. Thus, a merger that would likely be anticompetitive if these market factors were not present might well be unlikely to be so if these factors are present. However, some factors that impede oligopolistic coordination, like product heterogeneity, may also make unilateral effects more likely.

Oligopolistic coordination may also occur on matters other than price, including output, market divisions, or innovation. In a differentiated market, coordinating on a policy of not invading the market positions of others can be an effective strategy. As noted in Chapter 6, the recent Supreme Court decision in *Twombly* recognizes the plausibility of such coordination on maintaining market differentiation, and thus indicates that theories of oligopolistic coordination and market differentiation are not at all mutually exclusive.

As we shall see, U.S. and EU merger guidelines consider both unilateral and oligopoly effects. However, they both use HHI thresholds that are economically relevant to Cournot effects, but have no relevance to unilateral effects and no clear relationship to oligopolistic coordination, which turns instead on the collective market power of oligopolists and their ability to coordinate with each other. The use of HHI thresholds in all cases may simply be a historical holdover from the focus of earlier analysis on concentration levels.

Proper antitrust analysis does not stop with identification of possible anticompetitive concerns. Such concerns may be offset by low entry barriers, merger-created efficiencies, or because one of the firms was failing and would have exited the market without the merger. Both U.S. and EU law thus take those factors into account before blocking a merger. The following will separately discuss each major element of horizontal merger analysis: the two major anticompetitive theories—(1) unilateral effects or (2) oligopoly effects—and the three major offsetting factors—(3) post-merger entry, (4) efficiencies, and (5) the failing firm defense. We end this section with factor (6), which is the extent to which buyer power, sophistication or views should affect merger analysis.

1.   UNILATERAL EFFECTS

U.S. DOJ/FTC, Horizontal Merger Guidelines
(2010).

1. Overview. . . .

The Agencies seek to identify and challenge competitively harmful mergers while avoiding unnecessary interference with mergers that are either competitively beneficial or neutral. Most merger analysis is necessarily predictive, requiring an assessment of what will likely happen if a merger proceeds as compared to what will likely happen if it does not. Given this inherent need for prediction, these Guidelines reflect the congressional intent that merger enforcement should interdict competitive problems in their incipiency and that certainty about anticompetitive effect is seldom possible and not required for a merger to be illegal.

These Guidelines describe the principal analytical techniques and the main types of evidence on which the Agencies usually rely to predict whether a horizontal merger may substantially lessen competition. They are not intended to describe how the Agencies analyze cases other than horizontal mergers. These Guidelines are intended to assist the business community and antitrust practitioners by increasing the transparency of the analytical process underlying the Agencies' enforcement decisions. They may also assist the courts in developing an appropriate framework for interpreting and applying the antitrust laws in the horizontal merger context. . . . [2]

The unifying theme of these Guidelines is that mergers should not be permitted to create, enhance, or entrench market power or to facilitate its exercise. For simplicity of exposition, these Guidelines generally refer to all of these effects as enhancing market power. A merger enhances market power if it is likely to encourage one or more firms to raise price, reduce output, diminish innovation, or otherwise harm customers as a result of diminished competitive constraints or incentives. In evaluating how a merger will likely change a firm's behavior, the Agencies focus primarily on how the merger affects conduct that would be most profitable for the firm.

A merger can enhance market power simply by eliminating competition between the merging parties. This effect can arise even if the merger causes no changes in the way other firms behave. Adverse competitive effects arising in this manner are referred to as "unilateral effects." A merger also can enhance market power by increasing the risk of coordinated, accommodating, or interdependent behavior among rivals. Adverse competitive effects arising in this manner are referred to as "coordinated effects." In any given case, either or both types of effects may be present, and the distinction between them may be blurred.

These Guidelines principally describe how the Agencies analyze mergers between rival suppliers that may enhance their market power as sellers. Enhancement of market power by sellers often elevates the prices charged to customers. For simplicity of exposition, these Guidelines generally discuss the analysis in terms of such price effects. Enhanced market power can also be manifested in non-price terms and conditions that adversely affect customers, including reduced product quality, reduced product variety, reduced service, or diminished innovation. Such non-price effects may coexist with price effects, or can arise in their absence. When the Agencies investigate whether a merger may lead to a substantial lessening of non-price competition, they employ an approach analogous to that used to evaluate price competition. Enhanced market power may also make it more likely that the merged entity can profitably and effectively engage in exclusionary conduct. Regardless of how enhanced market power likely

---

2. These Guidelines are not intended to describe how the Agencies will conduct the litigation of cases they decide to bring. Although relevant in that context, these Guidelines neither dictate nor exhaust the range of evidence the Agencies may introduce in litigation.

would be manifested, the Agencies normally evaluate mergers based on their impact on customers. The Agencies examine effects on either or both of the direct customers and the final consumers. The Agencies presume, absent convincing evidence to the contrary, that adverse effects on direct customers also cause adverse effects on final consumers. . . .

2. Evidence of Adverse Competitive Effects

The Agencies consider any reasonably available and reliable evidence to address the central question of whether a merger may substantially lessen competition. This section discusses several categories and sources of evidence that the Agencies, in their experience, have found most informative in predicting the likely competitive effects of mergers. The list provided here is not exhaustive. In any given case, reliable evidence may be available in only some categories or from some sources. For each category of evidence, the Agencies consider evidence indicating that the merger may enhance competition as well as evidence indicating that it may lessen competition.

2.1 Types of Evidence

2.1.1 Actual Effects Observed in Consummated Mergers

When evaluating a consummated merger, the ultimate issue is not only whether adverse competitive effects have already resulted from the merger, but also whether such effects are likely to arise in the future. Evidence of observed post-merger price increases or other changes adverse to customers is given substantial weight. The Agencies evaluate whether such changes are anticompetitive effects resulting from the merger, in which case they can be dispositive. However, a consummated merger may be anticompetitive even if such effects have not yet been observed, perhaps because the merged firm may be aware of the possibility of post-merger antitrust review and moderating its conduct. Consequently, the Agencies also consider the same types of evidence they consider when evaluating unconsummated mergers.

2.1.2 Direct Comparisons Based on Experience

The Agencies look for historical events, or "natural experiments," that are informative regarding the competitive effects of the merger. For example, the Agencies may examine the impact of recent mergers, entry, expansion, or exit in the relevant market. Effects of analogous events in similar markets may also be informative.

The Agencies also look for reliable evidence based on variations among similar markets. For example, if the merging firms compete in some locales but not others, comparisons of prices charged in regions where they do and do not compete may be informative regarding post-merger prices. In some cases, however, prices are set on such a broad geographic basis that such comparisons are not informative. The Agencies also may examine how prices in similar markets vary with the number of significant competitors in those markets.

2.1.3 Market Shares and Concentration in a Relevant Market

The Agencies give weight to the merging parties' market shares in a relevant market, the level of concentration, and the change in concentration caused by the merger. See Sections 4 and 5. Mergers that cause a significant increase in concentration and result in highly concentrated markets are presumed to be likely to enhance market power, but this presumption can be rebutted by persuasive evidence showing that the merger is unlikely to enhance market power.

2.1.4 Substantial Head-to-Head Competition

The Agencies consider whether the merging firms have been, or likely will become absent the merger, substantial head-to-head competitors. Such evidence can be especially relevant for evaluating adverse unilateral effects, which result directly from the loss of that competition. See Section 6. This evidence can also inform market definition. See Section 4. . . .

2.2 Sources of Evidence

The Agencies consider many sources of evidence in their merger analysis. The most common sources of reasonably available and reliable evidence are the merging parties, customers, other industry participants, and industry observers.

2.2.1 Merging Parties

The Agencies typically obtain substantial information from the merging parties. This information can take the form of documents, testimony, or data, and can consist of descriptions of competitively relevant conditions or reflect actual business conduct and decisions. Documents created in the normal course are more probative than documents created as advocacy materials in merger review. Documents describing industry conditions can be informative regarding the operation of the market and how a firm identifies and assesses its rivals, particularly when business decisions are made in reliance on the accuracy of those descriptions. The business decisions taken by the merging firms also can be informative about industry conditions. For example, if a firm sets price well above incremental cost, that normally indicates either that the firm believes its customers are not highly sensitive to price (not in itself of antitrust concern, see Section 4.1.3[3]) or that the firm and its rivals are engaged in coordinated interaction (see Section 7). Incremental cost depends on the relevant increment in output as well as on the time period involved, and in the case of large increments and sustained changes in output it may include some costs that would be fixed for smaller increments of output or shorter time periods.

Explicit or implicit evidence that the merging parties intend to raise prices, reduce output or capacity, reduce product quality or variety, withdraw products or delay their introduction, or curtail research and development efforts after the merger, or explicit or implicit evidence that the ability to engage in such conduct motivated the merger, can be highly informative in evaluating the likely effects of a merger. Likewise, the Agencies look for reliable evidence that the merger is likely to result in efficiencies. The Agencies give careful consideration to the views of individuals whose responsibilities, expertise, and experience relating to the issues

---

3. High margins commonly arise for products that are significantly differentiated. Products involving substantial fixed costs typically will be developed only if suppliers expect there to be enough differentiation to support margins sufficient to cover those fixed costs. High margins can be consistent with incumbent firms earning competitive returns.

in question provide particular indicia of reliability. The financial terms of the transaction may also be informative regarding competitive effects. For example, a purchase price in excess of the acquired firm's stand-alone market value may indicate that the acquiring firm is paying a premium because it expects to be able to reduce competition or to achieve efficiencies. . . .

4. Market Definition

When the Agencies identify a potential competitive concern with a horizontal merger, market definition plays two roles. First, market definition helps specify the line of commerce and section of the country in which the competitive concern arises. In any merger enforcement action, the Agencies will normally identify one or more relevant markets in which the merger may substantially lessen competition. Second, market definition allows the Agencies to identify market participants and measure market shares and market concentration. See Section 5. The measurement of market shares and market concentration is not an end in itself, but is useful to the extent it illuminates the merger's likely competitive effects.

The Agencies' analysis need not start with market definition. Some of the analytical tools used by the Agencies to assess competitive effects do not rely on market definition, although evaluation of competitive alternatives available to customers is always necessary at some point in the analysis.

Evidence of competitive effects can inform market definition, just as market definition can be informative regarding competitive effects. For example, evidence that a reduction in the number of significant rivals offering a group of products causes prices for those products to rise significantly can itself establish that those products form a relevant market. Such evidence also may more directly predict the competitive effects of a merger, reducing the role of inferences from market definition and market shares. Where analysis suggests alternative and reasonably plausible candidate markets, and where the resulting market shares lead to very different inferences regarding competitive effects, it is particularly valuable to examine more direct forms of evidence concerning those effects. . . .

[Other portions on market definition are excerpted in Chapter 3].

5. Market Participants, Market Shares, and Market Concentration

The Agencies normally consider measures of market shares and market concentration as part of their evaluation of competitive effects. The Agencies evaluate market shares and concentration in conjunction with other reasonably available and reliable evidence for the ultimate purpose of determining whether a merger may substantially lessen competition . . .

[Sections on identifying market participants and calculating market shares are excerpted in Chapter 3.]

5.3 Market Concentration

Market concentration is often one useful indicator of likely competitive effects of a merger. In evaluating market concentration, the Agencies consider both the post-merger level of market concentration and the change in concentration resulting from a merger. Market shares may not fully reflect the competitive significance of firms in the market or the impact of a merger. They are used in conjunction with other evidence of competitive effects. See Sections 6 and 7.

In analyzing mergers between an incumbent and a recent or potential entrant, to the extent the Agencies use the change in concentration to evaluate competitive effects, they will do so using projected market shares. A merger between an incumbent and a potential entrant can raise significant competitive concerns. The lessening of competition resulting from such a merger is more likely to be substantial, the larger is the market share of the incumbent, the greater is the competitive significance of the potential entrant, and the greater is the competitive threat posed by this potential entrant relative to others.

The Agencies give more weight to market concentration when market shares have been stable over time, especially in the face of historical changes in relative prices or costs. If a firm has retained its market share even after its price has increased relative to those of its rivals, that firm already faces limited competitive constraints, making it less likely that its remaining rivals will replace the competition lost if one of that firm's important rivals is eliminated due to a merger. By contrast, even a highly concentrated market can be very competitive if market shares fluctuate substantially over short periods of time in response to changes in competitive offerings. However, if competition by one of the merging firms has significantly contributed to these fluctuations, perhaps because it has acted as a maverick, the Agencies will consider whether the merger will enhance market power by combining that firm with one of its significant rivals.

The Agencies may measure market concentration using the number of significant competitors in the market. This measure is most useful when there is a gap in market share between significant competitors and smaller rivals or when it is difficult to measure revenues in the relevant market. The Agencies also may consider the combined market share of the merging firms as an indicator of the extent to which others in the market may not be able readily to replace competition between the merging firms that is lost through the merger.

The Agencies often calculate the Herfindahl–Hirschman Index ("HHI") of market concentration. The HHI is calculated by summing the squares of the individual firms' market shares,[9] and thus gives proportionately greater weight to the larger market shares. When using the HHI, the Agencies consider both the post-merger level of the HHI and the increase in the HHI resulting from the merger. The increase in the HHI is equal to twice the product of the market shares of the merging firms.[10]

---

9. For example, a market consisting of four firms with market shares of thirty percent, thirty percent, twenty percent, and twenty percent has an HHI of 2600 ($30^2 + 30_2 + 20^2 + 20^2 = 2600$). The HHI ranges from 10,000 (in the case of a pure monopoly) to a number approaching zero (in the case of an atomistic market). Although it is desirable to include all firms in the calculation, lack of information about firms with small shares is not critical because such firms do not affect the HHI significantly.

10. For example, the merger of firms with shares of five percent and ten percent of the market would increase the HHI by 100 ($5 \times 10 \times 2 = 100$).

Based on their experience, the Agencies generally classify markets into three types:[25]

- *Unconcentrated Markets*: HHI below 1500
- *Moderately Concentrated Markets*: HHI between 1500 and 2500
- *Highly Concentrated Markets*: HHI above 2500

The Agencies employ the following general standards for the relevant markets they have defined:

- *Small Change in Concentration:* Mergers involving an increase in the HHI of less than 100 points are unlikely to have adverse competitive effects and ordinarily require no further analysis.

- *Unconcentrated Markets:* Mergers resulting in unconcentrated markets are unlikely to have adverse competitive effects and ordinarily require no further analysis.

- *Moderately Concentrated Markets:* Mergers resulting in moderately concentrated markets that involve an increase in the HHI of more than 100 points potentially raise significant competitive concerns and often warrant scrutiny.

- *Highly Concentrated Markets:* Mergers resulting in highly concentrated markets that involve an increase in the HHI of between 100 points and 200 points potentially raise significant competitive concerns and often warrant scrutiny. Mergers resulting in highly concentrated markets that involve an increase in the HHI of more than 200 points will be presumed to be likely to enhance market power. The presumption may be rebutted by persuasive evidence showing that the merger is unlikely to enhance market power.[26]

The purpose of these thresholds is not to provide a rigid screen to separate competitively benign mergers from anticompetitive ones, although high levels of concentration do raise concerns. Rather, they provide one way to identify some mergers unlikely to raise competitive concerns and some others for which it is particularly important to examine whether other competitive factors confirm, reinforce, or counteract the potentially harmful effects of increased concentration. The higher the post-merger HHI and the increase in the HHI, the greater are the Agencies' potential competitive concerns and the greater is the likelihood that the Agencies will request additional information to conduct their analysis.

6. Unilateral Effects

The elimination of competition between two firms that results from their merger may alone constitute a substantial lessening of competition. Such unilateral effects are most apparent in a merger to monopoly in a relevant market, but are by no means limited to that case. Whether

---

25. [Editor's Note. The following changed the prior merger guidelines, which defined markets as unconcentrated for HHI less than 1000, moderately concentrated for HHI between 1000 and 1800, and highly concentrated for HHI over 1800.]

26. [Editor's Note: This changed prior merger guidelines, which not only set the highly concentrated threshold at 1800, but also stated that a HHI increase of between 50–100 potentially raised concerns and an HHI increase of over 100 would be presumed to be likely to be anticompetitive.]

cognizable efficiencies resulting from the merger are likely to reduce or reverse adverse unilateral effects is addressed in Section 10.

Several common types of unilateral effects are discussed in this section. Section 6.1 discusses unilateral price effects in markets with differentiated products. Section 6.2 discusses unilateral effects in markets where sellers negotiate with buyers or prices are determined through auctions. Section 6.3 discusses unilateral effects relating to reductions in output or capacity in markets for relatively homogeneous products. Section 6.4 discusses unilateral effects arising from diminished innovation or reduced product variety. These effects do not exhaust the types of possible unilateral effects; for example, exclusionary unilateral effects also can arise.

A merger may result in different unilateral effects along different dimensions of competition. For example, a merger may increase prices in the short term but not raise longer-term concerns about innovation, either because rivals will provide sufficient innovation competition or because the merger will generate cognizable research and development efficiencies. See Section 10.

6.1 Pricing of Differentiated Products

In differentiated product industries, some products can be very close substitutes and compete strongly with each other, while other products are more distant substitutes and compete less strongly. For example, one high-end product may compete much more directly with another high-end product than with any low-end product.

A merger between firms selling differentiated products may diminish competition by enabling the merged firm to profit by unilaterally raising the price of one or both products above the pre-merger level. Some of the sales lost due to the price rise will merely be diverted to the product of the merger partner and, depending on relative margins, capturing such sales loss through merger may make the price increase profitable even though it would not have been profitable prior to the merger.

The extent of direct competition between the products sold by the merging parties is central to the evaluation of unilateral price effects. Unilateral price effects are greater, the more the buyers of products sold by one merging firm consider products sold by the other merging firm to be their next choice. The Agencies consider any reasonably available and reliable information to evaluate the extent of direct competition between the products sold by the merging firms. This includes documentary and testimonial evidence, win/loss reports and evidence from discount approval processes, customer switching patterns, and customer surveys. The types of evidence relied on often overlap substantially with the types of evidence of customer substitution relevant to the hypothetical monopolist test. See Section 4.1.1.

Substantial unilateral price elevation post-merger for a product formerly sold by one of the merging firms normally requires that a significant fraction of the customers purchasing that product view products formerly sold by the other merging firm as their next-best choice. However, unless pre-merger margins between price and incremental cost are low, that significant fraction need not approach a majority. For this purpose, incremental cost is measured over the change in output that would be caused by the price change considered. A merger may produce significant unilateral effects for a given product even though many more sales are diverted to products sold by non-merging firms than to products previously sold by the merger partner.

Example 19: In Example 5, the merged entity controlling Products A and B would raise prices ten percent, given the product offerings and prices of other firms. In that example, one-third of the sales lost by Product A when its price alone is raised are diverted to Product B. Further analysis is required to account for repositioning, entry, and efficiencies.

In some cases, the Agencies may seek to quantify the extent of direct competition between a product sold by one merging firm and a second product sold by the other merging firm by estimating the diversion ratio from the first product to the second product. The diversion ratio is the fraction of unit sales lost by the first product due to an increase in its price that would be diverted to the second product. Diversion ratios between products sold by one merging firm and products sold by the other merging firm can be very informative for assessing unilateral price effects, with higher diversion ratios indicating a greater likelihood of such effects. Diversion ratios between products sold by merging firms and those sold by non-merging firms have at most secondary predictive value.

Adverse unilateral price effects can arise when the merger gives the merged entity an incentive to raise the price of a product previously sold by one merging firm and thereby divert sales to products previously sold by the other merging firm, boosting the profits on the latter products. Taking as given other prices and product offerings, that boost to profits is equal to the value to the merged firm of the sales diverted to those products. The value of sales diverted to a product is equal to the number of units diverted to that product multiplied by the margin between price and incremental cost on that product. In some cases, where sufficient information is available, the Agencies assess the value of diverted sales, which can serve as an indicator of the upward pricing pressure on the first product resulting from the merger. Diagnosing unilateral price effects based on the value of diverted sales need not rely on market definition or the calculation of market shares and concentration. The Agencies rely much more on the value of diverted sales than on the level of the HHI for diagnosing unilateral price effects in markets with differentiated products. If the value of diverted sales is proportionately small, significant unilateral price effects are unlikely.[11]

Where sufficient data are available, the Agencies may construct economic models designed to quantify the unilateral price effects resulting from the merger. These models often include independent price responses by non-merging firms. They also can incorporate merger-specific efficiencies. These merger simulation methods need not rely on market definition.

---

11. For this purpose, the value of diverted sales is measured in proportion to the lost revenues attributable to the reduction in unit sales resulting from the price increase. Those lost revenues equal the reduction in the number of units sold of that product multiplied by that product's price.

The Agencies do not treat merger simulation evidence as conclusive in itself, and they place more weight on whether their merger simulations consistently predict substantial price increases than on the precise prediction of any single simulation.

A merger is unlikely to generate substantial unilateral price increases if non-merging parties offer very close substitutes for the products offered by the merging firms. In some cases, non-merging firms may be able to reposition their products to offer close substitutes for the products offered by the merging firms. Repositioning is a supply-side response that is evaluated much like entry, with consideration given to timeliness, likelihood, and sufficiency. See Section 9. The Agencies consider whether repositioning would be sufficient to deter or counteract what otherwise would be significant anticompetitive unilateral effects from a differentiated products merger.

6.2 Bargaining and Auctions

In many industries, especially those involving intermediate goods and services, buyers and sellers negotiate to determine prices and other terms of trade. In that process, buyers commonly negotiate with more than one seller, and may play sellers off against one another. Some highly structured forms of such competition are known as auctions. Negotiations often combine aspects of an auction with aspects of one-on-one negotiation, although pure auctions are sometimes used in government procurement and elsewhere.

A merger between two competing sellers prevents buyers from playing those sellers off against each other in negotiations. This alone can significantly enhance the ability and incentive of the merged entity to obtain a result more favorable to it, and less favorable to the buyer, than the merging firms would have offered separately absent the merger. The Agencies analyze unilateral effects of this type using similar approaches to those described in Section 6.1.

Anticompetitive unilateral effects in these settings are likely in proportion to the frequency or probability with which, prior to the merger, one of the merging sellers had been the runner-up when the other won the business. These effects also are likely to be greater, the greater advantage the runner-up merging firm has over other suppliers in meeting customers' needs. These effects also tend to be greater, the more profitable were the pre-merger winning bids. All of these factors are likely to be small if there are many equally placed bidders.

The mechanisms of these anticompetitive unilateral effects, and the indicia of their likelihood, differ somewhat according to the bargaining practices used, the auction format, and the sellers' information about one another's costs and about buyers' preferences. For example, when the merging sellers are likely to know which buyers they are best and second best placed to serve, any anticompetitive unilateral effects are apt to be targeted at those buyers; when sellers are less well informed, such effects are more apt to be spread over a broader class of buyers.

6.3 Capacity and Output for Homogeneous Products

In markets involving relatively undifferentiated products, the Agencies may evaluate whether the merged firm will find it profitable unilaterally to suppress output and elevate the market price. A firm may leave capacity idle, refrain from building or obtaining capacity that would have been obtained absent the merger, or eliminate pre-existing production capabilities. A firm may also divert the use of capacity away from one relevant market and into another so as to raise the price in the former market. The competitive analyses of these alternative modes of output suppression may differ.

A unilateral output suppression strategy is more likely to be profitable when (1) the merged firm's market share is relatively high; (2) the share of the merged firm's output already committed for sale at prices unaffected by the output suppression is relatively low; (3) the margin on the suppressed output is relatively low; (4) the supply responses of rivals are relatively small; and (5) the market elasticity of demand is relatively low.

A merger may provide the merged firm a larger base of sales on which to benefit from the resulting price rise, or it may eliminate a competitor that otherwise could have expanded its output in response to the price rise.

> *Example 20*: Firms A and B both produce an industrial commodity and propose to merge. The demand for this commodity is insensitive to price. Firm A is the market leader. Firm B produces substantial output, but its operating margins are low because it operates high-cost plants. The other suppliers are operating very near capacity. The merged firm has an incentive to reduce output at the high-cost plants, perhaps shutting down some of that capacity, thus driving up the price it receives on the remainder of its output. The merger harms customers, notwithstanding that the merged firm shifts some output from high-cost plants to low-cost plants.

In some cases, a merger between a firm with a substantial share of the sales in the market and a firm with significant excess capacity to serve that market can make an output suppression strategy profitable.[12] This can occur even if the firm with the excess capacity has a relatively small share of sales, if that firm's ability to expand, and thus keep price from rising, has been making an output suppression strategy unprofitable for the firm with the larger market share.

6.4 Innovation and Product Variety

Competition often spurs firms to innovate. The Agencies may consider whether a merger is likely to diminish innovation competition by encouraging the merged firm to curtail its innovative efforts below the level that would prevail in the absence of the merger. That curtailment of innovation could take the form of reduced incentive to continue with an existing product-development effort or reduced incentive to initiate development of new products.

The first of these effects is most likely to occur if at least one of the merging firms is engaging in efforts to introduce new products that would

---

12. Such a merger also can cause adverse coordinated effects, especially if the acquired firm with excess capacity was disrupting effective coordination.

capture substantial revenues from the other merging firm. The second, longer-run effect is most likely to occur if at least one of the merging firms has capabilities that are likely to lead it to develop new products in the future that would capture substantial revenues from the other merging firm. The Agencies therefore also consider whether a merger will diminish innovation competition by combining two of a very small number of firms with the strongest capabilities to successfully innovate in a specific direction.

The Agencies evaluate the extent to which successful innovation by one merging firm is likely to take sales from the other, and the extent to which post-merger incentives for future innovation will be lower than those that would prevail in the absence of the merger. The Agencies also consider whether the merger is likely to enable innovation that would not otherwise take place, by bringing together complementary capabilities that cannot be otherwise combined or for some other merger-specific reason. See Section 10.

The Agencies also consider whether a merger is likely to give the merged firm an incentive to cease offering one of the relevant products sold by the merging parties. Reductions in variety following a merger may or may not be anticompetitive. Mergers can lead to the efficient consolidation of products when variety offers little in value to customers. In other cases, a merger may increase variety by encouraging the merged firm to reposition its products to be more differentiated from one another.

If the merged firm would withdraw a product that a significant number of customers strongly prefer to those products that would remain available, this can constitute a harm to customers over and above any effects on the price or quality of any given product. If there is evidence of such an effect, the Agencies may inquire whether the reduction in variety is largely due to a loss of competitive incentives attributable to the merger. An anticompetitive incentive to eliminate a product as a result of the merger is greater and more likely, the larger is the share of profits from that product coming at the expense of profits from products sold by the merger partner. Where a merger substantially reduces competition by bringing two close substitute products under common ownership, and one of those products is eliminated, the merger will often also lead to a price increase on the remaining product, but that is not a necessary condition for anticompetitive effect.

Example 21: Firm A sells a high-end product at a premium price. Firm B sells a mid-range product at a lower price, serving customers who are more price sensitive. Several other firms have low-end products. Firms A and B together have a large share of the relevant market. Firm A proposes to acquire Firm B and discontinue Firm B's product. Firm A expects to retain most of Firm B's customers. Firm A may not find it profitable to raise the price of its high-end product after the merger, because doing so would reduce its ability to retain Firm B's more price-sensitive customers. The Agencies may conclude that the withdrawal of Firm B's product results from a loss of competition and materially harms customers. . . .

EU Guidelines on the Assessment of Horizontal Mergers
O.J. 2004, C 31/5.

III. MARKET SHARE AND CONCENTRATION LEVELS. Market shares and concentration levels provide useful first indications of the market structure and of the competitive importance of both the merging parties and their competitors.

Normally, the Commission uses current market shares in its competitive analysis. However, current market shares may be adjusted to reflect reasonably certain future changes, for instance in the light of exit, entry or expansion. Post-merger market shares are calculated on the assumption that the post-merger combined market share of the merging parties is the sum of their pre-merger market shares. Historic data may be used if market shares have been volatile, for instance when the market is characterised by large, lumpy orders. Changes in historic market shares may provide useful information about the competitive process and the likely future importance of the various competitors, for instance, by indicating whether firms have been gaining or losing market shares. In any event, the Commission interprets market shares in the light of likely market conditions, for instance, if the market is highly dynamic in character and if the market structure is unstable due to innovation or growth.

The overall concentration level in a market may also provide useful information about the competitive situation. In order to measure concentration levels, the Commission often applies the Herfindahl–Hirschman Index (HHI). The HHI is calculated by summing the squares of the individual market shares of all the firms in the market. The HHI gives proportionately greater weight to the market shares of the larger firms. Although it is best to include all firms in the calculation, lack of information about very small firms may not be important because such firms do not affect the HHI significantly. While the absolute level of the HHI can give an initial indication of the competitive pressure in the market post-merger, the change in the HHI (known as the "delta") is a useful proxy for the change in concentration directly brought about by the merger.

Market share levels. According to well-established case law, very large market shares—50% or more—may in themselves be evidence of the existence of a dominant market position. However, smaller competitors may act as a sufficient constraining influence if, for example, they have the ability and incentive to increase their supplies. A merger involving a firm whose market share will remain below 50% after the merger may also raise competition concerns in view of other factors such as the strength and number of competitors, the presence of capacity constraints or the extent to which the products of the merging parties are close substitutes. The Commission has thus in several cases considered mergers resulting in firms holding market shares between 40% and 50%, and in some cases below 40%, to lead to the creation or the strengthening of a dominant position.

Concentrations which, by reason of the limited market share of the undertakings concerned, are not liable to impede effective competition may be presumed to be compatible with the common market. Without prejudice to Articles [101 and 102 TFEU], an indication to this effect exists, in particular, where the market share of the undertakings concerned does not exceed 25% either in the common market or in a substantial part of it.[24]

HHI levels. The Commission is unlikely to identify horizontal competition concerns in a market with a post-merger HHI below 1000. Such markets normally do not require extensive analysis.

The Commission is also unlikely to identify horizontal competition concerns in a merger with a post-merger HHI between 1000 and 2000 and a delta below 250, or a merger with a post-merger HHI above 2000 and a delta below 150, except where special circumstances such as, for instance, one or more of the following factors are present:

(a) a merger involves a potential entrant or a recent entrant with a small market share;

(b) one or more merging parties are important innovators in ways not reflected in market shares;

(c) there are significant cross-shareholdings among the market participants;

(d) one of the merging firms is a maverick firm with a high likelihood of disrupting coordinated conduct;

(e) indications of past or ongoing coordination, or facilitating practices, are present;

(f) one of the merging parties has a pre-merger market share of 50% of more.

Each of these HHI levels, in combination with the relevant deltas, may be used as an initial indicator of the absence of competition concerns. However, they do not give rise to a presumption of either the existence or the absence of such concerns....

IV. POSSIBLE ANTI-COMPETITIVE EFFECTS OF HORIZONTAL MERGERS. There are two main ways in which horizontal mergers may significantly impede effective competition, in particular by creating or strengthening a dominant position:

(a) by eliminating important competitive constraints on one or more firms, which consequently would have increased market power, without resorting to coordinated behaviour (non-coordinated effects);

(b) by changing the nature of competition in such a way that firms that previously were not coordinating their behaviour, are now significantly more likely to coordinate and raise prices or otherwise harm effective competition. A merger may also make coordination easier, more stable or more effective for firms which were coordinating prior to the merger (coordinated effects).

---

24. Recital 32 of the Merger Regulation. However, such an indication does not apply to cases where the proposed merger creates or strengthens a collective dominant position involving the "undertakings concerned" and other third parties (see Joined Cases C–68/94 and C–30/95, Kali and Salz, [1998] ECR I–1375, paragraphs 171 et seq.; and Case T–102/96, Gencor v. Commission, [1999] ECR II–753, paragraphs 134 et seq.).

The Commission assesses whether the changes brought about by the merger would result in any of these effects. Both instances mentioned above may be relevant when assessing a particular transaction.

Non-coordinated effects. A merger may significantly impede effective competition in a market by removing important competitive constraints on one or more sellers, who consequently have increased market power. The most direct effect of the merger will be the loss of competition between the merging firms. For example, if prior to the merger one of the merging firms had raised its price, it would have lost some sales to the other merging firm. The merger removes this particular constraint. Non-merging firms in the same market can also benefit from the reduction of competitive pressure that results from the merger, since the merging firms' price increase may switch some demand to the rival firms, which, in turn, may find it profitable to increase their prices. The reduction in these competitive constraints could lead to significant price increases in the relevant market.

Generally, a merger giving rise to such non-coordinated effects would significantly impede effective competition by creating or strengthening the dominant position of a single firm, one which, typically, would have an appreciably larger market share than the next competitor post-merger. Furthermore, mergers in oligopolistic markets involving the elimination of important competitive constraints that the merging parties previously exerted upon each other together with a reduction of competitive pressure on the remaining competitors may, even where there is little likelihood of coordination between the members of the oligopoly, also result in a significant impediment to competition. The Merger Regulation clarifies that all mergers giving rise to such non-coordinated effects shall also be declared incompatible with the common market.

A number of factors, which taken separately are not necessarily decisive, may influence whether significant non-coordinated effects are likely to result from a merger. Not all of these factors need to be present for such effects to be likely. Nor should this be considered an exhaustive list.

Merging firms have large market shares. The larger the market share, the more likely a firm is to possess market power. And the larger the addition of market share, the more likely it is that a merger will lead to a significant increase in market power. The larger the increase in the sales base on which to enjoy higher margins after a price increase, the more likely it is that the merging firms will find such a price increase profitable despite the accompanying reduction in output. Although market shares and additions of market shares only provide first indications of market power and increases in market power, they are normally important factors in the assessment.

Merging firms are close competitors. Products may be differentiated[32] within a relevant market such that some products are closer substitutes

---

32. Products may be differentiated in various ways. There may, for example, be differentiation in terms of geographic location, based on branch or stores location; location matters for retail distribution, banks, travel agencies, or petrol stations. Likewise, differentiation may be based on brand image, technical specifications, quality or level of service. The

than others. The higher the degree of substitutability between the merging firms' products, the more likely it is that the merging firms will raise prices significantly. For example, a merger between two producers offering products which a substantial number of customers regard as their first and second choices could generate a significant price increase. Thus, the fact that rivalry between the parties has been an important source of competition on the market may be a central factor in the analysis. High pre-merger margins[36] may also make significant price increases more likely. The merging firms' incentive to raise prices is more likely to be constrained when rival firms produce close substitutes to the products of the merging firms than when they offer less close substitutes. It is therefore less likely that a merger will significantly impede effective competition, in particular through the creation or strengthening of a dominant position, when there is a high degree of substitutability between the products of the merging firms and those supplied by rival producers.

When data are available, the degree of substitutability may be evaluated through customer preference surveys, analysis of purchasing patterns, estimation of the cross-price elasticities of the products involved,[38] or diversion ratios.[39] In bidding markets it may be possible to measure whether historically the submitted bids by one of the merging parties have been constrained by the presence of the other merging party.

In some markets it may be relatively easy and not too costly for the active firms to reposition their products or extend their product portfolio. In particular, the Commission examines whether the possibility of repositioning or product line extension by competitors or the merging parties may influence the incentive of the merged entity to raise prices. However, product repositioning or product line extension often entails risks and large sunk costs and may be less profitable than the current line.

Customers have limited possibilities of switching supplier. Customers of the merging parties may have difficulties switching to other suppliers because there are few alternative suppliers or because they face substantial switching costs. Such customers are particularly vulnerable to price increases. The merger may affect these customers' ability to protect themselves against price increases. In particular, this may be the case for customers that have used dual sourcing from the two merging firms as a means of obtaining competitive prices. Evidence of past customer switching patterns and reactions to price changes may provide important information in this respect.

---

level of advertising in a market may be an indicator of the firms' effort to differentiate their products. For other products, buyers may have to incur switching costs to use a competitor's product.

36. Typically, the relevant margin (m) is the difference between price (p) and the incremental cost (c) of supplying one more unit of output expressed as a percentage of price (m = ((p − c)/p)).

38. The cross-price elasticity of demand measures the extent to which the quantity of a product demanded changes in response to a change in the price of some other product, all other things remaining equal. The own-price elasticity measures the extent to which demand for a product changes in response to the change in the price of the product itself.

39. The diversion ratio from product A to product B measures the proportion of the sales of product A lost due to a price increase of A that are captured by product B.

Competitors are unlikely to increase supply if prices increase. When market conditions are such that the competitors of the merging parties are unlikely to increase their supply substantially if prices increase, the merging firms may have an incentive to reduce output below the combined pre-merger levels, thereby raising market prices. The merger increases the incentive to reduce output by giving the merged firm a larger base of sales on which to enjoy the higher margins resulting from an increase in prices induced by the output reduction.

Conversely, when market conditions are such that rival firms have enough capacity and find it profitable to expand output sufficiently, the Commission is unlikely to find that the merger will create or strengthen a dominant position or otherwise significantly impede effective competition. Such output expansion is, in particular, unlikely when competitors face binding capacity constraints and the expansion of capacity is costly or if existing excess capacity is significantly more costly to operate than capacity currently in use. Although capacity constraints are more likely to be important when goods are relatively homogeneous, they may also be important where firms offer differentiated products.

Merged entity able to hinder expansion by competitors. Some proposed mergers would, if allowed to proceed, significantly impede effective competition by leaving the merged firm in a position where it would have the ability and incentive to make the expansion of smaller firms and potential competitors more difficult or otherwise restrict the ability of rival firms to compete. In such a case, competitors may not, either individually or in the aggregate, be in a position to constrain the merged entity to such a degree that it would not increase prices or take other actions detrimental to competition. For instance, the merged entity may have such a degree of control, or influence over, the supply of inputs or distribution possibilities that expansion or entry by rival firms may be more costly. Similarly, the merged entity's control over patents or other types of intellectual property (e.g. brands) may make expansion or entry by rivals more difficult. In markets where interoperability between different infrastructures or platforms is important, a merger may give the merged entity the ability and incentive to raise the costs or decrease the quality of service of its rivals. In making this assessment the Commission may take into account, inter alia, the financial strength of the merged entity relative to its rivals.

Merger eliminates an important competitive force. Some firms have more of an influence on the competitive process than their market shares or similar measures would suggest. A merger involving such a firm may change the competitive dynamics in a significant, anti-competitive way, in particular when the market is already concentrated. For instance, a firm may be a recent entrant that is expected to exert significant competitive pressure in the future on the other firms in the market.

In markets where innovation is an important competitive force, a merger may increase the firms' ability and incentive to bring new innovations to the market and, thereby, the competitive pressure on rivals to innovate in that market. Alternatively, effective competition may be significantly impeded by a merger between two important innovators, for instance between two companies with "pipeline" products related to a specific product market. Similarly, a firm with a relatively small market share may nevertheless be an important competitive force if it has promising pipeline products. . . .

Questions on the U.S. and EU Guidelines on Unilateral Effects

1. Is there much difference between the U.S. and EU guidelines on unilateral effects?

2. Could unilateral effects resulting from capacity constraints or differentiated markets have been addressed under the old EU regulation that only prohibited mergers that created or strengthened a dominant position?

3. Given that HHIs are mainly relevant to Cournot effects, does it make sense to use them (as the U.S. and EU guidelines do) as a threshold to determine whether to consider unilateral effects? To use them to create presumptions about whether those effects exist?

4. Is market definition necessary to finding unilateral effects on a differentiated market? If market is sufficiently differentiated that the merger of firms close to each other in one market segment can have price effects, it is not clear why we should care about market definition, market shares, or HHIs levels. One might think that, if such price effects are possible, a market should be defined narrowly as the product space right around those firms. However, defining a narrow market will not produce accurate results if the merging firms are not the closest rivals to each other because such market definition treats all firms within the product space/market as identical even when they are not. In such cases, direct consideration of differentiated market effects is more accurate. There is also the reality that intuition often makes courts reluctant to define markets narrowly around certain brands even when that definition matches economic reality.

5. The EU guidelines indicate that unilateral effects are more likely if the market share of the merging parties is "large" and unlikely if the share is below 25%. Should the Commission and the courts use the same market share thresholds to determine whether a horizontal merger creates unilateral effects that they used to determine whether a dominant position exists under Article 102? Are there reasons to set a higher threshold under Article 102 because that determines when all of a firm's business conduct was subject to review, whereas here the threshold only applies to merger cases and can be used to prophylactically prevent adverse market structures from arising?

FTC v. Staples, Inc.
970 F.Supp. 1066 (D.D.C. 1997).

■ THOMAS F. HOGAN, DISTRICT JUDGE. [The FTC] . . . seeks a preliminary injunction . . . to enjoin the consummation of any acquisition by defendant Staples, Inc., of defendant Office Depot, Inc. . . . Defendants are both corporations which sell office products—including office supplies, business machines, computers and furniture—through retail stores, commonly described as office supply superstores, as well as through direct mail delivery and contract stationer operations. Staples is the second largest office superstore chain in the United States with approximately 550 retail stores located in 28 states and the District of Columbia, primarily in the Northeast and California. In 1996 Staples' revenues from those stores were approximately $4 billion through all operations. Office Depot, the largest office superstore chain, operates over 500 retail office supply superstores that are located in 38 states and the District of Columbia, primarily in the South and Midwest. Office Depot's 1996 sales were approximately $6.1 billion. OfficeMax, Inc., is the only other office supply superstore firm in the United States.

On September 4, 1996, defendants Staples and Office Depot ... entered into [a merger agreement. The FTC voted to challenge the merger and brought this suit.] ...

II. The Geographic Market

One of the few issue about which the parties to this case do not disagree is that metropolitan areas are the appropriate geographic markets for analyzing the competitive effects of the proposed merger....

III. The Relevant Product Market

... The Commission defines the relevant product market as "the sale of consumable office supplies through office superstores," with "consumable" meaning products that consumers buy recurrently, i.e., items which "get used up" or discarded. For example, under the Commission's definition, "consumable office supplies" would not include capital goods such as computers, fax machines, and other business machines or office furniture, but does include such products as paper, pens, file folders, post-it notes, computer disks, and toner cartridges. The defendants ... counter that the appropriate product market ... is simply the overall sale of office products, of which a combined Staples–Office Depot accounted for 5.5% of total sales in North America in 1996. ... [T]he Court finds that the appropriate relevant product market definition in this case is, as the Commission has argued, the sale of consumable office supplies through office supply superstores.

The general rule when determining a relevant product market is that "[t]he outer boundaries of a product market are determined by the reasonable interchangeability of use [by consumers] or the cross-elasticity of demand between the product itself and substitutes for it." *Brown Shoe,* 370 U.S. at 325; *see also du Pont.* ... This case, of course, is an example of perfect "functional interchangeability." The consumable office products at issue here are identical whether they are sold by Staples or Office Depot or another seller of office supplies. A legal pad sold by Staples or Office Depot is "functionally interchangeable" with a legal pad sold by Wal–Mart. ... A computer disk sold by Staples–Office Depot is "functionally interchangeable" with a computer disk sold by CompUSA. ... However, as the government has argued, functional interchangeability should not end the Court's analysis.

The Supreme Court did not stop after finding a high degree of functional interchangeability between cellophane and other wrapping materials in the *du Pont* case. . . . Following that reasoning in this case, the Commission has argued that a slight but significant increase in Staples–Office Depot's prices will not cause a considerable number of Staples–Office Depot's customers to purchase consumable office supplies from other non-superstore alternatives such as Wal–Mart, Best Buy, Quill, or Viking. On the other hand, the Commission has argued that an increase in price by Staples would result in consumers turning to another office superstore, especially Office Depot, if the consumers had that option. Therefore, the Commission concludes that the sale of consumable office supplies by office supply superstores is the appropriate relevant product market in this case, and products sold by competitors such as Wal–Mart, Best Buy, Viking, Quill, and others should be excluded. . . .

The Court acknowledges that there is, in fact, a broad market encompassing the sale of consumable office supplies by all sellers of such supplies, and that those sellers must, at some level, compete with one another. However, the mere fact that a firm may be termed a competitor in the overall marketplace does not necessarily require that it be included in the relevant product market for antitrust purposes. The Supreme Court has recognized that within a broad market, "well-defined submarkets may exist which, in themselves, constitute product markets for antitrust purposes." *Brown Shoe* . . . There is a possibility, therefore, that the sale of consumable office supplies by office superstores may qualify as a submarket within a larger market of retailers of office supplies in general.

The Court in *Brown Shoe* provided a series of factors or "practical indicia" for determining whether a submarket exists including "industry or public recognition of the submarket as a separate economic entity, the product's peculiar characteristics and uses, unique production facilities, distinct customers, distinct prices, sensitivity to price changes, and specialized vendors." Since the Court described these factors as "practical indicia" rather than requirements, subsequent cases have found that submarkets can exist even if only some of these factors are present. . . .

The Commission discussed several of the *Brown Shoe* "practical indicia" in its case, such as industry recognition, and the special characteristics of superstores which make them different from other sellers of office supplies, including distinct formats, customers, and prices. Primarily, however, the FTC focused on what it termed the "pricing evidence," which the Court finds corresponds with *Brown Shoe's* "sensitivity to price changes" factor. First, the FTC presented evidence comparing Staples' prices in geographic markets where Staples is the only office superstore, to markets where Staples competes with Office Depot or OfficeMax, or both. Based on the FTC's calculations, in markets where Staples faces no office superstore competition at all, something which was termed a one firm market during the hearing, prices are 13% higher than in three firm markets where it competes with both Office Depot and OfficeMax. . . . Similarly, the evidence showed that Office Depot's prices are significantly higher—well over 5% higher,[8] in Depot-only markets than they are in three firm markets. . . .

---

8. . . . The *Merger Guidelines* use 5% as the usual approximation of a "small but significant and nontransitory price increase." For this reason, the Court's analysis will often refer to this 5% number.

This evidence all suggests that office superstore prices are affected primarily by other office superstores and not by non-superstore competitors such as mass merchandisers like Wal–Mart, Kmart, or Target, wholesale clubs such as BJ's, Sam's, and Price Costco, computer or electronic stores such as Computer City and Best Buy, independent retail office supply stores, mail orders firms like Quill and Viking, and contract stationers. Though the FTC did not present the Court with evidence regarding the precise amount of non-superstore competition in each of Staples' and Office Depot's one, two, and three firm markets, it is clear to the Court that these competitors, albeit in different combinations and concentrations, are present in every one of these markets. For example, it is a certainty that the mail order competitors compete in all of the geographic markets at issue in this case. Office products are available through the mail in all 50 states, and have been for approximately 30 years. Despite this mail order competition, however, Staples and Office Depot are still able to charge higher prices in their one firm markets than they do in the two firm markets and the three firm markets without losing a significant number of customers to the mail order firms. The same appears to be true with respect to Wal–Mart. Bill Long, Vice President for Merchandising at Wal–Mart Stores, testifying through declaration, explained that price-checking by Wal–Mart of Staples' prices in areas where both Staples and Wal–Mart exist showed that, on average, Staples' prices were higher where there was a Staples and a Wal–Mart but no other superstore than where there was a Staples, a Wal–Mart, and another superstore.

The evidence with respect to the wholesale club stores is consistent. Mike Atkinson, Vice President, Division Merchandise Manager of BJ's Wholesale Club, testified at the hearing regarding BJ's price checking of Staples and Office Depot in areas where BJ's competes with one or both of those superstores.... BJ's price checking found that, in general, office supply superstore prices were lowest where there was both a Staples and an Office Depot. In addition, Staples' own pricing information shows that warehouse clubs have very little effect on Staples' prices. ... There is also consistent evidence with respect to computer and/or consumer electronics stores such as Best Buy....

There is similar evidence with respect to the defendants' behavior when faced with entry of another competitor. The evidence shows that the defendants change their price zones when faced with entry of another superstore, but do not do so for other retailers....

... [T]he Court finds this evidence a compelling showing that a small but significant increase in Staples' prices will not cause a significant number of consumers to turn to non-superstore alternatives for purchasing their consumable office supplies. Despite the high degree of functional interchangeability between consumable office supplies sold by the office superstores and other retailers of office supplies, the evidence presented by the Commission shows that even where Staples and Office Depot charge higher prices, certain consumers do not go elsewhere for their supplies. This further demonstrates that the sale of office supplies by non-superstore retailers are not responsive to the higher prices charged by Staples and Office Depot in the one firm markets. This indicates a low cross-elasticity of demand between the consumable office supplies sold by the superstores and those sold by other sellers.

Turning back to the other *Brown Shoe* "practical indicia" of submarkets ... the ... evidence shows that office superstores are, in fact, very different in appearance, physical size, format, the number and variety of SKU's offered, and the type of customers targeted and served than other sellers of office supplies. ... Office supply superstores are high volume, discount office supply chain stores averaging in excess of 20,000 square feet, with over 11,000 of those square feet devoted to traditional office supplies, and carrying over 5,000 SKUs of consumable office supplies in addition to computers, office furniture, and other non-consumables. In contrast, stores such as Kmart devote approximately 210 square feet to the sale of approximately 250 SKUs of consumable office supplies. Kinko's devotes approximately 50 square feet to the sale of 150 SKUs. Target sells only 400 SKUs. Both Sam's Club and Computer City each sell approximately 200 SKUs. ... The superstores' customer base overwhelmingly consists of small businesses with fewer than 20 employees and consumers with home offices. In contrast, mail order customers are typically mid-sized companies with more than 20 employees. . . .

Another of the "practical indicia" for determining the presence of a submarket suggested by *Brown Shoe* is "industry or public recognition of the submarket as a separate economic entity." The Commission offered abundant evidence on this factor from Staples' and Office Depot's documents which shows that both Staples and Office Depot focus primarily on competition from other superstores. . . . When assessing key trends and making long range plans, Staples and Office Depot focus on the plans of other superstores. In addition, when determining whether to enter a new metropolitan area, both Staples and Office Depot evaluate the extent of office superstore competition in the market and the number of office superstores the market can support. When selecting sites and markets for new store openings, defendants repeatedly refer to markets without office superstores as "non-competitive," even when the new store is adjacent to or near a warehouse club, consumer electronics store, or a mass merchandiser such as Wal–Mart. . . . In addition, it is clear from the evidence that Staples and Office Depot price check the other office superstores much more frequently and extensively than they price check other retailers such as BJ's or Best Buy, and that Staples and Office Depot are more concerned with keeping their prices in parity with the other office superstores in their geographic areas than in undercutting Best Buy or a warehouse club.

For the reasons set forth in the above analysis, the Court finds that the sale of consumable office supplies through office supply superstores is the appropriate relevant product market for purposes of considering the possible anti-competitive effects of the proposed merger between Staples and Office Depot. The pricing evidence indicates a low cross-elasticity of demand between consumable office products sold by Staples or Office Depot and those same products sold by other sellers of office supplies. This same evidence indicates that non-superstore sellers of office supplies are not able to effectively constrain the superstores prices, because a significant number of superstore customers do not turn to a non-superstore alternative when

faced with higher prices in the one firm markets. In addition, the factors or "practical indicia" of *Brown Shoe* support a finding of a "submarket" under the facts of this case, and "submarkets," as *Brown Shoe* established, may themselves be appropriate product markets for antitrust purposes[10]
. . . .

IV.   Probable Effect on Competition

After accepting the Commission's definition of the relevant product market, the Court next must consider the probable effect of a merger between Staples and Office Depot in the geographic markets previously identified. . . . Currently, the least concentrated market is that of Grand Rapids–Muskegon–Holland, Michigan, with an HHI of 3,597, while the most concentrated is Washington, D.C. with an HHI of 6,944. In contrast, after a merger of Staples and Office Depot, the least concentrated area would be Kalamazoo–Battle Creek Michigan, with an HHI of 5,003, and many areas would have HHIs of 10,000. The average increase in HHI caused by the merger would be 2,715 points. . . . The combined shares of Staples and Office Depot in the office superstore market would be 100% in 15 metropolitan areas. It is in these markets the post-merger HHI would be 10,000. In 27 other metropolitan areas, where the number of office super-store competitors would drop from three to two, the post-merger market shares would range from 45% to 94%, with post-merger HHIs ranging from 5,003 to 9,049. Even the lowest of these HHIs indicates a "highly concen-trated" market.

According to the Department of Justice Merger Guidelines, . . . an HHI over 1800 qualifies as "highly concentrated." Further, . . . unless mitigated by other factors . . . an increase in the HHI in excess of 50 points in a post-merger highly concentrated market may raise significant competitive con-cerns. . . . The *Merger Guidelines,* of course, are not binding on the Court, but, as this Circuit has stated, they do provide "a useful illustration of the application of the HHI," and the Court will use that guidance here. . . . With HHIs of this level, the Commission certainly has shown a "reasonable probability" that the proposed merger would have an anti-competitive effect.

The HHI calculations and market concentration evidence, however, are not the only indications that a merger between Staples and Office Depot may substantially lessen competition. Much of the evidence already dis-cussed with respect to defining the relevant product market also indicates that the merger would likely have an anti-competitive effect. The evidence of the defendants' own current pricing practices, for example, shows that an office superstore chain facing no competition from other superstores has the ability to profitably raise prices for consumable office supplies above competitive levels. . . . Since prices are significantly lower in markets where Staples and Office Depot compete, eliminating this competition with one

---

10.   As other courts have noted, use of the term "submarket" may be confusing. *See Allen–Myland v. IBM Corp.,* 33 F.3d 194, 208 n. 16 (3d Cir.1994) (finding it less confusing to speak in terms of the relevant product market rather than the submarket). *Olin Corp. v. FTC,* 986 F.2d 1295, 1299 (9th Cir.1993) ("'[E]very market that encompasses less than all products is, in a sense, a submarket"). Whatever term is used—market, submarket, relevant product market—the analysis is the same.

another would free the parties to charge higher prices in those markets, especially those in which the combined entity would be the sole office superstore. In addition, allowing the defendants to merge would eliminate significant future competition. Absent the merger, the firms are likely, and in fact have planned, to enter more of each other's markets, leading to a deconcentration of the market and, therefore, increased competition between the superstores.

In addition, direct evidence shows that by eliminating Staples' most significant, and in many markets only, rival, this merger would allow Staples to increase prices or otherwise maintain prices at an anti-competitive level.[14] The merger would eliminate significant head-to-head competition between the two lowest cost and lowest priced firms in the superstore market. Thus, the merger would result in the elimination of a particularly aggressive competitor in a highly concentrated market, a factor which is certainly an important consideration when analyzing possible anti-competitive effects. It is based on all of this evidence as well that the Court finds that the Commission has shown a likelihood of success on the merits and a "reasonable probability" that the proposed transaction will have an anti-competitive effect.

By showing that the proposed transaction between Staples and Office Depot will lead to undue concentration in the market for consumable office supplies sold by office superstores in the geographic markets agreed upon by the parties, the Commission establishes a presumption that the transaction will substantially lessen competition. Once such a presumption has been established, the burden of producing evidence to rebut the presumption shifts to the defendants. *See, e.g., United States v. Marine Bancorporation,* 418 U.S. 602, 631 (1974); *United States v. General Dynamics Corp.,* 415 U.S. 486, 496–504 (1974). To meet this burden, the defendants must show that the market-share statistics give an inaccurate prediction of the proposed acquisition's probable effect on competition. . . .

In their criticism of the Commission's pricing evidence, the defendants accused the FTC of "cherry-picking" its data and pointed to specific examples which contradict the Commission's conclusions. . . . However, the fact that there may be some examples with respect to individual items in individual cities which contradict the FTC's evidence does not overly concern the Court. A few examples of isolated products simply cannot refute the power of the FTC's evidence with respect to the overall trend over time, which is that Staples' and Office Depot's prices are lowest in three firm markets and highest where they do not compete with another office superstore. Neither does the fact that some two superstore areas have lower prices than some three firm markets. . . .

Defendants also argued that the regional price differences set forth in the FTC's pricing evidence do not reflect market power, because the reason for those differentials is not solely the presence or absence of other

---

14.   . . . This does not necessarily mean that prices would rise from the levels they are now. Instead, according to the Commission, prices would simply not decrease as much as they would have on their own absent the merger. . . . Therefore, when the Court discusses "raising" prices it is also with respect to raising prices with respect to where prices would have been absent the merger, not actually an increase from present price levels.

superstore competition. Instead, argued the defendants, these differentials are the result of a host of factors other than superstore competition. As examples of other factors which cause differences in pricing between geographic markets, the defendants offered sales volume, product mix, marketing or advertising costs, and distribution costs. Defendants also argued that there are differences in wages and rent which cause the differences in pricing between certain stores. The Court, however, cannot find that the evidence submitted by the defendants with respect to other reasons for the differences in pricing between one, two, and three firm markets is sufficient to rebut the Commission's evidence. . . .

[The portions of the opinion on entry, efficiencies, and balancing the equities are excerpted later in this chapter.]

Questions on *Staples*

1. Suppose the court had agreed with the defendants that the appropriate product market was all office products. Should the case have come out any differently? Wouldn't the price evidence introduced in this case still show unilateral effects from a merger of close firms on a differentiated market? Would the latter be altered by the fact that after a merger the firms would only have 5.5% of the market for all consumable office supplies? What does this suggest about the wisdom of the Guideline's use of HHI thresholds for unilateral effects?

2. Once the court found that prices were higher in markets with one office-superstore than in markets with two or three, did it matter what the HHIs were on the defined market?

3. Given the advent of computerized pricing data because of scanning bar codes, do you think antitrust will or should move towards proving cases more with direct evidence of price effects than by defining markets and proving high market shares? Which is more directly correlated to the relevant functional concern?

U.S. Agency Enforcement Activity

The 2010 U.S. guidelines increased the HHI thresholds because actual agency practice indicated that enforcement was not likely at the low levels suggested by the old thresholds. Outside of oil markets, the agencies virtually never challenged mergers that resulted in HHIs below 2000.[27] However, in suggesting that enforcement is presumptive for mergers that significantly increase HHI to a level over 2500, the new guidelines may still overstate the likelihood of enforcement if past agency enforcement practices continue. FTC data on mergers that significantly increase HHI indicate that, for post-merger HHIs less than 4000, the likelihood of enforcement is below 40% when the market is left with four significant rivals and below 50% when it is left with three.[28] Further, when the merger

---

27. *See* FTC–DOJ, Merger Challenges Data, Fiscal Years 1999–2003, at Tables 3–10.

28. *See* Coate & Ulrick, *Transparency at the Federal Trade Commission: The Horizontal Merger Review Process 1996–2003*, 73 ANTITRUST L.J. 531, 557 (2006).

leaves the market with only two significant rivals, it takes an HHI of over 3000 to make enforcement more likely than not.[29] Overall, the average HHI in a case that the FTC closed without challenge after a second request was 3055–3271 (with an HHI change of 703–825), whereas the average HHI in a case where the FTC did challenge was 5220–5833 (with a change of 1774–1903).[30] Enforcement odds were best predicted by HHIs when the relevant anticompetitive theory is oligopolistic effects and by the number of significant rivals when the relevant theory is unilateral effects.[31]

2. OLIGOPOLY EFFECTS & COLLECTIVE DOMINANCE

U.S. DOJ/FTC, Horizontal Merger Guidelines

(2010).

2.1 Types of Evidence. [In addition to types of evidence noted in excerpt under unilateral effects, the agencies also consider the following in a coordinated effects case.] . . .

2.1.5 Disruptive Role of a Merging Party

The Agencies consider whether a merger may lessen competition by eliminating a "maverick" firm, i.e., a firm that plays a disruptive role in the market to the benefit of customers. For example, if one of the merging firms has a strong incumbency position and the other merging firm threatens to disrupt market conditions with a new technology or business model, their merger can involve the loss of actual or potential competition. Likewise, one of the merging firms may have the incentive to take the lead in price cutting or other competitive conduct or to resist increases in industry prices. A firm that may discipline prices based on its ability and incentive to expand production rapidly using available capacity also can be a maverick, as can a firm that has often resisted otherwise prevailing industry norms to cooperate on price setting or other terms of competition. . . .

7. Coordinated Effects

A merger may diminish competition by enabling or encouraging post-merger coordinated interaction among firms in the relevant market that harms customers. Coordinated interaction involves conduct by multiple firms that is profitable for each of them only as a result of the accommodating reactions of the others. These reactions can blunt a firm's incentive to offer customers better deals by undercutting the extent to which such a move would win business away from rivals. They also can enhance a firm's incentive to raise prices, by assuaging the fear that such a move would lose customers to rivals.

---

29. *Id.*

30. *See id.* at 543.

31. *See* Coate, *Empirical Analysis of Merger Enforcement Under the 1992 Merger Guidelines*, 27 REV. INDUS. ORG. 279 (2005).

Coordinated interaction includes a range of conduct. Coordinated interaction can involve the explicit negotiation of a common understanding of how firms will compete or refrain from competing. Such conduct typically would itself violate the antitrust laws. Coordinated interaction also can involve a similar common understanding that is not explicitly negotiated but would be enforced by the detection and punishment of deviations that would undermine the coordinated interaction. Coordinated interaction alternatively can involve parallel accommodating conduct not pursuant to a prior understanding. Parallel accommodating conduct includes situations in which each rival's response to competitive moves made by others is individually rational, and not motivated by retaliation or deterrence nor intended to sustain an agreed-upon market outcome, but nevertheless emboldens price increases and weakens competitive incentives to reduce prices or offer customers better terms. Coordinated interaction includes conduct not otherwise condemned by the antitrust laws.

The ability of rival firms to engage in coordinated conduct depends on the strength and predictability of rivals' responses to a price change or other competitive initiative. Under some circumstances, a merger can result in market concentration sufficient to strengthen such responses or enable multiple firms in the market to predict them more confidently, thereby affecting the competitive incentives of multiple firms in the market, not just the merged firm.

7.1 Impact of Merger on Coordinated Interaction

The Agencies examine whether a merger is likely to change the manner in which market participants interact, inducing substantially more coordinated interaction. The Agencies seek to identify how a merger might significantly weaken competitive incentives through an increase in the strength, extent, or likelihood of coordinated conduct. There are, however, numerous forms of coordination, and the risk that a merger will induce adverse coordinated effects may not be susceptible to quantification or detailed proof. Therefore, the Agencies evaluate the risk of coordinated effects using measures of market concentration (see Section 5) in conjunction with an assessment of whether a market is vulnerable to coordinated conduct. See Section 7.2. The analysis in Section 7.2 applies to moderately and highly concentrated markets, as unconcentrated markets are unlikely to be vulnerable to coordinated conduct.

Pursuant to the Clayton Act's incipiency standard, the Agencies may challenge mergers that in their judgment pose a real danger of harm through coordinated effects, even without specific evidence showing precisely how the coordination likely would take place. The Agencies are likely to challenge a merger if the following three conditions are all met: (1) the merger would significantly increase concentration and lead to a moderately or highly concentrated market; (2) that market shows signs of vulnerability to coordinated conduct (see Section 7.2); and (3) the Agencies have a credible basis on which to conclude that the merger may enhance that vulnerability. An acquisition eliminating a maverick firm (see Section 2.1.5) in a market vulnerable to coordinated conduct is likely to cause adverse coordinated effects.

7.2 Evidence a Market is Vulnerable to Coordinated Conduct

The Agencies presume that market conditions are conducive to coordinated interaction if firms representing a substantial share in the relevant market appear to have previously engaged in express collusion affecting the relevant market, unless competitive conditions in the market have since changed significantly. Previous express collusion in another geographic market will have the same weight if the salient characteristics of that other market at the time of the collusion are comparable to those in the relevant market. Failed previous attempts at collusion in the relevant market suggest that successful collusion was difficult pre-merger but not so difficult as to deter attempts, and a merger may tend to make success more likely. Previous collusion or attempted collusion in another product market may also be given substantial weight if the salient characteristics of that other market at the time of the collusion are closely comparable to those in the relevant market.

A market typically is more vulnerable to coordinated conduct if each competitively important firm's significant competitive initiatives can be promptly and confidently observed by that firm's rivals. This is more likely to be the case if the terms offered to customers are relatively transparent. Price transparency can be greater for relatively homogeneous products. Even if terms of dealing are not transparent, transparency regarding the identities of the firms serving particular customers can give rise to coordination, e.g., through customer or territorial allocation. Regular monitoring by suppliers of one another's prices or customers can indicate that the terms offered to customers are relatively transparent.

A market typically is more vulnerable to coordinated conduct if a firm's prospective competitive reward from attracting customers away from its rivals will be significantly diminished by likely responses of those rivals. This is more likely to be the case, the stronger and faster are the responses the firm anticipates from its rivals. The firm is more likely to anticipate strong responses if there are few significant competitors, if products in the relevant market are relatively homogeneous, if customers find it relatively easy to switch between suppliers, or if suppliers use meeting-competition clauses.

A firm is more likely to be deterred from making competitive initiatives by whatever responses occur if sales are small and frequent rather than via occasional large and long-term contracts or if relatively few customers will switch to it before rivals are able to respond. A firm is less likely to be deterred by whatever responses occur if the firm has little stake in the status quo. For example, a firm with a small market share that can quickly and dramatically expand, constrained neither by limits on production nor by customer reluctance to switch providers or to entrust business to a historically small provider, is unlikely to be deterred. Firms are also less likely to be deterred by whatever responses occur if competition in the relevant market is marked by leapfrogging technological innovation, so that responses by competitors leave the gains from successful innovation largely intact.

A market is more apt to be vulnerable to coordinated conduct if the firm initiating a price increase will lose relatively few customers after rivals respond to the increase. Similarly, a market is more apt to be vulnerable to coordinated conduct if a firm that first offers a lower price or improved product to customers will retain relatively few customers thus attracted away from its rivals after those rivals respond.

The Agencies regard coordinated interaction as more likely, the more the participants stand to gain from successful coordination. Coordination generally is more profitable, the lower is the market elasticity of demand.

Coordinated conduct can harm customers even if not all firms in the relevant market engage in the coordination, but significant harm normally is likely only if a substantial part of the market is subject to such conduct. The prospect of harm depends on the collective market power, in the relevant market, of firms whose incentives to compete are substantially weakened by coordinated conduct. This collective market power is greater, the lower is the market elasticity of demand. This collective market power is diminished by the presence of other market participants with small market shares and little stake in the outcome resulting from the coordinated conduct, if these firms can rapidly expand their sales in the relevant market.

Buyer characteristics and the nature of the procurement process can affect coordination. For example, sellers may have the incentive to bid aggressively for a large contract even if they expect strong responses by rivals. This is especially the case for sellers with small market shares, if they can realistically win such large contracts. In some cases, a large buyer may be able to strategically undermine coordinated conduct, at least as it pertains to that buyer's needs, by choosing to put up for bid a few large contracts rather than many smaller ones, and by making its procurement decisions opaque to suppliers . . .

Questions on U.S. Guidelines on Oligopoly Effects

1. Why doesn't the likelihood of oligopolistic coordination turn solely on market concentration? Do you see how the above factors might affect the likelihood of such coordination?

2. Even if oligopolistic coordination were not possible, couldn't Cournot effects still occur if each firm individually chooses an output level rather than a price?

3. Should Cournot effects be considered "coordinated" even though they do not require settling on common terms or punishment of deviation from such common terms? Even if we call Cournot effects "coordinated", does it make sense to require evidence of factors like an ability to settle on common terms and to notice and punish rival deviations from common terms, when assessing alleged effects.

Qualitative v. Empirical Assessments

The U.S. guidelines take the approach of looking at the factors that theoretically affect the level of oligopolistic coordination and then reaching some qualitative assessment of how likely coordination seems given those factors. Such qualitative assessments seem to rest largely on subjective judgments about the weight of the factors. One might wonder why, instead of resting on such subjective judgments, agencies and courts don't simply examine directly the empirical evidence about the extent to which firms in the relevant market are able to price above marginal cost. If such evidence existed, then one might be able to infer the degree of coordination or unilateral effects that must be going on in a more rigorous and precise way.

The new empirical industrial organization (NEIO) models take this approach. See Chapter 1. Under this approach, the degree to which firms behave competitively is neither assumed nor made the subject of qualitative assessment. Instead, it is put into the equation as a "conduct parameter," which is then calculated by measuring the relevant elasticities, price-cost margins, and market concentration. For example, rather than assuming either Cournot effects or coordination, or their absence, one can use the equation $(P–MC)/P = (1+K)HHI/\epsilon$, where K is the conduct parameter, P is price, MC is marginal cost, and ϵ is marketwide demand elasticity. Past data on price, costs, market concentration and demand elasticity can then be examined to determine the remaining variable K. If K turns out to equal -1, then that suggests an absence of even Cournot effects. If K is zero, then that indicates pure Cournot effects because then the Lerner Index equals HHI/ϵ. If K is positive, it indicates oligopolistic coordination over and above mere Cournot effects.

FTC v. H.J. Heinz Co.

246 F.3d 708 (D.C. Cir. 2001).

■ KAREN LECRAFT HENDERSON, CIRCUIT JUDGE.

On February 28, 2000 H.J. Heinz ... and ... Beech–Nut ... entered into a merger agreement. The ... FTC ... sought a preliminary injunction ... The district court denied the preliminary injunction and the FTC appealed to this court. For the reasons set forth below, we reverse the district court and remand for entry of a preliminary injunction against Heinz and Beech–Nut.

I. Background

Four million infants in the United States consume 80 million cases of jarred baby food annually, representing a domestic market of $865 million to $1 billion. The baby food market is dominated by three firms, Gerber ..., Heinz and Beech–Nut. Gerber, the industry leader, enjoys a 65 per cent market share while Heinz and Beech–Nut come in second and third, with a 17.4 per cent and a 15.4 per cent share respectively. The district court found that Gerber enjoys unparalleled brand recognition with a brand loyalty greater than any other product sold in the United States. Gerber's products are found in over 90 per cent of all American supermarkets.

By contrast, Heinz is sold in approximately 40 per cent of all supermarkets. Its sales are nationwide but concentrated in northern New England, the Southeast and Deep South and the Midwest. Despite its second-place domestic market share, Heinz is the largest producer of baby food in the world with $1 billion in sales worldwide. Its domestic baby food products with annual net sales of $103 million are manufactured at its Pittsburgh, Pennsylvania plant, which was updated in 1991 at a cost of $120 million. The plant operates at 40 per cent of its production capacity and produces 12 million cases of baby food annually. Its baby food line includes about 130 SKUs (stock keeping units), that is, product varieties (*e.g.*, strained carrots, apple sauce, etc.). Heinz lacks Gerber's brand recognition; it markets itself as a "value brand" with a shelf price several cents below Gerber's.

Beech–Nut has a market share (15.4%) comparable to that of Heinz (17.4%), with $138.7 million in annual sales of baby food, of which 72 per cent is jarred baby food. Its jarred baby food line consists of 128 SKUs. Beech–Nut manufactures all of its baby food in Canajoharie, New York at a manufacturing plant that was built in 1907 and began manufacturing baby food in 1931. Beech–Nut maintains price parity with Gerber, selling at about one penny less. It markets its product as a premium brand. Consumers generally view its product as comparable in quality to Gerber's. Beech–Nut is carried in approximately 45 per cent of all grocery stores. Although its sales are nationwide, they are concentrated in New York, New Jersey, California and Florida.[3]

At the wholesale level Heinz and Beech–Nut both make lump-sum payments called "fixed trade spending" (also known as "slotting fees" or "pay-to-stay" arrangements) to grocery stores to obtain shelf placement. Gerber, with its strong name recognition and brand loyalty, does not make such pay-to-stay payments. The other type of wholesale trade spending is "variable trade spending," which typically consists of manufacturers' discounts and allowances to supermarkets to create retail price differentials that entice the consumer to purchase their product instead of a competitor's. . . .

[T]he district court . . . court concluded that it was "more probable than not that consummation of the Heinz/Beech–Nut merger will actually increase competition in jarred baby food in the United States." . . .

II. Analysis

. . . [In] Section 7 of the Clayton Act . . . "Congress used the words '*may* be substantially to lessen competition' (emphasis supplied), to indicate that its concern was with probabilities, not certainties." *Brown Shoe*, 370 U.S. at 323 (emphasis original); *see* S.Rep. No. 1775, at 6 (1950), U.S.Code Cong. & Admin. News at 4293, 4298 ("The use of these words ['may be'] means that the bill, if enacted, would not apply to the mere possibility but only to the reasonable probability of the pr[o]scribed effect. . . .") . . . .

1. *Likelihood of Success*

To determine likelihood of success on the merits we measure the probability that, after an administrative hearing on the merits, the Commission will succeed in proving that the effect of the Heinz/Beech–Nut merger "may be substantially to lessen competition, or to tend to create a

---

3. Although Heinz and Beech–Nut introduced evidence showing that in areas that account for 80% of Beech–Nut sales, Heinz has a market share of about 2% and in areas that account for about 72% of Heinz sales, Beech–Nut's share is about 4%, the FTC introduced evidence that Heinz and Beech–Nut are locked in an intense battle at the wholesale level to gain (and maintain) position as the second brand on retail shelves.

monopoly" in violation of section 7 of the Clayton Act. 15 U.S.C. § 18. This court and others have suggested that the standard for likelihood of success on the merits is met if the FTC "has raised questions going to the merits so serious, substantial, difficult and doubtful as to make them fair ground for thorough investigation, study, deliberation and determination by the FTC in the first instance and ultimately by the Court of Appeals." . . .

In *United States v. Baker Hughes Inc.*, 908 F.2d 981, 982–83 (D.C.Cir. 1990), we explained the analytical approach by which the government establishes a section 7 violation. First the government must show that the merger would produce "a firm controlling an undue percentage share of the relevant market, and [would] result[ ] in a significant increase in the concentration of firms in that market." *Philadelphia Nat'l Bank,* 374 U.S. at 363. Such a showing establishes a "presumption" that the merger will substantially lessen competition. *See Baker Hughes,* 908 F.2d at 982. To rebut the presumption, the defendants must produce evidence that "show[s] that the market-share statistics [give] an inaccurate account of the [merger's] probable effects on competition" in the relevant market. *United States v. Citizens & S. Nat'l Bank,* 422 U.S. 86, 120 (1975).[4] "If the defendant successfully rebuts the presumption [of illegality], the burden of producing additional evidence of anticompetitive effect shifts to the government, and merges with the ultimate burden of persuasion, which remains with the government at all times." *Baker Hughes Inc.,* 908 F.2d at 983. . . .

a. Prima Facie Case

Merger law "rests upon the theory that, where rivals are few, firms will be able to coordinate their behavior, either by overt collusion or implicit understanding, in order to restrict output and achieve profits above competitive levels." *FTC v. PPG Indus.,* 798 F.2d 1500, 1503 (D.C.Cir. 1986). Increases in concentration above certain levels are thought to "raise[ ] a likelihood of 'interdependent anticompetitive conduct.' " *Id.* (quoting *General Dynamics,* 415 U.S. at 497); *see FTC v. Elders Grain,* 868 F.2d 901, 905 (7th Cir.1989). Market concentration, or the lack thereof, is often measured by the Herfindahl–Hirschmann Index (HHI).[9]

---

4. To rebut the defendants may rely on "[n]onstatistical evidence which casts doubt on the persuasive quality of the statistics to predict future anticompetitive consequences" such as "ease of entry into the market, the trend of the market either toward or away from concentration, and the continuation of active price competition." *Kaiser Aluminum & Chem. Corp. v. FTC,* 652 F.2d 1324, 1341 (7th Cir.1981). In addition, the defendants may demonstrate unique economic circumstances that undermine the predictive value of the government's statistics. *See United States v. General Dynamics Corp.,* 415 U.S. 486, 506–10 (1974) (fundamental changes in structure of coal market made market concentration statistics inaccurate predictors of anticompetitive effect).

9. "The FTC and the Department of Justice, as well as most economists, consider the measure superior to such cruder measures as the four-or eight-firm concentration ratios which merely sum up the market shares of the largest four or eight firms." *PPG,* 798 F.2d at 1503. The Department of Justice and the FTC rely on the HHI in evaluating proposed horizontal mergers. *See Horizontal Merger Guidelines* §§ 1.5, 1.51. . . . Under the Merger Guidelines a market with a postmerger HHI above 1800 is considered "highly concentrated" and "mergers that increase the HHI in such a market by over . . . 100 points [in such markets] are [presumed] likely to create or enhance market power or facilitate its exercise." Although the Merger Guidelines are not binding on the court, they provide "a useful illustration of the application of the HHI." *PPG,* 798 F.2d at 1503 n. 4.

Sufficiently large HHI figures establish the FTC's prima facie case that a merger is anti-competitive. *See Baker Hughes,* 908 F.2d at 982–83 & n.3; *PPG,* 798 F.2d at 1503. The district court found that the pre-merger HHI "score for the baby food industry is 4775"—indicative of a highly concentrated industry.[10] The merger of Heinz and Beech–Nut will increase the HHI by 510 points. This creates, by a wide margin, a presumption that the merger will lessen competition in the domestic jarred baby food market. *See* Horizontal Merger Guidelines, *supra,* § 1.51 (stating that HHI increase of more than 100 points, where post-merger HHI exceeds 1800, is "presumed . . . likely to create or enhance market power or facilitate its exercise"); *see also Baker Hughes,* 908 F.2d at 982–83 & n.3; *PPG,* 798 F.2d at 1503. Here, the FTC's market concentration statistics[12] are bolstered by the indisputable fact that the merger will eliminate competition between the two merging parties at the wholesale level, where they are currently the only competitors for what the district court described as the "second position on the supermarket shelves." Heinz's own documents recognize the wholesale competition and anticipate that the merger will end it. . . .

Finally, the anticompetitive effect of the merger is further enhanced by high barriers to market entry. The district court found that there had been no significant entries in the baby food market in decades and that new entry was "difficult and improbable." This finding largely eliminates the possibility that the reduced competition caused by the merger will be ameliorated by new competition from outsiders and further strengthens the FTC's case.

As far as we can determine, no court has ever approved a merger to duopoly under similar circumstances.

b. Rebuttal Arguments

In response to the FTC's prima facie showing, the appellees make three rebuttal arguments, which the district court accepted . . . For the reasons discussed below, these arguments fail and thus were not a proper basis for denying the FTC injunctive relief.

1. Extent of Pre–Merger Competition. The appellees first contend . . . that Heinz and Beech–Nut do not really compete against each other at the retail level. Consumers do not regard the products of the two companies as substitutes, the appellees claim, and generally only one of the two brands is available on any given store's shelves. Hence, they argue, there is little competitive loss from the merger.

This argument has a number of flaws which render clearly erroneous the court's finding that Heinz and Beech–Nut have not engaged in significant pre-merger competition. First, in accepting the appellees' argument

---

10.   . . . The [district] court defined the product market as jarred baby food and the geographic market as the United States. The parties do not challenge the court's definition.

12. The Supreme Court has cautioned that statistics reflecting market share and concentration, while of great significance, are not conclusive indicators of anticompetitive effects. In *General Dynamics* the Supreme Court held that the market share statistics the government used to seek divestiture of the merged firm were insufficient because, in failing to take into account the acquired firm's long-term contractual commitments (coal contracts), the statistics overestimated the acquired firm's ability to compete in the relevant market in the future. *General Dynamics,* 415 U.S. at 500–504.

that Heinz and Beech–Nut do not compete, the district court failed to address the record evidence that the two do in fact price against each other, and that, where both are present in the same areas,[14] they depress each other's prices as well as those of Gerber even though they are virtually never all found in the same store. This evidence undermines the district court's factual finding.

Second, the district court's finding is inconsistent with its conclusion that there is a single, national market for jarred baby food in the United States. The Supreme Court has explained that "[t]he outer boundaries of a product market are determined by the reasonable interchangeability of use [by consumers] or the cross-elasticity of demand between the product itself and substitutes for it." *Brown Shoe*, 370 U.S. at 325; *see also du Pont*. The definition of product market thus "focuses solely on demand substitution factors," *i.e.*, that consumers regard the products as substitutes. Horizontal Merger Guidelines, *supra*, § 1.0. By defining the relevant product market generically as jarred baby food, the district court concluded that in areas where Heinz's and Beech–Nut's products are both sold, consumers will switch between them in response to a "small but significant and nontransitory increase in price (SSNIP)." Horizontal Merger Guidelines, *supra*, § 1.11. . . .

Third, and perhaps most important, the court's conclusion concerning pre-merger competition does not take into account the indisputable fact that the merger will eliminate competition at the wholesale level between the only two competitors for the "second shelf" position. Competition between Heinz and Beech–Nut to gain accounts at the wholesale level is fierce with each contest concluding in a winner-take-all result. The district court regarded this loss of competition as irrelevant because the FTC did not establish to its satisfaction that wholesale competition ultimately benefitted consumers through lower retail prices. The district court concluded that fixed trade spending did not affect consumer prices and that "the FTC's assertion that the proposed merger will affect variable trade spending levels and consumer prices is . . . at best, inconclusive." . . .

In rejecting the FTC's argument regarding the loss of wholesale competition, the court committed two legal errors. First, as the appellees conceded at oral argument, no court has ever held that a reduction in competition for wholesale purchasers is not relevant unless the plaintiff can prove impact at the consumer level. Second, it is, in any event, not the FTC's burden to prove such an impact with "certainty." To the contrary, the antitrust laws assume that a retailer faced with an increase in the cost of one of its inventory items "will try so far as competition allows to pass that cost on to its customers in the form of a higher price for its product."

2. *Post–Merger Efficiencies*. [Excerpted Below.]

3. *Innovation*. [Excerpted Below.]

4. *Structural Barriers to Collusion*. . . . Jonathan B. Baker, a former Director of the Bureau of Economics at the FTC, . . . testified that in order to coordinate successfully, firms must solve "cartel problems" such as

---

14. There are at least ten metropolitan areas in which Heinz and Beech–Nut both have more than a 10 per cent market share and their combined share exceeds 35 per cent.

reaching a consensus on price and market share and deterring each other from deviating from that consensus by either lowering price or increasing production. He opined that after the merger the merged entity would want to expand its market share at Gerber's expense, thereby decreasing the likelihood of consensus on price and market share. In his report, Baker elaborated on his theory, explaining that the efficiencies created by the merger will give the merged firm the ability and incentive to take on Gerber in price and product improvements. He also predicted that policing and monitoring of any agreement would be more difficult than it is now, due in part to a time lag in the ability of one firm to detect price cuts by another. But the district court made no finding that any of these "cartel problems" are so much greater in the baby food industry than in other industries that they rebut the normal presumption. In fact, Baker's testimony about "time lag" is refuted by the record which reflects that supermarket prices are available from industry-wide scanner data within 4–8 weeks. His testimony is further undermined by the record evidence of past price leadership in the baby food industry.

The combination of a concentrated market and barriers to entry is a recipe for price coordination. ... The creation of a durable duopoly affords both the opportunity and incentive for both firms to coordinate to increase prices. ... Because the district court failed to specify any "structural market barriers to collusion" that are unique to the baby food industry, its conclusion that the ordinary presumption of collusion in a merger to duopoly was rebutted is clearly erroneous....

Questions on *FTC v. Heinz*

1. Should the mere fact that this was a merger that would create a duopoly suffice to infer likely anticompetitive effects?

2. Absent oligopolistic coordination, do you think baby food makers are more likely to compete by choosing output levels, thus creating Cournot effects, or by choosing price levels and selling whatever output they can at that price, thus suggesting Bertrand competition that would drive prices down to marginal cost?

3. Did the evidence suggest it was likely that oligopolistic coordination would occur between Gerber and a merged Heinz–Beech–Nut?

a. Did the court apply the factors from merger guidelines § 7?

i. Was it easy here to settle on a common price and to notice deviations from it? Had the firms settled on a common price before the merger? Were they more likely to do so post-merger?

ii. What is wrong with the argument that a merged Heinz–Beech–Nut would likely be unwilling to coordinate because it would have half the market share of Gerber and have efficiencies it would want to exploit by cutting prices?

b. Did the court simply hold that the defendant had the burden of proof on these factors? Or did it alter the standard of proof by holding that the defendant had to show that factors undermining coordination were "so much greater in the baby food industry than in other industries that they rebut the normal presumption" that coordination is likely? Is it generally fair to presume oligopolistic coordination will occur on a concentrated market in a typical industry?

4. The lower court had found that: "It is undisputed that Heinz and Beech–Nut are virtually never found in the same supermarket; that Beech–Nut and Heinz do not price against the other or even consistently monitor one another's prices; and that the cross-elasticity of demand between Heinz and Beech–Nut is not statistically significant. Heinz and Beech–Nut asserted, and proved with econometric evidence, that they do not constrain one another's retail or consumer prices.... Defendant's expert, Dr. Jonathan Baker, was director of the FTC's Bureau of Economics from 1995 until 1998. Dr. Baker studied the markets where all three companies had a significant presence, and markets where only Heinz or Beech–Nut had a significant presence with Gerber, seeking to isolate the effects of competition on price.... Dr. Baker ... found no discernible differences in the price of baby food regardless of whether there were two or three competitors." *FTC v. H.J. Heinz, Co.,* 116 F.Supp.2d 190, 196 (D.D.C.2000).

a. The appellate court pointed to evidence that prices were depressed in the 10 metropolitan areas where the firms are both a significant presence even though not in the same store. Should such evidence be dismissed as involving only a few cities or if the evidence is anecdotal rather than econometric?

b. The appellate court also argued that this theory was inconsistent with the lower court's finding that the market was national and for all jarred baby food. Should this pricing evidence instead have lead the district court to conclude that the relevant markets were high-end baby food (where Gerber and Beech–Nut competed) and low-end baby food (where only Heinz competed) and that thus the merger did not decrease market competition at all? Is it possible that Heinz and Beech–Nut competed with Gerber but not with each other, so that defining separate markets would be inappropriate even though direct competition between Heinz and Beech–Nut is low?

c. Does the fact that Heinz and Beech–Nut do not price against each other and have a low cross-elasticity disprove anticompetitive effects?

i. Doesn't it disprove unilateral effects more effectively than coordinated effects? Couldn't the two have a low cross-elasticity yet also be more likely to coordinate with Gerber if they were one firm?

ii. Does the absence of cross-elasticity in retail prices necessarily mean the companies are not close competitors at wholesale? Is the relevant market here retail or wholesale or both?

d. If consumer prices are no higher in local markets where all three firms are significant players as where only two firms are, why would the merger have anticompetitive effects?

i. Does this evidence show that the move from three to two firms does not increase the likelihood of oligopolistic coordination?

ii. Given that such evidence is consistent with the possibility that oligopolistic coordination is already occurring both in the two-firm and three-firm markets, should courts ban the merger on the theory that coordination is more likely to break down in the future with three firms and that a merger would entrench such coordination?

iii. Isn't this evidence also equally consistent with the possibility that, in local markets where only two firms are significant, pricing is affected by the possibility of entry by the third firm?

e. The last possibility is related to the appellate court's point that Heinz and Beech–Nut compete at wholesale for the second shelf position even though they are rarely both in the same grocery stores at retail. The appellate court concluded that (1) this decrease in wholesale competition was sufficiently likely to increase wholesale prices (by reducing trade spending) to create anticompetitive effects and (2) it did not matter that there was no evidence that fixed or variable trade spending actually affected consumer prices, and that "Dr. Baker's econometric analysis revealed that trade spending levels had no effect on price, even in markets where all three firms are present." 116 F.Supp.2d at 197. Is the court right that mergers that increase wholesale prices should be deemed anticompetitive even if they do not raise retail prices charged to consumers?

Early EU Caselaw on Oligopolistic Coordination and Collective Dominance

The 2004 Regulation now makes the EMCR applicable to mergers that "significantly impede effective competition" even if the merger does not create a dominant position, and thus make it clearly applicable to mergers that create oligopoly effects. Before then, this was less clear because the regulation only banned mergers that created or strengthened a dominant position. Moreover, unlike Article 102 TFEU, the EMCR did not refer to a dominant position on the part of one *or more* undertakings. The Commission solved this problem by concluding that oligopolists held a collective dominant position in the 1992 case of *Nestlé/Perrier*.[32] In 1998, the ECJ concluded in *Kali & Salz* that the EMCR did extend to mergers that created a collective dominant position, stating that:

> A concentration which creates or strengthens a dominant position on the part of the parties concerned with an entity not involved in the concentration is liable to prove incompatible with the system of undistorted competition which the Treaty seeks to secure. Consequently, if it were accepted that only concentrations creating or strengthening a dominant position on the part of the parties to the concentration were covered by the Regulation, its purpose as indicated in particular by the abovementioned recitals would be partially frustrated. The Regulation would thus be deprived of a not insignificant aspect of its effectiveness, without that being necessary from the perspective of the general structure of the Community system of control of concentrations.[27]

---

32. Commission Decision 92/553 of 22 July 1992, Nestlé/Perrier, O.J. 1992 L 356.

27. Cases C–68/94 and C–30/95, France v. Commission, Société Commerciale des Potasses et de l'Azote (SCPA) v. Commission (Kali & Salz), [1998] E.C.R. I–1375, at ¶ 171.

In another part of the judgment, the ECJ also attempted to clarify when collective dominance existed, stating:

> In the case of an alleged collective dominant position, the Commission is ... obliged to assess, using a prospective analysis of the reference market, whether the concentration which has been referred to it leads to a situation in which effective competition in the relevant market is significantly impeded by the undertakings involved in the concentration and one or more other undertakings which together, in particular because of correlative factors which exist between them, are able to adopt a common policy on the market and act to a considerable extent independently of their competitors, their customers, and also of consumers.[28]

The central issue is thus whether "correlative factors" between the firms allows them to adopt a "common policy." The ECJ concluded that, in the case at hand, the "structural links" resulting from contractual and other arrangements between the parties were not sufficient to find collective dominance. It did not say, however, whether contractual or other structural links were a prerequisite to find collective dominance, and thus did not establish whether factors suggesting the merger was likely to enhance oligopolistic coordination could suffice. In *Gencor*, the General Court concluded that they could, and in the *Airtours* case the General Court clarified the proof necessary to establish such a likelihood.

Case T–102/96, Gencor Limited v. Commission
[1999] E.C.R. II–753.

In its judgment in the *Flat Glass* case, the Court referred to links of a structural nature only by way of example and did not lay down that such links must exist in order for a finding of collective dominance to be made.

It merely stated that there is nothing, in principle, to prevent two or more independent economic entities from being united by economic links in a specific market and, by virtue of that fact, from together holding a dominant position vis-à-vis the other operators on the same market. It added (in the same paragraph) that that could be the case, for example, where two or more independent undertakings jointly had, through agreements or licences, a technological lead affording them the power to behave to an appreciable extent independently of their competitors, their customers and, ultimately, of consumers.

Nor can it be deduced from the same judgment that the Court has restricted the notion of economic links to the notion of structural links referred to by the applicant.

Furthermore, there is no reason whatsoever in legal or economic terms to exclude from the notion of economic links the relationship of interdependence existing between the parties to a tight oligopoly within which, in a market with the appropriate characteristics, in particular in terms of market concentration, transparency and product homogeneity, those par-

---

28. *Id.* at ¶ 221.

ties are in a position to anticipate one another's behaviour and are therefore strongly encouraged to align their conduct in the market, in particular in such a way as to maximise their joint profits by restricting production with a view to increasing prices. In such a context, each trader is aware that highly competitive action on its part designed to increase its market share (for example a price cut) would provoke identical action by the others, so that it would derive no benefit from its initiative. All the traders would thus be affected by the reduction in price levels.

That conclusion is all the more pertinent with regard to the control of concentrations, whose objective is to prevent anti-competitive market structures from arising or being strengthened. Those structures may result from the existence of economic links in the strict sense argued by the applicant or from market structures of an oligopolistic kind where each undertaking may become aware of common interests and, in particular, cause prices to increase without having to enter into an agreement or resort to a concerted practice.

In the instant case, therefore, the applicant's ground of challenge alleging that the Commission failed to establish the existence of structural links is misplaced.

Case T–342/99, Airtours v. Commission

[2002] E.C.R. II–2585.

[This case concerned a proposed merger between Airtours and First Choice. The Commission concluded that the merger would create a collective dominant position because the merged firm and two other firms (Thomson and Thomas Cook) would be able to engage in oligopolistic coordination in the market for short-haul package holidays in the United Kingdom.]

Where, for the purposes of applying Regulation No 4064/89, the Commission examines a possible collective dominant position, it must ascertain whether the concentration would have the direct and immediate effect of creating or strengthening a position of that kind, which is such as significantly and lastingly to impede competition in the relevant market. If there is no substantial alteration to competition as it stands, the merger must be approved. . . .

A collective dominant position . . . may . . . arise as the result of a concentration where, in view of the actual characteristics of the relevant market and of the alteration in its structure that the transaction would entail, the latter would make each member of the dominant oligopoly, as it becomes aware of common interests, consider it possible, economically rational, and hence preferable, to adopt on a lasting basis a common policy on the market with the aim of selling at above competitive prices, without having to enter into an agreement or resort to a concerted practice within the meaning of Article 101 (see, to that effect, *Gencor*) and without any actual or potential competitors, let alone customers or consumers, being able to react effectively.

As the applicant has argued and as the Commission has accepted in its pleadings, three conditions are necessary for a finding of collective dominance as defined:

—first, each member of the dominant oligopoly must have the ability to know how the other members are behaving in order to monitor whether or not they are adopting the common policy. As the Commission specifically acknowledges, it is not enough for each member of the dominant oligopoly to be aware that interdependent market conduct is profitable for all of them but each member must also have a means of knowing whether the other operators are adopting the same strategy and whether they are maintaining it. There must, therefore, be sufficient market transparency for all members of the dominant oligopoly to be aware, sufficiently precisely and quickly, of the way in which the other members' market conduct is evolving;

—second, the situation of tacit coordination must be sustainable over time, that is to say, there must be an incentive not to depart from the common policy on the market. As the Commission observes, it is only if all the members of the dominant oligopoly maintain the parallel conduct that all can benefit. The notion of retaliation in respect of conduct deviating from the common policy is thus inherent in this condition. In this instance, the parties concur that, for a situation of collective dominance to be viable, there must be adequate deterrents to ensure that there is a long-term incentive in not departing from the common policy, which means that each member of the dominant oligopoly must be aware that highly competitive action on its part designed to increase its market share would provoke identical action by the others, so that it would derive no benefit from its initiative (see, to that effect, *Gencor*);

—third, to prove the existence of a collective dominant position to the requisite legal standard, the Commission must also establish that the foreseeable reaction of current and future competitors, as well as of consumers, would not jeopardise the results expected from the common policy.

. . . [I]t is also apparent from the judgment in *Kali and Salz* that, where the Commission takes the view that a merger should be prohibited because it will create a situation of collective dominance, it is incumbent upon it to produce convincing evidence thereof. . . .

The [Commission] Decision identifies two types of players on the relevant market, the large tour operators on the one hand, and the secondary or small tour operators on the other:

—the major tour operators are characterised by their relatively large size—each of them having a market share exceeding 10% (according to the Commission's data, Thomson accounts for 27% of sales, Airtours for 21%, Thomas Cook for 20% and First Choice for 11%, that is, overall for 79% of sales. . . .). A further characteristic is that they are all integrated both upstream (operation of charter airlines) and downstream (travel agencies);

—the secondary operators are smaller, none of them having a market share in excess of 5%, and in general they do not own either their own charter airlines or their own travel agencies. Apart from Cosmos (which, since it is linked to Monarch, one of the major charter airlines in the United Kingdom, is exceptional among secondary operators where there is no vertical integration), Manos and Kosmar, which are the fifth, sixth and seventh tour operators accounting respectively for 2.9%, 1.7% and 1.7% of sales, there are several hundred competing small tour operators, none of them accounting for more than 1% of sales. . . .

1. Preliminary observations . . . . The . . . Commission concluded that the proposed merger would create, rather than strengthen, a dominant position on the market. The Commission . . . does not contend that there was a situation of oligopolistic dominance at the time of the notification. . . . Thus, it does not deny that prior to the proposed merger the major tour operators did not find it possible or profitable to restrict capacity in order to increase prices and revenues.

It follows that in this instance the starting point for the Court's examination must be a situation in which—in the Commission's own view—the four major tour operators are not able to adopt a common policy on the market and hence do not face their competitors, their commercial associates and consumers as a single entity, and in which they thus do not enjoy the powers inherent in a collective dominant position.

In those circumstances, it was for the Commission to prove that . . . approval of the [merger] would have resulted in the creation of a collective dominant position restrictive of competition, inasmuch as Airtours/First Choice, Thomson and Thomas Cook would have had the ability, which they did not previously have, to adopt a common policy on the market by setting capacity lower than would normally be the case in a competitive market already distinguished by a degree of caution in matters of capacity.

2. The finding that were the merger to proceed, the three remaining large tour operators would have an incentive to cease competing with each other . . . .

The assessment of competition between the leading tour operators. . . . [O]ne of the questions which the Commission is required to address where there is alleged to be collective dominance is whether the concentration referred to it would result in effective competition in the relevant market being significantly impeded. If there is no significant change in the level of competition obtaining previously, the merger should be approved because it does not restrict competition. It follows that the level of competition obtaining in the relevant market at the time when the transaction is notified is a decisive factor in establishing whether a collective dominant position has been created for the purposes of Regulation No 4064/89. . . .

[T]he Commission explains that the large tour operators adopt a cautious approach to capacity planning and take particular note of the estimates of their main competitors . . . [S]ince it did not deny that the market was competitive, the Commission was not entitled to treat the cautious capacity planning characteristic of the market in normal circumstances as evidence substantiating its proposition that there was already a tendency to collective dominance in the industry. . . .

The assessment of the volatility of historic market shares. . . . [F]or the purpose of determining whether there is a collective dominant position, the stability of historic market shares is a factor conducive to the development of tacit collusion, inasmuch as it facilitates division of the market instead of fierce competition, each operator referring to its historic market share in order to fix its production in proportion thereto.

In the present case, the Commission's finding that the market shares of Thomson, Airtours, Thomas Cook and First Choice remained stable over the last five years is predicated on the assumption that growth by acquisition is to be ignored. . . . However, there is no justification in the present case for excluding growth by acquisition when assessing the volatility of market shares, inasmuch as in the relevant market the size of the undertakings and their degree of vertical integration are significant factors in competition. In such circumstances, the fact that the large operators have made numerous acquisitions in the past . . . may be taken to be indicative of strong competition between those operators, which make further acquisitions to avoid being outdistanced by their main competitors in key areas in order to take full advantage of economies of scale. . . . [I]f growth by acquisition is included, there is considerable variation in the major tour operators' shares of the foreign package holiday market.

. . . [I]t should be added that the applicant has claimed, and the Commission has not disputed, that the performances of the main tour operators may vary in a given season (with winners and losers) and may also vary from one season to another. That fact must be regarded as evidence that the market is competitive and consequently militates against any finding of collective dominance. . . .

Findings on low demand growth . . . [T]he Commission's interpretation of the data available to it concerning growth demand was inaccurate in its disregard for the fact that the market had been marked by a clear tendency to considerable growth over the last decade in general, despite the volatile nature of demand from one year to another, and that the pace of demand growth has increased during recent years in particular. . . . In that context of growth, . . . the Commission was not entitled to conclude that market development was characterised by low growth, which was, in this instance, a factor conducive to the creation of a collective dominant position by the three remaining large tour operators. . . .

Findings on demand volatility . . . [E]conomic theory regards volatility of demand as something which renders the creation of a collective dominant position more difficult. Conversely, stable demand, thus displaying low volatility, is a relevant factor indicative of the existence of a collective dominant position, in so far as it makes deviations from the common policy (that is, cheating) more easily detectable, by enabling them to be distinguished from capacity adjustments intended to respond to expansion or contraction in a volatile market.

. . . [T]here is a considerable degree of volatility in the market. . . . [T]he Commission is not entitled to rely on the fact that tour operators, to protect themselves against sudden downward volatility in demand, plan capacity cautiously, preferring to increase it later if demand proves to be particularly strong, for the purpose of denying the relevance in this instance of a factor which is significant as evidence of oligopolistic dominance, such as the degree of market stability and predictability. Although it is certainly the case that the caution inherent in the way the market normally operates means that account must be taken of the need to make the best possible estimates of the way in which demand will develop, the planning process remains difficult, because each operator must anticipate (some 18 months in advance because of the market's distinctive features) how demand will evolve—demand being distinguished by its considerable volatility and thus entailing a degree of speculation. Furthermore, the Commission did not regard either the operators' caution or demand volatility to be restrictive of competition in the pre-merger market. Caution cannot therefore be interpreted, as such, as evidence of a collective dominant position rather than as a characteristic of a competitive market of the kind that existed at the time of the notification. . . .

Finally, the Court must reject the Commission's argument that there is no difficulty in differentiating between a decline in demand and an increase in capacity by another operator because the latter can be observed directly. The Court rejects that argument on the ground that an integrated tour operator will, for the reasons set out below in the examination of market transparency, find it difficult to interpret with any accuracy capacity decisions taken by the other tour operators.

It follows from the foregoing that the Commission has failed to establish that economic theory is inapplicable in the present case, and that it was wrong in concluding that volatility of demand was conducive to the creation of a dominant oligopoly by the three remaining major tour operators.

The assessment of the degree of market transparency. . . . [The Commission contends] that in this instance the tacit coordination instancing the collective dominant position is focused not on prices but on the capacity put onto the market and . . . that, . . . the crucial capacity decisions for the coming season are taken during the planning period. . . . The approach thus taken by the Commission is borne out by its assertion . . . in response to the applicant's argument that, since each of the large integrated tour operators has to deal with several thousand different prices because of the various programmes offered, tacit agreement on all those prices would be impossible: the Commission asserts that it does not consider an agreement on prices to be necessary in this instance in order to reach a collective dominant position. It adds: "during the selling season, there is little incentive for any of the integrated operators to cut prices in order to gain market share, which is determined by the amount of capacity offered. . . ."

It follows that in this instance it is appropriate to ascertain, first, whether each of the large tour operators will be able, when making its crucial capacity decisions during the planning period, to find out with any degree of certainty what those of its main competitors are. Only if there is sufficient transparency will an operator be able to estimate the total capacity decided upon by the other members of the alleged oligopoly and then be in a position to be sure that by planning its capacity in a given way it is adopting the same policy as them and hence will have an incentive to do so. The degree of transparency is also important for the purposes of permitting each member of the oligopoly subsequently to detect alterations made by the others as regards capacity, to distinguish deviations from the common policy from mere adjustments consequent upon volatility of demand and, finally, to ascertain whether it is necessary to react to any such deviations by punishing them.

... [A]n examination of the data shows that the planning cycle does not simply run from year to year. By way of example, for the summer season 1999 ("Year N"), running from May 1999 to October 1999, capacity planning starts some 18 months before, in October or November 1997 ("Year N–2").... Within that time frame, overall capacity planning operates by reference to general and specific considerations which are refined over time. General considerations ("top-down considerations") take account of the key factors influencing holiday demand, such as economic activity, exchange rates and consumer confidence. Specific considerations ("bottom-up considerations") are based on a detailed analysis of existing product offerings, starting with, for example, consideration of gross and net margins by flight and accommodation unit for each resort. In that connection, each flight (by departure and destination airport and flight slot) is analysed, as are the available destinations and products and consumer demand for particular types of holiday, so that a comprehensive range of shorthaul foreign package holidays can be prepared. That range is also supplemented by new product offerings developed by the applicant.

.... [T]he crux of the planning process is not simply the renewal of capacity budgeted or sold in the past but is the attempt to predict how demand will develop on both a macroeconomic and microeconomic level.... In addition ..., it is necessary to mention the practical difficulties ... which make it very difficult to find out what capacity is projected by each of the other large tour operators during the planning period, inasmuch as their decisions on total capacity for a given season consolidate a whole range of individual decisions, taken on a resort-by-resort and flight-by-flight basis and varying from one season to the next.... [C]apacity decisions do not involve merely increasing or reducing overall capacity, without taking account of the differences between the various categories of package holidays, which are differentiated by destination, departure date, departure airport, aircraft model, type and quality of accommodation, length of stay and, finally, price. To be able to develop their package holidays, tour operators must take into account a series of variables, such as the availability of accommodation at the various destinations and the availability of airline seats on various dates and at different times of the year. As the applicant has argued, capacity decisions are necessarily taken on a "micro level."

The Commission's global approach ..., which regards the total number of package holidays offered by each operator as what is important, thus encounters some significant difficulties on a practical level, since, in order to ascertain total capacity—to the extent that it stems from a miscellaneous set of individual decisions—it is necessary to be able to identify those decisions.

It follows that, on the face of it, the complexity of the capacity planning procedure, the development of the product and its marketing is a major obstacle to any attempt at tacit coordination. In a market in which demand is on the whole increasing, but is volatile from one year to the next, an integrated tour operator will have difficulty in interpreting accurately capacity decisions taken by the other operators concerning holidays to be taken a year and a half later.

However, despite the fact that each tour operator takes capacity decisions on the basis of a miscellaneous set of factors, it is nevertheless necessary to consider whether, in practice, at the time when total capacity is set, each member of the oligopoly can know "the overall level of capacity (number of holidays) offered by the individual integrated tour operators."

The Commission alleges . . . that "each of the four integrated operators is . . . well able to monitor the total amount of holidays offered by each of the others [during the planning period]. . . ." However, the Commission fails to prove those allegations. . . .

It follows from all of the foregoing that the Commission . . . wrongly concluded that the degree of market transparency was a characteristic which made the market conducive to collective dominance . . .

3. The inadequate nature of the deterrents which the Commission alleges will secure unity within the alleged dominant oligopoly

. . . It is . . . important to ascertain whether the individual interests of each major tour operator (maximising profits while competing with the whole range of operators) outweigh the common interests of the members of the alleged dominant oligopoly (restricting capacity in order to increase prices and make supra-competitive profits). That would be the case if the absence of deterrents induced an operator to depart from the common policy, taking advantage of the absence of competition essential to that policy, so as to take competitive initiatives and derive benefit from the advantages inherent therein (see, to that effect, *Gencor* . . .).

The fact that there is scope for retaliation goes some way to ensuring that the members of the oligopoly do not in the long run break ranks by deterring each of them from departing from the common course of conduct.

In that context, the Commission must not necessarily prove that there is a specific "retaliation mechanism involving a degree of severity, but it must none the less establish that deterrents exist, which are such that it is not worth the while of any member of the dominant oligopoly to depart from the common course of conduct to the detriment of the other oligopolists. . . ."

In the first place, the Court finds that the Commission was wrong in concluding that the mere threat of reverting to a situation of oversupply acts as a deterrent. The Commission refers to the 1995 crisis to illustrate the effects of oversupply on the market. However, it should be made clear that the events of 1995 took place in a context different from that of the present case: then, all operators—regardless of whether they were large or small—boosted their capacity during the 1994 planning period in order to meet the increase in overall demand, which sectoral indicators and the preceding two years' growth suggested would occur. However, in this case the Commission anticipates that there will be a situation in which the three major tour operators, acting appreciably more cautiously than normal, will have reduced capacity below forecast demand and in which cheating has occurred. It is against that background, which differs markedly from the 1995 capacity surplus, that the Court must examine whether a possible return to oversupply acts as a deterrent. Oversupply could occur only one season later and only if the other members of the oligopoly decided to increase capacity above estimates of demand growth, that is very significantly in comparison with the level of under-supply that would exist in the context of tacit coordination envisaged by the Commission.

In the second place, the scope for increasing capacity in the selling season cannot act as a deterrent for the following reasons.

First, as the Decision itself emphasises, the market is distinguished by an innate tendency to caution as regards capacity decisions, given that matching capacity to demand is critical to profitability, since package holidays are perishable goods.

Second, in this market a decision to depart from the common policy by increasing capacity in the selling season would be taken at a stage when it would be difficult to detect it in sufficient time. Furthermore, even if the other members of the oligopoly managed to expose the deviating conduct, any reaction on their part involving a retaliatory capacity increase could not be sufficiently rapid or effective, inasmuch as it could be implemented only to a very limited extent in the same season ... and only subject to restrictions, which would become increasingly acute as the selling season progressed (in the best-case scenario, capacity for the forthcoming summer season could be increased by only 10% up until February).

Lastly, it may be assumed that, since they know that the perpetrators of any retaliatory measures are likely to find it difficult to sell late-added package holidays because of the low quality of such products (inconvenient flight times, poor-quality accommodation), the other members of the dominant oligopoly would be cautious about increasing capacity by way of retaliation. ...

In the third place, as regards the possibility of increasing capacity in the following season and the fact that capacity can be added between seasons ..., it is appropriate to observe that increasing capacity in that way is unlikely to be effective as a retaliatory measure, given the unpredictable way in which demand evolves from one year to the next and the time needed to implement such a measure ...

4.   Underestimation of the likely reaction of smaller tour operators, potential competitors and consumers as a counterbalance capable of destabilising the alleged dominant oligopoly.... [T]o prove conclusively the existence of a collective dominant position in this instance, the Commission should also have established that the foreseeable reactions of current and future competitors and consumers would not jeopardise the results expected from the large tour operators' common policy. In this case, that implies that where the large tour operators, for anti-competitive purposes, reduce available capacity to a level below what is required to adjust to anticipated trends in demand, such a reduction must not be offset by their current competitors, smaller operators, any potential competitors, tour operators with a presence in other countries or on the long-haul market, or their customers (United Kingdom consumers) reacting in such a way as to render the dominant oligopoly unviable....

The possible response of current competitors: smaller tour operators.... [T]he Commission states that the ability of the "fringe of smaller suppliers to compete effectively with the four large tour operators is further constrained by their lack of vertical integration and their small size, which means inter alia that they cannot make the same economies of scale and scope as the larger operators...."

However, it must be made clear that the issue here is not whether a small tour operator can reach the size necessary for it to compete effectively with the integrated tour operators by challenging them for their places as market leaders. Rather, it is a question of whether, in the anti-competitive situation anticipated by the Commission, the hundreds of small operators already present on the market, taken as a whole, can respond effectively to a reduction in capacity put on to the market by the large tour operators to a level below estimated demand by increasing their capacity to take advantage of the opportunities inherent in a situation of overall under-supply and whether they can thereby counteract the creation of a collective dominant position....

Furthermore, as the applicant has pointed out, despite the fact that over the last decade a number of small tour operators have been taken over by the larger ones, small operators still exist in large numbers (several hundred), with continuous regeneration by new players entering the market, and continue to account for a significant part of the market.

... [I]n the present case the members of the alleged dominant oligopoly do not control individually or collectively the markets for the raw materials or services necessary for preparing and distributing the product concerned....

First, ... [there are] several examples of small tour operators who have put on additional capacity in response to opportunities that have arisen as a result of unexpected developments in the market. In 1996 (following the difficulties associated with the 1995 crisis), the three largest tour operators at that time reduced or froze their capacity, whilst several of the smaller operators underwent significant expansion, for example Virgin Holidays (+ 28%), Kuoni Travel (+ 20%), Direct Holidays (+ 68%) and Sun Express (+ 109%).

Second, ... smaller tour operators tend to set capacity after the large operators have made their major capacity decisions and that they may still, to a certain extent and like any tour operator, increase their capacity subsequently.

Third, ... several small operators have made it clear that they intend to increase their market share, which suggests that they are, on any view, extremely keen to make the most of any opportunities afforded as a result of the leading tour operators making capacity reductions unconnected with foreseeable trends in demand. . . .

Fourth, it is appropriate to mention a study indicating which of a selected number (59) of smaller tour operators are also present at 12 of the most sought-after short-haul destinations served by the large tour operators, which was produced during the administrative procedure and was not challenged by the Commission. The study shows (i) that all those destinations are served by at least four small tour operators; (ii) that the most popular, such as Corfu, Rhodes, Majorca or mainland Spain, are served by a large number of them (20 to 30 small tour operators); and (iii) that several small operators (such as Cosmos, Manos or Virgin Holidays) serve practically all the destinations. That study also shows that the small tour operators offer similar products (as regards number of nights and services) at prices that are comparable to, or even better than, prices offered by the larger tour operators.

Fifth, . . . it is apparent from that study . . . that the smaller tour operators normally manage to obtain accommodation at short-haul destinations on conditions similar to those of the large operators. The study examines 20 hotels in popular short-haul resorts and compares the prices paid by Airtours with those paid by Panorama and Direct, two small independent operators which were subsequently taken over by Airtours, and shows that the prices are similar and that in some cases the smaller operators obtained more favourable terms than Airtours, even though Airtours reserved many more nights than the smaller operators. . . .

[The evidence also showed] that the Commission was wrong to conclude that smaller tour operators would not have access to airline seats on favourable enough terms to attempt to increase capacity . . . [and] was wrong to conclude that smaller tour operators would not have access to a channel through which to distribute their products to consumers on favourable enough conditions to enable them to expand their capacity significantly. . . .

Possible reactions of potential competitors: other tour operators. [Excerpted below in section on entry barriers.]

The possible reaction of consumers. In seeking to prove that the oligopoly emerging after the transaction would be able to act independently of consumers, it is necessary to determine what the reaction of United Kingdom consumers would be and to ascertain whether they would be prepared to look for other options if the price of significantly or if there were a dearth of such holidays.

. . . [I]t is appropriate to emphasise that the fact that consumers do not have significant buyer power because they act in isolation must not be confused with the question of whether they would be able to react to a price rise brought about by the large tour operators restricting capacity put onto the market to an anti-competitive level. As the applicant submits, it is not disputed that consumers make comparisons before purchasing a holiday. The Commission itself admits . . . that "consumers are sensitive to relatively small differences in the prices of similar holidays."

In that context, the Commission has underestimated the role that might be played by United Kingdom consumers, who are in a position to try to obtain better prices from small tour operators.

Furthermore, ... although the Commission, in the proper exercise of its discretion, concluded that the relevant product market should be narrowly defined, it nevertheless did not question either the fact that long-haul foreign package holidays are becoming increasingly attractive to consumers or the fact that the market studies ... draw attention to the tendency of United Kingdom consumers to go further afield for their holidays, in particular to the other side of the Atlantic. That fact lends weight to the applicant's proposition that demand might partly switch to other types of holidays if there were sufficient price convergence, inasmuch as the studies concerned clearly show that consumer tastes are evolving and that consumers do not appear in any way to regard the Mediterranean coast as the only place to go on holiday. . . .

5.   *The assessment of the impact of the transaction on competition* ... [T]he Commission was wrong to conclude that the degree of market transparency was sufficient to allow each of the major tour operators to be aware of the conduct of the others, to detect any deviations from the common policy and to see retaliatory measures for what they are. The Commission has failed to establish that the situation would be any different if there was a move from four major tour operators to three. . . .

Note and Questions on *Airtours*

Before *Airtours*, merger cases alleging collective dominance were limited to mergers that created a duopoly. *Airtours* was the first case where the Commission tried to block a merger that created a collective dominant position between three firms on the ground that oligopolistic coordination among them was likely. This 2002 General Court decision approved such a claim in theory, even before the 2004 amendments extended the regulation to any merger that significantly impeded competition. However, the General Court also set rigorous standards for showing that oligopolistic coordination was sufficiently likely to constitute collective dominance, requiring convincing evidence of: (1) transparency (firms can monitor each other); (2) deterrence (deviations from oligopoly conduct are likely to be punished) and (3) collective market power (the oligopoly price will not be undermined by rival expansion, new entry, or consumer responses).

The result has been to complete a remarkable convergence. EU and U.S. merger law started at opposite poles, and contrary to stereotype on convergence, it was the EU that began with the more conservative position. The EU initially condemned only mergers that created a single dominant firm, and U.S. cases historically condemned mergers that left markets with over ten firms because they increased market concentration. Over the decades, the law in both places has evolved until they have ended up in largely the same place. Now in both places, mergers to duopoly are condemned fairly routinely (though still contestable) and mergers that leave 3–5 major firms in the market are considered close cases, with decisions turning on detailed analysis of whether the relevant market conditions make oligopolistic coordination or unilateral effects likely.

1. Is the General Court right that volatile market shares indicate a likely absence of oligopolistic coordination even when the volatility resulted from past mergers rather than consumer shifts between the firms?

2. Why would high demand growth make oligopolistic coordination less likely? Does it make it harder to assess whether rival capacity increases reflect estimates of demand growth rather than deviations from oligopolistic coordination?

3. Why did coordination on price seem unlikely here?

4. Does it seem likely that firms could monitor the decisions each other made on capacity during a planning period that came about 18 months before the relevant season? How does the varied nature of that capacity affect the ability to monitor it?

5. What does the deterrence element add to the transparency element? Doesn't this element amount to the conclusion that, by the time other firms' capacity decisions are transparent, it is too late for fellow oligopolists to respond effectively?

6. The assessment of possible responses by smaller tour operators amounts to an inquiry into their elasticity of supply. Should that be measured directly rather than just qualitatively assessed? Is the General Court right that it does not matter that none of these small operators could achieve the same efficiencies as the larger tour operators? Wouldn't the lack of such efficiencies affect the likelihood of consumers switching to the smaller operators?

7. The assessment of consumer responses amounts to an inquiry into their demand elasticity for the relevant product. Shouldn't that already be taken into account when doing the market definition? If the market definition was done properly, doesn't it necessarily indicate that consumer responses would not restrain an oligopoly from charging at least 5–10% above competitive prices?

Proving That a Merger Would Worsen Oligopolistic Coordination

The General Court decision in *Airtours* requires proof not only that oligopolistic coordination was likely post-merger, but also that the merger increases the likelihood or effectiveness of oligopolistic coordination. Requiring rigorous proof of this can put enforcement agencies in a difficult spot. If they claim that there was no effective oligopolistic coordination before the merger, then it will be hard to prove that decreasing the number of firms by one would be the decisive factor that makes coordination likely. If they claim there was effective oligopolistic coordination before the merger, then it will be hard to prove that decreasing the number of firms by one will make matters any worse since pre-merger prices were already at oligopoly levels.

It is unclear how standards of proof will evolve to avoid such a Catch–22. The U.S. Merger Commentary suggests that, if there was coordination in the past, then the U.S. agencies rely on an assumption that reducing the number of firms will increase the effectiveness of coordination, unless something else has changed to make coordination less likely. If so, then this test does not really require concrete evidence that the merger would worsen coordination. If there wasn't oligopolistic coordination in the past, the Commentary suggests that it requires evidence the merger would increase the incentives to coordinate by eliminating a maverick firm or particular disruptive incentives held by a merging firm. But this does not capture the possibility that the simple reduction in the number of firms might make coordination more likely even without eliminating uniquely disruptive firms or incentives.

A more quantitative possibility might be to use the NEIO approach described above. One can use past data on market prices, costs, shares and elasticity to calculate the conduct parameter K using the equation (P–MC)/P = $(1+K)$HHI/e. One can then use this equation to determine what the price effect of a change in HHI might be, holding K constant on the assumption that the degree of competitiveness was unaffected by the merger. One might also examine past increases in market concentration to see whether they had any effect on the size of K, thus indicating increased effectiveness in coordination, which would further affect prices.

EU Guidelines on the Assessment of Horizontal Mergers

O.J. 2004, C 31/18.

IV. POSSIBLE ANTI-COMPETITIVE EFFECTS OF HORIZONTAL MERGERS....

Coordinated Effects. In some markets the structure may be such that firms would consider it possible, economically rational, and hence preferable, to adopt on a sustainable basis a course of action on the market aimed at selling at increased prices. A merger in a concentrated market may significantly impede effective competition, through the creation or the strengthening of a collective dominant position, because it increases the likelihood that firms are able to coordinate their behaviour in this way and raise prices, even without entering into an agreement or resorting to a concerted practice within the meaning of Article [101 TFEU]. A merger may also make coordination easier, more stable or more effective for firms, that were already coordinating before the merger, either by making the coordination more robust or by permitting firms to coordinate on even higher prices.

Coordination may take various forms. In some markets, the most likely coordination may involve keeping prices above the competitive level. In other markets, coordination may aim at limiting production or the amount of new capacity brought to the market. Firms may also coordinate by dividing the market, for instance by geographic area or other customer characteristics, or by allocating contracts in bidding markets.

Coordination is more likely to emerge in markets where it is relatively simple to reach a common understanding on the terms of coordination. In addition, three conditions are necessary for coordination to be sustainable. First, the coordinating firms must be able to monitor to a sufficient degree whether the terms of coordination are being adhered to. Second, discipline requires that there is some form of credible deterrent mechanism that can be activated if deviation is detected. Third, the reactions of outsiders, such as current and future competitors not participating in the coordination, as well as customers, should not be able to jeopardise the results expected from the coordination.

The Commission examines whether it would be possible to reach terms of coordination and whether the coordination is likely to be sustainable. In this respect, the Commission considers the changes that the merger brings about. The reduction in the number of firms in a market may, in itself, be a factor that facilitates coordination. However, a merger may also increase the likelihood or significance of coordinated effects in other ways. For instance, a merger may involve a "maverick" firm that has a history of preventing or disrupting coordination, for example by failing to follow price increases by its competitors, or has characteristics that gives it an incentive to favour different strategic choices than its coordinating competitors would prefer. If the merged firm were to adopt strategies similar to those of other competitors, the remaining firms would find it easier to coordinate, and the merger would increase the likelihood, stability or effectiveness of coordination.

In assessing the likelihood of coordinated effects, the Commission takes into account all available relevant information on the characteristics of the markets concerned, including both structural features and the past behaviour of firms. Evidence of past coordination is important if the relevant market characteristics have not changed appreciably or are not likely to do so in the near future. Likewise, evidence of coordination in similar markets may be useful information.

Reaching terms of coordination. Coordination is more likely to emerge if competitors can easily arrive at a common perception as to how the coordination should work. Coordinating firms should have similar views regarding which actions would be considered to be in accordance with the aligned behaviour and which actions would not.

Generally, the less complex and the more stable the economic environment, the easier it is for the firms to reach a common understanding on the terms of coordination. For instance, it is easier to coordinate among a few players than among many. It is also easier to coordinate on a price for a single, homogeneous product, than on hundreds of prices in a market with many differentiated products. Similarly, it is easier to coordinate on a price when demand and supply conditions are relatively stable than when they are continuously changing. In this context volatile demand, substantial internal growth by some firms in the market or frequent entry by new firms may indicate that the current situation is not sufficiently stable to make coordination likely. In markets where innovation is important, coordination may be more difficult since innovations, particularly significant ones, may allow one firm to gain a major advantage over its rivals.

Coordination by way of market division will be easier if customers have simple characteristics that allow the coordinating firms to readily allocate them. Such characteristics may be based on geography; on customer type or simply on the existence of customers who typically buy from one specific firm. Coordination by way of market division may be relatively straightforward if it is easy to identify each customer's supplier and the coordination device is the allocation of existing customers to their incumbent supplier.

Coordinating firms may, however, find other ways to overcome problems stemming from complex economic environments short of market division. They may, for instance, establish simple pricing rules that reduce the complexity of coordinating on a large number of prices. One example of such a rule is establishing a small number of pricing points, thus reducing the coordination problem. Another example is having a fixed relationship between certain base prices and a number of other prices, such that prices basically move in parallel. Publicly available key information, exchange of information through trade associations, or information received through cross-shareholdings or participation in joint ventures may also help firms reach terms of coordination. The more complex the market situation is, the more transparency or communication is likely to be needed to reach a common understanding on the terms of coordination.

Firms may find it easier to reach a common understanding on the terms of coordination if they are relatively symmetric, especially in terms of cost structures, market shares, capacity levels and levels of vertical integration. Structural links such as cross-shareholding or participation in joint ventures may also help in aligning incentives among the coordinating firms.

Monitoring deviations. Coordinating firms are often tempted to increase their share of the market by deviating from the terms of coordination, for instance by lowering prices, offering secret discounts, increasing product quality or capacity or trying to win new customers. Only the credible threat of timely and sufficient retaliation keeps firms from deviating. Markets therefore need to be sufficiently transparent to allow the coordinating firms to monitor to a sufficient degree whether other firms are deviating, and thus know when to retaliate.

Transparency in the market is often higher, the lower the number of active participants in the market. Further, the degree of transparency often depends on how market transactions take place in a particular market. For example, transparency is likely to be high in a market where transactions take place on a public exchange or in an open outcry auction. Conversely, transparency may be low in a market where transactions are confidentially negotiated between buyers and sellers on a bilateral basis. When evaluating the level of transparency in the market, the key element is to identify what firms can infer about the actions of other firms from the available information. Coordinating firms should be able to interpret with some certainty whether unexpected behaviour is the result of deviation from the terms of coordination. For instance, in unstable environments it may be difficult for a firm to know whether its lost sales are due to an overall low level of demand or due to a competitor offering particularly low prices. Similarly, when overall demand or cost conditions fluctuate, it may be difficult to interpret whether a competitor is lowering its price because it expects the coordinated prices to fall or because it is deviating.

In some markets where the general conditions may seem to make monitoring of deviations difficult, firms may nevertheless engage in practices which have the effect of easing the monitoring task, even when these practices are not necessarily entered into for such purposes. These practices, such as meeting-competition or most-favoured-customer clauses, voluntary publication of information, announcements, or exchange of information through trade associations, may increase transparency or help competitors interpret the choices made. Cross-directorships, participation in joint ventures and similar arrangements may also make monitoring easier.

Deterrent mechanisms. Coordination is not sustainable unless the consequences of deviation are sufficiently severe to convince coordinating firms that it is in their best interest to adhere to the terms of coordination. It is thus the threat of future retaliation that keeps the coordination sustainable. However the threat is only credible if, where deviation by one of the firms is detected, there is sufficient certainty that some deterrent mechanism will be activated.[70]

Retaliation that manifests itself after some significant time lag, or is not certain to be activated, is less likely to be sufficient to offset the benefits from deviating. For example, if a market is characterised by infrequent, large-volume orders, it may be difficult to establish a sufficiently severe deterrent mechanism, since the gain from deviating at the right time may be large, certain and immediate, whereas the losses from being punished may be small and uncertain and only materialise after some time. The speed with which deterrent mechanisms can be implemented is related to the issue of transparency. If firms are only able to observe their competitors' actions after a substantial delay, then retaliation will be similarly delayed and this may influence whether it is sufficient to deter deviation.

The credibility of the deterrence mechanism depends on whether the other coordinating firms have an incentive to retaliate. Some deterrent mechanisms, such as punishing the deviator by temporarily engaging in a price war or increasing output significantly, may entail a short-term economic loss for the firms carrying out the retaliation. This does not necessarily remove the incentive to retaliate since the short-term loss may be smaller than the long-term benefit of retaliating resulting from the return to the regime of coordination.

Retaliation need not necessarily take place in the same market as the deviation. If the coordinating firms have commercial interaction in other markets, these may offer various methods of retaliation. The retaliation could take many forms, including cancellation of joint ventures or other forms of cooperation or selling of shares in jointly owned companies.

Reactions of outsiders. For coordination to be successful, the actions of non-coordinating firms and potential competitors, as well as customers, should not be able to jeopardise the outcome expected from coordination.

---

70. Although deterrent mechanisms are sometimes called "punishment" mechanisms, this should not be understood in the strict sense that such a mechanism necessarily punishes individually a firm that has deviated. The expectation that coordination may break down for a certain period of time, if a deviation is identified as such, may in itself constitute a sufficient deterrent mechanism.

For example, if coordination aims at reducing overall capacity in the market, this will only hurt consumers if non-coordinating firms are unable or have no incentive to respond to this decrease by increasing their own capacity sufficiently to prevent a net decrease in capacity, or at least to render the coordinated capacity decrease unprofitable.

The effects of entry and countervailing buyer power of customers are analysed in later sections. However, special consideration is given to the possible impact of these elements on the stability of coordination. For instance, by concentrating a large amount of its requirements with one supplier or by offering long-term contracts, a large buyer may make coordination unstable by successfully tempting one of the coordinating firms to deviate in order to gain substantial new business.

Questions on the EU Guidelines on Coordinated Effects

1. In addition to the three conditions imposed by the General Court in *Airtours*, the EU Guidelines add another initial condition, which is that the firms are likely to be able to reach terms of coordination to begin with, which the U.S. agencies also require. The Commission identifies a series of market circumstances that make it more likely that coordination among firms will emerge. Such circumstances include a homogeneous product, stable demand and supply, and limited innovations. In today's economy, do many markets fit such circumstances? Can firms sometimes develop facilitating practices to aid coordination in more complex market environments? How?

2. Is this initial condition really separate from the rest, or are those the same items one would examine to determine whether firms can monitor each other and deter deviations?

3. Are there other factors that might affect the ease of reaching common terms of coordination?

a. Would variation in costs undermine the likelihood of coordination?

b. Would uniform market shares make coordination more likely because each firm expects similar terms or less likely because it means there is no natural price leader for the rest to follow?

4. Like the U.S. guidelines, the EU guidelines stress the importance of homogeneity as a factor facilitating coordination. But can't product differentiation also be used strategically to effectively coordinate on a division of the market?

Merger Assessments in Other Nations

In general, other nations use similar analytical steps to judge mergers, including defining the relevant markets, determining market shares and concentration levels, identifying potential anticompetitive effects in connection with the transaction, identifying entry conditions, and assessing whether economic efficiencies—and in some cases public interest goals—outweigh potential anticompetitive effects. For purposes of defining the relevant market, some nations expressly adopt the hypothetical monopolist

SSNIP test, while others are less clear in this regard, and those that do adopt it use hypothetical price increases that range from 5 to 15%.[33] Nations generally measure concentration levels using either HHIs or x-firm concentration indexes.

Mexico has a distinctive approach. It views HHIs alone as unsatisfactory because they always increase with any merger, even a merger between small firms, which the Mexican authorities apparently deem likely to be procompetitive on the theory that making the size of firms more equal tends to increase competitiveness.[34] Thus, Mexico also utilizes a "Dominance Index," which is calculated by squaring each firm's market share, dividing by the HHI, squaring the resulting fraction, and then adding the same for each other firm in the market.[35] This formula is designed to increase when the merging firms are large but not when they are small.

Some nations, including South Korea, presume mergers above certain thresholds are anticompetitive.[36] Most nations do not, and Canada even prohibits blocking a merger based solely on evidence of market shares.[37] Instead, most nations use market share thresholds only as presumptive safe-harbors. In Australia, a transaction is unlikely to be challenged if *either* the resulting HHI is below 2,000 or the HHI increase is below 100.[38] In Chile, mergers are presumptively legal if the resulting HHI is below 1000 or is between 1000–1800 and the increase is below 100, or if the resulting HHI is above 1800 and the increase is less than 50.[39] In Colombia, a merger can proceed without preapproval if the merged firm share would be less than 20%.[40] Japan presumes no anticompetitive effect if the post-merger HHI is (a) below 1,500, (b) between 1,500–2,500 with an HHI increase not more than 250, (c) over 2,500 with an HHI increase not more than 150.[41] The Japan guidelines also note the likelihood of anticompetitive effects is "usually ... small" when the post-merger HHI is not more than 2,500 and merged firm market share is not more than 35%.[42] In Mexico, a transaction is unlikely to be challenged if the increase in HHI is below 75, the resulting HHI is below 2,000, the dominance index decreases, or the resulting dominance index is below 2,500.[43] In New Zealand and Singapore, mergers are unlikely to be challenged if the merged firm has less than a

---

33. *See* Chapter 3.B.3.

34. ABA, II COMPETITION LAWS OUTSIDE THE UNITED STATES at Mexico–15 (2001).

35. ABA, COMPETITION LAWS OUTSIDE THE UNITED STATES at Mexico–10 (Supp. 2005). Thus, where S_i is the market share of each firm, the dominance index $= \Sigma \ (S_i^2/HHI)^2$.

36. South Korea Fair Trade Act Arts. 4, 7(4) provides that a merger is presumptively anticompetitive if the merged firm market share (a) is 50% or more (b) is 10% or more and three largest firms together are 75% or higher, or (c) exceeds the next largest firm by 25% or more.

37. Canada Competition Act § 92(2).

38. Australia Merger Guidelines § 7.14 (2008).

39. Chile, Internal Guidelines for the Analysis of Horizontal Concentration Operations, IV. 3.

40. Colombia Competition Law, Art. 9.

41. *See* Japan Business Combination Guidelines § IV.1(3) (2010).

42. *Id.*

43. *See* ABA, COMPETITION LAWS OUTSIDE THE UNITED STATES at Mexico–10 (Supp. 2005).

20% market share or less than a 40% market share in a market where the three largest firms have less than 70%.[44] South Africa is unlikely to challenge a merger if the merged firm share is below 15%, the HHI is below 1000, the increase in HHI is below 50, or the HHI is between 1000–1800 but the increase is below 100.[45] In addition to presuming some high concentration mergers to be anticompetitive, South Korea also has presumptive safe harbors if (a) the post-merger HHI is lower than 1,200, (b) the post-merger HHI is between 1,200 and 2,500 and the HHI increase is 250 or less, or (c) the post-merger HHI is higher than 2,500 and the HHI increase is 150 or lower.[46] Some nations, like Argentina and Venezuela, do not set thresholds for concern in their merger review guidelines.

Some nations use different presumptive safe-harbors for unilateral and coordinated effects cases. Canada is unlikely to bring a challenge alleging unilateral effects if the merged firm would have a market share less than 35% or a challenge alleging coordinated effects if the merged firm would have less than 10% or the four-firm concentration ratio is less than 65%.[47] In Brazil the safe harbors are 20% in unilateral cases and either a merged firm share of less than 10% or a four-firm concentration ratio of less than 75% in oligopoly cases.[48] Many nations also have provisions that note the greater likelihood of anticompetitive effects when a merger eliminates a maverick firm.[49]

1. Should other nations use a Mexican-style index that does not rise when small firms merge? Does allowing small firms to merge to a size similar to bigger firms increase competition? Or does it decrease it by making both unilateral and coordinated effects more likely? If a merger sometimes allows small firms to achieve efficiencies of size, won't those efficiencies be taken into account more directly with an efficiency defense?

2. Should nations use thresholds for either presumptive condemnation or presumptive safe harbors? Should they adopt only one of those presumptions, both, or neither?

3. Should the U.S. and EU join other nations in having different thresholds for unilateral and coordinated effects?

4. Should the unilateral effects threshold turn only on the single firm market shares rather than on HHIs? Does it make much sense to have a

---

44. New Zealand Mergers Guidelines § 5.3 (2007); Singapore Merger Guidelines § 5.15 (2007).

45. *Id.* ABA, COMPETITION LAWS OUTSIDE THE UNITED STATES at at South Africa–62 (Supp. 2005).

46. South Korea Merger Guidelines II.1.(5)(a) (2009).

47. *See* Canada Merger Guidelines § 4.12 (2004). The Competition Bureau has stated that mergers over 45% are likely be deemed to substantially lessen competition without adopting a presumption to that effect. *See* ABA, I COMPETITION LAWS OUTSIDE THE UNITED STATES at Canada–82 (2001).

48. *See* Brazil Horizontal Merger Guidelines § 36 (2001).

49. *See, e.g.,* Australia Trade Practices Act § 50(3)(h); Brazil Horizontal Merger Guidelines § 65 (2001); Canada Competition Act § 93(f); Canada Merger Guidelines §§ 5.31–5.32 (2004); India Competition Act § 20(4)(i); New Zealand Mergers Guidelines § 7.2 (2006). Other nations that consider the maverick factor include Argentina, South Africa, South Korea, and Venezuela.

single firm market share threshold when the concern is that the firms are close to each other on a differentiated market?

5. Should the coordinated effects threshold turn only on the three or four-firm concentration levels rather than on HHIs?

6. Doesn't it make sense to use HHIs as a threshold only when a nation is condemning mergers based on multi-firm Cournot effects?

3. POST-MERGER ENTRY

U.S. DOJ/FTC, Horizontal Merger Guidelines
(2010).

9. Entry

The analysis of competitive effects in Sections 6 and 7 focuses on current participants in the relevant market. That analysis may also include some forms of entry. Firms that would rapidly and easily enter the market in response to a SSNIP are market participants and may be assigned market shares. See Sections 5.1 and 5.2. Firms that have, prior to the merger, committed to entering the market also will normally be treated as market participants. See Section 5.1. This section concerns entry or adjustments to pre-existing entry plans that are induced by the merger.

As part of their full assessment of competitive effects, the Agencies consider entry into the relevant market. The prospect of entry into the relevant market will alleviate concerns about adverse competitive effects only if such entry will deter or counteract any competitive effects of concern so the merger will not substantially harm customers.

The Agencies consider the actual history of entry into the relevant market and give substantial weight to this evidence. Lack of successful and effective entry in the face of non-transitory increases in the margins earned on products in the relevant market tends to suggest that successful entry is slow or difficult. Market values of incumbent firms greatly exceeding the replacement costs of their tangible assets may indicate that these firms have valuable intangible assets, which may be difficult or time consuming for an entrant to replicate.

A merger is not likely to enhance market power if entry into the market is so easy that the merged firm and its remaining rivals in the market, either unilaterally or collectively, could not profitably raise price or otherwise reduce competition compared to the level that would prevail in the absence of the merger. Entry is that easy if entry would be timely, likely, and sufficient in its magnitude, character, and scope to deter or counteract the competitive effects of concern.

The Agencies examine the timeliness, likelihood, and sufficiency of the entry efforts an entrant might practically employ. An entry effort is defined by the actions the firm must undertake to produce and sell in the market. Various elements of the entry effort will be considered. These elements can include: planning, design, and management; permitting, licensing, or other approvals; construction, debugging, and operation of production facilities; and promotion (including necessary introductory discounts), marketing, distribution, and satisfaction of customer testing and qualification requirements. Recent examples of entry, whether successful or unsuccessful, generally provide the starting point for identifying the elements of practical entry efforts. They also can be informative regarding the scale necessary for an entrant to be successful, the presence or absence of entry barriers, the factors that influence the timing of entry, the costs and risk associated with entry, and the sales opportunities realistically available to entrants.

If the assets necessary for an effective and profitable entry effort are widely available, the Agencies will not necessarily attempt to identify which firms might enter. Where an identifiable set of firms appears to have necessary assets that others lack, or to have particularly strong incentives to enter, the Agencies focus their entry analysis on those firms. Firms operating in adjacent or complementary markets, or large customers themselves, may be best placed to enter. However, the Agencies will not presume that a powerful firm in an adjacent market or a large customer will enter the relevant market unless there is reliable evidence supporting that conclusion.

In assessing whether entry will be timely, likely, and sufficient, the Agencies recognize that precise and detailed information may be difficult or impossible to obtain. The Agencies consider reasonably available and reliable evidence bearing on whether entry will satisfy the conditions of timeliness, likelihood, and sufficiency.

9.1 Timeliness

In order to deter the competitive effects of concern, entry must be rapid enough to make unprofitable overall the actions causing those effects and thus leading to entry, even though those actions would be profitable until entry takes effect.

Even if the prospect of entry does not deter the competitive effects of concern, post-merger entry may counteract them. This requires that the impact of entrants in the relevant market be rapid enough that customers are not significantly harmed by the merger, despite any anticompetitive harm that occurs prior to the entry.

The Agencies will not presume that an entrant can have a significant impact on prices before that entrant is ready to provide the relevant product to customers unless there is reliable evidence that anticipated future entry would have such an effect on prices.

9.2 Likelihood

Entry is likely if it would be profitable, accounting for the assets, capabilities, and capital needed and the risks involved, including the need for the entrant to incur costs that would not be recovered if the entrant later exits. Profitability depends upon (a) the output level the entrant is likely to obtain, accounting for the obstacles facing new entrants; (b) the price the entrant would likely obtain in the post-merger market, accounting for the impact of that entry itself on prices; and (c) the cost per unit the entrant would likely incur, which may depend upon the scale at which the entrant would operate.

9.3 Sufficiency

Even where timely and likely, entry may not be sufficient to deter or counteract the competitive effects of concern. For example, in a differentiated product industry, entry may be insufficient because the products offered by entrants are not close enough substitutes to the products offered by the merged firm to render a price increase by the merged firm unprofitable. Entry may also be insufficient due to constraints that limit entrants' competitive effectiveness, such as limitations on the capabilities of the firms best placed to enter or reputational barriers to rapid expansion by new entrants. Entry by a single firm that will replicate at least the scale and strength of one of the merging firms is sufficient. Entry by one or more firms operating at a smaller scale may be sufficient if such firms are not at a significant competitive disadvantage . . .

Questions on U.S. Guidelines on Entry

1. The pre–2010 guidelines defined entry as timely if it occurs within two years, while the new guidelines define entry as timely if it is rapid enough to make it unprofitable to engage in the actions that cause the anticompetitive effects of concern. Which approach seems preferable?

2. The pre–2010 guidelines defined entry as likely if it would be profitable at premerger prices, whereas the new guidelines define entry as likely if it would be profitable at the price the entrant would likely obtain in the post-merger market. Which approach seems preferable? If entry would be profitable at premerger prices, wouldn't the firms already have entered?

FTC v. Staples, Inc.

970 F.Supp. 1066 (D.D.C. 1997).

■ THOMAS F. HOGAN, DISTRICT JUDGE. . . . [Portions of the opinion defining the market and finding likely anticompetitive effects are excerpted above.]

V. Entry Into the Market

"The existence and significance of barriers to entry are frequently, of course, crucial considerations in a rebuttal analysis [because] [i]n the absence of significant barriers, a company probably cannot maintain supracompetitive pricing for any length of time." *Baker Hughes, Inc.,* 908 F.2d at 987. . . . If the defendants' evidence regarding entry showed that the Commission's market-share statistics give an incorrect prediction of the proposed acquisition's probable effect on competition because entry into the market would likely avert any anti-competitive effect by acting as a constraint on Staples-Office Depot's prices, the Court would deny the FTC's motion. The Court, however, cannot make such a finding in this case.

... [W]hile it is true that all office superstore entrants have entered within the last 11 years, the recent trend for office superstores has actually been toward exiting the market rather than entering. Over the past few years, the number of office superstore chains has dramatically dropped from twenty-three to three. All but Staples, Office Depot, and OfficeMax have either closed or been acquired. The failed office superstore entrants include very large, well-known retail establishments such as Kmart, Montgomery Ward, Ames, and Zayres. A new office superstore would need to open a large number of stores nationally in order to achieve the purchasing and distribution economies of scale enjoyed by the three existing firms. Sunk costs would be extremely high. Economies of scale at the local level, such as in the costs of advertising and distribution, would also be difficult for a new superstore entrant to achieve since the three existing firms have saturated many important local markets....

For the reasons discussed above, the Court finds it extremely unlikely that a new office superstore will enter the market and thereby avert the anti-competitive effects from Staples' acquisition of Office Depot.... The Court also finds it unlikely that the expansions by U.S. Office Products and Wal–Mart would avert the anti-competitive effects which would result from the merger.

The problems with the defendants' evidence regarding U.S. Office Products are numerous. In contrast to Staples and Office Depot, U.S. Office Products is a company which is focused on a contract stationers business servicing primarily the medium corporate segment. The Mailboxes stores recently acquired by U.S. Office Products carry only 50–200 SKUs of office supplies in stores of approximately 1,000–4,000 square feet with no more than half of that area devoted to consumable office supplies. In addition to their small size and limited number of SKUs, the Mailboxes stores would not actually be new entrants. U.S. Office Products is acquiring existing stores, and, besides Mr. Ledecky's plans to put a U.S. Office Products catalogue in every Mailboxes store, there was no testimony regarding plans to expand the number of SKUs available in the retail stores themselves or to increase the size of the average Mailboxes store. Finally, though Mr. Ledecky testified that if Staples and Office Depot were to raise prices after the merger he would look on that as an opportunity to take business away from the combined entity, he later clarified that statement by explaining that he meant in the contract stationer field.

The defendants' evidence regarding Wal–Mart's expansion of Department 3 has similar weaknesses. While the total number of SKUs expected to be carried by the new Department 3 is impressive, Mr. Glass estimated it to be between 2,600 to 3,000 SKUs, the evidence shows that this is only an increase of approximately 400 SKUs. The Court has already found that Wal–Mart's sales of office supplies are outside the relevant product market in this case primarily because the pricing evidence shows that Wal–Mart does not presently effectively constrain the superstores' prices. The Court cannot conclude that an addition of 400 SKUs and reconfigured shelf space will significantly change Wal–Mart's ability to constrain Staples' and Office Depot's prices. The superstores will continue to offer significantly more SKUs of consumable office supplies. For these reasons, the Court cannot find that Wal–Mart's expansion through Department 3 is likely to avert anti-competitive effects resulting from Staples' acquisition of Office Depot.

The defendants' final argument with respect to entry was that existing retailers such as Sam's Club, Kmart, and Best Buy have the capability to reallocate their shelf space to include additional SKUs of office supplies. While stores such as these certainly do have the power to reallocate shelf space, there is no evidence that they will in fact do this if a combined Staples–Office Depot were to raise prices by 5% following a merger. In fact, the evidence indicates that it is more likely that they would not. For example, even in the superstores' anti-competitive zones where either Staples or Office Depot does not compete with other superstores, no retailer has successfully expanded its consumable office supplies to the extent that it constrains superstore pricing. Best Buy attempted such an expansion by creating an office supplies department in 1994, offering 2000 SKUs of office supplies, but found the expansion less profitable than hoped for and gave up after two years. For these reasons, the Court also cannot find that the ability of many sellers of office supplies to reconfigure shelf space and add SKUs of office supplies is likely to avert anti-competitive effects from Staples' acquisition of Office Depot. . . .

[Portions of the opinion addressing alleged efficiencies and balancing the equities are excerpted below.]

Questions on *Staples*

1. Should the fact that all the office superstores entered within the last 11 years dispositively show entry was likely? Should the fact that in the past few years all but 3 office superstores exited the market dispositively show entry was unlikely?

2. Should the plans of Walmart and Mailboxes, Etc to expand their office supply offerings have been deemed to show entry was likely? Should the fact that Sam's Club, Kmart, and Best Buy could reallocate shelf space to office supplies have been deemed to show entry was likely?

  a. Would either sort of entry be into the office superstore market?

  b. Would either be sufficient to eliminate any anticompetitive effects?

3. Doesn't the evidence that prices were higher in markets with one office-superstore than in markets with two or three alone show that entry must not be sufficient to curb price increases in markets with one office-superstore? Given this sort of hard price evidence, do courts need to rely on qualitative assessments about the likelihood of entry?

EU Guidelines on the Assessment of Horizontal Mergers
O.J. 2004, C 31/5.

VI. ENTRY. When entering a market is sufficiently easy, a merger is unlikely to pose any significant anti-competitive risk. Therefore, entry analysis constitutes an important element of the overall competitive assessment. For entry to be considered a sufficient competitive constraint on the merging parties, it must be shown to be likely, timely and sufficient to deter or defeat any potential anti-competitive effects of the merger.

Likelihood of entry. The Commission examines whether entry is likely or whether potential entry is likely to constrain the behaviour of incumbents post-merger. For entry to be likely, it must be sufficiently profitable taking into account the price effects of injecting additional output into the market and the potential responses of the incumbents. Entry is thus less likely if it would only be economically viable on a large scale, thereby resulting in significantly depressed price levels. And entry is likely to be more difficult if the incumbents are able to protect their market shares by offering long-term contracts or giving targeted pre-emptive price reductions to those customers that the entrant is trying to acquire. Furthermore, high risk and costs of failed entry may make entry less likely. The costs of failed entry will be higher, the higher is the level of sunk cost associated with entry.

Potential entrants may encounter barriers to entry which determine entry risks and costs and thus have an impact on the profitability of entry. Barriers to entry are specific features of the market, which give incumbent firms advantages over potential competitors. When entry barriers are low, the merging parties are more likely to be constrained by entry. Conversely, when entry barriers are high, price increases by the merging firms would not be significantly constrained by entry. Historical examples of entry and exit in the industry may provide useful information about the size of entry barriers.

Barriers to entry can take various forms:

(a) Legal advantages encompass situations where regulatory barriers limit the number of market participants by, for example, restricting the number of licences. They also cover tariff and non-tariff trade barriers.

(b) The incumbents may also enjoy technical advantages, such as preferential access to essential facilities, natural resources, innovation and R&D, or intellectual property rights, which make it difficult for any firm to compete successfully. For instance, in certain industries, it might be difficult to obtain essential input materials, or patents might protect products or processes. Other factors such as economies of scale and scope, distribution and sales networks, access to important technologies, may also constitute barriers to entry.

(c) Furthermore, barriers to entry may also exist because of the established position of the incumbent firms on the market. In particular, it may be difficult to enter a particular industry because experience or reputation is necessary to compete effectively, both of which may be difficult to obtain as an entrant. Factors such as consumer loyalty to a particular brand, the closeness of relationships between suppliers and customers, the importance of promotion or advertising, or other advantages relating to reputation will be taken into account in this context. Barriers to entry also encompass situations where the incumbents have already committed to building large excess capacity, or where the costs faced by customers in switching to a new supplier may inhibit entry.

The expected evolution of the market should be taken into account when assessing whether or not entry would be profitable. Entry is more likely to be profitable in a market that is expected to experience high growth in the future than in a market that is mature or expected to decline. Scale economies or network effects may make entry unprofitable unless the entrant can obtain a sufficiently large market share.

Entry is particularly likely if suppliers in other markets already possess production facilities that could be used to enter the market in question, thus reducing the sunk costs of entry. The smaller the difference in profitability between entry and non-entry prior to the merger, the more likely such a reallocation of production facilities.

Timeliness. The Commission examines whether entry would be sufficiently swift and sustained to deter or defeat the exercise of market power. What constitutes an appropriate time period depends on the characteristics and dynamics of the market, as well as on the specific capabilities of potential entrants. However, entry is normally only considered timely if it occurs within two years.

Sufficiency. Entry must be of sufficient scope and magnitude to deter or defeat the anti-competitive effects of the merger. Small-scale entry, for instance into some market "niche", may not be considered sufficient. . . .

Case T–342/99, Airtours v. Commission

[2002] E.C.R. II–2585.

[Other portions of this opinion are excerpted above].

Possible reactions of potential competitors: other tour operators. It is also necessary to consider whether, were the large tour operators to restrict capacity put on to the market to anti-competitive levels, tour operators in other countries of the Community or in the United Kingdom long-haul foreign package holiday market would be capable of entering the United Kingdom short-haul foreign package holiday market.

It is appropriate to recall the wording employed by the MMC [United Kingdom Monopolies and Mergers Commission] in its 1997 report:

> "Players come and go. There are no significant barriers to entering either the tour operator or the travel agent market" . . . if particular types of holidays, holidays from certain airports or holidays at particular times of year were overpriced, then tour operators would be able to move their business into each of those areas and undercut their prices.

[T]he Commission nevertheless notes that since the MMC's report was completed in 1997 there has been substantial consolidation in the industry and considers that henceforth barriers to market entry will be greater . . . and that they would increase still further if the proposed merger were implemented. The Commission then submits:

> "To be sufficient to remove the threat of creation of a dominant position, entry must, clearly, be more than merely possible. Among other things, it must be sustainable, which, in markets such as

this one, where scale is an important factor, means that it must be capable of being on, or quickly acquiring, a sufficient scale to offer a real competitive challenge to the dominant suppliers. In the Commission's view, this is unlikely to be the case here."

It should nevertheless be borne in mind that, as is the case with current competitors, what is important here is not whether there is scope for potential competitors to reach a sufficient size to compete on an equal footing with the large tour operators, but simply whether there is scope for such competitors to take advantage of opportunities afforded by the large operators restricting capacity put onto the relevant market to below a competitive level. In that context, the Commission cannot contend that, merely because they would have difficulty expanding beyond a certain size, tour operators offering other products (such as long-haul foreign package holidays) or carrying on business in other countries (such as Germany or the Netherlands) could not enter the United Kingdom short-haul foreign package holiday market fast and effectively if the large tour operators decided to restrict competition significantly....

Furthermore, ... the Decision does not examine competition at the level of holiday accommodation, although the supply of capacity of that type is very important if the dynamic of the relevant market is to be understood, in particular with regard, first, to the ability of members of the alleged dominant oligopoly to act independently of hotel owners at short-haul destinations, and, second and consequently, to the ability of current and potential competitors to react to a possible reduction in the capacity supplied by the large tour operators. It is unlikely that any hotel beds becoming available following a decision by the large tour operators to restrict capacity will not be immediately booked by other operators....

Questions on *Airtours* Analysis of Entry

1. Do you agree with the General Court that it does not matter that the potential entrants could not achieve the same efficiencies as the incumbent major firms? Doesn't that undermine the sufficiency of their entry? Or is it sufficient that they could inefficiently expand capacity?

2. Why is the availability of hotel accommodations relevant to entry by new tour operators? Is it likely hotels would be willing to have rooms remain vacant so that the incumbent tour operators could reduce the number of vacations?

Post–Merger Entry Analysis in Other Nations

Many other nations similarly consider whether low entry barriers undermine the likelihood that a merger might create anticompetitive effects.[50] The analysis elsewhere is similar to that in the U.S. and EU.

---

50. *See, e.g.,* Australia Trade Practices Act § 50(3)(b); Australia Merger Guidelines §§ 7.17–7.32 (2008); Brazil Horizontal Merger Guidelines §§ 45–59 (2001); Canada Competition Act § 93(d); Canada Merger Guidelines §§ 6.1–6.17 (2004); Chile, Horizontal Merger Guidelines IV. 3 (2006); India Competition Act § 20(4)(b); Japan Business Combination Guidelines 28–29 (2004); New Zealand Mergers Guidelines § 6.1 (2004); Singapore Merger

4. EFFICIENCIES & WEIGHING THE EQUITIES

U.S. DOJ/FTC, Horizontal Merger Guidelines
(2010).

10. Efficiencies

Competition usually spurs firms to achieve efficiencies internally. Nevertheless, a primary benefit of mergers to the economy is their potential to generate significant efficiencies and thus enhance the merged firm's ability and incentive to compete, which may result in lower prices, improved quality, enhanced service, or new products. For example, merger-generated efficiencies may enhance competition by permitting two ineffective competitors to form a more effective competitor, e.g., by combining complementary assets. In a unilateral effects context, incremental cost reductions may reduce or reverse any increases in the merged firm's incentive to elevate price. Efficiencies also may lead to new or improved products, even if they do not immediately and directly affect price. In a coordinated effects context, incremental cost reductions may make coordination less likely or effective by enhancing the incentive of a maverick to lower price or by creating a new maverick firm. Even when efficiencies generated through a merger enhance a firm's ability to compete, however, a merger may have other effects that may lessen competition and make the merger anticompetitive.

The Agencies credit only those efficiencies likely to be accomplished with the proposed merger and unlikely to be accomplished in the absence of either the proposed merger or another means having comparable anticompetitive effects. These are termed merger-specific efficiencies.[13] Only alternatives that are practical in the business situation faced by the merging firms are considered in making this determination. The Agencies do not insist upon a less restrictive alternative that is merely theoretical.

Efficiencies are difficult to verify and quantify, in part because much of the information relating to efficiencies is uniquely in the possession of the merging firms. Moreover, efficiencies projected reasonably and in good faith by the merging firms may not be realized. Therefore, it is incumbent upon the merging firms to substantiate efficiency claims so that the Agencies can verify by reasonable means the likelihood and magnitude of each asserted efficiency, how and when each would be achieved (and any costs of doing so), how each would enhance the merged firm's ability and incentive to compete, and why each would be merger-specific.

Efficiency claims will not be considered if they are vague, speculative, or otherwise cannot be verified by reasonable means. Projections of efficien-

---

Guidelines § 7.6 (2007); South Africa Competition Act § 12A(2)(b); South Korea Merger Guidelines VII.1.E (2009); Taiwan Merger Guidelines Art. IX.3 (2006); Turkey Merger Communiqué (No. 2010/4), Art. 13(1).

13. The Agencies will not deem efficiencies to be merger-specific if they could be attained by practical alternatives that mitigate competitive concerns, such as divestiture or licensing. If a merger affects not whether but only when an efficiency would be achieved, only the timing advantage is a merger-specific efficiency.

cies may be viewed with skepticism, particularly when generated outside of the usual business planning process. By contrast, efficiency claims substantiated by analogous past experience are those most likely to be credited.

Cognizable efficiencies are merger-specific efficiencies that have been verified and do not arise from anticompetitive reductions in output or service. Cognizable efficiencies are assessed net of costs produced by the merger or incurred in achieving those efficiencies.

The Agencies will not challenge a merger if cognizable efficiencies are of a character and magnitude such that the merger is not likely to be anticompetitive in any relevant market.[14] To make the requisite determination, the Agencies consider whether cognizable efficiencies likely would be sufficient to reverse the merger's potential to harm customers in the relevant market, e.g., by preventing price increases in that market.[15] In conducting this analysis, the Agencies will not simply compare the magnitude of the cognizable efficiencies with the magnitude of the likely harm to competition absent the efficiencies. The greater the potential adverse competitive effect of a merger, the greater must be the cognizable efficiencies, and the more they must be passed through to customers, for the Agencies to conclude that the merger will not have an anticompetitive effect in the relevant market. When the potential adverse competitive effect of a merger is likely to be particularly substantial, extraordinarily great cognizable efficiencies would be necessary to prevent the merger from being anticompetitive. In adhering to this approach, the Agencies are mindful that the antitrust laws give competition, not internal operational efficiency, primacy in protecting customers.

In the Agencies' experience, efficiencies are most likely to make a difference in merger analysis when the likely adverse competitive effects, absent the efficiencies, are not great. Efficiencies almost never justify a merger to monopoly or near-monopoly. Just as adverse competitive effects can arise along multiple dimensions of conduct, such as pricing and new product development, so too can efficiencies operate along multiple dimensions. Similarly, purported efficiency claims based on lower prices can be undermined if they rest on reductions in product quality or variety that customers value.

---

14. The Agencies normally assess competition in each relevant market affected by a merger independently and normally will challenge the merger if it is likely to be anticompetitive in any relevant market. In some cases, however, the Agencies in their prosecutorial discretion will consider efficiencies not strictly in the relevant market, but so inextricably linked with it that a partial divestiture or other remedy could not feasibly eliminate the anticompetitive effect in the relevant market without sacrificing the efficiencies in the other market(s). Inextricably linked efficiencies are most likely to make a difference when they are great and the likely anticompetitive effect in the relevant market(s) is small so the merger is likely to benefit customers overall.

15. The Agencies normally give the most weight to the results of this analysis over the short term. The Agencies also may consider the effects of cognizable efficiencies with no short-term, direct effect on prices in the relevant market. Delayed benefits from efficiencies (due to delay in the achievement of, or the realization of customer benefits from, the efficiencies) will be given less weight because they are less proximate and more difficult to predict. Efficiencies relating to costs that are fixed in the short term are unlikely to benefit customers in the short term, but can benefit customers in the longer run, e.g., if they make new product introduction less expensive.

The Agencies have found that certain types of efficiencies are more likely to be cognizable and substantial than others. For example, efficiencies resulting from shifting production among facilities formerly owned separately, which enable the merging firms to reduce the incremental cost of production, are more likely to be susceptible to verification and are less likely to result from anticompetitive reductions in output. Other efficiencies, such as those relating to research and development, are potentially substantial but are generally less susceptible to verification and may be the result of anticompetitive output reductions. Yet others, such as those relating to procurement, management, or capital cost, are less likely to be merger-specific or substantial, or may not be cognizable for other reasons.

When evaluating the effects of a merger on innovation, the Agencies consider the ability of the merged firm to conduct research or development more effectively. Such efficiencies may spur innovation but not affect short-term pricing. The Agencies also consider the ability of the merged firm to appropriate a greater fraction of the benefits resulting from its innovations. Licensing and intellectual property conditions may be important to this enquiry, as they affect the ability of a firm to appropriate the benefits of its innovation. Research and development cost savings may be substantial and yet not be cognizable efficiencies because they are difficult to verify or result from anticompetitive reductions in innovative activities ...

EU Guidelines on the Assessment of Horizontal Mergers
O.J. 2004, C 31/5.

VII. EFFICIENCIES ... The Commission considers any substantiated efficiency claim in the overall assessment of the merger. It may decide that, as a consequence of the efficiencies that the merger brings about, there are no grounds for declaring the merger incompatible with the common market pursuant to Article 2(3) of the Merger Regulation. This will be the case when the Commission is in a position to conclude on the basis of sufficient evidence that the efficiencies generated by the merger are likely to enhance the ability and incentive of the merged entity to act pro-competitively for the benefit of consumers, thereby counteracting the adverse effects on competition which the merger might otherwise have.

For the Commission to take account of efficiency claims in its assessment of the merger and be in a position to reach the conclusion that as a consequence of efficiencies, there are no grounds for declaring the merger to be incompatible with the common market, the efficiencies have to benefit consumers, be merger-specific and be verifiable. These conditions are cumulative.

Benefit to consumers. The relevant benchmark in assessing efficiency claims is that consumers will not be worse off as a result of the merger. For that purpose, efficiencies should be substantial and timely, and should, in principle, benefit consumers in those relevant markets where it is otherwise likely that competition concerns would occur.

Mergers may bring about various types of efficiency gains that can lead to lower prices or other benefits to consumers. For example, cost savings in production or distribution may give the merged entity the ability and incentive to charge lower prices following the merger. In line with the need to ascertain whether efficiencies will lead to a net benefit to consumers, cost efficiencies that lead to reductions in variable or marginal costs are more likely to be relevant to the assessment of efficiencies than reductions in fixed costs; the former are, in principle, more likely to result in lower prices for consumers. Cost reductions, which merely result from anti-competitive reductions in output, cannot be considered as efficiencies benefiting consumers.

Consumers may also benefit from new or improved products or services, for instance resulting from efficiency gains in the sphere of R&D and innovation. A joint venture company set up in order to develop a new product may bring about the type of efficiencies that the Commission can take into account.

In the context of coordinated effects, efficiencies may increase the merged entity's incentive to increase production and reduce prices, and thereby reduce its incentive to coordinate its market behaviour with other firms in the market. Efficiencies may therefore lead to a lower risk of coordinated effects in the relevant market.

In general, the later the efficiencies are expected to materialise in the future, the less weight the Commission can assign to them. This implies that, in order to be considered as a counteracting factor, the efficiencies must be timely.

The incentive on the part of the merged entity to pass efficiency gains on to consumers is often related to the existence of competitive pressure from the remaining firms in the market and from potential entry. The greater the possible negative effects on competition, the more the Commission has to be sure that the claimed efficiencies are substantial, likely to be realised, and to be passed on, to a sufficient degree, to the consumer. It is highly unlikely that a merger leading to a market position approaching that of a monopoly, or leading to a similar level of market power, can be declared compatible with the common market on the ground that efficiency gains would be sufficient to counteract its potential anti-competitive effects.

Merger specificity. Efficiencies are relevant to the competitive assessment when they are a direct consequence of the notified merger and cannot be achieved to a similar extent by less anticompetitive alternatives. In these circumstances, the efficiencies are deemed to be caused by the merger and thus, merger-specific. It is for the merging parties to provide in due time all the relevant information necessary to demonstrate that there are no less anti-competitive, realistic and attainable alternatives of a non-concentrative nature (e.g. a licensing agreement, or a cooperative joint venture) or of a concentrative nature (e.g. a concentrative joint venture, or a differently structured merger) than the notified merger which preserve the claimed efficiencies. The Commission only considers alternatives that are reasonably practical in the business situation faced by the merging parties having regard to established business practices in the industry concerned.

Verifiability. Efficiencies have to be verifiable such that the Commission can be reasonably certain that the efficiencies are likely to materialise, and be substantial enough to counteract a merger's potential harm to consumers. The more precise and convincing the efficiency claims are, the better the Commission can evaluate the claims. Where reasonably possible, efficiencies and the resulting benefit to consumers should therefore be quantified. When the necessary data are not available to allow for a precise quantitative analysis, it must be possible to foresee a clearly identifiable positive impact on consumers, not a marginal one. In general, the longer the start of the efficiencies is projected into the future, the less probability the Commission may be able to assign to the efficiencies actually being brought about.

Most of the information, allowing the Commission to assess whether the merger will bring about the sort of efficiencies that would enable it to clear a merger, is solely in the possession of the merging parties. It is, therefore, incumbent upon the notifying parties to provide in due time all the relevant information necessary to demonstrate that the claimed efficiencies are merger-specific and likely to be realized. Similarly, it is for the notifying parties to show to what extent the efficiencies are likely to counteract any adverse effects on competition that might otherwise result from the merger, and therefore benefit consumers.

Evidence relevant to the assessment of efficiency claims includes, in particular, internal documents that were used by the management to decide on the merger, statements from the management to the owners and financial markets about the expected efficiencies, historical examples of efficiencies and consumer benefit, and pre-merger external experts' studies on the type and size of efficiency gains, and on the extent to which consumers are likely to benefit.

Questions on U.S. and EU Guidelines

1. Suppose a merger decreases producer costs by $100 million but increases consumer prices by $10 million. Is such a merger condemned under these guidelines? What does that suggest about whether the standard is consumer welfare or total welfare? Which is the best standard?

2. Why is a merger that reduces variable or marginal costs more likely to lower consumer prices than reductions in fixed costs? Could a reduction in fixed costs also decrease consumer prices, especially in a market characterized by monopolistic competition? See Chapter 3.B.1.

3. The U.S. and EU guidelines also generally require that efficiencies must benefit consumers in the market where the mergers create anticompetitive concerns, and thus do not allow efficiencies in one product or geographic market to offset anticompetitive effects in another.[51]

a. Does this make sense on a consumer welfare standard? Is it unnecessarily rigid to forego large efficiencies and consumer gain in one market to avoid small consumer harm in another market? Or does a market-by-market inquiry make sense because firms can generally divest assets to avoid harm in particular markets and go ahead with the merger on other markets?

---

51. *See also Philadelphia National Bank*, 374 U.S. at 370–71.

b. Would it still make sense if effects in the two markets are inextricably linked with each other because any divestiture necessary to eliminate the anticompetitive effect in one market would prevent the economic integration necessary to achieve the efficiency in the other market? Does this explain U.S. Guidelines footnote 15?

4. The U.S. and EU guidelines both state that it is highly unlikely that a merger leading to monopoly or similar levels of market power can be justified by efficiency gains. Why should that be the case?

5. Given that decisions to merge reflect a calculated risk about merger synergies that often do not pan out in practice, won't it be hard for merging parties to prove those efficiencies are verifiable, merger-specific, and large enough to counteract any harm to consumers? In fact, it is not clear the agencies have ever concluded that an efficiency defense saved a merger that the agencies felt would be anticompetitive but for those efficiencies.

6. Wouldn't it be even harder for agencies to prove the absence of sufficient efficiencies? Who should bear the burden of production and persuasion on this issue?

Merger Efficiencies and Total v. Consumer Welfare

Efficiencies that lower fixed costs but not marginal costs are unlikely to lower prices charged to consumers, unless the fixed costs are recurring and the market reflects the sort of monopolistic competition discussed in Chapter 3. A merger that lowers marginal costs might also fail to lower consumer prices if it increases market power. Suppose, for example, the pre-merger firm-specific demand elasticity of a firm is 2 and a proposed merger would increase market power by lowering that elasticity by 10%. Without a marginal cost decrease, it would raise price by 12.5%.[52] Marginal costs would have to drop by over 11% to offset this additional power to raise prices and make the merger benefit consumer welfare.[53]

However, if one instead makes total welfare the standard, then modest cost decreases can offset larger price increases. If demand elasticity is 2, then a cost decrease of .25% suffices to offset the negative effect on total welfare of a price increase of 5%, and a cost decrease of 9% offsets a price increase of 30%.[54] The essential reason is that a cost decrease creates an efficiency gain over the producer's entire output. A price increase, in contrast, creates an efficiency loss only for the marginal output that is lost because some consumers will no longer buy the product. (The price increase for the remaining output is a transfer payment from consumers to producers that does not alter efficiency, though it obviously has a distributive effect.)

---

52. Recall from Chapter 3 that (P–MC)/P = 1/ϵ. An initial elasticity of 2 meant that P=2MC. If elasticity drops to 1.8, then that (P–MC)/P = 1/1.8, which implies P=2.25MC.

53. From the last footnote P=2.25MC. So to make the pre and post-merger prices the same, $2MC_{pre-merger} = 2.25MC_{post-merger}$. Thus, $MC_{post-merger} = 2/2.25MC_{pre-merger} = .888MC_{pre-merger}$

54. See Williamson, *Economies as an Antitrust Defense: The Welfare Tradeoffs*, 58 AMER. ECON. REV. 18, 22–23 (1968).

A merger law that prevents mergers that increase total welfare because they raise consumer prices can thus produce large amounts of inefficiency. Should merger law thus adopt a total welfare standard instead of consumer welfare standard? Or should it adopt some more complicated formula that considers the extent to which redistribution from consumers to shareholders is undesirable?

Commissioner of Competition v. Superior Propane Inc.

2000 Canada Comp. Trib. 16 (April 4, 2002).

[In an initial decision, the Canada Competition Tribunal concluded that the merger would raise propane prices by 8% but that under the Canada Competition Act § 96 efficiencies need only exceed the deadweight loss from a price increase, thus adopting a total surplus standard that excluded from consideration the transfer of wealth from consumers to the merging firms' shareholders.[47] The Federal Court of Appeal then set aside the Tribunal's findings, concluding that "the Tribunal erred in law when it interpreted § 96 as mandating that, in all cases, the only effects of an anticompetitive merger that may be balanced against the efficiencies created by the merger are those identified by the total surplus standard."[48] The Court said it was not competent to "prescribe the 'correct' methodology" but that

> "Whatever standard is selected (and, for all I know, the same standard may not be equally apposite for all mergers) must be more reflective than the total surplus standard of the different objectives of the Competition Act. It should also be sufficiently flexible in its application to enable the Tribunal fully to assess the particular fact situation before it. It seems to me that the balancing weights approach proposed by Professor Townley, and adopted by the Commissioner, meets those requirements."

The following opinion was then issued on remand to the Competition Tribunal.]

. . . Professor Townley adopts the following notation to describe the effects of the merger:

(a) the portion of lost consumer surplus (B) transferred to shareholders;

(b) the corresponding increase in the shareholder profit due to the higher price (B);

(c) the cost-savings (gains in efficiency) from the merger (A); and

(d) the loss of efficiency or deadweight loss (the remaining portion of lost consumer surplus) from the merger (C). . . .

---

47. Commissioner of Competition v. Superior Propane Inc., 2000 Comp. Trib. 15, at ¶¶ 252–53, 261, 451–58, 467 (August 30, 2000).

48. Commissioner of Competition v. Superior Propane Inc. (2001), 11 C.P.R. (4th) 289, at ¶¶ 139–41 (April 4, 2001).

According to Professor Townley, the Total Surplus Standard [provides that] a merger is approved if the loss of consumer surplus is exceeded by the increase in producer surplus. Using his notation, the merger is approved if: $(A+B) > (B+C)$. In this formulation, the income loss by consumers (B) equals the corresponding excess profit to shareholders due to the higher price (B). Unlike the Consumer Surplus Standard, the Total Surplus Standard includes the effect on shareholders but regards these gains and losses as exactly offsetting, so the test reduces to whether $A > C$. Accordingly, total surplus increases if the cost-savings exceed the deadweight (or efficiency) loss. . . .

Professor Townley's principal objection to the Total Surplus Standard is that it does not distinguish between shareholders of the merged firm and consumers of the product of the merged firm. If shareholders are uniformly better off than consumers, then the redistribution of income arising from the merger may be unfair to the less well-off group, and hence be socially adverse.

Presumably, however, if, . . . consumers were better off than the shareholders, Professor Townley would not be critical of a merger that was approved under a Total Surplus Standard. In that case, the redistribution of income would not be unfair to consumers because, by hypothesis, they are the better-off group to begin with. The merger would both increase efficiency and promote distributional fairness by transferring income to shareholders. Such redistributional effect would be socially positive.

The Tribunal notes that if the consumer and shareholder groups were each characterized by variability of income and wealth of their members, it might be difficult to characterize the redistribution of income arising from a merger as being unfair to one group or the other. . . .

In his Balancing Weights Approach, Professor Townley invites the Tribunal to attach a weight of unity to all producer gains from a merger. He proposes that a weight (w) be determined for all consumers ". . . because information on individual affected consumers is lacking . . .", such that the weighted surplus is zero, hence:

$$1(A+B) - w(B+C) = 0$$

where A, B and C are known quantitative estimates of the magnitudes of all of the effects of the merger. Solving this equation for w, the balancing weight, establishes the weight accorded to consumers as a group in order that the consumer loss and the producer gains are just balanced.

In the instant merger, the Commissioner submits that A equals $29.2 million, B equals $40.5 million, and C equals $3 million. On these figures, the balancing weight is found to be 1.6. Then, the Tribunal would decide whether the balancing weight was reasonable ". . . Based on whatever quantitative and qualitative information is available regarding the distributional impacts of a merger. . . ."

Using the Balancing Weights Approach to assess the distributional concerns in the instant case, the Tribunal must find that the weight that properly reflects the consumer loss is at least 60 percent higher than the weight on shareholder gains, assuming again that the consumer and shareholder groups are distinct and reasonably internally homogeneous. If it can so find, then that is a factor that counts against the merger, and must be considered with all other factors required to be considered. Indeed, if estimates of A, B, and C accurately described all of the effects of a merger, the appropriateness of the balancing weight would be determinative. Accordingly, if the Tribunal knew, or could derive, the correct weight, it would be able to determine whether or not that weight exceeded the balancing weight. . . .

In the Tribunal's view, the correct weight should be established by society or should reflect social attitudes toward equity among different income classes. There may be several sources from which the proper weighting can be inferred, one such being the tax system, which is explicitly, although not solely, concerned with equity. It is clear that the prevailing system of taxation in Canada does reflect a social consensus about the desirability of imposing burdens on different income classes. If tax rates are progressive with respect to income, then society has decided that the marginal dollar of income is worth less to the high-income taxpayer than it is to the low-income taxpayer. If, for example, the lowest tax rate is 20 percent and the highest is 50 percent, there is clear indication that low-income individuals are favoured over high-income individuals; assigning a weight of 1.0 to the latter group, the corresponding weight on the former would be 2.5. . . .

It appears to the Tribunal that if the proper weight is to be inferred from the tax system alone, then it is unlikely to be as high as 1.6 given the general proportionality of effective tax rates. However, the Tribunal would expect to have the benefit of expert opinion in matters as specialized as this. . . .

Differences Between Canadian and American Approaches to Mergers and Efficiencies. . . . It is clear that the Court has placed weight on the American approach to antitrust and on the views of American commentators who, in line with that approach, are antagonistic to the Total Surplus Standard. In so doing, the Court does not appear to take account of the historic and continuing hostility toward efficiencies in merger review under American antitrust law and the reasons for that hostility, and it may not have completely realized the several critical, and perhaps subtle, ways in which the merger provisions of Canada's Act differ from the antitrust statutes and the judicial histories thereof in the United States.

. . . [T]he Horizontal Merger Guidelines of the American enforcement agencies ("Horizontal Merger Guidelines") require that efficiency gains "cleanse" the merger of its harmful effects. In this way, the analysis of efficiencies is directly tied to the analysis of the merger's competitive effects on consumers. Only when the agencies are convinced that the negative effects have been eliminated will they decline to challenge the merger. The requirement that proven efficiency gains "cleanse" the anti-competitive merger arises in the United States from the absence of a specific affirmative statutory defence that would permit an anti-competitive merger to proceed.

The approach to efficiencies under subsection 96(1) of the Act is very different. There is no requirement for efficiency gains to prevent the effects of lessening or prevention of competition from occurring, and the Tribunal found accordingly.... Section 96 is worded accordingly by requiring that gains in efficiency be "greater than and offset" the effects of lessening or prevention of competition, rather than prevent those effects from occurring. Accordingly, "cleansing" of those effects is not required under the Act and, indeed, effects of lessening or prevention of competition may remain even when the test under section 96 is met.

[Under the U.S.] Horizontal Merger Guidelines note, ... in a merger where several relevant product and/or geographic markets have been delineated, the efficiency gains must reverse the harm in each such market. Accordingly, the insufficiency of those gains in even one relevant market can lead the enforcement agencies to disregard efficiency gains produced by the merger entirely.... [I]t is only when efficiencies are inextricably linked that inter-market trade-offs can be considered, but even that exception is rare and related to the inadequacy of the remedy.

By contrast, section 96 of the Act applies to the transaction in its entirety. There is no requirement that gains in efficiency in one market or area exceed and offset the effects in that market or area. Rather, the tests of "greater than" and "offset" in section 96 require a comparison of the aggregate gains in efficiency with the aggregate of the effects of lessening or prevention of competition across all markets and areas. Accordingly, the Act clearly contemplates that some markets or areas may experience gains in efficiency that exceed the effects therein, while others may not.

... Given the historical American concern with preventing increases in industrial concentration and the possible political ramifications of conjoining economic and political power, efficiency concerns have been given much less importance. The same cannot be said for Canada. Since industrial concentration was already high in certain sectors and because of the increased openness of the Canadian economy to foreign competition, further increases in domestic concentration were deemed less important than the gains in economic efficiency that could be obtained, if proven.... "... smallness of market also means a greater probability of the existence of non-captured scale and other economies...." Given the size of the American economy and the historic purpose of American antitrust laws, it is not surprising that the potential for losing scale economies was not a significant concern ... In a globally more liberal environment for international trade and investment, the efficiency defence in section 96 allows the possibility that mergers among major Canadian businesses may produce entities that may possibly compete more effectively with large foreign enterprises at home and abroad.

... [Under the U.S.] Horizontal Merger Guidelines, claimed efficiency gains must be "merger-specific". Although those Guidelines do not elaborate, this requirement appears to mean that a claimed efficiency gain is not cognizable if it could be achieved in another, presumably less anticompetitive, way. The Tribunal found that the gains in efficiency in the instant merger would not be achieved absent the merger (i.e. if the order were made) and hence could be included.... This requirement is not the same as the one used by the American enforcement agencies.... The Commissioner may require that efficiency gains be merger-specific when deciding whether to challenge a merger. However, once an application is brought under the Act, included efficiency gains are "order-driven" rather than "merger-specific"....

IS THE ENTIRE TRANSFER NECESSARILY INCLUDED? ... The Commissioner's position is that the measured redistributive effect must be taken into account in its entirety even when the consumers and shareholders are the same people.... In the Tribunal's view, there is no policy choice to favour consumers in the merger provisions of the Act. The Tribunal concluded that efficiency was the paramount objective of the merger provisions of the Act, and the Court agreed while requiring that the transfer be considered under subsection 96(1). A similar policy choice to favour efficiency is found in section 86 of the Act which permits higher prices to consumers if efficiencies are large enough to justify the specialization agreement.

A second reason for rejecting the necessity of including the entire amount of the transfer is that doing so vitiates the statutory efficiency defence.... [W]here the price elasticity of demand is–1.0 and the consequential price increase is 10 percent, the wealth transfer will be 20 times the deadweight loss (for constant elasticity of demand). Accordingly, proven efficiency gains would be insufficient unless they were at least 21 times greater than the deadweight loss. For linear demand under the same conditions, the wealth transfer will be 22 times the deadweight loss. Hence, proven efficiency gains would be insufficient unless they were at least 23 times greater than the deadweight loss.

By comparison, the proven efficiency gains in the instant merger ($29.2 million) are approximately 10 times the measured deadweight loss. Thus, even where the deadweight loss is relatively small and the proven efficiency gains are substantial in comparison, the latter will almost always be insufficient if the entire transfer were required to be included.... Accordingly, a second reason for not requiring the full inclusion of the transfer, as a matter of law, is that it would make the defence of efficiency in section 96 unavailable except in rare circumstances, hence vitiating a statutory provision the paramount objective of which is economic efficiency.

... [T]he Tribunal will not revisit its conclusions that the $3 million estimate of deadweight loss submitted by the Commissioner is probably overstated and that the total deadweight loss is most unlikely to exceed $6 million.... The Commissioner further quotes the American authors noted above who make the point that the redistributive effects can have additional negative implications for efficiency. Citing articles by R. Posner and by R. Lande, these authors argue that the redistributed income will eventually be transformed into efficiency losses because the merged firm may become complacent and allow costs to rise. To the Tribunal, this interesting observation suggests that the estimated deadweight loss from the instant merger is too low. However, these inferences are unsupported by anything on the record and the Tribunal will not consider them further....

TRIBUNAL'S ANALYSIS OF THE TRANSFER.... In the simplest analysis, the redistribution of income that results from an anti-competitive merger of producers has a negative effect on consumers (through loss of consumer surplus) and a corresponding positive effect on shareholders (excess profit). Whether these two effects are completely or only partially offsetting is a social decision that, in Professor Townley's words, requires a value judgment and will depend on the characteristics of those consumers and shareholders. In some cases, society may be more concerned about one group than the other. In that case, the redistribution of income will not be neutral to society but rather will be seen as a social cost of, or social gain from, the merger.

Yet it is rarely so clear where or how the redistributive effects are experienced. As Williamson notes:

> For some products, however, the interests of users might warrant greater weight than those of sellers; for other products, such as products produced by disadvantaged minorities and sold to the very rich, a reversal might be indicated. But a general case that user interests greatly outweigh seller interests is not easy to make and possibly reflects a failure to appreciate that profits ramify through the system in ways—such as taxes, dividends, and retained earnings—that greatly attenuate the notion that monolithic producer interests exist and are favored . . .

(O. Williamson, Economies as an Antitrust Defense Revisited, volume 125, No. 4, University of Pennsylvania Law Review, 1977,699, at 711)

When viewed in this light, the redistributive effects are generally difficult to identify correctly, and will involve multiple social decisions. Given the informational requirements of such assessments, the assumption of neutrality could be appropriate in many circumstances.

. . . [T]he Tribunal must accept that the redistributional effects can legitimately be considered neutral in some instances, but not in others. Fairness and equity require complete data on socio-economic profiles on consumers and shareholders of producers to know whether the redistributive effects are socially neutral, positive or adverse. While complete data may never be attainable, the Tribunal must be able to establish on the evidence the socially adverse effects of the transfer. . . .

Following the instruction of the Court, the Tribunal would adopt the Balancing Weights Approach if there were sufficient information in evidence to come to an assessment of whether the estimated balancing weight of 1.6 is reasonable given the socio-economic differences between and among consumers and shareholders. . . . [T]he Commissioner submits that in view of the record in its entirety, there is no basis for concluding that a weight of 1.6 or less is reasonable. There is, however, some limited information in the record that the Tribunal can use to reach a conclusion on the redistributive effects.

. . . [P]ropane expenditure constitutes 1.68 percent of the total expenditure of the 20 percent of households with the lowest income (i.e. the lowest-income quintile). For the 20 percent of households that have the highest income (the highest-income quintile), propane spending is only 0.07 percent thereof. Professor Townley notes that while absolute spending does not display this pattern, the fact that bottled propane expenditure decreases as a share of total expenditure as income rises indicates to him that a price increase would have a relatively larger impact the lower one's income.

. . . 4.7 percent of the households in the lowest-income quintile and 29.1 percent of households in the highest-income quintile consume bottled propane. Accordingly, consumption of bottled propane is not limited to low-income groups.... "... Although some consumers purchase propane for less than essential purposes, such as heating their swimming pools, most purchase it for home heating, automotive fuel and industrial purposes...." 53 percent of Superior's residential customers use propane for heating and 10 percent to heat a swimming pool.

The Tribunal cannot avoid the conclusion that the redistributive effect of the merger on low-income households that purchase propane will be socially adverse. As suggested above, however, the number of such households is quite small and some undetermined number of them may not be using propane for essential purposes.

The Tribunal places less weight on the redistributive effect on households which, as the respondents observe, use propane for swimming pools, barbeques, heating second homes, cottages and ski chalets. Many, although not necessarily all, of those households will presumably be in the higher income groups. The record is silent in this regard....

The Tribunal notes further that since 90 percent of the merged firm's sales will be to other businesses, the impact of the price increase will fall on the products of those firms and will, through interrelated markets, ultimately be borne by business owners and household purchasers throughout the economy, to the extent that they are not borne by the lower profits of owners of those businesses that purchase the propane directly from the merged company. How the burden of the price increase is ultimately shared across business owners in interrelated markets and by households is an important question that is difficult to answer. Certainly, however, shareholders of the merged firm will not escape the price increases.

Yet, having regard to the evidence of regressivity of the price increase on consumers of "bottled propane" discussed above, there is no basis for assuming that outcome generally. The price increase may hit higher income groups disproportionately depending on their consumption patterns and on the extent to which propane is involved in the production of those goods and services. There is no evidence according to which such incidence of the price increase on 90 percent of initial propane sales might be inferred.

There may well be some small and medium-sized businesses that are only marginally profitable and also unable to pass on the price increase. However, there is no information on the record that would allow the Tribunal to assess the number of such enterprises or to distinguish between them and those that are perhaps quite successful. In the former, the redistribution of profit to the shareholders of the merged firm might not be socially neutral; in the latter, perhaps, it would be....

Based on its review of the evidence, the Tribunal cannot agree with the respondents' position that the redistributive effects are completely neutral. It is our view that the gains and losses are not completely offsetting and that there is a social loss that requires consideration.

However, on the basis of the evidence, the Tribunal cannot find that such loss is measured by the Commissioner's measured transfer of $40.5 million per annum, because the Commissioner has not demonstrated that that amount is the socially adverse effect. There is considerable reason to think that portions, perhaps significant portions, of the measured transfer are redistributions of profit among shareholders that society would regard neutrally.

The evidence tends to support the socially adverse redistributive effects regarding low income households that use propane for essential purposes and have no good alternatives, but the number of such households appears to be small. In the Balancing Weights Approach of Professor Townley, the interests of those households should be weighted more heavily than the interests of the shareholders of the merged firm, but the higher weight is not determinable given the information on the record. In the Tribunal's view, the interests of other households and business owners should be weighted equally with shareholders of the merged firm in this case, particularly since, as the Commissioner has noted, all producers are, in a sense, consumers as well.

The Tribunal notes that it is possible to quantify the adverse redistributive effects of the transfer on household consumers of bottled propane in the lowest-income quintile ... As there are approximately 102,465 consuming households in that group, and as the average expenditure per consuming household in that group is $277 per year, total sales to that group are approximately $28.4 million per mum. Since the Commissioner's measured deadweight loss assumes a demand elasticity of –1.5 and a price increase to residential consumers in general of 11 percent, the transfer is 9.2 percent of sales. . . . Accordingly, on the Commissioner's evidence, the measured adverse redistributive effect on that group is approximately $2.6 million. This estimate assumes that all propane consumed by households in this group is for essential purposes.

CONCLUSIONS. It is clear, in our view, that the Court did not direct us to consider the entire amount of the wealth transfer as an "effect" of the lessening or prevention of competition. . . . Having assessed the measured adverse redistributive effect based on the evidence, it remains for the Tribunal to decide how to combine it with the measured deadweight loss of $3 million and the maximum deadweight loss attributable to changes in the merged company's product line of $3 million. Weighting redistributive effects equally with efficiency losses, the three effects would be added together to produce a maximum total effect of approximately $8.6 million.

However, there is no statutory basis under the Act (or in U.S. antitrust law) for assuming such equal weighting: perhaps the adverse redistributive effects should weigh twice as heavily as efficiency losses, in which case the three weighted effects would not exceed $11.2 million. Alternatively, since efficiency concerns are paramount in merger review, perhaps adverse redistributive effects should be weighted half as much as deadweight losses. In the instant case, it is clear that the adverse redistributive effects are, on the evidence, quite small. Accordingly, the Tribunal is of the view that any under any reasonable weighting scheme, the gains in efficiency of $29.2 million are greater than and offset all of the effects of lessening and prevention of competition attributable to the merger under review. . . .

This decision has been a very difficult exercise. [We agree with Professor Stanbury that § 96:]

"raises a number of difficult questions. The first and most important is the matter of incommensurability—namely, that the tribunal will be asked to deal and make a judgment between a lessening
of competition, which will probably result in higher prices, and
gains in efficiency, which are real savings to society. These are not
comparable kinds of things because one involves a redistribution of
income and the other involved real gains in terms of the savings of
resources.

*"Second, there is an inherent and unavoidable value judgment
that the tribunal must make in dealing with [§ 96]. The sad part is
that Parliament has given no guidance to the tribunal as to its
priorities, as to the weights to be applied to the lessening of
competition [effects] and gains in efficiency.... Parliament should
decide and give instructions to the tribunal as to what values it
wants the tribunals to adopt...."*

It was the Tribunal's initial view, on its acceptance of the Total
Surplus Standard, that the Act did not give rise to the difficulties to which
Professor Stanbury referred. However, in light of the Court's Appeal
Judgment, we feel that, as Professor Stanbury pointed out ..., subsection
96(1) requires the Tribunal to compare matters that cannot be easily, if at
all, compared. On the one hand, there are efficiencies, which are real
savings to society, and on the other hand, there are the redistribution
effects which arise by reason of a price increase. We have attempted to
render the incomparable "comparable" by, whenever possible, quantifying
the effects. We have not been totally successful in this endeavour but we
have come to the conclusion that the $29.2 million of efficiencies brought
about by the merger is greater than and outweighs the "effects" of the
lessening of competition....

[On re-appeal to the Federal Court of Appeal, it sustained this decision
in 2003, concluding that the Tribunal was right not to apply a consumer
surplus standard that would deem the entire welfare transfer as anticompetitive, and properly exercised discretion in deciding how much of the
welfare transfer to count an anticompetitive effect.[49] The Canada Competition Bureau then adopted merger guidelines in 2004 providing: "There is
currently no statutory basis for assuming any fixed set of weighting
between redistributive effects, deadweight losses and efficiency gains. Such
weighting depends on the facts of a particular case. Because all gains must
be weighed against all effects, the exercise of judgment is required when
combining measured gains (effects) with qualitative gains (effects) for the
purpose of performing the trade-off."[50]]

Note and Questions on *Superior Propane*

1. Do courts have any principled basis for determining how much
weight to give to redistributions of wealth?

---

49. Commissioner of Competition v. Superior Propane Inc., 2003 F.C.A. 53.

50. Canada Merger Guidelines § 8.34 (2004).

2. Is redistributing wealth from consumers to shareholders always bad?

3. Assuming courts had a principled basis for assessing redistributions, are there any administrable standards for deciding the extent to which a transfer of wealth from consumers to producers implicates undesirable redistributions for a particular merger?

4. If there are no real legal standards for deciding how much weight to give to redistributions in particular mergers, would it be better to either give no weight to such transfers (by adopting a total welfare standard) or 100% to them (by adopting a consumer welfare standard)?

5. As we will see in Chapter 8, the consumers affected by this merger were mainly outside of Canada. Do you think this might help explain why the Canadian courts were inclined to underweigh the interests of consumers? If mergers in a nation mainly affect export industries, will it be inclined more toward a total welfare standard than a consumer welfare standard?

6. One reason one might not want to adopt a total welfare standard is the theory that if a firm enjoys monopoly rents, those rents will tend to be dissipated by the costs of obtaining them or by managerial inefficiency.[55] If this is true, should we exclude producer surplus and thus adopt a consumer welfare standard? Or should courts engage in case-by-case inquiry of the extent to which this is true, as the Tribunal suggested and Canada Guideline 8.29 now provides?

7. Many of the most famous persons accused of anticompetitive conduct, such as Standard Oil's John Rockefeller and Microsoft's Bill Gates, devoted much of their monopoly profits to charities. Under a *Superior Propane* approach, must the distributional effects of such future donations be taken into account?

Consumer Trusts and Other Coasian Solutions to the Total v. Consumer Welfare Debate

If a merger would increase total welfare, couldn't merging parties always structure the deal in such a way as to satisfy a consumer welfare test too? That is, if the dollar gains to the merging parties exceed the dollar losses to consumers, one would think the merging parties could devise some mechanism to transfer enough of their gain to consumers to offset any losses to those consumers. One possibility is simply committing not to raise prices or lower output, though that may raise difficulties if market conditions indicate prices or output should change over time or if there are concerns firms might lower quality.

---

55. *See* Richard A. Posner, The Social Costs of Monopoly and Regulation, in James M. Buchanan, Robert D. Tollison, and Gordon Tullock, eds., Toward a Theory of the Rent–Seeking Society 71 (Texas A & M 1980) (arguing that the cost of competing to become a monopolist increases the deadweight loss of monopoly by eating up even the monopolist's surplus); Elhauge, *Defining Better Monopolization Standards*, 56 STANFORD LAW REVIEW 253, 299–300 (2003) (summarizing X-inefficiency theory that monopolists exhibit greater agency costs and other inefficiencies).

Another possibility would be to allow firms to create some sort of consumer trust. For example, if the objection to a merger efficiency is that it lowers fixed costs but not marginal costs, then merging firms could create a trust, funded out of their reduction in fixed costs, that pays merged firms a dollar sum for every unit they sell. In this way, the trust could convert a reduction in the firms' fixed costs into a reduction in their marginal costs. If the concern is that the merging firms will not pass on a sufficient share of the reduction in their marginal costs to make consumers better off, the trust could pay consumers a sum for every unit they purchase, though this would also cause shifts in the demand curve that would have to be taken into account. Whatever the details, one would think merging firms with large net efficiency gains in the offing could put together some sort of Coasian deal that makes them better off without harming consumers, unless the transaction costs of doing so are so large they exceed the net efficiency gains.

An additional benefit to this approach is that it helps avoid the problem that agencies may have a much harder time than merging firms in assessing the amount of efficiencies. If the merging parties are really confident that the size of their efficiencies offsets the consumer harm, then they should be willing to fund a plan to offset any consumer harm.

In short, the best justification for a consumer welfare test may not be that it is a better measure of social desirability than total welfare. It may rather be that a consumer welfare test allows mergers that increase total welfare as long as the merging firms are willing to compensate for any adverse effects on consumers, which forces merging firms to put their money where their mouth is on the claim that efficiency gains offset consumer harm.

Other Nations' Treatment of Efficiencies

Many other nations follow the U.S.–EU approach of considering efficiencies only to the extent they improve the welfare of consumers.[56] Some other nations similarly do not seem to weigh producer surplus in the balance, but do consider whether the efficiencies benefit the national economy more generally.[57] South Africa takes a distinctive position. It uses a sliding scale where the more the claimed efficiencies constitute "real" efficiencies like dynamic or productive efficiencies, the less compelling the evidence has to be that they were passed on to consumers, whereas the more the claimed efficiencies constitute less compelling efficiencies like "pecuniary" ones or "mere redistribution of income from customers, suppliers, or employees to the merged entity," the more compelling the proof has to be that they were sufficiently passed on to consumers.[58] Should the latter sort of efficiencies count at all?

56. These nations include Argentina, Brazil, Chile. Colombia, Israel, Japan, Mexico, Turkey, and Venezuela. *See, e.g.,* Brazil Horizontal Merger Guidelines § 87 (2001); Chile Horizontal Merger Guidelines IV. 6.1 (2006); Colombia Decree 2153/92, Art. 51; Turkey Merger Communiqué (No. 2010/4), art. 13(1).

57. *See* Australia Trade Practices Act § 90(9A); South Africa Competition § 12A(3); South Korea Merger Guidelines VIII.1 (2009).

58. *See* Trident Steel/Dorbyl, 89/LM/OCT00, ¶ 81 (South Africa Competition Tribunal).

FTC v. Staples, Inc.

970 F.Supp. 1066 (D.D.C. 1997).

... **I. SECTION 13(b) STANDARD FOR PRELIMINARY INJUNCTIVE RELIEF**

... [I]n a suit for preliminary relief, the FTC is not required to prove, nor is the Court required to find, that the proposed merger would in fact violate Section 7 of the Clayton Act.... Section 13(b) of the Federal Trade Commission Act, provides that "[u]pon a proper showing that, weighing the equities and considering the Commission's likelihood of ultimate success, such action would be in the public interest, and after notice to the defendant, a temporary restraining order or a preliminary injunction may be granted without bond."[2] Courts have interpreted this to mean that a court must engage in a two-part analysis in determining whether to grant an injunction under section 13(b). (1) First, the Court must determine the Commission's likelihood of success on the merits in its case under Section 7 of the Clayton Act, and (2) Second, the Court must balance the equities....

It is not enough for the FTC to show merely that it has a "fair and tenable chance" of ultimate success on the merits as has been argued and rejected in other cases. However, the FTC need not prove to a certainty that the merger will have an anti-competitive effect. That is a question left to the Commission after a full administrative hearing. Instead, in a suit for a preliminary injunction, the government need only show that there is a "reasonable probability" that the challenged transaction will substantially impair competition....

[Excerpts above contain the portions of the opinion defining the market, and finding likely anticompetitive effects that were not offset by low entry barriers.]

.... **VI. Efficiencies**

Whether an efficiencies defense showing that the intended merger would create significant efficiencies in the relevant market, thereby offsetting any anti-competitive effects, may be used by a defendant to rebut the government's prima facie case is not entirely clear. The newly revised efficiencies section of the *Merger Guidelines* recognizes that, "mergers have the potential to generate significant efficiencies by permitting a better utilization of existing assets, enabling the combined firm to achieve lower costs in producing a given quality and quantity than either firm could have achieved without the proposed transaction." This coincides with the view of some courts that "whether an acquisition would yield significant efficiencies in the relevant market is an important consideration in predicting whether the acquisition would substantially lessen competition.... [T]herefore, ... an efficiency defense to the government's prima facie case in section 7 challenges is appropriate in certain circumstances." *FTC v. University Health*, 938 F.2d 1206, 1222 (11th Cir.1991). The Supreme Court, however, in *FTC v. Procter & Gamble Co.*, 386 U.S. 568, 579 (1967), stated that "[p]ossible economics cannot be used as a defense to illegality in

---

2. The traditional "irreparable harm" element is absent from the Section 13(b) standard. In this respect, the section 13(b) standard is "lesser" than that which courts normally impose on private litigants seeking a preliminary injunction.

section 7 merger cases." There has been great disagreement regarding the meaning of this precedent and whether an efficiencies defense is permitted. *Compare RSR Corp. v. FTC,* 602 F.2d 1317, 1325 (9th Cir.1979) (finding that the efficiencies argument has been rejected repeatedly), *with University Health,* 938 F.2d at 1222 (recognizing the defense). Neither the Commission or the defendants could point to a case in which this Circuit has spoken on the issue. Assuming that it is a viable defense, however, the Court cannot find in this case that the defendants' efficiencies evidence rebuts the presumption that the merger may substantially lessen competition or shows that the Commission's evidence gives an inaccurate prediction of the proposed acquisition's probable effect.

The Court agrees with the defendants that where, as here, the merger has not yet been consummated, it is impossible to quantify precisely the efficiencies that it will generate. In addition, the Court recognizes a difference between efficiencies which are merely speculative and those which are based on a prediction backed by sound business judgment. Nor does the Court believe that the defendants must prove their efficiencies by "clear and convincing evidence" in order for those efficiencies to be considered by the Court. That would saddle Section 7 defendants with the nearly impossible task of rebutting a possibility with a certainty, a burden which was rejected in *Baker Hughes,* 908 F.2d at 992. Instead, like all rebuttal evidence in Section 7 cases, the defendants must simply rebut the presumption that the merger will substantially lessen competition by showing that the Commission's evidence gives an inaccurate prediction of the proposed acquisition's probable effect. Defendants, however, must do this with credible evidence, and the Court with respect to this issue did not find the defendants' evidence to be credible.

Defendants' submitted an "Efficiencies Analysis" which predicted that the combined company would achieve savings of between $4.9 and $6.5 billion over the next five years. In addition, the defendants argued that the merger would also generate dynamic efficiencies. For example, defendants argued that as suppliers become more efficient due to their increased sales volume to the combined Staples–Office Depot, they would be able to lower prices to their other retailers. Moreover, defendants argued that two-thirds of the savings realized by the combined company would be passed along to consumers.

  ... First, the Court notes that the cost savings estimate of $4.947 billion over five years which was submitted to the Court exceeds by almost 500% the figures presented to the two Boards of Directors in September 1996, when the Boards approved the transaction. ... The Court also finds that the defendants' projected "Base Case" savings of $5 billion are in large part unverified, or at least the defendants failed to produce the necessary documentation for verification.

  ... [T]he evidence shows that the defendants did not accurately calculate which projected cost savings were merger specific and which were, in fact, not related to the merger. For example, defendants' largest cost savings, over $2 billion or 40% of the total estimate, are projected as a result of their expectation of obtaining better prices from vendors. However, this figure was determined in relation to the cost savings enjoyed by

Staples at the end of 1996 without considering the additional cost savings that Staples would have received in the future as a stand-alone company. Since Staples has continuously sought and achieved cost savings on its own, clearly the comparison that should have been made was between the projected future cost savings of Staples as a stand-alone company, not its past rate of savings, and the projected future cost savings of the combined company. Thus, the calculation in the Efficiencies Analysis included product cost savings that Staples and Office Depot would likely have realized without the merger. In fact, [FTC expert] Mr. Painter testified that, by his calculation, 43% of the estimated savings are savings that Staples and Office Depot would likely have achieved as stand-alone entities. . . .

In addition to the problems that the Court has with the efficiencies estimates themselves, the Court also finds that the defendants' projected pass through rate—the amount of the projected savings that the combined company expects to pass on to customers in the form of lower prices—is unrealistic. The Court has no doubt that a portion of any efficiencies achieved through a merger of the defendants would be passed on to customers. Staples and Office Depot have a proven track record of achieving cost savings through efficiencies, and then passing those savings to customers in the form of lower prices. However, in this case the defendants have projected a pass through rate of two-thirds of the savings while the evidence shows that, historically, Staples has passed through only 15–17%. Based on the above evidence, the Court cannot find that the defendants have rebutted the presumption that the merger will substantially lessen competition by showing that, because of the efficiencies which will result from the merger, the Commission's evidence gives an inaccurate prediction of the proposed acquisition's probable effect. Therefore, the only remaining issue for the Court is the balancing of the equities.

VII. The Equities

Where, as in this case, the Court finds that the Commission has established a likelihood of success on the merits, a presumption in favor of a preliminary injunction arises. Despite this presumption, however, once the Court has determined the FTC's likelihood of success on the merits, it must still turn to and consider the equities. . . . The strong public interest in effective enforcement of the antitrust laws weighs heavily in favor of an injunction in this case, as does the need to preserve meaningful relief following a full administrative trial on the merits. "Unscrambling the eggs" after the fact is not a realistic option in this case. Both the plaintiff as well as the defendants introduced evidence regarding the combined company's post-merger plans, including the consolidation of warehouse and supply facilities in order to integrate the two distribution systems, the closing of 40 to 70 Office Depot and Staples stores, changing the name of the Office Depot stores, negotiating new contracts with manufacturers and suppliers, and, lastly, the consolidation of management which is likely to lead to the loss of employment for many of Office Depot's key personnel. As a result, the Court finds that it is extremely unlikely, if the Court denied the plaintiff's motion and the merger were to go through, that the merger could be effectively undone and the companies divided if the agency later found that the merger violated the antitrust laws. It would not simply be a matter of putting the old Office Depot signs back on the stores. Office Depot would have lost its name, many of its stores, its distribution centers, and key personnel. It would also be behind in future plans to open new stores and expand on its own.

More importantly, in addition to the practical difficulties in undoing the merger, consumers would be at risk of serious anti-competitive harm in the interim. Without an injunction, consumers in the 42 geographic markets where superstore competition would be eliminated or significantly reduced face the prospect of higher prices than they would have absent the merger. These higher charges could never be recouped even if the administrative proceeding resulted in a finding that the merger violated the antitrust laws. Failure to grant a preliminary injunction also would deny consumers the benefit of any new competition that would have occurred, absent the merger, between Staples and Office Depot as those stores continued to enter and compete in each other's markets. Both parties had aggressive expansion plans before the merger, many of which have been put on hold pending the outcome of this case. . . .

Note and Questions on *Staples*

As the court notes, there is no current U.S. Supreme Court caselaw that clearly recognizes an efficiency defense. Indeed, old U.S. Supreme Court cases (like old EU cases) tended to treat efficiencies as a ground for condemning a merger because it meant the merged firm would dominate other firms. But the new EU regulation overrides this, and an efficiency defense is commonly accepted in U.S. agencies and lower courts and it would be very surprising if the Supreme Court failed to recognize it given how its other antitrust caselaw has developed. However, efficiencies are not really a "defense" because establishing them does not suffice to eliminate liability. It is rather more accurate to say efficiencies are a factor considered in determining whether the merger will impose a net harm on consumers.

1. Was the court right to reject the offered efficiencies because they were exaggerated? Even discounted, weren't they quite high?

2. Was the court right to reject the offered efficiencies because it was not proven that most of them would be passed on to consumers? Even if the merged firms only followed Staples' historical practice of passing on 15–17% of cost savings, couldn't that be quite substantial?

FTC v. H.J. Heinz Co.

246 F.3d 708 (D.C. Cir. 2001).

■ KAREN LECRAFT HENDERSON, CIRCUIT JUDGE. . . . [Portions of the opinion finding presumptive anticompetitive effects are excerpted above].

    b.   Rebuttal Arguments . . .

2. Post-Merger Efficiencies. The appellees' second attempt to rebut the FTC's prima facie showing is their contention that the anticompetitive effects of the merger will be offset by efficiencies resulting from the union of the two companies, efficiencies which they assert will be used to compete more effectively against Gerber. It is true that a merger's primary benefit to the economy is its potential to generate efficiencies. As the *Merger Guidelines* now recognize, efficiencies "can enhance the merged firm's ability and incentive to compete, which may result in lower prices, improved quality, or new products."

Although the Supreme Court has not sanctioned the use of the efficiencies defense in a section 7 case, *see Procter & Gamble Co.,* 386 U.S. at 580,[18] the trend among lower courts is to recognize the defense. *See, e.g., FTC v. Tenet Health Care Corp.,* 186 F.3d 1045, 1054 (8th Cir.1999); *University Health,* 938 F.2d at 1222; *FTC v. Cardinal Health, Inc.,* 12 F.Supp.2d 34, 61 (D.D.C.1998); *Staples,* 970 F.Supp. at 1088–89; *see also* ABA Antitrust Section, *Mergers and Acquisitions: Understanding the Antitrust Issues* 152 (2000) ("The majority of courts have considered efficiencies as a means to rebut the government's prima facie case that a merger will lead to restricted output or increased prices. These courts, however, generally have found inadequate proof of efficiencies to sustain a rebuttal of the government's case."). In 1997 the Department of Justice and the FTC revised their Horizontal Merger Guidelines to recognize that "mergers have the potential to generate significant efficiencies by permitting a better utilization of existing assets, enabling the combined firm to achieve lower costs in producing a given quantity and quality than either firm could have achieved without the proposed transaction."

Nevertheless, the high market concentration levels present in this case require, in rebuttal, proof of extraordinary efficiencies, which the appellees failed to supply. *See University Health,* 938 F.2d at 1223 ("[A] defendant who seeks to overcome a presumption that a proposed acquisition would substantially lessen competition must demonstrate that the intended acquisition would result in significant economies and that these economies ultimately would benefit competition and, hence, consumers."); Horizontal Merger Guidelines § 4 (stating that "[e]fficiencies almost never justify a merger to monopoly or near-monopoly"); 4A Areeda, *et al., Antitrust Law* ¶ 971f, at 44 (requiring "extraordinary" efficiencies where the "HHI is well above 1800 and the HHI increase is well above 100"). Moreover, given the high concentration levels, the court must undertake a rigorous analysis of the kinds of efficiencies being urged by the parties in order to ensure that those "efficiencies" represent more than mere speculation and promises about post-merger behavior. The district court did not undertake that analysis here.

---

18. In *Procter & Gamble Co.,* 386 U.S. at 580 the Supreme Court stated that "[p]ossible economies cannot be used as a defense to illegality" in section 7 merger cases. The issue is, however, not a closed book. *See Staples,* 970 F.Supp. at 1088 (collecting cases). Areeda and Turner explain that "[i]n interpreting the *Clorox* language, moreover, observe that the court referred only to 'possible' economies and to economies that 'may' result from mergers that lessen competition. To reject an economies defense based on mere possibilities does not mean that one should reject such a defense based on more convincing proof." 4 Phillip Areeda & Donald Turner, *Antitrust Law* ¶ 941b, at 154 (1980). They conclude that "[t]he Court's brief and unelaborated language [in *Clorox*] cannot reasonably be taken as a definitive disposition of so important and complex an issue as the role of economies in analyzing legality of a merger." *Id.*

In support of its conclusion that post-merger efficiencies will outweigh the merger's anticompetitive effects, the district court found that the consolidation of baby food production in Heinz's under-utilized Pittsburgh plant "will achieve substantial cost savings in salaries and operating costs." The court also credited the appellees' promise of improved product quality as a result of recipe consolidation.[19] The only cost reduction the court quantified as a percentage of pre-merger costs, however, was the so called "variable conversion cost": the cost of processing the volume of baby food now processed by Beech–Nut. The court accepted the appellees' claim that this cost would be reduced by 43% if the Beech–Nut production were shifted to Heinz's plant, a reduction the appellees' expert characterized as "extraordinary."

The district court's analysis falls short of the findings necessary for a successful efficiencies defense in the circumstances of this case. We mention only three of the most important deficiencies here. First, "variable conversion cost" is only a percentage of the total variable manufacturing cost. A large percentage reduction in only a small portion of the company's overall variable manufacturing cost does not necessarily translate into a significant cost advantage to the merger. Thus, for cost reduction to be relevant, we must at least consider the percentage of Beech–Nut's total variable manufacturing cost that would be reduced as a consequence of the merger. At oral argument, the appellees' counsel agreed. This correction immediately cuts the asserted efficiency gain in half since, according to the appellees' evidence, using total variable manufacturing cost as the measure cuts the cost savings from 43% to 22.3%.

Second, the percentage reduction in *Beech–Nut's* cost is still not the relevant figure. After the merger, the two entities will be combined, and to determine whether the merged entity will be a significantly more efficient competitor, cost reductions must be measured across the new entity's combined production—not just across the pre-merger output of Beech–Nut. The district court, however, did not consider the cost reduction over the merged firm's combined output. At oral argument the appellees' counsel was unable to suggest a formula that could be used for determining that cost reduction.

Finally, and as the district court recognized, the asserted efficiencies must be "merger-specific" to be cognizable as a defense. That is, they must be efficiencies that cannot be achieved by either company alone because, if they can, the merger's asserted benefits can be achieved without the concomitant loss of a competitor. Yet the district court never explained why Heinz could not achieve the kind of efficiencies urged without merger. As noted, the principal merger benefit asserted for Heinz is the acquisition of Beech–Nut's better recipes, which will allegedly make its product more attractive and permit expanded sales at prices lower than those charged by

---

19. In addition, the district court described Heinz's distribution network as much more efficient than Beech–Nut's. It failed to find, however, a significant diseconomy of scale in distribution from which either Heinz or Beech–Nut suffers. In other words, although Beech–Nut has an inefficient distribution system, it can make that system more efficient without merger. Heinz's own efficient distribution network illustrates that a firm the size of Beech–Nut does not need to merge in order to attain an efficient distribution system.

Beech–Nut, which produces at an inefficient plant. Yet, neither the district court nor the appellees addressed the question whether Heinz could obtain the benefit of better recipes by investing more money in product development and promotion—say, by an amount less than the amount Heinz would spend to acquire Beech–Nut. At oral argument, Heinz's counsel agreed that the taste of Heinz's products was not so bad that no amount of money could improve the brand's consumer appeal. That being the case, the question is how much Heinz would have to spend to make its product equivalent to the Beech–Nut product and hence whether Heinz could achieve the efficiencies of merger without eliminating Beech–Nut as a competitor. The district court, however, undertook no inquiry in this regard. In short, the district court failed to make the kind of factual determinations necessary to render the appellees' efficiency defense sufficiently concrete to offset the FTC's prima facie showing.

3.   *Innovation.* The appellees claim next that the merger is required to enable Heinz to innovate, and thus to improve its competitive position against Gerber. Heinz and Beech–Nut asserted, and the district court found, that without the merger the two firms are unable to launch new products to compete with Gerber because they lack a sufficient shelf presence or ACV. This kind of defense is often a speculative proposition. *See* 4A Areeda, *et al., supra,* ¶ 975g (noting "truly formidable" proof problems in determining innovation economies). In this case, given the old-economy nature of the industry as well as Heinz's position as the world's largest baby food manufacturer, it is a particularly difficult defense to prove. The court below accepted the appellees' argument principally on the basis of their expert's testimony that new product launches are cost-effective only when a firm's ACV is 70% or greater (Heinz's is presently 40%; Beech–Nut's is 45%). That testimony, in turn, was based on a graph that plotted revenue against ACV. According to the expert, the graph showed that only four out of 27 new products launched in 1995 had been successful—all for companies with an ACV of 70% or greater.

The chart, however, does not establish this proposition and the court's consequent finding that the merger is necessary for innovation is thus unsupported and clearly erroneous. All the chart plotted was revenue against ACV and hence all it showed was the unsurprising fact that the greater a company's ACV, the greater the revenue it received. Because the graph did not plot the profitability (or any measure of "cost-effectiveness"), there is no way to know whether the expert's claim—that a 70% ACV is required for a launch to be "successful" in an economic sense—is true.[21] Moreover, the number of data points on the chart were few; they were limited to launches in a single year; and they involved launches of all new grocery products rather than of baby food alone. Assessing such data's statistical significance in establishing the proposition at issue, *i.e.,* the necessity of 70% ACV penetration, is thus highly speculative. The district court did not even address the question of the data's statistical significance

---

21.   For example, a 5 cent piece of bubble gum introduced with a 90% ACV could appear as a failure on the graph because of low revenue but nonetheless be profitable. On the other hand, a high priced grocery product introduced with the same ACV could generate a lot of revenue (and thus appear as a "success" on the graph) yet be unprofitable.

and the appellees' counsel could offer no help at oral argument. In the absence of reliable and significant evidence that the merger will permit innovation that otherwise could not be accomplished, the district court had no basis to conclude that the FTC's showing was rebutted by an innovation defense.

Moreover, Heinz's insistence on a 70–plus ACV before it brings a new product to market may be largely to persuade the court to recognize promotional economies as a defense. Heinz argues that to profitably launch a new product, it must have nationwide market penetration to recoup the money spent on advertising and promotion. It wants to spread advertising costs out among as many product units as possible, thereby lowering the advertising cost per unit. It does not want to "waste" promotional expenditures in markets where its products are not on the shelf or where they are on only a few shelves. For example, in a metropolitan area in which Heinz has a 75 per cent ACV, every dollar spent on advertising is two or three times more "effective" than in a market in which it has only a 25 per cent ACV. As one authority notes, however, "[t]he case for recognizing a defense based on promotional economies is relatively weak." 4A Areeda, *et al.*, *supra*, ¶ 975f, at 77. The district court accepted Heinz's claim that it could not introduce new products without at least a 70 per cent ACV because it would be unable to adequately diffuse its advertising and promotional expenditures. But the court failed to determine whether substantial promotional scale economies exist now and, if they do, whether Heinz and Beech–Nut "for that reason operate at a substantial competitive disadvantage in the market or markets in which they sell" or whether there are effective alternatives to merger by which the disadvantage can be overcome. *Id*. at ¶ 975f2, at 78. . . .

Although we recognize that, post-hearing, the FTC may accept the rebuttal arguments proffered by the appellees, including their efficiencies defense, and permit the merger to proceed, we conclude that the FTC succeeded in "rais[ing] questions going to the merits so serious, substantial, difficult and doubtful as to make them fair ground for thorough investigation, study, deliberation and determination by the FTC." . . .

2. Weighing of the Equities

Although the FTC's showing of likelihood of success creates a presumption in favor of preliminary injunctive relief, we must still weigh the equities in order to decide whether enjoining the merger would be in the public interest. 15 U.S.C. § 53(b); *see PPG*, 798 F.2d at 1507; *Weyerhaeuser*, 665 F.2d at 1081–83. The principal public equity weighing in favor of issuance of preliminary injunctive relief is the public interest in effective enforcement of the antitrust laws. *University Health*, 938 F.2d at 1225. The Congress specifically had this public equity consideration in mind when it enacted section 13(b). *See Food Town Stores*, 539 F.2d at 1346 (Congress enacted section 13(b) to preserve status quo until FTC can perform its function). The district court found, and there is no dispute, that if the merger were allowed to proceed, subsequent administrative and judicial proceedings on the merits "will not matter" because Beech–Nut's manufacturing facility "will be closed, the Beech–Nut distribution channels will be closed, the new label and recipes will be in place, and it will be impossible as a practical matter to undo the transaction." *H.J. Heinz,* 116 F.Supp.2d at 201. Hence, if the merger were ultimately found to violate the Clayton Act, it would be impossible to recreate pre-merger competition. Section 13(b) itself embodies congressional recognition of the fact that divestiture is an inadequate and unsatisfactory remedy in a merger case, 119 Cong. Rec. 36612 (1973), a point that has been emphasized by the United States Supreme Court. *See, e.g., FTC v. Dean Foods Co.,* 384 U.S. 597, 606 n.5 ("Administrative experience shows that the Commission's inability to unscramble merged assets frequently prevents entry of an effective order of divestiture.").

On the other side of the ledger, the appellees claim that the injunction would deny consumers the procompetitive advantages of the merger. The district court found that if the merger were preliminarily enjoined, the injury to competition would also be irreversible, that is, the merger would be abandoned and could not be consummated if ultimately found lawful. By contrast to its first finding, however, for the latter conclusion the court relied not on the facts of this case but on our statement in *Exxon* that—as a general matter—temporarily blocking a tender offer is likely to end an attempted acquisition, "as a result of the short life-span of most tender offers." In their brief in this court, the appellees offer nothing more to support the finding that the merger would never be consummated were an injunction to issue. Indeed, they devote only a single sentence, without any citation, to the point. The district court's finding that an injunction would "kill this merger" is thus not a factual finding supported by record evidence. This case does not involve a short-lived tender offer as did the case cited by the court for its "kill the merger" conclusion. The appellees acknowledge that there is no alternative buyer for Beech–Nut and the court found that it is not a failing company but rather a "profitable and ongoing enterprise." If the merger makes economic sense now, the appellees have offered no reason why it would not do so later. Moreover, Beech–Nut's principal assets of value to Heinz are, assertedly, its recipes and brand name. Nothing in the record leads us to believe that both will not still exist when the FTC completes its work. It may be that Beech–Nut will have to sell its recipes to Heinz at a lower price than the price of today's merger. But that is at best a "private" equity which does not affect our analysis of the impact on the market of the two options now before us and which has not in any event been urged by the appellees.[25]

In sum, weighing of the equities favors the FTC. If the merger is ultimately found to violate section 7 of the Clayton Act, it will be too late to preserve competition if no preliminary injunction has issued. On the other hand, if the merger is found not to lessen competition substantially, the efficiencies that the appellees urge can be reclaimed by a renewed transac-

---

25. ... "While it is proper to consider private equities in deciding whether to enjoin a particular transaction, we must afford such concerns little weight, lest we undermine section 13(b)'s purpose of protecting the "public-at-large, rather than the individual private competitors." *University Health,* 938 F.2d at 1225 (citation omitted); *cf. Weyerhaeuser,* 665 F.2d at 1083 ("Private equities do not outweigh effective enforcement of the antitrust laws. When the Commission demonstrates a likelihood of ultimate success, a countershowing of private equities alone would not suffice to justify denial of a preliminary injunction barring the merger.").

tion. Our conclusion with respect to the equities necessarily lightens the burden on the FTC to show likelihood of success on the merits, a burden which the FTC has met here. . . .

Questions on *FTC v. Heinz*

1. The major efficiency defense was that Heinz had a new plant at 40% capacity but had bad baby food that did not compete well with Gerber, whereas Beech–Nut had better baby food that did compete directly with Gerber but made it in an antiquated plant built in 1907 with higher variable production costs. Thus a merged firm could produce all the baby-food at lower cost at the Heinz plant and create a firm that would combine low costs and better quality and be able to compete better with Gerber. Do you agree with the appellate court's rejection of the argument that it was efficient to transfer Beech–Nut's production to the 60% of underused capacity at Heinz's new plant?

a. Even if Beech–Nut's variable costs were reduced by only 22.3% rather than 43%, and the cost savings were only 10–11% of the combined Heinz–Beechnut, weren't the cost savings still pretty high? Does it seem likely that the merger would have created an ability to increase prices that offset the tendency of those cost savings to decrease prices?

b. Do you agree with the court that this is not a merger-specific efficiency because Heinz could simply develop some better baby food recipes itself? Even if it did improve its quality, would it likely be easy to develop a brand reputation for being nearly equal to Gerber?

c. Isn't the current existence of substantial underutilized capacity consistent with the proposition that the firms are already engaged in oligopolistic coordination?[59]

d. Doesn't this efficiency defense inherently mean that the plan was to close the existing Beech–Nut plant? Is such a reduction in capacity likely to improve pricing? Could it do so if the Heinz plant would still not be at full capacity and marginal costs would be lower for the Beech–Nut brands?

e. If this argument were accepted, wouldn't it create an incentive to build excess capacity in order to justify mergers that eliminate competition?

2. Do you agree with the appellate court's rejection of the defense that the merged firm would be more likely to innovate if it had shelf space at a greater percentage of stores because it would then get greater returns for any investment in innovation? Does such a claim seem likely to be very provable? How much innovation would one expect in baby food anyway?

How to Balance the Equities in Merger Cases

Although courts generally talk about balancing the equities, in fact the harm to defendants from blocking a merger is only deemed legitimate if it

---

59. *See* IV AREEDA, ANTITRUST LAW at 217 (a "merger might be even more dangerous with industrywide excess capacity, which can (1) indicate that the firms have already successfully coordinated their prices at high levels and thereby reduced output in relation to existing capacity and (2) deter new entry and thereby shelter incumbents from potential competitors currently outside the market.") (summarizing *FTC v. Elders Grain*, 868 F.2d 901, 905 (7th Cir. 1989)).

reflects the denial of a procompetitive benefit. Thus, the real issues on preliminary injunction are the likelihoods and magnitudes of procompetitive versus anticompetitive effects, and which of them would last longer because they would be irreparable at trial. For example, suppose the odds are 50–50 whether a trial will deem a merger to have net procompetitive or anticompetitive effects, each of which is the same in expected magnitude. If a consummated merger could not be undone after trial (because it is too difficult to unscramble the eggs as the *Staples* and *Heinz* courts found), then preliminarily allowing the merger will have a 50% chance of producing anticompetitive effects that last forever. If an unconsummated merger could still be done after trial (as the *Heinz* appellate court found), then preliminarily blocking the merger has a 50% chance of denying procompetitive benefits but only for the period until the trial is completed. On the other hand, if the unconsummated merger could not be done after trial (because it would be abandoned given the difficulty of maintaining financing, as the *Heinz* district court found), then preliminarily blocking the merger has a 50% chance of denying procompetitive benefits forever. Thus, whether preliminarily blocking the merger creates net benefits or harms turns on the likelihoods, magnitudes, and reversibilities of possible anticompetitive effects and denied procompetitive benefits.[60]

5. THE FAILING FIRM DEFENSE

International Shoe v. FTC

280 U.S. 291 (1930).

■ MR. JUSTICE SUTHERLAND delivered the opinion of the Court.

[International Shoe acquired the capital stock of McElwain Company. The FTC found the merger anticompetitive and ordered divestiture of that capital stock.] . . .

Beginning in 1920 there was a marked falling off in prices and sales of shoes, as there was in other commodities; and, because of excessive commit-

---

60. Mathematically, a court should preliminarily block a merger if

$$P_{ac}M_{ac\text{-}pre} + P_{ac}P_{ac\text{-}irr}M_{ac\text{-}post} > P_{pc}M_{pc\text{-}pre} + P_{pc}P_{pc\text{-}irr}M_{pc\text{-}post}$$

where P_{ac} is the probability of net anticompetitive effects, $M_{ac\text{-}pre}$ is the expected magnitude of anticompetitive effects pre-trial, $P_{ac\text{-}irr}$ is the probability anticompetitive effects will be irreversible (eggs cannot be unscrambled), $M_{ac\text{-}post}$ is the expected magnitude of anticompetitive effects post-trial, P_{pc} is the probability of net procompetitive effects, $M_{pc\text{-}pre}$ is the expected magnitude of procompetitive effects pre-trial, $P_{pc\text{-}irr}$ is the probability procompetitive effects will be irreversible (merger will be abandoned), and $M_{pc\text{-}post}$ is the expected magnitude of procompetitive effects post-trial. Given that all the variables are difficult to quantify, such formulas cannot be expected to produce precise answers but are useful in helping to frame the analysis and see the tradeoffs. Because the post-trial periods will last much longer, the magnitudes of post-trial effects are likely larger, though they may also be discounted to present value.

If damage remedies were adequate, then even pre-trial harms might be reversible. But for mergers that are procompetitive, there is no mechanism for allowing consumers and defendants to recover any lost procompetitive benefits. And for mergers that are anticompetitive, it is difficult to quantify the anticompetitive harm and distribute any damages to consumers, as the *Staples* court noted.

ments which the McElwain Company had made for the purchase of hides as well as the possession of large stocks of shoes and an inability to meet its indebtedness for large sums of borrowed money, the financial condition of the company became such that its officers, after long and careful consideration of the situation, concluded that the company was faced with financial ruin, and that the only alternatives presented were liquidation through a receiver or an outright sale.... In the spring of 1921 the company owed approximately $15,000,000 to some 60 or 70 banks and trust companies, and, in addition, nearly $2,000,000 on current account. Its factories, which had a capacity of 38,000 to 40,000 pairs of shoes per day, in 1921 were producing only 6,000 or 7,000 pairs. An examination of its balance sheets and statements and the testimony of its officers and others conversant with the situation, clearly shows that the company had reached the point where it could no longer pay its debts as they became due. In the face of these adverse circumstances it became necessary, under the laws of Massachusetts, to make up its annual financial statement, which, when filed, would disclose a condition of insolvency, as that term is defined by the statute and decisions of the State, and thus bring the company to the point of involuntary liquidation....

The condition of the International Company, on the contrary, notwithstanding these adverse conditions in the shoe trade generally, was excellent. That company had so conducted its affairs that its surplus stock was not excessive, and it was able to reduce prices. Instead of a decrease, it had an increase of business of about 25 per cent in the number of shoes made and sold. During the early months of 1921, orders exceeded the ability of the company to produce, so that approximately one-third of them were necessarily canceled. In this situation, with demands for its products so much in excess of its ability to fill them, the International was approached by officers of the McElwain Company with a view to a sale of its property. After some negotiation, the purchase was agreed upon. The transaction took the form of a sale of the stock instead of the assets, not, as the evidence clearly establishes, because of any desire or intention to thereby affect competition, but because by that means the personnel and organization of the McElwain factories could be retained, which, for reasons that seem satisfactory, was regarded as vitally important. It is perfectly plain from all the evidence that the controlling purpose of the International in making the purchase in question was to secure additional factories, which it could not itself build with sufficient speed to meet the pressing requirements of its business.

Shortly stated, the evidence establishes the case of a corporation in failing circumstances, the recovery of which to a normal condition was, to say the least, in gravest doubt, selling its capital to the only available purchaser in order to avoid what its officers fairly concluded was a more disastrous fate. It was suggested by the court below, and also here in argument, that instead of an outright sale, any one of several alternatives might have been adopted which would have saved the property and preserved competition; but, as it seems to us, all of these may be dismissed as lying wholly within the realm of speculation. The company might, as suggested, have obtained further financial help from the banks, with a resulting increased load of indebtedness which the company might have carried and finally paid, or, on the other hand, by the addition of which, it might more certainly have been crushed. As to that, one guess is as good as the other. It might have availed itself of a receivership, but no one is wise enough to predict with any degree of certainty whether such a course would have meant ultimate recovery or final and complete collapse. If it had proceeded, or been proceeded against, under the Bankruptcy Act, holders of the preferred stock might have paid or assumed the debts and gone forward with the business; or they might have considered it more prudent to accept whatever could be salvaged from the wreck and abandon the enterprise as a bad risk.

As between these and all other alternatives, and the alternative of a sale such as was made, the officers, stockholders and creditors, thoroughly familiar with the factors of a critical situation and more able than commission or court to foresee future contingencies, after much consideration, felt compelled to choose the latter alternative. There is no reason to doubt that in so doing they exercised a judgment which was both honest and well informed; and if aid be needed to fortify their conclusion, it may be found in the familiar presumption of rightfulness which attaches to human conduct in general. Aside from these considerations, the soundness of the conclusion which they reached finds ample confirmation in the facts already discussed and others disclosed by the record.

In the light of the case thus disclosed of a corporation with resources so depleted and the prospect of rehabilitation so remote that it faced the grave probability of a business failure with resulting loss to its stockholders and injury to the communities where its plants were operated, we hold that the purchase of its capital stock by a competitor (there being no other prospective purchaser), not with a purpose to lessen competition, but to facilitate the accumulated business of the purchaser and with the effect of mitigating seriously injurious consequences otherwise probable, is not in contemplation of law prejudicial to the public and does not substantially lessen competition or restrain commerce within the intent of the Clayton Act. . . . *Reversed.*

■ MR. JUSTICE STONE, [Joined by JUSTICES HOLMES and BRANDEIS,] dissenting. . . . Nor am I able to say that the McElwain Company, for the stock of which petitioner gave its own stock having a market value of $9,460,000, was then in such financial straits as to preclude the reasonable inference by the Commission that its business, conducted either through a receivership or a reorganized company, would probably continue to compete with that of petitioner. It plainly had large value as a going concern, there was no evidence that it would have been worth more or as much if dismantled, and there was evidence that the depression in the shoe trade in 1920–1921 was then a passing phase of the business. . . .

Note and Questions on *International Shoe v. FTC*

International Shoe required two elements to satisfy the failing company defense: (1) the acquired firm would go bankrupt but for the merger; and (2) the acquirer was the only available purchaser.

1. If the McElwain Company was going to go bankrupt without the merger, would a merger necessarily only increase market output? Does that depend on whether the McElwain Company would have had its assets liquidated, sold as a going concern, or just reorganized in a way that eliminated its debts without ending the business? Even if the assets were liquidated, wouldn't they likely be used to make shoes for some firm?

2. Given that International Shoe was willing to pay almost $10 million for the McElwain Company, does it seem likely that absent the merger the company would have been liquidated in a way that eliminated its business? Or is it likely International Shoe would be willing to pay much more than anyone else, either because it had particular problems of undercapacity or because it would earn particular profits from ending competition?

3. Is the court right that the corporate participants of the McElwain Company were best placed to decide whether to sell the business to International Shoe, get new loans, or reorganize in bankruptcy? Aren't their incentives to make the decision that maximizes the value of the McElwain Company rather the decision that minimizes the anticompetitive effect? And won't making a sale that gives another firm market power generally be the profit-maximizing move since such a buyer should be willing to pay more than other buyers?

Citizen Publishing v. United States

394 U.S. 131 (1969).

■ MR. JUSTICE DOUGLAS delivered the opinion of the Court.

Tucson, Arizona, has only two daily newspapers of general circulation, the Star and the Citizen. The Citizen ... is an evening paper published six times a week. The Star ... has a Sunday as well as a daily issue. Prior to 1940 the two papers vigorously competed with each other. While their circulation was about equal, the Star sold 50% more advertising space than the Citizen and operated at a profit, while the Citizen sustained losses. Indeed the Star's annual profits averaged about $25,825, while the Citizen's annual losses averaged about $23,550....

[Beginning in 1940, a] joint operating agreement between the two papers ... provided that each paper should retain its own news and editorial department, as well as its corporate identity. It provided for the formation of Tucson Newspapers, Inc. (TNI), which was to be owned in equal shares by the Star and Citizen and which was to manage all departments of their business except the news and editorial units. The production and distribution equipment of each paper was transferred to TNI. The latter had five directors—two named by the Star, two by the Citizen, and the fifth chosen by the Citizen out of three named by the Star.

The purpose of the agreement was to end any business or commercial competition between the two papers and to that end three types of controls were imposed. First was *price fixing*. The newspapers were sold and distributed by the circulation department of TNI; commercial advertising placed in the papers was sold only by the advertising department of TNI;

the subscription and advertising rates were set jointly. Second was *profit pooling*. All profits realized were pooled and distributed to the Star and the Citizen by TNI pursuant to an agreed ratio. Third was a *market control*. It was agreed that neither the Star nor the Citizen nor any of their stockholders, officers, and executives would engage in any other business in Pima County—the metropolitan area of Tucson—in conflict with the agreement. Thus competing publishing operations were foreclosed.

All commercial rivalry between the papers ceased. Combined profits before taxes rose from $27,531 in 1940 to $1,727,217 in 1964.

[The District Court found violations of Sherman Act §§ 1 and 2, and Clayton Act § 7.] . . . The only real defense of appellants was the "failing company" defense—a judicially created doctrine. The facts tendered . . . mak[e] plain that the requirements of the failing company doctrine were not met. That defense was before the Court in *International Shoe* v. *FTC*, where § 7 of the Clayton Act was in issue. The evidence showed that the resources of one company were so depleted and the prospect of rehabilitation so remote that "it faced the grave probability of a business failure." There was, moreover, "no other prospective purchaser." It was in that setting that the Court held that the acquisition of that company by another did not substantially lessen competition within the meaning of § 7.

In the present case the District Court found: "At the time Star Publishing and Citizen Publishing entered into the operating agreement, and at the time the agreement became effective, Citizen Publishing was not then on the verge of going out of business, nor was there a serious probability at that time that Citizen Publishing would terminate its business and liquidate its assets unless Star Publishing and Citizen Publishing entered into the operating agreement." The evidence sustains that finding. There is no indication that the owners of the Citizen were contemplating a liquidation. They never sought to sell the Citizen and there is no evidence that the joint operating agreement was the last straw at which the Citizen grasped. Indeed the Citizen continued to be a significant threat to the Star. How otherwise is one to explain the Star's willingness to enter into an agreement to share its profits with the Citizen? Would that be true if as now claimed the Citizen was on the brink of collapse?

The failing company doctrine plainly cannot be applied in a merger or in any other case unless it is established that the company that acquires the failing company or brings it under dominion is the only available purchaser. For if another person or group could be interested, a unit in the competitive system would be preserved and not lost to monopoly power. So even if we assume, *arguendo*, that in 1940 the then owners of the Citizen could not long keep the enterprise afloat, no effort was made to sell the Citizen; its properties and franchise were not put in the hands of a broker; and the record is silent on what the market, if any, for the Citizen might have been.

Moreover, we know from the broad experience of the business community since 1930, the year when the *International Shoe* case was decided, that companies reorganized through receivership, or through Chapter X or Chapter XI of the Bankruptcy Act often emerged as strong competitive companies. The prospects of reorganization of the Citizen in 1940 would have had to be dim or nonexistent to make the failing company doctrine applicable to this case.

The burden of proving that the conditions of the failing company doctrine[4] have been satisfied is on those who seek refuge under it. That burden has not been satisfied in this case.

We confine the failing company doctrine to its present narrow scope. . . .

Note and Questions on *Citizen's Publishing*

Citizen's Publishing appears to clarify that under the failing firm defense, the merging firms have the burden of showing three requirements. (1) The firm was on the verge of bankruptcy. (2) There was no other available purchaser. (3) Bankruptcy would almost certainly have led to liquidation of assets because the prospects for reorganization were "dim or nonexistent." Is this test really consistent with *International Shoe*?

1.   Did the merging firms in *International Shoe* show bankruptcy was imminent?

2.   Although the court there said there was no other purchaser, did it require evidence (like here) that the allegedly failing firm was put in the hands of a broker or otherwise marketed?

3.   Didn't the court there reject the option of reorganization?

4.   Is the major difference that this case puts the burden squarely on the merging firms and thus resolves any uncertainty in the opposite direction as *International Shoe*?

5.   Does it make sense to impose tougher requirements where (as here) the merger is one to monopoly?

In footnote 4, *Citizen's Publishing* noted that Congress was considering enacting a bill to create an antitrust exemption for newspaper joint operating agreements in cases of economic distress, but declined to adopt one judicially. The next year Congress enacted a statute providing an antitrust exemption for a "joint newspaper operating arrangement" if "not more than one of the newspaper publications . . . was likely to remain or become a financially sound publication," and requiring approval by the Attorney General under this standard for future joint newspaper operating arrangements.[61] This appears to substantially weaken the general standards for the failing firm defense articulated in *Citizen's Publishing* for cases of newspaper joint operating agreements by requiring proof of only

---

4.   Bills were introduced both in the 90th Congress . . . and in the 91st Congress . . . to exempt from the antitrust laws joint operating agreements between newspapers because of economic distress. Extensive hearings were held in 1967 and 1968. The hearings reflect all shades of opinion. As stated by the House Subcommittee: "The antitrust laws embody concepts and principles which long have been considered to be the bedrock of our economic institutions. Piecemeal exemptions from the antitrust laws to cope with problems of particular industries have been given reluctantly and only after there has been a clear showing of overriding need." As of this date Congress has taken no action on any of those bills.

61.   Newspaper Preservation Act, 84 Stat. 466 (1970), 15 U.S.C. § 1803.

insolvency, rather than proof of likely liquidation, absence of other purchasers, and inability to reorganize in bankruptcy.

1. Does it make sense to weaken those standards? Aren't they all relevant to the competitive impact?

2. Is there any sound policy reason to make those standards weaker in the case of newspapers than in other industries? Are the political risks of an editorial monopoly so great that they outweigh the economic risks of approving a joint operating agreement that may raise prices but preserves editorial competition?

3. Given the pending bills, should the Court have tried to anticipate legislative preferences and adopted such a special rule for newspapers itself? Or was it better to force the issue in the legislature and make clear just how much political clout the newspapers had? Could the Court have anticipated just what standard Congress would want? Could it have interpreted the statute to create an administrative approval process with the Attorney General?[62]

U.S. DOJ/FTC, Horizontal Merger Guidelines

(2010).

11. Failure and Exiting Assets

Notwithstanding the analysis above, a merger is not likely to enhance market power if imminent failure, as defined below, of one of the merging firms would cause the assets of that firm to exit the relevant market. This is an extreme instance of the more general circumstance in which the competitive significance of one of the merging firms is declining: the projected market share and significance of the exiting firm is zero. If the relevant assets would otherwise exit the market, customers are not worse off after the merger than they would have been had the merger been enjoined.

The Agencies do not normally credit claims that the assets of the failing firm would exit the relevant market unless all of the following circumstances are met: (1) the allegedly failing firm would be unable to meet its financial obligations in the near future; (2) it would not be able to reorganize successfully under Chapter 11 of the Bankruptcy Act; and (3) it has made unsuccessful good-faith efforts to elicit reasonable alternative offers that would keep its tangible and intangible assets in the relevant market and pose a less severe danger to competition than does the proposed merger.[16]

---

62. See Elhauge, Statutory Default Rules 181–183 (Harvard University Press 2008) (arguing that the presumption against antitrust exemptions in cases where legislative preferences are unclear is justified when decisions that conflict with actual legislative preferences are more likely to provoke statutory overrides that make those preferences clear when the decisions deny an exemption than when they recognize an exemption.)

16. Any offer to purchase the assets of the failing firm for a price above the liquidation value of those assets will be regarded as a reasonable alternative offer. Liquidation value is the highest value the assets could command for use outside the relevant market.

Similarly, a merger is unlikely to cause competitive harm if the risks to competition arise from the acquisition of a failing division. The Agencies do not normally credit claims that the assets of a division would exit the relevant market in the near future unless both of the following conditions are met: (1) applying cost allocation rules that reflect true economic costs, the division has a persistently negative cash flow on an operating basis, and such negative cash flow is not economically justified for the firm by benefits such as added sales in complementary markets or enhanced customer goodwill;[17] and (2) the owner of the failing division has made unsuccessful good-faith efforts to elicit reasonable alternative offers that would keep its tangible and intangible assets in the relevant market and pose a less severe danger to competition than does the proposed acquisition. . . .

Note and Questions on Merger Guidelines on the Failing Firm Defense

1. The 2010 Guidelines follow the same three-part test as *Citizen's Publishing*, but while the guidelines makes those three elements normally necessary to prove a failing firm defense, it makes the ultimate test whether the assets of the failing firm would otherwise exit the market. Meeting the three elements may not suffice to satisfy that ultimate test if, without the merger, the failing firm would be liquidated, with those assets sold piecemeal to firms within the market. A liquidation that kept the failing firm's assets in the market, even on a piecemeal basis, would likely be less anticompetitive than having those assets all transferred to a single firm with market power. On the other hand, forcing liquidation in such a case risks inefficiently sacrificing the going-concern value of the firm. How should such cases be handled? Perhaps the best solution is to say that although the failing firm defense is not met in such cases, agencies and courts should consider any efficiencies from maintaining going-concern value directly in a way that is balanced against any anticompetitive effects.

2. Is it likely many firms can show that it would be impossible to reorganize in bankruptcy? Won't that always be possible if the firm is worth more as a going concern than as liquidated assets?

3. How can one decide what constitutes a good faith effort to sell a company or a reasonable alternative offer?

a. Is it good faith to sell to the highest bidder? Wouldn't the buyer who would gain the most market power likely be the highest bidder?

b. If the company can't sell to the highest bidder, how much below that bid still constitutes a reasonable alternative offer? Won't there always be some alternative buyer who is preferable from a competitive standpoint if the price is lowered far enough, especially if the test is (as footnote 7 says) the value of the assets outside the market?

---

17. Because the parent firm can allocate costs, revenues, and intra-company transactions among itself and its subsidiaries and divisions, the Agencies require evidence on these two points that is not solely based on management plans that could have been prepared for the purpose of demonstrating negative cash flow or the prospect of exit from the relevant market.

4. If the failing firm doctrine were not an absolute defense, but instead a factor that could be weighed against any anticompetitive effects, do you think the doctrine would be as narrow?

Joined Cases C–68/94 and C–30/95, French Republic and Société commerciale des potasses et de l'azote (SCPA) and Entreprise minière et chimique (EMC) v. Commission (Commission v. France)

1998 E.C.R. I–1375.

[Kali und Salz (K + S) and Mitteldeutsche Kali (Mdk) sought to merge. Collectively the firms would have a de facto monopoly in the potash sector. MdK, which had considerable financial difficulties, was owned by Treuhand.]

The Court observes at the outset that under Article 2(2) of the Regulation, a "concentration which does not create or strengthen a dominant position as a result of which effective competition would be significantly impeded in the common market or in a substantial part of it shall be declared compatible with the common market".

Thus if a concentration is not the cause of the creation or strengthening of a dominant position which has a significant impact on the competitive situation on the relevant market, it must be declared compatible with the common market.

It appears from ... the contested decision [in *Kali und Salz*] that, in the Commission's opinion, a concentration which would normally be considered as leading to the creation or reinforcement of a dominant position on the part of the acquiring undertaking may be regarded as not being the cause of it if, even in the event of the concentration being prohibited, that undertaking would inevitably achieve or reinforce a dominant position. [The decision] goes on to state that, as a general matter, a concentration is not the cause of the deterioration of the competitive structure if it is clear that:

—the acquired undertaking would in the near future be forced out of the market if not taken over by another undertaking,

—the acquiring undertaking would gain the market share of the acquired undertaking if it were forced out of the market,

—there is no less anticompetitive alternative purchase.

It must be observed, first of all, that the fact that the conditions set by the Commission for concluding that there was no causal link between the concentration and the deterioration of the competitive structure do not entirely coincide with the conditions applied in connection with the United States "failing company defence" is not in itself a ground of invalidity of the contested decision. Solely the fact that the conditions set by the Commission were not capable of excluding the possibility that a concentration might be the cause of the deterioration in the competitive structure of the market could constitute a ground of invalidity of the decision.

In the present case, the French Government disputes the relevance of the criterion that it must be verified that the acquiring undertaking would in any event obtain the acquired undertaking's share of the market if the latter were to be forced out of the market.

However, in the absence of that criterion, a concentration could, provided the other criteria were satisfied, be considered as not being the cause of the deterioration of the competitive structure of the market even though it appeared that, in the event of the concentration not proceeding, the acquiring undertaking would not gain the entire market share of the acquired undertaking. Thus, it would be possible to deny the existence of a causal link between the concentration and the deterioration of the competitive structure of the market even though the competitive structure of the market would deteriorate to a lesser extent if the concentration did not proceed.

The introduction of that criterion is intended to ensure that the existence of a causal link between the concentration and the deterioration of the competitive structure of the market can be excluded only if the competitive structure resulting from the concentration would deteriorate in similar fashion even if the concentration did not proceed.

The criterion of absorption of market shares, although not considered by the Commission as sufficient in itself to preclude any adverse effect of the concentration on competition, therefore helps to ensure the neutral effects of the concentration as regards the deterioration of the competitive structure of the market. This is consistent with the concept of causal connection set out in Article 2(2) of the Regulation.

Questions on *Kali und Salz/Commission v. France*

As the European Court of Justice noted, the EU failing firm test differs from the U.S. test by adding the second condition that the acquiring firm would take over the market share of the acquired firm if it failed.

1. Does this second condition have a sound economic rationale?

2. On any market with at least two nonfailing firms, isn't it likely that at least some of the market share of the failing firm would go to each firm? Doesn't this make the defense effectively applicable only to mergers to monopoly, or at least much easier to prove in such cases? Is that a perverse result? Or does it make sense because in such cases a monopoly would result without the merger, whereas in markets with at least two nonfailing firms, the market shares would likely be more deconcentrated if the failing firm's share would be distributed across the nonfailing firms without the merger?

3. Suppose there are three firms with 33% market share, one of which is failing, and if it exits, the two remaining firms will split its market share and thus each obtain 50% of the market. A merger between the failing firm and one of the healthy firms would instead create a firm with 66% market share. Is that necessarily more anticompetitive than the first scenario? Although the 66% scenario is more likely to be deemed to have created a dominant firm, the 50% scenario means that the failing firm's capacity exits the market, and may thus mean lower output and higher prices.

Commission Decision 2002/365, BASF/Eurodiol/Pantochim

O.J. 2002, L 132/45.

The approach taken by the Court of Justice is wider than the criteria set out in the Commission's decision in *Kali + Salz*. According to the Court of Justice, a merger can be regarded as a rescue merger if the competitive structure resulting from the concentration would deteriorate in similar fashion even if the concentration did not proceed, that is to say, even if the concentration was prohibited.

In general terms, the concept of the "rescue merger" requires that the undertakings to be acquired can be regarded as "failing firms" and that the merger is not the cause of the deterioration of the competitive structure. Thus, for the application of the rescue merger, two conditions must be satisfied:

(a) the acquired undertaking would in the near future be forced out of the market if not taken over by another undertaking; and

(b) there is no less anti-competitive alternative purchase.

However, the application of these two criteria does not completely rule out the possibility of a takeover by third parties of the assets of the undertakings concerned in the event of their bankruptcy. If such assets were taken over by competitors in the course of bankruptcy proceedings, the economic effects would be similar to a takeover of the failing firms themselves by an alternative purchaser.

Thus it needs to be established in addition to the first two criteria, that the assets to be purchased would inevitably disappear from the market in the absence of the merger.

Given this general framework, the Commission regards the following criteria as relevant for the application of the concept of the "rescue merger":

(a) the acquired undertaking would in the near future be forced out of the market if not taken over by another undertaking;

(b) there is no less anti-competitive alternative purchase; and

(c) the assets to be acquired would inevitably exit the market if not taken over by another undertaking.

In any event, the application of the concept of the "rescue merger" requires that the deterioration of the competitive structure through the merger is at least no worse than in the absence of the merger.

EU Guidelines on the Assessment of Horizontal Mergers

O.J. 2004, C 31/5.

VIII. FAILING FIRM. The Commission may decide that an otherwise problematic merger is nevertheless compatible with the common market if one of the merging parties is a failing firm. The basic requirement is that the deterioration of the competitive structure that follows the merger cannot be said to be caused by the merger. This will arise where the competitive structure of the market would deteriorate to at least the same extent in the absence of the merger.

The Commission considers the following three criteria to be especially relevant for the application of a "failing firm defence". First, the allegedly failing firm would in the near future be forced out of the market because of financial difficulties if not taken over by another undertaking. Second, there is no less anti-competitive alternative purchase than the notified merger. Third, in the absence of a merger, the assets of the failing firm would inevitably exit the market.[111]

It is for the notifying parties to provide in due time all the relevant information necessary to demonstrate that the deterioration of the competitive structure that follows the merger is not caused by the merger.

Questions on *BASF/Pantochim/Eurodiol* and the Commission Guidelines on the Assessment of Horizontal Mergers

In *Commission v. France*, the ECJ confirmed the relevance of the condition that the acquiring firm would in any event obtain the acquired firm's market share if it failed. However, in *BASF/Pantochim/Eurediol*, the Commission relied on the fact that the ECJ's more general test was whether the competitive structure of the market in question would deteriorate to a similar extent if the merger were not to take place, and cited this as a justification for abandoning the condition sustained in *Commission v. France*.

1. Do you have the same reading of *Commission v. France* as the Commission?

2. The Commission has now replaced the old second condition of *Kali und Salz* with a new condition requiring evidence that "the assets to be acquired would inevitably exit the market if not taken over by another undertaking." This makes the EU failing firm test parallel the U.S. guidelines. Is this change in conditions desirable? Does it make the test easier or harder to meet?

Treatment of Failing Firms in Other Nations

Many other nations recognize failing firm arguments, requiring a showing to varying degrees that (1) the firm is insolvent and (2) there is no competitively preferable alternative like bankruptcy reorganization or selling the firm or assets to other buyers.[63] Taiwan and Turkey add to those two elements the explicit requirement that without the merger the assets would leave the market, though the other nations may regard that as the

---

111. The inevitability of the assets of the failing firm leaving the market in question may, in particular in a case of merger to monopoly, underlie a finding that the market share of the failing firm would in any event accrue to the other merging party. See *Kali and Salz*.

63. *See* Canada Competition Act § 93(b); Canada Merger Guidelines § 9.1–9.10 (2004); Chile Merger Guidelines at IV. 6.2 (2006); Colombia SIC Resolution 13544 of 26 May 2006; Japan Business Combination Guidelines 31 (2004); New Zealand Supplementary Merger Guidelines on Failing Firms (2009); Singapore Merger Guidelines § 7.24 (2007); South Africa

implicit conclusion if the first two elements are met.[64] Most nations do not deem failing firm status a true "defense," but rather they deem it a factor relevant to determining whether the merger is likely to be anticompetitive.[65] Australia also allows its Commission to authorize an anticompetitive merger with a failing firm based on general public benefit grounds: like the retention of technical or productive assets, avoidance of social dislocation and unemployment, or the achievement of resource savings through rationalization and economies of scale.[66]

If its elements are shown, doesn't proving the failing firm "defense" show the merger will have no anticompetitive effects? If so, is there anything to weigh it against?

6.   THE RELEVANCE OF BUYER POWER, SOPHISTICATION, OR VIEWS

a.   MERGERS BETWEEN BUYERS THAT CREATE BUYER POWER

It has long been understood that: "The exercise of market power by buyers, or monopsony, can impose social costs equivalent to those imposed by monopoly."[67] This point was strongly reaffirmed in the *Weyerhaeuser* case excerpted for Chapter 3. It is no defense that the creation of monopsony power lowers prices in the purchasing market. Those lower prices are *sub*competitive prices and thus (like *supra*competitive prices) produce a lower and subcompetitive market output. This will be true even if sellers have no fixed costs as long as they have increasing marginal costs.[68] A buyer with market power will maximize profits by paying only a subcompetitive price even though that lowers output because it will take into account the fact that any additional marginal purchases it can make by increasing the price will increase the market price it pays for all inframarginal purchases.[69]

The adverse effects of buyer market power may seem counter-intuitive because the consequence is lower prices in the purchasing market. But

Competition Act § 12A(2)(g); South Korea Fair Trade Act Art. 7(2)(iii); South Korea Merger Guidelines VIII.2 (2009); Schumann Sasol Ltd./Price's Daelite Ltd., 23/LM/MAY01 (South Africa Competition Tribunal). Failing firm arguments are also deemed relevant in Argentina, Australia, Brazil, and Mexico.

64.   Taiwan Merger Guidelines Art. XIII (2006); Turkey Competition Board Decision No. 08–23/237–75 (2008).

65.   *See,* Australia Merger Guidelines §§ 3.22–3.23 (2008); Canada Merger Guidelines § 9.2 (2004);; India Competition Act § 20(4)(k); Japan Business Combination Guidelines 31 (2004); New Zealand Supplementary Merger Guidelines on Failing Firms (2009); South Africa Competition Act § 12A(2)(g); Iscor Ltd./Saldanha Steel Ltd., 67/LM/DEC01, at ¶¶ 104–05 (South Africa Competition Tribunal).

66.   See OECD, Failing Firm Defense, Contribution from Australia, OCDE/GD(96)23 (1996).

67.   IV AREEDA, HOVENKAMP & SOLOW, ANTITRUST LAW ¶ 980 (rev. ed. 1998); *see generally* BLAIR & HARRISON, MONOPSONY (1993).

68.   *See, e.g.,* HOVENKAMP, FEDERAL ANTITRUST POLICY § 1.2b (1994).

69.   For a seller with market power, its marginal revenue is lower than the price it charges to make the marginal sale because it has to take into account that any price cut lowers the prices it makes on the inframarginal sales. Thus, the seller with market power does not

these lower prices are *sub*competitive prices and thus (like *supra*competitive prices) produce a lower and subcompetitive market output and quality. Thus, the intuition proves false for at least three reasons.

(1) Where the firm with buyer market power also has selling market power in a downstream market, the predictable result of upstream monopsony power is lower downstream output, and thus *higher* (supracompetitive) prices in the downstream market in which the powerful buyer sells.[70]

(2) Even without higher prices in a downstream market, the creation of monopsony power remains anticompetitive in the upstream market and harmful to sellers in it.[71]

(3) Even if an upstream exercise of buyer market power did turn out to lower downstream consumer prices, those lower prices would remain *sub*competitive prices that create *sub*competitive levels of market output and quality downstream. These subcompetitive levels of output and quality would remain harmful to consumers, who by definition would have been willing to pay more for the output and quality level that a competitive market would have afforded them.

Further, if price discrimination is possible, then a buyer with market power that wants to gain a competitive advantage downstream may be able to insist on a large discount compared to what the sellers charge other buyers who compete with the powerful buyer downstream. This may distort downstream competition. Further, the upstream result can be that the powerful buyer pays a *sub*competitive price on its purchases whereas rival buyers pay a *supra*competitive price for their purchases. Both *sub*competitive and *supra*competitive prices lead to lower output than the competitive price. The *sub*competitive prices will lower output by making sellers less willing to produce for the powerful buyer; the *supra*competitive prices will lower output by making rival buyers less willing to purchase.

---

produce the output where price equals its marginal costs but rather the lower output where its marginal revenue equals its marginal costs. Likewise, for a buyer with market power, its marginal outlay is higher than the price it pays to make the marginal purchase because it has to take into account that any price increase raises the prices it pays on inframarginal purchases. Thus, the buyer with market power does not offer prices high enough to result in an output where price equals its marginal demand, but rather demands subcompetitive prices that produce a lower output where its marginal outlay equals its marginal demand.

70. *Id.*; Roger D. Blair & Jeffery L. Harrison, *Antitrust Policy and Monopsony*, 76 CORNELL L. REV. 297, 335 (1991) ("Substantive economic analysis reveals that it is an error to infer that the lower prices a monopsonist obtains translate into lower ultimate prices for the monopsonists' customers.").

71. *See* Weyerhaeuser Co. v. Ross–Simmons Hardwood Lumber, 549 U.S. 312 (2007) (articulating test for predatory overbuying that imposes liability for enhancing upstream monopsony power in a local market rather than requiring anticompetitive effects in the downstream national market); Mandeville Island Farms v. American Crystal Sugar, 334 U.S. 219 (1948) (condemning a buying cartel in a regional sugar beet market without any proof that it would have a price effect on the downstream national market in refined sugar); United States v. Pennzoil, 252 F.Supp. 962 (W.D.Pa. 1965) (condemning merger that created local monopsony power in Pennsylvania crude oil market even though it seemed unlikely to affect output in downstream worldwide market for refined oil); United States v. Rice Growers Ass'n, 1986-2 Trade Cas. (CCH) ¶ 67,288 (E.D. Cal.) (condemning merger that created local monopsony power in California paddy rice market even though it seemed unlikely to affect output in downstream worldwide market for milled rice).

U.S. DOJ/FTC, Horizontal Merger Guidelines

(2010).

12. Mergers of Competing Buyers

Mergers of competing buyers can enhance market power on the buying side of the market, just as mergers of competing sellers can enhance market power on the selling side of the market. Buyer market power is sometimes called "monopsony power."

To evaluate whether a merger is likely to enhance market power on the buying side of the market, the Agencies employ essentially the framework described above for evaluating whether a merger is likely to enhance market power on the selling side of the market. In defining relevant markets, the Agencies focus on the alternatives available to sellers in the face of a decrease in the price paid by a hypothetical monopsonist.

Market power on the buying side of the market is not a significant concern if suppliers have numerous attractive outlets for their goods or services. However, when that is not the case, the Agencies may conclude that the merger of competing buyers is likely to lessen competition in a manner harmful to sellers.

The Agencies distinguish between effects on sellers arising from a lessening of competition and effects arising in other ways. A merger that does not enhance market power on the buying side of the market can nevertheless lead to a reduction in prices paid by the merged firm, for example, by reducing transactions costs or allowing the merged firm to take advantage of volume-based discounts. Reduction in prices paid by the merging firms not arising from the enhancement of market power can be significant in the evaluation of efficiencies from a merger, as discussed in Section 10.

The Agencies do not view a short-run reduction in the quantity purchased as the only, or best, indicator of whether a merger enhances buyer market power. Nor do the Agencies evaluate the competitive effects of mergers between competing buyers strictly, or even primarily, on the basis of effects in the downstream markets in which the merging firms sell.

> *Example 24*: Merging Firms A and B are the only two buyers in the relevant geographic market for an agricultural product. Their merger will enhance buyer power and depress the price paid to farmers for this product, causing a transfer of wealth from farmers to the merged firm and inefficiently reducing supply. These effects can arise even if the merger will not lead to any increase in the price charged by the merged firm for its output....

EU Notice on the Definition of the Relevant Market for the Purposes of Community Competition Law

1997 O.J. C 372.

... The equivalent analysis is applicable in cases concerning the concentration of buying power, where the starting point would then be the supplier and the price test allows to identify the alternative distribution channels or outlets for the supplier's products . . .

EU Guidelines on the Assessment of Horizontal Mergers

O.J. 2004, C 31/5.

IV. POSSIBLE ANTI-COMPETITIVE EFFECTS OF HORIZONTAL MERGERS. . . . *Mergers creating or strengthening buyer power in upstream markets*. The Commission may also analyse to what extent a merged entity will increase its buyer power in upstream markets. On the one hand, a merger that creates or strengthens the market power of a buyer may significantly impede effective competition, in particular by creating or strengthening a dominant position. The merged firm may be in a position to obtain lower prices by reducing its purchase of inputs. This may, in turn, lead it also to lower its level of output in the final product market, and thus harm consumer welfare. Such effects may in particular arise when upstream sellers are relatively fragmented. Competition in the downstream markets could also be adversely affected if, in particular, the merged entity were likely to use its buyer power vis-à-vis its suppliers to foreclose its rivals.

On the other hand, increased buyer power may be beneficial for competition. If increased buyer power lowers input costs without restricting downstream competition or total output, then a proportion of these cost reductions are likely to be passed onto consumers in the form of lower prices.

In order to assess whether a merger would significantly impede effective competition by creating or strengthening buyer power, an analysis of the competitive conditions in upstream markets and an evaluation of the possible positive and negative effects described above are therefore required. . . .

Questions on U.S.–EU Agency Materials on Buyers That Enhance Buyer Power

1. Do the U.S. and EU agency approaches differ on assessments of mergers between buyers that may create buyer power?

2. Is the EU right to allow the defense that increased buyer power might lower input prices without lowering downstream output?

a. Is that very likely?

b. If output were not affected by lower prices, isn't it likely that quality would be?

c. Is it likely an adjudicator could determine in which cases buyer power would not have anticompetitive effects downstream?

d. Even if downstream output were not affected, isn't the effect on upstream sellers anticompetitive?

3. If a merger lowers prices by creating buyer power, does that really count as a procompetitive effect?

Case No. IV/M.784—Kesko/Tuko

O.J. 1997, L 110/53.

[This case involved a merger between Kesko and Tuko, Finnish firms active in the retail sales of daily consumer goods and/or speciality goods. The Commission concluded that the merger would have an impact on the following markets: (1) the retail market for daily consumer goods; (2) the market for cash-and-carry sales of daily consumer goods (a cash-and-carry outlet is a shop that does not provide delivery services); and (3) the markets for procurement of daily consumer goods. One of the concerns was that, due to the combined size, these two firms could acquire substantial buyer power.]

The most important distribution channel for daily consumer goods is clearly through retail supermarkets ... [T]he combined ... share of Kesko and Tuko of the [Finnish] retail market for daily consumer goods is at least 55%. The second most important channel is sales at cash-and-carry outlets. In this market, the combined national market share of Kesko and Tuko is about 80%. Kesko's and Tuko's total sales in the cash-and-carry market equal more than 25% of their retail sales. This guarantees Kesko an extremely powerful negotiating position vis-à-vis the producers of daily consumer goods.

Although distribution channels other than supermarkets, e.g. pharmacies, are available to some producers, mainly in the non-food sector it is clear that distribution channels other than those dominated by Kesko and Tuko are not viable alternative distribution channels for the majority of producers ...

As an indication of the magnitude of the buying power of Kesko and Tuko, the majority of the suppliers (including several major multinationals) who replied to the Commission's investigation indicated that they depend on Kesko and Tuko for approximately 50 to 75% of their total sales in Finland. The dependency of different suppliers will differ according to the nature and size of their business and consumer perception regarding their products. Thus, although some very large producers of highly regarded brand products may have some countervailing power vis-à-vis Kesko, it will be of vital importance for most small and medium-sized producers to maintain sales through Kesko at the present level.

Kesko will not be dependent on any individual supplier to the same extent. Kesko has provided a series of statistics purporting to show its dependence on producers in terms of percentages of individual products purchased from individual producers. However, the percentages are not particularly high, exceeding 50% for one supplier in only four of 10 product groups cited. In any event, for any one product group Kesko will normally be able to switch from one supplier to another, since there will nearly always be an alternative large producer with adequate capacity to meet increased short-term demand. The producers, on the other hand, will not have a similar possibility to switch from Kesko post-merger, since Kesko's retailing competitors will not have the capacity (with only about 40% of the market) and additional retailing capacity can only be brought on-stream in the medium or even long term.

Moreover, recent developments in retailing will enhance the buying power of the merged entity. In particular, private label development is a key element in the power wielded by retailers vis-à-vis branded daily consumer-goods producers. It enables retailers, who are inevitably privy to commercially sensitive details regarding the branded goods producers' product launches and promotional strategies, to act as competitors as well as key customers of the producers. This privileged position increases the leverage enjoyed by retailers over branded-goods producers. Both Kesko and Tuko already market successful private label products. Again, a new dimension in retailers' control over information is emerging with the increased use of store payment cards and "loyalty" cards, which enable retailers to make targeted appeals to individual consumers based on known patterns of past purchases and socio-demographic profiles. The potential combination and expansion of Kesko's and Tuko's card schemes will enhance their negotiating power vis-à-vis producers, who do not enjoy the same immediate access to information as consumer behaviour.

For these reasons, and given that the concentration would lead to dominant positions on the retail and cash-and-carry markets, the Commission is of the opinion that the increased buying power of Kesko would further reinforce the dominant position of Kesko on the retail and cash-and-carry markets. In particular Kesko would be able to use its buying power to employ different strategies, the long-term effects of which would be to further weaken the position of its competitors....

Questions on Kesko/Tuko

1. Do you agree with the European Commission's view that buyer market power would be all right if countervailing seller market power existed?

2. Could the SSNIP test be of any help in assessing the presence of buyer market power?

3. Is the European Commission right to think that the existence of private labels worsens matters or increases retailer leverage over sellers? Similarly, is the European Commission right right to think that enhanced consumer information increases anticompetitive leverage?

b. SHOULD MERGERS BETWEEN SELLERS BE DEEMED CONSTRAINED BY BUYER POWER?

U.S. DOJ/FTC, Horizontal Merger Guidelines

(2010).

8. Powerful Buyers

Powerful buyers are often able to negotiate favorable terms with their suppliers. Such terms may reflect the lower costs of serving these buyers, but they also can reflect price discrimination in their favor.

The Agencies consider the possibility that powerful buyers may constrain the ability of the merging parties to raise prices. This can occur, for example, if powerful buyers have the ability and incentive to vertically integrate upstream or sponsor entry, or if the conduct or presence of large buyers undermines coordinated effects. However, the Agencies do not presume that the presence of powerful buyers alone forestalls adverse competitive effects flowing from the merger. Even buyers that can negotiate favorable terms may be harmed by an increase in market power. The Agencies examine the choices available to powerful buyers and how those choices likely would change due to the merger. Normally, a merger that eliminates a supplier whose presence contributed significantly to a buyer's negotiating leverage will harm that buyer.

Example 22: Customer C has been able to negotiate lower pre-merger prices than other customers by threatening to shift its large volume of purchases from one merging firm to the other. No other suppliers are as well placed to meet Customer C's needs for volume and reliability. The merger is likely to harm Customer C. In this situation, the Agencies could identify a price discrimination market consisting of Customer C and similarly placed customers. The merger threatens to end previous price discrimination in their favor.

Furthermore, even if some powerful buyers could protect themselves, the Agencies also consider whether market power can be exercised against other buyers.

Example 23: In Example 22, if Customer C instead obtained the lower pre-merger prices based on a credible threat to supply its own needs, or to sponsor new entry, Customer C might not be harmed. However, even in this case, other customers may still be harmed. . . .

EU Guidelines on the Assessment of Horizontal Mergers
O.J. 2004, C 31/5.

V. COUNTERVAILING BUYER POWER. The competitive pressure on a supplier is not only exercised by competitors but can also come from its customers. Even firms with very high market shares may not be in a position, post-merger, to significantly impede effective competition, in particular by acting to an appreciable extent independently of their customers, if the latter possess countervailing buyer power. Countervailing buyer power in this context should be understood as the bargaining strength that the buyer has vis-à-vis the seller in commercial negotiations due to its size, its commercial significance to the seller and its ability to switch to alternative suppliers.

The Commission considers, when relevant, to what extent customers will be in a position to counter the increase in market power that a merger would otherwise be likely to create. One source of countervailing buyer power would be if a customer could credibly threaten to resort, within a reasonable timeframe, to alternative sources of supply should the supplier decide to increase prices or to otherwise deteriorate quality or the conditions of delivery. This would be the case if the buyer could immediately switch to other suppliers, credibly threaten to vertically integrate into the upstream market or to sponsor upstream expansion or entry for instance by persuading a potential entrant to enter by committing to placing large orders with this company. It is more likely that large and sophisticated customers will possess this kind of countervailing buyer power than smaller firms in a fragmented industry. A buyer may also exercise countervailing buying power by refusing to buy other products produced by the supplier or, particularly in the case of durable goods, delaying purchases.

In some cases, it may be important to pay particular attention to the incentives of buyers to utilise their buyer power. For example, a downstream firm may not wish to make an investment in sponsoring new entry if the benefits of such entry in terms of lower input costs could also be reaped by its competitors.

Countervailing buyer power cannot be found to sufficiently off-set potential adverse effects of a merger if it only ensures that a particular segment of customers, with particular bargaining strength, is shielded from significantly higher prices or deteriorated conditions after the merger. Furthermore, it is not sufficient that buyer power exists prior to the merger, it must also exist and remain effective following the merger. This is because a merger of two suppliers may reduce buyer power if it thereby removes a credible alternative.

Questions on Whether Buyer Power Should Alter Assessments of Mergers That Otherwise Create Seller Market Power

1.   Where a merger would create a seller with market power, is it clear that the existence of buyer market power will prevent the merger from raising prices or lowering output? See Chapter 2.H.

2.   Wouldn't it be better to allow the buyer market power to be corrected by market forces rather than to entrench market power on both sides?

3.   Doesn't a powerful buyer have incentives not to exercise its countervailing market power to reduce seller maker power but rather to collude with the seller to preserve and enhance seller market power in exchange for a share of the sellers' supracompetitive profits?

4.   Even when the powerful buyer does try to exercise countervailing market power, isn't it indeterminate whether this will raise or lower prices?

United States v. Baker Hughes, Inc.

908 F.2d 981 (D.C. Cir. 1990).

■ CLARENCE THOMAS, CIRCUIT JUDGE:

Appellee Oy Tampella AB, a Finnish corporation, through its subsidiary Tamrock AG, manufactures and sells hardrock hydraulic underground drilling rigs (HHUDRs) in the United States and throughout the world. Appellee Baker Hughes Inc., a corporation based in Houston, Texas, owned a French subsidiary, Eimco Secoma, S.A. (Secoma), that was similarly involved in the HHUDR industry. In 1989, Tamrock proposed to acquire Secoma.

The United States challenged the proposed acquisition, charging that it would substantially lessen competition in the United States HHUDR market in violation of section 7 of the Clayton Act, . . . [T]he district court held a bench trial and issued a decision rejecting the government's request for a permanent injunction and dismissing the section 7 claim. . . .

The basic outline of a section 7 horizontal acquisition case is familiar. By showing that a transaction will lead to undue concentration in the market for a particular product in a particular geographic area,[2] the government establishes a presumption that the transaction will substantially lessen competition. *See United States v. Citizens & Southern Nat'l Bank,* 422 U.S. 86, 120–22 (1975); *Philadelphia Nat'l Bank,* 374 U.S. at 363. The burden of producing evidence to rebut this presumption then shifts to the defendant. *See, e.g., Marine Bancorporation,* 418 U.S. at 631; *General Dynamics,* 415 U.S. at 496–504; *Philadelphia Bank,* 374 U.S. at 363. If the defendant successfully rebuts the presumption, the burden of producing additional evidence of anticompetitive effect shifts to the government, and merges with the ultimate burden of persuasion, which remains with the government at all times. *See Kaiser Aluminum & Chem. Corp. v. FTC,* 652 F.2d 1324, 1340 & n.12 (7th Cir.1981).

By presenting statistics showing that combining the market shares of Tamrock and Secoma would significantly increase concentration in the already highly concentrated United States HHUDR market, the government established a prima facie case of anticompetitive effect.[3] The district court, however, found sufficient evidence that the merger would not substantially lessen competition to conclude that the defendants had rebutted this prima facie case. The government did not produce any additional evidence showing a probability of substantially lessened competition, and thus failed to carry its ultimate burden of persuasion. . . .

The district . . . court gave particular weight to two non-entry factors: the flawed underpinnings of the government's prima facie case and the sophistication of HHUDR consumers. The court's consideration of these factors was not only appropriate, but imperative, because in this case these factors significantly affected the probability that the acquisition would have anticompetitive effects.

---

2. The parties in this case do not seriously contest the district court's definition of the relevant markets. The court defined the geographic market as the entire United States, and the relevant product as three types of HHUDRs: face drills ("jumbos"), long-hole drills, and roof-bolting drills, as well as associated spare parts, components, and accessories, and used drills. . . .

3. From 1986 through 1988, Tamrock had an average 40.8% share of the United States HHUDR market, while Secoma's share averaged 17.5%. In 1988 alone, the two firms enjoyed a combined share of 76% of the market. . . . The acquisition thus has brought about a dramatic increase in the Herfindahl–Hirschman Index (HHI)—a yardstick of concentration—for this market. The Department of Justice's Merger Guidelines characterize as "highly concentrated" any market in which the HHI exceeds 1800. This acquisition has increased the HHI in this market from 2878 to 4303.

With respect to the first factor, the statistical basis of the prima facie case, the court accepted the defendants' argument that the government's statistics were misleading. Because the United States HHUDR market is minuscule, market share statistics are "volatile and shifting," and easily skewed. In 1986, for instance, only 22 HHUDRs were sold in the United States. In 1987, the number rose to 43, and in 1988 it fell to 38. Every HHUDR sold during this period, thus, increased the seller's market share by two to five percent. A contract to provide multiple HHUDRs could catapult a firm from last to first place. The district court found that, in this unusual market, "at any given point in time an individual seller's future competitive strength may not be accurately reflected." While acknowledging that the HHUDR market would be highly concentrated after Tamrock acquired Secoma, the court found that such concentration in and of itself would not doom competition. High concentration has long been the norm in this market. For example, only four firms sold HHUDRs in the United States between 1986 and 1989. Nor is concentration surprising where, as here, a product is esoteric and its market small. Indeed, the trial judge found that "[c]oncentration has existed for some time [in the United States HHUDR market] but there is no proof of overpricing, excessive profit or any decline in quality, service or diminishing innovation."

The second non-entry factor that the district court considered was the sophistication of HHUDR consumers. HHUDRs currently cost hundreds of thousands of dollars, and orders can exceed $1 million. These products are hardly trinkets sold to small consumers who may possess imperfect information and limited bargaining power. HHUDR buyers closely examine available options and typically insist on receiving multiple, confidential bids for each order. This sophistication, the court found, was likely to promote competition even in a highly concentrated market.

.... These findings provide considerable support for the district court's conclusion that the defendants successfully rebutted the government's prima facie case. Because the defendants also provided compelling evidence on ease of entry into this market, we need not decide whether these findings, without more, are sufficient to rebut the government's prima facie case. The foregoing analysis of non-entry factors is intended merely to underscore that ... these factors are relevant, and can even be dispositive, in a section 7 rebuttal analysis....

Note and Questions on *Baker Hughes*

Another way to state *Baker Hughes'* first factor is that in bid markets, where firms bid for the same jobs and market shares turn on which firms won the bids in any given year, it may not make sense to get too fixated on those market shares rather than on the number of firms able to make such bids. But even if this is so, does it alter the fact that a merger between two of the few firms in the market is likely to significantly increase concentration?

The second factor *Baker Hughes* relied on was the sophistication of buyers in that market. Does this factor make sense? Would the ability of a merged firm with market power to raise prices be offset if buyers are sophisticated? Perhaps the court simply meant that, where such buyers procure secret bids for large contracts, they are likely to disrupt oligopolistic coordination. But if so, this would only seem relevant if the anticompetitive theory were that oligopolistic coordination would occur post-merger, which is unclear given that the merged firm would have 76% of the market. Further, such a rebuttal would require the more detailed sort of inquiry indicated in U.S. Horizontal Merger Guideline § 2.11 for assessing claims that such large buyers can disrupt oligopolistic coordination.

Baker Hughes did not hold that the above factors sufficed to rebut the government's prima facie case because it also found that entry barriers were low. Should those factors have sufficed without evidence of low entry barriers? Are they necessary if entry barriers are low? Do those factors really add much to the inquiry if the answers to these questions are "no"?

Commission Decision 1999/641/EC, Enso/Stora

O.J. 1999, L 254/9.

... The liquid packaging board market is characterised by few large producers and few large buyers. In addition to Stora and Enso, the producers of liquid packaging board in Europe include only Korsnäs and AssiDomän. Buyers of liquid packaging board are few and the market is dominated by Tetra Pak, which represents an estimated market share of close to [between 60 and 80%]*.[72] The other main buyers of liquid packaging board are Elopak and SIG Combibloc with about [between 10 and 20%]* of the EEA market each. After the merger the structure of the supply-side will mirror the structure of the demand-side of the market for liquid packaging board, with one large supplier and two smaller suppliers facing one large buyer and two smaller buyers.

According to the parties, the three large customers, and Tetra Pak in particular, exercise considerable buyer power that prevents the producers of liquid packaging board from increasing prices.

The investigation showed that the relationship between the suppliers and the customers is one of mutual dependency. In the liquid packaging board market the relationships between suppliers and buyer are of a long-term nature and switching supplier of liquid packaging board is rare. The customers have indicated that switching the supplier would lead to delays, is costly and technically demanding due to the fact that the evaluation process for liquid packaging board is complex and time-consuming. In particular, the investigation showed that to become a supplier for a specific type of liquid packaging board requires considerable investment from both the producer and the customer in terms of machinery, technical support production and product trials as well as human resources.

As evidence regarding the long-term relationship between the producers and the buyers, it is noted that in the case of Enso the longest customer relationship goes back 40 years. Further evidence of the long-term and mutually dependent supplier-buyer relationships in the industry is the fact

---

72. [Editor's Note: The " * " in this opinion means that the precise figures are subject to confidentiality restrictions.]

that Enso has divided its research and development activities into units, which specialise in developing boards for Tetra Pak, Elopak and SIG Combibloc respectively.

An examination of each of the main buyers confirms that the demand-side has countervailing buyer power.

Tetra Pak buys about [more than 500000 tonnes] of liquid packaging board per year for use in the EEA. This volume is bought from Enso, Stora, AssiDomän and Korsnäs. Outside the EEA, Tetra Pak also uses other local suppliers. Tetra Pak has in the past been instrumental in developing several of its current suppliers into producers of liquid packaging board.

Tetra Pak buys about [more than 50%] of its requirements in the EEA from Stora Enso. The purchases of Tetra Pak represent the whole output of several board machines and about [more than 50%] of the parties' total output for the EEA. Furthermore, it has to be considered that the production of liquid packaging board is a high fixed-cost industry, where high rates of capacity utilisation are necessary in order to achieve satisfactory levels of profitability. To lose the large volumes purchased by Tetra Pak would therefore mean that the parties would have to find other customers in order to fill the capacity. This would not be an easy task in the short term.

Tetra Pak, on the other hand, buys such volumes of liquid packaging board that it would have the option of developing new capacity with other existing or new suppliers, should the parties attempt to exercise market power. In addition, Tetra Pak, through close cooperation with the producers of liquid packaging board, has an intimate knowledge of the cost structure of the parties. Furthermore, the liquid packaging board represents about [more than 50%] of the cost of the blank supplied by Tetra Pak to its customers. The Commission has also noted that plastic may to a certain extent be a substitute for liquid packaging board in the long term in the downstream market for the packaging of liquids. Tetra Pak, therefore, has every incentive to seek to exercise its countervailing buyer power.

Consequently, for all the reasons stated above, it is concluded that Tetra Pak has countervailing buyer power to such an extent that it will neutralise the potential increase in market power of the merger between Stora and Enso.

Elopak and SIG Combibloc are buying much smaller volumes of liquid packaging board than Tetra Pak. Furthermore, in particular where Elopak is concerned, it is noted that Elopak and Enso's subsidiary Pakenso at present run joint converting activities in Lahti in Finland [. . .]. These joint converting activities represent a significant proportion of the total amount of cartons converted by Elopak. This link to the parties could weaken the buyer power of Elopak following the merger.

However, it also has to be considered that both companies place orders large enough to fill the capacity of a board machine. This would in itself make it difficult for Elopak and SIG Combibloc to switch a significant proportion of volumes sourced to alternative suppliers at short notice. However, it also means that a large shift of volumes to alternative suppliers such as AssiDomän and Korsnäs, who could in principle switch WTL capacity to the production of liquid packaging board, could hurt Stora Enso significantly, should the parties attempt to exercise market power. Elopak and SIG Combibloc both also source strategic volumes from the United States, which strengthens their countervailing buyer power. Both of them also have significant operations outside the EEA. Finally, as for Tetra Pak, both Elopak and SIG Combibloc have detailed knowledge of the cost structure of the parties. They also have the same incentives as Tetra Pak to exercise their buyer power.

Compared to Tetra Pak, both companies are, nevertheless, in a weaker position in the short to medium term vis-à-vis Stora Enso, since they will have only one EEA supplier after the merger, whereas Tetra Pak will have three. Furthermore, Elopak and SIG Combibloc source much smaller volumes than Tetra Pak. Therefore, while it is true that Elopak and SIG Combibloc are not without any means to counter a price increase, it seems that the proposed merger will shift the balance of power towards Stora Enso in its relationship with Elopak and SIG Combibloc.

Furthermore, in the case of Elopak and SIG Combibloc, it also has to be considered that the parties will have an incentive to have both companies as major players in the market in order to not to become completely dependent on Tetra Pak. Therefore, while the concern that Elopak and SIG Combibloc could be disadvantaged by the merger in comparison with Tetra Pak is not completely removed, it also has to be recognised that the countervailing buyer power of Tetra Pak will for this reason, to a certain extent, spill over to Elopak and SIG Combibloc as well. In addition, the undertakings given by the parties are an attempt by the parties to address these concerns. It is in particular noted that Enso's divestiture of its share in the joint converting activities with Elopak in Lahti in Finland will remove any concerns that this link could have given the parties an increased leverage over Elopak.

In conclusion, the merger will result in a market structure with one large and two smaller suppliers facing one large and two smaller buyers. This is a rather exceptional market structure. On balance, the Commission considers that the buyers in these rather special market circumstances have sufficient countervailing buyer power to remove the possibility of the parties' exercising market power. . . .

Based on the above, it may be concluded that the parties will have a large market position in the market for liquid packaging board. There will be only limited potential competition. However, the demand-side is as concentrated as the supply-side, and the countervailing buyer power of the main buyers, in particular Tetra Pak, means that the operation will not lead to the creation or strengthening of a dominant position in the market for liquid packaging board.

Questions on *Enso Stora*

1. In this case, Tetra Pak buys 60–80% of the available quantities of liquid packaging board. The two other main buyers have together a 10–20% market share. This gives Tetra Pak significant countervailing buyer power over the merging firms. How would the situation be different if Tetra Pak, Elopak and SIG Combibloc each had an equivalent market share of 33%?

a. Would this weaken or strengthen the claim of the merging firms that they faced significant countervailing buyer?

b. Is there a specific degree of buyer concentration below which a countervailing buyer power argument will be denied or does it depend on the circumstances?

c. Is the degree of buyer concentration the only relevant factor when assessing countervailing buyer power?

i. What is the relevance of significant buyer switching costs?

ii. What is the relevance of buyer knowledge of the merging firms' cost structure?

2. Could smaller buyers be affected by the merger in ways that Tetra Pak wouldn't be?

a. Does the merger reduce the smaller buyers' bargaining position vis-à-vis the merged firm? Why?

b. Does the merger also create a risk that, as far as their supplies of liquid packaging board are concerned, they will be placed at a cost disadvantage compared to Tetra Pak? How so?

3. *Enso Stora* involves a homogeneous product (liquid packaging board) where brand does not matter. How is the strength of the countervailing power defense affected when the merging parties hold powerful (must-carry) brands?

4. *Enso Stora* is a single firm dominance case and the Commission guidelines seem also to refer to single firm dominance cases.

a. How would analysis of a countervailing buyer power argument be affected if it did not involve single firm dominance but collective dominance?

b. All things being equal, is a large buyer better able to exercise its countervailing buyer power when faced with a firm holding a single dominant position or several firms holding a collective dominant position?

Commissioner of Competition v. Superior Propane Inc.

2000 Canada Comp. Trib. 16 (April 4, 2002).

Pre-existing Monopsony ... Where consumers have organized to extract a subcompetitive price from producers in an industry, the gain in consumer surplus is not a gain to society because it comes at the expense of a corresponding loss in producers' profits. A subsequent merger that conferred market power on producers might be allowed to proceed in light of efficiency gains by ignoring the loss of the consumer surplus due to the pre-existing monopsony; only that portion of the wealth transfer that resulted from the increase in price above the competitive level would be considered.

The Tribunal agrees that, if it is to consider redistributional effects under a standard other than the Total Surplus Standard, it should not automatically count the loss of consumer surplus attributable to pre-existing monopsony power against the merger if section 96 is invoked. The appropriate treatment of the various redistributional effects depends on the evidence presented, and that portion of the wealth transfer from consumers to producers may not be an adverse effect of the merger.

Although the Tribunal agrees with the submission of counsel, it notes that a merger policy that favours consumers over producers/shareholders would object to the loss of pre-existing monopsony benefits and, hence, in the scenario offered by counsel, the loss to consumers of their monopsony benefits would be counted against a merger that offered countervailing market power. Yet this is not the approach offered by counsel for the Commissioner, presumably because it is not what the Act requires. As noted previously, the Tribunal held and the Court agreed that the paramount objective of the merger provisions of the Act is efficiency....

In the Tribunal's view, the monopsony example raises a critical issue. Why should the merger provisions of the Act deny the consumer benefit in that instance? There must be some reason why merger policy concerns itself with the competitive price, even when achieving that price harms consumers by denying their monopsonistic gains.

The answer to that question ... is, clearly, economic efficiency itself. Competitive prices are desirable, not because they are low or fair to consumers-indeed, they may be quite the opposite-but rather because, in a wide range of circumstances, they promote economic efficiency quite generally. If this were not true, then there would be no particular reason to favour competitive markets....

Note and Questions on *Superior Propane*

Many other nations also consider countervailing bargaining power to be a factor that lessens the anticompetitive effect of a merger.[73]

1. Do you agree that merger analysis should exclude any harm to consumer welfare that results from a rise in prices from subcompetitive levels (that resulted from pre-merger monopsony levels) to competitive levels?

2. If so, do you agree that this means consumer welfare cannot be the ultimate test?

3. Is it clear that prices will move closer to competitive levels when a merger creates seller market power and monopsony power existed pre-merger?

4. Would it be better to block the merger and have the monopsony power undone by market or legal forces?

---

73. *See, e.g.,* Australia Trade Practices Act § 50(3)(d); Brazil Horizontal Merger Guidelines § 84 (2001); South Africa Competition Act § 12A(2)(d); South Korea Merger Guidelines VII.1.B(4) (2009).

c. SHOULD BUYER VIEWS ALTER ASSESSMENTS OF MERGERS BETWEEN SELLERS?

Commission Decision 1999/641/EC, Enso/Stora
O.J. 1999, L 254/9.

... Reactions from third parties. The customers, in particular, have ranged from neutral to positive in their reaction. According to customers a major long-term strategic issue for the liquid packaging board industry is the possibility that plastic will over time replace paper for more and more applications. The liquid packaging board industry as such, therefore, needs to become more competitive. The merger between Stora and Enso should allow a more efficient production of liquid packaging board and will, therefore, contribute to improving the long-term competitiveness of liquid packaging board vis-à-vis plastic packaging materials....

Questions on *Enso Stora*

1. Should it matter that buyers were not complaining about the merger in *Enso Stora*?

2. Should that be dispositive or just a relevant factor?

U.S. DOJ/FTC, Horizontal Merger Guidelines
(2010).

2.2 Sources of Evidence ....

2.2.2 Customers

Customers can provide a variety of information to the Agencies, ranging from information about their own purchasing behavior and choices to their views about the effects of the merger itself.

Information from customers about how they would likely respond to a price increase, and the relative attractiveness of different products or suppliers, may be highly relevant, especially when corroborated by other evidence such as historical purchasing patterns and practices. Customers also can provide valuable information about the impact of historical events such as entry by a new supplier.

The conclusions of well-informed and sophisticated customers on the likely impact of the merger itself can also help the Agencies investigate competitive effects, because customers typically feel the consequences of both competitively beneficial and competitively harmful mergers. In evaluating such evidence, the Agencies are mindful that customers may oppose, or favor, a merger for reasons unrelated to the antitrust issues raised by that merger.

When some customers express concerns about the competitive effects of a merger while others view the merger as beneficial or neutral, the Agencies take account of this divergence in using the information provided by customers and consider the likely reasons for such divergence of views.

For example, if for regulatory reasons some customers cannot buy imported products, while others can, a merger between domestic suppliers may harm the former customers even if it leaves the more flexible customers unharmed. See Section 3.

When direct customers of the merging firms compete against one another in a downstream market, their interests may not be aligned with the interests of final consumers, especially if the direct customers expect to pass on any anticompetitive price increase. A customer that is protected from adverse competitive effects by a long-term contract, or otherwise relatively immune from the merger's harmful effects, may even welcome an anticompetitive merger that provides that customer with a competitive advantage over its downstream rivals.

> *Example 1:* As a result of the merger, Customer C will experience a price increase for an input used in producing its final product, raising its costs. Customer C's rivals use this input more intensively than Customer C, and the same price increase applied to them will raise their costs more than it raises Customer C's costs. On balance, Customer C may benefit from the merger even though the merger involves a substantial lessening of competition.

2.2.3   Other Industry Participants and Observers

Suppliers, indirect customers, distributors, other industry participants, and industry analysts can also provide information helpful to a merger inquiry. The interests of firms selling products complementary to those offered by the merging firms often are well aligned with those of customers, making their informed views valuable.

Information from firms that are rivals to the merging parties can help illuminate how the market operates. The interests of rival firms often diverge from the interests of customers, since customers normally lose, but rival firms gain, if the merged entity raises its prices. For that reason, the Agencies do not routinely rely on the overall views of rival firms regarding the competitive effects of the merger. However, rival firms may provide relevant facts, and even their overall views may be instructive, especially in cases where the Agencies are concerned that the merged entity may engage in exclusionary conduct.

> *Example 2:* Merging Firms A and B operate in a market in which network effects are significant, implying that any firm's product is significantly more valuable if it commands a large market share or if it is interconnected with others that in aggregate command such a share. Prior to the merger, they and their rivals voluntarily interconnect with one another. The merger would create an entity with a large enough share that a strategy of ending voluntary interconnection would have a dangerous probability of creating monopoly power in this market. The interests of rivals and of consumers would be broadly aligned in preventing such a merger.

3.   Targeted Customers and Price Discrimination

When examining possible adverse competitive effects from a merger, the Agencies consider whether those effects vary significantly for different customers purchasing the same or similar products. Such differential impacts are possible when sellers can discriminate, e.g., by profitably raising price to certain targeted customers but not to others. The possibility of price discrimination influences market definition (see Section 4), the measurement of market shares (see Section 5), and the evaluation of competitive effects (see Sections 6 and 7).

When price discrimination is feasible, adverse competitive effects on targeted customers can arise, even if such effects will not arise for other customers. A price increase for targeted customers may be profitable even if a price increase for all customers would not be profitable because too many other customers would substitute away. When discrimination is reasonably likely, the Agencies may evaluate competitive effects separately by type of customer. The Agencies may have access to information unavailable to customers that is relevant to evaluating whether discrimination is reasonably likely.

For price discrimination to be feasible, two conditions typically must be met: differential pricing and limited arbitrage.

First, the suppliers engaging in price discrimination must be able to price differently to targeted customers than to other customers. This may involve identification of individual customers to which different prices are offered or offering different prices to different types of customers based on observable characteristics.

Example 3: Suppliers can distinguish large buyers from small buyers. Large buyers are more likely than small buyers to self-supply in response to a significant price increase. The merger may lead to price discrimination against small buyers, harming them, even if large buyers are not harmed. Such discrimination can occur even if there is no discrete gap in size between the classes of large and small buyers.

In other cases, suppliers may be unable to distinguish among different types of customers but can offer multiple products that sort customers based on their purchase decisions.

Second, the targeted customers must not be able to defeat the price increase of concern by arbitrage, e.g., by purchasing indirectly from or through other customers. Arbitrage may be difficult if it would void warranties or make service more difficult or costly for customers. Arbitrage is inherently impossible for many services. Arbitrage between customers at different geographic locations may be impractical due to transportation costs. Arbitrage on a modest scale may be possible but sufficiently costly or limited that it would not deter or defeat a discriminatory pricing strategy
. . .

Buyer Noncomplaints

In practice, one of the most influential factors in determining whether U.S. enforcement agencies move to block a merger is whether buyers are complaining. For mergers that resulted in a post-merger HHI between 2000–3999, the FTC was 93% likely to challenge the merger if there were strong (that is, economically sophisticated) buyer complaints, but only 32%

likely to challenge without them.[74] With strong buyer complaints, the FTC was 100% likely to challenge a merger that left the market with between three to five significant competitors; without such buyer complaints, if the number of significant competitors was three, the likelihood was only 50%; if it was four, the likelihood was only 7%; and if it was five, the likelihood was 0%.[75] Moreover, the latter statistics include mergers where the only buyers are consumers, when the agencies clearly do not expect strong complaints given each buyer's low stake. These statistics thus probably overstate the likelihood of a challenge when a merger has business buyers who have all declined to complain. Other nations also put great weight on the existence or absence of buyer complaints.[76]

Buyers have such strong influence on merger enforcement for three main reasons. First, they often have the information that the agencies need to decide whether a merger is likely to create anticompetitive problems. Second, having buyers as witnesses is often thought necessary to putting on an effective case at trial, though that would seem to depend on whether courts treat their absence as problematic. Third, and most important, buyers are often thought to have incentives that align them well with competitive concerns, unlike rivals of the merging parties, who generally should benefit from an anticompetitive merger and be hurt by an efficient one. If a merger is likely to create unilateral or oligopoly effects that raise prices, then buyers have incentives to complain. If the merger were not likely to create such anticompetitive effects, or generated efficiencies that offset them enough to lower prices, then buyers would not have incentives to complain. Or so the logic goes.

However, buyer noncomplaints may provide a poor signal. One reason is that buyers may be uninformed or unsophisticated about the facts or the substance or procedure of antitrust merger analysis. The more important reason is that their incentives may be skewed. This skew means a buyer may fail to complain even though it does believe the merger is anticompetitive, or would believe so if it expended the resources to investigate the issue.[77]

Where there are many buyers, they face a collective action problem that may prevent buyers from complaining about an inefficient merger. To complain to an antitrust enforcement agency, firms must incur significant individual costs. These include not only the considerable economic cost of doing serious economic and legal analysis, but often more important the cost of possible retaliation or maltreatment by the firms that wish to merge, which those firms will have even more power to do if the merger succeeds. In contrast, the benefits of successfully complaining are collective and nonexclusive because each buyer benefits if an inefficient merger is

74.   *See* FTC, Horizontal Merger Investigation Data: Fiscal Years 1996–2003, at Tables 7.1–7.2 (2004).

75.   *Id.* at 8.1–8.2. *See also* Coate & Ulrick, *supra* note 22, at 549, 561.

76.   *See* ABA, I COMPETITION LAWS OUTSIDE THE UNITED STATES at Canada–84–85 (2001).

77.   In contrast, the existence of complaints by a credible buyer (that is not also a rival) provides a stronger signal, for if the buyer really thought the merger was likely to lower prices, it would have no incentive to expend the considerable resources it takes to mount a credible complaint in a merger case.

blocked whether it complained or not. Moreover, each buyer likely realizes that its single decision whether or not to complain is unlikely to affect the outcome. Thus, each buyer has individual incentives to free ride on the possible complaints of other buyers because the costs of complaining are borne individually whereas the benefits are collective. The result can be that no buyer complains even though the merger is in fact inefficient.

Where some buyers are large and have buyer market power, collective action problems may be less important. But this market structure creates other incentive problems. The powerful buyers may figure that their purchasing power will get them discounts from the supracompetitive prices inflicted on rivals or potential entrants.[78] Such special discounts may fully offset any price increase expected from the merger, or go beyond such an offset to give the powerful buyers a share of the seller's supracompetitive profits, but even if they don't, the competitive advantage the powerful buyers gain against their less powerful rivals may give them additional downstream profits that offset the cost of any merger-caused price increase. Indeed, firms seeking to merge are generally advised to go to all their buyers before proposing their merger to give them whatever assurances are necessary to get them to refrain from complaining, which often take the form of special long-term contracts guaranteeing that the prices of such powerful buyers will not be raised if the merger goes through, which effectively guarantees them precisely just a special discount.

Further, just as a few firms in an oligopolistic industry can coordinate on price, perhaps a few firms in an industry can also coordinate on a policy of not objecting to each other's mergers. True, this requires coordination across levels of production and over time. But if the firms in the industry are few enough, they can develop a social norm against complaining about each others' mergers. Anecdotal evidence suggests such a norm exists in many industries, and a firm that deviated from it might well expect others to complain about its mergers. Any firm that thinks it might want to merge down the line thus may have incentives not to object to mergers by others.

Further, business buyers are generally corporations, and corporations cannot speak for themselves—only their managers can. A firm's managers may benefit from a short-term price reduction, or by avoiding the costs of complaining, even if the firm's long-term costs increase because the merger enhanced seller market power that harms their successors. That is, agency costs might mean that no corporate buyer complains about an anticompetitive merger.

Finally, other buyers might have special reasons why they might not oppose an inefficient merger. Some buyers may plan to enter the relevant market themselves, like HMOs who do not object to hospital mergers because the HMOs themselves plan to enter the market for providing some medical-surgical services. Increased market concentration makes such entry easier and more profitable for such buyers. Other buyers are governmental actors who do not face market discipline but do face political pressure, and thus may lack sufficient incentives to oppose inefficient mergers. Moreover, to the extent any increased monopoly profits are

---

78. *See* Elhauge, supra note 51, at 288–92.

garnered in-state, whereas much of the anticompetitive costs are external-ized outside the state, state buying agencies may have incentives not to oppose inefficient mergers.

One might imagine coupling evidence of a lack of buyer complaints with economic analysis rebutting all the above concerns. But the economic analysis that would be necessary to determine whether buyer noncomp-laints are reliable indicators of merger efficiency is probably more compli-cated and less accurate than the economic analysis employed to analyze directly the merger on structural grounds. Thus, even though buyer non-complaints may not be irrelevant, they do not appear to offer a useful screen for avoiding traditional analysis of market structure.

B.   Vertical Mergers

Vertical mergers have several possible anticompetitive effects. General-ly, these effects are similar to the possible anticompetitive effects from exclusive dealing. That is, the concern is that the vertical merger might foreclose a sufficient share of suppliers or buyers to rivals that it impairs the ability of rivals to compete, and may even effectively require two-level entry to compete. If there are few firms in the market, vertical mergers might also facilitate oligopolistic coordination among them by making their pricing more noticeable (such as when a manufacturer merges into retail) or because the merged firm can, as buyer, better monitor rival upstream pricing.

Vertical mergers also raise the concern that they might eliminate potential horizontal competition, such as when the merging firms are likely to have entered each others' market absent the merger. We will, however, defer those issues to the section on conglomerate mergers, which centers more directly on that issue. Finally, vertical integration might facilitate price discrimination if the integrated firm is more able to stop any buyer resales that would otherwise undermine such price discrimination. As usual, such price discrimination might decrease or increase consumer or total welfare, but usually it decreases consumer welfare and increases total welfare, efficiency, and market output.

Absent one of those anticompetitive effects, even firms with market power generally have no incentive to use vertical mergers to prevent vigorous competition upstream or downstream because their market power at any given stage is greater if other production or distribution stages are more efficient because that increases the value of the ultimate product to consumers. Vertical mergers can also have affirmatively procompetitive effects. In part, these are similar to the possible procompetitive effects from exclusive dealing. Vertical mergers can reduce uncertainty, eliminate free riding incentives between manufacturers and dealers in promoting a brand, or more generally encourage firm-specific investments, but do so in a way that systematically restricts opportunism rather than being limited to specific deals. Vertical mergers can also create other important additional efficiencies. Like horizontal mergers, they can create efficiencies from integration like synergies, economies of scale or scope, or lowered administrative costs. Further, where vertical mergers combine firms that have market or monopoly power in successive markets, they avoid the lower output or inefficient substitution that such successive market power causes.

In the United States, the current law on vertical mergers is obscure. *Brown Shoe* did condemn a vertical merger that foreclosed only 1.2% of the relevant market. But, while that case has never been overruled, it clearly does not reflect modern antitrust practice. The U.S. agencies issued guidelines in 1984 that covered vertical mergers. These certainly come closer to reflecting current law than does *Brown Shoe*. But although the parts of the guidelines dealing with horizontal mergers have repeatedly been updated since 1984, the portions on vertical and conglomerate mergers never have been. Further, former FTC Chairman Professor Pitofsky has stated, "Unlike the horizontal merger guidelines which may be the most influential piece of government regulation in the past fifty years, and the conglomerate merger guidelines which seem to have caught the direction the law was going, the vertical merger guidelines have been widely ignored."[79]

Modern U.S. antitrust enforcement policy clearly deems vertical mergers far less likely than horizontal mergers to raise anticompetitive concerns.[80] From 1996–2003, the FTC's second requests included 17 vertical cases and 162 horizontal cases.[81] Moreover, actual U.S. enforcement action against vertical mergers is nearly non-existent. "The FTC successfully challenged three vertical mergers during the Clinton administration, and the FTC during the second Bush administration has challenged one and closely examined a second. In every one of the challenged cases the merger was abandoned or substantially restructured before it was allowed to proceed so there is no court opinion elaborating on theory."[82] There is thus little concrete guidance available about the content of modern U.S. antitrust law on vertical mergers. Further complicating matters is the fact that, unlike with horizontal mergers, vertical merger enforcement in the U.S. is strongly influenced by whether Democrats or Republicans are in office. For horizontal mergers, the change from the Clinton to Bush Administration had no statistically significant effect on FTC enforcement odds.[83] In contrast, that same shift caused the odds of vertical merger challenges to drop sharply.[84] To reveal where the two varying enforcement policies currently lie, we excerpt an FTC consent decree on a vertical merger that produced divided statements by FTC commissioners.

---

79. *See* Robert Pitofsky, *Past, Present, and Future of Antitrust Enforcement at the Federal Trade Commission*, 72 U. CHIC. L. REV. 209, 220 (2005).

80. *Id.*

81. *See* FTC, Horizontal Merger Investigation Data: Fiscal Years 1996–2003, at Table 1 (2004). The figure of 162 includes not only the 151 the FTC classified as "horizontal" but also the 11 it classified as involving either buyer power or joint ventures since both of those also involve horizontal combinations.

82. *Id.*

83. *See* Coate & Ulrick, *supra* note 22, at 546–47, 554.

84. *See* Coate, *Twenty Years of Federal Trade Commission Merger Enforcement Activity* (1985–2004), Potomac Working Paper in Law and Economics 05–02, at 4 & Table 1 (Oct. 2005).

In the EU, the Commission has on a number of occasions prohibited vertical mergers or authorized such mergers with corrective remedies because of their effects of possible exclusion of competitors. While the Commission has expressed concerns on the foreclosure of vertical mergers in a variety of fields, it is in the media and aviation sectors that it has taken particularly drastic measures (including several decisions of prohibitions) to avoid the potentially exclusionary effects of vertical concentrations. The current view of the Commission on vertical mergers can be found in its recently published guidelines on non-horizontal mergers.[85]

Like horizontal mergers, vertical mergers are also subject to efficiency and failing firm defenses. Entry barriers are also relevant at both the upstream and downstream levels.

U.S. DOJ, 1984 Merger Guidelines

4.21 Barriers to Entry from Vertical Mergers. In certain circumstances, the vertical integration resulting from vertical mergers could create competitively objectionable barriers to entry. Stated generally, three conditions are necessary (but not sufficient) for this problem to exist. First, the degree of vertical integration between the two markets must be so extensive that entrants to one market (the "primary market") also would have to enter the other market (the "secondary market")[30] simultaneously. Second, the requirement of entry at the secondary level must make entry at the primary level significantly more difficult and less likely to occur. Finally, the structure and other characteristics of the primary market must be otherwise so conducive to non-competitive performance that the increased difficulty of entry is likely to affect its performance. The following standards state the criteria by which the Department will determine whether these conditions are satisfied.

4.211 Need for Two–Level Entry. If there is sufficient unintegrated capacity in the secondary market, new entrants to the primary market would not have to enter both markets simultaneously. The Department is unlikely to challenge a merger on this ground where post-merger sales (purchases) by unintegrated firms in the secondary market would be sufficient to service two minimum-efficient-scale plants in the primary market. When the other conditions are satisfied, the Department is increasingly likely to challenge a merger as the unintegrated capacity declines below this level.

4.212 Increased Difficulty of Simultaneous Entry to Both Markets. The relevant question is whether the need for simultaneous entry to the secondary market gives rise to a substantial incremental difficulty as compared to entry into the primary market alone. If entry at the secondary

---

85. Guidelines on the assessment of non-horizontal mergers under the Council Regulation on the control of concentrations between undertakings, O.J. 2008, C 165/1.

30. This competitive problem could result from either upstream or downstream integration, and could affect competition in either the upstream market or the downstream market. In the text, the term "primary market" refers to the market in which the competitive concerns are being considered, and the term "secondary market" refers to the adjacent market.

level is easy in absolute terms, the requirement of simultaneous entry to that market is unlikely adversely to affect entry to the primary market. Whatever the difficulties of entry into the primary market may be, the Department is unlikely to challenge a merger on this ground if new entry into the secondary market can be accomplished under the conditions stated in Section [3]. When entry is not possible under those conditions, the Department is increasingly concerned about vertical mergers as the difficulty of entering the secondary market increases. The Department, however, will invoke this theory only where the need for secondary market entry significantly increases the costs (which may take the form of risks) of primary market entry.

More capital is necessary to enter two market than to enter one. Standing alone, however, this additional capital requirement does not constitute a barrier to entry to the primary market. If the necessary funds were available at a cost commensurate with the level of risk in the secondary market, there would be no adverse effect. In some cases, however, lenders may doubt that would-be entrants to the primary market have the necessary skills and knowledge to succeed in the secondary market and, therefore, in the primary market. In order to compensate for this rick of failure, lenders might charge a higher rate for the necessary capital. This problem becomes increasingly significant as a higher percentage of the capital assets in the secondary market are long-lived and specialized to that market and, therefore, difficult to recover in the event of failure. In evaluating the likelihood of increased barriers to entry resulting from increased cost of capital, therefore, the Department will consider both the degree of similarity in the essential skills in the primary and secondary markets and the economic life and degree of specialization of the capital assets in the secondary market.

Economies of scale in the secondary market may constitute an additional barrier to entry to the primary market in some situations requiring two-level entry. The problem could arise if the capacities of minimum-efficient-scale plants in the primary and secondary markets differ significantly. For example, if the capacity of a minimum-efficient-scale plant in the secondary market were significantly greater than the needs of a minimum-efficient-scale plant in the primary market, entrants would have to choose between inefficient operation at the secondary level (because of operating an efficient plant at an inefficient output or because of operating an efficiently small plant) or a larger than necessary scale at the primary level. Either of these effects could cause a significant increase in the operating costs of the entering firm.[33]

4.213 Structure and Performance of the Primary Market. Barriers to entry are unlikely to affect performance if the structure of the primary market is otherwise not conducive to monopolization or collusion.[34] The Department is unlikely to challenge a merger on this ground unless overall

---

33. It is important to note, however, that this problem would not exist if a significant outside market exists at the secondary level. In that case, entrants could enter with the appropriately scaled plants at both levels, and sell or buy in the market as necessary.

34. For example, a market with 100 firms of equal size would perform competitively despite a significant increase in entry barriers.

concentration of the primary market is above 1800 HHI (a somewhat lower concentration will suffice if one or more of the factors discussed in Section [2.1] indicate that effective collusion is particularly likely). Above that threshold, the Department is increasingly likely to challenge a merger that meets the other criteria set forth above as the concentration increases.

4.22   Facilitating Collusion Through Vertical Mergers.

4.221   Vertical Integration to the Retail Level. A high level of vertical integration by upstream firms into the associated retail market may facilitate collusion in the upstream market by making it easier to monitor price. Retail prices are generally more visible than prices in upstream markets, and vertical mergers may increase the level of vertical integration to the point at which the monitoring effect becomes significant. Adverse competitive consequences are unlikely unless the upstream market is generally conducive to collusion and a large percentage of the products produced there are sold through vertically integrated retail outlets.

The Department is unlikely to challenge a merger on this ground unless (1) overall concentration of the upstream market is above 1800 HHI (a somewhat lower concentration will suffice if one or more of the factors discussed in Section [2.1] indicate that effective collusion is particularly likely), and (2) a large percentage of the upstream product would be sold through vertically-integrated retail outlets after the merger. Where the stated thresholds are met or exceeded, the Department's decision whether to challenge a merger on this ground will depend upon an individual evaluation of its likely competitive effect.

4.222   Elimination of a Disruptive Buyer. The elimination by vertical merger of a particularly disruptive buyer in a downstream market may facilitate collusion in the upstream market. If upstream firms view sales to a particular buyer as sufficiently important, they may deviate from the terms of a collusive agreement in an effort to secure that business, thereby disrupting the operation of the agreement. The merger of such a buyer with an upstream firm may eliminate that rivalry, making it easier for the upstream firms to collude effectively. Adverse competitive consequences are unlikely unless the upstream market is generally conducive to collusion and the disruptive firm is significantly more attractive to sellers than the other firms in its market.

The Department is unlikely to challenge a merger on this ground unless (1) overall concentration of the upstream market is 1800 HHI or above (a somewhat lower concentration will suffice if one or more of the factors discussed in Section [2.1] indicate that effective collusion is particularly likely), and (2) the allegedly disruptive firm differs substantially in volume of purchases or other relevant characteristics from the other firms in its market. . . .

4.23   Evasion of Rate Regulation. Non-horizontal mergers may be used by monopoly public utilities subject to rate regulation as a tool for circumventing that regulation. The clearest example is the acquisition by a regulated utility of a supplier of its fixed or variable inputs. After the merger, the utility would be selling to itself and might be able arbitrarily to inflate the prices of internal transactions. Regulators may have great difficulty in policing these practices, particularly if there is no independent market for the product (or service) purchased from the affiliate. As a result, inflated prices could be passed along to consumers as "legitimate" costs. In extreme cases, the regulated firm may effectively preempt the adjacent market, perhaps for the purpose of suppressing observable market transactions, and may distort resource allocation in that adjacent market as well as in the regulated market. In such cases, however, the Department recognizes that genuine economies of integration may be involved. The Department will consider challenging mergers that create substantial opportunities for such abuses.[36]

4.24 Efficiencies. As in the case of horizontal mergers, the Department will consider expected efficiencies in determining whether to challenge a vertical merger. An extensive pattern of vertical integration may constitute evidence that substantial economies are afforded by vertical integration. Therefore, the Department will give relatively more weight to expected efficiencies in determining whether to challenge a vertical merger than in determining whether to challenge a horizontal merger.

Note and Questions on U.S. Vertical Merger Guidelines

The 1984 U.S. guidelines require that the primary market have an HHI above 1800 and that the merger either (1) anticompetitively raises entry barriers because (a) the unforeclosed market could support fewer than two firms at minimum efficient scale and (b) two-level entry is significantly harder than one-level entry into the primary market, *or* (2) facilitates oligopolistic coordination because (a) the upstream market is sufficiently concentrated and a large percentage of the upstream product would be sold through vertically-integrated outlets after the merger or (b) the merger would eliminate a disruptive buyer. Although these guidelines have not yet been updated, presumably the HHI level would now be increased to 2500 given the 2010 Horizontal Merger Guidelines.

These guidelines are clearly far more narrow than the decision in *Brown Shoe*. The guidelines approve a merger if the unforeclosed market could support two firms. In *Brown Shoe*, the Supreme Court condemned a merger where the unforeclosed market supported 70,000 other retail outlets. There was no evidence that the merger significantly raised entry barriers in *Brown Shoe*, and the shoe markets there were not oligopolistic but rather highly fragmented. Further, the trend toward vertical mergers that *Brown Shoe* thought increased anticompetitive concerns is taken as a sign that those mergers are efficient in the guidelines. Suppose one believes that *Brown Shoe* more accurately reflects the intent of the 1950 Congress that amended Clayton Act § 7, given that the 1962 *Brown Shoe* decision was more contemporaneous with that legislature and conducted an extensive analysis of the legislative history.

1. Is it legitimate for the guidelines to take an approach so much narrower than the only Supreme Court authority interpreting the statute's application to vertical mergers?

---

36. Where a regulatory agency has the responsibility for approving such mergers, the Department may express its concerns to that agency in its role as competition advocate.

2. If Congress doesn't like the more narrow interpretation given by the guidelines, why doesn't it override them with a new statute? Does the failure to override probably reflect the fact that the views of the current Congress differ from those of the enacting Congress? Can an agency legitimately take such a drift in Congressional views into account when, as here, the statutory text itself is ambiguous?[86]

3. Former FTC Chairman Professor Pitofsky has stated that "The important point about these guidelines is they completely ignore any formulation of foreclosure theory—old fashioned or modern—that could lead to anticompetitive effects."[87] But doesn't Guideline § 4.211 require sufficient foreclosure to create a need for two-level entry? Or is Professor Pitofsky instead complaining that the guidelines do not address whether a firm would have incentives to engage in foreclosure and seem to ignore the possibility that vertical mergers might reduce the competitiveness of rivals without actually eliminating them or affecting their ability to enter the market?

In the Matter of Cadence Design Systems, Inc.

124 F.T.C. 131 (1997).

[Cadence, which made integrated circuit layout environments, wanted to acquire CCT, which made integrated circuit routing tools. The FTC charged the following in a complaint.] Integrated circuit layout environments are software infrastructures within which integrated circuit designers access integrated circuit layout tools, including ... routing tools.... CCT is currently the only firm with a commercially viable ... integrated circuit routing tool. At least one other firm with ... routing-technology is in the process of developing [an] integrated circuit routing tool. Cadence is the dominant supplier of integrated circuit layout environments. Cadence's leading competitor in the supply of integrated circuit layout environments is the Avant! Corporation. Avant! and several of its top executives have been charged criminally with conspiracy and theft of trade secrets from Cadence.

There are substantial barriers to entry in the market for ... integrated circuit routing tools, [which] ... are technologically complex and difficult to develop. De novo entry takes approximately two to three and a half years for a company that already possesses certain underlying core technology that can be used to develop [an] integrated circuit router ... Entry is likely to take even longer for a company that does not possess such technology.

In order to achieve the necessary compatibility between the integrated circuit layout tools that they use, integrated circuit designers select integrated circuit layout tools that have interfaces to a common integrated circuit layout environment. Since Cadence is the dominant supplier of integrated circuit layout environments, [an] integrated circuit routing tool

---

86. See Elhauge, *supra* note 58, at Chapter 3 (arguing that when statutory meaning is ambiguous, the enacting legislature itself would prefer that agencies track current legislative preferences).

87. *See* Pitofsky, *supra* note 74, at 220.

that lacks an interface into a Cadence integrated circuit layout environment is less likely to be selected by integrated circuit designers than [an] integrated circuit routing tool that possesses an interface into a Cadence integrated circuit layout environment.

An integrated circuit layout environment is not likely to be selected by integrated circuit designers unless a full set of compatible integrated circuit layout tools is available. A full set of integrated circuit layout tools includes at least placement, routing, and analysis and verification tools, each of which must be able to interface into the integrated circuit layout environment that the integrated circuit designer has selected.

It is in Cadence's interest to make available to users of a Cadence integrated circuit layout environment a complete a set of integrated circuit layout tools, because to do so makes the Cadence integrated circuit layout environment more valuable to integrated circuit designers. Cadence historically has provided access to Cadence integrated circuit layout environments to suppliers of complementary integrated circuit layout tools that Cadence does not supply.

Cadence does not, however, have incentives to provide access to a Cadence integrated circuit layout environment to suppliers of integrated circuit layout tools that compete with Cadence products. Cadence historically has been reluctant to provide access to Cadence integrated circuit layout environments to suppliers of integrated circuit layout tools that compete with Cadence products.

Prior to the Proposed Merger, Cadence did not have a commercially viable . . . integrated circuit routing tool. As a result of the Proposed Merger, Cadence will own the only currently available commercially viable . . . integrated circuit routing tool. For this reason, the Proposed Merger will make Cadence less likely to permit potential suppliers of competing . . . integrated circuit routing tools to obtain access to Cadence integrated circuit layout environments. Without access to Cadence integrated circuit layout environments, developers are less likely to gain successful entry into the market for . . . integrated circuit routing tools.

The Proposed Merger will make it more likely that successful entry into the . . . integrated circuit routing tool market would require simultaneous entry into the market for integrated circuit layout environments. This need for dual-level entry will decrease the likelihood of entry into the market for . . . integrated circuit routing tools.

The Proposed Merger may substantially lessen competition or tend to create a monopoly in the market for . . . integrated circuit routing tools. The Proposed Merger may, among other things, lead to higher prices, reduced service, and less innovation. . . .

DECISION AND ORDER

[Based on the above complaint, the FTC and merging parties entered into a consent order approving the merger on the conditions that for the next ten years Cadence: (1) had to provide other integrated circuit router tool companies with equal access to Cadence's "Connections Program," which provided independent software developers with the interfaces necessary to work with Cadence's integrated circuit layout, and (2) notify the FTC before acquiring another integrated circuit routing tool company.] . . .

STATEMENT OF CHAIRMAN ROBERT PITOFSKY & COMMISSIONER JANET D. STEIGER.[88] . . . The Commission's complaint alleges a well-established vertical theory of competitive harm, laid out in the 1984 Merger Guidelines. The Guidelines explain that a vertical merger can produce horizontal anticompetitive effects by making competitive entry less likely if (1) as a result of the merger, there is a need for simultaneous entry into two or more markets and (2) such simultaneous entry would make entry into the single market less likely to occur. While the dissenting Commissioners may take issue in this case with the "dual-level entry" theory of vertical mergers that the 1984 Guidelines articulate, the available evidence suggests that the Cadence/CCT merger, which combines Cadence's dominant position in integrated circuit layout environments with CCT's current monopolistic position in . . . integrated circuit routers, presents a straightforward case of anticompetitive effects caused by vertical integration. We believe that this type of competitive harm merits our attention.[4]

. . . [U]nless a would-be supplier of routing tools had the ability to develop an interface to the Cadence integrated circuit layout environment, it would not be able to market its routing product effectively to the vast majority of potential customers which use the Cadence layout environment. Without an expectation that it could design software compatible with Cadence's installed base, a would-be entrant might well decide not to compete.

After the Cadence/CCT merger, Cadence would have had an incentive to impede attempts by companies developing routing technology competitive with CCT's . . . router technology, IC Craftsman, to gain access to the Cadence integrated circuit layout environment. Following the merger, successful entry into the routing tool market is more likely to require simultaneous entry into the market for integrated circuit layout environments. Without a consent order that mandates access to Cadence's layout environment, and thus lowers the barriers to entry in the market, a combined Cadence/CCT will face less competitive pressure to innovate or to price aggressively. Thus, competition would likely be reduced as a result of the acquisition.

The remedy in this matter preserves opportunities for new entrants with integrated circuit routers competitive with IC Craftsman by allowing them to interface with Cadence's layout environments on the same terms as developers of complementary design tools. Specifically, the order requires Cadence to allow independent commercial router developers to build interfaces between their design tools and the Cadence layout environment through Cadence's "Connections Program." The Connections Program is

---

88. [Editor's Note: Commissioner Varney initially joined this statement when it was issued for public comment, but left the FTC before this statement was finalized.]

4. Contrary to Commissioner Starek's assertions that enforcement action here, in the context of a merger, leads logically to enforcement action against internal vertical expansion, . . . such unilateral action has been known to present a completely different set of questions under the antitrust laws for more than one hundred years.

in place now and has more than one hundred participants who have all entered a standard form contract with Cadence. . . .

The dissenting statements fail to give full weight to all the incentives at work in the vertical case. It is true that Cadence would be motivated by the entry of new, promising routing technology to allow an interface to its layout environment to sell more of its complementary products. And absent the merger, that would be its only incentive. But with the merger, Cadence clearly also has an incentive to prevent loss of sales in its competing products. And while these two incentives may compete as a theoretical matter, the evidence in this case indicated that Cadence has acted historically according to the latter incentive. There is some reason to believe that Cadence in the past has thwarted attempts by firms offering potentially competitive technology to develop interfaces to its layout environment (including at one point, CCT). Now that it has a satisfactory router to offer its customers, there is no reason to think that absent the consent order, Cadence would treat developers of routers that would compete with IC Craftsman any differently than it once treated CCT.

Commissioner Azcuenaga also suggests that the consent order is unnecessary because a company developing a router to compete with IC Craftsman could proceed, as CCT did, without an interface to Cadence's design layout environment. The evidence showed, however, that CCT's management thought that ensuring compatibility with Cadence's layout environment was critical and that marketing without that compatibility, which it had done, was not sufficient. It took the extreme measure of inducing a third party to write software for CCT to interface IC Craftsman with the Cadence layout environment without Cadence's knowledge. Moreover, despite CCT's success in developing a routing program, its sales of IC Craftsman were quite modest before it obtained an authorized interface with the Cadence environment.

Commissioner Azcuenaga is further concerned that mandating access to the Connections Program for developers of routing software on terms as favorable as for other Connections participants might have unintended consequences. In particular, she is concerned that the order may prompt Cadence to charge higher prices to all Connections partners. But the Connections Program is an existing program with over one hundred members, and Cadence would have significant logistical difficulties, and would risk injuring its reputation, if it suddenly altered the terms of the program. Also, Cadence has good reasons for having so many Connections partners— they offer Cadence customers valuable tools, most of which do not compete with Cadence products. It seems unlikely that Cadence would be motivated to make the Connections Program less appealing to those partners.

Both Commissioners Azcuenaga and Starek suggest that the remedy may be difficult to enforce. Any time this Commission enters an order, it takes upon itself the burden of enforcing the order, which requires use of our scarce resources. However, we think the order, which simply requires Cadence to allow competitors and potential competitors developing routing technology to participate in independent software interface programs on terms no less favorable than the terms applicable to any other participants in such programs, is a workable approach.[10] Connections partners all sign the same standard-form contract and there has been a consistent pattern of conduct with respect to the program to use as a baseline for future comparisons. Moreover, the Commission has had experience with such non-discrimination provisions, and can rely on respondent's compliance reports required under the order as well as complaints from independent software developers to ensure compliance with the consent order. We think the dissenting Commissioners' scenarios about intractable compliance issues are unfounded. . . .

STATEMENT OF COMMISSIONER MARY L. AZCUENAGA CONCURRING IN PART AND DISSENTING IN PART. The acquisition of [CCT] by Cadence . . . combines the only firm currently marketing [an] integrated circuit routing tool with a firm that was, at least until the acquisition, on the verge of entry into this market. I find reason to believe that the proposed merger would violate Section 7 of the Clayton Act under a horizontal, potential competition theory [because Cadence was likely to enter the tool market, and thus I concur in the part of the order requiring notification of future acquisitions of tool companies.]. . . .

The vertical theory of violation alleged in the complaint is that the acquisition of [CCT] by Cadence will make it more difficult for another firm to introduce [an] IC router because such an entrant would need its own IC layout environment to enter the market, and that dual level entry is more difficult. Although this is a recognized theory, I question whether it applies in this case and whether a firm needs to enter both the routing and the environment markets simultaneously.

[CCT] was successful in developing and marketing its routing program before it gained access to Cadence's environment. In a separate statement, Chairman Pitofsky and Commissioners Varney and Steiger assert that [CCT's] "sales were modest before the merger announcement." I disagree based on [CCT's] penetration of the market. Cadence's willingness to pay more that $400 million in stock for [CCT] also suggests a greater competitive significance than the majority concedes. [CCT's] record indicates that access to a layout environment is not a precondition to successful entry in the market for . . . integrated circuit routers. It appears, based on the available information, that dual level entry theory does not apply in this market.

In addition, although Cadence initially denied [CCT] access to its connections program, it subsequently reversed course and granted the access. This suggests that Cadence capitulated to pressure from customers to grant [CCT] access and that Cadence has little or no power to deny access to its connections program if granting access is the only way to enable its customers to use a product they want to use. Finally, . . . the order is premised on the allegation in . . . the complaint that "Cadence does not, however, have incentives to provide access to a Cadence integrated circuit layout environment to suppliers of integrated circuit layout tools

---

10. The language of the consent order is clear in requiring that terms for routing companies be no less favorable than for any other participant in the Connections Program. Thus, we do not understand Commissioner Starek's conclusion that the order could be interpreted to require routing companies to pay a "fee no higher than the highest fee." . . .

that compete with Cadence products." The incentives appear to be at least as likely to go the other way. If another company develops an innovative, advanced router, one would assume that Cadence would have incentives to welcome the innovative product to its suite of connected design tools, thereby enhancing the suite's utility to customers.

[T]he order [requiring equal access to interfaces] may be counterproductive and may result in substantial enforcement costs for the Commission. Because [this order] bars Cadence from charging developers of "Commercial Integrated Circuit Routing Tools" a higher access fee than developers of other design tools, one possible, unintended consequence of the order is that Cadence may reduce or eliminate discounting of access fees. In addition, enforcement of the provision of the order requiring Cadence to provide access to the connections program to developers of "Commercial Integrated Circuit Routing Tools" on terms "no less favorable than the terms applicable to any other participants" may embroil the Commission unnecessarily in complex commercial disputes. . . .

DISSENTING STATEMENT OF COMMISSIONER ROSCOE B. STAREK, III. . . . To justify the complaint and order, the Commission once again invokes the specter of anticompetitive "foreclosure" as a direct consequence of the transaction. As I have made clear on previous occasions, foreclosure theories are generally unconvincing as a rationale for antitrust enforcement. The current case provides scant basis for revising this conclusion. . . .

The logic of the complaint is fundamentally flawed. Even if we assume arguendo—as the complaint in this case does—that Cadence is "dominant" in the supply of software components complementary to the router,[4] the fact remains that it has no incentive to restrict the supply of routers . . .[5] The same is true here: the introduction of a lower-priced or higher-quality routing program increases the value of Cadence's "dominant" position in the sale of software complementary to the router, because it increases the demand for Cadence design software, thereby allowing Cadence to increase the price and/or the output of these programs. Despite the assertions of Chairman Pitofsky and Commissioner Steiger to the contrary,[6] this is true

---

4. The anticompetitive theory requires Cadence to have substantial monopoly power: if there were numerous good alternatives to Cadence's suite, other independent vendors of routing software could affiliate with them and there would be no "foreclosure."

5. Moreover, . . . the description of the premerger state of competition set forth in the complaint itself tends to exclude the possibility of substantial postmerger foreclosure. . . . [T]he . . . complaint alleges that there are substantial premerger barriers to entry into the market for the kind of "router" software that CCT produces. But one cannot find both that the premerger supply elasticity of substitutable software is virtually zero and that the merger would result in the substantial postmerger foreclosure of independent software producers. If entry into . . . IC router software is effectively blocked premerger, as the complaint contends, it cannot also be the case that the merger would cause a substantial incremental reduction in entry opportunities.

6. Chairman Pitofsky and Commissioner Steiger assert that "Cadence clearly also has an incentive to prevent loss of sales in its competing products." . . . Because [they never describe] . . . how this conclusion was reached, it is difficult to identify precisely the source of the erroneous reasoning. Chiefly, however, it seems to reflect a manifestation of the "sunk cost fallacy," whereby it is argued that because Cadence has now sunk a large sum of money into acquiring CCT, this in and of itself would provide Cadence with an incentive not to deal with independent vendors of complements. This reasoning, of course, is fallacious: the cost incurred

whether or not Cadence has vertically integrated into the sale of routing software, for efficient entry into the production of routing software increases the joint profits of the entrant and Cadence. If the Commission is correct that Cadence is "dominant" in the supply of software components complementary to routers, then of course Cadence may be in a position to expropriate—e.g., via royalties paid to Cadence by the entrant for the right to "connect" to Cadence's software—some or all of the "efficiency rents" that otherwise would accrue to an efficient entrant. This, however, would constitute harm to a competitor, not to competition, and Cadence would have no incentive to set any such rates so high as to preclude entry. . . .

Contrary to the analysis presented above, suppose that somehow Cadence could profit anticompetitively from denying interconnection rights to independent router vendors. If that were so, then it would not be sufficient merely to prevent Cadence from acquiring producers of complementary software. Rather, the Commission would have to take the further step of preventing Cadence from developing its own routers; for under the anticompetitive theory advanced in the complaint, any vertical integration by Cadence into routers, whether accomplished by acquisition or through internal expansion, would engender equivalent post-integration incentives to "foreclosure" independent vendors of routing software.[7] Of course, . . . there is likely to be little enthusiasm for such a policy because there is a general predisposition to regard internal capacity expansion as procompetitive.[8]

Not only am I unpersuaded that Cadence's acquisition of CCT is likely to reduce competition in any relevant market, but . . . I would find the order unacceptable even were I convinced as to liability. . . . [T]he Commission imposes a "most favored nations" clause that requires Cadence to allow all independent router developers to participate in its software interface programs on terms that are "no less favorable than the terms applicable to any other participants in" those interface programs. Even apart from the usual problems with "most favored nations" clauses in

---

by Cadence in acquiring CCT—whether a large or a small sum—is irrelevant to profit-maximizing behavior once incurred, for bygones are forever bygones. The introduction of a superior new router, even if by an independent vendor, will increase the joint profits of Cadence and this vendor (irrespective of the amount spent in acquiring CCT), and both parties will have a profit incentive to facilitate its introduction.

7. Thus, it is unclear how the Commission should respond, under the logic of its complaint, were Cadence to introduce an internally developed software program (now provided by one or more independent vendors) that is complementary to its "dominant" suite of programs. Obviously Cadence would be in a position (similar to that alleged in the Commission's complaint) to block access to the Cadence design software if it wanted to. Even if Cadence did not terminate the independent vendors, consistent application of the economic logic of the present complaint seemingly would require the Commission to seek a prophylactic "open access" order against Cadence similar to the order sought here. This enforcement policy would of course have a number of adverse competitive consequences, including deterrence of Cadence from efficiently entering complementary software lines through internal expansion.

8. . . . [T]he Commission has alleged the existence of substantial pre-acquisition market power in both vertically related matters (routing software and the rest of the IC layout "suite" . . .). Under these circumstances, there is a straightforward reason why vertical integration is both profitable and procompetitive (i.e., likely to result in lower prices to consumers): vertical integration would yield only one monopoly markup by the integrated firm, rather than separate markups (as in the pre-integration situation) by Cadence and CCT.

consent orders,[9] this order ... will require that the Commission continuously regulate the prices and other conditions of access.

... What does it mean to mandate treatment "no less favorable than" that granted to others, when Cadence's current Connections Program—with well over 100 participants—allows access prices to differ substantially across participants and imposes substantial restrictions on the breadth and scope of the permitted connection rights?[10] Does it mean that router vendors pay a connection fee no higher than the highest fee paid by an existing participant? Or would they pay a fee no higher than the current lowest fee? Or does it mean something else? Router vendors surely will argue for the second interpretation—a view also apparently shared by Chairman Pitofsky and Commission Steiger—yet there is no obvious reason why router vendors should be entitled to such a Commission-mandated preferential pricing arrangement ... Similarly, does the "no less favorable" requirement mandate that the vendors of routing software obtain access rights as broad as the broadest rights now granted, or simply no worse than the narrowest now granted? ...

The preceding suggests strongly that the real (albeit unstated) goal of the order is not to nullify any actual anticompetitive effects from the transaction, but rather to invalidate the principal aspects of Cadence's "Connections Program" (i.e., the ability to charge different connection fees and to terminate vendors at will) without demonstrating that the program's provisions violate the law. There is little reason to believe that this program is harmful to competition, and there are strong efficiency reasons for allowing Cadence to set different fees for different vendors. Moreover, setting a uniform fee would result in price increases to at least some vendors.

Because I do not accept the Commission's theory of liability in this case, and because I find the prescribed remedy at best unenforceable and at worst competitively harmful, I dissent.

Questions on *Cadence*

1. Notwithstanding his opinion above that this case could be brought under the vertical merger guidelines, Professor Pitofsky later stated in a 2005 article that "none of [the] five [vertical merger] cases [including *Cadence*] could have been brought if the vertical merger guidelines were controlling."[89] Was he right in his opinion or in his article?

2. Isn't it reasonable to think that the merger of the dominant supplier of integrated circuit layout with the only firm with a commercially viable integrated circuit routing tool would foreclose other firms from that layout and require them to produce both products to compete?

---

9. ... [T]hese clauses have the capacity to cause all prices to rise rather than to fall. The Chairman and Commissioner Steiger seem comfortable with this outcome, provided that all vendors pay the same price.

10. For example, CCT had been permitted to participate in the Connections Program with its printed circuit board router but not with its IC router.

89. *See* Pitofsky, *supra* note 74, at 221.

3. Is the Starek dissent correct that the merged firm would have no incentive to deny access to its integrated circuit layout to rival producers of integrated circuit routing tools?

a. Would the Starek dissent be right if the foreclosure did not create a need for two-level entry that increased entry barriers in a way that increased the degree of market power in either market? Isn't the Starek dissent ignoring this possibility? Doesn't ignoring this possibility conflict with the guidelines?

b. Aren't there conflicting economic incentives at work: one to possibly increase entry barriers and the other to have the most efficient complementary product?

i. Is there any way to figure out which incentive will outweigh the other?

ii. Are you persuaded by the majority that the former incentive must be the stronger one because Cadence in fact denied access to its layout to vertical firms like CCT before the merger? Isn't that logic inconsistent with the majority's statement: "It is true that Cadence would be motivated by the entry of new, promising routing technology to allow an interface to its layout environment to sell more of its complementary products. And absent the merger, that would be its only incentive"? That is, doesn't the statement that the only pre-merger incentive of Cadence was efficient suggest that any pre-merger denial of access to its interface must have been efficiently motivated? And if so, doesn't that cast doubt on the remedy of providing all routing tool companies with equal access to its interfaces?

4. Is the Starek dissent correct in footnote 5 when it says that the existence of entry barriers to the routing tool market means that the merger cannot increase entry barriers? Would Starek be correct if the entry barriers were infinite?

5. Is Commissioner Azcuenaga correct that a routing tool company must not need access to integrated circuit layouts because CCT itself successfully entered the tool market without it? Or is the majority right because CCT ultimately obtained access to the relevant interface?

6. Is the Starek dissent correct that blocking this merger implies the FTC should also ban internal expansion into vertical markets? Isn't there a difference between (a) acquiring and foreclosing existing firms and (b) adding new capacity and output to the downstream market without foreclosing any existing capacity and output?

7. Isn't the Starek dissent correct in footnote 9 that the existence of market power in both layouts and routing tools suggests the merger must eliminate a successive monopoly problem and thus increase efficiency? *See* Chapter 3.C.4. Isn't that likely to be true for most vertical mergers that meet the guideline conditions? How can adjudicators weigh this procompetitive benefit against the possible anticompetitive effects?

8. Is the equal access order enforceable? How will the FTC decide when differences among firms requesting access justify treating firms differently under an equally-applicable principle?

9. Couldn't the FTC have allowed the merger and then policed the feared post-merger conduct under the unilateral refusal to deal doctrine?

a. If the post-merger refusal involved discrimination among outsiders, wouldn't it be covered by the *Aspen* duty to deal? Isn't this what the consent order basically imposes?

b. If the layout environment were truly essential, wouldn't refusals to provide it be covered by the essential facilities doctrine?

T-210/01, General Electric v. Commission

2005 E.C.R. II-5575.

[The Commission had found a proposed merger of GE and Honeywell illegal on several grounds. This portion of the opinion addressed the Commission's condemnation of the vertical combination of GE's dominant position in large jet engines with Honeywell's leading position in engine starters. Both were worldwide markets.]

... Honeywell had a market share of [50–60]% on the market for ... engine starters, Hamilton Sundstrand, a sister company of P & W, being the second largest manufacturer with a market share of [40–50]%.... The Commission held that ... the proposed merger will strengthen GE's dominant position on the market for large commercial aircraft engines as a result of the vertical foreclosure of the competing engine manufacturers that will result from the vertical relationship between GE as an engine manufacturer and Honeywell as a supplier of engine starters to GE and its competitors. In its view, "[f]ollowing the proposed merger, the merged entity would have an incentive to delay or disrupt the supply of Honeywell engine starters to competing engine manufacturers, which would result in damaging supply, distribution, profitability and competitiveness of GE's engine competitors. Likewise, the merged entity could increase the prices of engine starters or their spares, thereby increasing rival engine manufacturers' costs and reducing even further their ability to compete against the merged entity" ...

The Commission ... stated ... that Hamilton Sundstrand at present manufactures engine starters exclusively for P & W engines and contended that it had no commercial interest in selling its engine starters to other engine manufacturers, even if there were to be a price increase. Consequently, the Commission took the view that Hamilton Sundstrand was not to be considered a competitor of Honeywell. The Commission stated that no other competitor was capable of exerting effective competitive constraints on Honeywell on the market and that the barriers to entry were significant and that therefore the possibility of new market entry was not a real constraint either.... [The General Court agreed that this evidence meant] Honeywell's market share of [50–60]% thus does not adequately reflect the scale of the commercial influence which it would wield ...

The effects of the merger at issue in this part of the judgment are not conglomerate effects inasmuch as they result from a direct vertical relationship of supplier and customer. However, it is clear from the above description that the Commission's case concerning the anti-competitive effects of the merger that would result from that relationship hinges on the merged entity's future behaviour, without which this aspect of the merger would not have any harmful effect. The onus was thus on the Commission to produce convincing evidence as to the likelihood of that behaviour (see, by analogy, *Tetra Laval*).

In some cases, such evidence may consist of economic studies establishing the likely development of the market situation and demonstrating that there is an incentive for the merged entity to behave in a particular way. As the applicant points out, the Commission has not produced any such evidence in this case.... [H]owever ..., since in Community law it is an overriding principle that the evaluation of evidence should be unfettered, the absence of evidence of that type is not in itself decisive. In particular, in a situation in which it is obvious that the commercial interests of an undertaking militate predominantly in favour of a given course of conduct, such as making use of an opportunity to disrupt a competitor's business, the Commission does not commit a manifest error of assessment in holding that it is likely that the merged entity will actually engage in the conduct foreseen. In such a case, the simple economic and commercial realities of the particular case may constitute the convincing evidence required by the case-law.

... Leaving aside at this stage any potential legal constraints capable of having an impact in that regard, it ... would be in the commercial interest of the merged entity to use its power as the unavoidable supplier, in certain cases, of a relatively low-cost component, which is however essential for the operation of an engine, as a means of disrupting its competitors' engine production.... [E]ven in the absence of economic studies, ... it is clear that the conduct foreseen, allowing the merged entity to harm its competitors' interests significantly, would have been in its commercial interests. The parties agree that an engine starter represents only a tiny fraction of the cost of the engine, 0.2%.... Consequently, the profits which the merged entity could make by selling that product to Rolls–Royce and P & W are necessarily minimal in comparison with those which it could make by increasing its share of the market for large commercial aircraft engines at the expense of Rolls–Royce and P & W. ...[Thus] there would be an incentive for the merged entity to limit or disrupt supplies to its competitors of starters for large commercial aircraft engines....

However, ... the Commission should have taken account of the obligations to which the merged entity would be subject under Article [102 TFEU] ... [T]he Court of Justice held in ... *Tetra Laval* ... that the likelihood of the adoption of certain conduct must be examined comprehensively, that is to say, taking account both of the incentives to adopt such conduct and the factors liable to reduce, or even eliminate, those incentives, including the possibility that the conduct is unlawful. However, the Court of Justice also held that it would run counter to the preventive purpose of Regulation No 4064/89 to require the Commission to examine, for each proposed merger, the extent to which the incentives to adopt anti-competitive conduct would be reduced, or even eliminated, as a result of the unlawfulness of the conduct in question, the likelihood of its detection and the action taken by the competent authorities.

It follows that the Commission must, as a rule, take into account the potentially unlawful, and thus sanctionable, nature of certain conduct as a factor which might diminish, or even eliminate, incentives for an undertaking to engage in particular conduct. However, it is not required to establish that the conduct foreseen in the future will actually constitute an infringement of Article [102 TFEU] or that, if that were to be the case, that infringement would be detected and punished, the Commission being able to limit itself in that regard to a summary analysis based on the evidence available to it.

In the present case, the Commission has predicted future conduct on the engine-starter market the object and—were it to prove effective—effect of which would be to strengthen the dominant position on the market for large commercial jet aircraft engines specifically by weakening the merged entity's competitors on that market. The conduct in question, namely interrupting the supply of engine starters to competitors, even refusing to sell them, and price increases, would produce an effect on the market for large commercial jet aircraft engines only in so far as it significantly harmed the jet-engine manufacturing activities of the merged entity's competitors.

... [A] refusal by an undertaking in a dominant position to sell an essential component to its competitors ... constitutes an abuse of that position. *Commercial Solvents.*

As to the possibility of the merged entity increasing the price of its engine starters, it should be observed that, in order to have a tangible effect on Rolls–Royce's competitiveness on the market for large commercial jet aircraft engines, such an increase would have to be so large that it would clearly amount to abuse. A possible 50% increase in the price of engine starters, without any apparent commercial justification, would represent only a 0.1% increase in the price of a jet engine and would therefore have virtually no effect on the jet-engine market. Moreover, if a price increase for engine starters were applied in a non-discriminatory way, it would be liable adversely to affect some of the merged entity's customers, and accordingly would have harmful commercial effects for it. Such an increase could, in particular, affect its relations with airlines, which are customers for engine starters both indirectly as purchasers of aircraft and directly on the aftermarket for services and which are also likely to be customers of the merged entity for both engines and avionics and non-avionics products. Conversely, if such an increase were applied in a discriminatory way vis-à-vis its competitors, it would be clear that the object of the increase was to foreclose those competitors from the market and it would therefore constitute abuse.

Likewise, a disruption of supplies by the merged entity following the merger would adversely affect its own customers if the disruption was general and would clearly constitute abuse if the disruption was discriminatory, in particular with regard to Rolls–Royce.

It follows from the foregoing that the conduct predicted by the Commission in this instance is liable to amount to an abuse of a dominant position. In the present case, the more convincing the Commission's case as to the effectiveness of the conduct in question and thus the clearer the commercial incentive to engage in it, the greater the likelihood of the conduct being classified as anti-competitive. It is precisely the most extreme forms of the conduct foreseen by the Commission which would be both the most effective for the purposes of harming competitors' businesses and the most likely to constitute visible and obvious—and therefore the most likely to be penalised—abuses of the merged entity's dominant position.

In that regard, the fact that the abuse takes place on a particular market (in this instance the engine-starter market) does not mean that the relevant market for the purposes of appraising dominance cannot be the related downstream market (in this instance the market for large commercial jet aircraft engines), given that the conduct foreseen by the Commission on the first market is specifically intended to maintain or strengthen the undertaking's dominant position on the second market. *AKZO; British Airways*.

Thus, in view of its finding that the applicant was in a dominant position on the market for large commercial jet aircraft engines prior to the merger, the Commission necessarily had available all the evidence required in this case to assess, without the need to carry out a detailed investigation in that regard, to what extent the conduct which it itself anticipated on the engine-starter market would constitute infringements of Article [102 TFEU] and be sanctioned as such. It therefore made an error of law in failing to take into account the deterrent effect which that factor might have had on the merged entity.

It is also clear that, if the deterrent effect had been taken into account, it could materially have influenced the Commission's appraisal of how likely it was that the conduct in question would be adopted. In these circumstances, it is not for the Court to substitute its own appraisal for that of the Commission, by seeking to establish what the latter would have decided if it had taken into account the deterrent effect of Article [102 TFEU]. Accordingly, the Commission's analysis of this aspect of the case, since it did not include any consideration of the deterrent effect of Article [102 TFEU]—notwithstanding its relevance—, is necessarily vitiated by a manifest error of assessment.

. . . The Court therefore holds that the [parts] of the contested decision relating to the strengthening of the applicant's pre-merger dominant position on the market for large commercial jet aircraft engines, resulting from the vertical overlap between its engine-manufacturing business and Honeywell's manufacture of starters for those engines, is not sufficiently established. . . .

Questions on Vertical Merger Issues in *GE v. Commission*

1. Are you persuaded by the GC's holding that the Commission sufficiently showed that the merged firm would have incentives to deny engine starters to engine rivals? Can one establish such commercial incentives without a clear economic model? What would FTC Commissioner Starek have said?

2. Should the merger be allowed because refusal-to-deal law can adequately address the feared post-merger conduct?

a. Why wasn't this a big argument in the U.S. *Cadence* case?

b. Does the analysis here suggest that the EU should be less likely to block vertical mergers than the U.S. because the EU restricts refusals to deal more whereas the U.S. may need to block the vertical merger to prevent the feared post-merger refusal to deal?

c. Does the way the General Court describes the prohibited post-merger conduct suggest that the General Court also imposes a nondiscrimination requirement similar to *Aspen*?

EU Guidelines on the Assessment of Non–Horizontal Mergers Under the Council Regulation on the Control of Concentrations Between Undertakings (2008)

II. OVERVIEW

. . . Non-horizontal mergers are generally less likely to significantly impede effective competition than horizontal mergers.

First, unlike horizontal mergers, vertical or conglomerate mergers do not entail the loss of direct competition between the merging firms in the same relevant market. As a result, the main source of anti-competitive effect in horizontal mergers is absent from vertical and conglomerate mergers.

Second, vertical and conglomerate mergers provide substantial scope for efficiencies. A characteristic of vertical mergers and certain conglomerate mergers is that the activities and/or the products of the companies involved are complementary to each other. The integration of complementary activities or products within a single firm may produce significant efficiencies and be pro-competitive. In vertical relationships for instance, as a result of the complementarity, a decrease in mark-ups downstream will lead to higher demand also upstream. A part of the benefit of this increase in demand will accrue to the upstream suppliers. An integrated firm will take this benefit into account. Vertical integration may thus provide an increased incentive to seek to decrease prices and increase output because the integrated firm can capture a larger fraction of the benefits. This is often referred to as the "internalisation of double mark-ups". Similarly, other efforts to increase sales at one level (e.g. improve service or stepping up innovation) may provide a greater reward for an integrated firm that will take into account the benefits accruing at other levels.

Integration may also decrease transaction costs and allow for a better co-ordination in terms of product design, the organisation of the production process, and the way in which the products are sold. Similarly, mergers which involve products belonging to a range or portfolio of products that are generally sold to the same set of customers (be they complementary products or not) may give rise to customer benefits such as one-stop-shopping.

However, there are circumstances in which non-horizontal mergers may significantly impede effective competition, in particular as a result of the creation or strengthening of a dominant position. This is essentially because a non-horizontal merger may change the ability and incentive to compete on the part of the merging companies and their competitors in ways that cause harm to consumers. . . .

In assessing the competitive effects of a merger, the Commission compares the competitive conditions that would result from the notified merger with the conditions that would have prevailed without the merger. . . .

In its assessment, the Commission will consider both the possible anti-competitive effects arising from the merger and the possible pro-competitive effects stemming from substantiated efficiencies benefiting consumers. . . .

III. MARKET SHARE AND CONCENTRATION LEVELS

Non-horizontal mergers pose no threat to effective competition unless the merged entity has a significant degree of market power (which does not necessarily amount to dominance) in at least one of the markets concerned. The Commission will examine this issue before proceeding to assess the impact of the merger on competition.

Market shares and concentration levels provide useful first indications of the market power and the competitive importance of both the merging parties and their competitors.

The Commission is unlikely to find concern in non-horizontal mergers, be it of a coordinated or of a non-coordinated nature, where the market share post-merger of the new entity in each of the markets concerned is below 30% and the post-merger HHI is below 2000.

In practice, the Commission will not extensively investigate such mergers, except where special circumstances such as, for instance, one or more of the following factors are present:

(a) a merger involves a company that is likely to expand significantly in the near future, e.g. because of a recent innovation;

(b) there are significant cross-shareholdings or cross-directorships among the market participants;

(c) one of the merging firms is a firm with a high likelihood of disrupting coordinated conduct;

(d) indications of past or ongoing coordination, or facilitating practices, are present.

The Commission will use the above market share and HHI thresholds as an initial indicator of the absence of competition concerns. However, these thresholds do not give rise to a legal presumption. The Commission is of the opinion that it is less appropriate in this context to present market share and concentration levels above which competition concerns would be deemed to be likely, as the existence of a significant degree of market power in at least one of the markets concerned is a necessary condition for competitive harm, but is not a sufficient condition.

IV. VERTICAL MERGERS

... In its assessment, the Commission will consider both the possible anti-competitive effects arising from vertical mergers and the possible pro-competitive effects stemming from efficiencies substantiated by the parties.

A. *Non-coordinated effects: foreclosure*

A merger is said to result in foreclosure where actual or potential rivals' access to supplies or markets is hampered or eliminated as a result of the merger, thereby reducing these companies' ability and/or incentive to compete. Such foreclosure may discourage entry or expansion of rivals or encourage their exit. Foreclosure thus can be found even if the foreclosed rivals are not forced to exit the market: It is sufficient that the rivals are disadvantaged and consequently led to compete less effectively. Such fore-closure is regarded as anti-competitive where the merging companies—and, possibly, some of its competitors as well—are as a result able to profitably increase the price charged to consumers.

Two forms of foreclosure can be distinguished. The first is where the merger is likely to raise the costs of downstream rivals by restricting their access to an important input (input foreclosure). The second is where the merger is likely to foreclose upstream rivals by restricting their access to a sufficient customer base (customer foreclosure).

1. **Input foreclosure**

Input foreclosure arises where, post-merger, the new entity would be likely to restrict access to the products or services that it would have otherwise supplied absent the merger, thereby raising its downstream rivals' costs by making it harder for them to obtain supplies of the input under similar prices and conditions as absent the merger. This may lead the merged entity to profitably increase the price charged to consumers, resulting in a significant impediment to effective competition. As indicated above, for input foreclosure to lead to consumer harm, it is not necessary that the merged firm's rivals are forced to exit the market. The relevant benchmark is whether the increased input costs would lead to higher prices for consumers. Any efficiencies resulting from the merger may, however, lead the merged entity to reduce price, so that the overall likely impact on consumers is neutral or positive. . . .

In assessing the likelihood of an anticompetitive input foreclosure scenario, the Commission examines, first, whether the merged entity would have, post-merger, the ability to substantially foreclose access to inputs, second, whether it would have the incentive to do so, and third, whether a foreclosure strategy would have a significant detrimental effect on competition downstream. In practice, these factors are often examined together since they are closely intertwined.

A. *Ability to foreclose access to inputs*

Input foreclosure may occur in various forms. The merged entity may decide not to deal with its actual or potential competitors in the vertically related market. Alternatively, the merged firm may decide to restrict supplies and/or to raise the price it charges when supplying competitors and/or to otherwise make the conditions of supply less favourable than they would have been absent the merger. Further, the merged entity may opt for a specific choice of technology within the new firm which is not compatible with the technologies chosen by rival firms. Foreclosure may also take more subtle forms, such as the degradation of the quality of input supplied. In its assessment, the Commission may consider a series of alternative or complementary possible strategies.

Input foreclosure may raise competition problems only if it concerns an important input for the downstream product. This is the case, for example, when the input concerned represents a significant cost factor relative to the price of the downstream product. Irrespective of its cost, an input may also be sufficiently important for other reasons. For instance, the input may be a critical component without which the downstream product could not be manufactured or effectively sold on the market, or it may represent a significant source of product differentiation for the downstream product. It may also be that the cost of switching to alternative inputs is relatively high.

For input foreclosure to be a concern, the vertically integrated firm resulting from the merger must have a significant degree of market power in the upstream market. It is only in these circumstances that the merged firm can be expected to have a significant influence on the conditions of competition in the upstream market and thus, possibly, on prices and supply conditions in the downstream market.

The merged entity would only have the ability to foreclose downstream competitors if, by reducing access to its own upstream products or services, it could negatively affect the overall availability of inputs for the downstream market in terms of price or quality. This may be the case where the remaining upstream suppliers are less efficient, offer less preferred alternatives, or lack the ability to expand output in response to the supply restriction, for example because they face capacity constraints or, more generally, face decreasing returns to scale. Also, the presence of exclusive contracts between the merged entity and independent input providers may limit the ability of downstream rivals to have adequate access to inputs.

When determining the extent to which input foreclosure may occur, it must be taken into account that the decision of the merged entity to rely on its upstream division's supply of inputs may also free up capacity on the part of the remaining input suppliers from which the downstream division used to purchase before. In fact, the merger may merely realign purchase patterns among competing firms.

When competition in the input market is oligopolistic, a decision of the merged entity to restrict access to its inputs reduces the competitive pressure exercised on remaining input suppliers, which may allow them to raise the input price they charge to non-integrated downstream competitors. In essence, input foreclosure by the merged entity may expose its downstream rivals to non-vertically integrated suppliers with increased market power. This increase in third-party market power will be greater the lower the degree of product differentiation between the merged entity and other upstream suppliers and the higher the degree of upstream concentration. However, the attempt to raise the input price may fail when independent input suppliers, faced with a reduction in the demand for their products (from the downstream division of the merged entity or from independent downstream firms), respond by pricing more aggressively.

In its assessment, the Commission will consider, on the basis of the information available, whether there are effective and timely counter-strategies that the rival firms would be likely to deploy. Such counterstrategies include the possibility of changing their production process so as to be less reliant on the input concerned or sponsoring the entry of new suppliers upstream.

B.   *Incentive to foreclose access to inputs*

The incentive to foreclose depends on the degree to which foreclosure would be profitable. The vertically integrated firm will take into account how its supplies of inputs to competitors downstream will affect not only the profits of its upstream division, but also of its downstream division. Essentially, the merged entity faces a trade-off between the profit lost in the upstream market due to a reduction of input sales to (actual or potential) rivals and the profit gain, in the short or longer term, from expanding sales downstream or, as the case may be, being able to raise prices to consumers.

The trade-off is likely to depend on the level of profits the merged entity obtains upstream and downstream. Other things constant, the lower the margins upstream, the lower the loss from restricting input sales. Similarly, the higher the downstream margins, the higher the profit gain from increasing market share downstream at the expense of foreclosed rivals.

The incentive for the integrated firm to raise rivals' costs further depends on the extent to which downstream demand is likely to be diverted away from foreclosed rivals and the share of that diverted demand that the downstream division of the integrated firm can capture. This share will normally be higher the less capacity constrained the merged entity will be relative to non-foreclosed downstream rivals and the more the products of the merged entity and foreclosed competitors are close substitutes. The effect on downstream demand will also be higher if the affected input represents a significant proportion of downstream rivals' costs or if the affected input represents a critical component of the downstream product.

The incentive to foreclose actual or potential rivals may also depend on the extent to which the downstream division of the integrated firm can be expected to benefit from higher price levels downstream as a result of a strategy to raise rivals' costs. The greater the market shares of the merged entity downstream, the greater the base of sales on which to enjoy increased margins.

An upstream monopolist that is already able to fully extract all available profits in vertically related markets may not have any incentive to foreclose rivals following a vertical merger. The ability to extract available profits from the consumers does not follow immediately from a very high market share. Such a finding would require a more thorough analysis of the actual and future constraints under which the monopolist operates.

When all available profits cannot be extracted, a vertical merger—even if it involves an upstream monopolist—may give the merged entity the incentive to raise the costs of downstream rivals, thereby reducing the competitive constraint they exert on the merged entity in the downstream market.

In its assessment of the likely incentives of the merged firm, the Commission may take into account various considerations such as the ownership structure of the merged entity, the type of strategies adopted on the market in the past or the content of internal strategic documents such as business plans.

In addition, when the adoption of a specific course of conduct by the merged entity is an essential step in foreclosure, the Commission examines both the incentives to adopt such conduct and the factors liable to reduce, or even eliminate, those incentives, including the possibility that the conduct is unlawful. Conduct may be unlawful inter alia because of competition rules or sector-specific rules at the EU or national levels. This appraisal, however, does not require an exhaustive and detailed examination of the rules of the various legal orders which might be applicable and of the enforcement policy practised within them. Moreover, the illegality of a conduct may be likely to provide significant disincentives for the merged entity to engage in such conduct only in certain circumstances. In particular, the Commission will consider, on the basis of a summary analysis: (i) the likelihood that this conduct would be clearly, or highly probably, unlawful under Community law, (ii) the likelihood that this illegal conduct could be detected, and (iii) the penalties which could be imposed.

C.   Overall likely impact on effective competition

In general, a merger will raise competition concerns because of input foreclosure when it would lead to increased prices in the downstream market thereby significantly impeding effective competition.

First, anticompetitive foreclosure may occur when a vertical merger allows the merging parties to increase the costs of downstream rivals in the market thereby leading to an upward pressure on their sales prices. Significant harm to effective competition normally requires that the foreclosed firms play a sufficiently important role in the competitive process on the downstream market. The higher the proportion of rivals which would be foreclosed on the downstream market, the more likely the merger can be expected to result in a significant price increase in the downstream market and, therefore, to significantly impede effective competition therein. Despite a relatively small market share compared to other players, a specific firm may play a significant competitive role compared to other players, for instance because it is a close competitor of the vertically integrated firm or because it is a particularly aggressive competitor.

Second, effective competition may be significantly impeded by raising barriers to entry to potential competitors. A vertical merger may foreclose potential competition on the downstream market when the merged entity would be likely not to supply potential downstream entrants, or only on less favourable terms than absent the merger. The mere likelihood that the merged entity would carry out a foreclosure strategy post-merger may already create a strong deterrent effect on potential entrants. Effective competition on the downstream market may be significantly impeded by raising barriers to entry, in particular if input foreclosure would entail for such potential competitors the need to enter at both the downstream and the upstream level in order to compete effectively on either market. The concern of raising entry barriers is particularly relevant in those industries that are opening up to competition or are expected to do so in the foreseeable future.

If there remain sufficient credible downstream competitors whose costs are not likely to be raised, for example because they are themselves vertically integrated or they are capable of switching to adequate alternative inputs, competition from those firms may constitute a sufficient constraint on the merged entity and therefore prevent output prices from rising above pre-merger levels.

The effect on competition on the downstream market must also be assessed in light of countervailing factors such as the presence of buyer power or the likelihood that entry upstream would maintain effective competition.

Further, the effect on competition needs to be assessed in light of efficiencies substantiated by the merging parties The Commission may decide that, as a consequence of the efficiencies that the merger brings about, there are no grounds for declaring the merger incompatible with the common market pursuant to Article 2(3) of the Merger Regulation. This will be the case when the Commission is in a position to conclude on the basis of sufficient evidence that the efficiencies generated by the merger are likely to enhance the ability and incentive of the merged entity to act pro-competitively for the benefit of consumers, thereby counteracting the adverse effects on competition which the merger might otherwise have. . . .

Vertical mergers may entail some specific sources of efficiencies, the list of which is not exhaustive.

In particular, a vertical merger allows the merged entity to internalise any pre-existing double mark-ups resulting from both parties setting their prices independently pre-merger. Depending on the market conditions, reducing the combined mark-up (relative to a situation where pricing decisions at both levels are not aligned) may allow the vertically integrated firm to profitably expand output on the downstream market.

A vertical merger may further allow the parties to better coordinate the production and distribution process, and therefore to save on inventories costs.

More generally, a vertical merger may align the incentives of the parties with regard to investments in new products, new production processes and in the marketing of products. For instance, whereas before the merger, a downstream distributor entity might have been reluctant to invest in advertising and informing customers about the qualities of products of the upstream entity when such investment would also have benefited the sale of other downstream firms, the merged entity may reduce such incentive problems.

2. Customer foreclosure

Customer foreclosure may occur when a supplier integrates with an important customer in the downstream market. Because of this downstream presence, the merged entity may foreclose access to a sufficient customer base to its actual or potential rivals in the upstream market (the input market) and reduce their ability or incentive to compete. In turn, this may raise downstream rivals' costs by making it harder for them to obtain supplies of the input under similar prices and conditions as absent the merger. This may allow the merged entity profitably to establish higher prices on the downstream market. Any efficiencies resulting from the merger, however, may lead the merged entity to reduce price, so that there is overall not a negative impact on consumers. For customer foreclosure to lead to consumer harm, it is thus not necessary that the merged firm's rivals are forced to exit the market. The relevant benchmark is whether the increased input costs would lead to higher prices for consumers.

In assessing the likelihood of an anticompetitive customer foreclosure scenario, the Commission examines, first, whether the merged entity would have the ability to foreclose access to downstream markets by reducing its purchases from its upstream rivals, second, whether it would have the incentive to reduce its purchases upstream, and third, whether a foreclosure strategy would have a significant detrimental effect on consumers in the downstream market.

A. *Ability to foreclose access to downstream markets*

A vertical merger may affect upstream competitors by increasing their cost to access downstream customers or by restricting access to a significant customer base. Customer foreclosure may take various forms. For instance, the merged entity may decide to source all of its required goods or services from its upstream division and, as a result, may stop purchasing from its upstream competitors. It may also reduce its purchases from upstream rivals, or purchase from those rivals on less favourable terms than it would have done absent the merger.

When considering whether the merged entity would have the ability to foreclose access to downstream markets, the Commission examines whether there are sufficient economic alternatives in the downstream market for the upstream rivals (actual or potential) to sell their output. For customer foreclosure to be a concern, it must be the case that the vertical merger involves a company which is an important customer with a significant degree of market power in the downstream market. If, on the contrary, there is a sufficiently large customer base, at present or in the future, that is likely to turn to independent suppliers, the Commission is unlikely to raise competition concerns on that ground.

Customer foreclosure can lead to higher input prices in particular if there are significant economies of scale or scope in the input market or when demand is characterised by network effects. It is mainly in such circumstances that the ability to compete of upstream rivals, be they actual or potential, can be impaired. . . .

In the presence of economies of scale or scope, customer foreclosure may also render entry upstream by potential entrants unattractive by significantly reducing the revenue prospects of potential entrants. When customer foreclosure effectively results in entry deterrence, input prices may remain at a higher level than otherwise would have been the case, thereby raising the cost of input supply to downstream competitors of the merged firm.

Further, when customer foreclosure primarily impacts upon the revenue streams of upstream rivals, it may significantly reduce their ability and incentive to invest in cost reduction, R&D and product quality. This may reduce their ability to compete in the long run and possibly even cause their exit from the market.

In its assessment, the Commission may take into account the existence of different markets corresponding to different uses for the input. If a substantial part of the downstream market is foreclosed, an upstream supplier may fail to reach efficient scale and may also operate at higher costs in the other market(s). Conversely, an upstream supplier may continue to operate efficiently if it finds other uses or secondary markets for its input without incurring significantly higher costs.

In its assessment, the Commission will consider, on the basis of the information available, whether there are effective and timely counterstrategies, sustainable over time, that the rival firms would be likely to deploy. Such counterstrategies include the possibility that upstream rivals decide to price more aggressively to maintain sales levels in the downstream market, so as to mitigate the effect of foreclosure.

B. *Incentive to foreclose access to downstream markets*

The incentive to foreclose depends on the degree to which it is profitable. The merged entity faces a trade-off between the possible costs associated with not procuring products from upstream rivals and the possible gains from doing so, for instance, because it allows the merged entity to raise price in the upstream or downstream markets.

The costs associated with reducing purchases from rival upstream suppliers are higher, when the upstream division of the integrated firm is less efficient than the foreclosed suppliers. Such costs are also higher if the upstream division of the merged firm is capacity constrained or rivals' products are more attractive due to product differentiation.

The incentive to engage in customer foreclosure further depends on the extent to which the upstream division of the merged entity can benefit from possibly higher price levels in the upstream market arising as a result of upstream rivals being foreclosed. The incentive to engage in customer foreclosure also becomes higher, the more the downstream division of the integrated firm can be expected to enjoy the benefits of higher price levels downstream resulting from the foreclosure strategy. In this context, the greater the market shares of the merged entity's downstream operations, the greater the base of sales on which to enjoy increased margins.

When the adoption of a specific conduct by the merged entity is an essential step in foreclosure, the Commission examines both the incentives to adopt such conduct and the factors liable to reduce, or even eliminate, those incentives, including the possibility that the conduct is unlawful.

C.   *Overall likely impact on effective competition*

Foreclosing rivals in the upstream market may have an adverse impact in the downstream market and harm consumers. By denying competitive access to a significant customer base for the foreclosed rivals' (upstream) products, the merger may reduce their ability to compete in the foreseeable future. As a result, rivals downstream are likely to be put at a competitive disadvantage, for example in the form of raised input costs. In turn, this may allow the merged entity to profitably raise prices or reduce the overall output on the downstream market.

The negative impact on consumers may take some time to materialise when the primary impact of customer foreclosure is on the revenue streams of upstream rivals, reducing their incentives to make investments in cost reduction, product quality or in other competitive dimensions so as to remain competitive.

It is only when a sufficiently large fraction of upstream output is affected by the revenue decreases resulting from the vertical merger that the merger may significantly impede effective competition on the upstream market. If there remain a number of upstream competitors that are not affected, competition from those firms may be sufficient to prevent prices from rising in the upstream market and, consequently, in the downstream market. Sufficient competition from these non-foreclosed upstream firms requires that they do not face barriers to expansion e.g. through capacity constraints or product differentiation. When the reduction of competition upstream affects a significant fraction of output downstream, the merger is likely, as with input foreclosure, to result in a significant increase of the price level in the downstream market and, therefore, to significantly impede effective competition.

Effective competition on the upstream market may also be significantly impeded by raising barriers to entry to potential competitors. This may be so in particular if customer foreclosure would entail for such potential competitors the need to enter at both the downstream and the upstream level in order to compete effectively on either market. In such a context, customer foreclosure and input foreclosure may thus be part of the same strategy. The concern of raising entry barriers is particularly relevant in those industries that are opening up to competition or are expected to do so in the foreseeable future.

The effect on competition must be assessed in light of countervailing factors such as the presence of countervailing buyer power or the likelihood that entry would maintain effective competition in the upstream or down-stream markets.

Further, the effect on competition needs to be assessed in light of efficiencies substantiated by the merging parties.

B.   *Other non-coordinated effects*

The merged entity may, by vertically integrating, gain access to com-mercially sensitive information regarding the upstream or downstream activities of rivals. For instance, by becoming the supplier of a downstream competitor, a company may obtain critical information, which allows it to price less aggressively in the downstream market to the detriment of consumers. It may also put competitors at a competitive disadvantage, thereby dissuading them to enter or expand in the market.

C. Coordinated effects

As set out in Section IV of the Notice on Horizontal Mergers, a merger may change the nature of competition in such a way that firms that previously were not coordinating their behaviour, are now significantly more likely to coordinate and raise prices or otherwise harm effective competition. A merger may also make coordination easier, more stable or more effective for firms which were coordinating prior to the merger.

Market coordination may arise where competitors are able, without entering into an agreement or resorting to a concerted practice within the meaning of Article 81 of the Treaty, to identify and pursue common objectives, avoiding the normal mutual competitive pressure by a coherent system of implicit threats. In a normal competitive setting, each firm constantly has an incentive to compete. This incentive is ultimately what keeps prices low, and what prevents firms from jointly maximising their profits. Coordination involves a departure from normal competitive conditions in that firms are able to sustain prices in excess of what independent short term profit maximisation would yield. Firms will refrain from undercutting the high prices charged by their competitors in a coordinated way because they anticipate that such behaviour would jeopardise coordination in the future. For coordinated effects to arise, the profit that firms could make by competing aggressively in the short term ("deviating") has to be less than the expected reduction in revenues that this behaviour would entail in the longer term, as it would be expected to trigger an aggressive response by competitors ("a punishment").

Coordination is more likely to emerge in markets where it is relatively simple to reach a common understanding on the terms of coordination. In addition, three conditions are necessary for coordination to be sustainable. First, the coordinating firms must be able to monitor to a sufficient degree whether the terms of coordination are being adhered to. Second, discipline requires that there is some form of deterrent mechanism that can be activated if deviation is detected. Third, the reactions of outsiders, such as current and future competitors not participating in the coordination, as well as customers, should not be able to jeopardise the results expected from the coordination.

Reaching terms of coordination

A vertical merger may make it easier for the firms in the upstream or downstream market to reach a common understanding on the terms of coordination.

For instance, when a vertical merger leads to foreclosure, it results in a reduction in the number of effective competitors in the market. Generally speaking, a reduction in the number of players makes it easier to coordinate among the remaining market players.

Vertical mergers may also increase the degree of symmetry between firms active in the market. This may increase the likelihood of coordination by making it easier to reach a common understanding on the terms of coordination. Likewise, vertical integration may increase the level of market transparency, making it easier to coordinate among the remaining market players.

Further, a merger may involve the elimination of a maverick in a market. A maverick is a supplier that for its own reasons is unwilling to accept the co-ordinated outcome and thus maintains aggressive competition. The vertical integration of the maverick may alter its incentives to such an extent that co-ordination will no longer be prevented.

Monitoring deviations

Vertical integration may facilitate coordination by increasing the level of market transparency between firms through access to sensitive information on rivals or by making it easier to monitor pricing. Such concerns may arise, for example, if the level of price transparency is higher downstream than upstream. This could be the case when prices to final consumers are public, while transactions at the intermediate market are confidential. Vertical integration may give upstream producers control over final prices and thus monitor deviations more effectively.

When it leads to foreclosure, a vertical merger may also induce a reduction in the number of effective competitors in a market. A reduction in the number of players may make it easier to monitor each other's actions in the market.

Deterrent mechanisms

Vertical mergers may affect coordinating firms' incentives to adhere to the terms of coordination. For instance, a vertically integrated company may be in a position to more effectively punish rival companies when they choose to deviate from the terms of coordination, because it is either a crucial customer or supplier to them.

Reactions of outsiders

Vertical mergers may reduce the scope for outsiders to destabilise the coordination by increasing barriers to enter the market or otherwise limiting the ability to compete on the part of outsiders to the coordination.

A vertical merger may also involve the elimination of a disruptive buyer in a market. If upstream firms view sales to a particular buyer as sufficiently important, they may be tempted to deviate from the terms of co-ordination in an effort to secure their business. Similarly, a large buyer may be able to tempt the co-ordinating firms to deviate from these terms by concentrating a large amount of its requirements on one supplier or by offering long term contracts. The acquisition of such a buyer may increase the risk of co-ordination in a market.

Question on the EU Guidelines on Non–Horizontal Merger Guidelines

1. Is the approach taken by the Commission in the guidelines in line with the US merger guidelines?

2. The EU guidelines state that "non-horizontal mergers pose no threat to effective competition unless the merged entity has a significant degree of market power (which does not necessarily amount to dominance) in at least one of the markets concerned."

   a.   Why is it so?

   b.   Does it make any difference whether the market power is held downstream or upstream? Is downstream market power more likely to create anti-competitive concerns or vice-versa? Or does it depend on the facts in question?

   3.   What is likely to be the main source of concerns in vertical mergers: coordinated or non-coordinated effects? Is the situation similar with respect to horizontal mergers?

   4.   The guidelines state that "when the adoption of a specific course of conduct by the merged entity is an essential step in foreclosure, the Commission examines both the incentives to adopt such conduct and the factors liable to reduce, or even eliminate, those incentives, including the possibility that the conduct is unlawful."

   a.   But isn't input foreclosure prohibited under Article 102 TFEU?

   b.   If so, why is the Commission analyzing the ability and incentives of the merged parties to engage in input foreclosure?

   5.   What is the third step of the Commission's analysis of input (or customer) foreclosure? Is the balancing analysis to be carried out by the Commission easy to perform?

   6.   Do you think that the Commission would have reached a different outcome in GE/Honeywell if it had followed the analytical framework proposed in its non-horizontal guidelines?

Vertical Mergers in Other Nations

   Other nations likewise treat vertical mergers more leniently than horizontal mergers, and generally give them much less attention in merger guidelines.[90] The Canadian Bureau is not likely to challenge a vertical merger on grounds that it forecloses rivals from upstream supply or downstream buyers unless: (1) the need to enter both markets makes it unlikely entry could constrain a "material price increase within two years" in the market of concern; and, (2) this increased entry barrier will facilitate "the exercise of market power" in that market.[91] It is also unlikely to challenge a vertical merger on grounds that it aids oligopolistic coordination unless (1) downstream prices are more transparent; (2) oligopolistic coordination is otherwise likely upstream; and (3) unintegrated firms are unlikely to constrain "a material price increase" for two years.[92] Japan emphasizes vertical mergers are much less likely to have anticompetitive effects than horizontal mergers, and apply a larger presumptive safe harbor to vertical mergers that makes them presumptively legal if the market share in all of the combined markets is less than 10% or it is less than 25%

---

   90.   Brazil limits its guidelines to horizontal mergers even though the statute may also regulate vertical mergers. *See* Brazil Horizontal Merger Guidelines § 4 (2001).

   91.   *See* Canada Merger Guidelines § 10.3 (2004).

   92.   *Id.* § 10.6.

and the HHI is less than 2,500.[93] South Korea applies the same concentration thresholds to judge vertical mergers as horizontal mergers, but requires that they be met both at the upstream and downstream levels, and applies a rule of reason that considers the extent of foreclosure and possibility of collusive behavior among rivals.[94] Taiwan raises the expedited simplified review threshold of 15% for horizontal mergers to 25% for vertical mergers.[95] Other nations simply note that vertical mergers can raise concerns when they facilitate foreclosure or coordination.[96]

C. CONGLOMERATE MERGERS

Any merger that is not a horizontal or vertical merger falls by default into the category of conglomerate merger. Conglomerate mergers raise two sorts of concerns: (1) that they might eliminate potential horizontal competition; and (2) that the merger will enable the merged firm to engage in vertical exclusionary conduct post-merger. Like horizontal and vertical mergers, either theory of anticompetitive harm can be rebutted by establishing low entry barriers, offsetting efficiencies, or the failing firm defense.

Eliminating Potential Competition. The acquisition of a potential competitor who is not already in the market might have economic relevance for two sorts of reasons. First, the perception that the potential competitor might enter a market can constrain current market pricing and behavior. Acquiring the potential competitor can lift this constraint and thus directly raise market prices above current levels. Second, it might be that the potential competitor actually would have entered the market. Acquiring the potential competitor then would eliminate actual future competition and market deconcentration that otherwise would have occurred and lowered prices below current levels. The first is known in the literature as the elimination of "perceived potential competition"; the latter as the elimination of "actual potential competition." In the first, what matters is the perception of incumbent firms about the likelihood of entry in response to a price increase. In the second, what matters is the likelihood that the acquired firm actually would have entered at current prices.

To a large extent, the economic theory on mergers that eliminate perceived potential competitors is simply the flip side of the economic theories on limit pricing. The theory of limit pricing indicates that the possibility of entry often induces firms with dominant market power not to price to the full profit-maximizing monopoly level, but instead to engage in limit pricing that keeps perceived likely entrants out. It follows from this theory that mergers with perceived potential competitors can exacerbate the dominant firm's power to exploit consumers.

The economic theory on mergers that eliminate actual potential competitors is likewise the same as the general economic theory supporting the

93. Japan Business Combination Guidelines at V.1(3) (2010).

94. *See* South Korea Merger Guidelines VII.2 (1999); Chapter 7.A.2.

95. Taiwan Merger Guidelines Art. VII (2006)

96. *See, e.g.,* Singapore Merger Guidelines §§ 8.3–8.10 (2007).

proposition that firms with dominant market power will charge more than they would without such power, or the various theories about why concentrated oligopoly markets can have worse economic performance than deconcentrated ones. Since the grounds for concern here are that the acquired firm would (absent the merger) have actually entered and offered independent competition, the theoretical and empirical grounds for thinking such mergers harm the market are the same as that for thinking that mergers that increase market concentration will harm the market. The only grounds for distinction are greater uncertainty about whether the entry would have actually occurred and how extensive it would have been. But similar uncertainties are entertained all the time in considering *defensive* uses of potential competition, that is in considering the argument that the possibility of supplier entry lessens the anticompetitive implications one might otherwise infer from high market shares. *See* Chapter 7.A.3. Under a neutral regulatory approach, there does not appear to be any reason to entertain greater uncertainty in such *defensive* uses of the potential competition argument than in *offensive* uses of the potential competition argument to condemn a merger.

The U.S. Supreme Court has sustained blocking a conglomerate merger that eliminated perceived potential competition but not yet one that eliminated only actual potential competition, although the logic of its opinions would seem to extend to the latter as well. U.S. enforcement guidelines have provided that the elimination of either perceived or actual potential competition can trigger an agency enforcement action. Actual U.S. enforcement is, however, relatively rare. From 1996–2003, the FTC issued second requests in 12 potential competition cases compared to 162 horizontal cases and 17 vertical ones.[97] The willingness to challenge mergers that raise potential competition issues is much lower if the FTC chair is a Republican.[98] Thus, U.S. enforcement of potential competition theories exhibit the same sort of political division that afflicts vertical merger enforcement, rather than the nonpartisan enforcement that governs horizontal mergers. EC merger law is likewise clearer about blocking a conglomerate merger that eliminates perceived potential competition than one that eliminates only actual potential competition.

Enabling Post–Merger Exclusionary Conduct. Another concern with conglomerate mergers is that they might enable the merged firm to engage in post-merger conduct that anticompetitively forecloses rivals. For example, a merger of a firm that sells product *A* with one that sells product *B* might enable the merged firm to engage in anticompetitive bundling of products *A* and *B*. In several conglomerate merger cases, the concern has instead been the related one that a merger of a firm that *buys* product *A* with a firm that sells product *B* might enable the merged to engage in reciprocity: buying product *A* from other businesses only if they buy product *B* from it. This is similar to tying with the difference that here it is the willingness to buy (rather than sell) product *A* that is conditioned on the other firm buying product *B*.

---

97. *See* FTC, Horizontal Merger Investigation Data: Fiscal Years 1996–2003, at Table 1 (2004).

98. *See* Coate, *Twenty Years, supra* note 79, at 5 & Table 1.

Although a 1965 U.S. Supreme Court sustained blocking a conglomerate merger on the grounds that it would enable the merged firm to engage in reciprocity,[99] modern U.S. antitrust practice generally refuses to block a conglomerate merger on the theory that it will enable the merged firm to engage in post-merger exclusionary conduct. The typical reason given is that the proper remedy is not to block the merger but to wait to see if the feared post-merger conduct actually occurs, which may resolve uncertainties about whether it is actually anticompetitive, and then to penalize the post-merger conduct directly when appropriate. This is clearest when the post-merger conduct is something like tying, which is covered by Sherman Act § 1 and Clayton Act § 3 and subject to treble damages.

The availability of adequate post-merger penalties is less clear for reciprocity for two reasons. First, reciprocity may not be sufficiently concrete to constitute an agreement, and the merged firm may have market power that falls short of monopoly power. Such reciprocity might still be challengeable under FTC § 5 if it were anticompetitive, but that might be viewed as an insufficient deterrent given its weak penalties. Second, even under FTC Act, it would be hard to define and remedy reciprocity post-merger. Doing so would require ascertaining whether a firm is refusing to buy one product from a seller because the seller does not buy another product from it, or instead is refusing for other reasons regarding the merits of the first product. This may be particularly hard to ascertain when the firm is buying a product from the seller that is made using a component that the first firm sells and believes is the best product on that component market. Moreover, even when reciprocity can be identified, prohibiting it would require obligating the firm to buy from a seller it does not want to buy from, which would require defining how much it has to buy from that seller and at what terms. Thus, it may be hard to police reciprocity post-merger, which argues for trying to prevent the sorts of market structures that create incentives to engage in it.

This probably explains why conglomerate merger cases have been more concerned with reciprocity. However, the theory that a merger should be blocked because it creates an opportunity for reciprocity has not been pursued by modern U.S. enforcement agencies, and it is not clear that current U.S. courts would approve it. Nor does it seem likely that modern U.S. agencies or courts would find reciprocity itself worrisome absent stronger proof than was offered in the 1965 case that the buyer market power and resulting foreclosure were significant enough to have anticompetitive effects that were not outweighed by any procompetitive effects.

In contrast, in the EU, the Commission has sought to block several conglomerate mergers on the theory that they might enable the merged firm to engage in post-merger exclusionary conduct like bundling or reciprocity. As we will see below, this culminated in a famous conflict between EU and U.S. regulators in the *GE/Honeywell* case, where the European Commission condemned the merger largely based on the fear that the merged firm would engage in bundling and reciprocity, theories that were unconvincing to the U.S. authorities that wanted to approve the merger.

---

99. *See* FTC v. Consolidated Foods, 380 U.S. 592 (1965).

This post-merger misconduct theory has been sustained in principle by the CFI and ECJ, but those courts have required more rigorous proof that the merger would really create or increase incentives to engage in such misconduct and that other laws would not adequately deter the post-merger conduct. The Commission's current position on conglomerate mergers can be found in its guidelines on non-horizontal mergers, the relevant part of which will be discussed below.

U.S. DOJ, 1984 Merger Guidelines

4.11 The Theory of Potential Competition. In some circumstances, the non-horizontal merger[25] of a firm already in a market (the "acquired firm") with a potential entrant to that market (the "acquiring firm")[26] may adversely affect competition in the market. If the merger effectively removes the acquiring firm from the edge of the market, it could have either of the following effects:

4.111 Harm to "Perceived Potential Competition." By eliminating a significant present competitive threat that constrains the behavior of the firms already in the market, the merger could result in an immediate deterioration in market performance. The economic theory of limit pricing suggests that monopolists and groups of colluding firms may find it profitable to restrain their pricing in order to deter new entry that is likely to push prices even lower by adding capacity to the market. If the acquiring firm had unique advantages in entering the market, the firms in the market might be able to set a new and higher price after the threat of entry by the acquiring firm was eliminated by the merger.

4.112 Harm to "Actual Potential Competition." By eliminating the possibility of entry by the acquiring firm in a more procompetitive manner, the merger could result in a lost opportunity for improvement in market performance resulting from the addition of a significant competitor. The more procompetitive alternatives include both new entry and entry through a "toehold" acquisition of a present small competitor.

4.12 Relation Between Perceived and Actual Potential Competition. If it were always profit-maximizing for incumbent firms to set price in such a way that all entry was deterred and if information and coordination were sufficient to implement this strategy, harm to perceived potential competition would be the only competitive problem to address. In practice, however, actual potential competition has independent importance. Firms already in the market may not find it optimal to set price low enough to deter all entry; moreover, those firms may misjudge the entry advantages of a particular firm and, therefore, the price necessary to deter its entry.[27]

---

25. Under traditional usage, such a merger could be characterized as either "vertical" or "conglomerate," but the label adds nothing to the analysis.

26. The terms "acquired" and "acquiring" refer to the relationship of the firms to the market of interest, not to the way the particular transaction is formally structured.

27. When collusion is only tacit, the problem of arriving at and enforcing the correct limit price is likely to be particularly difficult.

4.13 Enforcement Standards. Because of the close relationship between perceived potential competition and actual potential competition, the Department will evaluate mergers that raise either type of potential competition concern under a single structural analysis analogous to that applied to horizontal mergers. The Department first will consider a set of objective factors designed to identify cases in which harmful effects are plausible. In such cases, the Department then will conduct a more focused inquiry to determine whether the likelihood and magnitude of the possible harm justify a challenge to the merger. In this context, the Department will consider any specific evidence presented by the merging parties to show that the inferences of competitive harm drawn from the objective factors are unreliable.

The factors that the Department will consider are as follows:

4.131 Market Concentration. Barriers to entry are unlikely to affect market performance if the structure of the market is otherwise not conducive to monopolization or collusion. Adverse competitive effects are likely only if overall concentration, or the largest firms's market share, is high. The Department is unlikely to challenge a potential competition merger unless overall concentration of the acquired firm's market is above 1800 HHI (a somewhat lower concentration will suffice if one or more of the factors discussed in [other parts of the guidelines] indicate that effective collusion in the market is particularly likely). Other things being equal, the Department is increasingly likely to challenge a merger as this threshold is exceeded.

4.132 Conditions of Entry Generally. If entry to the market is generally easy, the fact that entry is marginally easier for one or more firms is unlikely to affect the behavior of the firms in the market. The Department is unlikely to challenge a potential competition merger when new entry into the acquired firm's market can be accomplished by firms without any specific entry advantages under the conditions stated in [other parts of the guidelines]. Other things being equal, the Department is increasingly likely to challenge a merger as the difficulty of entry increases above that threshold.

4.133 The Acquiring Firm's Entry Advantage. If more than a few firms have the same or a comparable advantage in entering the acquired firm's market, the elimination of one firm is unlikely to have any adverse competitive effect. The other similarly situated firm(s) would continue to exert a present restraining influence, or, if entry would be profitable, would recognize the opportunity and enter. The Department is unlikely to challenge a potential competition merger if the entry advantage ascribed to the acquiring firm (or another advantage of comparable importance) is also possessed by three or more other firms. Other things being equal, the Department is increasingly likely to challenge a merger as the number of other similarly situated firms decreases below three and as the extent of the entry advantage over non-advantaged firms increases.

If the evidence of likely actual entry by the acquiring firm is particularly strong,[28] however, the Department may challenge a potential competition

---

28. For example, the firm already may have moved beyond the stage of consideration and have made significant investments demonstrating an actual decision to enter.

merger, notwithstanding the presence of three or more firms that are objectively similarly situated. In such cases, the Department will determine the likely scale of entry, using either the firm's own documents or the minimum efficient scale in the industry. The Department will then evaluate the merger much as it would a horizontal merger between a firm the size of the likely scale of entry and the acquired firm.

4.134 The Market Share of the Acquired Firm. Entry through the acquisition of a relatively small firm in the market may have a competitive effect comparable to new entry. Small firms frequently play peripheral roles in collusive interactions, and the particular advantages of the acquiring firm may convert a fringe firm into a significant factor in the market. The Department is unlikely to challenge a potential competition merger when the acquired firm has a market share of five percent or less. Other things being equal, the Department is increasingly likely to challenge a merger as the market share of the acquired firm increases above that threshold. The Department is likely to challenge any merger satisfying the other conditions in which the acquired firm has market share of 20 percent or more.

4.135 Efficiencies. As in the case of horizontal mergers, the Department will consider expected efficiencies in determining whether to challenge a potential competition merger....

U.S. DOJ/FTC, Horizontal Merger Guidelines

(2010).

... These Guidelines outline the principal analytical techniques, practices, and the enforcement policy of the Department of Justice and the Federal Trade Commission (the "Agencies") with respect to mergers and acquisitions involving actual or potential competitors ("horizontal mergers") under the federal antitrust laws....

5.1 Market Participants

All firms that currently earn revenues in the relevant market are considered market participants. ... Firms not currently earning revenues in the relevant market, but that have committed to entering the market in the near future, are also considered market participants.

Firms that are not current producers in a relevant market, but that would very likely provide rapid supply responses with direct competitive impact in the event of a SSNIP, without incurring significant sunk costs, are also considered market participants. These firms are termed "rapid entrants." Sunk costs are entry or exit costs that cannot be recovered outside the relevant market. Entry that would take place more slowly in response to adverse competitive effects, or that requires firms to incur significant sunk costs, is considered in Section 9.

Firms that produce the relevant product but do not sell it in the relevant geographic market may be rapid entrants. Other things equal, such firms are most likely to be rapid entrants if they are close to the geographic market ...

5.2 Market Shares

The Agencies normally calculate market shares for all firms that currently produce products in the relevant market, subject to the availability of data. The Agencies also calculate market shares for other market participants if this can be done to reliably reflect their competitive significance ... The Agencies measure market shares based on the best available indicator of firms' future competitive significance in the relevant market. . . .

In most contexts, the Agencies measure each firm's market share based on its actual or projected revenues in the relevant market. . . .

5.3 Market Concentration ...

In analyzing mergers between an incumbent and a recent or potential entrant, to the extent the Agencies use the change in concentration to evaluate competitive effects, they will do so using projected market shares. A merger between an incumbent and a potential entrant can raise significant competitive concerns. The lessening of competition resulting from such a merger is more likely to be substantial, the larger is the market share of the incumbent, the greater is the competitive significance of the potential entrant, and the greater is the competitive threat posed by this potential entrant relative to others ...

Note and Questions on U.S. Guidelines on Mergers Affecting Potential Competition

The 1984 U.S. merger guidelines embrace theories of both potential and perceived competition in highly concentrated markets, and make clear that the DOJ is unlikely to pursue cases where entry barriers are too low and focuses more on whether the acquiring firm has significant entry advantages over all but a few firms. The merger guidelines also presumptively exclude "toehold" mergers with firms holding less than 5% of the market, in part because some cases had condemned conglomerate mergers with larger firms on the grounds that the acquiring firm should instead have acquired a smaller toehold firm.

The 2010 Horizontal Merger Guidelines also address mergers between potential competitors, but take a simpler approach. They simply project a future market share for the potential entrant, and then apply the standard horizontal merger guidelines given those projections. The 1984 guidelines projected market shares, but only when the likelihood of entry was "particularly strong." The 2010 guidelines, however, effectively always require strong evidence of likely entry by narrowing who counts as a potential entrant, requiring evidence that the firm either (1) has already "committed" to entry or (2) would very likely enter rapidly in response to a SSNIP without incurring significant sunk costs. Firms already committed to enter seem to correspond to actual potential competition, and firms likely to enter rapidly seem to correspond to perceived potential competition, though on the latter the 2010 guidelines focus more on actual responsiveness to price increases rather than incumbent perceptions of it. The 2010 guidelines approach also seems to avoid the 1984 guideline approach of counting how many other firms have similar entry advantages, by simply taking any entry advantages into account in projecting future shares.

1. Should the 2010 guidelines be reviewed as replacing or supplementing the 1984 guidelines on potential competition? The problem is that if the 1984 guidelines remain operative on potential competition, they would seem to circumvent the 2010 guidelines limits on how sure entry must be by effectively including in the market firms that have not committed to enter or would not be likely to rapidly enter in response to a price increase because they would have to incur significant sunk costs to enter. Perhaps the 2010 guidelines meant to narrowly construe who was in the market for defensive purposes (to prevent merging firms from diluting their market shares with less likely entrants) without being so narrow on assessing potential entrants for offensive purposes (to assess whether mergers with potential entrants might have anticompetitive effects). However, the 2010 guidelines state that they "outline the principal analytical techniques, practices, and the enforcement policy" of the agencies "with respect to mergers and acquisitions involving actual or *potential* competitors ('horizontal mergers')," which seems to define "horizontal" mergers to include conglomerate mergers with potential competitors, and suggests the 2010 guidelines intend to replace the prior ones.

The differences between the 1984 and 2010 guidelines boil down to the fact that the former would block mergers with potential entrants who have entry advantages possessed by few other firms if they: (a) have not committed to enter but are actually likely to do so; (b) would have to incur significant sunk costs to enter but are likely enough to enter in response to price increases that they would constrain those price increases from ever occurring; (c) are not actually likely to enter in response to price increases, but are wrongly perceived to be likely to do so by incumbents. Should claims in such cases be pursued? Note that claim (b) would be consistent with neutral treatment of defensive and offensive uses of potential entry, because the existence of such potential entrants (if not part of the merger) could eliminate anticompetitive concerns under 2010 guidelines § 9, even though such potential entrants are not quite likely enough to enter to be deemed market participants already.

2. Even if the 1984 guidelines on potential competition survive, given that modern U.S. agencies often do not challenge mergers that leave only three firms in a market, does it seem likely they would ever apply the 1984 guideline approach of challenging a merger that eliminates one of three possible entrants? In practice, it seems unlikely that the potential competition argument will have much impact on current U.S. agency action unless the merger is with a firm that has unique entry advantages or is more likely than others to enter.

3. Suppose two firms form a joint venture to enter into a market that neither of them are in now. Can their venture be challenged on the ground that, without their joint venture, both of them would have entered that market? Can it be challenged on the ground that, without their joint venture, one of them would have entered the market with the other remaining a significant potential competitor? A 1964 Supreme Court decision held both are viable claims.[100] Do you think that remains good law today? Would the agencies be likely to bring such a claim?

United States v. Marine Bancorporation

418 U.S. 602 (1974).

■ Mr. Justice Powell delivered the opinion of the Court.

The United States brought this civil antitrust action ... to challenge a proposed merger between two commercial banks. The acquiring bank is a large, nationally chartered bank based in Seattle, Washington, and the acquired bank is a medium-size, state-chartered bank located at the opposite end of the State in Spokane. The banks are not direct competitors to any significant degree in Spokane or any other part of the State. They have no banking offices in each other's home cities. The merger agreement would substitute the acquiring bank for the acquired bank in Spokane and would permit the former for the first time to operate as a direct participant in the Spokane market.

The proposed merger would have no effect on the number of banks in Spokane. The United States bases its case exclusively on the potential-competition doctrine under § 7 of the Clayton Act. It contends that if the merger is prohibited, the acquiring bank would find an alternative and more competitive means for entering the Spokane area and that the acquired bank would ultimately develop by internal expansion or mergers with smaller banks into an actual competitor of the acquiring bank and other large banks in sections of the State outside Spokane. The Government further submits that the merger would terminate the alleged procompetitive influence that the acquiring bank presently exerts over Spokane banks due to the potential for its entry into that market.

After a full trial, the District Court held against the Government on all aspects of the case. We affirm that court's judgment. We hold that in applying the potential-competition doctrine to commercial banking, courts must take into account the extensive federal and state regulation of banks, particularly the legal restraints on entry unique to this line of commerce. The legal barriers to entry in the instant case, notably state-law prohibitions against *de novo* branching, against branching from a branch office, and against multibank holding companies, compel us to conclude that the challenged merger is not in violation of § 7.

I. Background ...

The acquiring bank, National Bank of Commerce (NBC), [has] ... its principal office in Seattle, [and] ... is a wholly owned subsidiary of a registered bank holding company, Marine Bancorporation, Inc. (Marine).... The target bank, Washington Trust Bank (WTB), ... [has] ... headquarters in Spokane. Spokane is located in the extreme eastern part of the State, approximately 280 road miles from Seattle.... WTB has seven branch offices, six in the city of Spokane and one in ... a Spokane suburb.... It controls 17.4% of the 46 commercial banking offices in the

---

100. *See* United States v. Penn–Olin Chemical, 378 U.S. 158 (1964).

Spokane metropolitan area.... Although WTB has exhibited a pattern of moderate growth, at no time during its 70–year history has it expanded outside the Spokane metropolitan area.

... There are six banking organizations operating in the Spokane metropolitan area. One organization, Washington Bancshares, ... held 42.1% of total deposits in the area. Seattle–First National Bank ... held 31.6%. The target bank held 18.6% of total deposits at that time, placing it third in the Spokane area ... Thus, taken together, Washington Bancshares, Seattle–First National Bank, and WTB hold approximately 92% of total deposits in the Spokane area. None of the remaining three commercial banks in Spokane holds a market share larger than 3.1%.

... The United States sought to establish that the merger "may ... substantially ... lessen competition" within the meaning of § 7 in three ways: by eliminating the prospect that NBC, absent acquisition of the market share represented by WTB, would enter Spokane *de novo* or through acquisition of a smaller bank and thus would assist in deconcentrating that market over the long run; by ending present procompetitive effects allegedly produced in Spokane by NBC's perceived presence on the fringe of the Spokane market; and by terminating the alleged probability that WTB as an independent entity would develop through internal growth or through mergers with other medium-size banks into a regional or ultimately statewide counterweight to the market power of the State's largest banks. The Government's first theory—alleged likelihood of *de novo* or foothold entry by NBC if the challenged merger were blocked—was the primary basis upon which this case was presented to the District Court.

II. THE RELEVANT MARKETS

... The ... relevant product market ... is the "business of commercial banking ..." ... The ... relevant geographic market is the Spokane metropolitan area ...

III. POTENTIAL-COMPETITION DOCTRINE

... The potential-competition doctrine has been defined in major part by ... cases, particularly *United States v. Falstaff Brewing Corp., 410 U.S. 526 (1973)*. Unequivocal proof that an acquiring firm actually would have entered *de novo* but for a merger is rarely available. Thus, as *Falstaff* indicates, the principal focus of the doctrine is on the likely effects of the premerger position of the acquiring firm on the fringe of the target market. In developing and applying the doctrine, the Court has recognized that a market extension merger may be unlawful if the target market is substantially concentrated, if the acquiring firm has the characteristics, capabilities, and economic incentive to render it a perceived potential *de novo* entrant, and if the acquiring firm's premerger presence on the fringe of the target market in fact tempered oligopolistic behavior on the part of existing participants in that market. In other words, the Court has interpreted § 7 as encompassing what is commonly known as the "wings effect"—the probability that the acquiring firm prompted premerger procompetitive effects within the target market by being perceived by the existing firms in that market as likely to enter *de novo*. *Falstaff*. The elimination of such present procompetitive effects may render a merger unlawful under § 7.

Although the concept of perceived potential entry has been accepted in the Court's prior § 7 cases, the potential-competition theory upon which the Government places principal reliance in the instant case has not. The Court has not previously resolved whether the potential-competition doctrine proscribes a market extension merger solely on the ground that such a merger eliminates the prospect for long-term deconcentration of an oligopolistic market that in theory might result if the acquiring firm were forbidden to enter except through a *de novo* undertaking or through the acquisition of a small existing entrant (a so-called foothold or toehold acquisition). *Falstaff* expressly reserved this issue. . . .

B.   Structure of the Spokane Market.

. . . The potential-competition doctrine has meaning only as applied to concentrated markets. That is, the doctrine comes into play only where there are dominant participants in the target market engaging in interdependent or parallel behavior and with the capacity effectively to determine price and total output of goods or services. If the target market performs as a competitive market in traditional antitrust terms, the participants in the market will have no occasion to fashion their behavior to take into account the presence of a potential entrant. The present procompetitive effects that a perceived potential entrant may produce in an oligopolistic market will already have been accomplished if the target market is performing competitively. Likewise, there would be no need for concern about the prospects of long-term deconcentration of a market which is in fact genuinely competitive.

In an effort to establish that the Spokane commercial banking market is oligopolistic, the Government relied primarily on concentration ratios indicating that three banking organizations (including WTB) control approximately 92% of total deposits in Spokane. . . . We conclude that by introducing evidence of concentration ratios of the magnitude of those present here the Government established a prima facie case that the Spokane market was a candidate for the potential-competition doctrine. On this aspect of the case, the burden was then upon appellees to show that the concentration ratios, which can be unreliable indicators of actual market behavior, did not accurately depict the economic characteristics of the Spokane market. In our view, appellees did not carry this burden, and the District Court erred in holding to the contrary. Appellees introduced no significant evidence of the absence of parallel behavior in the pricing or providing of commercial bank services in Spokane. . . .

C.   Potential De Novo or Foothold Entry.

. . . . The Government contends that the challenged merger violates § 7 because it eliminates the alleged likelihood that, but for the merger, NBC would enter Spokane *de novo* or through a foothold acquisition. Utilization of one of these methods of entry, it is argued, would be likely to produce deconcentration of the Spokane market over the long run or other procompetitive effects, because NBC would be required to compete vigorously to expand its initially insignificant market share.

Two essential preconditions must exist before it is possible to resolve whether the Government's theory, if proved, establishes a violation of § 7.

It must be determined: (i) that in fact NBC has available feasible means for entering the Spokane market other than by acquiring WTB; and (ii) that those means offer a substantial likelihood of ultimately producing deconcentration of that market or other significant procompetitive effects.... There is no dispute that NBC possesses the financial capability and incentive to enter. The controversy turns on what methods of entry are realistically possible and on the likely effect of various methods on the characteristics of the Spokane commercial banking market.

It is undisputed that under state law NBC cannot establish *de novo* branches in Spokane and that its parent holding company cannot hold more than 25% of the stock of any other bank. Entry for NBC into Spokane therefore must be by acquisition of an existing bank. The Government contends that NBC has two distinct alternatives for acquisition of banks smaller than WTB and that either alternative would be likely to benefit the Spokane commercial banking market.

First, the Government contends that NBC could arrange for the formation of a new bank (a concept known as "sponsorship"), insure that the stock for such a new bank is placed in friendly hands, and then ultimately acquire that bank. Appellees respond that this approach would violate the spirit if not the letter of state-law restrictions on bank branching. ... [W]e will assume, *arguendo*, that NBC conceivably could succeed in sponsoring and then acquiring a new bank in Spokane at some indefinite time in the future. It does not follow from this assumption, however, that this method of entry would be reasonably likely to produce any significant procompetitive benefits in the Spokane commercial banking market. To the contrary, it appears likely that such a method of entry would not significantly affect that market.

State law would not allow NBC to branch from a sponsored bank after it was acquired. NBC's entry into Spokane therefore would be frozen at the level of its initial acquisition. Thus, if NBC were to enter Spokane by sponsoring and acquiring a small bank, it would be trapped into a position of operating a single branch office in a large metropolitan area with no reasonable likelihood of developing a significant share of that market.[8] This assumed method of entry therefore would offer little realistic hope of ultimately producing deconcentration of the Spokane market. Moreover, it is unlikely that a single new bank in Spokane with a small market share, and forbidden to branch, would have any other significant procompetitive effect on that market. The Government introduced no evidence, for example, establishing that the three small banks presently in Spokane have had any meaningful effect on the economic behavior of the large Spokane banks. In sum, it blinks reality to conclude that the opportunity for entry

---

8. NBC's acquisition of WTB, by comparison, will give it eight banking offices in Spokane and a significant market share. From this position, NBC will be able to have a substantial impact on the Spokane market. The Government suggests that a sponsored bank could create a number of branches before being acquired. The Government offered no proof that this has ever occurred in Washington. Undertaking sponsorship on such a scale is probably unrealistic, and it would multiply the problems of obtaining approval of a sponsorship plan from bank regulatory agencies. In any event, nothing in § 7 of the Clayton Act requires a firm to go to such lengths in order to avoid a merger that has no effect on concentration in the relevant market in the first place.

through sponsorship, assuming its availability, is comparable to the entry alternatives open to unregulated industries such as those involved in this Court's prior potential-competition cases or would be likely to produce the competitive effects of a truly unfettered method of entry. Since there is no substantial likelihood of procompetitive loss if the challenged merger is undertaken in place of the Government's sponsorship theory, we are unable to conclude that the effect of the former "may be substantially to lessen competition" within the meaning of the Clayton Act.

As a second alternative method of entry, the Government proposed that NBC could enter by a foothold acquisition of one of two small, state-chartered commercial banks that operate in the Spokane metropolitan area. . . . Granting the Government the benefit of the doubt that these two small banks were available merger partners for NBC, or were available at some not too distant time, it again does not follow that an acquisition of either would produce the long-term market-structure benefits predicted by the Government. Once NBC acquired either of these banks, it could not branch from the acquired bank. This limitation strongly suggests that NBC would not develop into a significant participant in the Spokane market . . .

In sum, with regard to either of its proposed alternative methods of entry, the Government has offered an unpersuasive case on the first precondition of the question reserved in *Falstaff*—that feasible alternative methods of entry in fact existed. Putting these difficulties aside, the Government simply did not establish the second precondition. It failed to demonstrate that the alternative means offer a reasonable prospect of long-term structural improvement or other benefits in the target market. In fact, insofar as competitive benefits are concerned, the Government is in the anomalous position of opposing a geographic market extension merger that will introduce a third full-service banking organization to the Spokane market, where only two are now operating, in reliance on alternative means of entry that appear unlikely to have any significant procompetitive effect. Accordingly, we cannot hold for the Government on its principal potential-competition theory. Indeed, since the preconditions for that theory are not present, we do not reach it, and therefore we express no view on the appropriate resolution of the question reserved in *Falstaff*. . . .

D. *Perceived Potential Entry.*

. . . Rational commercial bankers in Spokane, it must be assumed, are aware of the regulatory barriers that render NBC an unlikely or an insignificant potential entrant except by merger with WTB. In light of those barriers, it is improbable that NBC exerts any meaningful procompetitive influence over Spokane banks by "standing in the wings." Moreover, the District Court found as a fact that "the threat of entry by NBC into the Spokane market by any means other than the consummation of the merger, to the extent any such threat exists, does not have any significant effect on the competitive practices of commercial banks in that market nor any significant effect on the level of competition therein." . . .

E. *Elimination of WTB's Potential for Growth.*

[T]he Government [also] challenges the merger on the ground that it will eliminate the prospect that WTB may expand outside its base in

Spokane and eventually develop into a direct competitor with large Washington banks in other areas of the State. The District Court found, however, that the Government had "failed to establish . . . that there is any reasonable probability that WTB will expand into other banking markets. . . ." The record amply supports this finding. At no time in its 70–year history has WTB established branches outside the Spokane metropolitan area. Nor has it ever acquired another bank or received a merger offer other than the one at issue here. In sum, the Government's argument about the elimination of WTB's potential for expansion outside Spokane is little more than speculation. . . .

IV. CONCLUSION

In applying the doctrine of potential competition to commercial banking, courts must, as we have noted, take into account the extensive federal and state regulation of banks. Our affirmance of the District Court's judgment in this case rests primarily on state statutory barriers to *de novo* entry and to expansion following entry into a new geographic market. In States where such stringent barriers exist and in the absence of a likelihood of entrenchment, the potential-competition doctrine—grounded as it is on relative freedom of entry on the part of the acquiring firm—will seldom bar a geographic market extension merger by a commercial bank. In States that permit free branching or multibank holding companies, courts hearing cases involving such mergers should take into account all relevant factors, including the barriers to entry created by state and federal control over the issuance of new bank charters. Testimony by responsible regulatory officials that they will not grant new charters in the target market is entitled to great weight, although it is not determinative. To avoid the danger of subjecting the enforcement of the antitrust laws to the policies of a particular bank regulatory official or agency, courts should look also to the size and growth prospects of the target market, the size and number of banking organizations participating in it, and past practices of regulatory agencies in granting charters. If regulatory restraints are not determinative, courts should consider the factors that are pertinent to any potential-competition case, including the economic feasibility and likelihood of *de novo* entry, the capabilities and expansion history of the acquiring firm, and the performance as well as the structural characteristics of the target market. . . .

Note and Questions on *Marine Bancorp*

While Marine Bancorp did not rule on whether a conglomerate merger could be condemned on grounds that it prevented actual potential competition, it did rule that (if valid) any such claim would require proof that: (1) the market was sufficiently concentrated that the elimination of an entrant mattered; (2) entry outside the merger was feasible; and (3) entry would have a substantial likelihood of having a significant procompetitive impact. The latter seems to include inquiry into how timely the entry would have been.

1. Is there much difference between actual potential competition and perceived potential competition?

    a. Didn't the Court rely on the same evidence for both conclusions?

    b. Wouldn't it make equal sense to inquire into those three factors under either theory?

    c. Is this a distinction that only comes up when the court's predictions about what would have happened differ from firm perceptions? If so, which are more likely to be accurate in such a case? Should there only be a difference when there are internal corporate documents indicating entry plans about which the market was unaware?

    d. Couldn't one ground for divergence be that the actual likelihood of future entry may be low precisely because firms are keeping prices low enough to dissuade it because they perceive entry would be likely if they raised prices?

    e. Might there also be a difference because firms may not have sufficient incentives (especially in an oligopoly market) to constrain present prices in order to restrain future entry, even though they perceive it is likely?

    2. Are these three factors the right inquiry? *Marine Bancorp* holds that, if entry barriers are very high, then potential competition theory should not bar a merger because entry would not have occurred without the merger. But if entry barriers were very low, shouldn't we conclude that potential competition theory should not bar a merger because the threat of entry will render the market competitive regardless of whether the merger occurs. Does the potential competition theory only work for mid-range levels of entry barriers, where it is not so difficult to enter that the merging party would not have done so, but not so easy to enter that others could not have entered too?

    3. Shouldn't it matter how many other entrants exist who could equally restrain any increase in market prices, and whether those other entrants could enter as easily as the firm merging into the market? That is, shouldn't the focus be on the degree to which the firm merging into the market has lower entry barriers than other firms, rather than on the absolute size of entry barriers?

EU Guidelines on the Assessment of Horizontal Mergers

O.J. 2004, C 31/5.

    Merger with a potential competitor. Concentrations where an undertaking already active on a relevant market merges with a potential competitor in this market can have similar anti-competitive effects to mergers between two undertakings already active on the same relevant market and, thus, significantly impede effective competition, in particular through the creation or the strengthening of a dominant position.

    A merger with a potential competitor can generate horizontal anti-competitive effects, whether coordinated or non-coordinated, if the potential competitor significantly constrains the behaviour of the firms active in the market. This is the case if the potential competitor possesses assets that could easily be used to enter the market without incurring significant sunk costs. Anticompetitive effects may also occur where the merging partner is very likely to incur the necessary sunk costs to enter the market in a relatively short period of time after which this company would constrain the behaviour of the firms currently active in the market.

For a merger with a potential competitor to have significant anti-competitive effects, two basic conditions must be fulfilled. First, the potential competitor must already exert a significant constraining influence or there must be a significant likelihood that it would grow into an effective competitive force. Evidence that a potential competitor has plans to enter a market in a significant way could help the Commission to reach such a conclusion. Second, there must not be a sufficient number of other potential competitors, which could maintain sufficient competitive pressure after the merger.

Questions on EU Horizontal Merger Guidelines Regarding Potential Competition

These guidelines cover mergers with a firm that already constrains or could enter and constrain existing firms, which seems to cover both perceived and actual potential competition. But are the EU merger guidelines too vague about how many other potential entrants can exist under this theory?

Commission Decision 98/602/EC, Guinness/Grand Metropolitan

O.J. 1998, L 288/24.

... [The proposed merger of GrandMet and Guinness (GMG)] will combine the activities of the two largest spirits suppliers in the world (and, on the basis of sales figures by value, the two largest in the Community) creating a company approximately twice the size of its nearest rival, Allied Domecq. However ... competition takes place principally within each different spirit type, and at national level. ...

In addition to horizontal overlaps [in certain spirit markets], a key result of the merger, recognised as a major part of its rationale by the parties and by third parties, is that it combines the two parties' ranges or portfolios of products and brands. The holder of a portfolio of leading spirit brands may enjoy a number of advantages. In particular, his position in relation to his customers is stronger since he is able to provide a range of products and will account for a greater proportion of their business, he will have greater flexibility to structure his prices, promotions and discounts, he will have greater potential for tying, and he will be able to realise economies of scale and scope in his sales and marketing activities. Finally the implicit (or explicit) threat of a refusal to supply is more potent.

The strength of these advantages, and their potential effect on the competitive structure of the market, depends on a number of factors, including: whether the holder of the portfolio has the brand leader or one or more leading brands in a particular market; the market shares of the various brands, particularly in relation to the shares of competitors; the relative importance of the individual markets in which the parties have significant shares and brands across the range of product markets in which the portfolio is held; and/or the number of markets in which the portfolio holder has a brand leader or leading brand. In addition the strength of a portfolio effect has to be considered in the context of the relative strength of competitors' brands and their portfolios.

The portfolio effect has been recognised in two recent cases in the soft drinks sector. Furthermore in response to the Commission's enquiries, competitors and customers recognised the portfolio effect in practice; for example, of ten firms responding to the question "does possession of a leading brand in all or most spirit categories help sales of spirits in general?" eight replied that it would help a lot. At the hearing, major competitors of the parties confirmed the existence of a portfolio effect and provided evidence of how their portfolio could be used.

The parties have said that consumers buy brands and not portfolios. That is true. However, the parties do not sell their products to the final consumers. They sell them to intermediaries, multiple retailers, wholesalers and others. Those customers would buy a range of products from GMG, and the fact that GMG would be able to offer in many national markets a wide and deep portfolio of leading brands would give the combined entity advantages in dealing with its clients. The strength of any portfolio effect will vary from geographic market to geographic market. In the present case, the only market in which it has been considered to be a significant feature in the context of the assessment is Greece. . . .

Relevant product markets. The relevant product markets under consideration in the Greek market are the internationally recognised categories of spirits, that is whiskey, vodka, gin, rum, brandy, the various liqueurs (each of which may constitute a separate niche product market), and the local ouzo aperitif. Scotch whisky accounts for 95% of all whiskey consumed in Greece. However, on the basis of the market shares of the parties, the assessment of the operation would be similar no matter whether Scotch whisky or all whiskey is used. Therefore, the assessment below is made on the basis of all whiskey. . . .

Market profile and position of the parties. (a) Position in the market— . . . The major brands of the parties [in Greece] are: Johnnie Walker Red Label, Dewar's, White Horse, Bell's, Haig, VAT 69 (Guinness) and J & B (GrandMet) in Scotch whisky; Smirnoff (GrandMet) in vodka; Metaxa (GrandMet) in brandy; Gordon's (Guinness) in gin; Ouzo 12 (GrandMet) in ouzo; and Baileys, Malibu and Archer's (GrandMet) in liqueurs and fruit schnapps. In addition, Guinness distributes Bacardi rum and Wyborowa and Finlandia vodkas, whereas GrandMet distributes tequila Cuervo, both on a brand agency basis. . . .

(b) Categories and brands of the parties— . . . [T]he combined entity will cover a broad range of spirits categories, in fact all the major and popular types of spirits. Taken separately, Guinness has currently a strong position in whiskey, gin and rum, whereas GrandMet is strong in brandy, ouzo, tequila and liqueurs. The merger thus fills the gaps in the respective portfolios of each party. The resulting combined portfolio will be by far wider and deeper than that of competitors. After the proposed operation has been completed, the combined entity will account for above [45–55%] of the overall trade of spirits ([20–30%] from Guinness and [10–20%] from GrandMet), covering all the major categories of spirits marketed in Greece. The next largest competitors, Karoulias/Berry Brothers and Allied Domecq, have shares of [5–15%] and [5–15%] respectively. More specifically, GMG will be the driving force in the whiskey market, with a market share above [45–55%]. In addition, it will be the largest supplier in categories such as gin with a market share above [75–85%] (Gordon's), brandy, with a market share above [75–85%] (Metaxa), and rum with a market share of [75–85%] (Bacardi). Moreover, GMG will supply other categories, such as tequila (Cuervo), ouzo (Ouzo 12), cream liqueurs (Baileys and Malibu) and fruit schnapps (Archer's).

(c) Aggregation—In so far as it concerns horizontal overlap in the individual categories, . . . the combined entity's share in [the Greek Whiskey] market would amount to [45–55%] (that is [40–50%] from Guinness and [10%] from GrandMet). The . . . Commission considers this accretion significant. . . .

(d) Portfolio effects—Although there is no horizontal aggregation in other categories, the merger will bring together existing high market shares in gin, brandy and rum. Guinness' Gordon's gin accounts for over [75–85%] of the gin market and is complemented by two premium quality brands, that is Tanqueray (Guinness) and Bombay Sapphire (GrandMet). Competing brands in this market include Allied Domecq's Beefeater [10%] and Four Seasons [10%], Amvyx's Nicholson's [10%], and Seagram's Burnetts [10%]. In brandy, Metaxa is the uncontested market leader with a market share of [70–80%], whereas competitors offer Remy Martin [2%], Martell [2%], Courvoisier [2%] and Hennessy with an insignificant market share. In rum, Bacardi is the leading brand with a [75–85%] market share, whereas its only potential competitor is Seagram's Captain Morgan [5–15%]. For the rest of the rum market, an industry report (Canadean) makes reference to "cheap imitations of Bacardi". Apart from the leading brands in their respective categories, GMG would also have a number of second-string brands including White Horse, Black & White, Bell's, Haig, VAT 69, Mackenzie, Crawford's, Dimple and Cardhu Scotch whiskies, Finlandia and Wyborowa vodkas, Grand Marnier and Sheridans liqueurs, Tanqueray gin and Karavaki and Kaloyannis ouzo.

Accordingly, and given that market entry and countervailing buyer power are not significant constraints, as explained below, the Commission considers that the parties have existing dominant positions in the markets for gin, rum and brandy.

Overall, GMG will be at least four times as big as the next largest competitors, none of whom account for more than [5–15%] of the spirits market. It will therefore become the largest spirits importer and distributor in Greece. . . .

The issue of portfolio power is of particular relevance in the assessment of the operation with regard to the Greek market. This is mainly due to the fact that the combined entity will be present across the major categories of spirits, that is whiskey, gin, rum and brandy, where it will be able to supply the leading brands, with the exception of vodka.

To date, the Greek market has been characterised by the presence of various suppliers, none of which was strong across all the categories of spirits. As a result, customers, whether wholesalers or retailers, have obtained their spirits from a variety of suppliers, according to the latter's strength in the various categories. It is precisely in those market conditions that the combination of the most important spirits categories in one single supplier's portfolio is expected to enhance that supplier's market power in individual categories. . . .

As stated above, whiskey is by far the largest category of spirits sold in Greece. However, the fact that GMG will include brands with very significant market shares in smaller categories is also important. For example, even if gin or rum have lower sales than whiskey, the presence of Gordon's and Bacardi is of crucial importance to a particular outlet, as these brands have been driving their respective categories for a long time and are identified with the category to which they belong. According to Canadean 1996 on Greece, "gin continues to grow, largely due to a strong performance by Gordon's". The same industry report refers to the rum market as consisting essentially of Bacardi.

It is true that other competitors supply important brands, some of which have achieved high sales volumes. For instance, on the merits of their sales performance, Cutty Sark whisky and Stolichnaya vodka would not face particular problems in access to the trade. However, the potential power of those brands is significantly reduced by the fact that they are spread out among different suppliers. That fragmentation of the market, as contrasted to the combined portfolio of GMG, deprives such brands of their potential portfolio power.

More particularly, a deep portfolio of whiskey brands, spread out across the various quality and price segments, confers considerable price flexibility and marketing opportunities. Therefore, the supplier is shielded from market pressures, as he is able to face price competition from other suppliers' brands by positioning and pricing his various brands within the category. For instance, with its secure high market performance of the best-selling whiskey brands, GMG will be able to devote as many resources as necessary in order to maintain its secondary brands in their position or to reposition the weaker brands upwards by expanding their share at the expense of competing brands, or in order to counter eventual competitive pressure coming from those brands. The parties have argued that such "pull-through" has not occurred in the past and is accordingly unlikely to occur in the future. However, this argument ignores the substantial increase in the parties' market shares and resources that the merger will create.

Moreover, a wide portfolio of categories confers major marketing advantages, giving GMG the possibility of bundling sales or increasing the sales volume of one category by tying it to the sale of another category. Both Guinness and GrandMet have made use of their portfolios of brands in bundling deals. . . .

In the on-trade, where spirits producers build a brand's strength and image, GMG, through its broad portfolio of brands, would be able to influence what products are stocked or displayed in the limited space available behind the bar, (the so-called back-bar), thus further strengthening its market power. For small outlets which have smaller back-bars, or for Greek night-clubs which concentrate on whiskey, the combined entity would be an attractive solution for one-stop-shopping considerations. In addition, larger modern outlets, which usually stock a much broader variety of brands, may also become a target of the combined entity, should it attempt to gain more back-bar space or use the image of fashionable clubs in order to launch its brands. GMG could afford to make substantial offers, discounts and credits or organise and finance promotional events, that would also accrue to the outlet itself, and use its strength in leading brands, such as Johnnie Walker Red Label, Gordon's gin and Bacardi rum, in order to induce bars to list brands in the same or another category. Given that those premises could not afford not to stock the brands set out above, the negotiating power of GMG would be significantly strengthened. Therefore, it would be much easier for GMG to induce bartenders to adopt GMG brands as pouring brands (that is, the brand offered when a customer fails to specify a brand by name), thus increasing their sales volumes and public awareness.

In the off-trade, the elimination of competition between Guinness and GrandMet for in-store promotions will serve to enable GMG to plan jointly the timing of promotions, negotiate jointly the terms of promotions and coordinate any price changes. Moreover, through its variety of brands, GMG could also alternate branded products promoted over a period of time, thus occupying long promotion periods and excluding competitors from access to the promotion calendar for long periods.

By comparison, competitors have weaker portfolios and fewer strong brands, the most important being Cutty Sark, accounting for [15–25%] of whiskey sales, and Stolichnaya and Serkova vodkas, accounting for [20–30%] and [15–25%] of vodka sales respectively. As stated in the preceding paragraphs, although those brands may have performed well, they lack the support of a strong portfolio of brands. Indeed, in contrast to the complete GMG portfolio, the discontinuity of the competitors' portfolios would deprive them of price flexibility and make them more vulnerable to market pressures. For example, when their brands start losing sales volume, they will have to commit disproportionately stronger resources in order to avoid situations that could in the long run restrict their competitive scope.

Questions on *Guinness/Grand Metropolitan*

1. To the extent the relevant portfolio effect is that the portfolio will give the merged firm greater potential to tie products in the portfolio, is this a valid reason to ban the merger?

a. Can we be sure the merged firm will engage in tying post-merger?

b. If it does engage in tying, can we be sure that tying will be anticompetitive?

c. If the merged firm does engage in post-merger tying that is anticompetitive, can't the Commission prohibit it under Articles 101 or 102?

d. If the concern is really tying, shouldn't the merger be approved conditional on a ban on post-merger tying?

2. To the extent the relevant portfolio effect is that the portfolio will give the merged firm "economies of scale and scope in his sales and marketing activities," shouldn't that constitute an efficiency defense rather than grounds to condemn the merger? Does this part of the opinion thus fail to survive the regulation amendments making clear that efficiencies constitute a defense?

3. Might the portfolio effect concern instead be that, while not in the same market, these various liquors are partial substitutes so that the merger might increase incentives to raise prices on particular types of liquor? Suppose, for example, that a monopolist in whiskey could only raise prices by 20% over the competitive price because at that level too many consumers started to switch to vodka. Wouldn't a merger of the whiskey monopolist with a vodka monopolist raise anticompetitive concerns? But shouldn't such concerns have to be validated with actual evidence on the relevant cross-elasticities under a conventional horizontal merger theory?

Case T–5/02, Tetra Laval BV v. Commission
2002 E.C.R. II–04381.

[Many liquids like milk or orange juice are sold both in cartons and in plastic bottles. Tetra Laval owned Tetra Pak, which made carton packaging for liquids and had a dominant position in aseptic carton packaging market and a leading position in non-aseptic carton packaging, both of which were global, but a limited presence in market for plastic packaging of liquids. Tetra Laval sought to acquire Sidel, which was the world-wide leader in producing the stretch blow moulding (SBM) equipment that is used to make plastic polyethylene terephthalate (PET) bottles for packaging liquids. The Commission declared the proposed merger illegal and Tetra appealed to the [General Court]

It is common ground between the parties that the modified merger is conglomerate in type, that is, a merger of undertakings which, essentially, do not have a pre-existing competitive relationship, either as direct competitors or as suppliers and customers. Mergers of this type do not give rise to true horizontal overlaps between the activities of the parties to the merger or to a vertical relationship between the parties in the strict sense of the term. Thus it cannot be presumed as a general rule that such mergers produce anti-competitive effects. However, they may have anti-competitive effects in certain cases.

. . . [The Commission's conclusion] that the modified merger will have foreseeable anti-competitive conglomerate effects [rests on two pillars]. First, the merger would enable the merged entity to use its dominant position on the global carton packaging market as a lever in order to achieve a dominant position on the PET packaging equipment markets.

Second, the merger would reinforce the current dominant position of Tetra on the markets for aseptic carton packaging equipment and aseptic cartons, because it would eliminate the competitive constraint, represented by Sidel, coming from the neighbouring PET markets . . .

The first pillar: leveraging . . . . [A] merger having a conglomerate effect must, like any other merger, be authorised by the Commission if it is not established that it creates or strengthens a dominant position in the common market or in a substantial part of it and that, as a result, effective competition will be significantly impeded . . . .

(i) *Temporal aspects of conglomerate effects.* . . . [I]f the Commission is able to conclude that a dominant position would, in all likelihood, be created or strengthened in the relatively near future and would lead to effective competition on the market being significantly impeded, it must prohibit it. *Kali & Salz*; *Gencor; Airtours.*

(ii) *Aspects concerning the specific nature of the conglomerate effects.* . . . The Commission's analysis of a merger producing a conglomerate effect is conditioned by requirements similar to those defined by the Court with regard to the creation of a situation of collective dominance. *Kali & Salz; Airtours.* . . . Since the effects of a conglomerate-type merger are generally considered to be neutral, or even beneficial, for competition on the markets concerned, as is recognised in the present case by the economic writings cited in the analyses annexed to the parties' written pleadings, the proof of anti-competitive conglomerate effects of such a merger calls for a precise examination, supported by convincing evidence, of the circumstances which allegedly produce those effects. *Airtours.*

In the present case, the leveraging from the aseptic carton market, as described in the contested decision, would manifest itself—in addition to the possibility of the merged entity engaging in practices such as tying sales of carton packaging equipment and consumables to sales of PET packaging equipment and forced sales—firstly, by the probability of predatory pricing by the merged entity; secondly, by price wars; and, thirdly, by the granting of loyalty rebates. Engaging in these practices would enable the merged entity to ensure, as far as possible, that its customers on the carton markets obtain from Sidel any PET equipment they may require. The contested decision finds that Tetra holds a dominant position on the aseptic carton markets, that is to say, the markets for aseptic carton packaging systems and aseptic cartons, a finding which is not disputed by the applicant.

. . . [T]he Commission did not deny that leveraging by Tetra through the conduct described above could constitute abuse of Tetra's pre-existing dominant position in the aseptic carton markets. . . . However, the Commission went on to state that the fact that a type of conduct may constitute an independent infringement of [Article 102 TFEU] does not preclude that conduct from being taken into account in the Commission's assessment of all forms of leveraging made possible by a merger transaction.

. . . [A]lthough the Regulation provides for the prohibition of a merger creating or strengthening a dominant position which has significant anti-competitive effects, these conditions do not require it to be demonstrated that the merged entity will, as a result of the merger, engage in abusive, and consequently unlawful, conduct. Although it cannot therefore be presumed that Community law will not be complied with by the parties to a conglomerate-type merger transaction, such a possibility cannot be excluded by the Commission when it carries out its control of mergers. Accordingly, when the Commission, in assessing the effects of such a merger, relies on foreseeable conduct which in itself is likely to constitute abuse of an existing dominant position, it is required to assess whether, despite the prohibition of such conduct, it is none the less likely that the entity resulting from the merger will act in such a manner or whether, on the contrary, the illegal nature of the conduct and/or the risk of detection will make such a strategy unlikely. While it is appropriate to take account, in its assessment, of incentives to engage in anti-competitive practices, such as those resulting in the present case for Tetra from the commercial advantages which may be foreseen on the PET equipment markets, the Commission must also consider the extent to which those incentives would be reduced, or even eliminated, owing to the illegality of the conduct in question, the likelihood of its detection, action taken by the competent authorities, both at Community and national level, and the financial penalties which could ensue.

Since the Commission did not carry out such an assessment in the contested decision, it follows that, in so far as the Commission's assessment is based on the possibility, or even the probability, that Tetra will engage in such conduct in the aseptic carton markets, its findings in this respect cannot be upheld.

Moreover, the fact that the applicant offered commitments regarding its future conduct is also a factor which the Commission should have taken into account in assessing whether it was likely that the merged entity would act in a manner which could result in the creation of a dominant position on one or more of the relevant PET equipment markets. . . .

The second pillar: reduction of potential competition on the carton markets . . . . The contested decision finds that the modified merger would enable Tetra to strengthen its current dominant position in carton packaging by eliminating a source of significant competitive constraint. . . . The Court finds . . . that when the Commission relies on the elimination or significant reduction of potential competition, even of competition which will tend to grow, in order to justify the prohibition of a notified merger, the factors which it identifies to show the strengthening of a dominant position must be based on convincing evidence. The mere fact that the acquiring undertaking already holds a clear dominant position on the relevant market may constitute an important factor, as the contested decision finds, but does not in itself suffice to justify a finding that a reduction in the potential competition which that undertaking must face constitutes a strengthening of its position. . . .

According to the applicant, the contested decision finds that the PET and carton packaging equipment markets are distinct owing in particular to the current weak cross-elasticity of demand by reference to price between the two materials. The applicant maintains that marketing-and barrier technology-related factors are, and will remain, decisive for the choice of packaging and prevent a future increase in such cross-elasticity of price between PET and carton . . .

The Commission maintains that, notwithstanding the fact that carton and PET packaging systems do not belong to the same market, they may converge in future and there is already significant interaction between them. In the present case, since the aseptic carton markets are highly concentrated, competition on them is already weakened to such an extent that any further reduction, even from external sources, could have a significant impact. The Commission asserts that carton and PET will be used in future to package the same products. PET would thus exert pressure on the aseptic carton markets; it is not necessary for the two materials to belong to the same relevant product market. . . .

In maintaining that significant competitive pressure will be eliminated as a result of the modified merger, the Commission relies principally on the considerable growth it foresees in PET use for packaging sensitive products. [The Court concludes that this growth was likely to be too small] to determine, with the certainty required to justify the prohibition of a merger, whether the implementation of the modified merger would place Tetra in a situation where it could be more independent than in the past in relation to its competitors on the aseptic carton markets. . . .

. . . [Nor has it] been shown that, in the event of elimination or significant reduction of competitive pressure from the PET markets, Tetra would have an incentive not to reduce its carton packaging prices and would stop innovating.

As regards price competition, the contested decision does not call into question the finding of the independent Warrick Report, to which it refers and according to which PET is 30–40% more expensive than carton currently and that, to be competitive on total cost, the packaging price of PET would need to be 5–10% lower than aseptic carton cost, to compensate for the lower distribution cost of carton systems.

As regards the more price-sensitive carton customers who indicated to the Commission, during its market investigation, that they would only consider a switch from carton to PET if carton prices rose by a significant amount of 20% or more, it is clear that a lowering of carton prices is not necessary to keep them in the carton markets. In finding simply that "[t]hese same price-sensitive customers would presumably be dissuaded from making a switch from carton to PET if a carton-price reduction increased the price difference between a carton and PET packaging line," the contested decision does not explain why, without the merger, Tetra would be obliged to make such price reductions in order to keep those customers. These customers would not switch to PET unless carton prices rose by at least 20% or there was a corresponding reduction in PET prices. The finding that, in the absence of the merger, "Tetra would [. . .] defend its position fiercely [. . .] in some cases, [by] lowering carton prices" is, therefore, not based on convincing evidence. Inasmuch as the Commission pleads before the Court that, once the merger is implemented, it is possible that Tetra might find it more easy to raise its prices on the aseptic carton markets for those customers, it does not explain, in particular, why this would not enable Tetra's competitors on the carton markets who are also active on the PET market, such as SIG and Elopak, to benefit from this.

As for beverage producers who will switch from carton to PET for commercial reasons despite the fact that PET is considerably more costly than carton, a reduction in carton prices would not necessarily persuade those non-price-sensitive customers to keep carton packaging. The contested decision does not show why companies active in the PET equipment markets which, without the modified merger, would be expected to compete vigorously to gain market share from carton, would modify their behaviour following the transaction in question here. If the pressure from Sidel were to disappear, the contested decision does not explain why, if Sidel's competitors had not been marginalised through successful leveraging, the other companies active in the PET equipment markets would no longer be able to promote the advantages of PET to Tetra's customers on the carton markets. The finding in the contested decision that Tetra would be exposed to less pressure to lower its carton prices if it could acquire Sidel is, therefore, not based on convincing evidence.

Turning to the allegedly diminished need for Tetra to innovate following implementation of the modified merger, both the contested decision and the explanations given in the Commission's written and oral pleadings show that, at present, competition on the various carton markets takes place principally through innovation. According to the Commission, Tetra's introduction in the past of new carton packages with more user-friendly features such as the carton top package with screw top closure shows that innovation is a practical necessity. According to Tetra's pleadings at the hearing, which were not disputed on this point by the Commission, these innovations were not due to pressure from the PET equipment markets, but rather to the demands of consumers of carton-packaged products. Even if the acquisition of Sidel were to reduce the pressure on innovation emanating from the indirect, but growing, competition from the PET equipment markets, ... the contested decision does not state why demand from customers wishing to remain with carton would not continue in the future to be the driving force behind innovation, especially on the aseptic carton markets. Although the Commission correctly points out, in particular, that Tetra can improve the production rate of its carton packaging equipment, the contested decision does not show that the incentive to do so would disappear simply because of the acquisition of Sidel. This is even less likely given that it is not disputed that Tetra's activities in the carton markets are very profitable. Consequently, it is unlikely that Tetra, following the modified merger, would be less inclined to continue investing in any innovation possible for the range of equipment and products it offers its customers on the carton markets.

This finding is supported by the continued presence of competitors of the merged entity on the aseptic carton markets. Although Tetra's share of that market is very strong at present, the Commission recognises that its position is slightly lower compared with 1991. No explanation whatsoever is given of why Tetra's competitors, particularly SIG, its main competitor, with a market share of [10–20%], could not benefit from a decision by the merged entity to innovate less. Such an explanation was all the more necessary in the light of the fact that SIG is active in particular on the carton packaging equipment and PET packaging equipment markets and, unlike the merged entity, would not be subject to any constraints as to joint offers of carton and SBM machines. . . . The Commission was also incorrect in finding that, apart from Tetra, the SIG group is the only other company in the world that manufactures and sells both carton and PET packaging equipment, since, as is apparent from the contested decision, the Elopak group can also do this, under agreements with other companies active on the PET equipment markets. . . .

Consequently, the contested decision has not established to the requisite legal standard that the merged entity would have less incentive than Tetra currently has to innovate in the carton sector.

It follows that the evidence relied on in the contested decision does not establish to the requisite legal standard that the effects of the modified merger on Tetra's position, principally on the aseptic carton markets, would, by eliminating Sidel as a potential competitor, be such as to fulfil the conditions of Article 2(3) of the Regulation. . . .

Case C–12/03 P, Commission v. Tetra Laval BV

[2005] E.C.R. I–987.

. . . *The first ground of appeal* . . . By its first ground of appeal, the Commission [argues that] the Court of First Instance required it . . . to satisfy a standard of proof and to provide a quality of evidence in support of its line of argument which are incompatible with the wide discretion which it enjoys in assessing economic matters. . . . Whilst the Court recognises that the Commission has a margin of discretion with regard to economic matters, that does not mean that the Community Courts must refrain from reviewing the Commission's interpretation of information of an economic nature. Not only must the Community Courts, inter alia, establish whether the evidence relied on is factually accurate, reliable and consistent but also whether that evidence contains all the information which must be taken into account in order to assess a complex situation and whether it is capable of substantiating the conclusions drawn from it. Such a review is all the more necessary in the case of a prospective analysis required when examining a planned merger with conglomerate effect.

Thus, the Court of First Instance was right to find . . . that the Commission's analysis of a merger producing a conglomerate effect is subject to requirements similar to those defined by the Court with regard to the creation of a situation of collective dominance and that it calls for a close examination of the circumstances which are relevant for an assessment of that effect on the conditions of competition on the reference market.

Although the Court of First Instance stated . . . that proof of anti-competitive conglomerate effects of a merger of the kind notified calls for a precise examination, supported by convincing evidence, of the circumstances which allegedly produce those effects, it by no means added a condition relating to the requisite standard of proof but merely drew attention to the essential function of evidence, which is to establish convincingly the merits of an argument or, as in the present case, of a decision on a merger....

The analysis of a conglomerate-type' concentration is a prospective analysis in which, first, the consideration of a lengthy period of time in the future and, secondly, the leveraging necessary to give rise to a significant impediment to effective competition mean that the chains of cause and effect are dimly discernible, uncertain and difficult to establish. That being so, the quality of the evidence produced by the Commission in order to establish that it is necessary to adopt a decision declaring the concentration incompatible with the common market is particularly important, since that evidence must support the Commission's conclusion that, if such a decision were not adopted, the economic development envisaged by it would be plausible....

The second ground of appeal. By its second ground of appeal, the Commission complains that the [General Court] [wrongly] ... required the Commission to take account of the impact which the illegality of certain conduct would have on the incentives for the merged entity to engage in leveraging and to assess, as a possible remedy, the commitment not to engage in abusive conduct....

Since the view is taken in the contested decision that [this] conduct ... is an essential step in leveraging, the [General Court] was right to hold that the likelihood of its adoption must be examined comprehensively, ... taking account ... both of the incentives to adopt such conduct and the factors liable to reduce, or even eliminate, those incentives, including the possibility that the conduct is unlawful.

However, it would run counter to the Regulation's purpose of prevention to require the Commission, as was held [by the General Court], to examine, for each proposed merger, the extent to which the incentives to adopt anti-competitive conduct would be reduced, or even eliminated, as a result of the unlawfulness of the conduct in question, the likelihood of its detection, the action taken by the competent authorities, both at Community and national level, and the financial penalties which could ensue. An assessment such as that required by the [General Court] would make it necessary to carry out an exhaustive and detailed examination of the rules of the various legal orders which might be applicable and of the enforcement policy practised in them. Moreover, if it is to be relevant, such an assessment calls for a high probability of the occurrence of the acts envisaged as capable of giving rise to objections on the ground that they are part of anti-competitive conduct.

It follows that, at the stage of assessing a proposed merger, an assessment intended to establish whether an infringement of Article [102 TFEU] is likely and to ascertain that it will be penalised in several legal orders would be too speculative and would not allow the Commission to base its assessment on all of the relevant facts with a view to establishing whether they support an economic scenario in which a development such as leveraging will occur.

Consequently, the [General Court] erred in law in rejecting the Commission's conclusions as to the adoption by the merged entity of anticompetitive conduct capable of resulting in leveraging on the sole ground that the Commission had, when assessing the likelihood that such conduct might be adopted, failed to take account of the unlawfulness of that conduct and, consequently, of the likelihood of its detection, of action by the competent authorities, both at Community and national level, and of the financial penalties which might ensue....

[T]he Court of First Instance ... was nevertheless right to hold ... that the Commission ought to have taken account of the commitments submitted by Tetra with regard to that entity's future conduct. Accordingly, whilst the ground of appeal is well founded in part, it cannot call into question the judgment under appeal in so far as it annulled the contested decision since that annulment was based, inter alia, on the Commission's refusal to take account of those commitments.

The fourth ground of appeal. By its fourth ground of appeal, the Commission [challenged the GC's rejection of its potential competition theory.] ...

As is clear from Article 2(1) of the Regulation, the Commission, when assessing the compatibility of a concentration with the common market, must take account of a number of factors, such as the structure of the relevant markets, actual or potential competition from undertakings, the position of the undertakings concerned and their economic and financial power, possible options available to suppliers and users, any barriers to entry and trends in supply and demand. The [General Court] was therefore right to point out ... that, although constituting an important factor, as the contested decision finds, the mere fact that the acquiring undertaking already holds a clear dominant position on the relevant market does not in itself suffice to justify a finding that a reduction in the potential competition which that undertaking must face constitutes a strengthening of its position.

The potential competition represented by a producer of substitute products on a segment of the relevant market (namely in the present case the competition, in relation to aseptic carton packaging, from Sidel, as a supplier of PET packaging, on the market segment for sensitive products) is only one of the set of factors which must be taken into account when assessing whether there is a risk that a concentration might strengthen a dominant position. It cannot be ruled out that a reduction in that potential competition might be compensated by other factors, with the result that the competitive position of the already dominant undertaking remains unchanged.

.... The Court of First Instance was therefore right to ... rel[y] on the potential reactions of Tetra's competitors on the carton markets, which are also active on the PET market, as a basis for refuting ... the Commission's argument that Tetra might be encouraged, once the merger has been completed, to increase its prices on the aseptic carton markets and ... the argument that the merged entity might decide to innovate less....

... [T]he Commission's line of argument with respect to the likely growth in the use of PET for packaging sensitive products was examined in connection with the first ground of appeal [above] ... In so far as the Commission, by this part of the ground of appeal, contests the [General Court]'s findings in that regard, it must be held that it calls into question the [General Court]'s assessment of the evidence, which is not subject to review by the Court in appeal proceedings. The same applies to the part of the ground of appeal by which the Commission challenges how ... the [General Court] assessed the evidence submitted by the Commission in relation to the effect on prices of the elimination of Sidel and to the lesser incentive for the merged entity to innovate in the carton sector.

It follows ... that the fourth ground of appeal is, in part, inadmissible and, in part, unfounded.

Questions on *Tetra Laval*

1. When the claim is that a conglomerate merger would enable the merged firm to engage in exclusionary post-merger conduct, the ECJ agreed with the General Court that the Commission must provide convincing evidence that this conduct is likely based on a comprehensive examination of the incentives to engage in it and factors that might offset those incentives like legal penalties. However, it held that the General Court was wrong to require a detailed examination of the extent to which the conduct would violate EU or national law, the likelihood of detection and enforcement and the penalties that would apply. Without such a showing, just how is the Commission supposed to establish the likelihood of the post-merger conduct?

2. If Articles 101 and 102 do not suffice to deter anticompetitive post-merger conduct, is the solution to change how they are applied rather than to block mergers by firms that might engage in such conduct?

3. Should the fact that Tetra Pak has already been condemned for abuses of its dominant position (see Chapter 3) be deemed relevant here?

4. The General Court accepted on principle the Commission theory that the merger would anticompetitively reduce potential competition because plastic and cartons were likely to be closer substitutes in the future, but concluded it was factually unfounded in the case at hand, and was sustained by the ECJ on this.

a. What does this suggest about whether the EU courts recognize an actual potential competition theory?

b. Was the General Court right to second-guess the factual basis of the Commission's theory?

    i. Given the size of the price gap, does it seem likely that plastic and carton packaging would converge soon enough to make them reasonable substitutes in the "relatively near future"?

    ii. But if some set of customers would switch from carton to plastic in response to a price increase in cartons, wouldn't the merger reduce the disincentive to raise carton prices because part of the switching would accrue to the financial benefit of Tetra in plastic packaging? Do you agree that this effect will necessarily be offset by the existence of carton rivals who are or could be active in the plastic market too?

c. Was the ECJ right to hold it could not review the General Court's second-guessing? If second-guessing the Commission's Fact Finding is a question of law, why isn't reviewing that second-guessing a legal question too?

5. Was the ECJ right to hold that the General Court's scrutiny of the economic evidence was consistent with the Commission's discretion on economic matters?

a. Are courts sufficiently qualified to review complex economic evidence?

b. Do U.S. courts show any hesitation to second-guess the economic evidence provided by enforcement agencies?

c. Should courts appoint experts to compensate for their lack of expertise?

6. The ECJ stated that thorough judicial review was particularly necessary in conglomerate merger cases because they required a prospective analysis.

a. Why isn't judicial review particularly inappropriate in such a case because reversal cannot rest on the existence of past evidence that courts can ascertain, but must instead rest on future projections that require the sort of expert judgment the Commission is more likely to have?

b. Does this holding mean that the Commission should enjoy greater discretion in its assessment of horizontal and vertical mergers?

When to Block a Merger Based on a Risk of Post–Merger Misconduct

The EU courts hold that blocking a merger based on post-merger misconduct requires proof that the post-merger misconduct will be likely, given the profitability of that conduct and the factors deterring it. It is tempting to say that other laws can always deter any post-merger misconduct and should be changed or reinterpreted if they do not. However, as we have emphasized throughout this book, uncertainties in information and adjudication mean that any rule that regulates conduct optimally cannot eliminate underdeterrence, but rather can only minimize the sum of harm from under-and overdeterrence. Thus, other laws will, even if optimally designed, always leave some bad post-merger conduct underdeterred, raising the question whether it is better to tackle the problem by blocking the merger that creates the ability or incentives to engage in that misconduct.

Presumably, if efficiency gains are shown, the Commission must go on to determine whether that efficiency exceeds the likelihood of post-merger misconduct times the magnitude of the anticompetitive harm it would create. Thus, the ultimate question is whether the Merger–Specific Efficiency Gain > (Probability Post–Merger Misconduct is Profitable)x(Probability Post–Merger Misconduct Will Be Undeterred by Other Laws)x(Magnitude of Anticompetitive Harm from Post–Merger Misconduct). Although the relevant variables may not be susceptible of precise quantification, this sort of formula usefully helps to frame analysis.

Indeed, we can use the above formula to map the general pattern of merger enforcement. It makes sense that the areas of most vigorous merger enforcement are blocking mergers that create unilateral or oligopoly effects because there the bad post-merger misconduct is high unilateral or oligopoly pricing, which is highly profitable, hard to effectively regulate post-merger, and causes great anticompetitive harm. *See* Chapters 3, 6. Conglomerate mergers that eliminate potential competition manifest more mixed enforcement because the potential competition may not be profitable and eliminating it may not be that harmful, but any anticompetitive problem cannot be deterred post-merger because there is no effective way to force the merged firm to enter a market and compete with itself. Vertical mergers manifest even weaker enforcement because there the feared post-merger misconduct is refusing to deal with rivals, which may not be profitable, is subject to at least some (though fairly deferential) antitrust review, and may not be that anticompetitive when it occurs. And conglomerate mergers that enable post-merger exclusionary conduct manifest the weakest enforcement because there the feared conduct is vertical exclusionary conduct that may not be profitable, is subject to the strictest antitrust scrutiny of any post-merger conduct here discussed, and may not be anticompetitive if it occurs. Not surprisingly, conglomerate mergers that enable post-merger exclusionary conduct are most likely to be blocked when the post-merger conduct is something relatively hard to regulate, like reciprocity.

Damien Geradin and Nicolas Petit, Article 230 EC Annulment Proceedings Against Competition Law Decisions in the Light of the "Modernisation" Process

in Barry Hawk, Ed., International Antitrust and Policy, 2005 Corporate Law Institute, at p. 383.

The growing role of economic analysis inherent to the recent reforms has meant that competition law has become so technical that there is a worry that the [General Court], in its role as a generalist Court may not be in a position to exercise a thorough review of the legality of an act in cases put before it. This development could result in an increase in the discretionary powers of the Commission.

The [EU] courts have, however, shown themselves to be anxious to reaffirm the scope of the principle of judicial review of Commission decisions within the framework of Article [263 TFEU] (1.1.). In practice, more frequent recourse to outside expertise would certainly assist the Community Court in exercising more extensive review of complex economic arguments put forward by the parties (1.2).

1.1. The scope of the principle of judicial review by the [General Court]. Drawing inspiration from principles found in French administrative law, the ECJ was reticent, in the initial years of the implementation of competition law, to exercise its review of Commission decisions beyond an assessment of errors of law or manifest errors of appraisal that the latter may have committed in its analysis of a supposedly anti-competitive practice. The ECJ thus held in *Remia*:

"The Court must therefore limit its review of such an appraisal to verifying whether the relevant procedural rules have been complied with, whether the statement of the reasons for the decision is adequate, whether the facts have been accurately stated and whether there has been any manifest error of appraisal or a misuse of powers".

This jurisprudence was equally continued in *Matra/Hachette* where the [General Court] recalled that:

"judicial review of the legal characterization of the facts is limited to the possibility of the Commission having committed a manifest error of assessment".

Notwithstanding this restrictive interpretation of the principle, both the [General Court] and ECJ were prepared to undertake a thorough examination of the Commission's analyses (including the facts, their assessment and their qualification), as is witnessed by the *Woodpulp* case where the ECJ verified whether the alignment of prices as found by the Commission could be explained by economic circumstances unrelated to a concerted practice forbidden by Article [101 TFEU].

The question of the scope of judicial review was further discussed within the field of merger control. In *Kali und Salz*, the ECJ seemed to refuse to undertake a thorough analysis of the economic analysis carried out by the Commission as the merger control regulation was deemed to confer on the latter a "certain discretion, especially with respect to assessments of an economic nature" which the Courts had to respect.

Within this context, the three annulment judgments handed down by the General Court in *Airtours, Schneider Electric* and *Tetra Laval* could be interpreted as an encroachment on the margin of discretion attributed to the Commission by the regulation. In its appeal against the General Court's *Tetra Laval* judgment, the Commission criticised the General Court for having exceeded the standard in *Kali und Salz* by examining the Commission's economic analysis too closely.... The ECJ [rejected this view, concluding] that the scope of judicial review carried out by the General Court encompasses an evaluation of any given economic data within the confines of an examination of their veracity, their relevance and their coherence. This solution should be positively welcomed. First, it reduces the risk that the competition authority will succumb to arbitrariness and stray away from its assigned duty. This objective is all the more urgent given that the economic theories currently appreciated by competition authorities are often malleable instruments which can conceal, while simulating analytical rigour, purely opportunistic goals. Further this solution also assures the parties that there will be a real review of their legal situation, in line with the principle laid down by the European Court of Human Rights which requires that everyone have the right to appeal.

1.2. Recourse to outside expertise when dealing with matters of an economic nature. The growing technical nature of the economic arguments put forward by parties in competition law litigation complicates the Court's mission to such an extent that it sometimes may prefer to hold back from examining whether the theories advanced by the parties are well-grounded. Admittedly, we have just seen that the Court pronounced itself in favour of a control of any given economic arguments put forward by the parties. In order to ensure that this jurisprudence does not remain a *de facto* declaration of intention, we consider that more frequent recourse to outside experts could usefully assist the Court in carrying out this delicate mission.

Article 70 of the General Court's Rules of Procedure allows the General Court to order third party expertise. An independent expert operating under the control of the Court reporter can be nominated. He compiles an expert report covering all the points asked of him. Within the field of competition law, the Court has only sparingly used outside expertise. The *Woodpulp* case represents a rare example. The ECJ ordered two expert evaluations on the question whether the structure of the woodpulp market inevitably led to price harmonisation through parallel behaviour or to different prices. The Court explicitly relied on the experts' reports in order to conclude that the parallel behaviour observed on the woodpulp market could not be explained by concertation as the Commission had found, but could be satisfactorily explained by the oligopolistic nature of the market.

The infrequency of the General Court's recourse to outside expertise contrasts with the growing tendency for parties before the Commission or General Court to employ outside expertise. This development makes it all the more pressing for the General Court to nominate an independent expert who is able to arbitrate on the often opposing views of the experts in economics employed by the parties in a given case. Such a solution was used in the U.S. *Microsoft* case. The Court nominated Larry Lessig, a law professor at Harvard University (now at Stanford) as "Special Master" and charged him with the preparation of a report on questions of a technological nature as well as requiring him to assist it on questions of law and fact which came up before it. The General Court could most certainly make more extensive use of a power which is attributed to it by its regulation in cases involving complex economic questions.

T–210/01, General Electric v. Commission
[2005] ECR II–5575.

[The proposed merger between General Electric (GE) and Honeywell raised vertical issues that were excerpted above, and also created horizontal overlaps in various markets that the General Court held supported blocking the merger because the divestitures proposed were inadequate. But the thrust of the opinion focused on the conglomerate effects theory that was the basis for a more wholesale condemnation of the merger and the following focuses on the facts and analysis relative to them.

GE had a dominant position in the markets for making jet engines for large commercial and regional aircraft. GE's subsidiary GECAS, was the biggest leaser of aircrafts to airlines and bought 10% of the world's aircraft, more than any other purchaser. The Commission found that GE's dominant position in the above engine markets was reinforced by GECAS's reciprocity policy of buying only planes with GE engines. GE sought to merge with Honeywell, which had a leading position in avionics and non–avionic equipment. Avionics are used for aircraft control, navigation, communication, monitoring flying conditions. Unless they are integrated into systems, avionics constitute Buyer–Furnished–Equipment (BFE) because buyers purchase it for installation in the aircraft they buy. BFE is selected by aircraft buyers out of the two or three products certified by the airframe manufacturer. Non-avionics include auxiliary power units, environmental control systems, electric power, wheels and brakes, landing gear and aircraft lighting. With exception of highly consumable parts such as wheels and brakes, non-avionics constitute Supplier–Furnished–Equipment (SFE) because aircraft makers purchase it for incorporation in the aircraft they sell.

The Commission held that this merger would create a dominant position in avionics and non-avionics because of two conglomerate effects. First, the Commission found that the merged firm would extend the reciprocity GECAS already exercised on engines by buying only Honeywell BFE and buying only aircraft that contained Honeywell SFE. The Commission concluded this had a more significant effect than GECAS's 10% buyer market share might alone suggest because airlines were relatively indifferent to the brand of SFE and the prospect of selling one or two additional aircraft would offset any inducements Honeywell rivals could offer to aircraft makers, and GECAS leased aircraft to airlines that liked to standardize the equipment used on the aircraft they flew. Second, the Commission found that the merged firm would extend the bundling that Honeywell already practiced in avionics and non-avionics to bundle GE engines with Honeywell equipment. This might take the form of pure bundling (refusing to sell one product to those who do not buy the other), technical bundling (selling them as a physically integrated system), or mixed bundling (bundled discounts). Such bundling would occur in sales to aircraft makers for SFE and in sales to aircraft buyers for BFE. The Commission found insufficient commitments by the merged firm not to engage in reciprocity involving Honeywell equipment, nor to bundle GE engines with Honeywell equipment, unless rivals were bundling the same sort of equipment or buyers requested such a bundle.]

... *Treatment of conglomerate effects*. Conglomerate-type concentrations do not give rise to horizontal overlaps between the activities of the parties to the merger or to a vertical relationship between the parties in the strict sense of the term. Even though, as a general rule, such concentrations do not produce anti-competitive effects, they may none the less have such effects in some cases. *Tetra Laval*. In a prospective analysis of the effects of a conglomerate-type concentration, if the Commission is able to conclude that by reason of the conglomerate effects a dominant position would, in all likelihood, be created or strengthened in the relatively near future and would lead to effective competition on the market being significantly impeded as a result of the concentration, it must prohibit the concentration. *Tetra Laval*.

... [T]he Commission had the onus to provide convincing evidence to support its conclusion that the merged entity would probably behave in the way foreseen. If it did not behave in that way, the combination of the positions of the two parties to the merger on neighbouring but distinct markets could not have led to the creation or strengthening of dominant positions, since those respective positions of the parties would not have had any commercial impact on one another.

Treatment of factors which might deter the merged entity from behaving in the ways predicted in the contested decision .... It follows from [*Tetra Laval*] that the Commission must, in principle, take into account the potentially unlawful, and thus sanctionable, nature of certain conduct as a factor which might diminish, or even eliminate, incentives for an undertaking to engage in particular conduct. That appraisal does not, however, require an exhaustive and detailed examination of the rules of the various legal orders which might be applicable and of the enforcement policy practised within them, given that an assessment intended to establish whether an infringement is likely and to ascertain that it will be penalised in several legal orders would be too speculative.

Thus, where the Commission, without undertaking a specific and detailed investigation into the matter, can identify the unlawful nature of the conduct in question, in the light of Article[102 TFEU]or of other provisions of Community law which it is competent to enforce, it is its responsibility to make a finding to that effect and take account of it in its assessment of the likelihood that the merged entity will engage in such conduct; *Tetra Laval*

It follows that, although the Commission is entitled to take as its basis a summary analysis, based on the evidence available to it at the time when it adopts its merger-control decision, of the lawfulness of the conduct in question and of the likelihood that it will be punished, it must none the less, in the course of its appraisal, identify the conduct foreseen and, where appropriate, evaluate and take into account the possible deterrent effect represented by the fact that the conduct would be clearly, or highly probably, unlawful under Community law....

D—CONGLOMERATE EFFECTS

1. Financial strength and vertical integration [Reciprocity]

... In accordance with ... *Tetra Laval* ..., it was for the Commission to establish not only that the merged entity had the ability to transfer [its reciprocity in the engine market] ... to the markets for avionics and non-avionics products but also, on the basis of convincing evidence, that it was likely that the merged entity would engage in such conduct. Furthermore, the Commission was required to establish that those practices would have created, in the relatively near future, a dominant position, at the very least on some of the markets for the avionics and non-avionics products concerned. *Tetra Laval*. These two aspects of the analysis which was required of the Commission will be examined in turn below.

The likelihood of the future conduct foreseen by the Commission .... SFE-standard products—... The Commission was required to establish, on the basis of convincing evidence, that ... a likelihood existed [the merged entity would use reciprocity on SFE products]. Given that this involved establishing, before the merger had taken place, how the merged entity would behave after the merger on markets where, prior to the merger, there was no scope for behaviour of the type foreseen by the Commission, such evidence cannot, as a general rule, consist exclusively of evidence of past conduct. It follows that the Commission's findings ... [that GE used] GECAS and GE Capital [to engage in reciprocity] on the market for large commercial jet aircraft engines, are not sufficient on their own to satisfy that requirement, even though they may play a part in doing so.

That said, convincing evidence could, in principle, consist of documents attesting to the settled intention of the board of directors of the applicant and/or Honeywell to exploit commercially the strength of GECAS and GE Capital on the avionics and non-avionics markets after the merger, in the same manner as described above in relation to the market for large commercial jet aircraft engines, or an economic assessment showing that such behaviour would objectively have been in the merged entity's commercial interests. Since the Commission failed to put forward any evidence capable of establishing that there was such an intention to transpose GE's practices on the market for large commercial jet aircraft engines to the markets for avionics and non-avionics products after the merger, it is necessary to consider whether the contested decision establishes that such a transposition would have been in the merged entity's commercial interests.

The applicant submits that it is not in the merged entity's commercial interests to insist that airframe manufacturers select SFE avionics and non-avionics products from the former Honeywell. It points out that there is a huge difference in price between jet engines manufactured by the applicant for large regional aircraft and large commercial aircraft and each avionics and non-avionics product. It therefore submits that the merged entity would have had no commercial interest in promoting avionics and non-avionics products in that way....

In the present context, the merger might have had an effect on the situation on the market for avionics and non-avionics products but only to the extent that the merged entity persuaded airframe manufacturers to select the former Honeywell's products in situations in which they would not have selected them in the absence of such commercial pressure. Given that the applicant's securing of the exclusive engine supply for the B777X involved some commercial "cost", it cannot be ruled out that an airframe manufacturer could have demanded [some compensation] if the merged entity had also insisted on the selection of SFE avionics and non-avionics products.... The contested decision does not address the question whether, if the merged entity had insisted on its SFE products being selected, that would have involved an additional commercial cost for it nor, indeed, the question whether the revenue deriving from the airframe manufacturers' selection of those products would have outweighed that possible cost. In the absence of such information, it is impossible in the circumstances of this case to determine whether the merged entity would have chosen to extend the practices concerned to the markets for SFE-standard avionics and non-avionics products if the merger had taken place. . . .

BFE ... products—. . . [A]s far as BFE products are concerned, the Commission acknowledges, [in] the contested decision, the existence of customer preferences and commonality effects. It does not consider these to be significant in this case because "the airlines are, due to their limited profit margins, not in a position to reject commercial offers that represent short-term cost savings" and that "for the airlines short-term cost reduction outweighs the possibility of longer-term reduction in competition". The Commission, however, puts forward no proof in support of its assertion as to the financial weakness of airlines. Nor does it put forward any specific evidence capable of supporting its assessment that preferences and cost reductions resulting from BFE-component commonality within an airline's fleet are less important factors in determining the airline's choices of BFE products than "short-term cost savings" represented by the purchasing or leasing terms which will, according to its argument, be offered by GECAS. In the absence of an economic appraisal, or at the very least an estimate, of the advantage represented by such terms, it is impossible to assess how plausible is the Commission's case in that regard.

Thus, as with SFE-standard products, the Commission's case is based on the notion that GECAS will offer favourable terms to airlines as an incentive to them to accept aircraft equipped with the merged entity's BFE products, which they would not have chosen had they been able to make an independent choice. The creation of such an incentive is liable to entail some "cost" to the merged entity inasmuch as an airline will not, as a general rule, accept equipment or, as the case may be, a pre-equipped aircraft already purchased by GECAS, unless the merged entity's overall offer is sufficiently attractive for that choice to be in the airline's commercial interests.

Since the Commission has recognised that airlines have preferences for certain products, the merged entity would, in such cases, have to overcome the obstacle represented by an airline's preference for another manufacturer's avionics and non-avionics products. It might be the case that the cost concerned is negligible in relation to the revenues accruing to the merged entity from the sale of the BFE components in question, in which case that course of action would be rational commercial behaviour on the part of the merged entity. However, it was for the Commission to examine that issue, in the light of the circumstances of the present case. . . .

Conclusion. . . . [T]he Commission has not established to a sufficient degree of probability that, following the merger, the merged entity would have extended to the markets for avionics and non-avionics products the [reciprocity] practices found by the Commission on the market for large commercial jet aircraft engines, by which the applicant exploited the financial strength of the GE group attributable to GE Capital and the commercial lever represented by GECAS's aircraft purchases in order to promote sales of its products. . . .

2. Bundling. . . . [T]he Court must determine whether the Commission has established that the merged entity would not only have the capability to engage in the bundling practices described in the contested decision but also, on the basis of convincing evidence, that it would have been likely to engage in those practices after the merger and that, in consequence, a dominant position would have been created or strengthened on one or more of the relevant markets in the relatively near future. *Tetra Laval* ...

Bundling in general. One practical problem with the Commission's analysis of bundling is that the final customer for the various engines, avionics products and non-avionics products is not always the same. Where an airframer selects an engine on an exclusive basis and consequently the platform is sole-source, the airframer is in essence the manufacturer's customer and the same is true as regards SFE-standard avionics and non-avionics products. In that situation, the only choice left to the airline is, logically, whether or not to purchase the aircraft. By contrast, in cases in which the airframe manufacturer approves a number of engines for its platform (to make it a multi-source platform), it is the airline that selects the engine from those available, and it does the same in relation to BFE ... avionics and non-avionics products. It follows from the foregoing that, logically, bundling is possible, in the case of airframe manufacturers, only between GE engines and Honeywell SFE-standard products on sole-source platforms and, in the case of airlines, only between GE engines and Honeywell BFE ... products on multi-source platforms. Those findings preclude, in principle, the possibility of pure bundling in cases other than those mentioned above: i.e. it is precluded in cases in which the customer who selects the engine and the customer who selects the avionics or non-avionics product concerned are not one and the same person. . . .

Pure bundling. So far as pure bundling is concerned, the Commission anticipates that the engine or one of the avionics products or non-avionics products could be the tying product, that is to say the vital component, or component of choice, which the merged entity would refuse to sell independently of its other products ...

Given that ... pure bundling is conceivable only where the customers are the same for each product, it should also be noted that, in cases in which a platform is multi-source as to its engine and the avionics products concerned are BFE ... products, the scope for pure bundling is very limited. It would only be where, for technical or other reasons, an airline had a marked preference for the merged entity's engine that such a strategy might conceivably drive it to purchase a BFE avionics or non-avionics product from the merged entity. It must be noted that, in the contested decision, the Commission did not carry out a specific examination to ascertain for which platforms and/or particular products such a commercial strategy could have proved effective.

[The Commission decision also lacked] ... any analysis of the effects of the merger on the individual markets for avionics and non-avionics products defined by the Commission. Moreover, given that preferences for a product are, more often than not, relative rather than absolute, account should also have been taken, in the course of such an analysis, of any harmful commercial effects which pure bundling might have. Indeed, such an approach could deter a potential purchaser of one of the merged entity's engines, notwithstanding its preference—which might only be slight—for that engine. Since the Commission failed to carry out a detailed examination of that kind in the contested decision, it did not establish that it would have been viable for the merged entity to engage in pure bundling in cases in which one of its engines on a multi-source platform was the tying product.

With regard to the possibility of tying the sales of an engine on sole-source aircraft and of SFE-standard avionics and non-avionics products, the Commission did not put forward any concrete examples of how the future behaviour foreseen by it would operate. Again, the lack of any specific analysis of the markets means that its reasoning is not sufficiently precise to substantiate the conclusion which it reaches. Although the Commission concluded that there was a dominant position on the market for large commercial jet aircraft engines, it still found there to be a degree of residual competition on that market. Therefore if the merged entity were to "compel" an airframe manufacturer to select its SFE avionics and non-avionics products, that could have harmful commercial consequences for it in that an airframer might be prompted to choose another manufacturer's product in certain cases. Since the Commission failed to consider that possibility in the contested decision, it did not establish that pure bundling would have made it possible to place SFE products on large commercial aircraft platforms.

As regards the possibility that either the avionics products or the non-avionics products of the former Honeywell could act as a tying product and compel customers to purchase the merged entity's engines, the Commission puts forward, ... [in] the contested decision, a single concrete example as to where pure bundling might be possible. It states that "the merged entity will have the ability to render the sale of products where Honeywell has 100% market share (such as EGPWS [Enhanced Ground Proximity Warning System] for example), conditional on the sale of its engine. In order to obtain such products, airlines will have no other choice than to buy the engine offered by the merged entity." In relation to the possibility of exerting similar pressure on airframe manufacturers, the Commission is less categoric, merely stating ... that "GE may strengthen its dominant position through package offers or tying vis-à-vis airframers".

It should be observed that the Commission's case in this regard assumes that the merged entity would be able to engage in a type of commercial blackmail vis-à-vis its customers by refusing to sell them a relatively inexpensive but vital avionics product, unless the customers agreed to purchase its engines. Although the power of the applicant's customers on the market for large commercial jet aircraft engines (both airframers and airlines) to stand up to the applicant may be limited ..., and would be even more limited vis-à-vis the merged entity following the merger, the Commission did not establish in the present case that customers would have lost all residual power to hold out against the imposition of such a practice.

As for the specific product to which the Commission refers, the EGPWS, it is apparent ... that there were other products which could be substituted for the former Honeywell's device. The Commission notes that none of those products has been sold in significant quantities on the market and observes that, according to Thales, the fact that its product does not have an established reputation has proved to be a major barrier to market entry. However, if the merged entity were to adopt the extreme commercial stance represented by pure bundling, which is tantamount to a threat to refuse to supply, customers might prefer to use another product, even an inferior one, instead of the former Honeywell's EGPWS, rather than accept an engine which is not their engine of choice. In any event, it was for the Commission to examine that possibility. In particular, it did not consider and reject the possibility that customers might select Universal Avionics' TAWS system (Terrain Avoidance Warning System), as Airborne did in January 2001, merely noting that, according to Rockwell, Universal Avionics did not team up with it in order to win that bid ... The latter fact is not relevant to the question whether Universal Airborne's product is a viable alternative to Honeywell's.

Finally, in accordance with *Tetra Laval*, the Commission was also required to take account of the possible impact, on the markets in question, of the potentially deterrent effect of the prohibition on abuses of a dominant position laid down in Article [102 TFEU].

Given the extreme nature, from a commercial perspective, of the behaviour described above, which would have been necessary in this instance for the merged entity to implement a strategy based on pure bundling, it was incumbent on the Commission to take into account the effect which the Community-law prohibition on abuses of a dominant position might have had on the merged entity's incentive to implement such practices. Since the Commission failed to do that, it made an error of law, as a result of which its analysis is distorted and, accordingly, vitiated by a manifest error of assessment.

In the light of the foregoing, it must be held that the Commission has not sufficiently established that the merged entity would have engaged in pure bundling following the merger, and its analysis is vitiated in that regard by a number of manifest errors of assessment.

Technical bundling. In relation to technical bundling, the Commission relies on the integration between the various avionics products and on the future development of the More Electric Aircraft Engine project ..., whilst itself admitting that "explicit integration of the engine and systems has not occurred yet". It submits that such integration is likely to take place "in the near future" as part of that project but it does not provide any details about the project and does not indicate a date by which that integration is in its view foreseeable. Nevertheless, it relies exclusively on the future development of that project to conclude that Honeywell's elimination as a potential innovation partner will further strengthen the applicant's dominant position on the market for large commercial jet aircraft engines ...

That basic description of the way the market might evolve, without even a brief account of those specific aspects of the project which would make such evolution likely, is not sufficient to establish that the Commission's case on this point is well founded. According to *Tetra Laval* ... the Commission's task is to show in relation to the future development of the market, on the basis of convincing evidence and with a sufficient degree of probability, not only that any conduct foreseen by it will take place in the relatively near future but also that the conduct will result in the creation or strengthening of a dominant position in the relatively near future; this the Commission has not done. The lack of any detailed analysis of the technical integration which might be achieved as between engines, on the one hand, and avionics and non-avionics products, on the other, and of the likely influence of such integration on the way the different markets concerned might evolve, also makes the Commission's case less credible. It is not enough for the Commission to put forward a series of logical but hypothetical developments which, were they to materialise, it fears would have harmful effects for competition on a number of different markets. Rather, the onus is on it to carry out a specific analysis of the likely evolution of each market on which it seeks to show that a dominant position would be created or strengthened as a result of the merger and to produce convincing evidence to bear out that conclusion.

In view of the foregoing, the Commission has not adequately established that the merged entity would actually have the capability, immediately after the merger, or indeed in the relatively near future, to tie sales of its avionics products and/or its non-avionics products to sales of its engines by means of technical constraints.

Mixed bundling. So far as mixed bundling is concerned, ... such an offer will have economic effects on the market only in so far as customers accept it and, in particular, do not demand that the offer is unbundled product by product. The onus was thus on the Commission to show that the merged entity would have been able to insist that the package it was offering its customers was not unbundled. Furthermore, as has been held above, the Commission was required to establish that there was a likelihood of the merged entity actually exploiting the possibility of engaging in mixed bundling. . . .

In this instance, the Commission in effect employed three distinct lines of reasoning in the contested decision in order to establish the likelihood that the merged entity would actually engage in mixed bundling. First, it claimed that practices analogous to those which it anticipates have already been used in the past on the relevant markets, in particular by Honeywell ... Second, it argued that it follows from well-established economic theories, particularly the "Cournot effect" ..., that the merged entity would have an economic incentive to engage in the practices foreseen by the Commission and that there was no need to rely on a specific economic model in that regard. Third, the Commission alleged that the merged entity's strategic objective would be to increase its power on the different markets on which it is present and that, given that intention, bundling would be economically rational behaviour on its part and, therefore, likely behaviour ...

Previous practice—It must first be noted that the examples of previous practices put forward by the Commission relate in essence to alleged bundling offered by Honeywell of avionics and non-avionics products ... Even assuming that those examples are sufficiently established, they are of little relevance for the purpose of establishing that after the merger the merged entity was likely to have the ability to bundle engines sales with sales of avionics and non-avionics products and that it was likely to have the commercial incentive to do that. It is not disputed that the price of the engine is markedly higher than that of each avionics or non-avionics component and that therefore the commercial dynamic of a mixed bundle is very different depending on whether it consists (i) solely of avionics and non-avionics products or (ii) of those products and an engine. Thus, it cannot be established, on the basis of examples relating to avionics and non-avionics products alone, that mixed bundling covering engines as well would have been viable and commercially advantageous for the merged entity following the merger.

The Commission also states [in] the contested decision that Honeywell's ability to engage in extensive bundled deals, including engines and avionics/non-avionics products, arose only recently, in particular after the merger of Honeywell and AlliedSignal in 1999. Even though that factor might explain why the Commission could find only one example of such bundling, it cannot make up for the absence of convincing examples on the basis of which the Court might ultimately conclude that previous practice shows that there is a likelihood of similar practices occurring in future.

Furthermore, there are significant differences between the large commercial aircraft sector, where the merger would in future allow the merged entity to offer bundled sales for the first time, and the corporate aircraft sector, notably in so far as large commercial aircraft are sometimes multisource platforms as regards engines, where the engine manufacturer's customer is the airline, whilst corporate aircraft are always sole-source platforms, where the customer is the airframer.

In the light of the above, the examples put forward by the Commission relating to Honeywell's previous practice do not establish that it was likely that after the merger the merged entity would have engaged in mixed bundling including the former GE's engines, on the one hand, and the former Honeywell's avionics and non-avionics products, on the other hand.

Economic analyses—... Wherever the Commission refers ..., to the incentive, as opposed to the mere ability, which the merged entity would have to engage in those practices, no evidence or analysis is put forward which is such that it might establish that there was a real likelihood of such an incentive existing after the merger.... However, the Commission puts forward other considerations under the heading ... entitled "The Cournot effect of bundling". The Cournot effect is an economic theory dealing, in substance, with the advantages which a firm that sells a wide range of products, in contrast to its competitors whose range is more restricted, may derive from the fact that, if it offers discounts on all the products in the range, thereby reducing its profit margin on each, it none the less benefits overall from that practice because it sells a larger quantity of all the products in its range....

However, ..., the establishment of such a case on the basis of the Cournot effect requires detailed empirical analysis—both of the size of the price cuts and the shifts in sales that would be expected, as well as the costs and the profit margins of the various market participants. ... ['T']he Commission itself seems to have considered, at the stage of the administrative procedure, that such an economic analysis was necessary for it to make out its case ..... [T]he Commission state[d] that Professor Choi had developed a model analysing the situation in which demand for the products concerned was inelastic, which showed that bundling was liable to have anti-competitive effects. Furthermore, the applicant cites the reports of other economists, in particular those of Professors Nalebuff, Rey and Shapiro, appended to the reply to the SO and to the application, which indicate, in substance, that the merged entity was not likely to have had an incentive, following the transaction, to engage in mixed bundling, at least to any significant degree, contrary to Professor Choi's conclusion. In particular, Professors Nalebuff and Rey criticise Professor Choi's underlying assumptions about the nature of the market and Professor Rey observes, in particular, that the Choi model was capable of producing (validly on its own calibration conditions) different results depending on the range of starting parameters used.

It may therefore be concluded—without a detailed assessment in these proceedings of either the merits of the conclusions reached by the various economists or of the relative weight of the respective analyses of Professors Nalebuff, Rey and Shapiro in comparison with that of Professor Choi—that the question as to whether the Cournot effect would have given the merged entity an incentive to engage in mixed bundling in the present case is a matter of controversy. The Commission's conclusion as to the likelihood of there being such an incentive is thus certainly not a direct and automatic consequence of the economic theory of Cournot effect.

Moreover, there is a further consideration relating to the implementation of bundled sales which indicates that in this instance the Commission's case cannot be established by reference to the Cournot effect.... [GE made its large CFMI jet engines in a joint venture with Snecma.] Snecma would have had no interest in sacrificing a part of its profits by granting discounts in order to promote the former Honeywell's profits, and ... therefore mixed bundling including CFMI engines would have been impossible.... Consequently, discounts on engine prices offered to customers as part of a mixed bundle including a CFMI engine would, in principle, have to be financed exclusively by GE.... Consequently, mixed bundling including CFMI engines would have been markedly less profitable commercially from the merged entity's standpoint than it would have been if the applicant were the sole manufacturer of those engines. Even supposing that the Cournot effect could have been found to exist here for mixed bundles including the former GE's engines, the Commission would have needed to carry out a separate analysis, which took account of the factor noted in the previous paragraph, in order to ascertain whether such an effect existed in the case of mixed bundling including CFMI engines.

Bearing in mind all of the foregoing, in the absence of a detailed economic analysis applying the Cournot effect theory to the particular circumstances of the present case, it cannot be concluded from the Commission's brief mention of that theory in the contested decision that the merged entity would have been likely to engage in mixed bundling after the merger. The Commission could produce convincing evidence within the meaning of *Tetra Laval* ... by relying on the Cournot effect only if it demonstrated its applicability to this specific case. Accordingly, by merely describing the economic conditions which would in its view exist on the market after the merger, the Commission did not succeed in demonstrating, with a sufficient degree of probability, that the merged entity would have engaged in mixed bundling after the merger.

The strategic nature of the behaviour foreseen—Third, the Commission argued before the Court that its description of bundling and of the likelihood that it would actually occur must be read in the light of the fact that the merged entity will use its ability to offer bundled deals strategically as a "lever" specifically in order to marginalise its competitors.... [I]t has already been held ... above ... that the Commission did not establish, by reference to the objective commercial and economic circumstances of the case, that it would necessarily have been in the interests of the merged entity to engage in mixed bundling following the merger. Thus, from the commercial standpoint, various strategies would have been open to the merged entity after the merger. Although the strategic choice anticipated by the Commission would certainly have been among the options available to it, the short-term maximisation of profits by obtaining the largest possible profit margin on each individual product would also have been an option.

Therefore, and given that it had not been sufficiently established that the merged entity had an economic incentive, the onus was on the Commission to put forward in the contested decision other evidence suggesting that the merged entity would make the strategic decision to sacrifice profits in the short term with a view to reaping larger profits in the future. By way of example, internal documents showing that the applicant's Board of Directors had that objective on the launch of their bid to acquire Honeywell could, depending on the circumstances, have constituted such evidence. The ... Commission did not put forward any evidence of such a nature that it might establish that the merged entity would in fact make that strategic decision. It merely asserts in the contested decision that the merged entity would have had the ability to price its proposed bundled deals strategically and to engage in cross-subsidisation, and that it would have actually employed those practices, but does not put forward the reasons which justify that assertion. However, the fact that the merged entity could have made a strategic decision to such effect is not sufficient to establish that it would in fact have done so, and that dominant positions would have been created on the various avionics and non-avionics markets as a result.

Finally, before the [General Court], the Commission claimed that the strategic purpose of the applicant's anticipated future conduct had itself to be taken into account when assessing the likelihood of that conduct. Although such an argument might explain why the Commission did not rely on a specific economic model, once again it cannot make up for the lack of evidence as to the likely adoption by the applicant of a commercial policy with such strategic purpose.

It is appropriate to add that, according to *Tetra Laval*, the Commission should indeed have taken into account the deterrent effect which the possibility of penalties imposed for an abuse of a dominant position under Article [102 TFEU] might have on a merged entity. The failure to take that factor into account in the contested decision further undermines its assessment with regard to mixed bundling.

In view of the foregoing, the Court must conclude that the Commission's reasoning based on the future adoption of a "strategic" commercial policy cannot be accepted, since convincing evidence attesting to the likelihood of that hypothesis has not been adduced. . . .

It follows from all the foregoing that the Commission has not sufficiently established that, following the merger, the merged entity would have engaged in bundling including both the former GE's engines and the former Honeywell's avionics and non-avionics products. In the absence of such sales, the mere fact that the merged entity would have had a wider range of products than its competitors is not sufficient to justify the conclusion that dominant positions would have been created or strengthened for it on the different markets concerned.

In view of the conclusion in the previous paragraph, there is no need to examine the applicant's argument concerning the foreclosure of competitors from the market, alleged by the Commission, since the Commission's conclusions on bundling are in any event not sufficiently established. Nor is there any need to consider the Commission's treatment of the commitments relating to this aspect of the case, and in particular the Commission's rejection of the behavioural commitment relating to bundling. . . .

Questions on *GE/Honeywell*

The General Court held that pre-merger reciprocity and bundling was alone insufficient to show the merged firm here was likely to extend those practices to other markets post-merger, so that the Commission had to show either (a) that documents indicated the merged firm intended the feared post-merger conduct or (b) that economic analysis indicated the merged firm would profit from the feared post-merger conduct and would not be sufficiently deterred by legal prohibitions.

1. *Pre–Merger Conduct as a Basis for Inferring Post–Merger Conduct.*

a. Why isn't it enough to show that GE used reciprocity previously in engines? Does the fact that Honeywell components are less expensive than engines affect the likelihood GECAS would refuse to buy jets without them?

b. Why isn't it enough to show that Honeywell used bundling previously between avionics and non-avionics?

2. *Documentary Proof of Intent to Engage in Post–Merger Conduct.*

a. Given this decision, does it seem likely any well-advised firm would ever create documentary evidence of an intent to engage in post-merger exclusionary conduct?

b. Where such document evidence nonetheless exists, shouldn't adjudicators nonetheless base decisions on it?

c. Should any weight be given to corporate documents disavowing an intent to engage in post-merger misconduct?

3. *Economic Analysis of Profitability.*

a. In its analysis, the General Court seems to assume that any insistence on Honeywell components would, if the aircraft maker or airline would not otherwise choose them, necessarily require GE to bear some cost. Is the General Court thus accepting the single monopoly profit theory, at least presumptively, for reciprocity and tying? Does such a presumption seem warranted, at least in the short run? Did the Commission offer any economic model to show it was not warranted?

b. *Post–Merger Reciprocity.* Does it seem plausible that a purchaser with 10% of the market could create sufficient foreclosure in the avionics or non-avionics markets to make reciprocity profitable?

    i.   One theory offered for why 10% of purchases could be leveraged into larger foreclosure was that GECAS leased aircraft to airlines that liked to standardize the equipment used on the aircraft they flew. Is this theory persuasive? Does the answer depend on how strong the economic incentives to standardization are?

    ii.   The other theory is that aircraft sellers care only about selling planes and most buyers are indifferent on components so that, if a buyer of 10% of aircraft does care about the components, that will dictate what the seller installs in all aircraft. Barry Nalebuff, one of the economists retained by GE, and co-author David Majerus compared this theory to the Kosher certification process:

"Observant Jews will not eat food that has not been certified Kosher. While the population or market share of observant Jews is small, under 1%, a typical manufacturer will still go through the expense of Kosher certification (when it is possible to do so). The reason is simple. If the food is not certified, then the entire Kosher market is guaranteed to be lost. If it is certified, then the company can compete for these customers.... Because they care and others are indifferent, manufacturers make choices based on the preferences of less than 1% of the market. Reynolds and Ordover suggest that GECAS's favouritism towards GE products (and Honeywell post merger) will play a similar role. For GECAS, a plane is only 'Kosher' if all of the parts that could be are, indeed, supplied by GE and Honeywell. Thus, the airframer knows that it would sacrifice all of GECAS's business if it does not equip the plane with GE/Honeywell parts where possible. If other customers don't care, then GECAS's preferences would determine the results for all of the market and competitors will be foreclosed."

Why didn't the General Court accept this argument? What proof did the Commission fail to offer to prove that the choice of components by aircraft makers was economically similar to the Kosher process?

    (1)   Doesn't this theory work only if (a) the benefits of Kosher food or airplanes to the buyers who care exceed the costs of catering to them and (b) no other buyer is affected? If those conditions were met, wouldn't Kosher food or airplanes be efficient? Or is the problem that the practice imposes an externality on GE rivals, and then ultimately on the markets as a whole, that

no individual participant has incentives to resist given collective action problems?

(2) Would this theory work if the avionics or non-avionics markets were differentiated in quality and price? Given such differentiation, is it clear it would be in GE's best interest to apply a Honeywell components-only policy in the purchases of aircraft made by GECAS? Wouldn't such a policy risk losing the profits made by the sale/leasing of aircraft powered by GE engines in order to try to impose Honeywell components the buyer would not otherwise have wanted?

iii. Couldn't an insistence on buying only planes with GE equipment have procompetitive efficiencies like:

(1) reducing the successive monopolies problem?

(2) giving the buyer better assurances on the quality of the parts or an ability to do its own maintenance more easily?

(3) reducing contracting problems by reducing any future incentive gaps?

c. *Post–Merger Bundling.*

i. Was the General Court right to hold that the Commission failed to provide sufficient evidence the merged firm would bundle GE engines and Honeywell avionics and non-avionic products? Did it show pure bundling would produce additional revenue that would exceed the costs? That technical bundling was feasible? That mixed bundling (bundled discounts) would be profitable either in the short run or in the long-run if it foreclosed rivals?

ii. Even if such post-merger bundling would have occurred, might it not be efficient and desirable?

iii. If the post-merger conduct was anticompetitive and undesirable, couldn't tying and loyalty discount law adequately deter it?

4. *Stock Market Event Studies.* In their paper, Nalebuff and Majerus report that from the time of the announced merger, almost all of the rivals firms of the merging parties had a gain in stock that exceeded the S & P index. In contrast, GE's stock under-performed the index.

a. Does this prove the stock market must not have thought the planned merger could harm GE/Honeywell's rivals? If so, should antitrust enforcers or adjudicators take that into account?

b. Isn't that stock data equally consistent with the hypothesis that the stock market thought

i. the merger would ultimately get blocked and in the meantime take up GE attention?

ii. the horizontal overlaps would increase prices in a way that benefited rivals but the merger was not good for GE because it overpaid?

5. *Future Enforcement.* Some observers argue that, after *Tetra Laval* and *GE*, it will be very hard for the Commission in future cases to prohibit a conglomerate merger on the ground that it enables post-merger misconduct.

    a. Do you agree with this analysis or do you consider that in this case, the Commission just did a sloppy job in its attempt to show the existence of such effects?

    b. If the proof is highly demanding, would it be better for the Commission to stop trying to control such effects?

        i. Wouldn't this be a way to save scarce enforcement resources and align EU practice with U.S. practice?

        ii. Wouldn't this also increase the risk of underenforcement for post-merger misconduct that cannot adequately be regulated with other laws?

William J. Kolasky, Deputy Assistant Attorney General Antitrust Division, U.S. Department of Justice, "Conglomerate Mergers and Range Effects: It's a Long Way From Chicago to Brussels"

(2001).

    . . . [L]et me turn to GE/Honeywell. The [U.S. DOJ] has previously provided an explanation for our decision not to challenge that merger, except with respect to a couple of horizontal overlaps. Now that the [initial European Commission] decision is public, we can examine its reasoning in order . . . to deconstruct the reasons for our divergent outcomes.

    . . . [T]he theory that GE and Honeywell would engage in "mixed bundling" by offering a package of GE engines and Honeywell avionics and nonavionics systems at discounted prices because of the so-called Cournot effect . . . was originally based largely on a model developed by Jay Pil Choi for one of the complainants, based on previous work by Barry Nalebuff. The parties retained Nalebuff to evaluate Choi's model. His conclusions, which he has now incorporated in an article, were that the model simply did not fit the competitive realities of aerospace markets, with highly differentiated products, powerful buyers, and individually negotiated transactions. Nalebuff further found that "[w]hen a model is built that takes into account the nature of competition in this industry, we do not find that product bundling creates an advantage."

    In its final decision, the EU eschews further reliance on Choi's model, but nevertheless inexplicably concludes (with no other support) that "bundling would lead to a re-allocation and therefore to a shift of market share in favour of the merged entity" to such an extent that over the longer term GE's competitors would be unable to cover their fixed costs and would exit the market. Blocking a $42 billion merger on this basis, with neither theoretical or empirical support, is difficult to understand, to say the least.

    . . . The second key factor contributing to GE's dominance in engines, according to the EU, was its vertical integration into aircraft purchasing, financing and leasing through GECAS, which EU describes as the largest purchaser of aircraft in the world. With its GE-only procurement policy, the

EU argued, GECAS has been able to influence the selection of engines by serving as a launch customer and by causing airlines to standardize fleets around GE-powered aircraft. The merger would enable GECAS to extend this influence to the markets in which Honeywell competes.

The problem with this story is that the facts didn't support it. GECAS's share of aircraft purchases is less than 10%, substantially less than what U.S. antitrust courts typically require to support a finding of potential foreclosure. Given its small share of aircraft purchases, we found no evidence that GECAS's policy of purchasing only aircraft equipped with GE engines had or could foreclose rivals from the market. Given GECAS's small share, unless its policy could somehow change equipment preferences of ultimate customers, the likely Nash equilibrium response by rival leasing companies should be to purchase proportionately more non-GE engines, in part to differentiate themselves from GE. We found several examples of rival leasing companies doing exactly that.

Our investigation also found that GECAS was not a significant launch customer and that the claims GECAS could "seed" airlines with GE engines because of the importance of commonality were seriously over-stated; in fact, 90% of the world's aircraft are in mixed fleets. To the extent seeding was even a possibility, we could see no reason why rival engine manufacturers could not do the same simply by offering discounts off their engines. It makes no difference analytically whether GE is able to sell engines based on (1) a low lease rate from GECAS or (2) a low engine price. A low lease rate is simply another form of discount. To the extent airlines prefer discounts in this form, rival equipment suppliers could partner with leasing companies to offer favorable lease term for aircraft equipped with their engines. Once again the EU's theory fails the Nash equilibrium test.

We also examined the argument that GECAS could cause "share shifting" by inducing airframe manufacturers to sole source engines from GE. We examined each of the four transactions in which GECAS allegedly used its buying power to get GE engines sole source on new aircraft platforms. In each, we found that GECAS played no role in the customer's decision to sole source and that in each case GE had won the competition on the merits, by offering the best engines for the customer needs at the best price.

Rival Exit. All the EU's theories of competitive harm are crucially dependent on its prediction that rivals would be forced to exit in the face of a strengthened Honeywell. These claims were, in our view, simply not credible. Honeywell's competitors include large, financially healthy compa-nies like United Technologies, BF Goodrich, and Thales, each with impor-tant competitive advantages of its own. These companies are all more than holding their own currently. In addition, these aerospace markets are characterized by powerful buyers, Boeing and Airbus being the two best examples, with a strong incentive to maintain competition in the supply of avionics and nonavionics systems. These strong rivals, either independently or with the support of these powerful buyers, have a wide range of counter-strategies available, including mergers and teaming arrangements among themselves. The EU's dismissal of teaming arrangements as an effective counter-strategy is particularly ironic, given that GE's allegedly dominant position in engines results from just such a teaming arrangement with SNECMA and that the Commission found that teaming arrangements were an effective counter-strategy in this industry just one year earlier in its decision approving the Allied Signal/Honeywell merger. Indeed, immediately after the announcement of the merger, Rockwell announced that it was spinning off its avionics division, Collins, prompting speculation that it was positioning Collins to be a merger partner for another aerospace company. Again, the EU's theory fails the Nash equilibrium test. . . .

Why Do We Care? That's enough about GE/Honeywell. That merger is history. Our reason for discussing it is based on concern for the future, not the past. From that perspective, the type of divergence between the two largest antitrust jurisdictions in the world we experienced in this case is very troubling for at least three reasons.

First, in cases involving mergers in global markets, there are serious externalities associated with one jurisdiction blocking a merger on the basis of theories that other jurisdictions believe risk sacrificing important efficiencies to prevent speculative future harm to competition. By so doing, that jurisdiction denies consumers around the world the benefits the merger might have delivered.

Second, divergent substantive standards between the U.S. and Europe are almost certain to increase the transactions costs associated with the merger clearance process. The result may well be to deter mergers that would have been pro-competitive and efficiency-enhancing.

Third, such a sharp divergence undermines the strong political consensus supporting vigorous antitrust enforcement, something none of us wants.

We recognize that the EU is entitled to make and interpret its own laws. We also recognize that we and the EU will not always agree and that our way is not always best. We have no power to change EU law, other than by persuasion. For this reason, we believe it is important that we discuss this issue in depth, both in private and in public. We also encourage the business community, the private bar, and the academy to participate in this debate.

Questions on the EU–U.S. Difference on GE–Honeywell

1. Are you persuaded by William Kolasky's arguments about . . .

a. why post-merger bundling wouldn't occur? Does the fact that a party pays the author of a theory to opine against its application necessarily mean the theory does not properly apply? Are the reasons given for the nonapplication persuasive?

b. why post-merger reciprocity is unlikely and would not produce much foreclosure? Is he right that . . .

i. rival leasing companies would respond to reciprocity by buying more planes without GE components to satisfy the existing mix of customer preferences? Doesn't this depend on customers caring about the brand, that is on product differentiation?

ii. the fact of mixed fleets undermines the argument about standardization?

iii. if standardization is important, rival engine makers would just discount their engines to compete with any GECAS lowering of lease rates to compete in seeding airlines with their brand?

iv. GECAS's failure to cause aircraft makers to sole source engines from GE indicated it was unlikely to be able to do so in the future?

c. why rival exit was unlikely or why rivals would team with powerful buyers?

2. Is the U.S. approach in the end that different from the EU's given the General Court decision? Does this indicate we are already seeing convergence? Should we have convergence between the U.S. and EU on merger law despite the divergence between U.S. and EU laws regulating post-merger conduct?

EU Guidelines on the Assessment of Non-horizontal Mergers Under the Council Regulation on the Control of Concentrations Between Undertakings (2008)

V. CONGLOMERATE MERGERS

Conglomerate mergers are mergers between firms that are in a relationship which is neither purely horizontal (as competitors in the same relevant market) nor vertical (as supplier and customer). In practice, the focus is on mergers between companies that are active in closely related markets (e.g. mergers involving suppliers of complementary products or of products which belong to a range of products that is generally purchased by the same set of customers for the same end use).

Whereas it is acknowledged that conglomerate mergers in the majority of circumstances will not lead to any competition problems, in certain specific cases there may be harm to competition. In its assessment, the Commission will consider both the possible anti-competitive effects arising from conglomerate mergers and the possible pro-competitive effects stemming from efficiencies substantiated by the parties.

A. Non-coordinated effects: foreclosure

The main concern in the context of conglomerate mergers is that of foreclosure. The combination of products in related markets may confer on the merged entity the ability and incentive to leverage a strong market position from one market to another by means of tying or bundling or other exclusionary practices. Tying and bundling as such are common practices that often have no anticompetitive consequences. Companies engage in tying and bundling in order to provide their customers with better products or offerings in cost-effective ways. Nevertheless, in certain circumstances, these practices may lead to a reduction in actual or potential rivals' ability or incentive to compete. This may reduce the competitive pressure on the merged entity allowing it to increase prices.

In assessing the likelihood of such a scenario, the Commission examines, first, whether the merged firm would have the ability to foreclose its rivals, second, whether it would have the economic incentive to do so and, third, whether a foreclosure strategy would have a significant detrimental effect on competition, thus causing harm to consumers. In practice, these factors are often examined together as they are closely intertwined.

A. *Ability to foreclose*

The most immediate way in which the merged entity may be able to use its market power in one market to foreclose competitors in another is by conditioning sales in a way that links the products in the separate markets together. This is done most directly either by tying or bundling.

"Bundling" usually refers to the way products are offered and priced by the merged entity. One can distinguish in this respect between pure bundling and mixed bundling. In the case of pure bundling the products are only sold jointly in fixed proportions. With mixed bundling the products are also available separately, but the sum of the stand-alone prices is higher than the bundled price. Rebates, when made dependent on the purchase of other goods, may be considered a form of mixed bundling. "Tying" usually refers to situations where customers that purchase one good (the tying good) are required to also purchase another good from the producer (the tied good). Tying can take place on a technical or contractual basis. For instance, technical tying occurs when the tying product is designed in such a way that it only works with the tied product (and not with the alternatives offered by competitors). Contractual tying entails that the customer when purchasing the tying good undertakes only to purchase the tied product (and not the alternatives offered by competitors).

The specific characteristics of the products may be relevant for determining whether any of these means of linking sales between separate markets are available to the merged entity. For instance, pure bundling is very unlikely to be possible if products are not bought simultaneously or by the same customers. Similarly, technical tying is only an option in certain industries.

In order to be able to foreclose competitors, the new entity must have a significant degree of market power, which does not necessarily amount to dominance, in one of the markets concerned. The effects of bundling or tying can only be expected to be substantial when at least one of the merging parties' products is viewed by many customers as particularly important and there are few relevant alternatives for that product, e.g. because of product differentiation or capacity constraints on the part of rivals.

Further, for foreclosure to be a potential concern it must be the case that there is a large common pool of customers for the individual products concerned. The more customers tend to buy both products (instead of only one of the products), the more demand for the individual products may be affected through bundling or tying. Such a correspondence in purchasing behaviour is more likely to be significant when the products in question are complementary.

Generally speaking, the foreclosure effects of bundling and tying are likely to be more pronounced in industries where there are economies of scale and the demand pattern at any given point in time has dynamic implications for the conditions of supply in the market in the future. Notably, where a supplier of complementary goods has market power in one of the products (product A), the decision to bundle or tie may result in reduced sales by the non-integrated suppliers of the complementary good (product B). If further there are network externalities at play this will significantly reduce these rivals' scope for expanding sales of product B in the future. Alternatively, where entry into the market for the complementary product is contemplated by potential entrants, the decision to bundle by the merged entity may have the effect of deterring such entry. The limited availability of complementary products with which to combine may, in turn, discourage potential entrants to enter market A.

It can also be noted that the scope for foreclosure tends to be smaller where the merging parties cannot commit to making their tying or bundling strategy a lasting one, for example through technical tying or bundling which is costly to reverse.

In its assessment, the Commission considers, on the basis of the information available, whether there are effective and timely counter-strategies that the rival firms may deploy. One such example is when a strategy of bundling would be defeated by single-product companies combining their offers so as to make them more attractive to customers. Bundling is further less likely to lead to foreclosure if a company in the market would purchase the bundled products and profitably resell them unbundled. In addition, rivals may decide to price more aggressively to maintain market share, mitigating the effect of foreclosure.

Customers may have a strong incentive to buy the range of products concerned from a single source (one-stop-shopping) rather than from many suppliers, e.g. because it saves on transaction costs. The fact that the merged entity will have a broad range or portfolio of products does not, as such, raise competition concerns.

B.   Incentive to foreclose

The incentive to foreclose rivals through bundling or tying depends on the degree to which this strategy is profitable. The merged entity faces a trade-off between the possible costs associated with bundling or tying its products and the possible gains from expanding market shares in the market(s) concerned or, as the case may be, being able to raise price in those market(s) due to its market power.

Pure bundling and tying may entail losses for the merged company itself. For instance, if a significant number of customers are not interested in buying the bundle, but instead prefers to buy only one product (e.g. the product used to leverage), sales of that product (as contained in the bundle) may significantly fall. Furthermore, losses on the leveraging product may arise where customers who, before the merger, used to "mix and match" the leveraging product of a merging party with the product of another company, decide to purchase the bundle offered by rivals or no longer to purchase at all.

In this context it may thus be relevant to assess the relative value of the different products. By way of example, it is unlikely that the merged entity would be willing to forego sales on one highly profitable market in order to gain market shares on another market where turnover is relatively small and profits are modest.

However, the decision to bundle and tie may also increase profits by gaining market power in the tied goods market, protecting market power in the tying goods market, or a combination of the two (see Section C below).

In its assessment of the likely incentives of the merged firm, the Commission may take into account other factors such as the ownership structure of the merged entity [95], the type of strategies adopted on the market in the past or the content of internal strategic documents such as business plans.

When the adoption of a specific conduct by the merged entity is an essential step in foreclosure, the Commission examines both the incentives to adopt such conduct and the factors liable to reduce, or even eliminate, those incentives, including the possibility that the conduct is unlawful.

C. Overall likely impact on prices and choice

Bundling or tying may result in a significant reduction of sales prospects faced by single-component rivals in the market. The reduction in sales by competitors is not in and of itself a problem. Yet, in particular industries, if this reduction is significant enough, it may lead to a reduction in rivals' ability or incentive to compete. This may allow the merged entity to subsequently acquire market power (in the market for the tied or bundled good) and/or to maintain market power (in the market for the tying or leveraging good).

In particular, foreclosure practices may deter entry by potential competitors. They may do so for a specific market by reducing sales prospects for potential rivals in that market to a level below minimum viable scale. In the case of complementary products, deterring entry in one market through bundling or tying may also allow the merged entity to deter entry in another market if the bundling or tying forces potential competitors to enter both product markets at the same time rather than entering only one of them or entering them sequentially. The latter may have a significant impact in particular in those industries where the demand pattern at any given point in time has dynamic implications for the conditions of supply in the market in the future.

It is only when a sufficiently large fraction of market output is affected by foreclosure resulting from the merger that the merger may significantly impede effective competition. If there remain effective single-product players in either market, competition is unlikely to deteriorate following a conglomerate merger. The same holds when few single-product rivals remain, but these have the ability and incentive to expand output.

The effect on competition needs to be assessed in light of countervailing factors such as the presence of countervailing buyer power or the likelihood that entry would maintain effective competition in the upstream or downstream markets.

Further, the effect on competition needs to be assessed in light of the efficiencies substantiated by the merging parties.

Many of the efficiencies identified in the context of vertical mergers may, mutatis mutandis, also apply to conglomerate mergers involving complementary products.

Notably, when producers of complementary goods are pricing independently, they will not take into account the positive effect of a drop in the price of their product on the sales of the other product. Depending on the market conditions, a merged firm may internalise this effect and may have a certain incentive to lower margins if this leads to higher overall profits (this incentive is often referred to as the "Cournot effect"). In most cases, the merged firm will make the most out of this effect by means of mixed bundling, i.e. by making the price drop conditional upon whether or not the customer buys both products from the merged entity.

Specific to conglomerate mergers is that they may produce cost savings in the form of economies of scope (either on the production or the consumption side), yielding an inherent advantage to supplying the goods together rather than apart. For instance, it may be more efficient that certain components are marketed together as a bundle rather than separately. Value enhancements for the customer can result from better compatibility and quality assurance of complementary components. Such economies of scope however are necessary but not sufficient to provide an efficiency justification for bundling or tying. Indeed, benefits from economies of scope frequently can be realised without any need for technical or contractual bundling.

B. Co-ordinated effects

Conglomerate mergers may in certain circumstances facilitate anticompetitive co-ordination in markets, even in the absence of an agreement or a concerted practice within the meaning of Article 81 of the Treaty. The framework set out in Section IV of the Notice on Horizontal Mergers also applies in this context. In particular, co-ordination is more likely to emerge in markets where it is fairly easy to identify the terms of co-ordination and where such co-ordination is sustainable. One way in which a conglomerate merger may influence the likelihood of a coordinated outcome in a given market is by reducing the number of effective competitors to such an extent that tacit coordination becomes a real possibility. Also when rivals are not excluded from the market, they may find themselves in a more vulnerable situation. As a result, foreclosed rivals may choose not to contest the situation of co-ordination, but may prefer instead to live under the shelter of the increased price level.

Further, a conglomerate merger may increase the extent and importance of multi-market competition. Competitive interaction on several markets may increase the scope and effectiveness of disciplining mechanisms in ensuring that the terms of co-ordination are being adhered to.

Questions on EU Guidelines on Conglomerate Mergers

1. The guidelines say: "In order to be able to foreclose competitors, the new entity must have a significant degree of market power, which does not necessarily amount to dominance, in one of the markets concerned."

a.   Isn't this statement confusing? Can a firm hold a "significant degree of market power" and not be dominant?

b.   Doesn't the application of Article 102 TFEU require the presence of dominance in at least one market? Why should the test be different here?

2.   Is the analytical approach promoted by the Commission in line with the case-law of the European courts?

3.   The guidelines say that: "The fact that the merged entity will have a broad range or portfolio of products does not, as such, raise competition concerns." But wasn't this "portfolio effect" a problem in the Guinness/Grand Metropolitan merger discussed above?

4.   The Commission states that: "The incentive to foreclose rivals through bundling or tying depends on the degree to which this strategy is profitable."

a.   But isn't it really difficult (and speculative) to examine ex ante the merger whether a strategy of bundling or tying would be ex post profitable?

b.   Given the uncertainty and the fact that anti-competitive bundling and tying are prohibited under Article 102 TFEU with a very test being applied, does it make sense to prohibit mergers on the basis that the parties may find it subsequently profitable to bundle or tie?

5.   Pursuant to the guidelines "[b]undling or tying may result in a significant reduction of sales prospects faced by single-component rivals in the market. The reduction in sales by competitors is not in and of itself a problem. Yet, in particular industries, if this reduction is significant enough, it may lead to a reduction in rivals' ability or incentive to compete." In which kind of industries would a reduction in sales be a problem? Why?

Conglomerate Mergers in Other Nations

In other nations, conglomerate mergers receive less attention, usually even less than vertical mergers. Some nations address conglomerate issues separately in their guidelines or together with vertical issues, while others do not address the issue specifically. Guidelines on conglomerate mergers in Japan and South Korea consider both potential competition and post-merger foreclosure theories, and apply a larger presumptive safe harbor for conglomerate mergers than for horizontal mergers. Japan makes conglomerate mergers presumptively legal if the market share in all of the combined markets is less than 10% or if it is less than 25% and the HHI is less than 2,500.[101] South Korea makes conglomerate mergers presumptively legal if (a) the HHI in the particular area of trade is less than 2,500 and the merged market share is less than 25% or (b) the market ranking of each party in its respective area of trade is fourth or lower.[102] Guidelines regarding conglomerate mergers in Argentina, Canada, New Zealand, Taiwan, and Venezuela focus on actual potential competition rather than on

---

101.   Japan Business Combination Guidelines at V.1(3) (2010).

102.   South Korea Merger Guidelines VII.3 (2009).

post-merger exclusionary conduct.[103] Singapore focuses instead on post-merger exclusionary conduct or coordination.[104] Although Turkey guidelines do not specifically refer to conglomerate mergers, some of its decisions do, and have focused on post-merger exclusionary conduct.[105]

---

103. *See, e.g.,* Canada Merger Guidelines § 11.1–11.2 (2004); New Zealand Merger Guidelines § 10.2 (2004); Taiwan Merger Guidelines Art. XII (2006).

104. Singapore Merger Guidelines §§ 8.11–8.17 (2007).

105. See Turkey Competition Board Decision No. 07–65/804–299 (2007).

CHAPTER 8

MARKETS THAT SPAN MULTIPLE ANTITRUST REGIMES

In today's world, firms operate on global markets and thus their conduct can have effects throughout the world. The U.S. and EU, and many other nations, each exert jurisdiction over anticompetitive conduct that raises prices within their borders even when that conduct occurs on foreign soil. This leaves firms on global markets regulated by a potentially divergent set of rules. Although the chapters above indicate that U.S. and EU doctrine are closer than they might appear and probably converging over time, there remain important differences. Those differences include divergent rules on: (1) excessive unilateral pricing; (2) above-cost predatory pricing; (3) a recoupment requirement for below-cost predatory pricing; (4) unilateral duties to deal; (5) loyalty and volume-based discounts; (6) vertical territorial restraints; and (6) vertical and conglomerate mergers. Moreover, even when the doctrines do not differ, their application can lead to conflicting conclusions if the courts or agencies in the U.S. and EU differ in their assessment of the facts of particular cases or how the law applies to those facts. And even when the U.S. and EU agree, other affected nations may not.

This conflict is not just theoretical. It led to conflicting U.S. and EU judgments on the GE/Honeywell merger. *See* Chapter 7. Similarly, the DeHavilland–ATR merger was approved by Canada but prohibited by the EU. Nor are international conflicts limited to mergers. On the loyalty discount dispute between Virgin Airlines and British Airways, the EU condemned the very conduct that deemed permissible under U.S. antitrust law.[1] And sometimes a conflict in remedial approaches can result. Thus, although Microsoft's efforts to bundle other software into its operating system have been condemned both in the U.S. and EU, *see* Chapter 4, the U.S. was not willing to impose the sort of extensive remedies the EU has imposed. More systematically, the U.S. imposes treble damages and criminal penalties that the EU does not.

In general, this sort of jurisdictional conflict does not impose conflicting obligations on firms. They need simply conform their conduct to whichever antitrust regime is most restrictive: thus if their merger is approved in the U.S. and banned in the EU, they can comply with the law in both places by simply refraining from the merger. However, this leads to the global problem that the most aggressive antitrust regime always wins. If we assume each antitrust regime is likely to err equally toward over-and

---

1. *Compare* Case T–219/99 British Airways PLC v. Commission [2003] ECR II–5917, *with* Virgin Atl. Airways Ltd. v. British Airways PLC, 257 F.3d 256 (2d Cir.2001).

underregulation, the net effect is to encourage global overregulation. To the extent that EU law is generally more restrictive than U.S. law, it means largely ceding to the EU the antitrust regulation of global markets. Moreover, even when such conflicts do not result in firms facing inconsistent legal obligations, they can lead to an important conflict in policy objectives because decisions by one nation to allow certain conduct generally proceed on the conclusion that its procompetitive consequences likely outweigh its anticompetitive effects. For another nation to prohibit that conduct is thus to deny those beneficial procompetitive effects to the first nation contrary to its policy preferences. This can lead to serious policy conflicts where nations differ on what counts as a procompetitive effect and on the extent to which it exists in particular cases.

Another concern is that each nation's antitrust enforcement or policy choices might be biased to the extent that the conduct's effects are distributed unequally across nations. If the conduct imposes anticompetitive costs mainly on nation A, and the supracompetitive profits and/or efficiency gains are mainly enjoyed by nation B, then one might fear that nation A will have incentives to underweigh the benefits of the conduct, causing it to condemn conduct that is on balance beneficial, and that nation B will have incentives to underweigh the costs, causing it to approve conduct that is on balance harmful. This might distort antitrust enforcement in particular cases that involve those products that nation B exports to A, for which producer effects are likely to dominate decisions in nation B while consumer effects dominate decisions in nation A. Or it might distort the nation's overall choice of antitrust regime, so that nations that are net importers would be more likely to choose pro-consumer antitrust standards, whereas nations that are net exporters would be more likely to choose pro-producer antitrust standards.[2]

However, it is not clear this is a serious problem. True, the U.S., EU and other jurisdictions decline to penalize export cartels within their borders, which has often been cited as evidence that the above bias concerns are very real. But such export cartels are penalized under the antitrust laws of the importing jurisdiction that suffers the anticompetitive effects. Thus, a U.S. cartel that exports to the EU is regulated by EU competition law, while an EU cartel that exports to the U.S. is regulated by U.S. competition law. From a global perspective, this may not be discriminatory enforcement but a sensible allocation of enforcement authority to the jurisdiction that has the best incentives to punish anticompetitive conduct. One might fear the regulating jurisdiction would have incentive to overenforce their antitrust laws, but both the U.S. and EU use a consumer welfare standard that allows conduct with efficiency benefits only to the extent it provides a net gain to consumers, and being a consuming nation would not distort incentives in applying such a standard.[3]

---

2.   *See* Andrew Guzman, *The Case for International Antitrust*, 22 BERKELEY J INTL. L 355 (2004).

3.   Likewise, for products that are both produced and consumed in both jurisdictions, the fact that most production occurs in jurisdiction *A* and most consumption occurs in jurisdiction *B* may cause *A* to underenforce but *B* can cure this through its own enforcement.

Nonetheless, even if enforcement incentives are adequate, the ability of the consuming jurisdiction to prosecute antitrust cases can be compromised if the case requires evidence within the exporting jurisdiction or remedies that only that exporting jurisdiction can impose because of where firm assets or personnel are located. Thus, making this allocation of enforcement authority effective requires that the exporting jurisdictions assist foreign antitrust authorities in discovering evidence about firms within their borders and in enforcing foreign judgments. As we shall see, this has been the main focus on international antitrust cooperation so far.

Nor is it clear that distributional effects would bias the overall choice of antitrust regimes. The U.S. and EU are exporters on some products but importers on others, and thus each knows that any pro-producer antitrust policy will harm them on products they import. True, nations run trade deficits or surpluses that make them overall net importers or exporters. However, the percentages of those deficits or surpluses are quite small in relation to each nation's GDP, and most nations change back and forth over time from being net exporters to net importers, with the trade flows in theory balancing over the long run. Thus, trade deficits or surpluses seem unlikely to greatly affect the overall choice of antitrust policy even to the extent they do create a bias.

Nor is it clear that being a net exporter or importer creates a bias. A net exporter would be tempted to choose an unduly lax antitrust regime *if* it thought it was the only regulator, but in fact it knows that net importers will be vigorously enforcing their antitrust laws against anticompetitive conduct that occurs in the net exporters. Because the net exporter is effectively not the decisive regulator on the products it exports, it would make more sense for it to adopt a consumer welfare standard to govern the products it either imports or produces for domestic consumption, where its regulation actually is decisive.[4] A net importer might be tempted to choose an overly aggressive antitrust regime, but that would just hurt its own consumers to the extent it fails to consider efficiencies that are passed on to consumers.

The more serious concern might be that, because decisive antitrust enforcement of global markets rests largely in the hands of net importers, each nation might have incentives to choose a consumer welfare standard (which ignores gains to producers that are not passed on to consumers) rather than a total surplus standard (which allows losses to consumers to be offset by gains to producers). This might help explain why consumer welfare standards tend to dominate antitrust policy in most nations. But in the U.S. and EU, consumer welfare standards were adopted in cases where this possible distortion was irrelevant because they were mainly domestic. Further, the EU has often had trade surpluses making it a net exporter, and both U.S. and EU trade deficits and surpluses remain so small in relation to overall GDP that they seem unlikely to be a significant influence.

---

4. Again, this may require that nations assist foreign nations in procuring evidence and enforcing antitrust judgments, or else a net exporter might effectively become the decisive regulator because other nations cannot get access to the necessary evidence or impose the necessary remedies.

Moreover, a consumer welfare standard is, if anything, more optimal in the international context because, compared to domestic markets, the arguments are weaker both (a) that any business profits will redound to the benefit of consumers in their roles as the firm's employees or stockholders or as citizens that benefit from taxes on the firm's profits and (b) that it would be better to allow the increase in total surplus and achieve any redistributive goal by increasing taxes on business profits and transferring the funds to consumers. In the international case, it is less likely that consumers will be employees or stockholders of the foreign producers or that the importing nations will be able to effectively tax the foreign firms to achieve such redistribution. Nor need a consumer welfare standard ban conduct that would increase total welfare. Firms that want to engage in conduct whose benefits to them outweigh the costs to consumers need only commit to some mechanism for passing on a sufficient share of those benefits to consumers to outweigh the costs.[5]

Another possible concern is that the fact that firms span many nations may sometimes mean that many of the affected nations have inadequate incentives, ability, or evidence to stop their anticompetitive conduct. A collective action problem might result if, for example, a cartel spans many small or developing nations, each of which hopes to free ride off of the enforcement efforts of others, and does not want to discourage the cartel from selling, investing, or employing within its borders by trying to enforce competition law on its own. If such collective action problems exist, they can make it in each small nation's individual interests to underregulate anticompetitive conduct even though such underregulation is harmful to all of them collectively.

However, it is again unclear how serious this concern is. The direct costs of antitrust enforcement seem relatively small compared to the possible financial costs of anticompetitive conduct. If antitrust regulation discouraged firms from selling, investing or employing in a nation, that would be a more significant cost. But if it is profitable to sell to consumers in that nation, it is hard to see why a firm would forgo sales to them because that nation had antitrust laws. Nor is it clear why a lack of antitrust laws would significantly induce firms to invest or employ in the nation. To the extent firms want to exploit that nation's consumers, they could take advantage of the lack of antitrust laws to do so from abroad without investing or employing in that nation. To the extent firms want to exploit consumers in other nations, it is also unclear why they would favor investing or employing in nations that underregulate anticompetitive conduct. After all, if their aim is to avoid home country antitrust review of their exports, they would also get that if they invested in the U.S. or EU. And no matter where they are located, their anticompetitive export practices would still be subject to antitrust review in the importing nations. This strategy is thus likely to work only if the underregulating nations (unlike the U.S. and EU) also protect those firms by refusing to cooperate with foreign antitrust authorities on evidence and remedies. Moreover, even in such cases, such a strategy to attract firms that want to earn

---

5. *See* Chapter 7.A.4 (describing how firms could make such commitments to get merger approval).

supracompetitive profits on exports from those nations may not be effective if those firms compete in a global market with firms located in nations that do enforce their antitrust laws.

Special problems are raised when foreign nations are themselves involved in the anticompetitive conduct adjudicated by other nations. Foreign nations may enjoy sovereign immunity or benefit from rules that forbid inquiry into the validity of their actions. Private parties may also enjoy immunity when their conduct is either compelled by foreign government action or involves petitioning for such action. We address those below as well as more general issues of extraterritorial conflict and coordination.

A.   EXTRATERRITORIAL CONDUCT AFFECTING DOMESTIC COMMERCE

Background on the Extraterritorial Application of U.S. Antitrust Statutes

Personal Jurisdiction. U.S. antitrust laws provide for worldwide service of process and personal jurisdiction over any foreign firm or person as long as it has minimum contacts with the United States and foreign prohibitions do not restrict service. *See* Chapter 1. Because creating any anticompetitive market effect suffices to create minimum contacts and foreign firms are generally subject to service for other purposes, in practice this is not much of a bar to exercising personal jurisdiction over foreign firms.

Substantive Reach. The Sherman, Clayton, and FTC Acts all apply to "commerce . . . with foreign nations."[6] Further, the Wilson Tariff Act of 1894 expressly prohibited agreements that restrained import trade. 15 U.S.C. § 8. Notwithstanding this general language, in 1909 the Supreme Court held that the canon against interpreting statutes to apply to foreign conduct meant that the Sherman Act did not apply to conduct occurring on foreign soil even though the conduct in that case in fact had, and was intended to have, an anticompetitive effect on both U.S. consumers and a U.S. firm.[7] However, later decisions effectively reversed this ruling, extending the U.S. antitrust laws to just about any extraterritorial conduct with effects on U.S. commerce that are direct, substantial, and reasonably foreseeable.

Decisions as early as 1911–13 cut back on the location-of-conduct test by holding that extraterritorial conduct could be reached when coupled with U.S. conduct,[8] and decisions in 1917 and 1927 extended this concept to hold that trivial or incidental U.S. acts by the defendant or its agents were sufficient in cases where there were substantial effects in the United States.[9] In the 1945 *Alcoa* decision, Judge Hand converted this line of authority into a general effects test with the following reasoning:

---

6.   *See* 15 U.S.C. §§ 1–2, 12, 44.

7.   American Banana Co. v. United Fruit Co., 213 U.S. 347, 356–57 (1909).

8.   *See* United States v. American Tobacco, 221 U.S. 106 (1911); United States v. Pacific & Artic Ry., 228 U.S. 87 (1913).

9.   Thomsen v. Cayser, 243 U.S. 66 (1917); United States v. Sisal Sales Corporation, 274 U.S. 268 (1927). Part of the reason for this switch in interpretation of the Sherman Act may

"... [W]e are concerned only with whether Congress chose to attach liability to the conduct outside the United States of persons not in allegiance to it. That being so, the only question open is whether Congress intended to impose the liability, and whether our own Constitution permitted it to do so: as a court of the United States, we cannot look beyond our own law. Nevertheless, it is quite true that we are not to read general words, such as those in this Act, without regard to the limitations customarily observed by nations upon the exercise of their powers; limitations which generally correspond to those fixed by the 'Conflict of Laws.' We should not impute to Congress an intent to punish all whom its courts can catch, for conduct which has no consequences within the United States. On the other hand, it is settled law that any state may impose liabilities, even upon persons not within its allegiance, for conduct outside its borders that has consequences within its borders which the state reprehends; and these liabilities other states will ordinarily recognize.

It may be argued that this Act extends further. Two situations are possible. There may be agreements made beyond our borders not intended to affect imports, which do affect them, or which affect exports. Almost any limitation of the supply of goods in Europe, for example, or in South America, may have repercussions in the United States if there is trade between the two. Yet when one considers the international complications likely to arise from an effort in this country to treat such agreements as unlawful, it is safe to assume that Congress certainly did not intend the Act to cover them. Such agreements may on the other hand intend to include imports into the United States, and yet it may appear that they had no effect upon them. That situation might be thought to fall within the doctrine that intent may be a substitute for performance in the case of a contract made within the United States; or it might be thought to fall within the doctrine that a statute should not be interpreted to cover acts abroad which have no consequence here. We shall not choose between these alternatives; but for argument we shall assume that the Act does not cover agreements, even though intended to affect imports or exports, unless its performance is shown actually to have had some effect upon them. Where both conditions are satisfied, the situation

---

be that Congress signaled its desire for a broader extraterritorial application with its 1913 amendment to the Wilson Tariff Act, which extended the ban on import conspiracies to include defendants acting as importers either directly or through agents, 15 U.S.C. § 8 (2000), and in 1914 enacted the Clayton Act, which took the approach of extending the statute to foreign commerce as long as it had the requisite anticompetitive effects within the United States. The Clayton Act defined the covered "commerce" to include "commerce ... with foreign nations" or between any part of the U.S. and a foreign nation. See 15 U.S.C. § 12. However, the Clayton Act limited the provisions regulating price discrimination and conditioned sales to those involving commodities that are "for use, consumption, or resale within the United States." 15 U.S.C. § 13(a), 14. It also limited the merger provision to mergers that may substantially lessen competition "affecting commerce in any section of the country." 15 U.S.C. § 18. This may have suggested the advisability of a parallel treatment of the Sherman Act.

certainly falls within such decisions as *Pacific, Thomsen,* and *Sisal....* It is true that in those cases the persons held liable had sent agents into the United States to perform part of the agreement; but an agent is merely an animate means of executing his principal's purposes, and, for the purposes of this case, he does not differ from an inanimate means; besides, only human agents can import and sell ingot.

"Both agreements would clearly have been unlawful, had they been made within the United States; and it follows from what we have just said that both were unlawful, though made abroad, if they were intended to affect imports and did affect them."[10]

Thus, by treating products sold in the United States as the inanimate agents of foreign firms who were creating anticompetitive effects in the United States, *Alcoa* converted a test that focused on the conduct's location into a test that focused on the location of its effect and whether those effects were intended. Proving intent in antitrust generally requires proving only the objective intent implied by the conduct, as Judge Hand himself held when he said "no monopolist monopolizes unconscious of what he is doing," which suggests the intent requirement would be deemed met in any case where it was reasonably foreseeable the conduct would have an effect in the United States.[11] However, proof of a subjective intent to affect U.S. markets remains relevant because it shifts the burden of proof to the defendant to disprove effects in the United States.[12] Further, Hand's assumption that an intent could not be shown when firms limited the supply of goods in Europe or in South America in a way that indirectly affected U.S. markets suggests he meant the intent requirement to embrace some showing that the U.S. effects were relatively direct and substantial. Thus, *Alcoa* suggested that U.S. antitrust laws applied to any foreign conduct that had direct substantial foreseeable effects in the United States.

After *Alcoa,* some courts went so far as to conclude that any effect in the United States might suffice, but most courts concluded the U.S. effect had to be direct, substantial, and foreseeable, as did the Second Restatement of Foreign Relations.[13] This latter line of authority was effectively codified in the Foreign Trade Antitrust Improvements Act (FTAIA) of 1982, which stated that the Sherman and FTC Acts "shall not apply to conduct involving trade or commerce (other than import trade or import commerce) with foreign nations unless ... (1) such conduct has a direct, substantial, and reasonably foreseeable effect" on U.S. commerce or on

---

10.   U.S. v. Alcoa, 148 F.2d 416, 443–44 (2d Cir. 1945).

11.   *Id.* at 432.

12.   *Id.* at 444.

13.   *See* Hartford Fire Insur. v. California, 509 U.S. 764, 796 (1993); Matsushita Elec. Industrial Co. v. Zenith Radio Corp., 475 U.S. 574, 582 n.6 (1986); Timberlane Lumber Co. v. Bank of America, 549 F.2d 597, 610–11 (9th Cir. 1976) (collecting cases); ALI, Restatement of the Foreign Relations Law of the United States 2d, § 18 (1965). Although Continental Ore v. Union Carbide, 370 U.S. 690 (1962), is often cited for the same proposition, in fact it held only that such effects sufficed when some conduct was foreign but other conduct occurred in the United States, *id.* at 704–05.

U.S. exporters *and* "(2) such effect gives rise to a claim" under the Sherman or FTC Acts.[14] Although some have suggested the FTAIA exemption is limited to restraints on "exports," that interpretation is not supported by the text, which (leaving aside imports) uses the same "commerce ... with foreign nations" language as the Sherman Act uses to describe the foreign conduct it might reach, nor by the legislative history and Supreme Court interpretation.[15] Further, although the FTAIA exemption does not apply to restraints on U.S. imports, one might think such any such restraint would always meet the test that U.S. effects would be direct, substantial, and reasonably foreseeable. Thus, the statute does seem to dictate when the Sherman and FTC Acts do *not* apply to foreign conduct. Of course, that does not alone affirmatively indicate when the U.S. antitrust laws *do* apply. However, given the precedent leading up to the FTAIA, and the desire to keep extraterritorial application of the Clayton Act (which is not affected by the FTAIA) parallel with that the Sherman and FTC Acts, it makes sense to read the FTAIA as codifying the affirmative substantive reach of the U.S. antitrust laws.

The FTAIA thus usefully breaks Hand's intent requirement into the separate requirements of directness, substantiality and reasonable foreseeability. The directness element adds little to damage claims, which must already show directness to show proximate causation. *See* Chapter 1. However, it remains important because it effectively adds a proximate causation requirement for non-damage claims against foreign conduct, including those brought by the government. In addition, the FTAIA adds the new requirement (which was perhaps simply assumed in the prior cases where it was always met) that the requisite U.S. effect gives rise to the relevant antitrust claim. This requirement adds little to the typical suit by private plaintiffs operating in the U.S. because they must already prove antitrust injury. *See id.* But it too is important because it effectively adds the requirement of proving antitrust injury to U.S. commerce or exports in suits brought by a U.S. agency and requires private plaintiffs to show that their antitrust injury was connected to such U.S. effects, which precludes cases by plaintiffs claiming injuries suffered in foreign nations that were independent of the U.S. effects.[16]

Comity Limits. Although the U.S. antitrust statutes can reach any foreign anticompetitive conduct with a direct, substantial, foreseeable effect

---

14. *See* 15 U.S.C §§ 6a, 45(a)(3).

15. *See* F. Hoffmann-la Roche Ltd. v. Empagran S.A., 542 U.S. 155, 162–63 (2004). In 1987, the Third Restatement of Foreign Relations Law concluded that U.S. antitrust jurisdiction continued to apply if either (a) the conduct had a "principal purpose" of affecting U.S. commerce and "some effect" on it ("even if the actual effect proves to be insubstantial") or (b) a "substantial effect" on U.S. commerce and the exercise of jurisdiction was not unreasonable under the following comity principles. Restatement (Third) of Foreign Relations Law of the United States § 415, and Comment a (1987). Further, and in some contradiction with the text of its own rule, the Restatement Comments indicated that it took no position on whether an intent to affect U.S. commerce should suffice even without any evidence of effects and that it sufficed if a substantial effect was "likely" even if not effectuated. See id. Comments a & d. However, some of these conclusions appear to be inconsistent with the FTAIA and its interpretation in *Empagran*.

16. *See Empagran*, 542 U.S. at 166–75.

in the United States, many cases have also held that this authority should not be exercised when it would violate principles of international comity. Several cases have held that this comity doctrine means that courts must weigh the substantiality of the effects in the U.S. against the interests of foreign nations using a multi-factor balancing test. For example, one leading case held that the "elements to be weighed include the degree of conflict with foreign law or policy, the nationality or allegiance of the parties and the locations or principal places of businesses or corporations, the extent to which enforcement by either state can be expected to achieve compliance, the relative significance of effects on the United States as compared with those elsewhere, the extent to which there is explicit purpose to harm or affect American commerce, the foreseeability of such effect, and the relative importance to the violations charged of conduct within the United States as compared with conduct abroad."[17] The Third Restatement of Foreign Relations Law likewise adopted a multi-factor balancing approach, providing that: (a) a state may not exercise substantive jurisdiction when doing so would be "unreasonable" considering "all relevant factors" which include, but are not limited to, whether foreign conduct has a "substantial, direct, and foreseeable effect" in the state exercising jurisdiction; and (b) if two states reasonably could exercise substantive jurisdiction but their laws are in conflict, then jurisdiction should be exercised by whichever state has a "clearly greater" interest.[18]

---

17. *Timberlane*, 549 at 611–15; *see also* Mannington Mills v. Congoleum Corp., 595 F.2d 1287, 1297 (3d Cir. 1979) (listing its own multi-factor balancing test).

18. Restatement (Third) of Foreign Relations Law § 403 (1987) provides:

(1) Even when one of the bases for jurisdiction under § 402 is present, a state may not exercise jurisdiction to prescribe law with respect to a person or activity having connections with another state when the exercise of such jurisdiction is unreasonable.

(2) Whether exercise of jurisdiction over a person or activity is unreasonable is determined by evaluating all relevant factors, including, where appropriate:

(a) the link of the activity to the territory of the regulating state, i.e., the extent to which the activity takes place within the territory, or has substantial, direct, and foreseeable effect upon or in the territory;

(b) the connections, such as nationality, residence, or economic activity, between the regulating state and the person principally responsible for the activity to be regulated, or between that state and those whom the regulation is designed to protect;

(c) the character of the activity to be regulated, the importance of regulation to the regulating state, the extent to which other states regulate such activities, and the degree to which the desirability of such regulation is generally accepted.

(d) the existence of justified expectations that might be protected or hurt by the regulation;

(e) the importance of the regulation to the international political, legal, or economic system;

(f) the extent to which the regulation is consistent with the traditions of the international system;

(g) the extent to which another state may have an interest in regulating the activity; and

(h) the likelihood of conflict with regulation by another state.

(3) When it would not be unreasonable for each of two states to exercise jurisdiction over a person or activity, but the prescriptions by the two states are in conflict, each state has an obligation to evaluate its own as well as the other state's interest in exercising jurisdiction, in

Consider whether such a balancing approach to comity issues has been altered by the next case.

Hartford Fire Insur. v. California

509 U.S. 764 (1993).

■ JUSTICE SOUTER . . . delivered the opinion of the Court with respect to [all parts excerpted below.]

The plaintiffs (respondents here) allege that both domestic and foreign defendants (petitioners here) violated the Sherman Act by engaging in various conspiracies to affect the American insurance market. We hold that . . . the principle of international comity does not preclude District Court jurisdiction over the foreign conduct alleged. . . .

The two petitions before us stem from consolidated litigation comprising the complaints of 19 States and many private plaintiffs alleging that the defendants, members of the insurance industry, conspired in violation of § 1 of the Sherman Act to restrict the terms of coverage of commercial general liability (CGL) insurance available in the United States. Because the cases come to us on motions to dismiss, we take the allegations of the complaints as true. . . . According to the complaints, the object of the conspiracies was to force certain primary insurers (insurers who sell insurance directly to consumers) to change the terms of their standard CGL insurance policies to conform with the policies the defendant insurers wanted to sell. The defendants wanted four changes.

First, CGL insurance has traditionally been sold in the United States on an "occurrence" basis, through a policy obligating the insurer "to pay or defend claims, whenever made, resulting from an accident or 'injurious exposure to conditions' that occurred during the [specific time] period the policy was in effect." In place of this traditional "occurrence" trigger of coverage, the defendants wanted a "claims-made" trigger, obligating the insurer to pay or defend only those claims made during the policy period. Such a policy has the distinct advantage for the insurer that when the policy period ends without a claim having been made, the insurer can be certain that the policy will not expose it to any further liability. Second, the defendants wanted the "claims-made" policy to have a "retroactive date" provision, which would further restrict coverage to claims based on incidents that occurred after a certain date. Such a provision eliminates the risk that an insurer, by issuing a claims-made policy, would assume liability arising from incidents that occurred before the policy's effective date, but remained undiscovered or caused no immediate harm. Third, CGL insurance has traditionally covered "sudden and accidental" pollution; the defendants wanted to eliminate that coverage. Finally, CGL insurance has traditionally provided that the insurer would bear the legal costs of defending covered claims against the insured without regard to the policy's stated limits of coverage; the defendants wanted legal defense costs to be counted against the stated limits (providing a "legal defense cost cap"). . . .

---

light of all the relevant factors, including those set out in Subsection (2); a state should defer to the other state if that state's interest is clearly greater.

The Fifth Claim for Relief in the California Complaint alleges a violation of § 1 of the Sherman Act by certain London reinsurers who conspired to coerce primary insurers in the United States to offer CGL coverage on a claims-made basis, thereby making "occurrence CGL coverage ... unavailable in the State of California for many risks." The Sixth Claim for Relief in the California Complaint alleges that the London reinsurers violated § 1 by a conspiracy to limit coverage of pollution risks in North America, thereby rendering "pollution liability coverage ... almost entirely unavailable for the vast majority of casualty insurance purchasers in the State of California." The Eighth Claim for Relief in the California Complaint alleges a further § 1 violation by the London reinsurers who, along with domestic retrocessional reinsurers, conspired to limit coverage of seepage, pollution, and property contamination risks in North America, thereby eliminating such coverage in the State of California.

At the outset, we note that the District Court undoubtedly had jurisdiction of these Sherman Act claims, as the London reinsurers apparently concede. Although the proposition was perhaps not always free from doubt, see *American Banana*, it is well established by now that the Sherman Act applies to foreign conduct that was meant to produce and did in fact produce some substantial effect in the United States. See *Matsushita; Alcoa*; Restatement (Third) of Foreign Relations Law of the United States § 415, and Reporters' Note 3 (1987) (hereinafter Restatement (Third) Foreign Relations Law); 1 P. Areeda & D. Turner, Antitrust Law ¶ 236 (1978); cf. Continental Ore Co. v. Union Carbide & Carbon Corp., 370 U.S. 690, 704 (1962); Steele v. Bulova Watch Co., 344 U.S. 280, 288, (1952); United States v. Sisal Sales Corp., 274 U.S. 268, 275–276 (1927).[22] Such is the conduct alleged here: that the London reinsurers engaged in unlawful conspiracies to affect the market for insurance in the United States and that their conduct in fact produced substantial effect.[23]

According to the London reinsurers, the District Court should have declined to exercise such jurisdiction under the principle of international comity.[24] The Court of Appeals agreed that courts should look to that

---

22. JUSTICE SCALIA believes that what is at issue in this litigation is prescriptive, as opposed to subject-matter, jurisdiction. The parties do not question prescriptive jurisdiction, however, and for good reason: it is well established that Congress has exercised such jurisdiction under the Sherman Act. See G. Born & D. Westin, International Civil Litigation in United States Courts 542, n. 5 (2d ed. 1992) (Sherman Act is a "prime example of the simultaneous exercise of prescriptive jurisdiction and grant of subject matter jurisdiction").

23. Under § 402 of the Foreign Trade Antitrust Improvements Act of 1982 (FTAIA), 15 U.S.C. § 6a, the Sherman Act does not apply to conduct involving foreign trade or commerce, other than import trade or import commerce, unless "such conduct has a direct, substantial, and reasonably foreseeable effect" on domestic or import commerce. § 6a(1)(A). The FTAIA was intended to exempt from the Sherman Act export transactions that did not injure the United States economy, see H. R. Rep. No. 97–686, pp. 2–3, 9–10 (1982); P. Areeda & H. Hovenkamp, Antitrust Law P236'a, pp. 296–297 (Supp. 1992), and it is unclear how it might apply to the conduct alleged here. Also unclear is whether the Act's "direct, substantial, and reasonably foreseeable effect" standard amends existing law or merely codifies it. *See id.*, P236'a, p. 297. We need not address these questions here. Assuming that the FTAIA's standard affects this litigation, and assuming further that that standard differs from the prior law, the conduct alleged plainly meets its requirements.

24. JUSTICE SCALIA contends that comity concerns figure into the prior analysis whether jurisdiction exists under the Sherman Act. This contention is inconsistent with the

principle in deciding whether to exercise jurisdiction under the Sherman Act. This availed the London reinsurers nothing, however. To be sure, the Court of Appeals believed that "application of [American] antitrust laws to the London reinsurance market 'would lead to significant conflict with English law and policy,' " and that "[s]uch a conflict, unless out-weighed by other factors, would by itself be reason to decline exercise of jurisdiction." But other factors, in the court's view, including the London reinsurers' express purpose to affect United States commerce and the substantial nature of the effect produced, out-weighed the supposed conflict and required the exercise of jurisdiction in this litigation.

When it enacted the FTAIA, Congress expressed no view on the question whether a court with Sherman Act jurisdiction should ever decline to exercise such jurisdiction on grounds of international comity. See H. R. Rep. No. 97–686, p. 13 (1982) ("If a court determines that the requirements for subject matter jurisdiction are met, [the FTAIA] would have no effect on the court['s] ability to employ notions of comity . . . or otherwise to take account of the international character of the transaction") (citing *Timberlane*). We need not decide that question here, however, for even assuming that in a proper case a court may decline to exercise Sherman Act jurisdiction over foreign conduct (or, as JUSTICE SCALIA would put it, may conclude by the employment of comity analysis in the first instance that there is no jurisdiction), international comity would not counsel against exercising jurisdiction in the circumstances alleged here.

The only substantial question in this litigation is whether "there is in fact a true conflict between domestic and foreign law." The London reinsurers contend that applying the Act to their conduct would conflict significantly with British law, and the British Government, appearing before us as *amicus curiae*, concurs. They assert that Parliament has established a comprehensive regulatory regime over the London reinsurance market and that the conduct alleged here was perfectly consistent with British law and policy. But this is not to state a conflict. "The fact that conduct is lawful in the state in which it took place will not, of itself, bar application of the United States antitrust laws," even where the foreign state has a strong policy to permit or encourage such conduct. Restatement (Third) Foreign Relations Law § 415, Comment *j*; see *Continental Ore Co., supra, at 706–707*. No conflict exists, for these purposes, "where a person subject to regulation by two states can comply with the laws of both." Restatement (Third) Foreign Relations Law § 403, Comment *e*.[25] Since the London reinsurers do not argue that British law requires them to act in some fashion prohibited by the law of the United States, or claim that their compliance with the laws of both countries is otherwise impossible, we see

---

general understanding that the Sherman Act covers foreign conduct producing a substantial intended effect in the United States, and that concerns of comity come into play, if at all, only after a court has determined that the acts complained of are subject to Sherman Act jurisdiction. In any event, the parties conceded jurisdiction at oral argument, and we see no need to address this contention here.

25. JUSTICE SCALIA says that we put the cart before the horse in citing this authority, for he argues it may be apposite only after a determination that jurisdiction over the foreign acts is reasonable. But whatever the order of cart and horse, conflict in this sense is the only substantial issue before the Court.

no conflict with British law. See *Restatement (Third) Foreign Relations Law § 403*, Comment *e*, § 415, Comment *j*. We have no need in this litigation to address other considerations that might inform a decision to refrain from the exercise of jurisdiction on grounds of international comity. . . . *It is so ordered.* . . .

■ SCALIA, J., delivered a dissenting opinion . . ., in which O'CONNOR, KENNEDY, and THOMAS, JJ., joined . . .

It is important to distinguish two distinct questions raised by this petition: whether the District Court had jurisdiction, and whether the Sherman Act reaches the extraterritorial conduct alleged here. On the first question, I believe that the District Court had subject-matter jurisdiction over the Sherman Act claims against all the defendants (personal jurisdiction is not contested). Respondents asserted nonfrivolous claims under the Sherman Act, and 28 U.S.C. § 1331 vests district courts with subject-matter jurisdiction over cases "arising under" federal statutes. . . .

The second question—the extraterritorial reach of the Sherman Act—has nothing to do with the jurisdiction of the courts. It is a question of substantive law turning on whether, in enacting the Sherman Act, Congress asserted regulatory power over the challenged conduct. If a plaintiff fails to prevail on this issue, the court does not dismiss the claim for want of subject-matter jurisdiction—want of power to adjudicate; rather, it decides the claim, ruling on the merits that the plaintiff has failed to state a cause of action under the relevant statute. There is, however, a type of "jurisdiction" relevant to determining the extraterritorial reach of a statute; it is known as "legislative jurisdiction," *Aramco*; Restatement (First) Conflict of Laws § 60 (1934), or "jurisdiction to prescribe," 1 Restatement (Third) of Foreign Relations Law of the United States 235 (1987). This refers to "the authority of a state to make its law applicable to persons or activities," and is quite a separate matter from "jurisdiction to adjudicate." There is no doubt, of course, that Congress possesses legislative jurisdiction over the acts alleged in this complaint: Congress has broad power under Article I, § 8, cl. 3, "to regulate Commerce with foreign Nations," and this Court has repeatedly upheld its power to make laws applicable to persons or activities beyond our territorial boundaries where United States interests are affected. But the question in this litigation is whether, and to what extent, Congress *has* exercised that undoubted legislative jurisdiction in enacting the Sherman Act.

Two canons of statutory construction are relevant in this inquiry. The first is the "longstanding principle of American law 'that legislation of Congress, unless a contrary intent appears, is meant to apply only within the territorial jurisdiction of the United States.' " *Aramco*. Applying that canon in *Aramco*, we held that the version of Title VII of the Civil Rights Act of 1964 then in force did not extend outside the territory of the United States even though the statute contained broad provisions extending its prohibitions to, for example, " 'any activity, business, or industry in commerce.' " We held such "boilerplate language" to be an insufficient indication to override the presumption against extraterritoriality. The Sherman Act contains similar "boilerplate language," and if the question were not governed by precedent, it would be worth considering whether that presumption controls the outcome here. We have, however, found the presumption to be overcome with respect to our antitrust laws; it is now well established that the Sherman Act applies extraterritorially. See *Matsushita Elec.; Continental Ore; ALCOA.*

But if the presumption against extraterritoriality has been overcome or is otherwise inapplicable, a second canon of statutory construction becomes relevant: "An act of congress ought never to be construed to violate the law of nations if any other possible construction remains." Murray v. Schooner Charming Betsy, 6 U.S. 64 (1804) (Marshall, C.J.). This canon is "wholly independent" of the presumption against extraterritoriality. *Aramco* (Marshall, J., dissenting). It is relevant to determining the substantive reach of a statute because "the law of nations," or customary international law, includes limitations on a nation's exercise of its jurisdiction to prescribe. See Restatement (Third) §§ 401–416. Though it clearly has constitutional authority to do so, Congress is generally presumed not to have exceeded those customary international-law limits on jurisdiction to prescribe.

Consistent with that presumption, this and other courts have frequently recognized that, even where the presumption against extraterritoriality does not apply, statutes should not be interpreted to regulate foreign persons or conduct if that regulation would conflict with principles of international law. . . . More recent lower court precedent has also tempered the extraterritorial application of the Sherman Act with considerations of "international comity." The "comity" they refer to is not the comity of courts, whereby judges decline to exercise jurisdiction over matters more appropriately adjudged elsewhere, but rather what might be termed "prescriptive comity": the respect sovereign nations afford each other by limiting the reach of their laws. That comity is exercised by legislatures when they enact laws, and courts assume it has been exercised when they come to interpreting the scope of laws their legislatures have enacted. It is a traditional component of choice-of-law theory. Comity in this sense includes the choice-of-law principles that, "in the absence of contrary congressional direction," are assumed to be incorporated into our substantive laws having extraterritorial reach. Considering comity in this way is just part of determining whether the Sherman Act prohibits the conduct at issue.

In sum, the practice of using international law to limit the extraterritorial reach of statutes is firmly established in our jurisprudence. In proceeding to apply that practice to the present cases, I shall rely on the Restatement (Third) for the relevant principles of international law. Its standards appear fairly supported in the decisions of this Court construing international choice-of-law principles . . . and in the decisions of other federal courts, especially *Timberlane*. Whether the Restatement precisely reflects international law in every detail matters little here, as I believe this litigation would be resolved the same way under virtually any conceivable test that takes account of foreign regulatory interests.

Under the Restatement, a nation having some "basis" for jurisdiction to prescribe law should nonetheless refrain from exercising that jurisdiction "with respect to a person or activity having connections with another state when the exercise of such jurisdiction is unreasonable." Restatement (Third) § 403(1). The "reasonableness" inquiry turns on a number of factors including, but not limited to: "the extent to which the activity takes place within the territory [of the regulating state]," *id.*, § 403(2)(a); "the connections, such as nationality, residence, or economic activity, between the regulating state and the person principally responsible for the activity to be regulated," *id.*, § 403(2)(b); "the character of the activity to be regulated, the importance of regulation to the regulating state, the extent to which other states regulate such activities, and the degree to which the desirability of such regulation is generally accepted," *id.*, § 403(2)(c); "the extent to which another state may have an interest in regulating the activity," *id.*, § 403(2)(g); and "the likelihood of conflict with regulation by another state," *id.*, § 403(2)(h). Rarely would these factors point more clearly against application of United States law. The activity relevant to the counts at issue here took place primarily in the United Kingdom, and the defendants in these counts are British corporations and British subjects having their principal place of business or residence outside the United States.[10] Great Britain has established a comprehensive regulatory scheme governing the London reinsurance markets, and clearly has a heavy "interest in regulating the activity," *id.*, § 403(2)(g). Finally, § 2(b) of the McCarran–Ferguson Act allows state regulatory statutes to override the Sherman Act in the insurance field, subject only to the narrow "boycott" exception set forth in § 3(b)—suggesting that "the importance of regulation to the [United States]," Restatement (Third) § 403(2)(c), is slight. Considering these factors, I think it unimaginable that an assertion of legislative jurisdiction by the United States would be considered reasonable, and therefore it is inappropriate to assume, in the absence of statutory indication to the contrary, that Congress has made such an assertion.

It is evident from what I have said that the Court's comity analysis, which proceeds as though the issue is whether the courts should "decline to exercise   jurisdiction," rather than whether the Sherman Act covers this conduct, is simply misdirected. I do not at all agree, moreover, with the Court's conclusion that the issue of the substantive scope of the Sherman Act is not in the cases. To be sure, the parties did not make a clear distinction between adjudicative jurisdiction and the scope of the statute. Parties often do not, as we have observed (and have declined to punish with procedural default) before. It is not realistic, and also not helpful, to pretend that the only really relevant issue in this litigation is not before us. In any event, if one erroneously chooses, as the Court does, to make adjudicative jurisdiction (or, more precisely, abstention) the vehicle for taking account of the needs of prescriptive comity, the Court still gets it wrong. It concludes that no "true conflict" counseling nonapplication of United States law (or rather, as it thinks, United States judicial jurisdiction) exists unless compliance with United States law would constitute a *violation* of another country's law. That breathtakingly broad proposition, which contradicts the many cases discussed earlier, will bring the Sherman Act and other laws into sharp and unnecessary conflict with the legitimate interests of other countries—particularly our closest trading partners.

---

10. Some of the British corporations are subsidiaries of American corporations, and the Court of Appeals held that "the interests of Britain are at least diminished where the parties are subsidiaries of American corporations." In effect, the Court of Appeals pierced the corporate veil in weighing the interests at stake. I do not think that was proper.

In the sense in which the term "conflict" ... is generally understood in the field of conflicts of laws, there is clearly a conflict in this litigation. The petitioners here ... were not compelled by any foreign law to take their allegedly wrongful actions, but that no more precludes a conflict-of-laws analysis here than it did there. Where applicable foreign and domestic law provide different substantive rules of decision to govern the parties' dispute, a conflict-of-laws analysis is necessary. See generally R. Weintraub, Commentary on Conflict of Laws 2–3 (1980); Restatement (First) of Conflict of Laws § 1, Comment *c* and Illustrations (1934).

Literally the *only* support that the Court adduces for its position is § 403 of the Restatement (Third)—or more precisely Comment *e* to that provision, which states:

> "Subsection (3) [which says that a State should defer to another state if that State's interest is clearly greater] applies only when one state requires what another prohibits, or where compliance with the regulations of two states exercising jurisdiction consistently with this section is otherwise impossible. It does not apply where a person subject to regulation by two states can comply with the laws of both...."

The Court has completely misinterpreted this provision. Subsection (3) of § 403 (requiring one State to defer to another in the limited circumstances just described) comes into play only after subsection (1) of § 403 has been complied with—*i.e.*, after it has been determined that the exercise of jurisdiction by *both* of the two States is not "unreasonable." That prior question is answered by applying the factors (*inter alia*) set forth in subsection (2) of § 403, that is, precisely the factors that I have discussed in text and that the Court rejects....

Questions on *Hartford Fire*

1. Would it make sense to give antitrust authority to the nation in which conduct occurred rather than the nation in which the effects of that conduct were felt?

a. If producers in nation *A* formed a cartel in nation *A* to raise prices charged in nation *B*, would nation *A* have the right incentives to police such misconduct?

b. What does the U.S. statute exempting restraints affecting exports suggest about national enforcement incentives in such a case?

c. Did Great Britain have adequate incentives to police the alleged anticompetitive conduct that its insurers engaged in here?

d. Is Justice Scalia right to suggest that, absent precedent, the applicability of antitrust statutes to extraterritorial conduct should be limited in the same way as the EEOC? Even if the canon against extraterritorial application is equally applicable to both statutes, don't the express references in the U.S. antitrust statutes to "foreign commerce" involve the sort of non-boilerplate language that suggests an affirmative Congressional desire for some extraterritorial application?

2. Would it be easier to solve the above problem by giving the sole regulatory authority to the nation in which the effects were felt?

a. If a nation is a net importer, will it have incentives to overenforce antitrust law? Does the answer turn on whether the right antitrust standard is consumer welfare or total welfare?

b. In an increasingly globalized world where markets span multiple nations, won't anticompetitive conduct affecting such markets necessarily have substantial effect on every nation within the multinational market?

3. If two nations are reasonably interested in regulating anticompetitive conduct that affects them, what should be the presumed limits on any one nation exercising such a regulatory power?

a. Should both nations regulate the conduct unless their laws conflict in the sense that firms could not simultaneously obey both?

    i. This is how Justice Scalia and many commentators read the Court opinion in *Hartford Fire.* But is this what the Court held? Or was its holding limited to the proposition that because the only comity claim raised was such a regulatory conflict, it sufficed that such a conflict did not exist?

    ii. Is this a sensible way to determine when the laws of two nations are in conflict? Doesn't this bias international law against nations that either (1) choose a deregulatory policy in their nation or (2) make a deliberate choice to adopt a more narrow antitrust regime because they believe that much of the conduct condemned by other nations' antitrust regimes is affirmatively procompetitive?

b. Should the answer turn on judicial balancing of all the relevant state interests?

    i. Does such a test provide any guidance to firms about which regulatory regime they have to comply with?

    ii. Once everything is relevant, do we really have any test?

    iii. Won't the judge adjudicating such a balancing test be biased in favor of its own nation?

c. Which is more likely to satisfy Congressional desires about how far to extend its antitrust laws in cases where U.S. antitrust policy conflicts with foreign policy: (1) a rule that applies U.S. antitrust law other than in cases where foreign law compels the opposite conduct; or (2) a comity balancing test that considers all the factors that Congress would want weighed?

    i. If judicial balancing often misassesses Congressional desires, might not the first rule satisfy Congressional desires better overall than a judicial balancing test?[19]

    ii. If judicial balancing does do a better job than the first rule of satisfying Congressional desires but is sometimes inaccurate, would it still be better to use the first rule in order to provoke the sort of

---

19. *See* Elhauge, Statutory Default Rules 204–210 (Harvard University Press 2008).

international policy conflict that is likely to produce an international treaty, which provides an even more accurate assessment of U.S. governmental preferences and can resolve the need for international coordination?[20]

4. Assuming one does apply a general balancing test, is it clear Justice Scalia is correct that it clearly counsels for nonapplication of U.S. antitrust law to a London insurance conspiracy that restrains the insurance offered in the United States?

a. If this conspiracy were anticompetitive, wouldn't the supracompetitive profits be reaped in Great Britain while the costs would be suffered in the United States? Is Great Britain the best nation to enforce antitrust rules against such a conspiracy?

b. Does the McCarran–Ferguson Act indicate a lack of U.S. interest in the matter? Why would a U.S. decision to rely on state rather than federal regulation of insurance indicate that the U.S. lacks a significant interest in matters affecting domestic insurance?[21] Is being pro-federalism the same as being uninterested?

5. Justice Scalia indicates that he would find U.S. antitrust law inapplicable even as to foreign corporations that are subsidiaries of U.S. corporations. Wouldn't exempting such subsidiaries make it easy to evade U.S. antitrust law by just setting up foreign subsidiaries and having them meet in foreign nations that have no antitrust laws in order to reach agreements to cartelize U.S. markets?

U.S. DOJ–FTC, Antitrust Enforcement Guidelines for International Operations

(April 1995).

3.   THRESHOLD INTERNATIONAL ENFORCEMENT ISSUES

3.1   Jurisdiction. .... Anticompetitive conduct that affects U.S. domestic or foreign commerce may violate the U.S. antitrust laws regardless of where such conduct occurs or the nationality of the parties involved. Under the Sherman Act and the FTC Act, there are two principal tests for subject matter jurisdiction in foreign commerce cases. With respect to foreign import commerce, the Supreme Court has recently stated in *Hartford Fire* that "the Sherman Act applies to foreign conduct that was meant to produce and did in fact produce some substantial effect in the United States." There has been no such authoritative ruling on the scope of the FTC Act, but both Acts apply to commerce "with foreign nations" and the Commission has held that terms used by both Acts should be construed together. Second, with respect to foreign commerce other than imports, the Foreign Trade Antitrust Improvements Act of 1982 ("FTAIA") applies to

---

20. *See id.*

21. Because he was focused only on the boycott exception to the McCarran–Ferguson Act (which was the other issue adjudicated in that case), Justice Scalia appears to have also failed to appreciate that several other limitations make the McCarran–Ferguson exemption more narrow than he supposed. *See* Chapter 1.

foreign conduct that has a direct, substantial, and reasonably foreseeable effect on U.S. commerce.

3.11 Jurisdiction Over Conduct Involving Import Commerce. Imports into the United States by definition affect the U.S. domestic market directly, and will, therefore, almost invariably satisfy the intent part of the *Hartford Fire* test. Whether they in fact produce the requisite substantial effects will depend on the facts of each case.

ILLUSTRATIVE EXAMPLE A

Situation: A, B, C, and D are foreign companies that produce a product in various foreign countries. None has any U.S. production, nor any U.S. subsidiaries. They organize a cartel for the purpose of raising the price for the product in question. Collectively, the cartel members make substantial sales into the United States, both in absolute terms and relative to total U.S. consumption.

Discussion: These facts present the straightforward case of cartel participants selling products directly into the United States. In this situation, the transaction is unambiguously an import into the U.S. market, and the sale is not complete until the goods reach the United States. Thus, U.S. subject matter jurisdiction is clear under the general principles of antitrust law expressed most recently in *Hartford Fire*. The facts presented here demonstrate actual and intended participation in U.S. commerce. The separate question of personal jurisdiction under the facts presented here would be analyzed using the principles discussed infra in Section 4.1.

3.12 Jurisdiction Over Conduct Involving Other Foreign Commerce. With respect to foreign commerce other than imports, the jurisdictional limits of the Sherman Act and the FTC Act are delineated in the FTAIA.... To the extent that conduct in foreign countries does not "involve" import commerce but does have an "effect" on either import transactions or commerce within the United States, the Agencies apply the "direct, substantial, and reasonably foreseeable" standard of the FTAIA. That standard is applied, for example, in cases in which a cartel of foreign enterprises, or a foreign monopolist, reaches the U.S. market through any mechanism that goes beyond direct sales, such as the use of an unrelated intermediary, as well as in cases in which foreign vertical restrictions or intellectual property licensing arrangements have an anticompetitive effect on U.S. commerce.

ILLUSTRATIVE EXAMPLE B

Situation: As in Illustrative Example A, the foreign cartel produces a product in several foreign countries. None of its members has any U.S. production, nor do any of them have U.S. subsidiaries. They organize a cartel for the purpose of raising the price for the product in question. Rather than selling directly into the United States, however, the cartel sells to an intermediary outside the United States, which they know will resell the product in the United States. The intermediary is not part of the cartel.

Discussion: The jurisdictional analysis would change slightly from the one presented in Example A, because not only is the conduct being challenged entered into by cartelists in a foreign country, but it is also initially implemented through a sale made in a foreign country. Despite the different test, however, the outcome on these facts would in all likelihood remain the same. The fact that the illegal conduct occurs prior to the import would trigger the application of the FTAIA. The Agencies would have to determine whether the challenged conduct had "direct, substantial and reasonably foreseeable effects" on U.S. domestic or import commerce. Furthermore, since "the essence of any violation of Section 1 [of the Sherman Act] is the illegal agreement itself—rather than the overt acts performed in furtherance of it," the Agencies would focus on the potential harm that would ensue if the conspiracy were successful, not on whether the actual conduct in furtherance of the conspiracy had in fact the prohibited effect upon interstate or foreign commerce.

ILLUSTRATIVE EXAMPLE C

Situation:

Variant (1): Widgets are manufactured in both the United States and various other countries around the world. The non-U.S. manufacturers meet privately outside the United States and agree among themselves to raise prices to specified levels. Their agreement clearly indicates that sales in or into the United States are not within the scope of the agreement, and thus that each participant is free independently to set its prices for the U.S. market. Over time, the cartel members begin to sell excess production into the United States. These sales have the effect of stabilizing the cartel for the foreign markets. In the U.S. market, these "excess" sales are priced at levels below those that would have prevailed in the U.S. market but for the cartel, but there is no evidence that the prices are predatory. As a result of these events, several U.S. widget manufacturers curtail their production, overall domestic output falls, and remaining manufacturers fail to invest in new or improved capacity.

Variant (2): Assume now that the cartel agreement specifically provides that cartel members will set agreed prices for the U.S. market at levels designed to soak up excess quantities that arise as a result of price increases in foreign markets. The U.S. price level is set at periodic meetings where each participant indicates how much it must off-load in this way. Thus, the cartel members sell goods in the U.S. market at fixed prices that undercut prevailing U.S. price levels, with consequences similar to those in Variant 1.

Discussion:

Variant (1): The jurisdictional issue is whether the predictable economic consequences of the original cartel agreement and the independent sales into the United States are sufficient to support jurisdiction. The mere fact that the existence of U.S. sales or the level of U.S. prices may ultimately be affected by the cartel agreement is not enough for either *Hartford Fire* jurisdiction or the FTAIA.[59] Furthermore, in the absence

---

59.   If the Agencies lack jurisdiction under the FTAIA to challenge the cartel, the facts of this example would nonetheless lend themselves well to cooperative enforcement action among

of an agreement with respect to the U.S. market, sales into the U.S. market at non-predatory levels do not raise antitrust concerns.

Variant (2): The critical element of a foreign price-fixing agreement with direct, intended effects in the United States is now present. The fact that the cartel believes its U.S. prices are "reasonable," or that it may be exerting downward pressure on U.S. price levels, does not exonerate it. Variant 2 presents a case where the Agencies would need clear evidence of the prohibited agreement before they would consider moving forward. They would be particularly cautious if the apparent effects in the U.S. market appeared to be beneficial to consumers. . . .

3.13   Jurisdiction When U.S. Government Finances or Purchases. The Agencies may, in appropriate cases, take enforcement action when the U.S. Government is a purchaser, or substantially funds the purchase, of goods or services for consumption or use abroad. Cases in which the effect of anticompetitive conduct with respect to the sale of these goods or services falls primarily on U.S. taxpayers may qualify for redress under the federal antitrust laws. As a general matter, the Agencies consider there to be a sufficient effect on U.S. commerce to support the assertion of jurisdiction if, as a result of its payment or financing, the U.S. Government bears more than half the cost of the transaction [even though the relevant product is bought and used in a foreign nation]. . . .

3.14   Jurisdiction Under Section 7 of the Clayton Act. Section 7 of the Clayton Act applies to mergers and acquisitions between firms that are engaged in commerce or in any activity affecting commerce. The Agencies would apply the same principles regarding their foreign commerce jurisdiction to Clayton Section 7 cases as they would apply in Sherman Act cases.

ILLUSTRATIVE EXAMPLE H

Situation: Two foreign firms, one in Europe and the other in Canada, account together for a substantial percentage of U.S. sales of a particular product through direct imports. Both firms have sales offices and are subject to personal jurisdiction in the United States, although neither has productive assets in the United States. They enter into an agreement to merge.

Discussion: The express language of Section 7 of the Clayton Act reaches the stock and asset acquisitions of persons engaged in trade and commerce "with foreign nations." Thus, in assessing jurisdiction for this merger outside the United States the Agencies could establish U.S. subject matter jurisdiction based on its effect on U.S. imports. If the facts stated above were modified to show that the proposed merger would have effects on U.S. export commerce, as opposed to import trade, then in assessing jurisdiction under the Clayton Act the Agencies would analyze the question of effects on commerce in a manner consistent with the FTAIA: that is, they would look to see whether the

---

antitrust agencies. Virtually every country with an antitrust law prohibits horizontal cartels and the Agencies would willingly cooperate with foreign authorities taking direct action against the cartel in the countries where the agreement has raised the price of widgets to the extent such cooperation is allowed under U.S. law and any agreement executed pursuant to U.S. law with foreign agencies or governments.

effects on U.S. domestic or import commerce are direct, substantial, and reasonably foreseeable. It is appropriate to do so because the FTAIA sheds light on the type of effects Congress considered necessary for foreign commerce cases, even though the FTAIA did not amend the Clayton Act.

In both these situations, the Agencies would conclude that Section 7 jurisdiction technically exists. However, if effective relief is difficult to obtain, the case may be one in which the Agencies would seek to coordinate their efforts with other authorities who are examining the transaction.

3.2 Comity. In enforcing the antitrust laws, the Agencies consider international comity. Comity itself reflects the broad concept of respect among co-equal sovereign nations and plays a role in determining "the recognition which one nation allows within its territory to the legislative, executive or judicial acts of another nation." Thus, in determining whether to assert jurisdiction to investigate or bring an action, or to seek particular remedies in a given case, each Agency takes into account whether significant interests of any foreign sovereign would be affected.

In performing a comity analysis, the Agencies take into account all relevant factors. Among others, these may include

1.   the relative significance to the alleged violation of conduct within the United States, as compared to conduct abroad;

2.   the nationality of the persons involved in or affected by the conduct;

3.   the presence or absence of a purpose to affect U.S. consumers, markets, or exporters;

4.   the relative significance and foreseeability of the effects of the conduct on the United States as compared to the effects abroad;

5.   the existence of reasonable expectations that would be furthered or defeated by the action;

6.   the degree of conflict with foreign law or articulated foreign economic policies;

7.   the extent to which the enforcement activities of another country with respect to the same persons, including remedies resulting from those activities, may be affected; and

8.   the effectiveness of foreign enforcement as compared to U.S. enforcement action.

The relative weight that each factor should be given depends on the facts and circumstances of each case. With respect to the factor concerning conflict with foreign law, the Supreme Court made clear in *Hartford Fire* that no conflict exists for purposes of an international comity analysis in the courts if the person subject to regulation by two states can comply with the laws of both. Bearing this in mind, the Agencies first ask what laws or policies of the arguably interested foreign jurisdictions are implicated by the conduct in question. There may be no actual conflict between the antitrust enforcement interests of the United States and the laws or policies of a foreign sovereign. This is increasingly true as more countries adopt antitrust or competition laws that are compatible with those of the United States. In these cases, the anticompetitive conduct in question may also be prohibited under the pertinent foreign laws, and thus the possible conflict would relate to enforcement practices or remedy. If the laws or policies of a foreign nation are neutral, it is again possible for the parties in question to comply with the U.S. prohibition without violating foreign law.

The Agencies also take full account of comity factors beyond whether there is a conflict with foreign law. In deciding whether or not to challenge an alleged antitrust violation, the Agencies would, as part of a comity analysis, consider whether one country encourages a certain course of conduct, leaves parties free to choose among different strategies, or prohibits some of those strategies. In addition, the Agencies take into account the effect of their enforcement activities on related enforcement activities of a foreign antitrust authority. For example, the Agencies would consider whether their activities would interfere with or reinforce the objectives of the foreign proceeding, including any remedies contemplated or obtained by the foreign antitrust authority.

The Agencies also will consider whether the objectives sought to be obtained by the assertion of U.S. law would be achieved in a particular instance by foreign enforcement. In lieu of bringing an enforcement action, the Agencies may consult with interested foreign sovereigns through appropriate diplomatic channels to attempt to eliminate anticompetitive effects in the United States. In cases where the United States decides to prosecute an antitrust action, such a decision represents a determination by the Executive Branch that the importance of antitrust enforcement outweighs any relevant foreign policy concerns. The Department does not believe that it is the role of the courts to "second-guess the executive branch's judgment as to the proper role of comity concerns under these circumstances."[77] To date, no Commission cases have presented the issue of the degree of deference that courts should give to the Commission's comity decisions.[78] It is important also to note that in disputes between private parties, many courts are willing to undertake a comity analysis.

ILLUSTRATIVE EXAMPLE I

Situation: A group of buyers in one foreign country decide that they will agree on the price that they will offer to U.S. suppliers of a particular product. The agreement results in substantial loss of sales and capacity reductions in the United States.

Discussion: From a jurisdictional point of view, the FTAIA standard appears to be satisfied because the effects on U.S. exporters presented here are direct and the percentage of supply accounted for by the buyers' cartel is substantial given the fact that the U.S. suppliers are "major." The Agencies, however, would also take into consideration

---

77. United States v. Baker Hughes, 731 F. Supp. 3, 6 n.5 (D.D.C. 1990), aff'd, 908 F.2d 981 (D.C. Cir. 1990).

78. Like the Department, the Commission considers comity issues and consults with foreign antitrust authorities, but the Commission is not part of the Executive Branch.

the comity aspects presented before deciding whether or not to proceed.

Consistent with their consideration of comity and its obligations under various international agreements, the Agencies would ordinarily notify the antitrust authority in the cartel's home country. If that authority were in a better position to address the competitive problem, and were prepared to take effective action to address the adverse effects on U.S. commerce, the Agencies would consider working cooperatively with the foreign authority or staying their own remedy pending enforcement efforts by the foreign country. In deciding whether to proceed, the Agencies would weigh the factors relating to comity set forth above. Factors weighing in favor of bringing such an action include the substantial and purposeful harm caused by the cartel to the United States. . . .

Questions on U.S. International Enforcement Guidelines

1.   In example A, could the Department of Justice bring even a criminal case against an agreement that was made on foreign soil by foreign firms about the prices they would charge everywhere in the world, including the United States?[22] Does this interfere with the judgment of any foreign nations that have concluded criminal penalties are inappropriate for antitrust violations?

2.   Why should example B be covered by U.S. antitrust law?

a.   If the foreign cartel is selling to an intermediary who doesn't belong to the cartel, isn't any injury to the domestic buyers from that intermediary "indirect"?

b.   For purposes of antitrust standing, U.S. law determines whether an injury is "indirect" by asking functionally whether statutory enforcement would be more vigorous if the claim were concentrated in the hands of a more directly injured party. *See* Chapter 1. Are foreign antitrust enforcement authorities likely to vigorously enforce rules against cartels that affect intermediaries who resell all the product to the United States?

3.   In example B, the guidelines also state that potential harm to U.S. commerce suffices even absent evidence of actual U.S. effects.

a.   Is this a fair reading of the FTAIA? Should the U.S. agencies be exercising antitrust enforcement against such a conspiracy? Does this exception to the need to prove actual effect to U.S. commerce only apply to per se violations?

b.   If substantial U.S. effects must be shown, would that mean that per se rules never apply to foreign agreements?[23]

   i.   Wouldn't an answer of "yes" be inconsistent with the weaker standard used to judge whether there are sufficient effects on interstate commerce to make the federal antitrust laws applicable to a local restraint? Where, as here, the issue is jurisdictional, does it make sense

---

22.   *See* United States v. Nippon Paper Indus., 109 F.3d 1 (1st Cir. 1997) (holding "yes").

23.   *See* Metro Indus. v. Sammi Corp., 82 F.3d 839 (9th Cir. 1996) (holding "yes").

to require the sort of detailed proof of effects the Rule of Reason requires on the merits? Or does it suffice that the restraint is the sort that, if it had anticompetitive effects at all, would be likely to have them in the U.S.?

ii. Even if detailed proof on U.S. effects were required, wouldn't a per se rule still mean that procompetitive justifications cannot be introduced? Or do considerations of international comity require allowing their introduction, especially because they are sometimes allowed in per se cases within the U.S.? See Chapter 2.

c. Even if detailed proof of substantial effects were not required under FTAIA, would it be required under the comity balancing test in any case where foreign interests were conflicting because one cannot determine the weight to give the U.S. effects without knowing how large they are? Is this a good reason not to adopt a balancing test of comity?

4. Suppose a foreign cartel fixes the price of a local product that is consumed entirely within that foreign nation. If the U.S. government is the purchaser that consumes the product within that foreign nation, do the U.S. antitrust laws apply? Why should they? Why shouldn't the same principle apply when a U.S. corporation or citizen is the purchaser who consumes the product in the foreign nation?

5. The guidelines indicate a very open-ended balancing test on comity.

a. Does it make more sense for such an open-ended balancing test to be applied by executive agencies than by the courts? Which is more likely to accurately weigh the foreign policy interests of the United States?

b. Do you agree with the guidelines and the court opinion they cite that, if a U.S. executive agency does bring an action, then a court should automatically conclude that comity is satisfied? Why would a court ever be justified in concluding that it could weigh the comity factors better than the agency?

c. Do your answers to the last two questions change if the enforcing agency is the FTC, which is an independent agency rather than an executive agency?

d. Should a court enforce comity concerns where, as in *Hartford Fire*, a state government has brought a case? Is there any reason to think state governments might reflect U.S. foreign policy interests less well than U.S. government agencies?

F. Hoffmann–La Roche Ltd. v. Empagran S.A.

542 U.S. 155 (2004).

■ Justice Breyer delivered the opinion of the Court.

The Foreign Trade Antitrust Improvements Act of 1982 (FTAIA) excludes from the Sherman Act's reach much anticompetitive conduct that causes only foreign injury. It does so by setting forth a general rule stating that the Sherman Act "shall not apply to conduct involving trade or commerce ... with foreign nations." 15 U.S.C. § 6a. It then creates exceptions to the general rule, applicable where (roughly speaking) that conduct significantly harms imports, domestic commerce, or American exporters.

We here focus upon anticompetitive price-fixing activity that is in significant part foreign, that causes some domestic antitrust injury, and that independently causes separate foreign injury. We ask two questions about the price-fixing conduct and the foreign injury that it causes. First, does that conduct fall within the FTAIA's general rule excluding the Sherman Act's application? That is to say, does the price-fixing activity constitute "conduct involving trade or commerce ... with foreign nations"? We conclude that it does.

Second, we ask whether the conduct nonetheless falls within a domestic-injury exception to the general rule, an exception that applies (and makes the Sherman Act nonetheless applicable) where the conduct (1) has a "direct, substantial, and reasonably foreseeable effect" on domestic commerce, and (2) "such effect gives rise to a [Sherman Act] claim." §§ 6a(1)(A), (2). We conclude that the exception does not apply where the plaintiff's claim rests solely on the independent foreign harm.

To clarify: The issue before us concerns (1) significant foreign anticompetitive conduct with (2) an adverse domestic effect and (3) an independent foreign effect giving rise to the claim. In more concrete terms, this case involves vitamin sellers around the world that agreed to fix prices, leading to higher vitamin prices in the United States and independently leading to higher vitamin prices in other countries such as Ecuador. We conclude that, in this scenario, a purchaser in the United States could bring a Sherman Act claim under the FTAIA based on domestic injury, but a purchaser in Ecuador could not bring a Sherman Act claim based on foreign harm.

I

The plaintiffs in this case originally filed a class-action suit on behalf of foreign and domestic purchasers of vitamins under, *inter alia*, § 1 of the Sherman Act.... Their complaint alleged that petitioners, foreign and domestic vitamin manufacturers and distributors, had engaged in a price-fixing conspiracy, raising the price of vitamin products to customers in the United States and to customers in foreign countries.

... [P]etitioners moved to dismiss the suit as to the *foreign* purchasers (the respondents here), five foreign vitamin distributors located in Ukraine, Australia, Ecuador, and Panama, each of which bought vitamins from petitioners for delivery outside the United States. Respondents have never asserted that they purchased any vitamins in the United States or in transactions in United States commerce, and the question presented assumes that the relevant "transactions occurr[ed] entirely outside U.S. commerce." The District Court dismissed their claims. It applied the FTAIA and found none of the exceptions applicable. Thereafter, the *domestic* purchasers transferred their claims to another pending suit and did not take part in the subsequent appeal.

A divided panel of the Court of Appeals reversed. The panel concluded that the FTAIA's general exclusionary rule applied to the case, but that its domestic-injury exception also applied. It basically read the plaintiffs' complaint to allege that the vitamin manufacturers' price-fixing conspiracy (1) had "a direct, substantial, and reasonably foreseeable effect" on ordinary domestic trade or commerce, *i.e.,* the conspiracy brought about higher domestic vitamin prices, and (2) "such effect" gave "rise to a [Sherman Act] claim," *i.e.,* an injured *domestic* customer could have brought a Sherman Act suit, 15 U.S.C. §§ 6a(1), (2). Those allegations, the court held, are sufficient to meet the exception's requirements.

The court assumed that the foreign effect, *i.e.,* higher prices in Ukraine, Panama, Australia, and Ecuador, was independent of the domestic effect, *i.e.,* higher domestic prices. But it concluded that, in light of the FTAIA's text, legislative history, and the policy goal of deterring harmful price-fixing activity, this lack of connection does not matter. The District of Columbia Circuit denied rehearing *en banc* by a 4–to–3 vote. . . .

II

The FTAIA seeks to make clear to American exporters (and to firms doing business abroad) that the Sherman Act does not prevent them from entering into business arrangements (say, joint-selling arrangements), however anticompetitive, as long as those arrangements adversely affect only foreign markets. It does so by removing from the Sherman Act's reach, (1) export activities and (2) other commercial activities taking place abroad, *unless* those activities adversely affect domestic commerce, imports to the United States, or exporting activities of one engaged in such activities within the United States.

The FTAIA says:

"Sections 1 to 7 of this title [the Sherman Act] shall not apply to conduct involving trade or commerce (other than import trade or import commerce) with foreign nations unless—

"(1) such conduct has a direct, substantial, and reasonably foreseeable effect—

"(A) on trade or commerce which is not trade or commerce with foreign nations [*i.e.,* domestic trade or commerce], or on import trade or import commerce with foreign nations; or

"(B) on export trade or export commerce with foreign nations, of a person engaged in such trade or commerce in the United States [*i.e.,* on an American export competitor]; and

(2) such effect gives rise to a claim under the provisions of sections 1 to 7 of this title, other than this section.

"If sections 1 to 7 of this title apply to such conduct only because of the operation of paragraph (1)(B), then sections 1 to 7 of this title shall apply to such conduct only for injury to export business in the United States." 15 U.S.C. § 6a.

This technical language initially lays down a general rule placing *all* (non-import) activity involving foreign commerce outside the Sherman Act's reach. It then brings such conduct back within the Sherman Act's reach *provided that* the conduct *both* (1) sufficiently affects American commerce, *i.e.,* it has a "direct, substantial, and reasonably foreseeable effect" on American domestic, import, or (certain) export commerce, *and* (2) has an effect of a kind that antitrust law considers harmful, *i.e.,* the "effect" must "giv[e] rise to a [Sherman Act] claim." §§ 6a(1), (2).

We ask here how this language applies to price-fixing activity that is in significant part foreign, that has the requisite domestic effect, and that also has independent foreign effects giving rise to the plaintiff's claim.

III

Respondents make a threshold argument. They say that the transactions here at issue fall outside the FTAIA because the FTAIA's general exclusionary rule applies only to conduct involving exports. The rule says that the Sherman Act "shall not apply to conduct involving trade or commerce (other than import trade or import commerce) *with* foreign nations." § 6a (emphasis added). The word "with" means *between* the United States and foreign nations. And, they contend, commerce between the United States and foreign nations that is not import commerce must consist of export commerce—a kind of commerce irrelevant to the case at hand.

The difficulty with respondents' argument is that the FTAIA originated in a bill that initially referred only to "export trade or export commerce." H.R. 5235, 97th Cong., 1st Sess., § 1 (1981). But the House Judiciary Committee subsequently changed that language to "trade or commerce (other than import trade or import commerce)." 15 U.S.C. § 6a. And it did so deliberately to include commerce that did not involve American exports but which was wholly foreign. . . .

IV

We turn now to the basic question presented, that of the exception's application. Because the underlying antitrust action is complex, potentially raising questions not directly at issue here, we reemphasize that we base our decision upon the following: The price-fixing conduct significantly and adversely affects both customers outside the United States and customers within the United States, but the adverse foreign effect is independent of any adverse domestic effect. In these circumstances, we find that the FTAIA exception does not apply (and thus the Sherman Act does not apply) for two main reasons.

First, this Court ordinarily construes ambiguous statutes to avoid unreasonable interference with the sovereign authority of other nations. This rule of construction reflects principles of customary international law—law that (we must assume) Congress ordinarily seeks to follow. See Restatement (Third) of Foreign Relations Law of the United States §§ 403(1), 403(2) (1986) (hereinafter Restatement) (limiting the unreasonable exercise of prescriptive jurisdiction with respect to a person or activity having connections with another State); *Murray v. Schooner Charming Betsy,* 2 Cranch 64, 118 (1804) ("[A]n act of Congress ought never to be construed to violate the law of nations if any other possible construction remains"); *Hartford Fire* (SCALIA, J., dissenting) (identifying rule of construction as derived from the principle of "prescriptive comity").

This rule of statutory construction cautions courts to assume that legislators take account of the legitimate sovereign interests of other nations when they write American laws. It thereby helps the potentially conflicting laws of different nations work together in harmony—a harmony particularly needed in today's highly interdependent commercial world.

No one denies that America's antitrust laws, when applied to foreign conduct, can interfere with a foreign nation's ability independently to regulate its own commercial affairs. But our courts have long held that application of our antitrust laws to foreign anticompetitive conduct is nonetheless reasonable, and hence consistent with principles of prescriptive comity, insofar as they reflect a legislative effort to redress *domestic* antitrust injury that foreign anticompetitive conduct has caused.

But why is it reasonable to apply those laws to foreign conduct *insofar as that conduct causes independent foreign harm and that foreign harm alone gives rise to the plaintiff's claim?* Like the former case, application of those laws creates a serious risk of interference with a foreign nation's ability independently to regulate its own commercial affairs. But, unlike the former case, the justification for that interference seems insubstantial. See Restatement § 403(2) (determining reasonableness on basis of such factors as connections with regulating nation, harm to that nation's interests, extent to which other nations regulate, and the potential for conflict). Why should American law supplant, for example, Canada's or Great Britain's or Japan's own determination about how best to protect Canadian or British or Japanese customers from anticompetitive conduct engaged in significant part by Canadian or British or Japanese or other foreign companies?

We recognize that principles of comity provide Congress greater leeway when it seeks to control through legislation the actions of *American* companies, see Restatement § 402; and some of the anticompetitive price-fixing conduct alleged here took place in *America.* But the higher foreign prices of which the foreign plaintiffs here complain are not the consequence of any domestic anticompetitive conduct *that Congress sought to forbid,* for Congress did not seek to forbid any such conduct insofar as it is here relevant, *i.e.,* insofar as it is intertwined with foreign conduct that causes independent foreign harm. Rather Congress sought to *release* domestic (and foreign) anticompetitive conduct from Sherman Act constraints when that conduct causes foreign harm. Congress, of course, did make an exception where that conduct also causes domestic harm. See House Report 13, U.S.Code Cong. & Admin.News 1982, 2487, 2498 (concerns about American firms' participation in international cartels addressed through "domestic injury" exception). But any independent domestic harm the foreign conduct causes here has, by definition, little or nothing to do with the matter.

We thus repeat the basic question: Why is it reasonable to apply this law to conduct that is significantly foreign *insofar as that conduct causes independent foreign harm and that foreign harm alone gives rise to the plaintiff's claim?* We can find no good answer to the question.

The Areeda and Hovenkamp treatise notes that under the Court of Appeals' interpretation of the statute "a Malaysian customer could ... maintain an action under United States law in a United States court against its own Malaysian supplier, another cartel member, simply by noting that unnamed third parties injured [in the United States] by the American [cartel member's] conduct would also have a cause of action. Effectively, the United States courts would provide worldwide subject matter jurisdiction to any foreign suitor wishing to sue its own local supplier, but unhappy with its own sovereign's provisions for private antitrust enforcement, provided that a different plaintiff had a cause of action against a different firm for injuries that were within U.S. [other-than-import] commerce. It does not seem excessively rigid to infer that Congress would not have intended that result." P. Areeda & H. Hovenkamp, Antitrust Law ¶ 273, pp. 51–52 (Supp.2003).

We agree with the comment. We can find no convincing justification for the extension of the Sherman Act's scope that it describes.

Respondents reply that many nations have adopted antitrust laws similar to our own, to the point where the practical likelihood of interference with the relevant interests of other nations is minimal. Leaving price fixing to the side, however, this Court has found to the contrary. See, *e.g., Hartford Fire* (noting that the alleged conduct in the London reinsurance market, while illegal under United States antitrust laws, was assumed to be perfectly consistent with British law and policy); see also, *e.g.,* 2 W. Fugate, Foreign Commerce and the Antitrust Laws § 16.6 (5th ed.1996) (noting differences between European Union and United States law on vertical restraints).

Regardless, even where nations agree about primary conduct, say price fixing, they disagree dramatically about appropriate remedies. The application, for example, of American private treble-damages remedies to anticompetitive conduct taking place abroad has generated considerable controversy. And several foreign nations have filed briefs here arguing that to apply our remedies would unjustifiably permit their citizens to bypass their own less generous remedial schemes, thereby upsetting a balance of competing considerations that their own domestic antitrust laws embody. *E.g.,* Brief for Federal Republic of Germany et al. as *Amici Curiae* 2 (setting forth German interest "in seeing that German companies are not subject to the extraterritorial reach of the United States' antitrust laws by private foreign plaintiffs—whose injuries were sustained in transactions entirely outside United States commerce—seeking treble damages in private lawsuits against German companies"); Brief for Government of Canada as *Amicus Curiae* 14 ("treble damages remedy would supersede" Canada's "national policy decision"); Brief for Government of Japan as *Amicus Curiae* 10 (finding "particularly troublesome" the potential "interfere[nce] with Japanese governmental regulation of the Japanese market").

These briefs add that a decision permitting independently injured foreign plaintiffs to pursue private treble-damages remedies would undermine foreign nations' own antitrust enforcement policies by diminishing foreign firms' incentive to cooperate with antitrust authorities in return for prosecutorial amnesty. Brief for Federal Republic of Germany et al. as *Amici Curiae* 28–30; Brief for Government of Canada as *Amicus Curiae* 11–

14. See also Brief for United States as *Amicus Curiae* 19–21 (arguing the same in respect to American antitrust enforcement).

Respondents alternatively argue that comity does not demand an interpretation of the FTAIA that would exclude independent foreign injury cases *across the board.* Rather, courts can take (and sometimes have taken) account of comity considerations case by case, abstaining where comity considerations so dictate. Cf., *e.g., Hartford Fire, supra,* at 797, n. 24.

In our view, however, this approach is too complex to prove workable. The Sherman Act covers many different kinds of anticompetitive agreements. Courts would have to examine how foreign law, compared with American law, treats not only price fixing but also, say, information-sharing agreements, patent-licensing price conditions, territorial product resale limitations, and various forms of joint venture, in respect to both primary conduct and remedy. The legally and economically technical nature of that enterprise means lengthier proceedings, appeals, and more proceedings—to the point where procedural costs and delays could themselves threaten interference with a foreign nation's ability to maintain the integrity of its own antitrust enforcement system. Even in this relatively simple price-fixing case, for example, competing briefs tell us (1) that potential treble-damage liability would help enforce widespread anti-price-fixing norms (through added deterrence) and (2) the opposite, namely that such liability would hinder antitrust enforcement (by reducing incentives to enter amnesty programs). Compare, *e.g.,* Brief for Certain Professors of Economics as *Amici Curiae* 2–4 with Brief for United States as *Amicus Curiae* 19–21. How could a court seriously interested in resolving so empirical a matter—a matter potentially related to impact on foreign interests—do so simply and expeditiously?

We conclude that principles of prescriptive comity counsel against the Court of Appeals' interpretation of the FTAIA. Where foreign anticompetitive conduct plays a significant role and where foreign injury is independent of domestic effects, Congress might have hoped that America's antitrust laws, so fundamental a component of our own economic system, would commend themselves to other nations as well. But, if America's antitrust policies could not win their own way in the international marketplace for such ideas, Congress, we must assume, would not have tried to impose them, in an act of legal imperialism, through legislative fiat.

Second, the FTAIA's language and history suggest that Congress designed the FTAIA to clarify, perhaps to limit, but not *to expand* in any significant way, the Sherman Act's scope as applied to foreign commerce. See House Report 2–3, U.S.Code Cong. & Admin.News 1982, 2487, 2487–2488. And we have found no significant indication that at the time Congress wrote this statute courts would have thought the Sherman Act applicable in these circumstances.

The Solicitor General and petitioners tell us that they have found no case in which any court applied the Sherman Act to redress foreign injury in such circumstances. And respondents themselves apparently conceded as much at a May 23, 2001, hearing before the District Court below.

Nevertheless, respondents now have called to our attention six cases, three decided by this Court and three decided by lower courts. In the first three cases the defendants included both American companies and foreign companies jointly engaged in anticompetitive behavior having both foreign and domestic effects. See *Timken Roller Bearing Co. v. United States,* 341 U.S. 593, 595 (1951) (agreements among American, British, and French corporations to eliminate competition in the manufacture and sale of anti-friction bearings in world, including United States, markets); *United States v. National Lead Co.,* 332 U.S. 319, 325–328 (1947) (international cartels with American and foreign members, restraining international commerce, including United States commerce, in titanium pigments); *United States v. American Tobacco Co.,* 221 U.S. 106, 171–172 (1911) (American tobacco corporations agreed in England with British company to divide world markets). In all three cases the plaintiff sought relief, including relief that might have helped to protect those injured abroad.

In all three cases, however, the plaintiff was the Government of the United States. A Government plaintiff, unlike a private plaintiff, must seek to obtain the relief necessary to protect the public from further anticompetitive conduct and to redress anticompetitive harm. And a Government plaintiff has legal authority broad enough to allow it to carry out this mission. Private plaintiffs, by way of contrast, are far less likely to be able to secure broad relief. This difference means that the Government's ability, in these three cases, to obtain relief helpful to those injured abroad tells us little or nothing about whether this Court would have awarded similar relief at the request of private plaintiffs.

Neither did the Court focus explicitly in its opinions on a claim that the remedies sought to cure only independently caused foreign harm. Thus the three cases tell us even less about whether this Court then thought that foreign private plaintiffs could have obtained foreign relief based solely upon such independently caused foreign injury.

Respondents also refer to three lower court cases brought by private plaintiffs. In the first, *Industria Siciliana Asfalti, Bitumi, S.p.A. v. Exxon Research & Engineering Co.,* 1977 WL 1353 (S.D.N.Y., Jan. 18, 1977), a District Court permitted an Italian firm to proceed against an American firm with a Sherman Act claim based upon a purely foreign injury, *i.e.,* an injury suffered in Italy. The court made clear, however, that the foreign injury was *"inextricably bound up with ... domestic restraints of trade,"* and that the plaintiff *"was injured ... by reason of an alleged restraint of our domestic trade,"* id., at *11, *12 (emphasis added), *i.e.,* the foreign injury was dependent upon, *not independent of,* domestic harm.

In the second case, *Dominicus Americana Bohio v. Gulf & Western Industries, Inc.,* 473 F.Supp. 680 (S.D.N.Y.1979), a District Court permitted Dominican and American firms to proceed against a competing American firm and the Dominican Tourist Information Center with a Sherman Act claim based upon injury apparently suffered in the Dominican Republic. The court, in finding the Sherman Act applicable, weighed several different factors, including the participation of American firms in the unlawful conduct, the partly domestic nature of both conduct and harm (to American tourists, a kind of "export"), and the fact that the domestic harm depended in part upon the foreign injury. *Id.,* at 688. The court did not separately analyze the legal problem before it in terms of independently caused foreign injury. Its opinion simply does not discuss the matter. It consequently cannot be taken as significant support for application of the Sherman Act here.

The third case, *Hunt v. Mobil Oil Corp.,* 550 F.2d 68, 72 (C.A.2 1977), . . . was about the "act of state" doctrine.

The upshot is that no pre–1982 case provides significant authority for application of the Sherman Act in the circumstances we here assume. Indeed, a leading contemporaneous lower court case contains language suggesting the contrary. See *Timberlane Lumber Co. v. Bank of America,* 549 F.2d 597, 613 (C.A.9 1976) (insisting that the foreign conduct's domestic effect be "sufficiently large to present a cognizable injury *to the plaintiffs*" (emphasis added)).

Taken together, these two sets of considerations, the one derived from comity and the other reflecting history, convince us that Congress would not have intended the FTAIA's exception to bring independently caused foreign injury within the Sherman Act's reach.

V

Respondents point to several considerations that point the other way. For one thing, the FTAIA's language speaks in terms of the Sherman Act's *applicability* to certain kinds of *conduct.* The FTAIA says that the Sherman Act applies to foreign "conduct" with a certain kind of harmful domestic effect. Why isn't that the end of the matter? How can the Sherman Act both *apply to the conduct* when one person sues but *not apply to the same conduct* when another person sues? The question of who can or cannot sue is a matter for other statutes (namely, the Clayton Act) to determine.

Moreover, the exception says that it applies if the conduct's domestic effect gives rise to "*a claim,*" not to "*the plaintiff's claim*" or "*the claim at issue.*" 15 U.S.C. § 6a(2) (emphasis added). The alleged conduct here did have domestic effects, and those effects were harmful enough to give rise to "a" claim. Respondents concede that this claim is not their own claim; it is someone else's claim. But, linguistically speaking, they say, that is beside the point. Nor did Congress place the relevant words "gives rise to a claim" in the FTAIA to suggest any geographical limitation; rather it did so for a here neutral reason, namely, in order to make clear that the domestic effect must be an *adverse* (as opposed to a beneficial) effect. See House Report 11, U.S.Code Cong. & Admin.News 1982, 2487, 2496.

Despite their linguistic logic, these arguments are not convincing. Linguistically speaking, a statute can apply and not apply to the same conduct, depending upon other circumstances; and those other circumstances may include the nature of the lawsuit (or of the related underlying harm). It also makes linguistic sense to read the words "a claim" as if they refer to the "plaintiff's claim" or "the claim at issue."

At most, respondents' linguistic arguments might show that respondents' reading is the more natural reading of the statutory language. But those arguments do not show that we *must* accept that reading. And that is the critical point. The considerations previously mentioned—those of comity and history—make clear that the respondents' reading is not consistent with the FTAIA's basic intent. If the statute's language reasonably permits an interpretation consistent with that intent, we should adopt it. And, for the reasons stated, we believe that the statute's language permits the reading that we give it.

Finally, respondents point to policy considerations that we have previously discussed, namely, that application of the Sherman Act in present circumstances will (through increased deterrence) help protect Americans against foreign-caused anticompetitive injury. As we have explained, however, the plaintiffs and supporting enforcement-agency *amici* have made important experience-backed arguments (based upon amnesty-seeking incentives) to the contrary. We cannot say whether, on balance, respondents' side of this empirically based argument or the enforcement agencies' side is correct. But we can say that the answer to the dispute is neither clear enough, nor of such likely empirical significance, that it could overcome the considerations we have previously discussed and change our conclusion.

For these reasons, we conclude that petitioners' reading of the statute's language is correct. That reading furthers the statute's basic purposes, it properly reflects considerations of comity, and it is consistent with Sherman Act history.

VI

We have assumed that the anticompetitive conduct here independently caused foreign injury; that is, the conduct's domestic effects did not help to bring about that foreign injury. Respondents argue, in the alternative, that the foreign injury was not independent. Rather, they say, the anticompetitive conduct's domestic effects were linked to that foreign harm. Respondents contend that, because vitamins are fungible and readily transportable, without an adverse domestic effect (*i.e.*, higher prices in the United States), the sellers could not have maintained their international price-fixing arrangement and respondents would not have suffered their foreign injury. They add that this "but for" condition is sufficient to bring the price-fixing conduct within the scope of the FTAIA's exception.

The Court of Appeals, however, did not address this argument, and, for that reason, neither shall we. Respondents remain free to ask the Court of Appeals to consider the claim. The Court of Appeals may determine whether respondents properly preserved the argument, and, if so, it may consider it and decide the related claim.

For these reasons, the judgment of the Court of Appeals is vacated, and the case is remanded for further proceedings consistent with this opinion. *It is so ordered.*

Note and Questions on *Empagran*

While *Hartford Fire* holds that U.S. antitrust law applies to remedy the U.S. effects of extraterritorial conduct (subject to comity limits), *Empagran* holds that U.S. antitrust law does not apply to remedy the independent foreign effects of that same conduct. Because *Empagran* justifies its decision with the comity canon against interpreting statutory ambiguities to unreasonably interfere with the regulatory authority of foreign nations, it confirms that *Hartford Fire* did not hold that the only comity limit was when foreign law compelled conduct in violation of U.S. antitrust law, but rather held that this was the only comity issue raised in that case. *Empagran* also indicates a willingness to apply comity principles not just case-by-case but to reach a general statutory interpretation.

The big issue *Empagran* did not resolve was what to do when the foreign effects are not independent of the U.S. effects. The appellate courts have so far held that the requisite causal link between the foreign and U.S. effects was not "but for" causation but rather "proximate" causation.[24] More controversially, the appellate courts have concluded that the causal link is not proximate when a foreign plaintiff offers to prove that the existence of a global market meant that fixing U.S. prices was necessary to fix the foreign prices paid by the foreign plaintiff. On the other hand, at least one district court has held that the causal link *is* proximate if the foreign plaintiff argues that the fixing of foreign prices caused an increase in U.S. prices,[25] and other cases have held that this holding is consistent with the circuit court holdings.[26] The apparent distinction is that causation is not deemed proximate when the foreign effects are alleged to be the *result* of fixing U.S. price but is deemed proximate when the foreign price-fixing is alleged to be the *means* for the U.S. effects. But if so, any restriction could be avoided by careful pleading because, in any global market, one could allege that anticompetitive foreign price effects caused U.S. effects just as easily as alleging that anticompetitive U.S. effects caused foreign effects. Or perhaps the district court holding will ultimately be overruled, and courts will hold that, where the only causal link comes from the reality that international markets make prices in one nation depend on prices in another nation, the foreign effects must be remedied under foreign law, with the U.S. effects remedied under U.S. law.

1. Should a foreign plaintiff be able to bring a U.S. antitrust claim if it can show that an anticompetitive effect in the U.S. was necessary to cause its foreign injury?

2. If the properly defined geographic market is global, won't it always be the case that foreign prices cannot be increased unless domestic prices are raised given that such a global market definition means foreign and domestic sales must be reasonably interchangeable?

3. Would it be a bad thing if any global price-fixing cartel could be challenged in a single global class action in the U.S. courts?

a. Wouldn't that be an efficient way to adjudicate global price-fixing conspiracies? Isn't the relevant activity in such a case the global price-fixing agreement rather than the individual sales in particular nations?

---

24. See Empagran S.A. v. F. Hoffman–LaRoche, Ltd., 417 F.3d 1267 (D.C. Cir. 2005); In re Monosodium Glutamate Antitrust Litig., 477 F.3d 535, 539–40 (8th Cir.2007); In re Dynamic Random Access Memory (DRAM) Antitrust Litig., 546 F.3d 981, 987 (9th Cir.2008).

25. See MM Global Servs. v. Dow Chem. Co., 329 F.Supp.2d 337 (D.Conn.2004).

26. *In re DRAM Antitrust Litig.*, 546 F.3d at 989 n.9; In re Hydrogen Peroxide Antitrust Litigation, 702 F.Supp.2d 548 (E.D. Pa.2010); Latino Quimica–Amtex S.A. v. Akzo Nobel Chem. B.V., 2005 WL 2207017, at *13 (S.D.N.Y.2005).

b. Would such a global class action interfere with foreign antitrust laws that have decided on different remedies than private treble damage suits? With foreign nation's decisions to settle or seek different sorts of injunctive relief for harm to their nation's consumers than the U.S. court might order?

4. If foreign plaintiffs could bring U.S. antitrust claims whenever they can show their injury depends on anticompetitive effects in the United States, wouldn't they be able to bring U.S. antitrust claims whenever any conduct (not just cartels) anticompetitively affected a global market?

a. Would that be an efficient way to resolve global misconduct?

b. Might that interfere with foreign antitrust laws that differ from U.S. antitrust law on whether the relevant conduct is considered anticompetitive?

5. If the U.S. claimed jurisdiction over all global anticompetitive effects on the grounds that they are necessarily linked to U.S. effects, couldn't every foreign nation equally claim global jurisdiction that included the U.S. effects because any U.S. effects could not have resulted unless foreign prices were increased?

6. Is the statutory language requiring that the requisite U.S. "effect gives rise to a claim under" U.S. antitrust law sufficiently ambiguous to allow an interpretation that precludes claims of foreign injuries that depend on U.S. effects? The Supreme Court above held that "a claim" could be understood to mean "the plaintiff's claim." Could one also reasonably interpret the language to mean that in a case of joint causation, where both U.S. and foreign effects were necessary to create global effects, the U.S. effects do not "give rise" to the foreign claim? Could one reasonably interpret the language the other way?

7. If the statutory language could be read either way, should the issue be resolved by:

a. the statutory default rule against interpretations that may interfere with the regulatory authority of foreign nations? Why not instead rely on the case-by-case application of comity principles to deal with that concern?

b. the Congressional purpose not to greatly expand the extraterritorial scope of the Sherman Act coupled by the dearth of prior cases interpreting it to apply to such linked foreign claims? Was there much caselaw either way on this issue? Doesn't this likely reflect the fact that markets were less global in the past?

c. whether the plaintiff is the U.S. government?

    i. Is this because a decision by the U.S. government to sue means it has weighed any effects on foreign relations in a way that should bind the courts? Is this consistent with the Court's reading that the connection to U.S. effects is necessary under the FTAIA?

    ii. Or is this relevant only to the extent that the U.S. government only seeks to remedy U.S. effects?

8. Suppose the correct interpretation is, where conduct causes anti-competitive effects on a global market, each nation's antitrust law states the relevant legal rules that can remedy harms caused in that nation.

a. Won't international conflicts still arise if:

i. one nation orders injunctive relief that varies with that ordered by another nation?

ii. one nation prohibits or deters conduct that another nation deems procompetitive and desirable?

iii. one nation uses sanctions like treble damages or criminal punishment that other nations deem excessively overdeterring of desirable conduct that might mistakenly be thought anticompetitive?

b. Should such potential interferences with the regulatory authority of foreign nations suggest that each nation's antitrust laws should be deemed inapplicable to global anticompetitive conduct? Wouldn't this leave global anticompetitive conduct completely unregulated? Is it likely each nation would want that given the harm it suffers from global anticompetitive effects?

c. Is the case-by-case application of comity principles sufficient to avoid such interferences with the regulatory authority of foreign nations? If so, why aren't they sufficient to avoid them if U.S. antitrust laws were deemed to reach all global anticompetitive effects?

d. Couldn't plaintiffs still bring all global claims into a single U.S. lawsuit because a district court with jurisdiction over the U.S. claims against conduct affecting a global market could take supplemental jurisdiction over the foreign antitrust claims under 28 U.S.C. § 1367?

i. Where the effects are on a global market, wouldn't the U.S. and foreign claims all be sufficiently related to be part of the same case or controversy?

ii. Would having a U.S. court adjudicate claims to remedy foreign harms based on foreign competition law interfere with international relations?

9. If global anticompetitive effects must be separated into the harms caused in each nation and then remedied separately by each nation's antitrust laws, won't this disadvantage small nations that may lack the necessary expertise or access to the relevant evidence?

a. Won't underenforcement by small nations lead to underdeterrence of global cartels by increasing the profit-liability ratio experienced by cartelists? Isn't this particularly important given the difficulty of detecting and punishing global cartels?

b. Won't any underdeterrence of global cartels harm U.S. consumers?

c. Could any doctrine about anticompetitive conduct affecting global markets be limited to cartels or would it have to extend to more ambiguous conduct where overdeterrence concerns may be as significant as underdeterrence?

10. Is the best solution to have a global antitrust court to adjudicate any conduct alleged to have anticompetitive effects on a global market?

11. Suppose producers in a small Caribbean Island nation decide to fix the prices of some souvenir that is sold within that nation but bought 80% by U.S. tourists.

a. Could the U.S. tourists bring a U.S. antitrust claim against the souvenir cartel? Would this souvenir cartel amount to a restraint on imports because the tourists bring the souvenirs back?

b. If instead the Caribbean cartel fixed the prices of margaritas that were 80% purchased by U.S. tourists who consumed them while on the island, would there be a U.S. antitrust claim? Would this still amount to a restraint on something imported to U.S. purchasers?

c. If instead the Caribbean cartel fixed the prices of hotel rooms that were 80% occupied by U.S. tourists, would U.S. antitrust law apply? Would the answer turn on whether the hotels were advertised within the United States and reserved from there?

Background on the Extraterritorial Application of EU Competition Law

Substantive Reach. In conformity with public international law principles, the EU competition regime follows a system of "territorial jurisdiction."[27] The wording of the TFEU requires, for both Article 101 and 102 to apply, that the conduct at hand "has an impact within the common market." A similar condition is included in the EU merger regulation, which only applies to mergers between companies that achieve a given level of turnover within the EU.[28] Anticompetitive practices of non-European firms may thus fall within the reach of EU competition law to the extent that they produce an impact within the EU.

The apparent analogy between this approach and U.S. law is, however, not complete. Instead of proclaiming a U.S.-like "effects doctrine", the EU courts initially showed reluctance to apply competition rules to non European firms on the sole basis that their conduct had an effect within the EU. Rather, the first pronouncements of the ECJ rested on a material link between the non-EU company and the EU territory. The 1972 *Dyestuffs* judgment, in which the ECJ introduced the so-called *single economic unit* doctrine, is illustrative of that approach. In that case, the ECJ was asked to rule on an application for annulment against a Commission decision imposing fines on non-EU companies which had—together with EU companies—entered into illicit price fixing practices within the EU. In its decision, the Commission had concluded that the showing of an effect on the EC territory was sufficient to apply Article 101 to firms located outside Europe. ICI, a firm located in the United Kingdom (at the time not a Member State of the EU), appealed the Commission's decision. It sought, *inter alia*, to contest the Commission's jurisdiction. In his opinion, Advo-

---

27. See the famous *Lotus* case, Permanent Court of International Justice, 7 September 1927, Series A. NĖ10.

28. See Recital 10 of the ECMR which states that it is applicable to companies "irrespective of whether or not the undertakings effecting the concentration have their seat or their principal fields of activity in the Community, provided they have substantial operations there."

cate General Mayras supported the application of a U.S.-like "effects doctrine" insofar as the effects within the EU were direct and immediate, reasonably foreseeable and substantial.[29] The Court managed to escape tackling this issue by observing that the conduct had an impact within the EU because the price increase decisions of ICI were implemented in the EU through an EU subsidiary that it actively controlled.

In later cases under Article 82, the Court followed a similar approach. In *Continental Can v. Commission,* the Court found the U.S. company Continental Can guilty of an abuse of a dominant position.[30] Europemballage, its European subsidiary, had as a result of the acquisition of a competitor, eliminated all competition on the packaging markets. As a result of the structural links existing between Europemballage and Continental Can, the Court applied the single economic unit doctrine to uphold the fine imposed on the latter.

The question whether firms not located within the EU could be held guilty of infringing EU competition rules simply on the basis that their conduct produced effects in the Community arose again in the *Wood Pulp* case. In a decision adopted in 1987, the Commission found that forty wood pulp producers and three of their trade associations had infringed Article 101 TFEU by concerting on prices for bleached sulphate pulp sold within the EU territory. These producers were established outside the Community. They exported in the EU either directly to purchasers within the Community or were doing business through branches, subsidiaries, agencies or other establishments in the Community. Several wood pulp producers appealed the Commission decision before the ECJ on the ground that the Commission lacked territorial jurisdiction to apply Article 101 to them.

The ECJ again declined to apply the "effects doctrine", in spite of the support of the Commission and Advocate General Darmon.[31] Rather, the *Wood Pulp* Court relied on what has since then been called the "implementation doctrine." The fact that a cartel agreement is implemented on the EU territory is sufficient to trigger the jurisdiction of EU competition rules. In adopting this judgment, the Court extended the territorial reach further than allowed under the *single economic unit* doctrine. Non–European firms can be held liable of an infringement to Article 101 absent any subsidiary, agents, sub-agents or branches in the EU. However, the implementation doctrine seems to require that the companies in question have taken affirmative steps to market products within the EU. There are thus doubts as to whether non-European firms engaged in collective refusals to sell to the EU territory (including perhaps as part of a horizontal market division) can be brought within the ambit of Article 101. These firms are (by hypothesis) not implementing any commercial practice within the EU. Former Advocate General Van Gerven, for instance, concludes that this distinguishes the implementation doctrine from the effects doctrine known

---

29. See Opinion of Advocate General Mayras in *ICI & others v. Commission,* ECR [1972] 619.

30. See ECJ, 6/72, *Europemballage Corporation and Continental Can Company v. Commission,* ECR [1973] 215.

31. See Opinion of Mr. Advocate General Darmon delivered on 25 May 1988, A. *Ahlström Osakeyhtiö and others v. Commission,* ECR [1988] 5193 at § 58.

under U.S. law.[32] Other authors in contrast tend to include that any refusal to sell that creates a competitive restriction within the EU territory can be deemed to be implemented in the EU.[33]

Comity limits and non-interference principles. The origins of the so-called comity principle are found in public international law. Pursuant to this principle (sometimes labeled "non interference" principle), competition authorities undertaking enforcement action against an anticompetitive practice have to take due account of other countries' important interests.[34] This principle thus places some limits to the scope for intervention of a competition authority.[35] In practice, a direct implication of the comity principle is that antitrust agencies contemplating enforcement action have to take due account of the enforcement steps already taken by other agencies elsewhere in the world. However, the scope of the comity principle is not limited to the antitrust enforcement initiatives of third countries. The "important interests" of third countries indeed encompass all sorts of strategic issues. In the *Boeing/McDonnell–Douglas* merger, for instance, the Commission took into account the U.S. government concerns with respect to "important U.S. defence interests."[36]

Traditionally, the Commission has shown deference to the comity principle when asserting its jurisdiction over international anti-competitive practices. In its Eleventh Annual Report on Competition Policy, the Commission for instance observed that "active cooperation between the authorities concerned should iron out certain difficulties and at the same time help maintain fair competition in the interest of the continuing growth of international trade".[37]

However, on several occasions, the Commission, the ECJ and the GC have also stressed that the comity principle would only apply in a narrow set of exceptional circumstances. In *Aluminium imports from Eastern Europe*,[38] the Commission examined the application of the comity principle to the commercial conduct of the foreign trade organization of the USSR, Poland, Hungary, Czechoslovakia and the German Democratic Republic. It held that:

---

32. See Walter Van Gerven, "EC Jurisdiction in Antitrust Matters: The Wood Pulp Judgement," in Barry E. Hawk, ed., 1989 Annual Proceedings of the Fordham Corporate Law Institute International Law and Policy Conference (New York: Fordham Corporate Law Institute, 1990), pp. 451–467.

33. See Michel Waelbroeck et Aldo Frignani, Commentaire J. Mégret, Droit de la CE, Volume 4, Concurrence, Editions de l'Université Libre de Bruxelles, 2ème Edition, 1997, p. 89.

34. See M. Janow, Antitrust Goes Global, Brookings Institution, 2000, at p. 33.

35. See OECD, CLP Report on Positive Comity, DAFFE/CLP(99)19, 6–7 May 1999 at § 16 speaking of a "principle of voluntary abstention".

36. See Commission Decision, of 30 July 1997, Boeing/McDonnell–Douglas, Case No. IV/1.877.

37. See XIth Report on Competition Policy, at § 37. In its Fourteenth Annual Report, the Commission further mentioned cases where it had consulted third countries authorities to "ensure that proposed decisions did not affect important interests of the countries and, possibly, to look for mutually acceptable compromises." See XIVth Report on Competition Policy, at § 21.

38. See Commission Decision 85/206/EEC of 19 December 1984, IV/26.870—Aluminium imports from eastern Europe, O.J. L 92 of 30 March 1985, pp. 1–76.

"... There is no prohibitive rule of international law which prevents the application of Community law to all the participants in the [relevant] arrangements. Moreover there are no reasons of comity which militate in favour of self restraint in the exercise of jurisdiction by the Commission. The exercise of jurisdiction by the Commission does not require any of the undertakings concerned to act in any way contrary to the requirements of their domestic laws, nor would the application of Community law adversely affect important interests of a non-member State. Such an interest would have to be so important as to prevail over the fundamental interest of the Community that competition within the common market is not distorted ..., for that is an essential means under the Treaty for achieving the objectives of the Community."

A similar restrictive approach to the comity principle was used in the *Wood Pulp* and *Gencor* cases excerpted below.

Imperial Chemical Industries Ltd. v. Commission of the European Communities *(Dyestuffs)*, Case 48–69

ECR 1972 [619] (ECJ).

... The applicant, whose registered office is outside the Community, argues that the Commission is not empowered to impose fines on it by reason merely of the effects produced in the Common Market by actions which it is alleged to have taken outside the Community.

Since a concerted practice is involved, it is first necessary to ascertain whether the conduct of the applicant has had effects within the Common Market.... [T]he increases at issue were put into effect within the Common Market and concerned competition between producers operating within it. Therefore the actions for which the fine at issue has been imposed constitute practices carried on directly within the Common Market. ... [T]he applicant company decided on increases in the selling prices of its products to users in the Common Market, and that these increases were of a uniform nature in line with increases decided upon by the other producers involved.

By making use of its power to control its subsidiaries established in the Community, the applicant was able to ensure that its decision was implemented on that market. The applicant objects that this conduct is to be imputed to its subsidiaries and not to itself. The fact that a subsidiary has separate legal personality is not sufficient to exclude the possibility of imputing its conduct to the parent company. Such may be the case in particular where the subsidiary, although having separate legal personality, does not decide independently upon its own conduct on the market, but carries out, in all material respects, the instructions given to it by the parent company. Where a subsidiary does not enjoy real autonomy in determining its course of action in the market, the prohibitions set out in Article [101(1)] may be considered inapplicable in the relationship between it and the parent company with which it forms one economic unit. In view of the unity of the group thus formed, the actions of the subsidiaries may in certain circumstances be attributed to the parent company.

It is well-known that at the time the applicant held all or at any rate the majority of the shares in those subsidiaries. The applicant was able to exercise decisive influence over the policy of the subsidiaries as regards selling prices in the Common Market and in fact used this power upon the occasion of the three price increases in question. In effect the telex messages relating to the 1964 increase, which the applicant sent to its subsidiaries in the common market, gave the addressees orders as to the prices which they were to charge and the other conditions of sale which they were to apply in dealing with their customers. In the absence of evidence to the contrary, it must be assumed that on the occasion of the increases of 1965 and 1967 the applicant acted in a similar fashion in its relations with its subsidiaries established in the Common Market.

In the circumstances the formal separation between these companies, resulting from their separate legal personality, cannot outweigh the unity of their conduct on the market for the purposes of applying the rules on competition. It was in fact the applicant undertaking which brought the concerted practice into being within the Common Market.

The submission as to lack of jurisdiction raised by the applicant must therefore be declared to be unfounded. . . .

A. Ahlström Osakeyhtiö and Others v. Commission of the European Communities (Wood Pulp), joined Cases 89, 104, 114, 116, 117 and 125 to 129/85

27 September 1988, ECR, [1988] 5193 (ECJ).

. . . [Th]e applicants which have made submissions regarding jurisdiction maintain first of all that by applying the [EU]competition rules to them the Commission has misconstrued the territorial scope of Article [101]. They note that in *Dyestuffs* . . . the Court did not adopt the "effects doctrine" but emphasized that the case involved conduct restricting competition within the common market because of the activities of subsidiaries which could be imputed to the parent companies. The applicants add that even if there is a basis in Community law for applying Article [101] to them, the action of applying the rule interpreted in that way would be contrary to public international law which precludes any claim by the Community to regulate conduct restricting competition adopted outside the territory of the Community merely by reason of the economic repercussions which that conduct produces within the Community.

The applicants which are members of the KEA further submit that the application of Community competition rules to them is contrary to public international law in so far as it is in breach of the principle of non-interference. They maintain that in this case the application of Article [101] harmed the interest of the United States in promoting exports by United States undertakings as recognized in the Webb Pomerene Act of 1918 under which export associations, like the KEA, are exempt from United States anti-trust laws.

Certain Canadian applicants also maintain that by imposing fines on them and making reduction of those fines conditional on the producers giving undertakings as to their future conduct the Commission has infringed Canada's sovereignty and thus breached the principle of international comity.

The Finnish applicants [(at the time, Finland was not a Member State of the EU)] consider that in any event it is only the rules on competition contained in the Free Trade Agreement between the Community and Finland that may be applied to their conduct, to the exclusion of Article [101 TFEU], and that the Community should therefore have consulted Finland on the measures which it envisaged adopting regarding the agreement in question in accordance with the procedure provided for in Article 27 of that agreement. . . .

Incorrect assessment of the territorial scope of Article [101] TFEU and incompatibility of the decision with public international law

. . . Article [101] . . . prohibits all agreements between undertakings and concerted practices which may affect trade between Member States and which have as their object or effect the restriction of competition within the common market.

. . . [T]he main sources of supply of wood pulp are outside the Community, in Canada, the United States, Sweden and Finland and . . . the market therefore has global dimensions. Where wood pulp producers established in those countries sell directly to purchasers established in the Community and engage in price competition in order to win orders from those customers, that constitutes competition within the common market.

It follows that where those producers concert on the prices to be charged to their customers in the Community and put that concertation into effect by selling at prices which are actually coordinated, they are taking part in concertation which has the object and effect of restricting competition within the common market within the meaning of Article [101 TFEU].

Accordingly, it must be concluded that by applying the [EU] competition rules in the circumstances of this case to undertakings whose registered offices are situated outside the Community, the Commission has not made an incorrect assessment of the territorial scope of Article [101].

The applicants have submitted that the decision is incompatible with public international law on the grounds that the application of the competition rules in this case was founded exclusively on the economic repercussions within the common market of conduct restricting competition which was adopted outside the Community.

It should be observed that an infringement of Article [101], such as the conclusion of an agreement which has had the effect of restricting competition within the common market, consists of conduct made up of two elements, the formation of the agreement, decision or concerted practice and the implementation thereof. If the applicability of prohibitions laid down under competition law were made to depend on the place where the agreement, decision or concerted practice was formed, the result would obviously be to give undertakings an easy means of evading those prohibitions. The decisive factor is therefore the place where it is implemented.

The producers in this case implemented their pricing agreement within the common market. It is immaterial in that respect whether or not they had recourse to subsidiaries, agents, sub-agents, or branches within the Community in order to make their contacts with purchasers within the Community. Accordingly the Community's jurisdiction to apply its competition rules to such conduct is covered by the territoriality principle as universally recognized in public international law ...

[The Court also rejected the argument that imposing fines on non EU firms was a breach of international comity with the following analysis.] As regards the argument based on the infringement of the principle of non-interference, it should be pointed out that the applicants who are members of KEA have referred to a rule according to which where two States have jurisdiction to lay down and enforce rules and the effect of those rules is that a person finds himself subject to contradictory orders as to the conduct he must adopt, each State is obliged to exercise its jurisdiction with moderation. The applicants have concluded that by disregarding that rule in applying its competition rules the Community has infringed the principle of non-interference.

There is no need to enquire into the existence in international law of such a rule since it suffices to observe that the conditions for its application are in any event not satisfied. There is not, in this case, any contradiction between the conduct required by the United States and that required by the Community since the Webb Pomerene Act merely exempts the conclusion of export cartels from the application of United States anti-trust laws but does not require such cartels to be concluded.

It should further be pointed out that the United States authorities raised no objections regarding any conflict of jurisdiction when consulted by the Commission pursuant to the OECD Council Recommendation of 25 October 1979 concerning Cooperation between Member Countries on Restrictive Business Practices affecting International Trade (Acts of the Organization, Vol. 19, p. 376).

As regards the argument relating to disregard of international comity, it suffices to observe that it amounts to calling in question the Community's jurisdiction to apply its competition rules to conduct such as that found to exist in this case and that, as such, that argument has already been rejected. Accordingly it must be concluded that the Commission's decision is not contrary to Article [101 TFEU] or to the rules of public international law relied on by the applicants.

Questions on *Dyestuffs and Wood Pulp*

1. Why was the ECJ so afraid to recognize the "effects doctrine" in these cases?

a. Wouldn't that be a simpler and clearer approach?

b. Wouldn't recognition of the effects doctrine allow the Commission to extend the jurisdiction of EU competition law? What are the benefits and downsides of such an extension of jurisdiction?

c. Would recognizing the effects doctrine violate international law? Why, then, were Advocate Generals Mayras and Darmon in favor of recognizing this doctrine?

d. Do the early EU cases resemble the early history of U.S. extraterritorial application of antitrust law, which required some conduct by the defendant or its agents within the United States even though that conduct might not be central to the violation?

2. From an enforcement standpoint, what is the added value of the "implementation" doctrine (*Wood Pulp*) in comparison to the *single economic unit* doctrine (*Dyestuffs*)?

3. Does the "implementation" doctrine reach any case the effects doctrine reaches? Does it allow EU competition rules to catch all anticompetitive behaviors conceived in foreign jurisdictions?

4. Suppose U.S. and EU producers of widgets decided to divide the worldwide market so that U.S. producers sold only in the U.S. and EU producers sold only in the EU.

a. Would this horizontal market division likely have anticompetitive effects in the U.S. and EU?

b. Would the U.S. producers be engaged in any conduct within the EU that implements this market division? Would they thus be immune from suit under the implementation doctrine?

c. Would the agreement of the EU producers to sell only within the EU cause any anticompetitive harm within the EU? Doesn't that agreement, standing alone, only increase EU output and advance EU consumer welfare? Isn't the real harm to the EU caused by the agreement by U.S. producers not to sell in the EU?

5. Does the comity analysis in *Wood Pulp* resemble that used by the U.S. Supreme Court in *Hartford Fire*?

The Application of EU Merger Law to Foreign Firms

In the field of merger control, extraterritoriality has also been an issue of debate. Pursuant to the EU Merger Regulation, only those concentrations that have a "Community dimension" fall within the regulatory oversight of the Commission.[39] In order to determine whether a merger has a Community dimension, the Regulation provides a set of Community turnover thresholds relating to "products sold or services provided to undertakings or consumers in the Community of a Member State."[40] Therefore, a merger between non-EU firms that both achieve a European turnover in excess of the thresholds will undisputably fall within the purview of the EU merger regulation, irrespective of whether they have

---

39. See Article 1 of the EU Merger Regulation.

40. Id. at Article 5(1).

subsidiaries or branches in Europe. This explains why the Merger Regulation has been applied to mergers between U.S. firms in the *Boeing/McDonnell–Douglas* and *General Electric/Honeywell* cases,[41] or between South African companies in the *Gencor/Lonrho* decision.[42] In the latter case, the Commission opposed the merger of two companies incorporated in South Africa. The companies challenged the Commission's jurisdiction before the General Court.

Gencor Ltd v. Commission

T–102/96 ECR, [1999] II–753 (CFI).

... The applicant submits, as its main argument, that the [Merger Control] Regulation does not confer jurisdiction on the Commission to examine the compatibility of the concentration with the common market. In the alternative, if the Regulation does confer such jurisdiction, it is unlawful and therefore inapplicable pursuant to Article [277 TFEU]. The Regulation was not applicable to the concentration at issue since it related to economic activities conducted within the territory of a non-member country, the Republic of South Africa, and had been approved by the authorities of that country. The Regulation applies only to concentrations carried out within the Community. That analysis is consistent with the principle of territoriality, a general principle of public international law which the Community must observe in the exercise of its powers. *Wood Pulp*....

The applicant explains that its analysis does not mean that the Regulation can apply only to concentrations between undertakings established in the Community. It is in fact not so much the place of establishment of the undertakings concerned which matters, but rather the place or places where the concentration is carried out. The applicant relies in that regard on *Continental Can*, in which the Court of Justice held that the Commission was competent to apply Article [102 TFEU] to a concentration effected by an undertaking located outside the Community since the case concerned the acquisition of an interest in a Community undertaking. The Regulation is thus applicable only if the activities forming the subject-matter of the concentration are located within the Community. More particularly, ..., it applies to undertakings which have substantial operations in the Community. In the instant case, the location of the concentration notified to the Commission is South Africa, where the undertakings carrying it out have their main field of activity, namely the mining and refining of PGMs [Platinum Group Metals]. Neither the fact that Lonrho has a subsidiary with an office in the Community through which it sells its entire PGM production nor the fact that it carries on other activities in the Community in the hotel and general trading fields means that it can be considered to have substantial operations in the Community within the meaning of the 11th recital in the preamble....

---

41. See Commission decision of 30 July 1997, *Boeing/McDonnell–Douglas*, Case No IV/M.877; Commission Decision of 3 July 2001, *General Electric/Honeywell*, Case COMP/M.2220.

42. See Commission decision of 24 April 1996, *Gencor/Lonrho*, Case No. IV/M.619.

Findings of the Court

It is necessary first of all to reject the Commission's argument that, by notifying the concentration agreement for examination and by making clearance a condition precedent to its implementation, the applicant voluntarily submitted to the Commission's jurisdiction. Infringement of the obligations regarding notification and suspension laid down in Articles 4 and 7 of the Regulation for all concentrations with a Community dimension is punishable by severe financial penalties under Article 14. No voluntary submission whatever by the applicant to the jurisdiction of the Community can therefore be inferred from the notification of the concentration agreement or from the suspension of its implementation. Besides, in order for the Commission to assess whether a concentration is within its purview, it must first be in a position to examine that concentration, a fact which justifies requiring the parties to the concentration to notify the agreement. That obligation does not predetermine the question whether the Commission is competent to rule on the concentration.

In the instant case, two questions must be examined. It must be ascertained first whether the Regulation covers concentrations such as the one at issue and then, if it does, whether its application to concentrations of that kind is contrary to public international law on State jurisdiction.

1. Assessment of the territorial scope of the Regulation

The Regulation, in accordance with Article 1 thereof, applies to all concentrations with a Community dimension, that is to say to all concentrations between undertakings which do not each achieve more than two-thirds of their aggregate Community-wide turnover within one and the same Member State, where the combined aggregate worldwide turnover of those undertakings is more than [Euro] 5,000 million and the aggregate Community-wide turnover of at least two of them is more than [Euro] 250 million.

Article 1 does not require that, in order for a concentration to be regarded as having a Community dimension, the undertakings in question must be established in the Community or that the production activities covered by the concentration must be carried out within Community territory.

With regard to the criterion of turnover, ... the concentration at issue has a Community dimension within the meaning of Article 1(2) of the Regulation. The undertakings concerned have an aggregate worldwide turnover of more than [Euro] 10,000 million, above the [Euro] 5,000 million threshold laid down by the Regulation. Gencor and Lonrho each had a Community-wide turnover of more than [Euro] 250 million in the latest financial year. Finally, they do not each achieve more than two-thirds of their aggregate Community-wide turnover within one and the same Member State.

The applicant's arguments to the effect that the legal bases for the Regulation and the wording of its preamble and substantive provisions preclude its application to the concentration at issue cannot be accepted. The legal bases for the Regulation, namely Articles [103 and 352 TFEU], and more particularly the provisions to which they are intended to give effect, that is to say Articles [3(1)(g) of the EC Treaty, now repealed] and [101 and 102 TFEU], as well as the first to fifth, ninth and eleventh recitals in the preamble to the Regulation, merely point to the need to ensure that competition is not distorted in the common market, in particular by concentrations which result in the creation or strengthening of a dominant position. They in no way exclude from the Regulation's field of application concentrations which, while relating to mining and/or production activities outside the Community, have the effect of creating or strengthening a dominant position as a result of which effective competition in the common market is significantly impeded.

In particular, the applicant's view cannot be founded on the closing words of the 11th recital in the preamble to the Regulation. That recital states that "a concentration with a Community dimension exists ... where the concentrations are effected by undertakings which do not have their principal fields of activities in the Community but which have substantial operations there."

By that reference, in general terms, to the concept of substantial operations, the Regulation does not, for the purpose of defining its territorial scope, ascribe greater importance to production operations than to sales operations. On the contrary, by setting quantitative thresholds in Article 1 which are based on the worldwide and Community turnover of the undertakings concerned, it rather ascribes greater importance to sales operations within the common market as a factor linking the concentration to the Community. It is common ground that Gencor and Lonrho each carry out significant sales in the Community (valued in excess of [Euro] 250 million).

Nor is it borne out by either the 30th recital in the preamble to the Regulation or Article 24 thereof that the criterion based on the location of production activities is well founded. Far from laying down a criterion for defining the territorial scope of the Regulation, Article 24 merely regulates the procedures to be followed in order to deal with situations in which non-member countries do not grant Community undertakings treatment comparable to that accorded by the Community to undertakings from those non-member countries in relation to the control of concentrations.

The applicant cannot, by reference to the judgment in *Wood Pulp*, rely on the criterion as to the implementation of an agreement to support its interpretation of the territorial scope of the Regulation. Far from supporting the applicant's view, that criterion for assessing the link between an agreement and Community territory in fact precludes it. According to *Wood Pulp*, the criterion as to the implementation of an agreement is satisfied by mere sale within the Community, irrespective of the location of the sources of supply and the production plant. It is not disputed that Gencor and Lonrho carried out sales in the Community before the concentration and would have continued to do so thereafter.

Accordingly, the Commission did not err in its assessment of the territorial scope of the Regulation by applying it in this case to a proposed concentration notified by undertakings whose registered offices and mining and production operations are outside the Community.

2. *Compatibility of the contested decision with public international law*

Following the concentration agreement, the previously existing competitive relationship between Implats and LPD, in particular so far as concerns their sales in the Community, would have come to an end. That would have altered the competitive structure within the common market since, instead of three South African PGM suppliers, there would have remained only two. The implementation of the proposed concentration would have led to the merger not only of the parties' PGM mining and production operations in South Africa but also of their marketing operations throughout the world, particularly in the Community where Implats and LPD achieved significant sales.

Application of the Regulation is justified under public international law when it is foreseeable that a proposed concentration will have an immediate and substantial effect in the Community.

In that regard, the concentration would, according to the contested decision, have led to the creation of a dominant duopoly on the part of Amplats and Implats/LPD in the platinum and rhodium markets, as a result of which effective competition would have been significantly impeded in the common market within the meaning of Article 2(3) of the Regulation. It is therefore necessary to verify whether the three criteria of immediate, substantial and foreseeable effect are satisfied in this case. With regard, specifically, to the criterion of immediate effect, the words "medium term" used in ... the contested decision in relation to the creation of a dominant duopoly position are, contrary to the applicant's assertion, entirely unambiguous. They clearly refer to the time when it is envisaged that Russian stocks will be exhausted, enabling a dominant duopoly on the part of Amplats and Implats/LPD to be created on the world platinum and rhodium markets and, by the same token, in the Community as a substantial part of those world markets.

That dominant position would not be dependent, as the applicant asserts, on the future conduct of the undertaking arising from the concentration and of Amplats but would result, in particular, from the very characteristics of the market and the alteration of its structure. In referring to the future conduct of the parties to the duopoly, the applicant fails to distinguish between abuses of dominant position which those parties might commit in the near or more distant future, which might or might not be controlled by means of Articles [101 and/or 102 TFEU], and the alteration to the structure of the undertakings and of the market to which the concentration would give rise. It is true that the concentration would not necessarily lead to abuses immediately, since that depends on decisions which the parties to the duopoly may or may not take in the future. However, the concentration would have had the direct and immediate effect of creating the conditions in which abuses were not only possible but economically rational, given that the concentration would have significantly impeded effective competition in the market by giving rise to a lasting alteration to the structure of the markets concerned.

Accordingly, the concentration would have had an immediate effect in the Community.

So far as concerns the criterion of substantial effect, ... the Commission established to the requisite legal standard that the concentration would have created a lasting dominant duopoly position in the world platinum and rhodium markets.

The applicant cannot maintain that the concentration would not have a substantial effect in the Community in view of the low sales and small market share of the parties to the concentration in the EEA. While the level of sales in western Europe (20% of world demand) and the Community market share of the entity arising from the concentration ((...)% in respect of platinum) were already sufficient grounds for the Community to have jurisdiction in respect of the concentration, the potential impact of the concentration proved even higher than those figures suggested. Given that the concentration would have had the effect of creating a dominant duopoly position in the world platinum and rhodium markets, it is clear that the sales in the Community potentially affected by the concentration would have included not only those of the Implats/LPD undertaking but also those of Amplats (approximately 35% to 50%), which would have represented a more than substantial proportion of platinum and rhodium sales in western Europe and a much higher combined market share held by Implats/LPD and Amplats (approximately (...)% to 65%).

Finally, it is not possible to accept the applicant's argument that the creation of the dominant position referred to by the Commission in the contested decision is not of greater concern to the Community than to any other competent body and is even of less concern to it than to others. The fact that, in a world market, other parts of the world are affected by the concentration cannot prevent the Community from exercising its control over a concentration which substantially affects competition within the common market by creating a dominant position.

The arguments by which the applicant denies that the concentration would have a substantial effect in the Community must therefore be rejected.

As for the criterion of foreseeable effect, it follows from all of the foregoing that it was in fact foreseeable that the effect of creating a dominant duopoly position in a world market would also be to impede competition significantly in the Community, an integral part of that market.

It follows that the application of the Regulation to the proposed concentration was consistent with public international law....

[On the comity issue, the court stated the following.] It is necessary to examine next whether the Community violated a principle of non-interference or the principle of proportionality in exercising that jurisdiction.

The applicant's argument that, by virtue of a principle of non-interference, the Commission should have refrained from prohibiting the concentration in order to avoid a conflict of jurisdiction with the South African authorities must be rejected, without it being necessary to consider whether such a rule exists in international law. Suffice it to note that there was no conflict between the course of action required by the South African Government and that required by the Community given that, in their letter of 22 August 1995, the South African competition authorities simply concluded that the concentration agreement did not give rise to any competition policy concerns, without requiring that such an agreement be entered into. . . .

In its letter of 19 April 1996 the South African Government, far from calling into question the Community's jurisdiction to rule on the concentration at issue, first simply expressed a general preference, having regard to the strategic importance of mineral exploitation in South Africa, for intervention in specific cases of collusion when they arose and did not specifically comment on the industrial or other merits of the concentration proposed by Gencor and Lonrho. It then merely expressed the view that the proposed concentration might not impede competition, having regard to the economic power of Amplats, the existence of other sources of supply of PGMs and the opportunities for other producers to enter the South African market through the grant of new mining concessions.

Finally, neither the applicant nor, indeed, the South African Government in its letter of 19 April 1996 have shown, beyond making mere statements of principle, in what way the proposed concentration would affect the vital economic and/or commercial interests of the Republic of South Africa.

Questions on *Gencor*

1. The General Court states that "application of the Regulation is justified under public international law when it is foreseeable that a proposed concentration will have an immediate and substantial effect in the Community."

a. Does this mean that the General Court has adopted the "effects" doctrine?

b. Are the conditions imposed by the General Court for the EU to assert its jurisdiction similar to those applied by U.S. courts?

2. Is the difference between the position of the ECJ vis-à-vis restrictive agreements and the one of the General Court vis-à-vis mergers justified? When it comes to asserting jurisdiction, should restrictive agreements and mergers be subject to different treatment?

3. When global firms merge they generally have to notify their transaction in a large number of jurisdictions.

a. Isn't there a risk that such mergers could be blocked by a small nation prohibiting the merger on the ground that it would have negative effects on the conditions of competition within its borders?

b. Isn't this making global mergers excessively vulnerable?

4. Is the court's comity analysis similar to that used in *Hartford Fire?*

The Treatment of Extraterritorial Conduct in Other Nations

Other nations generally apply their antitrust laws to extraterritorial conduct that has effects in their nations.[43] For example, South Africa

---

43. *See, e.g.,* Argentina Competition Law Art. 3; Brazil Competition Law Article 2; ABA, I COMPETITION LAWS OUTSIDE THE UNITED STATES at Canada–112–13 (2001) (also recognizing

exercised such jurisdiction to address a U.S. export cartel.[44] However, in practice, some nations lack the resources to adequately enforce their provisions extraterritorially or find enforcement stymied by an inability to obtain evidence located abroad. Also, extraterritorial application by the U.S. and EU of their antitrust laws has caused frictions in other nations, and the reactions include blocking statutes that deny discovery to aid foreign proceedings and clawback statutes entitling firms to recover any excess over single damages paid, which generally affects only U.S. judgments for treble damages.[45]

B.   SPECIAL TREATMENT OF CONDUCT AFFECTING EXPORTS

In the United States, as noted above, the FTAIA provides that conduct having an anticompetitive effect on exports enjoys antitrust immunity unless it has a "direct, substantial, and reasonably foreseeable effect" on U.S. commerce domestic trade or on U.S. exporters. In addition, there are other special U.S. statutes on exports like the Webb–Pomerene Act, 15 U.S.C. §§ 61–65. Their content is described in the following guidelines.

U.S. DOJ–FTC, Antitrust Enforcement Guidelines for International Operations

(April 1995).

2.   ANTITRUST LAWS ENFORCED BY THE AGENCIES . . .

The Webb–Pomerene Act, 15 U.S.C. 61–65, provides a limited antitrust exemption for the formation and operation of associations of otherwise competing businesses to engage in collective export sales. The exemption applies only to the export of "goods, wares, or merchandise." It does not apply to conduct that has an anticompetitive effect in the United States or that injures domestic competitors of the members of an export association. Nor does it provide any immunity from prosecution under foreign antitrust laws. Associations seeking an exemption under the Webb–Pomerene Act must file their articles of agreement and annual reports with the [Federal Trade] Commission, but pre-formation approval from the Commission is not required. . . .

---

comity limits); China Anti–Monopoly Law Art. 2; Egypt Competition Law Art. 5; India Competition Act § 32; OECD, Directorate for Financial, Fiscal and Enterprise Affairs, Annual Report on Competition Policy Developments in Korea 2000–2001 (2001); New Zealand Commerce Act § 4; Peru Competition Law, Art. 4; Saudi Arabia Implementing Regulations Art. 3; South Africa Competition Act § 3(1); Singapore Competition Act § 33(1); Taiwan Guidelines on Extraterritorial Mergers (2005); Turkey Competition Act Art. 2.

44. *See* American Nat'l Soda Ash Corp. v. South Africa Competition Commission, 12/CAC/DEC01.

45. *See, e.g.,* Australia Foreign Proceedings (Excess of Jurisdiction) Act No. 3 of 1984; Canada (Foreign Extraterritorial Measures Act of 1984, c. 49, § 1).

The Export Trading Company Act of 1982 (the "ETC Act"), Pub. L. No. 97–290, 96 Stat. 1234, is designed to increase U.S. exports of goods and services. It addresses that goal in several ways. . . . [I]n Title III, it reduces uncertainty concerning the application of the U.S. antitrust laws to export trade through the creation of a procedure by which persons engaged in U.S. export trade may obtain an export trade certificate of review ("ETCR"). . . . [I]n Title IV, it clarifies [in the FTAIA] the jurisdictional rules applicable to non-import cases brought under the Sherman Act and the FTC Act. . . .

Export trade certificates of review [under Title III] are issued by the Secretary of Commerce with the concurrence of the Attorney General. Persons named in the ETCR obtain limited immunity from suit under both state and federal antitrust laws for activities that are specified in the certificate and that comply with the terms of the certificate. To obtain an ETCR, an applicant must show that proposed export conduct will:

    1.   result in neither a substantial lessening of competition or restraint of trade within the United States nor a substantial restraint of the export trade of any competitor of the applicant;

    2.   not unreasonably enhance, stabilize, or depress prices in the United States of the class of goods or services covered by the application;

    3.   not constitute unfair methods of competition against competitors engaged in the export of the class of goods or services exported by the applicant; and

    4.   not include any act that may reasonably be expected to result in the sale for consumption or resale in the United States of such goods or services.

Congress intended that these standards "encompass the full range of the antitrust laws," as defined in the ETC Act.

Although an ETCR provides significant protection under the antitrust laws, it has certain limitations. First, conduct that falls outside the scope of a certificate remains fully subject to private and governmental enforcement actions. Second, an ETCR that is obtained by fraud is void from the outset and thus offers no protection under the antitrust laws. Third, any person that has been injured by certified conduct may recover actual (though not treble) damages if that conduct is found to violate any of the statutory criteria described above. In any such action, certified conduct enjoys a presumption of legality, and the prevailing party is entitled to recover costs and attorneys' fees. Fourth, an ETCR does not constitute, explicitly or implicitly, an endorsement or opinion by the Secretary of Commerce or by the Attorney General concerning the legality of such business plans under the laws of any foreign country.

The Secretary of Commerce may revoke or modify an ETCR if the Secretary or the Attorney General determines that the applicant's export activities have ceased to comply with the statutory criteria for obtaining a certificate. The Attorney General may also bring suit under Section 15 of the Clayton Act to enjoin conduct that threatens "a clear and irreparable harm to the national interest," even if the conduct has been pre-approved as part of an ETCR. The Commerce Department, in consultation with the Department, has issued guidelines setting forth the standards used in reviewing ETCR applications. . . .

3.122   Jurisdiction in Cases Under Subsection 1(B) of the FTAIA

Two categories of "export cases" fall within the FTAIA's jurisdictional test. First, the Agencies may, in appropriate cases, take enforcement action against anticompetitive conduct, wherever occurring, that restrains U.S. exports, if

    1.   the conduct has a direct, substantial, and reasonably foreseeable effect on exports of goods or services from the United States, and

    2.   the U.S. courts can obtain jurisdiction over persons or corporations engaged in such conduct.

As Section 3.2 below explains more fully, if the conduct is unlawful under the importing country's antitrust laws as well, the Agencies are also prepared to work with that country's authorities if they are better situated to remedy the conduct, and if they are prepared to take action that will address the U.S. concerns, pursuant to their antitrust laws.

Second, the Agencies may in appropriate cases take enforcement action against conduct by U.S. exporters that has a direct, substantial, and reasonably foreseeable effect on trade or commerce within the United States, or on import trade or commerce. This can arise in two principal ways. First, if U.S. supply and demand were not particularly elastic, an agreement among U.S. firms accounting for a substantial share of the relevant market, regarding the level of their exports, could reduce supply and raise prices in the United States. Second, conduct ostensibly export-related could affect the price of products sold or resold in the United States. This kind of effect could occur if, for example, U.S. firms fixed the price of an input used to manufacture a product overseas for ultimate resale in the United States.

ILLUSTRATIVE EXAMPLE D

Situation: Companies E and F are the only producers of product Q in country Epsilon, one of the biggest markets for sales of Q in the world. E and F together account for 99 percent of the sales of product Q in Epsilon. In order to prevent a competing U.S. producer from entering the market in Epsilon, E and F agree that neither one of them will purchase or distribute the U.S. product, and that they will take "all feasible" measures to keep the U.S. company out of their market. Without specifically discussing what other measures they will take to carry out this plan, E and F meet with their distributors and, through a variety of threats and inducements, obtain agreement of all of the distributors not to carry the U.S. product. There are no commercially feasible substitute distribution channels available to the U.S. producer. Because of the actions of E and F, the U.S. producer cannot find any distributors to carry its product and is unable to make any sales in Epsilon.

Discussion: The agreement between E and F not to purchase or distribute the U.S. product would clearly have a direct and reasonably foreseeable effect on U.S. export commerce, since it is aimed at a U.S. exporter. The substantiality of the effects on U.S. exports would depend on the significance of E and F as purchasers and distributors of Q, although on these facts the virtually total foreclosure from Epsilon would almost certainly qualify as a substantial effect for jurisdictional purposes. However, if the Agencies believe that they may encounter difficulties in establishing personal jurisdiction or in obtaining effective relief, the case may be one in which the Agencies would seek to resolve their concerns by working with other authorities who are examining the transaction.

ILLUSTRATIVE EXAMPLE E

Situation: Companies P, Q, R, and S, organized under the laws of country Alpha, all manufacture and distribute construction equipment. Much of that equipment is protected by patents in the various countries where it is sold, including Alpha. The companies all belong to a private trade association, which develops industry standards that are often (although not always) adopted by Alpha's regulatory authorities. Feeling threatened by competition from the United States, the companies agree at a trade association meeting

    1. to refuse to adopt any U.S. company technology as an industry standard, and

    2. to boycott the distribution of U.S. construction equipment.

The U.S. companies have taken all necessary steps to protect their intellectual property under the law of Alpha.

Discussion: In this example, the collective activity impedes U.S. companies in two ways: their technology is boycotted (even if U.S. companies are willing to license their intellectual property) and they are foreclosed from access to distribution channels. The jurisdictional question is whether these actions create a direct, substantial, and reasonably foreseeable effect on the exports of U.S. companies. The mere fact that only the market of Alpha appears to be foreclosed is not enough to defeat such an effect. Only if exclusion from Alpha as a quantitative measure were so de minimis in terms of actual volume of trade that there would not be a substantial effect on U.S. export commerce would jurisdiction be lacking. Given that this example involves construction equipment, a generally highly priced capital good, the exclusion from Alpha would probably satisfy the substantiality requirement for FTAIA jurisdiction. This arrangement appears to have been created with particular reference to competition from the United States, which indicates that the effects on U.S. exports are both direct and foreseeable. . . .

Questions on U.S. Guidelines Regarding Exports

    1. Is it legitimate for the United States to immunize conduct on its soil that it would otherwise find an antitrust violation just because its anticompetitive effects are only felt in foreign nations? Does the United States have any legitimate interest in protecting foreign firms or consumers from those effects? Are foreign nations better placed to protect against such anticompetitive effects?

2. Suppose U.S. firms agree to raise prices or reduce output on an exported product.

a. Isn't the only likely effect on the domestic market for that product to leave more output for domestic consumption and thus to reduce domestic prices? Does the U.S. suffer any antitrust injury from such an effect? The guidelines elsewhere suggest such an effect may exist if domestic prices are driven below cost, but would an export cartel ever cause below-cost pricing domestically?

b. Won't another effect of such an export cartel be to reduce output (and raise prices) for any domestic inputs used to make the exported product? Isn't such an effect too indirect under U.S. antitrust law to be the basis of suit?

3. Suppose foreign firms exclude a U.S. firm from an export market.

a. Is such an exclusion in fact covered by U.S. antitrust law?

b. Who is harmed by such an exclusion—foreign consumers or domestic consumers?

c. Isn't the only effect on domestic consumers likely to be that the firm has more output to sell domestically, which should if anything reduce domestic prices without driving them below cost? Given the lack of harm to domestic consumer welfare, should U.S. antitrust law apply?

d. Given the harm to foreign consumers, can we just trust that foreign antitrust authorities will have adequate incentives to bring suit?

4. Given the FTAIA, is any substantive role left for the Webb–Pomerene Act and the rest of the Export Trading Company Act?

a. Don't both of the latter require the sort of showing that would in any event put exporters with the immunity provided by the FTAIA?

b. Does the registration and certification process provide more prospective protection against a latter determination that the firms exceed that immunity?

c. Given the information disclosures necessary to register an association under the Webb–Pomerene Act or to apply for a certificate under the Export Trading Company Act, does either seem on balance that attractive to pursue?

5. Does the rest of the Export Trading Company Act moot the Webb–Pomerene Act?

a. Is there any reason why the benefits on the Webb–Pomerene Act should be limited to goods while the Export Trading Company Act applies to goods and services?

b. Why should a registered export association involving goods enjoy complete immunity under the Webb–Pomerene Act while a certified export practice involving goods or services is still subject to single damages under the Export Trading Company Act?

EU Law Regarding Exports

A consequence of the "territorial jurisdiction" principle applied in the EU is that practices by European firms whose only impact is outside the EU fall short of the substantive reach of European competition law. The case law of the European Court of Justice has, however, recognized important exceptions to the implicit exemption this gives export cartels.

Export cartels which create artificial product scarcity on domestic markets. One exception can be found in the *Cement* decision. In this case, the Commission punished a number of collective export practices that, as part of a complex cartel agreement, sought to divert quantities from the Community markets in order to prevent the shipment of quantities within the EU from disrupting the collusive scheme.[46]

Export practices which directly or incidentally limit imports within the European Territory. In the 80s and 90s, European and third countries manufacturers (especially from Asia) often entered into "orderly marketing agreements" with a view to soften the aggressive commercial practices of the latter, through a direct or indirect limitation of their imports on the European territory. The applicability of Article 101 was confirmed by the Court in the *EMI/CBS* case:

"... A restrictive agreement between traders within the common market and competitors in third countries that would bring about an isolation of the common market as a whole which, in the territory of the Community, would reduce the supply of products originating in third countries and similar to those protected by a mark within the community, might be of such a nature as to affect adversely the conditions of competition within the common market."[47]

In *Javico*, Article 101 was applied to a vertical export agreement which restricted competition outside the Community, but could have indirect effects on the conditions of competition with the common market. Yves Saint Laurent (YSLP), a perfumes manufacturer, had concluded with Javico International two contracts for the distribution of its products, one covering Russia and Ukraine and the other Slovenia.

Javico International and Javico Ag v. Yves Saint Laurent Parfums SA (YSLP)

C–306/96, ECR [1998] I–1983 (ECJ).

... The distribution contract for Russia and Ukraine provides: "Our products are intended for sale solely in the territory of the Republics of Russia and Ukraine. In no circumstances may they leave the territory of the Republics of Russia and Ukraine. Your company promises and guarantees that the final destination of the products will be in the territory of the

---

46. See Commission Decision 94/815/EC of 30 November 1994, Cases IV/33.126 and 33.322–*Cement*, O.J. L 343, 30 December 1994 pp. 1–158.

47. See ECJ, 51–75, 15 June 1976, *EMI Records Limited v. CBS United Kingdom Limited*, ECR [1976] 811.

Republics of Russia and Ukraine, and that it will sell the products only to traders situated in the territory of the Republics of Russia and Ukraine. Consequently, your company will provide the addresses of the distribution points of the products in the territory of the Republics of Russia and Ukraine and details of the products by distribution point."

The distribution contract for Slovenia provides: "In order to protect the high quality of the distribution of the products in other countries of the world, the distributor agrees not to sell the products outside the territory or to unauthorised dealers in the territory."

Shortly after the conclusion of those contracts, YSLP discovered in the United Kingdom, Belgium and the Netherlands products sold to Javico which should have been distributed in Russia, Ukraine and Slovenia. YSLP therefore terminated the contracts and instituted proceedings before the Tribunal de Commerce, Nanterre, which ... upheld the termination of the two contracts and YSLP's claim for contractual compensation and damages.

Javico appealed against that decision to the Cour d'Appel, Versailles, which considered that the validity of the provisions in the distribution contracts at issue had to be appraised in the light of Article [101(1) TFEU], the appellants having contended that those contractual provisions were void by virtue of Article [101(2) TFEU].

In those circumstances, the Cour d'Appel stayed proceedings pending a ruling from the Court of Justice on [various] questions: .... By its first question, the national court asks whether Article [101(1) TFEU] precludes a supplier established in a Member State from prohibiting a distributor established in another Member State to which it entrusts the distribution of its products in a territory outside the Community from making any sales in a territory other than the contractual territory, including the territory of the Community, either by means of direct sales or by means of re-exportation from the contractual territory.

According to settled case-law ..., agreements between economic operators at different levels of the economic process may be caught by the prohibition contained in Article [101(1) TFEU].

In order to determine whether agreements such as those concluded by YSLP with Javico fall within the prohibition laid down by that provision it is necessary to consider whether the purpose or effect of the ban on supplies which they entail is to restrict to an appreciable extent competition within the common market and whether the ban may affect trade between Member States. ...

[T]he provisions of the agreements in question, in that they prohibit direct sales within the Community and re-exports of the contractual product to the Community, cannot be contrary, by their very nature, to Article [101(1) TFEU].

Although the contested provisions of those agreements do not, by their very nature, have as their object the prevention, restriction or distortion of competition within the common market within the meaning of Article [101(1) TFEU], it is, however, for the national court to determine whether they have that effect. Appraisal of the effects of those agreements necessarily implies taking account of their economic and legal context ... and, in particular, of the fact that YSLP has established in the Community a selective distribution system enjoying an exemption.

In that regard, it is first necessary to determine whether the structure of the Community market in the relevant products is oligopolistic, allowing only limited competition within the Community network for the distribution of those products.

It must then be established whether there is an appreciable difference between the prices of the contractual products charged in the Community and those charged outside the Community. Such a difference is not, however, liable to affect competition if it is eroded by the level of customs duties and transport costs resulting from the export of the product to a non-member country followed by its re-import into the Community.

If that examination were to disclose that the contested provisions of the agreements concerned had the effect of undermining competition within the meaning of Article [101(1) TFEU], it would also be necessary to determine whether, having regard to YSLP's position on the Community market and the extent of its production and its sales in the Member States, the contested provisions designed to prevent direct sales of the contractual products in the Community and re-exports of them to the Community entail any risk of an appreciable effect on the pattern of trade between the Member States such as to undermine attainment of the objectives of the common market.

In that regard, intra-Community trade cannot be appreciably affected if the products intended for markets outside the Community account for only a very small percentage of the total market for those products in the territory of the common market.

It is for the national court, on the basis of all the information available to it, to determine whether the conditions are in fact fulfilled for the agreements at issue to be caught by the prohibition laid down in Article [101(1) TFEU]. . . .

Questions on *Javico*

1. According to the ECJ, what are the factors that make it likely that the EU market will suffer anticompetitive effects from a vertical agreement between two EU firms requiring one of the firms to resell only in a foreign nation?

2. Why does the ECJ refer to the presence of an oligopolistic structure of the European market or price difference between the European and foreign market?

3. Are re-exports to the EU territory more likely to occur for high-value products or for low-value ones? In particular, were the luxury products at stake likely to be re-imported in the EU territory?

Other Nations' Antitrust Treatment of Exports

Most other nations either explicitly exempt exports or implicitly do so by making their antitrust laws inapplicable unless the conduct affects that nation's domestic market. A recent survey of 55 nations found 17 had explicit exemptions, 34 had implicit ones, and only 4 had no statutory exemption.[48] And one suspects that at least some of the latter four nations might interpret their antitrust laws not to apply to exports if the issue arose. Some nations, like Australia and Israel, require notification to obtain an export exemption.[49] Others do not. For example, India exempts agreements that relate exclusively to exports from India.[50] Canada exempts agreements that relate only to exports form Canada, unless the agreement (i) has or likely will reduce those exports; (ii) has or likely will restrict export opportunities; or (iii) affects (or for per se violations, relates to) the supply of services that facilitate exports.[51] Mexico exempts voluntary associations that exclusively export products that are their region's main income source and are not dire need products.[52]

C. THE TRADE–ANTITRUST INTERSECTION

Commissioner of Competition v. Superior Propane Inc.
2000 Canada Comp. Trib. 16 (April 4, 2002).

[The main portions of this opinion are excerpted in Chapter 7].

. . . *Redistribution to Foreigners.* While advocating that the entire amount of the redistributed income be included as an effect for the analysis under subsection 96(1), counsel for the Commissioner suggests . . . that there may be circumstances where the Tribunal should use its discretion to do otherwise. One instance is a merger of Canadian exporters following which the price increase is paid very largely by foreign consumers. In this case, counsel submits that the domestic component of the wealth transfer may be quite modest and the large component falling on foreign consumers could be ignored. The Tribunal should use its discretion to disregard the latter and therefore give the total wealth transfer less weight; accordingly, significant efficiency gains in comparison with the loss of efficiency (i.e. a small deadweight loss) and other effects could well allow the anti-competitive merger to proceed.

The respondents argue, similarly, that many of Superior's largest customers are foreign-owned companies and that the effect of the transfer on these foreign shareholders is not an adverse effect that should be considered. . . .

The international ramifications of section 96 have been discussed by the American Professor Ross whose article was cited with approval by the Court. He posits an anti-competitive acquisition under the Act in Canada of a Canadian-owned firm by an American-owned firm where efficiency gains

---

48.   Levenstein & Suslow, *The Changing International Status of Export Cartel Exemptions,* 20 Am. U. Int'l L. Rev. 785, 819–20 (2005).

49.   *Id.* at 801–02, 819–20.

50.   India Competition Act § 3(5)(ii).

51.   Canada Competition Act §§ 45(5), 90.1(8)

52.   Mexico Federal Economic Competition Law Art. 6.

are large but accrue only in the United States; yet consumers pay higher prices, there are significant layoffs in Canada, and the deadweight loss is small. He concludes that under a "... total world welfare" standard, such merger would be approved, but under the "... consumer surplus model (roughly followed in the United States)", it would be blocked. He further concludes that under a "... total Canadian welfare model", the merger could be blocked by excluding the efficiency gains in the United States, but this raises serious questions of discrimination under Canada's international obligations under NAFTA and GATT. Accordingly, for this reason, and because he endorses the American approach to efficiencies generally, he doubts that the Canadian Parliament intended a standard other than the Consumer Surplus Standard.

Under the purpose clause of the Act, the purpose thereof is to maintain and encourage competition in Canada in order, inter alia, to promote the efficiency and adaptability of the Canadian economy. Accordingly, in the Tribunal's view, efficiency gains and deadweight loss (i.e. losses in efficiency) in foreign markets resulting from an anti-competitive merger in Canada are to be excluded in the application of section 96. This is clearly stated in the statute and is not a discretionary matter for the Tribunal. Accordingly, if the deadweight loss in foreign markets is an excluded effect, so are all other effects in foreign markets. In the Tribunal's view, the Act does not endorse a "total world welfare" standard.

A "total Canadian welfare standard" as defined by Professor Ross may or may not be discriminatory under Canada's international obligations, but the Act is not. In the Tribunal's understanding, those obligations require "national treatment" in the application of Canadian laws. Accordingly, if efficiency gains and effects in foreign markets are excluded when reviewing an anti-competitive merger of two Canadian-owned firms in Canada, the same exclusion must be accorded if those merging firms are owned by non-residents. In Professor Ross' hypothetical, the anti-competitive merger of an American-owned and a Canadian-owned firm would be blocked under the Total Surplus Standard (even if consideration of the layoffs was excluded) because there are no gains in efficiency in Canada.

Accordingly, the Tribunal agrees with counsel for the Commissioner that the portion of the transfer experienced by foreign consumers should be excluded in the section 96 analysis. However, the Tribunal does not agree that so doing is a matter of discretion.

The Applicability of Trade Law's Nondiscrimination Rule

The General Agreement on Tariffs and Trade (GATT) 1947, Article III(4) provides that imported goods "shall be accorded treatment no less favourable than that accorded to like products of national origin in respect of all laws, regulations and requirements affecting their internal sale, offering for sale, purchase, transportation, distribution or use." The General Agreement on Trade in Services (GATS) is more limited, providing a similar nondiscrimination principle for like services (including insurance) but only for those areas where the member state made a specific commitment.[53]

1.   Do you agree with the Canadian Tribunal that this nondiscrimination principle can be complied with by ignoring foreign effects whether or not the firms are foreign-owned? Doesn't it categorize efficiency effects as foreign if they inure to the benefit of foreign shareholders?

2.   If a nation's antitrust standards did not vary with who owned the firm, would such a nondiscrimination principle suffice to eliminate the problem that exporting nations have an incentive to underenforce antitrust law and thus justify giving exclusive jurisdiction to the nation where the conduct occurred?

a.   Given that the rule only governs discrimination in treatment of "like products," couldn't a nation that exports cars and imports steel comply with this rule by having an antitrust exemption for the car industry that applied evenhandedly to foreign and domestic car makers but no antitrust exemption for steel? Couldn't it thus discriminate by thus adopting antitrust exemptions for any products it mainly exports but not for products that it mainly imports?

b.   Given that the nondiscrimination principle applies only to laws affecting "internal sale ... or use," couldn't a nation comply with this law by generally having an antitrust exemption for anticompetitive conduct affecting exports? Isn't this what U.S. and EU law actually do?

c.   Does limiting the nondiscrimination principle to discrimination between imported products that compete with "like" domestic products make more sense for trade laws designed to prevent protectionism and protect foreign firms than for any rule designed to prevent discriminatory antitrust enforcement and protect consumer welfare?

3.   Would the problem be solved by changing the nondiscrimination trade rule to prohibit treating foreign *consumers* worse than domestic consumers? Won't the "like products" limitation still likely make this nondiscrimination rule ineffective because a nation could just be lax on antitrust enforcement for any product that it mainly exports?

4.   Could the problem be solved by a more general nondiscrimination rule that requires nations to apply their antitrust laws equally to every industry?[54]

a.   Wouldn't nations that are net exporters of overall products and services still have incentives to adopt unduly lax but nondiscriminatory

---

53.   See GATS Art. VI ("In sectors where specific commitments are undertaken, each Member shall ensure that all measures of general application affecting trade in services are administered in a reasonable, objective and impartial manner."); *id.* Art. XVII ("In the sectors inscribed in its Schedule, and subject to any conditions and qualifications set out therein, each Member shall accord to services and service suppliers of any other Member, in respect of all measures affecting the supply of services, treatment no less favourable than that it accords to its own like services and service suppliers.")

54.   For proposals to adopt such a nondiscrimination rule for antitrust policy, see the essays of John McGinnis and Trebilcock & Iacobucci in COMPETITION LAWS IN CONFLICT (Epster & Greve, eds. 2004).

antitrust doctrines if they had exclusive jurisdiction over exporters acting within their borders?

b. Would it be easy to monitor whether a nation is discriminating against antitrust enforcement in those cases where the anticompetitive effects are mainly externalized? Would a nation be adequately deterred from doing so by the prospect of WTO trade sanctions?

5. Given that in fact the importing nations affected by foreign anti-competitive conduct can bring their own antitrust suits against such conduct, should we care whether the nation where the exporters are located discriminatorily underenforces its antitrust laws against them?

a. Is antitrust enforcement by the importing nation always feasible without the cooperation of the exporting nation where the conduct occurred and the defendants may reside? Would this problem be solved by treaties to share evidence and enforce foreign judgments?

b. Should we be concerned that the importing nations would engage in discriminatory overenforcement of antitrust laws?

    i. If we assume the consumer welfare standard is optimal, would importing nations have any incentive to overenforce their antitrust laws?

    ii. If we instead assume the optimal rule is a total welfare standard that considers both consumer and producer welfare, would importing nations have incentives to overenforce antitrust laws by choosing the consumer welfare standard instead? Is this likely to be a major problem given that trade deficits are normally a small percentage of GDP?

    iii. Is a total welfare standard in fact the optimal rule on international markets?

        (1) Are there any international mechanisms for offsetting the adverse distributional effects such a rule might have on consumers in one nation by taxing the profits by producers in other nations?

        (2) Would a consumer welfare standard prevent foreign firms from engaging in conduct that increases total welfare if they are willing to commit a share of the benefits they receive to offset any harm to consumers?

c. If nations differed on whether they preferred a consumer or total welfare standard, wouldn't antitrust laws in any nations that adopted a consumer welfare standard effectively trump those in nations that adopted a total welfare standard for any conduct affecting global markets, because the former standard would condemn some conduct the latter standard would approve?

Introduction to the Tension Between Antitrust and Antidumping Law

According to Article VI of the GATT:

"…. dumping, by which products of one country are introduced into the commerce of another country at less than the normal value of the products, is to be condemned if it causes or threatens material injury to an established industry in the territory of a contracting party or materially retards the establishment of a domestic industry. For the purposes of this Article, a product is to be considered as being introduced into the commerce of an importing country at less than its normal value, if the price of the product exported from one country to another: (a) is less than the comparable price, in the ordinary course of trade, for the like product when destined for consumption in the exporting country, or; (b) in the absence of such domestic price, is less than either (i) the highest comparable price for the like product for export to any third country in the ordinary course of trade, or (ii) the cost of production of the product in the country of origin plus a reasonable addition for selling cost and profit. . . ."

Antidumping is thus a trade remedy for industries injured by imports' competition. In most antidumping cases, however, imports' low prices are not the result of predatory strategies but rather the consequence of the superior cost efficiency of foreign production.[55] Hence, if one sees competition policy as a driver for economic efficiency, there is an apparent tension between antidumping and competition policies.

U.S. DOJ–FTC, Antitrust Enforcement Guidelines for International Operations

(April 1995).

. . . The Revenue Act of 1916, better known as the Antidumping Act, 15 U.S.C. 71–74, is not an antitrust statute, but its subject matter is closely related to the antitrust rules regarding predation. It is a trade statute that creates a private claim against importers who sell goods into the United States at prices substantially below the prices charged for the same goods in their home market. In order to state a claim, a plaintiff must show both that such lower prices were commonly and systematically charged, and that the importer had the specific intent to injure or destroy an industry in the United States, or to prevent the establishment of an industry. Dumping cases are more commonly brought using the administrative procedures of the Tariff Act of 1930, discussed below.

2.83   Tariff Act of 1930 . . . .

2.831   Countervailing Duties. Pursuant to Title VII.A of the Tariff Act, U.S. manufacturers, producers, wholesalers, unions, and trade associations may petition for the imposition of offsetting duties on subsidized foreign imports. The Department of Commerce's International Trade Administration ("ITA") must make a determination that the foreign government in question is subsidizing the imports, and in almost all cases the International Trade Commission ("ITC") must determine that a domestic industry is materially injured or threatened with material injury by reason of these imports.

---

55. See Vandenbussche, Hylke & Veugelers, Reinhilde, 1996. "European Anti-dumping Policy and the Profitability of National and International Collusion", CEPR Discussion Papers 1469, C.E.P.R. Discussion Papers.

2.832 Antidumping Duties. Pursuant to Title VII.B of the Tariff Act, parties designated in the statute (the same parties as in the countervailing duties provision) may petition for antidumping duties, which must be imposed on foreign merchandise that is being, or is likely to be, sold in the United States at "less than fair value" ("LTFV"), if the U.S. industry is materially injured or threatened with material injury by imports of the foreign merchandise. The ITA makes the LTFV determination, and the ITC is responsible for the injury decision.

2.833 Section 337. Section 337 of the Tariff Act, 19 U.S.C. 1337, prohibits "unfair methods of competition and unfair acts in the importation of articles into the United States," if the effect is to destroy or substantially injure a U.S. industry, or where the acts relate to importation of articles infringing U.S. patents, copyrights, trademarks, or registered mask works. Complaints are filed with the ITC. The principal remedies under Section 337 are an exclusion order directing that any offending goods be excluded from entry into the United States, and a cease and desist order directed toward any offending U.S. firms and individuals. The ITC is required to give the Agencies an opportunity to comment before making a final determination. In addition, the Department participates in the interagency group that prepares recommendations for the President to approve, disapprove, or allow to take effect the import relief proposed by the ITC.

2.84 Trade Act of 1974.

2.841 Section 201. Section 201 of the Trade Act of 1974, 19 U.S.C. 2251 et seq., provides that American businesses claiming serious injury due to significant increases in imports may petition the ITC for relief or modification under the so-called "escape clause." If the ITC makes a determination that "an article is being imported into the United States in such increased quantities as to be a substantial cause of serious injury, or the threat thereof, to the domestic industry producing an article like or directly competitive with the imported article," and formulates its recommendation for appropriate relief, the Department participates in the interagency committee that conducts the investigations and advises the President whether to adopt, modify, or reject the import relief recommended by the ITC.

2.842 Section 301. Section 301 of the Trade Act of 1974, 19 U.S.C. 2411, provides that the U.S. Trade Representative ("USTR"), subject to the specific direction, if any, of the President, may take action, including restricting imports, to enforce rights of the United States under any trade agreement, to address acts inconsistent with the international legal rights of the United States, or to respond to unjustifiable, unreasonable or discriminatory practices of foreign governments that burden or restrict U.S. commerce. Interested parties may initiate such actions through petitions to the USTR, or the USTR may itself initiate proceedings. Of particular interest to antitrust enforcement is Section 301(d)(3)(B)(i)(IV), which includes among the "unreasonable" practices of foreign governments that might justify a proceeding the "toleration by a foreign government of systematic anticompetitive activities by enterprises or among enterprises in the foreign country that have the effect of restricting . . . access of United States goods or services to a foreign market." The Department participates in the interagency committee that makes recommendations to the President on what actions, if any, should be taken. . . .

3.4 Antitrust Enforcement and International Trade Regulation. There has always been a close relationship between the international application of the antitrust laws and the policies and rules governing the international trade of the United States. Restrictions such as tariffs or quotas on the free flow of goods affect market definition, consumer choice, and supply options for U.S. producers. In certain instances, the U.S. trade laws set forth specific procedures for settling disputes under those laws, which can involve price and quantity agreements by the foreign firms involved. When those procedures are followed, an implied antitrust immunity results. However, agreements among competitors that do not comply with the law, or go beyond the measures authorized by the law, do not enjoy antitrust immunity. In the absence of legal authority, the fact, without more, that U.S. or foreign government officials were involved in or encouraged measures that would otherwise violate the antitrust laws does not immunize such arrangements.

If a particular voluntary export restraint does not qualify for express or implied immunity from the antitrust laws, then the legality of the arrangement would depend upon the existence of the ordinary elements of an antitrust offense, such as whether or not a prohibited agreement exists or whether defenses such as foreign sovereign compulsion can be invoked.

ILLUSTRATIVE EXAMPLE M

Situation: Six U.S. producers of product Q have initiated an antidumping action alleging that imports of Q from country Sigma at less than fair value are causing material injury to the U.S. Q industry. The ITC has made a preliminary decision that there is a reasonable indication that the U.S. industry is suffering material injury from Q imported from Sigma. The Department of Commerce has preliminarily concluded that the foreign market value of Q imported into the United States by Sigma's Q producers exceeds the price at which they are selling Q in this country by margins of 10 to 40 percent. Sigma's Q producers jointly initiate discussions with the Department of Commerce that lead to suspension of the investigation in accordance with Section 734 of the Tariff Act of 1930, 19 U.S.C. 1673c. The suspension agreement provides that each of Sigma's Q producers will sell product Q in the United States at no less than its individual foreign market value, as determined periodically by the Department of Commerce in accordance with the Tariff Act. Before determining to suspend the investigation, the Department of Commerce provides copies of the proposed agreement to the U.S. Q producers, who jointly advise the Department that they do not object to the suspension of the investigation on the terms proposed. The Department also determines that suspension of the investigation would be in the public interest. As a result of the suspension agreement, prices in the United States of Q imported from Sigma rise by an average of 25 percent from the prices that prevailed before the antidumping action was initiated.

Discussion: While an unsupervised agreement among foreign firms to raise their U.S. sales prices ordinarily would violate the Sherman Act, the suspension agreement outlined above qualifies for an implied immunity from the antitrust laws. As demonstrated here, the parties have engaged only in conduct contemplated by the Tariff Act and none of the participants have engaged in conduct beyond what is necessary to implement that statutory scheme. . . .

Questions on the Competitive Implications of U.S. Trade Laws

1. From the standpoint of competition law, does it make any sense to have antidumping statutes that prevent firms from charging much less in the United States than abroad unless the U.S. prices are predatory under competition standards?

a. Isn't nonpredatory price discrimination of this type favorable to U.S. consumers? Doesn't the sort of suspension agreement described in Example M to enforce such antidumping law amount to the U.S. government requiring and enforcing a foreign cartel against U.S. consumers?

b. Are the requirements to show a "specific intent to injure or destroy an industry in the United States" or that "U.S. industry is materially injured or threatened with material injury" the same as requiring proof of predation? Does either meet the modern standards for showing predation or primary-line price discrimination under U.S. law? *See* Chapters 3, 5.

c. Doesn't this sort of antidumping law effectively amount to having a much lower standard for proving predatory pricing or primary-line price discrimination when the seller is a foreign firm than when the seller is a U.S. firm? If antidumping rules were not themselves part of GATT (Article VI), would antidumping laws themselves violate the trade law ban on discriminating against foreign producers?

d. What does this sort of trade law suggest about the relative political influence of U.S. producers and consumers on trade law?

2. Aren't all international trade agreements based on a similar premise that the political systems in most nations typically weigh domestic producer interests more heavily than domestic consumer interests? If nations didn't do that, wouldn't they each unilaterally suspend tariffs against foreign imports without any need for an international trade agreement?

3. Suppose a foreign nation allows its producers to anticompetitively exclude U.S. firms from entering a foreign market for making some product.

a. Would FTAIA prevent a U.S. antitrust claim against the foreign firms that engaged in such an anticompetitive exclusion? Does it count as a restraint on U.S. exports if, absent the exclusion, the U.S. firm would have produced the product in the foreign nation?

b. Could the foreign nation itself be pursued under U.S. antitrust law?

c. Would the foreign nation's refusal to enforce its antitrust laws against its firms' exclusion of U.S. entrants in the foreign market amount to a violation of the nondiscrimination GATT rule? Or does the "like product" requirement mean it would have to be shown that the foreign nation's application of antitrust law to the relevant market discriminates between foreign and domestic firms?[56]

i. Doesn't the latter allow a foreign nation to enforce its antitrust laws in a way that effectively discriminates against markets where imports are a concern?

ii. Is it feasible to police this concern by determining whether the foreign nation applies its competition law equally to all industries? Couldn't the foreign nation always plausibly say that the anticompetitive and procompetitive effects differed in different markets, making different treatment a nondiscriminatory application of the same test?

d. Would a foreign nation's decision to allow such an anticompetitive exclusion of U.S. entrants from its market be potentially actionable under SEUtion 301 of the Trade Act of 1974?

e. Would a foreign nation have any incentives to allow the exclusion of U.S. entrants unless it weighed the interests of its producers more heavily than those of its consumers?

Background on EU Antidumping Legislation

The EU antidumping regime can be found in Regulation 1225/2003, commonly referred to as the Anti–Dumping Regulation.[57] This Regulation closely follows a set of measures that were agreed during the Uruguay Round negotiations in the context of the GATT. The Anti–Dumping Regulation enables the EU to impose anti-dumping duties when the following conditions are met:

1. A finding of dumping: the export price at which the product is sold on the Community market is lower than the price on the producer's home market;

2. A material injury to the European industry: the imports have caused or threaten to cause damage to a substantial part of the industry within the EU (*e.g.*, market share losses, reduced prices for producers and increased pressure on production, sales, profits, productivity etc.);

3. The interests of the EU: the costs for the EU of taking measures must not be disproportionate to the benefits.

The European Commission is responsible for investigating complaints and assessing whether they are founded. When European operators consider that dumped imports from non-EU countries are causing them material injury, they may submit a complaint to the European Commission, either directly or through their national government. The Commission then has

---

56. A WTO panel ruled the latter, holding that Japan did not discriminate in violation of trade law by allowing its photo film makers to engage in practices that excluded U.S. firms because everyone making photo film was allowed to engage in the same practices, without considering whether Japan applied its competition law in the same way in other industries. See Japan–Measures Affecting Consumer Photographic Film and Paper: Report of the Panel, WT/DS44/R, ¶¶ 10.378–10.382 (Mar. 31, 1998).

57. See Council Regulation 1225/2003 of 30 November 2003 on protection against dumped imports from countries not members of the European Community O.J. L 30 22 December 2003 pp. 51/73.

45 days to examine the complaint, consult the member states (represented in an Advisory Committee) and decide whether or not there is enough evidence to initiate a formal investigation. Complaints are rejected (i) absent cogent evidence of industry injury or (ii) if the complainants do not represent at least 25% of the total EU production of the product in question.

The Commission's formal investigation assesses whether dumping is taking place (leading to complex price assessments) as well as whether dumped imports are causing material injury to Community industry. The investigation must be completed within 15 months. The Commission can impose provisional duties.

Once the Commission has completed its full investigation and consulted stakeholders (producers, consumers and member states), it lies on the Council of Ministers (an organ composed of the relevant ministers/secretary of states of each EU Member States) to decide the adoption of definitive anti-dumping duties. Definitive duties are valid for five years, but can be removed before that term under specific conditions. The Council's decisions (in the form of regulations) to impose anti-dumping duties can be challenged before the Court of First Instance. The WTO dispute settlement procedure may be used to settle disputes between WTO Member States with respect to anti-dumping duties.

The conceptual conflicts between antidumping and competition policies have given rise to a number of practical difficulties in the EU. Its antidumping practice has, for instance, been found to conflict with the goal of protecting a competitive market structure enclosed in Article 82. In the *Soda Ash–ICI* case, the Commission noted *inter alia* that the anti-dumping rights imposed on United States and Eastern European producers afforded ICI a significant protection from competitive pressures on the UK market and thus contributed to sustaining its dominance and the possibility of abusive conducts.[58] The conflicts between antidumping legislation and competition policy were further discussed in the *Extramet* case that is excerpted next.

Extramet Industrie SA v. Council, C–358/89

ECR [1992] 3813 (ECJ).

... Extramet is the largest importer in the Community of calcium metal, essentially from the People's Republic of China and the Soviet Union. Imports of calcium metal constitute the principal source of supply of Extramet, which uses it to produce, by a redistillation process which it has developed and patented, granules of pure calcium which are used mainly in the metallurgical industry.

Following a complaint lodged ... on behalf of Péchiney ..., the sole producer of calcium metal in the Community, which processes pure calcium metal by its own distillation process, the Commission adopted ... a definitive anti-dumping duty of 21.8% and 22% on imports of calcium metal

---

58. See Commission Decision 91/300/EEC of 19 December 1990, IV/33.133–D: Soda-ash—ICI, O.J. L 152, 15 June 1991 pp. 40–53 at para. 48.

originating in the People's Republic of China and the Soviet Union respectively and definitively collecting the provisional anti-dumping duty imposed on such imports.

According to the recitals in the preamble to [the] regulation [imposing this antidumping duty], the Community producer, namely Péchiney, and an independent importer (which also processes the product), namely Extramet, had, after the introduction of the provisional anti-dumping duty, requested and been granted an opportunity to be heard by the Commission and had submitted written observations to it. It is apparent from those recitals that the importer had claimed in particular that the Community producer suffered self-inflicted injury in refusing to supply calcium metal to it, prompting the importer to lodge a complaint with the competent French authorities alleging abuse of a dominant position. . . .

In support of its application, Extramet . . . contends . . . that Péchiney itself caused the injury suffered since it refused to supply calcium metal to Extramet. According to Extramet, if Péchiney had agreed to deliver calcium metal to it, it would not have suffered, during the period chosen for consideration of the injury, any loss of production and Soviet and Chinese imports into the Community would have fallen by half and thereafter accounted for only a minimal share of the Community market.

Extramet also states that, following Péchiney's refusal to sell calcium metal to it, it commenced legal proceedings against Péchiney before the competent French authorities for abuse of a dominant position. It considers that, in anti-dumping proceedings, account must be taken of such anti-competitive practices and that an anti-dumping duty must not be imposed if its effect would be to maintain an unjustified advantage in the Community market resulting from a cartel or an abuse of a dominant position, provided that formal evidence of such practices is produced and an action is brought on the basis of the Community competition rules.

In that connection, it must first be recalled that, pursuant to Article 4(1) of Council Regulation (EEC) No 2423/88 of 11 July 1988 on protection against dumped or subsidized imports from countries not members of the European Economic Community, "a determination of injury shall be made only if the dumped or subsidized imports are. . . . causing injury" to Community producers and "injuries caused by other factors . . . must not be attributed to the dumped or subsidized imports."

In determining the injury, the Council and the Commission are thus under an obligation to consider whether the injury on which they intend to base their conclusions actually derived from dumped imports and must disregard any injury deriving from other factors, in particular from the conduct of Community producers themselves.

It must next be noted that, in order to refute Extramet's argument, the Council merely referred, in the proceedings before the Court, to recital 15 in the preamble to the contested regulation, contending that, because of its specific nature, an anti-dumping procedure cannot prevent other actions from being brought in order to penalize anti-competitive conduct.

In recital 15 in the preamble to the contested regulation, however, the Council had merely stated that, according to the Commission, first, Péchiney had denied Extramet's allegations and no final judgment had yet been reached by the French authorities before which Extramet had commenced proceedings and, secondly, an anti-dumping investigation could not prejudice the outcome of proceedings brought under Article [101 or 102 TFEU] and, if an infringement of those rules were discovered, Article 14(1) of Regulation No 2423/88 would enable the anti-dumping procedure in question to be reviewed.

None of those statements shows that the Community institutions actually considered whether Péchiney itself contributed, by its refusal to sell, to the injury suffered and established that the injury on which they based their conclusions did not derive from the factors mentioned by Extramet. They did not therefore follow the proper procedure in determining the injury. Consequently, the plea as to errors made in the determination of the injury suffered by the Community industry must be upheld and the contested regulation must be annulled, without its being necessary to consider the other pleas and arguments put forward by the applicant. . . .

Questions on *Extramet*

1. What is the interaction between the antidumping duties and the competition rules in this case? Does the ECJ conclude that the imposition of anti-dumping duties is against EU competition law or does it say something more narrow?

2. Does the imposition of anti-dumping duties serve to prevent predatory pricing from foreign firms or is it rather a political mechanism designed to protect local industries from cheap imports?

    a. If the former, why not instead rely on competition law?

    b. If the latter, is this a sensible policy?

        i. Aren't cheap imports a good thing for consumers?

        ii. Are they necessarily a bad thing for local industries taken as a whole?

        iii. Should cheap imports be prohibited when they drive local producers from the market?

        iv. Does competition law seek to protect consumer welfare or competitors' welfare?

        v. Why should it be different for trade law?

3. Aren't the practical difficulties of applying anti-dumping rules likely to lead to serious mistakes?

Trade–Antitrust Intersection in Other Nations

A great majority of other nations also have antidumping legislation following the set of measures agreed during the Uruguay Round negotiations in the context of the GATT.[59] Sometimes a case is brought in one nation under an antitrust statute and in another nation under an anti-

---

59. Examples include Australia, Brazil, Canada, Egypt, Mexico, and Turkey.

dumping statute.[60] Trade disputes involving competition issues are often brought before the World Trade Organization.[61] Also, a growing number of regional trade agreements, a significant portion of them involving developing nations, contain provisions on competition law.[62]

D.   ANTICOMPETITIVE CONDUCT INVOLVING FOREIGN SOVEREIGNS

When foreign nations engage in anticompetitive acts, they may enjoy sovereign immunity from antitrust liability or benefit from an act of state doctrine that forbids inquiry into the validity of their actions. Immunity may also extend to private parties when the foreign government has compelled their actions, or when those private parties are simply petitioning the foreign governments for action. The U.S. law on these doctrines is summarized in the following excerpt.

U.S. DOJ–FTC, Antitrust Enforcement Guidelines for International Operations

(April 1995).

.... *3.3 Effects of Foreign Government Involvement.* Foreign governments may be involved in a variety of ways in conduct that may have antitrust consequences. To address the implications of such foreign governmental involvement, Congress and the courts have developed four special doctrines: the doctrine of foreign sovereign immunity; the doctrine of foreign sovereign compulsion; the act of state doctrine; and the application of the Noerr–Pennington doctrine to immunize the lobbying of foreign governments. Although these doctrines are interrelated, for purposes of discussion the Guidelines discuss each one individually.

3.31   Foreign Sovereign Immunity. The scope of immunity of a foreign government or its agencies and instrumentalities (hereinafter foreign government)[81] from the jurisdiction of the U.S. courts for all causes of action,

---

60. For example, the allegedly anticompetitive behavior of the American Natural Soda Ash Corp. (ANSAC), a registered Webb–Pomerene Association, was challenged by the antitrust authorities of India and South Africa based upon predatory pricing theories, and before the Brazilian trade authorities under the anti-dumping statute. *See* Ana Paula Martinez, *Competition Policy in Developing Societies*, at 86–88 (Harvard Law School LLM Paper 2006).

61. For example, the United States has brought trade disputes involving competition issues against both Canada (Measures Relating to Exports of Wheat and Treatment of Imported Grain, DS 276; Panel Report: April 6, 2004; Appellate Body Report: August 30, 2004) and Japan (Measures Affecting Consumer Photographic Film and Paper, DS 44; Panel Report: June 13, 1996; Appellate Body Report: March 31, 1998).

62. *See* UNCTAD, *Competition Provisions in Regional Trade Agreements*, UNCTAD/DITC/CLP/2005/1 (2005); Oliver Solano & Andreas Sennekamp, *Competition Provisions in Regional Trade Agreements*, OECD Trade Policy Working Paper No. 31, COM/DAF/TD(2005)3/FINAL (2006).

81. Section 1603(b) of the Foreign Sovereign Immunities Act of 1976 defines an "agency or instrumentality of a foreign state" to be any entity "(1) which is a separate legal person, corporate or otherwise; and (2) which is an organ of a foreign state or political subdivision

including antitrust, is governed by the Foreign Sovereign Immunities Act of 1976 ("FSIA").[82] Subject to the treaties in place at the time of FSIA's enactment, a foreign government is immune from suit except where designated in the FSIA.[83]

Under the FSIA, a U.S. court has jurisdiction if the foreign government has:

1. waived its immunity explicitly or by implication,

2. engaged in commercial activity as described in the statute,

3. expropriated property in violation of international law,

4. acquired rights to U.S. property,

5. committed certain torts within the United States, or agreed to arbitration of a dispute.[84]

The commercial activities exception is a frequently invoked exception to sovereign immunity under the FSIA. Under the FSIA, a foreign government is not immune in any case: "in which the action is based upon a commercial activity carried on in the United States by the foreign state; or upon an act performed in the United States in connection with a commercial activity of the foreign state elsewhere; or upon an act outside the territory of the United States in connection with a commercial activity of the foreign state elsewhere and that act causes a direct effect in the United States."[85]

"Commercial activity of the foreign state" is not defined in the FSIA, but is to be determined by the "nature of the course of conduct or particular transaction or act, rather than by reference to its purpose."[86] In attempting to differentiate commercial from sovereign activity, courts have considered whether the conduct being challenged is customarily performed for profit[87] and whether the conduct is of a type that only a sovereign government can perform.[88] As a practical matter, most activities of foreign government-owned corporations operating in the commercial marketplace will be subject to U.S. antitrust laws to the same extent as the activities of foreign privately-owned firms.

The commercial activity also must have a substantial nexus with the United States before a foreign government is subject to suit. The FSIA sets out three different standards for meeting this requirement. First, the challenged conduct by the foreign government may occur in the United

---

thereof, or a majority of whose shares or other ownership interest is owned by a foreign state or political subdivision thereof; and (3) which is neither a citizen of a State of the United States as defined in Section 1332(c) and (d) of [Title 28, U.S. Code], nor created under the laws of any third country." 28 U.S.C. 1603(b) (1988). It is not uncommon in antitrust cases to see state-owned enterprises meeting this definition.

82. 28 U.S.C. 1602, et seq. (1988).

83. 28 U.S.C. 1604 (1988 & Supp. 1993).

84. 28 U.S.C. 1605(a)(1–6) (1988).

85. 28 U.S.C. 1605(a)(2) (1988).

86. 28 U.S.C. 1603(d) (1988).

87. See, e.g., Republic of Argentina v. Weltover, Inc., 112 S.Ct. 2160 (1992) . . .

88. See, e.g., Saudi Arabia v. Nelson, 113 S.Ct. 1471 (1993) . . .

States.[89] Alternatively, the challenged commercial activity may entail an act performed in the United States in connection with a commercial activity of the foreign government elsewhere. Or, finally, the challenged commercial activity of a foreign government outside of the United States may produce a direct effect within the United States, i.e., an effect which follows "as an immediate consequence of the defendant's . . . activity."[91]

3.32   Foreign Sovereign Compulsion. Although U.S. antitrust jurisdiction extends to conduct and parties in foreign countries whose actions have the required effects on U.S. commerce, as discussed above, those parties may find themselves subject to conflicting requirements from the other country (or countries) where they are located. Under *Hartford Fire*, if it is possible for the party to comply both with the foreign law and the U.S. antitrust laws, the existence of the foreign law does not provide any legal excuse for actions that do not comply with U.S. law. However, a direct conflict may arise when the facts demonstrate that the foreign sovereign has compelled the very conduct that the U.S. antitrust law prohibits.

In these circumstances, at least one court has recognized a defense under the U.S. antitrust laws, and the Agencies will also recognize it.[93] There are two rationales underlying the defense of foreign sovereign compulsion. First, Congress enacted the U.S. antitrust laws against the background of well recognized principles of international law and comity among nations, pursuant to which U.S. authorities give due deference to the official acts of foreign governments. A defense for actions taken under the circumstances spelled out below serves to accommodate two equal sovereigns. Second, important considerations of fairness to the defendant require some mechanism that provides a predictable rule of decision for those seeking to conform their behavior to all pertinent laws.

Because of the limited scope of the defense, the Agencies will refrain from enforcement actions on the ground of foreign sovereign compulsion only when certain criteria are satisfied. First, the foreign government must have compelled the anticompetitive conduct under circumstances in which a refusal to comply with the foreign government's command would give rise to the imposition of penal or other severe sanctions. As a general matter, the Agencies regard the foreign government's formal representation that refusal to comply with its command would have such a result as being sufficient to establish that the conduct in question has been compelled, as long as that representation contains sufficient detail to enable the Agencies to see precisely how the compulsion would be accomplished under local law.

---

89.   28 U.S.C. 1603(e) (1988).

91.   *Republic of Argentina*, 112 S.Ct. at 2168.

93.   Interamerican Refining Corp. v. Texaco Maracaibo, Inc., 307 F. Supp. 1291 (D. Del. 1970) (defendant, having been ordered by the government of Venezuela not to sell oil to a particular refiner out of favor with the current political regime, held not subject to antitrust liability under the Sherman Act for an illegal group boycott). The defense of foreign sovereign compulsion is distinguished from the federalism-based state action doctrine. The state action doctrine applies not just to the actions of states and their subdivisions, but also to private anticompetitive conduct that is both undertaken pursuant to clearly articulated state policies, and is actively supervised by the state. . . . [See Chapter 1].

Foreign government measures short of compulsion do not suffice for this defense, although they can be relevant in a comity analysis.

Second, although there can be no strict territorial test for this defense, the defense normally applies only when the foreign government compels conduct which can be accomplished entirely within its own territory. If the compelled conduct occurs in the United States, the Agencies will not recognize the defense. For example, no defense arises when a foreign government requires the U.S. subsidiaries of several firms to organize a cartel in the United States to fix the price at which products would be sold in the United States, or when it requires its firms to fix mandatory resale prices for their U.S. distributors to use in the United States. Third, with reference to the discussion of foreign sovereign immunity in Section 3.31 above, the order must come from the foreign government acting in its governmental capacity. The defense does not arise from conduct that would fall within the FSIA commercial activity exception.

ILLUSTRATIVE EXAMPLE K

Situation: Greatly increased quantities of commodity X have flooded into the world market over the last two or three years, including substantial amounts indirectly coming into the United States. Because they are unsure whether they would prevail in an antidumping and countervailing duty case, U.S. industry participants have refrained from filing trade law petitions. The officials of three foreign countries meet with their respective domestic firms and urge them to "rationalize" production by cooperatively cutting back. Going one step further, one of the interested governments orders cutbacks from its firms, subject to substantial penalties for non-compliance. Producers from the other two countries agree among themselves to institute comparable cutbacks, but their governments do not require them to do so.

Discussion: Assume for the purpose of this example that the overseas production cutbacks have the necessary effects on U.S. commerce to support jurisdiction. As for the participants from the two countries that did not impose any penalty for a failure to reduce production, the Agencies would not find that sovereign compulsion precluded prosecution of this agreement. As for participants from the country that did compel production cut-backs through the imposition of severe penalties, the Agencies would acknowledge a defense of sovereign compulsion.

3.33 Acts of State. The act of state doctrine is a judge-made rule of federal common law.[97] It is a doctrine of judicial abstention based on considerations of international comity and separation of powers, and applies only if the specific conduct complained of is a public act of the foreign sovereign within its territorial jurisdiction on matters pertaining to its governmental sovereignty. The act of state doctrine arises when the validity of the acts of a foreign government is an unavoidable issue in a case.[98]

---

97. Banco Nacional de Cuba v. Sabbatino, 376 U.S. 398, 421–22 n.21 (1964) (noting that other countries do not adhere in any formulaic way to an act of state doctrine).

98. See W.S. Kirkpatrick & Co. v. Environmental Tectonics, 493 U.S. 400 (1990).

Courts have refused to adjudicate claims or issues that would require the court to judge the legality (as a matter of U.S. law or international law) of the sovereign act of a foreign state. Although in some cases the sovereign act in question may compel private behavior, such compulsion is not required by the doctrine. While the act of state doctrine does not compel dismissal as a matter of course, judicial abstention is appropriate in a case where the court must "declare invalid, and thus ineffective as a rule of decision in the U.S. courts, . . . the official act of a foreign sovereign."[101]

When a restraint on competition arises directly from the act of a foreign sovereign, such as the grant of a license, award of a contract, expropriation of property, or the like, the Agencies may refrain from bringing an enforcement action based on the act of state doctrine. For example, the Agencies will not challenge foreign acts of state if the facts and circumstances indicate that: (1) the specific conduct complained of is a public act of the sovereign, (2) the act was taken within the territorial jurisdiction of the sovereign, and (3) the matter is governmental, rather than commercial.

3.34   Petitioning of Sovereigns. Under the *Noerr–Pennington* doctrine, a genuine effort to obtain or influence action by governmental entities in the United States is immune from application of the Sherman Act, even if the intent or effect of that effort is to restrain or monopolize trade. [See Chapter 1]. Whatever the basis asserted for *Noerr–Pennington* immunity (either as an application of the First Amendment or as a limit on the statutory reach of the Sherman Act, or both), the Agencies will apply it in the same manner to the petitioning of foreign governments and the U.S. Government.

ILLUSTRATIVE EXAMPLE L

Situation: In the course of preparing an antidumping case, which requires the U.S. industry to demonstrate that it has been injured through the effects of the dumped imports, producers representing 75 percent of U.S. output exchange the information required for the adjudication. All the information is exchanged indirectly through third parties and in an aggregated form that makes the identity of any particular producer's information impossible to discern.

Discussion: Information exchanged by competitors within the context of an antidumping proceeding implicates the *Noerr–Pennington* petitioning immunity. To the extent that these exchanges are reasonably necessary in order for them to prepare their joint petition, which is permitted under the trade laws, *Noerr* is available to protect against antitrust liability that would otherwise arise. On these facts the parties are likely to be immunized by *Noerr* if they have taken the necessary measures to ensure that the provision of sensitive information called for by the Commerce Department and the ITC cannot be used for anticompetitive purposes. In such a situation, the information exchange is incidental to genuine petitioning and is not subject to the antitrust laws. Conversely, were the parties directly to exchange exten-

---

101. *Kirkpatrick*, 493 U.S. at 405, quoting Ricaud v. American Metal Co., 246 U.S. 304, 310 (1918).

sive information relating to their costs, the prices each has charged for the product, pricing trends, and profitability, including information about specific transactions that went beyond the scope of those facts required for the adjudication, such conduct would go beyond the contemplated protection of *Noerr* immunity....

Questions on U.S. Doctrines Where Foreign Sovereigns Are Involved

1. Why should foreign sovereign immunity turn on whether the action involves commercial activity?

a. Does this have a parallel in the application of state action immunity to conduct by state agencies or municipalities? See Chapter 1.

b. Suppose the foreign government is purchasing products on a commercial marketplace for government use and agrees to participate in a buyer cartel. Would it enjoy foreign sovereign immunity?

c. Should foreign sovereign immunity apply when a government issues bonds?[63]

2. Suppose a foreign government compels its firms to engage in a price-fixing cartel.

a. If those firms fix the prices of products they sell in a foreign nation for export to the United States, would they be immune from a U.S. antitrust claim? Would any immunity be consistent with the fact that state action immunity would not immunize a price-fixing agreement that was compelled by state law unless the state or a state agency was the one fixing the prices? See Chapter 1. Should foreign compulsion immunity likewise require proof that the foreign government not only compelled price-fixing but fixed the price levels?

b. If those compelled foreign firms fix the prices of products they sell in the United States, would they be immune from a U.S. antitrust claim? What are firms supposed to do when they are faced with a choice between severe sanctions from the foreign government or severe sanctions under U.S. antitrust law?

c. Does it make sense to have the compulsion doctrine differ so much based on the location of the conduct when the location of the effects is the same in cases *a* and *b*? Is this distinction consistent with the general movement of doctrine in this area from a conduct-location test to an effects-location test?

3. Should the scope of petitioning immunity differ at all when firms are petitioning a foreign government than when they are petitioning a U.S. state or federal entity?

Foreign Nations as U.S. Antitrust Plaintiffs

If foreign nations enjoy sovereign immunity as defendants, should they be able to bring suit as plaintiffs? The Supreme Court has held they can,

---

63. *See* Republic of Argentina v. Weltover, Inc., 504 U.S. 607 (1992) (holding "no").

but Congress then enacted a statute providing that a foreign nation can recover only single (not treble) damages unless it would be denied sovereign immunity either because it waived that immunity or it is engaged in a commercial activity.[64] This differs from U.S. states and municipalities, both of which can sue for treble damages even though the states enjoy state action immunity and the municipalities enjoy immunity when their conduct is authorized by the state and are subject to only single-damages as a defendant when they are not. *See* Chapter 1. Is it justifiable to treat foreign nations differently than U.S. states? Is this difference in treatment justified by the fact that foreign nations generally do not allow treble damages under their own competition laws?

W.S. Kirkpatrick & Co. v. Environmental Tectonics

493 U.S. 400 (1990).

■ JUSTICE SCALIA delivered the opinion of the Court.

In this case we must decide whether the act of state doctrine bars a court in the United States from entertaining a cause of action that does not rest upon the asserted invalidity of an official act of a foreign sovereign, but that does require imputing to foreign officials an unlawful motivation (the obtaining of bribes) in the performance of such an official act.

I

The facts as alleged in respondent's complaint are as follows: In 1981, Harry Carpenter, who was then chairman of the board and chief executive officer of petitioner ... Kirkpatrick ..., learned that the Republic of Nigeria was interested in contracting for the construction and equipment of an aeromedical center at Kaduna Air Force Base in Nigeria. He made arrangements with Benson "Tunde" Akindele, a Nigerian citizen, whereby Akindele would endeavor to secure the contract for Kirkpatrick. It was agreed that, in the event the contract was awarded to Kirkpatrick, Kirkpatrick would pay to two Panamanian entities controlled by Akindele a "commission" equal to 20% of the contract price, which would in turn be given as a bribe to officials of the Nigerian Government. In accordance with this plan, the contract was awarded to ... Kirkpatrick International ..., a wholly owned subsidiary of Kirkpatrick; Kirkpatrick paid the promised "commission" to the appointed Panamanian entities; and those funds were disbursed as bribes. All parties agree that Nigerian law prohibits both the payment and the receipt of bribes in connection with the award of a government contract.

Respondent Environmental Tectonics ..., an unsuccessful bidder for the Kaduna contract, learned of the 20% "commission" and brought the matter to the attention of the Nigerian Air Force and the United States Embassy in Lagos. Following an investigation by the Federal Bureau of

---

64. *See* Pfizer, Inc. v. Government of India, 434 U.S. 308 (1978); 15 U.S.C. § 15(b), 96 Stat. 1964 (1982).

Investigation, the United States Attorney for the District of New Jersey brought charges against both Kirkpatrick and Carpenter for violations of the Foreign Corrupt Practices Act of 1977, and both pleaded guilty.

Respondent then brought this civil action in ... United States District Court ... against Carpenter, Akindele, petitioners, and others, seeking damages under the Racketeer Influenced and Corrupt Organizations Act, the Robinson–Patman Act, and the New Jersey Anti–Racketeering Act. The defendants moved to dismiss the complaint under Rule 12(b)(6) of the Federal Rules of Civil Procedure on the ground that the action was barred by the act of state doctrine.

... The District Court concluded that the act of state doctrine applies "if the inquiry presented for judicial determination includes the motivation of a sovereign act which would result in embarrassment to the sovereign or constitute interference in the conduct of foreign policy of the United States." Applying that principle to the facts at hand, the court held that respondent's suit had to be dismissed ... The Court of Appeals for the Third Circuit reversed.... The Court of Appeals found particularly persuasive the letter to the District Court from the legal adviser to the Department of State, which had stated that in the opinion of the Department judicial inquiry into the purpose behind the act of a foreign sovereign would not produce the "unique embarrassment, and the particular interference with the conduct of foreign affairs, that may result from the judicial determination that a foreign sovereign's acts are invalid." The Court of Appeals acknowledged that "the Department's legal conclusions as to the reach of the act of state doctrine are not controlling on the courts," but concluded that "the Department's factual assessment of whether fulfillment of its responsibilities will be prejudiced by the course of civil litigation is entitled to substantial respect." ...

II

This Court's description of the jurisprudential foundation for the act of state doctrine has undergone some evolution over the years. We once viewed the doctrine as an expression of international law, resting upon "the highest considerations of international comity and expediency," *Oetjen v. Central Leather Co.,* 246 U.S. 297, 303–304 (1918). We have more recently described it, however, as a consequence of domestic separation of powers, reflecting "the strong sense of the Judicial Branch that its engagement in the task of passing on the validity of foreign acts of state may hinder" the conduct of foreign affairs, *Banco Nacional de Cuba v. Sabbatino,* 376 U.S. 398, 423 (1964). Some Justices have suggested possible exceptions to application of the doctrine, where one or both of the foregoing policies would seemingly not be served: an exception, for example, for acts of state that consist of commercial transactions, since neither modern international comity nor the current position of our Executive Branch accorded sovereign immunity to such acts, see *Alfred Dunhill of London, Inc. v. Republic of Cuba,* 425 U.S. 682, 695–706 (1976) (opinion of WHITE, J.); or an exception for cases in which the Executive Branch has represented that it has no objection to denying validity to the foreign sovereign act, since then the courts would be impeding no foreign policy goals, see *First National City Bank v. Banco Nacional de Cuba,* 406 U.S. 759, 768–770 (1972) (opinion of REHNQUIST, J.).

The parties have argued at length about the applicability of these possible exceptions, and, more generally, about whether the purpose of the act of state doctrine would be furthered by its application in this case. We find it unnecessary, however, to pursue those inquiries, since the factual predicate for application of the act of state doctrine does not exist. Nothing in the present suit requires the Court to declare invalid, and thus ineffective as "a rule of decision for the courts of this country," Ricaud v. American Metal Co., 246 U.S. 304, 310 (1918), the official act of a foreign sovereign.

In every case in which we have held the act of state doctrine applicable, the relief sought or the defense interposed would have required a court in the United States to declare invalid the official act of a foreign sovereign performed within its own territory. In *Underhill v. Hernandez,* 168 U.S. 250, 254 (1897), holding the defendant's detention of the plaintiff to be tortious would have required denying legal effect to "acts of a military commander representing the authority of the revolutionary party as government, which afterwards succeeded and was recognized by the United States." In *Oetjen* and in *Ricaud,* denying title to the party who claimed through purchase from Mexico would have required declaring that government's prior seizure of the property, within its own territory, legally ineffective. In *Sabbatino,* upholding the defendant's claim to the funds would have required a holding that Cuba's expropriation of goods located in Havana was null and void. In the present case, by contrast, neither the claim nor any asserted defense requires a determination that Nigeria's contract with Kirkpatrick International was, or was not, effective.

Petitioners point out, however, that the facts necessary to establish respondent's claim will also establish that the contract was unlawful. Specifically, they note that in order to prevail respondent must prove that petitioner Kirkpatrick made, and Nigerian officials received, payments that violate Nigerian law, which would, they assert, support a finding that the contract is invalid under Nigerian law. Assuming that to be true, it still does not suffice. The act of state doctrine is not some vague doctrine of abstention but a *"principle of decision* binding on federal and state courts alike." *Sabbatino.* As we said in *Ricaud,* "the act within its own boundaries of one sovereign State . . . becomes . . . a rule of decision for the courts of this country." Act of state issues only arise when a court *must decide*—that is, when the outcome of the case turns upon—the effect of official action by a foreign sovereign. When that question is not in the case, neither is the act of state doctrine. That is the situation here. Regardless of what the court's factual findings may suggest as to the legality of the Nigerian contract, its legality is simply not a question to be decided in the present suit, and there is thus no occasion to apply the rule of decision that the act of state doctrine requires. Cf. *Sharon v. Time, Inc.,* 599 F.Supp. 538, 546 (SDNY

1984) ("The issue in this litigation is not whether [the alleged] acts are valid, but whether they occurred").

In support of their position that the act of state doctrine bars any factual findings that may cast doubt upon the validity of foreign sovereign acts, petitioners cite Justice Holmes' opinion for the Court in *American Banana Co. v. United Fruit Co.*, 213 U.S. 347 (1909). That was a suit under the United States antitrust laws, alleging that Costa Rica's seizure of the plaintiff's property had been induced by an unlawful conspiracy. In the course of a lengthy opinion Justice Holmes observed, citing *Underhill,* that "a seizure by a state is not a thing that can be complained of elsewhere in the courts." The statement is concededly puzzling. *Underhill* does indeed stand for the proposition that a seizure by a state cannot be complained of elsewhere—in the sense of being sought to be declared *ineffective* elsewhere. The plaintiff in *American Banana,* however, like the plaintiff here, was not trying to undo or disregard the governmental action, but only to obtain damages from private parties who had procured it. Arguably, then, the statement did imply that suit would not lie if a foreign state's actions would be, though not invalidated, impugned.

Whatever Justice Holmes may have had in mind, his statement lends inadequate support to petitioners' position here, for two reasons. First, it was a brief aside, entirely unnecessary to the decision. *American Banana* was squarely decided on the ground (later substantially overruled, see *Continental Ore*) that the antitrust laws had no extraterritorial application, so that "what the defendant did in Panama or Costa Rica is not within the scope of the statute." Second, whatever support the dictum might provide for petitioners' position is more than overcome by our later holding in *United States v. Sisal Sales Corp.*, 274 U.S. 268 (1927). There we held that, *American Banana* notwithstanding, the defendant's actions in obtaining Mexico's enactment of "discriminating legislation" could form part of the basis for suit under the United States antitrust laws. Simply put, *American Banana* was not an act of state case; and whatever it said by way of dictum that might be relevant to the present case has not survived *Sisal Sales.*

Petitioners insist, however, that the policies underlying our act of state cases—international comity, respect for the sovereignty of foreign nations on their own territory, and the avoidance of embarrassment to the Executive Branch in its conduct of foreign relations—are implicated in the present case because, as the District Court found, a determination that Nigerian officials demanded and accepted a bribe "would impugn or question the nobility of a foreign nation's motivations," and would "result in embarrassment to the sovereign or constitute interference in the conduct of foreign policy of the United States." The United States, as *amicus curiae,* favors the same approach to the act of state doctrine, though disagreeing with petitioners as to the outcome it produces in the present case. We should not, the United States urges, "attach dispositive significance to the fact that this suit involves only the 'motivation' for, rather than the 'validity' of, a foreign sovereign act," and should eschew "any rigid formula for the resolution of act of state cases generally." In some future case, perhaps, "litigation ... based on alleged corruption in the award of contracts or other commercially oriented activities of foreign governments could sufficiently touch on 'national nerves' that the act of state doctrine or related principles of abstention would appropriately be found to bar the suit," and we should therefore resolve this case on the narrowest possible ground, viz., that the letter from the legal adviser to the District Court gives sufficient indication that, "in the setting of this case," the act of state doctrine poses no bar to adjudication.*

These urgings are deceptively similar to what we said in *Sabbatino,* where we observed that sometimes, even though the validity of the act of a foreign sovereign within its own territory is called into question, the policies underlying the act of state doctrine may not justify its application. We suggested that a sort of balancing approach could be applied—the balance shifting against application of the doctrine, for example, if the government that committed the "challenged act of state" is no longer in existence. But what is appropriate in order to avoid unquestioning judicial acceptance of the acts of foreign sovereigns is not similarly appropriate for the quite opposite purpose of expanding judicial incapacities where such acts are not directly (or even indirectly) involved. It is one thing to suggest, as we have, that the policies underlying the act of state doctrine should be considered in deciding whether, despite the doctrine's technical availability, it should nonetheless not be invoked; it is something quite different to suggest that those underlying policies are a doctrine unto themselves, justifying expansion of the act of state doctrine (or, as the United States puts it, unspecified "related principles of abstention") into new and uncharted fields.

The short of the matter is this: Courts in the United States have the power, and ordinarily the obligation, to decide cases and controversies properly presented to them. The act of state doctrine does not establish an exception for cases and controversies that may embarrass foreign governments, but merely requires that, in the process of deciding, the acts of foreign sovereigns taken within their own jurisdictions shall be deemed valid. That doctrine has no application to the present case because the validity of no foreign sovereign act is at issue.

The judgment of the Court of Appeals for the Third Circuit is affirmed.

Questions on *Kirkpatrick*

1.   Could this case have been resolved by the doctrines of foreign sovereign immunity or foreign compulsion?

2.   Doesn't a conclusion that a foreign government was bribed into an action necessarily call the validity of that action into question? Is the Court saying that as long as that action is treated as legally binding, the act of

---

* Even if we agreed with the Government's fundamental approach, we would question its characterization of the legal adviser's letter as reflecting the absence of any policy objection to the adjudication. The letter ... did not purport to say whether the State Department would like the suit to proceed, but rather responded (correctly, as we hold today) to the question whether the act of state doctrine was applicable.

state doctrine poses no bar to imposing penalties on the private party that illegally procured it?

3. Should the act of state doctrine instead consist of (or be limited by) a case-by-case determination of whether the suit is likely to adversely affect the foreign relations of the United States? If so, what would it add to the doctrine of comity?

4. Should the act of state doctrine ever bar a claim that the U.S. government indicates should proceed? Should it ever bar a claim brought by the U.S. government itself?

5. Suppose a U.S. antitrust claim were brought against the OPEC nations for their oil cartel.

a. Isn't selling oil a commercial activity? Given this, shouldn't foreign sovereign immunity be denied under the FSIA? Should act of state immunity also be denied under the *Dunhill* plurality's exception for commercial activities even though such an action necessarily call into question the validity of the foreign state action of agreeing to fix production as part of OPEC? Given doctrinal developments, is it time to rethink old lower court caselaw finding OPEC immune under one of these theories?[65]

b. Should the validity of such a U.S. antitrust claim instead turn on questions of comity? Would comity pose any bar if the U.S. agencies themselves decided to sue OPEC in antitrust?

6. Suppose a foreign nation made a private corporation its official agent. Would the actions of such an official agent enjoy act of state immunity?[66]

7. Does the Robinson–Patman Act claim turn on whether the 20% commission paid was an illegal bribe or not? Doesn't the Robinson–Patman Act apply to discriminatory prices that are otherwise legal?

8. Why doesn't petitioning immunity apply to this effort to procure foreign government action? Is it because bribery constitutes an exception to petitioning immunity?[67] If so, that might explain why it was thought necessary in this case to prove the commission was an illegal bribe.

---

65. *See* International Association of Machinists and Aerospace Workers v. OPEC, 477 F.Supp. 553 (C.D.Cal 1979) (finding OPEC immune under sovereign immunity), *affirmed on different grounds*, 649 F.2d 1354 (9th Cir.1981) (finding OPEC was immune under act of state doctrine). The most recent case to address the substance concluded that the commercial activities exception defeated both these immunity doctrines and entered a default judgment against OPEC. *See* Prewitt Enterprises, Inc. v. OPEC, 2001 WL 624789 (N.D. Ala. 2001). However, the case was transferred to another judge who dismissed the case for faulty service of process because federal rules require that international service comply with foreign law, and OPEC was headquartered in Austria, which had a special rule that prohibited service on OPEC without the consent of OPEC's Secretary General. This decision was affirmed on appeal with reasoning that indicated the outcome might be different if suit were sought against the nations belonging to the OPEC cartel rather than against OPEC itself. *See* 353 F.3d 916, 922 n.9 (11th Cir. 2003).

66. *See* Continental Ore v. Union Carbide, 370 U.S. 690, 706–07 (1962) (rejecting act of state immunity).

67. *See* Einer Elhauge, *Making Sense of Antitrust Petitioning Immunity*, 80 CALIF. L.REV. 1177, 1243–46 (1992) (collecting the conflicting caselaw and dicta on this issue and arguing that bribery should be an exception).

Opinion of Advocate General Fennelly Delivered on 29 October 1998, Joined Cases C–395/96 P and C–396/96 P Compagnie Maritime Melge NV and Dafra–Lines v. Commission of the European Communities

[2000] ECR I–136.

[The Commission penalized the members of CEWAL, a liner conference, for a series of abusive practices on the market for freight between Zaire (now Congo) and Northern Europe. One of those practices was that the members of the liner conference had concluded a cooperation agreement with the Zairean public authorities (Ogefrem), whereby the latter would ensure that no goods would be shipped by competitors of the CEWAL liner conference (a form of exclusivity arrangement).]

. . . [T]he Commission found that, in order to eliminate its competitor, Cewal had, *inter alia*, abused its joint dominant position by "participating in the implementation of the cooperation agreement with Ogefrem and by repeatedly [requesting] by a variety of means that it be strictly complied with. . . ." [The CFI affirmed.] . . .

—*The relevance of the "Act of State" doctrine.* The appellants contend that their behaviour should be characterised as amounting to no more than an attempt to lobby the Zaïrean authorities regarding the fulfilment of a State concession. . . . The appellants rely, in particular, on certain principles developed in the anti-trust case-law of the United States of America. They accept that no such principles have been established in Community law. In essence, this part of the appellants' argument depends on their showing that the Ogefrem Agreement represents an act exercising the sovereign power of the Government of Zaïre.

. . . Under an "Act of State" doctrine associated with the principle of comity of nations, it appears that the courts of the United States have held that acts of inducement or persuasion (even unlawful ones) of a foreign sovereign power fall outside the scope of the anti-trust rules. In the view that I take of the nature of the Ogefrem Agreement, it is unnecessary for me to discuss this doctrine further. It is, of course, clear that the simple fact that a Member State creates a legal monopoly by granting exclusive rights does not infringe Article [102]. It is, no doubt, a corollary of this that acting so as to persuade a Member State to create such a monopoly also falls outside Article [102]. The Court has, however, equally made it clear that "the [TFEU] rules on competition and in particular those contained in Article [102] apply to such undertakings." It can be supposed that, by extension, these principles also apply to the establishment of legal monopolies by foreign governments. . . .

The "Act of State" principle will not apply, however, if the Ogefrem Agreement is not the unilateral act of a sovereign power but, as found by the Commission, in substance and reality a consensual agreement. For that purpose, it does not seem to me to matter that, as no doubt correctly urged by the appellants, Ogefrem is not an undertaking for the purposes of Articles [101] and [102]. First, the abuse alleged consists of the acts of insistence on implementation of the exclusivity conferred by the agreement and not of its conclusion. Secondly, the application of Article [102] to an undertaking in a position such as that of Cewal is not dependant on the Ogefrem Agreement being an agreement for the purposes of Article [101].

In that light, I shall summarise the appellants' case regarding the "Act of State" character of the agreement as made in very extensive pleadings before the Court of First Instance and before this Court.

First, the appellants attach great importance to the UNCTAD Code of 1974, which [was ratified by the EU] ... The Code provided, at Article 2, for the distribution of conference shipping trade between any two States covered by such conference according to a 40: 40: 20 rule. Such trade should be shared as to 40% each between the national shipping lines of the two States between which the trade was conducted with 20% being allocated to any third-country conference-member shipping line. It is common case that there were, from an early date, seriously divergent views as to the correct interpretation of the Code between the OECD signatory States and a number of African States, among them Zaïre. The former maintained that both the clear wording of the Code and its context show that it applies only to conference-liner trade. The latter claimed that it extends to all liner traffic.

The applicants have recounted at length the steps taken by a number of African States and Zaïre in particular to impose their interpretation with a view to protecting their national shipping lines. Zaïre incorporated Ogefrem as a public body in 1980.... It became operational in 1983 pursuant to "Ordonnance Presidentielle No. 80–256". Its tasks included the control of cargo and negotiation of freight rates, the protection of the profitability of the national shipping line, Compagnie Maritime Zaïroise (hereinafter "CMZ") and the defence of Zaïrean shipping interests.

A further legislative act, an "arrêté d'exécution" No. 001–83 of 17 January 1983, applied the UNCTAD 40: 40: 20 rule to the distribution of all cargo. Cewal and other European shipping interests, Member States and the Commission made extensive but unsuccessful efforts politically and otherwise to secure the reversal or modification of this policy.

Ogefrem from 1984 imposed a number of additional financial and administrative burdens on Cewal including the payment by each Cewal member of a deposit of U.S. $10,000 to Ogefrem, and payment of a 3% commission on the freight rate in supposed protection of CMZ's participation in 40% of the cargo.

In these circumstances, Cewal says that the Ogefrem Agreement was "imposed upon it." It cites the terms of the agreement to demonstrate, in particular, that it results from, inter alia, "Ordonnance 80–256", and claims that it could not resist the imposition by a government whose policy was vital to its trade of an agreement which implemented that policy.

The Commission, while not disputing most of the recited facts, maintains that the Ogefrem Agreement does not have the character of an imposed "Act of State" but constitutes an agreement imposing mutual obligations and granting reciprocal benefits.

In the first instance, it says that the appellants commit a fundamental error of logic with regard to the Code. It points out that the application of the UNCTAD 40: 40: 20 rule to all liner traffic and the proportion of liner traffic carried by conferences are completely separate issues, so that there is no logical connection between the participation of the African national lines in their full share of the market and any exclusivity for conferences. In short, the guarantee of the 40% of all cargo to those lines does not mean that all of the remaining 60% should go to members of the conference lines.

As to the terms of the Ogefrem Agreement, the Commission refers to the provision for unilateral termination by either party on one year's notice, the provision for reference of disputes to arbitration and the apparent success of Cewal in negotiating the rate of commission down from 3% to 0.5%. Furthermore, the Commission repudiates the description of the agreement as a State concession. That would presuppose legislation providing for the grant of an exclusive right and for its grant through an administrative procedure.

—*The true nature of the Ogefrem Agreement.* It must be accepted that it was the policy of the Government of Zaïre, in common with those of several other African States, to apply the UNCTAD 40: 40: 20 rule, by law if necessary, to all cargo and not merely to conference traffic. To that end, it established Ogefrem with extensive powers to regulate and supervise shipping into and out of Zaïre. However, I agree with the Commission that Zaïre's approach to the UNCTAD 40: 40: 20 rule does not justify Cewal's attempt to exclude non-conference traffic. . . .

Nor do the difficulties described by the appellants in dealing with Ogefrem go further than to establish a certain inequality of bargaining power. In spite of many problems described, Cewal wished to continue to operate the conference line on which it had, as it concedes, a de facto monopoly. It had already, if reluctantly, agreed to concede 40% of the traffic to CMZ, which became a member of the Cewal conference.

Next, it is necessary to turn to the text of the Ogefrem Agreement, drawn up in French. I do not agree that the introductory recital in the agreement of the several Zaïrean legal acts and instruments is enough to give it the character of a sovereign act of the State of Zaïre. For example, it recites a resolution of the Ministerial Conference of Central and West Africa inviting the shipowner companies of the member states of that conference to undertake concerted action with the maritime conferences serving Central and West Africa with a view to stabilising freight rates and adapting their statutes to conform with the Code of Conduct for Maritime Conferences. Nor does its recital of Ogefrem's own principal objectives limit the character of the agreement itself. The introductory recitals explain Ogefrem's status and objectives. They do not show the contents of the "cooperation agreement to be an act of State with the character of a legal act conferring a monopoly right."

In its operative part, the Ogefrem Agreement is just that, i.e. an agreement. The exclusivity clause in Article 1 is the heart of the matter. It does not purport to exercise any legal or administrative power. I agree with the Commission that it does not identify any particular basis for the grant, by way of State concession, of a legal right. It is, in fact, expressed in the simple terms of a joint or mutual obligation. The remainder of the operative part of the agreement imposes respective obligations of a general kind regarding the maintenance and exchange of statistics (Article 6), the deduction of an agreed percentage from the freight for payment to Ogefrem (Article 7), the maintenance of accounting records (Articles 8 and 9) and the observance of negotiated rates (Article 10). By Article 11, the agreement was concluded for a single year, but automatically renewed in default of one year's notice of termination by either party. Finally, Article 12 contains provision for obligatory reference of disputes to an arbitral college of three persons, one to be chosen by each party and the third by the persons so chosen.

In my view, neither the terms of the Ogefrem Agreement, the legal background recounted by the appellants nor the circumstances of its conclusion give it the character of the act of a sovereign power granting any form of State concession as claimed by the appellants. It is, accordingly, unnecessary for the purposes of this appeal, to determine the role to be allowed in Community law to the State-action doctrine. Accordingly, I would dismiss the second head of the ground of appeal relating to the Ogefrem Agreement. . . .

A similar fate must befall the appellants' [last] argument, namely that Article [102] does not prohibit an undertaking which has been lawfully granted a legal exclusivity from insisting that it be respected. The appellants rely on the constant case-law of the Court to the effect that "[i]t is not incompatible with Article [102] for an undertaking to which a Member State has granted exclusive rights within the meaning of Article [106 TFEU] to enjoy a monopoly." Since we are not dealing with such a monopoly, the issue simply does not arise. Moreover, it is here appropriate to recall the view of the [General Court] . . . that Cewal members had, under the very terms of the Ogefrem Agreement, a mechanism for opening up competition. They chose to insist on not availing of this possibility. Consequently, I would also dismiss the [last] argument and, therefore, the entire ground of appeal relating to the finding of abuse in respect of the Ogefrem Agreement. . . .

Compagnie Maritime Belge Transports SA, Compagnie Maritime Belge SA and Dafra–Lines A/S v. Commission, Joined Cases C–395/96 P and C–396/96 P

ECR [2000] 1365 (ECJ).

. . . . It is clear from . . . the contested judgment that the first paragraph of Article 1 of the Ogefrem Agreement provided for exclusivity for the benefit of members of Cewal in respect of all cargoes to be carried within the field of activity of the conference. The second paragraph of that article made express provision for possible derogations, subject to agreement of the two parties. Ogefrem unilaterally granted approval to an independent shipping operation, in principle to the extent of 2% of aggregate Zairean trade, although its share subsequently increased. Thereupon, the members of Cewal made approaches to Ogefrem in order to have Grimaldi and Cobelfret (G & C) removed from the market. In particular, the members of Cewal reminded Ogefrem of its obligations and requested that they be strictly complied with.

The first question is whether the fact that the appellants insisted, in the context of an agreement concluded with the Zairean authorities, that the terms of that agreement be strictly complied with is to be treated in the same way as mere inducement to government action. If so, the next question is whether such inducement can itself constitute an abuse.

It cannot be disputed that there is a difference between a request to a public authority to comply with a specific contractual obligation and mere incitement or inducement of the authority to take action. In the latter case, there is a simple attempt to influence the authority concerned in the exercise of its discretion. The purpose of a request to comply with a specific contractual obligation, by contrast, is to enforce legal rights which the authority concerned is, by definition, bound to observe.

It follows that the appellants' insistence that the terms of the Ogefrem Agreement be complied with cannot be treated in the same way as mere incitement of the Zairean authorities to take government action. It is therefore unnecessary to consider whether, and in what circumstances, mere incitement of a government to take action may constitute abuse within the meaning of Article [102 TFEU].

As has been stated, the Court of First Instance and the Commission considered that the abuse consisted in the fact that Cewal had repeatedly insisted that the Zairean authorities strictly observe its exclusive right.

It should be remembered that the existence of a dominant position means that, irrespective of the reasons which have led to such a position, the dominant undertaking or undertakings have a special responsibility not to allow their conduct to impair genuine undistorted competition on the common market (*Michelin*).

It is established, in the present case, that Cewal sought to rely on the contractual exclusivity provided for in the Ogefrem Agreement in order to remove its only competitor from the market. Such conduct was in no way required by that agreement, since, under the second paragraph of Article 1 thereof, express provision is made for possible derogations, so that the requirements of Article [102 TFEU] could be met.

Accordingly, the ... argument [that appellants merely were inciting government action] must be rejected and the [other argument], that the appellants were criticised for not having waived their exclusive rights, is irrelevant. . . .

Questions on *Compagnie Maritime Belge*

1. According to Advocate General Fennelly, is there an Act of State Doctrine under EU law?

a. Under which conditions could an agreement concluded between an EU company and a foreign government fall under the Act of State Doctrine?

b. Why doesn't the agreement in question fall under the Act of State Doctrine?

2.   Can the simple fact of lobbying a public authority for exclusivity violate Article 102? Does this case involve anything more?

3.   Is the Article 102 violation Cewal's exclusive agreement with a foreign public authority?

a.   If not, what is the violation? Is it the fact Cewal tried to enforce a veto the agreement gave it against the introduction of some competition by the foreign authority?

b.   But if the conclusion of an exclusive agreement with a foreign government is compatible with Article 102, why does Cewal violate Article 102 by exerting a veto right it holds pursuant to the agreement against Article 102?

4.   Suppose Cewal and Zaire responded to this decision by adopting the terms of the agreement into a Zaire regulation giving Cewal exclusive rights.

a.   Would such a regulation violate Article 102? Even if the regulation itself were not the violation, would the ECJ say that any effort by Cewal to enforce the veto right the regulation gives it is a violation? Doesn't this amount to interfering with the regulatory acts of foreign states?

b.   If such a regulation would not amount to an Article 102 violation, why should the mere difference in form between it and the agreement in the case at hand matter? Why should the ability to secure exclusive rights from foreign governments turn on whether the parties and foreign government received good legal advice about what legal formality to use?

E.   INTERNATIONAL COOPERATION IN ANTITRUST ENFORCEMENT

U.S. DOJ–FTC, Antitrust Enforcement Guidelines for International Operations

(April 1995).

. . . *2.9 Relevant International Agreements*. . . . To further the twin goals of promoting enforcement cooperation between the United States and foreign governments and of reducing any tensions that may arise in particular proceedings, the Agencies have developed close relationships with antitrust and competition policy officials of many different countries. In some instances, understandings have been reached with respect to notifications, consultations, and cooperation in antitrust matters. In other instances, more general rules endorsed by multilateral organizations such as the Organization for Economic Cooperation and Development ("OECD") provide the basis for the Agencies' cooperative policies. Finally, even in the absence of specific or general international understandings or recommendations, the Agencies often seek cooperation with foreign authorities.

2.91   Bilateral Cooperation Agreements . . . Formal written bilateral arrangements exist between the United States and the Federal Republic of Germany, Australia, and Canada. International antitrust cooperation can also occur through mutual legal assistance treaties ("MLATs"), which are treaties of general application pursuant to which the United States and a foreign country agree to assist one another in criminal law enforcement matters. MLATs currently are in force with over one dozen countries, and many more are in the process of ratification or negotiation. However, only the MLAT with Canada has been used to date to obtain assistance in antitrust investigations. The Agencies also hold regular consultations with the antitrust officials of Canada, the European Commission, and Japan, and have close, informal ties with the antitrust authorities of many other countries. Since 1990, the Agencies have cooperated closely with countries in the process of establishing competition agencies, assisted by funding provided by the Agency for International Development.

On November 2, 1994, President Clinton signed into law the International Antitrust Enforcement Assistance Act of 1994, which authorizes the Agencies to enter into antitrust mutual assistance agreements in accordance with the legislation.[68]

2.92   International Guidelines and Recommendations. The Agencies have agreed with respect to member countries of the OECD to consider the legitimate interests of other nations in accordance with relevant OECD recommendations. Under the terms of a 1986 recommendation, the United States agency with responsibility for a particular case notifies a member country whenever an antitrust enforcement action may affect important interests of that country or its nationals. Examples of potentially notifiable actions include requests for documents located outside the United States, attempts to obtain information from potential witnesses located outside the United States, and cases or investigations with significant foreign conduct or involvement of foreign persons. . . .

Background on U.S.–EU Antitrust Cooperation

The cooperation between the European Commission and the U.S. antitrust authorities is primarily based on the 1991 Cooperation Agreement and the 1998 "Positive Comity Agreement."

The 1991 Co-operation Agreement essentially provides for: (i) the notification of cases being handled by the authorities of one Party, to the extent that these cases concern the "important interests" of the other Party (Article II); (ii) the exchange of information between the Parties on general matters relating to the implementation of the competition rules (Article III); (iii) the co-operation and co-ordination of the actions of both Parties' competition authorities (Article IV); (iv) a "traditional comity" procedure pursuant to which each Party undertakes to take into account the "important interests" of the other Party in its enforcement actions (Article VI); and (v) a "positive comity" procedure by virtue of which either Party can invite the other Party to take, on the basis of the latter's legislation, appropriate measures regarding anticompetitive behavior imple-

---

68. [Editor's Note: The U.S. agencies subsequently entered into a mutual assistance agreement with Australia and cooperation agreements with Brazil, Israel, Japan, and Mexico, and updated agreements with Canada and the EC. *See* http://www.usdoj.gov/atr/public/international/int_arrangements.htm.]

mented on its territory and which affects the important interests of the requesting Party (Article V).

The 1998 Positive Comity Agreement clarifies the mechanics of the positive comity co-operation instrument, as well the circumstances in which it can be called to operate. In principle, one party may request the other party to remedy anticompetitive behaviour which originates in its jurisdiction but affects the requesting party as well.

In addition to the 1991 and 1998 agreements, the EU and U.S. antitrust authorities issued in 2002 a set of best practices on co-operation in reviewing mergers, which require approval on both sides of the Atlantic. The best practices put in place a more structured basis for co-operation in reviews of individual merger cases. They recognize that cooperation is most effective when the investigation timetables of the reviewing agencies run more or less in parallel. Merging companies will therefore be offered the possibility of meeting at an early stage with the agencies to discuss timing issues. Companies are also encouraged to permit the agencies to exchange information which they have submitted during the course of an investigation and, where appropriate, to allow joint EU/U.S. interviews of the companies concerned.

Agreement Between the Government of the United States of America and the Commission of the European Communities Regarding the Application of their Competition Laws

(1991).

... Article II. Notification

1. Each Party shall notify the other whenever its competition authorities become aware that their enforcement activities may affect important interests of the other Party.

2. Enforcement activities as to which notification ordinarily will be appropriate include those that:

a) Are relevant to enforcement activities of the other Party;

b) Involve anticompetitive activities (other than a merger or acquisition) carried out in significant part in the other Party's territory;

c) Involve a merger or acquisition in which one or more of the parties to the transaction, or a company controlling one or more of the parties to the transaction, is a company incorporated or organized under the laws of the other Party or one of its states or member states;

d) Involve conduct believed to have been required, encouraged or approved by the other Party; or

e) Involve remedies that would, in significant respects, require or prohibit conduct in the other Party's territory....

Article III. Exchange of Information ...

2.   ... [A]ppropriate officials from the competition authorities of each Party shall meet at least twice each year, unless otherwise agreed, to (a) exchange information on their current enforcement activities and priorities, (b) exchange information on economic sectors of common interest, (c) discuss policy changes which they are considering, and (d) discuss other matters of mutual interest relating to the application of competition laws.

3.   Each Party will provide the other Party with any significant information that comes to the attention of its competition authorities about anticompetitive activities that its competition authorities believe is relevant to, or may warrant, enforcement activity by the other Party's competition authorities.

4.   Upon receiving a request from the other Party, and within the limits of Articles VIII and IX, a Party will provide to the requesting Party such information within its possession as the requesting Party may describe that is relevant to an enforcement activity being considered or conducted by the requesting Party's competition authorities.

Article IV. Cooperation and Coordination in Enforcement Activities

1.   The competition authorities of each Party will render assistance to the competition authorities of the other Party in their enforcement activities, to the extent compatible with the assisting Party's laws and important interests, and within its reasonably available resources.

2.   In cases where both Parties have an interest in pursuing enforcement activities with regard to related situations, they may agree that it is in their mutual interest to coordinate their enforcement activities....

Article V. Cooperation Regarding Anticompetitive Activities
in the Territory of One Party That Adversely Affect
the Interests of the Other Party

1.   The Parties note that anticompetitive activities may occur within the territory of one Party that, in addition to violating that Party's competition laws, adversely affect important interests of the other Party. The Parties agree that it is in both their interests to address anticompetitive activities of this nature.

2.   If a Party believes that anticompetitive activities carried out on the territory of the other Party are adversely affecting its important interests, the first Party may notify the other Party and may request that the other Party's competition authorities initiate appropriate enforcement activities. The notification shall be as specific as possible about the nature of the anticompetitive activities and their effects on the interests of the notifying Party, and shall include an offer of such further information and other cooperation as the notifying Party is able to provide.

3.   Upon receipt of a notification under paragraph 2, and after such other discussion between the Parties as may be appropriate and useful in the circumstances, the competition authorities of the notified Party will consider whether or not to initiate enforcement activities, or to expand ongoing enforcement activities, with respect to the anticompetitive activi-

ties identified in the notification. The notified Party will advise the notifying Party of its decision. If enforcement activities are initiated, the notified Party will advise the notifying Party of their outcome and, to the extent possible, of significant interim developments.

4. Nothing in this Article limits the discretion of the notified Party under its competition laws and enforcement policies as to whether or not to undertake enforcement activities with respect to the notified anticompetitive activities, or precludes the notifying Party from undertaking enforcement activities with respect to such anticompetitive activities.

Article VI. Avoidance of Conflicts over Enforcement Activities

Within the framework of its own laws and to the extent compatible with its important interests, each Party will seek, at all stages in its enforcement activities, to take into account the important interests of the other Party. Each Party shall consider important interests of the other Party in decisions as to whether or not to initiate an investigation or proceeding, the scope of an investigation or proceeding, the nature of the remedies or penalties sought, and in other ways, as appropriate. In considering one another's important interests in the course of their enforcement activities, the Parties will take account of, but will not be limited to, the following principles:

1. While an important interest of a Party may exist in the absence of official involvement by the Party with the activity in question, it is recognized that such interests would normally be reflected in antecedent laws, decisions or statements of policy by its competent authorities.

2. A Party's important interests may be affected at any stage of enforcement activity by the other Party. The Parties recognize, however, that as a general matter the potential for adverse impact on one Party's important interests arising from enforcement activity by the other Party is less at the investigative stage and greater at the stage at which conduct is prohibited or penalized, or at which other forms of remedial orders are imposed.

3. Where it appears that one Party's enforcement activities may adversely affect important interests of the other Party, the Parties will consider the following factors, in addition to any other factors that appear relevant in the circumstances, in seeking an appropriate accommodation of the competing interests:

　　a) the relative significance to the anticompetitive activities involved of conduct within the enforcing Party's territory as compared to conduct within the other Party's territory;

　　b) the presence or absence of a purpose on the part of those engaged in the anticompetitive activities to affect consumers, suppliers, or competitors within the enforcing Party's territory;

　　c) the relative significance of the effects of the anticompetitive activities on the enforcing Party's interests as compared to the effects on the other Party's interests;

d) the existence or absence of reasonable expectations that would be furthered or defeated by the enforcement activities;

e) the degree of conflict or consistency between the enforcement activities and the other Party's laws or articulated economic policies; and

f) the extent to which enforcement activities of the other Party with respect to the same persons, including judgments or undertakings resulting from such activities, may be affected.

Article VII. Consultation

1. Each Party agrees to consult promptly with the other Party in response to a request by the other Party for consultations regarding any matter related to this Agreement and to attempt to conclude consultations expeditiously with a view to reaching mutually satisfactory conclusions. Any request for consultations shall include the reasons therefor and shall state whether procedural time limits or other considerations require the consultations to be expedited.

These consultations shall take place at the appropriate level, which may include consultations between the heads of the competition authorities concerned.

2. In each consultation under paragraph 1, each Party shall take into account the principles of cooperation set forth in this Agreement and shall be prepared to explain to the other Party the specific results of its application of those principles to the issue that is the subject of consultation.

Article VIII. Confidentiality of Information

1. Notwithstanding any other provision of this Agreement, neither Party is required to provide information to the other Party if disclosure of that information to the requesting Party (a) is prohibited by the law of the Party possessing the information, or (b) would be incompatible with important interests of the Party possessing the information.

2. Each Party agrees to maintain, to the fullest extent possible, the confidentiality of any information provided to it in confidence by the other Party under this Agreement and to oppose, to the fullest extent possible, any application for disclosure of such information by a third party that is not authorized by the Party that supplied the information.

Article IX. Existing Law

Nothing in this Agreement shall be interpreted in a manner inconsistent with the existing laws, or as requiring any change in the laws, of the United States of America or the European Communities or of their respective states or member states. . . .

Questions on the 1991 U.S.–EU Coordination Agreement

1. Does it seem likely that this sort of Agreement will suffice to eliminate conflicts in antitrust policy between the U.S. and the EU? Does

this Agreement help eliminating substantive divergences between U.S. and EU's approaches in areas such as, for instance, abuses of dominant position? Can it at least help prevent inadvertent conflicts?

2. Can such agreements also aid enforcement actions where there is no policy conflict by helping provide information and enforcement assistance to the other jurisdiction?

3. Can such agreements to procure information and aid foreign enforcement also ameliorate the incentives each jurisdiction might otherwise have to underenforce antitrust law for any industries where it is mainly an exporter by arming the importing jurisdiction with the tools it needs to be an effective enforcer?

4. What would you expect to be the area of antitrust in which the cooperation between the U.S. and EU antitrust agencies has been particularly intense? Why?

5. Sharing of information between antitrust agencies is always a very sensitive issue.

a. What does this Agreement say about exchanges of confidential information between the Parties?

b. Does the agreement places limitations on such information exchanges?

    i. Are these limitations enunciated in the Agreement or do they essentiality depend on the laws of the Parties?

    ii. Do limitations on the exchange of confidential information between the Parties constrain the effectiveness of the Agreement?

Agreement Between the Government of the United States of America and the European Communities on the Application of Positive Comity Principles in the Enforcement of Their Competition Laws

(1998).

... Article I. Scope and Purpose of this Agreement

1. This Agreement applies where a Party satisfies the other that there is reason to believe that the following circumstances are present:

a. Anticompetitive activities are occurring in whole or in substantial part in the territory of one of the Parties and are adversely affecting the interests of the other Party; and

b. The activities in question are impermissible under the competition laws of the Party in the territory of which the activities are occurring.

2. The purposes of this Agreement are to:

a. Help ensure that trade and investment flows between the Parties and competition and consumer welfare within the territories of the Parties are not impeded by anticompetitive activities for which the competition laws of one or both Parties can provide a remedy, and

b.   Establish cooperative procedures to achieve the most effective and efficient enforcement of competition law, whereby the competition authorities of each Party will normally avoid allocating enforcement resources to dealing with anticompetitive activities that occur principally in and are directed principally towards the other Party's territory, where the competition authorities of the other Party are able and prepared to examine and take effective sanctions under their law to deal with those activities. . . .

ARTICLE III. POSITIVE COMITY

The competition authorities of a Requesting Party may request the competition authorities of a Requested Party to investigate and, if warranted, to remedy anticompetitive activities in accordance with the Requested Party's competition laws. Such a request may be made regardless of whether the activities also violate the Requesting Party's competition laws, and regardless of whether the competition authorities of the Requesting Party have commenced or contemplate taking enforcement activities under their own competition laws.

ARTICLE IV. DEFERRAL OR SUSPENSION OF INVESTIGATIONS IN RELIANCE ON ENFORCEMENT ACTIVITY BY THE REQUESTED PARTY

1.   The competition authorities of the Parties may agree that the competition authorities of the Requesting Party will defer or suspend pending or contemplated enforcement activities during the pendency of enforcement activities of the Requested Party.

2.   The competition authorities of a Requesting Party will normally defer or suspend their own enforcement activities in favor of enforcement activities by the competition authorities of the Requested Party when the following conditions are satisfied:

a.   The anticompetitive activities at issue:

i.   do not have a direct, substantial and reasonably foreseeable impact on consumers in the Requesting Party's territory, or

ii.   where the anticompetitive activities do have such an impact on the Requesting Party's consumers, they occur principally in and are directed principally towards the other Party's territory;

b.   The adverse effects on the interests of the Requesting Party can be and are likely to be fully and adequately investigated and, as appropriate, eliminated or adequately remedied pursuant to the laws, procedures, and available remedies of the Requested Party. The Parties recognize that it may be appropriate to pursue separate enforcement activities where anticompetitive activities affecting both territories justify the imposition of penalties within both jurisdictions; and

c.   The competition authorities of the Requested Party agree that in conducting their own enforcement activities, they will:

i.   devote adequate resources to investigate the anticompetitive activities and, where appropriate, promptly pursue adequate enforcement activities;

ii.   use their best efforts to pursue all reasonably available sources of information, including such sources of information as may be suggested by the competition authorities of the Requesting Party;

iii.   inform the competition authorities of the Requesting Party, on request or at reasonable intervals, of the status of their enforcement activities and intentions, and where appropriate provide to the competition authorities of the Requesting Party relevant confidential information if consent has been obtained from the source concerned. The use and disclosure of such information shall be governed by Article V;

iv.   promptly notify the competition authorities of the Requesting Party of any change in their intentions with respect to investigation or enforcement;

v.   use their best efforts to complete their investigation and to obtain a remedy or initiate proceedings within six months, or such other time as agreed to by the competition authorities of the Parties, of the deferral or suspension of enforcement activities by the competition authorities of the Requesting Party;

vi.   fully inform the competition authorities of the Requesting Party of the results of their investigation, and take into account the views of the competition authorities of the Requesting Party, prior to any settlement, initiation of proceedings, adoption of remedies, or termination of the investigation; and

vii.   comply with any reasonable request that may be made by the competition authorities of the Requesting Party.

When the above conditions are satisfied, a Requesting Party which chooses not to defer or suspend its enforcement activities shall inform the competition authorities of the Requested Party of its reasons.

3.   The competition authorities of the Requesting Party may defer or suspend their own enforcement activities if fewer than all of the conditions set out in paragraph 2 are satisfied.

4.   Nothing in this Agreement precludes the competition authorities of a Requesting Party that choose to defer or suspend independent enforcement activities from later initiating or reinstituting such activities. In such circumstances, the competition authorities of the Requesting Party will promptly inform the competition authorities of the Requested Party of their intentions and reasons. If the competition authorities of the Requested Party continue with their own investigation, the competition authorities of the two Parties shall, where appropriate, coordinate their respective investigations under the criteria and procedures of Article IV of the 1991 Agreement.

Article V. Confidentiality and Use of Information

Where pursuant to this Agreement the competition authorities of one Party provide information to the competition authorities of the other Party for the purpose of implementing this Agreement, that information shall be used by the latter competition authorities only for that purpose. However, the competition authorities that provided the information may consent to another use, on condition that where confidential information has been provided pursuant to Article IV.2 (c) (iii) on the basis of the consent of the source concerned, that source also agrees to the other use. Disclosure of such information shall be governed by the provisions of Article VIII of the 1991 Agreement and the exchange of interpretative letters dated 31 May and 31 July 1995.

ARTICLE VI. RELATIONSHIP TO THE 1991 AGREEMENT

This Agreement shall supplement and be interpreted consistently with the 1991 Agreement, which remains fully in force.

ARTICLE VII. EXISTING LAW

Nothing in this Agreement shall be interpreted in a manner inconsistent with the existing laws, or as requiring any change in the laws, of the United States of America or the European Communities or of their respective states or Member States....

Questions on the 1998 U.S.–EU Positive Comity Agreement

1. What is the purpose of this Agreement? In which way does it strengthen the 1991 Agreement discussed above?

2. Does this Agreement completely prevent parallel investigations by the U.S. and EU antitrust authorities?

3. Does this Agreement provide for the exchange of confidential business information between U.S. and EU antitrust authorities absent consent by the firm(s) targeted by the investigation? Isn't the lack of provisions allowing the U.S. and EU antitrust authorities to share confidential information absent consent of the investigated firms the main limitation to the effectiveness of the 1991 and 1998 cooperation agreements?

Intel Corp. v. Advanced Micro Devices, Inc.

542 U.S. 241 (2004).

■ JUSTICE GINSBURG delivered the opinion of the Court.

This case concerns the authority of federal district courts to assist in the production of evidence for use in a foreign or international tribunal. In the matter before us, respondent Advanced Micro Devices, Inc. (AMD) filed an antitrust complaint against petitioner Intel ... with the ... European Commission.... In pursuit of that complaint, AMD applied to [a] United States District Court ..., invoking 28 U.S.C. § 1782(a), for an order requiring Intel to produce potentially relevant documents. Section 1782(a) provides that a federal district court "may order" a person "resid[ing]" or "found" in the district to give testimony or produce documents "for use in a proceeding in a foreign or international tribunal ... upon the application of any interested person."

Concluding that § 1782(a) did not authorize the requested discovery, the District Court denied AMD's application. The Court of Appeals for the Ninth Circuit reversed that determination and remanded the case, instructing the District Court to rule on the merits of AMD's application. In accord with the Court of Appeals, we hold that the District Court had authority under § 1782(a) to entertain AMD's discovery request. The statute, we rule, does not categorically bar the assistance AMD seeks: (1) A complainant before the European Commission, such as AMD, qualifies as an "interested person" within § 1782(a)'s compass; (2) the Commission is a § 1782(a) "tribunal" when it acts as a first-instance decisionmaker; (3) the "proceeding" for which discovery is sought under § 1782(a) must be in reasonable contemplation, but need not be "pending" or "imminent"; and (4) § 1782(a) contains no threshold requirement that evidence sought from a federal district court would be discoverable under the law governing the foreign proceeding. We caution, however, that § 1782(a) authorizes, but does not require, a federal district court to provide judicial assistance to foreign or international tribunals or to "interested person[s]" in proceedings abroad. Whether such assistance is appropriate in this case is a question yet unresolved. To guide the District Court on remand, we suggest considerations relevant to the disposition of that question. . . .

. . . Although lacking formal "party" or "litigant" status in Commission proceedings, the complainant has significant procedural rights. Most prominently, the complainant may submit to the DG–Competition information in support of its allegations, and may seek judicial review of the Commission's disposition of a complaint. . . .

We turn first to Intel's contention that the catalog of "interested person[s]" authorized to apply for judicial assistance under § 1782(a) includes only "litigants, foreign sovereigns, and the designated agents of those sovereigns," and excludes AMD, a mere complainant before the Commission, accorded only "limited rights." Highlighting § 1782's caption, "[a]ssistance to foreign and international tribunals and to *litigants* before such tribunals," Intel urges that the statutory phrase "any interested person" should be read, correspondingly, to reach only "litigants."

The caption of a statute, this Court has cautioned, "cannot undo or limit that which the [statute's] text makes plain." The text of § 1782(a), "upon the application of any interested person," plainly reaches beyond the universe of persons designated "litigant." No doubt litigants are included among, and may be the most common example of, the "interested person [s]" who may invoke § 1782; we read § 1782's caption to convey no more.

The complainant who triggers a European Commission investigation has a significant role in the process. . . . [I]n addition to prompting an investigation, the complainant has the right to submit information for the DG–Competition's consideration, and may proceed to court if the Commission discontinues the investigation or dismisses the complaint. Given these participation rights, a complainant "possess[es] a reasonable interest in obtaining [judicial] assistance," and therefore qualifies as an "interested person" within any fair construction of that term. . . .

We next consider whether the assistance in obtaining documents here sought by an "interested person" meets the specification "for use in a foreign or international tribunal." Beyond question the reviewing authorities, both the Court of First Instance and the European Court of Justice, qualify as tribunals. But those courts are not proof-taking instances. Their review is limited to the record before the Commission. Hence, AMD could "use" evidence in the reviewing courts only by submitting it to the Commission in the current, investigative stage.... We have no warrant to exclude the European Commission, to the extent that it acts as a first-instance decisionmaker, from § 1782(a)'s ambit....

Intel also urges that AMD's complaint has not progressed beyond the investigative stage; therefore, no adjudicative action is currently or even imminently on the Commission's agenda. Section 1782(a) does not limit the provision of judicial assistance to "pending" adjudicative proceedings. In 1964, when Congress eliminated the requirement that a proceeding be "judicial," Congress also deleted the requirement that a proceeding be "pending." ... [W]e reject the view ... that § 1782 comes into play only when adjudicative proceedings are "pending" or "imminent." Instead, we hold that § 1782(a) requires only that a dispositive ruling by the Commission, reviewable by the European courts, be within reasonable contemplation....

We take up next the foreign-discoverability rule on which lower courts have divided: Does § 1782(a) categorically bar a district court from ordering production of documents when the foreign tribunal or the "interested person" would not be able to obtain the documents if they were located in the foreign jurisdiction?

We note at the outset, and count it significant, that § 1782(a) expressly shields privileged material: "A person may not be compelled to give his testimony or statement or to produce a document or other thing in violation of any legally applicable privilege." Beyond shielding material safeguarded by an applicable privilege, however, nothing in the text of § 1782 limits a district court's production-order authority to materials that could be discovered in the foreign jurisdiction if the materials were located there. "If Congress had intended to impose such a sweeping restriction on the district court's discretion, at a time when it was enacting liberalizing amendments to the statute, it would have included statutory language to that effect."

Nor does § 1782(a)'s legislative history suggest that Congress intended to impose a blanket foreign-discoverability rule on the provision of assistance under § 1782(a). The Senate Report observes in this regard that § 1782(a) "leaves the issuance of an appropriate order to the discretion of the court which, in proper cases, may refuse to issue an order or may impose conditions it deems desirable."

Intel raises two policy concerns in support of a foreign-discoverability limitation on § 1782(a) aid—avoiding offense to foreign governments, and maintaining parity between litigants. While comity and parity concerns may be important as touchstones for a district court's exercise of discretion in particular cases, they do not permit our insertion of a generally applicable foreign-discoverability rule into the text of § 1782(a).

We question whether foreign governments would in fact be offended by a domestic prescription permitting, but not requiring, judicial assistance. A foreign nation may limit discovery within its domain for reasons peculiar to its own legal practices, culture, or traditions—reasons that do not necessarily signal objection to aid from United States federal courts.[12] A foreign tribunal's reluctance to order production of materials present in the United States similarly may signal no resistance to the receipt of evidence gathered pursuant to § 1782(a). See *South Carolina Ins. Co. v. Assurantie Maatschappij "De Zeven Provincien" N.V.*, [1987] 1 App. Cas. 24 (House of Lords ruled that nondiscoverability under English law did not stand in the way of a litigant in English proceedings seeking assistance in the United States under § 1782). When the foreign tribunal would readily accept relevant information discovered in the United States, application of a foreign-discoverability rule would be senseless. The rule in that situation would serve only to thwart § 1782(a)'s objective to assist foreign tribunals in obtaining relevant information that the tribunals may find useful but, for reasons having no bearing on international comity, they cannot obtain under their own laws.

Concerns about maintaining parity among adversaries in litigation likewise do not provide a sound basis for across-the-board foreign-discoverability rule. When information is sought by an "interested person," a district court could condition relief upon that person's reciprocal exchange of information. Moreover, the foreign tribunal can place conditions on its acceptance of the information to maintain whatever measure of parity it concludes is appropriate.

We also reject Intel's suggestion that a § 1782(a) applicant must show that United States law would allow discovery in domestic litigation analogous to the foreign proceeding. Section 1782 is a provision for assistance to tribunals abroad. It does not direct United States courts to engage in comparative analysis to determine whether analogous proceedings exist here. Comparisons of that order can be fraught with danger. For example, we have in the United States no close analogue to the European Commission regime under which AMD is not free to mount its own case in the Court of First Instance or the European Court of Justice, but can participate only as complainant, an "interested person," in Commission-steered proceedings. . . .

As earlier emphasized, a district court is not required to grant a § 1782(a) discovery application simply because it has the authority to do so. We note below factors that bear consideration in ruling on a § 1782(a) request.

First, when the person from whom discovery is sought is a participant in the foreign proceeding (as Intel is here), the need for § 1782(a) aid generally is not as apparent as it ordinarily is when evidence is sought from a nonparticipant in the matter arising abroad. A foreign tribunal has jurisdiction over those appearing before it, and can itself order them to produce evidence. In contrast, nonparticipants in the foreign proceeding

---

12. Most civil-law systems lack procedures analogous to the pretrial discovery regime operative under the Federal Rules of Civil Procedure.

may be outside the foreign tribunal's jurisdictional reach; hence, their evidence, available in the United States, may be unobtainable absent § 1782(a) aid.

Second, as the 1964 Senate Report suggests, a court presented with a § 1782(a) request may take into account the nature of the foreign tribunal, the character of the proceedings underway abroad, and the receptivity of the foreign government or the court or agency abroad to U.S. federal-court judicial assistance. Further, the grounds Intel urged for categorical limitations on § 1782(a)'s scope may be relevant in determining whether a discovery order should be granted in a particular case. Specifically, a district court could consider whether the § 1782(a) request conceals an attempt to circumvent foreign proof-gathering restrictions or other policies of a foreign country or the United States. Also, unduly intrusive or burdensome requests may be rejected or trimmed.

Intel maintains that, if we do not accept the categorical limitations it proposes, then, at least, we should exercise our supervisory authority to adopt rules barring § 1782(a) discovery here. We decline, at this juncture, to adopt supervisory rules. Any such endeavor at least should await further experience with § 1782(a) applications in the lower courts. The European Commission has stated in *amicus curiae* briefs to this Court that it does not need or want the District Court's assistance. It is not altogether clear, however, whether the Commission, which may itself invoke § 1782(a) aid, means to say "never" or "hardly ever" to judicial assistance from United States courts. Nor do we know whether the European Commission's views on § 1782(a)'s utility are widely shared in the international community by entities with similarly blended adjudicative and prosecutorial functions.

Several facets of this case remain largely unexplored. Intel and its *amici* have expressed concerns that AMD's application, if granted in any part, may yield disclosure of confidential information, encourage "fishing expeditions," and undermine the European Commission's Leniency Program. Yet no one has suggested that AMD's complaint to the Commission is pretextual. Nor has it been shown that § 1782(a)'s preservation of legally applicable privileges, and the controls on discovery available to the District Court, see, *e.g.*, Fed. Rule Civ. Proc. 26(b)(2) and (c), would be ineffective to prevent discovery of Intel's business secrets and other confidential information.

On the merits, this case bears closer scrutiny than it has received to date. Having held that § 1782(a) authorizes, but does not require, discovery assistance, we leave it to the courts below to assure an airing adequate to determine what, if any, assistance is appropriate. . . .

Questions on *Intel v. AMD*

As this case indicates, coordination can occur not only between enforcement agencies but between proceedings in different nations, with that coordination sometimes orchestrated by private parties, whom this opinion allows to sometimes obtain discovery using U.S. civil procedure in order to support complaints before the European Commission.

1. Why should litigants ever be able to obtain discovery in the United States for use in a foreign proceeding when:

a. such discovery could not be obtained in a similar U.S. litigation?

b. such discovery would not be permitted under the discovery rules of the foreign nation? Doesn't this undermine the discovery limits imposed by that nation? Even if the foreign nation is willing to accept this information, doesn't this result in U.S. litigants being treated worse than other litigants in that nation?

c. the foreign tribunal (like the Commission here) states it does not want the assistance of U.S. discovery? Are parties likely to be able to get the Commission to weigh in on every U.S. discovery request made to support an EU complainant? If the EU itself invokes its right to § 1782 assistance, should it categorically be given the discovery?

d. the party from whom the information is sought is (as here) a defendant before the foreign proceeding and thus could be ordered to produce the relevant discovery by the foreign tribunal if it wanted it?

2. Is the Court right to treat each of the above as discretionary factors cutting against discovery rather than as a categorical bar?

3. Should the U.S. courts compel the discovery of documents to aid foreign antitrust proceedings even when those foreign nations refuse to reciprocate by compelling discovery to aid U.S. antitrust proceedings?

International Cooperation Involving Other Nations

Many other nations have entered into antitrust cooperation agreements with the U.S. or EU or into similar bilateral or regional agreements involving other nations.[69] The level of cooperation that derives from such agreements varies widely. Some are much more detailed than others. Some include positive comity or technical assistant provisions, whereas others do not. Nations with legal and cultural similarities, like Australia and New Zealand, seem particularly successful at cooperation. Most cooperation is bilateral, but regional trade pacts that contain provisions for some level of cooperation on competition law include: NAFTA, MERCOSUR, the Free Trade Area of the Americas, the Common Market for Eastern and Southern Africa, and the Asia–Pacific Economic Cooperation.[70] Sometimes formal cooperation is restricted due to confidentiality constraints. Informal cooperation between agency officials is also common, though not always successful.

F. THE PROSPECTS FOR INTERNATIONAL ANTITRUST LAW

Almost since the end World War II, a number of prominent academics, practitioners, and policy-makers have argued that there is a need for

---

69. For agreements with the U.S., see http://www.justice.gov/atr/public/international/int_arrangements.htm. For agreements with the EU, see http://ec.europa.eu/competition/international/bilateral/index.html. For other agreements, see, *e.g.*, the Canada–Mexico Agreement (2001); the Australia–New Zealand–UK Cooperation and Coordination Agreement (2003), and the Australia–New Zealand–Canada Agreement (2000).

70. *See* ABA, I COMPETITION LAWS OUTSIDE THE UNITED STATES at Overview—125–29 (2001).

international antitrust rules combined, according to some, with a global antitrust authority. Some of the reasons, raised throughout the discussion in this chapter, include fears that regulating anticompetitive practices that occur on international markets through independent national antitrust authorities leads to inconsistent judgments, biased enforcement against foreigners, underincentives to incur the costs of enforcement because of free rider problems, obstacles to effective enforcement because evidence or assets are located abroad, and high transaction costs because of multi-jurisdictional filings. Others have, however, disputed the necessity of an international antitrust regime and argued that it is not desirable or achievable given (a) the reality that any international rules would have to deviate somewhat from the diverging antitrust views of each nation and (b) the risk that any independent antitrust agency or tribunal would itself be biased toward certain nations or adopt interpretations or enforcement policies that deviate from the preferences of most nations. The main actors on the global antitrust scene have also held opposing views on the subject. While the EU has traditionally been favorable to the setting up of a global antitrust regime, the U.S. have been opposed to such an approach.

Notwithstanding these objections, in 2001 a Doha Ministerial declaration committed to try to negotiate international competition rules on at least some topics during the Doha Round of multilateral trade negotiations. However, efforts to negotiate such an international agreement foundered, with much of the opposition coming from small or developing nations. In 2004, the Doha Work Program adopted by the General Council of the WTO abandoned any effort to negotiate the adoption of competition rules. The following explores some of the history and issues.

Damien Geradin and Michel Kerf, "Levelling the Playing Field: Is the World Trade Organization Adequately Equipped to Prevent Anti–Competitive Practices in Telecommunications?"

in D. Geradin and D. Luff, Eds., *The WTO and Global Convergence in Telecommunications and Audio–Visual Services* 130–62 (Cambridge University Press 2004).

Whether or not the multilateral trading system should comprise competition rules is hardly a new issue in international trade law. By 1947, the Havana Charter and the International Trade Organization contemplated it, envisaging a chapter containing provisions for the regulation of restrictive business practices. The ITO failed, however, in part because of objections of the U.S. Government to its antitrust policy provisions. No competition-related rules were eventually included in the original GATT. Discussions over multilateral competition rules continued in a variety of international fora. For instance, in the early 1950s, the Economic and Social Council (ECOSOC) of the United Nations attempted to formulate an international agreement on restrictive business practices, which was also rejected by the United States. In the 1970s, developing countries decided to pursue the negotiation of a multilateral code on restrictive business practices. These efforts led to the adoption in 1980 of a "Set of Multilaterally Agreed Equitable Principles and Rules for the Control of Restrictive Business

Practices." The practical importance of this code was, however, limited by its purely voluntary nature. While efforts to develop binding international competition rules remain fruitless, many States engaged in bilateral cooperation agreements. Pursuant to these agreements, the parties agree to cooperate in the context of international antitrust investigations (e.g., by providing that each party notify the other of a pending enforcement action that could impact upon important interests of the other party). Some of these agreements also identify a set of negative and positive comity principles that can guide both parties as they decide whether or not to exercise or forgo jurisdiction over a case. These agreements do not lead, however, to any coordination of substantive competition laws. In the absence of multilateral competition rules, some nations also started to coordinate their competition policy on a regional basis. Examples include the EU, NAFTA, and Mercosur.

In the 1990s, internationalization of competition rules remained at the forefront of international trade discussions. The European Union in particular pressed its trading partners for the adoption of a competition law framework in the context of the WTO. This approach was supported by some major trading nations. It was, however, opposed by the United States. As a result, while the Uruguay Round negotiations led to the adoption of specific agreements over issues, such as intellectual property rights (TRIPs) and international investments (TRIMs), these negotiations did not lead to the adoption of global competition rules. Several agreements that are part of the WTO framework contain, however, competition-related provisions. For instance, the TRIPs authorizes Members to specify, in their legislation, licensing practices or conditions that may, in particular cases, constitute an abuse of intellectual property rights having an averse effect on competition in the relevant market. The TRIMs requires, within five years from the date at which it becomes enforceable, consideration of whether the agreement should be complemented with provisions on investment and competition policy.

In 1996, the WTO Ministerial Meeting held in Singapore created a Working Group on the Interaction between Trade and Competition Policy. The mission of this Working Group was to "study issues raised by Members relating to the interaction between trade and competition policy, including anti-competitive practices, in order to identify any areas that may merit further consideration in the WTO framework". This Working Group has produced several reports, which will provide support to further WTO initiatives in the competition field. In this regard, the recent Doha Ministerial Declaration represented another major step as it provided that negotiations over competition will take place after the next WTO Ministerial Meeting, probably in 2003, based on modalities to be decided at the time. It is, of course, too early at this stage to predict whether these negotiations will lead to the adoption of a WTO competition law framework.

Doha Ministerial Declaration

Adopted on 14 November 2001.

   . . . Recognizing the case for a multilateral framework to enhance the contribution of competition policy to international trade and development, and the need for enhanced technical assistance and capacity-building in this area . . ., we agree that negotiations will take place after the Fifth Session of the Ministerial Conference on the basis of a decision to be taken, by explicit consensus, at that Session on modalities of negotiations.

We recognize the needs of developing and least-developed countries for enhanced support for technical assistance and capacity building in this area, including policy analysis and development so that they may better evaluate the implications of closer multilateral cooperation for their development policies and objectives, and human and institutional development. To this end, we shall work in cooperation with other relevant intergovernmental organisations, including UNCTAD, and through appropriate regional and bilateral channels, to provide strengthened and adequately resourced assistance to respond to these needs.

In the period until the Fifth Session, further work in the Working Group on the Interaction between Trade and Competition Policy will focus on the clarification of: core principles, including transparency, non-discrimination and procedural fairness, and provisions on hardcore cartels; modalities for voluntary cooperation; and support for progressive reinforcement of competition institutions in developing countries through capacity building. Full account shall be taken of the needs of developing and least-developed country participants and appropriate flexibility provided to address them.

Doha Work Programme Decision Adopted by the General Council on 1 August 2004

. . . Relationship between Trade and Investment, Interaction between Trade and Competition Policy and Transparency in Government Procurement: the Council agrees that these issues, mentioned in the Doha Ministerial Declaration . . . will not form part of the Work Programme set out in that Declaration and therefore no work towards negotiations on any of these issues will take place within the WTO during the Doha Round.

Explaining the Inability to Negotiate International Antitrust Rules So Far

As the last excerpt indicates, the Doha negotiations on international antitrust rules collapsed. A major reason for the collapse was the opposition of small or developing nations that feared overly intrusive antitrust enforcement. In some ways this is surprising because one might have thought (a) those are the nations that suffer most from the U.S.–EU unwillingness to police international cartels to the extent they harm consumers in other nations[71] and (b) that any preference of small or developing nations for lax antitrust rules to govern their exporters would be hard to effectuate, given U.S.–EU antitrust enforcement against extraterritorial conduct that affects consumers in the U.S. and EU. Perhaps developing nations have collective

---

71. For evidence of the extent to which international cartels harm developing nations, see Margaret Levenstein and Valerie Y. Suslow, Contemporary International Cartels and Developing Countries: Economic Effects and Implications for Competition Policy, 71 Antitrust L. J. 801 (2004).

action problems that cause them to choose to underenforce antitrust laws against global anticompetitive conduct, but if so they should benefit all the more from a collective international agreement to overcome those collective action problems. Unless the developed nations are unable to effectively enforce their antitrust laws against export cartels in small or developing nations because of problems in procuring evidence or penalizing assets in the latter nations, small or developing nations would seem to lack any strategic reason to oppose international antitrust enforcement.

One possible explanation for the opposition of small or developing nations is that antitrust enforcement is costly and difficult, and that small or developing nations lack the budget or expertise to do it effectively. However, this is one reason the initial Doha declaration stressed the need for technical assistance for such nations, and this would seem to be the easiest issue to resolve with funding or transfer payments. Still, small nations may well have feared that the technical assistance might not actually materialize or that the expertise gap and need to accept foreign funding on regulatory policy would inevitably deprive them of equal influence on policy decisions.

A more intriguing possibility is that the antitrust policies that are optimal for developed nations might differ from those that are optimal for developing nations, so that the latter would suffer from the adoption of international antitrust rules that are designed to be optimal for more developed economies. Some have suggested that small or developing nations might want to have laxer antitrust rules because economies of scale mean that it is efficient for such nations to have more concentrated markets.[72] But if the markets are truly limited to small nations, then they would be unaffected by international rules that govern international markets. And if the markets are international, then there is no reason to presuppose that those markets are small or are especially likely to require high concentrations to achieve efficient economies of scale. Nor does it make much sense to adopt any categorical presumption that economies of scale will require high concentrations in markets within small or developing nations and low concentrations in larger developed nations or global markets. A market may be small, but have few economies of scale given how the product is produced, or any economies of scale may not be relevant to the alleged anticompetitive activities. A nation may be large and developed, yet the relevant market within it may be quite small in any given case. Or a market may be large and even global, and yet have economies of scale that justify high concentration levels.

Further, to the extent economies of scale are more significant in small and developing nations and lead to more concentrated markets, that would seem to only increase the risk that firms might be able to collude or have market power they can protect with anticompetitive conduct, especially since greater economies of scale also imply greater entry barriers. If anything, this just increases the benefits of effective antitrust enforcement. In short, economies of scale and increased concentration levels do not really justify laxer antitrust policy in small nations rather than having similar

---

72. *See* MICHAL GAL, COMPETITION POLICY FOR SMALL MARKET ECONOMIES (2003).

antitrust rules in every nation whose criteria include the relevance of economies of scale, entry barriers, and market concentration levels to any particular market and alleged anticompetitive conduct.

Developing nations might also be thought to reasonably differ from developed nations by giving relatively more weight to productive efficiency than allocative efficiency.[73] Because production in developing nations is often much less efficient than in developed nations, developing nations might benefit more often by allowing the sort of conduct or combinations likely to increase productive efficiency even when it leads to market power that decreases allocative efficiency. Competition to increase productive efficiency over time might thus be relatively more important in developing nations than static competition to lower prices at any one time. But it is unclear whether this argument really holds. Given its premise, firms in developing nations can improve productive efficiency simply by copying techniques already used in developed nations, whereas firms in developed nations can improve productive efficiency only by innovating to create new techniques. One might thus think that competition to increase productive efficiency over time will, if anything, be more important in developed nations. Nor is at all clear that lax antitrust enforcement increases innovation or that firms with market power are more likely to innovate than firms that have to innovate to survive in competitive markets.[74] In any event, even if the point is generally valid, it does not justify a categorical distinction since productive efficiency concerns will hardly be paramount in every market or case in developing nations. Instead, the point would seem to merely justify taking proper account of whether any allocative inefficiencies might be offset by productive efficiencies in each case.

Moreover, any disagreement based on the above differences does not explain why developed and developing nations could not agree on things like an international law against hard core cartels that cannot be justified by economies of scale. This is presumably why the initial Doha declaration stressed it would focus on clear issues like cartels, on which it should have been easier to reach consensus. But small and developing nations may reasonably have feared that once any international antitrust authority was created, it would be hard to stop its expansion to cover the full range of competition law issues.

Also undercutting the theory that small or developing nations actually benefit from laxer antitrust policy is the evidence that adopting and effectively enforcing antitrust laws is positively correlated with higher GDP.[75] True, such correlations may simply mean that richer nations can afford more antitrust enforcement, which is expensive and requires the sort of expertise rich nations have. Such correlations may also reflect the fact

---

73. *See* Ajit Singh and Rahul Dhumale, *Competition Policy, Development And Developing Countries*, 7 T.R.A.D.E. WORKING PAPERS 12–14 (Nov. 1999).

74. Patrick Rey, *Competition Policy and Economic Development* 1–21 (September 1997) available at dei.fr/doc/by/rey/competition.pdf.

75. *See* Michael W. Nicholson, *Quantifying Antitrust Regimes*, 267 FTC Working Paper 17 (February 2004) (correlation of antitrust adoption with GDP levels); WORLD BANK, WORLD DEVELOPMENT REPORT: BUILDING INSTITUTIONS FOR MARKETS 141 (2002) (correlation of effective antitrust enforcement with GDP).

that often nations, especially the EU, make the adoption of antitrust laws a condition to obtain trade agreements. If those trade agreements lead to increased growth, then such a correlation would exist even if the antitrust laws did not increase growth at all, and in fact many of the small and developing nations that adopt antitrust laws in order to get trade agreements engage in little effective enforcement of those antitrust laws.[76] However, these alternative hypotheses seem rebutted by other evidence that more effective implementation of antitrust laws in developing nations also correlates positively with increased economic growth, greater intensity of competition, and the expansion of more efficient private firms.[77] Moreover, because national antitrust enforcement is generally designed to maximize consumer welfare and excludes producer surplus, it is not clear one would expect desirable antitrust enforcement to increase GDP, unless it were adjusted with some purchasing power index.

A final possibility is that even if the optimal antitrust laws do not differ much for developed and developing nations, their political economies may differ significantly. If small or developing nations have political systems that are more dominated by existing producers, then they might be unwilling to enforce antitrust laws that harm the interests of such producers to benefit consumers or potential entrants even if doing so would enhance total or consumer welfare within those nations. It might make little policy sense to have antitrust rules that allow anticompetitive conduct that is both inefficient and distributionally regressive because it harms consumers and entrants to benefit existing producers. But it might make a lot of political sense to do so if those producers dominate decisions about what antitrust rules to adopt in those nations.

Still, other than the treaty forming the EU itself, even developed nations have not entered into treaties creating international antitrust laws to govern conduct on their overlapping markets, and the U.S. has historically opposed EU efforts to do so. This suggests that something other than differences between developed and developing nations is causing or contrib-

---

76. *See* Dina Waked, *Antitrust Law Adoption/Enforcement in Developing Countries Compared to the U.S. & EC* (Harvard Law School LLM paper, 2006). This hypothesis seems supported by a study finding that the mere existence of competition law has no statistically significant effect on the difference between market prices and marginal cost after one controls for import competition and the number of domestic firms in the market. See Hiau Looi Kee and Bernard Hoekman, *Imports, Entry, and Competition Law as Market Disciplines*, 3031 World Bank Policy Research Working Paper 3, 20–21 (April 2003). This finding seems to suggest that free trade agreements matter more than the adoption of antitrust laws. But even this study found that the existence of competition law did tend to increase the number of domestic firms in the market, which led to lower prices. *See id.* at 3–4, 22–23. And this study did not purport to measure whether the antitrust laws were being effectively implemented.

77. *See* Aydin Hayri and Mark Dutz, *Does More Intense Competition Lead to Higher Growth?*, 2320 World Bank Policy Research Working Paper 2, 9–12 (Nov.30, 1999); Maria Vagliasindi, *Competition Across Transition Economies: An Enterprise-level Analysis of the Main Policy and Structural Determinants*, 68 European Bank Working Paper 1, 13–20 (December 2001); Mark A. Dutz and Maria Vagliasindi, *Competition Policy Implementation in Transition Economies: An Empirical Assessment*, 13 OECD GLOBAL FORUM ON COMPETITION 1, 7–9 (2002). *See also* John Preston, *Investment Climate Reform Competition Policy and Economic Development: Some Country Experiences*, DIFID Case Study for WDR 6–9 (November 2003) (describing positive effects on economic development in Australia, Japan, Korea, Mexico and Peru).

uting to the failure to agree on international antitrust laws. There are at least three possible explanations about what this might be.

First, it may be that while some form of international antitrust law would be beneficial for all nations (or at least the developed ones), certain forms would be more beneficial for some nations and others more beneficial for other nations, so that the nations are unable to agree on which form to adopt. In the lingo of international relations, bargaining on international antitrust rules may be a coordination game.[78] If so, once the nations do coordinate on common antitrust rules, the result will be stable because no nation would benefit from unilaterally deviating from those rules. However each nation will prefer to coordinate on a different set of rules. If each nation could predict and quantify the benefit of adopting their preferred international regime, then transfer payments or concessions on other international trade issues might be able to overcome any reluctance to adopt another regime. However if those benefits are hard to predict or quantify, then this may be hard to do because the amount of transfer payments will be difficult to set.

Second, it may just be a question of timing. Nations may believe that while they could strike a favorable international bargain today, they could strike an even more favorable one tomorrow because other nations are converging towards their systems over time. Many in the U.S., for example, believe that EU competition law is evolving towards something closer to U.S. antitrust law, which may mean the bargain they could strike today would be further from the U.S. ideal position than the bargain they could strike in a few decades. This might explain why the U.S. has been more reluctant than the EU to adopt international antitrust rules. However, a countervailing consideration is the fact that recently the EU has been much more successful in exporting its version of competition law to other nations, in part because (unlike the U.S.) it links the adoption of similar competition laws to trade agreements. At some point, the greater success of the EU on the international market for competition law may make it harder to strike an international agreement close to the U.S. ideal point because more nations will already have EU versions of competition law. Further, the increasing adoption of competition laws by developing nations may give them the sort of experience and expertise that increases their comfort level with international antitrust rules.

Third, it may be that an international antitrust agreement is simply unnecessary, or that the gains that it could achieve are not worth the costs. One might, for example, believe that the current system already adequately deals with problems of biased or inconsistent enforcement by effectively allocating regulatory power to the nations where consumers are affected rather than to the nations where the producers reside. Under this regime it is not clear that either net importers or exporters have incentives to deviate from the antitrust law that is optimal under a consumer welfare standard. One might further think that free rider problems are not severe because the costs of enforcement are relatively low compared to the benefits to each nation's consumers and because it is difficult to attract firms to invest or

---

78. *See* Piilola, *International Antitrust Negotiations and the Failed Promise of the WTO* (June 15, 2006 draft).

employ within a nation by underregulating antitrust issues. If so, all that may be necessary is a commitment to assist foreign antitrust authorities in procuring evidence and enforcing remedies, which is what has in fact been the focus of international cooperation between the U.S. and EU and with other developed nations.

Or one might think that although the current system does create some problems, the benefits from their elimination are small in relation to the costs of an international regime. Those costs include the fact that each nation would have to deviate from its ideal antitrust policy to compromise on a common international regime. They also include the risk that an independent international antitrust agency or tribunal that might itself be biased toward certain nations in a way that would be much harder to correct than is the case under the current decentralized regime. To address that problem, one might want to make the international antitrust agency or tribunal independent of all political influence by affected nations, but that increases the risk that it might adopt interpretations or enforcement policies that deviate from the views of most or all nations.

INDEX

References are to Pages.

†